TYPICAL SUPPLY CHAINS

A typical manufacturing supply chain.

A typical service supply chain.

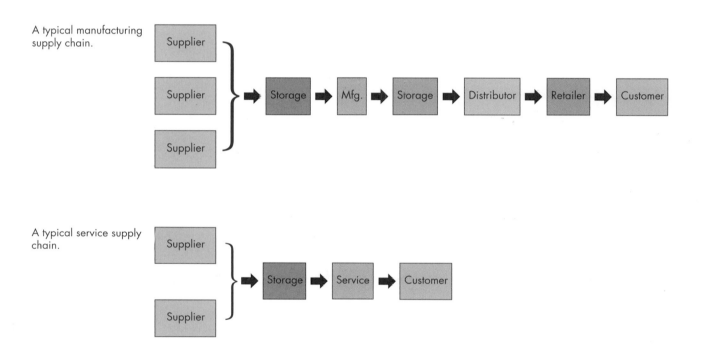

Operations Management

Operations Management

William J. Stevenson
Rochester Institute of Technology

Mehran Hojati
University of Saskatchewan

Toronto   Montréal   Boston   Burr Ridge, IL   Dubuque, IA   Madison, WI   New York
San Francisco   St. Louis   Bangkok   Bogotá   Caracas   Kuala Lumpur   Lisbon   London
Madrid   Mexico City   Milan   New Delhi   Santiago   Seoul   Singapore   Sydney   Taipei

OPERATIONS MANAGEMENT
Third Canadian Edition

Statistics Canada information is used with the permission of the Minister of Industry, as Minister responsible for Statistics Canada. Information on the availability of the wide range of data from Statistics Canada can be obtained from Statistics Canada's Regional Offices, its World Wide Web site at http://www.statcan.ca, and its toll-free access number 1-800-263-1136.

ISBN-13: 978-0-07-095167-9
ISBN-10: 0-07-095167-5

4 5 6 7 8 9 10 CTPS 0 9

Printed and bound in China

Care has been taken to trace ownership of copyright material contained in this text; however, the publisher will welcome any information that enables them to rectify any reference or credit for subsequent editions.

President, Higher Education: Patrick Ferrier
Editorial Director: Joanna Cotton
Publisher, Business and Economics: Lynn Fisher
Marketing Manager: Joy Armitage-Taylor
Developmental Editor: Jennifer Bastarache
Freelance Editor: Tracey Haggert
Freelance Photo/Permission Editor: Christina Beamish
Editorial Associate: Stephanie Hess
Senior Supervising Editor: Margaret Henderson
Copy Editors: Shirley Corriveau, Jim Zimmerman
Senior Production Coordinator: Paula Brown
Cover Design: Sharon Lucas
Cover Images: Technician sampling & Large gears © Jeff Sherman & J Price/Taxi;
Auto plant © Monty Rakusen/Digital Vision; Pharmacist & Construction © Stockbyte;
Departure board © Tom Hussey/Workbook Stock
Interior Design: Greg Devitt
Page Layout: SR Nova Pvt Ltd, Bangalore, India
Printer: China Translation Printing Services Ltd.

National Library of Canada Cataloguing in Publication

Stevenson, William J.
   Operations management / William J. Stevenson, Mehran Hojati.—3rd Canadian ed.

First ed. had title: Production/operations management.
Includes bibliographical references and indexes.
ISBN 0-07-095167-5

1. Production management—Textbooks. I. Hojati, Mehran, 1958-
II. Stevenson, William J. Production/operations management. III. Title.

TS155.S785 2006   658.5   C2006-904843-6

About the Authors

William Stevenson

Rochester Institute of Technology

This book is dedicated to you.

Dr. William Stevenson is an associate professor of Decision Sciences in the College of Business at Rochester Institute of Technology. He teaches graduate and undergraduate courses in operations management, management science, quality concepts, and quality applications.

He is the author of textbooks in management science and statistics as well as operations management. His articles have appeared in *Management Science* and *Decision Sciences, Quality Progress*, and other journals.

Dr. Stevenson received a bachelor's degree in industrial engineering, an M.B.A. and a Ph.D. in production/operations management from Syracuse University.

Mehran Hojati

University of Saskatchewan

I dedicate this book to my dear mother, Mahvash Hedayati.

Dr. Hojati is an associate professor of management science in the College of Commerce at the University of Saskatchewan. He teaches operations management and purchasing and supply management. He has taught and prepared teaching materials for the Purchasing Management Association of Canada. His articles have appeared in *International Journal of Production Economics, Production & Inventory Management Journal*, and others. His research interests are in applications of operations research techniques in management.

Dr. Hojati received a bachelor's degree in economics and a master's degree in operational research from the London School of Economics, and a Ph.D. in management science from the University of British Columbia.

Tejal Govande

Brief Contents

Contents

PART THREE

System Design

CHAPTER FOUR

Product and Service Design   116

SUPPLEMENT TO CHAPTER FOUR

Reliability   144

CHAPTER FIVE

Strategic Capacity Planning   159

Preface

The field of operations management is dynamic and an integral part of many of the good things that are happening in business organizations. The material in this book is intended as an introduction to the field of operations management and to show its interesting, realistic, and practical applications to service and manufacturing operations.

The subject matter represents a blend of concepts from industrial engineering, cost accounting, marketing, general management, management science, quantitative methods, and statistics. The topics covered include both strategic issues and operational decisions. Operations activities such as forecasting, designing products and services, choosing a location for an office or plant, allocating resources, scheduling activities, and assuring and improving quality are core activities and important issues in business organizations. Some of you are or will be employed directly in these areas, while others will have jobs that are indirectly related. So, whether this is your field of study or not, knowledge of this field will certainly benefit you and the organization you work for.

The advantages of using a Canadian version of an Operations Management textbook are numerous, including:

- Canadian data for employment, productivity, etc., are used
- Canadian location decisions are described
- Examples of small- and medium-sized Canadian companies are more familiar and interesting to students
- Issues important for Canadian instructors and reviewers are addressed

APPROACHES TO STUDY

The text contains more material than one could normally hope to study in a one-term course. Rather than rely on the authors' personal biases, each instructor can choose those topics that are most suited to his or her own interests. Those who prefer an analytic/ quantitative emphasis, for example, will be quite comfortable with the abundance of examples and problems. Those who prefer a more qualitative approach will welcome the fact that most of the more quantitative material is placed in chapter supplements and that there are questions, readings, operations tours, and mini-cases for assignment. Obviously, there are many possibilities between these two extremes.

WHAT'S NEW IN THE THIRD CANADIAN EDITION?

The Third Canadian Edition of *Operations Management* has been developed for the Canadian market with an eye toward several key features:

New and Updated Canadian and International Content—A new selection of relevant Canadian and international readings, mini-cases, and problems fill the text with real-world applications. There are approximately 70 new readings and mini-cases, replacing old material; all the other readings and mini-cases have been updated. Canadian-specific employment and productivity data have also been updated.

Profiles of such diverse companies as WestJet, Great Western Brewing Company, and Amazon.com provide students with a realistic understanding of the manufacturing and service companies inside and outside Canada.

Updated Coverage and Organization—The Third Canadian Edition features increased coverage of topics requested by the Canadian reviewers and other material deemed necessary by the Canadian author. Some of the important additions/changes are as follows.

Chapter	Title	Important Changes/Additions
2	Competitiveness, Strategy, and Productivity	Expands the description of Operations Strategy.
3	Forecasting	Gives complete steps in time series decomposition of data with trend and seasonality.
4	Product and Service Design	Adds the stage-gate model and expanded service design.
6	Process Design and Facility Layout	Adds a detailed example (operations tour) of each process type (job shop, batch, assembly, continuous).
7	Design of Work Systems	Includes a simplified Methods-Time Measurement table and Maynard Operation Sequence Technique (MOST).
9	Management of Quality	Combines Introduction to Quality and Total Quality Management chapters. Updates ISO 9000 principles and introduces Hazard Analysis and Critical Control Point (HACCP) system.
10	Quality Control	Describes in detail Six Sigma and Design of Experiments.
11	Inventory Management	Includes the Economic Order Quantity with Planned Shortage.
12	Aggregate Operations Planning	Covers Sales & Operations Planning and Aggregate Planning in Services.
14	Just-in-Time and Lean Manufacturing	Describes Shingo Prize for lean manufacturing. Replaces the solution method for mixed model sequencing. Also, adds Hyundai's mixed model sequencing.
15	Scheduling and Control	Describes cyclical staff scheduling for determining two consecutive days off and expanded within-the-day staff scheduling.
16	Supply Chain Management	Supply Chain Management now includes the Purchasing supplement. Expands the Bullwhip Effect.
17	Project Management	Expands description of project planning, scheduling, execution, and monitoring and control. Describes in detail how to use Microsoft Project. Also describes features of another popular software, Deltek's Welcom.
18	Waiting Lines Analysis	Adds approximate solution to the general arrival, general service time queues.

All chapter supplements have been updated and all except Reliability (which is located in the text) are available in PDF format on the student DVD or the Online Learning Centre at www.mcgrawhill.ca/olc/stevenson.

Tightened Exposition—The Third Canadian Edition of *Operations Management* has been further revised to bring you a tighter, shortened text while maintaining the wide topical coverage and student-friendly style.

HIGHLIGHTS OF THE THIRD CANADIAN EDITION

Balanced Content—The text strives to achieve a careful balance in the presentation of operations management. Care has been taken to balance definitions and concepts with quantitative, hands-on problems; to balance theoretical material with real life applications, and to balance classical topics in operations management with new developments that particularly interest students.

Problem-Solving Approach—To further students' hands-on experience of OM, the text contains examples with solutions throughout. At the end of most chapters there is a group of solved problems to illustrate concepts and techniques. Some of the end-of-chapter problems have answers at the end of the book.

Renowned Style—Always favoured among instructors, the writing style in *Operations Management* is clear, concise, and student-friendly, while maintaining the technical rigour necessary for the subject matter. From step-by-step problem solving, to theoretical exposition, to in-depth mini-cases and readings, the book is designed to promote student understanding of the role of operations management in successful businesses— which, in turn, promotes student success in class.

MAJOR STUDY AND LEARNING FEATURES

A number of key features in this textbook have been specifically designed to help introductory students learn, understand, and apply Operations concepts and problem solving techniques. All of these have been carefully developed over three Canadian editions and nine U.S. editions and have proven to be successful.

Learning Objectives. Every chapter and supplement lists the learning objectives as a short guide to studying the chapter. These objectives are also incorporated in study outline questions on the student DVD.

Chapter Outlines. Every chapter and supplement includes an outline of the topics covered.

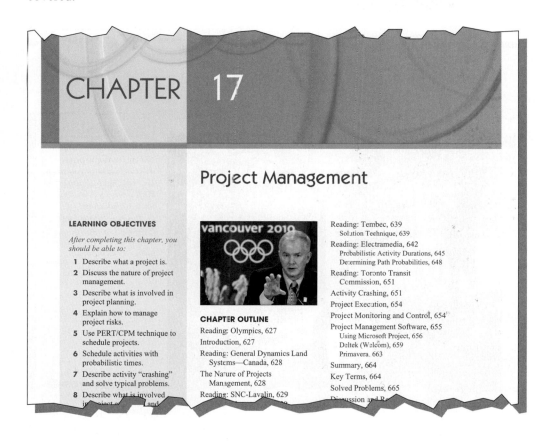

CHAPTER 17

Project Management

LEARNING OBJECTIVES

After completing this chapter, you should be able to:

1 Describe what a project is.
2 Discuss the nature of project management.
3 Describe what is involved in project planning.
4 Explain how to manage project risks.
5 Use PERT/CPM technique to schedule projects.
6 Schedule activities with probabilistic times.
7 Describe activity "crashing" and solve typical problems.
8 Describe what is involved in project execution and control.

CHAPTER OUTLINE

Reading: Olympics, 627
Introduction, 627
Reading: General Dynamics Land Systems—Canada, 628
The Nature of Projects Management, 628
Reading: SNC-Lavalin, 629

Reading: Tembec, 639
  Solution Technique, 639
Reading: Electramedia, 642
  Probabilistic Activity Durations, 645
  Determining Path Probabilities, 648
Reading: Toronto Transit Commission, 651
Activity Crashing, 651
Project Execution, 654
Project Monitoring and Control, 654
Project Management Software, 655
  Using Microsoft Project, 656
  Deltek (Welcom), 659
  Primavera, 663
Summary, 664
Key Terms, 664
Solved Problems, 665
Discussion and R...

Figures and Photos. The Third Canadian Edition includes extensive photographs and graphic illustrations to support student study and provide interest and motivation.

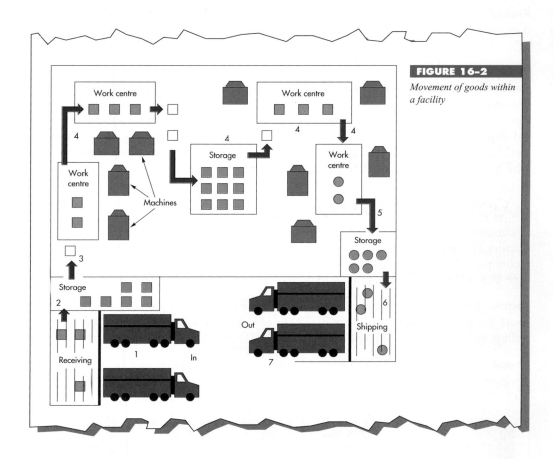

Movement of goods within a facility

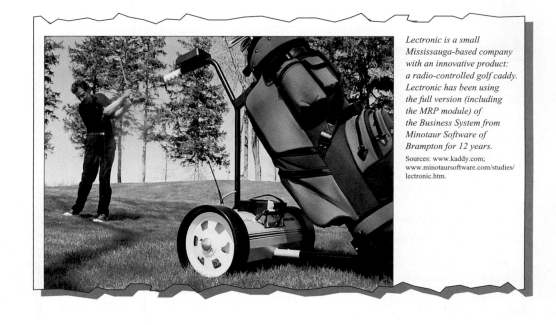

Lectronic is a small Mississauga-based company with an innovative product: a radio-controlled golf caddy. Lectronic has been using the full version (including the MRP module) of the Business System from Minotaur Software of Brampton for 12 years.

Sources: www.kaddy.com; www.minotaursoftware.com/studies/lectronic.htm.

Readings and Newsclips. Throughout the textbook, and in the assignment sections of some chapters, are newsclips as well as readings. These highlight important real-world applications, provide examples of operations issues, and offer further elaboration of the textbook material. They also provide a basis for classroom discussion and generate interest in the subject matter.

 READING

Garrison Guitars

Garrison Guitars of Mount Pearl, Newfoundland, was founded only six years ago, but it has already become a big success. It employs 63 people and produces 12,000 guitars per year, exporting most of them. The reason for this success is the single-unit fiberglass brace module which replaces the tens of separate small wood pieces previously used inside the body of the guitar to hold the top, bottom, and side veneers together. As a result, assembly is easier and faster. There is no need for linings (Kerfing) to be attached to the wood pieces in order to facilitate gluing of the veneer together. Also, there is no need for fine-tuning the wood pieces by a skilled person. The production time has been reduced from 2 hours down to 12 minutes. In addition, the quality has improved because all parts vibrate in unison. You can watch a video of factory operations at www.garrisonguitars.com.

 NEWSCLIP

A QFD Snapshot

How a pencilmaker sharpened up its product by listening to "the voice of the customer" through quality function deployment.

Devised by Japan's Professor Yoji Akao, QFD has been winning adherents since it was transplanted to North America in the late 1980s. In this example of how it works, Writesharp Inc. is imaginary, but the technique in the accompanying diagram is real.

First, Writesharp's customers were surveyed to determine what they value in a pencil and how they rate the leading brands. Each wish list item was correlated with a pencil's physical and functional characteristics. "Reverse engineering"—tearing down a competitors' product to see what makes it tick—produced the competitive evaluation of technical requirements.

An analysis of the plots quickly revealed that the improvement with the biggest potential was "point lasts," to be of customer requirements). An interdepartmental team was assigned the task of evaluating new lead formulations that would last longer and generate less dust. Another team ran tests to determine whether substituting cedar for oak in the wood casing would improve shape quality, or hexagonality, and thus reduce the pencil's tendency to roll down slanted desktops.

The lead-formulation team organized its work with a similar matrix chart, segmented to show the physical and functional contributions of the ingredients in pencil lead. This revealed that the binder, or glue, used in forming the lead was the key variable. Tests found a polymer that dramatically reduced dusting by retaining more moisture and also wore down more slowly. While this binder was more expensive, better production controls promised to reduce waste enough to trim total per-pencil manufacturing costs by 1¢.

Changing the wood, meanwhile, yielded only marginal enhancements.

Source: Reprinted from October 25, 1991, issue of *Business Week* by special permission, copyright © 1991 by The McGraw-Hill

Operations Strategy. Throughout the textbook, whenever the concepts being presented have significant strategic implications for companies, these issues are stated briefly under the Operations Strategy heading.

Operations Strategy

Product and service design is a fertile area for achieving competitive advantage and/or increasing customer satisfaction. Potential sources of such benefits include:

1. Shortening the time to market using concurrent engineering, QFD, and design for manufacturing and assembly.
2. Designing environmentally friendly products.
3. Increasing emphasis on component commonality and standardization such as using multiple-use platforms. Auto manufacturers use the same platform (basic chassis, say) for several modules (e.g., Jaguar S type, Lincoln LS, and Ford Thunderbird have a shared platform).
4. Implementing tactics that will achieve the benefits of high volume while satisfying customer needs for variety (such as mass customization).
5. Continually monitoring products and services for small improvements.

Mini-Cases. Many chapters include short cases, selected to provide a broader, more integrated thinking opportunity for students.

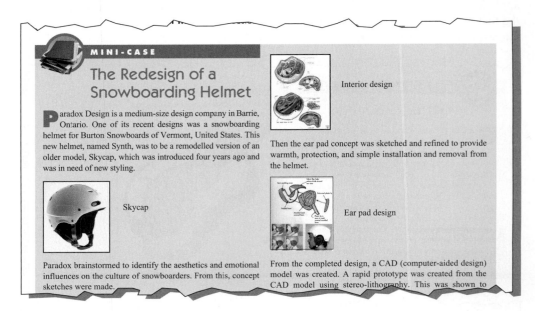

MINI-CASE

The Redesign of a Snowboarding Helmet

Paradox Design is a medium-size design company in Barrie, Ontario. One of its recent designs was a snowboarding helmet for Burton Snowboards of Vermont, United States. This new helmet, named Synth, was to be a remodelled version of an older model, Skycap, which was introduced four years ago and was in need of new styling.

Skycap

Paradox brainstormed to identify the aesthetics and emotional influences on the culture of snowboarders. From this, concept sketches were made.

Interior design

Then the ear pad concept was sketched and refined to provide warmth, protection, and simple installation and removal from the helmet.

Ear pad design

From the completed design, a CAD (computer-aided design) model was created. A rapid prototype was created from the CAD model using stereo-lithography. This was shown to

Examples with Solutions. Throughout the textbook, wherever a quantitative technique is introduced, an example is included to illustrate the application of that technique. These are designed to be easy to follow.

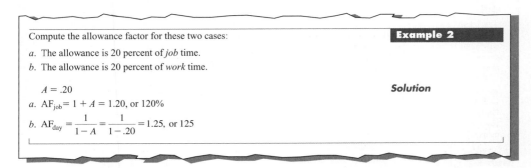

Compute the allowance factor for these two cases:

Example 2

a. The allowance is 20 percent of *job* time.

b. The allowance is 20 percent of *work* time.

Solution

$A = .20$

a. $AF_{job} = 1 + A = 1.20$, or 120%

b. $AF_{day} = \dfrac{1}{1-A} = \dfrac{1}{1-.20} = 1.25$, or 125

Service Icons. Where service topics are addressed in the textbook, a service "S" icon appears in the corresponding margin to flag the attention of both students and instructors.

Web Links. Web addresses of relevant Web sites are highlighted in the margin with a Web icon.

Global Icons. Where a concept or example has worldwide effect, it is flagged with a globe.

Foreign Locations. Some firms are attracted to foreign locations to exploit foreign natural resources. Other firms view foreign locations as a way to expand their markets, and still others are attracted by ample supplies of labour. Many developing countries offer an abundant supply of cheap labour. For example, many North American companies have plants in China.

A firm contemplating a foreign location must carefully weigh the potential benefits against the potential problems. A major factor is the stability of a country's government and its attitude toward foreign firms. Some of the problems of a foreign location can be caused by language and cultural differences. One factor that has negatively impacted the bottom line of some Canadian firms' operating plants in foreign countries is the level of corruption present, and having to deal with politics. For example, Manulife Financial

END OF CHAPTER RESOURCES

For student study and review, the following items are provided at the end of each chapter or chapter supplement.

Summaries. Chapters contain summaries that provide an overview of the material covered.

Key Terms. Key terms are highlighted in the text, and then repeated in the margin with brief definitions for emphasis, and they are listed at the end of each chapter (along with page references) to aid in reviewing.

Solved Problems. At the end of some chapters and chapter supplements, "solved problems" are provided to illustrate problem solving and the core concepts in the chapter. These have been carefully prepared to enhance student understanding as well as to provide additional examples of problem solving.

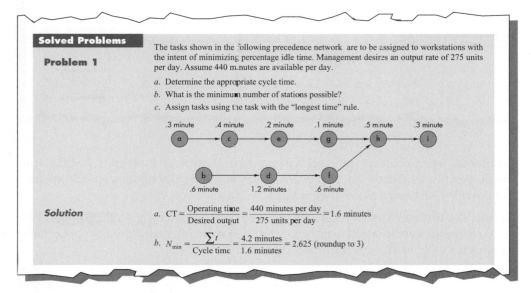

Solved Problems

Problem 1

The tasks shown in the following precedence network are to be assigned to workstations with the intent of minimizing percentage idle time. Management desires an output rate of 275 units per day. Assume 440 minutes are available per day.

   a. Determine the appropriate cycle time.

   b. What is the minimum number of stations possible?

   c. Assign tasks using the task with the "longest time" rule.

Solution

   a. $CT = \dfrac{\text{Operating time}}{\text{Desired output}} = \dfrac{440 \text{ minutes per day}}{275 \text{ units per day}} = 1.6 \text{ minutes}$

   b. $N_{\min} = \dfrac{\sum t}{\text{Cycle time}} = \dfrac{4.2 \text{ minutes}}{1.6 \text{ minutes}} = 2.625 \text{ (roundup to 3)}$

Excel Spreadsheet Solutions. Where applicable, the solved problems include screen shots of a spreadsheet solution. These are taken from the Excel templates, which are on the student DVD included in the back of the textbook.

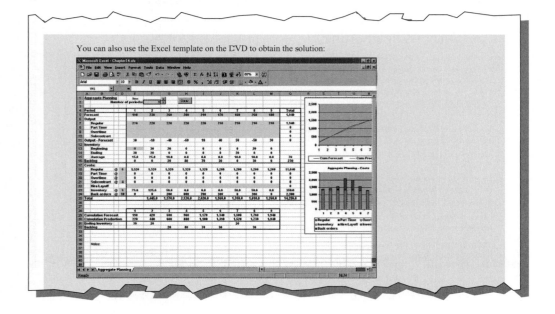

You can also use the Excel template on the DVD to obtain the solution:

Discussion and Review Questions. Each chapter and each supplement has a list of discussion and review questions. These are intended to serve as a student self-review or as class discussion starters.

Taking Stock, Critical Thinking Exercises, and Internet Exercises. These activities encourage analytical thinking and help broaden conceptual understanding.

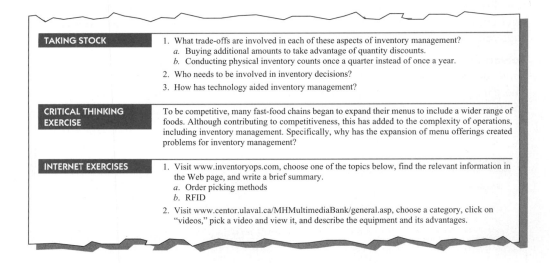

TAKING STOCK	1. What trade-offs are involved in each of these aspects of inventory management?
	a. Buying additional amounts to take advantage of quantity discounts.
	b. Conducting physical inventory counts once a quarter instead of once a year.
	2. Who needs to be involved in inventory decisions?
	3. How has technology aided inventory management?
CRITICAL THINKING EXERCISE	To be competitive, many fast-food chains began to expand their menus to include a wider range of foods. Although contributing to competitiveness, this has added to the complexity of operations, including inventory management. Specifically, why has the expansion of menu offerings created problems for inventory management?
INTERNET EXERCISES	1. Visit www.inventoryops.com, choose one of the topics below, find the relevant information in the Web page, and write a brief summary.
	a. Order picking methods
	b. RFID
	2. Visit www.centor.ulaval.ca/MHMultimediaBank/general.asp, choose a category, click on "videos," pick a video and view it, and describe the equipment and its advantages.

Problems. Most chapters and supplements have numerous Problems, ranging from simple practice problems that apply techniques to more difficult conceptual problems that provide a challenge and require students to integrate concepts.

Cases. The text includes short cases for most chapters, including several new ones, 30 in total. The cases were selected to provide a broader, more integrated thinking opportunity for students without taking a full "case" approach.

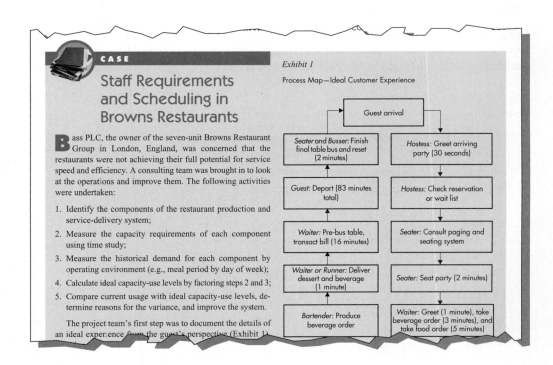

CASE

Staff Requirements and Scheduling in Browns Restaurants

Bass PLC, the owner of the seven-unit Browns Restaurant Group in London, England, was concerned that the restaurants were not achieving their full potential for service speed and efficiency. A consulting team was brought in to look at the operations and improve them. The following activities were undertaken:

1. Identify the components of the restaurant production and service-delivery system;

2. Measure the capacity requirements of each component using time study;

3. Measure the historical demand for each component by operating environment (e.g., meal period by day of week);

4. Calculate ideal capacity-use levels by factoring steps 2 and 3;

5. Compare current usage with ideal capacity-use levels, determine reasons for the variance, and improve the system.

The project team's first step was to document the details of an ideal experience from the guest's perspective (Exhibit 1).

Exhibit 1

Process Map—Ideal Customer Experience

Guest arrival

Seater and *Busser:* Finish final table bus and reset (2 minutes)

Guest: Depart (83 minutes total)

Waiter: Pre-bus table, transact bill (16 minutes)

Waiter or Runner: Deliver dessert and beverage (1 minute)

Bartender: Produce beverage order

Hostess: Greet arriving party (30 seconds)

Hostess: Check reservation or wait list

Seater: Consult paging and seating system

Seater: Seat party (2 minutes)

Waiter: Greet (1 minute), take beverage order (3 minutes), and take food order (5 minutes)

Operations Tours. These readings give students a descriptive look at operations in action at manufacturers or service organizations. These real-life illustrations show direct application to reinforce the importance of the concepts described in the textbook.

OPERATIONS TOUR

Sobeys

www.sobeys.com

Up until 1998, Sobeys was a privately owned chain of grocery stores in the Atlantic provinces. Sobeys grew out of a butcher shop in Stellarton, Nova Scotia, opened by the Sobey family in 1907. When Loblaw, Canada's largest national grocery chain, expanded into Sobeys' territories, competition heated up. Sobeys' directors decided on a bold move in order to gain sufficient economies of scale to be able to compete with Loblaw. Sobeys took over the larger Oshawa Group (at a purchase price of $1.5 billion), then Canada's second largest national grocery chain, which included (mostly franchised) IGA and Price Chopper stores and the wholesale food cistribution company SERCA.

Since 1998, Sobeys has worked hard and successfully to integrate the supermarket chains. It has divided the country into four regions (Atlantic, Quebec, Ontario, and the West), has aligned each store's size and merchandise to its market, centralized purchasing and merchandising, improved its logistics and distribution, and focused on its core grocery retail

names Sobeys, Garden Market IGA (in Western Canada), and IGA Extra (in Quebec). These stores are over 60,000 square feet in size and feature farm-fresh produce, full-line bakeries, extensive home-style meal selections, and a variety of innovative in-store retail services such as photo finishing, florist, Western Union money wiring, dry-cleaning and banking (TD Canada Trust). They usually have between 12 and 16 checkout lanes. A Sobeys store of this size typically employs from 200 to 250 people.

IGA stores (approximately 400) are designed primarily for mid-sized communities with store sizes in the range of 15,000–40,000 square feet. The emphasis in these stores is on fresh produce, meat, dairy, and bakery goods, and on highly personalized service. Stores of this size often have 10 to 12 checkout lanes and employ 50 to 120 people. Price Choppers stores (more than 100) are also approximately the same size as IGA stores, but are for value-conscious consumers.

In smaller communities, Sobeys runs over 300 stores under the banners Foodland, Food Town, Les Marchés Tradition, and Marché Boni choix, which offer consumers convenient, full-service supermarkets on a smaller scale.

Sobeys also runs 128 Needs Convenience Stores, and 58 Lawton Drugstores in Atlantic Canada. Recently, Sobeys

SUPERIOR SERVICE

Service takes on a whole new meaning with McGraw-Hill Ryerson and *Operations Management*. More than just bringing you the textbook, we have consistently raised the bar in terms of innovation and educational research—both in operations management and in education in general. These investments in learning and the education community have helped us to understand the needs of students and educators across the country, and allowed us to foster the growth of truly innovative, integrated learning.

Integrated Learning. Your Integrated Learning Sales Specialist is a McGraw-Hill Ryerson representative who has the experience, product knowledge, training, and support to help you assess and integrate any of our products, technology, and services into your course for optimum teaching and learning performance. Whether it's helping your students improve their grades, or putting your entire course online, your *i*Learning Sales Specialist is there to help you do it. Contact your *i*Learning Sales Specialist today to learn how to maximize all of McGraw-Hill Ryerson's resources!

iLearning Services. McGraw-Hill Ryerson offers a unique *i*Services package designed for Canadian faculty. Our mission is to equip providers of higher education with superior tools and resources required for excellence in teaching. For additional information, visit www.mcgrawhill.ca/highereducation/iservices.

Teaching, Learning & Technology Conference Series. The educational environment has changed tremendously in recent years, and McGraw-Hill Ryerson continues to be committed to helping you acquire the skills you need to succeed in this new milieu. Our innovative Teaching, Learning & Technology Conference Series brings faculty together from across Canada with 3M Teaching Excellence award winners to share teaching and learning best practices in a collaborative and stimulating environment. Pre-conference work-shops on general topics, such as teaching large classes and technology integration, will also be offered. We will also work with you at your own institution to customize workshops that best suit the needs of your faculty.

Research Reports on Technology and Student Success in Higher Education. These landmark reports, undertaken in conjunction with academic and private sector advisory boards, are the result of research studies into the challenges professors face in helping students succeed and the opportunities that new technology presents to impact teaching and learning.

COMPREHENSIVE TEACHING AND LEARNING PACKAGE

We have developed a number of supplements for both teaching and learning to accompany this text:

Instructor's CD-ROM. The Instructor's CD-ROM provides the necessary Instructor Supplements including:

- **Instructor's Manual.** Prepared by the authors, this manual includes a brief description of the McGraw-Hill OM video series, "teaching notes" for each chapter and supplement, complete solutions to all text problems, and teaching hints for the readings and cases. Also included are several enrichment modules that provide coverage of such topics as Vogel's approximation, distance measurement, and Emergency Facility Location.

- **Computerized Test Bank.** Prepared by Laurel Donaldson, Douglas College, includes over 2,000 questions and problems for exams.

- **PowerPoint Lecture Slides.** Prepared by Romulus Cismaru, University of Regina, the PowerPoint slides draw on the highlights of each chapter and provide an opportunity for the instructor to emphasize the most relevant visuals in class discussions.

- **Additional Content.** Data files, Lekin scheduling software, videos and Excel Templates are also available.

Video Library. The MH OM Video Series includes professionally developed videotapes showing students real applications of key manufacturing and service topics. Each tape or DVD contains plant tours to help students see how companies are using operations management concepts and techniques to be productive and competitive. For full descriptions of all 12 volumes, visit mcgrawhill.ca/olc/stevenson.

McGraw-Hill's Homework Manager™. McGraw-Hill's Homework Manager is an online electronic homework system customized to the textbook and is available as an option for students. The system utilizes the exercises from the text both in a static one-problem-at-a-time fashion as well as algorithmically where problems can generate multiple data possibilities and answers.

You choose the problems. Assignments are graded automatically and the results are stored in your private gradebook. Detailed results show you at a glance how each student does on an assignment or even on an individual problem. You can also monitor progress to see which students need extra help.

Course Management

Pageout. McGraw-Hill Ryerson's course management system, PageOut, is the easiest way to create a Web site for your *Operations Management* course. There is no need for HTML coding, graphic design, or a thick how-to book. Just fill in a series of boxes in plain English and click on one of our professional designs. In no time, your course is online!

For the integrated instructor, we offer *Operations Management* content for complete online courses. Whatever your needs, you can customize the *Operations Management* Online Learning Centre content and author your own online course materials. It is entirely up to you. You can offer online discussion and message boards that will complement your office hours, and reduce the lines outside your door. Content cartridges are also available for course management systems, such as **WebCT** and **Blackboard**. Ask your *i*Learning Sales Specialist for details.

FOR STUDENTS

Student DVD

The Student DVD packaged with each new copy of the textbook includes Chapter Supplements, Excel Templates and data files, Screencam Tutorials, self quizzes, study outlines, Lekin interactive scheduling software, developed by Michael Pinedo and Andrew Feldman at New York University, Leonard N. Stern Business School, video segments, 12 full-length videos, and a Web link file.

Excel Templates. Templates created by Lee Tangedahl, University of Montana, are included on the student DVD. The templates, over 70 in total, organized in chapter folders all include dynamically linked graphics and variable controls. They allow students to solve a number of problems in the textbook or additional problems you may assign. All templates have been revised to allow formatting of all cells, hiding rows or columns, and entering data or calculations in blank cells. Many of the templates have been expanded to accommodate solving larger problems and cases.

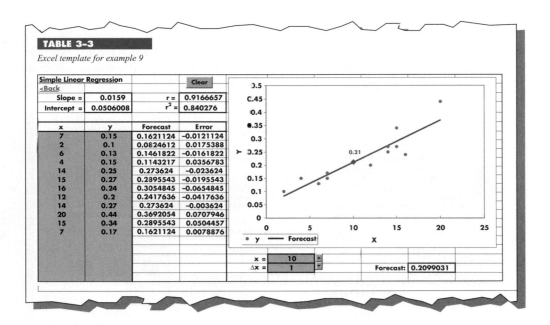

TABLE 3-3

Excel template for example 9

SOLUTIONS/TECHNOLOGY

Operations Management Center (OMC)

The OM Center, edited and maintained by Byron Finch, provides additional operations management resources for both students and instructors. Please consider this as your site for pedagogical support or reference and for students seeking current OM information. Among its features, the site covers OM resources by topic, contains links to the "top 50" company tours, offers Internet published articles and business news, and lists OM publications and organizations. The site also contains articles from *BusinessWeek* and other journals available exclusively to users of the site, daily news feeds on topics such as supply chain management, and links to many other McGraw-Hill operations management resources. To explore, visit www.mcgrawhill.ca/olc/stevenson and follow the links.

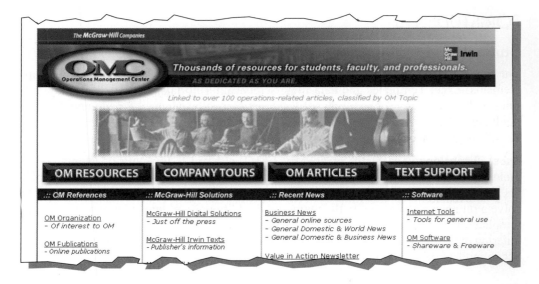

Online Learning Centre (OLC)

The Online Learning Centre located at www.mcgrawhill.ca/olc/stevenson is the text Web site with online content for both instructors and students. It provides text-specific resources such as key points, a glossary, self-grading quizzes, and solved problems for each chapter of the text.

In addition, students can open or download Excel datafiles, and use and review the dynamic Interactive Operations Management modules (such as the sample shown below).

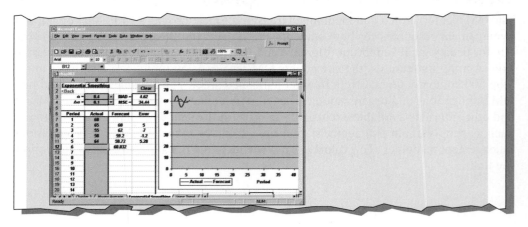

Acknowledgements

We gratefully acknowledge the input of reviewers and contributors who so vitally helped to shape the Third Canadian Edition of *Operations Management*, including:

Kirk Bailey,
Ryerson University

Walid Belassi,
Athabasca University

George Dracalopoulos,
Vanier College

Brent McKenzie,
University of Western Ontario

Ron McLachlin,
University of Manitoba

Saibal Ray,
McGill University

Mahesh C. Sharma,
Concordia University

Rob Shepherd,
Niagara College

Manish Verma,
Memorial University

We also appreciate the work of reviewers and contributors for the Second Canadian Edition:

Mitali De,
Wilfrid Laurier University

Conrad D'Souza,
Centennial College

Stephen Dudra,
British Columbia Institute of Technology

Albert Ersser,
Mohawk College

Wieslaw Kubiak,
Memorial University of Newfoundland

Shanling Li,
McGill University

Jim Mason,
University of Regina

Dave Meston,
Ryerson University

Ragu Nayak,
Centennial College

Saibal Ray,
McGill University

Austin Redlack,
Memorial University

Jane Rotering,
George Brown College

Mahesh Sharma,
Concordia University

Bill Wedley,
Simon Fraser University

Sajjad Zahir,
University of Lethbridge

We would like to thank the McGraw-Hill Ryerson staff, including Publisher Lynn Fisher, Sponsoring Editor Rhondda McNabb, the development editors Jennifer Bastarache and Tracey Haggert, Senior Supervising Editor Margaret Henderson, copy editor Shirley Corriveau, and other production staff for their good work.

Mehran Hojati
William J. Stevenson

PART ONE

Introduction

Chapter 1 introduces you to the field of operations management. It describes the nature and scope of operations management, and how operations management relates to other parts of the organization. Among the other important topics it covers are a comparison of manufacturing and service operations, a brief history of operations management, and a list of trends in business that relate to operations. After you have read this chapter, you will have a good understanding of what the operations function of a business organization encompasses.

Chapter 2 discusses operations management in a broader context, and presents the issues of competition, strategy, and productivity. After you have read Chapter 2, you will understand the importance of the operations function relative to the goals of a business organization, and how performance of production function can be measured.

Introduction includes two chapters:

Chapter 1   Introduction to Operations Management

Chapter 2   Competitiveness, Strategy, and Productivity

CHAPTER 1

Introduction to Operations Management

LEARNING OBJECTIVES

After completing this chapter, you should be able to:

1 Define the term *operations management*.

2 Identify the three major functional areas of organizations and describe how they interrelate.

3 Describe the operations function and the nature of the operations manager's job.

4 Differentiate between design and operation of production systems.

5 Compare and contrast service and manufacturing operations.

6 Briefly describe the historical evolution of operations management.

7 Describe the key aspects of operations management decision making.

8 Identify some of the current trends in business that impact operations management.

U p until the late 1990s, Sobeys was a regional chain of supermarkets in Atlantic Canada. Then, Loblaw started opening up stores in Sobeys' backyard. Sobeys' top management decided that the only way they could compete was to expand nationally. The company is now the second largest grocery chain in Canada, competing well with Loblaw.

When Wal-Mart expanded into Canada in the mid-1990s, it caught Zellers by surprise. Zellers had been operating with almost no competition, carrying old merchandize, and offering little customer service. Profits shrank and losses piled up. The parent company, Hudson's Bay Company, had to change the strategic and operations direction of Zellers with the result that Zellers is now more competitive.

This book is about operations management. The subject matter is fascinating and timely: productivity, quality, e-business, global competition, and customer service are very much in the news. All are part of operations management. This first chapter presents an introduction and overview of operations management. Among the issues it addresses are: What is operations management? Why is it important? What do operations managers do? The chapter also provides a brief description of the historical evolution of operations management and a discussion of the trends that impact operations management.

INTRODUCTION

Operations management is the management of processes or systems that create goods and/or provide services. It encompasses forecasting, capacity planning, scheduling, managing inventories, assuring quality, motivating employees, deciding where to locate facilities, buying material and equipment and maintaining them, and more.

operations management The management of processes or systems that *create goods and/or provide services.*

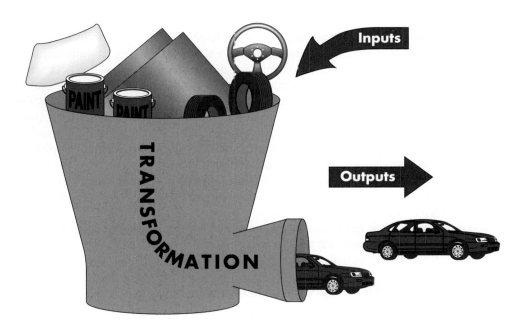

We can use an airline company to illustrate an operations system. The system includes staff and airplanes, airport facilities, and maintenance facilities, sometimes spread out over a wide territory. Most of the activities performed by management and employees fall into the realm of operations management:

Forecasting such things as seat demand for flights, the growth in air travel, and weather and landing conditions.

Capacity planning, deciding the number of planes and where to use them.

Scheduling of planes for flights and for routine maintenance; scheduling of pilots and flight attendants; and scheduling of ground crews, counter staff, and baggage handlers.

Managing inventories of such items as food and beverages and spare parts.

Assuring quality, essential in flying and maintenance operations, where the emphasis is on safety. Also important in dealing with customers at ticket counters, check-in, telephone and electronic reservations, and in-flight service, where the emphasis is on efficiency and courtesy.

Employee motivation and training in all phases of operations.

Location of facilities according to top managers' decisions on which cities to provide service for, where to locate maintenance facilities, and where to locate major and minor hubs.

Buying materials such as fuel, food, bags, and spare parts. Buying aircraft and maintaining it.

Now consider a bicycle factory. This might be primarily an *assembly* operation: buying components such as frames, tires, wheels, gears, and other items from suppliers, and then assembling bicycles. The factory might also do some of the *fabrication* work itself (forming frames, making the gears and chains) and buy mainly raw materials and a few parts and materials such as paint, nuts and bolts, and tires. Among the key operations management tasks in either case are scheduling production, deciding which components to make and which to buy, ordering parts and materials, deciding on the style of bicycle to produce and how many, purchasing new equipment to replace old or worn-out equipment, maintaining equipment, motivating workers, and ensuring that quality standards are met.

Obviously, an airline company and a bicycle factory are completely different types of operations. One is primarily a service operation, the other a producer of goods. Nonetheless, these two operations have much in common. Both involve scheduling of activities, motivating employees, ordering and managing supplies, selecting and maintaining equipment, and satisfying quality standards. And in both businesses, the success of the business depends on planning.

Many companies use operations management strategies, tactics, and actions in order to improve their efficiency and effectiveness. *Efficiency* refers to operating at minimum cost and fast, whereas *effectiveness* refers to achieving the intended goals (quality). This text contains many practical and real-life examples of operations management in the form of tours, readings, cases, photos and captions, news clips, and video clips (on the DVD). For example, there is a description of how Stone Consolidated, the paper manufacturer (now part of Abitibi Consolidated), chose a location for a landfill (Chapter 8), how Standard Aero (a small aircraft engine repairer) started its total quality management process (Chapter 9), how various food companies such as Good Humor Breyers use supply chain tools to improve their operation (Chapter 16), how various companies such as Eli Lilly Canada use warehouse management systems to operate efficiently (Chapter 11), how companies such as Celestica use just-in-time systems to work efficiently (Chapter 14), and how companies such as General Dynamics Land Systems use project management techniques and software to operate effectively (Chapter 17).

WHY STUDY OPERATIONS MANAGEMENT?

You may be wondering why you need to study operations management. Actually, there are a number of very good reasons. One is that operations management activities are at the core of *all* business organizations, regardless of what business they are in. Because a large percentage of a company's expenses occur in the operations area, such as purchasing materials and workforce salaries, more efficient operations—even a small reduction in operations costs—can result in large increases in profit. Second, a large number of all jobs are in operations management—such areas as purchasing, quality assurance, production planning and control, scheduling, logistics, inventory management, and many more (see for example, Operations Management Job Ads on the next page.) Third, activities in all of the other areas of business organizations, such as finance, accounting, human resources, management information systems (MIS), and marketing are all

Operations Management Job Ads

Purchasing Coordinator

Responsibilities

We require an experienced purchaser to manage the daily procurement of materials, tooling and shop supplies for a very busy custom machine shop. The role requires an understanding of the time constraints in the purchasing cycle including "on-demand" purchasing. Specific duties include negotiating pricing on regular purchases, following up on outstanding orders, building strong relationships with vendors, maintaining the integrity of data in the ERP system and developing strong processes and procedures for the role. The candidate must be able to deal with multiple deadlines and on-going requests for purchases from various internal sources.

Qualifications

Business Administration Diploma with 4 years experience in a manufacturing environment along with enrolment in a related certification program (PMAC or APICS). Custom machine shop experience is a definite asset. Strong computer skills with MS Office are required. Prior experience with Made2Manage ERP system is an asset.

Source: Alberta Institute of Purchasing Management Association of Canada (AIPMAC), extracted from www.aipmac.ab.ca/Employmentreferral.htm, January 25, 2005.

Materials Analyst/Coordinator

Responsibilities

- Analyze MRP and MPS to requisition purchase orders for Purchasing and creation of work orders

- Responsible for MPS of machines and parts sales
- Accountable for inventory turns, inventory levels and all inventory transactions
- Controls item master information related to min/max levels, source codes and lead times
- Responsible for cycle count program and all cycle count reconciliation and recording
- Creating various reports for inventory accuracy and open work orders
- Responsible for new parts log and maintaining accuracy
- Coordinate changes through engineering specification and engineering order changes
- Supervise Inventory Clerk

Qualifications

- Education/Experience: College diploma in Business Administration where Inventory Management and Purchasing were instructed
- Minimum College Degree in Business Administration and 8 years related experience. Good mathematical aptitude and attention to details for accuracy
- Preference given to C.P.I.M. designations
- Excellent interpersonal skills
- Proficient in the use of computer applications such as word processing and spreadsheets, as well as MRP material related system
- Ability to be a self-starter and professionally react to different situations
- Ability to manage multiple priorities in a fast paced environment

Source: http://www.apics-durham.org/cgi-bin/jobs/jobs_view.pl/index=27, extracted August 26, 2005.

interrelated with operations management activities. So it is essential for people who work in these areas to have a basic understanding of operations management.

Beyond all of this is the reality that operations management is about *management*, and *all managers* need to possess the knowledge and skills in the content areas you will learn about here. Among them are productivity, strategy, forecasting, quality, inventory control, and scheduling. Also, you will learn how to use a range of quantitative tools that enhance managerial decision making.

Careers in Operations Management

If you are thinking of a career in operations management, you can benefit by joining one or more of the following associations.

Purchasing Management Association of Canada (PMAC)

Supply Chain & Logistics Canada (SCL)

American Production and Inventory Control Society (APICS) (now called the Association for Operations Management)

www.pmac.ca

www.sclcanada.org

www.apics.org

American Society for Quality (ASQ)

Canadian Operational Research Society (CORS)

Production & Operations Management Society (POMS)

Project Management Institute (PMI)

APICS, PMAC, and ASQ all offer certification examination that can enhance your qualifications. Information about job opportunities can be obtained from all of these societies as well as from other sources, such as Decision Sciences Institute and the Institute of Industrial Engineers.

FUNCTIONS WITHIN ORGANIZATIONS

Organizations are formed to pursue goals that are achieved more efficiently and effectively by the concerted efforts of a group of people than by individuals working alone. Organizations are devoted to producing goods and/or providing services. They may be for-profit (i.e., business) or nonprofit organizations. Their goals, products, and services may be similar or quite different. Nonetheless, their functions and the way they operate are similar.

A typical organization has three basic functions: operations, finance, and marketing (see Figure 1–1). These three functions, and other supporting functions, perform different but *related* activities necessary for the operation of the organization. The functions must interact to achieve the goals and objectives of the organization, and each makes an important contribution. For instance, unless operations and marketing work together, marketing may promote goods or services that operations cannot profitably deliver, or operations may turn out goods or services for which there is no demand. Similarly, unless finance and operations work closely, funds for materials, expansion, and new equipment may not be available when needed.

Let's take a closer look at these functions.

Operations

The operations function performs all the activities *directly* related to producing goods or providing services. Hence, it exists both in fabrication and assembly operations, which are *goods-oriented*, and in areas such as health care, transportation, restaurant, and retailing, which are primarily *service-oriented* (see Table 1–1).

FIGURE 1-1

The three basic functions of business organizations and flows between them

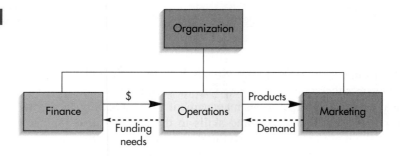

TABLE 1-1

Examples of types of operations

Type of Operations	Examples
Goods producing	Farming, mining, construction, manufacturing, power generation
Services	Warehousing, trucking, airlines
	Retailing, wholesaling, banking
	Films, radio and television
	Telephone

The operations function is the core of most organizations; it is responsible for the creation of an organization's goods or services. Inputs are used to obtain finished goods or services using one or more *transformation processes* (e.g., storing, transporting, cutting). To ensure that the desired outputs are obtained, measurements are taken at various points in the transformation process (*feedback*) and then compared with previously established standards to determine whether corrective action is needed (*control*). Figure 1–2 shows the conversion process. Table 1–2 provides two examples of inputs, transformation processes, and outputs.

It is important to note that goods and services often occur jointly. For example, having the oil changed in your car is a service, but the new oil is a good. Similarly, house painting is a service, but the paint is a good. The goods–service package is a continuum. It can range from primarily goods, with little service, to primarily service, with few goods (see Figure 1–3).

The essence of the operations function is to *add value* during the transformation process: **Value-added** is the term used to describe the difference between the cost of inputs and the value or price of outputs. In nonprofit organizations, the value of outputs (e.g., highway construction, police, and fire protection) is their value to society; the greater the value added, the greater the efficiency of these operations. In for-profit organizations, the value of outputs is measured by the prices that customers are willing to pay for those

value-added The difference between the cost of inputs and the value or price of outputs.

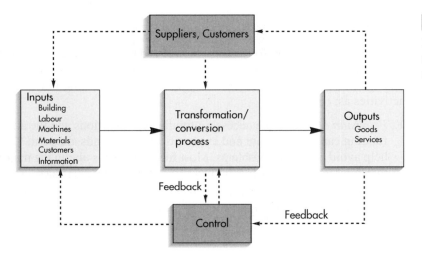

FIGURE 1–2

The operations function involves the conversion of inputs into outputs

Food Processor	Inputs	Process	Output
	Raw vegetables	Cleaning	Canned vegetables
	Metal sheets	Making cans	
	Water	Cutting	
	Energy	Cooking	
	Labour	Packing	
	Building	Labelling	
	Equipment		
Hospital	**Inputs**	**Process**	**Output**
	Doctors, nurses	Examination	Healthy patients
	Building	Surgery	
	Medical supplies	Monitoring	
	Equipment	Medication	
	Laboratories	Therapy	

TABLE 1–2

Illustrations of the transformation process

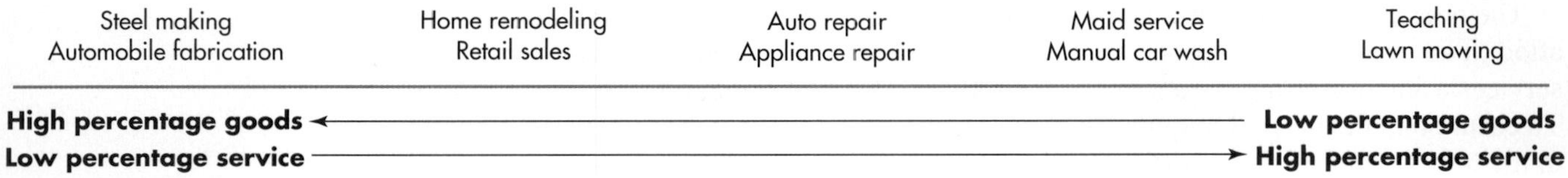

Steel making	Home remodeling	Auto repair	Maid service	Teaching
Automobile fabrication	Retail sales	Appliance repair	Manual car wash	Lawn mowing

High percentage goods ◄——————————————————————————— **Low percentage goods**

Low percentage service ———————————————————————————► **High percentage service**

FIGURE 1-3

The goods–service continuum

goods or services. Firms use the money generated by value-added for research and development, investment in new facilities and equipment, paying workers, and *profits*. Consequently, the greater the value-added, the greater the amount of funds available for these purposes.

One way that businesses attempt to become more productive (i.e., making more output with same or less inputs) is to examine critically whether the operations performed by their workers add value. Businesses consider those that do not add value wasteful. Eliminating or improving such operations decreases the cost of inputs or processing, thereby increasing the value-added. For instance, a firm may discover it is producing an item much earlier than the scheduled delivery date to a customer, thus requiring the storage of the item in a warehouse until delivery. In effect, additional costs are incurred by storing the item without adding to the value of the item. Reducing storage time would reduce the transformation cost and, hence, increase the value-added.

Finance

The finance function performs activities related to securing resources at favourable prices and allocating those resources throughout the organization. Finance and operations management personnel cooperate by exchanging information and expertise in such activities as:

1. *Provision of funds*. The necessary funding of operations and the amount and timing of funding can be important and even critical when funds are tight. Careful planning can help avoid cash-flow problems. Most for-profit firms obtain the majority of their funds through the revenues generated by sales of goods and services.

2. *Economic analysis of investment proposals*. Evaluation of alternative investments in plant and equipment requires inputs from both operations and finance people.

Marketing

Marketing's focus is on selling and/or promoting the goods or services of an organization. Marketing is also responsible for assessing customer wants and needs, and for communicating those needs and feedback to operations people and to product design people (usually engineers in manufacturing companies). That is, operations needs information about demand so that it can plan accordingly (e.g., purchase materials or schedule work), while product design people need information that relates to improving current products and services, and designing new ones. Marketing, design, and production must work closely together to successfully implement design changes and to develop and produce new products. Marketing can provide valuable insight on what competitors are doing. One important piece of information marketing needs from operations is the manufacturing or service **lead time** in order to give customers realistic estimates of how long it will take to fill their orders.

lead time The time between ordering a good or service and receiving it.

Thus, marketing, operations, and finance must interface on product and process design, forecasting, setting realistic schedules, and quality and quantity decisions.

Other Functions

There are a host of other supporting functions that interface with operations (see Figure 1–4).

FIGURE 1-4

Operations interfaces with a number of supporting functions

Accounting supplies information to management on costs of labour, materials, and overhead, and may provide reports on items such as scrap, downtime, and inventories. Accounting includes accounts payables and accounts receivables. Accountants gather the information needed for financial statements as well.

Management information systems (*MIS*) is concerned with providing management with the information it needs to effectively manage. This occurs mainly through designing systems (hardware and software) to capture relevant information and preparing reports.

Purchasing has responsibility for procurement of materials, supplies, equipment, and services. Close contact with operations is necessary to ensure correct quantities and timing of purchases. The purchasing department is often called on to evaluate vendors for quality, delivery time reliability, service, price, and flexibility. Purchasing may also be involved in arranging incoming transportation, receiving, and inspecting the purchased goods.

The *personnel* or *human resources* department is concerned with recruitment and training of personnel, labour relations, contract negotiations, wage and salary administration, and ensuring the health and safety of employees.

Product design in manufacturing companies usually is done by engineers, but in other companies it could be done by architects, scientists, chemists, and chefs. Designers create goods and services from information given to them on markets by marketing and provide product specifications to operations to make the products.

Maintenance is responsible for general upkeep and repair of equipment, buildings and grounds, heating and air-conditioning; removing toxic wastes; parking; and perhaps security.

Manufacturing engineering is responsible for design or purchase of the machines and equipment needed in the production process. Also called process engineers, they are mainly trained as mechanical engineers, but other fields like electrical and chemical may also be needed.

Logistics involves the transportation of raw material to the plant, storage, and shipping of goods to warehouses, retail outlets, or final customers.

Many of these interfaces are elaborated on in later chapters.

THE SCOPE OF OPERATIONS MANAGEMENT

We have already noted that the operations manager is responsible for the creation of goods and services. This encompasses acquisition of resources and the conversion of raw material into outputs using one or more transformation processes. This involves designing, planning, executing, and controlling the elements that make up the process.

A primary function of an operations manager is to guide the system by decision making. Certain decisions affect the *design* of the system, and others affect the *operation* (planning, execution, control) of the system. Design decisions are usually strategic and long term (1–5 years ahead), whereas planning decisions are tactical and medium term (1–12 months ahead), and execution and control decisions are short-term (1–12 weeks ahead).

System design involves decisions that relate to system capacity, the geographic location of facilities, arrangement of departments and placement of equipment within physical structures, product and service planning, and acquisition of equipment. *System operation* involves management of personnel, inventory planning and control, production planning, scheduling, project management, and quality assurance. In many instances, the operations manager is more involved in day-to-day operating decisions than with decisions relating to system design. However, the operations manager has a vital stake in system design because *system design essentially determines many of the parameters of system operation*. For example, costs, space, capacities, and quality are directly affected by design decisions. Even though the operations manager is not solely responsible for making all design decisions, he or she can provide those decision makers with a wide range of information that will have a bearing on their decisions. Table 1–3 provides additional details on the nature and scope of operations decisions, and indicates where the topics are discussed in this textbook.

TABLE 1–3	Decision Area	Basic Questions	Chapter
Design and operation decisions	Forecasting	What will the demand be?	3
	Design		
	Product and service design	What do customers want? How can products and services be improved?	4
	Capacity (long term)	How much capacity will be needed? How can the organization best meet capacity requirements?	5
	Process selection	What processes should the organization use?	6
	Layout	What is the best arrangement for departments, machines and equipment, in terms of work flow?	6
	Design of work systems	What is the best way to motivate employees? How can productivity be improved? How to measure work? How to improve work methods?	7
	Location	What is a satisfactory location for a facility (factory, store, etc.)?	8
	Operation (planning, execution and control)		
	Quality	How is quality defined? How are quality goods and services achieved and improved?	9
	Quality control	Are processes performing adequately? What standards should be used? Are standards being met?	10
	Inventory management	How much to order? When to reorder? Which items should get the most attention?	11
	Aggregate planning	How much capacity will be needed over the medium term? How can capacity needs best be met?	12
	Material requirements planning	What material, parts, and subassemblies will be needed, and when?	13
	Just-in-time manufacturing	How to manage production so that it is fast and lean?	14
	Scheduling	How can jobs best be scheduled? When to schedule staff?	15
	Supply chain management	Which supplier to choose? How to transport goods?	16
	Project management	Which activities are the most critical to the success of a project? What resources will be needed, and when will they be needed?	17
	Waiting lines	What service capacity is appropriate?	18

DIFFERENTIATING FEATURES OF OPERATIONS SYSTEMS

A number of features differentiate operations systems. A brief discussion of some of these features will help you develop a better understanding of the nature and scope of operations management. The three described are degree of product standardization, type of process, and production of goods versus services.

Degree of Product Standardization

The output of production systems can range from highly standardized to highly customized. *Standardized output* means that there is a high degree of uniformity (i.e., little variety) in goods or services. Standardized goods include radios, televisions, computers, newspapers, canned foods, automobile tires, pens and pencils, and commodities such as steel, sugar, and paper. Standardized services include automatic car washes, televised newscasts, taped lectures, commercial airline service, fast food service, motels, utilities, and education. *Customized output* means that the product or service is designed for a specific case or individual. Customized goods include eyeglasses, custom-fitted clothing, window glass (cut to order), and customized draperies. Customized services include tailoring, taxi rides, and surgery.

Systems with standardized output can generally take advantage of standardized methods, less-skilled workers, materials, and mechanization, all of which contribute to higher volumes and lower unit costs. In custom systems, on the other hand, each job is sufficiently different so that workers must be more skilled, the work moves slower, and the work is less susceptible to mechanization.

Type of Process

The degree of product standardization and the volume (quantity) of output of a product or service influence the way a firm organizes its production process. On one end of the scale is a single, large-scale project such as the launching of a space shuttle (service) or the construction of a skyscraper (product). On the other end is a continuous process, such as oil refining. Between these extremes are customized individual units of output (job shop), such as custom-made furniture and auto repair; batches, such as paint and food products; and mass production (repetitive process), such as automobiles, personal computers, and appliances.

You will learn more about these different types of operations in later chapters.

Production of Goods versus Services

Production of goods results in a *tangible output*, such as an automobile, a clock radio, a golf ball, a refrigerator—anything that we can see or touch. It may take place in a factory, but can occur elsewhere. Service, on the other hand, generally implies an *act*. A physician's examination, TV and auto repair, lawn care, and projecting a film in a theatre are examples of services. The majority of service jobs fall into these categories:

Government services (federal, provincial, municipal).

Wholesale/retail (clothing, food, appliances, stationery, toys, etc.).

Financial services (banking, stock brokerage, insurance, etc.).

Health care (doctors, dentists, hospitals, etc.).

Professional services (lawyers, accountants, architects)

Personal services (laundry, dry cleaning, hair/beauty, gardening, etc.).

Business services (data processing, e-business, advertising, employment agencies, etc.).

Education (schools, colleges, universities, etc.).

Hotels and restaurants

Recreation

Transportation and warehousing

Utilities

Manufacturing and service are often similar in terms of *what* is done but different in terms of *how* it is done. For example, both involve design and operation decisions. Manufacturers must decide what size factory is needed. Service organizations (e.g., hospitals) must decide what size building is needed. Both must make decisions on location, scheduling and control of operations, and allocation of scarce resources.

Manufacturing and service organizations differ chiefly because manufacturing is goods-oriented and service is act-oriented. The differences involve the following:

1. Customer contact, use of inventories, and demand variability
2. Uniformity of input
3. Labour content of jobs
4. Uniformity of output
5. Measurement of productivity
6. Quality assurance

Let us consider each of these differences.

 1. Often, by its nature, service involves a much higher degree of customer contact than manufacturing. The performance of a service often occurs at the point of consumption. For example, repairing a leaky roof must take place where the roof is, and surgery requires the presence of the patient. On the other hand, manufacturing allows a separation between production and consumption, so that manufacturing may occur away from the consumer. This permits a fair degree of latitude in selecting work methods, assigning jobs, scheduling work, and exercising control over operations. In addition, product-oriented operations can build up inventories of finished goods (e.g., cars, refrigerators), enabling them to absorb some of the shocks caused by variable demand. Service operations, however, cannot build up inventories and are much more sensitive to demand variability—banks and supermarkets alternate between lines of customers waiting for service and idle tellers or cashiers waiting for customers.

 2. Service operations are subject to greater variability of inputs than typical manufacturing operations. Each patient, each lawn, and each auto repair presents a specific problem that often must be diagnosed before it can be remedied. Manufacturing operations often have the ability to carefully control the amount of variability of inputs.

3. Services often require a higher labour content whereas manufacturing can be more capital-intensive (i.e., mechanized).

4. Because high mechanization generates products with low variability, manufacturing tends to be smooth and efficient; service activities sometimes appear to be slow and awkward, and output is more variable. Automated services are an exception to this.

5. Measurement of productivity (i.e., output per unit time) is more straightforward in manufacturing due to the high degree of uniformity of most manufactured items. In service operations, variations in demand intensity and in requirements from job to job make productivity measurement considerably more difficult. For example, compare the productivity of two doctors. One may have a large number of routine cases while the other does not, so their productivity appears to differ unless a very careful analysis is made.

6. Quality assurance is more challenging in services when production and consumption occur at the same time. In manufacturing, errors can be corrected before the customer receives the output.

Although it is convenient to think in terms of systems devoted exclusively to goods or services, most real systems are a blend of both. For instance, maintenance and repair of equipment are services performed by virtually every manufacturing firm. Similarly, most service organizations typically sell goods that complement their services. Thus, a lawn-care firm usually sells goods such as weed killers, fertilizers, and grass seed. Hospitals dispense drugs along with health services. Restaurants sell food. Movie theatres sell popcorn, candy, and beverages.

The service sector and the manufacturing sector are both important to the economy. The service sector has been growing and now accounts for more than 70 percent of jobs in Canada. See Figure 1–5.

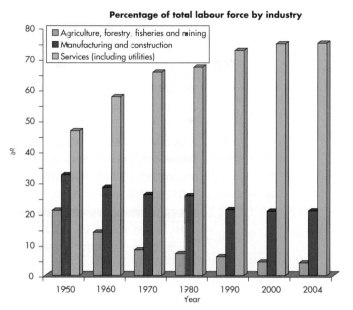

Percentage of total labour force by industry

FIGURE 1-5

Percentage of total labour force by industry

Source: Adapted from Statistics Canada CANSIM database, http://cansim2.statcan.ca, Table 282–0094, various series, January 24, 2005; and census data.

THE OPERATIONS MANAGER'S JOB

The operations manager is the key figure in the system: he or she has the ultimate responsibility for the creation of goods or provision of services.

The kinds of jobs that operations managers oversee vary tremendously from organization to organization largely because of the different products or services involved. Thus, managing a banking operation obviously requires a different kind of expertise than managing a steelmaking operation. However, in a very important respect, the jobs are the same: They are both essentially *managerial.* In every case, the operations manager must coordinate the use of resources through the management processes of planning, organizing, directing, and controlling.

Examples of the responsibilities of operations managers according to these classifications are given in Table 1–4. Note that operations managers require both technical and behavioural competence.

In a survey of production/operations managers of approximately 250 Australian companies (two-thirds manufacturing), the following characteristics were discovered: approximately half joined the company after trade school and were promoted through ranks; thus, they were deficient in business management, accounting/finance, and computer skills. Approximately half had total responsibility over planning, quality, and maintenance, whereas the other half provided major inputs into these decisions. Approximately half would like more control over planning, information systems, personnel, and quality decisions. Most production/operations managers were given targets for cost reduction and

Planning	Organizing
Capacity	Degree of centralization
Location	Departments
Mix of products and services	Subcontracting
Production process	Suppliers
Layout	Staffing
Controlling	Directing
Inventory control	Scheduling
Quality control	Issuance of work orders
Production pace	Job assignments
Motivation	Purchasing
Cost control	Logistics

TABLE 1-4

Responsibilities of operations managers

FIGURE 1-6

Level of job satisfaction

Source: B. D'Netto, A. S. Sohal, and J. Trevillyan, "An Empirical Assessment of the Production/Operations Manager's Job," *Production and Inventory Management Journal*, 1st Quarter 1998, 39(1), pp. 57–61. Reprinted with permission of APICS, The Association for Operations Management.

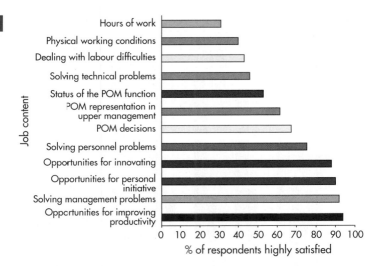

productivity improvement. A list of job content and satisfaction of respondents for each is given in Figure 1–6. Most enjoy these challenges, whereas more than half are not happy with the heavy hours of work, working conditions, dealing with labour difficulty, and solving technical problems. Further questions revealed that most are happy with their compensation, work variety, work importance, and autonomy, whereas most are unhappy with their benefits and feedback from top management.

OPERATIONS MANAGERS AND DECISION MAKING

The chief role of an operations manager is that of a decision maker. In this capacity, the operations manager exerts considerable influence over the degree to which the goals and objectives of the organization are realized.

Throughout this book, you will encounter the broad range of decisions that operations managers must make, and you will be introduced to the tools necessary to handle those decisions. This section describes general approaches to decision making, including the use of models, quantitative approaches, analysis of trade-offs, the systems approach, establishing priorities, and ethics.

Models

model An abstraction of reality; a simplified representation of something.

A **model** is an abstraction of reality, a simplified representation of something. For example, a child's toy car is a physical model of a real automobile. Mathematical models represent important characteristics of the object by mathematical symbols and their relationship by mathematical equations and inequalities. Examples of mathematical models include formulas and sets of equations. Schematic models are graphs, charts, and drawings. Common statistical models include Normal distribution and regression equations.

Real life involves an overwhelming amount of detail, much of which is irrelevant for any particular problem. Models ignore the unimportant details so that attention can be concentrated on the most important aspects of a situation, thus increasing the opportunity to understand a problem and its solution.

Because schematic, mathematical, and statistical models play a significant role in operations management decision making, they are heavily integrated into the material of this text. For each model, try to learn (1) its purpose, (2) how it is used to generate results, (3) how these results are interpreted and used, and (4) what assumptions and limitations apply.

Quantitative Approaches

Quantitative approaches to problem solving often embody an attempt to obtain optimum solutions to the mathematical models of managerial problems. This is sometimes done by solving a set of equations. A popular example is *linear programming*, which is widely used for optimum allocation of scarce resources. *Queuing techniques* are useful for analyzing situations in which waiting lines form. *Inventory techniques* are widely used to control inventories. *Project scheduling techniques* such as PERT (program evaluation and review technique) are useful for planning, coordinating, and controlling large-scale projects. *Forecasting techniques* are widely used in forecasting demand. *Statistical techniques* are currently used in many areas of decision making, including quality control.

Many of these quantitative techniques require computers, and are somewhat time-consuming. In contrast, a heuristic approach is a quick way to find a good solution. For many decisions, heuristic may be the only practical solution.

Analysis of Trade-offs

One type of heuristic approach is *trade-off* analysis. For example, (a) in deciding on the amount of inventory to stock, the manager may take into account the trade-off between the increased level of customer service that the additional inventory would yield and the increased costs required to stock that inventory, (b) in selecting a piece of equipment, a manager may evaluate the merits of extra features relative to the cost of those extra features, (c) in the scheduling of overtime to increase output, the manager may weigh the value of the increased output against the higher costs of overtime (e.g., higher labour costs, lower productivity, lower quality, and greater risk of accidents).

Throughout this book you will be presented with solution methods that reflect these kinds of trade-offs. Managers sometimes deal with these decisions by listing the advantages and disadvantages—the pros and cons—of a course of action to better understand the consequences of the decisions they must make. In some instances, managers add weights to the items on their list that reflect the relative importance of various factors. This can help them "net out" the potential impacts of the trade-offs on their decision. An example of this is the factor-rating approach described in Chapter 8 on facilities location.

The Systems Approach

A **system** can be defined as a set of interrelated parts that must work together. In a business organization, the organization can be thought of as a system composed of subsystems (e.g., marketing subsystem, operations subsystem, finance subsystems), which in turn are composed of lower subsystems. The systems approach emphasizes interrelationships among subsystems. Hence, from a systems viewpoint, the output and objectives of the organization as a whole take precedence over those of any one subsystem.

system A set of interrelated parts that must work together.

The systems approach is essential whenever something is being designed, redesigned, implemented, improved, or otherwise changed. It is important to take into account the impact on all parts of the system. For example, to investigate if the upcoming model of an automobile will have antilock brakes, a designer must take into account how customers will view the change, instructions for using the brakes, chances for misuse, the cost of producing the new brakes, installation procedures, recycling worn-out brakes, and repair procedures. In addition, workers will need training to make and/or assemble the brakes, production scheduling may change, inventory procedures may have to change, quality standards will have to be established, advertising must be informed of the new features, and parts suppliers must be selected.

Establishing Priorities

In virtually every situation, managers discover that certain elements are more important than others. Recognizing this fact of life enables the managers to direct their efforts to where they will do the most good and to avoid wasting time and energy on insignificant elements.

It is axiomatic that a relatively few factors are often most important, so that dealing with those factors will generally have a disproportionately larger impact on the results achieved. This is referred to as the **Pareto phenomenon**, which means some things (a few) will be very important for achieving an objective or solving a problem, and other

Pareto phenomenon A few factors account for a high percentage of the occurrence of some event(s).

things (many) will not. The implication is that a manager should examine each situation, searching for the few factors that will have the greatest impact, and give them the highest priority. This is one of the most important and pervasive concepts in operations management. In fact, this concept can be applied at all levels of management and to every aspect of decision making, both professional and personal.

Ethics

Operations managers, like all managers, have the responsibility to make ethical decisions. Ethical issues arise in many aspects of operations management, including:

- worker safety: providing adequate training, maintaining equipment in good working condition, maintaining a safe working environment;
- product safety: providing products that minimize the risk of injury to users or damage to property or the environment;
- the environment: not doing things that will harm the environment;
- closing facilities: taking into account the impact on a community, and honouring commitments that have been made.

In making decisions, managers must consider how their decisions will affect shareholders, employees, customers, the community at large, and the environment. Finding solutions that will be in the best interests of all of these stakeholders is not always easy, but it is a goal that all managers should strive to achieve.

THE HISTORICAL EVOLUTION OF OPERATIONS MANAGEMENT

Systems for production have existed since ancient times. The Great Wall of China, the Egyptian pyramids, the ships of the Spanish empire, and the roads and aqueducts of the Romans provide examples of the human ability to organize for production. Even so, most of these examples could be classified as "public works" projects.

craft production System in which highly skilled workers use simple, flexible tools to produce small quantities of customized goods.

In the earliest days of manufacturing, goods were produced using **craft production**: highly skilled workers using simple, flexible tools produced goods according to customer specifications. Goods were produced in small shops by craftsmen and their apprentices. Under that system, it was common for one person to be responsible for making a product, such as a horse-drawn wagon or a piece of furniture, from start to finish. Only simple tools were available; the machines that we use today had not been invented.

Craft production had major shortcomings. Because products were made by skilled craftsmen who custom-fitted parts, production was slow and costly. And when parts failed, the replacements also had to be custom made, which was also slow and costly. Another shortcoming was that production costs did not decrease as volume increased; there were no *economies of scale*, which would have provided a major incentive for companies to expand. Instead, many small companies emerged, each with its own set of standards.

Prior to the 1700s, business activities in Canada were limited to fishing and fur trade. Under a practice called *mercantilism*, raw materials were exported to Europe for further processing and manufacturing. Companies such as the Hudson's Bay Company were importing British-made goods to trade with local populations. All manufactured products came from Europe. The production of goods for sale, at least in the modern sense, and the modern factory system had their roots in the Industrial Revolution.

The Industrial Revolution

The Industrial Revolution began in the 1770s in England and spread to the rest of Europe and to North America during the nineteenth century. A number of innovations changed the face of production forever by substituting machine power for human power. Perhaps the most significant of these was the steam engine, made practical by James Watt around 1764, because it provided a source of power to operate machines in factories. The spinning jenny (1770) and power loom (1785) revolutionized the textile industry. Supplies of coal and iron ore provided material for generating power and making machinery. The new machines, made of iron, were much stronger and more durable than the simple wooden machines they replaced. Two concepts assisted in mass production: division of labour and interchangeable parts.

Division of labour, which Adam Smith wrote about in *The Wealth of Nations* (1776), means that an operation is divided up into a series of many small tasks and individual workers are assigned to one of those tasks. Unlike craft production, where each worker was responsible for doing many tasks and thus required skill, with division of labour the tasks were so narrow that virtually no skill was required.

division of labour Breaking up a production process into small tasks so that each worker performs a small portion of the overall job.

Interchangeable parts is sometimes attributed to Eli Whitney, an American inventor who applied the concept to assembling muskets in the late 1700s. The basis for interchangeable parts is to standardize parts so that any part in a batch of parts would fit. This meant that parts did not have to be custom fitted, as they were in craft production. The standardized parts could also be used for replacement parts. The result was a tremendous decrease in assembly time and cost.

interchangeable parts Parts of a product made to such precision that they do not have to be custom fitted.

Soon after their invention in Britain, the iron-making and steam engine technologies were imported into North America. In Canada, a few small mills began operating in the first half of the 1800s. By the second half of the 1800s, canals and railways were built, and timber was being exported.

The discovery of electricity by Edison in the late 1800s allowed replacement of electricity for steam as a power source, improving the efficiency and working environment of factories.

Despite the major changes that were taking place, management theory and practice had not progressed much from early days. What was needed was an enlightened and more systematic approach to management.

Scientific Management

The scientific management era brought widespread changes to the management of factories. The movement was spearheaded by the American efficiency engineer and inventor Frederick Taylor, who is often referred to as the father of scientific management. Taylor believed in a "science of management" based on observation, measurement, analysis and improvement of work methods, and economic incentives. He studied work methods in great detail to identify the best method for doing each job. Taylor also believed that management should be responsible for planning, carefully selecting and training workers, finding the best way to perform each job, achieving cooperation between management and workers, and separating management activities from work activities.

Taylor's methods emphasized maximizing output. They were not always popular with workers, who sometimes thought the methods were used to unfairly increase output without a corresponding increase in compensation. Certainly some companies did abuse workers in their quest for efficiency. Eventually, the public outcry reached the halls of the U.S. Congress, and hearings were held on the matter. Taylor himself was called to testify in 1911, the same year in which his classic book *The Principles of Scientific Management* was published. The publicity from those hearings actually helped scientific management principles to achieve wide acceptance in industry.

A number of other pioneers also contributed heavily to this movement, including the following:

Frank Gilbreth was an industrial engineer who is often referred to as the father of motion study. He developed the principles of motion economy that could be applied to incredibly small portions of a task.

Lillian Gilbreth, a psychologist and the wife of Frank Gilbreth, worked with her husband, focusing on the human factor in work. (The Gilbreths were the subject of a classic 1950s film, *Cheaper by the Dozen*.) Many of her studies in the 1920s dealt with worker fatigue.

Henry Gantt recognized the value of nonmonetary rewards to motivate workers, and developed a widely used system for scheduling, called Gantt charts.

Henry Ford, the great industrialist, employed scientific management techniques in his factories.

During the early part of the twentieth century, automobiles were just coming into vogue in North America. Ford's Model T was such a success that the company had trouble keeping up with orders for the cars. In an effort to improve the efficiency of operations, Ford adopted the scientific management principles espoused by Frederick Taylor. He also introduced the *moving assembly line*.

mass production System in which lower-skilled workers use specialized machinery to produce high volumes of standardized goods.

Among Ford's many contributions was the introduction of **mass production** to the automotive industry, a system of production in which large volumes of standardized goods are produced by low-skilled or semiskilled workers using highly specialized, and often costly, equipment. Ford was able to do this by taking advantage of a number of important concepts. Perhaps the key concept that launched mass production was interchangeable parts. Ford accomplished this by standardizing the gauges used to measure parts during production and by using newly developed processes to produce uniform parts. A second concept used by Ford was the division of labour. Together, these concepts enabled Ford to tremendously increase the production rate at his factories using readily available inexpensive labour.

The Industrial Revolution and scientific management allowed some industrialization in Canada in the beginning of the twentieth century. These changes allowed for more effective exploitation of Canada's resources, such as minerals and agriculture. The National Policy import tariffs encouraged foreign entrepreneurs and companies, mainly Americans, to set up factories and sales offices in Canada; the transfer of technology helped both countries. For an example, see the book *Harvest Triumphant*, which describes the establishment and growth of Massey Ferguson as one of the world leaders in agricultural harvesting machinery. The United States replaced Britain as the largest trading partner and investor in Canada in 1926.

The Human Relations Movement

Both Taylor and Ford expected workers to perform like robots. This paved the way for the human relations movement. Whereas the scientific management movement heavily emphasized the technical aspects of work design, the human relations movement emphasized the importance of the human element in job design. In the following decades, there was much emphasis on motivation. During the 1930s, Elton Mayo conducted studies at the Hawthorne division of Western Electric. His studies revealed that in addition to the physical and technical aspects of work, giving special attention to workers is critical for improving productivity. During the 1940s, Abraham Maslow developed motivational theories, which Frederick Hertzberg refined in the 1950s. Douglas McGregor added to this in the 1960s. In the 1970s, William Ouchi combined the Japanese approach, with such features as lifetime employment, employee problem solving, and consensus building, and the traditional Western approach that features short-term employment, specialists, and individual decision making and responsibility.

Decision Models and Computers

The factory movement was accompanied by the development of several quantitative techniques. F. W. Harris developed one of the first models in 1915: a mathematical model for inventory management. In the 1930s, three co-workers at Bell Telephone Labs developed statistical procedures for sampling and quality control.

At first, these quantitative models were not widely used in industry. However, the onset of the Second World War changed that. The war generated tremendous pressures on manufacturing output, and specialists from many disciplines combined efforts to achieve advancements in the military and in manufacturing. This area became known as operations research. After the war, efforts to develop and refine quantitative tools for decision making continued, facilitated by the advent of the mainframe computer in 1951.

This resulted in decision models for forecasting, production planning (using the linear program of Dantzig), project management, and other areas of operations management.

During the 1960s and 1970s, quantitative techniques were highly regarded (these modelling and solutions for business are called *management science*); in the 1980s, they lost some favour. However, the widespread use of personal computers (invented in the late 1970s by Apple Computers) and user-friendly software in the workplace is causing a resurgence in the popularity of these techniques. In 1975, Orlicky proposed Material Requirements Planning (MRP), mainly for assembly operations.

In the middle to late 1980s, network computing began to increase, with applications such as electronic data interchange (EDI) and the ability to instantaneously receive point-of-sale data. This has led to more cooperation with the suppliers in the form of partnering, and formation of supply chains. In the mid-1990s, the Internet began to play a major role in business operations, and more and more companies are using enterprise resources planning (ERP) software to coordinate their sales, materials management, production planning/manufacturing, and accounting/finance activities.

The Influence of Japanese Manufacturers

A number of Japanese manufacturers developed or refined management practices that increased the productivity of their operations and the quality of their products. This made them very competitive, sparking interest in their approaches by companies outside Japan. Their approaches emphasized quality and continual improvement, worker teams and empowerment, and achieving customer satisfaction. The Japanese can be credited with spawning the "quality revolution" that occurred in industrialized countries, and with generating widespread interest in just-in-time production.

The influence of the Japanese on North American manufacturing and service companies has been enormous and promises to continue for the foreseeable future. Because of that influence, this book will provide considerable information about Japanese methods and successes.

Lean production systems are so named because they use much less of certain resources than mass production systems use—less space, less inventory, and fewer workers—to produce a comparable amount of output. Lean production systems use a

lean production System that uses minimal amounts of resources to produce a high volume of high-quality goods with some variety.

New Balance Athletic Shoe, Inc., Lawrence, Massachusetts facility. This facility handles the entire manufacturing process, from cutting raw materials to assembly. While New Balance employs more than 2,400 associates over 120 countries, it is the only company manufacturing athletic shoes in the U.S.

www.newbalance.com

highly skilled workforce and flexible equipment. In effect, they incorporate advantages of both mass production (high volume, low unit cost) and craft production (variety and flexibility). And quality is higher than in mass production. Lean production is a broad approach to just-in-time.

The skilled workers in lean production systems are more involved in maintaining and improving the system than their mass production counterparts. They are taught to stop production if they discover a defect, and to work with other employees to find and correct the cause of the defect so that it won't recur. This results in an increasing level of quality over time, and eliminates the need to inspect and rework at the end of the line.

Because lean production systems operate with lower amounts of inventory, additional emphasis is placed on anticipating when problems might occur *before* they arise, and avoiding those problems through careful planning. Even so, problems still occur at times, and quick resolution is important. Workers participate in both the planning and correction stages. Technical experts are still used, but more as consultants rather than substitutes for workers. The focus is on designing a system (products and process) so that workers will be able to achieve high levels of quality and quantity.

Compared to workers in traditional systems, much more is expected of workers in lean production systems. They must be able to function in teams, playing active roles in operating and improving the system. Individual creativity is much less important than team success. Responsibilities also are much greater, which can lead to pressure and anxiety not present in traditional systems. Moreover, a flatter organizational structure means career paths are not as steep in lean production organizations. Workers tend to become generalists rather than specialists, another contrast to more traditional organizations.

Unions often oppose conversion from a traditional system to a lean system because they view the added responsibility and multiple tasks as an expansion of job requirements without comparable increases in pay. In addition, workers sometimes complain that the company is the primary beneficiary of employee-generated improvements.

Table 1–5 provides a comparison of craft production, mass production, and lean production. Keep in mind that all three of these modes of production are in existence today.

Table 1–6 provides a chronological summary of some of the key developments in the evolution of operations management.

TABLE 1-5

A comparison of craft, mass, and lean production

	Craft Production	Mass Production	Lean Production
Description	High variety, customized output, with one or a few skilled workers responsible for an entire unit of output.	High volume of standardized output, emphasis on volume. Capitalizes on division of labour, specialized equipment, and interchangeable parts.	Moderate to high volume of output, with more variety than mass production. Fewer mass production buffers such as extra workers, inventory, or time. Emphasis on quality. Employee involvement and teamwork are important.
Examples of Goods and Services	Home remodelling and landscaping, tailoring, portrait painting, diagnosis and treatment of injuries, surgery.	Automobiles, computers, calculators, sewing machines, compact discs, mail sorting, cheque clearing.	Similar to mass production.
Advantages	Wide range of choice, output tailored to customer needs.	Low cost per unit, requires mostly low-skilled workers.	Flexibility, variety, high quality of goods.
Disadvantages	Slow, requires skilled workers, few economies of scale, high cost, and low standardization.	Rigid system, difficult to accommodate changes in output volume, product design, or process design. Volume may be emphasized at the expense of quality.	No safety nets to offset any system breakdowns, fewer opportunities for employee advancement, more worker stress, requires higher-skilled workers than mass production.

Approximate Date	Contribution/Concept	Originator
1764	Steam engine	James Watt
1776	Division of labour	Adam Smith
1790	Interchangeable parts	Eli Whitney
1911	Principles of scientific management	Frederick W. Taylor
1911	Motion study; use of industrial psychology	Frank and Lillian Gilbreth
1912	Chart for scheduling activities	Henry Gantt
1913	Moving assembly line	Henry Ford
1915	Mathematical model for inventory management	F. W. Harris
1930	Hawthorne studies on worker motivation	Elton Mayo
1935	Statistical procedures for sampling and quality control	H. F. Dodge, H. G. Romig, W. Shewhart, L. H. C. Tippett
1940	Operations research applications in warfare	Operations research groups
1947	Linear programming	George Dantzig
1951	Commercial digital computers	Sperry Univac
1960s	Computer-aided automation	Numerous
1970s	Personal computers	Apple
1975	Material requirements planning	Orlicky
1980s	Emphasis on quality and time-based competition	Japanese manufacturers, especially Toyota, and Taiichi Ohno
1990s	Internet, supply chains	Numerous
2000s	E-business	Numerous

TABLE 1-6

Historical summary of operations management

TRENDS IN BUSINESS

Businesses must constantly monitor current trends and take them into account in their strategies and operations management. In this section we touch on some of the key trends that are occurring in businesses around the world.

Major Trends

1. *The Internet and e-business*. The *Internet* offers great potential for business organizations, but the potential as well as the risks must be clearly understood in order to determine if and how to exploit this potential. In many cases, the Internet has altered the way companies compete in the marketplace.

Electronic business, or **e-business**, involves the use of the Internet to transact business. E-business is changing the way business organizations interact with their customers and their suppliers. Most familiar to the general public is e-commerce, consumer–business transactions such as buying online or requesting information. However, business-to-business transactions, such as e-procurement, represent an increasing share of e-business. E-business is receiving increased attention from business owners and managers in developing strategies, planning, and decision making.

e-business Use of the Internet to transact business.

2. *Technology and technology management*. Technological advances have led to a vast array of new products and processes. Undoubtedly the computer has had—and will continue to have—the greatest impact on business organizations. It has revolutionized the way companies operate. Applications include product design, processing technology, information processing, and communication. Obviously there have been—and will continue to be—many benefits from technological advances. However, technological advance also places a burden on management. For example, management must keep abreast of changes and quickly assess both their benefits and risks. Predicting advances can be tricky at best, and new technologies often carry a high price tag and usually a high cost to operate or repair. And in the case of computer operating systems, as new systems are introduced, support for older versions is discontinued, making periodic upgrades

necessary. Conflicting technologies can exist that make technological choices even more difficult. Technological innovations in both *products* and *processes* will continue to change the way businesses operate, and hence, require continuing attention.

3. *Globalization*. Global competition, global markets, global supply chains, and global operations are having a growing impact on the strategies and operations of businesses, large and small, around the world. The General Agreement on Tariffs and Trade (GATT) of 1994 and later agreements of the World Trade Organization reduced the tariffs and subsidies in many countries, expanding world trade.

In addition, the Free Trade Agreement and NAFTA have increased trade with the U.S. to as much as 80 percent of total foreign trade of Canada. The implication is the need for improved efficiency and increased quality. However, occasionally there is protectionism, such as U.S. tariffs on Canadian softwood lumber.

supply chain A sequence of activities and organizations involved in producing and delivering a good or service.

4. *Supply chain management.* A **supply chain** is the sequence of organizations—their facilities and activities—that are involved in producing and delivering a product or service. The sequence begins with basic suppliers of raw materials and extends all the way to the final customer. Facilities might include warehouses, factories, processing centres, offices, distribution centres, and retail outlets. Activities include forecasting, purchasing, inventory management, information management, quality assurance, scheduling, production, distribution, delivery, and customer service.

Figure 1.7 provides an illustration of a supply chain: a chain that begins with wheat growing on a farm and ends with a customer buying a loaf of bread in a supermarket. Notice that the value of the product increases as it moves through the supply chain.

FIGURE 1-7

A supply chain for bread

A growing aspect of supply chain management is *outsourcing*—that is, buying goods or services rather than producing goods or performing services within the organization.

5. *Agility* is the ability of an organization to respond quickly to demands or opportunities. The Toyota production system (just-in-time) and rapid new product development are examples of agility. A major requirement for this is flexibility.

6. *Quality and process improvement*. Given a boost by the "quality revolution" of the 1980s and 1990s, quality is now ingrained in business. Where once quality was a criterion for being an "order winner," it has now become a criterion for being an "order qualifier." Some businesses use the term *total quality management (TQM)* to describe their quality efforts which emphasize *customer satisfaction* and involve *teamwork*. Process improvement can result in improved quality, cost reduction, and *time reduction*.

7. *Environmental issues*. Pollution control and reduction in waste and energy use are key issues managers must contend with. There is increasing emphasis on reducing waste, using less-toxic chemicals (e.g., lawncare services shifting to environmentally friendly approaches), recycling, making it easier for consumers to recycle products (e.g., including a shipping container for returning used laser printer cartridges), and designing products and parts that can be reused (remanufacturing products such as copying machines). The term *environmentally responsible manufacturing* is sometimes used to describe these policies.

Canada is a signatory to the Kyoto agreement which is to reduce greenhouse gases, including CO_2, to 6 percent below the 1990 level, by the year 2012. Some companies such as Dofasco Steel have implemented voluntary measures to achieve this.

8. *Working with fewer resources* due to layoffs, corporate downsizing, and general cost cutting is forcing managers to make trade-off decisions on resource allocation, and to place increased emphasis on cost control and productivity improvement.

Cost control has always been at least somewhat important, but lately it has taken on added significance due to a combination of economic pressures and increased competition. And *productivity*—output relative to input—is gaining added attention as organizations attempt to remain competitive while they tighten their belts.

9. *Ethical issues* are commanding increased attention of management at all levels. Accounting scandals, stockbrokers releasing misleading information of stocks, product liability claims, breaches in privacy and security of computer files, and sharing personal customer information among financial and other businesses are just some of the behaviours that have led to public outcries and government investigations.

These trends are having a major influence on business (including accounting, finance, international business, marketing, and MIS), as well as on operations management. Their impact on operations management is discussed throughout this text.

agility The ability of an organization to respond quickly to demands or opportunities.

SUMMARY

Operations management is that part of an organization responsible for planning and coordinating the use of the organization's resources to convert inputs into outputs. The operations function is one of three primary functions of business organizations; the other two are marketing and finance.

The operations function is present in both service and product-producing organizations. Operations decisions involve design decisions and operation decisions. Design decisions relate to capacity planning, product design, process design, layout of facilities, and selecting locations for facilities. Operation decisions relate to quality assurance, production planning and scheduling, inventory management, and project management.

The chapter provides a brief discussion of the historical evolution of operations management and recent trends in the field. Among those trends are e-business and supply chain management; increasing emphasis on quality; integrating technology into production systems; global competition; increasing attention to environmental issues; and increasing emphasis on agility, cost reduction, and ethical issues.

<table>
<tr><td>

KEY TERMS
</td><td>

agility, 23
craft production, 16
division of labour, 17
e-business, 21
interchangeable parts, 17
lead time, 8
lean production, 19
</td><td>

mass production, 18
model, 14
operations management, 3
Pareto phenomenon, 15
supply chain, 22
system, 15
value-added, 7
</td></tr>
</table>

DISCUSSION AND REVIEW QUESTIONS

1. Briefly describe the term *operations management*.
2. Identify the three major functional areas of business organizations and briefly describe how they interrelate.
3. Describe the operations function and the nature of the operations manager's job.
4. List five important differences between producing goods and performing services.
5. Briefly discuss each of these terms related to the historical evolution of operations management:
   a. Industrial Revolution
   b. Scientific management
   c. Interchangeable parts
   d. Division of labour
6. Why are services important? Why is manufacturing important?
7. What are models and why are they important?
8. Can you think of a business that doesn't need operations management?
9. List the trade-offs you would consider for each of these decisions:
   a. Driving your own car versus public transportation.
   b. Buying a computer now versus waiting for an improved model.
   c. Buying a new car versus buying a used car.
   d. Speaking up in class versus waiting to get called on by the instructor.
10. Describe each of these systems: craft production, mass production, and lean production.
11. Pick any business/organization you are familiar with, for example a restaurant or a store. State its name and the products or services it provides. Briefly describe the operations management activities necessary to design and operate this business/organization. You may use Table 1–3 on p. 10 as a source of ideas (there's no need to answer each basic question in the table).
12. How have technological changes affected you? Are there any downsides to technological change? Explain.
13. Identify some of the current trends in operations management and relate them to recent news or to your personal experience.
14. Why do people do things that are unethical?
15. Explain the term *value-added*.
16. Load the DVD that accompanies this book. Which items do you think will be most useful to you?

TAKING STOCK

This item appears at the end of each chapter. It is intended to focus your attention on three key issues for business organizations in general, and operations management in particular. Those issues are trade-off decisions, collaboration among various functional areas of the organization, and the impact of technology. You will see three or more questions relating to these issues. Here is the first set of questions:

1. What are trade-offs? Why is careful consideration of trade-offs important in decision making?
2. Why is it important for the various functional areas of a business organization to collaborate?
3. In what general ways does technology have an impact on operations management decision making?

This item also will appear in every chapter. It allows you to critically apply information you learned in the chapter to a practical situation. Here is the first exercise:

CRITICAL THINKING EXERCISE

Many organizations offer a combination of goods and services to their customers. As you learned in this chapter, there are some key differences between production of goods and delivery of services. What are the implications of these differences relative to managing operations?

This item will appear in most chapters. It allows you to use the Internet to gain additional knowledge about chapter material. Here is the first exercise.

INTERNET EXERCISE

Visit the Web page of one of the associations listed on pp. 5, 6 and briefly list the targetted members and the services that they provide to their members.

MINI-CASE

Lynn

Lynn had worked for the same major Canadian company for almost 15 years. Although the company had gone through some tough times, things were starting to turn around. Customer orders were up, and quality and productivity had improved dramatically from what they had been only a few years earlier due to a companywide quality improvement program. So it came as a real shock to Lynn and about 400 of her co-workers when they were suddenly terminated following the new CEO's decision to downsize the company.

After recovering from the initial shock, Lynn tried to find employment elsewhere. Despite her efforts, after eight months of searching she was no closer to finding a job than the day she started. Her funds were being depleted and she was getting more discouraged. There was one bright spot, though: She was able to bring in a little money by mowing lawns for her neighbours. She got involved quite by chance when she heard one neighbour remark that now that his children were on their own, nobody was around to cut the grass. Almost jokingly, Lynn asked him how much he'd be willing to pay. Soon Lynn was mowing the lawns of five neighbours. Other neighbours wanted her to work on their lawns, but she didn't feel that she could spare any more time from her job search.

However, as the rejection letters began to pile up, Lynn knew she had to make an important decision in her life. On a rainy Tuesday morning, she decided to go into business for herself—taking care of neighbourhood lawns. She was relieved to give up the stress of job hunting, and she was excited about the prospect of being her own boss. But she was also fearful of being completely on her own. Nevertheless, Lynn was determined to make a go of it.

At first, business was a little slow, but once people realized Lynn was available, many asked her to take care of their lawns. Some people were simply glad to turn the work over to her; others switched from professional lawn care services. By the end of her first year in business, Lynn knew she could earn a living this way. She also performed other services such as fertilizing lawns, weeding gardens, and trimming shrubbery. Business became so good that Lynn hired two part-time workers to assist her and, even then, she believed she could expand further if she wanted to. During winter months (January and February), Lynn takes her vacation in Florida.

Questions

1. Lynn is the operations manager of her business. Among her responsibilities are forecasting, inventory management, scheduling, quality assurance, and maintenance.

    a. What kinds of things would likely require forecasts?

    b. What inventory items does Lynn probably have? Name one inventory decision she has to make periodically.

    c. What scheduling must she do? What things might occur to disrupt schedules and cause Lynn to reschedule?

    d. How important is quality assurance to Lynn's business? Explain.

    e. What kinds of maintenance must be performed?

2. What are some of the trade-offs that Lynn probably considered relative to:

    a. Working for a company instead of for herself?

    b. Expanding the business?

    c. Launching a Web site?

3. Lynn decided to offer the students who worked for her a bonus of $25 for ideas on how to improve the business, and they provided several good ideas. One idea that she initially rejected now appears to hold great promise. The student who proposed the idea has left, and is currently working for a competitor. Should Lynn send that student a cheque for the idea?

Sobeys

www.sobeys.com

U p until 1998, Sobeys was a privately owned chain of grocery stores in the Atlantic provinces. Sobeys grew out of a butcher shop in Stellarton, Nova Scotia, opened by the Sobey family in 1907. When Loblaw, Canada's largest national grocery chain, expanded into Sobeys' territories, competition heated up. Sobeys' directors decided on a bold move in order to gain sufficient economies of scale to be able to compete with Loblaw. Sobeys took over the larger Oshawa Group (at a purchase price of $1.5 billion), then Canada's second largest national grocery chain, which included (mostly franchised) IGA and Price Chopper stores and the wholesale food distribution company SERCA.

Since 1998, Sobeys has worked hard and successfully to integrate the supermarket chains. It has divided the country into four regions (Atlantic, Quebec, Ontario, and the West), has aligned each store's size and merchandise to its market, centralized purchasing and merchandising, improved its logistics and distribution, and focused on its core grocery retailing business by selling SERCA to Sysco, the giant food distribution company. Sobeys now manages more than 1,300 grocery stores, has annual revenue of more than $11 billion, and employs 75,000 people. Sobeys' strategy is to emphasize ready-to-serve, quality food and fresh produce along with exceptional customer service in attractive stores.

Sobeys operates grocery stores of varying sizes in every region of Canada with a range of services suitable for the market. It runs more than 290 full-service supermarkets under the

names Sobeys, Garden Market IGA (in Western Canada), and IGA Extra (in Quebec). These stores are over 60,000 square feet in size and feature farm-fresh produce, full-line bakeries, extensive home-style meal selections, and a variety of innovative in-store retail services such as photo finishing, florist, Western Union money wiring, dry-cleaning and banking (TD Canada Trust). They usually have between 12 and 16 checkout lanes. A Sobeys store of this size typically employs from 200 to 250 people.

IGA stores (approximately 400) are designed primarily for mid-sized communities with store sizes in the range of 15,000–40,000 square feet. The emphasis in these stores is on fresh produce, meat, dairy, and bakery goods, and on highly personalized service. Stores of this size often have 10 to 12 checkout lanes and employ 50 to 120 people. Price Choppers stores (more than 100) are also approximately the same size as IGA stores, but are for value-conscious consumers.

In smaller communities, Sobeys runs over 300 stores under the banners Foodland, Food Town, Les Marchés Tradition, and Marché Boni choix, which offer consumers convenient, full-service supermarkets on a smaller scale.

Sobeys also runs 128 Needs Convenience Stores, and 58 Lawton's Drugstores in Atlantic Canada. Recently, Sobeys bought 15 Commisso's stores in the Niagara region.

Produce

A full-service Sobeys store's produce department is set up in a farmers' market style, with most of its produce unpacked and available for customer evaluation and selection. Its produce is sourced mainly nationally, but sometimes locally. As part of its wide produce selection, Sobeys also sells organically grown foods. Two features of the store's deli are the hot case foods, such as Grade A whole chickens, and the service case, which holds a wide variety of fresh salads and sliced meats. In addition, it carries a wide variety of international cheeses and sliced meats.

One characteristic of its East Coast origin is Sobeys' fresh seafood market. It stocks a number of fresh fish and seafood delicacies such as whole, portioned, and fillet fish, shellfish, store-made chowder ingredients, and live lobster cooked at a customer's request. Sobeys offers a wide assortment of premium-cut meats available from the service case and boxed meats that it sells under its private label. As well, a meat cutter is on duty to provide personalized service for special-order needs. Years ago Sobeys raised the standard of quality beef by introducing the "Aged for Flavour" program. It has gone a step further with its new "Canadian Select Beef." Sobeys now provides only the highest quality Certified AAA and AA grades of beef.

Sobeys' private-label products number more than 3,500, bringing in 20 percent of sales. Sobeys' premium private

label is "Our Compliments," adopted from IGA. Its value private label is "Smart Choice," also adopted from the IGA stores.

The Meals Made Easy program offers time-pressed shoppers a variety of ready-to-serve, home-cooked meals. At the Courtyard Café, shoppers can take the time to sample an appetizing range of premium-quality foods including fresh baked pizza, rotisserie chicken, hot and cold pasta entrées, a wide selection of fruit and vegetables, gourmet coffees, and a variety of desserts.

Technology and Operations

At Sobeys, using new technology is part of its approach to doing business. In the 1990s, both Sobeys and IGA started using Electronic Data Interchange (EDI) to communicate with their major suppliers, food manufacturers. This helped with information accuracy and speed. The acquisition of IGA stores has provided Sobeys the opportunity of streamlining all operations. Sobeys renovated the Milton warehouse (west of Toronto)

and built a large state-of-the-art warehouse in Whitby (east of Toronto), closed five old warehouses in Ontario, installed a warehouse management system (Exceed, by EXE) in its warehouses, used automated ordering systems, used productivity standards in the warehouses, reduced costs of transportation and distribution to its more than 25 regional distribution centres by using a truck-route optimization software by Manugistics, started using multi-temperature trucks to save on number of trips, and outsourced operations of the Milton and Whitby distribution centres to Axis (a member of Tibbett & Britten) and Ryder Logistics, respectively. Deliveries vary from one to two a week for the smaller stores to daily for the largest stores.

In 2000, Sobeys tried to install SAP's Enterprise Resources Planning software to integrate all its stores, warehouses, and headquarters. However, the system crashed in late November 2000 for five days, resulting in lost sales of more than $20 million. As a result, Sobeys' new CEO Bill McEwan decided to discontinue use of SAP (for more information on SAP, see Chapter 13).

First launched in 1997, the IGA Cybermarket is Canada's first home grocery shopping site on the Internet (www.iga.net), with the trial participation of some 130 stores in the province of Quebec. This service provides a new level of convenience by allowing customers to place their orders from home or work, with the local IGA store serving as the point of pick-up or delivery.

Recently, Sobeys has agreed to supply all inventory needs of Grocery Gateway, the independent Toronto-area e-tailer (Internet-based retailer).

In addition to its store services, Sobeys maintains a Web site that features much useful information including information on health and body, recipes, weekly flyer, and store locations. (www.sobeys.ca).

Questions

1. What are the inputs, processes, outputs, and feedback/control for a grocery store such as Sobeys or IGA?

2. What are the operations decisions involved in running a grocery store such as Sobeys or IGA?

Sources: Sobeys Annual Reports, 1999–2004; "Sobeys Reports Efficiencies from EDI," *Canadian Grocer* 109(7), July 95, p. 5; P. D'Souza and S. Silcoff, "On Special This Week: Supermarkets," *Canadian Business* 71(21), December 24, 1998–January 8, 1999, pp. 32–40; R. Robertson "Delivering Food Value," *Materials Management and Distribution* 45(4), May 2000, p. 18; M. Evans, "Grocery Gateway Inks Supply Deal with Sobeys: 'It Allows Us to Be Aggressive,'" *Financial Post* (*National Post*), October 23, 2002, p. FP4; J. Tutunjian, "The Passion of Bill McEwan," *Canadian Grocer* 118(4), May 2004, pp. 22–23.

SELECTED BIBLIOGRAPHY AND FURTHER READING

Bounds, Gregory, H. Dobbins, and Oscar S. Fowler. *Management: A Total Quality Perspective*. Cincinnati: South-Western Publishing, 1995.

Colvin, Geoffrey. "Managing in the Info Era." *Fortune*, March 6, 2000, pp. F6–F9.

Crainer, Stuart. *The Management Century*. New York: Jossey-Bass, 2000.

Denison, Merrill. *Harvest Triumphant: The Story of Massey Harris*. Toronto: McClelland and Stewart Ltd., 1948.

Hopp, William J., and Mark Spearman. *Factory Physics: Foundations of Manufacturing Management*. 2nd ed. Burr Ridge, IL: Irwin, 2001.

Owens, James. *Business Ethics*. Arlington, VA: Executive Publications, 1989.

Pfeiffer, Raymond S. *Ethics on the Job: Cases and Strategies*. Belmont, CA: Wadsworth Publishing Co., 1999.

Schmenner, Roger W. "Looking Ahead by Looking Back, Even Flow in the History of Manufacturing." *Production and Operations Management*, Spring 2001, pp. 87–96.

Taylor, Graham D., and Peter A. Baskerville. *A Concise History of Business in Canada*. Toronto: Oxford University Press, 1994.

Womack, James P., Daniel Jones, and Daniel Roos. *The Machine that Changed the World*. New York: Harper Perennial, 1991.

2 CHAPTER

Competitiveness, Strategy, and Productivity

CHAPTER OUTLINE

LEARNING OBJECTIVES

After completing this chapter, you should be able to:

1 List and briefly discuss the primary ways that business organizations compete.

2 Describe a company's mission/vision.

3 Describe operations strategy.

4 List steps involved in formulating an operations strategy.

5 Define and measure the term *productivity* and explain why it is important to organizations and to countries.

6 Identify the difference between manufacturing and service productivity.

7 List some of the reasons for poor productivity and some ways of improving it.

When Richard Currie was appointed as the president of Loblaw in 1976, Loblaw was only a regional chain of grocery stores in Ontario, making low profits and having cash flow problems. Now, Loblaw is Canada's largest national grocery store chain. How did Loblaw accomplish this?

Westjet was founded in 1996, but is now challenging Air Canada as the leading airline in Canada. Westjet's operating costs are almost half Air Canada's. How did Westjet achieve this when so many other airlines couldn't?

These are the types of questions answered in this chapter.

INTRODUCTION

This chapter discusses competitiveness, strategy, and productivity: three separate but related topics that are vitally important to business organizations. *Competitiveness* relates to how effective an organization is in the marketplace compared to other organizations that offer similar products or services; *strategy* is the plans that determine the direction an organization takes in pursuing its goals; *operations strategy* is the strategy used by the operations function; and *productivity* relates to better use of resources.

Slumping productivity gains in the late 1980s and the impressive successes of foreign competition in the marketplace caused many North American companies to rethink their strategies and to place increased emphasis on *operations strategy*.

COMPETITIVENESS

competitiveness How effectively an organization meets the needs of customers relative to others that offer similar goods or services.

Companies must be competitive to sell their goods and services in the marketplace. **Competitiveness** is an important factor in determining whether a company prospers, barely gets by, or fails. Business organizations compete with one another in a variety of ways. These are based on product or service attributes customers want, including price, quality, product or service differentiation, variety, timeliness, customer service, and location.

1. *Price* is the amount a customer must pay for the product or service. If all other factors are equal, customers will choose the product or service that has the lowest price. Organizations that compete based on price focus on lowering costs of goods or services.

2. *Quality* refers to design, material, workmanship, performance and consistency. Usually, it relates to how well the product or service will serve its intended purpose.

3. *Product* or *service differentiation* refers to any additional features that cause a product or service to be perceived by the buyer as more suitable than a competitor's product or service.

4. *Variety* refers to the choices of models and options available to customers. The more variety, the wider the range of potential customers. A company's operations has to be flexible in order to produce a variety of products.

5. *Timeliness* or *fast delivery* refers to a number of different things. One is how quickly a product or service is delivered to a customer. This can be facilitated by faster movement of information backward through the supply chain. Another is how quickly new products or services are developed or redesigned and brought to the market. Still another is the ability for on-time delivery, no sooner or later than when needed, required for just-in-time operation.

6. *Customer service* might involve after-sale activities that are perceived by customers as value-added, such as delivery, setup, warranty work, technical support, or extra attention while work is in progress, such as courtesy, keeping the customer informed, and attention to little details.

At Hertz, there is no paperwork and no waiting line once the customer is enrolled in their "Gold" services. Car keys to a pre-selected vehicle are provided, along with a copy of the rental agreement, as soon as the driver's license is shown. Hertz emphasizes timeliness and customer service attributes.

7. *Location* is being conveniently situated for the customers, essential in providing services.

Some of these dimensions overlap. For example, several of the items on the list may come under the heading of *quality*. Table 2–1 lists most of these competitive attributes and examples of companies that emphasize them.

Customers choose the "best buy" or best "value":

$$value = \frac{quality, timeliness, etc.}{price}$$

The key to successfully competing is to determine what customers want and then direct efforts toward meeting (or even exceeding) customer expectations.

In formulating a successful strategy, organizations must take into account both order qualifiers and order winners. Terry Hill, in his book *Manufacturing Strategy*, describes **order qualifiers** as those characteristics that potential customers perceive as minimum standards of acceptability to be considered as a potential for purchase. However, that may not be sufficient to get a potential customer to purchase from the organization. **Order winners** are those characteristics of an organization's goods or services that cause them to be perceived as better than the competition.

Characteristics such as price, delivery reliability (on time), delivery speed, and quality can be order qualifiers or order winners. Thus, quality may be an order winner in some situations, whereas in others it may be an order qualifier. Over time, a characteristic that once was an order winner may become an order qualifier, and vice versa.

Obviously, it is important to determine the set of order qualifier characteristics and the set of order winner characteristics, and it is also necessary to decide on the relative importance of each characteristic so that appropriate attention can be given to the various

order qualifiers Characteristics that customers perceive as minimum standards of acceptability to be considered as a potential for purchase.

order winners Characteristics of an organization's goods or services that cause it to be perceived as better than the competition.

TABLE 2–1

Examples of competitive attributes used by companies

	Competency	Examples of Companies Goods, or Services
Price	Low cost	Real Canadian Superstore (no name products) Westjet
Quality	High-performance	Sony TV Lexus, Cadillac Five-star restaurants or hotels
	Consistent quality	Coca-Cola, Pepsi Cola Kodak, Xerox, Bombardier Electrical power, Pizza Hut
Variety	Customization	Metal work (machine) shop Hospital emergency room
Timeliness	Rapid delivery	McDonald's, Burger King Purolator Domino's Pizza
	On-time delivery	Airlines Just-in-time suppliers
Customer service	Superior customer service	CP/Delta Hotels IBM London Drugs
Location	Convenience	Supermarkets, convenience stores Gas stations Branch banks, automated banking machines

Costco's mission is to provide a carefully selected number of quality products at low prices to loyal customers in a warehouse setting.

www.costco.ca

characteristics. Marketing must make that determination and communicate it to operations. Quality consistency and on-time delivery are order qualifiers for most companies.

Understanding competitive issues can help managers develop successful strategies.

STRATEGY

strategy A plan for achieving organizational mission/vision/goals.

A **strategy** is a plan for achieving mission/vision/goals. An organization's strategy has a long-term impact on the nature and characteristics of the organization. A strategy affects the ability of an organization to compete or, in the case of a nonprofit organization, the ability to serve its intended purpose.

In this section, you will learn about both organization strategy and operations strategy, and how they influence an organization. The nature of an organization's strategy depends on its mission/vision.

Mission/Vision

mission The reason for existence of an organization.

An organization's **mission** is the basis of the organization—the reason for its existence, and its products and markets. Missions vary from organization to organization, depending on the nature of their business. *Vision* is the shared perception of the organization's future, what it will achieve, and a supporting philosophy.

mission/vision statement A statement of purpose, products, and markets.

It is important that an organization have a clear and simple **mission/vision statement**, one that answers the question, "What business are we in?" The mission statement should serve to guide formulation of strategy for the organization as well as decision making at all levels. Table 2–2 provides some sample mission/vision statements.

One way to create a vision is "Future State Visioning."[1] Its main steps are:

- Identify the stakeholders of company and their vision of future, disassociated with any current problems.

- Develop a common vision in a participatory way. This will develop understanding and commitment. Ensure that the common vision is expressed in actionable terms.

- Develop values (fundamental beliefs and motivations) that will guide the company to achieve its vision. Avoid planning strategy and action programs until vision and values are developed.

---

[1]J. M. Stewart, "Future State Visioning Technique at National Rubber Company," *Planning Review* 22(2), March/April 1994, pp. 20–24, 33.

Loblaw	Loblaw believes that to be successful it must provide consumers with the best in one-stop shopping and continually introduce innovative products and convenient services that meet their everyday household needs.
	Looking ahead, Loblaw's long-term goal is to be known for:

- offering the highest-quality fresh foods
- its compelling value proposition and food assortment
- leading in the development of unique, high-quality control label products and services
- its powerful and compelling non-food offering
- delivering sustainable growth through distinct but integrated approaches to the marketplace
- providing a great place to work and grow (Source: Loblaw Companies Limited, *2003 Annual Report*, p. 23)

WestJet	WestJet Spirit: There is something special about WestJet's culture. It's a company with a unique corporate spirit ... a close knit family that's building something legendary ... and in the process changing the world.
	Our mission: To enrich the lives of everyone in WestJet's world by providing safe, friendly, affordable air travel.
	Our vision: WestJet will be the leading low-fare airline that people want to work with ... customers want to fly with ... and shareholders want to invest with. (Source: http://c3dsp.westjet.com/guest/about/westJetMissionTemplate.jsp., extracted March 2, 2005.)

McDonald's Restaurants	McDonald's vision is to be the world's best quick service restaurant experience. Being the best means providing outstanding quality, service, cleanliness and value, so that we make every customer in every restaurant smile. To achieve our vision, we are focused on three worldwide strategies:

- Be the best employer for our people in each community around the world.
- Deliver operational excellence to our customers in each of our restaurants.
- Achieve enduring profitable growth by expanding the brand and leveraging the strength of the McDonald's system through innovation and technology. (Used with permission from McDonald's Corporation.)

TABLE 2-2

Selected company mission/vision statements

www.loblaw.ca

www.westjet.ca

www.mcdonalds.com

Goals. A mission/vision statement provides a general direction for an organization and should lead to organizational *goals* or *objectives* which provide substance to the overall mission. For example, one goal of an organization may be to capture more market share for a product; another goal may be to achieve profitability. Taken together, the goals and the mission establish a destination for the organization.

Strategies. If you think of mission/vision/goals as destination, then strategy is the roadmap for reaching the destinations. A strategy is a set of coordinated broad long-term policies, objectives, and action programs to achieve goals/mission/vision and secure long-term sustainable advantage over competitors. Organizations have overall strategies called *organization* or *business strategies*, which relate to the entire organization, and they also have *functional strategies*, which relate to each of the functional areas of the organization. The functional strategies should support the overall strategy of the organization, just as the organizational strategy should support the goals/vision/mission of the organization.

Tactics are medium-term objectives, methods, and actions used to accomplish strategies. They are more specific in nature than strategies, and they provide guidance and direction for carrying out actual *operations*, which need the most specific and detailed plans and decision making in an organization.

It should be apparent that the overall relationship that exists from the mission/vision down to actual operations is *hierarchical* in nature. This is illustrated in Figure 2–1.

A simple example may help to put this hierarchy into perspective.

tactics The medium-term objectives, methods, and actions taken to accomplish strategies.

FIGURE 2-1

Strategic planning is hierarchical in organizations

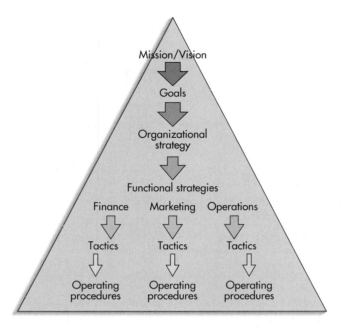

Example 1

Ashley is a high school student in Saskatoon. She would like to live comfortably. A possible scenario for achieving her mission/vision might look something like this:

Mission/vision: Live a good life.

Goal: Successful career, good income.

Strategy: Obtain a college/university education.

Tactics: Select a college/university and a major; decide how to finance the education.

Operations: Register, buy books, take courses, study.

Operations Strategy

operations strategy The approach, consistent with the organization strategy, that is used to guide the operations function.

The organization strategy provides the overall direction for the organization. It is broad in scope, covering the entire organization. **Operations strategy** is narrower in scope, dealing with guiding the operations aspect of the organization, but aligned with organization strategy and goals.

Operations strategy comprises a set of well-coordinated policies, objectives, and action programs, directly affecting the operations function, which is aimed at securing a long-term sustainable advantage over the competition.[2] In order to formulate an operations strategy, the operations function has to cooperate with all the other functions of the business and these functions should collectively monitor the external markets. For example, marketing should be aware of competitors' new product development and customers' expectations in the product markets, and engineering/R&D should be aware of new processing technologies in the technology markets.

The creation of operations strategy occurs both at the company level and at the functional level. At the company level, the role of operations should be identified. Usually, operations' objectives/performance measures are given in terms of competitive attributes such as cost (e.g., unit cost, labour productivity, inventory turnover), quality (e.g., percentage of products defective, cost of quality), timeliness (e.g., percentage of on-time deliveries, lead time), and variety (e.g., response to product/quantity changes,

---

[2]C. H. Fine and A. C. Hax, "Manufacturing Strategy: A Methodology and an Illustration," *Interfaces* 15(6), November/December 1985, pp. 28–46.

i.e., flexibility). Trade-offs must be made among these objectives because operations cannot excel in all of them simultaneously. For example, a flexible operation cannot produce the products at minimum cost.

Usually, the operations policies, objectives, and action programs are classified into nine major decision-making categories:

Facility: A major decision for multi-facility organizations is how to specialize or focus each facility: by market, product group, or process type. This usually depends on the economics of production and distribution.

Capacity: This decision is related to facility decision. Long-term capacity decisions relate to size of plants and major equipment. The main issue is how to change the capacity in anticipation of future demand.

Vertical Integration: This is the ownership of a major part or the whole of the supply chain. Cost, coordination, and control are the important factors.

Vendor Relations: The two extremes are using competitive arm's-length or cooperative close relationships. This decision also determines how the quality of purchased goods will be assured: either work with a supplier to assure/control its process or inspect the incoming parts.

Product Mix: The challenge of operations management increases as the variety of products and the rate of new product introduction increase. These require flexible production systems.

Process Types and Technology: There are four generic process types: job shop, batch, assembly line, and continuous flow. The product-process matrix (described in Chapter 6) can be used to relate product characteristics to process characteristics (and technologies). The matrix also shows the important trade-offs required in process choice. The process type determines the appropriate degree of process automation.

Human Resources: With cooperation of the Personnel Department, workers/staff are appraised, selected, developed, motivated, promoted, and rewarded to work as a team to achieve the company's goals. There are various types of compensation and incentive decisions that can be used.

Product Quality: Product's quality is determined during the design and production. Conformance to specification during production requires quality assurance, control, and improvement. The tools that can be used include cost of quality, statistical quality control, and continuous improvement/six-sigma. A major decision is whether to assign the responsibility of quality control to the workers.

Operations Infrastructure: These decisions include choosing a computerized planning and control system (including forecasting, material requirements planning, and scheduling), whether to use just-in-time, and the type of production/delivery system used: make-to-stock or make-to-order. Aggregate production planning involves tactical decisions faced by companies with seasonal demand—choices include carrying inventory, hiring temp workers, using overtime, etc.

The Steps for Formulation of an Operations Strategy

1. Link the business strategy to the operations strategy: determine operations requirements of the business strategy.

2. Conduct an operations audit to determine the strengths/weaknesses of the current operations strategy in each of the nine decision-making categories. Also, assess the relative standing of each product line against those of most relevant competitors.

3. Categorize the customers into types: for example, major customers (with whom closer relationship is desirable) and others (with whom transactional relationship is adequate).

4. Group product lines into types: for example, classify the product lines into low-volume and high-volume.

5. Assess the degree of focus at each plant: note that a focused plant is more efficient. We can use the product-process matrix to detect the degree of congruence between a product line and its "natural" process. For example, a low volume–high variety product line should be produced using a job shop process.

6. Develop an operations strategy and allocate product lines to plants: for each of the nine decision-making categories, state the objectives, policies, and broad action programs to achieve them. Deploy these policies and broad programs using a set of specific action programs.

Example 2

A Business Objective
Introduce a new product line, e.g., KFC offering ribs.

A Business Program
Identify and develop the product line.

Operations Strategy
Determine the relative importance of the product's cost, quality, timeliness, variety, etc. Determine the objectives and/or programs related to

- Facility, e.g., program: study whether to produce it in existing facilities.
- Capacity, e.g., program: study the space requirements.
- Vertical integration and vendor relations, e.g., program: either buy or set up partnership with major supplier(s).
- Product mix, e.g., objective: keep the number of varieties in the product line to 2.
- Process type and technology, e.g., program: determine the process type and design the process.
- Human resources, e.g., program: train employees.
- Quality, e.g., program: set up quality assurance and control plans.
- Infrastructure, e.g., objective: produce make-to-stock; program: set up a production planning and control system.

Example 3

Wilson Sporting Goods' management decided in the late 1980s to become the leader in the special-order golf-ball business (golf balls that have customized and personalized logos). This mission was to be accomplished over a five-year period by improving quality, response time, and customer service. Specific improvement targets were decided for each attribute, and these goals were cascaded down the organization to appropriate departmental teams, where action plans were established for each needed activity. The goals and an example of an action plan are shown in Figure 2–2.[3]

Operations strategy can have a major influence on the competitiveness of an organization. If it is well designed and well executed, there is a good chance that the organization will be successful; if it is not well designed or executed, the chances are much less that the organization will be successful.

In the 1970s and early 80s, operations strategy was often neglected in favour of marketing and financial strategies. That may have occurred because many chief executive officers did not come from operations backgrounds and perhaps did not fully appreciate

---

[3]Based on J. H. Sheridan, "America's Best Plants: Wilson Sporting Goods," *Industry Week* 241(20), October 19, 1992, pp. 59–62.

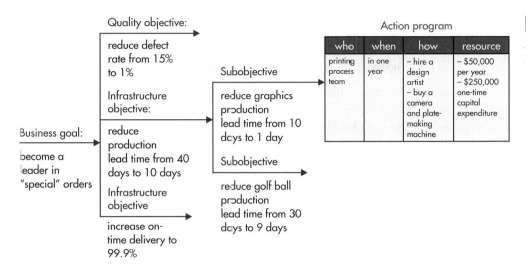

FIGURE 2-2

An example of implementing an operations strategy

the importance of the operations function. Mergers and acquisitions were common; leveraged buyouts were used, and conglomerates were formed that joined dissimilar operations. These did little to add value to the organization; they were purely financial in nature. Decisions were often made by individuals who were unfamiliar with the business, frequently to the detriment of that business. Meanwhile, foreign competitors began to fill the resulting vacuum with a careful focus on operations strategy.

In the late 1980s and early 90s, many companies began to realize this approach was not working. They recognized that they were less competitive than other companies. This caused them to focus attention on operations strategy. Toward that end, many firms are developing strategies that have *quality* or *time* as their central concern.

This correlates with a survey of manufacturing executives and managers who were asked to identify strategic and tactical issues that North American manufacturers must focus on to be competitive on a global basis.[4] The top two strategic issues were quality management and manufacturing strategy. The top two tactical issues were quality control and manufacturing planning and control systems. Successful companies use a coherent set of strategies over time in order to develop a distinctive competency.

Distinctive competencies are those special attributes or abilities possessed by an organization that give it a *competitive edge*. Competency can be developed over time by focusing on a limited range of products or services, and/or on a technology. Using teamwork and rewards, an organization can develop its capabilities to surpass the sum of the capabilities of its employees. Companies should use strategic "hinges" in order to add to or change their products or services. This involves using past experience and expertise in design, manufacturing, or marketing, and leveraging it in a similar new product or service.[5]

distinctive competencies The special attributes or abilities that give an organization a competitive edge.

It is important to realize that a company cannot become the best in every competitive attribute. Companies need to develop and stay with a core competency, including choice of the products and services. This hard decision involves trade-offs and setting priorities. The following is an example of a company that strayed from its core competency.

In the early 1990s, the Potash Corporation of Saskatchewan was already the largest potash mining and milling company in the world. But in the mid-1990s, the management decided to expand into phosphor and nitrogen, to become a fertilizer company. However, nitrogen production is very different from potash and phosphor. Nitrogen is produced from natural gas, and it is produced in many countries. The result was huge losses in the

[4]Manoj K. Malhotra, Daniel C. Steele, and Varun Grover, "Important Strategic and Tactical Manufacturing Issues in the 1990s" Decision Sciences 25(2), March/April 1994, pp. 189–214.
[5]R. H. Hayes, et al., *Strategic Operations—Competing through Capabilities* (New York: The Free Press, 1996).

late 1990s. The management decided to close many nitrogen plants it had bought in the U.S., and wrote off approximately $0.5 billion.

Some of the operations strategies various Japanese manufacturing companies have employed since the Second World War are:

- *Low labour cost strategy.* Immediately after the war, exploited the (then) inexpensive labour pool.
- *Scale-based strategy.* During the 1960s, used capital-intensive methods to achieve higher labour productivity and lower unit costs.
- *Focused factories strategy.* During the 1970s, used smaller factories that focused on narrow product lines to take advantage of specialization and achieve higher quality.
- *Flexible factories strategy.* During the 1980s, reduced the time needed to incorporate new product and process designs. Used flexible equipment that allowed volume and design changes, as well as product variety. Continued to stress quality.
- *Continuous improvement strategy.* In the 1990s, the leading Japanese manufacturers adopted an approach that incorporates introducing new product features and practising continuous improvement of both products and processes.[6]

Traditional strategies of business organizations have tended to emphasize cost minimization or product differentiation. While not abandoning those strategies, many organizations have embraced strategies based on *quality* and/or *time*. These two approaches are rapidly gaining favour throughout the business world. They are exciting and challenging, for they promise to significantly change the way business organizations operate.

quality-based strategy Strategy that focuses on quality in all phases of an organization.

Quality-based strategies focus on maintaining or improving the quality of an organization's products or services. Quality is generally a factor in both attracting and retaining customers. Quality-based strategies may be motivated by a variety of factors. They may reflect an effort to overcome an image of poor quality, a desire to catch up with the competition, a desire to maintain an existing image of high quality, or some

---

READING

Dell Computers

www.dell.ca

In 1984, Michael Dell, then a college student, started selling personal computers from his dorm room. He didn't have the resources to make computer components, so he let others do that, choosing instead to concentrate on selling the computers. And, unlike the major computer producers, he didn't sell to dealers. Instead, he sold directly to customers, eliminating intermediaries, which allowed for lower cost and faster delivery. Although direct selling of PCs is fairly commonplace now, in those days it was a major departure from the norm.

He had little inventory, little capital cost, no R&D expenditures, and relatively few employees. This allowed Dell to grow. Because he was in direct contact with his customers, he gained tremendous insight into their expectations and needs, which he communicated to his suppliers.

Having little inventory gave Dell several advantages over his competitors. Aside from the lower costs of inventory, when new, faster computer chips became available, there was little inventory to work off, so he was able to offer the newer models much sooner than competitors with larger inventories. Also, when the prices of various components dropped, as they frequently did, he was able to take advantage of the lower prices, which kept his average costs lower than competitors'.

Dell uses the Internet to sell its computers directly to customers. Dell allows customers to choose their options which appear to be a lot. This is an example of mass customization. Dell makes the computer to order and uses couriers to send it to the customer.

Today the company is worth billions, and so is Michael Dell.

Source: J. Magretta, "The Power of Virtual Integration: An Interview with Dell Computer's Michael Dell," *Harvard Business Review*, March/April 1998, pp. 73–84.

---

[6]George Stalk Jr. and Thomas Hout, "Competing Against Time," *Research and Technology Management* 33(2), March–April 1990, pp. 19–24.

combination of these and other factors. Quality-based strategies are the rule rather than the exception. Interestingly enough, quality-based strategies can be part of another strategy such as cost reduction or increased productivity, both of which benefit from higher quality.

Time-based strategies focus on reducing the time required to accomplish various activities (e.g., develop new products or services and market them, respond to a change in customer demand, change-over time or deliver a product or perform a service). By doing so, organizations seek to improve service to the customer and gain a competitive advantage over rivals who take more time to accomplish the same tasks. Also costs are generally less, productivity is higher, and quality tends to be higher.

time-based strategy Strategy that focuses on reduction of time needed to accomplish tasks.

An example of a Canadian company using a time-based strategy is Standard Aero, based in Winnipeg. By redesigning its processes into cells, and controlling the activities using a visual system, Standard Aero performs repairs/overhauls of small airplane engines in only two weeks, much faster than its competitors.

Many companies are increasing their use of outsourcing to reduce overhead, gain flexibility, and take advantage of suppliers' expertise. Dell Computers provides a great example of some of the potential benefits of outsourcing and using the supply chain as part of an operations strategy. As well, Dell has become the largest computer producer by using the Internet to reach and do business with its customers (called mass customization). See the reading on Dell Computers.

PRODUCTIVITY

One of the primary responsibilities of a manager is to achieve *productive use* of an organization's resources. The term *productivity* is used to describe this. **Productivity** is an index that measures output (goods and services) relative to the input (machine, labour, materials, energy) used to produce them. It is usually expressed as the ratio of output to input:

productivity A measure of efficient use of resources, usually expressed as the ratio of output to input.

$$\text{Productivity} = \frac{\text{Output}}{\text{Input}} \tag{2–1}$$

A productivity ratio can be computed for a worker, a department, an organization, or an entire country.

A related measure is the rate of *productivity growth*. Productivity growth is the increase in productivity from one period to the next relative to the productivity in the preceding period. Thus,

Productivity growth

$$= \frac{\text{Current period productivity} - \text{Previous period productivity}}{\text{Previous period productivity}} \tag{2–2}$$

For example, if productivity increased from 80 to 84, the growth rate would be

$$\frac{84 - 80}{80} = .05 \text{ or } 5\%$$

Productivity growth is a key factor in a country's standard of living. Productivity increases add value to the economy while keeping inflation in check.

Calculating Productivity

Productivity measures can be based on a single input (partial productivity), on more than one input (multifactor productivity), or on all inputs (total productivity). Table 2–3 lists some examples of productivity measures. The choice of productivity measure depends primarily on the purpose of the measurement. If the purpose is to track improvements in labour productivity, then labour becomes the obvious input measure.

Partial measures are often of greatest use in operations management. Table 2–4 provides some examples of partial productivity measures.

TABLE 2-3

Some examples of different types of productivity measures

Partial measures	$\dfrac{\text{Output}}{\text{Labour}}$	$\dfrac{\text{Output}}{\text{Machine}}$	$\dfrac{\text{Output}}{\text{Material}}$	$\dfrac{\text{Output}}{\text{Energy}}$
Multifactor measures	$\dfrac{\text{Output}}{\text{Labour} + \text{Machine}}$		$\dfrac{\text{Output}}{\text{Labour} + \text{Material} + \text{Energy}}$	
Total measure	$\dfrac{\text{Goods or services produced}}{\text{All inputs used to produce them}}$			

TABLE 2-4

Some examples of partial productivity measures

Labour Productivity	Units of output per labour hour
	Units of output per shift
	Value-added per labour hour
	Dollar value of output per labour hour
Machine Productivity	Units of output per machine hour
	Dollar value of output per machine hour
Material Productivity	Units of output per unit material input
	Dollar value of output per unit material input
Energy Productivity	Units of output per kilowatt-hour
	Dollar value of output per kilowatt-hour

The units of output used in productivity measure depends on the type of job performed. The following are examples of labour productivity:

$$\frac{\text{Square metres of carpet installed}}{\text{Labour hours}} = \text{Square metres of carpet installed per labour hour}$$

$$\frac{\text{Number of offices cleaned}}{\text{Number of shifts}} = \text{Number of offices cleaned per shift}$$

$$\frac{\text{Board feet of lumber cut}}{\text{Number of weeks}} = \text{Board feet of lumber cut per week (Board foot} = \text{volume of lumber which covers 1 foot} \times 1 \text{ foot} \times 1 \text{ inch)}$$

Similar examples can be listed for *machine productivity* (e.g., the number of pieces per hour turned out by a machine).

Example 4

Determine the productivity for these cases:

a. Four workers installed 720 square metres of carpet in eight hours.

b. A machine produced 68 usable (i.e., good quality) pieces in two hours.

Solution

a. Productivity $= \dfrac{\text{Square metres of carpet installed}}{\text{Labour hours worked}}$

$= \dfrac{720 \text{ square metres}}{4 \text{ workers} \times 8 \text{ hours}}$

$= \dfrac{720 \text{ square metres}}{32 \text{ worker hours}}$

$= 22.5$ square metres/worker hour

b. $\text{Productivity} = \dfrac{\text{Usable pieces}}{\text{Production time}}$

$= \dfrac{68 \text{ pieces}}{2 \text{ hours}}$

$= 34 \text{ pieces/hour}$

Calculations of multifactor productivity measure inputs using a common unit of measurement, such as dollars.

$$\frac{\text{Quantity of production}}{\text{Labour cost} + \text{Materials cost} + \text{Overhead}} \qquad (2\text{–}3)$$

Determine the multifactor productivity for the combined inputs of labour, materials, and machine time using the following data: **Example 5**

Output: 7,040 units

Input costs:

Labour (line and support staff, including benefits): $1,000

Materials: $520

Machine Overhead: $2,000

$\dfrac{\text{Multifactor}}{\text{productivity}} = \dfrac{\text{Output}}{\text{Labour} + \text{Materials} + \text{Machine Overhead}} = \dfrac{7{,}040 \text{ units}}{\$1{,}000 + \$520 + \$2{,}000}$ **Solution**

$= 2 \text{ units/dollar}$

See the reading, "Measuring Total Productivity Growth" for a simple method of determining total productivity growth.

Even though labour cost as a proportion of total cost has been decreasing in manufacturing companies, labour productivity is still the main measure being used to gauge the performance of individuals and plants. In addition, its use in services has been increasing as services are employing more workers.

Labour productivity and average operation time for tasks are related concepts. For example, if a task has an average time of five minutes, it implies a productivity of $60/5 = 12$ units per hour.

Productivity measures are useful on a number of levels. For an individual, department, or organization, productivity measures can be used to track performance *over time*. This allows managers to judge performance and to decide where improvements are needed. For example, if a manager finds that productivity has slipped in a certain area, the manager can examine the factors used to compute productivity to determine what has changed and then devise a means of improving productivity in subsequent periods. Another application of labour productivity is in labour wage negotiations where wage raises are sometimes tied to productivity growth.

Productivity measures can also be used to judge the performance of an entire industry or the productivity of a country as a whole. These productivity measures are *aggregate* measures.

In essence, productivity measurements serve as scorecards of the efficient use of resources. Business leaders are concerned with productivity as it relates to *competitiveness*: if two firms both have the same level of output, but one requires less input because of higher productivity, that one will be able to charge a lower price and consequently increase its share of the market, or it might elect to charge the same price, thereby reaping a greater profit.

Government leaders are concerned with national productivity because of the close relationship between productivity and a nation's *standard of living.* High levels of productivity (usually measured by gross domestic product per hour worked) are largely responsible for the high standards of living enjoyed by people in Canada. Furthermore, wage and price increases not accompanied by productivity increases tend to create inflationary pressures on the economy. (See the newsclip "Productivity Gains Curb Inflation.")

Labour productivity growth in Canada averaged to approximately 3 percent per year after the Second World War due to the postwar boom, but dropped to an average of approximately 1 percent per year from the late 1970s until now (see Figure 2–3). This productivity growth, though it is good relative to most countries, lags behind that of some other industrial countries, most notably the United States (see Figure 2–4).

Because of the large amount of trade with the United States, it is important not to lose ground on productivity to the U.S.. The current average productivity gap with the United States is approximately 18 percent. To explain the Canada–U.S. productivity gap, the following reasons have been given:

1. Increasing government regulations in Canada add to the administrative (and non-productive) burden of many companies.

2. The increasingly larger service sector in Canada is less productive than the U.S. service sector because of slower adoption of new technology.

3. Low funding for research and development (R&D), despite Canada's high R&D tax credit, results in a low level of innovation. A long-time criticism of Canadian manufacturing industries is that Canada's economy is dominated by "branch" plants whose parent companies do R&D in their own foreign headquarters.

4. Not using enough computers and advanced manufacturing technologies also puts Canada at a comparative productivity disadvantage.

5. Higher percentage of unionized labour and labour relations problems in Canada result in lower productivity.

FIGURE 2-3

Productivity Growth in Canada, 1962–2004 (annual percentage change in business sector GDP per hours worked)

Source: Adapted from Statistics Canada CANSIM 1 database, Series i602502, for pre-1987 data, and CANSIM 2, Table 383–0008, Series v1409154 and v1409155 for 1987 and after. March 6, 2005.

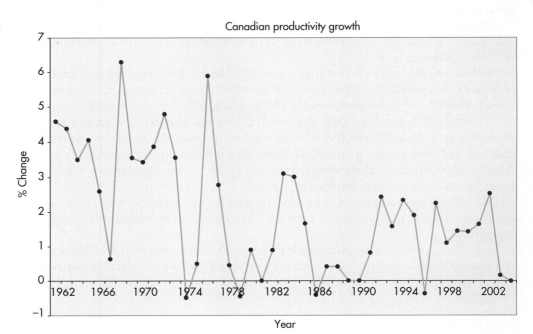

FIGURE 2-4

Labour productivity growth in the business sector of selected industrialized countries, 2002

Source: The Conference Board of Canada; OECD.

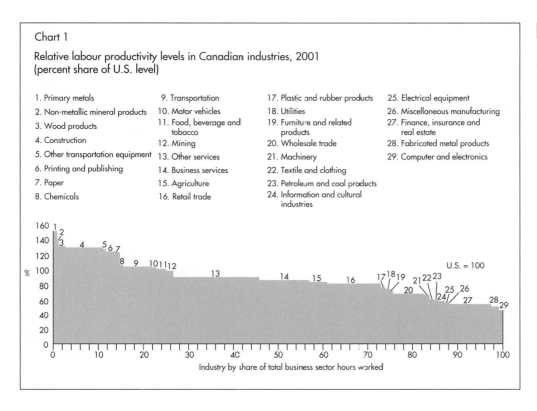

FIGURE 2-5

Source: The Conference Board of Canada.

Chart 1

Relative labour productivity levels in Canadian industries, 2001
(percent share of U.S. level)

1. Primary metals
2. Non-metallic mineral products
3. Wood products
4. Construction
5. Other transportation equipment
6. Printing and publishing
7. Paper
8. Chemicals

9. Transportation
10. Motor vehicles
11. Food, beverage and tobacco
12. Mining
13. Other services
14. Business services
15. Agriculture
16. Retail trade

17. Plastic and rubber products
18. Utilities
19. Furniture and related products
20. Wholesale trade
21. Machinery
22. Textile and clothing
23. Petroleum and coal products
24. Information and cultural industries

25. Electrical equipment
26. Miscellaneous manufacturing
27. Finance, insurance and real estate
28. Fabricated metal products
29. Computer and electronics

Industry by share of total business sector hours worked

6. Canada's smaller population and larger geographic area has resulted in a more dispersed population and smaller markets, hence lower competition and lower economies of scale.

7. The flow of foreign investment in Canada has halved since the mid-1980s. Investment in plants, machines, and equipment is an important factor in productivity growth.

8. Canada's infrastructure (roads, pipelines, etc.) is in need of renovation.

9. Commercialization of new technology in Canada lags behind many industrialized countries including the U.S.

To further investigate this, Figure 2–5 displays the gap in labour productivity growth between Canada and the United States in each major industry.[7] As can be seen, services (finance, wholesale and retail, business services) and many manufacturing sectors, such as computer and electronics, and the fabricated metal products, electrical equipment, and

[7]Conference Board of Canada, *Performance and Potential 2004–05*, www.conferenceboard.ca.

Measuring Total Productivity Growth

An interesting and simple method to measure the total productivity growth of the whole economy and its sectors has been suggested by Statistics Canada (see Productivity Growth in Canada, 2001, Stats Canada Catalogue no. 15-204-XIE, p. 17). In this method, the percentage growth rate of capital (value of plants and equipment) and labour are subtracted from the percentage growth rate of output (GDP) to arrive at the percentage growth rate due to productivity. Table 2–5 shows the calculations for the productivity growth rates for service and manufacturing sectors for various periods since 1961. To illustrate the results, in the 11 years of the 1989–99 period, the services sectors grew 3 percent in GDP, 1.4 percent in capital, and 1.4 percent in labour each year. The total productivity growth rate for services is therefore 3.0 − 1.4 − 1.4 = 0.2 percent per year during this period. As evident from the table, productivity growth has slowed down in recent years, and for services the growth rate has been at a slower pace.

TABLE 2–5

Annualized rates of growth of output, capital, and labour, and total productivity growth

	1961–66	1967–72	1973–78	1979–88	1989–99
			%		
Services					
Output growth	6.2	5.6	4.7	3.7	3.0
Capital growth	1.6	1.5	1.6	1.6	1.4
Labour growth	2.7	1.8	2.3	2.0	1.4
Productivity growth	1.9	2.3	.8	.2	.2
Manufacturing					
Output growth	8.9	4.9	2.5	2.5	2.3
Capital growth	1.3	1.4	.6	.9	.7
Labour growth	2.9	.7	.2	.2	.0
Productivity growth	4.6	2.7	1.7	1.4	1.6

machinery sectors have a relative labour productivity level much less than 100 percent, hence are less productive in Canada than the United States. On the other hand, primary metals, nonmetallic mineral, wood products, and construction have a relative labour productivity level much more than 100 percent, hence are more productive in Canada.

Productivity in the Service Sector

Service productivity measurement is more problematic than manufacturing productivity. In some services, a measure of output can be found. For example, in the transport sector ton-miles is used, in the power sector KWH is used, and in the communication sector number of phone calls is used. In other situations, it is more difficult to measure productivity, and thus to manage, because it involves intellectual activities and a high degree of variability in both output and input. Think about medical diagnosis, surgery, consulting, legal services, arts, painting, ballet, and orchestras. Quality is also hard to measure in these cases. This makes productivity improvements more difficult to achieve.

Sometimes measures of output used in services could result in misleading conclusions about productivity growth. For example, a hospital's output is usually measured by the number of patient-days of care provided. Suppose that the hospital becomes more productive, resulting in faster patient discharge. This reduces number of patient-days, which will reduce the productivity measure of the hospital!

In many cases, output has to be divided into types, and a weighted measure or "equivalent" unit needs to be determined and calculated. This is further illustrated in Chapter 12 in Aggregate Operations Planning.

Factors that Affect Productivity

Numerous factors affect productivity. Generally, they are methods, capital (building and machines), quality, technology, and management. Consider a student who plans to type a lengthy term paper. The student is an average typist and can turn out about three pages per hour. How could the student increase productivity (i.e., turn out more pages per hour)? One way would be to enroll in a short course to improve typing skills (method). Another way might be to replace her old computer with a more expensive computer and word-processing package (capital) to gain the speed of automatic features such as spell checking and grammar correction (quality). Still other productivity improvements might be achieved through improving organization and preparation for the actual typing (management). The incentive of receiving a good grade and the pride of doing a good job might also be important. The point is that all these factors are potential sources of productivity, not only for typing papers but for any kind of work, and it is generally up to the manager to see that they are fully exploited.

A commonly held misconception is that workers are the main determinant of productivity. According to that theory, the route to productivity gains involves getting employees to work harder. However, the fact is that many productivity gains in the past have come from *technological* improvements. Familiar examples include:

Fax machines	Automation and computers
Copying machines	Bar codes and scanners
Microwave ovens	Satellite and fibre optics
The Internet and e-mail	Text processing, spreadsheets,
Answering machines/voice mail/fax	and CAD software

However, technology alone won't guarantee productivity gains; it must be used wisely and thoughtfully. Without careful planning, technology can actually *reduce* productivity, especially if it leads to inflexibility, high costs, or mismatched operations. Another current productivity pitfall results from employees' use of computers for non-work-related activities (e.g., playing games or checking stock prices or sports scores on the Internet). Beyond all of these is the dip in productivity that results while employees learn to use new equipment or procedures that will eventually lead to productivity gains after the learning phase ends. *Computer viruses* can have an immense negative impact on productivity.

Standardizing processes and procedures wherever possible can have a significant impact on both productivity and quality. Note that only good quality output should be counted in productivity measurement. Therefore, *quality differences* may distort productivity measurements. One way this can happen is when comparisons are made over time, such as comparing the productivity of a factory now with one in the 1970s. Quality is now much higher than it was then, but there is no simple way to incorporate quality into productivity measurements.

Searching for lost or misplaced items wastes time, hence negatively affecting productivity. *Scrap rates* have an adverse effect on productivity, implying inefficient use of resources. *Safety* should be addressed. Accidents can take a toll on productivity. They tend to especially increase the costs. For example, a typical lost-time injury may cost $30,000, and a serious injury or fatality may cost $1 million.

Design of the workspace can impact productivity. For example, having tools and other work items within easy reach can positively impact productivity. *Incentive plans that reward productivity increases* can boost productivity.

FIGURE 2-6

Bottleneck operation

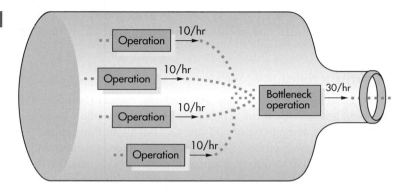

Improving Productivity

A company or a department can take a number of key steps toward improving productivity:

1. Develop productivity measures for all operations; measurement is the first step in managing and controlling an operation.

2. Look at the system as a whole in deciding which operations are most critical; it is overall productivity that is important. This concept is illustrated in Figure 2–6, which shows several operations feeding their output into a *bottleneck* operation. The capacity of the bottleneck operation is less than the combined capacities of the operations that provide input, so units queue up waiting to be processed; hence the term bottleneck. Productivity improvements to any *non*-bottleneck operation will not affect the productivity of the system. Improvements in the bottleneck operation *will* lead to increased productivity, up to the point where the output rate of the bottleneck equals the sum of output rate of the operations feeding it.

3. Develop methods for achieving productivity improvements, such as soliciting ideas from workers (perhaps organizing teams of workers, engineers, and managers), studying how other firms have increased productivity, and re-examining the way work is done.

4. Establish reasonable goals for improvement.

5. Make it clear that management supports and encourages productivity improvement. Consider incentives to reward workers for contributions.

6. Measure improvements and publicize them.

7. Use technology and capital as appropriate. Don't confuse productivity with *efficiency*. Efficiency is a narrower concept that pertains to getting the most out of a *fixed* set of resources; productivity is a broader concept that pertains to better use of overall resources. For example, an efficiency perspective on mowing a lawn if given a hand

NEWSCLIP

Productivity Gains Curb Inflation

www.burgerking.ca

Wage increases can lead to inflationary pressure—they can cause the prices consumers pay for products and services to rise. Unless, that is, they are offset by gains in productivity, which lead to an increase in profits. If that happens, a portion of the resulting profits can be used to cover the wage increases without having to raise prices. An example follows.

Some Burger Kings were able to increase the starting pay of new workers by $1 by achieving productivity gains. The restaurants restructured the menu, combining items into meal packages such as a burger, fries, and soft drink. This enabled the counter staff to enter orders with a single key stroke instead of multiple key strokes on their point-of-sale machines, reducing the time needed to take an order. That, in turn, enabled them to take orders more quickly, increasing productivity and, consequently, reducing labour requirements, which produced higher profits.

Source: Based on "Despite Pay Increases, Gains in Productivity, Profits Curb Inflation," *The Wall Street Journal*, May 22, 1997, p. A1.

mower would focus on the best way to use the hand mower; a productivity perspective would include the possibility of using a power mower.

Improving productivity is part of most chapters of this book.

SUMMARY

Competition is the driving force in many organizations. It involves emphasis on product attributes such as price, quality, variety, special features, customer service, timeliness, and location. To develop effective strategies for business, it is essential for organizations to determine what combinations of the attributes are important to customers, which attributes are order qualifiers, and which are order winners.

Strategies are plans for achieving organizational mission/vision/goals. Mission/vision is what the company wants to achieve, its products and services, and its markets. Organizations generally have overall strategies that pertain to the entire organization and strategies that pertain to each of the functional areas. Functional strategies are narrower in scope and should be linked to overall strategy. An operations strategy is a coordinated set of policies, objectives, and long-term action programs directly affecting the operations function, in order to gain a sustainable advantage over the competitors. Operations strategy is formed by the top executives. It includes setting performance measures for cost, quality, delivery, and flexibility, determining the operations requirements of the business strategy, determining the strengths and weaknesses of current operations policies and performance of product lines, grouping the product lines, assessing the focus of each plant, and developing objectives and broad and specific action programs in the categories of facilities, capacity, vertical integration, process types, product mix, human resources, product quality, operations infrastructure, and vendor relations. Time-based strategies and quality-based strategies are among the most widely used strategies business organizations employ to serve their customers and to become more productive.

Productivity is a measure of the use of resources. There is considerable interest in productivity both from an organizational standpoint and from a national standpoint. Business organizations want higher productivity because it yields lower costs and higher profits and helps them to become more competitive. Nations want higher productivity because it makes their goods and services more attractive, offsets inflationary pressures associated with higher wages, and results in a higher standard of living for their people.

KEY TERMS

competitiveness, 30	order winners, 31
distinctive competencies, 37	productivity, 39
mission, 32	quality-based strategy, 38
mission/vision statement, 32	strategy, 32
operations strategy, 34	tactics, 33
order qualifiers, 31	time-based strategy, 39

Solved Problems

Problem 1

A company that processes fruits and vegetables is able to produce 400 cases of canned peaches in one-half hour with four workers. What is labour productivity?

Solution

$$\text{Labour productivity} = \frac{\text{Quantity produced}}{\text{Labour hours}} = \frac{400 \text{ cases}}{4 \text{ workers} \times 1/2 \text{ hour}}$$

$$= 200 \text{ cases per worker hour}$$

Problem 2

A wrapping paper company produced 2,000 rolls of paper in one day. Labour cost was $160, material cost was $50, and overhead was $320. Determine the multifactor productivity.

Solution

$$\text{Multifactor productivity} = \frac{\text{Quantity produced}}{\text{Labour cost} + \text{Material cost} + \text{Overhead}}$$

$$= \frac{2,000 \text{ rolls}}{\$160 + \$50 + \$320}$$

$$= 3.77 \text{ rolls per dollar input}$$

A variation of the multifactor productivity calculation incorporates the price in the numerator by multiplying the units by the price.

DISCUSSION AND REVIEW QUESTIONS	

1. From time to time, the U.S. government imposes import restrictions or tariffs on Canadian-produced goods. What is the best way to handle this?
2. List the key ways that organizations compete.
3. Explain order qualifiers and order winners.
4. Select two stores you shop at, and state how they compete.
5. Describe what operations strategy is.
6. List the nine major operations decision-making categories.
7. Describe how an operating strategy is formulated.
8. Explain the term *time-based strategies* and give two examples.
9. What is productivity and why is it important? Who is primarily responsible for productivity in an organization?
10. List some factors that can affect productivity and some ways that productivity can be improved.
11. A typical Japanese automobile manufacturer produces more cars with fewer workers than its North American counterpart. What are some possible explanations for this, assuming that North American workers are as hardworking as Japanese workers?
12. A century ago, most people worked in agriculture, but now less than 4 percent of workers work in agriculture. Yet due to mechanization and automation, the agricultural output is much more now than a century ago. The majority of people now work in other industries making other products and rendering services. Also, the standard of living is much higher than a century ago. Discuss the statement "if productivity increases, fewer workers will be needed."
13. Boeing's strategy appears to focus on its 777 mid-size plane's ability to fly into smaller, non-hub airports. Rival European Airbus's strategy appears to focus on large planes. Compare the advantages and disadvantages of these two strategies.
14. Name five ways that banks compete for customers.
15. Explain the rationale of an operations strategy that seeks to increase the opportunity for use of technology by reducing variability in processing requirements.

TAKING STOCK	

1. Who needs to be involved in formulating operations strategy?
2. Name some of the competitive trade-offs that might arise in a fast-food restaurant.
3. How does technology improve each of these?
   a. Competitiveness
   b. Productivity

CRITICAL THINKING EXERCISE	

A company has two manufacturing plants, one in Canada and another in China. Both produce the same item. However, their labour productivity figures are quite different. The analyst thinks this is because the Canadian plant uses more automated equipment for processing while the other plant uses a higher percentage of labour. Explain how that factor can cause productivity figures to be misleading. Is there another way to compare the two plants that would be more meaningful?

INTERNET EXERCISE	

Pick a company, find its Web page, and search for its mission/vision statement. Does it contain their products and target market segment? Long-term goals? Explain.

PROBLEMS	

1. Suppose that a company produced 300 standard bookcases last week using seven workers and it produced 240 standard bookcases this week using five workers. In which period was labour productivity higher? Explain.
2. The manager of a crew that installs carpeting has tracked the crew's output over the past several weeks, obtaining these figures:

Week	Crew Size	Square Metres Installed
1	4	960
2	3	702
3	4	968
4	2	500
5	3	696
6	2	500

Calculate the labour productivity for each of the weeks. On the basis of your calculations, what can you conclude about crew size and productivity?

3. Calculate the multifactor productivity measure for each of the weeks shown below. What do the productivity figures suggest? Assume 40-hour weeks and an hourly wage of $12. Overhead is 1.5 times weekly labour cost. Material cost is $6 per kilogram. Selling price is $140 per unit.

Week	Output (units)	Workers	Material (kg)
1	300	6	45
2	338	7	46
3	322	7	46
4	354	8	48

4. A company that makes shopping carts for supermarkets and other stores recently purchased some new equipment that reduces the labour content of the jobs needed to produce the shopping carts. Prior to buying the new equipment, the company used four workers, who produced an average of 80 carts per hour. Labour cost was $10 per hour and machine cost was $40 per hour. With the new equipment, it was possible to transfer one of the workers to another department, and equipment cost increased by $10 per hour while output increased by four carts per hour.

   a. Calculate labour productivity before and after the new equipment. Use carts per worker per hour as the measure of labour productivity.

   b. Calculate the multifactor productivity before and after the new equipment. Use carts per dollar cost (labour plus equipment) as the measure.

   c. Comment on the changes in productivity according to the two measures, and on which one you believe is the more pertinent for this situation.

5. An operation has a 10-percent scrap rate. As a result, only 82 good pieces per hour are produced. What is the potential increase in labour productivity that could be achieved by eliminating the scrap?

6. A manager checked production records and found that a worker produced 160 units while working 40 hours. In the previous week, the same worker produced 138 units while working 36 hours. Did the worker's productivity increase, decrease, or remain the same? Explain.

7. Teradyne Connection Systems makes "backplanes" (large printed circuit-board assemblies) for communication and storages devices. Recently, they converted their production process from batch into assembly line. They also used computers to assist the workers at workstations. As a result, productivity has shot up. The site manager, Mark Galvin, says: "Operators made 300 backplanes in seven days using three shifts by a batch process (i.e., 7 days, 24 hours a day). Later, they assembled 500 backplanes in five days using just two shifts with the new assembly-line approach (i.e., 5 days, 16 hours a day)." Assuming the same number of workers worked during each shift, and before and after the conversion, what is the growth in labour productivity?

8. A land title search office has a staff of three, each working eight hours per day (for a total payroll cost of $480/day) and overhead costs of $300 per day. This office processes an average of 7 titles each day. The office recently purchased a computerized title-search system that will

allow the processing of an average of 12 titles per day. Although the staff, work hours, and pay will be the same, the overhead costs are now $600 per day.

    a. Calculate the labour productivity in the old and the new systems. How much (in percentage) has the labour productivity grown?

    b. Calculate the multifactor productivity in the old and the new systems. How much (in percentage) has the multifactor productivity grown?

    c. Which productivity measure is more appropriate?

9. When Henry Ford introduced moving assembly lines in his Ford Motor Company plants in 1913, the productivity soared.[8] An example of this is the Coil Line. A coil is an electrical component which makes high voltage for ignition. Before, a skilled worker took approximately 20 minutes to make a coil from start to finish. After an assembly line was set up and the job was divided into 29 different operations performed by 29 workers, it took only approximately 13 minutes to assemble one coil. (Note: Because workers work simultaneously, approximately every 0.5 minute a coil is produced.)

    a. Calculate the labour productivity before and after the conversion of the line into an assembly line.

    b. Calculate the percentage increase in productivity due to the assembly line.

10. (i) One person using a hammer will take five days to attach new shingles on the roof of a 1,000 ft² house.

  (ii) Two persons using a hammer but working together (one holds a shingle, the other swings the hammer) will take two days to do the same job.

 (iii) One person using a nail gun will take one day to do the same job.

    a. Define a labour productivity measure and determine its value for each of the above cases.

    b. Calculate the percentage increase in productivity due to method improvement, i.e., from (i) to (ii).

    c. Calculate the percentage increase in productivity due to using technology, i.e., from (i) to (iii).

11. Southwest Tube of Oklahoma[9] is a small fabricator of specialty tubes used in boilers and other equipment. Southwest buys the tubes in long segments and cuts, bends, cold draws, and welds the pieces to make what is needed for the products. A few years ago Southwest Tube was facing tough competition. The prices were falling while the costs were rising. To improve productivity, consultants were brought in. They pointed out problems with labour turnover, absenteeism, weak supervision, staffing mismatch, lack of performance goals, and dislike for weekly rotating schedule as causes of the problem. One of the solutions tried, in addition to other improvements, was changing the work schedule to four 12-hour days followed by three days off. The productivity seemed to improve gradually. To ascertain this, the following data for two physically demanding work-centres were collected starting the year before the change in work schedule.

Question: Has workers' productivity in the two work-centres increased? (Hint: Calculate the average productivity growth for each work-centre and interpret your results.)

Cold Draw Dept				**Weld Mill Dept**		
	Labour	Output			Labour	Output
Year	(1,000 hr)	(1,000 ft)		Year	(1,000 hr)	(1,000 ft)
0	228	18,269		0	132	22,434
1	234	19,576		1	157	34,777
2	183	17,633		2	102	26,715
3	150	18,870		3	77	25,227

---

[8]J. C. Wood and M. C. Wood, eds., *Henry Ford: Critical Evaluations in Business and Management* (London: Routledge, 2003).

[9]J. M. Shirley and T. M. Box, "Productivity Gains at Southwest Tube," *Production and Inventory Management Journal*, Fourth Quarter 1987, 28(4), pp. 57–60. Also see *www.webcoindustries.com*. Reprinted with permission of the APICS The Association for Operations Management.

READING

Zellers

www.hbc.com/zellers

Zellers is Canada's largest mass merchandise discount store chain. It has approximately 300 stores throughout Canada with annual sales of approximately $4.6 billion. Zellers is owned by the Hudson's Bay Company (HBC), which also owns The Bay, a major department store with approximately 100 stores. Prior to the late 1990s, Zellers targeted the budget-minded customer with the slogan, "Lowest Price is the Law."

Zellers was doing well up until 1993 when its earnings (before interest and tax) started to steadily decline from $256 million to $73 million in 1998, mainly due to stiff competition from Wal-Mart. Wal-Mart entered Canada in 1994 by purchasing more than 100 Woolco stores. Wal-Mart's efficient operations involve an integrated computerized inventory record-keeping system, which is accessed by suppliers regularly, and an efficient supply and distribution network. In addition, Wal-Mart has the broadest selection of merchandise, purchased in large volumes at discounted prices.

In addition to competition from Wal-Mart, Zellers had numerous operations problems, including having too many outdated products but being frequently out of stock on popular products, slow checkout lines due to missing product bar codes or having the wrong price in the computer, and lack of customer assistants on the store floor (making the stores essentially serve-service).

The dive in profits forced management to take some drastic actions starting in 1998:

- HBC purchased the more than 100 Kmart Canada stores. Based on location, size, performance, lease arrangements, and local market considerations, HBC closed approximately 40 of these stores and converted the remaining into Zellers.

- A major program to clean up inventories was undertaken. Substantial quantities of excessive or aged merchandise were cleared out of the system through heavy promotion and high markdowns. A program was put in place to regularly review stocks at the end of each month.

- The Zellers mission was changed to becoming "Mom's store" (with children under 12 years old) and providing "fair value," not the lowest price.

- Exclusive contracts are signed to sell famous brands such as Cherokee, Mossimo, Hillary Duff, and private brands such as Truly and ToGo were added.

- Larger store sizes, over 100,000 ft^2, were used for the new stores (as opposed to approximately 50,000 ft^2 previously). Zellers has now expanded and renovated approximately half its stores. Smaller stores were converted to a different name, Zellers-Select, carrying only high-demand products.

Zellers continuously experiments with new store locations (and closes many existing ones), sizes, and the merchandise each store carries.

- The layout and decoration of larger stores were redesigned to give a more open feel by removing tables and other obstructions from the aisles and widening them, instituting new and clearer colour-coded signage, and removing out of reach merchandise from the perimeter walls. Checkout is centralized.

- HBC combined the purchasing functions of The Bay and Zellers and created the position of VP merchandising. Zellers' headquarters was moved from Montreal into Bay headquarters in Toronto. Also, an "opportunity buys" business unit has been created to take advantage of one-time manufacturer sales.

- Zellers started to sell large appliances and furniture (like The Bay). Some prototype large stores even sell food. The idea is to cater to busy moms, who would save time buying milk and apparel in the same store.

- Zellers installed an integrated computer system (IBM) and merchandising software (Retek) and inventory-control software (Inforem), and financial enterprise resources planning software (Oracle) at a cost of approximately $50 million.

- HBC combined the credit cards and reward cards of Zellers and The Bay, encouraging the customers of one to shop in the other.

- Zellers has moved away from promotions (discounts) and uses everyday low pricing (like Wal-Mart) on 95 percent of its merchandise. It intends to use its advertising dollars more on radio and TV commercials and less on flyers.

- Zellers has moved away from its policy of self-service to one of having several customer service assistants available in the aisles.

Even though in the early 2000s, profit (before interest and tax) had crept back up to approximately $150 million per year, it has again declined to approximately $70 M per year.

Questions

1. State what competitive attributes (operations performance measures) are important for Zellers, and briefly explain why.

2. Determine if any of the action programs described in the case relate to any of the nine decision-making categories of operations strategy and identify which one.

Sources: HBC Annual Reports, 1998–2003; M. Duff, "Zellers Reorganizes Stores, Adopts EDLP Strategy," *DSN Retailing Today*, February 25, 2002, pp. 3, 27; M. Duff, "Zellers Debuts Marketing Driven, 'Airy' Prototype," *Discount Store News*, September 6, 1999, pp. 3, 17; D. Gill, "Zellers Fashions Its New Format," *Home Textiles Today*, August 9, 1999, pp. 1, 8 ff; V. L. Facenda, "At Zellers, Mom's the Word," *Discount Merchandiser*, August 99, pp. 87–91.

MINI-CASE

Lynn Revisited

(Refer to p. 25 for the Lynn case.)

1. What competitive advantage does Lynn have over a professional lawn care service?

2. Lynn would like to increase her profits, but she doesn't believe that it would be wise to raise her prices considering the current state of the local economy. Instead, she has given some thought to increasing productivity.

   a. Explain how increased productivity could be an alternative to increased prices.

   b. What are some ways that Lynn could increase productivity?

3. Lynn is thinking about the purchase of new equipment. One piece of equipment would be power sidewalk edgers. She believes edgers will lead to an increase in productivity.

Another piece of equipment would be a chain saw, which would be used for tree pruning. What trade-offs should she consider in her analysis?

4. Lynn has been fairly successful in her neighbourhood, and now wants to expand to other neighbourhoods, including some that are five kilometres away. What would be the advantages and disadvantages of doing this?

5. Lynn does not have a mission/vision statement or a set of objectives (goals). Which one of the following positions is correct? Explain.

   a. Lynn doesn't need a formal mission/vision statement and objectives. Many small businesses don't have them.

   b. She definitely needs a mission/vision statement and a set of objectives. They would be extremely beneficial.

   c. These may be of some benefit to Lynn's business, and she should consider developing them.

READING

Competing the Loblaw Way

www.loblaw.ca

Loblaw is Canada's largest food distributor, with operations across the country. It concentrates on food retailing with the objective of providing consumers with the best in one-stop shopping for everyday household needs. Loblaw is one of the largest companies in Canada, with over 119,000 employees.

When Richard J. Currie was appointed the president of Loblaw in 1976, Loblaw was only a regional chain (mainly in Ontario), with low profits and cash-flow problems. Most store buildings were leased on a long-term basis and the company had no strategic direction.

Currie closed some unprofitable stores and concentrated on maximizing sales per square foot of the other stores. Loblaw did not open new stores. Although it appeared weak to its competitors, this tactic allowed Loblaw to survive.

Currie believed that Loblaw should own its stores, rather than lease them. The leases were long-term and inflexible. This frequently resulted in the company having to pay for the building well after the store was closed. Also, changing a leased building to accommodate new departments was problematic. So, Loblaw gradually reduced its leases and increased its real estate ownership, investing its earnings. In fact, Loblaw now owns more lots and buildings than it uses.

Currie also believed that controlling the buying activities and labour costs was most important. Given that cost of goods is approximately 90 percent of the selling price in the grocery business, there is not much margin for labour and overhead costs. Also, he believed that union workers were much more costly than non-union workers. Given that most stores were already unionized, the way around the low margin was to expand the high-volume large stores.

Another problem in the food retailing business was that competitors competed using periodic sales (promotions), following a "high-low" strategy. Currie believed that selling anything below cost was absurd, but he could not convince his competitors. He believed that customers just needed "quality products, reliably available, and priced competitively."

His solution was to introduce the No-Name private label brand in 1978. This way, Loblaw could provide reasonable quality products at reduced prices every day. This was very successful. Later Loblaw continued its private brand with President's Choice in 1984, Club Pack in 1992, and recently Exact and Green.

Currie also believed in the advantage of an online in-store computerized information system. The use of bar codes and scanners allowed efficient data gathering that was used to identify profitability of items. This allowed Loblaw to control costs back up its supply chain.

Throughout the years, Loblaw has grown immensely through buying smaller regional chains and opening new stores. It now owns or franchises approximately 1,050 grocery stores in Canada, including The Real Canadian Superstore and Extra Foods in the West, Provigo in Quebec, and Atlantic Superstore in the Maritimes.

Other stores include Zehrs Markets, Valu-Mart, Maxi, Fortinos, Independent, and Cash & Carry. Approximately 650 stores are company owned and 400 of the smaller ones are franchised. It also supplies many independent small grocers such as Lucky Dollar Stores.

The relations with unions are fairly good. Loblaw has obtained wage decreases from its employees several times.

Loblaw pursues a multiformat approach on a market-by-market basis. Its stores vary in size from less than 20,000 ft² to more than 100,000 ft². Also, Loblaw has introduced non-food departments such as pharmacy, film development, and even a financial department with its own MasterCard (pays back 1 percent of charges).

Loblaw's supply and distribution network is efficient. It has 33 warehouses throughout Canada. It also has buying offices in the southern U.S. and recently built a huge 630,000 ft² distribution centre in Cambridge, Ontario.

In Ontario, Loblaw has combined its eight brand store chains and is also converting more stores into large Real Canadian superstore format.

Recently, Loblaw started to use the Internet for displaying current flyers, etc. Loblaw's sales revenue is growing at a phenomenal rate (more than 10 percent per year). Relative to 1997, Loblaw's revenue has doubled; its revenue was more than $25 billion in 2003, and its net margin was more than 2.5 percent—high for a grocery chain.

Questions

1. What competitive attributes does Loblaw emphasize?

2. What operations strategy does Loblaw use? Use the nine decision-making categories.

Sources: Loblaw Annual Reports 1998, 2001, and 2003. www.loblaw.ca; Richard J. Curry, "Loblaws: Putting the Super in Supermarket," *Business Quarterly*, Summer 1994, pp. 24–30; D. Kosub, "Discipline =Leadership: CCGD Conference," *Canadian Grocer* 116(5), June/July 2002, p. 88; N. Kuyumca, "The Duel of the Titans Continues Unabated," *Canadian Grocer* 117(6), August 2003, p. 13.

READING

WestJet's Strategy

www.westjet.ca

WestJet is the fast growing Canadian discount airline headquartered in Calgary. It started in 1996 targeting short trips in Western Canada (between Calgary, Edmonton, Kelowna, Winnipeg, and Vancouver). Clive Beddoe, one of the founders of WestJet, got the idea for WestJet after having to pay exorbitant fares to Air Canada and Canadian Airline (now part of Air Canada) for his frequent flights between Calgary (his hometown) and Edmonton and Vancouver, where he owned plastic manufacturing plants. According to Beddoe, "the key to expanding the market and luring masses of people who don't travel and those who drive is to charge them bargain-basement fares." He called this market the "visiting friends and relatives" market. In order to be able to offer low prices, WestJet needed to run a low-cost operation. WestJet studied successful discount airlines in the U.S. such as Southwest Airlines, and copied most of their operations' characteristics.

How could WestJet have planned for an operating cost approximately half that of Air Canada? The main aspects of WestJet's plan were:

- Short-distance flights. Advantage: no need for food for passengers, just a snack and juice.

- Purchase only one type of aircraft: Boeing 737. Advantages: made training of pilots and maintenance of aircrafts cheaper. WestJet bought three used (more than 20 years old) 737s.

- Fly to smaller cities such as Hamilton (rather than Toronto). Advantages: faster turn-round time (half-hour versus Air Canada's one hour) resulted in high aircraft utilization. Also, the airport fees are lower.

- Recruit young enthusiastic employees whose salary is slightly lower than average, but receive profit-sharing bonuses (the same percentage of the profit margin is distributed to staff, e.g., if the profit margin is 15 percent, then 15 percent of it is distributed). Advantage: the interests of employees and company are aligned; therefore the employees are more productive. For example, WestJet uses approximately 80 employees to operate and maintain one plane (versus approximately 140 by Air Canada).

- Emphasize "fun and friendly culture" and empower the employees (i.e., bottom-up management). Advantages: WestJet is nonunionized. Flexible work rules increase productivity; e.g., pilots help clean the planes between flights. Pro-Active Communication Team (PACT) acts as a company-sponsored association to hear and address staff concerns. Empowered frontline employees can give away company money to satisfy disgruntled customers. For example, when a wedding dress was lost, the employee went and purchased a replacement dress for the customer.

- Use equity financing. Initially the founders of WestJet solicited approximately $8 million from investors. Advantage: WestJet pays little interest for loans.

- Use paperless tickets, just the confirmation number. Advantage: saves costs. Now, over 70 percent of bookings are through Internet, which costs WestJet only approximately $2 per reservation versus approximately $20 when using travel agents.

- No connecting flights and no baggage transfers. Advantage: saves costs and allows on-time flights (no need to wait for late passengers).
- No frequent flyer program. Advantage: saves on the administration cost.

WestJet's growth has not been easy. Just six months after first flight, Transport Canada threatened to ground WestJet planes due to use of a modified version of Boeing's maintenance manual. WestJet stopped all its operations for approximately two weeks and scrambled to change its maintenance records to adhere to Boeing's standard manual.

Almost from the beginning, Air Canada tried to force West-Jet out of business. Air Canada introduced discount airline subsidiaries with flights between the same pairs of cities as WestJet, at around the same time of the day, and at approximately the same price. Even though this is not illegal, it has been found to be predatory. For example, after WestJet started to offer flights to Abbotsford, B.C., Air Canada started flights out of Abbotsford as well.

WestJet went public, i.e., offered shares in 1999 (brought in $24 million), and 2002 (brought in $82.5 million), and 2003. The proceeds were invested back in the company, mainly to buy new planes.

To further motivate its employees, WestJet introduced an employee share purchase program. Each employee can allocate a maximum of 20 percent of their salary to purchase WestJet shares and WestJet matches it dollar for dollar. Given WestJet's increased share price and the fact that the shares have split three times, many employees are quite wealthy now.

WestJet has gradually and carefully added to its flights. In 2000 WestJet expanded eastwards to Hamilton, Ontario (because the airport there is less crowded than Toronto's Pearson), then to Windsor, Halifax, Montreal, Gander, St. John's, and in 2002 to Toronto. Now, WestJet has flights to approximately 22 Canadian cities, and approximately 8 U.S. cities.

In 2000, WestJet partially hedged the price of its jet fuel needs by contracting with Petro-Canada, guaranteeing a price cap until 2003, based on $18 U.S. per barrel for crude oil.

WestJet has been gradually adding to its fleet of planes. Now it has approximately fifty-three 737 planes, most of them the new, slightly bigger but more efficient (by 30 percent) 737-700 model. The new planes have leather seats and individual live Satellite TV for each passenger. WestJet owns most of its planes.

In 2003, WestJet started accepting and giving Air Miles rewards. It has also started to sell sandwiches on flights longer than 2.5 hours.

WestJet is not afraid to spend money on useful technology. An example is the installation of blended winglets on the end of the wings of new planes which will increase fuel economy by approximately 5 percent. The approximately $600,000 investment per plane will pay back in about four years.

WestJet now employs approximately 4,800 employees and has about 30 percent of the air travel market in Canada. WestJet has one of the best on-time (within 15 minutes of the scheduled time) departure performances and is one of the most profitable airlines in North America.

Questions

1. What competitive attributes does WestJet use?
2. Determine if any of the actions described in the case relate to any of the nine decision-making categories of operations strategy, and identify which ones.

Sources: WestJet's 2003 Annual Report, *www.WestJet.ca*; P. Verburg, "A Dogfight Worth Watching," *Canadian Business,* August 30–September 12, 2004, 77, p. 19; A. A. Davis, "Sky High," *Profit* 23(1), March 2004, pp. 20–23; Anonymous, "WestJet Calls for 'Leap of Faith' in Upgrading Hamilton Airport," *Canadian Press Newswire*, January 29, 2002; P. Verburg, "Prepare to Take off," *Canadian Business* 73(24), December 25, 2000, pp. 94–98; P. Verburg, "Reach for the Bottom," *Canadian Business* 73(4), March 6, 2000, pp. 42–46; P. Verburg, "The Little Airline That Could," *Canadian Business*, April 1997, pp. 34–40; M. Nemeth, "Down, But Not Out," *MacLean's* 109(40), September 30, 1996, p. 38; M. Nemeth, "Upstairs in the Air," *MacLean's* 109(11), March 11, 1996, pp. 34–35.

Rohm and Haas' Operations Strategy

Rohm and Haas (R&H), based in Philadelphia, is a major producer of specialty chemicals such as polymer emulsions used in water-based paint. In the-mid 1990s, R&H was being squeezed between suppliers (petrochemical companies) and major customers such as Wal-Mart and Home Depot. Furthermore, competitors such as Dow Chemicals and BASF were taking market share. R&H's selling price had remained the same for five years whereas costs were going up. In addition, the production and order fulfillment was chaotic and stressful. The 11 U.S. plants each made all of the approximately 800 products. All customers, approximately 4,000, received the same service such as customized certificate of analysis or packaging/labelling. There was no fixed lead time; the due date was negotiated between the customer service rep (CSR) and the schedulers. The production schedule kept changing, with less than a day's notice.

To fix these problems, R&H spent $100 million on a Enterprise Resource Planning software, but after three years of implementation, there was no real change to its business processes. Then, a management team was formed consisting of Sales, Marketing, Manufacturing, Operations, and Logistics managers, and some internal consultants. The team analyzed R&H's customer base, dividing them into four categories: (1) partners or potential partners, (2) strategically important, (3) important, and (4) others.

It was decided that the approximately 3,200 customers in Tier 4 would be supplied by three exclusive distributors and not by R&H directly. This would save CSRs/schedulers' time and save production/transportation costs as larger batches to the distributors would be cheaper per unit.

Sales and Marketing people interviewed Tier 1 customers to find out what service they valued most and what R&H's competitors were offering. The services were categorized, their cost estimated, and a matrix was formed which relates each tier with standard service categories it would receive. For example, Tier 1 customers would receive customized packaging/labelling (see table below).

Also, the team studied the demand characteristic of the approximate 800 products. The results showed that most high-volume products were ordered regularly, whereas most low-volume products were ordered irregularly. The team modelled one of the facilities and performed a simulation study to find out the effect of dedicating chemical reactors to either high-volume or low-volume products, given various lead times. The results showed that the capacity would increase by 20 percent and on-time delivery will improve.

The team recommended specializing some of the plants/reactors to make the high-volume products and the others to make the low-volume products. Also, the high-volume products, which can be forecasted accurately, are to be made to stock, with a lead time of two days. On the other hand, it was decided not to carry any stocks of the low-volume variable-demand products. These are made to order with a lead time of seven days, and a minimum order quantity equal to the production batch size. Tier 1 customers have accepted the increase in lead time for low-volume products because it is certain.

As a result of these changes, R&H has saved millions of dollars, increased its production capacity, and improved its on-time delivery rates.

Questions

1. What competitive attributes (i.e., operations performance measures) does Rohm and Haas use?

2. Compare the above steps with the steps of operations strategy formulation recommended in the chapter? What are the similarities and differences?

3. What more could Rohm and Haas have done?

Source: A. J. D'Alessandro and A. Baveja, "Divide and Conquer: Rohm and Haas' Response to a Changing Specialty Chemicals Market," *Interfaces* 30(6), November/December 2000, pp. 1–16.

Customer Tier	Attributes and services	No. (%) of Customers	Percent Volume	Percentage of Gross Profit
1	Partners or potential partners Will drive business in the future Receive special services	82 (2%)	59	55
2	Strategic customers Critical to business Receive standard services	266 (6%)	26	24
3	Important customers based on a volume threshold Receive limited services	750 (17%)	11	14
4	Important as a class Not individually critical to the business Customers better served by high quality, exclusive distributors Receive defined services	3 serving 3,200 (75%)	4	7

SELECTED BIBLIOGRAPHY AND FURTHER READING

Bartlett, Christopher A., and Sumantra Ghoshal. "Going Global: Lessons from Late Movers." *Harvard Business Review,* March–April 2000, pp. 132–42.

Bernstein, Aaron. "Backlash: Behind the Anxiety of Globalization." *Business Week,* April 24, 2000, pp. 38–44.

Blackburn, Joseph D., ed. *Time-Based Competition.* Burr Ridge, IL: Business One Irwin, 1991.

Colvin, Geoffrey, "Managing in the Info Era." *Fortune,* March 6, 2000, pp. F6–F9.

Conference Board of Canada, "Performance and potential 2004–05." www.conferenceboard.ca.

Greenberg, L. *A Practical Guide to Productivity Measurement.* Washington. D.C.: Bureau of National Affairs, 1973.

Hachman, Mark. "Supply-Chain Program Boosts Productivity at Seagate Tech." *Electronic Buyers News,* January 17, 2000, p. 5.

Hill, Terry. *Manufacturing Strategy: Text and Cases,* 3rd ed. New York: McGraw-Hill, 2000.

Holstein, William J. "Are Raises Bad for America?" *U.S. News & World Report,* August 30, 1999, pp. 48–50.

Margretta, Joan. "The Power of Virtual Integration: An Interview with Dell Computer's Michael Dell." *Harvard Business Review,* March–April 1998, pp. 73–84.

Roach, Stephen. "In Search of Productivity." *Harvard Business Review,* September–October 1998, p. 153.

Ross, D. F. *Competing Through Supply Chain Management.* New York: Chapman and Hall, 1998.

Stalk, George, P. Evans, and L. E. Shulman. "Competing on Capabilities: The New Rules of Corporate Strategy." *Harvard Business Review,* March–April 1992, pp. 57–69.

PART TWO

Forecasting

This part is devoted solely to forecasting. It is presented early in the book because forecasts are the basis for a wide range of decisions that are described in the following chapters. In fact, forecasts are basic inputs for many kinds of decisions in business organizations. Consequently, it is important for *all* managers to be able to understand and use forecasts.

Although sales forecasts are typically developed by the sales/marketing function, the operations function, through production planning, will receive and use the forecasts. Also, operations develops forecasts for supplies and spare parts.

Chapter 3 provides important insights on forecasting as well as information on how to develop and monitor forecasts.

Forecasting

Before 1998, Ocean Spray, the cranberry cooperative, had some problems meeting retailer orders because it was not able to plan production effectively. Sales and operations in effect had two different forecasts of each product. Then, Ocean Spray changed its forecasting process. This improved the accuracy of forecasts from 55 percent to 75 percent, resulting in much improved customer service. How did Ocean Spray do this?

Spare parts are required for machines and equipment. They break down randomly. When they do, the spare part should be available soon to reduce the shut-down period. How do companies such as Caterpillar's Spare Parts Distribution or the maintenance warehouse of a chemical company such as Sterling Pulp Chemicals forecast the need for their spare parts?

These are the types of questions answered in this chapter.

INTRODUCTION

Many new-car buyers have a thing or two in common. Once they make the decision to buy a new car, they want it as soon as possible. They certainly don't want to order it and then have to wait six weeks or more for delivery. If the car dealer they visit doesn't have the car they want, they may look elsewhere. Hence, it is important for a dealer to *anticipate* what buyers want and to have those models, with the necessary options, in stock. The dealer who can correctly forecast what buyers want, and have those cars available, is going to be much more successful than a competitor who guesses instead of forecasting—and guesses wrong—and gets stuck with cars customers don't want. So how does the dealer know how many cars of each type to stock? The answer is, the dealer *doesn't* know for sure, but based on analysis of previous buying patterns, and perhaps making allowances for current conditions, the dealer can come up with a reasonable *approximation* of what buyers will want.

Planning is an integral part of a manager's job. If uncertainties cloud the planning process, managers will find it difficult to plan effectively. Forecasts help managers by reducing some of the uncertainty, thereby enabling them to develop more meaningful plans. A **forecast** is a statement about the future.

forecast A statement about the future.

This chapter provides a survey of business forecasting. It describes the necessary steps in preparing a forecast, basic forecasting techniques, and how to monitor a forecast.

People make and use forecasts all the time, both in their jobs and in everyday life. In everyday life, they forecast answers to questions. Typical questions they may ask are: "How much food and drink will I need?" "How much cash or gas will I need?" To make these forecasts, they may take into account two kinds of information. One is current factors or conditions. The other is past experience in a similar situation. Sometimes they will rely more on one than the other, depending on which approach seems more relevant at the time.

Forecasting for business purposes involves similar approaches. In business, however, more formal methods are used to make forecasts and to assess forecast accuracy.

There are three uses for forecasts in operations. One is to help managers *design the system*, the other is to help them *plan the medium-term use of the system*, and the third is to *schedule the short-term use of the system*. Designing the system involves long-term plans about the types of products and services to offer, capacities, what facilities and equipment to have, where to locate, and so on. Planning the medium-term use of the system involves tasks such as planning inventory and workforce levels, planning purchasing and production at the aggregate product family level. See the readings "Duracell Forecasting," for an example of the use of long- and medium-term forecasting, and "Colgate-Palmolive Co.," for an example of medium-term forecasting. Scheduling the short-term use of the system involves production, purchasing of supplies, and staff scheduling. (See Figure 3–1.)

Business forecasting pertains to more than predicting demand. Financial and economic forecasts are also used to predict profits, revenues, costs, and GDP. This chapter will focus on the forecasting of demand (sales or usage of supplies). Keep in mind, however, that the concepts and techniques apply equally well to the other variables.

FIGURE 3-1

*The uses of forecasts
in operations*

Source: Steven Nahmias, *Production
and Operations Analysis* (Irwin, 1997)
p. 61. Reprinted with permission of
The McGraw-Hill Companies.

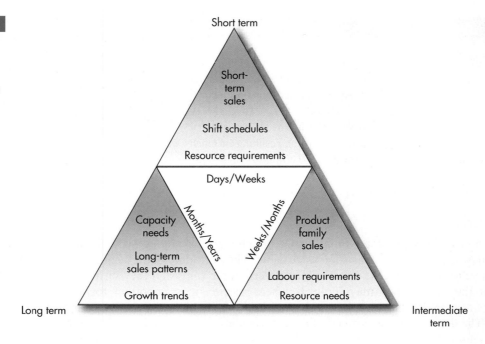

In spite of its use of computers and sophisticated mathematical models, forecasting is not an exact science. Instead, successful forecasting often requires a skillful blending of art and science. Experience, judgment, and technical expertise all play a role in developing useful forecasts. Along with these, a certain amount of luck and a dash of humility can be helpful, because the worst forecasters occasionally produce a very good forecast, and even the best forecasters sometimes miss completely. An example of a case where most forecasters got it wrong is the "crash" of high-tech companies such as Nortel Networks in the early 2000s.

Generally speaking, the responsibility for preparing sales forecasts lies with the marketing or sales department rather than operations. Nonetheless, because sales forecasts are major inputs for many operations decisions, operations managers and staff must be knowledgeable about the kinds of forecasting techniques available, the assumptions that underlie their use, and their limitations. Also the operations function provides feedback about the feasibility of producing the sales forecasts. See the reading, "Forecasting in Ocean Spray Cranberries." In addition, production planners (see Chapter 12) and inventory managers (see Chapter 11) make forecast of usage of supplies and spare parts.

Features Common to All Forecasts

A wide variety of forecasting techniques are in use. In many respects, they are quite different from one another, as you shall soon discover. Nonetheless, certain features are common to all, and it is important to recognize them.

1. Forecasting techniques generally assume that the same underlying causal system that existed in the past will continue to exist in the future.

Comment. A manager cannot simply delegate forecasting to models or computers and then forget about it, because unplanned or special occurrences can wreak havoc with forecasts. For instance, weather-related events, sales promotions, and changes in features or prices of own and competing products or services can have a major impact on demand. Consequently, a manager must be alert to such occurrences and be ready to override forecasts.

2. Forecasts are rarely perfect; actual results usually differ from predicted values. No one can predict *precisely* how related factors will impinge upon the variable in question; this, and the presence of randomness, preclude a perfect forecast. Allowances should be made for inaccuracies.

3. Forecasts for groups of items tend to be more accurate than forecasts for individual items because forecasting errors among items in a group usually have a cancelling effect. For example, the forecast for total sales of a new make of t-shirt will be more accurate than a forecast for each size and colour.

4. Forecast accuracy decreases as the time period covered by the forecast—the *time horizon*—increases. Generally speaking, short-term forecasts must contend with fewer uncertainties than longer-term forecasts, so they tend to be more accurate.

An important consequence of the last point is that flexible business organizations—those that can respond quickly to changes in demand—require a shorter forecasting horizon and, hence, benefit from more accurate short-term forecasts than competitors who are less flexible and who must therefore use longer forecast horizons.

READING

Forecasting in Ocean Spray Cranberries

www.oceanspray.com

Ocean Spray is an agricultural cooperative owned by approximately 800 cranberry growers and 100 grapefruit growers in the United States and Canada. It produces juices in bottles and cans in different flavour mixes and container sizes. When all the combination of products, sizes, and types of containers are taken into account, the number of different products ranges in the hundreds. For example, a case of eight 1.89 litre CranApple juice drink bottles is a product. The company also keeps track of groups of similar products, called categories and groups of same size products, e.g., a group of all 1.89 litre cranberry drink bottles. Also, the products and groups in each of company's four manufacturing plants and for the major customers, the retail chains, are tracked separately.

Forecasting is performed by the Demand Planning group which is located in the Logistics and Planning department. It consists of a manager and five demand planners, each responsible for a combination of approximately 300 different products and categories/size/manufacturing plant/major customer groupings. Forecasts are primarily used for production planning, purchasing, and shipment of the products. The planning process is called Sales and Operations Planning, discussed in more detail later in the text under the heading Aggregate Operations Planning in Chapter 12.

Every month during the first week, the demand planners use a software by Manugistics which uses the past three years' history of shipments and time series techniques to forecast shipments for the next six months. These forecasts are shared with local sales managers to check and adjust based on local knowledge of customer intentions, inventory, and promotions. During the second week, the adjusted forecasts are further examined and adjusted by regional and divisional marketing managers in a group meeting, called the Forecast Alignment meeting. During the third week, the aligned forecasts are

passed to the production/supply planning for review in the Supply Alignment meeting. Finally, during the last week of the month, upper management from Sales, Marketing, Operations, and Finance, and demand planners meet (called Sales and Operations Planning meeting) to review and implement the results of the alignment meetings.

Before setting up the above formal process and using Manugistics in 1998, Ocean Spray did not have one unique forecast for each product and groupings. The accuracy of forecasts was low—mean absolute percentage error (MAPE) was approximately 45 percent at the product level. Now, MAPE is approximately 25 percent.

Some of the challenges of the Demand Planners include the seasonally of sales of cranberries. Approximately 90 percent of sales occur during the fall, primarily before Thanksgiving and Christmas. Ocean Spray constantly introduces new products such as a new mix of another fruit with cranberry. If a similar product had been introduced before, this product's sales history will be used as a guide for the new product. Otherwise, the services of the Consumer Research department will be needed.

Sources: www.oceanspray.com; www.oceanspray.ca; P. Gelly, "Managing Bottom Up and Top Down Approaches: Ocean Spray's Experience," *Journal of Business Forecasting Methods & Systems* 18(4), Winter 1999/2000, pp. 3–5; J. Malehorn, "Forecasting at Ocean Spray Cranberries," *Journal of Business Forecasting Methods & Systems* 20(2), Summer 2001, pp. 6–8; http://www.manugistics.com/documents/collateral/Ocean_Spray_ManuCS.pdf.

Elements of a Good Forecast

A forecast should fulfill certain requirements:

1. The forecasting horizon must cover the time necessary to implement possible changes.
2. The degree of accuracy of the forecast should be stated.
3. The forecasting method/software chosen should be *reliable*; it should work consistently.
4. The forecast should be expressed in *meaningful units*. Financial planners need to know how many *dollars* will be needed, whereas demand and production planners need to know how many *units* will be needed.
5. All functions of an organization should be using the same forecast.
6. The forecasting technique should be *simple to understand and use*.

Steps in the Forecasting Process

There are six basic steps in the forecasting process (only steps 4 to 6 are used on a continuing basis):

1. *Determine the purpose of the forecast*, the level of detail required, the amount of resources (personnel, computer time, dollars) that can be justified, and the level of accuracy necessary.
2. *Establish a time horizon*.
3. *Select a forecasting technique*.
4. *Gather and analyze relevant historical data*. Identify any assumptions that are made.
5. *Prepare the forecast*.
6. *Monitor the forecast*. If it is not performing in a satisfactory manner, re-examine the parameters of the technique or use a different technique.

Approaches to Forecasting

There are two general approaches to forecasting: judgmental and quantitative. Judgmental methods consist mainly of subjective inputs, which often defy precise numerical description (but may still depend on historical data). Quantitative methods involve either the use of a time series model to extend the historical pattern of data or the development of associative models that attempt to utilize *causal (explanatory) variables* to make a forecast.

Judgmental techniques permit inclusion of *soft* information (e.g., human factors, personal opinions, hunches) in the forecasting process. Those factors are often omitted or downplayed when quantitative techniques are used because they are difficult to quantify. Quantitative techniques consist mainly of analyzing objective, or *hard*, data. They usually avoid personal biases that sometimes contaminate judgmental methods. In practice, either or both approaches might be used to develop a forecast.

judgmental methods Use subjective inputs such as opinions from consumer surveys, sales staff, managers, executives, historical analogies, and experts to help develop a forecast.

Judgmental methods rely on non-quantitative analysis of historical data and/or analysis of subjective inputs obtained from various sources, such as consumer surveys, historical analogies, the sales staff, managers and executives, and panels of experts. Quite frequently, these sources provide insights that are not otherwise available, e.g., for new product development, promotions, etc. Long-term forecasting uses judgments because quantitive techniques are inaccurate in this case.

time series models Extend the pattern of data into the future.

Some forecasting techniques simply attempt to project past data into the future. These techniques use historical, or time series, data with the assumption that the future will be like the past. **Time series models** identify specific patterns in the data and project or extrapolate those patterns into the future, without trying to identify causes of the patterns.

associative models Use explanatory variables to predict future demand.

Associative models use equations that consist of one or more *explanatory* variables that can be used to predict future demand. For example, demand for paint might be explained by variables such as the price, the amount spent on advertising, and the season, as well as specific characteristics of the paint (e.g., quality).

READING

McCormick

www.mccormick.com

McCormick is the largest spice manufacturer in North America. The sales (in units) of approximately 2,500 spices are forecasted by the production forecaster (located in the marketing/sales department) every month for the next two years. The functions that use these forecasts are purchasing, material management, and production. The production forecaster uses strictly judgmental forecasting. First, he looks at the past three years of sales history and from that he develops a base forecast. Then, he considers any sales/marketing information on price increases, promotions, fads, and trends, and modifies the base forecast. These forecasts are reviewed (for some products monthly and for others quarterly) by marketing/sales and production staff during regular monthly meetings.

To forecast sales during promotion of a spice, sales during past promotions of the same product are used. To forecast sales of new products, past sales of a similar product are used.

The production forecaster finds the forecast of new items and low-volume items most challenging because their sales are dependent on only few customers. Items being promoted and those subject to price change are also hard to forecast. The forecast errors range from approximately 20 percent for high-volume items to as high as 45 percent for low-volume and new items.

Sources: C. L. Jain, "Forecasting at McCormick & Company," *Journal of Business Forecasting Methods & Systems* 10(4), Winter 1991–92, pp. 3–5.

JUDGMENTAL METHODS

In some situations, forecasters may rely solely on judgment and opinion to make forecasts. The introduction of new products, the redesign of existing products, or sales promotions are situations where judgmental forecasting is needed, as well as when analyzing future actions of customers and competitors. In such instances, forecasts may be based on collective executive opinions, opinions of the sales staff, consumer surveys, historical analogies, or opinions of experts. See the McCormick reading for a case where the forecaster uses his own judgment to determine the base forecast.

Executive Opinions

A small group of upper-level managers (e.g., VPs of Marketing, Operations, and Finance) may meet and collectively develop a forecast. This approach is often used as a part of long-term planning and new-product development. It has the advantage of bringing together the considerable knowledge and talents of various managers.

Salesforce Opinions

The sales staff or the customer service staff is often a good source of information because of their direct contact with customers. They are often aware of any plans the customers may be considering for the future, including the current level of customer inventory.

Consumer Surveys

Because it is the potential consumers who ultimately determine sales, it seems natural to solicit input from them. This could be in the form of questionnaires conducted by mail or phone to a large sample of potential consumers. It also could be through group meetings with a small number of potential consumers (focus groups).

Historical Analogies

Sometimes the demand for a similar product in the past, after some adjustment, can be used to forecast a new product's demand. For example, the demand for cranberry-apple drink can be used to forecast the demand for cranberry-grape drink.

Expert Opinions

The forecaster may solicit opinions from a number of experts. One way of doing this is called the **Delphi method**. It involves circulating a series of questionnaires among experts. Responses are kept anonymous, which tends to encourage honest responses and reduces the

Delphi method Experts complete a series of questionnaires, each developed from the previous one, to achieve a consensus forecast.

Duracell Forecasting

Duracell is the largest manufacturer of alkaline batteries in the world. Although it has a limited number of common (e.g., AA, C) and specialty (e.g., for cameras, watches) batteries, the various regular pack sizes (e.g., 2, 4, etc.) and special promotions packs result in hundreds of different stock keeping units (SKUs). Forecasting is performed by the Market and Sales Forecasting group located in the finance department. There are a manager and six forecasters. The forecasting group performs two types of forecasting: strategic and tactical.

Strategic forecasting involves both projecting competitors' sales and Duracell's sales, by pack size and trade channel, for the next three years. Size of market and its growth, share of Duracell and its growth, and retail inventory changes are forecasted and used to arrive at Duracell's shipment forecasts. Marketing approves the growth plan and view of marketplace. Duracell finds the Point Of Sale (POS) data and Nielsen's market information valuable. Also used are economic data and industry data on battery-powered devices. Scenarios based on competitor and Duracell actions are developed and their effect on forecasts is examined using techniques such as regression. The strategic plan becomes the basis for the tactical plan.

In tactical planning, monthly forecasts (called Latest Estimates) are made at the SKU level for the next 12 months. Performance in the market during the previous month is reviewed, issues and assumptions are analyzed, and forecasts are updated. Information from salespeople regarding future promotions, in-store display changes, and competitors' actions are used in this process. The aggregate forecasts are approved by VPs of Marketing, Sales, and Finance by the fourth day of each month. By the sixth day, manufacturing also approves the plan. Later, SKU level forecasts are discussed with middle-level managers responsible for the required actions.

Source: R. Gordon, "A Role for the Forecasting Function," *Journal of Business Forecasting Methods & Systems* 16(4), Winter 1997/98, pp. 3–7; www.Duracell.com.

risk that one person's opinion will prevail. Each new questionnaire is developed using the information extracted from the previous one, thus enlarging the scope of information on which participants can base their judgments. The goal is to achieve a consensus forecast.

One application of the Delphi method is for *technological* forecasting, i.e., assessing changes in technology and their impact on an organization. Often the goal is to predict *when* a certain event will occur. For instance, the goal of a Delphi forecast might be to predict when video telephones might be installed in at least 50 percent of residential homes or when a vaccine for a disease might be developed. For the most part, these are long-term, single-time forecasts, which usually have very little hard information to go by.

TIME SERIES MODELS

time series A time-ordered sequence of observations taken at regular intervals of time.

A **time series** is a time-ordered sequence of observations taken at regular intervals over a period of time (e.g., hourly, daily, weekly, monthly, quarterly, annually). Forecasting techniques based on time series data are made on the assumption that future values of the series can be estimated from its own past values. Although no attempt is made to identify variables that influence the series, these methods are widely used, often with quite satisfactory results.

Analysis of time series data requires the analyst to identify the underlying behaviour of the series. This can often be accomplished by merely *plotting* the data and visually examining the plot. One or more patterns might appear: changes in level (i.e., average),

level (average) A short-term upward or downward movement in data or a step change.

trend, seasonal variation, and cycle. In addition, there can be random and irregular (one-time) variations. These behaviours can be described as follows:

1. **Level (average)** refers to either a short-term, upward or downward movement in the data, or a step change (jump).

trend A long-term upward or downward movement in data.

2. **Trend** refers to a long-term upward or downward movement in the data. Population growth, increasing incomes, and cultural changes often account for such movements.

seasonality Regular wavelike variations related to the calendar.

3. **Seasonality** refers to fairly regular repeating wavelike variations generally related to factors such as the calendar. For example, sales of ice cream are higher in the summer. Restaurants, supermarkets, and theatres experience weekly and even daily "seasonal" variations.

4. **Cycles** are wavelike variations of more than one year's duration. These are often related to a variety of economic, political, and even agricultural conditions, such as supply of cattle.

5. **Irregular variations** are due to unusual circumstances such as severe weather conditions, strikes, or a one-time event. They do not reflect typical behaviour, and whenever possible should be identified and removed from the data.

6. **Random variations** are residual variations that remain after all other behaviours have been accounted for.

Some of these behaviours are illustrated in Figure 3–2. The small "bumps" in the plots represent random variability.

cycle Wavelike variation lasting more than one year.

irregular variation Caused by unusual circumstances, not reflective of typical behaviour.

random variation Residual variations after all other behaviours are accounted for.

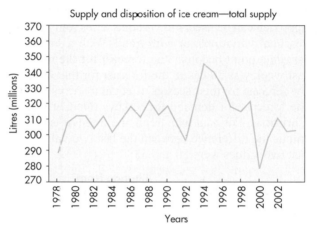

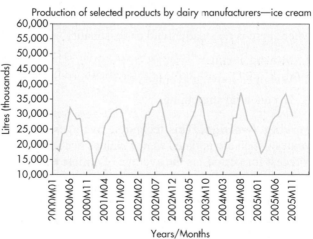

FIGURE 3–2

Level, trend, and seasonal variations

Source: Adapted from the Statistics Canada CANSIM 2 database <http://cansim2.statcan.ca>, Table 20010, Series v108517; January 23, 2006.

Source: Adapted from the Statistics Canada CANSIM 2 database <http://cansim2.statcan.ca>, Table 20010, Series v108612; January 23, 2006.

Source: Adapted from the Statistics Canada CANSIM 2 database <http://cansim2.statcan.ca>, Table 30010, Series v382696; January 23, 2006.

Historical data typically contain a certain amount of random variation, or *noise*, that tends to obscure systematic movements in the data. This randomness arises from the combined influence of many—perhaps a great many—relatively unimportant factors, and it cannot be reliably predicted. Time series techniques smooth random variations in the data.

The remainder of this section has descriptions of the various approaches to the analysis of time series data. Before turning to those discussions, one point should be emphasized: a demand forecast should ideally be based on a time series of past *demand* rather than sales or shipments. Sales or shipments would not truly reflect demand if *stockouts* occurred.

Naive Methods

naive forecast The forecast for any period equals the previous period's actual value.

A simple, but widely used approach to forecasting is the naive approach. A **naive forecast** uses a single previous value of a time series as the basis of a forecast. The naive approach can be used with a stable series (only possible changes in level or average), with seasonal variations, or with trend. With a stable series or with only level changes, the last data point becomes the forecast for the next period. Thus, if demand for a product last week was 20 cases, the forecast for this week is 20 cases. With seasonal variations, the forecast for this "season" is equal to the value of the series last "season." For example, the forecast for demand for turkeys this Christmas is equal to demand for turkeys last Christmas. For data with trend, the forecast is equal to the last value of the series plus or minus the difference between the last two values of the series. For example, suppose the last two values were 50 and 53:

Period	Actual	Change from Previous Value	Forecast
$t - 1$	50		
t	53	+ 3	
$t + 1$			$53 + 3 = 56$

Although at first glance the naive approach may appear *too* simplistic, it is nonetheless a legitimate forecasting tool used by some businesses such as restaurants and retail stores. Consider the advantages: It has virtually no cost, it is quick and easy to prepare, and it is easily understandable. The main objection to this method is its inability to provide highly accurate forecasts. The accuracy of a naive forecast can serve as a standard of comparison against which to judge the cost and accuracy of other techniques.

One weakness of the naive method is that the forecast just *traces* the actual data, with a lag of one period; it does not smooth the random variations out at all. But by expanding the amount of historical data a forecast is based on, this difficulty can be overcome.

Averaging Methods

Averaging techniques generate forecasts that reflect recent changes in level (i.e., average) of a time series. They can handle stable series (i.e., no change in level) as well as step changes and short-term changes in the level of the series. Three techniques for averaging, when there is no steady trend or seasonality, are described in this section:

1. Moving average
2. Weighted moving average
3. Exponential smoothing

moving average Technique that averages a number of recent actual values, updated as new values become available.

Moving Average. This technique averages a *number* of the most recent actual data values which are updated as new values become available. The *n*-period moving average forecast for period *t* is the average of *n* most recent actual values.

$$F_t = MA_n = \frac{\sum\limits_{i=t-1}^{t-n} A_i}{n} \tag{3–1}$$

where

i = An index that corresponds to age of the period ($i = t - 1$: last period; $i = t - 2$: two periods back, …)

n = Number of periods (data points) in the moving average

A_i = Actual value in period i

MA = Moving average

F_t = Forecast for this period (i.e., period t)

For example, MA_3 would refer to a three-period moving average forecast, and MA_5 would refer to a five-period moving average forecast.

Compute a three-period moving average forecast given demand for shopping carts for the last five periods.

Example 1

Period	Demand
1	42
2	40
3	43 ⎫
4	40 ⎬ the 3 most recent demands
5	41 ⎭

$$F_6 = \frac{43 + 40 + 41}{3} = 41.33$$

Solution

If actual demand in period 6 turns out to be 39, the moving average forecast for period 7 would be

$$F_7 = \frac{40 + 41 + 39}{3} = 40.00$$

Note that in a moving average, as each new actual value becomes available, the forecast is updated by adding the newest value and dropping the oldest and then calculating the average. Consequently, the forecast "moves" by reflecting only the most recent values.

Figure 3–3 illustrates a three-period moving average forecast plotted against actual demand during 31 periods. Note how the moving average forecast *lags* behind the actual values and how smooth the forecasted values are compared with the actual values.

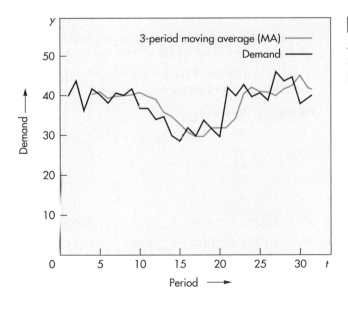

FIGURE 3-3

A moving average forecast tends to smooth the data but lags behind the data

FIGURE 3-4

The fewer periods in a moving average, the greater the forecast will be responsive to the most recent data

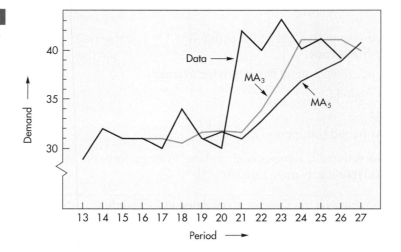

The moving average can incorporate as many data points as desired. In selecting the number of periods to include, the decision maker must take into account that the number of data points in the average determines its sensitivity to each new data point: the fewer the data points in an average, the more sensitive (responsive) to most recent data the average tends to be. (See Figure 3–4.) If responsiveness is important, a moving average with relatively few data points should be used. This will permit quick adjustment to, say, a step change in the data, but it will also cause the forecast to be somewhat responsive even to random variations. Conversely, moving averages based on more data points will be smoother but less responsive to "real" changes. Hence, the decision maker must weigh the cost of responding more slowly to changes in the data against the cost of responding to what might simply be random variations. A review of forecast errors can help in this decision.

The advantages of a moving average forecast are that it is easy to compute and easy to understand. A possible disadvantage is that all values in the average are weighted equally. For instance, in a 5-period moving average, each value has a weight of 1/5. Hence, the oldest value has the *same weight* as the most recent value.

weighted moving average

A variation of moving average where more recent values in the series are given more weight in calculating a forecast.

Weighted Moving Average is similar to a moving average, except that it assigns more weight to the most recent values in a time series. For instance, the most recent value might be assigned a weight of .40, the next most recent value a weight of .30, the next after that a weight of .20, and the next after that a weight of .10. Note that the weights sum to 1.00, and that the heaviest weights are assigned to the most recent values.

Example 2

Given the following demand data,

a. Calculate a weighted average forecast using a weight of .40 for the most recent period, .30 for the next most recent, .20 for the next, and .10 for the next.

b. If the actual demand for period 6 is 39, forecast the demand for period 7 using the same weights as in part *a.*

Period	Demand
1	42
2	40
3	43
4	40
5	41

Solution

a. $F_6 = .40(41) + .30(40) + .20(43) + .10(40) = 41.0$

b. $F_7 = .40(39) + .30(41) + .20(40) + .10(43) = 40.2$

Note that if four weights are used, only the *four most recent* demand values are used to prepare the forecast.

The advantage of a weighted average over a simple moving average is that the weighted average is more reflective of the most recent observations. However, the choice of weights is somewhat arbitrary and generally involves the use of trial and error to find a suitable weighting scheme.

Exponential Smoothing is a sophisticated weighted averaging method where a new forecast is based on the previous forecast plus a percentage of the difference between that forecast and the previous actual value. That is:

> Forecast = Previous forecast + α(Previous actual − Previous forecast)

exponential smoothing
Weighted averaging method based on previous forecast plus a percentage of the forecast error.

where (Previous actual − Previous forecast) represents the forecast error and α is a proportion less than one. More concisely,

$$F_t = F_{t-1} + \alpha(A_{t-1} - F_{t-1}) \tag{3–2a}$$

where

> F_t = Forecast for period t
> F_{t-1} = Forecast for period $t - 1$
> α = Smoothing constant, $0 < \alpha < 1$
> A_{t-1} = Actual demand in period $t - 1$

For example, suppose that the previous forecast was 42 units, previous actual demand was 40 units, and α = .10. The new forecast would be computed as follows:

$$F_t = 42 + .10(40 - 42) = 41.8$$

Then, if the actual demand turns out to be 43, the next forecast would be:

$$F_t = 41.8 + .10(43 - 41.8) = 41.92$$

An alternate form of formula 3–2a reveals the weighting of the previous forecast and the previous actual demand:

$$F_i = (1 - \alpha)F_{t-1} + \alpha A_{t-1} \tag{3–2b}$$

For example, if α = .10, this would be

$$F_t = .90F_{t-1} + .10A_{t-1}$$

The quickness of adjustment by forecast error is determined by the smoothing constant, α. The closer its value is to zero, the slower the forecast will adjust by forecast error (i.e., the greater the smoothing). Conversely, the closer the value of α is to 1.0, the greater the responsiveness and the less the smoothing. This is illustrated in Example 3.

The following table illustrates two series of exponential smoothing forecasts for a data set, and the resulting (Actual − Forecast) = Error, for each period. One forecast uses α = .10 and the other uses α = .40. The following figure plots the actual data and both sets of forecasts.

Example 3

Period (*t*)	Actual Demand	α = .10 Forecast	α = .10 Error	α = .40 Forecast	α = .40 Error
1	42	—	—	—	—
2	40	42	− 2	42	− 2
3	43	41.8	1.2	41.2	1.8
4	40	41.92	− 1.92	41.92	− 1.92
5	41	41.73	− 0.73	41.15	− 0.15
6	39	41.66	− 2.66	41.09	− 2.09
7	46	41.39	4.61	40.25	5.75
8	44	41.85	2.15	42.55	1.45
9	45	42.07	2.93	43.13	1.87
10	38	42.36	− 4.36	43.88	− 5.88
11	40	41.92	− 1.92	41.53	− 1.53
12		41.73		40.92	

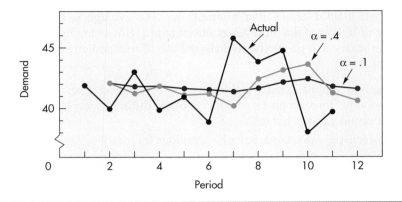

Selecting a smoothing constant is basically a matter of judgment or trial and error (or one can use the forecast errors to guide the decision). The goal is to select a smoothing constant that balances the benefits of smoothing random variations with the benefits of responding to real changes if and when they occur. Commonly used values of α range from .05 to .50. Low values of α are used when the underlying average tends to be stable; higher values are used when the underlying average is susceptible to change.

Some computer packages include a feature that permits automatic modification of the smoothing constant if the forecast errors become unacceptably large. This method is called adaptive or variable response exponential smoothing.

Exponential smoothing is one of the most widely used techniques in forecasting, partly because of its ease of calculation, and partly because of the ease with which the weighting scheme can be altered—simply by changing the value of α.

Note. A number of different approaches can be used to obtain a *starting forecast* for period 2, such as the average of the first several periods, a subjective estimate, or the first actual value (i.e., the naive approach). For simplicity, the naive approach is used in this book. In practice, using an average of, say, the first three values as a forecast for period 4 would provide a better starting forecast because that would tend to be more stable.

Techniques for Trend

Analysis of trend involves developing an equation that will suitably describe trend (assuming that trend is present in the data). The trend component may be linear, or it may be nonlinear. Some commonly encountered nonlinear trend types are illustrated in Figure 3–5. A simple plot of the data can often reveal the existence and nature of a trend.

FIGURE 3–5

Graphs of some nonlinear trends

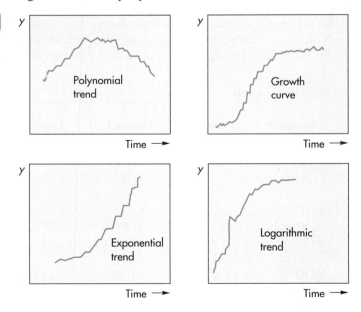

We will first focus on *linear* trends because these are fairly common. These trend models are usually fitted using regression. Excel facilitates this, in addition to many types of nonlinear trend. A more sophisticated method that combines trend and exponential smoothing will be described later.

Linear Trend Equation. This equation has the form

$$\hat{y}_t = a + bt \qquad (3\text{--}3)$$

where

t = Index of time periods, starting from $t = 1$ for the first period

$\hat{y}_t$ = Value of trend line at period t

a = Value of $\hat{y}_t$ at $t = 0$ (intercept)

b = Slope of the line

linear trend equation
$\hat{y}_t = a + bt$, used to develop forecasts when linear trend is present.

Forecast for period t: $F_t = a + bt$

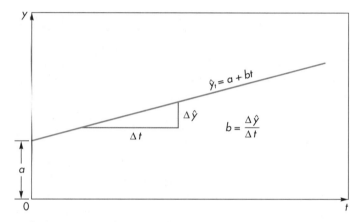

The line intersects the y axis where $\hat{y}_t = a$. The slope of the line $= b$.

For example, consider the trend equation $\hat{y}_t = 45 + 5t$. The value of $\hat{y}_t$ when $t = 0$ is 45, and the slope of the line is 5, which means that, on the average, the value of estimate of demand $\hat{y}_t$ will increase by five units for each time period. If $t = 10$, the forecast, F_t, is $45 + 5(10) = 95$ units. The equation can be plotted by finding two points on the line. One can be found by substituting some value of t into the equation (e.g., $t = 10$) and then solving for $\hat{y}_t$. The other point is a (i.e., $\hat{y}_t$ at $t = 0$). Plotting those two points and drawing a line through them yields a graph of the linear trend line.

The coefficients of the line, a and b, can be calculated from data using these two equations:

$$b = \frac{n\sum ty - \sum t \sum y}{n\sum t^2 - \left(\sum t\right)^2} \qquad (3\text{--}4)$$

$$a = \frac{\sum y - b\sum t}{n} \quad \text{or} \quad \bar{y} - b\bar{t} \qquad (3\text{--}5)$$

where

n = Total number of periods

y = Value of the demand time series

Note that these equations are identical to those used for computing a linear regression line, except that t replaces x in the equations.

Example 4

Cell phone sales for a company over the last 10 weeks are shown below. The data appear to have a linear trend. Determine the equation of the linear trend, and predict the sales of cell phones for weeks 11 and 12. Plot the data and trend line.

Week	Unit Sales
1	700
2	724
3	720
4	728
5	740
6	742
7	758
8	750
9	770
10	775

Solution

Week (t)	y	ty	t^2
1	700	700	1
2	724	1,448	4
3	720	2,160	9
4	728	2,912	16
5	740	3,700	25
6	742	4,452	36
7	758	5,306	49
8	750	6,000	64
9	770	6,930	81
10	775	7,750	100
55	7,407	41,358	385

Using formulas 3–4 and 3–5, we can calculate the coefficients of the trend line:

$$b = \frac{10(41,358) - 55(7,407)}{10(385) - 55(55)} = \frac{6,195}{825} = 7.51$$

$$a = \frac{7,407 - 7.51(55)}{10} = 699.40$$

Thus, the trend line is $\hat{y}_t = 699.40 + 7.51t$, where $t = 1$ for week 1.

Substituting values of t into this equation, the forecasts for the next two weeks (i.e., $t = 11$ and $t = 12$) are:

$F_{11} = 699.40 + 7.51(11) = 782.01$

$F_{12} = 699.40 + 7.51(12) = 789.52$

The original data (in black), the trend line (in blue), and the two projections (forecasts) are shown on the following graph. It is evident that the data exhibit a linear trend.

We can use the Excel template on the DVD to solve this problem. Alternatively, we can set up our own Excel template. In fact, Excel has a feature which makes fitting a trend line very easy. After charting the time series as a line plot, from the "Chart" pull-down menu, choose "Add Trendline ...," which can fit six types of trends to the data. The following is the result of choosing the default, the "Linear trend." Use the option "Display equation on chart."

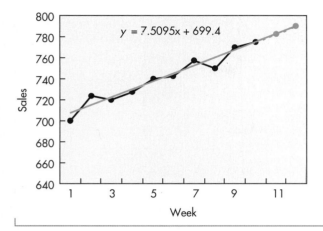

Although linear trend is appropriate for some series, it is inadequate for others such as demand for a new product that has a faster growth or for an old product that has a slower growth (i.e., a decline). Example 5 illustrates an exponential trend.

PHH Fantus Corp. is involved in facility location and capacity planning consulting work.[1] One project involved a manufacturer of audio products with a production facility in the United Kingdom that needed more production capacity. From this plant, the company was supplying all of Europe. The question was where to locate a second plant and what capacity to build it for. The historical sales for all major European countries were available. From these, Fantus forecasted 1991–95 sales. The largest sales market was in Germany, and it had exponential trend (see the graph on the next page). We wish to find out the equation for this trend and extend it one year further.

Example 5

Year (x)	Projected sales in Germany (in million units)
1991	11.3
1992	13.4
1993	16.1
1994	19.2
1995	22.9

Solution

After entering the data in Excel and drawing the time series line plot using "Chart," we use the "Add Trendline" function to fit the best exponential trend to the data. The equation will also be displayed if you select the "Display equation on chart" option in the "Options" tab in the "Add Trendline" mini window. The exponential trend equation is approximately, $\hat{y}_t = 9.44e^{0.177x}$, where $e = 2.7183$. Note that this exponential trend assumes a constant *percentage* increase in sales from one year to the next. This constant growth rate can be determined as follows: take the coefficient of year index x from regression, raise it to the power of e, subtract 1, and multiply by 100. For this example, $e^{0.177} = 1.194$, so the constant percentage yearly increase in sales is 19.4 percent. This can be confirmed by subtracting any year's sales from the following year's sales and dividing by the same year's sales. For example (forecast sales 1995 − forecast sales 1994)/forecast sales 1994 = (22.9 − 19.2)/19.2 = 0.193, or 19.3 percent (the difference to 19.4 percent is rounding error). The forecast for 1996 is $F_{96} = 9.44e^{0.177(6)} = 27.3$.

---

[1]M. P. Butler, "Facility and Capacity Planning Using Sales Forecasting by Today's Industrial Engineer," *Industrial Engineering* 22(6), June 1990, pp. 52–55.

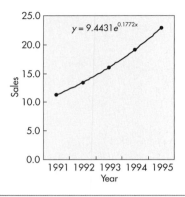

Trend-Adjusted Exponential Smoothing

trend-adjusted exponential smoothing Variation of exponential smoothing used when a time series exhibits trend.

A variation of simple exponential smoothing can be used when a time series exhibits trend. It is called **trend-adjusted exponential smoothing** or (Brown's) *double exponential smoothing*, to differentiate it from simple exponential smoothing. If a series exhibits trend, and simple smoothing is used on it, the forecasts will all lag behind the trend: if the data are increasing, each forecast will be too low; if decreasing, each forecast will be too high.

The trend-adjusted forecast (TAF) is composed of two elements: a smoothed average and a trend factor.

$$\text{TAF}_{t+1} = S_t + T_t \tag{3-6}$$

where

S_t = Smoothed average

T_t = Current trend estimate

and

$$S_t = \text{TAF}_t + \alpha(A_t - \text{TAF}_t) \tag{3-7}$$
$$T_t = T_{t-1} + \beta(\text{TAF}_t - \text{TAF}_{t-1} - T_{t-1})$$

where α and β are smoothing constants, and A_t = actual value in period t. In order to use this method, one must select values of α and β (usually through trial and error) and make a starting trend-adjusted forecast and an estimate of starting trend.

Example 6

Using the cell phone data from Example 4 (where it was concluded that the data exhibited a linear trend), use trend-adjusted exponential smoothing to prepare forecasts for periods 5 through 11, with $\alpha = .4$ and $\beta = .3$. Use the first four weeks to estimate starting trend and use week four's actual value as a smooth average in week four.

Solution

The initial estimate of trend is based on the net change of 28 for the *three* changes from week 1 to week 4, for an average of 9.33. The data and calculations are shown in Table 3–1. Notice that the starting trend-adjusted forecast (week 5) is developed using the previous (week 4) actual value of 728 plus the initial trend estimate:

$$\text{TAF}_5 = 728 + 9.33 = 737.33$$

After observing the actual sales in week 5 (740 units), we can forecast the smoothed average for week 5:

$$S_5 = \text{TAF}_5 + \alpha(A_5 - \text{TAF}_5)$$
$$= 737.33 + .4(740 - 737.33)$$
$$= 738.40$$

Given that the forecast for trend in week 5, T_5, was estimated to be 9.33, the trend-adjusted forecast for week 6 is:

$$\text{TAF}_6 = S_5 + T_5 = 738.40 + 9.33 = 747.73.$$

	t (Week)	A_t (Actual)				
Model development	1	700	Trend estimate $T_5 = \dfrac{728-700}{3} = \dfrac{28}{3} = 9.33$			
	2	724				
	3	720	Starting forecast $\text{TAF}_5 = 728 + 9.33 = 737.33$			
	4	728				

			$\text{TAF}_t + \alpha(A_t - \text{TAF}_t) = S_t$	$T_{t-1} + \beta(\text{TAF}_t - \text{TAF}_{t-1} - T_{t-1}) = T_t$	$\text{TAF}_{t+1} = S_t + T_t$
Model test	5	740	$737.33 + .4(740 - 737.33) = 738.40$	$= 9.33$	747.73
	6	742	$747.73 + .4(742 - 747.73) = 745.44$	$9.33 + .3(747.73 - 737.33 - 9.33) = 9.65$	755.09
	7	758	$755.09 + .4(758 - 755.09) = 756.25$	$9.65 + .3(755.09 - 747.73 - 9.65) = 8.96$	765.22
	8	750	$765.22 + .4(750 - 765.22) = 759.13$	$8.96 + .3(765.22 - 755.09 - 8.96) = 9.31$	768.45
	9	770	$768.45 + .4(770 - 768.45) = 769.07$	$9.31 + .3(768.45 - 765.22 - 9.31) = 7.49$	776.56
	10	775	$776.56 + .4(775 - 776.56) = 775.94$	$7.49 + .3(776.56 - 768.45 - 7.49) = 7.68$	783.61

Note: Some numbers don't add exactly due to rounding.

TABLE 3–1

Trend-adjusted forecast calculations for example 6.

After observing the actual sales in week 6 (742 units), we can forecast the smoothed average for week 6:

$$S_6 = \text{TAF}_6 + \alpha(A_6 - \text{TAF}_6)$$
$$= 747.73 + .4(742 - 747.73)$$
$$= 745.44$$

and the forecast for trend in week 6 is:

$$T_6 = T_5 + \beta(\text{TAF}_6 - \text{TAF}_5 - T_5)$$
$$= 9.33 + .3(747.73 - 737.33 - 9.33)$$
$$= 9.65.$$

Therefore, the trend-adjusted forecast for week 7 is:

$$\text{TAF}_7 = S_6 + T_6 = 745.44 + 9.65 = 755.09.$$

This process is continued until the trend-adjusted forecast for week eleven, 783.61, is determined (see Table 3–1).

Although calculations are somewhat more involved for trend-adjusted smoothing than for a linear trend line, trend-adjusted smoothing has the ability to adjust to *changes* in trend. A manager must decide if this benefit justifies the extra calculations.

Table 3–2 illustrates the solution obtained using the Excel template on the DVD for the trend-adjusted smoothing.

TABLE 3–2

Using the Excel template on the DVD for trend-adjusted smoothing. Note that forecast for week 5 is not shown.

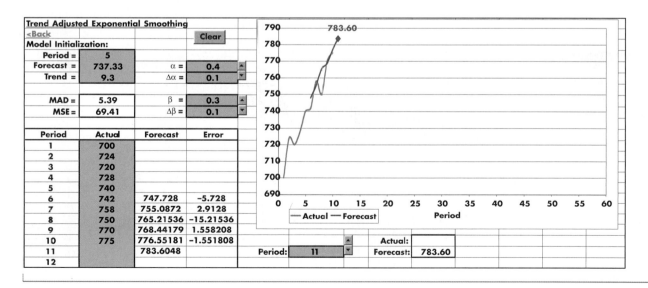

Demand for products such as Sea-doos and Ski-doos is subject to seasonal fluctuations. Bombardier matches these fluctuations by alternating its recreational vehicles division's manufacturing capacity between the two products.

Techniques for Seasonality

seasonal variations Regularly repeating movements in series values that can be tied to recurring events, weather, or calendar.

Seasonal variations in time series data or seasonality are regularly repeating upward or downward movements in series values that can be tied to recurring events, weather or calendar. Familiar examples of data with seasonality are airline travel, greeting card sales, and visitors at tourist and resort centres. The term *seasonal variation* is also applied to hourly, daily, weekly, and monthly seasons with a set of seasons. For example, rush hour traffic occurs twice a day—incoming in the morning and outgoing in the late afternoon. Theatres and restaurants often experience weekly demand patterns, with demand higher on Fridays. Banks may experience daily seasonal variations (heavier traffic during the noon hour and just before closing), weekly variations (heavier toward the end of the week), and monthly variations (heavier around the beginning of the month because of payroll cheques being cashed or deposited). Most products and services have seasonality.

Seasonality in a time series is expressed in terms of the amount that actual values deviate from the *average* value of a series. If the series tends to vary around an average value, then seasonality is expressed in terms of that average; if trend is present, seasonality is expressed in terms of the trend value.

There are two different models of seasonality: additive and multiplicative. In the *additive* model, seasonality is expressed as a *quantity* (e.g., 20 units), which is added or subtracted from the series average (or trend) in order to incorporate seasonality. In the *multiplicative* model, seasonality is expressed as a *proportion* of the average (or trend) amount (e.g., 1.10), which is then multiplied by the average (or trend) of the series. Figure 3–6 illustrates the two models for a linear trend line. In practice, businesses use the multiplicative model much more widely than the additive model, so we shall focus exclusively on the multiplicative model.

seasonal relative Proportion of average or trend for a season in the multiplicative model.

The seasonal proportions in the multiplicative model are referred to as **seasonal relatives** or *seasonal indexes*. Suppose that the seasonal relative for the quantity of toys sold in November at a store is 1.20. This indicates that toy sales for that month are

Seasonality: the additive and multiplicative models compared using a linear trend

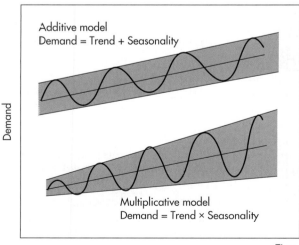

Some Examples of Seasonal Demand

There are many products whose demand/sales vary based on temperature and/or calendar events such as holidays. For example, demand for heating fuel such as natural gas

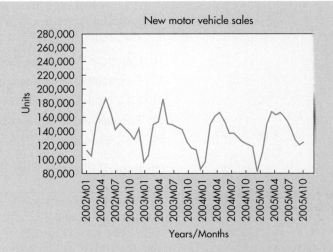

New motor vehicle sales

Source: Adapted from the Statistics Canada CANSIM 2 database <http://cansim2.statcan.ca>, Series v2452; January 23, 2006.

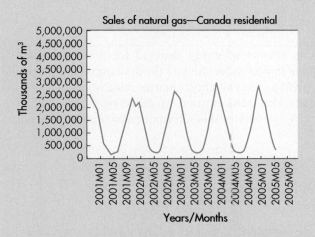

Sales of natural gas—Canada residential

Source: Adapted from the Statistics Canada CANSIM 2 database <http://cansim2.statcan.ca>, Series v47719; January 23, 2006.

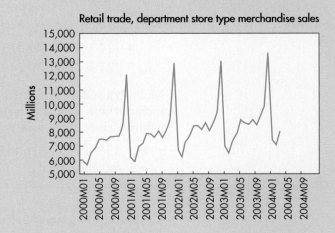

Retail trade, department store type merchandise sales

Source: Adapted from the Statistics Canada CANSIM 2 database <http://cansim2.statcan.ca>, Series v115563; January 23, 2006.

20 percent above the monthly average. A seasonal relative of .90 for July indicates that July sales are 90 percent of the monthly average.

Knowledge of seasonal variations is an important factor in retail planning and scheduling. Moreover, seasonality can be an important factor in capacity planning for systems that must be designed to handle peak loads (e.g., public transportation, electric power plants, highways, and bridges). Knowledge of the extent of seasonality in a time series can enable one to *remove* seasonality from the data (i.e., to seasonally adjust or deseasonalize the data) in order to discern other patterns. Thus, one frequently reads or hears about, for example, "seasonally adjusted unemployment."

The next section briefly describes how seasonal relatives are used, and the following section describes how seasonal relatives are computed.

Using Seasonal Relatives. Seasonal relatives are used first to *deseasonalize* the data, and then to *incorporate seasonality* in the forecast of deseasonalized data (i.e., to re-seasonalize the data).

To deseasonalize the data is to remove the seasonal component from the data in order to get a clearer picture of the nonseasonal components. Deseasonalizing data is accomplished by *dividing* each data point by its corresponding seasonal relative (e.g., divide November demand by the November relative, divide December demand by the December relative, and so on).

Re-seasonalizing the forecasts of the deseasonalized demand is accomplished by multiplying each forecast by its corresponding seasonal relative.

The steps of forecasting seasonal demand are as follows:

1. Compute the seasonal relatives
2. Deseasonalize the demand
3. Fit a model to the deseasonalized demand, e.g., moving average or trend
4. Forecast using this model and the deseasonalized demand
5. Re-seasonalize the deseasonalized forecasts

Example 7 illustrates steps 3 to 5 of this approach.

Example 7	A furniture manufacturer wants to predict quarterly demand for a certain loveseat for periods 15 and 16, which happen to be the second and third quarters of a particular year. The series consists of both trend and seasonality. Quarter relatives are $Q_1 = 1.20$, $Q_2 = 1.10$, $Q_3 = .75$, and $Q_4 = .95$. The trend portion of deseasonalized demand is projected using the equation $\hat{y}_t = 124 + 7.5t$. Use this information to predict demand for periods 15 and 16.
Solution	The trend values at $t = 15$ and $t = 16$ are:

$$\hat{y}_{15} = 124 + 7.5(15) = 236.5$$
$$\hat{y}_{16} = 124 + 7.5(16) = 244.0$$

Multiplying the trend value by the appropriate quarter relative yields a forecast that includes both trend and seasonality. Given that $t = 15$ is a second quarter and $t = 16$ is a third quarter, the forecasts are:

$$F_{15}: \ 236.5(1.10) = 260.15$$
$$F_{16}: \ 244.0(0.75) = 183.00$$

Computing Seasonal Relatives. We need to compute each period's typical proportion relative to the average (or trend) amount of all periods. A simple method is to just use the average of all periods. However, this ignores any trends. If there is a linear trend, then regression can be used to model it. However, seasonality could influence the slope of the line. A better way is to use **centred moving average**. Computations are similar to those for a moving average forecast. However, the values are not projected as in a forecast; instead, they are *positioned in the middle* of the periods used to compute the moving average. The implication is that the average is most representative of that point in the series. For example, consider the following time series data:

centred moving average
A moving average positioned at the centre of the data that were used to compute it.

Period	Demand	Three-Period Centred Average	
1	40		
2	46	42.67	$\text{Average} = \dfrac{40 + 46 + 42}{3} = 42.67$
3	42		

The three-period average is 42.67. As a centred average, it is positioned at period 2; the average is most representative of the series at that point.

The ratio of demand at period 2 to this centred average at period 2 is an estimate of the seasonal relative at that point. Because the ratio is $46/42.67 = 1.08$, the series is about 8 percent above average at that point. To achieve a reliable estimate of seasonality for any season, it is usually necessary to compute seasonal ratios for a number of seasons and then average these ratios. For example, average the ratios of three or four Fridays for the Friday relative, average three or four Saturdays for the Saturday relative, and so on.

Example 8

The manager of a parking lot has computed daily relatives for the number of cars per day in the lot. The computations are repeated here (about three weeks are shown for illustration). A seven-period centred moving average is used because there are seven days (seasons) per week.

Day	Volume	Centred MA$_7$	Volume/MA$_7$
Tues	67		
Wed	75		
Thur	82		
Fri	98	71.86	98/71.86 = 1.36 (Friday)
Sat	90	70.86	90/70.86 = 1.27
Sun	36	70.57	36/70.57 = .51
Mon	55	71.00	55/71.00 = .77
Tues	60	71.14	60/71.14 = .84 (Tuesday)
Wed	73	70.57	73/70.57 = 1.03
Thur	85	71.14	85/71.14 = 1.19
Fri	99	70.71	99/70.71 = 1.40 (Friday)
Sat	86	71.29	86/71.29 = 1.21
Sun	40	71.71	40/71.71 = .56
Mon	52	72.00	52/72.00 = .72
Tues	64	71.57	64/71.57 = .89 (Tuesday)
Wed	76	71.86	76/71.86 = 1.06
Thur	87	72.43	87/72.43 = 1.20
Fri	96	72.14	96/72.14 = 1.33 (Friday)
Sat	88		
Sun	44		
Mon	50		

The estimated Friday relative is (1.36 + 1.40 + 1.33)/3 = 1.36. Relatives for other days can be computed in a similar manner. For example, the estimated Tuesday relative is (.84 + .89)/2 = .87. The sum of average ratios of the seven days of the week should be 7. If it is not, they should be adjusted by rescaling them.

The number of periods needed in a centred moving average is equal to the number of "seasons" involved. For example, with quarterly data, a four-period moving average is needed. When the number of periods is even, one additional step is needed because the middle of an even set falls between two periods. The additional step requires taking a centred two-period moving average of the even-numbered centred moving average, which results in averages that "line up" with data points and, hence, permit determination of seasonal ratios.

Example 9

Below are quarterly data for production of ice cream in Canada from quarter 1 of 1999 to quarter 1 of 2002. (Source: CANSIM 2, Series v382696. Note that production of a perishable product such as ice cream is close to its sales.)

a. Calculate quarterly relatives using the centred moving average method.

b. Deseasonalize the data, fit an appropriate model, project it four quarters ahead, and re-seasonalize to obtain forecasts for ice cream demand from the second quarter of 2002 until the first quarter of 2003.

a.

Quarter	Production (million litres)	MA₄	MA₂	Production/CMA
1999,Q1	72			
2	101			
3	90	80	78.50	90/78.5 = 1.15
4	57	77	75.13	57/75.13 = .76
2000,Q1	60	73.25	71.75	.84
2	86	70.25	69.63	1.24
3	78	69	69.00	1.13
4	52	69	69.38	.75
2001,Q1	60	69.75	70.75	.85
2	89	71.75	72.88	1.22
3	86	74	74.63	1.15
4	61	75.25		
2002,Q1	65			

Year	Q1	Q2	Q3	Q4	
1999			1.15	.76	
2000	.84	1.24	1.13	.75	
2001	.85	1.22	1.15		
					Total
Average:	.84	1.23	1.14	.75	3.97
Adjusted:	.84*4/3.97	1.23*4/3.97			
	=.85	=1.24	1.15	.76	4.00

b.

Quarter	Production (million litres)	Seasonal relatives	Deseasonalized production
1999, Q1	72	.85	84.80
2	101	1.24	81.57
3	90	1.15	78.09
4	57	.76	74.97
2000, Q1	60	.85	70.67
2	86	1.24	69.45
3	78	1.15	67.68
4	52	.76	68.39
2001, Q1	60	.85	70.67
2	89	1.24	71.88
3	86	1.15	74.62
4	61	.76	80.23
2002, Q1	65	.85	76.56

$y = -0.4416x + 77.676$

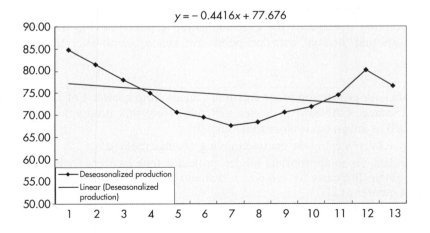

The deseasonalized data seems to have a non-linear trend. However, the trend seems to be changing at observation 13 (Q1 of 2002). Therefore, a linear trend is fitted to the deseasonalized data, and its equation is displayed at the top of the chart.

Using the regression equation, the trend forecasts for periods 14 to 17 (Q2 of 2002 to Q1 of 2003) are:

$$Y_{14} = -.4416*(14) + 77.676 = 71.49$$

$$Y_{15} = -.4416*(15) + 77.676 = 71.05$$

$$Y_{16} = -.4416*(16) + 77.676 = 70.61$$

$$Y_{17} = -.4416*(17) + 77.676 = 70.17$$

The re-seasonalized forecasts for the second quarter of 2002 until the first quarter of 2003 are:

$$F_{14} = 71.49 * 1.24 = 88.53$$

$$F_{15} = 71.05 * 1.15 = 81.88$$

$$F_{16} = 70.61 * .76 = 53.68$$

$$F_{17} = 70.17 * .85 = 59.57$$

If the data does not have trend, a simpler forecasting method in the presence of seasonality is: forecast using annual data, divide it equally into periods, and re-seasonalize.

Techniques for Cycles

Cycles are up and down movements similar to seasonal variations but of longer duration—say, two to six years between peaks. When cycles occur in time series data, their frequent irregularity makes it difficult or impossible to project them from past data because turning points are difficult to identify. A short moving average or a naive approach may be of some value, although both will produce forecasts that lag cyclical movements by one or several periods.

The most commonly used approach is associative models: Search for another variable that relates to, and *leads*, the variable of interest. For example, the number of housing starts (i.e., permits to build houses) in a given month often is an indicator of demand a few months later for products and services directly tied to construction of new homes (e.g., sales of dishwashers). Thus, if an organization is able to establish a high correlation with such a *leading variable*, it can develop an equation that describes the relationship, enabling forecasts to be made. It is important that a persistent relationship exists between the two variables. Moreover, the higher the correlation, the better the chances that the forecast will be on target.

ASSOCIATIVE MODELS

Associative models rely on identification of related variables that can be used to predict values of the variable of interest. For example, sales of beef may be related to the price for beef and the prices of substitutes such as chicken, pork, and lamb; sales during promotions depend on the discount and size of the ad; and crop yields are related to soil conditions and the amounts and timing of rain and fertilizer applications.

The essence of associative models is the development of an equation that summarizes the effects of **predictor variables** on the variable of interest. The primary method of analysis is **regression**.

predictor variables Variables that can be used to predict values of the variable of interest.

regression Technique for fitting a line to a set of points.

FIGURE 3-7

A straight line is fitted to a set of points, each a pair (x, y)

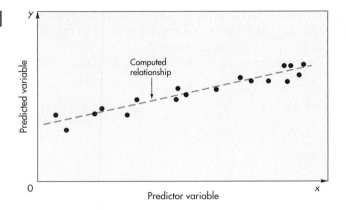

Simple Linear Regression

The simplest and most widely used form of regression involves a linear relationship between two variables. A plot of the values might appear like that in Figure 3–7. The objective in linear regression is to obtain an equation of a straight line that minimizes the sum of squared vertical deviations of data points (x, y) from the line. This **least squares line** has the equation

least squares line Minimizes the sum of the squared deviations around the line.

$$\hat{y} = a + bx \tag{3–8}$$

where

$\hat{y}$ = Predicted (dependent) variable
x = Predictor (independent) variable
b = Slope of the line
a = Value of $\hat{y}$ when $x = 0$ (i.e., the height of the line at the y intercept)

(Note: It is conventional to represent values of the predicted variable on the y axis and values of the predictor variable on the x axis.) Figure 3–8 is a graph of a linear regression line.

The coefficients a and b of the line are computed using these two equations:

$$b = \frac{n\left(\sum xy\right) - \left(\sum x\right)\left(\sum y\right)}{n\left(\sum x^2\right) - \left(\sum x\right)^2} \tag{3–9}$$

$$a = \frac{\sum y - b\sum x}{n} \quad \text{or} \quad \bar{y} - b\bar{x} \tag{3–10}$$

where

n = Number of paired observations
(x, y) = Pairs of data

FIGURE 3-8

Equation of a straight line

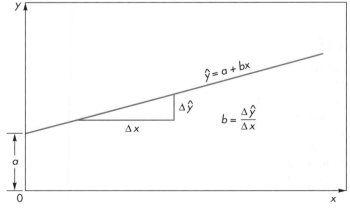

The line intersects the y axis where $\hat{y} = a$. The slope of the line $= b$.

Healthy Hamburgers has a chain of 12 stores. Revenue and profit for the stores are given below. Obtain a regression line for the data, and predict profit for a store with revenue of $10 million.

Example 10

Revenue, x	Profit, y
(in millions of dollars)	
7	.15
2	.10
6	.13
4	.15
14	.25
15	.27
16	.24
12	.20
14	.27
20	.44
15	.34
7	.17

First, plot the data and decide if a linear model is reasonable (i.e., do the points seem to scatter around a straight line? Figure 3–9 suggests they do). Next, compute the quantities Σx, Σy, Σxy and Σx^2 and substitute into the equation to find:

Solution

$$b = \frac{n\left(\sum xy\right) - \left(\sum x\right)\left(\sum y\right)}{n\left(\sum x^2\right) - \left(\sum x\right)^2} = \frac{12(35.29) - 132(2.71)}{12(1,796) - 132(132)} = .01593$$

$$a = \frac{\sum y - b\left(\sum x\right)}{n} = \frac{2.71 - 0.01593(132)}{12} = .0506$$

Thus, the regression equation is: $\hat{y} = .0506 + .01593x$. For revenue of $x = 10$ (i.e., $10 million), estimated profit is: $\hat{y} = .0506 + .01593(10) = .2099$, or $209,900. (It may appear strange that substituting $x = 0$ into the equation produces a predicted profit of $50,600 because it seems to suggest that amount of profit will occur with no sales. However, the value of $x = 0$ is *outside the range of observed values*. The regression line should be used only for the range of values from which it was developed; the relationship may be nonlinear outside that range. The purpose of the a value is simply to establish the height of the line where it crosses the y axis.) The Excel template of this problem on the DVD is shown in Table 3–3.

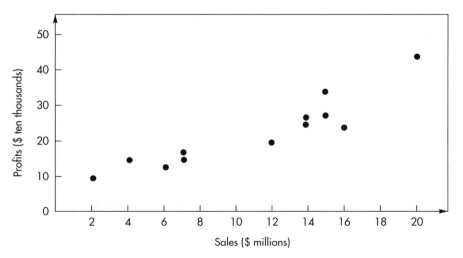

FIGURE 3-9

A linear model seems reasonable for Example 10

TABLE 3-3

Excel template for example 10

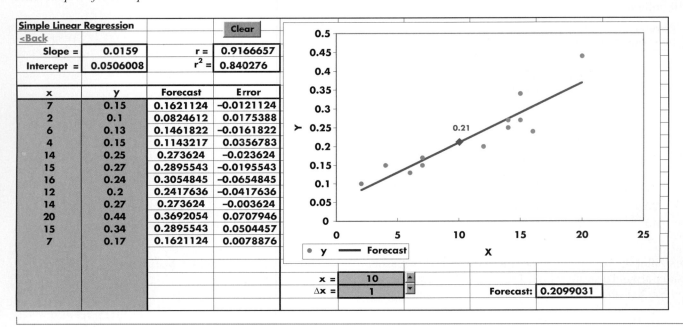

Simple Linear Regression				
<Back			Clear	
Slope =	0.0159	r =	0.9166657	
Intercept =	0.0506008	r^2 =	0.840276	
x	y	Forecast	Error	
7	0.15	0.1621124	−0.0121124	
2	0.1	0.0824612	0.0175388	
6	0.13	0.1461822	−0.0161822	
4	0.15	0.1143217	0.0356783	
14	0.25	0.273624	−0.023624	
15	0.27	0.2895543	−0.0195543	
16	0.24	0.3054845	−0.0654845	
12	0.2	0.2417636	−0.0417636	
14	0.27	0.273624	−0.003624	
20	0.44	0.3692054	0.0707946	
15	0.34	0.2895543	0.0504457	
7	0.17	0.1621124	0.0078876	

x = 10   Δx = 1   Forecast: 0.2099031

One application of regression in forecasting relates to the use of leading indicators. For example, changes in the Bank of Canada's discount rate may influence certain business activities. There are numerous published indicators from which to choose.[2] A fairly high correlation should exist between the leading variable and the variable of interest for it to be useful.

correlation A measure of the strength of relationship between two variables.

Correlation measures the strength of relationship between two variables. Correlation can range from −1.00 to +1.00. A correlation of +1.00 indicates that changes in one variable are always matched by changes in the other in the same direction; a correlation of −1.00 indicates that increases in one variable are matched by decreases in the other; and a correlation close to zero indicates little *linear* relationship between two variables. The correlation between two variables can be computed using the equation

$$r = \frac{n(\sum xy) - (\sum x)(\sum y)}{\sqrt{n(\sum x^2) - (\sum x)^2} \cdot \sqrt{n(\sum y^2) - (\sum y)^2}} \tag{3–11}$$

The square of the correlation coefficient, r^2, provides a measure of the proportion of variability in the values of y that is "explained" by the independent variable. The possible values of r^2 range from 0 to 1.00. The closer r^2 is to 1.00, the greater the proportion of explained variation. A high value of r^2, say .80 or more, would indicate that the independent variable is a good predictor of values of the dependent variable. A low value, say .25 or less, would indicate a poor predictor, and a value between .25 and .80 would indicate a moderate predictor.

---

[2]See Statistics Canada's CANSIM 2 database, also available through the Online Learning Centre at www.mcgrawhill.ca/olc/stevenson. For U.S. data see, for example, *The National Bureau of Economic Research's Economic Indicators*, *The Survey of Current Business*, and *The Monthly Labor Review*.

Mary Kay Cosmetics

www.marykay.com

The Financial Planning & Analysis office performs monthly sales forecasts, both in dollars and in individual units. The individual unit data are sent to the distribution function, which modifies them as new information is received. The revenue are forecast using a set of regression equations, in which the explanatory variables include the size of salesforce, each salesperson's order size, economic conditions, promotion, pricing, and seasonality. The individual units are forecast using naive and moving average techniques. The total of individual units is reconciled with revenue forecasts. A committee forecasts the new-product sales using analogies and market research.

Source: *Journal of Business Forecasting Methods & Systems*, Fall 1995, pp. 26–27.

Example 11

Monthly sales of 19-inch colour television sets in a store and the unemployment rate in the region are shown below. Determine if unemployment levels can be used to predict demand for 19-inch colour TVs and, if so, derive the correlation coefficient and the predictive equation.

Month	1	2	3	4	5	6	7	8	9	10	11
Units sold (y)	20	41	17	35	25	31	38	50	15	19	14
Unemployment % (x)	7.2	4.0	7.3	5.5	6.8	6.0	5.4	3.6	8.4	7.0	9.0

Solution

1. Plot the data to see if a linear model seems reasonable. In this case, a linear model seems appropriate.

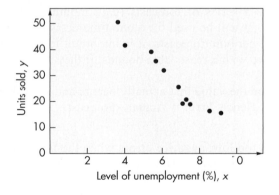

2. Compute the correlation coefficient:

$$r = \frac{11(1,750.8) - 70.2(305)}{\sqrt{11(476.3) - (70.2)^2} \cdot \sqrt{11(9,907) - (305)^2}} = -.966$$

This is a high negative correlation, indicating a strong downward-sloping linear relationship.

3. Compute the regression line:

$$b = \frac{11(1,750.8) - 70.2(305)}{11(476.4) - 70.2(70.2)} = -6.91$$

$$a = \frac{305 - (-6.9145)(70.2)}{11} = 71.85$$

$$y = 71.85 - 6.91x$$

Note that the equation pertains only to unemployment levels in the range 3.6 to 9.0 percent, because sample observations cover only that range.

Multiple Regression Analysis

Simple linear regression may prove inadequate to handle certain problems because more than one predictor variable is needed. Models that involve more than one predictor require the use of multiple regression analysis. While this is beyond the scope of this text, you should be aware that it is often used. The computations lend themselves more to computers than to hand calculation. It is necessary to weigh the additional cost and effort against potential improvements in accuracy of predictions. For an example of the use of multiple regression, see the reading, "Mary Kay Cosmetics."

ACCURACY AND CONTROL OF FORECASTS

Accuracy and control of forecasts is a vital aspect of forecasting. The complex nature of most real-world variables makes it almost impossible to correctly predict future values of those variables on a regular basis. Consequently, it is important to include an indication of the extent to which the forecast might deviate from the value of the variable that actually occurs. This will provide the forecast user with a better perspective on how far off a forecast might be.

Accurate forecasts are necessary for the success of daily activities of every business organization. Forecasts are the basis for an organization's schedules, and unless the forecasts are accurate, schedules will be generated that may provide for too few or too many resources, too little or too much output, the wrong output, or the wrong timing of output, all of which can lead to additional costs, dissatisfied customers, and headaches for managers.

Some forecasting applications involve a series of forecasts (e.g., monthly sales), whereas others involve a single forecast that will be used for a one-time decision (e.g., the size of a power plant). When making periodic forecasts, it is important to monitor forecast errors to determine if the errors are within reasonable bounds. If they are not, it will be necessary to take corrective action.

error Difference between the actual value and the value that was predicted for a given period.

Forecast **error** is the difference between the value that actually occurs and the value that was predicted for a given time period. Hence, Error = Actual − Forecast:

$$e_t = A_t - F_t \tag{3–12}$$

Positive errors result when the forecast is too low, negative errors when the forecast is too high. For example, if actual demand for a month is 100 units and forecast demand was 90 units, the forecast was too low; the error is $100 - 90 = +10$.

mean absolute deviation (MAD) The average of absolute value of forecast errors.

Forecast errors influence decisions in two somewhat different ways. One is in making a choice among various forecasting techniques, and the other is in controlling the forecasting process. We shall begin by examining ways to summarize forecast error over time, and see how that information can be applied for controlling forecasts. Then we will discuss choosing a forecasting technique.

mean squared error (MSE) The average of square of forecast errors.

Summarizing Forecast Errors

mean absolute percent error (MAPE) The average of absolute value of forecast error relative to actual.

Three commonly used measures for summarizing forecast errors are **mean absolute deviation (MAD)**, **mean squared error (MSE)**, and **mean absolute percent error (MAPE)**.

MAD is the average absolute error, MSE is the average of squared errors, and MAPE is the average absolute percent error. The formulas used to compute MAD[3], MSE, and MAPE are:

$$\text{MAD} = \frac{\sum |\text{Actual} - \text{Forecast}|}{n} \tag{3-13}$$

$$\text{MSE} = \frac{\sum (\text{Actual} - \text{Forecast})^2}{n} \tag{3-14}$$

$$\text{MAPE} = \frac{\sum \left[\dfrac{|\text{Actual} - \text{Forecast}|}{\text{Actual}} \right] \times 100}{n} \tag{3-15}$$

Example 12 illustrates the calculation of MAD, MSE, and MAPE.

Calculate MAD, MSE, and MAPE for the following data.

Example 12

Period	Actual	Forecast	(A – F) Error	|Error|	Error²	$\frac{\|Error\|}{Actual} * 100$
1	217	215	2	2	4	.92%
2	213	216	– 3	3	9	1.41
3	216	215	1	1	1	.46
4	210	214	– 4	4	16	1.90
5	213	211	2	2	4	.94
6	219	214	5	5	25	2.28
7	216	217	– 1	1	1	.46
8	212	216	– 4	4	16	1.89
			– 2	22	76	10.26%

Using the numbers shown in the table,

Solution

$$\text{MAD} = \frac{\sum |e|}{n} = \frac{22}{8} = 2.75$$

$$\text{MSE} = \frac{\sum e^2}{n} = \frac{76}{8} = 9.5$$

$$\text{MAPE} = \frac{\sum \left[\dfrac{|e|}{\text{Actual}} \times 100 \right]}{n} = \frac{10.26\%}{8} = 1.28\%$$

From a computational standpoint, the difference between these three measures is that MAD weighs all errors equally, MSE weighs errors according to their *squared* values, and MAPE weighs errors relative to actual values.

One use for these measures is to compare the accuracy of alternative forecasting methods. For instance, using MAD, MSE, or MAPE, a manager could compare the results of exponential smoothing with α values of .1, .2, and .3, to determine the one which yields the *lowest* MAD, MSE, or MAPE for a given set of data.

Controlling the Forecast

It is necessary to monitor forecast errors to ensure that the forecasting technique is performing adequately.

---

[3]The absolute value, represented by the two vertical lines in formula 3–13, ignores minus signs; all data are treated as positive values. For example, –2 becomes +2.

There are a variety of possible causes of large forecast errors, including:

1. The model may be inadequate due to (*a*) the omission of an important variable, (*b*) a change or shift in the variable that the model cannot deal with (e.g., sudden appearance of a trend), or (*c*) the appearance of a new variable (e.g., new competitor).

2. Irregular variations may occur due to severe weather or other natural phenomena, temporary shortages or breakdowns.

control chart A time series plot of forecast errors that has limits for individual forecast errors.

Monitoring forecast errors is accomplished by comparing forecast errors to predetermined values, or *action limits*, as illustrated in Figure 3–10. This is called a **control chart**. Errors that fall outside of either limit signal that corrective action is needed.

Also, corrective action is needed if there is strong evidence against the following assumptions:

1. Forecast errors are randomly distributed around a mean of zero.

2. The distribution of errors is Normal. See Figure 3–11.

The limits are multiples of the standard deviation of forecast errors. The square root of MSE is used in practice as an estimate of the standard deviation of errors.[4] That is,

$$s = \sqrt{\text{MSE}} \tag{3–16}$$

Recall from your stats course that for a Normal distribution, approximately 95 percent of the values (errors in this case) can be expected to fall within limits of $0 \pm 2s$ (i.e., 0 ± 2 standard deviations), and approximately 99.7 percent of the values can be expected to fall within $\pm 3s$ of zero. Hence, if the forecast is "in control," 99.7 percent or 95 percent of the errors should fall within the limits, depending on whether $3s$ or $2s$ limits are used. Points that fall outside these limits could be regarded as evidence that corrective action is needed (i.e., the forecasting technique is not performing adequately).

FIGURE 3–10

Monitoring forecast errors

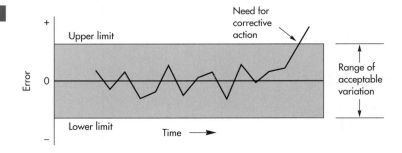

FIGURE 3–11

Conceptual representation of a control chart

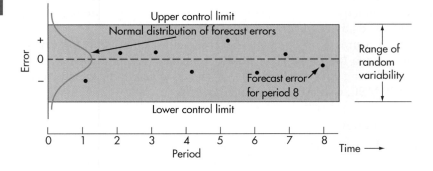

---

[4] The actual value could be computed as $s = \sqrt{\dfrac{\sum (e - \bar{e})^2}{n - 1}}$.

Monthly sales of leather jackets at the Lucky Leather Shoppe for the past 24 months, and forecasts and forecast errors for those months, are shown below. Determine if the forecasting technique is satisfactory using a control chart with $2s$ limits. Use data from the first eight months to develop the control chart, then evaluate the remaining data with the control chart.

Example 13

Month	A (Sales)	F (Forecast)	A − F (Error)
1	47	43	4
2	51	44	7
3	54	50	4
4	55	51	4
5	49	54	− 5
6	46	48	− 2
7	38	46	− 8
8	32	44	− 12
9	25	35	− 10
10	24	26	− 2
11	30	25	5
12	35	32	3
13	44	34	10
14	57	50	7
15	60	51	9
16	55	54	1
17	51	55	− 4
18	48	51	− 3
19	42	50	− 8
20	30	43	− 13
21	28	38	− 10
22	25	27	−2
23	35	27	8
24	38	32	6
			− 11

Solution

(1) Make sure that the average error is approximately zero:

$$\text{Average error} = \frac{\sum \text{errors}}{n} = \frac{-11}{24} = -0.46 \sim 0 \text{ relative to magnitude of sales.}$$

(2) Compute the standard deviation using the first 8 months:

$$s = \sqrt{\text{MSE}} = \sqrt{\frac{\sum e^2}{n}}$$

$$= \sqrt{\frac{4^2 + 7^2 + 4^2 + 4^2 + (-5)^2 + (-2)^2 + (-8)^2 + (-12)^2}{8}} = 6.46$$

(3) Determine $2s$ control limits:

$$0 \pm 2s = 0 \pm 2(6.46) = -12.92 \text{ to } +12.92$$

(4) i. Check that all errors are within the limits. Month 20's forecast error (−13) is just below the lower control limit (−12.92).

ii. Check for nonrandom patterns. Note the runs of positive and negative errors in the following plot. This suggests nonrandomness (and that a better forecasting technique is possible).[5]

---

[5]The theory and application of control charts and the various methods for detecting patterns in the data are covered in more detail in Chapter 10, on quality control.

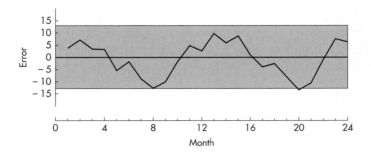

READING

Colgate-Palmolive Co.

www.colgate.com

The sales forecasting office in Colgate-Palmolive's finance department performs monthly sales forecasts of shipments for the next year, using the past two years' data. There are five regional sales forecasters in the U.S., who report to four national forecast managers, each responsible for one product line. Colgate-Palmolive uses a sophisticated software package called STSC to forecast individual item sales. The sales forecasters then aggregate the individual products into families, and evaluate each family's reasonableness in consultation with marketing/sales using information on promotion, price, economic trends, Nielsen data, and competition, making adjustments if necessary. The adjusted family sales forecasts are then disaggregated into individual-item forecasts. Monthly sales and forecast meetings are held with sales/marketing people to evaluate the forecasts. Separate monthly production planning meetings are held with the production people. Because forecasting promotion sales is more difficult, these are monitored daily. For brand items that have loyal customers and are not promoted, the forecast accuracy is better than 5 percent. For forecasting sales of a new product, first a panel of potential consumers is used to estimate the market size, then the market share for the product is estimated and finally the annual sales are estimated. These are further tested using selected test markets. However, the actions of the competitors may drastically affect the sales.

Source: C. L. Jain, "Forecasting at Colgate-Palmolive Company," *Journal of Business Forecasting Methods & Systems* 11(1), Spring 1992, pp. 16–20.

An alternative measure to control the forecasting performance is tracking signal:

$$Ts = \frac{\sum e}{\text{MAD}}.$$

When *Ts* values exceed 4 in absolute value, the analyst will study the model and make changes.

CHOOSING A FORECASTING TECHNIQUE

Many different kinds of forecasting techniques are available, and no single technique works best in every situation. When selecting a technique for a given situation, the manager or analyst must take a number of factors into consideration.

The two most important factors are *cost* and *accuracy*. Cost is affected by the preparation time and complexity. How much money is budgeted for generating the forecast? What are the possible costs of errors, and what are the benefits that might accrue from an accurate forecast? Generally speaking, the higher the accuracy, the higher the cost, so it is important to weigh cost–accuracy trade-offs carefully. The best forecast is not necessarily the most accurate or the least costly; rather, it is some combination of accuracy and cost deemed best by management.

Other factors to consider in selecting a forecasting technique include the availability of historical data, complexity, availability of computers, the forecast horizon, and pattern of data.

Some techniques are more suited to long-term forecasts while others work best for the shorter-term. For example, moving averages and exponential smoothing are essentially short-term techniques, since they produce forecasts for the *next* period. Trend equations can be used to project over much longer time periods. If there is strong and stable cause and effect relationship, then regression could be used. Also, if the objective of forecast is to understand what drives sales, then regression should be used. Several of the judgmental techniques are well suited to long-term forecasts because they do not require historical data. The Delphi method and executive opinion methods are often used for long-term planning. New products and services lack historical data, so forecasts for them must be based on subjective estimates. Table 3–4 provides a guide for selecting a forecasting method. Table 3–5 provides additional perspectives on forecasts in terms of the time horizon.

In some instances, a manager might use more than one forecasting technique to obtain independent forecasts. If the different techniques produced approximately the same predictions, that would give increased confidence in the results; disagreement among the forecasts would indicate that additional analysis may be needed. The chosen forecasting technique should be tested before use to ascertain the level of accuracy.

The Institute of Business Forecasting (www.IBF.org) annually surveys over 5,000 companies. Figures 3–12 to 3–15 show the results of a recent survey. As evident, time series techniques are popular, especially moving average, exponential smoothing, and linear trend. Also used are regression and surveys.[6] PERT forecasting involves asking an expert for three elements: optimistic, most likely, pessimistic. See Chapter 17.

TABLE 3-4

A guide to selecting an appropriate forecasting method

Forecasting Method	Amount of Historical Data	Data Pattern	Forecast Horizon	Preparation Time (reflects cost)	Complexity
Simple exponential smoothing	5 to 10 observations	Data should be stationary	Short	Short	Little sophistication
Trend-adjusted exponential smoothing	At least 4 or 5 observations per season	Trend	Short to medium	Short	Moderate sophistication
Trend models	10 to 20; for seasonality at least 5 per season	Trend	Short, medium, long	Short	Moderate sophistication
Seasonal	Enough to see 2 peaks and troughs	Handles cyclical and seasonal patterns	Short to medium	Short to moderate	Little sophistication
Causal regression models	10 observations per independent variable	Can handle complex patterns	Medium or long	Long development time, short time for implementation	Considerable sophistication

Source: J. Holton Wilson and Deborah Allison-Koerber, "Combining Subjective and Objective Forecasts Improves Results," *Journal of Business Forecasting Methods & Systems,* Fall 1992, p. 4.

TABLE 3-5

Forecast factors, by range of forecast

Factor	Short Term	Medium Term	Long Term
1. Frequency	Often	Occasional	Infrequent
2. Level of aggregation	Item	Product family	Total output Type of product/service
3. Type of model	Smoothing Trend Regression	Trend Seasonal Regression	Managerial Judgment
4. Degree of management involvement	Low	Moderate	High
5. Cost per forecast	Low	Moderate	High

[6]C. L. Jain, "Benchmarking Forecasting Models," *Journal of Business Forecasting Methods & Systems* 21(3), Fall 2002, pp. 18–20, 30.

FIGURE 3-12

Forecasting models used

Source: C. L. Jain, "Benchmarking Forecasting Models," *Journal of Business Forecasting Methods & Systems*, Fall 2002, pp. 18–20, 30.

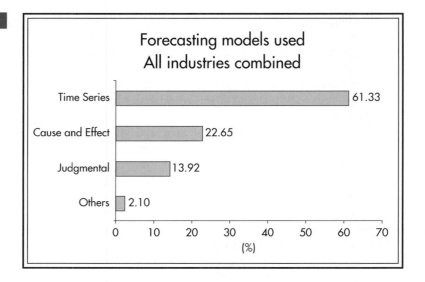

FIGURE 3-13

Time series models

Source: C. L. Jain, "Benchmarking Forecasting Models," *Journal of Business Forecasting Methods & Systems*, Fall 2002, pp. 18–20, 30.

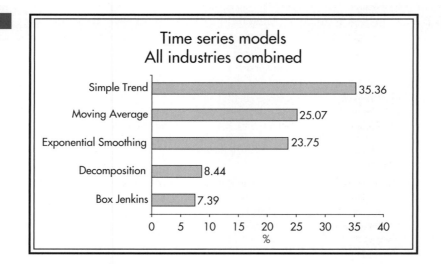

FIGURE 3-14

Cause and effect models

Source: C. L. Jain, "Benchmarking Forecasting Models," *Journal of Business Forecasting Methods & Systems*, Fall 2002, pp. 18–20, 30.

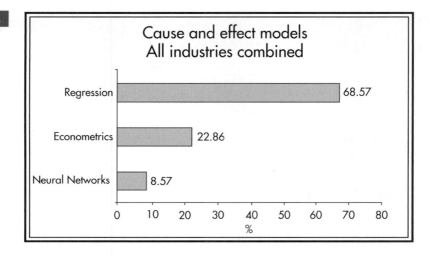

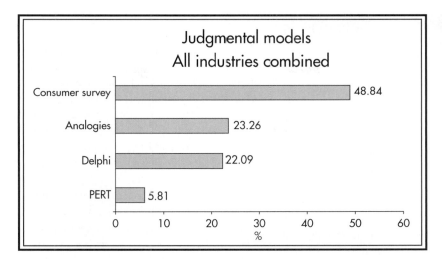

FIGURE 3-15

Judgmental models

Source: C. L. Jain, "Benchmarking Forecasting Models," *Journal of Business Forecasting Methods & Systems*, Fall 2002, pp. 18–20, 30.

Using Forecast Information

A manager can take a *reactive* or a *proactive* approach to a forecast. A reactive approach views forecasts as probable descriptions of future demand, and a manager reacts to meet that demand (e.g., adjusts production rates, inventories, the workforce). Conversely, a proactive approach seeks to actively influence demand (e.g., by means of advertising, pricing, or product/service changes).

Generally speaking, a proactive approach requires either an explanatory model (e.g., regression) or a subjective assessment of the influence on demand. It is possible that a manager might use two forecasts: one to predict what will happen under the status quo and a second one based on a "what-if" approach, if the results of the status quo forecast are unacceptable.

Computers in Forecasting

Computers play an important role in preparing forecasts based on quantitative data. Their use allows managers to develop and revise forecasts quickly, and without the burden of manual calculations. There is a wide range of software packages available for forecasting. The Excel templates on your DVD are an example of a spreadsheet approach.

A growing Canadian software company is Alt-C Systems of Montreal, whose TimeTrends forecasting software and some of its uses in industry are illustrated in the reading on page 94.

Operations Strategy

Forecasts are the basis for many decisions. Clearly, the more accurate an organization's forecasts, the better prepared it will be to take advantage of future opportunities and to reduce potential risks. Maintaining accurate, up-to-date information on demand, and other variables can have a significant impact on forecast accuracy.

An organization also can do other things to improve forecasts. These do not involve searching for improved techniques but relate to the inverse relation of accuracy to the forecast horizon: forecasts that cover shorter time frames tend to be more accurate than longer-term forecasts. Recognizing this, management might choose to devote efforts to *shortening the time horizon that forecasts must cover*. Essentially, this means shortening the *lead time* needed to respond to a forecast. This might involve building *flexibility* into operations to permit rapid response to changing demands for products and services, or to changing volumes in quantities demanded; shortening the lead time required to obtain supplies, equipment, and raw materials or the time needed to train or retrain employees; or shortening the time needed to *develop* new products and services.

READING

TimeTrends

www.alt-c.com

Alt-C Systems Inc. is a Montreal-based software company whose forecasting software, TimeTrends, is being used by some large companies. The software is simple, flexible, and easy to use. It performs all the techniques we have described in this chapter and some more. It can access SQL, Access, and other databases. It allows grouping of items for aggregate product family forecasting. For a given time series data, it can automatically determine the most appropriate technique and its parameter(s). In addition to forecasting, TimeTrends assists in replenishment (inventory control) decisions. An optional module assists in forecasting sales promotions.

Another optional module, e-forecasting, allows use of the software over the Internet. This feature was the reason Compaq Direct bought TimeTrends. Compact Direct is Compaq Computer's direct fulfillment subsidiary that sells customized computer solutions (configurations) to large accounts. The forecasting software is used by sales people (client service personnel) located in three call centres (in Indiana, California, and Nebraska) to forecast their customers' future demand. In the headquarters these forecasts are gathered and then sent to Compaq's assembly facility in California for production planning.

Molson Canada also purchased TimeTrends. It is used by three regional forecasters who forecast each product's demand in each market. Then the manager of demand planning accumulates the forecasts and sends them to be used in the planning of production and sales. They forecast 80 weeks into the future, and update the forecasts every week. TimeTrends automatically identifies the start and stop forecast dates for products that are offered only part of the year. It allows override of forecasts and automatically updates all the groups of products affected.

Parmalat Canada, the largest producer and distributor of dairy products in Canada (formed from Ault Foods and Beatrice), also uses TimeTrends to forecast demand. The forecast coordinator in the trade marketing office in Etobicoke, Ontario, especially likes the ability of TimeTrends to import the seasonal relatives from Excel. The forecasts are transmitted to the production plant in Belleville, Ontario, for use in sales and operations planning, and then purchase planning. TimeTrends is installed on a desktop computer that is connected to the sales database on the AS/400 server. The computer regularly updates the data from the server. The use of TimeTrends has resulted in 10 percent more of the products (from 40 to 50 percent) having forecasts that are accurate within plus or minus 30 percent of actual demand.

Sources: "Forecasting in the Field: Compaq Leverages the Web with Canadian Solution," *Manufacturing Automation* 16(5), September 2001, pp. 12–15; Molson case study, www.Alt-C.com; and Parmalat case study, www.Alt-C.com.

SUMMARY

Forecasts are vital inputs for the design and operation of the productive systems because they help managers to anticipate the future.

Forecasting techniques can be classified as judgmental or quantitative. Judgmental methods rely on judgment, experience, and expertise to formulate forecasts; quantitative techniques use precise numerical calculations to develop forecasts. Some of the techniques are simple and others are complex. Some work better than others, but no technique works all the time. Moreover, all forecasts include a certain degree of inaccuracy, and allowance should be made for this. All techniques assume that the same underlying system that existed in the past will continue to exist in the future.

The judgmental methods described in this chapter include executive opinions, salesforce estimates, consumer surveys, historical analogies, and expert opinions. Two major quantitative approaches are described: analysis of time series data and associative techniques. The time series techniques rely strictly on the examination of historical data; predictions are made by projecting past pattern of a variable into the future without considering specific factors that might influence the variable. Associative techniques attempt to explicitly identify influencing factors and to incorporate that information into equations that can be used for predictive purposes.

All forecasts tend to be inaccurate; therefore, it is important to provide a measure of accuracy. It is possible to compute several measures of forecast accuracy that help managers evaluate the performance of a given technique and to choose among alternative forecasting techniques. Control of forecasts involves deciding whether a forecast is performing adequately, using, for example, a control chart.

When selecting a forecasting technique, a manager must choose a technique that will serve the intended purpose at an acceptable level of cost and accuracy.

Table 3–6 lists the formulas used in the forecasting techniques and in the methods of measuring their accuracy.

Technique	Formula	Definitions
Naive forecast for stable data	$F_t = A_{t-1}$	F = Forecast A = Actual data t = Current period
Moving average forecast	$F = \dfrac{\sum\limits_{i=1}^{n} A_i}{n}$	n = Number of periods
Exponential smoothing forecast	$F_t = F_{t-1} + \alpha(A_{t-1} - F_{t-1})$	α = Smoothing factor
Linear trend forecast	$\hat{y} = a + bt$ where $b = \dfrac{n\sum ty - \sum t \sum y}{n\sum t^2 - \left(\sum t\right)^2}$ $a = \dfrac{\sum y - b\sum t}{n}$ or $\bar{y} - bt$	a = y intercept b = Slope y = Demand value $\hat{y}$ = Trend line value t = Index of time period
Trend-adjusted (exponential smoothing) forecast	$TAF_{t+1} = S_t + T_t$ where $S_t = TAF_t + \alpha(A_t - TAF_t)$ $T_t = T_{t-1} + \beta(TAF_t - TAF_{t-1} - T_{t-1})$	TAF_{t+1} = Trend-adjusted forecast for next period S = Smoothed average T = Trend component β = Smoothing factor for trend
Linear regression forecast	$\hat{y} = a + bx$ where $b = \dfrac{n\left(\sum xy\right) - \left(\sum x\right)\left(\sum y\right)}{n\left(\sum x^2\right) - \left(\sum x\right)^2}$ $a = \dfrac{\sum y - b\sum x}{n}$ or $\bar{y} - b\bar{x}$	x = Predictor (independent) variable
MAD	$MAD = \dfrac{\sum\limits^{n} |e|}{n}$	MAD = Mean absolute deviation e = Error = $A - F$
MSE	$MSE = \dfrac{\sum\limits^{n} e^2}{n}$	MSE = Mean squared error
MAPE	$MAPE = \dfrac{\sum\left[\dfrac{|e|}{Actual}\times 100\right]}{n}$	$MAPE$ = Mean absolute percent error
Control limits	$UCL = 0 + z\sqrt{MSE}$ $LCL = 0 - z\sqrt{MSE}$	$\sqrt{MSE}$ = standard deviation z = Number of standard deviations; 2 and 3 are typical values

TABLE 3-6

Summary of formulas

Solved Problems

Forecasts based on averages. Given the following data:

Problem 1

Period	Number of Complaints
1	60
2	65
3	55
4	58
5	64

Prepare a forecast using each of these approaches:

a. The appropriate naive approach.

b. A three-period moving average.

c. A weighted average using weights of .50 (most recent), .30, and .20.

d. Exponential smoothing with a smoothing constant of .40.

Solution

a. The values are stable. Therefore, the most recent value of the series can be used as the next forecast: 64.

b. $MA_3 = \dfrac{55 + 58 + 64}{3} = 59$

c. $F_6 = .50(64) + .30(58) + .20(55) = 60.4$

d.

Period	Number of Complaints	Forecast	Calculations
1	60		[The previous value of series is used
2	65	60	as the starting forecast.]
3	55	62	$60 + .40(65 - 60) = 62$
4	58	59.2	$62 + .40(55 - 62) = 59.2$
5	64	58.72	$59.2 + .40(58 - 59.2) = 58.72$
6		60.83	$58.72 + .40(64 - 58.72) = 60.83$

You can also obtain the forecasts and a plot using an Excel template, as shown:

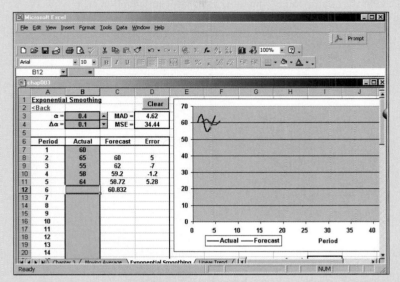

Using *seasonal relatives*. Apple's Citrus Fruit Farm ships boxed fruit anywhere in North America. Using the following information, forecast shipments for the first four months of next year.

Problem 2

Month	Seasonal Relative	Month	Seasonal Relative
Jan.	1.2	Jul.	.8
Feb.	1.3	Aug.	.6
Mar.	1.3	Sep.	.7
Apr.	1.1	Oct.	1.0
May	.8	Nov.	1.1
Jun.	.7	Dec.	1.4

The monthly forecast equation being used is:

$$y_t = 402 + 3t$$

where

$t = 0$ corresponds to January of two years ago

y_t = Number of boxes of fruit expected to ship in month t

a. Determine trend amounts for the first four months of *next* year: January, $t = 24$; February, $t = 25$; etc. Thus,

Solution

$$Y_{Jan} = 402 + 3(24) = 474$$
$$Y_{Feb} = 402 + 3(25) = 477$$
$$Y_{Mar} = 402 + 3(26) = 480$$
$$Y_{Apr} = 402 + 3(27) = 483$$

b. Multiply each monthly trend by the corresponding seasonal relative for that month.

Month	Seasonal Relative	Forecast
Jan.	1.2	474(1.2) = 568.8
Feb.	1.3	477(1.3) = 620.1
Mar.	1.3	480(1.3) = 624.0
Apr.	1.1	483(1.1) = 531.3

Problem 3

Linear trend line. Plot the following data on a graph, and verify visually that a linear trend line is appropriate. Develop a line or trend equation. Then use the equation to predict the next two values of the series.

Solution

Period	Demand
1	44
2	52
3	50
4	54
5	55
6	55
7	60
8	56
9	62

A plot of the data indicates that a linear trend line is appropriate:

Period, t	Demand, y	ty	t^2
1	44	44	1
2	52	104	4
3	50	150	9
4	54	216	16
5	55	275	25
6	55	330	36
7	60	420	49
8	56	448	64
9	62	558	81
45	488	2,545	285

$$b = \frac{n\sum ty - \sum t \sum y}{n\sum t^2 - \left(\sum t\right)^2} = \frac{9(2,545) - 45(488)}{9(285) - 45(45)} = 1.75$$

$$a = \frac{\sum y - b\sum t}{n} = \frac{488 - 1.75(45)}{9} = 45.47$$

Thus, the trend equation is $y_t = 45.47 + 1.75t$. The next two forecasts are:

$$y_{10} = 45.47 + 1.75(10) = 62.97$$

$$y_{11} = 45.47 + 1.75(11) = 64.72$$

You can also use an Excel template to obtain the coefficients and plot. Simply replace the existing data in the template with your data.

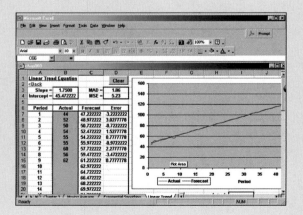

Calculating seasonal relatives. Obtain estimates of quarter relatives for these data:

Year:		1				2				3			4
Quarter:	1	2	3	4	1	2	3	4	1	2	3	4	1
Demand:	14	18	35	46	28	36	60	71	45	54	84	88	58

Solution

Note that each season has an *even* number of data points. When an even-numbered centred moving average is used (in this case, a four-period centred moving average), the "centred value" will not correspond to an actual data point; the centre of 4 is *between* the second and third data points. To correct for this, a *second* set of moving averages must be computed using the MA_4 values. The MA_2 values are centred between the MA_4 and "line up" with actual data points. For example, the first MA_4 value is 28.25. It should be centred between 18 and 35 (i.e., between quarter 2 and quarter 3). When the average of the first two MA_4 values is taken (i.e., MA_2) and centred, it lines up with the 35 and, hence, with quarter 3.

So, whenever an even-numbered moving average is used as a centred moving average (e.g., MA_4, MA_{12}), a second moving average, a two-period moving average, is used to achieve correspondence with periods. This procedure is not needed when the number of periods in the centred moving average is odd. See Example 8 in this chapter for an example with an odd number of periods.

Year	Quarter	Demand	MA₄	MA₂	Demand/MA₂
1	1	14			
	2	18	28.25		
	3	35	31.75	30.00	1.17
	4	46	36.25	34.00	1.35
2	1	28	42.50	39.38	.71
	2	36	48.75	45.63	.79
	3	60	53.00	50.88	1.18
	4	71	57.50	55.25	1.29
3	1	45	63.50	60.50	.74
	2	54	67.75	65.63	.82
	3	84	71.00	69.38	1.21
	4	88			
4	1	58			

	Quarter		
1	2	3	4
		1.17	1.35
.71	.79	1.18	1.29
.74	.82	1.21	____
1.45	1.61	3.56	2.64
Average for the quarter: .725	.805	1.187	1.320

The sum of these relatives is 4.037. Multiplying each by 4.00/4.037 will scale the relatives, making their total equal 4.00. The resulting relatives are: quarter 1, 0.718; quarter 2, .798; quarter 3, 1.176; quarter 4, 1.308.

Regression analysis. A large retailer has developed a graph that summarizes the effect of advertising expenditures on sales volume. Using the graph, determine an equation of the form $y = a + bx$ that describes this relationship.

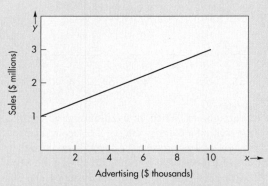

Solution

The linear equation has the form $\hat{y} = a + bx$, where a is the value of $\hat{y}$ when $x = 0$ (i.e., where the line intersects the y axis) and b is the slope of the line (the amount by which $\hat{y}$ changes for a one-unit change in x).

Accordingly, $a = 1$ and considering the points $(x = 0, y = 1)$ and $(x = 10, y = 3)$, $b = (3 - 1)/(10 - 0) = .2$, so $\hat{y} = a + bx$ becomes $\hat{y} = 1 + .2x$. [*Note:* $(3 - 1)$ is the change in y, and $(10 - 0)$ is the change in x.]

Problem 6

Regression analysis. The owner of a small hardware store has noted a sales pattern for door locks that seems to parallel the number of break-ins reported each week in the newspaper. The data are:

Sales:	46	18	20	22	27	34	14	37	30
Break-ins:	9	3	3	5	4	7	2	6	4

a. Plot the data to determine which type of equation, linear or nonlinear, is appropriate.

b. Obtain a regression equation for the data.

c. Estimate sales when the number of break-ins in a week is five.

Solution

a.

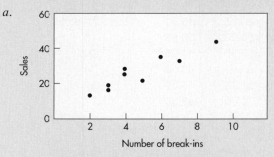

The graph supports a linear relationship.

b. The computations for a straight line are:

x	y	xy	x²	y²
9	46	414	81	2,116
3	18	54	9	324
3	20	60	9	400
5	22	110	25	484
4	27	108	16	729
7	34	238	49	1,156
2	14	28	4	196
6	37	222	36	1,369
4	30	120	16	900
43	248	1,354	245	7,674

$$b = \frac{n\left(\sum xy\right) - \left(\sum x\right)\left(\sum y\right)}{n\left(\sum x^2\right) - \left(\sum x\right)^2} = \frac{9(1,354) - 43(248)}{9(245) - 43(43)} = 4.275$$

$$a = \frac{\sum y - b\left(\sum x\right)}{n} = \frac{248 - 4.275(43)}{9} = 7.129$$

Hence, the equation is: $\hat{y} = 7.129 + 4.275x$.

You can obtain the regression coefficients using the appropriate Excel template. Simply replace the existing data for x and y with your data. Note: be careful to enter the values for the variable you want to predict as y values. In this problem, the objective is to predict sales, so the sales values are entered in the y column.

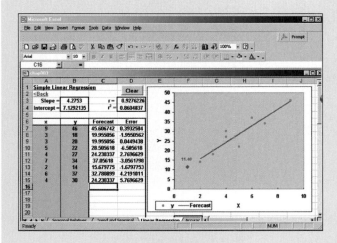

c. For $x = 5$, $\hat{y} = 7.129 + 4.275(5) = 28.50$.

Accuracy and control of forecasts. The manager of a large manufacturer of industrial pumps must choose between two alternative forecasting techniques. Both techniques have been used to prepare forecasts for a six-month period. Using MAD as a criterion, which technique has the better performance record?   **Problem 7**

		FORECAST	
Month	**Demand**	**Technique 1**	**Technique 2**
1	492	488	495
2	470	484	482
3	485	480	478
4	493	490	488
5	498	497	492
6	492	493	493

Check that each forecast has an average error of approximately zero. (See computations that follow.)   *Solution*

Month	**Demand**	**Technique 1**	**e**	**|e|**	**Technique 2**	**e**	**|e|**
1	492	488	4	4	495	−3	3
2	470	484	−14	14	482	−12	12
3	485	480	5	5	478	7	7
4	493	490	3	3	488	5	5
5	498	497	1	1	492	6	6
6	492	493	−1	1	493	−1	1
			−2	28		+2	34

$$\text{MAD}_1 = \frac{\sum |e|}{n} = \frac{28}{6} = 4.67$$

$$\text{MAD}_2 = \frac{\sum |e|}{n} = \frac{34}{6} = 5.67$$

Technique 1 is superior in this comparison because its MAD is smaller, although six observations would generally be too few on which to base a realistic comparison.

Problem 8

Control chart. Given the demand data that follow, prepare a naive forecast for periods 2 through 10. Then determine each forecast error, and use those values to obtain $2s$ control limits. If demand in the next two periods turns out to be 125 and 130, can you conclude that the forecasts are in control?

Period:	1	2	3	4	5	6	7	8	9	10
Demand:	118	117	120	119	126	122	117	123	121	124

Solution

For a naive forecast, each period's demand becomes the forecast for the next period. Hence, the forecasts and errors are:

Period	Demand	Forecast	Error	Error²
1	118	—	—	—
2	117	118	−1	1
3	120	117	3	9
4	119	120	−1	1
5	126	119	7	49
6	122	126	−4	16
7	117	122	−5	25
8	123	117	6	36
9	121	123	−2	4
10	124	121	3	9
			+6	150

$$s = \sqrt{\frac{\sum \text{error}^2}{n}} = \sqrt{\frac{150}{9}} = 4.08 \quad (n = \text{Number of errors})$$

The control limits are $\pm 2(4.08) = \pm 8.16$

The forecast for period 11 was 124. Demand turned out to be 125, for an error of $125 - 124 = +1$. This is within the limits of ± 8.16. If the next demand is 130 and the naive forecast is 125 (based on the period 11 demand of 125), the error is $+5$. Again, this is within the limits, so you cannot conclude the forecasting technique is not working properly. With more values—at least five or six—you could plot the errors to see whether you could detect any patterns suggesting the presence of nonrandomness.

DISCUSSION AND REVIEW QUESTIONS

1. What are the main advantages that quantitative techniques for forecasting have over qualitative methods? What limitations do quantitative techniques have?
2. What are some of the consequences of poor forecasts?
3. List the specific weaknesses of each of these approaches to developing a forecast:
   a. Consumer surveys
   b. Salesforce opinions
   c. Executive opinions
4. Briefly describe the Delphi method.
5. What is the purpose of establishing control limits for forecast errors?
6. What factors would you consider in deciding whether to use wide or narrow control limits for a forecast?
7. Contrast MAD, MSE, and MAPE in evaluating forecasts.
8. What advantages as a forecasting tool does exponential smoothing have over moving average?
9. How does the number of periods in a moving average affect the responsiveness of the forecast?
10. What factors enter into the choice of a value for the smoothing constant in exponential smoothing?

11. How accurate is your local five-day weather forecast?

12. Explain how using a centred moving average with a length equal to the length of all seasons eliminates seasonality from a time series.

13. Contrast the terms *sales* and *demand*.

14. Explain how flexibility in production systems relates to the forecast horizon and forecast accuracy.

15. Suppose a software producer is about to release a new version of its popular software. What information do you think it should take into account in forecasting initial sales?

16. Contrast the reactive and proactive approaches to forecasting. Give an example of an organization or situation in which each type is used.

17. How is forecasting in the context of a supply chain different from forecasting for just a single organization? List possible supply chain benefits and discuss potential difficulties in doing supply chain forecasting.

18. Choose the type of forecasting technique (survey, Delphi, averaging, seasonal naive, trend, or associative) that would be most appropriate for predicting
    a. Demand for Mother's Day greeting cards
    b. Popularity of a new television series.
    c. Demand for vacations on the moon.
    d. The impact a price increase of 10 percent would have on sales of orange marmalade.
    e. Demand for toothpaste in a particular supermarket.

TAKING STOCK

1. Explain the trade-off between responsiveness and stability in a forecasting system that uses time series data.

2. Who needs to be involved in preparing forecasts?

3. How has technology had an impact on forecasting?

CRITICAL THINKING EXERCISE

It has been said that forecasting using exponential smoothing is like driving a car by looking in the rear-view mirror. What are the conditions that would have to exist for driving a car that are analogous to the assumptions made when using exponential smoothing?

INTERNET EXERCISE

Go to the Institute of Business Forecasting Web site www.IBF.org and look into jobs in forecasting. Select a job in Canada and briefly summarize it. You will have to fill in some information about yourself to access the job description.

PROBLEMS

1. A commercial bakery has recorded sales (in dozens) for three products, as shown below:

Workday	Blueberry Muffins	Cinnamon Buns	Cupcakes
1	30	18	45
2	34	17	26
3	32	19	27
4	34	19	23
5	35	22	22
6	30	23	48
7	34	23	29
8	36	25	20
9	29	24	14
10	31	26	18
11	35	27	47
12	31	28	26
13	37	29	27
14	34	31	24
15	33	33	22

 a. Predict sales for the following day for each of the products using an appropriate naive method.

 b. What does the use of *sales* data instead of *demand* presume?

2. National Mixer, Inc., sells can openers. Monthly sales for a seven-month period were as follows:

Month	Sales (000 units)
Feb.	19
Mar.	18
Apr.	15
May	20
Jun.	18
Jul.	22
Aug.	20

 a. Plot the data.

 b. Forecast September's sales volume using each of the following:

   (1) A linear trend equation.

   (2) A four-month moving average.

   (3) Exponential smoothing with a smoothing constant equal to .10, assuming a March forecast of 19(000).

   (4) The naive approach.

   (5) A weighted average using .50 for August, .30 for July, and .20 for June.

 c. Which method seems least appropriate? Why?

 d. What does use of the term *sales* rather than *demand* presume?

3. A dry cleaner uses exponential smoothing to forecast equipment usage as a percentage of capacity at its main plant. August usage was forecast to be 88 percent of capacity; actual usage was 89.6 percent of capacity. A smoothing constant of .2 is used.

 a. Prepare a forecast for September.

 b. Assuming actual September usage of 92 percent, prepare a forecast for October's usage.

4. An electrical contractor's records during the last five weeks indicate the following number of job requests:

Week:	1	2	3	4	5
Requests:	20	22	18	21	22

 Predict the number of requests for week 6 using each of these methods:

 a. Naive.

 b. A four-period moving average.

 c. Exponential smoothing with $\alpha = .30$.

5. A cosmetics manufacturer's marketing department has developed a linear trend equation that can be used to predict annual sales of its popular Hand & Foot Cream:

$$\hat{y}_t = 80 + 15t$$

 where

   $\hat{y}_t$ = Annual sales (000 bottles)
   $t = 0$ corresponds to 1990

 a. Are annual sales increasing or decreasing? By how much?

 b. Predict annual sales for the year 2003 using the equation.

6. From the following graph, determine the linear equation of the trend line using 1995 as the base year for Glib Sales, Inc.

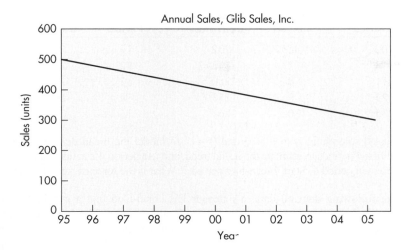

7. Freight car loadings over an 18-week period at a busy port are:

Week	Number	Week	Number	Week	Number
1	220	7	350	13	460
2	245	8	360	14	475
3	280	9	400	15	500
4	275	10	380	16	510
5	300	11	420	17	525
6	310	12	450	18	541

a. Compute a linear trend line for freight car loadings.

b. Use the trend equation to predict loadings for weeks 19 and 20.

c. The manager intends to install new equipment when the volume reaches 700 loadings per week. Assuming the current trend continues, the loading volume will reach that level in approximately what week?

8. Suppose it is the year 2001 and you are trying to assist the forecaster in Lennox Industries identify the trend in the heating equipment industry sales in Canada and forecast the total industry sales for 2001–2002. You have accessed Statistics Canada's CANSIM 2 database at http://cansim2.statcan.ca and found the heating equipment industry's GDP (in 1992 constant prices) in series v328689. This series is available between 1961 and 2000. You have observed its plot, and see a linear trend between 1992 and 2000.

Year	Heating Equipment Industry's GDP (in million 1992$)
1992	199
1993	223
1994	272
1995	305
1996	295
1997	312
1998	341
1999	346
2000	302

Fit a linear trend to the heating equipment industry's GDP data using Excel's "Add Trend Line" feature (under the "Chart" pull-down heading), and extend it for two years.

9. *a.* Develop a linear trend equation for the following data on bread deliveries, and use it to predict deliveries for periods 16 through 19.

Period	Dozen Deliveries	Period	Dozen Deliveries	Period	Dozen Deliveries
1	200	6	232	11	281
2	214	7	248	12	275
3	211	8	250	13	280
4	228	9	253	14	288
5	235	10	267	15	310

b. Use trend-adjusted smoothing with $\alpha = .3$ and $\beta = .2$ to model the bread delivery data in part a. Use the first 4 periods to estimate the initial trend, and use period 4's actual value as the smoothed average in period 4. Start forecasting period 5. What is the forecast for period 16?

10. After plotting the following demand data, a manager has concluded that a trend-adjusted exponential smoothing model is appropriate to predict future demand. The initial estimate of trend is based on the increase in demand of 30 from period 1 to period 4 for an average of +10 units of trend per period. Use $\alpha = .5$ and $\beta = .4$, and TAF of 250 for period 5. Develop forecasts for periods 6 through 10.

Period, t	A, Actual
1	210
2	224
3	229
4	240
5	255
6	265
7	272
8	285
9	294
10	

11. A manager of a store that sells and installs hot tubs wants to prepare a forecast for January, February, and March of next year. Her forecasts are a combination of trend and seasonality. She uses the following equation to estimate the trend component of monthly demand: $y_t = 70 + 6t$, where $t = 0$ in June of last year. Seasonal relatives are 1.10 for January, 1.02 for February, and .95 for March. What demands should she predict?

12. The following equation summarizes the trend portion of quarterly sales of automatic dishwashers over a long cycle. Sales also exhibit seasonal variations. Using the information given, prepare a forecast of sales for each quarter of 2004, and the first quarter of 2005.

$$y_t = 40 - 6.5t + 2t^2$$

where

y_t = Unit sales

$t = 0$ at the fourth quarter of 2001

Quarter	Seasonal Relative
1	1.1
2	1.0
3	.6
4	1.3

13. A gift shop in a tourist centre is open on weekends (Friday, Saturday, and Sunday). The owner–manager hopes to improve scheduling of part-time employees by determining seasonal relatives for each of these days. Data on recent activity at the store (sales transactions per day) have been tabulated and are shown in the following table.

	WEEK					
	1	**2**	**3**	**4**	**5**	**6**
Friday	149	154	152	150	159	163
Saturday	250	255	260	268	273	276
Sunday	166	162	171	173	176	183

a. Develop seasonal relatives for each day.

b. Using a naive trend approach to predict total sales transactions for the gift shop for the following week, the manager predicts a total of 636 sales transactions next week (Friday to Sunday). Using your seasonal relatives from part *a*, forecast the sales transactions for each day, Friday to Sunday, of next week.

14. The manager of a fashionable restaurant open Wednesday through Saturday, says that the restaurant does about 35 percent of its business on Friday night, 30 percent on Saturday night, and 20 percent on Thursday night. What seasonal relatives would describe this situation?

15. Coal shipments from Mountain Coal Company's no. 4 mine for the past 17 weeks are:

Week	Tonnes Shipped	Week	Tonnes Shipped
1	405	10	440
2	410	11	446
3	420	12	451
4	415	13	455
5	412	14	464
6	420	15	466
7	424	16	474
8	433	17	476
9	438		

a. Explain why an averaging technique would not be appropriate for forecasting tonnes shipped.

b. Use an appropriate technique to develop a forecast for the next three weeks.

16. Calculate estimates of daily relatives for the number of customers served at a restaurant, given the following data. (*Hint*: Use a seven-day centred moving average.)

Day	Number Served	Day	Number Served
1	80	15	84
2	75	16	77
3	78	17	83
4	95	18	96
5	130	19	135
6	136	20	140
7	40	21	37
8	82	22	87
9	77	23	82
10	80	24	98
11	94	25	103
12	125	26	144
13	135	27	144
14	42	28	48

17. Echlin Inc. is an after-market supplier of automotive spare parts.[7] A part is usually made specifically for a particular model of a car. In order to forecast the demand for this part, Echlin tries to use the following process: (a) determine the total number of new vehicles of this model sold each year, (b) determine the replacement probability by age for the first replacement, second replacement, and so on of the particular part for current and future years, (c) calculate the total number of replacement units for each year, (d) break this down into original equipment manufacturer market and aftermarket manufacturer market, (e) calculate Echlin's annual share using its market share, and, finally (f) break down the annual forecast into quarterly and monthly sales forecasts using seasonal relatives.

Consider a specific part. Echlin makes brake calipers for a particular model of a car, first introduced in 1986. Suppose it is now the end of 1992, and using steps *a* to *e* above Echlin has forecast its own sales of this caliper for 1993.

Year	Echlin's sales of calipers
1990	10,444
1991	10,319
1992	8,477
1993	6,334 (forecast)

Echlin also has quarterly sales of these calipers for the past three years.

Quarter	1990	1991	1992
Q_1	2370	2641	2281
Q_2	2058	2198	1814
Q_3	2778	2518	2127
Q_4	3238	2962	2255
Total	10,444	10,319	8,477

   a. Use the 1990–92 quarterly data above to determine the quarterly seasonal relatives.

   b. Use your answer to part *a* and 1993 forecast sales to forecast quarterly sales for 1993.

   c. Alternatively, use the steps outlined in the text. That is, deseasonalize the data, fit an appropriate model to the deseasonalized data, extend it 4 quarters, and re-seasonalize. Compare you results with part *b*.

18. A pharmacist has been monitoring sales of a certain over-the-counter pain reliever. Daily sales during the last 15 days were:

Day:	1	2	3	4	5	6	7	8	9
Number sold:	36	38	42	44	48	49	50	49	52

Day:	10	11	12	13	14	15
Number sold:	48	52	55	54	56	57

   a. If you learn that on some days the store ran out of this pain reliever, would that knowledge cause you any concern? Explain.

   b. Assume that the data refer to demand rather than sales. Using trend-adjusted exponential smoothing with an initial forecast of 50 for day 8, an initial trend estimate of 2, and $\alpha = \beta = .3$, develop forecasts for days 9 through 16.

19. New-car sales for a dealer for the past year are shown in the following table, along with monthly (seasonal) relatives.

[7]See J. A. G. Krupp, "Forecasting for the Automotive Aftermarket," *Journal of Business Forecasting Methods & Systems* 12(4), Winter 1993–94, pp. 8–12.

Month	Units Sold	Seasonal Relative	Month	Units Sold	Seasonal Relative
Jan.	640	0.80	Jul.	765	0.90
Feb.	648	0.80	Aug.	805	1.15
Mar.	630	0.70	Sept.	840	1.20
Apr.	761	0.94	Oct.	828	1.20
May	735	0.89	Nov.	840	1.25
Jun.	850	1.00	Dec.	800	1.25

a. Plot the data. Does there seem to be a trend?

b. Deseasonalize car sales.

c. Plot the deseasonalized data on the same graph as the original data. Comment on the two graphs.

20. The following table shows a tool and die company's quarterly sales for the current year. What sales would you predict for the first quarter of next year? Quarter relatives are $Q_1 = 1.10$, $Q_2 = .99$, $Q_3 = .90$, and $Q_4 = 1.01$. (*Hint:* First deseasonalize the data, then observe the trend and project it ahead, and finally re-seasonalize.)

Quarter	1	2	3	4
Sales	88	99	108	141

21. A farming cooperative's manager wants to forecast quarterly grain shipments, based on the data shown below (quantities are in metric tonnes):

	QUARTER			
Year	1	2	3	4
1	200	250	210	340
2	210	252	212	360
3	215	260	220	358
4	225	272	233	372
5	232	284	240	381

a. Determine quarter relatives (using the four-period centred moving average).

b. Deseasonalize the data, fit an appropriate model to the deseasonalized data, extend it 4 quarters, and finally re-seasonalize the projections.

22. Long-Life Insurance has developed a linear model that it uses to determine the amount of term life insurance a family of four should have, based on the current age of the head of the household. The equation is:

$y = 1,000 - 10x$

where

y = Insurance needed ($000)
x = Current age of head of household

a. Plot the relationship on a graph.

b. Use the equation to determine the amount of term life insurance to recommend for a family of four if the head of the household is 30 years old.

23. Timely Transport provides local delivery service for a number of businesses in a city. Delivery charges are based on distance and weight involved for each delivery: 11 cents per kg and 16 cents per km. Also, there is a $10 handling fee per parcel.

a. Develop an expression that summarizes delivery charges.

b. Determine the delivery charge for transporting a 40-kg parcel 26 kms.

24. The manager of a seafood restaurant was asked to establish a pricing policy on lobster dinners. Experimenting with prices produced the following data:

Average Number Sold per Day, y	Price, x	Average Number Sold per Day, y	Price, x
200.........	$6.00	155	$8.25
190.........	6.50	156	8.50
188.........	6.75	148	8.75
180.........	7.00	140	9.00
170.........	7.25	133	9.25
162.........	7.50		
160.........	8.00		

   a. Plot the data and a regression line on the same graph.
   b. Determine the correlation coefficient and interpret it.

25. The following data were collected during a study of consumer buying patterns.

Observation	x	y	Observation	x	y
1.......	15	74	8	18	78
2.......	25	80	9	14	70
3.......	40	84	10	15	72
4.......	32	81	11	22	85
5.......	51	96	12	24	88
6.......	47	95			
7.......	30	83			

   a. Plot the data.
   b. Obtain a linear regression line for the data.
   c. What percentage of the variation is explained by the regression line?
   d. Use the equation determined in part b to predict the value of y for $x = 41$.

26. Lovely Lawns, Inc., intends to use sales of lawn fertilizer to predict lawn mower sales. The store manager estimates a relationship between fertilizer sales and mower sales. The pertinent data are:

Period	Fertilizer Sales (tonnes)	Number of Mowers Sold	Period	Fertilizer Sales (tonnes)	Number of Mowers Sold
1	1.6	10	8	1.3	7
2	1.3	8	9	1.7	10
3	1.8	11	10	1.2	6
4	2.0	12	11	1.9	11
5	2.2	12	12	1.4	8
6	1.6	9	13	1.7	10
7	1.5	8			

   a. Determine the correlation between the two variables. Does it appear that a relationship between these variables will yield good predictions? Explain.
   b. Obtain a linear regression line for the data.
   c. Predict lawn mower sales, given fertilizer sales of 2 tonnes.

27. An analyst must decide between two different forecasting techniques for weekly sales of inline skates: a linear trend equation and the naive approach. The linear trend equation is $y_t = 124 + 2t$, and it was developed using data from periods 1 through 10. Based on data for

periods 11 through 19 as shown in the following table, which of these two methods has the greater accuracy?

t	Units Sold	t	Units Sold
11	147	16	152
12	148	17	155
13	151	18	157
14	145	19	160
15	155		

28. Two different forecasting techniques (F1 and F2) were used to forecast demand for cases of bottled water in a store. Actual demand and the two sets of forecasts are as follows:

		PREDICTED DEMAND	
Period	Demand	F1	F2
1	68	66	66
2	75	68	68
3	70	72	70
4	74	71	72
5	69	72	74
6	72	70	76
7	80	71	78

   a. Calculate the MAD for each set of forecasts. Given your results, which technique appears to be more accurate? Explain.

   b. Calculate the MSE for each set of forecasts. Given your results, which technique appears to be more accurate?

   c. Calculate the MAPE for each set of forecasts. Which technique appears to be more accurate?

   d. In practice, *either* MAD, MSE, or MAPE would be employed to compute a measure of forecast errors. What factors might lead a manager to favour one?

29. Two independent set of forecasts based on judgment and experience have been prepared each month for the past 10 months. The forecasts and actual demand are as follows:

Month	Demand	Forecast 1	Forecast 2
1....	770	771	769
2....	789	785	787
3....	794	790	792
4....	780	784	798
5....	768	770	774
6....	772	768	770
7....	760	761	759
8....	775	771	775
9....	786	784	788
10....	790	788	788

   a. Calculate the MSE, MAD, and MAPE for each forecast. Does one forecast seem superior? Explain.

   b. Calculate $2s$ control limits for each forecast and determine if it is in control.

30. The classified department of a monthly magazine has used a combination of quantitative and qualitative methods to forecast sales of advertising space. The forecast errors over an 18-month period are as follows:

Month	Error	Month	Error
1......	−8	11......	1
2......	−2	12......	6
3......	4	13......	8
4......	7	14......	4
5......	9	15......	1
6......	5	16......	−2
7......	0	17......	−4
8......	−3	18......	−8
9......	−9		
10......	−4		

a. Using the first half of the data, construct a control chart with $2s$ limits. What can you conclude?

b. Plot the last nine errors on the control chart. Are the errors random? What is the implication of this?

31. A textbook publishing company has compiled data on total annual sales of its business texts for the preceding eight years:

Year:	1	2	3	4	5	6	7	8
Scles (000):	40.2	44.5	48.0	52.3	55.8	57.1	62.4	69.0

a. Fit an appropriate model to the above data, and construct a $2s$ control chart.

b. Using the model, forecast textbook sales for each of the next five years.

c. Suppose actual sales for the next five years turn out as follows:

Year:	9	10	11	12	13
Sales (000):	73.7	77.2	82.1	87.8	90.6

Is the forecasting technique performing adequately? Explain.

32. A manager has just received an evaluation from an analyst on two potential forecasting alternatives. The analyst is indifferent between the two alternatives, saying that they should be equally effective.

Period:	1	2	3	4	5	6	7	8	9
Data:	37	39	37	39	45	49	47	49	51
Alt. 1:	36	38	40	42	46	46	46	48	52
Alt. 2:	36	37	38	38	41	52	47	48	52

a. What would cause the analyst to reach this conclusion? (*Hint*: Construct measures of forecast errors.)

b. Construct a $2s$ control chart for each alternative and interpret them.

33. A manager uses this equation to predict demand: $y_t = 10 + 5t$. Over the past seven periods, demand has been as follows.

Period, t:	1	2	3	4	5	6	7
Demand:	15	21	23	30	32	38	42

Is the forecasting technique performing adequately? Explain.

34. A manager uses a trend equation plus quarter relatives (seasonality) to predict demand. Quarter relatives are $Q_1 = .90$, $Q_2 = .95$, $Q_3 = 1.05$, and $Q_4 = 1.10$. The trend equation is: $y_t = 10 + 5t$. Over the past nine quarters, starting with $Q1$, demand has been as follows:

Period, t:	1	2	3	4	5	6	7	8	9
Demand:	14	20	24	31	31	37	43	48	52

Is the forecasting technique performing adequately? Explain.

35. Federated Cooperatives Limited (FCL) is the largest wholesaler of grocery, hardware, and agricultural supplies in Western Canada, and operates warehouses in Saskatoon, Edmonton,

Calgary, and Winnipeg. In the Calgary warehouse, a particular golf club is carried on stock. The demand for this golf club during each month of the period 1993–95 is listed below (note that FCL uses weekly time buckets, but for simplicity we have combined these into monthly data):

Month	1993	1994	1995
Jan	0	2	3
Feb	52	8	20
Mar	29	44	12
Apr	49	74	3¹
May	47	75	6¹
Jun	58	87	28
Jul	0	145	107
Aug	64	11	57
Sep	3	24	21
Oct	17	9	10
Nov	10	5	0
Dec	1	6	1
Total	330	490	351

Determine the monthly relatives, deseasonalize the data, fit an appropriate model to the deseasonalized data, project 12 months ahead, and re-seasonalize the projections to forecast monthly sales for 1996. (These figures are used to plan purchases of the golf club from the manufacturer.)

36. Consider the usage of item #14-46-506: 4 ft. Supersaver fluorescent lamps in Sterling Pulp Chemicals in the first 10 months of 1998.

Month	1998
Jan	10
Feb	10
Mar	66
Apr	32
May	34
June	18
July	24
Aug	9
Sep	14
Oct	48

Fit a model to the data using each of the following techniques and forecast the November usage in each case. Also, plot the two moving average forecasts and the actual, the two exponential smoothing forecasts and the actual, and the linear trend and the actual (three plots altogether).

  i. Three-month moving average
  ii. Five-month moving average
  iii. Exponential smoothing with smoothing constant = 0.1
  iv. Exponential smoothing with smoothing constant = 0.3
  v. Linear trend (regression)
  vi. Just by observing the plots, which of the above techniques would you use to forecast the usage of fluorescent lamps and why?

37. Consider the total production (and sales) of ice cream in Canada (in millions of litres) for the period 1995 until 2004 (from left to right; Series v108517 CANSIM 2 database):

      341, 331, 317, 315, 321, 278, 298, 311, 302, 302

Fit a model to ice cream production data using each of the following techniques and forecast the 2005 production in each case. Also, plot the two moving average forecasts and the actual, the two exponential smoothing forecasts and the actual, and the linear trend and the actual (three plots altogether).

    i. Two-year moving average

   ii. Four-year moving average

  iii. Exponential smoothing with smoothing constant = 0.2

  iv. Exponential smoothing with smoothing constant = 0.4

   v. Linear trend (regression)

  vi. Just by observing the plots, which of the above techniques would you use to forecast the ice cream production and why?

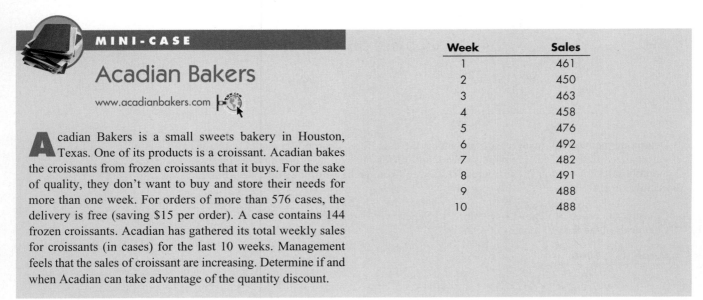

MINI-CASE

Acadian Bakers

www.acadianbakers.com

Acadian Bakers is a small sweets bakery in Houston, Texas. One of its products is a croissant. Acadian bakes the croissants from frozen croissants that it buys. For the sake of quality, they don't want to buy and store their needs for more than one week. For orders of more than 576 cases, the delivery is free (saving $15 per order). A case contains 144 frozen croissants. Acadian has gathered its total weekly sales for croissants (in cases) for the last 10 weeks. Management feels that the sales of croissant are increasing. Determine if and when Acadian can take advantage of the quantity discount.

Week	Sales
1	461
2	450
3	463
4	458
5	476
6	492
7	482
8	491
9	488
10	488

SELECTED BIBLIOGRAPHY AND FURTHER READING

Delurgio, Stephen. *Forecasting Principles and Applications*. Burr Ridge, IL: Irwin/McGraw-Hill, 1998.

Georgoff, D. M., and R. G. Murdick. "Manager's Guide to Forecasting." *Harvard Business Review*, January–February 1986, pp. 110–120.

Hopp, Wallace J., and Mark L. Spearman. *Factory Physics*, 2nd ed. Burr Ridge, IL: Irwin/McGraw-Hill, 2001.

Metzer, J.T., "The Impact of Forecasting on Return on Shareholder's Value." *Journal of Business Forecasting Methods & Systems*, Fall 1999, pp. 8–12.

Rowe, G., and G. Wright. "The Delphi Technique as a Forecasting Tool: Issues and Analysis." *International Journal of Forecasting* 15(4), October 1999. See also in the same issue: several commentaries on this article.

"Selecting the Appropriate Forecasting Method." *Journal of Business Forecasting*, Fall 1997.

Wilson, J. Holton, and Barry Keating. *Business Forecasting*. New York: McGraw-Hill, 1998.

PART THREE

System Design

Satisfying the customer begins with product and service design. Moreover, decisions made in this area impact on operations and on the organization's overall success.

Similarly, process design and capacity planning impact on the ability of the production system to perform and satisfy customers, in addition to cost of production. Flexibility, production time, and cost are key considerations in process design.

Process design and layout are closely related. Layout decisions involve the arrangement of the workplace, which affects the flow of work through the system. Layout impacts productivity, cost, and flexibility, in addition to being an important part of most services.

Work design focuses on the human element in production systems. Increasingly, managers are realizing that workers are a valuable asset and can contribute greatly to the organization's success.

Location decision influences operating costs and the ability to respond to customer demand. Location decision also impacts transportation costs, labour availability, material costs, and access to markets.

Design decisions have strategic significance for business organizations. Many of these decisions are made jointly with the CEO and top managers of other functional areas of the organization.

System design encompasses decisions involving:

CHAPTER 4

Product and Service Design

Nortel Networks is the premier high-tech company in Canada. Throughout its existence it invented and sold numerous products, especially the large switches in telephone company centres which direct incoming calls to their destinations.

How do some companies manage to introduce successful new products fast when others can't? This is the type of question we will be answering in this chapter.

The essence of any organization is the products or services it offers. There is an obvious link between the *design* of those products or services and the *success* of the organization. In addition, the quality of the product/service is mainly, perhaps as much as 80 percent, determined during the design stage. Hence, organizations have a vital stake in achieving good product and service design.

In this chapter you will find many insights into product and service design. Among the topics covered are the steps involved in product and service design or redesign; sources of ideas for design or redesign; design elements for manufacturing and service; and quality function deployment (QFD), a method for translating the "voice of customers" into design.

Product and service design—or redesign—should be closely tied to an organization's strategy. It is a major factor in customer satisfaction and competitive advantage.

INTRODUCTION

Successful organizations use four elements to create new products or services and bring them to the consumer (see Figure 4–1).

The product (or service) approval committee consists of top management and oversees and directs the development activities. It is responsible for authorizing new products (or services), reviewing the progress at phase review points, allocating resources across different projects, and ensuring consistency between company strategy and development projects.

Core teams are cross-functional teams empowered to plan and lead the development projects from concept to commercialization. This involves resolving issues and conflicts, making trade-off decisions, and directing other support staff. Every function involved should be represented in the core team, but it should not be large (maximum of eight members) in order to be effective. It is important to clearly define every core member's role and responsibility, and those of the functional managers, to ensure that the core team is empowered. The limits of authority of the core team should be defined. Many core teams also include a legal and regulatory member.

Phase reviews (or stage-gates) are milestones during a new product (or service) development project when the progress of the core team is reviewed by the product (or service) approval committee. The decision will be to approve, cancel, or redirect the project.

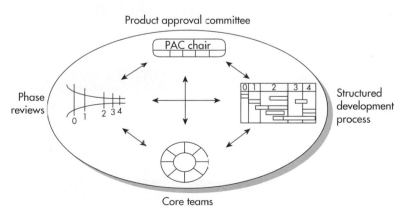

FIGURE 4–1

Four basic elements required to bring new services from concept to consumer

Source: J. Ong, "Rapid Telecommunication Service Development," *Telecommunications* 31(11), November 1997, pp. 40–44.

Reviews help top management acquire better understanding of the project and guide the project, and force closure of issues arising during each phase of the project.

The structured development process is the use of project management techniques. It involves breaking each phase into steps and each step into tasks, determining the precedence relationships, scheduling, and executing and control. The steps are most critical and are planned and managed by the core team. A task relates to one functional area and is planned and managed by the core team member from that function. Tasks may be broken down into day-to-day activities. It is important that the amount of structure is just right: too much structure results in bureaucracy and too little structure results in ineffective development process.

The usual phases for product or service design are:

1. Idea generation.

2. Build a business case: Market and competitor analysis; determine what customers want ("voice of the customer") and establish product/service goals (performance, cost, quality, etc.).

3. Development: Translate the "voice of the customer" into technical (physical) product/service specifications, such as product size/nature of service, features, and so on. As part of this, a concept is developed and/or chosen. A *concept* is an idea and a general way to materialize it. This may involve some (engineering) tests. Revise the target market/product goals if necessary. Build product prototypes; test; and revise the design if necessary.

4. Production process design: Design production/service delivery process, tooling/equipment, and quality control; revise product or service design if necessary. Conduct pilot production/service delivery runs; revise the process and/or product/service design if necessary.

5. Launch: Produce and distribute/render service.

A core team usually consists of a product manager, product designers (usually stylists and engineers), and manufacturing/operations representatives. The team is expanded during each phase of design with marketing representatives (at the start and at the end), accountants (to establish cost goals), process engineers (for process design, tooling/equipment), quality control, and purchasing and supplier representatives (component design and manufacturing).

This team-based approach of simultaneously designing the product and process is called *concurrent engineering*. In contrast, in the past, because of time pressure and the "silo" mentality, each functional area performed their part of design in isolation and "threw" their work "over the wall" to the next department in design. The order was (1) marketing, (2) product design/engineering, (3) manufacturing, and (4) purchasing. This frequently resulted in late launch dates and costly design revisions. Concurrent engineering is further discussed later in the chapter. The new product (or service) development process is illustrated in Figures 4–2a and b.

FIGURE 4–2A

The stage-gate model of new product design and development process

Source: R. G. Cooper, "Doing it Right," *Ivey Business Journal* 64(6), July/August 2000, pp. 54–60. Copyright © (2000) Ivey Management Services. One time permission to reproduce granted by Ivey Management Services on November 7, 2005.

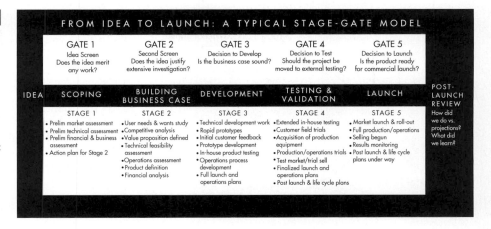

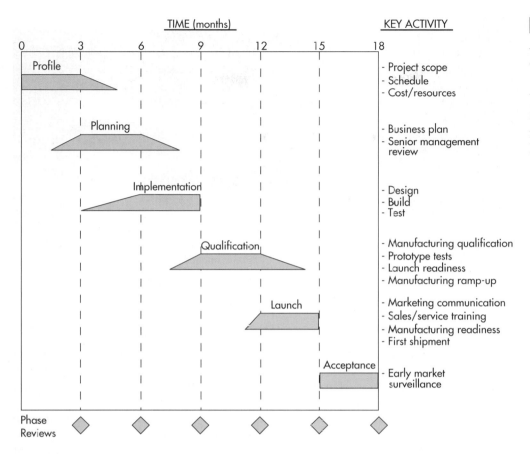

FIGURE 4-2B

Dell's new product development chart

Source: S. Thomke et al., *Product Development at Dell Computer Corporation*, Case no. 9-699-010. Boston: Harvard Business School, 2000. Copyright © 2000 by the President and Fellows of Harvard College. Reprinted by permission.

SOURCES OF IDEAS FOR NEW OR REDESIGNED PRODUCTS AND SERVICES

Ideas for new and improved products or services can come from a wide range of sources, both from within the organization and from outside it.

Employees—including those who make products or deliver services to customers, salespeople, and purchasing agents, can be a rich source of ideas, if they are motivated to offer suggestions. In addition to these are two more primary sources of ideas: marketing and research. Along with assessing current needs of customers, sales and marketing people typically are aware of problems with products or services. Similarly, product failures and warranty claims indicate where improvements are needed. Marketing people are often sources of ideas based on their studies of markets, buying patterns, and familiarity with demographics. Also, marketing can help craft a vision of what customers are likely to want in the future. Customers may submit suggestions for improvements or new products, or they may be queried through the use of surveys or focus groups.

One of the strongest motivators for new and improved products or services is competitors' products and services. Some companies purchase a competitor's product and then carefully dismantle and inspect it, searching for ways to improve their own product. This is called **reverse engineering**. The Ford Motor Company used this tactic in developing its highly successful Taurus model: it examined competitors' automobiles, searching for best-in-class components (e.g., best hood release, best dashboard display, best door handle). Sometimes reverse engineering can enable a company to "leapfrog" the competition by developing an even better product.

Suppliers are another source of ideas for the best way to design the components they make and the use of new technology.

reverse engineering Dismantling and inspecting a competitor's product to discover product improvements.

This Degree of Freedom Simulation Test is used in Ford Motor Company labs to simulate proving ground testing in the lab.

www.ford.com

Frontal impact crash test performed for the Honda S2000 by the New Car Assessment Program (NCAP) for the U. S. National Highway Safety Administration.

www.hondacars.com

research and development (R&D) Organized efforts for product innovation.

Research and development (R&D) refers to organized efforts that are directed toward product or process innovation. Most of the advances in semiconductors, medicine, communications, and space technology can be attributed to R&D efforts at colleges and universities, research foundations, government agencies, and private enterprises.

The costs of R&D can be high. Nortel Networks, for example, at its height spent more than $7 million *a day* on R&D. Large companies in the automotive, computer, communications, and pharmaceutical industries spend a lot, too. Canada spends only 1.5 percent of its GDP on R&D, in contrast with 3 percent by the United States, Japan, and Germany.

Hewlett-Packard is considered one of the most innovative companies in the world. In a study of innovative projects in HP, it was discovered that having skilled and helpful people who work well together, management support, and using a systematic product design process (to provide discipline and focus) are the required ingredients for a high degree of innovation.[1]

READING

Two Significant Canadian Contributions to World Technology

After the Second World War, the Canadian and Ontario governments supported research in the use of nuclear power for electricity generation, and in partnership with GE Canada set up a research lab in Chalk River, Ontario. This eventually led to the design of Candu reactors, which use heavy water and natural uranium to generate steam that is in turn transformed into electricity through turbines. Natural uranium bars are simpler to make than the enriched uranium used by U.S. reactors. This invention has been used in Canada and sold to several countries. Approximately half of Ontario's power comes from Candu reactors. Candu reactors are constantly redesigned in order to make them provide more power. See www.AECL.ca for more information.

Other highly recognized Canadian contributions are the Canadarm and Canadarm 2, the robotic arms for space shuttles and the space station, respectively. They both were made to work in a very inhospitable environment (space) with a high degree of reliability required. In addition to the arm-like motions, Canadarm 2 is expected to actually hop around the space station (i.e., it is not permanently anchored in one place, like the Canadarm). Both arms were made by Spar Aerospace, which was sold to MacDonald Dettwiler in 1999. See http://sm.mdacorporation.com for more information.

---

[1]R. Rivas and D. H. Gobeli, "Accelerating Innovation at Hewlett-Packard," *Research Technology Management* 48(1), January/February 2005, pp. 32–39.

Searching for New Product Ideas

What is the best way to find new product ideas? Consider the following approaches that have shown success in the past:

1. Listening to the Market Complaints

Many companies have made their products successful by listening to consumer complaints about products already on the market. Complaints about the inadequacies of two-ply tissues inspired Kimberly-Clark to create three-ply Cold Care Tissues, and Gillette found it could satisfy customers with complaints about white residue from their deodorants by creating the Clear Stick.

An equivalent complaint about lipstick smearing on coffee cups and shirt collars resulted in Lancome's transfer-resistant Rouge Idole lipsticks.

2. Gaps in the Market

3M used focus groups to create its Pop-up Tape Dispenser—it noticed consumers were one hand short of being able to hold wrapping paper, scissors, and tape when wrapping gifts. The new patented creation fit like a wristwatch, precutting tape strips and otherwise giving gift-wrappers a hand up. Black & Decker introduced its cordless DeWalt power tools for professionals who needed powerful equipment (such as drills) and could get this only from corded tools. The Black & Decker Snakelite twistable flashlight allows for hands-free use during repairs in tight-fitting spaces like bathrooms or furnaces.

John Deere Co.'s "Gator" is an inexpensive, six-wheel, off-road all-terrain personnel utility vehicle suitable for transporting everything from personnel and equipment to farming debris to wounded soldiers from the battlefield. The Gator simply doesn't have any direct competitors.

3. Exploring Niche Markets

For drivers who have been dropped by their insurance carriers because they are considered risky, Kingsway Financial Services Company of Mississauga, Ontario, provides an unparalleled service: offering car insurance to drivers like these, Kingsway has seen its annual revenue rocket from less than $20 million to more than $92 billion in a mere 10 years.

Coleman, traditionally a manufacturer of camping gear, found a lucrative niche in the market when it produced smoke detectors with large "broom button" alarm testers. Using a broom handle to shut off nuisance alarms triggered by burnt toast appealed especially to the elderly and gave Coleman a 40-percent market share as a result.

4. Using New Technology

Many new products have found that they could attract the attention of the market by exploiting a new science or art, whether it is a once-a-month pill to rid cats and dogs of fleas (Novartis), or frosted windows that clear up with the flip of a switch (3M). Research in Motion (RIM) founders managed to use their capability with pagers to invent Blackberry, a portable e-mail communicator, in the late 1990s at the peak of the high-tech boom.

5. Creating New Market Space

Westjet started by targeting a new market, the "friends and relatives" visitors who normally drive to visit. Sony Walkman created the new market of personal portable stereo market for joggers and commuters. Starbucks emphasizes the emotional value of drinking coffee providing a chic "caffeine-induced oasis." Body shop did the reverse by selling natural ingredients and healthy living instead of glamour and beauty.

Question

Can you name some more examples of the above sources of product ideas?

Sources: Adapted from Allan J. Magrath, "Mining for New Product Successes," *Business Quarterly* 62(2), Winter 1997, pp. 64–68; "The Edison Best New Product Awards," *Marketing News* 31(6), March 17, 1997, pp. E4–E12; W. C. Kim & R. Mauborgne, "Creating New Marketplace," *Harvard Business Review* 77(1), January/February 1999, pp. 83–93.

The readings on this and the previous page give two examples of Canadian high-tech products and illustrate some market-related sources of ideas for product and service design.

OTHER ISSUES IN PRODUCT AND SERVICE DESIGN

Designers must take into account product or service life cycles, how much standardization to incorporate, how to "customize" basically standard products, product or service reliability, robust design (wide range of operating conditions under which a product or service must function), and legal and ethical issues. These topics are discussed in this section. We begin with life cycles.

The LUKE Parking Meter by Digital Payment Technologies Corp. of Vancouver. The component on the top enables remote communication, for example, changing the parking rates. www.digitalpaytech.com

Life Cycles

life cycle Incubation, growth, maturity, saturation, and decline.

Most new products and services go through a **life cycle** in terms of demand. When an item is introduced, it may be treated as a curiosity. Demand is generally low because potential buyers are not yet familiar with the item. Many potential buyers recognize that all of the bugs have probably not been worked out and that the price may drop after the introductory period. Production methods are generally designed for low volume. With the passage of time, design improvements usually create a more reliable and less costly product. Demand then grows for these reasons and because of increasing awareness of the product or service. Higher production volume will involve different production methods and contribute to lower costs. At the next stage in the life cycle, the product or service reaches maturity: there are few, if any, design changes, and demand levels off. Eventually, the market becomes saturated, which leads to a decline in demand. In the last stage of a life cycle, some firms adopt a defensive research posture whereby they attempt to prolong the useful life of a product or service by improving its reliability, reducing costs of producing it (and, hence, the price), redesigning it, or changing the packaging. These stages are illustrated in Figure 4–3.

FIGURE 4-3

Most products or services exhibit life cycles over time

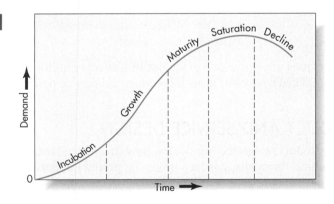

Consider the portable computer data storage products in various stages of the life cycle: DVDs and memory keys are in the introductory/growth stage, CDs are in the saturation stage, and 3.5" disks are in the decline stage.

Some products do not exhibit life cycles: wooden pencils, paper clips, nails, knives, forks and spoons, drinking glasses, and similar items. However, most new products do.

Services, too, experience life cycles. For example, in banking, using tellers is in saturation stage, using ABMs is in its maturity, and phone and Internet-banking are in their incubation stage.

Wide variations exist in the amount of time a particular product or service takes to pass through a given phase of its life cycle: some pass through various stages in a relatively short period; others take considerably longer. Often it is a matter of the basic *need* for the item and the *rate of technological change*. Some toys, novelty items, personal computers, and style items have a life cycle of less than one year, whereas other items, such as clothes washers and dryers, may last for decades before yielding to technological change.

Standardization

An important issue that often arises in product/service design is the degree of standardization. **Standardization** refers to the extent to which there is absence of variety in a part, product, or service, that is, having limited types, sizes, and colours. Standardized products are made in large quantities of identical items; paper, gasoline, and 2 percent milk are examples. Standardized service implies that every customer or item processed receives essentially the same service. An automatic car wash is a good example; each car, regardless of how clean or dirty it is, receives the same service.

Standardization carries a number of important benefits as well as certain disadvantages. Standardized components and parts are *interchangeable*, which greatly lowers the cost of production while increasing productivity and making replacement or repair relatively easy. Large-volume production and purchase of only a few types of standardized parts would reduce costs due to economies of scale. For example, General Motors has attempted to standardize key components of its automobiles across similar product lines; components such as brakes, electrical systems, and other "under-the-skin" parts would be the same. By reducing variety, GM saves time and money while increasing quality and reliability in its products.

Another benefit of standardization is reduced time and cost to train employees. Similarly, inventory, handling and purchasing, and accounting activities become much more routine. WestJet using only Boeing 737 airplanes is an example, where cost of training the pilots and maintenance workers, and inventory of spare parts are reduced.

Lack of standardization can at times lead to serious difficulties and competitive struggles, particularly when systems are incompatible. Consider a few examples: when VCRs were first introduced, there were two formats for tapes, VHS and Beta. Machines could play one or the other, but not both. This meant that producers needed to make two sets of tapes. High-definition television might have been introduced much earlier, but three competing—and incompatible—systems were proposed, which led to prolonged debate and study before one system could be agreed upon. The lack of standardization in computer software and operating systems (Apple versus IBM) has presented users with hard choices because of the difficulty in switching from one system to the other.

Standardization also has disadvantages. A major one relates to the reduction in variety. This can limit the range of customers to whom a product or service appeals. Customers may reluctantly accept a product only because nothing else suits their needs. But that creates a risk that a competitor will introduce a product with greater variety and realize a competitive advantage. Another disadvantage is that a manufacturer may freeze (standardize) a design prematurely and, once frozen, it may resist

standardization Extent to which there is absence of variety in a part, product, or service.

www.gm.com

modification. A familiar example of this is the keyboard arrangement of computers. Studies have demonstrated that another arrangement of keys would be more efficient, but the cost of retraining millions of typists may not be worth the benefit.

Designing for Mass Customization

Companies like standardization because it enables them to produce high volumes of relatively low-cost products, albeit products with little variety. Customers, on the other hand, typically prefer more variety, although they like the low cost. The question for producers is how to resolve these issues without (1) losing the benefits of standardization and (2) incurring the problems that are often linked to variety. The answer, at least for some companies, is **mass customization**, a strategy of producing standardized goods or services but incorporating some degree of customization in the final product or service. Several tactics make this possible. One is *delayed differentiation*, and another is *modular design*.

Delayed differentiation is a *postponement* tactic: the process of producing but not quite completing a product or service until customer preferences or specifications are known. In the case of goods, almost-finished units might be held in inventory until customer orders are received, at which time customized features are incorporated according to customer requests. For example, furniture makers can produce dining room sets but not apply stain, allowing customers a choice of stains. Once the choice is made, the stain can be applied in a relatively short time, thus eliminating a long wait for customers, giving the seller a competitive advantage. Another example is HP printers made in Singapore for the European market. By postponing country-specific customization, e.g., labels, packaging, and manuals, and doing this in its distribution centre in Stuttgart, HP saved 25 percent in total costs of manufacturing, shipping, and inventory costs. The result of delayed differentiation is a product or service with customized features that can be quickly produced, appealing to the customers' desire for variety and speed of delivery, and yet one that for the most part is standardized, enabling the producer to realize the benefits of standardized production. This technique is not new. Manufacturers of men's clothing, for example, produce suits with pants that have legs that are unfinished, allowing customers to tailor choices as to the exact length.

Modular design is grouping of parts into components that are easily interchanged or replaced. One familiar example of modular design is computers that have modular components that can be replaced if they become defective. By arranging modules in different configurations, different computer capabilities can be obtained. This is the major reason why Dell Computers can assemble and have delivered to its direct-sell Internet customers custom-ordered computers in a matter of days. For mass customization, modular design enables producers to quickly assemble modules to achieve a customized configuration for an individual customer, avoiding the long customer wait that would occur if individual parts had to be assembled.

One advantage of modular design of equipment compared with nonmodular design is that failures are often easier to diagnose and remedy because modules can be tested individually. The manufacture and assembly of modules generally involves simplification: fewer parts are involved, so purchasing and inventory control become more routine, fabrication and assembly operations become more standardized, and training costs often are relatively low.

The main disadvantage of modular design is the inability to disassemble some modules in order to replace a faulty part; the entire module must be scrapped—usually at a higher cost.

For two examples of modular design, see the readings, "Tesma's Engine Module" and "Garrison Guitars."

A relatively new way of mass customization uses computer technology. For example, Amazon.com uses a software program which analyzes a customer's browsing history and suggests other books that people with similar interests have bought.

---

mass customization Producing basically standardized goods or services but incorporating some degree of customization.

delayed differentiation Producing, but not quite completing, a product or service until customer preferences are known.

modular design Parts are grouped into modules that are easily replaced or interchanged.

Tesma's Engine Module

www.tesma.com

Automakers are increasingly looking to reduce the number of parts under the hood by moving to larger and more sophisticated engine modules. Tesma's front-engine cover module is one of the industry's most advanced and value-added engine modules. The module incorporates a wide range of components, including the front engine cover, water pump, oil pump, idler, tensioner, pulleys, and fasteners. The module provides vehicle manufacturers with one-stop shopping in terms of design, development, prototyping, testing, and manufacturing, as well as complete program management. The module also provides significant reductions in assembly time, which in turn results in cost savings.

Source: *Magna 2001 Annual Report*, pp. 12–13.

Reliability

Reliability is a measure of the ability of a product, a part, or an entire system to perform its intended function under normal conditions.

The term **failure** is used to describe a situation in which an item does not perform as intended. This includes not only instances in which the item does not function at all, but also instances in which the item's performance is substandard or it functions in a way not intended. For example, a smoke alarm might fail to respond to the presence of smoke (not operate at all), it might sound an alarm that is too faint to provide an adequate warning (substandard performance), or it might sound an alarm even though no smoke is present (unintended response).

New products are tested to find out their breaking points. If this is low, the reliability of the product must be improved. For example, laptop and notebook computers need to be tough enough to absorb unintentional drops, and trucks, cars, and bikes need to endure bumps in the roads for many years.

reliability The ability of a product, part, or system to perform its intended function under normal conditions.

failure Situation in which a product, part, or system does not perform as intended.

Robust Design

Some products or services will function as designed only within a narrow range of conditions, while others will perform over a much broader range of conditions. The latter have **robust design**. Consider a pair of fine leather boots—obviously not made for trekking through mud or snow. Now consider a pair of heavy rubber boots—just the thing for mud or snow. The rubber boots have a design that is more *robust* than the fine leather boots.

The more robust a product or service, the less likely it is to fail due to a change in the environment in which it is used or in which it is performed. Hence, the more designers can build robustness into the product or service, the better it should hold up, resulting in a higher level of customer satisfaction.

robust design Design that results in products or services that can function over a broad range of conditions.

Taguchi's Approach. Japanese engineer Genichi Taguchi's approach is based on the robust design. His premise is that it is often easier to design a product that is insensitive to environmental factors, either in manufacturing or in use, than to control the environmental factors.

The central feature of Taguchi's approach—and the feature used most often by North American companies—is *parameter design*. This involves determining the specification

Garrison Guitars

Garrison Guitars of Mount Pearl, Newfoundland, was founded only six years ago, but it has already become a big success. It employs 63 people and produces 12,000 guitars per year, exporting most of them. The reason for this success is the single-unit fiberglass brace module which replaces the tens of separate small wood pieces previously used inside the body of the guitar to hold the top, bottom, and side veneers together. As a result, assembly is easier and faster. There is no need for linings (Kerfing) to be attached to the wood pieces in order to facilitate gluing of the veneer together. Also, there is no need for fine-tuning the wood pieces by a skilled person. The production time has been reduced from 2 hours down to 12 minutes. In addition, the quality has improved because all parts vibrate in unison. You can watch a video of factory operations at www.garrisonguitars.com.

---

settings for the product that will result in robust design in terms of manufacturing variations, product deterioration, and conditions during use.

The Taguchi approach modifies the conventional statistical methods of experimental design. Consider this example. Suppose a company intends to use 11 chemicals in a new product. There are two suppliers for these chemicals, and the chemical concentrations vary slightly between the two suppliers. Classical design of experiments would require $2^{11} = 2,048$ test runs to determine which combination of chemicals would be optimum. Taguchi's approach would involve testing only 12 combinations.

Legal and Ethical Issues

Designers must be careful to take into account a wide array of legal and ethical considerations. Organizations have been faced with a large array of government (federal, provincial, municipal) acts and regulations, administered by government agencies and boards designed to regulate their activities. Among the more familiar ones are the Food and Drug Acts (Health Canada), the Canadian Environmental Protection Act (Environment Canada), the Motor Vehicle Safety Act (Transport Canada), and the Hazardous Products Act (Industry Canada). Bans or regulations on saccharin, CFC, phosphate, and asbestos have sent designers scurrying back to their drawing boards to find alternative designs acceptable to both government regulators and customers. Similarly, automobile pollution standards and safety features, such as seat belts, air bags, safety glass, and energy-absorbing bumpers and frames, have had a substantial impact on automotive design. Much attention also has been directed toward toy design to remove sharp edges, small pieces that can cause choking, and toxic materials. In construction, government (municipal) regulations require access to public buildings for persons with disabilities, and standards for insulation, electrical wiring, plumbing, and fire protection.

Product liability can be a strong incentive for design improvements. **Product liability** means that a manufacturer is liable for any injuries or damages caused by a faulty product because of poor workmanship or design. Product liability is more strictly enforced in the United States, where many businesses—including Ford and General Motors—have faced lawsuits related to their products. Manufacturers also are faced with the implied warranties provided in the **Sale of Goods Act**, which says that products carry an implication of *merchantability* and *fitness*; that is, a product must be usable for its intended purposes.

product liability A manufacturer is liable for any injuries or damages caused by a faulty product.

Sale of Goods Act Products carry an implication of merchantability and fitness.

www.gc.ca

Thus, it is extremely important to design products that are reasonably free of hazards. When hazards do exist, it is necessary to install safety guards or other devices for reducing accident potential, and to provide adequate warning notices of risks. Consumer groups, businesses, and various government agencies often work together to develop industrywide standards that help avoid some of the hazards.

Ethical issues often arise in the design of products and services; it is important for managers to be aware of these issues and for designers to adhere to ethical standards. Designers are often under pressure to speed up the design process and to cut costs. These pressures often require them to make trade-off decisions, many of which involve ethical considerations. One example is: should a software company release a product as scheduled when it struggles with bugs in the software, or wait until most of the bugs have been removed?

DESIGNING FOR MANUFACTURING

In this section, you will learn about design techniques that have greater applicability for design of products than services. Even so, you will see that they do have some relevance for service design. The topics include concurrent engineering, computer-aided design, designing for manufacturing and assembly, and component commonality.

Concurrent Engineering

To achieve a smoother transition from product design to production, and to decrease product development time, many companies are using *simultaneous development*, or concurrent engineering. In its narrowest sense, **concurrent engineering** means bringing design and manufacturing engineers together early in the design phase to simultaneously develop the product and the processes for creating the product. More recently, this concept has been enlarged to participative design/engineering which includes manufacturing personnel (e.g., materials specialists), marketing, and purchasing personnel in loosely integrated, cross-functional teams. In addition, the views of suppliers are frequently sought.

> **concurrent engineering** Bringing engineering design and manufacturing personnel together early in the design phase.

Traditionally, designers developed a new product without any input from manufacturing, and then turned over the design to manufacturing, which would then have to develop a process for making the new product. This "over-the-wall" approach created tremendous challenges for manufacturing, generating numerous conflicts and greatly increasing the time needed to successfully produce a new product. It also contributed to an "us versus them" mentality.

For these and similar reasons, the simultaneous development approach has great appeal. Among the key advantages of this approach are the following:

1. Manufacturing personnel are able to identify production capabilities. Very often, there is some latitude in design in terms of selecting suitable materials and processes. Knowledge of production capabilities can help in this selection. In addition, cost and quality considerations can be greatly influenced.

2. Early opportunities for design or procurement of critical machines or components, some of which might have long lead times. This can result in a major shortening of the product development process, which could be a key competitive advantage.

Computer-Aided Design (CAD)

Computers are increasingly used for product design. **Computer-aided design (CAD)** uses computer graphics for product design. The designer can modify an existing design or create a new one on a display unit by means of a light pen, a keyboard, a joystick, or a mouse. Once the design is entered into the computer, the designer can maneuver it on the screen: it can be rotated to provide the designer with different perspectives, it can be split apart to give the designer a view of the inside, and a portion of it can be enlarged for closer examination. The designer can obtain a printed version of the completed design and file it electronically, making it accessible to people in the firm who need this information (e.g., manufacturing).

> **computer-aided design (CAD)** Product design using computer graphics.

Computer-aided design (CAD) is used to design components and products to exact measurement and detail. This firehead sprinkler was designed to exact specifications.

A growing number of products are being designed in this way, including transformers, automobile parts, aircraft parts, integrated circuits, and electric motors.

A major benefit of CAD is the increased productivity of designers. No longer is it necessary to laboriously prepare manual drawings of products or parts and revise them repeatedly to correct errors or incorporate revisions. A rough estimate is that CAD increases the productivity of designers from 3 to 10 times. A second major benefit of CAD is the creation of a database for manufacturing that can supply needed information on product geometry and dimensions, tolerances, material specifications, and so on.

Some CAD systems allow the designer to perform engineering and cost analyses on proposed designs. For instance, the computer can determine the weight and volume of a part and do stress analysis as well. When there are a number of alternative designs, the computer can quickly go through the possibilities and identify the best one, given the designer's criteria.

Design for Manufacturing and Assembly

As noted earlier in the chapter, designers must take into account *production capabilities*. Designers need to clearly understand the capabilities of production (e.g., equipment, skills, types of materials, technologies). This will help in choosing designs that match capabilities. When opportunities and capabilities do not match, management must consider the potential for expanding or changing capabilities to take advantage of those opportunities.

Manufacturability is a key concern for manufactured goods: ease of fabrication and/or assembly is important for cost, productivity, and quality.

The term **design for manufacturing (DFM)** is used to indicate the designing of products that are compatible with manufacturing capabilities. A related concept is **design for assembly (DFA)**. A good design must take into account not only how a product will be fabricated, but also how it will be assembled. Design for assembly focuses on reducing the number of parts in an assembly, as well as on the assembly methods and sequence that will be employed. See Figure 4–4 for some examples.

Component Commonality

Companies often have multiple products or services to offer customers. Often, these products or services have a high degree of similarity of features and components. This is particularly true of *product families,* but it is also true of many services. Companies can realize significant benefits when a part can be used in multiple products. For example, car manufacturers employ this tactic by using chassis (platform) and internal components such as engines and transmissions on several models. In addition to the savings in design time, companies reap benefits through standard training for assembly and installation, increased opportunities for savings by buying in bulk from suppliers, and commonality of parts for repair, which reduces the inventory dealers and auto parts stores must carry. Similar benefits accrue in services. For example, in automobile repair, component commonality means less training is needed because the variety of jobs is reduced. The same applies to appliance repair, where commonality and *substitutability* of parts are typical. Multiple-use forms in financial and medical services is another example. Computer software often comprises a number of modules that are commonly used for similar applications, thereby saving the time and cost to write the code for major portions of the software. Tool manufacturers use a design that allows tool users to attach different power tools to a common power source. Similarly, Hewlett-Packard has a universal power source that can be used with a variety of computer hardware.

design for manufacturing (DFM) Designers take into account the organization's manufacturing capabilities when designing a product.

design for assembly (DFA) Designers focus on reducing the number of parts in a product and on assembly methods and sequence.

NEWSCLIP

RIM

www.rim.net

Research in Motion (RIM) of Waterloo, Ontario, is one of the most successful high-tech Canadian companies, even though it has only one product, the BlackBerry wireless handheld (e-mail) device. The continuous improvement of the technology of pagers for more than 15 years paid off in 1999 when RIM decided to convert its two-way pager to work with e-mail programs.

The market accepted BlackBerry as the best device of its kind, resulting in ever-increasing sales. One distinguishing feature of BlackBerry is that as it receives or sends e-mails, it automatically updates the e-mail program on the desktop using data communication lines. This eliminates the duplication of using the e-mail program. Similarly, the BlackBerry automatically updates the personal calendar on the desktop.

The competition in this market segment is fierce with most products converging to handle e-mail, voice, and video. Black-Berry was also modified in 2002 to work like a phone, and more recently to have a colour display.

Given the stiff competition, RIM is "protecting" itself by licensing its excellent wireless e-mail software to its competitors. This strategic move (i.e., if you can't beat them, join them) seems to be paying off. Also, RIM handles the subscription of its customers to a wireless telecommunication service.

RIM had revenues of more than half a billion dollars and employees of more than 2000 in 2004 (www.rim.net).

A BlackBerry is basically a portable e-mail device.

FIGURE 4-4

Examples of design for manufacturing and assembly

Source: J. G. Bralla, *Design for Manufacturability Handbook*, 2nd ed., New York: McGraw-Hill, 1999. Reprinted with permission from The McGraw-Hill Companies.

Feasible   Less expensive and therefore preferable

Avoid undercuts and reentrant angles in the cross-section of special cold-finished-steel stock if possible, since these are more costly to produce.

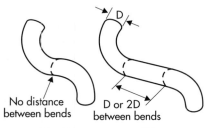

No distance between bends   D or 2D between bends

Not this   This

Allow a straight length between bends in tubes, because of metal fatigue as a result of bending.

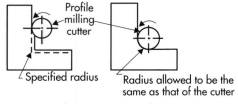

Feasible   Better

Minimize the number of fasteners by incorporating lips or other hooking elements in the basic parts. (Design for assembly.)

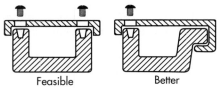

Profile milling cutter

Specified radius   Radius allowed to be the same as that of the cutter

Not this   This

Product design should permit the use of the radii provided by the cutting tools in milling machines.

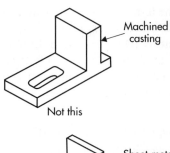

Machined casting

Not this

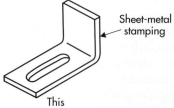

Sheet-metal stamping

This

Stampings are often less costly than machined castings.

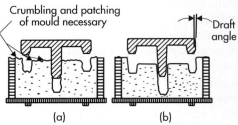

Crumbling and patching of mould necessary

Draft angle

(a)   (b)

(a) Poor stripping from the mould results when no allowance is made for draft.
(b) Ample draft permits easy and safe stripping for castings made in sand moulds.

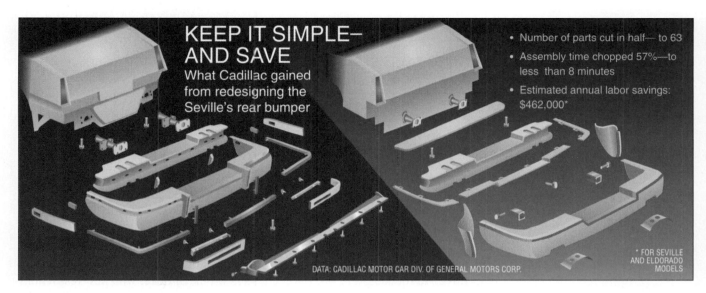

By redesigning the Seville's rear bumper for easy assembly, Cadillac cut the number of parts in half. The new design also led to high quality as there were fewer parts and steps that might be defective.

Reprinted by special permission of Business Week © *1991.* Art reprinted from October 25, 1991, issue of *Business Week* by special permission, copyright 1991 by McGraw-Hill, Inc.

DESIGNING SERVICES

As noted, some of the discussion on product design also applies to service design. This stems from the fact that goods and services often exist in combination. For example, getting an oil change for your car involves a service (draining the old oil and putting in new oil) and a good (the new oil). In some cases, what a customer receives is essentially a *pure* service, as in getting a haircut or your lawn mowed. However, the vast majority of cases involve some combination of goods and services. Because goods and services are so intertwined, managers must be knowledgeable about both in order to be able to manage effectively. However, there are some key differences between manufacturing and service that warrant special consideration for service design. This section outlines these key differences, gives an overview of service design, and provides a brief list of guidelines for service design.

Differences between Service Design and Product Design

1. Products are generally tangible; services are generally intangible. Consequently, service design often includes secondary factors such as peace of mind, ambiance, and convenience. Another consequence of this is that it is hard to sketch a service. Also, it implies that a new service must rely on faith and trust of customers; thus the importance of image.

2. In many instances services are created and delivered at the same time (e.g., a haircut, a car wash). In such instances, there is less latitude in finding and correcting errors *before* the customer has a chance to discover them. Consequently, training, process design, and customer relations are particularly important. Thus, the increased role of operations. Quality should be measured by measuring customer satisfaction.

3. Most services involve some degree of customization (variety). Because of this, there will be variability in length of service.

FIGURE 4–5

*Service variability and
customer contact relationship
in retail clothes selling*

Degree of Contact with Customer					
High	Customized clothing selling				Highly customized
Moderate		Department store selling			
Low			Telephone selling		
Minimal				Internet selling	Highly standardized
	High	Moderate	Low	Minimal	

Variability in Service

4. Services have lower barrier to entry and exit. Even in capital-intensive services such as air travel, introducing a new service, e.g., a new type of ticket with new restrictions on its use is relatively easy because it uses the current resources of the airline. The disadvantage of this is that the company cannot easily measure the cost of introducing the service because of the shared resources. Too many similar services will no doubt increase the complexity and cost of operations. This places pressure on service design to be innovative but selective. Because of its relative ease of introduction, many new services are an imitation of competitors' services.

5. Location is often important to service design, with convenience as a major factor. Hence, design of services and choice of location are often closely linked.

Let's consider some of these differences in more detail. When there is little or no contact, service can be much more standardized, whereas high contact provides the opportunity to tailor the service to the precise needs of individual customers. For examples of this relationship, see Figure 4–5, which shows different types of clothes retailing design. The customer contact also means that service design must incorporate *process*. The following example of service design illustrates the inseparable nature of the service/process connection when customers are a part of the system. If a refrigerator manufacturer changes the procedure it uses for assembling a refrigerator, that change will be hidden to the person who purchases the refrigerator. Conversely, if a bus company makes changes to the bus schedule, or the bus routes, or the types of buses used, those changes will not be hidden to the riders. Obviously, this service redesign could not be done realistically without considering the *process* for delivering the service.

Overview of Service Design

 Service design begins with the choice of a service strategy, which determines the nature and focus of the service and the target market. This requires an assessment by top management of the potential market and profitability (or need, in the case of a nonprofit organization) of a particular service, and an assessment of the organization's ability to provide the service. Once decisions on the focus of the service and the target market have been made, the customer requirements and expectations of the target market must be determined. The phases of service design are displayed in Table 4–1.

Financial services industry is one of the largest service sectors in Canada and introduces most new services. In a survey of 82 North American financial institutions (banks, insurance, trust, leasing, reinsurance, and mutual fund companies), in was discovered that financial institutions do not perform some of the above phases. In particular, most perform "preliminary market assessment" and "service activity development," but few do "market research" and "pre-commercialization business analysis." See Figure 4–6. The reason for this is that most new services offered by an organization are copies of successful services offered by a competitor or the organization itself.

Activity	Description
Idea screening	The initial go/no go decision where it is first decided to allocate funds to the proposed new service idea.
Preliminary market assessment	An initial quick look at the market.
Preliminary technical assessment	A quick assessment of the technical merits and difficulties of the project.
Detailed market study/ market research	Marketing research, involving a reasonable sample of respondents, a formal design, and consistent data collection procedure.
Business/financial analysis	A financial or business analysis leading to a go/no go decision prior to service development.
Service development	The actual design and development resulting in, e.g., a final service.
Process	Process (procedures) design and testing.
System design and testing	Computer systems are properly debugged.
Personnel training	All involved personnel are trained, e.g., training materials are prepared and people are trained in how to use and perform new service.
Test market/trial sell	A test market/trial sell is conducted to limited or test set of customers to test the plan for full launch.
Pre-commercialization business analysis	A financial or business analysis, after service development but prior to full-scale launch.
Full-scale launch	The launch of the service, on a full-scale and/or commercial basis: an identifiable set of marketing activities.
Post-launch review and analysis	Conduct a review and analysis after the new service is fully launched.

TABLE 4–1

New service design process activities

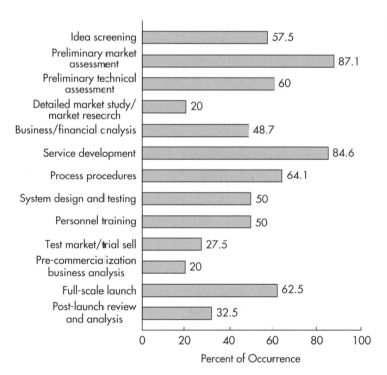

FIGURE 4–6

Frequency of new service design activities typically conducted by financial institutions

Table 4–1 and Figure 4–6 reprinted from *Industrial Marketing Management* 25, 1996, S. J. Edgett, "The New Product Development Process for Commercial Financial Services," pp. 507–515. Copyright 1996, with permission from Elsevier.

In comparing high and low performers, it was found that the difference is "better idea screening," "preliminary market assessment," "market research," "service development," and "post-launch review."

Design Guidelines

A number of simple but highly effective rules are often used to guide the design and development of service systems. The key rules are the following:

1. Have a single, unifying theme, such as convenience or speed. This will help personnel to work together rather than at cross-purposes.

2. Make sure the system has the capability to handle any expected variability in service requirements.

3. Include design features and checks to ensure that service will be reliable and will provide consistently high quality.

4. Design the system to be user-friendly. This is especially true for self-service systems.

QUALITY FUNCTION DEPLOYMENT

quality function deployment (QFD) An approach that integrates the "voice of the customer" into the product or service design.

Quality function deployment (QFD) is a structured approach for integrating the "voice of the customer" into the product or service design. Listening to and understanding the customer is the central feature of QFD. Requirements often take the form of a general statement such as, "It should be easy to adjust the cutting height of the lawn mower." Once the requirements are known, they must be translated into technical terms related to the product or service. For example, a statement about changing the height of the lawn mower may relate to the mechanism used to accomplish that, its position, instructions for use, tightness of the spring that controls the mechanism, or materials needed.

The structure of QFD is based on a set of matrices. The main matrix relates customer requirements (what) and their corresponding technical requirements (how). Technical requirements are the physical and functional characteristics of the product or service. This concept is illustrated in Figure 4–7. Additional features are usually added to the basic matrix to broaden the scope of analysis. Typical additional features include competitive evaluation of customer requirements. A correlation matrix is usually constructed for technical requirements; this can reveal conflicting technical requirements. Finally, target values for technical requirements are added. The matrix is often referred to as the *house of quality* because of its houselike appearance.

An example of QFD is shown in Figure 4–8. The data relate to a commercial printer (customer) and the company that supplies the paper rolls. To start, a key part is the list of customer requirements on the left side of the matrix. Next, note the technical requirements, listed vertically near the top. The key relationships are shown in the centre of the figure. The circle with a dot inside indicates the strongest positive relationship; that is, it denotes the most important technical requirements for satisfying the customer requirements (see the lower right-hand key for relationship weights). Now look at the

FIGURE 4–7

The house of quality

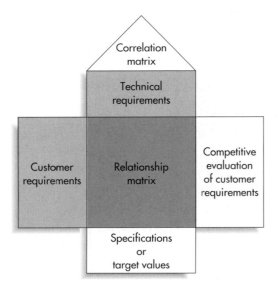

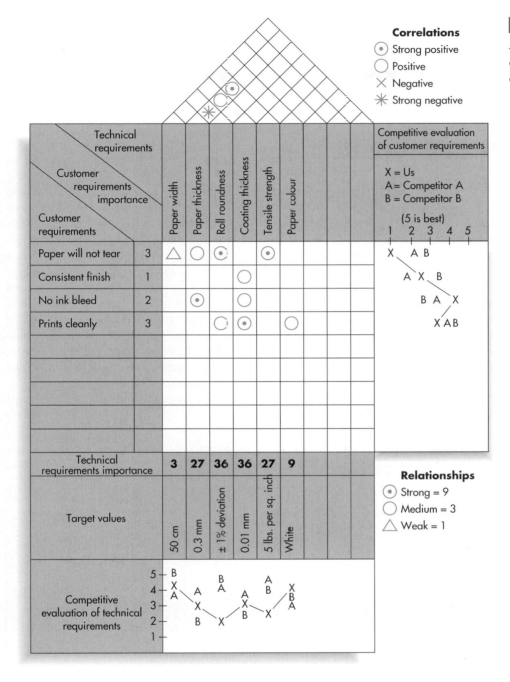

FIGURE 4–8

An example of the house of quality for paper rolls used by a commercial printer

"customer requirements importance" weights that are shown next to each customer requirement (3 is the most important).

Next, consider the correlation matrix at the top of the "house." Of special interest is the strong negative correlation between "paper thickness" and "roll roundness." Designers will have to find some way to overcome that or make a trade-off decision.

On the right side of the figure is a competitive evaluation of customer requirements comparing the company's performance on the customer requirements with each of the two key competitors (A and B). For example, the company (X) is worst on the first customer requirement and best on the third customer requirement. A line connects the X performances. Ideally, design will cause all of the Xs to be in the highest positions.

Across the bottom of Figure 4–8 are technical requirements importance weights, target values, and competitive evaluations of technical requirements. These can be interpreted in a manner similar to that of the competitive evaluations of customer requirements. The target values typically contain technical specifications that are the result of the design process. Technical requirements importance weights are the sums of values assigned to the relationships times customer requirements importance. For example, the 3 in the first column is the product of the importance to the customer, 3, and the weak ($\triangle$) relationship, 1. These help designers focus on important technical requirements. In this example, the first technical requirement has the lowest importance while the next four technical requirements all have high importance. The following newsclip contains another example of QFD.

NEWSCLIP

A QFD Snapshot

How a pencilmaker sharpened up its product by listening to "the voice of the customer" through quality function deployment.

Devised by Japan's Professor Yoji Akao, QFD has been winning adherents since it was transplanted to North America in the late 1980s. In this example of how it works, Writesharp Inc. is imaginary, but the technique in the accompanying diagram is real.

First, Writesharp's customers were surveyed to determine what they value in a pencil and how they rate the leading brands. Each wish list item was correlated with a pencil's physical and functional characteristics. "Reverse engineering"—tearing down a competitors' product to see what makes it tick—produced the competitive evaluation of technical requirements.

An analysis of the matrix quickly revealed that the improvement with the biggest potential was "point lasts," to be achieved by a better-quality lead (see competitive evaluation

of customer requirements). An interdepartmental team was assigned the task of evaluating new lead formulations that would last longer and generate less dust. Another team ran tests to determine whether substituting cedar for oak in the wood casing would improve shape quality, or hexagonality, and thus reduce the pencil's tendency to roll down slanted desktops.

The lead-formulation team organized its work with a similar matrix, segmented to show the physical and functional contributions of the ingredients in pencil lead. This revealed that the binder, or glue, used in forming the lead was the key variable. Tests found a polymer that dramatically reduced dusting by retaining more moisture and also wore down more slowly. While this binder was more expensive, better production controls promised to reduce waste enough to trim total per-pencil manufacturing costs by 1¢.

Changing the wood, meanwhile, yielded only marginal enhancements.

Source: Reprinted from October 25, 1991, issue of *Business Week* by special permission, copyright © 1991 by The McGraw-Hill Companies, Inc.

Example of the house of quality for a pencil.

Technical requirements
- ⊙ Strong correlation
- △ Possible correlation
- ○ Some correlation

Customer requirements	Pencil length (inches)	Time between sharpenings (written lines)	Lead dust (particles per line)	Hexagonality	Customer requirements importance rating (5 = highest)	Writesharp (now)	Competitor X	Competitor Y	Writesharp (target)
Easy to hold	○			○	3	4	3	3	4
Does not smear		○	⊙		4	5	4	5	5
Point lasts	△	⊙	○		5	4	5	3	5
Does not roll	△			⊙	2	3	3	3	4

Competitive evaluation of customer requirements — Scale: 1 to 5 (5 = best)

Competitive evaluation of technical requirements

	Pencil length	Time between sharpenings	Lead dust	Hexagonality
Writesharp (now)	5	56	10	70%
Competitor X	5	84	12	80%
Competitor Y	4	41	10	60%
Writesharp (target)	5.5	100	6	80%

	Writesharp (now)	Competitor X	Competitor Y	Writesharp (target)
Market price	15¢	18¢	14¢	16¢
Market share	16%	12%	32%	20%
Profit per unit	2¢	3¢	2¢	4¢

FIGURE 4-9

The Kano model

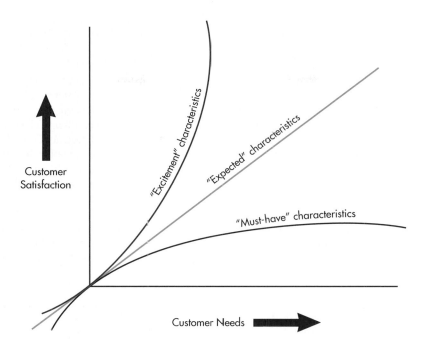

The Kano Model

The *Kano model* breaks down the customer requirements into three categories: basic or "must have" characteristics, spoken or "expected" characteristics, and "excitement" characteristics. The relationship between each category and customer satisfaction is illustrated in Figure 4–9.

The "must have" characteristics yield a basic level of satisfaction, but do not have the potential for increasing customer satisfaction beyond a certain level. For instance, air travellers expect, without expressing it, a safe, on-time trip with no lost luggage. Without these, customers will be very dissatisfied. In contrast, the "expected" characteristics are expressed and will yield a steady increase in customer satisfaction. For example, air travellers expect a minimum number of flights to different destinations, and enough arm and leg room. However, the greatest yield comes from "excitement" characteristics, perhaps evoking a "wow" from customers. These characteristics are not expressed or expected by customers. For example, air travellers will be delighted to have their own satellite TV. (This was recently introduced by Westjet.)

A possible design strategy would be to incorporate the "must have" characteristics, and then conduct a cost–benefit analysis of characteristics in the other two categories to decide which to provide.

Operations Strategy

Product and service design is a fertile area for achieving competitive advantage and/or increasing customer satisfaction. Potential sources of such benefits include:

1. Shortening the time to market using concurrent engineering, QFD, and design for manufacturing and assembly.

2. Designing environmentally friendly products.

3. Increasing emphasis on component commonality and standardization such as using multiple-use platforms. Auto manufacturers use the same platform (basic chassis, say) for several modules (e.g., Jaguar S type, Lincoln LS, and Ford Thunderbird have a shared platform).

4. Implementing tactics that will achieve the benefits of high volume while satisfying customer needs for variety (such as mass customization).

5. Continually monitoring products and services for small improvements.

SUMMARY

Product and service design is a key factor in satisfying the customer. To be successful, organizations must be continually aware of what customers want, what the competition is doing, what government regulations are, and what new technologies are available.

The design process involves market/competitor analysis, goal setting (performance, cost, quality), quality function deployment, concept development, product specification, and building and testing prototypes. The idea for a new product or a redesign can come from customers, employees, competitors, and the research and development department. The stage of life cycle of a product influences the nature of its redesign. Using standard parts and common modules saves operation costs, but it is possible to provide some mass customization by allowing customers options on modules. The reliability of well-designed products has to be extensively tested and improved. It may be cheaper to design robust products that perform consistently in varied production and use conditions. It is faster and less costly for the product team to perform both product and process designs concurrently. CAD has helped reduce the design time significantly. It is cheaper overall to design products that have fewer parts and are easier to manufacture and assemble. Services need to deal with customer presence and involvement, and the inherent variability in service requirements. QFD is a multi-functional process for design that starts with the "voice of the customer" and ends with its translation into product design.

KEY TERMS

computer-aided design (CAD), 127
concurrent engineering, 127
delayed differentiation, 124
design for assembly (DFA), 129
design for manufacturing
   (DFM), 129
failure, 125
life cycle, 122
mass customization, 124
modular design, 124

product liability, 126
quality function deployment (QFD), 134
reliability, 125
research and development (R&D), 120
reverse engineering, 119
robust design, 125
Sale of Goods Act, 126
standardization, 123

DISCUSSION AND REVIEW QUESTIONS

1. What are some of the factors that cause organizations to redesign their products or services?

2. What is involved in product/service design?

3. What is CAD? Describe some of the ways a product designer can use it.

4. Name some of the main advantages and disadvantages of standardization.

5. What is modular design? What are its main advantages and disadvantages?

6. Explain the term *design for manufacturing and assembly* and briefly explain why it is important.

7. What are some of the competitive advantages of concurrent engineering?

8. What is the *stage-gate* or *phase-review* model?

9. What is meant by the term *life cycle*? Why would this be a consideration in product or service design?

10. Name some ways the R&D department of a company contributes to produce design.

11. What is *mass customization*? What is *delayed differentiation*?

12. Name two factors that make service design different from product design.

13. Explain the term *robust design.*

14. Explain what *quality function deployment* is and how it can be useful.

15. What is reverse engineering? Do you feel this is unethical?

TAKING STOCK

1. Describe some of the trade-offs that are encountered in product or service design.

2. Who needs to be involved in the design of products or services? Explain.

3. How has technology had an impact on product and service design?

Think of a new or revised product or service that you would like to see on the market. Discuss the implications of designing and producing that product or service relative to legal, profitability, competitiveness, design, and production issues.

1. Using the following Web site, write a brief summary of important design concepts in product design of one of the following:

   a. Saturn (click on Main Menu)   *b.* Boeing 777
      http://bits.me.berkeley.edu/develop

2. Watch the Design Overview video in www.wescast.com/en/engineering_design. Summarize Wescast's engineering design process.

3. Visit www.baddesigns.com/examples.html and read about some bad designs. Describe one example from your own experience.

1. Prepare a matrix similar to Figure 4–5. Then place each of these banking transactions in the appropriate cell of the matrix:

   a. Make a cash withdrawal from an automated banking machine (ABM).

   b. Make a savings deposit using a teller.

   c. Open a savings account.

   d. Apply for a mortgage loan.

2. Prepare a matrix similar to Figure 4–5. Then place each of these transactions in the appropriate cell of the matrix:

   a. Buy stamps from a postal clerk.

   b. Mail a package that involves checking different rates.

   c. Send money using Western Union.

3. *a.* Refer to Figure 4–8. What two technical requirements have the highest impact on the customer requirement that the paper not tear?

   b. The following table presents some customer requirements and technical requirements for a copier. First, decide if any of the technical requirements relate to each customer requirement. Decide which technical requirement, if any, has the greatest impact on that customer requirement.

| | **TECHNICAL REQUIREMENTS** | | |
Customer requirements	**Feed mechanism for original papers**	**Feed mechanism for copy paper**	**Cylinder print element**
Copy paper doesn't jam			
Prints clearly			
Easy to use			

4. Prepare a table similar to that shown in Problem 3b for chocolate chip cookies made in a bakery. List what you believe are the three most important customer requirements (not including cost) and the three most relevant technical requirements (not including sanitary conditions). Next, indicate by a checkmark which customer requirements and which technical requirements are related. Finally, determine the target values.

5. Determine a QFD for a pen (such as a BIC pen), and fill it in as in Problem 4.

MINI-CASE

The Redesign of a Snowboarding Helmet

Paradox Design is a medium-size design company in Barrie, Ontario. One of its recent designs was a snowboarding helmet for Burton Snowboards of Vermont, United States. This new helmet, named Synth, was to be a remodelled version of an older model, Skycap, which was introduced four years ago and was in need of new styling.

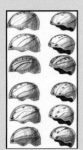

Skycap

Paradox brainstormed to identify the aesthetics and emotional influences on the culture of snowboarders. From this, concept sketches were made.

Concept sketches

A concept was chosen and the look was refined through feedback from marketing and snowboarder groups.

Detailed concept

Once the detailed design was finalized, a foam model was hand made to help visualize the shape and curves of the helmet.

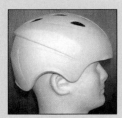

Foam model

Then, the interior of the helmet was designed to ensure comfort and ventilation.

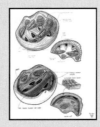

Interior design

Then the ear pad concept was sketched and refined to provide warmth, protection, and simple installation and removal from the helmet.

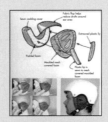

Ear pad design

From the completed design, a CAD (computer-aided design) model was created. A rapid prototype was created from the CAD model using stereo-lithography. This was shown to Burton for feedback.

Rapid prototype

The prototype was accepted by Burton, and Synth went into production. It is selling well.

Production model

Question

Compare the product design steps taken by Paradox Design with the steps given in the chapter. Is there any difference?

Source: www.paradoxdesign.net, accessed January 2005. Paradox Design merged with Spark Innovations of King City, Ontario, in 2005, www.sparkinnovations.com. Photos and figures courtesy of Steve Copeland and Roger Ball.

MINI-CASE

Open Wide and Say "Ultra"

www.harveys.ca

In fourth place behind McDonald's, A&W, and Burger King, Harvey's, the Canadian quick-service hamburger chain with more than 340 restaurants, needed a new idea in the mid-1990s. Harvey's is part of Cara Operations Ltd., the airline food-services company that also owns the Swiss Chalet chain of restaurants, approximately 100 Air Terminal Restaurants, and Summit Food Services Distributors. Harvey's had had new ideas before (open grill and fresh vegetables, for one), but these had become old hat by 1995. Gabe Tsampalieros, Cara's new president, who was a major franchisee with 60 Harvey's and Swiss Chalet restaurants, started working on the idea in October 1995, and by the following month the mission was clear: "Create Canada's best-selling hamburger." Tsampalieros and Harvey's vice-president planned the launch of the new burger for May 1996.

Harvey's began polling burger lovers across Canada in January 1996, first by telephone and later in focus groups of 8 to 12 people. While the tradition of burgers had so far led to flattened-out, Frisbee-like burgers that hung over the edges of the buns (giving customers the impression that they were getting more for their money), feedback from the market produced another idea: go thicker, juicier, chewier, and tastier. To bring this simple idea to life, Harvey's brought in chef Michael Bonacini, whose upscale Toronto restaurants had been a big hit.

Bonacini's challenge was not only to produce a tasty burger, but also to produce a burger that could handily survive the fast-food process (mechanically produced, frozen for weeks, and shipped around the country). Bonacini produced 12 "taste profiles"—from the bland to the bizarre—and introduced them to the Harvey's executives at a suburban Harvey's training centre. This would be the first in a long series of tasting exercises. (Bonacini thinks he ate 275 bite-sized burgers in a four-month period.)

Each of Harvey's executives tasted a portion of the 12 unlabelled patties and ranked it for "mouth feel," taste, linger, fill factor, and bite. Exotic offerings (Cajun, Oriental, falafel, and so forth) were rejected, leaving three simply seasoned burgers on the short list.

McCormick Canada Inc., Harvey's spice supplier, was employed to determine the final proportions of seasonings and secret ingredients to replicate the taste of Bonacini's samples in a way that could survive the fast-food process. "They [the meat packagers] would give us a 500-pound batch—that's 2,000 burgers—and we would taste them a couple of days after they had been mixed. Then we would also taste them at one-, two-, three-, and four-week intervals to see how the flavours would change," said Bonacini. McCormick's Food Technologists varied the seasonings by slight amounts with different results, and each change would follow with testing. For two months, all of Harvey's head-office workers gathered before breakfast to test the newest batches; it became clear that the May launch date was unrealistic, so they bumped back the launch to mid-September.

Though missing deadlines is rarely advisable, in this case it was fortuitous. On May 9, exactly one week before the original launch date, McDonald's introduced the Arch Deluxe with the most aggressive marketing campaign yet seen from McDonald's.

As the burger making neared completion, Harvey's turned its attention to choosing a name for the new burger. They considered several (the Ultimate, the Canadian, the Big Burger, the One and Only), but settled wisely on the Ultra, a bilingual name. They chose a foil packaging for better heat retention (and because the traditional box would appear larger than the burger itself), and reinitiated the advertising campaign, promoting a $1.88 price. Testing the burger in Calgary, Sudbury, and Quebec, Harvey's found customer reaction to be very positive ("It's more like a home-made burger," "It has a steak-like bite"), but went through five more adjustments to the amounts and mixing time of the ingredients.

On September 16, 1996, Ultra was launched and resulted in record sales, transaction counts, and restaurant visits. With over a million sold in the first two weeks, the Ultra resulted in more than 85 percent of Harvey's sales.

Since then, Harvey's has introduced other types of hamburgers such as bacon and cheese, veggie burger, Big Harv Angus, as well as a chicken sandwich.

Big Harv, introduced in 2003, was an attempt to bulk the trend of low-fat, low-calorie burgers offered by the other fast food restaurants. It had double the calories and fat of the Original burger. Big Harv targeted the male customers with craving for thick home-made barbequed burgers.

Also, Cara has expanded its full-service restaurant offerings by purchasing the Kelsey's chain and the Second Cup chain. In 2004, Cara bought back its outstanding shares and became a private company.

Questions

1. Identify the steps of the product design process used by Harvey's. (Specifically, consider market analysis, concept development, prototype development, and (external) testing and validation.

2. Did Harvey's use any other concepts discussed in the chapter?

3. Prepare a house of quality table similar to Figure 4–8 for the Ultra design. Fill it in as much as you can.

Sources: Adapted from P. Roy, "Open Wide and Say 'Ultra' (Harvey's Had a Brilliant Idea About Burgers)," *Canadian Business* 69(12), December 1996, pp. 26–30; "Stay Hungry: Gabe Tsampalieros Knows the Food Business from the Kitchen Floor Up (Will That Be Enough for Cara?)," *Canadian Business* 69(11), September 1996, pp. 104–110; Cara Operations Annual Reports, 1999–2003, www.cara.com.

Product Design and Development in Nortel Networks

Nortel is the largest high-tech company in Canada. Nortel's products range from Network access to network "transport" equipment. Its wireless business includes switches to receive cell phone calls and communication from other devices such as BlackBerry. Its enterprise products include Meridian Voice mail and data transmission systems such as VPN (Virtual Private Network) devices. Its digital switches are used by the telecommunication companies, and its optical devices are used in the fibre optics lines to help transmission of data (called broadband). It still has several research facilities such as in Silicon Valley (for VPN) and Ottawa (for wireless).

R & D in Nortel

The organization structure in Nortel Networks until the mid-1990s consisted of decentralized functions dominated by mechanical and electrical engineering functions. Product development teams were formed when needed by borrowing people from various functions as needed. However, most new products were simple revisions of old products, adding "bells and whistles." Telephone sets, especially, looked outdated. Nortel made industrial design (dealing with the form of

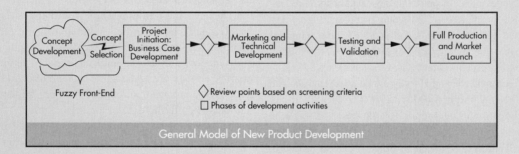

General Model of New Product Development

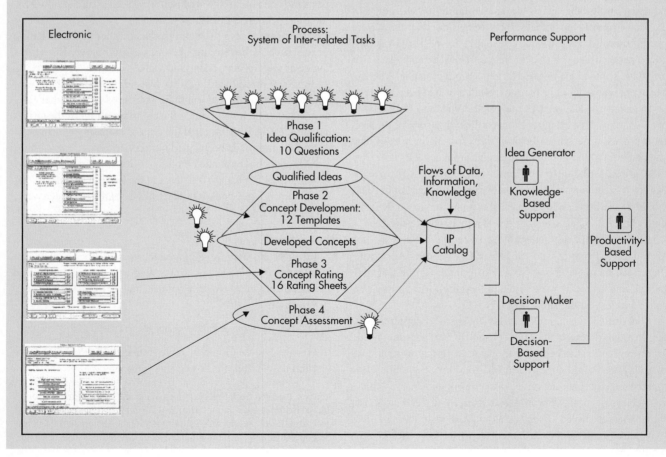

product) a priority. The objective was to make the product look good, with conspicuous value in the customers' eyes, as well as being easy to use.

Nortel did not have a systematic new product design process. In 1995, it adopted the phase-review (stage-gate) model (see the top design on the previous page). At a review point, a decision was made to either continue, revise, or terminate the concept or product.

In addition, before 1995, there was no assistance to the employees in order to develop their ideas and share them. Nortel commissioned the use of a decision support system to assist in idea generation and qualification, and concept development and selection. This electronic performance support system was called Virtual Mentor. It helps with marketing, business analysis, the human factor, and technical analysis issues (see the bottom diagram on the previous page).

In the late 1990s, Nortel changed the decentralized functional organization structure into lines of business e.g., wireless, optical, etc. Also, Nortel introduced a corporate learning officer position and a Business Venture Group to incubate the concepts.

Question

What are the advantages of Virtual Mentor?

Sources: Annual Reports, 1996–2003, www.nortel.com; A. P. Massey, et al., "Knowledge Management in Pursuit of Performance: Insights from Nortel Networks," *MIS Quarterly* 26(3) September 2002, pp. 269–289; J. Tyson, "User-centered Innovation," *Telesis* 100, October 1995, pp. 150. Figures copyright © 2002 by the Regents of the University of Minnesota. Used with permission.

SELECTED BIBLIOGRAPHY AND FURTHER READING

Baldwin, Carliss C., and Kim B. Clark. "Managing in the Age of Modularity." *Harvard Business Review*, September–October 1997, pp. 84–93.

Clausing, Don. Total Quality Development. New York: The American Society of Mechanical Engineers, 1995.

Cohen, Morris A., and Uday M. Apte. *Manufacturing Automation.* Chicago: McGraw-Hill, 1997.

Davis, Mark M., and Janelle Heineke. *Managing Services: Using Technology to Create Value.* New York: McGraw-Hill/Irwin, 2003.

Duray, Rebecca, and Glenn W. Milligan. "Improving Customer Satisfaction Through Mass Customization." *Quality Progress*, August 1999, pp. 60–66.

Easingwood, C. J., "New Product Development for Service Companies," *Journal of Product Innovation Management* 4, 1986, pp. 264–275.

Feitzinger, Edward, and Hau L. Lee. "Mass Customization at Hewlett-Packard: The Power of Postponement." *Harvard Business Review*, January–February 1997, pp. 116–121.

Fitzsimmons, James A., and Mona J. Fitzsimmons. *Service Management for Competitive Advantage.* New York: McGraw-Hill, 1994.

Gilmore, James, and B. Joseph Pine II. "The Four Faces of Mass Customization." *Harvard Business Review*, January–February 1997, pp. 91–101.

Gilmore, James, and B. Joseph Pine II. *Markets of One: Creating Customer-Unique Value Through Mass Customization.* Boston: Harvard Business School Press, 2000.

Gorman, Michael E. *Transforming Nature: Ethics, Invention, and Design.* Boston: Kluwer Academic Publishers, 1998.

Groover, Mikell P. *Automation, Production Systems, and Computer-Aided Manufacturing,* 2nd ed. Englewood Cliffs, NJ: Prentice Hall, 2001.

Heskett, James L., W. Earl Sasser Jr, and Leonard A. Schlesinger. *The Service Profit Chain.* New York: Free Press, 1997.

Lovelock, Christopher H. *Service Marketing: People, Technology, Strategy,* 2nd ed. Englewood Cliffs, NJ: Prentice Hall, 2001.

Peace, Glen Stuart. *Taguchi Methods—A Hands-On Approach.* Reading, MA: Addison-Wesley, 1993.

Prasad, Biren. *Concurrent Engineering Fundamentals: Integrated Product Development.* Englewood Cliffs, NJ: Prentice Hall PTR, 1997.

Rosenthal, Stephen R. *Effective Product Development.* Burr Ridge, IL: Irwin, 1992.

Shaw, John C. *The Service Focus.* Burr Ridge, IL: Irwin, 1990.

Smyth, J. E., D. A. Soberman, and A. J. Easson. *The Law and Business Administration in Canada,* 7th ed. Scarborough, ON: Prentice-Hall Canada, 1995.

Ternicko, John. *Step-by-Step QFD: Customer-Driven Product Design,* 2nd ed. Boca Raton, FL: CRC Press, 1997.

Ulrich, Karl T., and Steven D. Eppinger. *Product Design and Development.* New York: McGraw-Hill, 1995.

Reliability

INTRODUCTION

Reliability is a measure of the ability of a product, part, or system to perform its intended function under a prescribed set of conditions. In effect, reliability is a *probability*.

Suppose that an item has a reliability of .90. This means that it has a 90-percent probability of functioning as intended. The probability it will fail, i.e., its failure rate, is $1 - .90 = .10$, or 10 percent. Hence, it is expected that, on the average, 1 out of every 10 such items will fail or, equivalently, that the item will fail, on average, once in every 10 trials. Similarly, a reliability of .985 implies 15 failures per 1,000 parts or trials.

reliability The ability of a product, part, or system to perform its intended function under a prescribed set of conditions.

QUANTIFYING RELIABILITY

Reliability is used in two ways.

1. The probability that the product or system will function when activated (instantaneous reliability).
2. The probability that the product or system will function for a given length of time (continuous reliability).

The first of these focuses on *one point in time* and is often used when a product, part, or system must operate for one time or a relatively few number of times. The second of these focuses on the *length of service*. The distinction will become more apparent as each of these approaches is described in more detail.

The probability that a system, part, or product will operate as planned is an important concept in system and product design. Determining that probability when the product or system consists of a number of *independent* components requires the use of the rules of probability for independent events. Independent events have no relation to the occurrence or nonoccurrence of each other. What follows are three examples illustrating the use of probability rules to determine whether a given product or system will operate successfully.

Rule 1. If two or more events are independent and "success" is defined as the probability that all of the events occur, then the probability of success is equal to the product of the probabilities of the events.

Example. Suppose a room has two lamps, but to have adequate light both lamps must work (success) when turned on. One lamp has a probability of working of .90, and the other has a probability of working of .80. The probability that both will work is $.90 \times .80 = .72$. Note that the order of multiplication is unimportant: $.80 \times .90 = .72$ also. Also note that if the room had three lamps, three probabilities would have been multiplied.

This system can be represented by the following diagram:

Even though the individual components of a system might have high reliability, the system as a whole can have considerably less reliability because all components that are in series (as are the ones in the preceding example) must function. As the number of components in a series increases, the system reliability decreases. For example, a system that has eight components in series, each with a reliability of .99, has a reliability of only $.99^8 = .923$. See Figure 4S–1 for plots of product reliability as a function of number of its components for selected component reliability CR.

Obviously, many products and systems have a large number of component parts that must all operate, and some way to increase overall reliability is needed. One approach

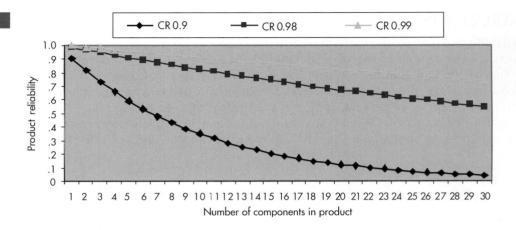

is to overdesign, i.e., enhancing the design to avoid a particular type of failure. For example, using a more durable and higher quality but more expensive material. Another is design simplification, i.e., reducing the number of parts in a product. The third approach is to use **redundancy** in the design. This involves providing backup components for some items.

redundancy The use of backup components to increase reliability.

Rule 2. If two events are independent and "success" is defined as the probability that *at least one* of the events will occur, the probability of success is equal to the probability of either one plus (1.00 − that probability) multiplied by the other probability.

Example. There are two lamps in a room. When turned on, one has a probability of working of .90 and the other has a probability of working of .80. Only a single lamp is needed to light for success. If one fails to light when turned on, the other lamp is turned on. Hence, one of the lamps is a backup in case the other one fails. Either lamp can be treated as the backup; the probability of success will be the same. The probability of success is $.90 + (1 - .90) \times .80 = .98$. If the .80 lamp is first, the calculation would be $.80 + (1 - .80) \times .90 = .98$.

This system can be represented by the following diagram.

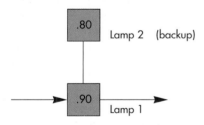

Rule 3. If three events are involved and success is defined as the probability that at least one of them occurs, the probability of success is equal to the probability of the first one (any of the events), plus the product of (1.00 − that probability) and the probability of the second event (any of the remaining events), plus the product of (1.00 − the first probability) and (1 − the second probability) and the probability of the third event. This rule can be expanded to cover more than three events.

Example. Three lamps have probabilities of .90, .80, and .70 of lighting when turned on. Only one lighted lamp is needed for success; hence, two of the lamps are considered to be backups. The probability of success is:

[#1 operates]		[#1 fails	and	#2 operates]		[#1 fails	and	#2 fails	and	#3 operates]	
.90	+	(1 − .90)	×	.80	+	(1.00 − .90)	×	(1.00 − .80)	×	.70	= .994

This system can be represented by the following diagram:

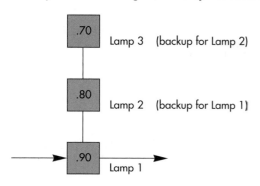

Alternatively, the system reliability = 1 − probability that none of the components work
$$= 1 - (1 - .90)(1 - .80)(1 - .70) = .994$$

Determine the reliability of the system shown below.   **Example S-1**

The system can be reduced to a series of three components: *Solution*

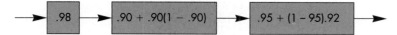

The system reliability is, then, the product of these:
.98 × .99 × .996 = .966

The second way of looking at reliability considers the incorporation of a time dimension: probabilities are determined relative to a specified length of time. This approach is commonly used in product warranties, which pertain to a given period of time after purchase of a product.

In this case, failure rate per unit is defined as the number of failures divided by total operating time.

Two hundred units of a particular component were subjected to an accelerated life test   **Example S-2**
equivalent to 2,500 hours of normal use. One failed after 1,000 hours and another after
2,000 hours. All others were working at the conclusion of the test.

The failure rate per unit = 2/[198 (2,500) + 1000 + 2000] = 0.000004 per hour

Note that this formula assumes constant failure rate over time.

A typical profile of product failure rate over time is illustrated in Figure 4S–2. Because of its shape, it is sometimes referred to as a bathtub curve. Usually, a number of products fail shortly after they are put into service, not because they wear out, but because they are defective to begin with. Examples include electronics components such as capacitators. The rate of failures decreases rapidly as the truly defective items are weeded out. During the second phase, there are fewer failures because most of the defective items have been eliminated, and it is too soon to encounter items that fail because they have worn out. In some cases, this phase covers a relatively long period of time. In the third phase, failures occur because the products are worn out, and the failure rate increases.

Failure rate is generally a function of time (the bathtub curve)

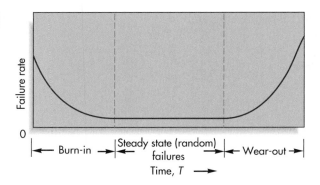

Number of light bulbs remaining over time

Source: S. M. Shafer and J. R. Meredith. *Operations Management* (New York: John Wiley & Sons Inc., 1998), p. 781. Reprinted with permission of John Wiley & Sons Inc.

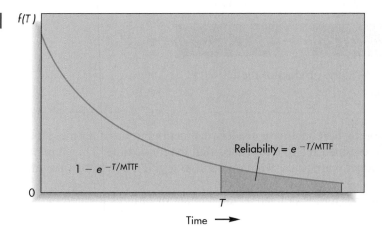

An Exponential distribution

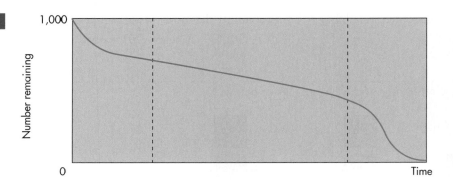

mean time to failure (MTTF)
The average length of time before failure of a product or component.

If 1,000 light bulbs are tested, the number remaining over time will be as shown in Figure 4S–3, where initially and at the end there are sharp drops in the number of bulbs working.

The inverse of failure rate per unit time is **Mean Time to Failure (MTTF)**. For data in Example S–2,

MTTF = 1/Failure rate per unit time = 1/0.000004 = 250,000 hours.

Note that this formula assumes that failure rate is constant and there is no wear-out period. In many cases, the useful life of the component restricts MTTF.

For repairable items, a similar term, Mean Time between Failure (MTBF), is usually used. MTBF is the average time from a failure to the next failure. It includes the repair time.

After the burn-in period and before the wear-out, it often turns out that the time to failure can be modelled by an Exponential distribution with an average equal to MTTF, such as that depicted in Figure 4S–4. Equipment failures as well as product failures may occur in this pattern. The probability that equipment or a product put into service at time 0 will fail *before* some specified time, T, is equal to the area under the curve between 0 and T. Reliability is specified as the probability that a product will last *at least until* time T; reliability is equal to the area under the curve *beyond T*. (Note that the total area under the curve is 100 percent.) Observe that as the specified length of service increases, the area under the curve to the right of that point (i.e., the reliability) decreases.

Determining values for the area under a curve to the right of a given point, T, becomes a relatively simple matter using a table of Exponential values. An Exponential distribution is completely described using a single parameter, the distribution mean, the mean time to failure. Using the symbol T to represent length of service, the probability that failure will not occur before time T (i.e., the area in the right tail) is easily determined:

$$P(\text{no failure before } T) = e^{-T/\text{MTTF}}$$

where

$$e = 2.7183$$

T = Length of service before failure

MTTF = Mean time to failure

The probability that failure will occur before time T is 1.00 minus that amount:

$$P(\text{failure before } T) = 1 - e^{-T/\text{MTTF}}$$

Selected values of $e^{-T/\text{MTTF}}$ are listed in Table 4S–1.

T/MTTF	$e^{-T/\text{MTTF}}$	T/MTTF	$e^{-T/\text{MTTF}}$	T/MTTF	$e^{-T/\text{MTTF}}$
.10	.9048	2.60	.0743	5.10	.0061
.20	.8187	2.70	.0672	5.20	.0055
.30	.7408	2.80	.0608	5.30	.0050
.40	.6703	2.90	.0550	5.40	.0045
.50	.6065	3.00	.0498	5.50	.0041
.60	.5488	3.10	.0450	5.60	.0037
.70	.4966	3.20	.0408	5.70	.0033
.80	.4493	3.30	.0369	5.80	.0030
.90	.4066	3.40	.0334	5.90	.0027
1.00	.3679	3.50	.0302	6.00	.0025
1.10	.3329	3.60	.0273	6.10	.0022
1.20	.3012	3.70	.0247	6.20	.0020
1.30	.2725	3.80	.0224	6.30	.0018
1.40	.2466	3.90	.0202	6.40	.0017
1.50	.2231	4.00	.0183	6.50	.0015
1.60	.2019	4.10	.0166	6.60	.0014
1.70	.1827	4.20	.0150	6.70	.0012
1.80	.1653	4.30	.0136	6.80	.0011
1.90	.1496	4.40	.0123	6.90	.0010
2.00	.1353	4.50	.0111	7.00	.0009
2.10	.1255	4.60	.0101		
2.20	.1108	4.70	.0091		
2.30	.1003	4.80	.0082		
2.40	.0907	4.90	.0074		
2.50	.0821	5.00	.0067		

TABLE 4S–1

Values of $e^{-T/\text{MTTF}}$

Example S-3

By means of extensive testing, a manufacturer has determined that its Super Sucker Vacuum Cleaner models have an expected life that is Exponential with a mean of four years and insignificant burn-in period. Find the probability that one of these cleaners will have a life that ends:

a. After the initial four years of service.

b. Before four years of service are completed.

c. Not before six years of service.

Solution

MTTF = 4 years

a. $T = 4$ years:

$$T/\text{MTTF} = \frac{4 \text{ years}}{4 \text{ years}} = 1.0$$

From Table 4S–1, $e^{-1.0} = .3679$.

b. The probability of failure before $T = 4$ years is $1 - e^{-1}$, or $1 - .3679 = .6321$.

c. $T = 6$ years:

$$T/\text{MTTF} = \frac{6 \text{ years}}{4 \text{ years}} = 1.50$$

From Table 4S–1, $e^{-1.5} = .2231$.

Mechanical items such as ball bearings, valves, and springs tend to have little burn-in and steady-state periods, and start to wear out right away.

Product failure due to wear-out can sometimes be modelled by a Normal distribution. Obtaining probabilities involves the use of a table (refer to Appendix B, Table B). The table provides areas under a Normal curve from the left end of the curve to a specified point z, where z is a *standardized* value computed using the formula:

$$z = \frac{T - \text{Mean wear-out time}}{\text{Standard deviation of wear-out time}}$$

Thus, to work with the Normal distribution, it is necessary to know the mean of the distribution and its standard deviation. A Normal distribution is illustrated in Figure 4S–5. Appendix B, Table B contains Normal probabilities (i.e., the area that lies to the left of z). To obtain a probability that service life will not exceed some value T, compute z and refer to the table. To find the reliability for time T, subtract this probability from 100 percent. To obtain the value of T that will provide a given probability, locate the nearest probability under the curve *to the left* in Table B. Then use the corresponding z in the preceding formula and solve for T.

FIGURE 4S-5

A Normal curve

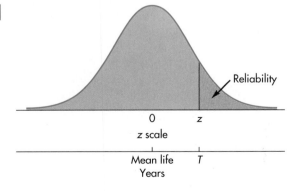

The mean life of a certain ball bearing can be modelled using a Normal distribution with a mean of six years and a standard deviation of one year. Determine each of the following:

Example S-4

a. The probability that a ball bearing will fail *before* seven years of service.

b. The probability that a ball bearing will fail *after* seven years of service (i.e., find its reliability).

c. The service life that will provide a failure probability of 10 percent.

Wear-out life mean = 6 years

Solution

Wear-out life standard deviation = 1 year

Wear-out life is Normally distributed

a. Compute z and use it to obtain the probability directly from Appendix B, Table B (see diagram).

$$z = \frac{7-6}{1} = +1.00$$

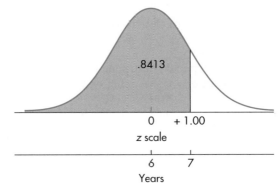

Thus, $P(T < 7) = .8413$.

b. Subtract the probability determined in part a from 100 percent (see diagram).

$$1.00 - .8413 = .1587$$

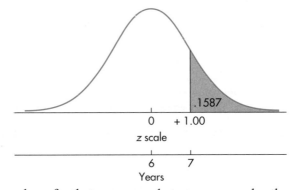

c. Use the Normal table and find the value of z that corresponds to an area under the curve (starting from the left side) of 10% (see diagram).

$$z = -1.28 = \frac{T-6}{1}$$

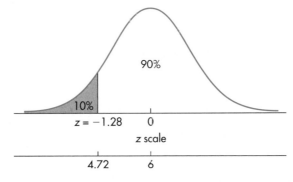

Solving for T, we find $T = 4.72$ years.

AVAILABILITY

availability The fraction of time a piece of equipment is expected to be available for operation.

A related measure of importance to customers, and hence to designers, is **availability**. It measures the fraction of time an equipment or a repairable product is expected to be operational (as opposed to being down for repairs). Availability can range from zero (never available) to 1.00 (always available). Companies that can offer equipment with high availability have a competitive advantage over companies that offer equipment with lower availability. Availability is a function of both the mean time to failure and the mean time to repair. We assume that there is little delay before a failed item begins to be repaired. The availability factor can be computed using the following formula:

$$Availability = \frac{MTTF}{MTTF + MTTR}$$

where

mean time to repair The average length of time to repair a failed item.

$MTTF$ = Mean time to failure

$MTTR$ = **Mean time to repair**

Example S–5	A copier is expected to be able to operate for 200 hours after repair, and the mean repair time is expected to be two hours. Determine the availability of the copier.

Solution

$MTTF$ = 200 hours, and $MTTR$ = 2 hours

$$Availability = \frac{MTTF}{MTTF + MTTR} = \frac{200}{200 + 2} = .99$$

Relex Software

Relex is a reliability software company based in Greensburg, Pennsylvania. Its software assists in designing products and parts in order to reduce chance of failure, reliability data collection, estimating failure rate and mean time between failures, finding the cause of failure, and many

other reliability activities. Below is a screenshot of the bill of materials of the processing unit of a computer, with component failure rate (per million hour) provided from the library of the software, based on quality and expected operating conditions such as temperature.

Source: www.relexsoftware.com/customers/cs/images/sciatl_pred_lg.gif. Image courtesy Relex Software Corporation.

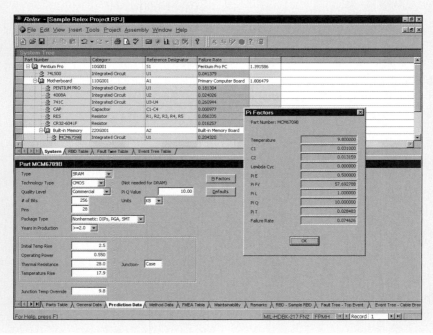

Two implications for design are revealed by the availability formula. One is that availability increases as the mean time to failure increases. The other is that availability also increases as the mean time to repair decreases. It would seem obvious that designers would want to design products that have a long time to failure. In addition, some design options enhance repairability. Laser printers, for example, are designed with print cartridges that can be easily replaced.

Solved Problems

Problem 1

A product design engineer must decide if a redundant component is cost-justified in a certain system. The system in question has a critical component with a probability of .98 of operating. System failure would involve a cost of $20,000. For a cost of $100, a switch and backup component could be added that would automatically transfer the control to the backup component in the event of a failure. Should the backup be added if the backup operating probability is also .98?

Solution

Because no probability is given for the switch, we will assume that its probability of operating when needed is 100 percent. The expected cost of failure (i.e., without the backup) is $20,000 $(1 - .98) = \$400$.

With the backup, the probability of *not* failing would be:

$.98 + .02(.98) = .9996$

Hence, the probability of failure would be $1 - .9996 = .0004$. The expected cost of failure with the backup would be the added cost of the backup plus the failure cost:

$\$100 + \$20,000(.0004) = \$108$

Because this is less than the cost without the backup, adding the backup is definitely cost justified.

Problem 2

Due to the extreme cost of interrupting production, a firm has two standby machines available in case a particular machine breaks down. The machine in use has a reliability of .94, and the backups have reliabilities of .90 and .80. In the event of a failure, either backup can be brought into service. If one fails, the other backup can be used. Compute the system reliability.

Solution

$R1 = .94,\quad R2 = .90,\quad \text{and}\quad R3 = .80$

The system can be depicted in this way:

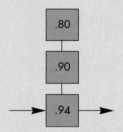

$R_{\text{system}} = R_1 + R_2(1 - R_1) + R_3(1 - R_2)(1 - R_1)$
$= .94 + .90(1 - .94) + .80(1 - .90)(1 - .94) = .9988$

Problem 3

A hospital has three *independent* fire alarm systems, with reliabilities of .95, .97, and .99. In the event of a fire, what is the probability that a warning would be given?

Solution

A warning would *not* be given if all three alarms failed. The probability that at least one alarm would operate is $1 - P(\text{none operate})$:

$P(\text{none operate}) = (1 - .95)(1 - .97)(1 - .99) = .000015$

$P(\text{warning}) = 1 - .000015 = .999985$

Alternatively, $P(\text{warning}) = .95 + .97(1 - .95) + .99(1 - .95)(1 - .97) = .999985$

Problem 4

A weather satellite has an expected life of 10 years from the time it is placed into earth's orbit. Determine its probability of failure after each of the following lengths of service. (Assume Exponential distribution is appropriate.)

a. 5 years.
b. 12 years.
c. 20 years.
d. 30 years.

Solution

MTTF = 10 years

Compute the ratio T/MTTF for $T = 5$, 12, 20, and 30, and obtain the values of $e^{-T/\mathrm{MTTF}}$ from Table 4S–1. The solutions are in the right column of the following table.

	T	MTTF	T/MTTF	$e^{-T/\mathrm{MTTF}}$
a.	5	10	.50	.6065
b.	12	10	1.20	.3012
c.	20	10	2.00	.1353
d.	30	10	3.00	.0498

Problem 5

What is the probability that the satellite described in Solved Problem 4 will fail between 5 and 12 years after being placed into earth's orbit?

Solution

$P(5 \text{ years} < \text{failure} < 12 \text{ years}) = P(\text{failure after 5 years})$
$$- P(\text{failure after 12 years})$$

Using the probabilities shown in the previous solution, you obtain:

$P(\text{failure after 5 years}) = .6065$
$- P(\text{failure after 12 years}) = \underline{.3012}$
$\phantom{- P(\text{failure after 12 years}) = } .3053$

The corresponding area under the curve is illustrated as follows:

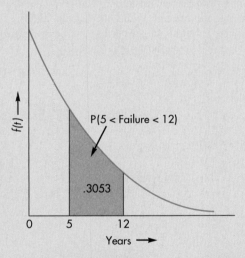

Problem 6

One line of radial tires produced by a large company has a wear-out life that can be modelled using a Normal distribution with a mean of 25,000 km and a standard deviation of 2,000 km. Determine each of the following:

a. The percentage of tires that can be expected to wear out within ±2,000 km of the average (i.e., between 23,000 km and 27,000 km).

b. The percentage of tires that can be expected to fail between 26,000 km and 29,000 km.

Solution

Notes: (1) Kilometres are analogous to time and are handled in exactly the same way; (2) *percentage* is probability times 100.

a. The phrase "within $\pm2,000$ km of the average" translates to within one standard deviation of the mean since the standard deviation equals 2,000 km. Therefore the range of z is $z = -1.00$ to $z = +1.00$, and the area under the curve between those points is found as the difference between $P(z < +1.00)$ and $P(z < -1.00)$, using values obtained from Appendix B, Table B.

$$P(z < +1.00) = .8413$$
$$\frac{-P(z < -1.00) = .1587}{P(-1.00 < z < +1.00) = .6826}$$

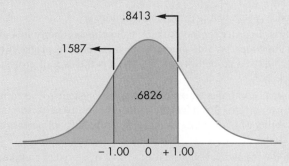

b. Wear-out mean $= 25,000$ km

Wear-out standard deviation $= 2,000$ km

$$P(26,000 < \text{Wear-out} < 29,000) = P(z < z_{29,000}) - P(z < z_{26,000})$$

$$z_{29,000} = \frac{29,000 - 25,000}{2,000} = +2.00 \to .9772$$

$$z_{26,000} = \frac{26,000 - 25,000}{2,000} = +.50 \to .6915$$

The difference is $.9772 - .6915 = .2857$, which means 28.57 percent of tires will wear out between 26,000 km and 29,000 km.

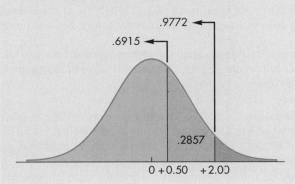

DISCUSSION AND REVIEW QUESTIONS

1. Define the term *reliability*.
2. Explain why a product or system might have an overall reliability that is low even though its components have fairly high reliabilities.
3. What is redundancy and how can it improve product reliability?

INTERNET EXERCISES

1. Visit either www.smrp.org/jobs.asp or www.sre.org/current/current.htm, pick a job announcement, and briefly summarize the duties involved.
2. Visit www.relex.com, choose a case (under "our clients"), and summarize the benefits of Relex software to the company. If there are new concepts or terms in the reading, use the Glossary under "Resources" on the Web page.

PROBLEMS

1. Consider the following system:

   Determine the probability that the system will operate under each of these conditions:
   a. The system as shown.
   b. Each system component has a backup with a reliability of .90 and a switch that is 100 percent reliable.
   c. Backups with .90 reliability and a switch that is 99 percent reliable.

2. A product is composed of four parts. In order for the product to function properly in a given situation, each of the parts must function. Two of the parts each have a .96 probability of functioning, and the other two each have a probability of .99. What is the overall probability that the product will function properly?

3. A system consists of three identical components. In order for the system to perform as intended, all of the components must perform. Each has the same probability of performance. If the system is to have a .92 probability of performing, what is the probability of performance needed by each of the individual components?

4. A product engineer has developed the following equation for the cost of a system component: $C = (10P)^2$, where C is the cost in dollars and P is the probability that the component will operate as expected. The system is composed of two identical components, both of which must operate for the system to operate. The engineer can spend $173 for the two components. To the nearest two decimal places, what is the largest component reliability that can be achieved?

5. The guidance system of a ship is controlled by a computer that has three major modules. In order for the computer to function properly, all three modules must function. Two of the modules have reliabilities of .97, and the other has a reliability of .99.
   a. What is the reliability of the computer?
   b. A backup computer identical to the one being used can be installed to improve overall reliability. Assuming that the new computer can automatically function if the main one fails, determine the resulting reliability.
   c. If the backup computer must be activated by a switch in the event that the first computer fails, and the switch has a reliability of .98, what is the overall reliability of the system? (*Both* the switch and the backup computer must function in order for the backup to take over.)

6. One of the industrial robots designed by a leading producer of servomechanisms has four major components. Components' reliabilities are .98, .95, .94, and .90. All of the components must function in order for the robot to operate effectively.
   a. Calculate the reliability of the robot.
   b. Designers want to improve the reliability by adding a backup component. Due to space limitations, only one backup can be added. The backup for any component will have the same reliability as the unit for which it is the backup. Which component should get the backup in order to achieve the highest reliability of robot?
   c. If one backup with a reliability of .92 can be added to any one of the main components, which component should get it to obtain the highest overall reliability?

7. A production line has three machines A, B, and C, with reliabilities of .99, .96, and .93, respectively. The machines are arranged so that if one breaks down, the others must shut down. Engineers are weighing two alternative designs for increasing the line's reliability. Plan 1 involves adding an identical backup line, and plan 2 involves providing a backup for each machine. In either case, three additional machines (A, B, and C) would be used with reliabilities equal to the original three.
   a. Which plan will provide the higher reliability?
   b. Explain why the two reliabilities are not the same.
   c. What other factors might enter into the decision of which plan to adopt?

8. Refer to the previous problem.
   a. Assume that the single switch used in plan 1 is 98 percent reliable, while reliabilities of the machines remain the same. Recalculate the reliability of plan 1. Compare the reliability of this plan with the reliability of the plan 1 calculated in solving the original problem. How much did reliability of plan 1 decrease as a result of a 98 percent reliable switch?

b. Assume that the three switches used in plan 2 are all 98 percent reliable, while reliabilities of the machines remain the same. Recalculate the reliability of plan 2. Compare the reliability of this plan with the reliability of the plan 2 calculated in solving the original problem. How much did reliability of plan 2 decrease?

9. A Web server has five major components which must all function in order for it to operate as intended. Assuming that each component of the system has the same reliability, what is the reliability each one must have in order for the overall system to have a reliability of .98?

10. Repeat Problem 9 under the condition that one of the components will have a backup with a reliability equal to that of any one of the other components.

11. Hoping to increase the chances of reaching a performance goal, the director of a research project has assigned three separate research teams the same task. The director estimates that the team probabilities are .9, .8, and .7 for successfully completing the task in the allotted time. Assuming that the teams work independently, what is the probability that the task will not be completed in time?

12. An electronic chess game has a useful life that is Exponential with a mean of 30 months. Determine each of the following:
   a. The probability that any given unit will operate for at least (1) 39 months, (2) 48 months, (3) 60 months.
   b. The probability that any given unit will fail sooner than (1) 33 months, (2) 15 months, (3) 6 months.
   c. The length of service time after which the percentage of failed units will approximately equal (1) 50 percent, (2) 85 percent, (3) 95 percent, (4) 99 percent.

13. A manufacturer of programmable calculators is attempting to determine a reasonable free-service period for a model it will introduce shortly. The manager of product testing has indicated that the calculators have an expected life of 30 months. Assume product life can be described by an Exponential distribution.
   a. If service contracts are offered for the expected life of the calculator, what percentage of those sold would be expected to fail during the service period?
   b. What service period would result in a failure chance of approximately 10 percent?

14. Lucky Lumen lightbulbs have a life that is Exponentially distributed with a mean of 5,000 hours. Determine the probability that one of these lightbulbs will last:
   a. At least 6,000 hours.
   b. No longer than 1,000 hours.
   c. Between 1,000 hours and 6,000 hours.

15. Planetary Communications, Inc., intends to launch a satellite that will enhance reception of television programs in Alaska. According to its designers, the satellite will have an expected life of six years. Assume that Exponential distribution applies. Determine the probability that it will function for each of the following time periods:
   a. More than 9 years.
   b. Less than 12 years.
   c. More than 9 years but less than 12 years.
   d. At least 21 years.

16. An office manager has received a report from a consultant that includes a section on equipment replacement. The report indicates that scanners have a service life that is Normally distributed with a mean of 41 months and a standard deviation of 4 months. On the basis of this information, determine the percentage of scanners that can be expected to fail in the following time periods:
   a. Before 38 months of service.
   b. Between 40 and 45 months of service.
   c. Within 2 months of the mean life.

17. A major television manufacturer has determined that its 19-inch colour TV picture tubes have a service life that can be modelled by a Normal distribution with a mean of six years and a standard deviation of a half year.
   a. What probability can you assign to service lives of (1) at least five years? (2) at least six years? (3) at most seven and a half years?
   b. If the manufacturer offers service contracts of four years on these picture tubes, what percentage can be expected to fail during the service period?

18. Refer to Problem 17. What service period would correspond to percentage failure of:
    a. 2 percent?
    b. 5 percent?

19. Determine the availability for each of these cases:
    a. MTTF = 40 days, average repair time = 3 days.
    b. MTTF = 300 hours, average repair time = 6 hours.

20. A machine can operate for an average of 50 days before it needs to be overhauled, a process which takes two days. Calculate the availability of this machine.

21. A manager must decide between two machines. Machine A has a projected average operating time of 142 hours and a projected average repair time of seven hours. Projected times for machine B are an average operating time of 65 hours and a repair time of 2 hours. What are the projected availabilities of each machine?

22. A designer estimates that she can (a) increase the average time to failure of a part by 5 percent at a cost of $450, or (b) reduce the average repair time by 10 percent at a cost of $200. Which option would be more cost-effective? Currently, the average time to failure is 100 hours and the average repair time is four hours.

23. Auto Batteries battery life is Normally distributed with a mean of 4.7 years and a standard deviation of .3 year. The batteries are warranteed to operate for a minimum of four years. If a battery fails within the warranty period, it will be replaced with a new battery at no charge.
    a. What percentage of batteries would you expect to fail before the warranty period expires?
    b. A competitor is offering a warranty of 54 months on its premium battery. The manager of Auto Batteries is toying with the idea of using the same battery with a different exterior, labelling it as a premium battery, and offering a 54-month warranty on it. How much more would the company have to charge on its "premium" battery to offset the additional cost of replacing batteries?

24. In practice, for a series system, the failure rate of a system is estimated by adding the failure rate of its components. For a system made of n identical components in series, each having a probability of failure = P_f, probability of system failure is approximately $n(P_f)$ provided that P_f is sufficiently small. Choose a value of $n > 1$ and $P_f < .05$ and show the above result.

25. The MTTF of the central processing unit (CPU) of a single board computer is 150,000 hours (Source: www.relex.com/customers/cs/versatel.asp). You can assume Exponential distribution for operating time of this component until failure. What is the probability that this component will operate without failure for
    a. 2.5 years
    b. 5 years
    c. 10 years
    (*Hint:* You may use a calculator, instead of Table 4S–1, to obtain more accurate probabilities.)

5 CHAPTER

Strategic Capacity Planning

LEARNING OBJECTIVES

After completing this chapter, you should be able to:

1 Explain the importance of long-term capacity planning.

2 Measure capacity and understand two related performance measures.

3 Describe factors influencing capacity.

4 Describe the capacity planning process in organizations.

5 Know how to determine capacity requirements.

6 Discuss the major considerations related to developing capacity alternatives.

7 Understand how the bottleneck segment of an operation affects capacity.

8 Understand how service capacity planning is different from manufacturing.

9 Briefly describe approaches for evaluating capacity alternatives.

10 Use the break-even analysis method.

hen Air Canada took over Canadian Airlines in 1999, the future looked bright: no competition, and lots of employees and planes on the way to profitability and expansion. Then came the dot.com bust and 9/11 attacks, and air travel took a dive. Even worse, a more efficient competitor, WestJet, started to expand nationally. Air Canada was left with excess planes and employees. Why is it that some companies make the right capacity decisions and some don't? This is the topic of this chapter.

In this chapter, you will learn about the importance of long-term capacity decisions, the measurement of capacity, how capacity requirements are determined, and the development and evaluation of capacity alternatives.

INTRODUCTION

capacity The upper limit on the load that an operating unit can handle.

Capacity refers to an upper limit on the load that an operating unit can handle. The operating unit might be a plant, department, machine, store, or worker.

Capacity is usually measured in terms of the output rate; e.g., the maximum number of motorcycles that can be assembled in a particular plant per day (running 2 shifts of 8 hours each) is 500, or the maximum number of customers that can be served in a particular restaurant per day is 200. If output is hard to measure, a major input can be used; e.g., maximum size of a particular restaurant is 100 seats or 25 tables of 4.

Capacity decisions have different time frames: long term, medium term, or short term. Long term usually refers to 2 to 5 years into the future. We need to make long-term capacity decisions such as determining the plant size and major machines and equipment. Medium-term usually refers to next 12 months, and medium-term capacity decisions include determining the nature and level of workforce which in turn determines the aggregate production plan. Short-term relates to the next few days and weeks, up to 12 weeks ahead, and short-term capacity decisions include determining nature and level of staffing and work shifts which in turn determines the production schedule of products or capacity of service.

In this chapter, we study mainly long-term capacity planning, while deferring medium-term capacity decisions to Chapter 12 (Aggregate Operations Planning) and short-term capacity decisions to Chapter 15 (Scheduling and Control) and Chapter 18 (Waiting Lines).

Importance of Long-Term Capacity Decisions

For a number of reasons, long-term capacity decisions are among the most fundamental of all the design decisions that managers must make.

1. Capacity decisions have a real impact on the ability of the organization to meet future demands for products and services; capacity essentially limits the rate of output possible. Having capacity to satisfy demand can allow a company to take advantage of opportunities.

2. Capacity decisions affect operating costs and ease of management. Ideally, capacity and demand requirements will be matched, which will tend to minimize operating costs. Production level too close to or exceeding capacity is costlier, requiring using overtime, expediting deliveries, lost sales, etc.

3. Capacity is usually a major determinant of initial capital cost. Typically, the greater the capacity of a productive unit, the greater its capital cost.

4. Capacity decisions involve long-term commitment of resources, and once they are implemented, it may be difficult to modify those decisions without incurring major costs.

5. Capacity can affect competitiveness. If a firm has excess capacity, or can quickly add capacity, that fact may serve as a barrier to entry by other firms. An example of this is

the Potash Corp of Saskatchewan, which, after expanding in the 1970s and 1980s, has been left with some idle potash-processing facilities. For example, the Lanigan mill's old side, after expansion, has been kept idle, and can be brought into operation if needed (at some expense). This excess capacity is a deterrant against new competition.

MEASURING CAPACITY AND TWO RELATED PERFORMANCE MEASURES

Capacity often refers to an upper limit on the *rate* of output. Even though this seems simple enough, there are subtle difficulties in actually measuring capacity in certain cases. These difficulties arise because of different interpretations of the term *capacity* and problems with identifying suitable measures for a specific situation.

In selecting a measure of capacity, it is better to choose one that does not require updating. For example, dollar amounts are often a poor measure of capacity (e.g., capacity of $30 million a year) because price changes over time necessitate updating of that measure.

Where only one product or service is involved, the capacity of the productive unit may be expressed in terms of that item. However, when multiple products or services are involved, as is often the case, using a simple measure of capacity based on units of output can be misleading. An appliance manufacturer may produce both refrigerators and freezers. If the output rates for these two products are different, it would not make sense to simply state capacity in units without reference to either refrigerators or freezers. The problem is compounded if the firm has other products. One possible solution is to state capacities in terms of each product. Thus, the firm may be able to produce 100 refrigerators per day *or* 80 freezers per day. Sometimes this approach is helpful, sometimes not. For instance, if an organization has many different products or services, it may not be practical to list all of the relevant capacities. A better way is to choose a major product, and represent each other product in equivalent units of the major product (more in Chapter 12). Alternatively, one can use the *availability of a major input.* Thus, a hospital has a certain number of beds, a job shop has a number of labour hours available, and a bus has a certain number of seats.

No single measure of capacity will be appropriate in every situation. Rather, the measure of capacity must be tailored to the situation. Table 5–1 provides some examples of commonly used measures of capacity.

There are two types of capacity:

1. **Design capacity**: the maximum output that can possibly be attained.
2. **Effective capacity**: the maximum possible output given operating hours, product mix, scheduling difficulties and expected delays, and machine maintenance.

Design capacity is the maximum rate of output achieved under ideal conditions. Effective capacity is less than design capacity owing to realities of working less than 24 hours per day, changing product mix, the need for periodic maintenance of equipment, lunch and coffee breaks, problems in scheduling and balancing operations, and similar circumstances. Actual output cannot exceed effective capacity and is often less because of

design capacity The maximum output that can possibly be attained.

effective capacity The maximum possible output given operating hours, product mix, scheduling difficulties and expected delays, and machine maintenance.

Business	Inputs	Outputs
Auto manufacturing		Number of cars per shift
Steel mill		Tonnes of steel per day
Oil refinery		Barrels of fuel per day
Farming	Number of acres	Bushels of grain per acres per year, litres of milk per day
Restaurant	Number of tables, seating capacity	Number of meals served per day
Theatre	Number of seats	Number of tickets sold per day
Retail sales	Square metres of floor space	Revenue generated per day

TABLE 5–1

Some examples of commonly used measures of capacity

READING

Utilization in Canadian Hospitals

Up until early 1990s, the Canadian healthcare system was the envy of the world. Then came a recession and the federal government deficits which were passed to provinces in the form of drastic cuts in social services transfer payments. In turn, provinces cut hospital budgets. The number of hospital beds in Canada dropped by 28 percent from 176,000 in 1989 to 126,000 in 1999. The bed reductions were followed by hospital closures and amalgamations. As a result, there is little slack in the system, especially during the peak flu season.

Most hospitals in Canada are examples of operations where utilization does exceed 100 percent during some days of the year. The Royal Columbian Hospital in Vancouver is an example. In peak season, the emergency room gets full because there are no beds in the hospital to move patients to. The average stay in the emergency room increases up to 3 days from the customary 2 hours. Utilization exceeds 100 percent of capacity because emergency stretchers are used as beds. The same story holds for most other hospitals such as the Foothills Hospital in Calgary, York Central of Toronto, and the Queen Elizabeth II Health Science Centre of Halifax.

As a result, nurses, physicians, and other healthcare providers are stressed out, and some people requiring emergency care are

dying. Examples include a heart attack victim in Weyburn, Saskatchewan, an asthmatic teenager in Toronto, and a construction worker who fell six stories in Mississauga. In all these cases, the ambulance was turned away by the hospitals because the emergency rooms were completely full.

Sources: B. Bergman, et al., "Pressure Point," *MacLean's* 113(6), February 7, 2000, pp. 48–53; W. McLellan, "Full Wards Mean ER Backups at BC Hospitals: Royal Columbian Hospital in New Westminster Operating at 104% Capacity," *Medical Post* 34(23), June 23, 1998, p. 41; B. Came, "Hospitals under the Knife," *MacLean's* 110(11), March 17, 1997, pp. 14–17.

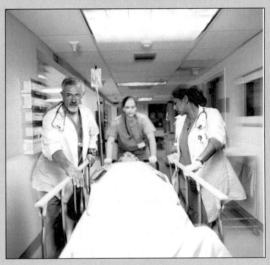

machine breakdowns, absenteeism, shortages of materials, and quality problems, as well as other factors that are outside the control of the operations managers.

These different measures of capacity are useful in defining two measures of operating unit performance: efficiency and utilization. **Efficiency** is the ratio of actual output to effective capacity. **Utilization** is the ratio of actual output to design capacity, or used time over available time.

efficiency The ratio of actual output to effective capacity.

utilization The ratio of actual output to design capacity, or used time over available time.

$$\text{Efficiency} = \frac{\text{Actual output}}{\text{Effective capacity}} \tag{5-1}$$

$$\text{Utilization} = \frac{\text{Actual output}}{\text{Design capacity}} \quad \text{or} \quad = \frac{\text{Used time}}{\text{Available time}} \tag{5-2}$$

Example 1

Given the information below, compute the efficiency and the utilization of a truck repair department:

Design capacity = 5 trucks per day (designed for 8 hours a day with 2 mechanics)

Effective capacity = 4 trucks per day (half hour coffee break and 1 hour expected delay)

Actual output = 3 trucks per day (1.5 hours of unexpected delays and break downs per day)

$$\text{Efficiency} = \frac{\text{Actual output}}{\text{Effective capacity}} = \frac{3 \text{ trucks per day}}{4 \text{ trucks per day}} = 75\%$$

$$\text{Utilization} = \frac{\text{Actual output}}{\text{Design capacity}} = \frac{3 \text{ trucks per day}}{5 \text{ trucks per day}} = 60\%$$

READING

Airline Capacity

Capacity in the airline industry is measured by available seat miles (the sum over all planes of the number of their seats multiplied by the number of miles each normally flies per year). The capacity utilization is measured by load factor, which is the average percentage of seats occupied. Air Canada, with approximately 290 planes and 724 flights per day, had approximately 54 billion available seat miles and a load factor of approximately 73 percent in 2003.

Source: *Air Canada's Annual Report, 2004*, www.aircanada.ca.

Both efficiency and utilization are normally less than 100 percent. For an example of a case where utilization is greater than 100 percent, see the reading, "Utilization in Canadian Hospitals." For capacity measure and utilization used by airlines, see the reading, "Airline Capacity."

Because effective capacity acts as a lid on actual output, the real key to improving capacity utilization is to increase effective capacity by identifying what is constraining it.

FACTORS INFLUENCING EFFECTIVE CAPACITY

Many decisions about system design have an impact on effective capacity. The same is true for many planning and operating decisions. This section briefly describes some of these factors. Note that increasing effective capacity is closely related to improving productivity.

Facilities Factors. The design of facilities, including floor space and layout directly influence effective capacity. Layout of the work area often determines how smoothly work can be performed, and environmental factors such as heating, lighting, and ventilation also play a significant role. Also, machine and equipment speed directly influence capacity.

Product/Service Factors. Product or service design can have a tremendous influence on effective capacity. For example, when items are similar, the ability of the system to produce those items is much greater than when successive items differ. Thus, a restaurant that offers a limited menu can usually prepare and serve meals at a faster rate than a restaurant with an extensive menu. The more uniform the output, the more opportunities there are for standardization of machines, methods and materials, which leads to greater effective capacity.

Human Factors. The tasks that make up a job, the variety of activities involved, and the training, skill, and experience required to perform a job all have an impact on the potential and actual output. In addition, employee motivation has a very basic relationship to effective capacity, as do absenteeism and labour turnover.

Planning and Operational Factors. Hours of operation influence effective capacity. A company using only one 8 hour shift in effect forgoes the use of its equipment 66 percent of the time. Scheduling problems may occur when an organization has differences in equipment capabilities or differences in job requirements. The effective capacity may be constrained by a bottleneck operation, inventory stocking decisions, late deliveries, acceptability of purchased materials and parts, and quality control procedures.

External Factors. Product standards, especially minimum quality and performance standards, can restrict management's options for increasing effective capacity. For example, pollution standards on products and equipment often reduce effective capacity, as does paperwork required by government regulatory agencies. A similar effect occurs when a union contract limits the number of hours and type of work an employee may do.

CAPACITY PLANNING PROCESS IN ORGANIZATIONS

Capacity decisions in organizations are usually part of the annual strategic planning process. They directly influence capital budgeting. The steps taken are as follows:

1. Forecast demand for products or services one to five years ahead.
2. Determine capacity requirements to make the products or provide the services one to five years ahead.
3. Measure capacity now, and decide if and how to bridge the gap in capacity in the future.
   a. Generate technically feasible alternatives varying in nature (plant, equipment, subcontract, lease), size, location, etc.
   b. Evaluate each alternative economically.
      i. Initial investment? Annual revenues? Annual operating expenses? Life of investment?
      ii. Method of evaluation:
         Break-even analysis, payback period, net present value.
   c. Consider noneconomic aspects too, e.g., ease of use, reliability, etc.
   d. Choose the best alternative and implement it.

For an example of a case where competitor capacity decisions influence a company's capacity decision, see the reading, "Building a New Plant vs Expansion at Shell Chemicals."

Determining Long-Term Capacity Requirements

We determine *long-term* capacity needs by forecasting demand over a long time horizon and then converting those forecasts into capacity requirements. Figure 5–1 illustrates some basic demand patterns that might be identified by a forecast. In addition to basic patterns there are more complex patterns, such as a combination of cycles and trends, and s-shaped product life cycle curves.

When trends are identified, the fundamental issues are (1) how long the trend might persist (because few things last forever) and (2) the shape and slope of the trend. If cycles are identified, interest focuses on (1) the approximate length of the cycles, and (2) the amplitude of the cycles (i.e., deviation from average). For an example of a case where technology changed a trend unexpectedly, see the reading, "Capacity in the Aluminum Industry."

The link between marketing and operations is crucial to realistic determination of capacity requirements. Through customer contacts, demographic analyses, and forecasts, marketing can supply vital information to operations for ascertaining capacity needs.

Calculating Processing Requirements

One must have reasonably accurate demand forecasts for each product, and know the standard processing time per unit for each product on the suggested process/machines, the number of workdays per year, and the number of shifts that will be used.

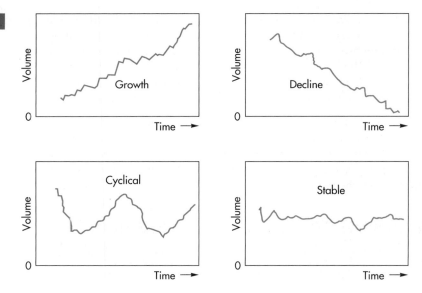

READING

Building a New Plant vs Expansion at Shell Chemicals

www.shellchemicals.com/scotford

When in 1995 Shell Chemicals was deciding on the possibility of expansion of its styrene plant in Scotford,

Alberta, near Edmonton, it decided to undertake only a modest upgrade of $25 million to increase its capacity of 825 million pounds per year by 165 million pounds per year, rather than building another plant. This is because 10 billion pounds per year capacity was already planned or under construction in China, North America's biggest export market for styrene. Therefore, any greater capacity in the Alberta factory would have been wasted.

Source: G. Morris, "Shell Canada Announces Modest Expansion," *Chemical Week*, 156(15), April 19, 1995, p. 10.

Example 2

A department works one eight-hour shift, 250 days a year, and has the following figures for product demands and expected usage of a type of machine that is currently being considered. How many machines are needed?

Product	Annual Demand	Standard Processing Time per Unit (Hr)	Processing Time Needed (Hr)
#1	400	5.0	2,000
#2	300	8.0	2,400
#3	700	2.0	1,400
			5,800

Solution

Working one eight-hour shift, 250 days a year provides an annual capacity of $8 \times 250 = 2,000$ hours per year. We can see that three of these machines would be needed to handle the required volume:

$$\frac{5,800 \text{ hours}}{2,000 \text{ hours/machine}} = 2.90 \text{ machines (round up to 3)}$$

DEVELOPING CAPACITY ALTERNATIVES

Aside from the general considerations about the development of alternatives (i.e., conduct a reasonable search for possible alternatives, consider doing nothing, take care not to overlook nonquantitative factors, analyze purchase versus lease, determine relative capacity of parts of operation dedicated to different products or services, consider capacity changes in phases overtime), there are other things that can be done to enhance capacity management:

1. Design flexibility into systems. The long-term nature of capacity decisions and the risks inherent in long-term forecasts suggest potential benefits from designing flexible systems. For example, provision for future expansion in the original design of a structure frequently can be obtained at a small price compared to what it would cost to remodel an existing structure that did not have such a provision. Hence, if future expansion of a restaurant seems likely, water lines, power hookups, and waste disposal lines can be put in place initially so that if expansion becomes a reality, modification to the existing structure can be minimized. Similarly, a new golf course may start as a nine-hole operation, but if provision is made for future expansion by obtaining options on adjacent land, it may progress to a larger (18-hole) course.

2. Differentiate between new and mature products or services. Mature products or services tend to be more predictable in terms of capacity requirements, and they may have limited life spans. The predictable demand pattern means less risk of choosing an incorrect capacity, but the possible limited life span of the product or service may necessitate finding an alternative use for the capacity at the end of the life span.

READING

Capacity in the Aluminum Industry

In the 1970s and 1980s, aluminum can sales were growing at over 10 percent per year. This occurred when aluminum cans grabbed market share from glass bottles as containers used to hold soft drinks. Companies such as Alcan saw no end to the market growth for aluminum cans. Therefore, they invested heavily in mills to make rolled sheets of aluminum from which pop cans are made. But in the early 1990s, market growth stopped because PET (PolyEthylene Terephthalate) plastic bottles grabbed market share from aluminum cans! The slowdown is partly responsible for mergers and takeovers in the aluminum industry: Alcoa has bought Reynolds metal, and Alcan has bought Pechiney.

Source: M. Brooks, President, Alcan Rolled Products, "Insights on the Global Aluminum Industry," www.alcan.com/web/publishing.nsf/Content/Insights+on+the+Global+Aluminum+Industry.

New products tend to carry higher risk because of the uncertainty often associated with predicting the quantity and duration of demand. These uncertainties are due to unknown and changing reaction of customers, evolving technologies, and uncertain competitor reaction.

3. Take a "big picture" approach to capacity changes. When developing capacity alternatives, it is important to consider how parts of the system interrelate. For example, when making a decision to increase the number of rooms in a motel, one should also take into account probable increased demands for parking, entertainment and food, and housekeeping. This is sometimes called *capacity balance*. Capacity *imbalance* results in *bottlenecks*, which restrict the capacity of the whole system. To increase the capacity of the system, the capacity of the bottleneck should be increased.

4. Prepare to deal with capacity "chunks." Capacity increases are often acquired in fairly large chunks rather than smooth increments, making it difficult to achieve a match between desired capacity and actual capacity. For instance, the desired capacity of a certain operation may be 55 units per hour; but machines used for this operation are able to produce 40 units per hour each. One machine by itself would cause capacity to be 15 units per hour short of what is needed, but two machines would result in an excess capacity of 25 units per hour. The illustration becomes even more extreme if we shift the topic to open-hearth furnaces or to the number of airplanes needed to provide a desired level of capacity.

5. Attempt to smooth out capacity requirements. Unevenness in capacity requirements also can create certain problems. For instance, during periods of inclement weather, public transportation ridership tends to increase substantially relative to periods of pleasant weather. Consequently, the system tends to alternate between underutilization and overutilization. Increasing the number of buses or trains will reduce the burden during periods of heavy demand, but this will aggravate the problem of overcapacity at other times and certainly add to the cost of operating the system. Spare capacity should be available or be arranged for peak periods.

Seasonal variations are generally easier to cope with than random variations (e.g., due to weather) because they are *predictable*. One possible solution to uneven demand is to identify products or services that have complementary demand patterns. For instance, demand for snow mobiles and demand for seados complement each other. (More solutions to this problem will be discussed in Chapter 12, Aggregate Operations Planning.)

6. Use Capacity Cushion. When demand is very variable, capacity is chosen well above the average (forecast) demand. The excess of capacity over the average demand is called **capacity cushion**. The size of capacity cushion depends on the tradeoff between cost of capacity shortage and cost of capacity excess. See Figure 5–2, where a Normal (bell-shaped) demand distribution is assumed. For vital services such as electricity, the

capacity cushion The excess of capacity over the average demand.

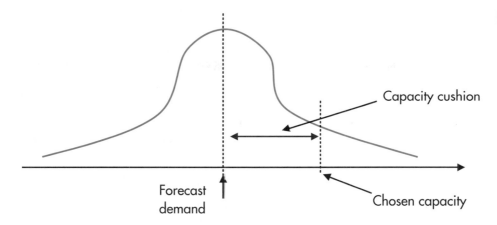

FIGURE 5-2

Capacity cushion

chosen capacity should be larger than *peak* demand, i.e., there should be a very large capacity cushion.

7. Identify the optimal operating level. Production units typically have an ideal or optimal level of operation in terms of average unit cost of output. At the ideal level, average cost per unit is the lowest for that production unit; larger or smaller rates of output will result in a higher unit cost.

The explanation for the shape of the cost curve is that at low levels of output, the investment costs of facilities and equipment must be absorbed (paid for) by very few units. Hence, the cost per unit is high. As output is increased, there are more units to absorb the "fixed" cost of facilities and equipment, so unit costs decrease. However, beyond a certain point, unit costs will start to rise. Reasons for this include worker fatigue; equipment breakdowns; the loss of flexibility, which leaves less of a margin for error; and, generally, greater difficulty in coordinating operations.

Both optimal operating rate and the amount of the minimum average unit cost tend to be a function of capacity of the operating unit. For example, as the capacity of a plant increases, the optimal output rate increases and the minimum cost for the optimal rate decreases. Thus, larger plants tend to have higher optimal output rates and lower minimum costs than smaller plants. Figure 5–3 illustrates this point, called **economies of scale**. Also see the reading, "Capacity Limitations," for an application.

In choosing the capacity of an operating unit, management must take these relationships into account along with the availability of financial and other resources and forecasts of expected demand.

economies of scale The economic conditions which favour mass production of a product by causing its price to decrease as production increases.

PLANNING SERVICE CAPACITY

Three very important factors in planning service capacity are (1) the need to be near customers, (2) the inability to store services, and (3) the degree of volatility of demand.

READING

Capacity Limitations

www.mitsubishi.ca

An example of a plant that was too small to compete was the TV tube factory of Mitsubishi, located in Midland,

Ontario, 150 km north of Toronto. With 575 employees, its capacity was 1 million picture tubes a year, whereas its competitor in the United States had an annual capacity of 3 million.

Source: "Capacity Limitations a Gloomy Picture for TV Factory," *Plant* 55(13), September 23, 1996, p. 2.

FIGURE 5-3

Average cost per unit and optimal operating rate are functions of size of a production unit (graph shows economies of scale)

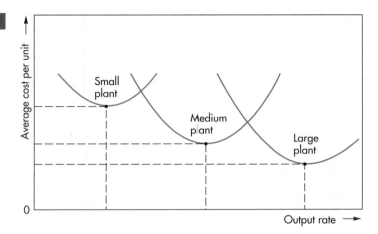

Convenience for customers is often an important aspect of service. Generally, a service must be located near customers. For example, hotel rooms must be where customers want to stay. Thus, capacity and location are closely tied.

Capacity must also be matched with the *timing* of demand. Unlike goods, services cannot be produced in one period and stored for use in a later period. Thus, an unsold seat on an airplane cannot be stored for use on a later trip. Similarly, inventories of goods allow customers to immediately satisfy wants, whereas a customer who wants a service may have to wait. This can result in a variety of negatives for an organization that provides the service. Thus, speed of delivery, or customer waiting time, becomes a major concern in service capacity planning. For example, deciding on the number of police officers and fire trucks to have on duty at any given time affects the speed of response. These issues are addressed in Chapter 18, Waiting Lines.

Demand volatility presents problems for capacity planners. Demand volatility tends to be higher for services than for goods, not only in timing of demand, but also in the time required to service individual customers. For example, banks tend to experience higher volumes of demand on certain days of the week or the month or the year, and the number and nature of transactions tend to vary for different individuals. Then, too, a wide range of social, cultural, and even weather factors can cause major peaks and valleys in demand. Essential service providers such as electric power companies need to meet peak demand. For some of the methods they use for capacity planning, see the reading, "Electricity Supply in Canada." Medium-term service capacity problems are addressed in Chapter 12, Aggregate Operations Planning, and short-term service capacity issues are addressed in Chapter 15, Scheduling and Control, and Chapter 18, Waiting Lines.

In some instances, *demand management* can be used to offset capacity limitations. Pricing, promotions, discounts, and similar tactics can help to shift some demand away from peak periods and into slow periods, allowing organizations to achieve a closer match in supply and demand.

EVALUATING ALTERNATIVES

An organization needs to examine alternatives for future capacity from a number of different perspectives. Most obvious are economic considerations: Will an alternative be economically feasible? How much will it cost? What will operating and maintenance costs be? What will be the revenue? What will its useful life be? Other considerations include: Will it be compatible with present personnel and operations? What is the personal preference of managers?

Less obvious, but nonetheless important, is possible negative public opinion. For instance, the decision to build a new power plant is almost sure to stir up reaction, whether the plant is coal-fired, hydroelectric, or nuclear. Any option that could disrupt lives and property (noise, traffic, pollution) is bound to generate hostile reactions.

Electricity Supply in Canada

Electricity generation is like a service operation because electricity cannot be stored in large quantities. The closest to inventoried electricity is having a water reservoir upstream from a dam (equipped with electricity-generating turbines).

Electricity demand is at its highest during hot summer days (when air conditioners are used) and during cold winter days (when room and car block heaters are used). Peak usage usually occurs between 4 and 8 p.m. when people return home, plug in the car, start cooking, possibly use the washing machine, and watch TV.

Most provinces have one power company (usually a Crown corporation; Alberta has three major electricity producers). The reason for this is that generating plants and transmission/distribution lines require significant investment; service to remote communities has to be subsidized, and reliable service is expected by all consumers. However, recently Alberta and Ontario moved toward privatization.

Privatization was first tried (successfully) in England in the late 1980s and later (unsuccessfully) by California in the late 1990s and early 2000s. Privatization aims to separate electricity generation from transmission/distribution, making generation subject to open competition (with an independent organization coordinating the buying and selling of electricity), but still regulating the transmission/distribution services. The proponents of privatization claim that savings of more than 5 percent can be achieved in electricity generation due to recent advances in gas turbine design, suitable for small facilities.

Ontario's experiment with privatization was a failure. The electricity price rose sharply in the summer of 2002. The government guaranteed a ceiling for the retail price of ¢4.7/kWh, paying the difference from the government budget, and has recently increased the ceiling to ¢5/kWh.

Up until the 1990s, provinces had invested heavily in power generation and transmission/distribution capacities. For example, many hydro dams are built in B.C. and Quebec, Alberta had built many coal-powered power plants and Ontario had built several nuclear power plants after the Second World War. Unfortunately, during the last decade there have been no new investments, letting the peak demands get close to total capacities. For example, Ontario had 30 gigawatts capacity and peak demand of 22 gigawatts in 1997, but in 2001 capacity was down to 27 gigawatts and peak demand was up to 25 gigawatts. And this is after four of the seven nuclear power plants, which were closed in 1997 for operating standards violations, have been brought back into operation (by British Energy under an 18-year lease contract).

The transmission network (the grid) within each province connects all power stations together and with demand points (cities, towns, and major factories).

The total capacity has almost always been sufficient to meet the demand. However, because of extreme temperatures, breakdowns (a typical generating plant has a 2-percent failure rate), and (simultaneous) maintenance shutdowns, the peak demand occasionally cannot be met. Power outage (blackouts) and voltage reduction (brownouts) do occur. For example, on May 15, 1998, there was a 3 percent voltage reduction (brownout) for about one hour in Ontario because the peak demand of 20 gigawatts could not be met (normal range for May is 13 to 17.5 gigawatts). Another example occurred on June 11, 1998, when four generating units in Alberta were offline for scheduled maintenance, and within 12 hours four more units crashed, resulting in blackout.

To reduce electricity shortages during peak periods, power companies have some temporary options. One is to encourage customers to conserve energy by, for example, charging higher prices for peak hours. This shifts some usage from peak to non-peak hours. Another option is to buy electricity from a neighbouring province or state. For example, Alberta can draw, if available, a maximum of 850 megawatts from B.C. and 150 megawatts from Saskatchewan to add to its 7.6-gigawatt capacity. As a last resort, blackouts can be rotated among various districts.

Question

Can you think of another option a power company can use to meet its peak demand?

Sources: "Energy Board Proposes Higher Electricity Prices," *Daily Commercial News and Construction Record*, 78(51), March 15, 2005, p 4; "Ontario Needs More Power—IMO Chief: Spade Yet to be Turned on Proposed New Plants," *Daily Commercial News*, 75(115), June 13, 2002, p. A5; B. Faught, "Nuclear Surprise: How Deregulation, Energy Shortages, Worries Over Global Warming and Tough Private-Sector Operators Like Duncan Hawthorne Have All Combined to Do What Many Would Have Once Thought Possible: Give Nuclear Power Back Its Glow," *National Post Business*, October 2001, pp. 96–106; M. Byfield, "The Struggle for Power: Electricity Blackouts Generate Industrial Feuds and a Worried Citizenry," *Alberta Report*, 25(45), October 26, 1998, pp. 12–15; G. Crone, "Ontario Hydro Prays for Cold, Wet Summer," *Financial Post Daily*, 11(79), June 19, 1998, p. 3; M. Jaccard, "California Shorts a Circuit: Should Canadians Trust the Wiring Diagram?" C. D. Howe Institute Commentary (159), February 2002.

Construction of new facilities may necessitate moving personnel to a new location. Embracing a new technology may mean retraining some people and terminating some jobs. Relocation can cause unfavourable reactions, particularly if a town is about to lose a major employer.

A number of techniques are useful for evaluating capacity alternatives from an economic standpoint. Some of the more common are break-even analysis, financial analysis, decision analysis, and waiting-line analysis. Break-even analysis is described in this chapter. Financial analysis is mentioned briefly (more in your Finance class); decision analysis is described in the chapter supplement and waiting-line analysis is described in Chapter 18.

Break-Even Analysis

Break-even analysis focuses on relationship between costs, revenue, and volume of output. The purpose of break-even analysis is to determine the volume at which the investment starts to make a profit. It is particularly useful as a tool for comparing capacity alternatives.

Use of the technique requires identification of all costs related to the production of a given product. These costs are then designated as fixed costs or variable costs. *Fixed costs* tend to remain constant regardless of volume of output. Examples include rental costs, property taxes, equipment costs, heating and cooling expenses, and certain administrative costs. *Variable costs* vary directly with volume of output. The major components of variable costs are generally materials and labour costs. We will assume that variable cost per unit remains the same regardless of volume of output.

Table 5–2 summarizes the symbols used in the break-even analysis formulas.

The total cost associated with a given volume of output is equal to the sum of the fixed cost and the variable cost per unit times volume:

$$TC = FC + VC \tag{5-3}$$
$$VC = Q \times v \tag{5-4}$$

Figure 5–4A shows the relationship between volume of output and fixed cost, total variable cost, and total (fixed plus variable) cost.

Revenue per unit, like variable cost per unit, is assumed to be the same regardless of quantity of output. Total revenue will have a linear relationship to output, as illustrated in Figure 5–4B. Assume that all output can be sold. The total revenue associated with a given quantity of output, Q, is:

$$TR = R \times Q \tag{5-5}$$

Figure 5–4C describes the relationship between profit—which is the difference between total revenue and total (i.e., fixed plus variable) cost—and volume of output. The volume at which total cost and total revenue are equal is referred to as the **break-even point (BEP)**. When volume is less than the break-even point, there is a loss; when volume is greater than the break-even point, there is a profit. The greater the deviation from this point, the greater the profit or loss. Total profit can be calculated using the formula:

$$P = TR - TC = R \times Q - (FC + v \times Q)$$

break-even point (BEP) The volume of output at which total cost and total revenue are equal.

TABLE 5-2

Break-even analysis symbols

FC = Fixed cost
VC = Total variable cost
 v = Variable cost per unit
TC = Total cost
TR = Total revenue
 R = Revenue per unit
 Q = Quantity or volume of output
Q_{BEP} = Break-even quantity
 P = Profit

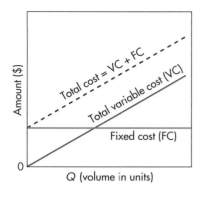

A. Fixed, variable, and total costs.

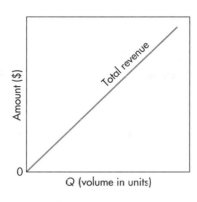

B. Total revenue increases linearly with output.

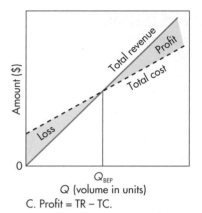

C. Profit = TR − TC.

FIGURE 5-4

Break-even relationships

Rearranging terms, we have

$$P = Q(R - v) - FC \tag{5-6}$$

The required volume, Q, needed to generate a specified profit is:

$$Q = \frac{P + FC}{R - v} \tag{5-7}$$

A special case of this is the volume of output needed for total revenue to equal total cost, i.e., when profit $P = 0$. This is the break-even point, computed using the formula:

$$Q_{BEP} = \frac{FC}{R - v} \tag{5-8}$$

The owner of Old-Fashioned Berry Pies is contemplating adding a new line of pies, which will require leasing new equipment for a monthly payment of $6,000. Variable costs would be $2.00 per pie, and pies would retail for $7.00 each.

Example 3

a. How many pies must be sold in order to break even?

b. What would the profit (loss) be if 1,000 pies are made and sold in a month?

c. How many pies must be sold to realize a profit of $4,000?

FC = $6,000 per month, v = $2 per pie, R = $7 per pie

a. $Q_{BEP} = \dfrac{FC}{R - v} = \dfrac{\$6,000}{\$7 - \$2} = 1,200$ pies/month

Solution

b. For $Q = 1,000$, $P = Q(R - v) - FC = 1,000(\$7 - \$2) - \$6,000 = -\$1,000$

c. $P = \$4,000$; solve for Q using formula 5–7:

$$Q = \frac{\$4,000 + \$6,000}{\$7 - \$2} = 2,000 \text{ pies}$$

Capacity alternatives may involve *step costs*, which are costs that increase stepwise as potential volume increases. For example, a firm may have the option of purchasing one, two, or three machines, with each additional machine increasing the fixed cost, although perhaps not linearly. (See Figure 5–5A.) Then fixed cost and potential volume would depend on the number of machines purchased. The implication is that *multiple break-even quantities* may occur, possibly one for each range. Note, however, that the total revenue line might not intersect the fixed-cost line in a particular range, meaning that there would be no

FIGURE 5-5

Break-even problem with step fixed cost

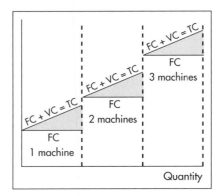

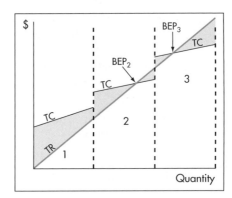

A. Step fixed costs and variable costs.   B. Multiple break-even points.

break-even point in that range. This possibility is illustrated in Figure 5–5B, where there is no break-even point in the first range. In order to decide how many machines to purchase, a manager must consider projected annual demand (volume) relative to the multiple break-even points and choose the most appropriate number of machines, as Example 4 shows.

Example 4

A manager has the option of purchasing one, two, or three machines. Fixed costs and potential volumes are as follows:

Number of Machines	Total Annual Fixed Cost	Corresponding Range of Output
1	$9,600	0 to 300
2	$15,000	301 to 600
3	$20,000	601 to 900

Variable cost is $10 per unit, and revenue is $40 per unit.

a. Determine the break-even point for each range.

b. If projected annual demand is between 580 and 660 units, how many machines should the manager purchase?

Solution

a. Compute the break-even point for each range using the formula $Q_{BEP} = FC/(R - v)$.

For one machine

$$Q_{BEP} = \frac{\$9,600}{\$40/\text{unit} - \$10/\text{unit}} = 320 \text{ units [not in the range, so there is no BEP]}$$

For two machines $Q_{BEP} = \dfrac{\$15,000}{\$40/\text{unit} - \$10/\text{unit}} = 500$ units

For three machines $Q_{BEP} = \dfrac{\$20,000}{\$40/\text{unit} - \$10/\text{unit}} = 666.67$ units

b. Comparing the projected range of demand to the two ranges for which a break-even point occurs, you can see that the correct break-even point is 500. This is because even if demand is at the low end of the range (580), it would be above the break-even point (500) and thus yield a profit. That is not true for 666.67. At the top end of projected demand (600), the volume would still be less than 666.67 units, so there would be no profit. Hence, the manager should choose two machines.

As with any quantitative tool, it is important to verify that the assumptions on which the technique is based are reasonably satisfied for a particular situation. For example, revenue per unit or variable cost per unit are not always constant. If demand is subject to random variations, one must take that into account in the analysis. Also, break-even analysis requires that fixed and variable costs can be separated, and this is sometimes exceedingly difficult to accomplish.

A notable benefit of break-even analysis is the conceptual framework it provides for integrating cost, revenue, and profit estimates into capacity decisions. If a proposal looks attractive using break-even analysis, the next step would be to develop cash flow models to see how it fares with the addition of time and more flexible cost functions.

Financial Analysis

A problem that is universally encountered by managers is how to allocate scarce funds. A common approach is to use *financial analysis* to rank investment proposals.

Two important terms in financial analysis are *cash flow* and *present value*:

Cash flow refers to the difference between the cash received from sales (of goods or services) and other sources (e.g., sale of old equipment) and the cash outflow for labour, materials, overhead, and taxes.

Present value expresses in current value the future cash flows of an investment proposal.

cash flow Difference between cash received from sales and other sources, and cash outflow for labour, material, overhead, and taxes.

present value The current value of future cash flows of an investment proposal.

The three most commonly used methods of financial analysis are payback period, net present value, and internal rate of return.

Payback period is a crude but widely used method that focuses on the length of time it will take for an investment to return its original cost. For example, an investment with an original cost of $6,000 and a monthly net cash flow of $1,000 has a payback period of six months. Payback period ignores the *time value of money*. Its use is easier to rationalize for short-term than for long-term projects.

The *net present value* (*NPV*) method summarizes the initial cost of an investment, its estimated annual cash flows, and any expected salvage value in a single value called the *net present value*, taking into account the time value of money (i.e., interest rates).

The *internal rate of return* (*IRR*) summarizes the initial, expected annual cash flows, and estimated future salvage value of an investment proposal in an *equivalent interest rate*. In other words, this method identifies the rate of return that equates the estimated future returns and the initial cost.

These techniques are appropriate when there is a high degree of *certainty* associated with estimates of future cash flows. In many instances, however, operations managers and other managers must deal with situations better described as risky or uncertain. When conditions of risk or uncertainty are present, decision analysis is often applied.

Decision Analysis

Decision analysis is a helpful tool for financial comparison of alternatives under conditions of risk or uncertainty. It is suited to capacity decisions and to a wide range of other decisions managers must make. Decision analysis is described in the supplement to this chapter.

Waiting-Line Analysis

Analysis of lines is often useful for designing service systems. Waiting lines have a tendency to form in a wide variety of service systems (e.g., airport ticket counters, hospital emergency rooms). The lines are symptoms of bottleneck operations. Analysis is useful in helping managers choose a capacity level that will be cost-effective through balancing the cost of having customers wait with the cost of providing additional capacity. This topic is described in Chapter 18.

Special service help when needed, such as transfers at the airport, can help keep lines moving at the ticket counter.

The strategic implications of capacity decisions can be enormous for an organization, impacting all areas of the organization. From an operations management standpoint, capacity decisions establish a set of conditions within which operations will be required to function. Hence, it is extremely important to include input from operations management people in making capacity decisions.

Flexibility can be a key issue in capacity decisions, although flexibility is not always an option, particularly in capital-intensive industries. However, where possible, flexibility allows an organization to be responsive (agile) to changes in the marketplace. Also, it reduces to a certain extent the dependence on long-range forecasts to accurately predict demand. And flexibility makes it easier for organizations to take advantage of technological and other innovations.

Bottleneck management can be a way to increase effective capacity, by scheduling non–bottleneck operations to achieve maximum utilization of bottleneck operation.

SUMMARY

Capacity refers to a system's potential for producing goods or delivering services over a specified time interval. Capacity decisions are important because capacity is a ceiling on output and a major determinant of costs.

The capacity decision is one of the most important decisions that managers make. The capacity decision is strategic and long-term in nature, often involving a significant initial investment of capital. Capacity planning is particularly difficult in cases where returns will accrue over a lengthy period and risk is a major consideration.

A variety of factors can interfere with capacity, so effective capacity is usually somewhat less than design capacity. These factors include facilities design and layout, human factors, product/service design, equipment maintenance, scheduling problems, and quality considerations.

Capacity planning involves long-term, medium-term, and short-term considerations. Long-term considerations relate to the overall level of capacity; medium-term considerations relate to seasonal demand; and short-term considerations relate to variations in capacity requirements due to random fluctuations in demand and within-day seasonality. Ideally, capacity will match demand. Thus, there is a close link between forecasting and capacity planning.

Development of capacity alternatives is enhanced by considering the life cycle of the product, by designing flexible systems, by taking a systems approach to planning, by recognizing that capacity increments are often acquired in chunks, by considering product/service complements as a way of dealing with various patterns of demand, by using capacity cushion, and by noting that large plants have lower average cost.

Service capacity should be where and when customers want it, and we need to meet the peak demand. In evaluating capacity alternatives a manager must consider both quantitative and qualitative aspects. Quantitative analysis usually reflects economic factors, and qualitative considerations include intangibles such as public opinion and personal preferences of managers. Break-even analysis can be useful for analyzing alternatives.

KEY TERMS

break-even point (BEP), 170
capacity, 160
capacity cushion, 166
cash flow, 173
design capacity, 161

economies of scale, 167
effective capacity, 161
efficiency, 162
present value, 173
utilization, 162

Solved Problems

Problem 1

A firm's manager must decide whether to make or buy a certain item used in the production of vending machines. Cost and volume estimates are as follows:

	Make	Buy
Annual fixed cost	$150,000	None
Variable cost/unit	$60	$80
Annual volume (units)	12,000	12,000

a. Given these numbers, should the firm buy or make this item?

b. There is a possibility that volume could change in the future. At what volume would the manager be indifferent between making and buying?

a. Determine the annual cost of each alternative:

Total cost = Fixed cost + Volume × Variable cost

Make: $150,000 + 12,000 ($60) = $870,000
Buy: 0   + 12,000 ($80) = $960,000

Because the annual cost of making the item is less than the annual cost of buying it, the manager should choose to make the item.

b. To determine the volume at which the two choices would be equivalent, set the two total costs equal to each other, and solve for volume: $TC_{make} = TC_{buy}$. Thus, $150,000 + Q($60) = 0 + Q($80)$. Solving, $Q = 7,500$ units. Therefore, at a volume of 7,500 units a year, the manager would be indifferent between making and buying. For lower volumes, the choice would be to buy, and for higher volumes, the choice would be to make.

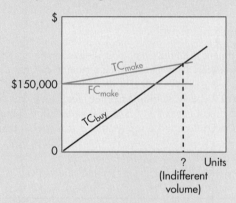

Solution

A small firm produces and sells novelty items. The firm expects to consolidate assembly of its electric turtle line at a single location. Currently, operations are in three widely scattered locations. The leading candidate for location will have a monthly fixed cost of $42,000 and variable costs of $3 per turtle. Turtles sell for $7 each. Prepare a table that shows total revenue, fixed cost, total variable cost, total cost, and profit for monthly volumes of 10,000, 12,000, and 15,000 units. What is the break-even point?

Problem 2

Revenue = $7 per unit
Variable cost = $3 per unit
Fixed cost = $42,000 per month
Profit = $Q(R - v) - FC$
Total cost = $FC + v \times Q$

Solution

Volume	Total Revenue	Total VC	Fixed Cost	Total Cost	Total Profit
10,000	$70,000	$30,000	$42,000	$72,000	$(2,000)
12,000	84,000	36,000	42,000	78,000	6,000
15,000	105,000	45,000	42,000	87,000	18,000

$$Q_{BEP} = \frac{FC}{R - v} = \frac{$42,000}{$7 - $3} = 10,500 \text{ units per month}$$

Refer to Problem 2. Develop an equation that can be used to compute profit for any volume. Use that equation to determine profit when volume equals 22,000 units.

Problem 3

Profit = $Q(R - v) - FC = Q($7 - $3) - $42,000 = $4Q - $42,000$
For $Q = 22,000$, profit is $4(22,000) - $42,000 = $46,000$

Solution

A manager must decide which type of equipment to buy, Type A or Type B. Type A equipment costs $15,000 each, and Type B costs $11,000 each. The equipment can be operated 8 hours a day, 250 days a year.
    Either machine can be used to perform two types of chemical analysis, C1 and C2. Annual service requirements and processing times are shown in the following table. Which type of

Problem 4

equipment should be purchased, and how many of that type will be needed? The goal is to minimize total purchase cost.

Analysis Type	Annual Volume	PROCESSING TIME PER ANALYSIS (HR) A	B
C1	1,200	1	2
C2	900	3	2

Solution

Total processing time (annual volume × processing time per analysis) needed by type of equipment:

Analysis Type		A	B
C1		1,200	2,400
C2		2,700	1,800
	Total	3,900	4,200

Total processing time available per piece of equipment is 8 hours/day × 250 days/year = 2,000. Hence, one piece can handle 2,000 hours of analysis, two pieces of equipment can handle 4,000 hours, etc.

Given the total processing requirements, two of Type A would be needed, for a total cost of 2 × $15,000 = $30,000, or three of Type B, for a total cost of 3 × $11,000 = $33,000. Thus, two pieces of Type A would have sufficient capacity to handle the load at a lower cost than three of Type B.

DISCUSSION AND REVIEW QUESTIONS

1. Contrast design capacity and effective capacity.
2. Propose measures of capacity for a hospital and for an airline. In what way are the measures similar and different?
3. How do long-term, medium-term, and short-term capacity decisions differ?
4. Contrast efficiency and utilization.
5. Give one example of building flexibility into system capacity.
6. Why is it important to adopt a "big picture" approach to capacity planning?
7. What is meant by "capacity in chunks," and why is that a factor in capacity planning?
8. What is economies of scale?
9. How do electrical utilities meet their peak demand?
10. What influences effective capacity?
11. Why is the optimal operating level usually less than design capacity?
12. What is capacity cushion?
13. Discuss how capacity planning for emergency services, such as ambulance service, or for utilities, such as electric power, differs from planning for other services.
14. Why is capacity planning one of the most critical decisions a manager has to make? What are the consequences of shortage or excess in capacity?
15. Why is capacity planning for services more challenging than it is for goods production?

TAKING STOCK

1. What are the major trade-offs in capacity planning?
2. Who needs to be involved in capacity planning?
3. In what ways does technology have an impact on capacity planning?

CRITICAL THINKING EXERCISE

A computer repair service has a design capacity of 80 repairs per day. Its effective capacity, however, is 64 repairs per day, and its actual output is 62 repairs per day. The manager would like to increase the number of repairs per day. Which of the following factors would you recommend that the manager investigate: quality problems, absenteeism, or scheduling and balancing? Explain your reasoning.

1. *a.* Determine the utilization and the efficiency for each of these situations:

      i A loan processing operation processes an average of 7 loans per day. The operation has a design capacity of 10 loans per day and an effective capacity of 8 loans per day.

      ii A furnace repair team services an average of four furnaces a day. The design capacity is six furnaces a day and the effective capacity is five furnaces a day.

   b. Would you say that systems that have higher efficiency ratios than other systems will always have higher utilization ratios than other systems? Explain.

2. In a job shop, effective capacity is only 50 percent of design capacity, and actual output is 80 percent of effective capacity. What design capacity would be needed to achieve an actual output of eight jobs per week?

3. A producer of pottery is considering the addition of a new factory to absorb the backlog of demand that now exists. The primary location being considered will have fixed cost of $10,000 per month and variable cost of $1 per unit produced. Each item is sold to retailers at a price that averages $2.

   a. What volume per month is required in order to break even?

   b. What profit would be realized on a monthly volume of 20,000 units?

   c. What volume is needed to obtain a profit of $16,000 per month?

   d. What volume is needed to provide a revenue of $23,000 per month?

   e. Plot the total cost and total revenue lines.

4. A small company intends to increase the capacity of a bottleneck operation by adding a new machine. Two alternatives, A and B, have been identified, and the associated costs and revenues have been estimated. Annual fixed costs would be $40,000 for A and $30,000 for B; variable costs per unit would be $10 for A and $12 for B; and revenue per unit would be $15 for A and $16 for B.

   a. Determine each alternative's break-even point.

   b. At what volume of output would the two alternatives yield the same profit?

   c. If expected annual demand is 12,000 units, which alternative would yield the higher profit?

5. A producer of felt-tip pens has received a forecast of demand of 90,000 pens for the coming month from its marketing department if the selling price is $1 per pen. Fixed cost of $25,000 per month is allocated to the felt-tip operation, and variable cost is 50 cents per pen.

   a. Find the break-even quantity.

   b. How many pens must be sold to obtain a monthly profit of $15,000?

6. A real estate agent is considering purchasing a cell phone and phone service plan. There are three service plans to choose from, all of which involve a monthly charge of $20. Plan A has a cost of $0.45 a minute for daytime calls and $0.20 a minute for evening/night/weekend calls. Plan B has a charge of $0.55 a minute for daytime calls and a charge of $0.15 a minute for evening/night/weekend calls. Plan C has a flat rate of $80 with 200 minutes of calls allowed per month and a cost of $0.40 per minute beyond that, day or evening/night/weekend.

   a. Determine the total charge under each plan for this case: 120 minutes of daytime calls and 40 minutes of evening/night/weekend calls in a month.

   b. Prepare a graph that shows total monthly daytime cost for each plan versus daytime call minutes.

   c. If the agent plans to use the service for only daytime calls, over what range of call minutes will each plan be optimal?

   d. Suppose that the agent expects both daytime and evening/night/weekend calls. At what point (i.e., percentage of call minutes for daytime calls) would she be indifferent between plans A and B?

7. A company plans to begin production of a new small appliance. The manager must decide whether to purchase the motors for the appliance from a vendor at $7 each or to produce them in-house. Either of two processes could be used for in-house production; one would have an annual fixed cost of $160,000 and a variable cost of $5 per unit, and the other would have an

annual fixed cost of $190,000 and a variable cost of $4 per unit. Determine the range of annual volume for which each of the alternatives would be best.

8. A manager is trying to decide whether to purchase a certain part or to have it produced internally. Internal production could use either of two processes. One would entail a variable cost of $16 per unit and an annual fixed cost of $200,000; the other would entail a variable cost of $14 per unit and an annual fixed cost of $240,000. Three vendors are willing to provide the part. Vendor A has a price of $20 per unit for any volume up to 30,000 units. Vendor B has a price of $22 per unit if demand is 1,000 units or less, but $18 per unit if demand is greater. Vendor C offers a price of $21 per unit for the first 1,000 units, and $19 per unit for additional units.

   a. If the manager anticipates an annual volume of 10,000 units, which alternative would be best from a cost standpoint? For 20,000 units, which alternative would be best?

   b. Determine the range for which each alternative is best. Are there any alternatives that are never best? Which?

9. A company manufactures a product using two identical machines. Each machine has a design capacity of 250 units per day and an effective capacity of 230 units per day. At present, actual output averages 200 units per machine, but the manager estimates that productivity improvements soon will increase output to 225 units per day. Annual demand is currently 50,000 units, but it is expected that within two years annual demand will triple. How many machines should the company plan to have to satisfy forecasted demand? Assume 240 workdays per year.

10. A manager must decide which type of machine to buy, A, B, or C. Machine costs are:

Machine	Cost/Year
A	$40,000
B	$30,000
C	$80,000

Product forecasts and processing times on the machines are as follows:

Product	Annual Demand	PROCESSING TIME PER UNIT (MINUTES)		
		A	B	C
1	16,000	3	4	2
2	12,000	4	4	3
3	6,000	5	6	4
4	30,000	2	2	1

   a. How many machines of each type would be needed in order to meet annual demand for all the products? Based on annual costs, which type of machine will cost least in satisfying the demand? Machines operate 8 hours a day, 250 days a year.

   b. Consider this additional information: The machines differ in terms of hourly operating costs: The A machines have an hourly operating cost of $10 each, B machines have an hourly operating cost of $11 each, and C machines have an hourly operating cost of $12 each. Which alternative should be selected, and how many machines would be necessary to minimize total cost while satisfying processing requirements?

11. A manager must decide how many machines of a certain type to purchase. Each machine can process 100 customers per day. One machine will result in a fixed cost of $2,000 per day, while two machines will result in a fixed cost of $3,800 per day. Variable costs will be $20 per customer, and revenue will be $45 per customer.

   a. Determine the break-even points for one machine and two machines.

   b. If estimated demand is 90 to 120 customers per day, how many machines should be purchased?

12. The manager of a car wash must decide whether to have one or two wash lines. One line will have a fixed cost of $6,000 a month, and two lines will have a fixed cost of $10,500 a month. Each line would be able to process 15 cars an hour. Variable costs will be $3 per car, and revenue will be $5.95 per car. The manager projects demand of between 14 and 18 cars an hour. Would you recommend one or two lines? The car wash will be open 300 hours a month.

13. The total demand for polypropylene in North America is approximately 11 billion pounds. H. Patrick Jack, VP of Fina Oil & Chemical Co., predicts (based on the previous 10 years) that total demand will grow anywhere between 5 and 8 percent annually. The total capacity is currently 12.3 billion pounds. In addition, a total of 4.5 billion pounds of new capacity is under construction by eight companies in eight locations and will be ready for production within the next four years. Would total capacity be enough to meet expected demand four years from now?[1]

14. A metal parts manufacturer plans to replace its existing facility with a new one. The management is considering two possible capacities for the new facility: 200,000 or 250,000 units per year. The 200,000-unit plant would have an annual fixed cost of $4.0 million and a per unit production cost of $20. The 250,000-unit plant would have an annual fixed cost of $6 million and a per unit cost of $15. The parts will be sold for an average price of $60 per unit.

    a. Calculate the break-even point for each capacity alternative.

    b. Suppose that the company projects its sales to be 160,000 units next year, and it expects sales to grow by 10 percent each year for the next four years. Calculate the total profit for each capacity alternative. Which alternative would you recommend? Explain. State your assumptions.

MINI-CASE

Air Canada

www.aircanada.com/en/about

Four years after its privatization in 1989, Air Canada started to make some profit. This lasted until 1999, when Air Canada took over Canadian Airlines, which was losing money and in debt (approximately $1 billion). Unfortunately, Air Canada had to agree to let Canadian Airlines operate almost independently for approximately two years. In particular, the Saber reservation system was to be kept and the employees were not to be dismissed or relocated. Initially, Air Canada started to coordinate its flights with those of Canadian Airlines, eliminating duplication (same time, same route) flights but using slightly larger planes. In addition, it started some new direct cross-country flights, such as Montreal to Vancouver, and some new international flights, such as Toronto to Melbourne. Then, the ticket counters and other facilities of the two airlines were combined. More than 100,000 person hours were spent to merge the two reservation systems.

In the autumn of 2000, Canadian Airlines joined Air Canada in Toronto's Pearson Airport, using Terminal 1 (for international) and 2 (for domestic flights). Due to the confusion and rise in demand, Air Canada had to hire an additional 3,000 customer sales and service representatives, flight attendants, and other employees. Before this, the total number of employees of Air Canada was approximately 23,000 and Canadian's was approximately 13,000 (excluding the Air Canada and Canadian regional airlines, totalling approximately 5,000).

In the meantime, Air Canada had to negotiate with the employees of Canadian Airlines and with its own employees.

The pilots, maintenance mechanics, flight attendants, ramp and cargo employees, and sales and service agents all had different unions representing them. During the hard negotiations, Air Canada guaranteed job security (in most cases until 2004) for most of these groups. It had to give salary raises to Canadian employees to bring their pay up to Air Canada's, and it had to give bonuses to its own employees in order for them to agree to this.

Pursuing an ambitious revitalization plan, Air Canada started ordering many new planes, all Airbus, to replace Canadian's aging DC9s (approximately 25 planes, with an average age of 30 years), as well as some Boeing 737s (approximately 45 planes, with an average age of 20 years), and nine 747s. In total, approximately 50 old planes were to be decommissioned, and approximately 40 new planes were to be mostly leased but some purchased. The leases were long-term; most were 5- to 10-year contracts. These would arrive within the next five years or so.

All this optimism was based on the boom in the economies of North America and most of the rest of the world. Unfortunately, the dot-com bubble burst in the fourth quarter of 2000 and as a result business travel was drastically reduced. Most airline profit came from business travellers, who bought the expensive last-minute and first-class seats.

Air Canada announced that it intended to reduce its workforce by 3,500 using voluntary early retirements. Then came the September 11 terrorist attacks in the United States. Air travel, especially international flights, was reduced by 15 to 20 percent. In October 2001, Air Canada president Robert Milton announced another 4,000 job cuts.

Despite soft demand for air travel and a $4-billion debt, Air Canada pushed ahead with its fleet modernization. To increase cash, it decided to sell and lease back approximately 30 of its owned planes; this move brought in approximately $1 billion.

---

[1]D. Richards, "Polypropylene Capacity Soars But All of It May Be Needed," *Chemical Market Reporter* 251(12), March 24, 1997, pp. 7, 9.

With some excess planes in hand and facing competition from WestJet, in 2002 Milton decided to introduce low-cost subsidiaries Tango (with long-range flights out of Toronto) and Zip (with short-range flights in western Canada). However, this only reduced Air Canada's revenues. Air Canada filed for bankruptcy protection in April 2003. The restructuring was completed in September 2004. Share price of Air Canada dropped to almost zero and unsecured creditors received less than 10 percent of their money. The cost of restructuring was more than $1 billion. Only recently has Air Canada started to make profit. The workforce has shrunk to a total of about 30,000 from approximately 40,000 in the year 2000.

Ever an optimist, Milton has ordered 59 Brazilian Embraer medium-size jets (to be delivered by 2007) to replace the aging planes and to expand North American flights, and 22 smaller Bombardier planes (delivered in 2005) to replace aging Air Canada's regional subsidiary's, Jazz, planes. Air Canada has given back to the lessees or removed from operation its nine 747s, some of its 767s, and most of its 737s (Jazz is using some). Recently Air Canada received two Airbus A340-500 very large planes which are used on the Toronto to Hong Kong direct flights.

Questions

1. For an airline, what are the advantages of having new modern planes? What are the disadvantages?

2. What are some of the difficulties in long-term forecasting for air travel?

3. What are some of the difficulties in workforce planning and change for Air Canada?

4. Were the introduction of Tango and Zip a good idea? Explain.

Sources: Air Canada Annual Reports, 2000 to 2004, and Air Canada press releases in http://micro.newswire.ca/13213-0.html.

MINI-CASE

Grocery Gateway

www.grocerygateway.com

In introducing a new product or service, (*a*) the fear of competitors catching up and (*b*) not knowing exactly what the customers want may result in making the wrong capacity decisions.

Such was the case for Grocery Gateway (GG), the grocery e-tailer in Toronto. In the height of the Internet craze of the late 1990s, GG managed to attract $30 million to start its business. Whereas a small grocery delivery business can just use a few trucks and shop at the local grocery stores, a larger outfit, having given guarantees of availability and quality to its thousands of customers, needs a warehouse. In 2000, GG managed to find investors to inject another $33 million into its business, thus enabling it to build a large (75,000 ft²) warehouse. Groceries were purchased from Longo Brothers wholesale and retail chain. GG would deliver a customer's order in a three-hour window specified by the customer at the cost of $6 per delivery.

By the end of year 2001, GG hadn't made any profit even though the number of its customers was increasing 30 percent per year and its revenue was $28 million in 2001. Was it because its market was too small or because its costs were too high? Thinking that it was the former reason, GG decided to expand its market to 10 urban centres as far away as Kitchener-Waterloo, moved into an even larger warehouse (280,000 ft²), and purchased Direct Home Deliver delivery services company (GG then had 140 delivery trucks).

The revenue in 2002 almost doubled ($51 million) but with the much higher overhead GG now needed $85 million revenue to break even. Was this because the purchased groceries were too expensive or because customers wanted to also buy other goods such as hardware and liquor? Thinking it was a little of both, GG changed its supplier from Longo Brothers to Sobeys (which had cheaper groceries but may be not as fresh), and started to offer products from Home Depot and some liquor. This move attracted another $12 million from investors.

However, the customers were not happy with the prices—some claimed that GG's prices were more than those of brick-and-mortar grocery stores, and others claimed that the quality of produce was lower than before. Business was not growing and losses were piling up. Finally in August of 2004 GG was sold to Longo Brothers for $7 million. Longo Brothers plans to close the warehouse and distribute the orders from its 14 retail stores.

Questions

1. What capacity mistakes did GG make?

2. Is the concept of grocery e-tailing a sound one? Explain.

Source: M. Snider, "Too Good to be True," *Profit* 23(5), November 2004, pp. 18–19.

MINI-CASE

Maritime Steel

Maritime Steel has to make a decision about its telephone switch and network: continue using the 14 year old PBX (Private Branch Exchange) enterprise phone exchange or buy a new VoIP (Voice over Internet Protocol) phone exchange system.

Maritime Steel and Foundries is a medium-size (400 employees) Nova Scotia steel castings maker whose products are used in bridges, railcars, overhead cranes, etc. Maritime's head office and structural engineering division are in Dartmouth and its foundry is in New Glasgow, 1.5 hours away. Maritime uses approximately 85 telephones in the three sites.

The old PBX system has two disadvantages: (*a*) Every time a new phone is required for a new employee or there is a change or problem, the phone company has to send a technician; this takes more than a week and costs around $75 on average; these add up to around $7,000 a year; (*b*) The phone calls between the remote sites are charged as long distance; this adds up to about $7,000 a year.

The VoIP system uses the Internet for the transmission of phone calls. It doesn't cost anything extra in monthly fees because there are already Internet lines to each site and to each office. There is a box which connects to the Internet (see photo), and each office will be connected to the box through a coaxial cable. The cable connects to a special phone in each office and the computer also connects to the phone. Up to eight outside phone lines can also be connected to the box to receive calls, and send calls over phone lines if needed.

Maritime is considering the NBX 100 from 3COM. They intend to purchase two boxes, one for Dartmouth, the other for New Glasgow, and 85 special phones. The total cost is $32,000, a one-time investment. They also have to lease an Internet line between the two remote facilities. This will enable people in the two facilities to call each other using just extension numbers. The lease of the line will cost $3,000 a year. One advantage of the NBX system is its ease of administration: a new phone can be hooked up to the system in five minutes. Another advantage is that phone calls can be routed to computers and laptops as e-mails. Otherwise, it will have all the features of a modern PBX system.

Question

Evaluate this investment decision. What is the payback period? [*Hint:* payback period (in years) = fixed one-time investment/(annual savings −annual costs)].

Sources: Based on D. Zimmer, "Stick it to the Telcos," *Profit* 23(1), March 2004, p. 85; http://www.3com.com/solutions/en_US/casestudy.jsp?caseid=154896

A VoIP (Voice over Internet Protocol) Exchange system from 3COM.

SELECTED BIBLIOGRAPHY AND FURTHER READING

Bakke, N. A., and R. Hellburg. "The Challenges of Capacity Planning." *International Journal of Production Economics* (1993), pp. 243–64.

Bolwijn, P. T., and T. Kumpe. "Manufacturing in the 1990's—Productivity, Flexibility, and Innovation." *Long Range Planning* 23, no. 4 (1990), pp. 44–57.

Cohen, Morris, and Uday M. Apte. *Manufacturing Automation.* Burr Ridge, IL: Richard D. Irwin, 1997.

Ettlie, John, and Henry Stoll. *Managing the Design-Manufacturing Process.* New York: McGraw-Hill, 1990.

Hill, Terry. *Manufacturing Strategy.* 2nd ed. Burr Ridge, IL: Richard D. Irwin, 1994.

Monroe, Joseph. "Strategic Use of Technology." *California Management Review,* Summer 1989, pp. 91–110.

Moore, Franklin, and Thomas E. Hendrick. *Production/Operations Management.* 9th ed. Burr Ridge, IL: Richard D. Irwin, 1985.

Upton, David. "The Management of Manufacturing Flexibility." *California Management Review* 36, no. 2, 1994, pp. 72–89.

Upton, David. "What Really Makes Factories Flexible." *Harvard Business Review,* July–August 1995, pp. 74–84.

To access "Decision Analysis," the supplement to Chapter 5, please visit the student **DVD** packaged with the text or the Online Learning Centre at **www.mcgrawhill.ca/olc/stevenson**

Process Design and Facility Layout

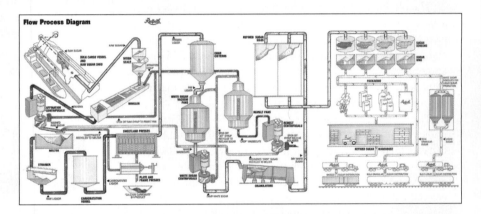

Flow Process Diagram

acing competition from other fast food restaurants such as Burger King and Wendy's and to improve its efficiency, McDonald's, in the late 1990s, after doing R&D for six years at the cost of $20 million, re-engineered its burger assembly process from make-to-stock to make-to-order. In the past, McDonald's would pre-make complete burgers and keep them on heated holding bins until they were either sold or discarded. The new "made for you" system is actually assemble-to-order, where the meat patties are pre-cooked and kept in special steamers; when a customer orders a burger, the buns are toasted and the burger is assembled. McDonald's implemented this system in most of its North American restaurants at a cost of $50,000 each. The result was a reduction of .25–.5 percent in the cost of wasted burgers. However, it was discovered that "made-for-you" was too slow for large restaurants during peak times, resulting in lost sales. Recently, McDonald's has modified the system to accommodate large restaurants. How do companies make good process decisions? This is the topic of this chapter.

INTRODUCTION

Product and service design, capacity planning, process design, and choices about location and layout are among the most basic decisions managers must make, because those decisions have long-term consequences for the organization.

Processes convert inputs into outputs; they are at the core of operations management. But the impact of process goes beyond operations management: it affects the entire organization and its ability to achieve its mission, and it affects the organization's supply chain. So process choices have strategic significance.

Process selection and facility layout (i.e., the arrangement of the workplace) are closely tied, and for that reason these two topics are presented in a single chapter. The first part of the chapter covers basic process types and design, whereas the second part is devoted to layout design.

Process design refers to how production of goods or services is to occur. It has major implications for layout of facilities, equipment, and design of work systems. Process design occurs as a matter of course when new products or services are being planned. However, process design occurs periodically due to technological changes in equipment and methods improvement.

The very first step in process planning is to consider whether to make or buy **(outsource)** some or all of a product or service. If a decision is made to buy a part or service, this eliminates the need to produce the part or service.

outsource Obtain a good or service from an external provider.

Make-or-buy decisions are often strategic, based on core capabilities or desired core capabilities. Other factors include available capacity, quality, whether demand is steady or temporary, the secrecy of technology, and cost.

Every production process is different, even in the same industry. However, there are certain similarities between operations based on quantity (volume) and variety of the products that are to be produced by the process.

The choice of operations used in a process depends on nature, shape, size, quantity, variety, and other competitive attributes of the products to be produced by the process. Examples of types of materials include metal, plastic, glass, wood, food ingredients, and yarn. Examples of shape include round, square, and with cavity. Examples of operations include forming (e.g., casting, forging), reshaping (e.g., drilling, cutting, bending, cold-drawing), and assembly (e.g., welding, bolting, gluing).

PROCESS TYPES

There are four basic process types: job shop, batch, repetitive (assembly line), and continuous. Projects are discussed in Chapter 17.

Job Shop. A **job shop** usually operates on a relatively small scale. It is used when a low volume of high-variety customized goods or services will be needed. Processing

job shop A process type used when a low volume of high-variety customized goods or services is needed.

is *intermittent*; work shifts from one small job to the next, each with somewhat different processing requirements. High flexibility of equipment and skilled workers are important characteristics of a job shop. A manufacturing example of a job shop is a tool and die shop that is able to produce one-of-a-kind tools and dies (a die is a metal "mould" used to form a part under a press, e.g., to make a coin). A service example is the emergency ward of a hospital, which is able to process a variety of injuries and diseases. For another example, see the Jubilee Ford reading at the end of this chapter.

The managerial challenge in a job shop is to schedule the jobs so that the due dates are met but the facility is utilized as much as possible.

Example 1

Hi-Bek Precision Spring Company is a small job shop located in the centre of Hamilton. Owned and operated by R. J. Hick, Hi-Bek fills a specialty niche in manufacturing, making custom springs for a variety of industrial customers.

Hi-Bek creates custom springs and wire forms for distributors and manufacturers, from the springs in Jolly Jumper baby exercisers, to Delta Faucet products, to Frost fences. Each spring requires a unique design.

Many of Hi-Bek's customers specify the design of the spring they need, sending a blueprint or a sample of the spring itself with their request for (1) a specific number of pieces desired (varying anywhere from 50 to 500,000), (2) the type of material required (the gauge of wire, any finishing required, etc.), and (3) the date by which the order is required. All of these factors are taken into consideration by Hick, who personally quotes on all orders. In some cases, a customer will require Hi-Bek to help create the actual design.

Naturally, it is easier for Hick to quote on projects Hi-Bek has done before. The various costs involved may fluctuate based on inflation and availability of raw material. (In 1994, 0.062-inch music wire—a very high grade of steel wire—cost 85¢ per pound. Today, it costs more than $1.00 per pound.) What will not change are the amounts of material required and the minimum amount of time required to run the job. In such a case as this, Hick consults the past record of production and adjusts it as required for the new order. Other factors that influence the quote include delivery dates (rush orders command higher margins) and the total number of units.

After a quote has been agreed on by the customer, the job order is then sent to the shop floor. The shop operates from 7:30 a.m. to 5:00 p.m., Monday to Friday, employing between six and nine workers depending on the demand. Hick handles prioritization of orders and scheduling of machines and personnel along with the shop foreman. Production on a given job begins with the setup of the appropriate machine. Coiling machines can be custom-configured for specific jobs, allowing for alterations to the gauge (thickness) and type of wire, the circumference and length of the spring, the number of coils in the spring, and the length of the spring ends. As well, the machine can be set to wind springs at varying speeds, depending on the level of quality required. Depending on the complexity of the product, a job being run in the machine may or may not require the full-time attention of an operator, and the time required for quality checking by the operator and foreman will vary accordingly. The setup of the job will cost the customer between $140 and $300, depending on complexity, and the skilled labour required to set up the job will cost $35 to $40 per hour. As well, customers are charged a "burden rate"— essentially a cost per hour for use of the machine during setup—of about $12 per hour. Finally, customers are charged for the operator's time to process the job, anywhere from $18 to $40 per hour.

Some jobs are quite simple, and springs are transported directly from the machine to the oven on large metal racks where the steel is heated to temper it, giving the spring its tension (its bounce, in the case of compression springs). Different springs require different temperatures (from 250°F for phosphor bronze—a low grade of wire—to 600°F for stainless steel), and a different length of time in the oven. The oven must also be scheduled for use for each individual job.

In the simplest jobs, after cooling the springs can then be packaged and arranged for shipping. In most cases, however, there are additional steps both before and after firing in the furnace.

Before firing, some springs require precision adjustments for their custom usage. The coiled springs are transported from the coiling machines to the precision-adjustment area of the shop in metal pails or large plastic drums, depending on the size of the job. An extension spring (the kind you stretch) or a torsion spring (the kind you twist) may require particularly crafted ends to suit its use. Each of these adjustments is made by hand, using a grinder or a press set for the specific job. Like the coiling machine, each press requires a certain amount of setup time and time for a shop worker to actually make the adjustments, all of which is factored into the price of the order. In the case of a press, a customer will be billed the same $140 to $300 per hour for setup though the customer is typically charged less for the labour required in the actual adjustment ($18 to 20 per hour) and the burden rate for the press (about $2 per hour).

Following the furnace springs may undergo grinding or finishing, for either practical or aesthetic reasons. In some cases, springs are electroplated with zinc. This is a complex process involving electricity and acid or alkaline solutions, and for this reason is outsourced. Depending on the needs of the job, it may be outsourced to a company as near as Cambridge, Ontario (60 km away), or as far as Buffalo, NY (more than 100 km away). In other cases, springs are coated with oil or painted with "Black Japan" (a coating of linseed oil and Gilsonite varnish) for durability, depending on their eventual use. Unlike electroplating, these processes can be done in-house at a competitive rate.

Finally, the product is packaged and readied to be shipped. This, too, can take a good deal of time (10,000 springs can take a half day or more to pack).

The illustration below shows the layout diagram and production process for three types of springs. The colours and icons correspond to the departments of the shop.

Job A is the type of compression spring used inside a ballpoint pen. Here, after setting up the coiling machine, the springs are wound, then heat-treated in the furnace and shipped to the customer.

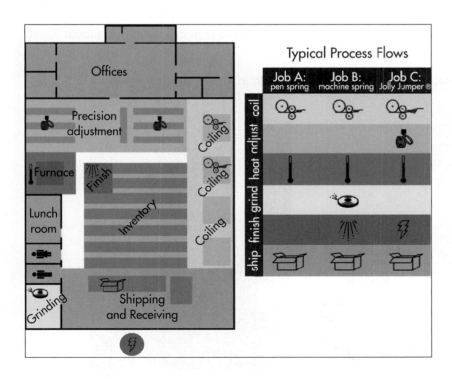

Job B is a typical machine spring, which undergoes the same basic steps as the ballpoint pen spring, but has its ends grinded and is coated with oil in the finishing stage to add durability to the spring before shipping.

Job C is Jolly Jumper® springs. In this case, the coiling machine requires a special setup, because the Jolly Jumper® springs require tapered ends. After this, each spring must be precision adjusted to give it a specially looped end. It is heat treated, but before shipping is sent to an outside company to be electroplated. The springs then return to Hi-Bek and are shipped to the customer.

batch processing A type of process used when a moderate volume or variety of goods or services is desired.

Batch. Batch processing is used when a moderate volume of goods or services is desired, and it can handle a moderate variety in products or services. The equipment need not be as flexible as in a job shop, but processing is still intermittent. The skill level of workers doesn't need to be as high as in a job shop because there is less variety in the jobs being processed. Examples of batch systems include small bakeries, which make bread, cakes, or cookies in batches; movie theatres, which show movies to groups (batches) of people; and airlines, which carry planeloads (batches) of people from airport to airport. Other examples of products that lend themselves to batch production are beer, paint, ice cream, clothes, magazines, and books. Other examples of services include plays, concerts, hotels, and restaurants. For more examples see the Great Canadian Bagel at the end of Chapter 11 and the Stickley Furniture at the end of Chapter 13.

The managerial challenge in a batch process is scheduling batches in order to meet planned production and demand while utilizing the facility at a high level. Capacity issues and technology management are more important than in job shops.

Example 2

Great Western Brewing Company was formed in 1989 when Molson Breweries of Canada decided to close the Saskatoon brewery and the employees reopened it as a private company. GWB produces light, regular, strong and specialty beers, and packages them in glass and plastic bottles, cans, and kegs. The main ingredient in beer is malt, which is partially sprouted barley. Other ingredients are grains such as corn or wheat, and hops which produces its bitter taste.

The production process can be divided into four stages: brewing, fermentation, finishing, and packaging. Brewing starts with mixing ground malt and water in the mash mixer.

The Brew Kettle.

The Lauter Tun.

Then, the mash (solid) and the wort (malt sugar liquid) are separated (by filtering) in the lauter tun. Next, the wort is boiled in the brew kettle for 1.5 hours while hops are added. Hops and other solids are separated from wort (by settlement) in the hot wort tank. So far the process has taken 5 hours. The batch size in the brewing part of the process is about 20,000 litres.

Fermentation starts when the settled wort is cooled in one of the many fermenters where GWB's brewers yeast is added. Yeast converts the wort sugars into alcohol and carbon dioxide (CO_2). The fermentation is complete in eight days and the fermented beer is now cooled and pumped into one of a many primary aging tanks. The yeast which settled in the fermenter is recovered and reused in subsequent batches.

Finishing involves cold aging of the beer for a minimum of one week in the primary aging tanks and then filtering and recooling it into secondary aging tanks where it rests a further week. The beer is then ready to be filtered and cooled again and pumped to the bright beer tanks where it is now ready to be packaged. CO_2 that has been collected during fermentation is injected into the beer each time it is moved, to ensure a very specific level in the final product.

The different types of beer differ in terms of taste, colour, and alcohol content. These are influenced by the ingredients, the temperature and times of each step of process, yeast, hops, separation, and filtration. The chemistry of brewing is very complex and is still not fully understood. The equipments are specialized, with all the products following the same processing route. Having remote-activated pumps and gauges, a central control room manages all the operations. Change over from one type of beer to another requires washing the tanks which takes approximately a half an hour. The plant floor plan (layout) is displayed below.

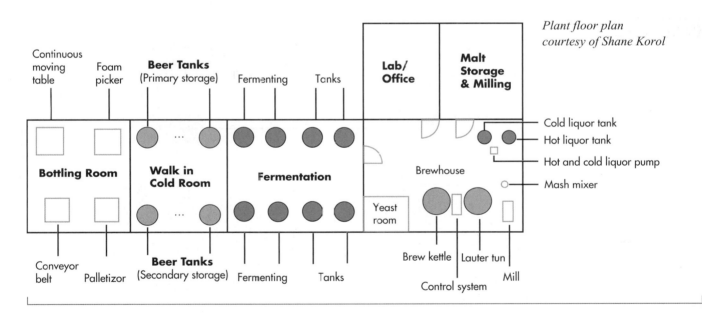

Plant floor plan courtesy of Shane Korol

Repetitive. When higher volumes of more standardized goods or services are needed, **repetitive processing** is used. The standardized output means only slight flexibility of equipment is needed. Skill of workers is generally low. Examples of this type of system include production lines and **assembly lines**. In fact, this type of process is sometimes referred to as *assembly*. The line can be either machine-paced (same speed) or worker-paced (variable speed). Familiar products made by these systems include automobiles, television sets, and computers. An example of repetitive service is an automatic carwash. Other examples of repetitive service include cafeteria lines and ticket collectors at sports events and concerts. For another example, see the Sylvania Lighting reading in this chapter.

The managerial challenges in an assembly line are capacity balance, technology management, quality, and materials management.

repetitive processing A type of process used when higher volumes of more standardized goods or services are needed.

assembly line An example of a repetitive system.

Example 3

Paccar Trucks builds Kenworth and Peterbilt trucks at its assembly plant in Sainte-Therese, Quebec. A truck has two major subassemblies: chassis and cab. The chassis is made up of the bottom frame, the engine and power train, wheels, etc. Paccar buys the major components from its suppliers and assembles them. Also, the cab and hood are purchased already fabricated. Paccar paints them and stores them in a buffer area on the second floor. This is to let the paint dry and because it is more efficient to use a batch process for painting (i.e., a large number of the same colours are pointed one after another). Sixty hoods and 30 cabs can be stored in the buffer area. Typically, a cab and hood are painted five days before they are used.

Four out of every five trucks are white. However, the different interior, motor, chassis length, and brand result in approximately 40 different products. The equipment is specialized but flexible enough. Most material handling is by overhead conveyors. Workers appreciate this in the frame shop where heavy (1–2.5 tonnes) and long (6–13 meters) beams are assembled. The overhead conveyors also save floor space.

The parts and components are received just-in-time and delivered straight to the point of use. There are 31 receiving docks near the points of use. The two subassembly lines (chassis and cab) join in the middle of the left side of the plant (see the process flow diagram below, drawn according to the actual plant layout) and the truck is hauled to the final assembly and test area on the right. Capacity of the plant is 40 trucks per eight-hour shift which means that every 12 minutes a truck moves up one workstation.

Process Flow Diagram for Paccar's Sainte-Therese, Quebec, Plant

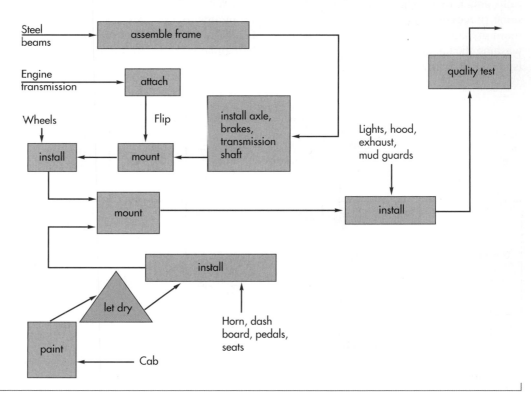

Continuous. When a very high volume of highly standardized output is desired, a continuous system is used. These systems have almost no variety in output and, hence, no need for equipment flexibility. As in assembly systems, workers are generally low skilled. Product is also continuous, i.e., it cannot be counted. Examples of products made in continuous systems include steel, paper, sugar, flour, and salt. Continuous services include utilities and the Internet.

continuous process Used when a high volume of highly standardized output is required.

The managerial challenges in a **continuous process** are the same as in an assembly line, but because of faster speed of production, greater care is required for automated control of the flow, and start and stop of production are more challenging.

Example 4

In 1854, the first sugar refinery in Canada was opened on the banks of the Lachine Canal in Montreal under the name of "The John Redpath, Canada Sugar Refinery." Today, the Redpath Sugar Refinery is part of the Tate & Lyle corporate group and the Redpath logo is Canada's oldest brand name for a Canadian food product. Production for Redpath sugar is centred on a refinery that is located on the Toronto waterfront. Designed for maximum output from minimal inputs of raw material, labour, and energy, (i.e., efficiency of operations), the refinery runs 24 hours a day, 7 days a week. Although individual stages of the following refining process use measured batches in separate machines, the use of multiple machines, running in a staggered sequence, creates a macro system that is practically continuous in its operations.

Raw Materials. Although all plants make some sugar (sucrose) through the process of photosynthesis, Sugar Cane makes the most and is therefore used as the world's primary source of sugar production. Grown in the tropics it is harvested and processed in huge mills, close to the field, by crushing the cane stalks and extracting the juice (sap). Boiling the juice produces a combination crystal of white sucrose, covered by a thin layer of brown molasses that is called "raw sugar." The raw sugar is then sold on the international commodities exchanges as a product and is purchased by refiners for shipment around the world in huge cargo vessels.

Cargos of raw sugar arrive at the refinery in volumes of up to 25,000 tonnes (this being the limit of vessels passing through the St. Lawrence Seaway) and are unloaded by the use of dockside cranes and then transferred by conveyor belt to the refinery's raw sugar shed. This building has a capacity of 65,000 tonnes and has a floor the size of two football fields, which is necessary because the seaway closes in the winter and all stocks of raw sugar must be brought in and stored to ensure a continuous flow of production year-round.

The Refining Process. Although the raw sugar purchased for processing is of a relatively high quality, it still contains a residue of original cane-trash, ash, waxes, as well as any additional solids or other impurities that might have contaminated the cargo during transportation. Refining is designed to remove all of these unwanted elements and leave only pure sucrose at the end.

The process commences with the transfer of the raw sugar into the refinery building, where it is weighed into specific quantities and fed into a mixing trough called a "mingler." Blended together with a solution of molasses and warm water, the resultant slurry ("magma") is spun at high speed in one of a set of oversized washing machines ("affination centrifugals") to separate the molasses coating from the central crystal. The spun off syrup is recycled, while the primary crystal ("washed raw sugar") is melted and dissolved in hot water to produce a syrup ("raw liquor") which is then passed through a succession of filters to remove the various impurities.

Starting with a simple mechanical sieve ("strainer") that removes the larger visible solids, the liquor passes through a "carbonation" and "sweetland" system, whereby chalk (calcium carbonate) encapsulates the remaining micro-solids, making them larger and able to be removed by fine cloth filters in the sweetland presses. The final filtration, to remove the undesirable yellow colouration in the liquor, is done by the use of absorption in large tanks filled with commercial resin and carbon-based filtration agents, similar to those used in municipal water purification systems. The end result of this series of filtrations is to produce a clear, colourless syrup ("fine liquor") consisting of nothing but sucrose and water.

The fine liquor is now recrystallized by boiling it for upwards of an hour under vacuum to prevent the syrup burning ("caramelizing"). The resultant "white massecuite" (a combination of recrystallized sucrose, uncrystallized sucrose syrup and water) is spun yet again in the "white sugar centrifugals" to separate the liquid phase from the crystals. While the syrups are recycled to create additional crystals, the semi-dry crystals of pure white sucrose are dried in large rotary driers to reduce the end moisture content to less than .03 percent.

The "mingler."

Vacuum vessels used for recrystalization.

Having manufactured a continuous flow of pure sucrose, the granular version of the product can now be either packaged in a range of volumes and weights that represent the Redpath retail line of products, or sold in larger "bulk" loads and shipped out in road or rail tanker loads (of up to 100 tonnes) for further use in a variety of industrial and commercial applications. Sugar can also be converted into a range of liquid or syrup formats and blends, which also have a wide range of industrial customers.

Table 6–1 provides an overview of these processing systems. The ideal is to have process capabilities such as equipment flexibility match product or service requirements such as product variety and quantity (volume). This relationship is also displayed in the product-process matrix of Figure 6–1. Failure to match product and process can result in inefficiencies and higher costs than are necessary, perhaps creating a competitive disadvantage. For example, using a batch process when there is only one product made on the process is inefficient. The process does not use the automated material movement of assembly or continuous processes. On the other hand, when there are many products produced on a continuous or assembly process, the frequent product switches will result in long change-over times which are nonproductive.

Another consideration is that products and services often go through *life cycles* that begin with low volume, which increases as products or services become better known. When that happens, a manager must know when to shift from one type of process (e.g., job shop) to the next (e.g., batch).

The type of process or processes used by an organization influences a great many activities of the organization. Table 6–2 briefly describes some of those influences.

TABLE 6–1

Characteristics of types of processes

	Job Shop	Batch	Repetitive/ Assembly	Continuous
Product Variety	Customized	Semi-standardized	Standardized	Highly standardized
Volume	Low	Low-moderate	High	Very high
Equipment flexibility	Very high	Moderate	Low	Very low

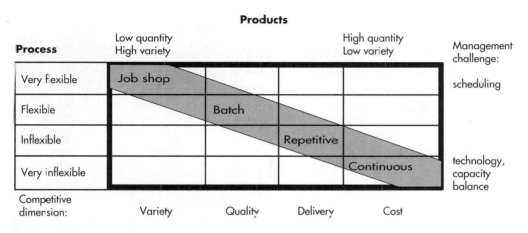

FIGURE 6-1

The product-process matrix

TABLE 6-2

Process choice affects numerous activities/functions

Characteristic	Job Shop	Batch	Repetitive	Continuous
Advantage	Able to handle a wide variety of work	Moderate flexibility	Low unit cost, high volume, efficient	Very efficient, very high volume
Disadvantages	Slow, high cost per unit, complex planning and scheduling	Moderate cost per unit, moderate scheduling complexity	Low flexibility, high cost of downtime	Very rigid, lack of variety, costly to change, very high cost of downtime
Cost estimation	Difficult	Somewhat routine	Routine	Routine
Cost per unit	High	Moderate	Low	Low
Equipment used	General purpose	General purpose	Special purpose	Special purpose
Fixed costs	Low	Moderate	High	Very high
Variable costs	High	Moderate	Low	Very low
Labour skills	High	Moderate	Low	Low
Marketing	Promote capabilities	Promote capabilities; semi-standard goods and services	Promote standardized goods/services	Promote standardized goods/services
Scheduling	Complex	Moderately complex	Routine	Routine
Work-in-process inventory	High	High	Low	Low

The processes discussed do not always exist in their "pure" forms. It is not unusual to find hybrid processes—processes that have elements of other process types embedded in them. For instance, if volume increases for some items, a process that began in, say, a job shop or batch mode may evolve into batch or repetitive. This may result in having some part of process in a job shop or batch mode and others in a repetitive mode.

Another point is that processes that produce high quantity of products specialize for these products, hence the low variety of products produced on the process. This concept is called "focused factory." Recently, however, some companies have managed to handle high quantity and high variety on the same process, e.g., the "made-for you" system of McDonald's or Dell Computer's Mass Customization.

Within each process, there are usually many individual operations which get performed. A list of some common metal-working and nonmetal-working operations is given in Table 6–3.

AUTOMATION

A key question in process design is whether to automate. **Automation** is using machinery that has sensing and control devices that enable it to operate automatically. If a

automation Using machinery that has sensing and control devices that enable it to operate automatically.

TABLE 6-3

Basic operations

	Some Metalworking Processes			
Assembly	**Casting and Molding**	**Cutting**	**Forming**	**Finishing**
Braze	Cast:	Broach	Draw	Blast
Cement	die, sand,	Drill	Extrude	Buff
Fasten	investment	Grind	Punch	Clean
Press-fit	Mold:	Hone	Roll	Debur
Shrink-fit	injection	Mill	Trim	Heat treat
Solder	powered metal	Shape	Swage	Paint
Weld	permanent mold	Turn	Spin	Polish

	Some Nonmetalworking Processes			
Chemicals	**Food**	**Mining**	**Textiles**	**Lumber**
Crack	Can	Dry	Braid	Debark
Cook	Cook	Crush	Knit	Cure
Cure	Crush	Excavate	Polish	Joint
Distill	Freeze	Extract	Shrink	Kiln
Evaporate	Pasteurize	Load	Spin	Plane
Grind	Press	Screen	Wash	Saw
Screen	Sterilize	Smelt	Weave	Turn

Source: PKG Operations Management W/OM Software CD-Rom, 9th edition by Gaither/Fraizer. © 2002. Reprinted with permission of South-Western, a division of Thomson Learning, www.thomsonrights.com. Fax 800-730-2215.

company decides to automate, the next question is how much. Automation can range from factories that are completely automated (including automated process control) to a single automated operation.

Automated services are also an option. Although not as plentiful as in manufacturing, automated services are becoming increasingly important. Examples range from ATMs to automated heating and air conditioning, automated inspection and vision systems, automated storage and retrieval systems, Automated Guided Vehicles, bar coding, package sorting, mail processing, and e-mail.

Automation offers a number of advantages over human labour. It has low variability, whereas it is difficult for a human to perform a task in exactly the same way, in the same amount of time, and on a repetitive basis. In a production setting, variability is detrimental to quality and to meeting schedules. Moreover, machines do not get bored or distracted, nor do they go out on strike, ask for higher wages, or file labour grievances. Still another advantage of automation is reduction of variable costs.

Automation is frequently touted as a strategy necessary for competitiveness. For example, in steel-making, some "mini" mills, controlled by an integrated computer system, produce an uninterrupted hot band of steel using scrap metal and electrical charge. Mini mills have a substantial productivity advantage over foundries which use iron ore in blast furnaces. An example of a mini-mill is the Direct Strip Production Complex of Algoma Steel. Another example of using automation for competing is the gigantic automated paper-making machines that automatically sense the width of paper and adjust to run at speeds of more than 60 km per hour.

Automation also has certain disadvantages and limitations compared to human labour. To begin with, it can be costly. Technology is expensive; usually it requires high volumes of output to offset high costs. In addition, automation is much less flexible than human labour. Once a process has been automated, it is hard to change it. Moreover, workers

www.algoma.com

sometimes fear automation because they may lose their jobs. That can have an adverse effect on morale and productivity.

Decision makers must carefully examine the issue of whether to automate or the degree to automate, so that they clearly understand all the ramifications. Also, much thought and careful planning are necessary to successfully *integrate* automation into a production system. Otherwise, it can lead to major problems. GM invested heavily in automation in the 1980s only to find its costs increasing while flexibility and productivity took a nosedive. Its market had shrunk while it was increasing its capacity! Moreover, automation has important implications not only for cost and flexibility, but also for the fit with overall strategic priorities.

An automated guided vehicle used in a John Deere factory.

Generally speaking, there are three kinds of automation: fixed, programmable, and flexible.

Fixed automation is the most rigid of the three types. The concept was perfected by the Ford Motor Company in the early 1900s, and it has been the cornerstone of mass production in the auto industry. Sometimes referred to as Detroit-type automation, it uses high-cost, specialized equipment for a fixed sequence of operations. Low unit cost and high volume are its primary advantages; minimal variety and the high cost of making major changes in either product or process are its primary limitations.

Programmable automation involves the use of high-cost, general-purpose equipment controlled by a computer program that provides both the sequence of operations and specific details about each operation. Changing the process is as easy (or difficult) as changing the computer program, and there is downtime while program changes are being made. This type of automation has the capability of economically producing a fairly wide variety of low-volume products in small batches. Numerically controlled (N/C) machines and some robots are examples of programmable automation.

Numerically controlled (N/C) machines are programmed to follow a set of processing instructions based on mathematical relationships that tell the machine the details of the operations to be performed. The instructions are stored on a device such as a computer

numerically controlled (N/C) machines Machines that perform operations by following mathematical processing instructions.

disk, magnetic tape, or microprocessor. Although N/C machines have been used for many years, they are an important part of new approaches to manufacturing. Individual machines may have their own computer; this is referred to as *computerized numerical control (CNC)*. Or one computer may control a number of N/C machines, which is referred to as *direct numerical control (DNC)*.

N/C machines are best used in cases where parts are processed frequently and in small batches, where part geometry is complex, close tolerances are required, mistakes are costly, and there is the possibility of frequent changes in design. The main limitations of N/C machines are the higher skill levels needed to program the machines and their high cost.

robot A machine consisting of a mechanical arm, a power supply, and a controller.

The use of robots in manufacturing is sometimes an option. A **robot** consists of three parts: a mechanical arm, a power supply, and a controller. Unlike movie versions of robots, which vaguely resemble human beings, industrial robots are much less glamorous and much less mobile; most robots are stationary except for their movable arms.

Robots can handle a wide variety of tasks, including welding, assembly (mainly surface-mounting for circuit boards), loading and unloading of machines, painting, and testing. They relieve humans from heavy, dirty, and unsafe work and often eliminate drudgery.

Some uses of robots are fairly simple, others are much more complex. At the lowest level are robots that follow a fixed set of instructions. Next are programmable robots, which can repeat a set of movements after being led through the sequence. These robots "play back" a mechanical sequence much as a video recorder plays back a visual sequence. At the next level up are robots that follow instructions from a computer. At the top are robots that can recognize objects and make certain simple decisions.

Robots can be powered pneumatically (by air), hydraulically (by fluids), or electrically. Figure 6–2 illustrates a robot.

Flexible automation evolved from programmable automation. It uses equipment that is more customized than that of programmable automation. A key difference between the two is that flexible automation requires significantly less changeover time. This permits almost continuous operation of equipment *and* product variety without the need to produce in batches.

FIGURE 6-2

Industrial robot

Source: Morris A. Cohen and Uday M. Apte, *Manufacturing Automation* (Burr Ridge, IL: Irwin/McGraw-Hill, 1997), p. 138.

www.milacron.com

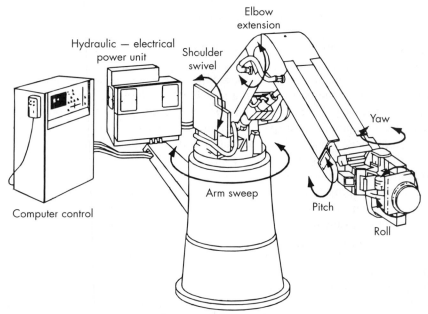

A computerized control room at a steel mini-mill.

In practice, flexible automation is used in several different formats.

A machining centre is a machine capable of performing a variety of operations on a part. The machine is numerically controlled.

A **flexible manufacturing system (FMS)** is a group of machining centres that include supervisory computer control, automatic material handling, and robots or other automated processing equipment. Reprogrammable controllers enable these systems to produce a variety of *similar* products. Systems may range from three or four machines to more than a dozen. They are designed to handle intermittent processing requirements with some of the benefits of automation and some of the flexibility of individual, or stand-alone, machines (e.g., N/C machines). Flexible manufacturing systems offer reduced labour costs and more consistent quality compared with more traditional manufacturing methods, lower capital investment and higher flexibility than "hard" automation, and relatively quick changeover time. Flexible manufacturing systems appeal to managers who hope to achieve both the flexibility of job shop processing and the productivity of repetitive processing systems.

Although these are important benefits, an FMS also has certain limitations. One is that this type of system can handle a relatively narrow range of part variety, so it must be used for a family of similar parts that all require similar machining. Also, an FMS requires longer planning and development times than more conventional processing equipment because of its increased complexity and cost. Furthermore, companies sometimes prefer a gradual approach to automation, but FMS represents a sizable chunk of technology.

The suitability of these systems to a production environment primarily depends on the variety and volume of products. See Figure 6–3.

Computer-integrated manufacturing (CIM) is a system that uses an integrating computer system to link a broad range of manufacturing activities, including engineering design, flexible manufacturing systems, and production planning and control. Not all elements are absolutely necessary. For instance, CIM might be as simple as linking two or more FMSs by a host computer. More encompassing systems can link order-taking, scheduling, purchasing, inventory control, shop control, and distribution. In effect, a CIM system integrates information from other areas of an organization with manufacturing.

flexible manufacturing system (FMS) A group of machining centres that include supervisory computer control, automatic material handling, and robots or other automated processing equipment.

computer-integrated manufacturing (CIM) A system for linking a broad range of manufacturing activities through an integrating computer system.

FIGURE 6-3

Applicability of automated systems based on product quantity and variety

Source: Roger G. Schroeder, *Operations Management,* 1st ed., (Boston: McGraw-Hill Irwin, 2000), p. 96. Reproduced with permission of the McGraw-Hill Companies.

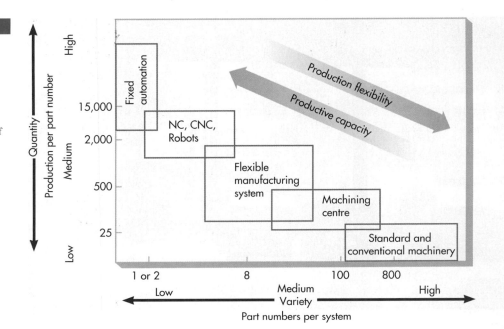

www.potashcorp.com

The overall goal of using CIM is to link various parts of an organization to achieve rapid response to customer orders and/or product changes, to allow rapid production, and to reduce *indirect* labour costs.

A shining example of how process choice can lead to competitive advantage can be found at the Rocanville facility of the Potash Corporation of Saskatchewan, one of the most automated mining and milling operations in North America. This facility operates as many as five huge mining machines one kilometre below the surface, tens of kilometres of conveyors underground, and a large mill on the surface. Allen-Bradley's computer-based information and management control system coordinates all of these operations. The mining machines run with no operators on-board, relying on Allen-Bradley programmable controllers. Tracking a laser beam, an on-board Allen-Bradley vision system maintains horizontal alignment of the machine as it cuts into the potash formation. The controller also uses an ore analyzer to adjust the machine vertically, following the potash formation. Above ground, 10 processors monitor and control a total of nearly 850 machines and equipment. In addition to reducing risks to mining machine operators, the Allen-Bradley system has simplified the operations and reduced reaction time to problems by giving operators immediate data. Furthermore, ore extraction and recovery have been maximized and operating costs are reduced.[1]

PROCESS DESIGN

Process design involves identifying the activities, resources, and controls needed in the production/service process. There are other activities in operating a business (besides the creation of goods and services) that should also be designed as processes, such as order taking and sales, planning, purchasing, and staffing.

We assume that this is a new process for a new product. More often, processes are only redesigned and this is done by either automating one part of the process or replacing a machine with a newer one. In this case, only some of the following steps need to be performed.

---

[1]See "Fully Integrated Control," *World Mining Equipment*, May 1997, pp. 36–37.

Methodology for Process Design

Given the product quantity, variety, cost, quality, delivery speed (lead time), and product specifications (nature, shape, size, components and how they fit together),

1. **Define the production process (process planning)**

   This involves the following:

   - Determine how completed the input materials should be. These are make or buy decisions.
   - Set production system objectives:
     - Capacity (or production speed), flexibility
     - Type of process (job shop, batch, assembly, continuous)
     - Cost (fixed, variable), process quality capability
     - Technology/extent of automation, production start date
   - Determine the nature of process in general.

2. **Conceptualize the design**

   This answers the question: How do you get from inputs (materials) to output? That is, what is the sequence of major operations (activities) needed?

   - Develop a few alternative process concepts (sketches). Two approaches can be used:

     a. Incremental: do one step at a time from start to end.

     b. Hierarchical (top down): break the whole job into two operations, then into suboperations, etc., until desired level of detail is reached.
   - Usually a process flow diagram is used to show the operations and movement of materials.
   - Evaluate each alternative process concept and choose the best.

3. **Make an embodiment of the design**

   - Choose one process concept and complete the design.
   - Build a prototype process (can use computer modelling) and test it.
     - Determine the resources (machines, equipment and labour) needed.
     - Estimate the costs, quality, etc., and compare with the objectives.
   - Refine the process and reevaluate it.
   - Choose the best process.

4. **Create a detailed design**

   - Finalize the process specifications
     - Determine the machines, equipment (their capacities and make), and labour.
     - Design the plant layout.
     - Design the work centres.

Drawing a **process flow diagram** starts with identifying the boundaries of the process (inputs and outputs) and the level of detail required. The incremental approach involves following the normal flow of materials (or customers, in services) through the transformation process, identifying the activities and resources (machines, labour, and their capabilities) required and their sequence. Experience with similar processing is used as a guide. For technical products, expertise of process/manufacturing engineers is required.

If the process is complex, the flow diagram needs to be redrawn, taking various processing options and technology into account.

process flow diagram
A diagram used to identify process boundaries and the level of detail required.

As an example, the process flow diagram for making a fast-food cheeseburger, similar to what might be found in McDonald's, is as follows:

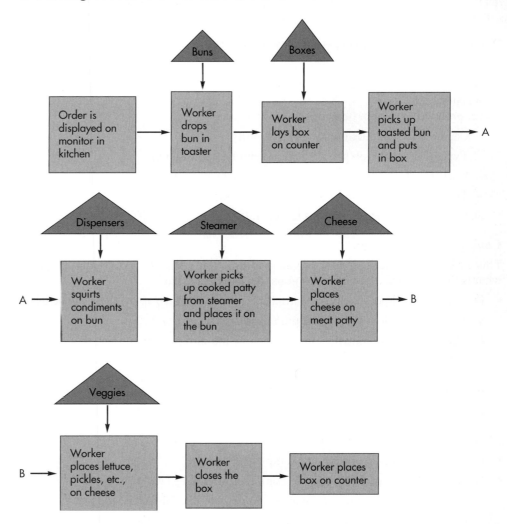

If there is a need to show the information flow, it could be shown as a dashed arrow.

Another example of the process flow diagram is given in the Sylvania Lighting reading.

| **Example 5** | A company wants to diversify into mass-producing bread. It requires a process flow diagram. |

Solution

The recipe for making a loaf of bread is:

1. Mix flour, salt, yeast, and water to obtain dough.
2. Knead the dough.
3. Shape the dough into a round chunk, put in a pan and leave to rise.
4. Bake in oven.
5. Let bread cool and remove from pan.

Because of the large quantity of ingredients (and the economy of quantity buying), a storage space will be used. Because mixing large quantities by hand is difficult, a mixing machine is required. The same reason applies to kneading. As it happens, there exists a machine that does both mixing and kneading. To automate the shaping, the easiest method is to dump the big lump of dough into a hopper that cuts and drops small pieces of dough in the bread pans, which are then transported on a conveyor belt into an open-ended oven (like a small automated carwash).

The following process flow diagram is a good first step:

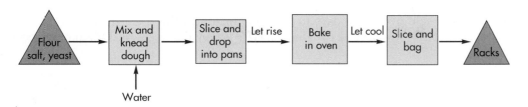

Suppose you wish to design a production process to make simple oak tables. The input material is oak planks approximately 2 inches thick by 6 inches wide by 6 feet long. The tables will have square tops with dimensions of 1 inch thick by 3 feet each side. Each of the four legs for a table should be round with a radius of 1 inch and length of 3 feet. All parts are sanded and varnished before assembly. The legs are assembled to the top using brackets. The low production quantity implies batch production. Design a production process to manufacture the tables by drawing a process flow diagram for the process. Identify the machines used for each operation. *Hint:* Saw the planks thickness-wise in half and glue them together to form part of a table top. Saw the planks into 2-inch wide segments and then use a lathe to make them round.

Example 6

Solution

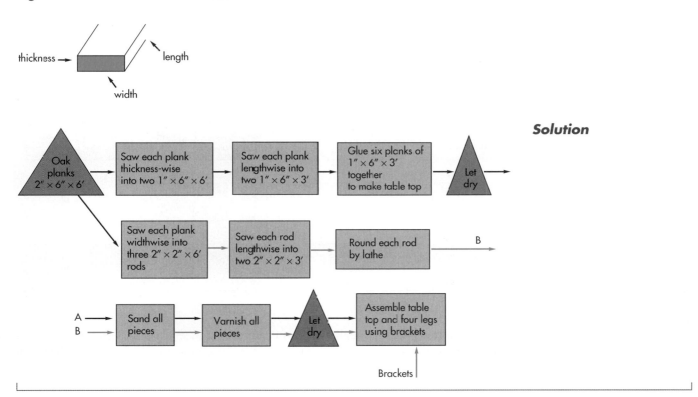

The Integrated DEFinition (IDEF) method is a hierarchical top-down approach to process design. Starting from the name/function of the process (e.g., "sell insurance"), the process design team decomposes it into its linked components step by step until the level of detail desired is reached. IDEF is a conceptual approach requiring brainstorming rather than recollection of past actual processes. At each stage, the team discusses and agrees to the decomposition, but it may be necessary to backtrack.[2]

---

[2]For more information, see www.idef.com. Example 7 is from J. Fulscher et al., "Anatomy of a Process Mapping Workshop," *Business Process Management Journal* 5(3), 1999, pp. 208ff.

Example 7

Secura Insurance Co. of Switzerland hired Coopers & Lybrand in 1997 to redesign its processes, one of which was the car insurance sales process. A workshop of the managers involved was held over three days to teach the managers the IDEF method. The "sell insurance" process was used as an example. Here is how the stages of IDEF progressed.

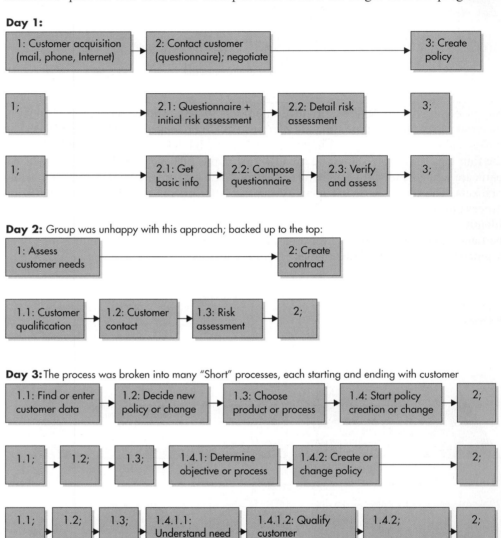

Day 1:

| 1: Customer acquisition (mail, phone, Internet) | → | 2: Contact customer (questionnaire); negotiate | → | 3: Create policy |

| 1; | → | 2.1: Questionnaire + initial risk assessment | 2.2: Detail risk assessment | 3; |

| 1; | → | 2.1: Get basic info | 2.2: Compose questionnaire | 2.3: Verify and assess | 3; |

Day 2: Group was unhappy with this approach; backed up to the top:

| 1: Assess customer needs | → | 2: Create contract |

| 1.1: Customer qualification | 1.2: Customer contact | 1.3: Risk assessment | 2; |

Day 3: The process was broken into many "Short" processes, each starting and ending with customer

| 1.1: Find or enter customer data | 1.2: Decide new policy or change | 1.3: Choose product or process | 1.4: Start policy creation or change | 2; |

| 1.1; | 1.2; | 1.3; | 1.4.1: Determine objective or process | 1.4.2: Create or change policy | 2; |

| 1.1; | 1.2; | 1.3; | 1.4.1.1: Understand need of customer | 1.4.1.2: Qualify customer | 1.4.2; | 2; |

Hierarchical design is frequently used in chemical engineering to design new chemical processing plants. To illustrate the methodology, in order to make ammonia (NH_3), in Stage 1 one can use a reactor to mix nitrogen (N) and hydrogen (H). But, the output of the reactor will also contain some unreacted hydrogen and nitrogen; these need to be separated out in order to obtain the desired purity of ammonia. This separation can be performed (in Stage 2) by a condenser, because the three gases have different boiling points. After separation, unreacted gases can be fed back into the reactor. But, the cold unreacted gases first have to be heated to room temperature. Here (in Stage 3) one can use a heat exchanger: the inputs and outputs of the condenser can exchange heat without mixing.

Service Process Design

Service process design is similar to manufacturing process design except that instead of material, the flow of the customer or something belonging to the customer is followed. Services are especially vulnerable to quality and delivery problems because the customer

Sylvania Lighting

www.sylvania.com

Sylvania Lighting's plants produce lightbulbs. One type of lightbulb they make is a family of fluorescent bulbs with a specific base type. A fluorescent lightbulb is a glass tube covered inside with phosphor. At each end there is a base, and connected to each base from inside there is a stem mount assembly that carries the electricity. The electricity activates the inert gas that is mixed with mercury vapour. "A" and "B"

stems differ in the brightness produced. The process flow diagram for assembling this type of lightbulb is shown below.

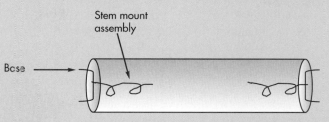

Source: D. T. Hubbard, et al., "Process Flow Scheduling in a High Volume Repetitive Manufacturing Environment," *Production and Inventory Management Journal*, Fourth Quarter, 1992, pp. 21–26.

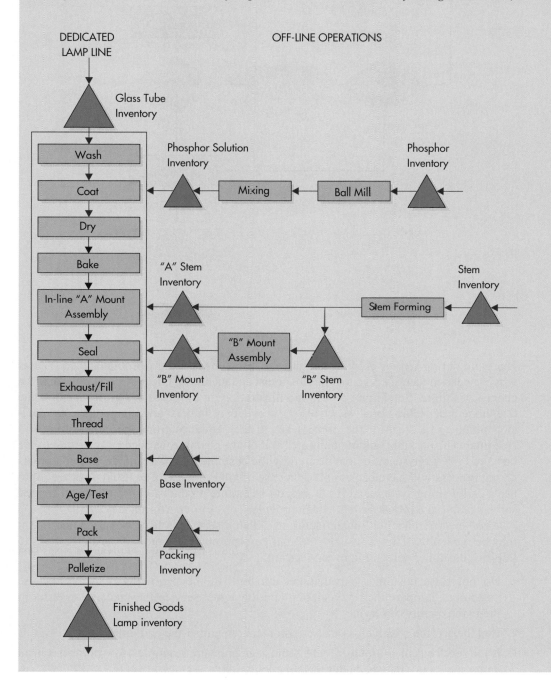

FIGURE 6-4

Process flow diagram of a catalogue call

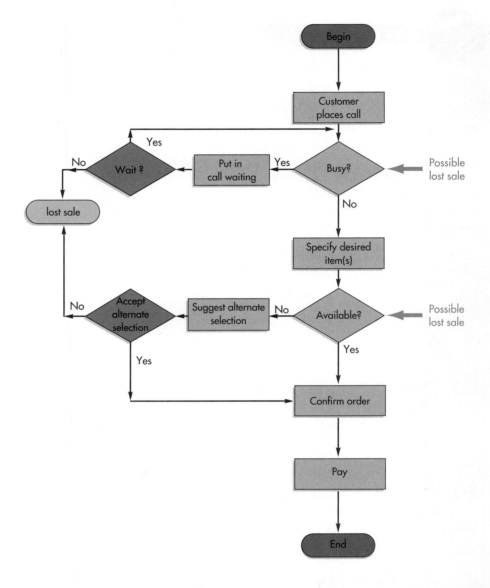

is present during service delivery and there is little time to fix any problems then. That is why we need to identify potential failure points and incorporate features that minimize the chance of failure. See Figure 6–4 for an illustration of a process design for a catalogue telephone order-taking process. Ovals show events of interest and diamonds show decision points. The steps of the process are in the sequence from the perspective of a customer. The possible failure points are (a) if all the customer service representatives are busy and (b) if the specific item desired by the customer is not available. A good order-taking process will have backup plans in case of either failure. The usual ones are (a) to use a call-waiting system and (b) to suggest substitute products. These plus well-trained servers result in a robust system which provides consistent performance.

Another difference with manufacturing is that a service is usually varied and that it may be intangible. This raises the customer perception issue. Some of the suggestions to improve customer perception in services are:

- Do not raise customer expectations too high in the beginning. This is because customers compare their expectation and the actual service they receive in order to judge the quality of service.
- End the service positively because customers remember the end more.
- If the service is pleasurable, divide it into segments. For example, two short rides in an amusement park may be better than one long ride.

- If the service is painful, combine the segments. For example, cleaning teeth in a one-hour session may be better than two half-hour sessions.

- Let customers control part or all of the process. For example, self-services such as ATMs are preferred by most people. In this case, it is important to make the process user-friendly.

- Communicate the evidence of quality to customers.

LAYOUT DESIGN

Layout refers to the configuration of departments, work centres, and equipment, with particular emphasis on movement of work through the system. A good layout facilitates flow of work, whereas a bad one results in congestion.

As in other areas of system design, layout decisions are important for three basic reasons: (1) they may require substantial investment of money and effort, (2) they may involve long-term commitment, which makes mistakes difficult to overcome, and (3) they may have a significant impact on the cost and efficiency of operations. This section describes the main types of layout designs and the models used to evaluate design alternatives.

The need for layout planning arises both in designing new facilities and in redesigning existing facilities. The most common reasons for redesign of layouts include inefficient operations (e.g., high cost, bottlenecks), accidents or safety hazards, changes in the design of products or services, changes in the volume of output or mix of outputs, changes in methods or equipment, changes in environmental or other legal requirements, and morale problems (e.g., lack of face-to-face contact).

TYPES OF LAYOUT

There are generally two types of layout—product layout (assembly, continuous) and process layout (job shop, batch).

Product Layouts

Product layouts are used to achieve a smooth and rapid flow of large volumes of goods or customers through a system. This is made possible by highly standardized goods or services that allow highly standardized, continual processing. The work is divided into a series of standardized tasks, permitting specialization of both labour and equipment. Because only one or a few very similar items are involved, it is feasible to arrange an entire layout to correspond to the processing requirements of the product or service. For instance, if a portion of a manufacturing operation required the sequence of cutting, sanding, and painting, the appropriate pieces of equipment would be arranged in that same sequence. And because each item follows the same sequence of operations, it is often possible to utilize fixed-path material-handling equipment such as conveyors to transport items between operations. The resulting arrangement forms a line like the one depicted in Figure 6–5. In manufacturing environments, lines refer to production lines or assembly lines, depending on the type of activity involved. In service processes, the term *line* may or may not be used. It is common to refer to a cafeteria line

product layout Uses standardized processing operations to achieve smooth, rapid, high-volume flow.

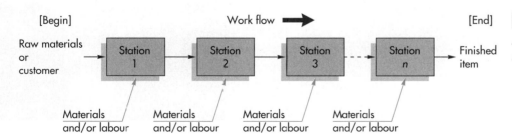

FIGURE 6–5

A flow line for production or service

[Begin]   Work flow ➡   [End]

Raw materials or customer → | Station 1 | → | Station 2 | → | Station 3 | ⋯→ | Station n | → Finished item

Materials and/or labour   Materials and/or labour   Materials and/or labour   Materials and/or labour

FIGURE 6-6

A cafeteria line

Tray → | Soup | Entree course | Vegetable | Drinks | Desserts | Cashier | →

as such but not a car wash, although from a conceptual standpoint the two are nearly identical. Figure 6–6 illustrates the layout of a typical cafeteria line. Examples of this type of layout are less plentiful in service environments because processing requirements usually exhibit too much variability to make standardization feasible. Without high standardization, many of the benefits of repetitive processing are lost. When lines are used, certain compromises must be made. For instance, an automatic car wash provides equal treatment to all cars—the same amount of soap, water, and scrubbing—even though cars may differ considerably in cleaning needs. As a result, very dirty cars may not come out completely clean, and relatively clean cars go through the same system with considerable waste of soap, water, and energy.

Product layouts achieve a high degree of labour and equipment utilization, which tends to offset their high equipment cost. Because items move quickly from operation to operation, the amount of work-in-process is often minimal. Consequently, operations are so closely tied to each other that the entire system is highly vulnerable to being shut down because of mechanical failure or absenteeism. Maintenance procedures are geared to this. *Preventive maintenance*—periodic inspection and replacement of worn parts or those with high failure rates—reduces the probability of breakdowns during the operations. Of course, no amount of preventive maintenance can completely eliminate failures, so management must take measures to provide quick repair. These include maintaining an inventory of spare parts and having repair personnel available to quickly restore equipment to normal operation.

Advantages of product layouts include simplified accounting, purchasing, and inventory control.

Disadvantages of product layouts include dull, repetitive jobs, repetitive stress injuries, inflexibility in response to changes in the volume of output or in product.

Cadillac assembly line.

Boeing

The Fabrication Division of Boeing in Auburn, Washington State, found itself under pressure to increase its capacity in the late 1990s. It was a large (475,000 square foot) machine shop organized into specific areas such as roughing, finishing, and hole-making. One of the parts it had to make was rib posts used to stiffen spars within wings of airplanes. Rib posts were all different sizes depending on their location within the wing, ranging from 15 cm to 1.5 m long. Depending on the type of aircraft, there were between 200 and 400 rib posts within a wing.

There was a lot of setups and movement of parts across the shop. Boeing decided to start a manufacturing cell dedicated to some of the rib posts. The cell consists of four numerically controlled machining centres, with a computer scheduling and controlling the operations within the cell. As a result of the change to manufacturing cell, the fabrication time for parts decreased by 60 percent.

Source: B. J. Hogan, "Cells Raise Boeing's Capacity," *Manufacturing Engineering* 120(3), March 1998, pp. 114–24.

Process Layouts

Process layouts are designed to process items or provide services that involve a variety of processing requirements. The variety of jobs that are processed requires frequent adjustments to equipment. This causes a discontinuous work flow, which is referred to as *intermittent processing*. The process (functional) layouts feature departments or other functional groupings in which similar kinds of activities are performed. A manufacturing example of a process layout is a *machine shop*, which has separate departments for milling, grinding, drilling, and so on. Items that require those operations are frequently moved in lots or batches to the departments in a sequence that varies from job to job. Consequently, variable-path material-handling equipment (forklift trucks, pallet-jacks, tote boxes, etc.) is needed. The use of *general-purpose equipment* provides the flexibility necessary to handle a wide range of processing requirements. Workers who operate the equipment are usually skilled or semiskilled. Figure 6–7 illustrates the departmental arrangement typical of a process layout.

process layout A layout that can handle varied processing requirements.

Process layouts are quite common in service environments. Examples include hospitals, colleges and universities, auto repair shops, and public libraries. For instance, hospitals have departments that specifically handle surgery, maternity, pediatrics, etc. And universities have separate colleges or departments that concentrate on one area of study such as business, engineering, etc.

Because equipment in a process layout is arranged by type rather than by processing sequence, the system is much less vulnerable to shutdown caused by mechanical failure or absenteeism. In manufacturing systems especially, idle equipment is usually available to replace machines that are temporarily out of service. Moreover, because items are often processed in lots, there is considerably less interdependence between successive operations than with a product layout. Maintenance costs tend to be lower because the equipment is less specialized than that of product layouts, and the grouping of machinery permits repair personnel to become skilled in handling that type of equipment. Machine similarity reduces the necessary investment in spare parts. On the negative side, routing

Process Layout
(functional)
Used for Intermittent Processing
Job Shop or **Batch**

Dept. A	Dept. C	Dept. E
Dept. B	Dept. D	Dept. F

FIGURE 6–7

Process layout

Standard Aero provides a variety of maintenance, repair and overhaul services to the Aviation Industry, including repair of gas turbine engines. They have locations in Canada, the United States, Europe and Asia. In the 1990s, among other things, it reorganized its repair facilities into manufacturing cells. Instead of a job shop layout where similar machines are bunched up together, they segmented the repair process and also grouped similar parts into cells. Each cell is operated by a self-managed team whose performance is measured and displayed in front of the cell. Standard Aero has become so proficient at conversion into manufacturing cells that they started a division that sells this service to other engine repair facilities.

and scheduling must be done on a continual basis to accommodate the variety of processing demands typically imposed on these systems. Material handling is inefficient, and unit handling costs are generally much higher than in product layouts. In-process inventories can be substantial due to batch processing. Furthermore, it is not uncommon for such systems to have equipment utilization rates under 50 percent because of routing and scheduling complexities related to the variety of processing demands being handled.

Cellular Layouts

manufacturing cell Layout in which machines are arranged in a cell that can process items that have similar processing requirements.

A **manufacturing cell** is a type of layout in which different machines are arranged in a *cell* that can process items with similar processing requirements called *part families*. The cells become, in effect, miniature versions of product layouts. The cells may have no conveyorized movement of parts between machines, or may have a flow line connected by a conveyor (automatic transfer). Figure 6–8 compares a typical functional (process) layout and a manufacturing cell layout. Observe that in the cellular layout, machines are arranged to handle all of the operations necessary for a group (family) of similar parts. Thus, all parts follow the same route although minor variations (e.g., skipping an operation) are possible. In contrast, the functional (process) layout involves multiple paths for parts.

Each cell may be U-shaped (see Figure 6–9). A U-shaped line permits increased communication among workers on the line because workers are clustered, thus facilitating teamwork. Flexibility in work assignments is increased because workers can handle not only adjacent stations but also stations on opposite sides of the line.

There are numerous benefits of manufacturing cells. These include faster processing time, increased capacity, less material handling, less work-in-process inventory, and reduced setup time.

group technology The grouping into part families of items with similar design or manufacturing characteristics.

Grouping of similar items is known as **group technology** and involves identifying items with similarities in either *design characteristics* or *manufacturing characteristics*, and grouping them into *part families*. Design characteristics include size, shape, and function; manufacturing characteristics involve the type and sequence of operations required. Figure 6–10 illustrates a group of parts with similar processing characteristics.

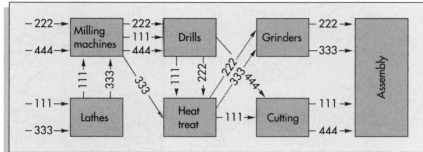

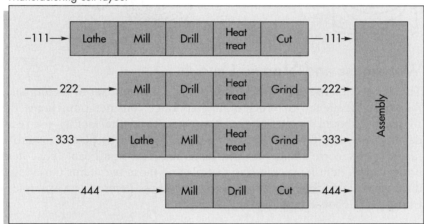

FIGURE 6-8

Comparison of functional (process) and manufacturing cell layouts

Source: Adapted from D. Fogarty and T. Hoffmann, *Production and Inventory Management* (Cincinnati: South-Western Publishing, 1983), p. 472.

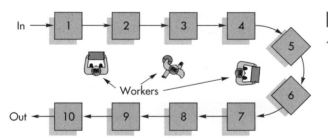

FIGURE 6-9

A U-shaped production line

Once similar items have been identified, items can be classified according to their families, then a system can be developed that facilitates retrieval of these codes from the database for purposes of design and manufacturing. For instance, a designer can use the system to determine if there is an existing part similar or identical to the one that needs to be designed. It may happen that an existing part, with some modification, is satisfactory. This greatly enhances the productivity of design. Similarly, planning the manufacturing of a new part can include matching it with one of the part families in existence, thereby alleviating much of the burden of specific processing details.

The conversion to group technology is often a major undertaking; it is a time-consuming job that involves the analysis of a considerable amount of data. Three primary methods for accomplishing this are visual inspection, examination of design and production data, and production flow sequence and routing analysis. For examples of manufacturing cells, see the reading, "Boeing," and the photo and caption on Standard Aero.

FIGURE 6-10

A group of parts with similar manufacturing requirements

Source: Mikell P. Groover, *Automation, Production Systems, and Computer-Aided Manufacturing* © 1980, p. 540. Reprinted by permission of Prentice Hall, Inc., Englewood Cliffs, New Jersey.

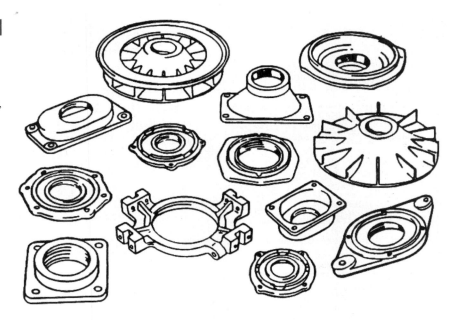

Warehouse and Storage Layouts

The design of storage facilities is based on a different set of factors than the design of factories. Frequency of order is an important consideration; items that are ordered frequently should be placed near the entrance to the facility (or receiving/shipping department), and those ordered infrequently should be placed toward the rear of the facility. Any correlations between items are also significant (e.g., item A is usually ordered with item B), suggesting that placing those two items close together would reduce the cost and time of *picking* (retrieving) those items. As an example, see "Federated Co-op's Warehouse" reading.

Retail Layouts

The objectives that guide design of manufacturing layouts often pertain to cost minimization and product flow. However, with retail layouts such as department stores, supermarkets, and specialty stores, designers take into account the presence of customers and the opportunity to influence sales. Traffic flow is an important factor to consider. See the reading, "Designing Supermarket Layout."

READING

Federated Co-op's Warehouse

www.fcl.ca

This 278,000 square foot warehouse/distribution centre in Saskatoon is a hub of activities 24 hours a day. Federated Co-operatives Ltd. is a wholesale grocery and hardware distributor in Western Canada. Most activities occur in the staging area on the north side of the warehouse. Shipments from manufacturers and producers arrive on pallets and get stored either on the dry grocery racks on the right, on the floor in the promotion area in the centre, or on racks in the produce, cooler, or freezer areas on the top left. Orders from customers, approximately 400 retail Co-op stores, get picked by order

pickers on pallet jacks and are collected in the staging area for trucking. Repack, in the bottom left, is a secure area for expensive items such as batteries and open cases of items.

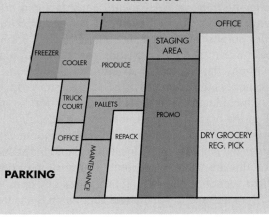

Designing Supermarket Layout

David Schardt

The produce is over here, the dairy's over there. The soft drink specials are at the end of the aisles, the candy's are at the checkout. Always.

A visit to your local supermarket isn't as haphazard as it seems. It's been laid out so that you spend as much as possible on what the store wants you to buy. And that's often more than you came in for, as we learned when we spoke to supermarket industry insiders. Here's how a typical supermarket is designed to maximize sales.

The more time you spend shopping along the sides and back of the supermarket, the more money the store makes. About half its profits come from perimeter items like fruits and veggies, milk and cheese, and meat, poultry, and fish. That's also where you'll find the bakery, the salad bar, and the deli.

Some foods are so profitable that they command their own aisles. Breakfast cereals bring in more dollars per square foot of shelf space than any other product in the interior of the store. So most supermarkets give cereals plenty of space.

Why are the dairy products usually as far away from the entrance as possible? Almost everybody buys milk when they shop. To reach it, they've got to walk through a good chunk of the supermarket, often along the perimeter. That's right where the store wants shoppers.

Also, stores like to "anchor" a display by putting popular items at each end. That's why milk, for example, is often at one end of the dairy case and margarine and butter at the other. You've got to run the gauntlet of cheese, yogurts, dips, etc. to get what you came for.

Every year, grocery chains are offered more than 15,000 new products, nearly all of which will fail. How do stores decide which ones to stock?

Large supermarkets often require manufacturers to pay for shelf space. "Slotting fees," as they're called, can range from $5,000 to $25,000 per supermarket chain for each new food.

Think it's a coincidence that you almost always have to walk through the produce department when you enter a supermarket? The look of those shiny, neatly stacked fruits and vegetables is *the* most important influence on where people decide to shop. It also doesn't hurt that produce is the second most profitable section (meat is first). While it occupies a little over 10 percent of the typical supermarket, it brings in close to 20 percent of the store's profits.

Source: Adapted from Copyright 1994, CSPI. Reprinted from *Nutrition Action Healthletter* (1875 Connecticut Avenue, N.W., Suite 300, Washington, D.C. 10009-5728).

Office Layouts

Office layouts underwent transformation as the flow of paperwork was replaced with electronic communication. That means that there is less need to place office workers in a layout that optimizes the physical transfer of information or paperwork. A new trend is to create an image of openness; office walls are giving way to low-rise partitions.

LAYOUT DESIGN PROCESS

Following are the steps of the manufacturing layout design process:

- Determine the location of receiving and shipping.
- For "product layout," fit the process flow diagram onto a sketch of the facility floor, starting from receiving and ending in shipping. Determine the approximate location of each part of the process.
- For "process layout," determine the expected work flow between each pair of departments, and place the two departments with the highest workflows closest to one another. Continue until all departments are located.
- Keep special requirements of machines in mind (e.g., heavy press needs strong ground, paint department needs clean environment).
- Allow space for machines, in-feeds, out-feeds, workers and carts/forklifts.
- Keep rearranging the plan until you find what works best.
- On the facility floor, paint an outline of machines, in-feed and out-feed spaces.
- Walk through the normal sequence of activities.
- Run the electricity and other lines, and move the machines in.

DESIGNING PRODUCT LAYOUTS: LINE BALANCING

Assembly lines range from fairly short, with just a few operations, to long lines that have a large number of operations. Automobile assembly lines are examples of long lines. At the assembly line for Ford Mustang, a Mustang travels about 14 kilometres from start to finish! Figure 6–11 illustrates the major steps involved in assembling an automobile.

Many of the benefits of a product layout relate to the ability to divide required work into a series of tasks (e.g., "assemble parts C and D") that can be performed quickly and routinely by low-skilled workers or specialized equipment. The durations of these tasks typically range from a few seconds to 15 minutes or more. Most time requirements are so

FIGURE 6–11

Auto assembly major steps

Source: "Computer Integrated Manufacturing," Vol. 1 in Revolution in Progress series, Chapman and Hall, London, 1990. Adapted from R. U. Ayres, Morris A. Cohen, and Uday M. Apte. *Manufacturing Automation* (Burr Ridge, IL: McGraw-Hill, 1997), p. 175.

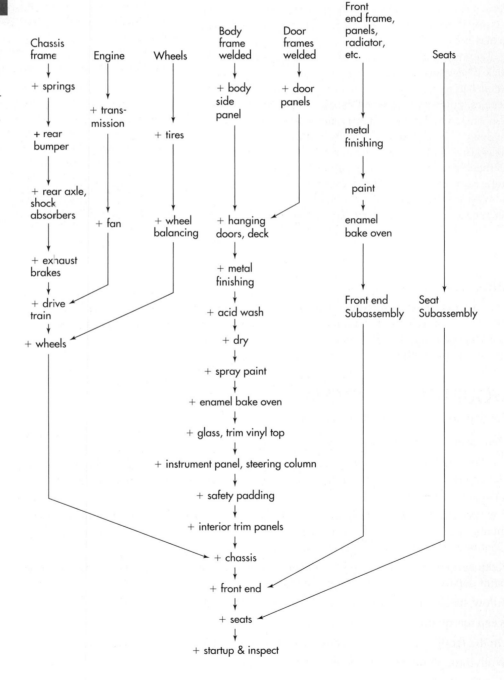

brief that it would be impractical to assign only one task to each worker. For one thing, most workers would quickly become bored by the limited job scope. For another, the number of workers required to complete even a simple product or service would be enormous. Instead, tasks are usually grouped into manageable bundles and assigned to workstations staffed by one or two operators.

The process of deciding how to assign tasks to workstations is referred to as **line balancing**. The goal of line balancing is to obtain task groupings that represent approximately equal time requirements. This minimizes the idle time along the line and results in a high utilization of labour and equipment. Idle time occurs if task times are not equal among workstations; some stations are capable of producing at higher rates than others. These "fast" stations will experience periodic waits for the output from slower stations or to avoid buildups of work in downstream stations. Unbalanced lines are undesirable in terms of inefficient utilization of labour and equipment and because they may create morale problems at the slower stations for workers who must work continuously.

line balancing The process of assigning tasks to workstations in such a way that the workstations have approximately equal time requirements.

Lines that are perfectly balanced will have a smooth flow of work as activities along the line are synchronized to achieve maximum utilization of labour and equipment. The major obstacle to attaining a perfectly balanced line is the difficulty of forming task bundles that have the same duration. One cause of this is that it may not be feasible to combine certain activities into the same bundle, either because of differences in equipment requirements or because the activities are not compatible (e.g., risk of contamination of paint from sanding). Another cause of difficulty is that differences among elemental task lengths cannot always be overcome by grouping tasks. A third cause of an inability to perfectly balance a line is that the technological sequence may prohibit otherwise desirable task combinations. Consider a series of three operations that have durations of two minutes, four minutes, and two minutes, as shown in the following diagram. Ideally, the first and third operations could be combined at one workstation and have a total time equal to that of the second operation. However, it may not be possible to combine the first and third operations. In the case of an automatic car wash, scrubbing and drying operations could not realistically be combined at the same workstation due to the need to rinse cars between the two operations.

```
┌─────────────┐      ┌─────────────┐      ┌─────────────┐
│  Scrubbing  │ ───► │   Rinsing   │ ───► │   Drying    │
│  2 minutes  │      │  4 minutes  │      │  2 minutes  │
└─────────────┘      └─────────────┘      └─────────────┘
```

Line balancing involves assigning tasks to workstations. Usually, each workstation has one worker who handles all of the tasks at that station, although an option is to have several workers at a single workstation. For purposes of illustration, however, all of the examples and problems in this chapter have workstations with one worker.

A manager could decide to use anywhere from one to five workstations to handle five tasks. With one workstation, all tasks would be done at that station; with five stations, one task would be assigned to each station. If two, three, or four workstations are used, some or all of the stations will have multiple tasks assigned to them. How does a manager decide how many stations to use?

The primary determinant is what the line's **cycle time** will be. The cycle time is the *maximum* time allowed at each workstation to perform assigned tasks before the work moves on. The cycle time also establishes the output rate of a line. For instance, if the cycle time is two minutes, units will come off the end of the line at the rate of one every two minutes.

cycle time The maximum time allowed at each workstation to complete its set of tasks on a unit.

We can gain some insight into task groupings and cycle time by considering a simple example. Suppose that the work required to fabricate a certain product can be divided into five tasks, with the task times and precedence relationships as shown in the following diagram.

```
→ │ .1 min │ → │ .7 min │ → │ 1.0 min │ → │ .5 min │ → │ .2 min │ →
```

The task times govern the range of possible cycle times. The *minimum* cycle time is equal to the *longest* task time (1.0 minute), and the *maximum* cycle time is equal to the sum of the task times (.1 + .7 + 1.0 + .5 + .2 = 2.5 minutes). The minimum cycle time would apply if there were five workstations. The maximum cycle time would apply if all tasks were performed at a single workstation. The minimum and maximum cycle times are important because they establish the potential range of output for the line, which we can compute using the following formula:

$$\text{Output capacity per day} = \frac{\text{OT}}{\text{CT}} \tag{6–1}$$

where

OT = Operating time per day

CT = Cycle time

Assume that the line will operate for eight hours per day (480 minutes). With a cycle time of 1.0 minute, output would be

$$\frac{480 \text{ minutes per day}}{1.0 \text{ minute per unit}} = 480 \text{ units per day}$$

With a cycle time of 2.5 minutes, the output would be

$$\frac{480 \text{ minutes per day}}{2.5 \text{ minutes per unit}} = 192 \text{ units per day}$$

The output selected for the line must fall in the range of 192 units per day to 480 units per day.

As a general rule, the cycle time is determined by the desired output; that is, a desired output level is selected, and the cycle time is computed. If the cycle time does not fall between the maximum and minimum bounds, the desired output rate must be revised. We can compute the cycle time using this formula:

$$\text{CT} = \frac{\text{OT}}{D} \tag{6–2}$$

where

D = Desired output per day (i.e., demand)

For example, suppose that the desired output rate is 480 units per day. Using Formula 6–2, the necessary cycle time is

$$\frac{480 \text{ minutes per day}}{480 \text{ units per day}} = 1.0 \text{ minute per unit}$$

The number of workstations that will be needed is a function of both the cycle time and our ability to combine tasks into workstations. We can determine the *theoretical minimum* number of stations necessary given a cycle time as follows:

$$N_{\text{min}} = \frac{\sum t}{\text{CT}} \tag{6–3}$$

where

N_{min} = Theoretical minimum number of stations

$\sum t$ = Sum of task times

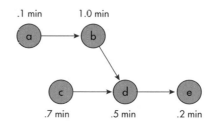

FIGURE 6-12

A simple precedence network

Suppose that the desired rate of output is 480 units per day. (This will require a cycle time of 1.0 minute.) The minimum number of stations required to achieve this goal is:

$$N_{\min} = \frac{2.5 \text{ minutes per unit}}{1 \text{ minute per unit per station}} = 2.5 \text{ stations}$$

Because 2.5 stations is not feasible, it is necessary to *round up* (because 2.5 is the minimum) to three stations. Thus, the actual number of stations used will equal or exceed three, depending on how successfully the tasks can be grouped into work bundles.

A very useful tool in line balancing is a **precedence network**. Figure 6–12 illustrates a simple precedence network. It visually portrays the tasks that are to be performed along with the *sequential* requirements; that is, the *order* in which tasks must be performed. The network is read from left to right, so the initial task(s) are on the left and the final task is on the right. In terms of precedence relationship, we can see from the diagram, for example, that the only requirement to begin task *b* is that task *a* must be finished. However, in order to begin task *d*, tasks *b* and *c* must *both* be finished. Note that the tasks are the same ones that we have been using.

precedence network
A diagram that shows the tasks and their precedence requirements.

Now let's see how a line is balanced. This involves assigning tasks to workstations. Generally, no techniques are available that guarantee an optimal set of assignments. Instead, managers employ rule of thumb or *heuristic (intuitive) rules*, which provide good and sometimes optimal sets of assignments. A number of line-balancing heuristics are in use, two of which are described here for purposes of illustration:

1. Assign the task with longest time.
2. Assign the task with the most followers.

The general procedure used in line balancing is described in Table 6–4.

TABLE 6-4

Line balancing procedure

1. Identify the cycle time and determine the minimum number of workstations.
2. Make assignments to workstations in order, beginning with Station 1. Tasks are assigned to workstations moving from left to right through the precedence network.
3. Before each assignment, use the following criteria to determine which tasks are *eligible* and will fit to be assigned:
   a. All its preceding tasks in the network have been assigned.
   b. The task time does not exceed the time left at the workstation.
   If no tasks will fit, move on to the next workstation.
4. After each task assignment, determine the time left at the current workstation by subtracting the sum of times for tasks already assigned to it from the cycle time.
5. Assign tasks (and break ties) using one of these heuristic rules:
   a. Assign the task with the longest time.
   b. Assign the task with the most followers.
6. Continue until all tasks have been assigned to workstations.
7. Compute appropriate measures (e.g., percentage idle time, efficiency) for the set of assignments.

				Assign	
Workstation	**Time Left**	**Eligible**	**Will fit**	**Task (time)**	**Idle Time**
1	1.0	a, c	a, c*	a (.1)	
	.9	b, c	c	c (.7)	
	.2	b	—		.2
2	1.0	b	b	b (1.0)	
	.0	d	—		.0
3	1.0	d	d	d (.5)	
	.5	e	e	e (.2)	
	.3	—	—		.3
					.5

Example 8

Arrange the tasks shown in Figure 6–12 into workstations using a cycle time of 1.0 minute. Assign the task with the most followers.

Solution

*Task a was assigned because it has more followers (three, vs. two for task c).

Comment: The initial "time left" for each workstation is equal to the cycle time. For a task to be eligible, tasks preceding it on the precedence network must have been assigned, and for it to fit, the task's time must not exceed the station's time left.

Example 8 was purposely simple; it was designed to illustrate the basic procedure. Example 9 will be a harder problem. Let us first consider some measures of effectiveness that can be used for evaluating a given set of assignments.

Two widely used measures of effectiveness are:

balance delay Percentage idle time of a line.

1. The *percentage idle time* of the line. This is sometimes referred to as the **balance delay**. It can be calculated as follows:

$$\text{Percentage idle time} = \frac{\text{Sum of Idle time per unit}}{N_{\text{actual}} \times \text{cycle time}} \times 100 \qquad (6\text{--}4)$$

where N_{actual} = Actual number of stations.

For the preceding example, the value is:

$$\text{Percentage idle time} = \frac{.5}{3 \times 1.0} \times 100 = 16.7\%$$

2. The *efficiency* of the line. This is calculated as follows:

$$\text{Efficiency} = 100 - \text{percent idle time} \qquad (6\text{--}5)$$

Here efficiency = 100% − 16.7% = 83.3%

Description of Line Balancing Procedure

In balancing an assembly line, tasks are assigned *one at a time* to the line, starting at the first workstation. At each step, the unassigned tasks are checked to determine which are eligible for assignment. Next, the eligible tasks are checked to see which of them will fit in the workstation being loaded. A heuristic is used to select one of the tasks that will fit, and the task is assigned. This process is repeated until there are no eligible tasks that will fit. Then the next workstation can be loaded. This continues until all tasks are assigned. The objective is to minimize the idle time for the line subject to precedence and cycle time constraints.

Precedence network tells us which tasks are *eligible* to be assigned at a particular position on the line. For example, in a car wash, the rinsing operation must be performed before the drying operation. The drying operation is not eligible for assignment until the rinsing operation has been assigned.

Cycle time constraint, on the other hand, determines the maximum amount of work that a manager can assign to each workstation, and this determines whether an eligible task *will fit* at a workstation. If a task can be assigned to a workstation without exceeding time left, then the task will fit.

Once it is known which tasks are *eligible* and *will fit*, the manager can select the task to be assigned (if there is more than one to choose from). This is where the heuristic rules help us decide which task to assign from among those that are eligible and will fit.

To clarify the terminology, *following tasks* are all tasks that you would encounter by following all paths from the task in question through the precedence network. *Preceding tasks* are all tasks you would encounter by tracing all paths *backward* from the task in question. In the precedence network below, tasks *b*, *d*, *e*, and *f* are followers of task *a*. Tasks *a*, *b*, and *c* are predecessors of *e*.

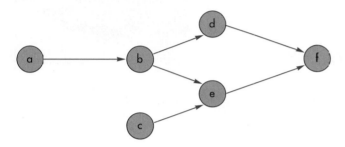

Neither of the heuristics *guarantees* the *best* solution to the line-balancing problem. It may be useful to apply several different heuristics to the same problem and pick the best (least percentage idle time) solution out of those developed.

Example 9

Suppose we were to design an assembly line for assembling the oak accessory table shown in the second photo on page 216 (shown upside down). The top and legs come as subassemblies (two leg subassemblies per table, each made of two legs already attached together). Note that both leg assemblies need to be screwed to the top before leg braces (cross-bars) can be assembled. The steps of assembly and their estimated times are:

Task	Time (seconds)
a. Place top subassembly upside down on the work surface.	4
b. Place a leg subassembly over the top subassembly as shown in the left-hand photo, insert a screw in the predrilled hole, align, and drive the screw in.	20
c. Insert another screw in the other predrilled hole and drive the screw in.	13
d. Place another leg subassembly over the other side of the top subassembly, insert a screw in the predrilled hole, align, and drive the screw in.	20
e. Insert another screw in the other predrilled hole and drive the screw in.	13
f. Place a leg brace between two leg subassemblies as shown in the right-hand photo, insert a screw in the predrilled hole, align, and drive the screw in.	20
g. Insert another screw in the other side's predrilled hole and drive the screw in.	13
h. Place another leg brace between two leg subassemblies on the other side, insert a screw in the predrilled hole, align, and drive the screw in.	20
i. Insert another screw in the other side's predrilled hole and drive the screw in.	13
j. Tighten all screws.	32

1. Draw the precedence network.

2. Assuming that we need to assemble one table per minute, assign the tasks to workstations using the task with longest time rule, breaking a tie with the task with the most

followers rule. If there is a further tie, break randomly (i.e., you can choose any one of the tasks tied).

Solution

1.

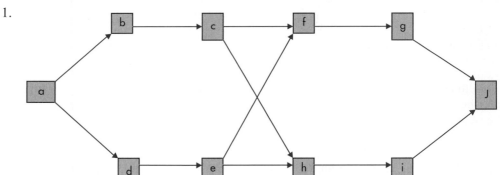

2.

WS	Time Left	Eligible	Will Fit	Assign (time)	Idle Time
1	60s	a	a	a(4)	
	56	b, d	b, d*	b(20)	
	36	c, d	c, d	d(20)	
	16	c, e	c, e**	c(13)	
	3	e	—	—	3
2	60s	e	e	e(13)	
	47	f, h	f, h***	f(20)	
	27	g, h	g, h	h(20)	
	7	g, i	—	—	7
3	60s	g, i	g, i****	g(13)	
	47	i	i	i(13)	
	34	J	J	J(32)	
	2	—	—	—	2
					12s

*b is assigned randomly—both b and d have 6 followers and their time is tied at 20s also.

**c is assigned randomly—both c and e have 5 followers and their time is tied at 13s also.

***f is assigned randomly—both f and h have 2 followers and their time is tied at 20s also.

****g is assigned randomly—both g and i have 1 follower and their time is tied at 13s also.

Other Factors

The preceding discussion on line balancing presents a relatively straightforward approach to approximating a balanced line. In practice, the ability to do this usually involves additional considerations.

Technical considerations include skill requirements of different tasks. If skill requirements of tasks are quite different, it may not be feasible to place the tasks in the same workstation. Similarly, if the tasks themselves are incompatible (e.g., the use of fire and flammable liquids), it may not be feasible even to place them in stations that are near to each other. There may also be space limitations.

Although it is convenient to treat assembly operations as if their time will be the same in each repetition, it is more realistic to assume that whenever humans are involved, task completion times will be variable. The reasons for the variations are numerous, including worker fatigue, boredom, and failure to concentrate on the task at hand.

There could also be material variations and shortages, defects, mechanical problems, and product differences.

The following example shows the effect of variation in task times. If three workstations each take 3 minutes to perform their activities, then the capacity of the line will be 20 units per hour, with percentage idle time = 0 percent (see case (a) below). However, if each workstation's time is random: 2 minutes with probability of .5 and 4 minutes with probability of .5, assuming that there is no room for inventory between the workstations, then it can be shown, using simulation, that the capacity of the line drops to 16.17 units per hour, with percentage idle time = 19.1 percent (see case (b) below). Note that the average workstation time is still 3 minutes; however, Workstations 1 and 2 can be left idle if their successor workstation is taking 4 minutes and Workstations 2 and 3 can be left idle if their predecessor workstation is taking 4 minutes.

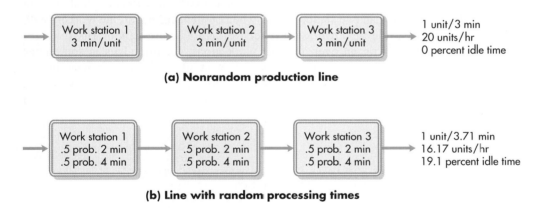

(a) Nonrandom production line

(b) Line with random processing times

Source: Adapted from Joseph S. Martinich, *Production and Operations Management: An Applied Modern Approach* (New York: John Wiley and Sons, Inc., 1997), p. 385. Reprinted with permission of John Wiley and Sons, Inc.

Solutions to the random task times include:

- Reduce the randomness, e.g., by designing the jobs better, by using high-quality material, and by doing preventative maintenance.
- Use buffer inventory between workstations.
- Leave some idle time in workstations which have random times.

Other Approaches

There are a number of other approaches companies use to achieve balance of the line. One approach is to use *parallel workstations*. These are beneficial for bottleneck operations that would otherwise disrupt the flow of product as it moves down the line. The bottlenecks may be the result of difficult or very long tasks. Parallel workstations increase the work flow and provide flexibility.

Consider the following example.[3] A job has four tasks; task times are 1 minute, 1 minute, 2 minutes, and 1 minute. Assume no buffer inventories between stations. The cycle time for the line would be 2 minutes per unit, and the output rate would be 30 units per hour:

$$\frac{60 \text{ minutes per hour}}{2 \text{ minutes per unit}} = 30 \text{ units per hour}$$

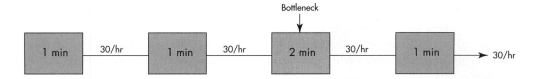

Using parallel stations for the third task would result in a cycle time of 1 minute per unit because the output rate at the parallel stations would total 60 units per hour, and allow an output rate for the line of 60 units per hour:

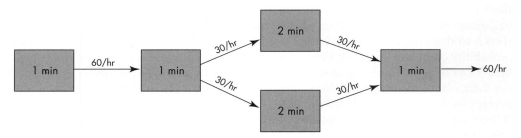

Another approach to achieving a balanced line is to *cross-train* workers so that they are able to perform in more than one station. Then, when bottlenecks occur, the workers with temporarily increased idle time can assist other workers who are temporarily overburdened, thereby maintaining an even flow of work along the line. This is sometimes referred to as *dynamic line balancing*, and it is used most often in just-in-time systems.

Sometimes a line needs to handle more than one product. This is referred to as a *mixed model line*. The following newsclip describes one solution to line balancing in mixed model lines:

---

[3]Adapted from Mikell P. Groover, *Automation, Production Systems, and Computer-Aided Manufacturing*, 2nd ed. (Englewood Cliffs, NJ: Prentice Hall, 1987), Chapter 6.

NEWSCLIP

Toyota Mixes and Matches

www.toyota.com

Toyota, long famous for producing quality cars and light trucks, decided to produce minivans in the U.S. in the late 1990s. Wanting to get into production quickly, Toyota took an ambitious step at its Georgetown, Kentucky, manufacturing plant, deciding to produce Sienna minivans at the same time—and at the same workstations—that produce Camry automobiles.

"Although Camry and Sienna are built from the same basic chassis, and share more than 50 percent of their parts, there are key differences. Sienna is five inches longer, three inches wider and a foot taller than Camry. Each Sienna takes up more space on the assembly line and requires more and bigger parts.

"Another automaker might shut down a plant for months to make the changes. But Toyota needed to move quickly. Delay could jeopardize sales of Sienna.

"Out of 300 stations on the assembly line, Sienna needs different parts at 26. But only seven new production steps are needed. ... To save time, Toyota decided not to add work-stations. Instead, it selected two teams of workers, one for each shift, that are responsible for attaching Sienna-only parts.

Meanwhile, engineers, working with Toyota workers, designed equipment intended to make those duties easy to perform."

As soon as a Sienna approaches one of the seven spots on the assembly line, a member of the Sienna team is there to take over. Some team members climb inside, where they scoot around on wheeled carts. Others attach roof racks by standing on platforms that put the van's top waist high, eliminating the need to reach, etc.

Toyota may have shortened the time needed to start production by three years by using this innovative approach to the assembly line.

Source: Based on "Camry Assembly Line Delivers New Minivan," *USA Today*, p. B3. Copyright 1997, *USA Today*. Adapted with permission.

DESIGNING PROCESS LAYOUTS

The main issue in design of process layouts concerns the relative positioning of the departments involved. As illustrated in Figure 6–13, departments must be assigned to locations. The challenge is to develop a reasonably good layout. Some departments may benefit from adjacent locations, whereas others should be separated. For example, a lab with delicate equipment should not be located near a department that has equipment with strong vibrations. Conversely, two departments that share some of the same equipment would benefit from being close together.

Layouts can also be influenced by external factors such as the location of entrances, loading docks, elevators, windows, and areas of reinforced flooring. Also important are noise levels, safety, and the size and locations of washrooms.

In a few instances (e.g., the layouts of supermarkets, gas stations, and fast-food restaurants), the development of standardized layouts is justified. For example, the use of the same basic patterns in McDonald's locations facilitates construction of new structures and employee training. Food preparation and order taking follow the same pattern throughout the chain. Installation and service of equipment are also standardized.

www.mcdonalds.com

The majority of layout problems involve single rather than multiple locations, and they present unique combinations of factors that do not lend themselves to a standardized approach. Consequently, these layouts require customized designs.

A major obstacle to finding the most efficient layout of departments is the large number of possible assignments. For example, there are more than 87 billion different ways that 14 departments can be assigned to 14 locations. However, special requirements (e.g., the stamping department may have to be assigned to a location with reinforced flooring) reduce the number of possibilities. Still, the remaining number of layout possibilities is quite large. Unfortunately, no algorithms exist to identify the best layout arrangements under all circumstances. Often planners must rely on heuristic rules to guide trial-and-error efforts for a satisfactory solution to each problem.

Measures of Effectiveness

One advantage of process layouts is their ability to satisfy a variety of processing requirements. Customers or materials in these systems require different operations and different sequences of operations, which causes them to follow different paths through the system. Material-oriented systems necessitate the use of variable-path material-handling equipment to move materials from department to department. In customer-oriented systems, people must travel or be transported from department to department. In both cases, transportation costs or time can be significant. Because of this factor, one of the

Locations

A	B	C
D	E	F

Departments to be assigned
1
2
3
4
5
6

FIGURE 6-13

Departments must be assigned to locations

major objectives in process layout is to minimize total transportation cost, distance, or time. This is usually accomplished by locating departments with relatively high inter-departmental work flow as close together as possible.

In situations that call for improvement of an existing layout, costs of relocating any department must be weighed against the potential benefits of the move.

Information Requirements

The design of process layouts requires the following information:

1. A list of departments or work centres to be arranged, their approximate dimensions, and the dimensions of the building that will house the departments.

2. A projection of future work flows between the various departments.

3. The distance between locations and the cost per unit of distance to move loads between locations.

4. A list of any special considerations (e.g., operations that must be close to each other or operations that must be separated).

The ideal situation is to first develop a layout and then design the physical structure around it, thus permitting maximum flexibility in design. This procedure is commonly followed when new facilities are constructed. Nonetheless, many layouts must be developed in existing structures where floor space, the dimensions of the building, location of entrances and elevators, and other similar factors must be carefully weighed in designing the layout. Note that multilevel structures pose special problems for layout planners.

Minimizing Total Transportation Cost or Distance

The most common goal in designing process layout is minimization of total transportation cost or distance. In such cases, it can be very helpful to summarize the necessary data in *from-to charts* like those in Tables 6–5 and 6–6. Table 6–5 indicates the distance between each pair of locations, and Table 6–6 indicates actual or projected work flow between each pair of departments. For instance, the distance chart reveals that a trip from location A to location B will involve a distance of 20 metres. (Distances are often measured between department centres.) Oddly enough, the length of a trip between locations A and B may differ depending on the *direction* of the trip, due to one-way routes, elevators, or other factors. To simplify the discussion, we assume a constant distance between any two locations regardless of direction. However, it is not realistic to assume that interdepartmental work flows are equal—there is no reason to suspect that department 1 will send as much work to department 2 as department 2 sends to 1. For example, several departments may send goods to packaging, but packaging may send goods only to the shipping department.

TABLE 6–5

Distance between locations (metres)

From \ To	LOCATION A	LOCATION B	LOCATION C
A	—	20	40
B	20	—	30
C	40	30	—

TABLE 6–6

Interdepartmental work flow (loads per day)

From \ To	DEPARTMENT 1	DEPARTMENT 2	DEPARTMENT 3
1	—	10	80
2	20	—	30
3	90	70	—

Transportation costs can also be summarized in from-to charts, but we shall avoid that complexity, assuming instead that costs are a direct, linear function of distance. We will use the following heuristic.

Heuristic

Assign the pair of departments with the greatest interdepartmental work flow to locations that are closest to each other, keeping the future assignments in mind. Then pick the pair with second highest work flow and assign them to the next two closest locations available, keeping their relationship with those already assigned and future assignments in mind. Continue until all departments have been assigned.

Example 10

Assign the three departments shown in Table 6–6 to locations A, B, and C, which are separated by the distances shown in Table 6–5, in such a way that total transportation cost is minimized.

Solution

Ranking departments according to highest work flow and locations according to lowest interlocation distances helps in making assignments. If interlocation distances are independent of direction of flow, work flow between two departments in each direction can be summed. Thus:

Department Pair	Work Flow	
3–1	90	}170
1–3	80	
3–2	70	}100
2–3	30	
2–1	20	} 30
1–2	10	

You can see that departments 1 and 3 have the highest interdepartmental work flow. Also note that locations A and B are the closest. Thus, it seems reasonable to consider assigning 1 and 3 to locations A and B, although it is not yet obvious which department should be assigned to which location. Further inspection of the work flow list reveals that 2 and 3 have higher work flow than 1 and 2, so 2 and 3 should be located more closely than 1 and 2. Hence, it would seem reasonable to place 3 between 1 and 2, or at least centralize that department with respect to the other two. The resulting assignments might appear as illustrated in Figure 6–14.

If the cost per metre to move any load is $1, you can compute the total daily transportation cost for this assignment by multiplying each department's number of loads by the trip distance, and summing those quantities:

Department	Number of Loads to:	Location	Distance to:	Loads × Distance
1	2: 10	A	C: 40	10 × 40 = 400
	3: 80		B: 20	80 × 20 = 1,600
2	1: 20	C	A: 40	20 × 40 = 800
	3: 30		B: 30	30 × 30 = 900
3	1: 90	B	A: 20	90 × 20 = 1,800
	2: 70		C: 30	70 × 30 = 2,100
				7,600

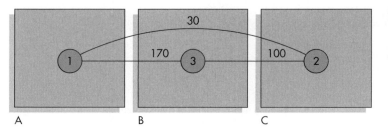

FIGURE 6-14

Interdepartmental work flows for assigned departments

At $1 per load metre, the cost for this plan is $7,600 per day. Even though it might appear that this arrangement yields the lowest transportation cost, you cannot be absolutely positive of that without actually calculating the total cost for every alternative and comparing it to this one. Although this could be done in this example, where the number of alternatives is quite small (i.e., there are 3!=6 possible arrangements), in problems with more departments, the number is likely to be too large to even consider examining every alternative. Instead, you can rely on reasonable heuristics such as that demonstrated above to arrive at a satisfactory, if not optimal, solution.

Closeness Ratings

The preceding approach suffers from the limitation of focusing on only one objective, but many situations involve multiple criteria. Richard Muther developed a more general approach to the problem, which allows for subjective input from managers to indicate the relative importance of closeness or remoteness of each department pairs.[4] That information is then summarized in a grid like that shown in Figure 6–15. The letters represent the importance of closeness for each department pair, with A being the most important and X represents an undesirable pairing. Thus, in the grid below it is "absolutely necessary" to locate 1 and 2 close to each other because there is an A at the intersection of those departments on the grid. On the other hand, 1 and 4 should not be close together because their intersection has an X. In practice, the letters on the grid are often accompanied by numbers that indicate the reason for each closeness rating: they are omitted here to simplify the illustration. Muther suggests the following list of reasons for closeness:

1. Use same equipment or facilities.
2. Share the same personnel.
3. Sequence of work flow.
4. Ease of communication.
5. Unsafe or unpleasant conditions.
6. Similar work performed.

Muther suggests that closeness ratings in the grid be first used to draw a relationship graph, using the A and X ratings, but keeping E ratings in mind. Then this graph is fitted into the floor plan. Example 11 illustrates the heuristic.

[4]Richard Muther and John Wheeler, "Simplified Systematic Layout Planning," *Factory* 120, nos. 8, 9, and 10 (August, September, October, 1962) pp. 68–77, 111–19, 101–13.

FIGURE 6-15

A simplified Muther grid

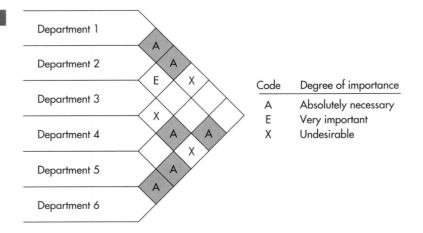

Code	Degree of importance
A	Absolutely necessary
E	Very important
X	Undesirable

Example 11

Assign the six departments in Figure 6–15 to a 2×3 set of locations.

Prepare a list of A and X ratings by referring to the grid in Figure 6–15:

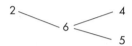

As	Xs
1–2	1–4
1–3	3–4
2–6	3–6
3–5	
4–6	
5–6	

Next, form a cluster of A links, beginning with the department that appears most frequently in the A list (in this case, 6):

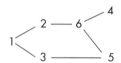

Take the remaining As in order of number of appearance in the list, and add them to this main cluster, rearranging the cluster as necessary. Form separate clusters for departments that do not link with the main cluster. In this case, all link with the main cluster.

Next, graphically portray the Xs:

Observe that, as it stands, the cluster of As also satisfies the X separations. It is a fairly simple exercise to fit the cluster into a 2 × 3 arrangement:

1	2	6
3	5	4

Note that alternative solutions are possible. For this solution, the E rating has also been satisfied with this arrangement, even though no attempt was made to explicitly consider it. Naturally, not every problem will yield the same results, so it may be necessary to do some additional adjusting to see if improvements can be made, keeping in mind that the A and X assignments deserve the greatest consideration.

Note that departments may be considered close not only when they touch side to side, but also when they touch corner to corner. However, side-by-side departments are closer. The distance is usually measured from the centres of departments.

Computer Software

The size and complexity of layout problems has led to the development of a number of computerized packages. An example of these is the e-Factory family of software by Unigraphics Solutions (UGS). This family (FactoryCAD, FactoryFlow, and Factory-Markup) provides icons for graphical display, calculates total material flow distances, uses several heuristics to determine a good layout, and provides 3-D walk-through displays. Another basically visualization software package is Intergraph's Smartplant family of products (including Plant Design System (PDS) and SmartSketch).

www.UGS.com/products/tecnomatix

www.intergraph.com

Process types include job shop, batch, repetitive, and continuous. Process type determines how work is organized, and it has implications for the entire organization and its supply chain. Process type and layout are closely related.

Job shops are used for many low-quantity customized products, whereas repetitive and continuous processes are used for one or two high-quantity standard products. Automation is used to reduce the variable production costs and improve quality. Examples include numerically controlled machining centres. Process design involves finding a conceptual sequence of operations to produce the good or service. Process flow diagram is used to display the sequence of operations.

Product layouts are geared to high-volume output of standardized items. Workers and equipment are arranged according to the technological sequence required by the product or service involved. Emphasis in design is on work flow through the system, and specialized processing and handling equipment is used.

Process layouts group similar activities into departments or work centres. These systems can handle a wide range of processing requirements. However, the variety of processing requirements necessitates continual routing and scheduling. The rate of output is generally much lower than that of product layouts.

A manufacturing cell processes a group of similar products or parts.

The main design effort in product layout development focuses on dividing the work required to produce a product or service into tasks and bundling them so that they are as nearly equal as possible in terms of time. The goal is to achieve a high degree of utilization of labour and equipment. In process layout, design efforts often focus on the relative positioning of departments to minimize total transportation cost or to meet other requirements concerning the proximity of certain department pairs.

KEY TERMS

assembly line, 187
automation, 191
balance delay, 214
batch processing, 186
computer-integrated manufacturing (CIM), 195
continuous process, 188
cycle time, 211
flexible manufacturing system (FMS), 195
group technology, 206
job shop, 183

line balancing, 211
manufacturing cell, 206
numerically controlled (N/C) machines, 193
outsource, 183
precedence network, 213
product layout, 203
process layout, 205
process flow diagram, 197
repetitive processing, 187
robot, 194

Solved Problems

Problem 1

The tasks shown in the following precedence network are to be assigned to workstations with the intent of minimizing percentage idle time. Management desires an output rate of 275 units per day. Assume 440 minutes are available per day.

a. Determine the appropriate cycle time.

b. What is the minimum number of stations possible?

c. Assign tasks using the task with the "longest time" rule.

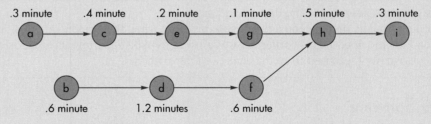

Solution

a. $\text{CT} = \dfrac{\text{Operating time}}{\text{Desired output}} = \dfrac{440 \text{ minutes per day}}{275 \text{ units per day}} = 1.6 \text{ minutes}$

b. $N_{\min} = \dfrac{\sum t}{\text{Cycle time}} = \dfrac{4.2 \text{ minutes}}{1.6 \text{ minutes}} = 2.625 \text{ (round up to 3)}$

Station	Time Left*	Eligible	Will Fit	Assign Task (Time)	Station Idle Time
1	1.6	a, b	a, b	b(.6)	
	1.0	a, d	a	a(.3)	
	.7	c, d	c	c(.4)	
	.3	e, d	e	e(.2)	
	.1	g, d	g	g(.1)	
	.0	d	—	—	.0
2	1.6	d	d	d(1.2)	
	.4	f	—	—	.4
3	1.6	f	f	f(.6)	
	1.0	h	h	h(.5)	
	.5	i	i	i(.3)	
	.2	—	—	—	.2
					.6

*The initial time for each station is the cycle time calculated in part *a*.

The resulting assignments are shown below.

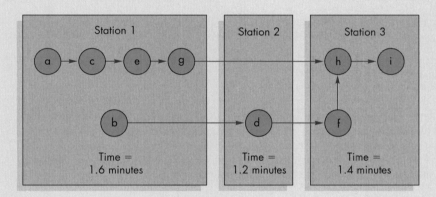

Assign nine automobile service departments to bays in a 3 × 3 grid so that the closeness ratings in the following matrix are satisfied. Only A and X ratings are shown. The location of department 4 must be in the middle right-hand side of the grid.   **Problem 2**

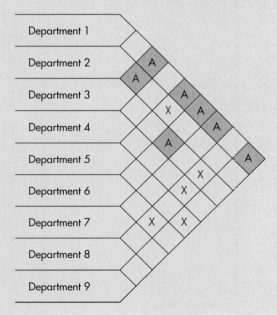

Solution

Note that department 1 has many A ratings, making it a strong candidate for the centre position in the graph. We can form a cluster of departments that should be close together:

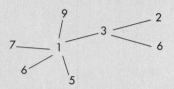

Next, we can identify departmental pairings that should be avoided:

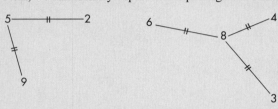

These departments should be spaced around the perimeter of the grid. After a bit of trial and error, the final grid shown below emerges. Check it against the graph to see if it satisfies the ratings.

2	3	6
9	1	4
8	7	5

Problem 3

Five departments are to be assigned to locations B–F in the grid below. (For technical reasons, department 6 must be assigned to location A.) Transportation cost is $2 per metre. The objective is to minimize total transportation cost. Information on from-to departmental work flows and distances between locations is shown in the following tables. Assign departments with the greatest interdepartmental work flow first. Calculate total transportation cost.

DISTANCE BETWEEN LOCATIONS (METRES)

From	To	A	B	C	D	E	F
A		—	50	100	50	80	130
B			—	50	90	40	70
C				—	140	60	50
D					—	50	120
E						—	50
F							—

NUMBER OF TRIPS PER DAY BETWEEN DEPARTMENTS

From	To	1	2	3	4	5	6
1		—	90	25	23	11	18
2		35	—	8	5	10	16
3		37	2	—	1	0	7
4		41	12	1	—	4	0
5		14	16	0	9	—	3
6		32	38	13	2	2	—

A Dept. 6	B	C
D	E	F

First, determine the total interdepartmental work flows (e.g., for 1–2 the flow is 90 + 35 = 125 *Solution* because the distances are symmetric). Then arrange them from high to low.

Pair of Dept.	Workflow
1–2	125
1–4	64
1–3	62
2–6	54
1–6	50
2–5	26
1–5	25
3–6	20
2–4	17
4–5	13
2–3	10
5–6	5
3–4	2
4–6	2
3–5	0

From this, we can see that departments 1 and 2 have the greatest interdepartmental work flow, so they should be closest, perhaps at B and E. However, since work flow between 2 and 6 is larger than between 1 and 6, place department 1 in location E and department 2 in location B. Next, work flow between 1 and 4 is highest. The work flow between 4 and 6 is low, suggesting that they need not be close. Therefore, place department 4 in F. Next, work flow between 1 and 3 is highest. Hence, place department 3 in location D. Finally, department 5 has to be placed at location C.

A Dept. 6	B Dept. 2	C Dept. 5
D Dept. 3	E Dept. 1	F Dept. 4

Total cost:

Pair of Dept.	b Distance		c Workflow	(b × c × $2) Cost
1–2	(B–E)	40	125	$10,000
1–3	(D–E)	50	62	6,200
1–4	(F–E)	50	64	6,400
1–5	(E–C)	60	25	3,000
1–6	(A–E)	80	50	8,000
2–3	(B–D)	90	10	1,800
2–4	(B–F)	70	17	2,380
2–5	(B–C)	50	26	2,600
2–6	(A–B)	50	54	5,400
3–4	(F–D)	120	2	480
3–5	(D–C)	140	0	0
3–6	(A–D)	50	20	2,000
4–5	(C–F)	50	13	1,300
4–6	(A–F)	130	2	520
5–6	(A–C)	100	5	1,000
				$51,080

DISCUSSION AND
REVIEW QUESTIONS

1. Explain the importance of process design.
2. Briefly describe the four basic process types and give a manufacturing example for each.
3. Give an example of each type of process in a service operation.
4. Briefly discuss the advantages and disadvantages of automation.
5. Briefly describe computer-aided approaches to production.
6. What is a numerically controlled machine?
7. What is the product-process matrix? What is its purpose?
8. Describe the approach for process design.
9. What is a process flow diagram?
10. What are the differences between product and service process design?
11. Describe the general approach for layout design.
12. Relate process and product layout to process types.
13. What are the main advantages of a product layout? The main disadvantages?
14. What are the main advantages of a process layout? The main disadvantages?
15. Why are routing and scheduling continual problems in process layouts?
16. Compare machine/equipment maintenance strategies in product and process layouts.
17. Briefly outline the impact that job processing sequence has on each of the layout types.
18. The City Transportation Planning Committee must decide whether to begin a long-term project to build a subway system or to upgrade the present bus service. Suppose you are an expert in fixed-path and variable-path material-handling equipment, and the committee seeks your counsel on this matter. What are the advantages and limitations of the subway and bus systems?
19. Why are product layouts atypical in service environments?
20. According to a study, it costs more than three times the original purchase price in parts and labour to replace a totally wrecked automobile. Explain the reasons for this large discrepancy in terms of the processes used to assemble the original car and those required to reconstruct the wrecked car.
21. Name some ways that a layout can help or hinder productivity.
22. What is a manufacturing cell? What are its main benefits and limitations?
23. What is group technology?
24. What is the goal of line balancing? What happens if a line is unbalanced?
25. Explain the consequences of task time variability on line balancing.
26. What is the objective of process layout?

TAKING STOCK

1. Name a major trade-off in process design.
2. What trade-offs are involved when deciding how often to rebalance an assembly line?
3. Who needs to be involved in process design?
4. Who needs to be involved in layout design?
5. In what ways does technology have an impact on process design? How can technology impact layout decisions?

CRITICAL THINKING EXERCISES

1. There are several factors that must exist in order to make automation feasible. Name one or two most important factors and briefly explain their importance.
2. Layout decisions affect a wide range of facilities, from factories, grocery stores, offices, department stores, and warehouses, to malls, parking lots and garages, and kitchens. Layout is also important in the design of some products such as the interiors of automobiles and the arrangement of components inside computers and other electronic devices. Select three different items from this list, or other similar items, and explain for each what the one or two key considerations for layout design are.

INTERNET EXERCISE

Visit the Web page of one of the following companies and draw their process flow diagram:

- Hershey's Chocolates   www.hersheys.com/discover/tour_video.asp
- Kalesnikoff Lumber   www.kalesnikoff.com/mill_tour/mill_tour1.htm
- Prestige Homes   www.prestigehomes.ca/homebuying/factory_tour/#photo-tour
- Guildcrest Homes   www.Guildcrest.com
- Tata Steel   www.tatasteel.com/steelmaking
- Dofasco   www.dofasco.ca/HOW_STEEL_IS_MADE/html
- Irving Paper   www.ifdn.com/paper/paper.htm
- CAMI   www.cami.ca/tour/camitour.shtml

PROBLEMS

1. An assembly line with 17 tasks is to be balanced. The longest task is 2.4 minutes, and the total time for all tasks is 18 minutes. The line will operate for 450 minutes per day.

   a. What are the minimum and maximum cycle times?

   b. What range of output is theoretically possible for the line?

   c. What is the minimum number of workstations needed if the maximum output rate is to be sought?

   d. What cycle time will provide an output rate of 125 units per day?

   e. What output will result if the cycle time is (1) 9 minutes? (2) 15 minutes?

2. A manager wants to assign tasks to workstations as efficiently as possible, and achieve an hourly output of $33\frac{1}{3}$ units. Assume that the shop works a 60-minute hour. Assign the tasks shown in the following precedence network (times are in minutes) to workstations using the following rules:

   a. In order of the task with most followers. Tiebreaker: the task with longest time.

   b. What is the efficiency?

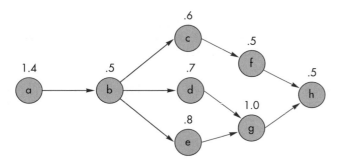

3. A manager wants to assign tasks to workstations as efficiently as possible, and achieve an hourly output of 4 units. The department uses a working time of 56 minutes per hour. Assign the tasks shown in the following precedence network (times are in minutes) to workstations using the following rules:

   a. In order of the task with most followers. Tiebreaker: the task with longest time. If a tie still exists, choose randomly.

   b. What is the efficiency?

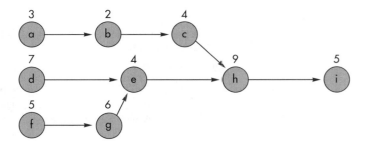

4. A large manufacturer of pencil sharpeners is planning to add a new line of sharpeners, and you have been asked to balance the process, given the following task times and precedence relationships. Assume that cycle time is to be the minimum possible.

Task	Length (minutes)	Immediate Follower
a	.2	b
b	.4	d
c	.3	d
d	1.3	g
e	.1	f
f	.8	g
g	.3	h
h	1.2	—

a. Do each of the following:
   (1) Draw the precedence network.
   (2) Assign tasks to stations in order of the task with most followers. Break ties using the task with longest time.
   (3) Determine the percentage idle time.
   (4) Calculate the rate of output that could be expected for this line assuming a 420-minute working day.

b. Answer these questions:
   (1) What is the shortest cycle time that will permit use of only two workstations? Is this cycle time feasible? Identify the tasks you would assign to each station.
   (2) Determine the percentage idle time that would result if two stations were used.
   (3) What is the daily output under this arrangement?

5. As part of a major plant renovation project, the industrial engineering department has been asked to balance a revised assembly operation to achieve an output of 240 units per eight-hour day. Task times and precedence relationships are as follows:

Task	Duration (minutes)	Precedes Task
a	.2	b
b	.4	c
c	.2	f
d	.4	e
e	1.2	g
f	1.2	g
g	1.0	—

Do each of the following:
a. Draw the precedence network.
b. Determine the required cycle time.
c. Determine the minimum number of stations needed.
d. Assign tasks to workstations on the basis of the task with most followers. Use the task with longest time as a tiebreaker. If a tie still exists, choose randomly.
e. Calculate the percentage idle time for the assignments in part d.

6. Twelve tasks, with times and precedence requirements as shown in the following table, are to be assigned to workstations using a cycle time of 1.5 minutes. Heuristic rule the task with most followers will be tried. The tiebreaker will be the task with longest time.

Task	Length (minutes)	Follows Task	Task	Length (minutes)	Follows Task
a	.1	—	g	.4	f
b	.2	a	h	.1	g
c	.9	b	i	.2	h
d	.6	c	j	.7	i
e	.1	—	k	.3	j
f	.2	d, e	l	.2	k

    a. Draw the precedence network for this line.

    b. Assign tasks to stations.

    c. Calculate the percentage idle time.

7. For the following tasks:

    a. Develop the precedence network.

    b. Determine the cycle time (in seconds) for a desired output of 500 units in a 7-hour day.

    c. Determine the minimum number of workstations for output of 500 units per day.

    d. Balance the line using the task with most followers heuristic. Break ties with the task with longest time heuristic. Use a cycle time of 50 seconds.

    e. Calculate the percentage idle time for the line.

Task	Task Time (seconds)	Immediate Predecessors
A	45	—
B	11	A
C	9	B
D	50	—
E	26	D
F	11	E
G	12	C
H	10	C
I	9	F, G, H
J	10	I
	193	

8. A shop works a 400-minute day. The manager of the shop wants an output of 200 units per day for the assembly line that has the tasks shown in the following table. Do the following:

    a. Construct the precedence network and calculate the cycle time.

    b. Assign tasks according to the task with most followers rule. In the case of a tie, use the task with longest time rule.

    c. Calculate the balance delay.

Task	Immediately Precedes Task(s)	Task Time
a	b, c, d	.5
b	e	1.4
c	e	1.2
d	f	.7
e	g, j	.5
f	i	1.0
g	h	.4
h	k	.3
i	j	.5
j	k	.8
k	m	.9
m	—	.3

9. Arrange six departments into a 2 × 3 grid so that these conditions are satisfied: 1 close to 2, 5 close to 2, 4, and 6, and 3 not close to 1 or 2.

10. Using the information given in the preceding problem, develop a Muther-type grid using the letters A and X. Leave any pair of combinations not mentioned blank.

11. Using the information in the following grid, determine the department locations on the following format. Note that departments 1 and 7 must be in the locations shown.

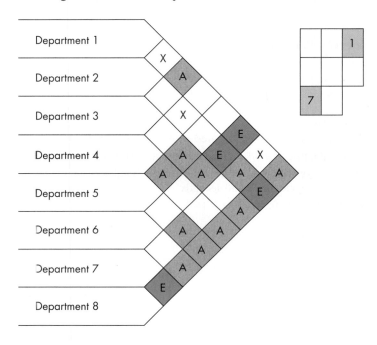

12. Arrange the eight departments shown in the following Muther grid into a 2 × 4 format. *Note*: Department 2 must be in the location shown.

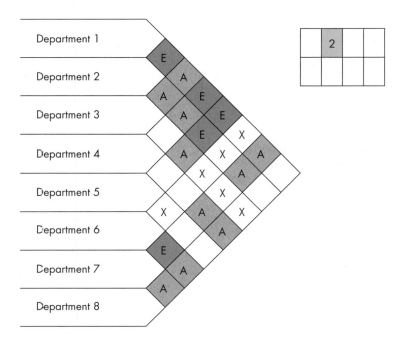

13. Arrange nine departments into a 3 × 3 format so they satisfy the conditions shown in the following Muther grid. Place department 5 in the lower left corner of the 3 × 3 grid.

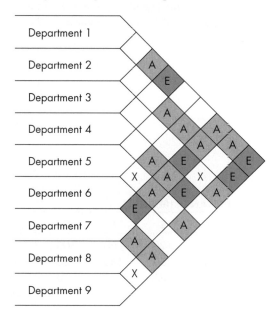

14. Determine the placement of departments for a newly designed facility that will minimize total transportation cost using the data in the following tables. Assume that reverse distances are the same. The locations are shown below. Use a cost of $1 per trip metre. Use the heuristic method of Example 10.

Location A	Location B	Location C
	Location D	

DISTANCE BETWEEN LOCATIONS (METRES)

From	To	A	B	C	D
A		—	40	80	70
B			—	40	50
C				—	60
D					—

NUMBER OF TRIPS PER DAY BETWEEN DEPARTMENTS

From	To	1	2	3	4
1		—	10	20	30
2			—	40	40
3				—	25
4		50	50	30	—

15. Eight work centres must be arranged in an L-shaped building. The locations of work centres 1 and 3 have already been assigned as shown in the following diagram. Assuming that transportation costs are $1 per load per metre, develop a suitable layout that minimizes total transportation cost using the information given below. (Assume the reverse distances are the same.) Use the heuristic method of Example 10.

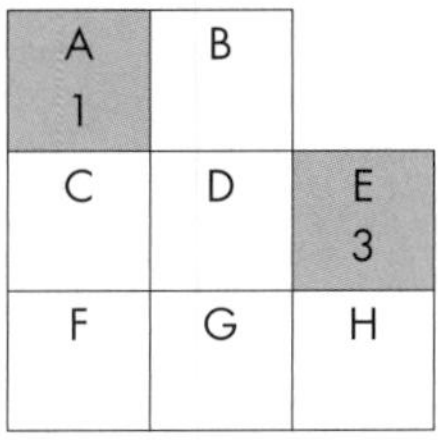

A 1	B	
C	D	E 3
F	G	H

DISTANCE (METRES)

From \ To	A	B	C	D	E	F	G	H
A	—	40	40	60	120	80	100	110
B		—	60	40	60	140	120	130
C			—	45	85	40	70	90
D				—	40	50	40	45
E					—	90	50	40
F						—	40	60
G							—	40
H								—

LOADS PER DAY

From \ To	1	2	3	4	5	6	7	8
1	—	10	5	90	365	135	125	0
2	0	—	140	10	0	35	0	120
3	0	220	—	110	10	0	0	200
4	0	110	240	—	10	0	0	170
5	5	40	100	180	—	10	40	10
6	0	80	40	70	0	—	10	20
7	0	45	20	50	0	40	—	20
8	0	0	0	20	0	0	0	—

16. Develop a process layout that will minimize the total distance travelled by patients at a medical clinic, using the following information on projected interdepartmental visits by patients and distance between locations. Assume a distance of 35 feet between the reception area and each other location A to F. Assume the reverse distances are the same. Use the floor space shown on the next page.

DISTANCE BETWEEN LOCATIONS (FEET)

From \ To	A	B	C	D	E	F
A	—	20	60	80	120	160
B		—	40	60	80	120
C			—	40	60	80
D				—	40	60
E					—	40
F						—

		TRIPS BETWEEN DEPARTMENTS (PER DAY)						
From	**To**	**1**	**2**	**3**	**4**	**5**	**6**	**Reception**
Reception		10	10	200	20	0	100	—
1		—	0	0	80	20	40	10
2		0	—	0	0	0	20	40
3		40	0	—	10	190	10	10
4		30	50	0	—	10	70	0
5		60	40	60	30	—	20	10
6		10	100	0	20	0	—	30

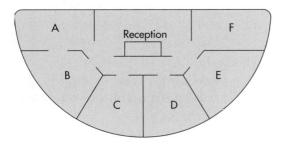

17. Ten labs should be assigned to the circular layout shown below. Recalling a similar layout's congestion in the halls, the new lab manager has requested an assignment that will minimize traffic between offices, but movement in the halls is restricted to a counterclockwise route. Develop a suitable layout using the following information. Assign Lab 1 to Location A, Lab 2 to Location I, and Lab 8 to Location E.

		NUMBER OF TRIPS PER DAY BETWEEN LABS									
From	**To**	**1**	**2**	**3**	**4**	**5**	**6**	**7**	**8**	**9**	**10**
1		—	40	1	20	20	4	0	2	6	5
2		0	—	2	15	25	10	2	12	13	6
3		50	35	—	10	13	4	0	4	7	1
4		6	1	8	—	0	14	10	20	22	11
5		3	2	7	35	—	22	5	9	19	10
6		5	5	10	0	2	—	15	0	1	20
7		20	16	50	4	9	2	—	1	3	0
8		10	6	14	2	4	44	13	—	1	25
9		5	5	18	1	2	40	30	42	—	32
10		30	30	35	20	15	5	40	10	15	—

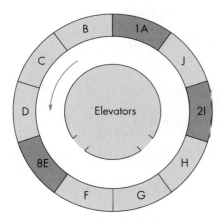

18. For the process of conducting a bank transaction using a teller in your bank:
    a. Draw a process flow diagram. Fail-safe this process.
    b. Use IDEF method to design this process.

19. Draw a process flow diagram for customer service/eating in a full-service restaurant.

20. Draw a process flow diagram for preparing a tax return.

21. Draw a process flow diagram for mass producing potato chips.

22. The tasks performed in a cafeteria and their average service times are as follows:

Tasks	Service Time Per Customer (seconds)
Serve vegetables	25
Serve entree	30
Serve soup	20
Serve dessert	15
Serve drink	10
Collect money	60

The only precedence relationship is that "collect money" has to be last. The current layout performs these tasks in the sequence given; each task is performed by one worker except that only one worker serves both dessert and drink.

  a. 1. Draw the precedence network.
      2. What is the maximum number of customers who can be served per hour (capacity) using the current layout?
      3. Assuming that capacity in 2 above equals desired output, what are the Cycle Time CT and minimum number of workstations (workers) N_{min} needed?
      4. Suppose that capacity has to be increased. Where can the sixth worker be employed, assuming that equipment is not a constraint?
      5. How can we keep the same number of workers (5) but change the process in order to increase the capacity?
  b. Using Cycle Time = 35 seconds and the task with longest time rule, balance the assembly line and calculate the percentage idle time.

23. Suppose you need to assemble 72 Quickline Guest tables in one hour (see photos on the next page). The assembly activities and their standard times are listed below. Using common sense, draw a precedence network and calculate the cycle time. Then, perform assembly line balancing using the task with longest time rule, breaking ties using the task with most followers rule. Any further ties can be broken randomnly.

Activity		Standard Time (seconds)
A.	Lay the top face down on a clean surface	10
B_1.	Attach a mounting bracket to a corner of the top using three screws	35
C_1.	Add a compression ring on the bracket	5
D_1.	Slide one end of a leg over the compression ring and turn it so that the hole is aligned with the Allen screw	10
E_1.	Tighten the screw with Allen wrench	15
B_2.	Attach another mounting bracket to another corner of top using three screws	35
C_2.	Add another compression ring	5
D_2.	Slide one end of another leg over the compression ring and turn it	10
E_2.	Tighten with Allen wrench	15
B_3.	Attach another mounting bracket to another corner of top using three screws	35
C_3.	Add another compression ring	5
D_3.	Slide end of another leg over the compression ring and turn it	10
E_3.	Tighten with Allen wrench	15
B_4.	Attach another mounting bracket to another corner of top using three screws	35
C_4.	Add another compression ring	5
D_4.	Slide end of another leg over the compression ring and turn it	10
E_4.	Tighten with Allen wrench	15
F.	Turn the table over on its legs	30

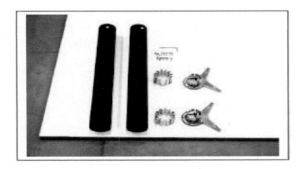

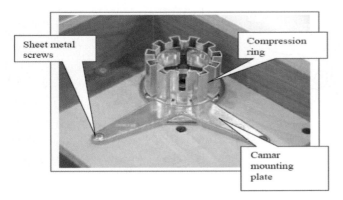

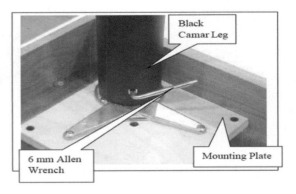

Images courtesy of Harris Corporation

24. Consider the Scoot & Go Rider shown on the next page) made by the Processed Plastic Company (PPC). Suppose that PPC has received a rush order from Wal-Mart for 8,800 units to be shipped in five days.

   a. Assuming 16 hour workdays, calculate the cycle time.

   b. Start with the body on the table, and assume all parts are within reach. Also assume that the steering wheel subassembly has already been made. Using common sense, draw a precedence network for the following activities which are required to assemble a Scoot & Go Rider.

	Activity	Standard time (seconds)
a.	Insert the steering wheel subassembly in the body	7
b.	Hammer the front (short) axle into a palnut (using the palnut tool)	10
c.	Slide a wheel in the component resulting from *b*	5
d.	Pass component resulting from *c* through the steering shaft hole	5
e.	Slide a wheel into component resulting from *d*	4
f.	Hammer the component resulting from *e* into a palnut (using the palnut tool)	12
g.	Hammer the rear (long) axle into a palnut (using the palnut tool)	10
h.	Slide a wheel in the component resulting from *g*	6
i.	Pass component resulting from *h* through the body's rear axle holes	7
j.	Slide a wheel into component resulting from *i*	4
k.	Hammer the component resulting from *j* into a palnut (using the palnut tool)	13
l.	Place walker bar on the body and attach using one screw	15
m.	Insert another screw into walker bar to attach it to the body	11
n.	Insert another screw into walker bar to attach it to the body	11
o.	Insert another screw into walker bar to attach it to the body	11
p.	Perform final quality check and box it	30

   c. If the Cycle time is 33 seconds, theoretically what is the minimum number of workstations needed?

d. Perform assembly line balancing using 33 seconds cycle time, the standard times and the precedence network from Part *b*. Use the task with longest time rule, breaking ties using the task with most followers rule. Any further ties can be broken arbitrarily.

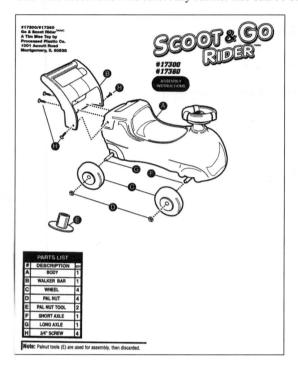

#	DESCRIPTION	qty
A	BODY	1
B	WALKER BAR	1
C	WHEEL	4
D	PAL NUT	4
E	PAL NUT TOOL	2
F	SHORT AXLE	1
G	LONG AXLE	1
H	3/4" SCREW	4

Note: Palnut tools (E) are used for assembly, then discarded.

READING

Jubilee Ford

www.jubileeford.com

Jubilee Ford is a large Ford dealer in Saskatoon. In addition to selling new cars, it services Ford cars and sells car parts. Jubilee Ford recently moved into a 68,000-ft² facility that has 39 stalls for service and 26 stalls for body shop; however, the building is shared with the Jaguar and Volvo dealerships.

In the service department, there are 23 stalls used by Ford, 1 service manager, 4 service advisers, 1 tower dispatcher, and 16 technicians. There are 15 skill groups such as electrical, mechanical, transmission, diesel, trim, front end, glass, remote starts, and so on.

The service process starts with the customer calling a service adviser to book an appointment. When the car is brought in (usually early in the morning), a service adviser obtains all personal customer information and car problem/work needed information from the customer. He/she can assist in discovering the problem, if any, but in some cases a technician will have to later diagnose the problem. The information is entered in Ford's Servus AS400 computer network, and a hard copy of the work order is printed, which the customer signs. The customer then leaves the car and its keys with the service adviser and departs.

The service adviser passes the work order to the tower dispatcher. He is the production controller in the service shop. The dispatcher enters the car information and the promised due date/time in System 2000 (a different software program used by the dispatcher to keep track of jobs in the shop). He assigns the job to the appropriate technician in the priority that he determines. After the job is done, a brief report is written on

the work order and this is passed back to the dispatcher, who will deliver it to the service adviser. The customer is contacted who will come to pay the bill and pick up his/her car.

At the end of the day, each technician will fill in a time ticket that lists all the jobs he/she performed. The technicians are paid according to a predetermined time standard for each job.

If there is a need for diagnosis of a problem, the technician will identify the problem and notify the service adviser, who will contact the customer and ask for a decision. The service manager is generally involved with the administration of the service department.

The parts department aims to carry about $600,000 worth of inventory and works toward turning over each part once a month. The regular automated weekly stock orders from Ford's Edmonton Depot receives a price discount. Rush next-day orders do not.

The body shop has 18 stalls, 3 painters, 4 body staff, 2 support staff, and 2 office staff. They use a different inventory system, and their inventory is worth approximately $25,000. Many items are used on consignment from the suppliers.

Jubilee Ford is working toward standardizing many procedures and processes such as order receiving and claims of warrantee repair expenses from Ford.

Questions

1. Draw the process flow diagram for a car service. Fail-safe it.

2. What is the process type for the service department?

3. What function does the dispatcher perform, and why is it important?

Source: Based on a term paper by Phillip Wyant and Grady Brown (Phillip is the son of Jubilee Ford owner Vaughn Wyant).

MINI-CASE

The Double-D Cell

Sometimes converting an assembly line into two or more manufacturing cells will actually reduce the manpower requirements. Such was the case in the hardware (mechanical parts) subassembly of recliners in the Franklin Corp. plant in Houston, Mississippi.

The Initial Subassembly Frames (ISF) were assembled by four workers. Then, the ISFs were stored in the ISF queue until they were needed by the circular line, at which time a material handler mounted ISFs on wheeled tables, which were secured to the outer ring of the line with rollers (see photo on the left). Five workers worked inside the ring. The cycle time in the ring was approximately 30 seconds, but there was a total of 35 seconds of idle time per subassembly assembled in the ring. There were four types of subassemblies but they were similar.

In order to improve the efficiency of the circular line, Double-D layout was proposed (see photo on the right):

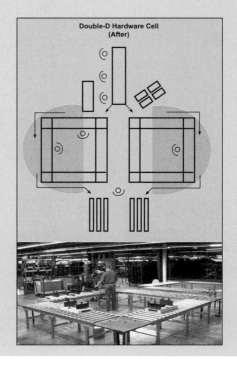

Questions

1. What are the advantages of the Double-D cells over the circular line?

2. Suppose that the task times of the five workstations in the ring were 30, 25, 20, 20, and 20 seconds, respectively.

Explain how four workers, two in each D, can produce the same output as the five workers in the ring.

Source: www.cfr.msstate.edu/fwrc/doubled.pdf

MINI-CASE

School Chairs

Recently school chairs are made of plastic and metal, costing anywhere from $30 to $100 each. You wish to evaluate the idea of manufacturing wooden chairs for sale to schools, churches, etc. You have found the following design for a chair.

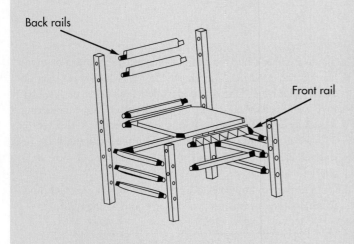

Back rails

Front rail

Most wooden chairs are made of hardwoods such as oak, maple, cherry, or cedar. Suppose that cedar is cheaper where you live. The dimensions of the parts of the chair are as follows:

Item	Number	Dimension (inches) (thickness, width, length)
Back post	2	2 × 2 × 36
Front post	2	2 × 2 × 18
Crossbar	10	1 × 1 × 14
Rails	3	2 × 1 × 14
Seat	1	1 × 16 ×16

The most economical size of cedar lumber is 2" × 4" × 8'. Therefore, you intend to buy only this size.

a. Calculate the number of this lumber you will need per chair.

b. Determine the operations needed to make the chair and draw a process flow diagram. Note that the crossbars and rails have a tenon (a small round tip) on each end which will go in the mortise (the hole) of the posts. These have to be made. Also, the seat's corners have to be cut to allow for the posts.

Source: Based on H. Quesada and R. Gazo, "Development of a Manufacturing System for Construction of School Furniture," *Forest Products Journal* 53(9), September 2003, pp. 47–54.

SELECTED BIBLIOGRAPHY AND FURTHER READING

Bolwijn, P. T., and T. Kumpe. "Manufacturing in the 1990's—Productivity, Flexibility, and Innovation." *Long Range Planning* 23(4), 1990, pp. 44–57.

Chase, R. B., et al. *Operations Management for Competitive Advantage*, 10th ed. New York: McGraw-Hill Irwin, 2004.

Cohen, Morris, and Uday M. Apte. *Manufacturing Automation*. Burr Ridge, IL: Richard D. Irwin, 1997.

Ettlie, John, and Henry Stoll. *Managing the Design-Manufacturing Process*. New York: McGraw-Hill, 1990.

Francis, Richard L., Leon F. McGinnis Jr., and John A. White. *Facility Layout and Location: An Analytical Approach*. 3rd ed. Englewood Cliffs, NJ: Prentice Hall, 1998.

Gaither, N., and G, Frazier. *Operations Management*, 9th ed. Cincinnati: South-Western, 2002.

Groover, Mikell P. *Automation, Production Systems, and Computer-Aided Manufacturing*, 2nd ed. Englewood Cliffs, NJ: Prentice Hall, 2001.

Hill, Terry. *Manufacturing Strategy*, 3rd ed. Burr Ridge, IL: Richard D. Irwin, 2001.

Kilbridge, M. D., and L. Wester. "A Heuristic Method of Assembly Line Balancing." *Journal of Industrial Engineering* 12, July–August 1961.

Mathaisel, D. F. X., et al. "Meeting the Competitive Challenge," *Industrial Engineering* 37(1), January 2005, pp. 39–45.

McDermott, J. "Effective Shop Layout." *Cabinetmaker* 14(8), July 2000, pp. 48–53.

Milas, Gene H. "Assembly Line Balancing ... Let's Remove the Mystery." *Industrial Engineering*, May 1990, pp. 31–36.

Monroe, Joseph. "Strategic Use of Technology." *California Management Review*, Summer 1989, pp. 91–110.

Muther, R., and K. McPherson. "Four Approaches to Computerized Layout Planning." *Industrial Engineering* 2, 1970, pp. 39–42.

Schmenner, R. G. *Production/Operations Management*, 5th ed. NY: Macmillan, 1993.

Shunk, Dan L. *Integrated Process Design and Development.* Burr Ridge, IL: Business One Irwin, 1992.

Stauffer, Robert. "Lessons Learned in Implementing New Technology." *Manufacturing Engineer*, June 1989.

Upton, David. "The Management of Manufacturing Flexibility." *California Management Review* 36(2), 1994, pp. 72–89.

Upton, David. "What Really Makes Factories Flexible." *Harvard Business Review*, July–August 1995, pp. 74–84.

To access "Linear Programming," the supplement to Chapter 6, please visit the student **DVD** packaged with the text or the Online Learning Centre at **www.mcgrawhill.ca/olc/stevenson**

Design of Work Systems

W ork required from an employee directly affects his/her satisfaction with the job, which in turn affects how he/she treats company's customers. Therefore, work design is very important. Companies such as Decoma have happy employees. On the other hand, efficiency and productivity also directly affect a company's competitiveness. Companies such as Bombardier are efficient and productive. How do these companies design work for their employees to achieve success? Questions such as this are answered in this chapter.

INTRODUCTION

This chapter covers work system design. Work system design involves *job design*, *work measurement* and establishment of time standards, and *compensation*.

As you read this chapter, note how decisions in other design areas have an impact on work systems, and how decisions on work systems have an impact on the other areas. For example, product or service design decisions (e.g., operate a coal mine, offer computer dating service, sell sports equipment) in large measure determine the kinds of activities workers will be involved with. Similarly, layout decisions often influence work systems. Process layouts tend to necessitate broader job content than product layouts. The implication of these interrelationships is that it is essential to adopt a systems approach to design; decisions in one area must be related to the overall system.

The importance of work system design is underscored by the organization's dependence on human efforts (i.e., work) to accomplish its goals. Work design is one of the oldest aspects of operations management. In the past, it has often been de-emphasized in operations management courses in favour of other topics. Recent years, however, have seen renewed interest that has come from somewhat different directions: Some of the interest has resulted from studies that reveal a general dissatisfaction felt by many workers with their jobs. And some of the interest has been sparked by increasing concerns over productivity.

JOB DESIGN

job design The act of specifying the contents and methods of job.

Job design involves specifying the content and methods of job. Job designers focus on *what* will be done in a job, and *how* the job will be done. The objectives of job design include productivity, safety, and quality of work life. In this section, we will describe two approaches to job design (the efficiency school and the behavioural school), explain behavioural approaches and teams. We will start the efficiency approach and describe specialization, methods analysis and motion study. Finally, effects of working conditions on work is explained.

The factors that affect job design and the implications of various alternatives are often so complex that a person without a good background in job design is likely to overlook important aspects of it. Workers and managers alike should be consulted in order to take advantage of their knowledge and to keep them informed. Because they are intimately involved with the work, employees can be a source of valuable ideas for job improvements. Managerial support for job design depends on the commitment and involvement of managers. It is usually easier to sell a design to these two groups if they have been included in the process.

Current practice in job design contains elements of two basic schools of thought. One might be called the *efficiency* school because it emphasizes a systematic, logical approach to job design emphasizing labour cost reduction; the other is called the *behavioural* school because it emphasizes satisfaction of wants and needs.

The efficiency approach, a refinement of Frederick Winslow Taylor's scientific management concepts, received considerable emphasis in the past. The behavioural approach emerged during the 1950s and has continued to make inroads into many aspects

TABLE 7-1

Major advantages and disadvantages of specialization in business

Advantages	
For management:	For blue-collar labour:
1. Simplifies training	1. Low education and skill requirements
2. High productivity	2. Minimum responsibilities
3. Low wage costs	3. Little mental effort needed

Disadvantages	
For management:	For blue-collar labour:
1. Difficult to motivate quality	1. Monotonous work
2. Worker dissatisfaction, possibly resulting in absenteeism, high turnover, disruptive tactics	2. Limited opportunities for advancement
	3. Little control over work
	4. Little opportunity for self-fulfillment

of job design. The main contribution of the behavioural approach is that it has reminded managers of the complexity of human beings, and that the efficiency approach may not be appropriate in every instance. It is noteworthy that specialization is a primary issue of disagreement between the efficiency and behavioural approaches.

specialization Work that concentrates on a narrow aspect of a product or service.

The term **specialization** describes jobs that have a very narrow scope. Examples range from assembly lines to medical specialties. College professors often specialize in teaching certain courses, some auto mechanics specialize in transmission repair, and some bakers specialize in wedding cakes. The main rationale for specialization is the ability to concentrate one's efforts and thereby become proficient at that type of work.

Sometimes the amount of knowledge or training required of a specialist and the complexity of the work suggest that individuals who choose such work are very happy with their jobs. This seems to be especially true in the "professions" (e.g., doctors, lawyers, professors). At the other end of the scale are assembly-line workers, who are also specialists, although their job is much less glamorous. The advantage of these highly specialized jobs is that they yield high productivity and low unit costs.

Unfortunately, many of these jobs can be monotonous or downright boring, and they are the source of much of the dissatisfaction among industrial workers today. Even so, it would be wrong to conclude that all workers oppose this type of work. Some workers undoubtedly prefer a job with limited requirements and responsibility for making decisions. The advantages and disadvantages of specialization are summarized in Table 7–1.

The seriousness of the problems with specialization caused job designers and others to seek ways of alleviating them. Some of those approaches are discussed in the following section.

Behavioural Approaches to Job Design

In an effort to make jobs more interesting and meaningful, job designers frequently consider job enlargement, job rotation, and job enrichment.

job enlargement Giving a worker a larger portion of the total task.

Job enlargement means giving a worker a larger portion of the total task. This constitutes *horizontal loading*—the additional work is on the same level of skill and responsibility as the original job. The goal is to make the job more interesting by increasing the variety of skills required and by providing the worker with a more recognizable contribution to the overall output. For example, a production worker's job might be expanded so that he or she is responsible for a *sequence* of activities instead of only one activity.

job rotation Workers periodically exchange jobs.

Job rotation means having workers periodically exchange jobs. A firm can use this approach to avoid having one or a few employees stuck in monotonous jobs. It works best when workers can be transferred to more interesting jobs; there is little advantage in having workers exchange one boring job for another. Job rotation allows workers to broaden their learning experience and enables them to fill in for others in the event of sickness or absenteeism.

READING

Examples of Workplace Innovation

Two examples of job enlargement are:

- H. J. Heinz Co. of Canada, Leamington, Ontario—Within the can fill, general fill, and cereal departments, established 13 new maintenance/line operator positions to perform normal maintenance work and replace a regular position on the line when required.

- City of Winnipeg—Eliminated the distinction between welders and blacksmiths by forming a single classification and expanded the scope of body repairman to include vehicle frame straightening and vehicle painting.

An example of job rotation is:

- Hershey Canada, Smiths Falls, Ontario—Operators in the wrapping, bagging, and Glosettes areas rotate jobs within their line team every half hour, and line teams rotate across these three areas every week.

An example of job enrichment is:

- Shell Refinery, East Montreal—Position of supervising operator became part of the operators. Thus, an operator performs minor maintenance work, completes time sheets, plans job rotation, decides on overtime, prepares vacation schedules, drafts operations and training manuals (replacing engineers), participates in reliability groups and planning of production shutdowns, and provides training.

Sources: S. Payette, "What's New in Workplace Innovations?," *Workplace Gazette* 3(1), 2000, pp. 110–118; Labour–Management Partnerships Program, "Workplace Innovation Experiences," *Workplace Gazette* 1(2), 1998, pp. 65–71; M. J. Delorme and J. G. Bergeron, "Work Reorganization at the East Montreal Shell Refinery, 1989–1998," *Workplace Gazette* 2(2), 1999, pp. 46–54.

Job enrichment involves an increase in the level of responsibility for planning and coordination. It is sometimes referred to as *vertical loading*. An example of this is to have stock clerks in supermarkets handle reordering of goods, thus increasing their responsibilities.

job enrichment Increasing responsibility for planning and coordination.

The importance of these approaches to job design is that they have the potential to increase the motivational power of jobs by increasing worker satisfaction through improvement in the *quality of work life*. For some examples of these approaches, see the readings, "Examples of Workplace Innovation" and "Flexible Working Time Arrangements."

People work for a variety of reasons. And although compensation is often the leading reason, it is not the only reason. Other reasons include socialization, self-actualization, status, the physiological aspects of work, and a sense of purpose and accomplishment. Awareness of these factors can help management develop a motivational framework that encourages workers to respond in a positive manner to the goals of the organization.

READING

Flexible Working Time Arrangements

Workers are demanding—and receiving—more flexible, family-friendly job arrangements. These include flexible work hours, using overtime, job sharing, and compressed workweeks. More workers are now entitled to use their overtime hours later for extended paid holidays (e.g., Hudson Bay Mining and Smelting, Dairyworld Foods). Some companies allow job sharing (e.g., Connaught Labs), where two employees performing similar duties can share one full-time position. Employees of some companies, such as Hydro Quebec and City of Montreal, are entitled to a flexible work schedule, with variable start and finish times, as long as core hours are covered. Full-time employees of some companies such as Bell Canada and Saskatchewan Crop Insurance are eligible for telework (i.e., working from home); the companies assume the cost of equipment and furniture if there is an enclosed and safe working area at home. Voluntary reduction in hours of the workweek is possible in some companies such as AT&T Canada. In BC Hydro, the workweek can be reduced to 35 hours.

Source: N. Boudreault and T. Plante, "Organization of Working Time—Job Sharing, Flexible Hours and Overtime, Right to Refuse and Compensatory Leave—in Major Collective Agreements, by Major Industry in Canada, in June 1988 and January 1998," *Workplace Gazette* 3(1), 2000, pp. 44–48.

Teams

The efforts of business organizations to become more productive, competitive, and customer-oriented have caused them to rethink how work is accomplished. A significant change in the structure of some work environments has been the increasing use of teams.

In the past, nonroutine job assignments, such as dealing with customer complaints or improving a process, were typically given to one individual. More recently, nonroutine assignments are being given to teams who develop and implement solutions to problems. Responsibility for the work is shared among team members, who often decide among themselves how the work is to be accomplished.

self-directed teams Groups empowered to make certain changes in their work processes.

Self-directed teams, sometimes referred to as *self-managed teams*, achieve a higher level of teamwork and employee involvement. Although such teams are not given absolute authority to make all decisions, they are typically empowered to make changes in the work processes under their control. The underlying concept is that the workers, who are close to the process and have the best knowledge of it, are better suited than management to make the most effective changes to improve the process. Moreover, because they have a vested interest and personal involvement in the changes, they tend to work harder to ensure that the desired results are achieved. For these teams to function properly, team members must be trained in new skills, including communication and leadership. Self-directed teams have a number of benefits. One is that fewer managers are necessary. Also, self-directed teams can provide improved responsiveness to problems, and they require less time to implement improvements.

Generally, the benefits of teams include higher quality, higher productivity, and greater worker satisfaction. However, middle managers often feel threatened as teams assume more of their traditional functions.

Methods Analysis

methods analysis Analyzing how a job is done.

Methods analysis focuses on how a job is done and tries to make it more efficient.

If methods analysis is done for an existing job, the procedure is to have the analyst observe the job as it is currently being performed and then devise improvements. For a new job, the analyst must rely on the method being used for similar jobs.

The basic procedure in methods analysis is:

1. Identify the job to be studied and gather all pertinent facts about operations, machines, equipment, materials, and so on.
2. Discuss the job with the operator and supervisor.
3. Study and document the present method of performing the job.
4. Analyze and question the present method.
5. Propose a new method.

Analyzing and questioning the method and proposing a new method requires careful thought about the what, why, when, where, and who of the job. Often, simply going through these questions will clarify the review process by encouraging the analyst to take a devil's advocate attitude toward both present and proposed methods. Frequently, technology assists in methods improvements; see the reading, "Sobeys Reorganizes" for two examples.

Analyzing and improving methods is facilitated by the use of various charts, such as *process charts* and *worker–machine charts*.

process chart Chart used to examine the overall sequence of an operation by focusing on movements of the operator or flow of materials.

Process charts are used to review and critically examine the overall sequence of an operation by focusing on the movements of the operator or the flow of materials. These charts are helpful in identifying nonproductive parts of the process (e.g., delays, temporary storages, distances travelled). Figure 7–1 illustrates a process chart for "Requisitioning of petty cash" in a company.

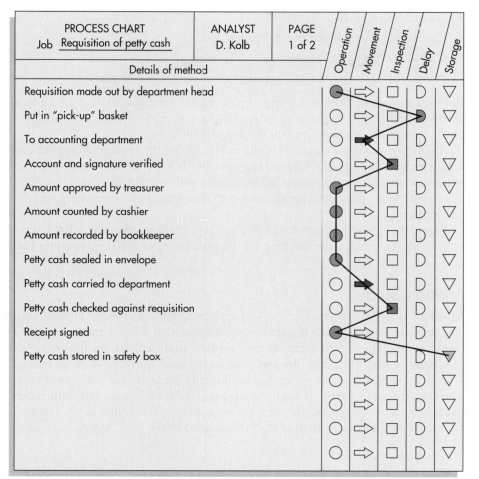

FIGURE 7-1

Example of a process chart

Source: Elias M. Awad, *Systems Analysis and Design,* 4th ed. (Burr Ridge, IL: Richard D. Irwin, 1985), p. 113. © 1985 by Richard D. Irwin, Inc. Reprinted by permission of the McGraw-Hill Companies Inc.

READING

Sobeys Reorganizes

When Sobeys bought the Oshawa Group in 1998, the food distribution centre in North Montreal, which supplies IGA and small independent chains, was already in the middle of work reorganization to streamline the supply chain and increase its operating efficiency. Five joint union–management improvement committees were formed: Technology Change and Working Methods; Perishable Sector; Non-perishable Sector; Transportation; and Occupational Health and Safety. One of the projects was the job assignment activity done at the beginning of each night shift. The assignment was done based on seniority; because the volume and type of work varied every night, it took approximately 30 minutes.

The new approach uses a job assignment software that takes only five minutes to run.

Another new work procedure concerns the job of order pickers. Before, they were given a customer order list showing the names of items and the number of cases to pick from each location in the warehouse. A minimum of 145 pickups per hour in the grocery section and 130 in the frozen section was required. The order pickers, using their pallet jacks, raced through the aisles of warehouse, following their own chosen routes; this resulted in accidents and errors. Sobeys installed a computer order-picking system that directs each order picker to his/her next pickup position and specifies the standard time for doing so.

Source: M. Brossard, "Reorganizing the Sobeys Distribution Centre in Montreal," *Workplace Gazette* 4(2), 2001, pp. 34–43.

Experienced analysts usually develop a checklist of questions they ask themselves to generate ideas for improvements. Some representative questions are:

1. Why is there a delay, storage, or inspection at this point?
2. How can travel distances be shortened or avoided?

3. Can an operation be eliminated?

4. Can the sequence of operations be changed?

5. Can similar activities be grouped?

6. Would the use of additional or improved equipment be helpful?

For the example of "Requisitioning of petty cash," after considering the amount of work involved and the high frequency of requisitions, a solution may be to issue a corporate credit card (with a certain limit) to the department head.

A **worker–machine chart** is helpful in visualizing the portions of a work cycle during which an operator and machine are busy or idle. The analyst can easily see when the operator and machine are working independently and when their work overlaps or is interdependent. One use of this type of chart is to determine how many machines the operator can manage.

Figure 7–2 presents an example of a worker–machine chart for weighing and pricing bulk food. As evident, the machine can be used by more than one operator because it is idle most of the time.

Motion Study

Motion study is the systematic study of the human motions used to perform an operation. The purpose is to eliminate unnecessary motions and to identify the best sequence of motions for maximum efficiency. Hence, motion study can be an important avenue for productivity improvements. Present practice evolved from the work of Frank Gilbreth, who originated the concepts in the bricklaying trade in the early twentieth century. Through the use of motion study techniques, Gilbreth is credited with increasing the average number of bricks laid per hour by a factor of 3. Usually, motion study is performed in conjunction with time study (described later).

worker–machine chart Used to determine portions of a work cycle during which an operator and equipment are busy or idle.

motion study Systematic study of the human motions used to perform an operation.

FIGURE 7–2

Example of a worker–machine chart

| Product: | Bulk Food | | Operator: | L.W. |
| Process: | Weigh/price | | Charted by: | R.G. |

Step	Employee	Time (seconds)	Machine
1	Accepts plastic bag from customer and places on scale	0 1	
2	Enters price/lb	2	
3		3	Calculates and displays total price. Dispenses price sticker.
4	Obtains price sticker and removes bag	4 5	
5	Places price sticker on bag	6 7	
6	Hands bag to customer	8	

Summary

	Employee Time (seconds)	%	Machine Time (seconds)	%
Work	7	87.5	1	12.5
Idle	1	12.5	7	87.5

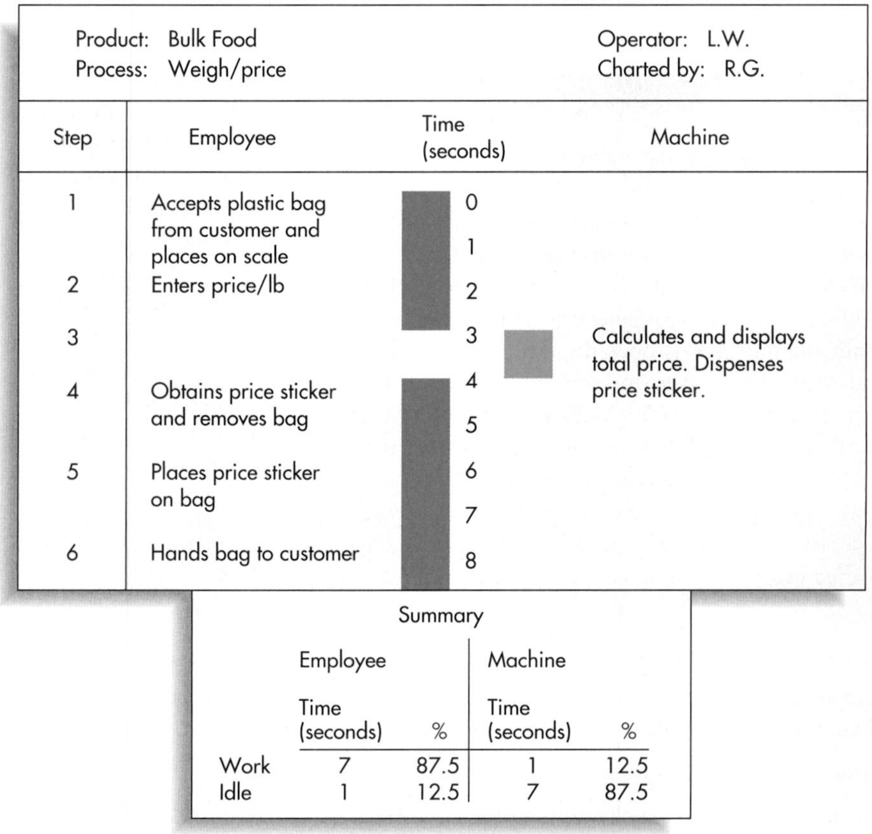

There are a number of different techniques that motion study analysts can use to develop efficient procedures. The most used techniques are:

1. Motion economy principles
2. Analysis of elementary motions: therbligs
3. Micromotion (slow-motion video) study
4. Simultaneous hands motion chart

Gilbreth's work laid the foundation for the development of **motion economy principles,** which are guidelines for designing motion-efficient work procedures. The guidelines are divided into three categories: principles for use of the body, principles for arrangement of the workplace, and principles for the design of tools and equipment. Table 7–2 lists some examples of the principles.

Therbligs are basic elementary motions. The term *therblig* is Gilbreth spelled backwards (except for the *th*). The idea behind the development of therbligs is to break jobs down into tiny elements and base improvements on an analysis of these basic elements by eliminating or reducing their difficulty, combining, or rearranging them.

A list of some common therbligs includes reach, grasp, position, and release. Describing a job using therbligs often takes a substantial amount of work. However, for short, repetitive jobs, therbligs analysis may be justified.

Frank Gilbreth and his wife, Lillian, an industrial psychologist, were also responsible for introducing motion pictures for studying motions, called **micromotion study**. This approach is applied not only in industry but also in some other areas such as sports. Use of camera and slow-motion replay enables analysts to study motions that would otherwise be too rapid to see. In addition, the resulting films provide a permanent record that can be referred to not only for training workers and analysts but also for settling job disputes involving work methods.

motion economy principles Guidelines for designing motion-efficient work procedures.

therbligs Basic elementary motions that make up a job.

micromotion study Use of motion pictures and slow motion to study motions that otherwise would be too rapid to analyze.

A. The use of the human body. Examples:
   1. Both hands should begin and end their activity simultaneously and should not be idle at the same instant, except during frequent but short rest periods.
   2. The motions made by the hands should be minimal and symmetrical.
   3. Momentum should assist workers wherever possible and should be minimized if it must be overcome by muscular effort.
   4. Continuous natural curved motions are preferable to straight-line motions involving sudden and sharp changes in direction.
   5. Strength requirements should be much less than the maximum available. Avoid lifting heavy objects. Use slow movements for maximum muscle strength.
   6. Eliminate bend and rise, awkward positions, and make the tasks easier to reduce fatigue.
   7. Eliminate eye travel and avoid losing eye focus.
B. The arrangement of the workplace. Examples:
   1. Fixed locations for all tools and material should be provided to permit the best sequence and to eliminate or reduce search and select.
   2. Gravity bins and drop delivery should reduce reach and move times; wherever possible, ejectors should remove finished parts automatically.
   3. All materials and tools should be located within easy reach.
   4. Provide a chair or stool if possible.
C. The design of tools and equipment. Examples:
   1. Where possible, power tools should replace hand tools.
   2. All levers, handles, wheels, and other control devices should be readily accessible to the operator and designed to give the best possible mechanical advantage and to utilize the strongest available muscle group.
   3. Parts should be held in position by fixtures.

TABLE 7–2

Examples of motion economy principles

Source: Adapted from Benjamin W. Niebel, *Motion and Time Economy* (Burr Ridge, IL: Richard D. Irwin, Inc., 1993), pp. 206–207. Reprinted with permission of the McGraw-Hill Companies Inc.

East Moline Plant

East Moline plant of Case (International Harvester) in Illinois, with approximately 900 employees, had 12 industrial engineers. The plant made combines and corn harvesters. The industrial engineers' responsibilities involved determining the best method for performing work, timing the elements of the work, and performing line balancing. Approximately 4,000 time standards were set each year, mostly as a result of changes in the method (combining or eliminating operations), but some were because of unusual parts and new products.

When an industrial engineer was assigned to set standard hours, he approached the work centre, and determined the cycle time, distances to load and unload the machines, type of machines used, and type of work done. He entered these data in the works management manual. He also determined the elements of the job and the right sequence for the elements to make it efficient, and assigned indices of difficulty to each element using the Maynard Operations Sequence Technique (MOST) to determine the (normal) time of each element.

These were added together, and then multiplied by the allowance factors for fatigue, personal time, and delays. These standard times were determined so that about 95 percent of workers were expected to perform better and received bonuses for doing so. There was a Union Works Standards representative who monitored this process and intervened when an operator challenged his standard hours. Most issues were solved between the industrial engineer and the union rep. However, a small portion went up as grievance, but in no case was there a strike based on dispute over time standards.

Other activities performed by industrial engineers included evaluating requests for additional staff by production units and participating in teams such as cost reduction teams, machine setup reduction teams, productivity task force, new product committee, and press guard safety committee. After New Holland took over Case in 1999 to form Case New Holland, CNH closed the East Moline plant in 2004 because of duplication of products.

Sources: http://www.nlrb.gov/nlrb/shared_files/decisions/304/304-152.txt; www.cnh.com.

---

simo chart A chart that shows the elements performed by each hand, side-by-side, over time.

Motion study analysts may use a **simo chart** (see Figure 7–3a) to study simultaneous motions of the hands. Here, the methods analyst studies a trim job on a hand-operated press with accompanying die. He breaks the job down in the form of a right- and left-hand process chart. A review of this process chart shows that delays are occurring because the motions of the right and left hand are not balanced: the left hand is waiting while the right hand raises the handle of the press, again while the right hand removes the part from the die, and again when the right hand regains control of the press handle. If the operator did not have to remove the finished piece from the die, he would be freed from the action of regrasping the press handle. The improved method is shown in Figure 7–3b. A fixture was developed to lift the part clear from the die while raising the press and eject it through the back of the press by an air blast. Simo charts are invaluable in studying operations such as data entry, sewing, surgical and dental procedures, and certain fabrication and assembly operations.

Working Conditions

Working conditions are an important aspect of job design. In many instances, government standards and regulations apply. Physical factors such as temperature and humidity, ventilation, illumination, noise and vibration, work breaks, safety, and ergonomics can have significant impacts on worker performance in terms of productivity and quality of output.

Brief History of Government Regulation of Workplace. It is well-known that some working conditions have been detrimental to the health of the workers and that work injuries and fatalities sometimes occur, although the numbers have been declining. Historically, the mechanization and creation of factories in the nineteenth century was the start of increasing health and safety problems. The government passed worker protection acts which required guards on the machines, fire safety, boiler and elevator inspection, sanitation, ventilation, and adequate heating and lighting. The Canadian Labour Code of 1966 included safety as well as other work standards such as minimum wage. In 1978, the

a. Right- and left-hand analysis of a blanking operation

THE AIRFELT MFG. CORP.
RIGHT AND LEFT HAND ANALYSIS

Operation *Blank supporting strip on hand arbor press*
Part No. *P-1107-7*   Dwg. No. *PB-1107*   Date *1-12-*
Drawn By *W. Eitele*   Dept. *13*   Plant *Bellefonte* Sheet *1* of *1*

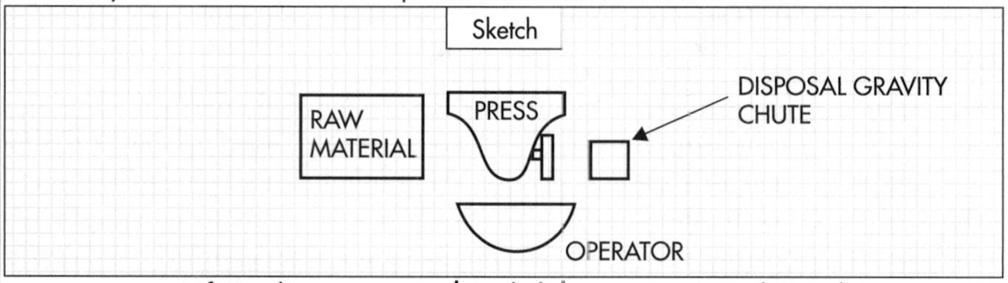

Sketch

RAW MATERIAL   PRESS   DISPOSAL GRAVITY CHUTE

OPERATOR

Left Hand	Symbols		Right Hand	
1. Pick up part from hopper			Pull press handle down	1.
Reach for part	Re	H	Hold handle	
Grasp part	G	H	Hold handle	
Move part adjacent to die	M	M	Move press handle down	
2. Wait for right hand			Raise press handle up	2.
Unavoidable delay	UD	M	Move press handle up	
Unavoidable delay	UD	RI	Release press handle	
3. Wait for right hand			Get part from die	3.
Unavoidable delay	UD	Re	Reach for part in die	
Unavoidable delay	UD	G	Grasp part	
4. Place part in die			Drop part in chute	4.
Move part to die	M	M	Move part to chute	
Position part in die	P	RI	Release part	
Release part	RI	UD	Wait for left hand	
5. Wait for right hand			Get press handle	5.
Unavoidable delay	UD	Re	Reach for handle	
Unavoidable delay	UD	G	Grasp handle	

b. Right- and left-hand analysis of a blanking operation in which unavoidable delays have been omitted

THE AIRFELT MFG. CORP.
RIGHT AND LEFT HAND ANALYSIS

Operation *Blank supporting strip on hand arbor press*
Part No. *P-1107-7*   Dwg. No. *PB-1107*   Date *1-12-*
Drawn By *W. Eitele*   Dept. *13*   Plant *Bellefonte* Sheet *1* of *1*

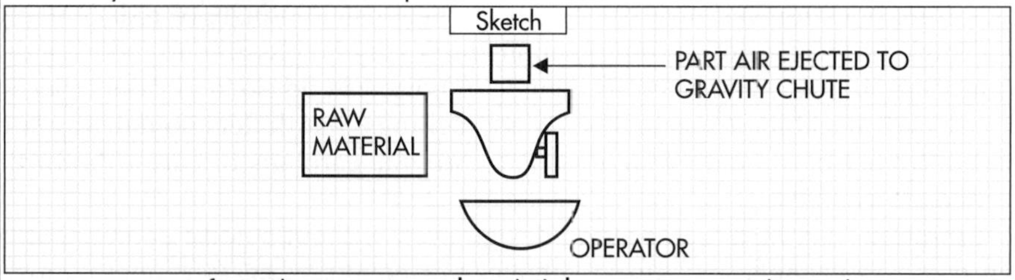

Sketch

PART AIR EJECTED TO GRAVITY CHUTE

RAW MATERIAL

OPERATOR

Left Hand	Symbols		Right Hand	
1. Get part from hopper			Pull press handle down	1.
Reach for part	RE	H	Hold handle	
Grasp part	G			
Move part to die	M	M	Move press handle down	
2. Place part in die				2.
Move part to die	M		Raise press handle up	
Position part	P	M	Move handle up	
Release part	RI	H	Hold handle	

FIGURE 7-3

A simultaneous hands motion chart

Source: B. W. Niebel, *Motion and Time Study*, 5th ed. (Homewood, IL: Richard D. Irwin, 1972). Reprinted by permission.

www.hc-sc.gc.ca/hecs-sesc/whmis

Labour Code was amended to give three rights to the workers: (a) to refuse dangerous work, (b) to participate in improving safety and health problems (through joint management/labour committees), and (c) to know about hazards in the workplace. Also created in 1978 was the Canadian Centre for Occupational Health and Safety. In 1988, the right to know about hazards in the workplace was shaped into the requirement for a Workplace Hazardous Materials Information System (WHMIS), which mandates proper labelling of hazardous material and making available the material safety data sheets.

Temperature and Humidity. Many operations need to be performed in high temperatures, such as in an iron foundry, and some others need to be performed in low temperatures, such as in a slaughterhouse. Although human beings can function under a fairly wide range of temperatures, work performance tends to be adversely affected if temperatures are outside a very narrow *comfort band*. That comfort band depends on how strenuous the work is; the more strenuous the work, the lower the comfort range.

For most work activities, the comfort band is about 10 °C to 21 °C at a relative humidity of between 30 to 80 percent. Productivity drops sharply below 0 °C and above 30 °C and at relative humidity close to 100 percent. Solutions range from selection of suitable clothing to space heating or cooling devices.

Ventilation. Some factories (such as lumber mills) create much dust, some others (such as pulp and paper mills) generate gases and foul odours. These are unhealthy and unpleasant. Large fans and air-conditioning equipment are commonly used to exchange and recondition the air.

Illumination. The amount of illumination required depends largely on the type of work being performed; the more detailed the work, the higher the level of illumination needed for adequate performance. Other important considerations are the amount of glare and contrast. From a safety standpoint, good lighting in halls, stairways, and other dangerous locations is important. However, because illumination is expensive, high illumination in all areas is not generally desirable.

Sometimes natural daylight can be used as a source of illumination. Not only is it free, but also it provides some psychological benefits. Workers in windowless rooms may feel cut off from the outside world and experience various psychological problems. On the down side, the inability to control natural light (e.g., cloudy days) can result in dramatic changes in light intensity.

Noise and Vibrations. Noise is caused by the movement and vibrations of machines or equipment. Noise can be annoying or distracting, leading to errors and accidents. It can also damage or impair hearing if it is loud enough.

Successful sound control begins with measurement of the offending sounds. In a new operation, selection and placement of equipment can eliminate or reduce many potential problems. In the case of existing equipment, it may be possible to redesign or substitute equipment. In some instances, the source of noise can be isolated from other work areas. If that isn't feasible, acoustical walls and ceilings that deflect sound waves may prove useful. Sometimes the only solution is to provide earplugs or earmuffs for those in the immediate vicinity.

Vibrations can be a factor in job design even without a noise component. Vibrations can come from tools, machines, vehicles, air-conditioning systems, pumps, and other sources. Corrective measures include padding, stabilizers, shock absorbers, cushioning, and rubber mountings.

Work Breaks. The frequency, length, and timing of work breaks (i.e., rests) can have a significant impact on both productivity and quality of output. One indication of the relationship between worker efficiency and work breaks is illustrated in Figure 7–4. It reveals that efficiency generally declines as the day wears on, but it also shows how breaks for lunch and rest can cause an upward shift in efficiency.

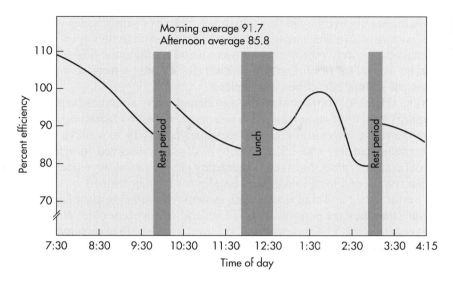

FIGURE 7-4

A typical relationship between worker efficiency and time of day

Source: Benjamin W. Niebel, *Motion and Time Study*, 8th ed. (Burr Ridge, IL: Richard D. Irwin, 1988), p. 270. © 1988 by Richard D. Irwin, Inc. Reprinted by permission of the McGraw-Hill Companies Inc.

An important variable in the rate of decline of efficiency and potential effects of work breaks is the amount of physical and/or mental requirements of the job. Steelworkers, for instance, may need rest breaks of 15 minutes per hour due to the strenuous nature of their jobs. In fact one of Taylor's experiments showed that for men carrying 92-pound pig-iron up a ramp, maximum output was quadrupled when the workers rested 58 percent of the time. For 40-pound pig-irons, optimal rest was 48 percent of the time. Physical effort is not the only condition that indicates the need for work breaks. People working at computer monitors also need periodic breaks, and students need study breaks.

Safety. Worker safety is one of the most basic issues in job design. This area needs constant attention from management, employees, and job designers. Workers cannot be effectively motivated if they feel they are in physical danger.

From an employer standpoint, accidents are undesirable because they are expensive (insurance and compensation); they usually involve damage to equipment and/or products; they require hiring, training, and makeup work; and they generally interrupt work.

The two basic causes of accidents are worker *carelessness* and unsafe conditions. Under the heading of carelessness come unsafe acts. Examples include failure to use protective equipment, overriding safety controls (e.g., taping control buttons down), disregarding safety procedures, improper use of tools and equipment, and failure to use reasonable caution in danger zones. Unsafe conditions include unprotected pulleys, chains, material-handling equipment, machinery, and so on. Also, poorly lit walkways, stairs, and loading docks constitute hazards. Toxic wastes, gases and vapours, and radiation hazards must be contained. In many instances, these cannot be detected without special equipment, so they would not be obvious to workers or emergency personnel. Protection against hazards involves use of proper lighting, clearly marked danger zones, use of protective equipment (hardhats, goggles, earmuffs, gloves, heavy shoes and clothing), safety devices (machine guards, dual-control switches that require an operator to use both hands), emergency equipment (emergency showers, fire extinguishers, fire escapes), and thorough instruction and training in safety procedures and use of regular and emergency equipment. Housekeeping (clean floors, open aisles, waste removal) is another important safety factor. Workers must be trained in proper procedures and attitudes. Management must enforce safety procedures and use of safety equipment.

The enactment of the Occupational Health and Safety regulations emphasizes the importance of safety considerations in work design. It provides specific safety regulations with inspectors to see that they are adhered to. Inspections are carried out both at random and to investigate complaints of unsafe conditions. The officials are empowered to issue warnings, to impose fines, and even to order shutdown for unsafe conditions.

www.bsi-global.com.

A more effective way to deal with management of safety issues is to incorporate it into the company's management planning and control activities, just as product quality is managed. A safety management system based on the guidelines of BSI OHSAS 18000 can be used. This is similar to ISO 9000 (for quality system) and ISO 14000 (for environment system), described in Chapter 9.

The OHSAS 18001 requires that health and safety activities be planned.[1] This process requires that, after an annual risk assessment, realistic objectives and targets be set and that the roles, responsibilities, and timelines necessary to achieve the targets be clearly communicated to—and understood by—all those involved in achieving them. Operational controls (procedures) and emergency plans must be developed and documented for those risks found to be intolerable. Employees must be trained.

Performance and compliance with system requirements must be measured in order to ensure that they are controlled. Any incident, accident, or other nonconformance within the system needs to be investigated at a level appropriate to its impact on the system. The resulting corrective and preventive action developed from this process ensures that the standards of practice are complied with and are adequate. Finally, senior management must periodically review the system (e.g., internal or external audits every six months) to ensure that it is meeting the objectives stated in its policy and that it is effectively implemented. Improvements in the overall system are identified and implemented through the planning process.

In March 2001, Compaq's Fremont, California, plant was one of the first plants in North America to implement OHSAS 18000. After obtaining its ISO 9002 and ISO 14000 registrations, it was rather easy for Compaq to use the same management systems to manage health and safety. In fact, the same person lead the environment, health, and safety systems. As a result, Compaq reduced its accident rate by 30 percent (twice its goal of 15 percent) in less than a year.[2]

ergonomics Fitting the job to the worker's capability and size.

Ergonomics. **Ergonomics** is the incorporation of human factors in the design of the workplace; that is, fitting the job to the worker's capability and size. It relates to the design of equipment, the design of work methods, and the overall design of the work space to remove awkward reaching and bending, forceful gripping of tools, heavy lifting, and endless repetition of motions. Among other things, ergonomics seeks to prevent

READING

Nexgen Ergonomics

www.nexgenergo.com

Nexgen Ergonomics is a well-known Canadian company, located in Montreal, involved in producing or reselling (under distribution agreement) software and products used in ergonomics. The products include a virtual mannequin which can be dimensioned according to average or extreme sizes of a male or female body, to be used in testing CAD drawings of products which directly interact with a human body. Also, Nexgen sells lumbar motion measurement products (see photos on the right), video analysis software, 2D to 3D conversion, and many medical and safety equipment.

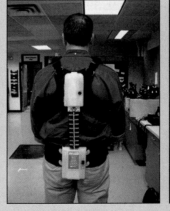 

[1] J. J. Janssen, "OHSAS 18001: Another @#$%& Standard?" *OH&S Canada* 18(1), January/February 2002, p 58.

[2] "Compaq Facility Reaps Benefits From OHSAS 18001," *OH&S Canada* 71(2), February 2002, p. 14. www.bsiamericas.com/OHS/OHSMSregistration/CompaqCaseStudy.pdf.

common workplace injuries such as back injuries and repetitive-motion injuries by taking into account the fact that people vary in their physical dimensions and capabilities, and that some activities, when continually repeated, result in strains in muscles and joints (called *musculoskeletal injuries, repetitive motion injuries,* or *cumulative trauma disorders*). Most ergonomic problems are unintentional mistakes that develop because no one had the knowledge or the time to design the task properly. Companies have compelling interests in reducing worker injuries: injuries result in lower productivity, lost workdays, and increases in workers' compensation and health premiums.

Some common examples of ergonomics problems in the office are as follows. A common problem in using the mouse is that it is usually placed beside the keyboard. This results in the need for constant reaching and stretching of the arm, which can result in long-term joint problems. A solution is using a rotating platform for the mouse so that it can be moved closer to the body. The arm should be at a right angle close to the body and the wrist should not be bent. Another common problem is bad sitting posture. An ergonomic chair should be used that can be adjusted for the user's body dimensions. After adjustment, the height of its back should fit in the "small" of the back of the user and the height of the seat should be just below the knees of the user (while standing). There should be about a 5-cm gap between the back of the knee and the chair (while sitting; see the illustration at right). The monitor should be just below the horizontal eyesight of the person so that there is no need for slouching. It should be approximately at a 60- to 80-cm distance from the eyes. Because monitors emit light, one should look away from the screen every few minutes for a few seconds (preferably at distant objects). If a document is being read, it, and not the monitor, should be lit using a lamp. Also, because monitors act like mirrors, their angle should be adjusted to avoid glare. For more information on ergonomics see the Canadian Centre for Occupational Health and Safety site at www.ccohs.ca.

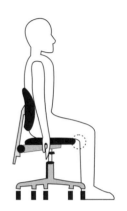

Some industrial applications of ergonomics are described in the following reading, and some ergonomics products are mentioned in the "Nexgen Ergonomics" reading on the preceding page.

READING

What Works to Cut CTD Risk, Improve Job Productivity?

A *panel of leading ergonomists offers case studies that show how workplace changes can cut CTDs [cumulative trauma disorders] and boost productivity. The ideas aren't complex or expensive, and are usually developed first by plant personnel.*

Improving the Tilt

The job: In this instance, the ergonomics team focused on the operator of a bench-mounted machine. The ergonomic problem was that the operator worked with a bent neck and bent wrists, in large part due to having to [compensate for] a flat work surface. The improvement was that the back legs of the machine were mounted on a small block of wood, thus tilting the machine forward. Both the wrist and neck were simultaneously placed in an improved posture, lowering the risk of CTDs. *Cost of the improvements: None.*

Meat Packing

The job was removing organs with a knife. The worker was using constant, static grasping force to hold the knife, as well as repetitive hand motions to both cut and hold the meat. The improvement was that a fixture was built and mounted to the work surface to hold the knife. With this knife in place, the meat could then be grasped with both hands and easily pulled through the cutting tool. *Cost of the improvements: Less than $50.*

Equipment Maintenance

Four hours a day were spent by a maintenance worker filling machines with fluids at an automotive-parts manufacturing company. Several 20-gallon pails were filled and pushed to the machines around the plant, and lifted to fill the various receptacles. The hard work and repetition (as well as an extra overtime shift added to the worker's schedule) resulted in shoulder and lower-back pain. An automated pumping system was installed to eliminate the lifting involved, and reduce the strain on the shoulders and lower back of the employee, resulting in increased comfort and an estimated 30 minutes a day in time saving.

Sources: *CTDNEWS Online* (www.ctdnews.com); C. McIntyre, "Task Design: The Multiplier Effect," *OH&S CANADA* 15(4), June 1999, pp. 54–55.

Healthy Workplace

www.nqi.ca

Many companies are realizing that safety and happiness of employees depend on their general health and well being. In fact, the National Quality Institute in cooperation with Health Canada developed the Healthy Workplace award in 1998 to recognize companies that have a holistic system for healthy workplace, including physical, mental, safety, personal, and social aspects. The criteria include four "drivers" of healthy workplace: leadership role (having a policy and being involved in healthy workplace); planning process (needs assessment, setting goals, designing programs); fostering worker involvement (respecting workers, training to use the programs); and process management (collecting and using feedback). The outcomes—the results of a healthy workplace system such as reduction in absenteeism, turnover, and accident rates—should be measured and compared with goals. The programs can affect the physical environment (safety, cleanliness, protective equipment, ergonomics, lighting, air quality, noise, violence, wheelchair accessibility, etc.), health practices (assistance to give up smoking and alcohol abuse, promoting healthy nutrition in the cafeteria, a fitness facility, etc.), and social environment (developing self-respect and a sense of belonging and control over work, protection against harassment, coping with stress, fairness in job assignment and evaluation, reasonable pace of work, flexible hours, benefits plan, etc.). Recent award winners include American Express Canada, Telus, Daimlerchrysler Canada, Delta Hotels, Statistics Canada, NCR, and Dofasco. For an application of Healthy Workplace, see the reading, "Decoma's Healthy Workplace Approach." For more information on the award and its criteria, see www.nqi.ca/HealthyWorkplace. For more cases on healthy workplaces, see www.clbc.ca/Research_and_Reports/Case_Studies.asp.

WORK MEASUREMENT

work measurement Determining how long it should take to do a job.

Job design determines the *content* of a job, and methods analysis and motion study determine *how* a job is to be performed. **Work measurement** is concerned with determining the *length of time* it should take to complete the job. Job times are vital inputs for personnel planning, estimating labour costs, assembly line balancing, and designing incentive systems. Moreover, from the workers' standpoint, time standards provide an indication of expected output. Time standards reflect the amount of time it should take an average worker to do a given job working under typical conditions. The standards include expected activity time plus allowances for probable delays, fatigue, personal needs and other reasons. For an application, see the reading, "Rebalancing at Ford's St. Thomas Plant."

standard time The amount of time it should take a qualified worker to complete a specified task, working at a sustainable rate, using given methods, tools and equipment, raw materials, and workplace arrangements.

A **standard time** is the amount of time it should take a qualified worker to complete a specified task, working at a sustainable rate, using given methods, tools and equipment, raw material inputs, and workplace arrangement. Whenever a standard time is developed for a job, it is essential to provide a complete description of the parameters of the job because the actual time to do the job is sensitive to all of these factors; changes in any one of the factors can materially affect time requirements. For instance, changes in product design or changes in job performance brought about by a methods analysis should trigger a new time study to update the standard time. As a practical matter, though, minor changes are occasionally made that do not justify the expense of restudying the job. Consequently, the standards for many jobs may be slightly inaccurate. Periodic time studies may be used to update the standards.

Organizations develop standard times in a number of different ways. Although some small manufacturers and service organizations rely on subjective estimates of job times, the most commonly used methods of work measurement are:

1. Stopwatch time study
2. Historical element times
3. Predetermined element times
4. Work sampling

READING

Decoma's Healthy Workplace Approach

www.decoma.com

Decoma designs and manufactures automotive exterior components. Until 1998, Decoma was part of Magna International. Decoma has approximately 13,500 employees in manufacturing and product development facilities in Canada and other countries. Fourteen of the 30 locations are in the Greater Toronto Area.

In Canada, each plant has a health program designed according to employee needs. Employees receive a bimonthly health and wellness newsletter. Health education and awareness are also developed through short, monthly seminars offered on a variety of topics (fitness, nutrition, back care, repetitive strain, shift work, etc.). The seminars are accompanied by corresponding screening clinics. For example, the Healthy Heart seminar is followed by a blood pressure clinic. Healthy workplace policies and programs such as discounts on local gyms, smoking cessation programs, and stretch break

programs further support employees as they move toward better health. There are intramural sports (hockey, baseball, and soccer) as well as social events such as the summer picnic and Christmas party. To encourage good nutrition, Decoma instituted a "Green Sticker" program—a means of identifying healthy choices in the vending machines and cafeterias.

Decoma is committed to an operating philosophy based on fairness and a concern for its people, put in the form of an Employee Charter. It includes the following principles: job security, a safe and healthful workplace, fair treatment, competitive wages and benefits, employee equity and profit participation, communication and information, a hotline, and an employee relations advisory board. Decoma offers a vast array of career training opportunities to employees at all levels. Employee input is encouraged through a process of anonymous suggestions, monthly meetings with the plant and human resources managers, and an employee satisfaction survey administered every 18 months.

Source: G. McKeown, "Case Study: Decoma International Inc.: Commitment to a Healthy Workplace, www.nqi.ca/articles/article_details.aspx?print=yes&id=55, July 28, 2001.

Stopwatch Time Study

Stopwatch time study was formally introduced by Frederick Winslow Taylor in the late nineteenth century. Today it is the most widely used method of work measurement. It is especially appropriate for short, repetitive tasks.

Stopwatch time study is used to develop a standard time for a job based on observations of one worker taken over a number of cycles. It is then applied to the work of all others in the organization who perform the same job. The basic steps in a stopwatch time study are:

1. Define the job to be studied, and inform the worker who will be studied.

2. Determine the number of cycles to observe.

3. Time the job, and rate the worker's performance.

4. Compute the standard time.

The analyst who studies the job should be thoroughly familiar with it because it is not unusual for workers to attempt to include extra motions during the study in the hope of gaining a standard that allows more time per piece (i.e., the worker will be able to work at a slower pace and still meet the standard). Furthermore, the analyst will need to check that the job is being performed efficiently (i.e., a methods analysis is first performed on the job) before setting the standard time.

In most instances, an analyst will break all but very short jobs down into basic elementary motions (e.g., reach, grasp) and obtain times for each element. There are several reasons for this: One is that some elements are not performed in every cycle, and the breakdown enables the analyst to get a better perspective on them. Another is that the worker's proficiency may not be the same for all elements of the job. A third reason is to build a file of element times that can be used to set times for other jobs.

Workers sometimes feel uneasy about being studied and fear changes that might result. The analyst should make an attempt to discuss these things with the worker prior to studying an operation to reduce such fears and to enlist the cooperation of the worker.

stopwatch time study
Development of a standard time based on observations of one worker taken over a number of cycles.

Rebalancing at Ford's St. Thomas Plant

One of the uses of standard time is in auto assembly plants, specifically in assembly line balancing. Because of work method and technology changes, the line needs to be rebalanced periodically. This work redistribution needs to be negotiated with the unions. At Ford's assembly plant in St. Thomas, Ontario, according to the collective agreement the management can rebalance the line during a four-month period every year (called the balance-out period). Ironically, many workers refuse their new work assignment using the right to refuse "unsafe" work.

Source: R. Sinclair, "Health and Safety Work Refusals: A Case Study of Ford of Canada's St. Thomas Assembly Plant," *Workplace Gazette* 1(4), 1998, pp. 54–58.

The number of cycles that must be timed is a function of three things: (1) the variability of observed times, (2) the desired accuracy, and (3) the desired level of confidence for the estimated job time. Very often the desired accuracy is expressed as a percentage of the mean of the observed times. For example, the goal of a stopwatch time study may be to achieve an estimate that is within 10 percent of the actual mean. The sample size needed to achieve that goal can be determined using:

$$n = \left(\frac{zs}{a\bar{x}}\right)^2 \tag{7–1}$$

where

z = Number of Normal standard deviations needed for desired confidence

s = Sample standard deviation

a = Desired accuracy percentage

$\bar{x}$ = Sample mean

Typical values of z used in this computation are:[3]

Desired Confidence (%)	z Value
90	1.65
95	1.96
95.5	2.00
98	2.33
99	2.58

Of course, the value of z for any desired confidence can be obtained from the Normal table in Appendix B, Table A (first divide the desired confidence by 2).

To make a preliminary estimate of sample size, it is typical to take a small number of observations (i.e., 10 to 20) and compute values of $\bar{x}$ and s to use in the formula for n. Toward the end of the study, the analyst may want to recompute n using revised estimates of $\bar{x}$ and s based on the increased data available.

An alternate formula used when the desired accuracy is stated as an *amount* (e.g., within one minute of the true mean) instead of a percentage is:

$$n = \left(\frac{zs}{e}\right)^2 \tag{7–2}$$

where

e = Accuracy amount or maximum acceptable error amount

---

[3]Theoretically, a t rather than a z value should be used because the population standard deviation is unknown. However, the use of z is simpler and provides reasonable results when the number of observations is 30 or more, as it generally is. In practice, z is used almost exclusively.

Note: These formulas may or may not be used in practice, depending on the person doing the time study. Often, an experienced analyst will rely on his or her judgment in deciding on the number of cycles to time.

A time study analyst wants to estimate the time required to perform a certain job. A preliminary study yielded a mean of 6.4 minutes and a standard deviation of 2.1 minutes. The desired confidence is 95 percent. How many observations will he need (including those already taken) if the desired maximum error is:

Example 1

a. $\pm$ 10 percent of the sample mean?

b. .5 minute?

a. $s = 2.1$ minutes $\qquad z = 1.96$

Solution

$\bar{x} = 6.4$ minutes $\qquad a = 10\%$

$$n = \left(\frac{zs}{a\bar{x}}\right)^2 = \left(\frac{1.96(2.1)}{.10(6.4)}\right)^2 = 41.36 \text{ (round up to 42)}$$

b. $e = .5$ $\quad n = \left(\frac{zs}{e}\right)^2 = \left(\frac{1.96(2.1)}{.5}\right)^2 = 67.77 \text{ (round up to 68)}$

Development of a standard time actually involves computation of three times: the *observed time* (OT), the *normal time* (NT), and the *standard time* (ST).

Observed Time. The average observed time is simply the average of the recorded times. Thus,

$$\text{OT} = \frac{\sum x_i}{n} \tag{7–3}$$

where

$\quad$ OT $=$ Average observed time

$\quad \sum x_i =$ Sum of recorded times

$\quad\quad n =$ Number of observations

Note: If a job element does not occur each cycle, its average time should be determined separately.

Normal Time. The normal time is the average observed time adjusted for worker's performance. It is computed by multiplying the average observed time by a *performance rating*. That is,

$$\text{NT} = \text{OT} \times \text{PR} \tag{7–4}$$

where

$\quad$ NT $=$ Normal time

$\quad$ PR $=$ Performance rating

This assumes that a single performance rating has been made for the entire job. If ratings are made on an element-by-element basis, the normal time is obtained by multiplying each element's average time by its performance rating and then summing those values:

$$\text{NT} = \sum (\bar{x}_j \times \text{PR}_j) \tag{7–5}$$

where

$\quad \bar{x}_j =$ Average time for element j

$\quad$ PR$_j =$ Performance rating for element j

The reason for including this adjustment factor is that the worker being observed may be working at a rate different from a "normal" rate, either to deliberately slow the pace or because his or her natural abilities differ from the norm. For this reason, the observer assigns a performance rating to adjust the observed times to an "average" pace. A normal rating is 1.00. A performance rating of .9 indicates a pace that is 90 percent of normal, whereas a rating of 1.05 indicates a pace that is slightly faster than normal. For long jobs, each element may be rated; for short jobs, a single rating may be made for an entire cycle.

When assessing performance, the analyst must compare the observed performance to his or her concept of normal. Obviously, there is room for debate about what constitutes normal performance, and performance ratings are sometimes the source of considerable conflict between labour and management. Although no one has been able to suggest a way around these subjective evaluations, sufficient training and periodic *recalibration* by analysts using training films can provide a high degree of consistency in the ratings of different analysts.

Standard Time. Normal time is the length of time a worker should take to perform a job if there are no delays or breaks. It does not take into account such factors as personal needs (getting a drink of water or going to the washroom), unavoidable delays (machine adjustments and repairs, talking to a supervisor, waiting for materials), or rest breaks to recover from fatigue. The standard time for a job is the normal time multiplied by an *allowance* for these factors.

The standard time is

$$ST = NT \times AF \tag{7–6}$$

where

ST = Standard time

AF = Allowance factor

Allowances can be based on either job time or time worked (e.g., a workday). If allowances are based on the *job time*, the allowance factor must be computed using the formula

$$AF_{job} = 1 + A; \quad A = \text{Allowance proportion based on job time} \tag{7–7}$$

This is used when different jobs have different allowances. If allowances are based on a proportion of the time worked (i.e., the *workday*), the appropriate formula is

$$AF_{day} = \frac{1}{1 - A}; \quad A = \text{Allowance proportion based on workday} \tag{7–8}$$

This is used when jobs are the same or similar and have the same allowance factors.

Time Study Observation Sheet

Usually a standard form is used to record the observations in a stopwatch time study. In the following example, the job is attaching 2 feet by 3 feet chart sheets together. The job has been decomposed into four elements (the left column). Under each element in parenthesis is the event which signifies the end of the element. For example, grasping the stapler signifies the end of element 1 and the start of element 2. Focusing on these events makes measuring the times easier. Also note that to the right of each element are two rows. The top row is the individual time of the element in each of the 10 cycles, whereas the bottom row is the cumulative times. For example, for element 2 in cycle 1, the cumulative time is .23 minutes. The individual time for this element is therefore .23 − .07 = .16 minutes, where .07 was the (cumulative) time at the end of element 1 in cycle 1. The cumulative time steadily advances as more cycles are timed. However, the minute digit of the cumulative time has been omitted in order to save recording time. For example, the cumulative time for element 4 in cycle 2 is actually 1.09, but only .09 is shown. It is clearly easier, faster, and more accurate to record the cumulative times first, and calculate the individual times after the completion of the study.

Source: R. B. Chase et al., *Operations Management for Competitive Advantage*, 10th ed. (Boston: McGraw-Hill, 2004). Reprinted with permission of the McGraw-Hill Companies.

Time Study Observation Sheet														
Identification of Operation		ASSEMBLE 24" x 36" CHART BLANKS							Date 10/9					
Began Timing: 9:26 Ended Timing: 9:32		Operator 109				Approval *BqR*			Observer *JDT.*					

Element Description and Breakpoint		1 .00	2	3	4	5	6	7	8	9	10	ΣT	T	PR	NT
1	Fold over end (grasp stapler)	.07	.07	.05	.07	.09	.06	.05	.08	.08	.06	.68	.07	.90	.06
		.07	.61	.14	.67	.24	.78	.33	.88	.47	.09				
2	Staple five times (drop stapler)	.16	.14	.14	.15	.16	.16	.14	.17	.14	.15	1.51	.15	1.05	.16
		.23	.75	.28	.82	.40	.94	.47	.05	.61	.24				
3	Bend and insert wire (drop pliers)	.22	.25	.22	.25	.23	.23	.21	.26	.25	.24	2.36	.24	1.00	.24
		.45	.00	.50	.07	.63	.17	.68	.31	.86	.48				
4	Dispose of finished chart (touch next sheet)	.09	.09	.10	.08	.09	.11	.12	.08	.17	.08	1.01	.10	.90	.09
		.54	.09	.60	.15	.72	.28	.80	.39	.03	.56			.55 normal minute for cycle	
5															
6															
10															

Normal cycle time _.55_ + Allowance _(.55 × .143)_ or _.08_ = Std. time _.63 min/pc._

Example 2

Compute the allowance factor for these two cases:

a. The allowance is 20 percent of *job* time.

b. The allowance is 20 percent of *work* time.

Solution

$$A = .20$$

a. $\text{AF}_{job} = 1 + A = 1.20$, or 120%

b. $\text{AF}_{day} = \dfrac{1}{1 - A} = \dfrac{1}{1 - .20} = 1.25$, or 125

Table 7–3 illustrates some typical allowances. In practice, allowances may be based on the judgment of the time study analyst, work sampling (described later in the chapter), or negotiations between labour unions and management.

Example 3 illustrates the time study process from observed times to the standard time.

Example 3

A time study of an assembly operation yielded the following observed times for one element of the job for which the analyst gave a performance rating of 1.13. Using an allowance of 20 percent of *job* time, determine the appropriate standard time for this element.

i Observation	Time, *x* (minutes)	Observation	Time (minutes)
1	1.12	6	1.18
2	1.15	7	1.14
3	1.16	8	1.14
4	1.12	9	1.19
5	1.15	Total	10.35

Solution

$n = 9$ $PR = 1.13$ $A = .20$

a. $\text{OT} = \dfrac{\sum x_i}{n} = \dfrac{10.35}{9} = 1.15$ minutes.

b. $\text{NT} = \text{OT} \times \text{PR} = 1.15(1.13) = 1.30$ minutes.

c. $\text{ST} = \text{NT} \times (1 + A) = 1.30(1.20) = 1.56$ minutes.

TABLE 7–3

Allowance percentages for working conditions recommended by the International Labour Organization

	Percent
A. Constant allowances for work breaks:	
1. Personal allowance	5
2. Basic fatigue allowances	4
B. Variable allowances:	
1. Standing allowance	2
2. Abnormal position allowance:	
a. Awkward (bending)	2
b. Very awkward (lying, stretching)	7
3. Use of force or muscular energy (lifting, pulling, or pushing):	
Weight lifted (in pounds):	
5	0
10	1
15	2
20	3
25	4
30	5
35	7
40	9
45	11
50	13
60	17
70	22
4. Bad light:	
a. Well below	2
b. Very inadequate	5
5. Atmospheric conditions (heat and humidity, cold)—variable	0–10
6. Close attention required:	
a. Fine or exacting	2
b. Very fine or very exacting	5
7. Noise level:	
a. Intermittent–loud	2
b. Intermittent–very loud	5
c. High-pitched–loud	5
8. Mental strain:	
a. Fairly complex process	1
b. Complex or wide span of attention	4
c. Very complex	8
9. Monotony:	
a. Medium	1
b. High	4
10. Tediousness:	
a. Tedious	2
b. Very tedious	5

Source: Benjamin W. Niebel, *Motion and Time Study,* 8th ed. (Burr Ridge, IL: Richard D. Irwin, 1988), p. 416. © 1988 by Richard D. Irwin, Inc. Reprinted with permission of the McGraw-Hill Companies Inc.

Note: If an abnormally short time has been recorded, it typically would be assumed to be observation error and thus discarded. If one of the observations in Example 3 had been .10, it would have been discarded. However, if an abnormally *long* time has been recorded, the analyst would want to investigate that observation to determine whether some irregularly occurring aspect of the task (e.g., retrieving a dropped tool or part) exists, which should legitimately be factored into the job time.

READING

Bombardier

Bombardier Aerospace's de Havilland plant in Toronto tried the AutoMOST software package from H. B. Maynard and Co. in order to become more efficient in its sheet metal, machining, and assembly operations. AutoMOST uses the MOST work measurement method. A Maynard consultant and five de Havilland methods engineers used some frame and ribs subassembly work centres as test areas for using AutoMOST. After getting the cooperation of the workers' union (Canadian Auto Workers union), they introduced the project and its goals to the work centres operators. Then, they identified the work elements performed in each work centre and improved the work methods to make them more efficient. They included activities such as locating inputs, verifying inputs, and deburring drilled holes as standard practices. The elements and their difficulty index were entered in AutoMOST which generated standard times for various operations. The project took about four months. Both the employees and the company were satisfied with the results. Later on, de Havilland methods engineers, having learned how to use AutoMOST, continued expanding the use of work measurement to other work centres.

Source: http://www.hbmaynard.com/ClientArticles/dehavilland.asp

Despite the obvious benefits that can be derived from work measurement using stopwatch time study, some limitations also must be mentioned. One limitation is the fact that only those jobs that can be observed can be studied. This eliminates most managerial and creative jobs, because these involve mental as well as physical aspects. Also, the cost of the study rules out its use for irregular operations and infrequently occurring jobs. Finally, it disrupts the normal work routine, and workers resent it in many cases.

Historical Element Times

Over the years, an Industrial engineering department can accumulate a file of element times that are common to many jobs. Many element times can be simply retrieved from the file, eliminating the need for analysts to go through a complete time study to obtain them.

The procedure for using historical element times consists of the following steps:

1. Analyze the job to identify the elements.
2. Check the file for elements that have historical times. Use stopwatch time study to obtain others if necessary.
3. Modify the file times if necessary (explained below).
4. Sum the element times to obtain the normal time, and factor in allowances to obtain the standard time.

In some cases, the file times may not pertain exactly to a specific task. For instance, standard element times might be on file for "move the tool 3 centimetres" and "move the tool 9 centimetres," when the task in question involves a move of 6 centimetres. However, it is often possible to interpolate between values to obtain the desired time estimate.

One obvious advantage of this approach is the potential savings in cost and effort created by not having to conduct a complete time study for each job. A second advantage is that there is less disruption of work, again because the analyst does not have to time the worker. A third advantage is that performance ratings do not have to be done; they are generally *averaged* in the file times. The main disadvantage of this approach is that times may not exist for enough elements to make it worthwhile, and the file times may be biased or inaccurate.

The method described in the following section is a variation of this approach, which helps avoid some of these problems.

Predetermined Element Times

predetermined element times
Published data based on extensive research on element times.

Predetermined element times are published data on element times. A commonly used system is *methods-time measurement* (MTM), which was developed in the late 1940s by the Methods Engineering Council. The MTM tables are based on extensive research of basic elementary motions and times. To use this approach, the analyst must divide the job into its basic elements (e.g., reach, grasp, move, turn, disengage), measure the distances involved (if applicable), rate the difficulty of the element (e.g., into three types of move: against stop; to approximate location; and to exact location), and then refer to the appropriate table of data to obtain the time for that element. The time for the job is obtained by adding the times for all of the basic elements. Times of the basic elements are measured in time measurement units (TMUs); one TMU equals .036 seconds. One minute of work may cover quite a few basic elements; a typical job may involve several tens or more of these basic elements. The analyst needs a considerable amount of skill to adequately describe the operation and develop realistic time estimates. Table 7–4 presents a portion of the MTM tables for "move" to give you an idea of the kind of information they provide.

For example, suppose that an element is to move a tape measure 12 inches to the end of a 2" × 4" × 8' plank of lumber. This is a Case B move: move object to approximate location. It is not an Exact move (Case C) because there are many possible locations at the

TABLE 7–4

The MTM table for move

Distance Moved (inches)	TIME (TMU) A	TIME (TMU) B	TIME (TMU) C	Hand in Motion B	WEIGHT ALLOWANCE Weight (pounds) up to:	Dynamic Factor	Static Constant TMU	Case and Description
¾ or less	2.0	2.0	2.0	1.7				
1	2.5	2.9	3.4	2.3	2.5	1.00	0	
2	3.6	4.6	5.2	2.9				**A.** Move object to other hand or against stop.
3	4.9	5.7	6.7	3.6	7.5	1.06	2.2	
4	6.1	6.9	8.0	4.3				
5	7.3	8.0	9.2	5.0	12.5	1.11	3.9	
6	8.1	8.9	10.3	5.7				
7	8.9	9.7	11.1	6.5	17.5	1.17	5.6	
8	9.7	10.6	11.8	7.2				
9	10.5	11.5	12.7	7.9	22.5	1.22	7.4	**B.** Move object to approximate or indefinite location.
10	11.3	12.2	13.5	8.6				
12	12.9	13.4	15.2	10.0	27.5	1.28	9.1	
14	14.4	14.6	16.9	11.4				
16	16.0	15.8	18.7	12.8	32.5	1.33	10.8	
18	17.6	17.0	20.4	14.2				
20	19.2	18.2	22.1	15.6	37.5	1.39	12.5	
22	20.8	19.4	23.8	17.0				**C.** Move object to exact location.
24	22.4	20.6	25.5	18.4	42.5	1.44	14.3	
26	24.0	21.8	27.3	19.8				
28	25.5	23.1	29.0	21.2	47.5	1.50	16.0	
30	27.1	24.3	30.7	22.7				

Source: MTM Association for Standards and Research. Copyrighted by the MTM Association for Standards and Research. No reprint permission without written consent from MTM Association, 16–01 Broadway, Fair Lawn, New Jersey 07410.

end of the plank. Note that the next element, not included here, will be position which is exact. The table says that this move should take 13.4 TMUs or approximately .5 seconds.

The weight allowances on the right of the table are for moving heavier objects. In this case, the formula for calculating the predetermined time is

Predetermined time = static constant + dynamic factor × time from the left of table.

For example, a hammer weighing 3 pounds is to be moved 12 inches. Because 2.5 < 3 < 7.5, the second category on the right of the table applies. Hence,

Predetermined time = 2.2 + 1.06 × 13.4 = 16.4 TMUs or .6 seconds.

A high level of skill is required to generate a predetermined element time. Analysts generally take training or certification courses to develop the necessary skills to do this kind of work.

Although proponents of predetermined element times claim that the approach provides much better accuracy than stopwatch time studies, not everyone agrees with that claim. Some argue that many activity times are too specific to a given operation to be generalized from published data. Others argue that different analysts perceive element activity breakdowns in different ways, and that this adversely affects the development of times and produces varying time estimates among analysts. Still others claim that analysts differ on the degree of difficulty they assign to a given task and thereby obtain different time.

There are many MTM tables. There is a table for reach, move, turn, apply pressure, grasp, position, release, disengage, eye travel and eye focus, and body, leg, and foot motions. Each table has various values depending on the distance, difficulty (e.g., reach to fixed location, or to variable location, etc.), whether the hand was in motion before or not, weight carried, degree turned, and size of object. Obviously, using the MTM tables is very time consuming and requires many years of experience.

Oglesby's Simplified MTM Table Oglesby et al. suggested the use of a simplified MTM table (see Table 7–5):

TABLE 7-5

Methods-time-measurement (MTM) simplified data

METHODS-TIME MEASUREMENT APPLICATION DATA

SIMPLIFIED DATA
(All times on this Simplified Data Table include 15% allowance)

HAND AND ARM MOTIONS			BODY, LEG, AND EYE MOTIONS	
REACH or MOVE		TMU		TMU
1"		2	Simple foot motion	10
2"		4	Foot motion with pressure	20
3" to 12" 4 + length of motion			Leg motion	10
over 12" 3 + length of motion				
(For TYPE 2 REACHES AND MOVES use length of motion only)			Side step case 1	20
			Side step case 2	40
POSITION				
Fit	Symmetrical	Other	Turn body case 1	20
Loose	10	15	Turn body case 2	45
Close	20	25		
Exact	50	55	Eye time	10
TURN—APPLY PRESSURE			Bend, stoop or kneel on one knee	35
TURN		6	Arise	35
APPLY PRESSURE		20		
			Kneel on both knees	80
			Arise	90
GRASP				
Simple		2	Sit	40
Regrasp or Transfer		6	Stand	50
Complex		10		
			Walk per pace	17
DISENGAGE				
Loose		5	1 TMU = .00001 hour	
Close		10	= .0006 minute	
Exact		30	= .036 second	

Source: Harold Maynard, *Industrial Engineering Handbook*, 2nd ed. (New York: McGraw-Hill, 1963). Reprinted with permission of the McGraw-Hill Companies.

Example 4	Suppose a carpenter needs a two-foot-long piece of a 2" × 4" × 8' plank of lumber which is located on his work table in front of him. First he needs to mark the two-foot location on the lumber. His retractable measurement tape is in one of his pockets, and his pencil is in the other pocket. After marking, both should be returned to the respective pockets. Decompose this marking activity into elements and determine a standard time for marking the wood using Table 7–5. Assume a right-handed person (i.e., mark with the right hand).

Solution

Element		Standard Time (TMU)
Reach for the measuring tape in pocket using the left hand (assume 12 inches)	4 + 12 =	16
Grasp simple		2
Move it to the end of the lumber (assume 12 inches)	4 + 12 =	16
Reach and grasp the end of the tape with the right hand (assume 12 inches)	(4 + 12) + 2 =	18
Position the end of the tape on the end of lumber (assume loose, symmetrical)		10
Move the measuring tape left across the lumber and locate (eye time) the two-foot mark	(3 + 24) + 10 =	37
Disengage the right hand, reach, and grasp pencil in the other pocket (assume 12 inches; assume complex grasp)	5 + (4 + 12) + 10 =	31
Move it close to the location of two-foot mark on the tape (assume 12 inches)	4 + 12 =	16
Position the pencil exactly and mark the location of two-foot mark (move 1 inch)	50 + 2 =	52
Put the pencil back into the pocket, disengage, and return hand	(4 + 12) + 5 + (4 + 12) =	37
Move the tape up 1 inch and wait until it retracts into its case (assume 1 second = 28 TMU retracting time)	2 + 28 =	30
Put the tape back into the pocket, disengage, and return hand	(4 + 12) + 5 + (4 + 12) =	37
		302 TMUs
		or 10.9 seconds

Maynard Operation Sequence Technique (MOST). MOST is a newer and simpler version of MTM that is used widely (www.hbmaynard.com). For applications, see the "East Moline Plant" reading earlier in this chapter and the "Bombardier" reading on page 263. The activities are categorized into only three sequences: General Move, Controlled Move, and Tool Use.

General Move (GM) consists of get, put, and return. Get consists of (horizontal) action distance (A), (vertical) body motion (B), and gain control (G). Put consists of A, B, and placement (P). Return is just A.

Controlled Move (CM) consists of get, move/actuate, and return. Get is A, B, G. Move/actuate consists of controlled move (M), process time (X), and alignment (I). Return is A.

Tool Use (TU) consists of get tool, put tool, use tool, put tool aside, and return. Get tool is A, B, G. Put tool is A, B, P. Use tool is fasten (F)/loosen (L), cut (C), surface treat (S), measure (M), record (R), or think (T). Put tool aside is A, B, P. Return is A.

The predetermined times for MOST, depending on distance, difficulty, etc., are given in Table 7–6 and Table 7–7.

Controlled Move

ABG MXI A
Get Move/Actuate Return

M — Move Controlled		X — Process Time			I — Alignment
Push/Pull/Pivot	Crank	Seconds	Minutes	Hours	
No Action	No Action	No Process Time			No Alignment
Push/Pull/Pivot ≤ 12 in. (30 cm.) / Push Button / Push or Pull Switch / Rotate Knob		.5 sec.	.01 min.	.0001 hr.	Align to 1 Point
Push/Pull/Pivot > 12 in. (30 cm.) / Push/Pull with Resistance / Seat / Unseat / Push/Pull with High Control / Push/Pull 2 Stages ≤ 12 in. (30 cm.) / Push/Pull 2 Stages ≤ 24 in. Total	1 Rev.	1.5 sec.	.02 min.	.0004 hr.	Align to 2 Points ≤ 4 in. (10 cm.)
Push/Pull 2 Stages > 12 in. (30 cm.) / Push/Pull 2 Stages > 24 in. Total / Push with 1 - 2 Steps	2 - 3 Revs.	2.5 sec.	.04 min.	.0007 hr.	Align to 2 Points > 4 in. (10 cm.)
Push/Pull 3 - 4 Stages / Push with 3 - 5 Steps	4 - 6 Revs.	4.5 sec.	.07 min.	.0012 hr.	
Push with 6 - 9 Steps	7 - 11 Revs.	7.0 sec.	.11 min.	.0019 hr.	Align with Precision

M — Push or Pull Extended Values

Index	Steps
24	10-13
32	14-17
42	18-22
54	23-28
67	29-34

Crank Extended Values

Index	Revs.
24	12-16
32	17-21
42	22-28
54	29-36

X — Process Time Extended Values

Index	Seconds	Minutes	Hours
24	9.5	.16	.0027
32	13.0	.21	.0036
42	17.0	.28	.0047
54	21.5	.36	.0060
67	26.0	.44	.0073
81	31.5	.52	.0088
96	37.0	.62	.0104
113	43.5	.72	.0121
131	50.5	.84	.0141
152	58.0	.97	.0162
173	66.0	1.10	.0184
196	74.5	1.24	.0207
220	83.5	1.39	.0232
245	92.5	1.54	.0257
270	102.0	1.70	.0284
300	113.0	1.88	.0314
330	124.0	2.06	.0344

TABLE 7-6

Maynard Operation Sequence Technique (MOST)—Controlled Move

Source: B. Niebel and A. Frivalds. *Methods, Standards, and Work Design*, 11th ed. (New York: McGraw-Hill, 2003). Reprinted with permission of the McGraw-Hill Companies Inc.

Tool Use and General Move

F L — Fasten or Loosen

Finger Action	Wrist Action					Arm Action					Tool Action
Spins	Turns	Strokes	Cranks	Taps	Turns		Strokes	Cranks	Strikes	Screw Dia.
Fingers, Screw-driver	Hand, Screw-driver, Ratchet, T-Wrench	Wrench, Allen key	Wrench, Allen key, Ratchet	Hand, Hammer	Ratchet	T-Wrench 2-Hands	Wrench, Allen key	Wrench, Allen key, Ratchet	Hand, Hammer	Power Wrench
1	-	-	-	1	-	-	-	-	-	
2	1	1	1	3	1	-	1	-	1	1/4" (6mm)
3	3	2	3	6	2	1	-	1	3	1" (25mm)
8	5	5	5	10	4	-	2	2	5	
16	9	5	8	16	6	3	3	3	8	
25	13	8	11	23	9	6	4	5	12	
35	17	10		30	12	8	6		16	
47	23	13		39	15	11	8		21	
61	29	17		50	20	15	10		27	

F — Fasten or Loosen

Tool	Index
Hammer	0 (a)
Finger or Hand	1 a or 6
Knife	1 (a)
Scissor	1 (a)
Pliers	1 (a)
Writing Instrument	1
Measuring Device	1
Surface Treating Device	1
Screwdriver	3
Ratchet	3
T-Wrench	3
Fixed End Wrench	3
Allen Wrench	3
Power Wrench	3
Adjustable Wrench	6

I — Alignment of Machining Tools

Index	Align to
3	Workpiece
6	Scale Mark
10	Indicator Dial

Alignment of Nontypical Objects

Index	Positioning Method
0	Against stop(s)
3	1 adjustment to stop
6	2 adjustments to stop(s) / 1 adjustment to 2 stops
10	3 adjustments to stop(s) / 2-3 adjustments to linemark

Nontypical Object Characteristics: Flat, Large, Flimsy, Sharp, Difficult to Handle

Tool Use

C Cut				S Surface Treat			M Measure	R Record			T Think	
Twist/Bend	Cutoff	Cut	Slice	Air-Clean	Brush-Clean	Wipe	Measure	Write		Mark	Inspect	Read
Pliers		Scissors	Knife	Nozzle	Brush	Cloth	Measuring Device	Pencil		Marker	Eyes, Fingers	Eyes
	Wire	Cut(s)	Slice(s)	sq. ft. (0, 1 m.²)	sq. ft. (0, 1 m.²)	sq. ft. (0, 1 m.²)	in.(cm.) ft.(m.)	Digits	Words	Digits	Points	Digits, Whole Words / Text of Words
Grip		1	-	-	-	-		1	-	Check Mark	1	1 / 3
	Soft	2	1	-	-	1/2		2	-	Scribe Line 1	3	3 / 8 Gauge
Twist Bend-Loop	Medium	4	-	Spot Point Cavity 1	Small Object 1	-		4	1	2	Touch or Feel 5	Scale Value 6 / 15 Date or Time
	Hard	7	3	-	-	1	Profile-Gauge	6	-	3	Feel for Defect 9	Vernier-Scale 12 / 24
Bend Cotter Pin		11	4	3	2	2	Fixed Scale / Caliper 12 in. (30 cm.)	9	Signature or Date 2	5		Table Value 38
		15	6	4	3	-	Feeler-Gauge	13	3	7		54
		20	9	7	5	5	Steel-Tape 6 ft. (2 m.) / Depth Micrometer	18	4	10		72
		27	11	10	7	7	OD-Micrometer 4 in. (10 cm.)	23	5	13		94
		33					ID-Micrometer 4 in. (10 cm.)	29	7	16		119

General Move

ABG ABP A
Get Put Return

A — Action Distance	B — Body Motion	G — Gain Control	P — Placement
≤ 2 in. (5 cm.)	No Body Motion	No Gain Control / Hold	No Placement / Hold / Toss
Within Reach		Grasp Light Object / Grasp Light Objects Simo	Lay Aside / Loose Fit
1 - 2 Steps	Sit without adjustments / Stand without adjustments / Bend and Arise 50% occ.	Get Non-simo / Get Heavy/Bulky / Get Blind / Get Obstructed / Free Interlocked / Disengage / Collect	Loose Fit Blind / Place with Adjustments / Place with Light Pressure / Place with Double Placement
3 - 4 Steps	Bend and Arise		Position with Care / Position with Precision / Position Blind / Position Obstructed / Position with Heavy Pressure / Position with Intermediate Moves
5 - 7 Steps	Sit / Stand		
8 - 10 Steps	Bend and Sit / Climb on / Climb off / Stand and Bend / Through Door		

A — Action Distance Extended Values

Index	Steps	Distance (ft.)	Distance (m.)
24	11-15	38	12
32	16-20	50	15
42	21-26	65	20
54	27-33	83	25
67	34-40	100	30
81	41-49	123	38
96	50-57	143	44
113	58-67	168	51
131	68-78	195	59
152	79-90	225	69
173	91-102	255	78
196	103-115	288	88
220	116-128	320	98
245	129-142	355	108
270	143-158	395	120
300	159-174	435	133
330	175-191	478	146

TABLE 7-7

Maynard Operation Sequence Technique (MOST) Continued—Tool Use and General Move

Source: B. Niebel and A. Frivalds. *Methods, Standards, and Work Design*, 11th ed. (New York: McGraw-Hill, 2003). Reprinted with permission of the McGraw-Hill Companies Inc.

Example 5	Consider the same activity (measuring and marking a two-foot piece of a plank) as in Example 4. Determine the standard time using MOST.

Solution

Activity	Operation Sequence	Time (TMU)
Get and put tape on the end of lumber (GM)	$A_1B_0G_1A_1B_0P_1A_0$	4×10
Grab end of tape and position (GM)	$A_1B_0G_1A_0B_0P_1A_0$	3×10
Move tape to right 2 feet (CM)	$A_0B_0G_0M_3X_0I_0A_0$	3×10
Pencil use (TU)	$A_1B_0G_1A_1B_0P_6R_1A_1B_0P_1A_1$	13×10
Let tape retract (CM)	$A_0B_0G_0M_1X_3I_0A_0$	4×10
Put tape back (CM)	$A_0B_0G_0A_1B_0P_1A_1$	3×10
		300 TMUs
		or 10.8 seconds

GM = General Move, CM = Controlled Move, and TU = Tool Use

Note: Time is the sum of the subscripts of the sequence times 10. For example, for the first sequence, time is $(1 + 0 + 1 + 1 + 0 + 1 + 0) \times 10 = 40$ TMUs.

Work Sampling

Work sampling is a technique for estimating the proportion of time that a worker spends on each activity or is idle.

Unlike time study, work sampling does not require timing an activity, nor does it even involve continuous observation of the activity. Instead, an observer makes brief observations of a worker at random intervals and simply notes the nature of the activity. For example, a secretary may be typing, filing, talking on the telephone, and so on; and a carpenter may be carrying supplies, taking measurements, cutting wood, and so on. The resulting data are *counts* of the number of times each category of activity or nonactivity was observed.

Although work sampling is occasionally used to set standard times, its primary use is for analysis of nonrepetitive jobs. In a nonrepetitive job, such as secretarial work or maintenance, it can be important to establish the percentage of time an employee is idle, find out the reason, and try to fix the problem. Work sampling can also be an important tool in developing the job description.

Work sampling estimates include some degree of error. Hence, it is important to treat work sampling estimates as *approximations* of the actual proportion of time devoted to a given activity. The goal of work sampling is to obtain an estimate that provides a specified confidence of not differing from the true value by more than a specified error. For example, we may desire an estimate of idle time that will provide a 95-percent confidence of being within 4 percent of the actual percentage. Hence, work sampling is designed to produce a value, $\hat{p}$, which estimates the true proportion, p, within some allowable error, e: $\hat{p} \pm e$. The variability associated with sample estimates of p tends to be approximately Normal for large sample sizes. The amount of maximum probable error is a function of the sample size, the desired level of confidence, and sample proportion.

For large samples, the maximum error e can be computed using the formula

$$e = z\sqrt{\frac{\hat{p}(1-\hat{p})}{n}} \tag{7–9}$$

where

z = Number of standard deviations needed to achieve desired confidence

$\hat{p}$ = Sample proportion (the number of occurrences divided by the sample size)

n = Sample size

In most instances, management will specify the desired confidence level and amount of allowable error, and the analyst will be required to determine a sample size sufficient to

READING

Eli Lilly

Work sampling can be performed in construction industry in order to identity opportunities for productivity improvements. This is in the interest of both the owner of the building and the construction company. An example of this is the work sampling study performed on a construction job on the land of the bulk manufacturing and lab of Eli Lilly Company in Tippecanoe, Indiana, in June 2002.

The trades involved were pipe fitters, electricians, sheet-metal workers, insulators, carpenters, and painters, working under the general contractor Shambaugh and Son. It was decided to classify the activities into three categories:

- Primary or productive (direct) work such as demolition, fabrication, installation, and inspection

- Supportive work such as material handling, clean-up, receiving instructions (called communication), reading blue-prints/making calculations/marking (called layout work), and doing safety work

- Recoverable (wasted) work such as late start/early finish, personal needs, waiting, and not being there (called missing in action)

Each day, a random start time was determined using the computer. A preplanned tour was followed through the job site,

recording the activity of each worker observed. Each tour took 25–30 minutes. The tours were repeated a few times each day, collecting 200–300 observations. Using two observers, approximately 5,000 observations were collected in 10 days.

The counts were summarized and are presented below. As can be observed, material handling (18 percent) and waiting (17 percent) are the largest supportive and recoverable components. To reduce these activities, a temporary building for material storage was set up on site and supervisors were trained in using scheduling techniques.

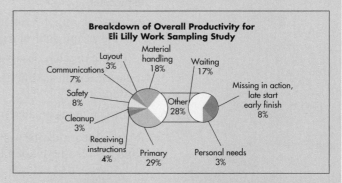

Breakdown of Overall Productivity for Eli Lilly Work Sampling Study

Layout 3%
Communications 7%
Safety 8%
Cleanup 3%
Receiving instructions 4%
Material handling 18%
Waiting 17%
Other 28%
Primary 29%
Missing in action, late start early finish 8%
Personal needs 3%

Source: J. L. Jenkins and D. L. Orth, "Productivity through Work Sampling," *AACE International Transactions* 2003, pp. CSC.05.1–7. Reprinted with the permission of AACE International, 209 Prairie Ave., Suite 100, Morgantown, WV 25601 USA. Phone 800-858-COST/304-296-8444. Fax: 304-291-5728. Internet: http://www.aacei.org E-mail: info@aacei.org. Copyright © by AACE International; all rights reserved.

obtain these results. The appropriate value for n can be determined by solving formula 7–9 for n, which yields

$$n = \left(\frac{z}{e}\right)^2 \hat{p}(1 - \hat{p}) \qquad (7\text{–}10)$$

Example 6

The manager of a small supermarket chain wants to estimate the proportion of time stock clerks spend making price changes on previously marked merchandise. The manager wants a 98-percent confidence that the resulting estimate will be within 5 percent of the true value. What sample size should she use?

$e = .05$ $z = 2.33$ (see p. 258) $\hat{p}$ is unknown

Solution

When no sample estimate of p is available, a preliminary estimate of sample size can be obtained using $\hat{p} = .50$. After 20 or so observations, a new estimate of $\hat{p}$ can be obtained from those observations and a revised value of n computed using the new $\hat{p}$. It would be prudent to recompute the value of n at two or three points during the study to obtain a better indication of the necessary sample size. Thus, the initial estimate of n is

$$n = \left(\frac{2.33}{.05}\right)^2 (.50)(1 - .50) = 542.89, \text{ or } 543 \text{ observations}$$

Suppose that, in the first 20 observations, stock clerks were found to be changing prices twice, making $\hat{p} = 2/20 = .10$. The revised estimate of n at that point would be

$$n = \left(\frac{2.33}{.05}\right)^2 (.10)(1 - .10) = 195.44, \text{ or } 196$$

Suppose a second check is made after a total of 100 observations, and $\hat{p} = .11$ at this point (including the initial 20 observations). Recomputing n yields

$$n = \left(\frac{2.33}{.05}\right)^2 (.11)(.89) = 212.60, \text{ or } 213$$

The overall procedure consists of the following steps:

1. Clearly identify the worker(s) to be studied.
2. Notify the workers and supervisors of the purpose of the study to avoid arousing suspicions.
3. Compute an initial estimate of sample size using a preliminary estimate of p, if available (e.g., from analyst experience or past data). Otherwise, use $\hat{p} = .50$.
4. Develop a random observation schedule.
5. Begin taking observations. Recompute the required sample size several times during the study.
6. Determine the estimated proportion of time spent on the specified activity.

Observations must be spread out over a period of time so that a true indication of variability is obtained. For an application of work sampling, see the reading, "Eli Lilly."

COMPENSATION

Compensation is a significant issue for the design of work systems. It is important for organizations to develop suitable compensation plans for their employees. If wages are too low, organizations may find it difficult to attract and hold competent workers and managers. If wages are too high, the increased costs may result in lower profits, or may force the organization to increase its prices, which might adversely affect demand for the organization's products or services.

time-based system
Compensation based on time an employee has worked during a pay period.

output-based (piece rate) system Compensation based on amount of output an employee produces during a pay period.

Organizations use two basic systems for compensating employees: *time-based systems* and *output-based systems*. **Time-based systems**, also known as *hourly* and *measured daywork* systems, compensate employees for the time the employee has worked during a pay period. Salaried workers also represent a form of time-based compensation. **Output-based (piece rate) systems** compensate employees according to the amount of output they produce during a pay period, thereby tying pay directly to performance.

Time-based systems are more widely used than output-based systems, particularly for office, administrative, and managerial employees, but also for blue-collar workers. One reason for this is that computation of wages is straightforward and managers can readily estimate labour costs for a given employee level. Employees often prefer time-based systems because the pay is steady and they know how much compensation they will receive for each pay period. In addition, employees may resent the pressures of an output-based system.

Another reason for using time-based systems is that many jobs do not lend themselves to the use of piece rate. In some cases, it may be difficult or impossible to measure output. For example, jobs that require creative or mental work cannot be easily measured on an output basis. Other jobs may include irregular activities or have so many different forms of output that measuring output and determining pay are fairly complex. Finally, *quality* considerations may be as important as *quantity* considerations. In health care, for example, emphasis is generally placed on both the quality of patient care and the number of patients processed.

On the other hand, situations exist where piece rate is desirable. Piece rate rewards workers for their output, causing some workers to produce more than they might under a time-based system. On the negative side, piece rate systems involve a considerable amount of paperwork. Calculation of wages is more difficult than under time-based systems, because output has to be measured and standards set.

In order to obtain maximum benefit from a piece rate plan, the plan should be:

1. Accurate
2. Easy to apply
3. Consistent
4. Easy to understand
5. Fair

In the past, piece rate plans were fairly popular. Now minimum-wage legislation makes them somewhat impractical. Even so, many of the plans currently in use represent variations of the piece rate plan. They typically incorporate a base rate that serves as a floor: workers are guaranteed that amount as a minimum, regardless of output. The base rate is tied to an output standard; a worker who produces less than the standard will be paid at the base rate. This protects workers from pay loss due to delays, breakdowns, and similar problems. In most cases, incentives are paid for output above standard, and the pay is referred to as a *bonus*.

Group Incentive Plans

A variety of group incentive plans, which stress sharing of productivity gains with employees, are in use. Some focus exclusively on output (called group incentive), while others reward employees for output and for reductions in costs (called gain sharing), or increases in profit (called profit sharing).

A survey of major collective agreements has shown that although (individual) piece rate plans are still popular, use of profit sharing is increasing.[4]

Skill/Knowledge-Based Pay Systems

As a result of increased competition and the need to reduce costs, companies are now putting increased emphasis on quality, productivity, and flexibility. Consequently, workers who can perform a variety of tasks are particularly valuable. Organizations are increasingly recognizing this, and they are setting up pay systems to reward workers who undergo training that increases their skill levels. This is sometimes referred to as **skill/knowledge-based pay**. It is a portion of a worker's pay that is based on the knowledge and skill that the worker possesses. Skill/knowledge-based pay has three dimensions: *horizontal skills* reflect the variety of tasks the worker is capable of performing; *vertical skills* reflect managerial tasks the worker is capable of; and *depth skills* reflect quality and productivity results.

An example of a skill/knowledge-based pay system is that used in the Molson Breweries (Montreal) plant, where a multiskill premium of $4 per day is paid to client service truck drivers and a $0.50 per hour premium is paid to multiskilled brewing operations employees. The team leaders in warehouse, shipping, and garage operations receive a team leader premium of $15 per week.[5]

skill/knowledge-based pay
A pay system to reward workers who undergo training that increases their skills/knowledge.

SUMMARY

The design of work systems involves job design, work measurement, and compensation.

Job design is concerned with the content of jobs and work methods. In the past, job design tended to focus on efficiency, but now there seems to be an increasing awareness and consideration of the behavioural aspects of work and worker satisfaction. These include job enlargement, rotation, enrichment, and teamwork.

Analysts often use methods analysis and motion study techniques to develop the "efficiency" aspects of jobs. Charts such as process charts, worker–machine charts, and simo charts are used. Working conditions are also a notable aspect of job design, not only because of the behavioural and efficiency factors but also because of concern for the health and safety of workers. Ergonomics is fitting the job to worker's capabilities.

---

[4]B. Fawcett, "Wage Incentive Plans—1988–1998," *Workplace Gazette* 1(3), 1998, pp. 41–44.

[5]S. Payette, "What's New in Workplace Innovations?" *Workplace Gazette* 3(1), 2000, pp. 110–119.

TABLE 7-8

Summary of formulas

Time Study		Work Sampling	
A. Sample size		A. Maximum error	
$n = \left(\dfrac{zs}{a\overline{x}}\right)^2$	(7–1)	$e = z\sqrt{\dfrac{\hat{p}(1-\hat{p})}{n}}$	(7–9)
$n = \left(\dfrac{zs}{e}\right)^2$	(7–2)	B. Sample size	
B. Average observed time		$n = \left(\dfrac{z}{e}\right)^2 \hat{p}(1-\hat{p})$	(7–10)
$OT = \dfrac{\sum x_i}{n}$	(7–3)		
C. Normal time		**Symbols:**	
$NT = OT \times PR$	(7–4)	a = Allowable error as a percentage of average time	
$NT = \sum(\overline{x}_i \times PR_i)$	(7–5)	A = Allowance proportion	
D. Standard time		e = Maximum acceptable error	
$ST = NT \times AF$	(7–6)	n = Number of observations needed	
E. Allowance factor		NT = Normal time	
$AF_{job} = 1 + A$	(7–7)	OT = Observed, or average, time	
$AF_{day} = \dfrac{1}{1 - A}$	(7–8)	PR = Performance rating	
		$\hat{p}$ = Sample proportion	
		s = Standard deviation of observed times	
		ST = Standard time	
		x_i = Time for ith observation ($i = 1, 2, 3, \ldots, n$)	
		z = No. of standard deviations needed to achieve desired confidence	

Work measurement is concerned with specifying the length of time needed to complete a job. Such information is vital for personnel planning, labour cost estimating, assembly line balancing, and worker compensation. Commonly used approaches include stopwatch time study and predetermined times. A related technique is work sampling which is used to estimate the proportion of time a worker spends on a certain aspect of the job. Table 7–8 provides a summary of the formulas used in time studies and work sampling.

Time-based (hourly, salaried) compensation is most common. Output-based (piece rate) compensation is used in some industries. Group incentive plans, such as profit sharing, and skill/knowledge-based compensation are becoming more common.

Organizations can choose from a variety of compensation plans. It is important to do so carefully, because compensation is key to both the worker and the organization, and, once adopted, it is usually difficult to substantially change a compensation plan.

KEY TERMS

ergonomics, 254
job design, 243
job enlargement, 244
job enrichment, 245
job rotation, 244
methods analysis, 246
micromotion study, 249
motion economy principles, 249
motion study, 248
output-based (piece rate) system, 270
predetermined element times, 264
process chart, 246

self-directed teams, 246
simo chart, 250
skill/knowledge-based pay, 271
specialization, 244
standard time, 256
stopwatch time study, 257
therbligs, 249
time-based system, 270
work measurement, 256
work sampling, 268
worker–machine chart, 248

Solved Problems

Problem 1

A time study analyst timed an assembly operation for 30 cycles, and then computed the average time per cycle, which was 18.75 minutes. The analyst assigned a performance rating of 96, and decided that an appropriate allowance was 15 percent. Assume that the allowance factor is based on the *workday*. Determine the following: the average observed time (OT), the normal time (NT), and the standard time (ST).

OT = Average observed time = 18.75 minutes

NT = OT $\times$ Performance rating = 18.75 minutes $\times$ .96 = 18 minutes

$$AF = \frac{1}{1-A} = \frac{1}{1-.15} = 1.176$$

ST = NT $\times$ AF = 18 $\times$ 1.176 = 21.17 minutes

Solution

A time study analyst wants to estimate the number of observations that will be needed to achieve a specified maximum error, with a confidence of 95.5 percent. A preliminary study yielded a mean of 5.2 minutes and a standard deviation of 1.1 minutes. Determine the total number of observations needed for these two cases:

Problem 2

a. A maximum error of $\pm$ 6% of the sample mean.

b. A maximum error of .40 minute.

a. $\bar{x} = 5.2$ minutes $z = 2.00$ for 95.5%
    $s = 1.1$ minutes $a = .06$

Solution

$$n = \left(\frac{zs}{a\bar{x}}\right)^2 = \left(\frac{2.00(1.1)}{.06(5.2)}\right)^2 = 49.72 \text{ (round up to 50 observations)}$$

b. $e = .40$

$$n = \left(\frac{zs}{e}\right)^2 = \left(\frac{2.00(1.1)}{.40}\right)^2 = 30.25 \text{ (round up to 31 observations)}$$

Work sampling. An analyst has been asked to prepare an estimate of the proportion of time that a turret lathe operator spends adjusting the machine, with a 90-percent confidence level. Based on previous experience, the analyst believes the proportion will be approximately 30 percent.

Problem 3

a. If the analyst uses a sample size of 400 observations, what is the maximum possible error that will be associated with the estimate?

b. What sample size would the analyst need in order to have maximum error of no more than $\pm$ 5 percent?

a. $\hat{p} = .30$ $z = 1.65$ (for 90-percent confidence)

Solution

$$e = z\sqrt{\frac{\hat{p}(1-\hat{p})}{n}} = 1.65\sqrt{\frac{.3(.7)}{400}} = .038 \text{ or } 3.8\%$$

b. $n = \left(\frac{z}{e}\right)^2 \hat{p}(1-\hat{p}) = \left(\frac{1.65}{.05}\right)^2 (.3)(.7) = 228.69, \text{ or } 229$

DISCUSSION AND REVIEW QUESTIONS

1. What is job design and why is it important?
2. What are some of the main advantages and disadvantages of specialization from management's perspective? From blue-collar workers' perspective?
3. Contrast the meanings of the terms *job enlargement* and *job enrichment*.
4. What is the purpose of behavioural approaches such as job enlargement and job enrichment?
5. What are self-directed work teams? What are some potential benefits of using these teams?
6. Some Japanese companies have a policy of rotating their managers among different managerial jobs. In contrast, North American managers are more likely to specialize in a certain area (e.g., finance or operations). Discuss the advantages and disadvantages of each of these approaches. Which do you prefer? Why?
7. Name some reasons why methods analysis is needed. How is methods analysis linked to productivity improvements?
8. How are aids such as process charts and worker–machine charts useful?

9. What are motion economy principles?

10. What is a standard time? What does it assume?

11. What are the main uses of time study information?

12. Could problems with determining performance rating be avoided by studying a group of workers and averaging their times? Explain briefly.

13. If an average worker could be identified, what advantage would there be in using that person for a stopwatch time study? What are some reasons why an average worker might not be studied?

14. What are the main limitations of stopwatch time study?

15. Comment on the following. "At any given instant, the standard times for many jobs will not be strictly correct."

    a. Why is this so?

    b. Does this mean that those standards are useless? Explain.

16. Why do workers sometimes resent time studies?

17. What is work sampling? How does it differ from time study?

18. What are the key advantages and disadvantages of:

    a. Time-based pay plans? i) for management and ii) workers?

    b. Piece rate (output-based) plans? i) for management and ii) workers?

19. Explain the term *skill/knowledge-based pay system*.

TAKING STOCK

1. What are the trade-offs in the following?

    a. Using self-directed teams instead of a more conventional approach with occasional use of teams.

    b. Deciding how often to update standard times due to minor changes in work methods.

2. Who uses the results of work measurement in an organization, and how do they use them?

3. In what ways does technology have an impact on job design?

CRITICAL THINKING EXERCISE

Can a work system be of strategic importance to a company? Explain and Give examples.

INTERNET EXERCISES

1. Look in the Web page of the Association of Canadian Ergonomists (www.ace-ergocanada.ca) and identify what types of activities ergonomists undertake.

2. Look in www.ergoweb.com/resources/casestudies to find an interesting ergonomics case study and summarize it.

PROBLEMS

1. An analyst has timed a metal-cutting operation for 50 cycles. The average time per cycle was 10.40 minutes, and the standard deviation was 1.20 minutes for a worker with a performance rating of 125 percent. Assume an allowance of 16 percent of job time. Find the standard time for this operation.

2. A job was timed for 60 cycles and had an average of 1.2 minutes per cycle. The performance rating was 95 percent, and workday allowance is 10 percent. Determine each of the following:

    a. Average observed time

    b. Normal time

    c. Standard time

3. A time study was conducted on a job that contains four elements. The observed times and performance ratings for six cycles are shown in the following table.

Element	Performance Rating	OBSERVATIONS (MINUTES PER CYCLE)					
		1	2	3	4	5	6
1........	90%	.44	.50	.43	.45	.48	.46
2........	85	1.50	1.54	1.47	1.51	1.49	1.52
3........	110	.84	.89	.77	.83	.85	.80
4........	100	1.10	1.14	1.08	1.20	1.16	1.26

    a. Determine the average time for each element.

    b. Find the normal time for each element.

    c. Assuming an allowance factor of 15 percent of workday, calculate the standard time for this job.

4. Given these observed times (in minutes) for four elements of a job, determine the average observed time (OT) for each element. Note: The second element occurs only every other cycle.

	CYCLE					
	1	2	3	4	5	6
Element 1	4.1	4.0	4.2	4.1	4.1	4.1
Element 2	—	1.5	—	1.6	—	1.4
Element 3	3.2	3.2	3.3	3.2	3.3	3.3
Element 4	2.7	2.8	2.7	2.8	2.8	2.8

5. Given these observed times (in minutes) for five elements of a job, determine the average observed time (OT) for each element. Note: Some of the elements occur only periodically. Also, using PR = .90 for each element and allowance of 15 percent of job time, calculate the standard time for the job.

	CYCLE					
	1	2	3	4	5	6
Element 1	2.1	2.0	2.2	2.1	2.1	—
Element 2	—	1.1	—	1.0	—	1.2
Element 3	3.4	3.5	3.3	3.5	3.4	3.3
Element 4	4.0	—	—	4.2	—	—
Element 5	1.4	1.4	1.5	1.5	1.5	1.4

6. Using Table 7–3 (on p. 264), develop an allowance percentage for a job element that requires the worker to lift a weight of 10 pounds while (1) standing, (2) in light that is well below recommended standards, and (3) with intermittent loud noises occurring. The monotony for this element is high. Include a personal allowance of 5 percent and a basic fatigue allowance of 4 percent.

7. A worker–machine operation was found to involve 3.3 minutes of machine time per cycle in the course of 40 cycles of a stopwatch time study. The worker's time loading and unloading the machine averaged 1.9 minutes per cycle, and the worker was given a rating of 120 percent (machine rating is 100 percent). Assuming an allowance factor of 12 percent of job time, determine the standard time for this job.

8. A recently negotiated union contract allows workers in a shipping department a total of 24 minutes for rest, 10 minutes for personal time, and 14 minutes for delays for each four hours worked. A time study analyst observed a job that is performed continuously and found an average time of 6.0 minutes per cycle for a worker she rated at 95 percent. What standard time is applicable for that operation?

9. The data in the following table represent time study observations for a woodworking operation.

    a. Based on the observations, determine the standard time for the operation, assuming an allowance of 20 percent of job times.

    b. How many observations would be needed to estimate the mean time for element 1 within 1 percent of its true value with a 95.5-percent confidence?

c. How many observations would be needed to estimate the mean time for element 1 within .01 minute of its true value with a 95.5-percent confidence?

Element	Performance Rating	OBSERVATIONS (MINUTES PER CYCLE)					
		1	2	3	4	5	6
1	110%	1.20	1.17	1.16	1.22	1.24	1.15
2	115	.83	.87	.78	.82	.85	1.32*
3	105	.58	.53	.52	.59	.60	.54

*Unusual delay, disregard time.

10. How many observations should a stopwatch time study analyst plan for in an operation that has a standard deviation of 1.5 minutes per piece if the goal is to estimate the mean time per piece to within .4 minute with a confidence of 95.5 percent?

11. How many work cycles should be timed to estimate the average cycle time to within 2 percent of the sample mean with a confidence of 99 percent if a pilot study yielded these times (in minutes): 5.2, 5.5, 5.8, 5.3, 5.5, and 5.1?

12. In an initial survey designed to estimate the percentage of time air-express cargo loaders are idle, an analyst found that loaders were idle in 6 of the 50 observations.
    a. What is the estimated percentage idle time?
    b. Based on the initial results, approximately how many observations would you require to estimate the actual percentage idle time to within 4 percent with a confidence of 95 percent?

13. A job in an insurance office involves telephone conversations with policyholders. The office manager estimates that about half of the employee's time is spent on the telephone. How many observations are needed in a work sampling study to estimate that time percentage to within 4 percent and have a confidence of 95 percent?

14. The killing and disassembly of a hog in a slaughter plant is very labour-intensive, because the tasks cannot easily be automated. This is because each hog is slightly different and the carcasses cannot in general be held in place in a consistent way in order to automate the work. To achieve the target production (which is high in order to make a profit), tasks need to be very specialized. For example, one task is called "snatching guts." Suppose you are helping the industrial engineer to determine the standard time for this task. The videotape of five cycles revealed the following task times (in seconds): 14, 13, 13, 12, and 14. Assume PR = .90 and allowance of 15 percent of job time. Calculate the standard time for this task.[6]

15. The following two activities are commonly used to train stopwatch time study observers to get a feel for an average performance rating, i.e., PR = 1.0.
    a. Walk at 3 miles per hour (= 80 metres per minute = 1.34 metres per second)
    b. Deal a deck of 52 cards into 4 equal piles in .5 minute

    Choose one of these and time yourself trying to achieve these times. If you are too slow, repeat the exercise faster until you reach these speeds. Do you believe that these times are sustainable? Explain.

16. We wish to time installing new shingles on our house. To start, we will try to time driving one nail into a shingle. Assume that the shingle is already in place. You have squatted on your roof facing the shingle. The hammer is on the roof next to the shingle. Nails are in your pocket. Use each of the following techniques to determine the time of driving one nail into the shingle:
    a. Oglesby's simplified MTM technique
    b. MOST

---

[6]Based on J. S. Moore and A. Garg, "Participatory Ergonomics in a Red Meat Packing Plant, Part II: Case Studies," *American Industrial Hygiene Association Journal* 58(7), July 1997, pp. 498–508.

CASE

Making Hotplates

A group of 10 workers were responsible for assembling hotplates (instruments for heating solutions to a given temperature) for hospital and medical laboratory use. A number of different models of hotplates were being manufactured. Some had a vibrating device so that the solution could be mixed while being heated. Others heated only test tubes. Still others could heat solutions in a variety of different containers.

With the appropriate small tools, each worker assembled part of a hotplate. The partially completed hotplate was placed on a moving belt, to be carried from one assembly station to the next. When the hotplate was completed, an inspector would check it over to ensure that it was working properly. Then the last worker would place it in a specially prepared cardboard box for shipping.

The assembly line had been carefully balanced by industrial engineers, who had broken the job down into subassembly tasks, each requiring about three minutes to accomplish. The workers were paid a straight hourly rate.

However, there were some problems. Morale seemed to be low, and the inspector was finding a relatively high percentage of badly assembled hotplates. Controllable rejects—those "caused" by the operator rather than by faulty materials—were running about 23 percent.

After discussing the situation, management decided to try something new. The workers were called together and asked if they would like to build the hotplates individually. The workers decided they would like to try this approach, provided they could go back to the old program if the new one did not work well. After several days of training, each worker began to assemble the entire hotplate.

The change was made at about the middle of the year. Productivity climbed quickly. By the end of the year, it had leveled off at about 84 percent higher than during the first half of the year, although no other changes had been made in the department or its personnel. Controllable rejects had dropped from 23 percent to 1 percent during the same period. Absenteeism had dropped from 8 percent to less than 1 percent. The workers had responded positively to the change, and their morale was higher. As one person put it, "Now, it is *my* hotplate." Eventually, the reject rate dropped so low that all routine final inspection was done by the assembly workers themselves. The full-time inspector was transferred to another job in the organization.

Questions

1. What might account for the increase in productivity, decrease in controllable rejects, drop in absenteeism, and the increase in morale?

2. Would you recommend changing the compensation from hourly rate to piece rate? Explain.

Barnes, Ralph M. *Motion and Time Study: Design and Measurement of Work*, 8th ed. New York: John Wiley & Sons, 1980.

Bridger, R. S. *Introduction to Ergonomics*. New York: McGraw-Hill, 1995.

Carlisle, Brian. "Job Design Implications for Operations Managers." *International Journal of Operations and Production Management*, no. 3 (1983), pp. 40–48.

Cunningham, J. Barton, and Ted Eberle. "A Guide to Job Enrichment and Redesign." *Personnel*, February 1990, pp. 56–61.

Jorgensen, Karen. *Pay for Results: A Practical Guide to Effective Employee Compensation*. Santa Monica, CA: Merritt Publishing, 1996.

Meyers, Fred E. *Motion and Time Study for Lean Manufacturing*, 2nd ed. Englewood Cliffs, NJ: Prentice Hall, 1999.

Mundel, Marvin E., and David L. Danner. *Motion and Time Study: Improving Productivity*, 7th ed. Englewood Cliffs, NJ: Prentice Hall, 1994.

Niebel, Benjamin, and Andris Freivalds. *Methods, Standards, and Work Design*, 11th ed. New York: McGraw-Hill, 2003.

Oglesby, C. H., et al. Productivity Improvement in Construction. New York: McGraw-Hill, 1989.

Osborn, Jack D., Linda Moran, Ed Musslewhite, and John Zenger. *Self-Directed Work Teams*. Burr Ridge, IL: Richard D. Irwin, 1990.

SELECTED BIBLIOGRAPHY AND FURTHER READING

To access "Learning Curves," the supplement to Chapter 7, please visit the student **DVD** packaged with the text or the Online Learning Centre at
www.mcgrawhill.ca/olc/stevenson

CHAPTER 8

Location Planning and Analysis

hen Cara Operations purchased five more chains of restaurants (in addition to Harvey's and Swiss Chalet) in the early 2000s, it needed to become more efficient in the site selection process. Fleetguard is a division of Cummins Engine Company, making filters, exhaust tubes, and mufflers. In the early 2000s, Fleetguard was looking for a site to make a new product. How do companies like these make location decisions? The answer to this and other questions is the topic of this chapter.

INTRODUCTION

When a well-known real estate agent was asked what the three most important determinants of the value of a property are, he said, "That's easy. Location, location, and location."

A house should be close to work, school, grocery store, mall, but not on a busy road. In many respects, the choice of location for a business organization is every bit as important as it is for a house, although for different reasons.

Location decisions represent a key part of the strategic planning process of virtually every organization. And, although it might appear that location decisions are one-time problems pertaining to new organizations, existing organizations often need to relocate too.

This chapter examines location planning and analysis. It covers the nature and importance of location decisions, a general procedure for location decision making, factors influencing the decision, reasons why a foreign company would want to locate in Canada, and techniques for evaluating the alternative locations.

NATURE AND IMPORTANCE OF LOCATION DECISIONS

New companies obviously need a plant or store/office in which to make or provide their new products or services. Existing organizations may need to make location decisions for a variety of reasons. Firms such as banks, fast-food chains, supermarkets, and retail stores view location as part of marketing strategy, and look for locations that will help them to expand their markets. Basically, the location decisions in those cases reflect the *addition* of new locations to an existing system.

A similar situation occurs when an organization experiences a growth in demand for its products or services that cannot be satisfied by expansion at an existing location.

Some firms face location decisions through depletion of basic inputs. For example, fishing and logging operations are often forced to relocate due to the exhaustion of fish or forests at a given location. Mining and petroleum operations face the same sort of situation.

For other firms, a shift in markets causes them to consider relocation, or the costs of doing business at a particular location reach a point where other locations begin to look more attractive. Another reason may be centralizing dispersed locations to gain economies of scale.

There are several reasons why location decisions are a highly important part of production or service systems design. One is that they entail a long-term commitment which makes mistakes difficult to overcome. A second is that location decisions impact investment requirements, operating costs, and revenues. Third, a poor choice of location might result in a shortage of qualified labour, inadequate supplies of raw materials, or some similar condition that is detrimental to operations.

Because, by its nature, location decision is usually based on many factors, no single location may be significantly better than the others. There may be numerous acceptable locations from which to choose, as shown by the wide variety of locations where successful organizations can be found.

Fleetguard

Fleetguard makes various types of filters, exhaust tubes, and mufflers. A subsidiary of Cummins Engine Company, Fleetguard employs 6,000 people working in 23 plants located in nine countries. In August 2002, Fleetguard was looking for a site, approximately 250,000 square feet for about 400 workers, to make exhaust products for small engines and recreational vehicles. Specifically, the objective was to be close to (within one-day truck delivery distance of) its customers (recreational vehicle manufacturers) who were mostly located in the southeast U.S. Fleetguard preferred a vacant building which required minimal structural changes.

A real estate advisor identified eight vacant buildings in various communities in the southeastern U.S. Then, WDG Consulting was hired to assist in site/building selection. Four green-field sites were to also be identified and evaluated for comparison. WDG collected preliminary information for each of 12 alternative sites/buildings to ensure that adequate qualified available workers live in the vicinity of each site, that

there is only a small threat of unionization, that retrofit or building permit application process would be short (less than six months), and that electricity supply would be stable. The information came from WDG files and local economic development agencies.

WDG chose three sites/buildings which satisfied the above requirements in order to investigate further. Interviews were conducted with managers of other plants, personnel agencies, real estate agents, and economic development officers in each area in order to determine the business climate and collect more accurate information. Government officials were asked to provide an incentive package. Each site/building was inspected in order to identify any site-related problems such as land pollution. The three alternatives were compared in terms of wage rates, labour turnover rate, land/building cost, transportation cost, tax rate, electricity rate, and incentive dollars. Waynesboro, Georgia, came up on top which was recommended to Fleetguard in August 2003.

Source: www.wdgconsulting.com/WDGC_project_case_studies_FleetguardNelson.htm

---

Location factors can depend on where a business is in the *supply chain*. For instance, at the retail end of a chain, site selection tends to focus more on accessibility, consumer demographics (population density, age distribution, average buyer income), and traffic patterns. Businesses at the beginning of a supply chain, supplying raw materials, are often located near the source of the raw materials. Businesses in the middle of the chain may locate near suppliers or near their customers, depending on a variety of circumstances. For example, businesses involved in storing and distributing goods often choose a central location to minimize distribution costs. Web-based and phone-based businesses are much less dependent on location decisions; they can exist just about anywhere.

Managers generally consider three options for capacity expansion. One is to expand an existing facility if there is adequate room for expansion. Expansion costs are often less than those of other alternatives. Another option is to add new locations while retaining existing ones, as is done in many retail operations. In such cases, it is essential to take into account what the impact will be on the total system—opening a new store in a shopping mall may simply draw customers who already patronize an existing store in the same chain. A third option is to shut down one location and move to another.

GENERAL PROCEDURE FOR MAKING LOCATION DECISIONS

The way an organization approaches location decisions often depends on its size and the nature or scope of its operations. New or small organizations tend to adopt a rather informal approach to location decisions. New firms typically locate in a certain area simply because the owner lives there. Similarly, managers of small firms often want to keep operations in their backyard, so they tend to focus almost exclusively on local alternatives. Large established companies, particularly those that already operate in more than one location, tend to take a more formal approach. Moreover, they usually consider a wider range of geographic locations. The discussion here pertains mainly to a formal approach to location decisions.

The general procedure for making location decisions usually consists of the following steps:

1. Identify important search parameters and factors, such as location of markets or raw materials.
2. Develop location alternatives:
   a. Identify the general region for a location.
   b. Identify a number of acceptable community/site alternatives.
3. Evaluate the alternatives and make a selection.

Whether a company chooses to use a location/site selection consultant or assign the project to someone in-house, the basic steps to a successful location decision will be similar. Once the company has defined its parameters for the search, the researcher will gather information on appropriate sites (e.g., through telephone and Internet inquiries, reading literature, etc.). Then she begins the process of elimination to achieve a list of three or four sites. Next, the researcher will usually visit those sites, meeting with local authorities and real estate agents. Company executives responsible for the decision may be involved at this stage. Then a final decision is made. Typically, the process will take six months to a year. For an application, see the reading, "Fleetguard."

FACTORS THAT AFFECT LOCATION DECISIONS

Many factors influence location decisions. However, it often happens that one or two factors are so important that they dominate the decision. For example, in manufacturing, the potentially dominating factors may include availability of an abundant energy and proximity to raw materials (e.g., aluminum production needs large amounts of electricity). Transportation to market costs can be a major factor (e.g., most soft drinks are produced in local bottling plants). In service organizations, possible dominating factors

READING

Two Examples of Closeness to Raw Material and Utilities

www.mccain.com
www.teckcominco.com

McCain Foods

The key to success for growing potatoes is the quality of the soil and good growing conditions. Because of their bulk and perishability, it is best to process potatoes where they are grown. The $20-billion world french fries market is growing at a rate to support three new factories per year.

McCain Foods represents about one-third of that market, so to keep its share of the global marketplace, the company has to build an average of one facility every year. By the late 1990s, it had potato-processing plants in PEI, New Brunswick (two), Manitoba, and several outside of Canada. In 1997, the Manitoba plant in Portage la Prairie was expanded, doubling its capacity. However, McCain soon realized that more capacity was needed to supply the Northwest U.S. and Asian markets.

McCain had been involved in southern Alberta for many years and purchased some of the potatoes for its Manitoba plant there. Alberta potatoes are firmer than their competitors from the northwestern United States and have lower water content, adding at least 1 percent to profitability.

McCain built a $94-million french fries plant near Coaldale, 30 km east of Lethbridge, Alberta. The company had owned land in the area for 25 years. According to Arnold Park, president of McCain Foods: "There are excellent farmers in southern Alberta and that particular area gives McCain good freight lanes to the ports of Vancouver and the markets of Asia Pacific."

Teck Cominco

Teck Cominco's zinc smelter and refinery in Trail, B.C., was built to process zinc from the nearby mine. Its source of electricity, a major expense, is its own dam on the nearby river. However, now, after a century, the supply of ore is running out. Instead of closing the facilities, Cominco is bringing in zinc from its other distant mines through port of Vancouver and by railway to Trail. This significant transportation cost is more than offset by the even cheaper electricity.

Source: J. Werniuk, "On the Trail to Continuous Improvement," *Canadian Mining Journal* 121(8), December 2000, pp. 9–13.

are market-related. For example, car rental agencies locate near airports and downtown, where their customers are.

This section contains a description of regional/country factors, community and site factors, and advantages of Canadian locations for foreign companies.

Regional/Country Factors

The primary regional factors involve raw materials, markets, and labour considerations.

Location of Raw Materials. Firms locate near or at the source of raw materials for three primary reasons: necessity, perishability, and transportation costs. Mining operations, farming, forestry, and fishing fall under *necessity*. Obviously, such operations must locate close to the raw materials. Firms involved in canning or freezing of fresh fruit and vegetables, processing of dairy and meat products, and so on must consider *perishability* when considering location. *Transportation costs* are important in industries where processing eliminates much of the bulk in a raw material, making it much less expensive to transport after processing. Examples include potash, lumber, and pulp and paper production. Being close to raw materials is the reason many forest-products companies such as MacMillan Bloedel (now part of Weyerhaeuser) and Canfor have plants in British Columbia. Many petrochemical plants are located in Alberta, many farmers are located in the prairies, and many fish-processing plants are located in the Maritimes. For two more examples, see the reading, "Two Examples of Closeness to Raw Material and Utilities" on the preceding page.

Location of Markets. Retail sales and services are usually found near the centre of the markets they serve. Examples include fast-food restaurants, gas stations, and supermarkets. Quite often their products and those of their competitors are so similar that they rely on convenience to attract customers. Hence, these businesses seek locations with high population densities or traffic. This is also true for banks, drugstores, convenience stores, and hair salons.

Competitive pressures at retail operations can be extremely high. In some cases, a market served by a particular location may be too small to justify two competitors (e.g., one burger franchise per block), so that a search for potential locations tends to concentrate on locations without competitors. The opposite also might be true; it could be desirable to locate near competitors. Large department stores often locate near each other, and small stores like to locate in shopping centres that have large department stores as anchors.

Some firms must locate close to their markets because of the perishability of their products. Examples include bakeries, flower shops, and fresh seafood stores. For other

High Liner Foods uses eight deep-sea trawlers to fish around Nova Scotia and Newfoundland. Its two primary processing plants are nearby in Lunenburg, NS, and Arnold's Cove, NF. This proximity is due to perishable fish.

www.highlinerfoods.com

READING

Provinces Compete for Companies

Provinces often compete to attract companies and hence create jobs. An example of this occurred when CIBC was looking for a Maritime call centre location in the mid-1990s. New Brunswick's government was very disappointed to find out that CIBC chose Halifax over Moncton. After all, Moncton is a bilingual city (a useful skill for call centre staff to have) and N.B. Telephone Company had lots of call-centre experience. Both governments offered similar "training" incentives (around $10,000 per worker). CIBC's reason for choosing Halifax was that they needed many part-time workers and felt that New Brunswick's labour market was already saturated. Also, they were looking for people who could speak Mandarin and Cantonese, as well as French and English. They believed that they would find these skills in Halifax.

Source: B. Banks and D. North, "1-800-Sour Grapes," *Canadian Business*, May 1995, pp. 22–23.

types of firms, distribution transportation costs are the main factor in closeness to market (for example, sand and gravel dealers and bottling plants). Another example is regional warehouses used by supermarkets and other retail operations to supply multiple outlets. Still other firms require close customer contact, so they too tend to locate within the area they expect to serve. Typical examples are tailor shops, home remodellers, home repair services, cabinetmakers, rug cleaners, lawn and garden services, and component suppliers to just-in-time manufacturers.

Location of many government services should be near the centre of the markets they are designed to serve. For instance, police patrols often concentrate on high-crime areas, and emergency health care facilities are usually found in central locations.

Labour Factors. Primary labour considerations are the wage rates and whether unions are a potential problem.

Labour costs are very important for labour-intensive organizations, and they can differ significantly across regions (see CANSIM II's "Labour Force Survey Estimates" Table #282-0074 for wage rates in each province). Labour rates are related to the cost of living, which also varies across regions. The significant contraction of furniture and apparel industries in Canada after the Free Trade Agreement with the U.S. in 1989 is likely due to higher labour costs in these industries in Canada.

Some companies target high unemployment regions in order to tap the large pool of unemployed workers. Presence of unions usually results in higher wages and less flexible work rules. Therefore, companies prefer to locate in regions where unions are not strong.

READING

Subsidies

An example of a company obtaining large subsidies is Ford of Canada when in 2003 it announced it would invest $1 billion to renovate and convert its Oakville assembly complex to flexible manufacturing and to start to assemble its new range of products there. At the time, Ford also announced it would seek government support for the venture. In return, Ford received $100 million from the Federal government and $100 from the Ontario government. Without the subsidies, the 51-year old Oakville site would have faced challenges from other Ford locations to build the new products. Some 3,800 employees at Ford's Oakville operations currently build Ford Freestar and Mercury Monterey models there. Earlier in

Ford's 5.4 million square feet Oakville Complex.

July 2004, Ford stopped producing F-Series pickup trucks in the same complex, laying off 1,200 workers. On January 8, 2006, Ford announced that, in addition to Freestar and

Monterey, it will start producing two new vehicles in the Oakville Complex: Ford Edge and Lincoln MKX. Subsidies are a fact of life in the auto industry with southern U.S. states being the prime example of securing auto investment by this means.

An example of a case in which government subsidies were inadequate was Alcoa's largest aluminum smelter in Baie-Comeau, 660 km northeast of Montreal. This facility employs about 1,800 workers. The previous provincial government had made a deal with Alcoa in late 2002 to renovate the 50 year old smelter, guaranteeing $128 million in interest-free loans, 10 years of tax holiday, and up to 175 megawatts of additional electricity at the low rate of 3.5 cents per kilowatt hour. (Electricity is a major cost in aluminum smelting—to make 1 tonne of aluminum, 15 megawatt hours of electricity is required). However, when Jean Charest became the premier in 2003, he changed the agreement to get a better deal for Quebec. In particular, he tried to tie the electricity price to the rate of inflation. Alcoa claimed that this would cost $10 billion over 40 years! The agreement was rescinded in June 2004 and Alcoa invested in Iceland and Brazil instead. Alcoa will

Alcoa's Baie-Comeau Aluminum refinery.

continue running the smelter until at least 2010 after which it may be closed down.

Sources: John Arnone, Corporate Affairs Manager, Ford of Canada, whose gracious assistance is hereby acknowledged; www.conway.com/ssinsider/bbdeal/bd041108.htm; www.conway.com/ssinsider/snapshot/sf040705.htm.

Other Factors. Electric power sometimes plays a role in location decisions. For instance, many aluminum-smelting plants are located in Quebec because such plants use a large amount of electricity, which is inexpensive in Quebec. The same is true for British Columbia.

Also, both business and personal taxes in some provinces can reduce or enhance a province's attractiveness to companies seeking new locations. Provinces such as Alberta and Quebec have used lower taxes to attract companies. Federal and provincial governments give tax incentives to encourage more research and development, manufacturing, and investment.

For examples, see the readings, "Provinces Compete for Companies" and "Subsidies." Land and building costs are also usually significant and can differ across regions.

Foreign Locations. Some firms are attracted to foreign locations to exploit foreign natural resources. Other firms view foreign locations as a way to expand their markets, and still others are attracted by ample supplies of labour. Many developing countries offer an abundant supply of cheap labour. For example, many North American companies have plants in China.

A firm contemplating a foreign location must carefully weigh the potential benefits against the potential problems. A major factor is the stability of a country's government and its attitude toward foreign firms. Some of the problems of a foreign location can be caused by language and cultural differences. One factor that has negatively impacted the bottom line of some Canadian firms' operating plants in foreign countries is the level of corruption present, and having to deal with politics. For example, Manulife Financial is having legal problems with its local partner in Indonesia, alleging corruption,[1] and Talisman Energy of Calgary has had to sell its share of an oil project in Sudan because of interest-groups' pressure and civil war.[2]

Further, it is much harder to coordinate the activities of foreign locations with domestic locations. The reading, "Should You Export, or Manufacture Overseas?" explores choice of foreign locations further.

---

[1]See P. Vieira, "Indonesia Has Tripped up Manulife Before," *Financial Post* (*National Post*), June 19, 2002, FP9.

[2]See "Talisman Confirms Sudan Sale," *Weekly Petroleum Argus* 32(43), November 4, 2002, p. 12; R. Hirsch, "Why Sudan Matters," *National Journal* 33(22), June 2, 2001, pp. 1640ff.

Should You Export, or Manufacture Overseas?

While exporting is often the least risky method of selling overseas, it frequently involves significant transportation and tariff costs that may make it uneconomical when compared with foreign manufacturing.

With exporting, a company must evaluate the various modes of transportation that would be involved in getting the goods there, and how this relates to the cycle time of putting the product in the marketplace. Some products are time-sensitive; others are less so.

Sometimes you run into government contracts where the only way to distribute a product in that country is to have it made locally. In China, for instance, you have to build something there in order to enter that market.

On the other hand, foreign manufacturing, while potentially a more competitive way of entering an overseas market, has its own problems. Political instability, fluctuating market conditions, and the huge capital costs to set up an overseas manufacturing operation are daunting challenges. For example, if you want to sell in Russia, you're facing political instability as your biggest single operating risk.

The maturity of a company's product affects this decision. A product expected to require design changes, for example, may not fit well with foreign manufacturing plans. Tactically, you want to be moving products offshore that are relatively stable.

Perhaps the best way for many companies to enter a foreign market is to first export there, but with an eye toward building there in the future. Exporting will give you a feel for the product and its market potential.

Such a strategy worked well for IPSCO, Inc. In the early 1980s, the Regina, Saskatchewan–based steel producer exported its steel pipes and flats to the United States from Canada—despite significant transportation costs. Once the company realized that there was significant U.S. demand for its products, it decided to set up shop there.

"Fundamentally it is very expensive to transport steel pipe from Canada to the United States," explained Mario Dalla-Vicenza, IPSCO senior vice-president. "Unlike flat steel, which you're able to transport up to the maximum load-bearing capability of a railcar, steel pipe—because it is hollow—fills the volume of a railcar before it fills the maximum load-bearing capability. So, there's a fundamental freight cost disadvantage." To overcome this drawback and make the company more competitive with U.S. pipe producers, IPSCO acquired pipe mills in Camanche, Iowa, and Geneva, Nebraska.

Later, IPSCO built three more pipe mills in Arkankas, Texas, and Minnesota, and two minimills in Alabama and Iowa.

Questions

1. What advantages does exporting have?

2. What advantages does foreign manufacturing have?

Source: Adapted from R. Banham, "Not-So-Clear Choices," *International Business*, November/December 1997, pp. 23–25.

Some Examples of Community Factors

Shuttle Craft

Shuttle Craft is a small Saskatoon-based company that manufactures a special type of a boat that a Sea-doo can hook into, thus enabling the Sea-doo to carry approximately four passengers. Shuttle Craft was started by three commerce graduates of the University of Saskatchewan who would like to stay in the community even though most of their products are sold in the United States. As the company has grown, Shuttle Craft has moved into larger plants. The latest plant is in Floral, a small town approximately 20 km southeast of Saskatoon, where the rent is even cheaper, but it is still close to family and friends.

Inco

Two geologists, looking for diamond, accidentally discovered the huge deposits of nickel ore in Voisey's Bay, Labrador, in 1993. In 1995, Inco bought a 30-percent share in the deposits for approximately $450 million. In 1996, Inco got into a bidding war with Falconbridge over the remaining share of deposits. It cost Inco another $4.6 billion to secure the other 70 percent. Then, a preliminary agreement with the province was made, promising to build a $2.7-billion smelter in Newfoundland to refine the ore. Next, there were claims by Innu and Inuit peoples of Labrador over the land. The negotiations, which also involved the provincial government, dragged on for years. In 1998, nickel prices plummeted and Inco reduced its production in its Sudbury, Ontario, and Thompson, Manitoba, smelters. This resulted in excess capacity, which forced Inco to withdraw its plan to build the smelter in Labrador. Inco found it cheaper to ship the nickel ore to Sudbury and Thompson to refine. The negotiation with the government of Newfoundland broke down. Even though Inco offered a compromise (to build a smaller plant), the government would not budge. Finally, after more than four years (a very long time for a company), the two sides came to an agreement. Inco will build a smelter by 2011, but during the construction can ship nickel out of the province for processing. The Innu and Inuit peoples got title to some land, some money, and some guarantee of employment in the mining and smelting operations.

Ganong

Ganong Brothers of St. Stephen, N.B., has manufactured chocolates there for about 130 years. When in 1990 the company needed more space and had to move, it found it difficult to leave St. Stephen—Ganong employs approximately 200 of the town's 4,000 population. In return, the employees are devoted to Ganong.

Sources: www.shuttlecraft.com; S. Reier, "The Treasure of Voisey Bay," *Financial World* 164(16), July 18, 1995, pp. 28–30; "Inco Taking Share of Voisey Bay," *American Metal Market* 103(111), June 9, 1995, pp. 1–2; "Will 90B Nickels or More Take the Voisey's Bay Nickel?" *Engineering & Mining Journal* 197(5), May 1996, pp. 10–11; B. Kelly, "Voisey's Startup Seen; Smelter Waits," *American Metal Market* 106(78), April 24, 1998, p. 2; "Voisey's Bay Gets Off the Ground," *Engineering & Mining Journal*, July 1, 2002; www.inco.com/about/development/voisey; "Ganong—A Committed Employer," *Candy Industry* 163(2), February 1998, p. 24; www.ganong.com

Community Considerations

Usually workers live close to their place of work. Blue-collar workers usually do not relocate to find a job. Therefore, companies should make sure that there are sufficient number of potential applicants living nearby a potential site. If there are other large employers in the vicinity, then the pool of available workers will be smaller. Large employers usually locate in or around a big city for this reason. Companies employing office workers, engineers, lab researchers, and specialized trades need the services of a college, university, or technical institution in the community. White-collar employees may relocate, but they usually require a high quality of life.

From a company standpoint, a number of factors determine the desirability of a community as a place for its workers and managers to live. They include facilities for education, shopping, recreation, transportation, entertainment, and medical services.

Many communities actively try to attract new businesses because they are viewed as potential sources of future tax revenues and new job opportunities. They offer tax abatements, low-cost loans and grants for worker training. However, communities do not, as a rule, want firms that will create pollution problems or otherwise lessen the quality of life in the community. Examples of this include community resistance to airport expansion, changes in zoning, construction of nuclear facilities, "factory farms," and highway construction.

For heavy industries, it is important to be close to a railway line, just at the outskirt of a city or town, usually on a green-field site (i.e., on a vacant out-of-town lot). Light industries usually need to be close to highways. Offices may want to be close to airports. Call centres and data centres need to be close to major telephone and data transmission lines.

Land and building prices may differ significantly across communities. See www.colliers.com/corporate/offices/Canada for commercial real estate prices in major cities in Canada. For examples of community factors, see the reading, "Some Examples of Community Factors."

Site-Related Factors

The primary considerations related to sites are land and access. Usually a company first estimates the size of land and building required. In many cases, both vacant buildings and undeveloped sites are considered. Because of the long-term commitment usually required, land costs may be secondary to other site-related factors, such as room for future expansion, utility and sewer capacities—and any limitations on these that could hinder future growth—and sufficient parking space for employees and customers. In addition, for many firms access roads for trucks or rail spurs are important.

Industrial parks may be worthy alternatives for firms involved in light manufacturing or assembly, warehouse operations, and customer-service facilities. Typically, the land is

Circles

Circles Inc. is an unusual Boston-based service company. Its employees provide personal assistance to staff and high-end customers of client companies using telephone and Internet (http://doit.circles.com). For example, they direct a person to the nearest wine glass engraving shop, suggest gifts, or make travel and event arrangements.

In 2004, Circles was looking for another call centre with 330 seats outside Boston to expand its capacity and also provide a backup centre in case of power or weather-related problems in Boston. The requirements were a location east of Rockies in the U.S. or Canada with educated labour force having strong written and verbal communication skills (because of high-end clients). With the help of a site selection/real estate company, Circles narrowed the list of potential cities/towns to 24 locations, many in Ontario. The final choice was Burlington, because it did not already have many call centres, and because it had a large pool of suitable applicants to choose from who are expected to stay with the company.

Ontario has over 3,500 call centres employing 255,000 people.

Source: www.siteselection.com/features/2005/mar/naCust

already developed—power, water, and sewer hookups have been attended to, and zoning restrictions do not require special attention.

For retailers and restaurants, customer access is a prime consideration. They tend to be revenue-focused, concerned with demographics such as age, income, education, population/drawing area, competition, traffic volume/patterns, and customer access/parking. They typically place traffic volume high on the list of important factors.

Downtown areas have a competitive disadvantage in attracting shoppers compared to malls because malls offer free parking and nearness to residential areas. The best store location in a mall is in the main aisle, between main doors and/or escalators receiving the highest traffic. It helps if it is near the top of an up escalator or near the bottom of a down escalator. Also, a large, visible, and accessible frontage is needed for people to see the shop and visit it. Of course, these locations cost more to lease![3]

WHY SHOULD FOREIGN COMPANIES LOCATE IN CANADA?

Foreign companies locate plants in Canada to shorten delivery time and reduce delivery costs to markets in Canada and the U.S., as well as to exploit Canadian natural resources and use Canadian skilled labour.

Canadian workers are educated and basic health care is free. Canada is generally safe and secure. Energy costs are low and governments provide R&D tax incentives. Canada has good phone and Internet infrastructure. Canada is considered politically stable. According to a study by KPMG, Canada is the cheapest of seven major industrialized countries in which to operate a plant. Many companies, mainly from the U.S., have set up plants in Canada over the last century, thus helping to industrialize Canada. One industry greatly benefiting Canada is the auto industry. The Big Three U.S. automakers, Toyota and Honda have several assembly and component plants in Canada, mainly in Southern Ontario.

---

[3]"How to Stand Out in a Crowd," *Canadian Business*, September 25, 1998, p. 30.

Ferrero

Ferrero is a privately owned Italian chocolate maker with 15 chocolate factories, mostly in Europe but one in New Jersey. In 2004 Ferrero was looking for a location for a chocolate factory in Canada. It chose the city of Brantford, between Toronto and London, Ontario. The $150 million,

600,000 square feet building on 160 acres (with plenty of room to grow) needed to be close to major Canadian and U.S. markets and close to highways. The available industrial land at a good price and a pro-business city hall also helped to attract Ferrero to Brantford.

Source: Official website for Economic Development Brantford-Brant "Your Advantage Point," www.brantfordbrant.com/publications/winter_2004.pdf.

Globeco

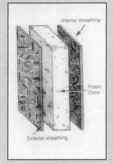

Globeco is a small Holland-based manufacturing and construction company with a special product: a sandwich-like wall panel. The two outer layers are Oriented Strand Board (OSB), whereas the inside is made of a wood frame, which creates a gap between the two outer sheaths, and insulation foam. The houses made by Globeco using these wall panels are simple but low cost, lightweight, and easy to put up. Globeco is constructing these buildings in several developing countries, working with Red Cross. The wall panels come in a 4′ by 8′ standard size, but Globeco has designed a new production process to make very large 8′ by 24′ panels. Globeco has located two small plants in western Ontario, in the small towns of Rainy River (to make the panels) and Barwick (to make the OSB), both close to the Manitoba and U.S. borders. The main reason

for locating the plants in Canada is the cheaper wood and labour costs (relative to Holland's). From Canada, the panels are shipped throughout the world.

Sources: K. McGowan, "Rainy River Attracts Foreign Investment," *Northern Ontario Business* 19(5), March 1, 1999, p. 8; http://globecotech.com.

Every province has something to offer. For example, Quebec has been promoting the development of its high-tech industries (which include e-commerce, multimedia, and biotech firms) for decades. It gives a 40-percent income tax credit for employee salaries of high-tech firms, and also a 40-percent tax credit on specialized machinery. This enables innovative companies to locate in Quebec and to take more risk in developing high-tech products. An example is a small French company, Trigonix, which is developing a scanner for very large documents. Another example is the French computer game maker Microids.

The readings on Circles, Ferrero, and Globeco provide three examples of foreign companies setting up shop in Canada.

EVALUATING LOCATION ALTERNATIVES

There are a number of techniques that are helpful in evaluating location alternatives: locational break-even analysis, the transportation method, factor rating, and the centre of gravity method.

Locational Break-Even Analysis

The economic comparison of location alternatives is facilitated by the use of break-even analysis. The analysis can be done numerically or graphically. The graphical approach will be demonstrated here because it enhances understanding of the concept and indicates the ranges over which one of the alternatives is superior to the others.

The procedure for **locational break-even analysis** involves these steps:

1. Determine the fixed and variable costs associated with each location alternative.
2. Plot the total-cost lines for all location alternatives on the same graph.
3. Determine which location will have the lowest total cost for the expected level of output.

locational break-even analysis Technique for evaluating location choices based on quantity to be produced.

This method assumes the following:

1. Fixed costs are constant for the range of probable output.
2. Variable costs are linear for the range of probable output.
3. The required level of output can be estimated.
4. Only one product is involved.

Compute the total cost for each location:

$$\text{Total cost} = FC + v \times Q \tag{8–1}$$

where

FC = Fixed cost

v = Variable cost per unit

Q = Quantity or volume of output

Fixed and variable costs for four potential plant locations are shown below:

Example 1

Location	Fixed Cost per Year	Variable Cost per Unit
A	$250,000	$11
B	100,000	30
C	150,000	20
D	200,000	35

a. Plot the total-cost lines for these locations on a single graph.

b. Identify the range of output for which each alternative is superior (i.e., has the lowest total cost).

c. If expected output at the selected location is to be 8,000 units per year, which location would provide the lowest total cost?

a. To plot the total-cost lines, select an output that is approximately equal to the expected output level (e.g., 10,000 units per year). Compute the total cost for each location at that level:

Solution

	Fixed Cost + Variable Cost = Total Cost
A ...	$250,000 + $11(10,000) = $360,000
B ...	100,000 + 30(10,000) = 400,000
C ...	150,000 + 20(10,000) = 350,000
D ...	200,000 + 35(10,000) = 550,000

Plot each location's fixed cost (at Output=0) and the total cost at 10,000 units; and connect the two points with a straight line. (See the following graph.)

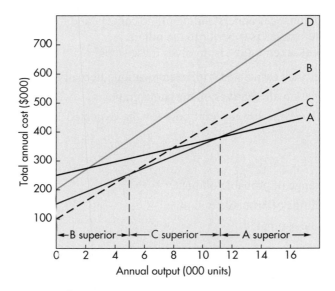

b. The *approximate* ranges for which the various alternatives will yield the lowest total cost are shown on the graph. Note that location D is never superior. The *exact* ranges can be determined by finding the output level at which lines B and C and lines C and A cross. To do this, set their total cost equations equal and solve for Q, the break-even output level. Thus, for B and C:

$$
\begin{array}{cc}
\text{(B)} & \text{(C)} \\
\$100,000 + \$30Q & = \$150,000 + \$20Q
\end{array}
$$

Solving, you find $Q = 5,000$ units per year.

  For C and A:

$$
\begin{array}{cc}
\text{(C)} & \text{(A)} \\
\$150,000 + \$20Q & = \$250,000 + \$11Q
\end{array}
$$

Solving, $Q = 11,111$ units per year.

c. From the graph, you can see that for 8,000 units per year, location C provides the lowest total cost.

Similar analysis can be performed using profit instead of total cost. Note that if the selling price and demand is the same across the sites, then the answer will be the same as when using total cost.

  For a profit analysis, compute the total profit for each location:

$$
\text{Total profit} = Q(R - v) - \text{FC} \tag{8–2}
$$

where

  $R =$ Revenue per unit

Solved Problem 2 at the end of the chapter illustrates profit analysis.

  Where the expected level of output is close to the middle of the range over which one alternative is superior, the choice is readily apparent. If the expected level of output is very close to the edge of a range, it means that the two alternatives will yield comparable annual costs, so management would be indifferent in choosing between the two *in terms of total cost*. However, it is important to recognize that, in most situations, other factors besides operations cost must also be considered (such as transportation cost and availability of labour). Below, a general scheme for including a broad range of factors is described (factor rating). First, let's consider another kind of cost often considered in location decisions: transportation costs.

The Transportation Method

Transportation costs sometimes play an important role in location decisions. These stem from the movement of raw materials and finished goods. If a facility will be the sole source or destination of shipments, the company can include the transportation costs in a locational break-even analysis by incorporating the transportation cost per unit into the variable cost per unit.

When a problem involves shipment of goods from multiple sending points to multiple receiving points, the company should use the *transportation method* of linear programming. It is a special-purpose algorithm used to determine the shipments in order to minimize total transportation cost subject to meeting the demand and not exceeding the capacities of supplies. Various models can be run, each adding one of the potential sites to the set of existing supply and demand points. The site resulting in minimum total transportation cost will be chosen. See the chapter supplement (available on the DVD) for further description of the transportation method.

Factor Rating

A typical location decision involves both qualitative and quantitative factors which tend to vary from situation to situation depending on the needs of each organization. **Factor rating** is a general approach that is useful for evaluating a given alternative and comparing alternatives. The value of factor rating is that it provides a rational basis for evaluation and facilitates comparison among alternatives by establishing a *composite* score for each alternative that summarizes all related factors. Factor rating enables decision makers to incorporate their personal opinions and quantitative information in the decision process.

factor rating General approach to evaluating locations that includes quantitative and qualitative factors.

The following procedure is used in a factor rating:

1. Determine which factors are relevant (e.g., location of market, labour supply, parking facilities, revenue potential).
2. Assign a weight to each factor that indicates its relative importance compared with all other factors. Typically, weights sum to 1.00.
3. Decide on a common scale for all factor scores (e.g., 0 to 100).
4. Score all factors for each location alternative.
5. Multiply the factor weight by the score for each factor, and sum the results for each location alternative.
6. Choose the alternative that has the highest composite score.

This procedure is illustrated by the next example.

A photo-processing company intends to open a new branch store. The table below contains information on two potential locations. Which is the better alternative?

Example 2

Solution

Factor	Weight	SCORES (OUT OF 100) Alt. 1	Alt. 2	WEIGHTED SCORES Alternative 1	Alternative 2
Distance from existing store[1]	.10	100	60	.10(100) = 10.0	.10(60) = 6.0
Traffic volume[1]	.05	80	80	.05(80) = 4.0	.05(80) = 4.0
Rental costs[2]	.40	70	90	.40(70) = 28.0	.40(90) = 36.0
Size[1]	.10	86	92	.10(86) = 8.6	.10(92) = 9.2
Renovation costs[2]	.20	40	70	.20(40) = 8.0	.20(70) = 14.0
Operating costs[2]	.15	80	90	.15(80) = 12.0	.15(90) = 13.5
	1.00			70.6	82.7

[1]Higher is better.
[2]Lower is better.

Alternative 2 is better because it has the higher composite score.

In some cases, managers may prefer to establish minimum *thresholds* for composite scores. If an alternative fails to meet that minimum, they can reject it without further consideration. If none of the alternatives meets the minimum, this means that either additional alternatives must be identified and evaluated or the minimum threshold must be re-evaluated.

The Centre of Gravity Method

centre of gravity method

Method for locating a distribution centre that minimizes total distribution cost.

The **centre of gravity method** is a method to determine the location of a distribution centre that will minimize total distribution cost. It treats distribution cost as a linear function of the distance and the quantity shipped.

The method includes the use of a map that shows the locations of destinations. The map must be accurate and drawn to scale. A coordinate system is overlaid on the map to determine relative locations. The location of the (0,0) point of the coordinate system, and its scale, is unimportant. Once the coordinate system is in place, you can determine the coordinates of each destination. (See Figure 8–1, parts a and b.)

If the quantities to be shipped to every location are *equal*, you can obtain the coordinates of the centre of gravity (i.e., the location of the distribution centre) by finding the average of the *x* coordinates and the average of the *y* coordinates (see Figure 8–1 part c).

FIGURE 8-1

Centre of gravity method
a. Map showing destinations
b. Add a coordinate system
c. Centre of gravity

a. Map showing destinations

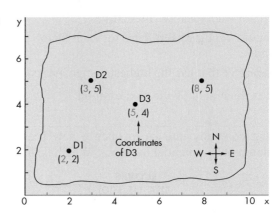

b. Add a coordinate system

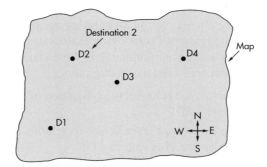

c. Centre of gravity

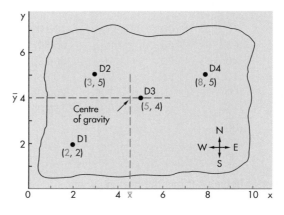

These averages can be easily determined using the following formulas:

$$\bar{x} = \frac{\sum x_i}{n}$$

$$\bar{y} = \frac{\sum y_i}{n}$$

(8–3)

where

$x_i = x$ coordinate of destination i

$y_i = y$ coordinate of destination i

n = number of destinations

When the number of units to be shipped is not the same for all destinations, which is usually the case, a *weighted average* must be used to determine the centre of gravity, with the weights being the *quantities* to be shipped.

The appropriate formulas are:

$$\bar{x} = \frac{\sum x_i Q_i}{\sum Q_i}$$

$$\bar{y} = \frac{\sum y_i Q_i}{\sum Q_i}$$

(8–4)

where

Q_i = Quantity to be shipped to destination i

Example 3

Determine the coordinates of the centre of gravity for the problem that is depicted in Figure 8–1a. Assume that the shipments from the centre of gravity to each of the four destinations will be equal quantities.

Solution

The coordinates of the destinations can be obtained from Figure 8–1b:

Destination	x, y
D1	2, 2
D2	3, 5
D3	5, 4
D4	8, 5
	18, 16

$$\bar{x} = \frac{\sum x_i}{n} = \frac{18}{4} = 4.5$$

$$\bar{y} = \frac{\sum y_i}{n} = \frac{16}{4} = 4$$

Hence, the centre of gravity is at (4.5, 4), which places it just west of destination D3 (see Figure 8–1c).

Example 4

Suppose that the shipments for the problem depicted in Figure 8–1a are not all equal, but instead are the following:

Destination	x, y	Weekly Quantity
D1	2, 2	800
D2	3, 5	900
D3	5, 4	200
D4	8, 5	100
		2,000

Determine the centre of gravity.

Solution

Because the quantities to be shipped differ among destinations, you must use the weighted average formulas.

FIGURE 8-2

Centre of gravity for Example 4

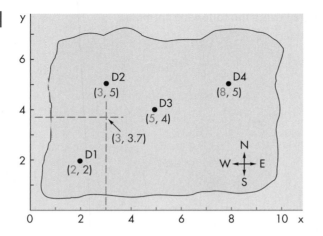

$$\bar{x} = \frac{\sum x_i Q_i}{\sum Q_i} = \frac{2(800) + 3(900) + 5(200) + 8(100)}{2,000} = \frac{6,100}{2,000} = 3.05 \text{ [round to 3]}$$

$$\bar{y} = \frac{\sum y_i Q_i}{\sum Q_i} = \frac{2(800) + 5(900) + 4(200) + 5(100)}{2,000} = \frac{7,400}{2,000} = 3.7$$

Hence, the coordinates of the centre of gravity are approximately (3, 3.7). This would place it south of destination D2. (See Figure 8–2.)

Location-Analysis Software

geographical information system (GIS) A computer-based tool for collecting, storing, retrieving, and displaying demographic data on maps.

Software can be helpful in location analysis. A **geographical information system (GIS)** is a computer-based tool for collecting, storing, retrieving, and displaying demographic data on maps. The data might involve age, incomes, type of employment, type of housing, or other similar data. The intuitive graphical maps facilitate communication of facts and hence decision making.

There are also optimization software packages available for location analysis. Many packages employ linear programming or a variation called mixed integer programming algorithms. In addition, some software packages use heuristic approaches to obtain reasonable solutions to location problems. Two companies producing location software are MicroAnalytics and MapInfo. For an application of MapInfo, see the reading, "Cara."

MicroAnalytics has a product called OptiSite which uses the transportation model to determine the optimal use and allocation of suppliers, warehouses, and customer demand points, as well as optimal location of plants and warehouses. Other software from Micro-Analytics are Bustops and TruckStops used for optimal routing (www.bestroutes.com).

A Geographic Information System (GIS) is a tool that can be used for location planning. This graphic of New York State combines information from different databases to answer demographic questions about the state. This information also can be broken down into smaller units, such as counties.

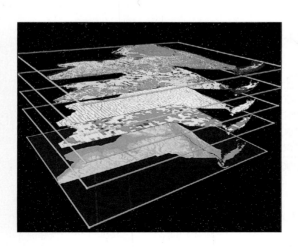

READING

Cara

When Cara Operations purchased five more restaurant chains in the beginning of the 2000s (in addition to Harvey's and Swiss Chalet), the Director of Market Planning in the Real Estate Department needed assistance to keep up. Cara purchased MapInfo's site selection software AnySite. The software not only provides electronic maps of trade areas but also provides demographic information such as the number of people and their spending habits for eating out. Cara also uses a plug-in software called Site Matcher that assists in matching a new trade area with a similar one which already has an existing restaurant in it. MapInfo has reduced the analysis time per site from half a day down to one hour.

Source: http://resource.mapinfo.com/static/files/document/1086796426697/Cara.5.7.pdf.

SUMMARY

Location decisions confront both new and existing organizations. Growth, market shifts, depletion of raw materials, and the introduction of new products and services are among the reasons organizations are concerned with location decisions. The importance of these decisions is underscored by the long-term commitment they typically involve and by their impact on costs. The primary location options available to existing organizations are to expand an existing location, move to a new location, and maintain existing facilities while adding another facility in a new location.

A common approach to location analysis is to first identify a country or region that seems to satisfy overall needs and then identify a number of community-site alternatives for more in-depth analysis.

In practice, the major influences on location decisions are location of raw materials, labour supply, market considerations, community-related factors, and site-related factors. Foreign locations may be attractive in terms of labour costs, abundance of raw materials, or as potential markets for a firm's products or services. Canada is one of the best locations for a foreign plant, because it is close to North American markets, has an educated labour force, and has abundant natural resources.

A variety of methods are used to evaluate location alternatives. Those described in the chapter include locational break-even analysis, factor rating, and the centre of gravity method. The transportation method was mentioned briefly; the chapter supplement on the DVD contains a more complete description of the transportation method.

KEY TERMS

centre of gravity method, 292
factor rating, 291

geographical information system (GIS), 294
locational break-even analysis, 289

Solved Problems

Cost analysis. A farm implements dealer is seeking a fourth warehouse location to complement three existing warehouses. There are three potential locations: Saskatoon, Regina, and Yorkton. Saskatoon would involve a fixed cost of $4,000 per month and a variable cost of $4 per unit; Regina would involve a fixed cost of $3,500 per month and a variable cost of $5 per unit; and Yorkton would involve a fixed cost of $5,000 per month and a variable cost of $6 per unit. Use of the Saskatoon location would increase system transportation costs by $19,000 per month, Regina by $22,000 per month, and Yorkton by $18,000 per month. Which location would result in the lowest total cost to handle 800 units per month?

Problem 1

Solution

Given: Volume = 800 units per month

	FC per Month	Variable Cost per Unit, v	Increase in Transportation Cost per Month
Saskatoon	$4,000	$4	$19,000
Regina	3,500	5	22,000
Yorkton	5,000	6	18,000

Monthly total cost = FC + VC + Increase in transportation cost

Saskatoon: $4,000 + $4 per unit × 800 units +$19,000 = $26,200
Regina: 3,500 + 5 per unit × 800 units + 22,000 = 29,500
Yorkton: 5,000 + 6 per unit × 800 units + 18,000 = 27,800

Hence, Saskatoon would have the lowest total cost for this monthly volume.

Problem 2

Profit analysis. A manufacturer of staplers is about to lose its lease, so it must move to another location. Two sites are currently under consideration. Fixed costs would be $8,000 per month at site A and $9,400 per month at site B. Variable costs are expected to be $5 per unit at site A and $4 per unit at site B. Monthly demand has been steady at 8,800 units for the last several years and is not expected to deviate from that amount in the foreseeable future. Assume staplers sell for $6 per unit. Determine which location would yield the higher profit under these conditions.

Solution

$$\text{Profit} = Q(R - v) - \text{FC}$$

Site	Revenue = QR	FC	Q.v	Monthly Profit
A	$52,800	$8,000	$44,000	$800
B	$52,800	$9,400	$35,200	$8,200

Hence, site B is expected to yield the higher monthly profit.

Problem 3

Factor rating. Determine which location has the higher composite score given the following information:

		SCORE	
Factor	Weight	A	B
Labour cost	.50	20	40
Material cost	.30	10	30
Supplier base	.20	50	10
	1.00		

Solution

Multiplying the weights with the location scores and adding, we can see that location B has the higher composite score:

		SCORE		WEIGHTED SCORES	
Factor	Weight	A	B	A	B
Labour cost	.50	20	40	.50(20) = 10	.50(40) = 20
Material cost	.30	10	30	.30(10) = 3	.30(30) = 9
Supplier base	.20	50	10	.20(50) = 10	.20(10) = 2
	1.00			23	31

DISCUSSION AND REVIEW QUESTIONS

1. In what ways can the location decision have an impact on the production system?
2. Respond to this statement: "The importance of the location decision is often vastly overrated; the fact that virtually every type of business is located in every region of the country means that there should be no problem in finding a suitable location."
3. What community factors influence location decisions?
4. How are manufacturing and service location decisions similar? Different?
5. What are the potential benefits of locating in foreign countries? Potential drawbacks?
6. What is factor rating, and how does it work?
7. Outline the general approach for developing location alternatives.
8. What are the basic assumptions in locational break-even analysis?
9. What is the centre-of-gravity method, and when should it be used?

10. The problem of finding a hub for an airline or a package delivery service such as FedEx (for which Memphis is the hub) can be modelled and solved by the centre-of-gravity method. Explain how.

11. Crude oil in Canada that was first explored near Sarnia, Ontario, is long gone by now. Still, Sarnia is known as the Chemical Capital of Canada, having 16 chemical and 3 major oil refineries.[4] Explain what advantage Sarnia has relative to locations in Alberta that are closer to oil and petrochemical feedstock production.

TAKING STOCK

1. What trade-offs are involved in deciding to have a single large, centrally located facility instead of several smaller, dispersed facilities?

2. Who needs to be involved in facility location decisions?

3. Name two ways that technology has had an impact on location decisions.

CRITICAL THINKING EXERCISE

The owner of a fast-food franchise has exclusive rights to operate in a city. The owner currently has a single outlet open, which has proved to be very popular, and there are often waiting lines of customers. The owner is therefore considering opening one or more outlets in the area. What are the key factors that the owner should investigate before making a final decision?

INTERNET EXERCISES

1. Visit www.MapInfo.com. Under "products and services," choose "software," then click on MapInfo Professional. Briefly summarize what it does. A useful article is "User-Friendly GIS," which is linked to the Web page.

2. Visit www.SiteSelection.com and search using "Canada" as the key word to find an article about a location decision involving Canada. Identify the company and the major factors they used to find a suitable site.

PROBLEMS

1. A newly formed company must decide on a plant location. There are two alternatives under consideration: locate near the major raw materials or locate near the major customers. Locating near the raw materials will result in lower fixed and variable costs than locating near the market, but the owners believe that there would be a loss in sales volume because customers tend to favour local suppliers. Revenue per unit will be $180 in either case. Using the following information, determine which location would produce the greater profit.

	Near raw materials	Near customers
Annual fixed costs ($ millions)	$1.2	$1.4
Variable cost per unit	$36	$47
Expected annual demand (units)	8,000	12,000

2. The owner of Genuine Subs, Inc., hopes to expand the present operation by adding one new outlet. She has studied three locations. Each would have the same labour and materials costs (food, serving containers, napkins, etc.) of $1.76 per sandwich. Sandwiches sell for $2.65 each in all locations. Rent and equipment costs would be $5,000 per month for location A, $5,500 per month for location B, and $5,800 per month for location C.

   a. Determine the volume necessary at each location to realize a monthly profit of $10,000.

   b. If expected sales at A, B, and C are 21,000, 22,000, and 23,000 sandwiches per month, respectively, which location would yield the greatest profit?

3. A small producer of machine tools wants to move to a larger building, and has identified two alternatives. Location A has annual fixed costs of $800,000 and variable costs of $14,000 per unit; location B has annual fixed costs of $920,000 and variable costs of $12,000 per unit.

---

[4]D. Richards, "Ontario Comes to Houston to Push Chemical Investment," *Chemical Marketing Reporter* 250(14), September 30, 1996, p. 7.

    a. At what volume of output would the two locations have the same total cost?

    b. For what range of output would location A be superior? For what range would B be superior (i.e., have lower total annual cost)?

4. A company that produces pleasure boats has decided to expand one of its lines. Current facilities are insufficient to handle the increased workload, so the company is considering three alternatives, A (new location), B (subcontract), and C (expand existing facilities).

    Alternative A would involve substantial fixed costs but relatively low variable costs: fixed costs would be $250,000 per year, and variable costs would be $500 per boat. Subcontracting would involve a cost per boat of $2,500, and expansion would require an annual fixed cost of $50,000 and a variable cost of $1,000 per boat.

    a. Find the range of output for each alternative that would yield the lowest total cost.

    b. Which alternative would yield the lowest total cost for an expected annual volume of 150 boats?

    c. What other factors might be considered in choosing between expansion and subcontracting?

5. Rework Problem 4*b* using this additional information: Expansion would result in an increase of $70,000 per year, subcontracting would result in an increase of $25,000 per year, and adding a new location would result in an increase of $40,000 per year in transportation costs.

6. A firm that has recently experienced an enormous growth rate is seeking to lease a small plant in Winnipeg, Montreal, or Toronto. Prepare an economic analysis of the three locations given the following information: annual costs for building, equipment, and administration would be $40,000 for Winnipeg, $60,000 for Montreal, and $100,000 for Toronto. Labour and materials are expected to be $8 per unit in Toronto, $4 per unit in Winnipeg, and $5 per unit in Montreal. The Montreal location would increase system transportation costs by $50,000 per year, the Winnipeg location by $60,000 per year, and the Toronto location by $25,000 per year. Expected annual volume is 10,000 units.

7. A retired auto mechanic hopes to open a rustproofing shop. Customers would be local new-car dealers. Two locations are being considered, one in the centre of the city and one on the outskirts. The central city location would involve fixed monthly costs of $7,000 and labour, materials, and transportation costs of $30 per car. The outside-city location would have fixed monthly costs of $4,700 and labour, materials, and transportation costs of $40 per car. Price at either location will be $90 per car.

    a. Which location will yield the greatest profit if monthly demand is (1) 200 cars? (2) 250 cars?

    b. At what volume of output will the two sites yield the same monthly profit?

8. For each of the four types of organizations shown below, rate the importance of each factor in terms of making location decisions using L = low importance, M = moderate importance, and H = high importance.

Factor	Local Bank	Steel Mill	Grocery Ware-house	Public School
Convenience for customers	____	____	____	____
Attractiveness of building	____	____	____	____
Nearness to raw materials	____	____	____	____
Large amounts of power	____	____	____	____
Labour cost and availability	____	____	____	____
Transportation costs	____	____	____	____
Construction costs	____	____	____	____

9. Using the following factor ratings (100 points is the maximum), determine which location alternative for a clothing store A, B, or C should be chosen on the basis of maximum composite score.

Factor	Weight	LOCATION A	B	C
Convenience of access . .	.15	80	70	60
Parking facilities	.20	72	76	92
Frontage	.18	88	90	90
Shopper traffic	.27	94	86	80
Operating costs	.10	98	90	82
Neighbourhood	.10	96	85	75
	1.00			

10. A manager has received an analysis of several cities being considered for a new office complex. The data (10 points is the maximum) are:

Factor	LOCATION A	B	C
Business services	9	5	5
Community services . .	7	6	7
Construction costs . . .	5	6	5
Cost of living	4	7	8
Personal taxes	5	5	4
Commuting ease	6	7	8

 a. If the manager weighs the factors equally, how would the locations stack up?

 b. If business services and construction costs are given weights that are double the weights of the other factors, how would the locations stack up?

11. A toy manufacturer distributes its toys from five distribution centres (DCs) throughout the country. A new plant is to be built for a new line of toys. The monthly quantities to be shipped to each DC are approximately the same. A coordinate system has been established, and the coordinates of each DC have been determined as shown. Determine the optimal coordinates of the plant.

Location	(x, y)
A	3, 7
B	8, 2
C	4, 6
D	4, 1
E	6, 4

12. A clothing manufacturer produces women's clothes at four locations. A coordinate system has been determined, as shown in the table below. The location of a central warehouse for bolts of cloth must now be determined. Weekly quantities to be shipped to each location are shown below. Determine the coordinates of the location that will minimize total transportation cost.

Location	(x, y)	Weekly Quantity
A	5, 8	15
B	6, 9	20
C	3, 9	25
D	9, 4	30

13. A company that handles hazardous waste wants to minimize the shipping cost for shipments to a new disposal centre from five receiving stations it operates. Given the locations of the receiving stations and the volumes to be shipped daily below, determine the location of the disposal centre.

Location of Receiving Station, (x, y)	Volume, Tonnes per Day
10, 4	26
4, 1	9
4, 7	25
2, 6	30
8, 7	40

14. Determine the centre of gravity for the destinations shown on the following map. Monthly shipments will be the quantities listed below.

Destination	Quantity
D1	900
D2	300
D3	700
D4	600
D5	800

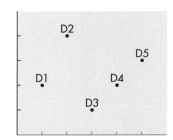

MINI-CASE

Acadian Bakers

Acadian Bakers is a small but well-known bakery making and selling cakes and croissants in Houston. Their major

customers, their location on a coordinated system, and their weekly purchases are listed below.

Acadian's coordinates are (27, 36). Is Acadian sufficiently centrally located to serve its customers?

	COORDINATES		
Customer	**X**	**Y**	**Weekly Purchases ($)**
B. Catering	22	31	80
B. Bar & Grill	38	38	70
H's	38	36	90
H Club	38	37	120
H. C. Club	30	33	90
J's Hideaway	−10	12	60
M's	38	36	140
M. Club	−10	44	140
N. M.	47	33	300
K. S. Catering	33	33	50

MINI-CASE

Stone Consolidated

In 1990 Stone Consolidated decided to develop new landfills for six of its seven mills in eastern Canada. Three of its mills in the St. Maurice Valley area of Quebec were closely situated: the Laurentide mill in Grand-Mere produced uncoated groundwood papers; the Belgo mill in Shawinigan (10 km south) produced newsprint and de-inked pulp; and the Wayagamack mill in Trois-Rivières (40 km further south) produced kraft specialty paper. Given their close proximity, Stone Consolidated began a search for a landfill site that could hold the combined waste generated by these three mills.

Stone Consolidated forecasted its total waste output over the next 25 years. It was calculated that the required landfill would need to take up a 58-hectare area.

Stone Consolidated began its search in a 45 × 60 km area containing the three mills, identifying all parcels of land that were at least 58 hectares and satisfied the Quebec Ministry of Environment's landfill guidelines; 175 potential sites were found. This number was reduced by consulting zoning restrictions affecting each of the potential sites, excluding sites within or close to residential and commercial areas as well as those in agricultural areas, which would have required zoning modification and a public hearing at the Quebec Commission for the Protection of Agricultural Territories. Still further sites were excluded for political reasons, being in municipalities that had negative histories with landfills. Of the original 175 potential sites, 67 were still viable after this initial exclusion phase.

To further exclude sites, Stone Consolidated consulted available geological and geotechnical reports and aerial photographs.

Sites predominantly of water-bearing sand and those with shallow bedrock were thus excluded because of risks of groundwater contamination and the costs of implementing measures in line with environmental protection. After this second exclusion phase, six potential sites remained.

Each of these six sites was subjected to tests to confirm viable subsoil conditions. No unexpected conditions were uncovered, so a decision matrix containing nine criteria was prepared to help select the optimum site: topography, road access, visual impact, weighted average distance to mills,

geology and soil condition, groundwater, surface water, actual or potential land use, and population density. Each criterion was assigned a weight varying between 3 and 8. For each evaluation criterion, a specific site was rated as follows:

– Favourable = 4
– Acceptable = 2
– Marginally acceptable = 1

The numerical ranking system is explained in Table 1. The scores of each of the six potential sites are shown in Table 2.

Table 1. Numerical ranking system

Criteria	Weighting	Favourable factor (4)	Acceptable (2)	Marginally acceptable (1)
Topography	5	Natural relief and slopes favourable to development	Acceptable relief and slopes —not seriously complicated for development	Abrupt relief—difficult or complicated development
Road access	6	Provincial highways bordered by few or no houses	Road network through areas with few houses	Road network through high-density population areas
Visual impact	3	Site not readily noticeable by passersby	Site could be readily visible to passersby; visual screening measures may be required	Site expected to be readily noticeable to passersby; screening measures necessary
Weighted avg. distance to mills	3	Average distance less than 15 km	Average distance less than 20 km	Average distance more than 20 km
Geology and soils	7	Low permeable soils	Moderately permeable soils	Permeable soils
Groundwater	8	Favourable depth to groundwater	Probably acceptable depth to groundwater	Potentially unacceptable depth to groundwater
Surface water	6	Drainage network a fair distance from the site	Drainage network at minimal distance from the site	Drainage network to be altered
Actual or potential land use	8	Forestry or industrial zoning—few or no houses	Adjacent to agricultural zoning	Site close to residential area
Population density	6	Minimal residential development	Scattered residential development	Moderate to dense residential development

Table 2. Site evaluation matrix

Criteria	Weight	St-Georges-de-Champlain	Ste-Geneviere	St-Barnabe	St-Mathieu	St-Gerard	Grandes-Piles
Topography	5	4	4	4	1	2	1
Road access	6	4	2	1	1	1	4
Visual impact	3	4	2	2	4	1	4
Weighted avg. distance to mills	3	4	1	2	2	4	2
Geology and soils	7	4	2	1	1	2	2
Groundwater	8	4	2	2	2	2	4
Surface water	6	1	2	2	4	2	2
Actual or potential land use	8	4	4	1	4	1	2
Population density	6	4	2	1	2	1	2

Question

Calculate the total weighted score for each site. Which one is the best?

Sources: Based on F. Villeneuve, D. Dallaire, and V. G. Fournier, "Site Location and Open Communications Are the Keys to a Successful Landfill Permitting: How One Company Handled Its Expansion Needs," *Pulp & Paper Canada* 99(2), February 1998, pp. 29–31 ff.

MINI-CASE

Marriott

Marriott is a leading world-wide hotel chain with approximately 2,600 hotels. In North America, it has approximately 180 hotels, with headquarters in Washington, D.C. Before the year 2000, each hotel had its own accountants who were responsible for arranging credit checks, receiving customer payments, and paying supplier invoices. In 2000, Marriott decided to centralize the accounting function for the North American hotels in one location. This would be called the shared services centre. The centre would house 300 people in a 50,000 square feet office space. PeopleSoft finance application would be used as the computer software. Each computer in the centre would run the client software, and the server, containing the database, would be located in Marriott's data centre in Frederick, Maryland. The data centre would also print and send the cheques, invoices, etc. The staff of each hotel, approximately 8,000, would access the centre by data lines.

Questions

1. What are the advantages of a shared services centre?

2. Name the most important factors to be used to decide the location of a centre.

Sources: www.wdgconsulting.com/WDGC_project_case_studies_Marriot.htm; C. A. Prescott, "Marriott Redefines the Shared Services Model," *Outlook* 1, 2002, pp. 86–89.

SELECTED BIBLIOGRAPHY AND FURTHER READING

Ballou, Ronald H. *Business Logistics Management*, 4th ed. Englewood Cliffs, NJ: Prentice Hall, 1999.

Ferdows, Kasra. "Making the Most of Foreign Factories." *Harvard Business Review*, March–April 1997, pp. 73–88

Francis, Richard L., Leon F. McGinnis Jr., and John A. White. *Layout and Location: An Analytical Approach*, 3rd ed. Englewood Cliffs, NJ: Prentice Hall, 1998.

Grimshaw, David J. *Bringing Geographical Information Systems into Business.* New York: John Wiley & Sons, 2000.

Lyne, Jack. "Quality-of-Life Factors Dominate Many Facility Location Decisions." *Site Selection Handbook,* August, 1988, pp. 868–70.

To access "The Transportation Model," the supplement to Chapter 8, please refer to the student **DVD** packaged with the text or the Online Learning Centre at
www.mcgrawhill.ca/olc/stevenson

PART FOUR

Quality

The topics in this part relate to quality. There are two chapters: Chapter 9 introduces quality concept, the thinking of quality "gurus," quality awards and certification, total quality management (TQM), and quality tools. Chapter 10 explains statistical quality control procedures.

Management of Quality

S tandard Aero is a small aircraft engine maintenance and repair company based in Winnipeg. Standard Aero is in tough competition with larger multinational aircraft engine repair companies, but it has managed to survive and grow.

Delta Hotels has become a leading Canadian hotel chain. How do companies like Standard Aero and Delta Hotels succeed? Focus on quality management is a major reason. This is the topic of this chapter.

T his chapter is the first of two chapters on quality. In this chapter you will learn about the evolution of quality management, definitions of quality, determinants of quality, the costs of quality and the consequences of poor quality, the philosophies of quality gurus, some quality awards and certification, total quality management (TQM), problem-solving and process improvement, and some quality tools.

INTRODUCTION

Broadly defined, **quality** refers to the ability of a product or service to consistently meet or exceed customer expectations. Prior to the increased level of Japanese competition in North American marketplace in the 1980s, quality was not uppermost in the minds of the management. They tended to focus on quantity, cost, and productivity rather than on quality. It wasn't that quality was *un*important, it just wasn't *very* important.

Partly because of this thinking, foreign companies, many of them Japanese, captured a significant share of the North American market. In the automotive sector, leading Japanese manufacturers Toyota, Honda, and Nissan became major players in the North American auto sales market. All three have built a reputation for quality and reliability in their vehicles.

Many North American companies changed their views about quality after that, and changed them drastically. Stung by the success of foreign competitors, they embraced quality in a big way. They hired consultants, sent their people (including top executives) to seminars, and initiated a vast array of quality improvement programs. These companies clearly recognized the importance of quality and the fact that quality isn't something that is tacked on as a special feature, but is an *integral part* of a product or service. In the 1990s, North American automakers began to close the quality gap.

quality The ability of a product or service to consistently meet or exceed customer expectations.

www.toyota.ca

www.honda.ca

www.nissan.ca

THE EVOLUTION OF QUALITY MANAGEMENT

Prior to the Industrial Revolution, in most cases skilled craftsmen performed all stages of production. Pride of workmanship and reputation often provided the motivation to see that a job was done right. Lengthy guild apprenticeships caused this attitude to carry over to new workers. Moreover, one person or a small group of people were responsible for an entire product.

Division of labour accompanied the Industrial Revolution; each worker was then responsible for only a small portion of each product. Pride of workmanship became less meaningful because workers could no longer identify readily with the final product. The responsibility for quality control shifted to the foremen and full-time quality inspectors. Inspection was either nonexistent or haphazard, although in some instances 100-percent inspection was used.

Frederick Winslow Taylor, the "father" of scientific management, gave new emphasis to quality by including product inspection and gauging in his list of fundamental areas of manufacturing management. In 1924, W. Shewhart of Bell Telephone Laboratories introduced statistical control charts that could be used to monitor production. Around 1930, H. F. Dodge and H. G. Romig, also of Bell Labs, introduced tables for acceptance sampling. Nevertheless, statistical quality control procedures were not widely used until the Second World War, when the U.S. government began to require vendors to use them.

The Second World War caused a dramatic increase in emphasis on quality control. About the same time, professional quality organizations were emerging throughout North America. One of these organizations was the American Society for Quality (ASQ). Over the years, the society has promoted quality with its publications, seminars and conferences, and training and certification programs.

During the 1950s, the quality movement started to evolve into quality assurance, which aims to prevent defects rather than finding them after they occur. Quality guru W. Edwards Deming encouraged Japanese manufacturers to adopt statistical quality control methods, promising that this would help them rebuild their manufacturing base and to compete in world markets.

At about the same time, another quality guru, Joseph Juran, began his "cost of quality" focus, emphasizing accurate and complete identification and measurement of the costs of quality. He stressed the desirability of lowering product failures.

In the mid-1950s, Armand Feigenbaum proposed *total quality control*, which enlarged the realm of quality efforts from its primary focus on manufacturing to include marketing, product design, and after-sale service. One important feature of his work was greater involvement of upper management in quality.

During the 1960s, the concept of "zero defects" gained favour. Championed by quality guru Philip Crosby, this approach focused on management's role, and the expectation of perfection from each employee.

The evolution of quality took a dramatic shift from quality control and assurance to a strategic management approach to quality in the 1980s. Quality and profits are closely linked. This approach places greater emphasis on customer satisfaction, and it involves all levels of management as well as workers in a continuing effort to increase quality (called total quality management). Recently, some companies are pursuing a variation of TQM called six sigma, which uses quality facilitators called Black Belts and more emphasis on statistics.

QUALITY: THE BASICS

Any serious effort to deal with quality must begin with a clear understanding of the meaning of the word *quality*.

The Dimensions of Quality

The term *quality* is used in a variety of ways. Sometimes it refers to the characteristics of material or grade of a product, such as "Canada Choice" or "grade A" eggs. At other times, it refers to workmanship, or performance, or reliability, or special features such as "waterproof" or "subtle aroma." We first describe product quality and then will focus on service quality.

The implication in these various connotations of quality is that customers value certain aspects of a product or service, and therefore associate those aspects with the quality that they perceive a product or service has.

dimensions of product quality Performance, aesthetics, special features, safety, reliability, durability, perceived quality, and service after sale.

Product Quality. The aspects or **dimensions of product quality** include:[1]

Performance—main characteristics or function of the product.

Aesthetics—appearance, feel, smell, taste.

Special features—extra characteristics or secondary functions.

Safety—reduction or elimination of risk of injury or harm.

Reliability—consistency of performance.

Durability—the useful life of the product or service.

Perceived quality—subjective evaluation of quality (e.g., reputation, image).

Service after sale—warrantees, maintenance, and handling of complaints.

---

[1] Adapted from David Garvin, "What Does Quality Really Mean?" *Sloan Management Review* 26(1), 1984, pp. 25–43.

Dimension	Example
1. Performance	Everything works; ride, handling, leg room
2. Aesthetics	Interior design, soft touch, fit and finish, grade of materials used
3. Special features	
Convenience	Placement of gauges and controls
High tech	GPS, DVD player
4. Safety	Antilock brakes, airbags
5. Reliability	Infrequency of breakdowns
6. Durability	Long life, resistance to rust and corrosion
7. Perceived quality	Top-rated car, e.g., Cadillac
8. Service after sale	Warrantee, handling of complaints, maintenance

TABLE 9–1

Examples of quality dimensions for a car

These dimensions are further described by the examples presented in Table 9–1. When a product fits a customer's defined purpose for it, the term *fitness for use* is used. Notice that price (or cost) is *not* a dimension of quality.

Service Quality. The dimensions of product quality don't adequately describe service quality. Instead, service quality is often described using these dimensions:[2]

Tangibles—the physical appearance of facilities, equipment, personnel, and communication materials.

Convenience—the availability and accessibility of the service.

Reliability—the ability to perform a service dependably, consistently, and accurately.

Responsiveness—the willingness of service providers to help customers in unusual situations and to deal with problems.

Time—the speed with which service is delivered.

Assurance—the knowledge exhibited by personnel who come into contact with a customer and their ability to convey trust and confidence.

Courtesy—the way customers are treated by employees who come into contact with them.

Table 9–2 illustrates how the dimensions of service quality might apply to having an automobile repaired.

The dimensions of both product and service quality establish a *conceptual* framework for thinking about quality, but even they are too abstract to be applied operationally for purposes of product or service design, or actually producing a product or delivering a service. They must be stated in terms of specific, *measurable* characteristics. For example,

---

[2]Adapted from Valerie A. Zeithhaml, A. Parasuraman, and Leonard L. Berry, *Delivering Quality Service and Balancing Customer Expectations* (New York: The Free Press, 1990), and J. R. Evans and W. M. Lindsey, *The Management and Control of Quality*, 3rd ed. (St. Paul, MN: West Publishing, 1996).

Dimension	Examples
1. Tangibles	Were the facilities clean? Were personnel neat?
2. Convenience	Was the service centre conveniently located?
3. Reliability	Was the problem fixed?
4. Responsiveness	Were customer service personnel willing and able to answer questions?
5. Time	How long did the customer have to wait?
6. Assurance	Did the customer service personnel seem knowledgeable about the repair?
7. Courtesy	Were customer service personnel and the cashier friendly and courteous?

TABLE 9–2

Example of service quality dimensions for having a car repaired

when buying a car, a customer would naturally be interested in the car's performance. But what does that mean? In more specific terms, it might refer to a car's estimated kilometres per litre, how quickly it can go from 0 to 100 km per hour, or its stopping distance when travelling at 100 kmph. Each of these can be stated in measurable terms (e.g., estimated kilometres per litre: city = 10, highway = 15). Similar measurable characteristics can often be identified for each of the other product dimensions, as well as for the service dimensions. This is the sort of detailed information that is needed to both design and produce high-quality goods and services.

Information on customer wants in service can sometimes be difficult to pin down, creating challenges for designing and managing service quality. For example customers may use words such as "friendly," "considerate," and "professional" to describe what they expect from service providers. These and similar descriptors are often difficult to translate into exact service specifications. Furthermore, in many instances, customer wants are often industry specific. Thus, the expectations for health care would be quite different than for dry cleaning. Furthermore, customer complaints may be due in part to unrelated factors (e.g., customer's mood or general health, the weather).

It should also be noted that in most instances, some quality dimensions of a product or service will be more important than others, so it is important to identify customer priorities, especially when it is likely that trade-off decisions will be made at various points in design and production. Quality function deployment (described in Chapter 4) is a tool that can be helpful for that purpose.

Finally, customers evaluate a product or services's quality relative to their expectation. If the quality, as perceived by a customer, is higher than expected, she will be delighted; if it is the same, the customer is satisfied, but if it is less, she will be dissatisfied.

The Determinants of Quality

The degree to which a product or a service successfully satisfies its intended purpose has four primary determinants. They are:

1. Design
2. How well it conforms to the design in production
3. Ease of use
4. Service after delivery

quality of design
Characteristics designers
specify for a product or
service.

The design phase is the starting point for the level of quality eventually achieved. Design involves decisions about the specific characteristics of a product or service such as size, shape, and material. **Quality of design** refers to the characteristics specified for a product or service. For example, many different models of automobiles are on the market today. They differ in size, appearance, roominess, fuel economy, comfort, and materials used. These differences reflect choices made by designers that determine the quality of the car. Design decisions must take into account customer wants, production or service capabilities, safety (both during production and after delivery), costs, and other similar considerations.

Designers may determine customer wants from information provided by marketing, perhaps through the use of consumer surveys or other market research. Marketing may organize focus groups of consumers to express their views on a product or service (what they like and don't like, and what they would like to have).

Designers must work closely with representatives of operations to ascertain that designs are manufacturable; that is, that production or service has the equipment and skills necessary to produce a particular design. A poor design can result in difficulties in production or service. For example, materials might be difficult to obtain, specifications difficult to meet, or procedures difficult to follow. Moreover, if a design is inadequate or inappropriate for the circumstances, the best workmanship in the world may not be enough to achieve the desired quality. Also, we cannot expect a worker to achieve good results if the given tools or procedures are inadequate. Similarly, a superior design usually cannot offset poor workmanship.

Ford's Protective Cover

Ford's Worldwide Direct Marketing Operations had a problem with surface scratches on its exported cars. A quality analyst, a so-called Six Sigma Black Belt, headed a team to find the cause and fix the problem. The team discovered that some corners of the protective plastic film installed on cars at the assembly plants became loose during the truck and rail transport. Further, the peelings let dirt and debris under the film, which in fact caused the majority of the defects. The team used a cause-and-effect diagram to identify possible causes. It was discovered that both the film and the operators installing them are at fault. The result of experiments showed that a better plastic film reduced the average number of defects (scratches, small dents, etc) per car from 2.89 to 1.29, and that better instructions and training reduced it further to 1.04 defects per car. Further study showed that in fact an etch-resistant coating applied at the factory was enough protection during the ground transportation in North America, and that the plastic film could be applied at the port just before shipping.

Source: "Ford Six Sigma Busts Surface Flaws," *Quality* 41(1), January 2002, pp. 40–41.

Quality of conformance refers to the degree to which goods and services conform to (i.e., *achieve*) the specification of the designers. This is affected by factors such as characteristics of materials; the capability of equipment used; the skills and training, the monitoring process to assess conformance; and the taking of corrective action (e.g., through problem solving) when necessary.

The determination of quality does not stop once the product or service has been sold or delivered. *Ease of use* and user instructions and labels are important. They increase the chances that a product will be used for its intended purposes and in such a way that it will continue to function properly and safely. Much of the same reasoning can be applied to services. Customers, patients, clients, or other users must be clearly informed on what they should or should not do; otherwise, there is the danger that they will take some action that will adversely affect quality. Some examples include the doctor who fails to specify that a medication should not be taken with certain other drugs and the attorney who neglects to inform a client of a deadline for filing a claim.

For a variety of reasons, products do not always perform as expected, and services do not always yield the desired results. Whatever the reason, it is important from a quality standpoint to remedy the situation—through recall and repair of the product, replacement, or refund—and do whatever is necessary to satisfy the customer.

The reasons for poor quality are numerous and relate to every step of product design, manufacture, use, and after-sale service. Examples of these are given in the cost of quality section after the following section.

quality of conformance The degree to which goods or services conform to the specification of the designers.

The Consequences of Poor Quality

It is important for management to recognize the different ways that poor quality of a company's products or services can affect the organization and to take these into account in developing and maintaining a quality control and assurance program. Some of the major ways that poor quality affects an organization are:

1. Loss of business
2. Liability
3. Productivity loss
4. Costs

A potentially...devastating consequence to the bottom line is the reaction of the consumer who receives a defective or otherwise unsatisfactory product or service. A recent study showed that, while a satisfied customer will tell a few people about his or her experience, a dissatisfied person will tell an average of 19 others.

Unfortunately, the company is usually the last to know of dissatisfaction. People rarely complain directly to the provider of poor quality goods and services. In fact, studies suggest that people usually complain, if at all, to their most immediate contact (e.g., a salesperson or service manager) and that these complaints are rarely transmitted further. A more common response is simply to switch to a competing product or service. Typically, formal complaints are received from less than 5 percent of dissatisfied customers.[3]

Organizations must pay special attention to their potential *liability* due to damages or injuries resulting from either faulty design or poor workmanship. This applies to both products and services. Thus, a poorly designed steering arm on a car might cause the driver to lose control of the car, but so could improper assembly of the steering arm. However, the net result is the same. Liability for poor quality has been well established in the courts, especially in the U.S. An organization's liability costs can often be substantial, especially if large numbers of items are involved, as in the automobile industry, or if potentially widespread injury or damage is involved (e.g., an accident at a nuclear power plant). Express written warranties as well as implied warranties generally guarantee the product as safe when used as intended. The courts, especially in the U.S., have tended to extend this to *foreseeable* uses, even if these uses were not intended by the producer. In the health care field, medical malpractice claims and insurance costs are a concern for physicians.

Productivity and quality are often closely related. Poor quality can adversely affect productivity during the manufacturing process if parts are defective and have to be reworked. Similarly, poor service can mean having to redo the service and reduces service productivity.

---

[3]The Ernst & Young Quality Improvement Consulting Group, *Total Quality: An Executive's Guide for the 1990s* (Burr Ridge, IL: Irwin Professional Publishing, 1990), pp. 6–7.

READING

Diversicare Canada Management Services

Achieving customer and employee satisfaction in the retirement and nursing home industry is no easy task. Diversicare operates 14 long-term-care homes and 23 retirement homes across Canada. In 1992, a committee of Diversicare employees met to identify how to expand and improve their programs. The result was "Continuous Quality Improvement" (CQI), designed to encourage employees to achieve excellence in quality of care.

CQI requires four crucial elements:

1. Key indicators: Continual measuring and monitoring of specific health care issues to ensure the effectiveness of programs and services.

2. Human resources: Training of management and staff, and development of management systems to achieve optimal use of human resources.

3. Commitment: Active encouragement of individual initiatives to implement improvements in the quality of care.

4. Empowerment: Empowering caregivers to review existing mechanisms and to make recommendations to improve the quality of life for residents.

CQI involves focus on customers, processes, and continuous improvement. In order to accomplish this, a common mission and vision is required. CQI is a management style with the central focus on knowing what customers need and want. At the same time, CQI examines the systems and processes used to achieve goals and the ways employees can improve them, either to improve present outcomes or to prevent future problems or risks. CQI means getting everyone involved. The company has invested heavily in its CQI program and focuses its quality initiatives on improving customer satisfaction and employee recruitment, development, and reward.

CQI has 15 key indicators that measure a host of employee and resident concerns such as safety. They have also added eight quality of life indicators. They constantly look for ways to improve these indicators. Information and initiatives from all levels within the organization are celebrated and shared through an annual CQI conference, which promotes the exchange of best practices within the organization. Diversicare, Ontario Region, won a 2001 Canada Award for Excellence Trophy.

Sources: 2001 Recipient Profiles: http://www.nqi.ca/articles/article_details.aspx?ID=47; http://www.diversicare.ca/corporate.html.

READING

Ford's Headliner

Also, the thick foam in the headliner contributed to variations. The headliner dimensions were adjusted and the amount of foam was reduced, solving the problem.

In the year 2000 Ford had a problem with its minivan headliners. A headliner is the plastic/foam fitting covering the ceiling of a minivan, 4 feet wide and 10 to 12 feet long (depending on the model). At the Oakville assembly plant, workers had difficulty preventing gaps of 1 to 5 millimetres occurring between the headliner and the adjacent components. An engineering team tried to identify the cause of the problem but couldn't. The difficulty is that the headliner, when installed, is hard to measure. The supplier, the Industrial Systems Division of Lear Canada couldn't find the cause of the gaps either. The team decided to bring in Applied Precision of Mississauga who had a sophisticated 3-D portable measurement system called Preseon 1000. The system generated a 3-D image by tracking the infrared hand-held touch probe. The PowerInspect Software compared this image with the CAD data files for the body. It was discovered that both the headliners and the body of the car contributed to the problem. There was variation in body dimensions emanating from the welding-assembly area.

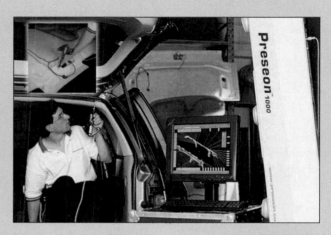

Sources: "Measurement System Solves Minivan Headliner Fit-up Problems," *Design Product News* 29(6), November 2001; "3-D Measurements Solve Fit Problem," *Quality* 41(3), March 2002, pp. 46, 48.

Poor quality increases certain *costs* incurred by the organization. The following section provides further detail on costs associated with quality.

The Costs of Quality

Any serious attempt to deal with quality issues must take into account the costs associated with quality. Those costs can be classified into four categories:

Internal failure costs   *Appraisal* costs

External failure costs   *Prevention* costs

Failure costs are incurred by defective parts or products or by faulty services. **Internal failures** are those discovered during the production process; **external failures** are those discovered after delivery to the customer.

Internal failures occur for a variety of reasons, including defective material from vendors, incorrect machine settings, faulty equipment, incorrect methods, incorrect processing, and faulty or improper material handling procedures. The costs of internal failures include lost production time, scrap and rework, investigation costs, possible equipment damage, and possible employee injury. Rework costs involve the salaries of workers and the additional resources needed to perform the rework (e.g., equipment, energy, raw materials). Other costs relate to inspection of reworked parts, disruption of schedules, the added costs of parts and materials in inventory waiting for reworked parts, and the paperwork needed to keep track of the items until they can be reintegrated into the process.

External failures are defective products or poor service that go undetected by the producer. Resulting costs include warranty work, handling of complaints, replacements, liability/litigation, payments to customers or discounts used to offset the inferior quality, loss of customer goodwill, and opportunity costs related to lost sales.

Appraisal costs relate to inspection, testing, and other activities intended to uncover defective products or services. They include the cost of inspectors, testing, test equipment, labs, quality audits, and field testing.

failure costs Costs caused by defective parts or products or by faulty services.

internal failures Failures discovered during production.

external failures Failures discovered after delivery to the customer.

appraisal costs Costs of inspection and testing.

READING

SKF Canada

www.skf.com/portal/skf.ca

The SKF name has been associated with rolling bearings for more than 90 years since a young Swedish maintenance engineer developed the angular contact bearing to solve a problem in the textile mill where he worked. Today one of every five bearings sold in the world is an SKF bearing. SKF Canada operates a sales and distribution centre in Scarborough, Ontario, from where it supplies bearings to industrial distributors and original equipment manufacturers for the pulp and paper, forestry, and mining industries.

SKF management realized the importance of costs of quality early in the 1990s: if prevention (training) costs $1, assessment (inspections and audits) costs $10, and fixing failures (giving credit notes to customers for shipment errors) costs $100.

After ISO 9000 certification in 1994, SKF Canada continued continuous improvement projects, and worked on business planning and customer and employee focus. SKF Canada received the Certificate of Merit of Canada Awards for Excellence in 2000.

Sources: "Canada Awards for Excellence," *Canadian Business*, December 11, 2000, pp. 93–96; www.skf.com.

---

prevention costs Costs of preventing defects from occurring.

Prevention costs relate to attempts to prevent defects from occurring. They include costs such as quality planning and administration systems, working with vendors, training, quality control procedures, and extra attention in both the design and production phases to decrease the probability of defective workmanship.

Internal and external failure costs represent costs related to poor quality, whereas appraisal and prevention costs represent investments for achieving good quality. For an example of Cost of Quality, see the SKF reading.

QUALITY GURUS

A core of quality experts has shaped modern quality practices. Among the most famous of this core of "gurus" are Deming, Juran, Feigenbaum, Crosby, Ishikawa, and Taguchi. Together, they have had a tremendous impact on the management and control of quality, and the way companies operate.

W. Edwards Deming

www.deming.org/Theman/
biography.html

A statistics professor at New York University in the 1940s, Deming went to Japan after the Second World War to assist the Japanese in improving quality and productivity. His contributions were so much appreciated that an annual quality prize, the Deming Prize, was established in 1951 in his name.

Although the Japanese revered Deming, he was largely unknown to business leaders in North America. In fact, he worked with the Japanese for almost 30 years before he gained recognition in North America. Before his death in 1993, North American companies turned their attention to Deming, embraced his philosophy, and requested his assistance in setting up quality improvement programs.

Deming compiled a famous list of 14 points he believed were the prescription needed to achieve quality in an organization (see Table 9–3). His message is basically that the cause of inefficiency and poor quality is the *system,* not the employees. Deming felt that it was *management's responsibility* to correct the system to achieve the desired results. Deming stressed the need to reduce variation in output, which can be accomplished by distinguishing between *special causes* of variation (i.e., correctable) and *common causes* of variation (i.e., random). This is the foundation of statistical process control (SPC). Deming also promoted the plan-do-study-act (PDSA) cycle of problem solving.

He believed that workers want to create and learn, but that management unintentionally often does things such as establishing rating systems that rob them of their internal motivation. He believed that management's greatest challenge in achieving quality was in motivating workers to contribute their collective efforts to achieve a common goal.

TABLE 9-3

Deming's 14 points

1. Create constancy of purpose toward improvement of product and service with a plan to become competitive and to stay in business. Decide to whom top management is responsible.
2. Adopt the new philosophy. We are in a new economic age. We can no longer live with commonly accepted levels of delays, mistakes, defective materials, and defective workmanship.
3. Cease dependence on mass inspection. Require, instead, statistical evidence that quality is built in. (*Prevent* defects rather than *detect* defects.)
4. End the practice of awarding business on the basis of price tag. Instead, depend on meaningful measures of quality along with price. Eliminate suppliers that cannot qualify with statistical evidence of quality.
5. Find problems. It is management's job to work continually on the system (design, incoming materials, composition of material, maintenance, improvement of machines, training, supervision, retraining).
6. Institute modern methods of training on the job.
7. The responsibility of foremen must be changed from sheer numbers to quality ... [which] will automatically improve productivity. Management must prepare to take immediate action on reports from foremen concerning quality barriers such as inherent defects, machines not maintained, poor tools, and fuzzy operational definitions.
8. Drive out fear so that everyone may work effectively for the company.
9. Break down barriers between departments. People in research, design, sales, and production must work as a team to foresee problems of production that may be encountered with various materials and specifications.
10. Eliminate numerical goals, posters, and slogans for the work force, asking for new levels of productivity without providing methods.
11. Eliminate work standards that prescribe numerical quotas.
12. Remove barriers that stand between the hourly worker and his right to pride of workmanship.
13. Institute a vigorous program of education and retraining.
14. Create a structure in top management that will push every day on the above 13 points.

Source: W. Edwards Deming, *Quality, Productivity, and Competitive Position* (Cambridge, MA: MIT, Center for Advanced Engineering Study, 1982), pp. 16–17.

Joseph M. Juran

Juran, like Deming, taught Japanese manufacturers how to improve the quality of their goods, and he, too, can be regarded as a major force in Japan's success in quality. He made his first trip to Japan a few years after the publication in 1951 of his *Quality Control Handbook.*

www.juran.com

Juran viewed quality as fitness-for-use. He also believed that roughly 80 percent of quality defects are controllable; thus, management has the responsibility to correct this deficiency. He described quality management in terms of a *trilogy* consisting of quality planning, quality control, and quality improvement. According to Juran, quality planning is necessary to establish processes that are *capable* of meeting quality standards; that quality control is necessary in order to know when corrective action is needed; and that quality improvement will help to find better ways of doing things. A key element of Juran's philosophy is the commitment of management to continual improvement.

Juran is credited as one of the first to measure the cost of quality, and he demonstrated the potential for increased profits that would result if costs of poor quality could be reduced.

Juran proposed 10 steps for quality improvement. These are shown in Table 9–4.

Armand Feigenbaum

Feigenbaum was General Electric's top expert on quality. He recognized that quality was not simply a collection of tools and techniques, but a "total field." He saw that when improvements were made in a process, other areas of the company also achieved improvements. Feigenbaum's understanding of systems theory led him to create an environment in which people could learn from each other's successes, and his leadership and open work environment led to cross-functional teamwork. Also, he introduced the

TABLE 9-4

Juran's 10 steps for quality improvement

1. Build awareness for the need and opportunity for improvement.
2. Set goals for improvement.
3. Organize people to reach the goals.
4. Provide training throughout the organization.
5. Carry out projects to solve problems.
6. Report progress.
7. Give recognition.
8. Communicate results.
9. Keep score.
10. Maintain momentum by making annual improvement part of the regular systems and processes of the company.

Source: Joseph M. Juran, ed. *Quality Control Handbook* (New York: McGraw-Hill, 1951).

TABLE 9-5

Key elements of Feigenbaum's philosophy of total quality control

1. Total quality control is a system for integrating quality development, maintenance, and improvement efforts in an organization that will enable engineering, marketing, production, and service to function at optimal economic levels while achieving customer satisfaction.
2. The "control" aspect of quality control should involve setting quality standards, appraising performance relative to these standards, taking corrective action when the standards are not met, and planning for improvement in the standards.
3. Factors that affect quality can be divided into two major categories: technological and human. The human factor is the more important one.
4. Operating quality costs can be divided into four categories: prevention costs, appraisal costs, internal failure costs, and external failure costs.
5. It is important to control quality at the source.

Source: Adapted from Peter Capezio and Debra Morehouse, *Taking the Mystery Out of TQM*, 2nd ed. (Franklin Lakes, NJ: Career Press, © 1995) pp. 100–101.

concept of quality at the source, meaning that every worker is responsible for his/her work. For example, a worker can stop the assembly line if there is a defect.

In 1961, his book *Total Quality Control* was published, in which he laid out quality principles in 40 steps. Table 9–5 lists some of his key ideas.

Philip B. Crosby

Crosby worked at Martin Marietta Company in the 1960s. While he was there, he developed the concept of *zero defects* and popularized the phrase "Do it right the first time." He stressed prevention, and he argued against the idea that "there will always be some level of defectives."

In accordance with the concept of zero defects, Crosby believes that any level of defects is too high, and that management must install programs that help the organization move toward that goal. Among some of his key points are the following:[4]

1. Top management must demonstrate its commitment to quality and its willingness to give support to achieve good quality.
2. Management must be persistent in efforts to achieve good quality.
3. Management must spell out clearly what it wants in terms of quality and what workers must do to achieve that.
4. Make it (or do it) right the first time.

Unlike the other gurus, Crosby maintains that achieving quality can be relatively easy. Crosby's quality-is-free concept is based on the following: costs of poor quality are much greater than traditionally defined, and these costs are so great that rather than viewing

---

[4]Philip Crosby, *Quality without Tears: The Art of Hassle-Free Management* (New York: McGraw-Hill, 1984).

READING

Delta Hotels

www.deltahotels.com

With 35 hotels and 7,500 employees working in hotels located in every major Canadian city, Delta is one of the top providers of first-class hotels. Delta Hotels is a subsidiary of Canadian Pacific Hotels & Resorts.

Since 1995 the company has developed formalized procedures for hotels' daily operations. These are based on the NQI's Criteria for Canada Awards for Excellence.

Delta Hotels trains internal assessors to conduct individual hotel assessments and develop a quality improvement plan. Every two years, a hotel will undergo an initial three-day assessment and a subsequent five-day assessment to ensure that ongoing quality measures are incorporated into Hotel's culture and all aspects of operations. External assessors are also invited to conduct assessments, ensuring that assessments meet the professional standards of NQI. According to the senior vice-president (people and quality), "Our goal is to ensure a seamless approach to quality, so that it is part of our culture."

Problem-solving teams regularly monitor processes for improvement opportunities. One result of these improvements is Delta's "one-minute check-in guarantee" for guests.

Delta has realized improved results in measuring guest satisfaction. Also, employee satisfaction and professional development have risen dramatically. Employee accomplishments are recognized during regular "town hall" meetings. As a result of all these improvements, Delta Hotels won a Canada Award for Excellence Trophy in 2000.

Sources: "Canada Awards for Excellence," *Canadian Business,* December 11, 2000, pp. 93–96; www.deltahotels.com.

---

quality efforts as costs, organizations should view them as a way to reduce costs, because the improvements generated by quality efforts will more than pay for themselves.

Kaoru Ishikawa

The late Japanese expert on quality was strongly influenced by both Deming and Juran, although he made significant contributions of his own to quality management. Among his key contributions were the development of the *cause-and-effect diagram* (also known as fishbone diagram) for problem-solving and the implementation of quality circles, which involves teams of workers in quality improvement. He was the first quality expert to call attention to the *internal customer*—the next employee in the process.

Genichi Taguchi

Taguchi is best known for the *Taguchi loss function*, which involves a formula for determining the cost of poor quality. The idea is that the deviation of a part's critical attribute from a specified target causes a loss, and the combined effect of deviations of all parts in a product from their targets can be large, even though each individual deviation is small.

A related concept is robust design, i.e., a design which results in acceptable product during manufacturing and use under varied conditions.

Building on this, Taguchi proposed the use of experiments to determine the best settings for the product and process parameter levels. He also devised efficient methods of experimental design. Taguchi's method is credited with helping the Ford Motor Company reduce its warranty losses by achieving less variation in the output of transmissions.

Table 9–6 provides a summary of the important contributions of the gurus to modern quality management.

Contributor	Key Contributions
Deming	14 points; special versus common causes of variation, SPC, PDSA cycle
Juran	Quality is fitness-for-use; quality trilogy
Feigenbaum	Quality is a total field; quality at the source
Crosby	Quality is free; zero defects
Ishikawa	Cause-and-effect diagrams; quality circles
Taguchi	Taguchi loss function, robust design, design of experiments

TABLE 9–6

A summary of key contributors to quality management

QUALITY AWARDS

Quality awards have been established to generate awareness and interest in quality. The Malcolm Baldrige Award (U.S.) and the Canada Awards for Excellence are two well-known awards given annually to firms that have integrated quality management in their operations.

The Baldrige Award

Baldrige Award Annual award given by the U.S. government to recognize quality achievement of U.S. companies.

The **Baldrige Award**, administered by the U.S. National Institute of Standards and Technology, intends to stimulate efforts to improve quality, to recognize quality achievements of U.S. companies, and to publicize successful programs.

Businesses that compete for the award are required to submit an application documenting their quality system. Applicants are evaluated in seven main areas: leadership, information and analysis, strategic planning, human resource management, process management, business results, and customer and market focus. These are basically the same as the requirements of total quality management.

The characteristics the examiners check include the extent to which top management incorporates quality values in daily management; whether products or services are at least as good as those of competitors; whether employees receive training in quality techniques; if the business works with suppliers to improve quality; and if customers are satisfied.

The Canada Awards for Excellence

Canada Awards for Excellence Canada's own awards recognizing outstanding quality achievement.

www.nqi.ca

The **Canada Awards for Excellence** are Canada's own awards recognizing outstanding quality achievement are administered by the National Quality Institute (NQI), an independent not-for-profit organization. NQI has investigated the workings of successful organizations and developed a set of criteria for business excellence. The criteria, similar to Baldrige Award criteria, are a comprehensive, practical, and well-tested framework for improvement. These criteria are given in the reading on the following page. Since 1989, the awards have honoured more than 50 Canadian organizations for outstanding quality achievement. Organizations such as IBM Canada, the Royal Bank, and Inco use the criteria as a framework for effectiveness. In addition to manufacturing and service sectors, more and more government, education, and health care organizations are putting the criteria into action and discovering the power of continuous improvement. For two applications, see the readings, "Diversicare Canada Management Services" earlier in the chapter and "Delta Hotels" on the preceding page.

QUALITY CERTIFICATION

Many firms that do business internationally recognize the importance of ISO 9000 quality certification.

ISO 9000

ISO 9000 A set of international standards on quality management and quality assurance, critical to international business.

www.iso.org

The purpose of the International Organization for Standardization (ISO) is to promote worldwide standards that will improve operating efficiency and productivity, and reduce costs. The ISO is composed of the national standards bodies of 91 countries. The Canadian representative body is the Standards Council of Canada. The work of the ISO is conducted by some 180 technical committees. ISO 9000 is the work of the Quality Management and Quality Assurance Committee.

The **ISO 9000** series is a set of international standards on quality management and quality assurance. These standards are critical for companies doing business internationally, particularly in Europe. They must go through a process that involves documenting quality procedures and on-site assessment. The process often takes 12 to 18 months. With certification comes *registration* in an ISO directory that companies seeking suppliers can refer to. They are generally given preference over unregistered companies. More than half a million companies are registered worldwide; three-fourths of them are located in Europe.

Criteria for Canada Awards for Excellence

The following is merely a summary of the criteria. For details, see Canadian Framework for Business Excellence which can be purchased from NQI.

1. Leadership

Creating the culture, values, and overall direction for lasting success.

1.1 Strategic Direction

1.2 Leadership Involvement

1.3 Continuous Improvement

> *Ongoing improvement cycle of Strategic Direction and Organizational Culture.*

2. Planning

Business planning (which incorporates improvement plans), the linkage of planning to strategic direction/intent, the implementation and the measurement of performance to assess progress.

2.1 Plan Development

2.2 Plan Implementation and Review

2.3 Continuous Improvement

> *Ongoing improvement cycle of Plan Development and Plan Implementation and Review.*

3. Customer Focus

Organization's focus on the customer and the marketplace and on the achievement of customer satisfaction and loyalty.

3.1 Customer, Market and Product Knowledge

3.2 Management of Customer Relationships

3.3 Continuous Improvement

> *Ongoing improvement cycle of Customer, Market and Product Knowledge and the Management of Customer Relationships.*

4. People Focus

How employees are encouraged, enabled, and involved to contribute to the achievement of the organization's goals, while reaching their full potential.

4.1 Human Resource Planning

4.2 Participatory Environment

4.3 Continuous Learning

4.4 Employee Satisfaction and Well-being

4.5 Continuous Improvement

> *Ongoing improvement cycle of Human Resource Management, Participatory Environment, Continuous Learning and Employee Satisfaction and Well-being.*

5. Process Management

How processes are managed to support the organization's strategic direction, with a specific focus on prevention (as against correction), as well as continuous improvement. Process management applies to all activities within the organization, in particular those that are critical (key) for success. Process improvement priorities are derived from goals established within other sections, notably Section Two (Planning) and Section Three (Customer Focus).

5.1 Process Development

5.2 Process Control

5.3 Process Improvement

5.4 Continuous Improvement

> *Ongoing improvement cycle of Process Development, Process Control and Process Improvement.*

6. Supplier/Partner Focus

Organization's external relationships with other organizations, institutions and/or alliances that are critical to it meeting its strategic objectives. Such working relationships may include suppliers, partnerships, distributors/dealers, joint ventures, in-sourcing/outsourcing, regulatory bodies and franchises. Suppliers can be external or internal (i.e., units of the parent organization that provides goods/services).

6.1 Partnering

6.2 Supplier/Partner Management

6.3 Continuous Improvement

> *Ongoing improvement cycle of Partnering and Supplier/ Partner Management*

7. Overall Business Performance

Outcomes from overall organizational achievements.

7.1 Customer Focus

7.2 People Focus

7.3 Process Management

7.4 Partnerships

7.5 Responsibility to Society

7.6 Owner/Shareholder Focus

The review process involves considerable self-appraisal, resulting in problem identification and improvement. Registered companies face an ongoing series of audits, and they must be re-registered every three years. A summary of standards (updated in the year 2000) is listed in Table 9–7.

ISO 9001:2000 Summary

1 Objectives
- To satisfy customers through the effective implementation of a quality system.
- To demonstrate consistent and effective application of a system aimed at prevention of nonconformity.
- To continually improve.

2 References

3 Definitions

4 Establishing a Quality Management System (QMS)

Create and document a quality policy, objectives, quality manual, quality planning, processes, procedures, and records. Also identify parts and processes outsourced and control their quality. Justify any exclusions. Describe the interaction between different processes. Control the issue and use of documents and records.

5 Management Responsibility
- Communicate the commitment to QMS to all employees, provide resources, establish a quality policy and deploy it as departments objective, and conduct management reviews of the QMS.
- Foster open communication and culture of employee involvement in the organization.
- Define and communicate the responsibilities and authority of all personnel. Ensure that customers' requirements are understood.
- Appoint a quality manager who ensures that the QMS is established and functions, reports its performance to top management, and promotes quality awareness.

6 Resource Management

Determine and provide the QMS resources needed. Provide education and training. All personnel must be competent. The infrastructure (building, equipment, etc.) and work environment must be appropriate to meet product requirements.

7 Product Realization

7.1 Planning of Product Realization

Plan and develop processes needed for producing the product, including quality requirements and inspection/testing requirements. This may include drawing process flow diagram, determining routing/process sheet, etc.

7.2 Customer-related Processes

Ensure that product requirements are defined (in sales order) and that the organization has the ability to meet the requirements. Establish effective communication with the customers.

7.3 Design and Development

Define the review and validation stages of product design and development. Review inputs, such as functional requirements, to ensure that all the requirements are complete, unambiguous and not in conflict with each other. Ensure that the design and development process meet the requirements, and provide clear information for the purchase of required material. Also, control the design and development changes.

7.4 Purchasing

Use a systematic supplier evaluation and selection procedure. Establish and implement inspection procedures for purchased parts. Ensure that purchased products conform to the specified purchase requirements (test them).

7.5 Production and Service Provision
- Plan the production.
- Produce under controlled conditions. Ensure product drawing, quality specifications, and work instructions are provided to the workers.
- Process the product on capable equipment. Make available suitable monitoring and measuring devices. Validate the process by approving the equipment, the qualification of personnel, and the use of specific methods and procedures. Define the inspection points within the process.
- Identify the parts and products (inventory control)
- Develop procedures for handling, storage, packaging, and delivery.

7.6 Control of Monitoring and Measurement Devices

Determine appropriate measurement and test equipment and calibrate them periodically.

8 Measurement, Analysis and Improvement

8.1 General

Determine the methods for measurement and analysis, including statistical techniques.

8.2 Monitoring and Measurement

Monitor and measure customer satisfaction, the processes, and the products. When results are unsatisfactory, corrective action must be undertaken. Conduct periodic and systematic audits of the QMS.

8.3 Control of Nonconforming Product

Segregate defective products. Repair, use as-is (with concession to the customer), or scrap the product. Keep records of the nonconformance and the action taken.

8.4 Analysis of Data

Collect and analyze appropriate data on customer satisfaction (and complaints), conformity to product requirements, characteristics and trends of processes, supplier performance, and the QMS.

8.5 Improvement

Continuously improve the QMS. Investigate the causes of actual or potential nonconformity and eliminate them.

Sources: www.conestogac.on.ca/~dmcintos/introduction.html; www.ulc.ca/downloads/ulc_management_RP2-2000.pdf; D. L. Goetsch and S. B. Davis. *Understanding and Implementing ISO 9000: 2000*, 2nd ed. (New Jersey: Pearson Prentice-Hall, 2002).

There are usually three types of documents created for ISO 9000: a quality policy, a procedures manual, and detailed work instructions and other supporting documents. The procedures manual lists all critical processes of the organization, and for each process describes (in general terms) how it is to be done (using a flow diagram), and what to do if there is a problem.

ISO 9000 (updated in the year 2000) is based on eight quality management principles:

Principle 1: Customer focus

Communicate customer requirements throughout the organization, measure customer satisfaction, act on the results, and maintain a good relationship with the customer.

Principle 2: Leadership

Establish unity of purpose and direction of the organization. Create and maintain the internal environment in which employees become fully involved in achieving the organization's objectives. Provide the employees the resources, responsibility, and authority to ensure customers' needs are met.

Principle 3: Involvement

Involve all the employees.

Principle 4: Process Approach

Identify, manage, and continually improve major organization activities as processes.

Principle 5: System approach to management

Identify and manage all the interrelated organization processes.

Principle 6: Continual improvement

Evaluate and improve all major processes.

Principle 7: Factual approach to decision making

Make decisions on the basis of actual data on products and processes.

Principle 8: Mutually beneficial supplier relationship

Create clear and open communications with the suppliers and jointly establish a clear understanding of customer needs.

ISO 14000

The International Organization for Standardization also introduced a set of environmental standards in 1996: **ISO 14000** is intended to assess a company's performance in terms of environmental responsibility. Initially, ISO 14000 began as a program of voluntary guidelines and certification. The standards for certification bear upon three major areas:

Management systems—Systems development and integration of environmental responsibilities into business planning.

Operations—Consumption of natural resources and energy.

Environmental systems—Measuring, assessing, and managing emissions, effluents, and other waste streams.

As with ISO 9000, the key to a successful ISO 14000 environmental management system (EMS) is to have documented procedures that are implemented and maintained. Required are environmental policy and environmental aspects and impacts of products, activities, and services, including legal requirements. Based on the prioritized environmental aspects and impacts, goals and objectives must be established that are consistent with

ISO 14000 A set of international standards for assessing a company's environmental performance.

the environmental policy. Specific programs and/or projects must be developed to achieve these goals and objectives, including integration of environmental aspects in product/service design, communicating environmental performance using labels, and devising emergency preparedness plans. The monitoring and evaluation of environmental performance and the EMS, and taking corrective actions, helps ensure continuous improvement by addressing root causes of non-conformance.

Honda Transmission Manufacturing plant in Russells Point, Ohio, is certified as ISO 14000.[5] The major challenges were the pressure to maintain production plan, conflicting duties for the environment coordinator and others, difficult-to-obtain funding, unrealistic initial environmental goals (due to lack of baseline environmental performance data), and problems with document control. The solutions included setting a process for goal setting (requiring information gathering), prioritizing the environmental goals, focusing on small investments first, educating staff as to the importance of environmental goals, allocating the cost of energy/water use and waste to the departments, establishing an e-team comprising one representative from each department and making them responsible for gathering data and reporting department progress, reviewing department performance, providing rewards for environmental achievements, and converting to electronic documentation.

HAZARD ANALYSIS CRITICAL CONTROL POINT (HACCP)

HACCP A quality control system designed for food processors.

HACCP is a quality control system, similar to ISO 9000, designed for food processors, especially meat, poultry, and fish processors. It originated with Pillsbury Company when they had to design and manufacture food for NASA space missions in 1960s. HACCP is mandatory for fish processors and is becoming mandatory for meat and poultry processors. Meat exporters to other countries such as the U.S. and Japan need to have HACCP certification too. HACCP is enforced by the Canadian Food Inspection Agency (CFIA). Other food related industries such as dairies, fruit and vegetable processors, and egg producers are also encouraged to implement HACCP.

HACCP deals with food safety, in particular, biological, chemical, and physical hazards.[6] HACCP is implemented by a multidisciplinary team, including a food biologist and sanitation expert in addition to representatives from production, engineering, quality assurance, etc. As in ISO 9000, top management's commitment is essential.

First, the HACCP team inspects various construction and/or sanitary aspects of the plant, equipment, and personnel. For example, the lot should have good drainage and water source, no garbage or odours. The building should have easy-to-clean walls, floors, and ceilings, sloped floors to drains, screened windows, close-fitting doors, self-closing washroom doors, good ventilation, and be pest proof.

If there is any short-coming, corrective action is implemented. Also, the team ensures that there is a regular system of work instructions, inspection, and prevention in place for the building, equipment, and personnel. Guidelines and Standard Operating Procedures (SOP) are provided by the CFIA and other government agencies. Further, there should be a procedure for product recall, i.e., a product coding system and records.

---

[5]A. M. C. McManus and L. A. Sanders, "The Real Value of an EMS," *Pollution Engineering* 33(5), June 2001, pp. 24–27

[6]www.inspection.gc.ca/english/fssa/polstrat/haccp/haccpe.shtml, www.omafra.gov.on.ca/OMAFRA/english/food/inspection/haccp/index.html.

The following product and process background information is required:

1. Describe the product, source of raw material, product characteristics, ingredients, packaging, how the product is used, shelf life, where the product will be sold, labelling instructions, and distribution control.

2. Draw the process flow diagram and number the steps of the process. Also, draw the plant layout diagram, identifying each operation by its number and showing the material flows by arrows.

3. Identify all the Regulatory Action Points (RAP), i.e., points in the process where safety control is mandated by the government. These usually include the receiving point(s) of raw material(s) and the shipping point of the product, but may include other critical points such as the thawing of fish and the labelling of fish cans. SOPs are provided for most of these activities, specifying parameters such as time and temperature. If there is no SOP for a RAP, the company needs to define one. The RAP plan specifies the control measure (such as a SOP), the monitoring procedure (what, how, frequency, and who), and corrective action.

There are three main HACCP steps:

1. Hazard Analysis:
   * For each ingredient/processing step, identify potential hazard(s). One can use the reference database of CFIA; books on microbiology, food processing, and plant sanitation; Health Canada reports on illnesses, recalls, and complaints; and scientific papers. Hazards are classified into: biological, chemical, and physical.
   * Determine if the potential hazard is significant and provide your justification.
   * Provide preventative measures for significant hazards.

2. Determine the Critical Control Points (CCP)
   * For every ingredient/processing step with one or more significant hazard(s), if there will not be a subsequent step that would eliminate the hazard, then this step is a CCP. The receiving point of raw material, the closing point of the cans, the sterilization point, and the point for checking the can weight are typical CCPs.

3. Establish the HACCP Plan
   * For each CCP/significant hazard, determine the control/preventative measure, the critical limits, the monitoring procedure (what, how, frequency, and who), the corrective action and records, and the verification procedures.

Example 1

The product description is chunk-style tuna, locally caught and canned in small cans sealed at the bottom and top, packaged in brine (salt water) or oil, ready-to-eat, with a five-year shelf life, no physical damage during distribution, and sold in retail stores.

A simplified process flow diagram is shown on the next page. The company buys the cans, with the bottom already sealed to the wall, but separate can tops. For simplicity, we assume that the tuna is canned fresh. The process briefly is as follows: after receiving, the fish's head and tail are cut off, and racks of fish are precooked in order to make skinning and deboning easier. Then, the automated canning line cuts the fish into chunks, fits a chunk in a can, adds ingredients, and vacuum-seals the top. Then, baskets of fish cans are sterilized and cooked further in pressurized steam rooms, washed, dried, weighed, and labelled.

Government regulations require that the tuna not be tainted or decomposed (should be safe and wholesome), and the can should be accurately labelled with a product code (including date canned). In addition to sanitation and hygiene at the plant, equipment, and operator levels, the HACCP requirements can be satisfied by the following critical control points and control plans:

Critical Control Point	Control Plan
Receiving	Vessel records of cooling
	Both visual inspection and tests for toxins (60 fish per lot)
Precooking	Standard operating procedures (SOP), cooking time and temperature
Cans and Tops	Manufacturing record of material and SOP
	Visual inspection
Close cans	Both visual (every half hour) and teardown test (every four hours) for seams
Pasteurize	SOP, temperature, time, pressure
Wash with chlorine	Test residual chlorine in water
Label	Inspect continuously for accuracy

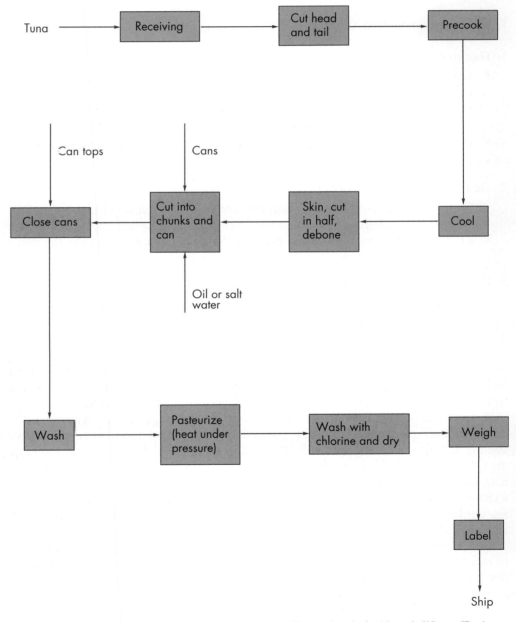

Sources: www.inspection.gc.ca/english/anima/fispoi/qmp/files/tuna.pdf; www.cloverleaf.ca/about.php?iContentID=4.

TOTAL QUALITY MANAGEMENT (TQM)

The term **total quality management (TQM)** refers to quest for quality in an organization. There are three key philosophies in this approach. One is a never-ending push to improve, which is referred to as *continuous improvement*; the second is the *involvement of everyone* in the organization; and the third is goal of *customer satisfaction*, which means meeting or exceeding customer expectations. TQM expands the traditional view of quality—looking only at the quality of the final product or service—to *looking at the quality of every aspect of the process* that produces the product or service. TQM systems are intended to prevent poor quality from occurring. The following reading describes some experiences with TQM.

total quality management (TQM) A philosophy that involves everyone in an organization in continual effort to improve quality and achieve customer satisfaction.

READING

Lessons from the Veterans of TQM

www.pwc.ca
www.amp.com
www.steelcase.com
www.cargill.com

Pratt & Whitney Canada, AMP Canada, Steelcase Canada, and Cargill Limited started their TQM programs in the late 1980s.

According to these companies, the road to effective and sustainable quality improvement lies in redefining traditional departmental boundaries and the communication channels that make up an organization.

These companies have redrawn departmental boundaries and redefined communication channels by supplanting some functions in favour of processes, by empowering teams of employees to achieve clearly defined goals, and by recognizing achievements.

Organizing by Process

These companies are paying attention to key processes such as order fulfillment, in contrast with internally focused functions such as sales, and manufacturing operations. As key processes begin to prevail over functions, organizational structures and internal boundaries are being redrawn, and the results are improved service quality and shorter cycle time. However, organizing around processes is not for the fainthearted—the change is painful.

At Pratt & Whitney, a major aircraft engine manufacturer, new-product development has gone from a series of over-the-departmental-wall transactions to an integrated effort with representatives from marketing, engineering, manufacturing, procurement, customer support, and finance working together. The result was that the product development cycle was reduced from five to two and a half years. A remarkable accomplishment, especially given the fact that the success of this project depended on the integrated efforts of some 5,000 people, including those working at four different stages: product definition, concept design, structural and performance design, and manufacturing engineering.

AMP is a major electrical and electronic connectors manufacturer, and is part of Tyco Electronics.

One of AMP's longest standing cross-functional teams is the "on-time delivery" team. This team, composed of representatives from quality, inside sales, warehouse, and inventory control, has steadily improved the order fulfillment process. On-time delivery has increased to 98 to 99 percent.

Steelcase is a major manufacturer of office furnishings. Steelcase's "Focus Factories" have cut cycle times of 8 to 10 weeks to 4 weeks and decreased inventory by 50 percent in two manufacturing areas. Focus Factories bring together all functions in production, inventory, procurement, and production scheduling. These cross-functional teams have had a direct effect on customer service through a "Quick Ship" program that ensures delivery of Steelcase's fast-moving items in 12 days or less.

Empowering Teams

Where these companies have been successful, teams have been instrumental in determining how boundaries are redrawn within the organization itself and beyond. In order to be confident about how and where the boundaries should lie and when they should be changed, these teams refer to clearly expressed goals. These goals are woven throughout the organization from overall corporate objectives to targets for specific teams.

Steelcase teams look to a set of clear aggressive targets for the corporation as a whole under the banner "Five-year Goals of World Class Performance." These goals are understood throughout the organization and enable all teams to set priorities and measure progress in areas such as waste, cycle times, safety, and product quality.

At Cargill's High River Boxed Meat Plant, members of the maintenance team set up preventive maintenance programs for the areas of the plant with the most costly history of downtime. They know weekly what their efforts are yielding and where resources would be better deployed.

AMP's progress toward team objectives is aggregated and posted in a company-wide "Excellence Index." Every team determines how it contributes to customer delight and determines how to measure that contribution. Each team posts performance data regularly.

Recognition of Achievements

Recognizing the hard work that goes into these changes is fundamental to redesigning the way the organization and its people work.

At Cargill, a team of employees has developed a comprehensive process to recognize both individual and team efforts.

At Steelcase, good teamwork is recognized in a number of ways. Some teams are invited to participate in outside events such as conferences where they present their successes to delegates and management. All teams are empowered to design their own celebration when they reach their objectives.

AMP celebrates all team accomplishments at its annual showcase. All teams that have implemented process improvement show their success story to their co-workers in a setting similar to that of a trade fair.

Source: Adapted from C. Bak, "Lessons from the Veterans of TQM," *Canadian Business Review* 19(4), Winter 1992, pp. 17–19.

We can describe the TQM approach as follows:

1. Find out what customers want. This might involve the use of surveys, focus groups, interviews, or some other technique that integrates the customer's voice in the decision-making process. Be sure to include the *internal customer* (the next person in the process) as well as the *external customer* (the final customer).

2. Design a product or service that will meet (or exceed) what customers want. Make it easy to use and easy to produce.

3. Design processes that facilitate doing the job right the first time. Determine where mistakes are likely to occur and try to prevent them. Involve and empower the workers. When mistakes do occur, find out why, so that they are less likely to occur again.

4. Keep track of results (TQM is data driven), and use them to guide improvement in the system. Never stop trying to improve.

5. Extend these concepts to suppliers and to distribution.

Many companies have successfully implemented TQM programs. Management from the top down must be totally committed and involved by becoming educated in quality, setting and enforcing improvement goals, providing resources, and reviewing progress. If it isn't, TQM will become just another fad that quickly dies and fades away.

The preceding description provides a good idea of what TQM is all about, but it doesn't tell the whole story. More detail on some of these and other elements of TQM follows.

1. *Continuous improvement.* The *philosophy* that seeks to improve all critical processes on an ongoing basis is called **continuous improvement**. This could be the order-filling process which cuts across sales, purchasing, and manufacturing. Under continuous improvement, the old adage "If it ain't broke, don't fix it" gets transformed into "Just because it isn't broken doesn't mean it can't be improved."

continuous improvement
Philosophy that seeks to make never-ending improvements to critical processes.

kaizen Japanese term for continuous improvement.

The concept of continuous improvement is not new, but it did not receive much interest in North America for a while, even though it originated here. However, many Japanese companies used it for years, and it became a cornerstone of the Japanese approach to production (i.e., JIT). The Japanese use the term **kaizen** to refer to continuous improvement. The successes of Japanese companies caused strong interest in continuous improvement.

2. *Competitive benchmarking.* This involves identifying other organizations that are the best at a process and studying how they do it to learn how to improve your operation. The company need not be in the same line of business. For example, Xerox used the mail-order company L.L.Bean to benchmark order filling.

3. *Employee empowerment.* Giving workers the responsibility for improvements and the authority to make changes to accomplish them provides strong motivation for employees. This puts decision making into the hands of those who are closest to the job and have considerable insight into problems and solutions. If the company is unionized, the union should be brought in for support. Frequently, the workers need assurance that there would be no layoffs as a result of productivity gains.

4. *Team approach.* The use of teams for problem solving and to achieve consensus takes advantage of group synergy, gets people involved, and promotes a spirit of

cooperation and shared values among employees. Respecting employees' opinions will encourage them to come forward with their ideas and suggestions. Some companies have permanently reorganized into manufacturing cells operated by teams.

5. *Decisions based on facts rather than opinions.* Data are gathered and analyzed as a basis for decision making.

6. *Training.* Employees and managers are extensively trained in the use of quality tools and change. The objective is to completely change the way employees think about their work.

7. *Quality at the source.* **Quality at the source** refers to the philosophy of making each worker responsible for the quality of his or her work. This incorporates the notions of "do it right the first time" and "if it isn't right, fix it." Workers are expected to provide goods or services that meet specifications and to find and correct mistakes that occur. In effect, each worker becomes a quality inspector for his or her work. When the work is passed on to the next operation in the process (the internal customer)—or, if that step is the last in the process, to the ultimate customer—the worker is "certifying" that it meets quality standards.

This accomplishes a number of things: (1) it places direct responsibility for quality on the person(s) who directly affect it; (2) it removes the adversarial relationship that often exists between quality control inspectors and production workers; and (3) it motivates workers by giving them control over their work as well as pride in it.

8. *Fail-safing.* Strive to make the process "mistake-proof." This is sometimes referred to as **fail-safing**: Elements are incorporated in product/service or process design that make it virtually impossible for an employee or process to do something incorrectly. The Japanese term for this is *pokayoke*. Examples include parts that fit together only one way and conveyors that stop if the next operation has stopped.

9. *Suppliers* are partners in the process, and long-term relationships are encouraged. This gives suppliers a vital stake in providing quality goods and services. Suppliers, too, are expected to provide quality at the source, thereby reducing or eliminating the need to inspect deliveries from suppliers.

The above elements should remind you of the criteria for Canada Awards for Excellence (or Baldrige Award), described earlier.

It would be incorrect to think of TQM as merely a collection of techniques. Rather, TQM reflects a whole new attitude toward quality. It is about the *culture* of an organization. To truly reap the benefits of TQM, the culture of an organization must change.

Table 9–8 illustrates the differences between cultures of a TQM organization and a more traditional organization. See the following two readings about implementing TQM.

quality at the source The philosophy of making each worker responsible for the quality of his or her work.

fail-safing Incorporating design elements that prevent mistakes.

Aspect	Traditional	TQM
Overall mission	Maximize return on investment	Meet or exceed customer expectations
Objectives	Emphasis on short term	Balance of long term and short term
Management	Not always open; sometimes inconsistent objectives	Open; encourages employee input; consistent objectives
Role of manager	Issue orders; enforce	Coach, remove barriers, build trust
Customer requirements	Not highest priority; may be unclear	Highest priority; important to identify and understand
Problems	Assign blame; punish	Identify and resolve
Problem solving	Not systematic; individuals	Systematic; teams
Improvement	Erratic	Continuous
Suppliers	Adversarial	Partners
Jobs	Narrow, specialized; much individual effort	Broad, more general; much team effort
Focus	Product-oriented	Process-oriented

TABLE 9–8

Comparing the cultures of TQM and traditional organizations

READING

TQM Implementation Problem at Alcan's Mill

www.cable.alcan.com

When the new manager in Alcan Cable's small mill in Saint-Maurice de Shawinigan, Quebec, introduced TQM, the mill already had gone through drastic job cuts due to shifting of some production to sister mills. The workers' union agreed to support the TQM program provided that there would be no more job cuts. Several improvement teams were set up and there was some progress such as simplification of duties and work methods, standardization of procedures, pooling of some trades, and some job enrichment. Approximately half the workers participated in improvement teams. However, then another mill (Saint Augustin) was shut down and the production and most employees were moved to the Saint-Maurice plant. This caused strong friction and distrust toward management because of problems in the amalgamation of the two workforces. Typical union issues such as seniority rights of transferred workers got in the way. Now, worker participation has decreased, and only occasional improvement teams are set up.

Source: R. Bourque, L. Hamel, and C. Julien, "Work Reorganization at the Alcan Mill in Saint-Maurice de Shawinigan, Quebec, From 1990 to 1997," *Workplace Gazette* 1(2), 1998, pp. 50–58.

READING

Introduction of TQM at Standard Aero

www.standardaero.com

In October 1988, when Bob Hamaberg became president, Standard Aero was a sleepy collection of 50-year-old machine shops.

In 1989, Standard Aero was purchased by the British company Hawker Siddeley Group, and Hamaberg was exposed to the concept of TQM, which had been used over the previous decade by Lucas Industries PLC, the former employer of Hawker Siddeley's managing director.

When Hawker Siddeley offered to fund six pilot projects for its corporate family, Hamaberg made certain Standard Aero secured one of these projects. He quickly put together a proposal and within a week outlined it to his management team. Selling the idea to Standard Aero's 670 employees wasn't easy. For example, Gil Blanchette, an inspector on the T56 line, said, "I was skeptical because we'd tried this sort of thing before, and it didn't seem to work. People were sick of trying new systems."

In January 1990, a Lucas engineer arrived in Winnipeg and the TQM process was underway—Hamaberg and five senior managers formed a "change council" to ensure availability of all the needed money and resources, and a "change manager" was hired from within to be the full-time TQM administrator. The company then selected a nine-member task group of employees from one of its major product lines, consisting of everyone from sales staff to mechanics, in order to redesign how Standard Aero repaired the T56 Allison turboprop engines.

The task group's first step was a $100,000 fact-finding mission that did something most TQM programs don't do—ask the customer what he or she wants. Two months were spent designing a questionnaire, working the phones, and visiting customers around the world. Customers were so impressed with Standard Aero's desire to learn their needs that the task force happened to pick up $7 million in new business.

"We had reactions everywhere from half an hour on the phone to eight hours in a boardroom with a senior management team saying, 'My God, we can't believe somebody's actually asking us!'" Hamaberg recalls. "Old theories were shattered. Beliefs in cost, quality, times, shipping distances and border issues—all the things we believed in—were shattered."

All of the data from the fact-finding mission were collated, and Standard Aero set targets that placed the company well ahead of the competition—literally twice as far ahead. If a competitor claimed it could overhaul a T56 engine in a month, Standard Aero set a target of two weeks. "We wanted to be twice as good as the perceived best anywhere in the world," says Hamaberg.

The first step toward this target was a systematic analysis of every person, machine, and activity associated with the T56 overhaul. The entire process was broken down into cells of 8–20 workers for shipping and receiving, disassembly, and so on, each of which was examined to streamline flow and processing. The task force cut out 93 percent of the 162 non-chargeable steps in a gearbox's journey through the plant, and cut the number of times the gearbox changed hands by 84 percent (as well as all of the paperwork associated with each step). All of this saved $150,000 a year just in paper costs.

Workers were trained in everything from statistics to operating lathes to teamwork. Even today, workers receive an average of 120 hours of training per year, a $1.5-million cost to the company that is well worth it.

The reorganization of T56 cells was completed in late 1991, resulting in 30 percent more engines passing through the shop. The shop floor had undergone a drastic makeover.

The production area was clean, and space was effectively laid out with painted lines on the floor. Each cell maintains bulletin boards that show each worker's progress toward training goals and keep track of performance indicators for the cell.

Business departments were also being overhauled as the shop floor was being redesigned. Rather than reporting through two levels of management and through several additional steps before speaking with a mechanic, a salesperson now reports directly to the shop floor, a change that is indicative of the entire company. Each product line essentially operates as a small business, with its own product unit director, accountant, engineers, and sales people.

The TQM task force worked 12–14 hours a day for a year and a half to implement the changes throughout the company—not an easy task, but if Standard Aero is any indication TQM may be one of the most effective changes to hit Canadian industry.

Why has TQM worked for Standard Aero, while it has not worked for some other companies? One big reason is that Standard Aero was dedicated to improving quality from the top down, talking to customers, and committing itself fully to the accomplishment of the goal. Standard Aero spent more than $13 million in its first three years of TQM implementation, and Hamaberg admits to firing several senior managers who opposed the change: "You must have senior management commitment. I had some obstacles. I removed the obstacles."

Sources: "No Pain, No Gain: How Do You Turn a Sleepy Bunch of Repair Shops into a Competition-crunching Money Machine? Get Ruthless about Quality," *Canadian Business* 66(1), January 1993, pp. 50–54; D. Luciani, "World Beaters," *Profit* 17(5), October 1, 1998, pp. 87ff; D. Kimmer, "Standard Aero Completes Expansion," *Business & Commercial Aviation* 91(2), August 2002, p. 40.

Step 1	**Define the problem and establish an improvement goal.** Give problem definition careful consideration; don't rush through this step because this will serve as the focal point of problem-solving efforts.
Step 2	**Collect data.** The solution must be based on *facts*. Possible tools include check sheet, scatter diagram, histogram, run chart, and control chart.
Step 3	**Analyze the problem.** Possible tools include Pareto chart and cause-and-effect diagram.
Step 4	**Generate potential solutions.** Methods include brainstorming, interviewing, and surveying.
Step 5	**Choose a solution.** Identify the criteria for choosing a solution. (Refer to the goal established in Step 1.) Apply criteria to potential solutions and select the best one.
Step 6	**Implement the solution.** Keep everyone informed.
Step 7	**Monitor the solution to see if it accomplishes the goal.** If not, modify the solution, or return to Step 1. Possible tools include control chart and run chart.

TABLE 9–9

Basic steps in TQM problem solving

PROBLEM SOLVING AND PROCESS IMPROVEMENT

Problem solving is one of the basic procedures of TQM. In order to be successful, problem-solving efforts should follow a standard approach. Table 9–9 describes the basic steps in the TQM problem-solving process.

An important aspect of problem solving in the TQM approach is *eliminating* the cause so that the problem does not recur. This is why users of the TQM approach often like to think of problems as "opportunities for improvement."

The Plan-Do-Study-Act Cycle

The **plan-do-study-act (PDSA) cycle**, also referred to as either the *Shewhart cycle* or the *Deming wheel*, is the conceptual basis for problem-solving activities. The cycle is illustrated in Figure 9–1. Representing the process with a circle underscores its continuing nature.

plan-do-study-act (PDSA) cycle A framework for problem solving and improvement activities.

FIGURE 9-1

A. The PDSA cycle

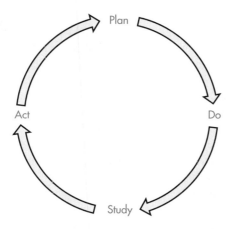

B. The PDSA cycle applied to problem solving

Source: Reprinted by permission of Prentice-Hall, Upper Saddle River, NJ. From Donna Summers, *Quality*, 2nd ed. (Upper Saddle River, NJ: Prentice Hall, 2000), p. 67.

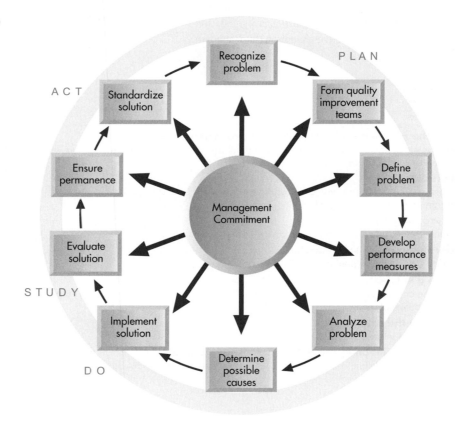

There are four basic steps in the cycle:

Plan. Begin by studying the current problem. Document the problem. Then collect data. Next, analyze the data and develop a plan for improvement. Specify measures for evaluating the plan.

Do. Implement the plan, on a small scale if possible. Document any changes made during this phase. Collect data systematically for evaluation.

Study. Evaluate the data collected during the *do* phase. Check how closely the results match the original goals of the *plan* phase.

Act. If the results are successful, *standardize* the new solution and communicate it to all people associated with the problem. Implement training for the new solution. If the results are unsuccessful, revise the plan and repeat the cycle or cease the project.

For an informal application of problem solving, see the reading, "Ford's Headliner" earlier in the chapter. Employing this sequence of steps provides a systematic approach to continuous improvement. A similar activity is process improvement.

A. Process mapping
1. Collect information about the process; identify each step in the process. For each step, determine:
   The inputs and outputs.
   The people involved.
   All decisions that are made, and activities performed.
   Document such measures as time, cost, space used, waste, employee morale and any employee turnover, accidents and/or safety hazards, working conditions, revenues and/or profits, quality, and customer satisfaction, as appropriate.
2. Prepare a flow diagram that *accurately* depicts the process; note that too little detail will not allow for meaningful analysis, and too much detail will overwhelm analysts and be counterproductive. Make sure that key activities and decisions are represented.

B. Analyze the process
1. Ask these questions about the process:
   Is the flow logical?
   Are any steps or activities missing?
   Are there any duplications?
2. Ask these questions about each step:
   Is the step necessary? Could it be eliminated?
   Does the step add value?
   Does any waste occur at this step?
   Could the time be shortened?
   Could the cost to perform the step be reduced?
   Could two (or more) steps be combined?

C. Redesign the process
Using the results of the analysis, redesign the process. Document the improvements; potential measures include reductions in time, cost, space, waste, employee turnover, accidents, safety hazards, and increases/improvements in employee morale, working conditions, revenues/profits, quality, and customer satisfaction.

TABLE 9–10

Overview of process improvement

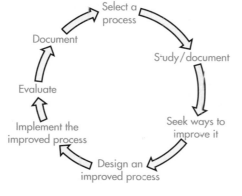

FIGURE 9–2

The process improvement cycle is another version of the plan-do-study-act cycle

Process improvement is a *systematic* approach to improving critical processes. It involves documentation, measurement, and analysis for the purpose of improving the functioning of a process. Typical goals of process improvement include increasing customer satisfaction, achieving higher quality, reducing waste, reducing cost, increasing productivity, and speeding up the process.

Table 9–10 provides an overview of process improvement, and Figure 9–2 shows its cyclical nature.

process improvement
A systematic approach to improving critical processes.

SIX SIGMA

Six sigma is the name given to a more advanced and effective version of problem solving/ process improvement. The methodology uses a five step approach: define, measure, analyze, improve, and control (DMAIC). The difference with PDSA is that more statistical techniques are used. In six sigma the best employees are trained to become full-time change agents, called Black Belts, who act like internal consultants with considerable power and resources at their disposal. Consequently, six sigma projects are more coordinated than the problem-solving/process-improvement projects of TQM. Each

six sigma The name given to a more advanced and effective version of TQM.

project chosen should significantly increase the value for customers, shareholders, or employees. In a narrower sense, six sigma refers to very capable processes which make only three or four defects per million parts produced. Companies such as GE, Allied Signal, Boeing, and American Express have implemented six sigma programs successfully.[7] For a brief application, see the reading, "Ford's Protective Cover" earlier in the chapter. There will be more on six sigma in the next chapter.

BASIC QUALITY TOOLS

There are a number of tools that an organization can use for problem solving and process improvement. This section describes some of these tools. The tools aid in data collection and interpretation and provide the basis for decision making.

The first seven tools are often referred to as the *seven basic quality tools*. Figure 9–3 provides a quick overview of the seven tools.

---

[7] T. Pyzdek, *The Six Sigma Handbook*, 2nd ed. (New York: McGraw-Hill, 2003).

FIGURE 9–3

The seven basic quality tools

Process flow diagram

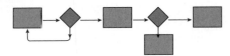

A diagram of the steps in a process

Check sheet

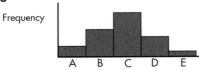

A tool for organizing and collecting data; a tally of problems or other events by category

Histogram

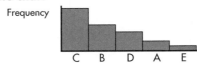

A chart that shows an empirical frequency distribution

Pareto chart

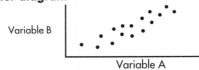

A diagram that arranges categories from highest to lowest frequency of occurrence

Scatter diagram

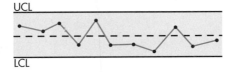

A graph that shows the degree and direction of the relationship between two variables

Control chart

A line plot of time-ordered values of a sample statistic (e.g., sample mean) with limits

Cause-and-effect diagram

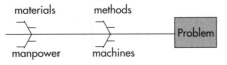

A diagram used to organize a search for the cause(s) of a problem; also known as a fishbone diagram

Process Flow diagram. A **process flow diagram** is a visual representation of a process. As a problem-solving tool, a process flow diagram can help investigators in identifying possible points in a process where problems occur.

Process flow diagram was described in Chapter 6. Any decision or checkpoint in the process is represented by a diamond shape.

process flow diagram A diagram of the steps in a process.

Check Sheets. A **check sheet** provides a format that enables users to record and organize data in a way that facilitates collection and analysis. Check sheets are designed on the basis of what the users are attempting to learn by collecting data. Many different formats can be used for a check sheet and there are many different types of sheets. One frequently used form of check sheet deals with types of defects and when they occur, another with location of defects. These are illustrated in Figures 9–4 and 9–5.

check sheet A tool for recording and organizing data to identify a problem.

Figure 9–4 shows tallies that denote the types of a product's label defects and the time of day each occurred. Problems with missing labels tend to occur early in the day and smeared print tends to occur late in the day, whereas offcentre labels are found throughout the day. Identifying types of defects and when they occur can help in pinpointing causes of the defects.

Figure 9–5 makes it easy to see where defects on the product are occurring. In this case, defects seem to be occurring on the tips of the thumb and first finger, in the finger valleys (especially between the thumb and first finger), and in the centre of the gloves. Again, this may help determine why the defects occur and lead to a solution.

Day	Time	Type of Defect					
		Missing label	Off-centre	Smeared print	Loose or folded	Other	
M	8–9	IIII	II				6
	9–10		III				3
	10–11	I	III	I			5
	11–12		I		I	I (Torn)	3
	1–2		I				1
	2–3		II	III	I		6
	3–4		II	HHI			8
Total		5	14	10	2	1	32

An example of a check sheet identifying the type and time of defect occurring in a product's labels

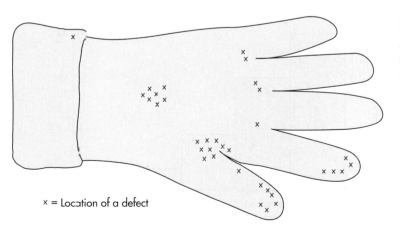

× = Location of a defect

A check sheet which identifies the location of defects on a rubber glove

histogram A chart of an empirical frequency distribution.

Histograms. A **histogram** is a graph of the frequency distribution of observed values. Among other things, one can see if the distribution is symmetrical, what the range of values is, and if there are any unusual values. Figure 9–6 illustrates a histogram for repair times for a machine. Note the two peaks. A possible cause might be that there are two types of breakdowns, requiring minor and major repairs.

Pareto analysis Technique for focusing on the most important problem.

Pareto Analysis. **Pareto analysis** is a technique for focusing attention on the most important problem. The Pareto concept, named after the nineteenth-century Italian economist Vilfredo Pareto, is that a relatively few factors generally account for a large percentage of the total problems (e.g., complaints, defects). The idea is to classify the factors according to degree of importance, and focus on resolving the most important, leaving the less important. Often referred to as the 80–20 rule, the Pareto concept states that approximately 80 percent of the problems are from 20 percent of the types of problems. For instance, 80 percent of machine breakdowns are from 20 percent of the types of breakdowns, and 80 percent of the product defects are from 20 percent of the types of defects.

Often, it is useful to prepare a chart that shows the number of occurrences by category (type), arranged in order of frequency. Figure 9–7 illustrates such a chart corresponding to the check sheet shown in Figure 9–4. The dominance of the problem with

FIGURE 9-6

A histogram of a machine's repair times

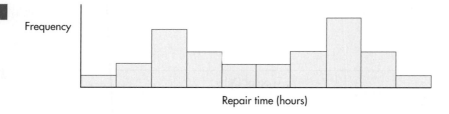

FIGURE 9-7

A Pareto chart based on data in Figure 9–4

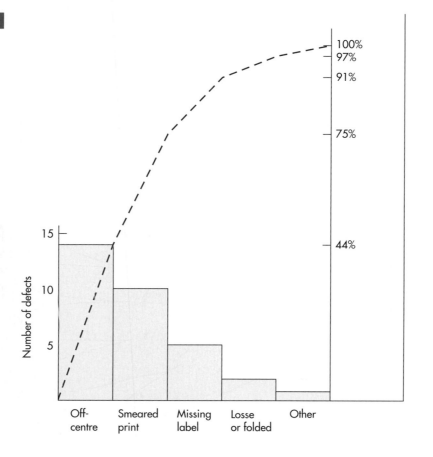

off-centre labels becomes apparent. Presumably, the manager and employees would first focus on trying to resolve this problem. Once they accomplish that, they could address the remaining defects in similar fashion; "smeared print" would be the next major category to be resolved, and so on. Additional check sheets would be used to collect data to verify that the defects in these categories have been eliminated or greatly reduced. Hence, in later Pareto diagrams, categories such as "off-centre" may still appear but would be much less prominent.

Sometimes each defect type has a different consequence, and the company may assign different weights to each. Then, the weighted value (weight × frequency) will be used in the Pareto analysis. For example, an overnight package delivery company such as FedEx has lower number of lost packages than number of abandoned calls to its call centres due to busy operators, but the lost package error is much more serious and should be dealt with first.

Scatter Diagrams. A **scatter diagram** is a plot of pairs of observations of two variables, and can show the correlation between the two variables. A correlation may point to a cause of a problem. Figure 9–8 shows an example of a scatter diagram. In this particular diagram, there is a *positive* (upward-sloping) relationship between the humidity and the number of errors per hour. High values of humidity result in high numbers of errors. On the other hand, a *negative* (downward-sloping) relationship would mean that when values of one variable are high, values of the other variable are low.

scatter diagram A plot that shows the degree and direction of the relationship between two variables.

The higher the correlation between the two variables, the less scatter in the points; the points will tend to line up. Conversely, if there were little or no relationship between two variables, the points would be completely scattered. In Figure 9–8, the correlation between humidity and errors seems strong, because the points appear to scatter along an imaginary line.

Control Charts. A **control chart**, a time-ordered plot of values of a sample statistic with limits, can be used to monitor a process to see if the process output is stable with random variation. It can help detect the presence of *correctable* causes of variation. Figure 9–9 illustrates a control chart. Control charts can also indicate when a problem occurred and thus give insight into what caused the problem. Control charts are described in detail in Chapter 10.

control chart A line plot of time-ordered values of a sample statistic with limits.

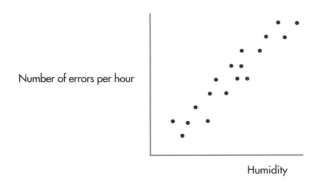

FIGURE 9–8

A scatter diagram

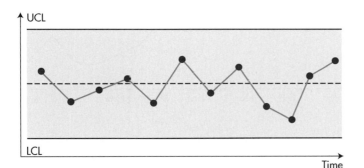

FIGURE 9–9

A control chart

cause-and-effect diagram
Used to search for the cause(s) of a problem; also called *fishbone diagram.*

Cause-and-Effect Diagrams. A **cause-and-effect diagram** offers a structured approach to the search for the possible cause(s) of a problem. It is also known as a **fishbone diagram** because of its shape, or an *Ishikawa diagram*, after the Japanese professor who developed the approach to aid workers overwhelmed by the number of possible sources of problems when problem solving. This tool helps to organize problem-solving efforts by identifying *categories* of factors that might be causing problems. Usually 4Ms—machine (and equipment), method, manpower, and materials—are included as categories. Often this tool is used after brainstorming sessions to organize the ideas generated.

An example of an application of such a cause-and-effect diagram is shown in Figure 9–10. Each of the factors listed in the diagram is a potential source of ticket defects. Note that related factors are bunched up, for example maintenance frequency and tension adjustment. Some factors are more likely causes than others, depending on the nature of the errors. If the cause is still not obvious at this point, additional investigation into the *root cause* may be necessary, involving a more in-depth data collection and analysis.

run chart Tool for tracking results over a period of time.

Run Charts. A **run chart** is a time plot that can be used to track the values of a variable over time. This can aid in identifying trends or other patterns that may be occurring. Figure 9–11 provides an example of a run chart showing a decreasing trend in accident frequency over time. The following three readings are applications of process improvement using basic quality tools.

FIGURE 9–10

Cause-and-effect diagram for airline ticket defects

Source: Reprinted from Howard Gitlow, Alan Oppenheim, and Rosa Oppenheim, *Quality Management: Tools and Methods for Improvement* (Burr Ridge, IL: Richard D. Irwin, 1995), p. 313, by permission.

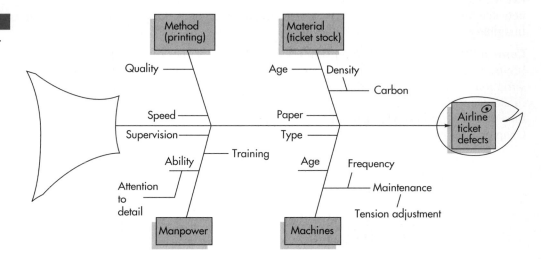

FIGURE 9–11

A run chart (shows performance over time)

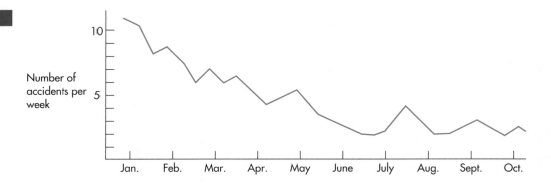

Process Improvement on the Free-Throw Line

Timothy Clark and Andrew Clark

In 1924, Walter Shewhart developed a problem-solving method to continually improve quality by reducing variation (the difference between the ideal outcome and the actual situation). To help guide improvement efforts, Shewhart outlined a process referred to as the plan-do-study-act (PDSA) cycle. The PDSA cycle is what my son and I used to continuously improve his basketball free-throw shooting.

Plan

Identify the facts. I had observed over a three-year period from 1991 to 1993 that in basketball games, my son Andrew's free-throw shooting percentage averaged between 45 percent and 50 percent.

Identify and define the process. Andrew's process for shooting free throws was simple: Go to the free-throw line, bounce the ball four times, aim, and shoot.

The desired outcome was a higher free-throw shooting percentage. An ideal outcome, or perfection, would be one in which 100 percent of the shots fall through the middle of the rim.

Plot the points. To confirm my observations on the results of the current process, we went to the YMCA and Andrew shot five sets of 10 free throws for a total of 50 shots. His average was 42 percent. Results were recorded on a run chart (see Figure 1). I concluded the process was stable.

Identify the causes. Causes of variation in any process can be identified through the general categories of manpower, machines/equipment, materials, methods, environment, and

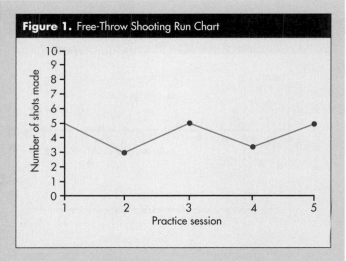

Figure 1. Free-Throw Shooting Run Chart

measurement. A cause-and-effect diagram is used to graphically illustrate the relationship between the effect—a low free-throw shooting percentage—and the principal causes (see Figure 2).

In analyzing my son's process, I noticed that he did not stand at the same place on the free-throw line every time. I believed his inconsistent shooting position affected the direction of the shot. If the shot goes left or right, there is a smaller probability that the ball will have a lucky bounce and go in. I also noticed that he didn't seem to have a consistent focal point.

Develop and select alternatives. The alternative selected for Andrew, a right-handed shooter, was for him to line up his right foot on the middle of the free-throw line, bounce the ball four times, focus on the middle of the front part of the rim, and visualize the perfect shot before he released the ball.

Develop an action plan. The course of action at this point was for Andrew to shoot five more sets of 10 free throws to test the effectiveness of the changes.

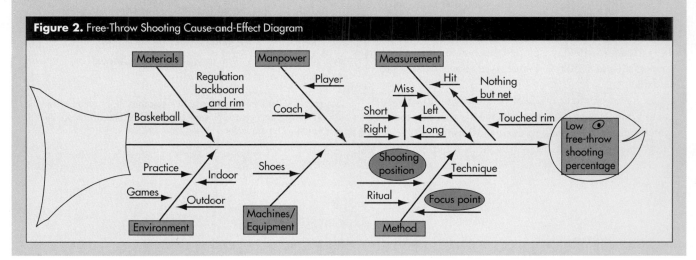

Figure 2. Free-Throw Shooting Cause-and-Effect Diagram

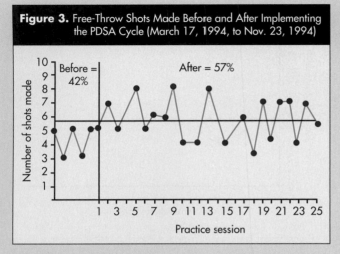

Figure 3. Free-Throw Shots Made Before and After Implementing the PDSA Cycle (March 17, 1994, to Nov. 23, 1994)

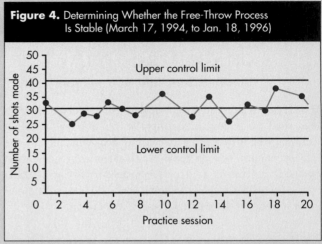

Figure 4. Determining Whether the Free-Throw Process Is Stable (March 17, 1994, to Jan. 18, 1996)

Do and Study

Implement the selected alternative and compare actual with expected results. The new process resulted in a 36-percent improvement in Andrew's average free-throw percentage at basketball practice, which raised his average to 57 percent. This and the results of another 20 practice sessions are compared with before-improvement results in Figure 3. The new process was first implemented in games toward the end of the 1994 season, and in the last three games, Andrew hit nine of his 13 free throws for a free-throw shooting average of 69 percent.

During the 1995 season, Andrew made 37 of his 52 free throws in games for an average of 71 percent. In one extremely close game where the other team was forced to foul Andrew's team in an effort to get the ball back, Andrew hit seven of his seven shots, which helped his team win the game. In team practices, the coaches had the players shoot two free throws and then rotate. For the entire season, Andrew hit 101 of 169 of his team practice free throws for an average of 60 percent.

As we monitored Andrew's process from March 17, 1994 to Jan. 18, 1996, we plotted the total number of practice shots made out of 50 (see Figure 4). It shows that the process is stable.

In the late summer of 1995, Andrew went to a basketball camp where he was advised to change his shooting technique, which reduced his shooting percentage during the 1996 season to 50 percent. We then reinstalled his old process, and his shooting percentage returned to its former level. In one series of 50 practice free throws, he hit 35 of 50 shots for an average of 70 percent and in another set, he hit an average of 64 percent. During the remaining team practices, Andrew hit 14 of 20 for an average of 70 percent.

During the 1996 and 1997 seasons, Andrew was a point guard and had fewer opportunities to shoot free throws, but he made nine of them for an average of 75 percent.

Overall benefits. In addition to the tangible results, such as improved free-throw shooting, the intangible benefits were also significant. For example, Andrew's confidence improved, and he learned how to determine when changes to his shooting technique resulted in improvement.

Act

Take appropriate action based on study results. In preparation for the 1998 season, Andrew's priorities for improvement are to continue to monitor his free-throw shooting to ensure it remains stable and to work on improving the shooting percentage of his two- and three-point shots.

Developing a knowledge and understanding of variation will change the way you look at the world forever and can lead to unprecedented levels of quality.

Source: T. Clark and A. Clark, "Continuous Improvement on the Free-Throw Line," *Quality Progress* 30(10), October 1997, pp. 78–80. Reprinted with permission.

Honda

At the Honda plant in Marysville, Ohio, an improvement project was undertaken to solve the excessive use of primer by Line 1. The problem was discovered by comparing Line 1 with Line 2. On both lines, primer was coated on the body of a car by first charging the body with electricity and then lowering it in a primer bath. To identify why there was a difference in primer thickness, data was collected on the two lines and compared.

Note from the histograms in Figure 1, the average thickness of primer in Line 1 is greater than Line 2. Also, the variability of primer thickness is higher in Line 1 than Line 2. Because every car's primer thickness should be higher than the minimum specification (shown by the dashed vertical line on the left), the higher variability forces the average primer thickness

for Line 1 to be greater than Line 2. To identify the cause for this, the team looked into factors such as time-in-bath, cleanliness of bath, and primer density. Measurements showed no significant difference between the two lines for these factors. Finally, the temperature of the primer solution was measured over four shifts.

As can be observed from the run charts and histograms in Figure 2, Line 1 has a higher temperature variability. Thus, temperature must be the cause of the primer thickness variability. A new temperature control device was purchased and installed on Line 1, lowering the variability in temperature, and therefore in primer thickness, allowing the improvement project goal of solving the excessive use of primer on Line 1 to be achieved.

Source: G. P. Maul and J. S. Gillard, "Solving Chronic Problems with Simple Tools," *Quality Progress*, July 1994, pp. 51–55. Figures reprinted with permission from Quality Progress, American Society for Quality.

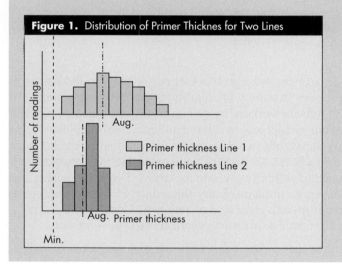

Figure 1. Distribution of Primer Thickness for Two Lines

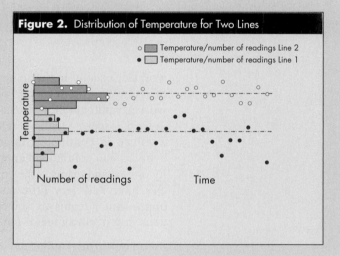

Figure 2. Distribution of Temperature for Two Lines

METHODS FOR GENERATING IDEAS AND REACHING CONSENSUS

Some additional tools that are useful for problem solving/process improvement are brainstorming, quality circles, interviewing, benchmarking, the 5W2H approach, and reaching consensus.

Brainstorming. Brainstorming is a technique in which a group of people share thoughts and ideas on problems in a relaxed atmosphere that encourages unrestrained collective thinking. The goal is to generate a free flow of ideas on identifying problems, and finding causes, solutions, and ways to implement solutions. In successful brainstorming, criticism is absent, no single member is allowed to dominate sessions, and all ideas are welcomed.

Quality Circles. One way companies have tapped employees for ideas concerning quality improvement is through **quality circles**. The circles comprise a number of

brainstorming Technique for generating a free flow of ideas in a group of people.

quality circles Groups of workers who meet to discuss ways of improving products or processes.

READING

University of Alberta Hospital

The University of Alberta Hospital started to try quality improvement projects in 2001. The first project was to study the time for a lab test required by emergency room patients. After studying the time before, during and after the test, it was discovered that the time before a lab test could be improved. This time was divided into three activities: (*a*) time from the doctor writing the order until the clerk received it (ORD/REC), (*b*) time from receiving the order until a sample is collected from the patient (REQ/COL), and (*c*) time from collection of the sample to delivering it to the lab (COL/REC). After observing the process for one week, it was recommended that the doctor actually hand the order to the clerk instead of leaving it on the patient's chart or clerk's desk, and also that the collection be done in batches of two instead

of three. Following these method's changes, the average pre-lab time was reduced from 48 to 33 minutes.

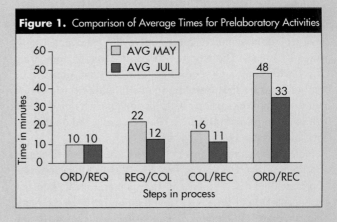

Figure 1. Comparison of Average Times for Prelaboratory Activities

Source: L. Lutes et al., "Clinical Quality Improvement Project: Finding a Repeatable Approach for Improving STAT Lab Testing," *International Journal of Health Care Quality Assurance* 16(2), 2003, pp. i–v. Reprinted with the permission of Emerald Group Publishing Limited.

workers, usually in the same department, who get together periodically to discuss ways of improving products and processes. Not only are quality circles a valuable source of worker input, but they also can motivate workers, by demonstrating management interest in worker ideas. Quality circles are usually less structured and more informal than teams involved in continuous improvement, but in some organizations quality circles have evolved into continuous improvement teams. Perhaps a major distinction between quality circles and teams is the amount of authority given to the teams. Typically, quality circles have had very little authority to implement any but minor changes; continuous improvement teams are sometimes given a great deal of authority. Consequently, continuous improvement teams have the added motivation generated by *empowerment*.

interviewing Technique for identifying problems and collecting information.

benchmarking Process of measuring performance against the best in the same or another industry.

Interviewing. Another technique that a firm can use to identify problems or collect information about a problem is **interviewing**. Internal problems may require interviewing employees or suppliers; external problems may require interviewing customers.

Benchmarking. Benchmarking is an approach that can inject new energy into improvement efforts. Benchmarking is the process of measuring an organization's performance against the best in the industry, or against the best in any industry. Its purpose is to establish a standard against which performance is judged, and to identify a model for learning how to improve. Once a benchmark has been identified, the goal is to meet or exceed that standard through improvements in appropriate processes.

Selecting an industry leader provides insight into what competitors are doing; however, competitors may be reluctant to share this information. Selecting organizations that are world leaders in other industries is another alternative. For example, Xerox uses many benchmarks: For employee involvement, Procter & Gamble; for quality process, Florida Power & Light and Toyota; for high-volume production, Kodak and Canon; for bill collection, American Express; for research and development, AT&T and Hewlett-Packard; for order filling and distribution, L.L.Bean and Hershey Foods; and for daily scheduling, Cummins Engine.

Category	5W2H	Typical Questions	Goal
Subject	What?	What is being done?	Identify the focus of analysis.
Purpose	Why?	Why is this necessary?	Eliminate unnecessary tasks.
Location	Where?	Where is it being done? Why is it done there? Would it be better to do it someplace else?	Improve the location.
Sequence	When?	When is it done? Would it be better to do it at another time?	Improve the sequence.
People	Who?	Who is doing it? Could someone else do it better?	Reduce the labour requirement.
Method	How?	How is it being done? Is there a better way?	Simplify tasks, improve productivity.
Cost	How much?	How much does it cost now? What would the new cost be?	Improve the cost.

TABLE 9–11

The 5W2H approach

Source: Adapted from Alan Robinson, *Continuous Improvement in Operations: A Systematic Approach to Waste Reduction* (Cambridge, MA: Productivity Press, 1991), p. 246.

READING

Motorola's Material Management Improvement

www.motorola.com

Motorola's group purchasing teams in its Materials Operations Department, Motorola Automotive and Industrial Electronics Group, Northbrook, Illinois, meet weekly to analyze material-related downtimes and develop root causes and action plans to reduce them. An effective way to collect downtime data is to have a material "advocate" on each production line who attends the daily production meetings. A form is completed for each downtime incident, indicating when, where and how many units were involved in the downtime, and their impact. The purchasing team finds the material-related cause for each downtime, classifies it (e.g., inventory inaccuracy, misusing the planning software, poor supplier quality, and design issues), chooses the most frequent cause using a Pareto chart, and finds a solution for it.

As a result, many problems—such as inventory record inaccuracies and supplier quality/flexibility problems—have been identified and solved. The number of "hot parts" at receiving has plummeted, and inventory accuracy is up. The downtime incidence rate is running at less than a third of its original rate.

Source: Q. B. Samelson, "World-class Materiel Flexibility: One Plant's Victory Over Materiel-related Downtime," *Hospital Materiel Management Quarterly* 18(4), May 1997, pp. 71–78.

The 5W2H Approach. Asking questions about the process/problem can lead to important insights about the cause of the problem, as well as potential ways to improve it. One method is called the **5W2H** (5 "w" words and 2 "h" words) **approach** (see Table 9–11). For an example using 5W2H, see the above reading on Motorola.

Sometimes posing the questions in a negative way may help. For example, in addition to asking, "Where is the defect on the object?" also ask, "Where else could the defect have been on the object, but isn't?" In addition to asking, "When did the defect occur?" also ask, "When else could the defect have occurred, but didn't?"

5W2H approach A method of asking questions about a process/problem that include what, why, where, when, who, how, and how much.

Reaching Consensus

The team approach works best when it reaches decisions based on consensus. This may be achieved using one or more of the following methods:

1. *List reduction* is applied to a list of possible problems or solutions. Its purpose is to clarify items and, in the *process*, reduce the list of items by posing questions about affordability, feasibility, and likelihood of solving the problem for each item.

2. A *balance sheet* approach lists the pros and cons of each item and focuses discussion on important issues.

3. *Paired comparisons* is a process by which each item on a list is compared with every other item, two at a time. For each pair, team members select the preferred item. This approach forces a choice between items. It works best when the list of items is small: say, five or fewer.

SUMMARY

Quality has evolved from artisan's workmanship to quality inspectors and to quality assurance and prevention of defects, and finally to incorporation of quality in company strategy as in Total Quality Management.

Quality is defined according to various dimensions that pertain to customer satisfaction. Determinants of quality are design, conformance to design, ease of use, and service after delivery. The consequences of poor quality include loss of market share, liability claims, decrease in productivity, and cost of quality.

Modern quality management is directed at preventing mistakes rather than finding them after they occur. Currently, the business community shows widespread interest in improving quality and competitiveness.

The chapter includes a description of the key contributors (gurus) to quality management. Two awards, the Baldrige Award and the Canada Awards for Excellence are given annually to organizations that have shown great achievement in quality management. ISO 9000:2000 is a standard for quality management, and HACCP is used in the food industry.

Total quality management (TQM) is a never-ending pursuit of higher quality that involves everyone in an organization. The driving force is customer satisfaction; a key philosophy is continuous improvement. Training of managers and workers in quality concepts, tools, and procedures is an important aspect of the approach. Teams are an integral part of TQM. Two major activities of the TQM approach are problem solving and process improvement.

KEY TERMS

appraisal costs, 311
Baldrige Award, 316
benchmarking, 338
brainstorming, 337
Canada Awards for Excellence, 316
cause-and-effect diagram, 334
check sheet, 331
continuous improvement, 324
control chart, 333
dimensions of product quality, 306
external failures, 311
fail-safing (*pokayoke*), 325
failure costs, 311
fishbone diagram, 334
5W2H approach, 339
HACCP, 320
histogram, 332
internal failures, 311

interviewing, 338
ISO 9000, 316
ISO 14000, 319
kaizen, 324
Pareto analysis, 332
plan-do-study-act (PDSA) cycle, 327
prevention costs, 312
process flow diagram, 331
process improvement, 329
quality, 305
quality at the source, 325
quality of conformance, 309
quality circles, 337
quality of design, 308
run chart, 334
scatter diagram, 333
six sigma, 329
total quality management (TQM), 323

A city's police department handed out the following traffic infractions on a summer weekend. Make a check sheet and a Pareto diagram for the types of infraction.

Ticket Number	Infraction	Ticket Number	Infraction
1	Excessive speed	11	Expired license
2	Expired license	12	DUI
3	Improper turn	13	Improper turn
4	Excessive speed	14	DUI
5	DUI	15	Excessive speed
6	DUI	16	DUI
7	Excessive speed	17	DUI
8	DUI	18	DUI
9	Improper turn	19	Excessive speed
10	DUI	20	DUI

Check sheet (list the types of infractions, tally, summarize frequencies):

Solution

Infraction	Tally	Frequency
Excessive speed	卌	5
Expired license	//	2
Improper turn	///	3
Driving under influence	卌 卌	10

Pareto diagram (array infractions from highest frequency to lowest):

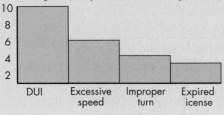

1. List and briefly explain the dimensions of product and service quality.

2. Explain the terms *quality of design* and *quality of conformance.*
3. What are some possible consequences of poor quality?
4. Use the dimensions of quality to describe typical characteristics of these products and services:
   a. A television set
   b. A restaurant meal (product)
   c. A restaurant meal (service)
   d. Painting a house
5. Describe the cost of quality.
6. Describe the evolution of quality management.
7. Select one of the quality gurus and briefly describe his major contributions to quality management.
8. What is ISO 9000, and why is it important for global businesses to have ISO 9000 certification?
9. Briefly explain how a company can achieve lower production costs by improving the quality of its products or services.
10. Briefly describe the criteria for Canada Awards for Excellence.
11. Describe HACCP.
12. What are the key elements of the TQM approach?
13. Briefly describe each of the seven basic quality tools.

14. Briefly define or explain each of these tools:
    a. Brainstorming
    b. Benchmarking
    c. Run chart
15. Explain each of these methods:
    a. The plan-do-study-act cycle
    b. The 5W2H approach
16. List the steps of problem solving.
17. Is there a specific set and sequence of quality tools used in problem solving/process improvement? Compare the two readings in the chapter "Process Improvement on the Free-throw Line," and "Honda" in this regard.
18. List the steps of process improvement.

TAKING STOCK

1. What trade-offs are involved in deciding on how much to spend on quality improvement?
2. Who needs to be involved in setting priorities for quality improvement?
3. Name one or two ways that technology has had an impact on quality.

CRITICAL THINKING EXERCISE

Consider an auto assembly operation. What kinds of quality problems can arise during assembly? Name one or two. How can each be fixed? Prevented?

INTERNET EXERCISES

1. Visit the Web site of Baldrige Award (www.quality.nist.gov).
    a. Choose a recent recipient of the award and identify what aspects of TQM that company emphasizes, *or*
    b. Briefly describe the Baldrige criteria for business companies and compare it with the criteria for Canada Awards for Excellence (given in the chapter).
2. Visit the Web site of the Canada Food Inspection Agency, Fish processing examples, www.inspection.gc.ca/english/animal/fispoi/qmp/files/planse.shtml. Choose a type of fish and describe the HACCP analysis for processing it.
3. Visit www.asq.org and describe a type of certification they offer.

PROBLEMS

1. Make a check sheet and then a Pareto chart for the following car service repair shop data.

Ticket No.	Work	Ticket No.	Work	Ticket No.	Work
1	Tires	11	Brakes	21	Lube & oil
2	Lube & oil	12	Lube & oil	22	Brakes
3	Tires	13	Battery	23	Transmission
4	Battery	14	Lube & oil	24	Brakes
5	Lube & oil	15	Lube & oil	25	Lube & oil
6	Lube & oil	16	Tires	26	Battery
7	Lube & oil	17	Lube & oil	27	Lube & oil
8	Brakes	18	Brakes	28	Battery
9	Lube & oil	19	Tires	29	Brakes
10	Tires	20	Brakes	30	Tires

2. An air-conditioning repair department manager has compiled data on the primary reason for 41 service calls during the previous week, as shown on the next page. Using the data, make a check sheet for the problem types for each customer type, and then construct a Pareto chart for each type of customer.

Job Number	Problem/Customer Type	Job Number	Problem/Customer Type	Job Number	Problem/Customer Type
301	F/R	315	F/C	329	O/C
302	O/R	316	O/C	330	N/R
303	N/C	317	W/C	331	N/R
304	N/R	318	N/R	332	W/R
305	W/C	319	O/C	333	O/R
306	N/R	320	F/R	334	O/C
307	F/R	321	F/R	335	N/R
308	N/C	322	O/R	336	W/R
309	W/R	323	F/R	337	O/C
310	N/R	324	N/C	338	O/R
311	N/R	325	F/R	339	F/R
312	F/C	326	O/R	340	N/R
313	N/R	327	W/C	341	O/C
314	W/C	328	O/C		

Key: Problem type:
N = Noisy
F = Equipment failure
W = Runs warm
O = Odour

Customer type:
C = Commercial customer
R = Residential customer

3. Prepare a run chart for the number of occurrences of defective computer monitors based on the following data, which an analyst obtained from the process for making the monitors. Workers are given a 15-minute break at 10:15 A.M. and 3:15 P.M., and a lunch break at noon. What can you conclude?

Interval Start Time	Number of Defects	Interval Start Time	Number of Defects
8:00	1	1:00	1
8:15	0	1:15	0
8:30	0	1:30	0
8:45	1	1:45	1
9:00	0	2:00	1
9:15	1	2:15	0
9:30	1	2:30	2
9:45	2	2:45	2
10:00	3	3:00	3
10:30	1	3:30	0
10:45	0	3:45	1
11:00	0	4:00	0
11:15	0	4:15	0
11:30	1	4:30	1
11:45	3	4:45	3

4. Prepare a run chart for this 911 call data. Use five-minute intervals (i.e., count the calls received in each five-minute interval. Use intervals of 0–4, 5–9, etc.). Note: Two or more calls may occur in the same minute; there were three operators on duty this night. What can you conclude from the run chart?

Call	Time	Call	Time	Call	Time
1	1:03	15	1:43	29	2:03
2	1:06	16	1:44	30	2:04
3	1:09	17	1:47	31	2:06
4	1:11	18	1:48	32	2:07
5	1:12	19	1:50	33	2:08
6	1:17	20	1:52	34	2:08
7	1:21	21	1:53	35	2:11
8	1:27	22	1:56	36	2:12
9	1:28	23	1:56	37	2:12
10	1:29	24	2:00	38	2:13
11	1:31	25	2:00	39	2:14
12	1:36	26	2:01	40	2:14
13	1:39	27	2:02	41	2:16
14	1:42	28	2:03	42	2:19

5. Suppose that a table lamp fails to light when turned on. Prepare a simple cause-and-effect diagram to analyze possible causes. Use categories such as lamp, chord, etc.

6. Prepare a cause-and-effect diagram to analyze why a machine has produced a defective part.

7. Prepare a scatter diagram for each of the following data sets and then express in words the apparent relationship between the two variables. Put the first variable on the horizontal axis and the second variable on the vertical axis.

a.
Age	24	30	22	25	33	27	36	58	37	47	54	28	42	55
Days absent	6	5	7	6	4	5	4	1	3	2	2	5	3	1

b.
Temperature (°C)	18	17	22	19	28	14	24	30	25	18	26
Error rate	1	2	0	0	3	3	1	5	2	1	3

8. The local police department has responded to a vehicle accident along a stretch of highway. Prepare a cause-and-effect diagram for this accident. Use categories such as vehicle, driver, weather, etc.

9. Suppose you are going to have a prescription filled at a local pharmacy. Referring to the dimensions of service quality, for each dimension, give an example of how you would judge the quality of the service.

10. Prepare a HACCP analysis for burgers made in a fast-food restaurant such as McDonald's.

READING

Flex-o-mark: Quality Manages Growth
Jane Rotering

www.flexomark.com

Flex-o-mark is a small Mississauga, Ontario, company that has been manufacturing and distributing in-house and purchased label-making systems and labelling services to its customers for more than 20 years. They became QS-9000 certified in December 1999. QS-9000 is a quality-certification program with specific requirements demanded by the automotive industry. While it encompasses the ISO 9000 requirements, QS-9000 has additional requirements, such as a production-part approval process. When a company becomes QS-9000 certified, they also gain the ISO 9000 certification.

Why would a small company that has 35 employees go through the expense and effort to become certified? The strongest reason was because their customers demanded it. While the demand came about very recently, Flex-o-mark had begun investigating certification five years earlier when it was even smaller. Management had the foresight to recognize that if the company were to grow, it would have to gain certification. As the company expanded, the number of employees reached critical mass, and more organization and specialization was required.

Tony Sharma, the general manager and son of the founder of the family-owned business, says the QS-9000 certification has "allowed us to have good management." He knew that the number-one reason for business failures was poor management, and he was determined that Flex-o-mark would make the growth transition successfully.

The first step was to set up a quality committee of employees representing all areas of the company. It was this group that would investigate how the QS-9000 certification could be implemented and be aligned with the future growth plans of Flex-o-mark.

According to Tony, the greatest benefit certification has given to Flex-o-mark is that there is now structure within the company. Traditionally, information and responsibilities in small companies are informally shared. This can work well until the company starts to grow, when there often becomes a lot of duplicated work and no one person is accountable for a job function. Prior to certification at Flex-o-mark, if a matter came up regarding, for example, transportation, three or four people would end up working on that problem at different times and with little coordination of effort. Now everyone—in both the office area and the manufacturing plant—has a position description with work instructions.

With the implementation of position descriptions, jobs are allocated to the correct person. The traffic manager now handles all functions related to transportation, and this is recognized as her area of expertise. The same happens in the plant. Tony says the plant press operators, for example, "now know what is expected of them and will ask questions rather than do something they are unsure of." They are able to perform better by focusing on their jobs. "In addition," says Tony "it takes pressure off me. I used to deal with all kinds of problems at all levels; now I just have to talk to the key people."

Another benefit is that there are fewer errors being made. Now, everyone in the company is aware of the procedures that have to be followed for an order to be processed. There are certain steps in place that allow employees to spot an error or defect before it goes out to the customer. If there is a mistake made, Tony knows that "nine times out of ten it is because someone didn't follow the process."

Also, employees are more aware of what is expected of them and how their jobs should be performed. They now have tools to guide them, such as performance reports that highlight errors. "Errors are costly, but if they can be spotted quickly, then we can fix them," says Tony. "But a program like this will never work if you don't have your employees onside and involved in the process right from the beginning."

Does certification help to increase the customer base? Tony noted that, in addition to those customers that require their suppliers to be certified, new customers want to do business with them because they know that Flex-o-mark has procedures in place, and the company has the ability to take proper corrective action if something should go wrong. While some new customers may not require QS-9000 certification, they know that a certain level of quality will be met because of certification.

Quality has come with a dollar cost, but the benefits far outweigh it. As Tony readily admits, some potential customers may go to another supplier who can supply the product for less cost than Flex-o-mark.

In order to continually improve their processes and products, and adhere to the QS quality standards, Flex-o-mark has hired a full-time quality control person. This person is responsible for monitoring and improving the standards within the company.

"The additional salary cost of a full-time quality manager is substantial for a company our size," says Tony "but we have the potential to grow to ten times our current size. It is the QS certification process that will allow us to handle that growth."

Questions

1. Identify the changes in Flex-o-mark's operation as a result of QS-9000 certification.

2. Identify some local companies which are QS-9000 or ISO 9000 certified.

(*Hint*: try www.qualitydigest.com/isodatabase/iso9000database. shtml)

Walkerton's Tragedy

In May 2000, seven residents of Walkerton, a small town in southern Ontario, died of E. coli poisoning transmitted through the town's water. The water had been drawn from a well which is usually a safe source of water supply. Although well water treatment is rather simple—just add chlorine to disinfect it—the town water works' manager, Stan Koebel, believed that the water was so safe that chlorine did not have to be used.

This conclusion may have been true under normal circumstances; however, during April 2000 the farm adjacent to the well fertilized its fields with cattle manure. Unfortunately, during the second week of May, the area received unusually high levels of rain which washed E. coli from the manure into the well. The usual level of chlorine was inadequate to kill the high level of the bacteria. Compounding this Koebel did not follow the Ontario Ministry of the Environment's guideline for checking the level of residual chlorine in treated water (in fact a minimum of .5 mg per litre should remain to continue disinfecting the water through the distribution pipes).

During the third week of May, people started to get sick. Water was finally tested and E. coli was found in the samples. Koebel kept quiet for a few days hoping the nightmare would go away. Unfortunately, the situation got worse: almost half the town's population got sick and eventually seven people died.

Questions

1. State the quality characteristics of drinking water.

2. Draw a process flow diagram for water treatment of a town like Walkerton which uses well water.

3. Apply the HACCP analysis to develop a quality system for water treatment of such a town.

Source: www.attorneygeneral.jus.gov.on.ca/english/about/pubs/walkerton/part1

MINI-CASE

North Battleford's *Cryptosporidium* Outbreak

In April 2001, approximately 50 residents of North Battleford, Saskatchewan, were hospitalized due to severe diarrhea resulting from drinking city water that was tainted with a waterborne parasite called *Cryptosporidium*. This protozoa grows in the excrement of cattle and humans who have been infected by it.

North Battleford has two treatment facilities: Plant 1 draws water from underground wells; Plant 2 uses the North Saskatchewan River's water. Surface water is more polluted than underground water because of microorganisms that get into it. In particular, *Cryptosporidium* was found in small amounts in the river water. The river originates in Alberta's Rocky Mountains and passes through cattle-raising areas. Edmonton and other towns along the river draw their drinking water from it, and some sewage, after treatment, is poured back into the river. The number of parasites in the river increases significantly (approximately 100 times) in the spring, when the ice and snow thaw and carry feces into the river.

The effects of *cryptosporidium* infection (cryptosporidiosis) are a new discovery. The largest outbreak of the infection in North America occurred in 1993 in Milwaukee, where more than 100 people died. *Cryptosporidium* is resistant to chlorine, the common chemical used in water treatment. However, by adding other substances to the water, coagulation can be induced causing the protozoae to be encysted and settle in the sedimentation stage of treatment. These can then be removed from the water as waste. The knowledge of cryptosporidiosis, and how to prevent it, is limited mainly to scientists. Not many water treatment operators know much about it.

The administration of the city of North Battleford, with a population of approximately 15,000, operates under fiscal restraints. Plant 2 was built more than 40 years ago and was technologically outdated. For example, it had no route to divert wastewater (created during the cleaning of filters) and only one tank for coagulation/flocculation/settlement. Most other water treatment facilities have separate tanks for each operation (coagulation needs rapid mixing, whereas flocculation needs slow mixing, and settlement needs no mixing). The process of coagulation/flocculation/settlement is very sensitive to the amount of chemicals added. In fact, too much coagulant will cause charge-reversal, resulting in failure of the process. In addition to this, the plant foreman retired in December 2000, citing work stress as reason, and a new foreman was not hired until June 2001.

After preliminary sand separation to remove sand, potassium permanganate was added to improve water taste and odour, liquid alum (aluminum sulfate) and Aluminex to help coagulation, and chlorine to disinfect the water. Lime was added to reduce acidity caused by alum, and polymer to help flocculation. The process of coagulation/flocculation/sedimentation all took place in one tank, the Solids Contact Unit (SCU). There was no rapid agitation during this process

Plant 2 Process Flow Diagram

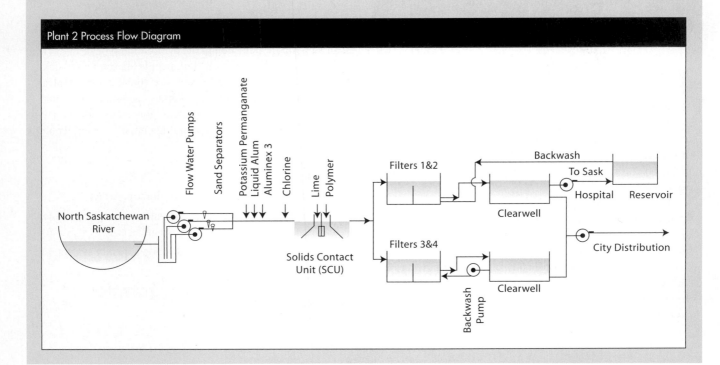

as is usually common for this process. The filters consisted of a layer of coal and a layer of sand. Periodic backwash cleaned the filters.

Annually, the SCU is thoroughly cleaned. On March 30, 2001, the SCU was cleaned. However, no sedimentation was forming after that day because water turbidity was low (i.e., it was very clear). Not realizing the significance of this, the plant kept on producing tainted drinking water. Eventually, after about three weeks, proper settling was re-established.

Questions

1. State the quality characteristics of drinking water.

2. Draw a process flow diagram for water treatment of river water.

3. Use the HACCP analysis to develop a quality system for water treatment of a city like North Battleford which uses river water.

Sources: The Honourable R. D. Laing, Commissioner, *Report of the Commission of Inquiry into Matters Relating to the Safety of the Public Drinking Water in the City of North Battleford, Saskatchewan* (Regina: Government of Saskatchewan, March 28, 2002); *Waterborne Cryptosporidiosis Outbreak, North Battleford, Saskatchewan* (Ottawa: Health Canada, September 24, 2001); www.NorthBattlefordwaterinquiry.ca.

MINI-CASE

Chick-n-Gravy Dinner Line

The operations manager of a company that produces frozen dinners had received numerous complaints from supermarkets about the company's Chick-n-Gravy dinners. The manager asked her assistant, Ann, to investigate the matter and to report her recommendations.

Ann's first task was to determine what problems were generating the complaints. The majority of complaints centred on five defects: underfilled packages, a missing item, spilled/mixed items, unacceptable taste, and improperly sealed packages.

Next, she took samples of dinners from the two production lines and examined each sample, making note of any defects that she found. A summary of those results is shown in the table below.

The data resulted from inspecting approximately 800 frozen dinners. What should Ann recommend to the manager?

				DEFECT OBSERVED			
Date	Time	Line	Underfilled	Missing Item	Spilled/ Mixed	Unacceptable Taste	Improperly Sealed
5/12	0900	1		√√	√	√√√	
5/12	1330	2			√√		√√
5/13	1000	2				√	√√√
5/13	1345	1	√√		√√		
5/13	1530	2		√√	√√√		√
5/14	0830	1		√√√		√√√	
5/14	1100	2	√		√	√√	
5/14	1400	1			√		√
5/15	1030	1		√√√		√√√√	
5/15	1145	2			√	√√	
5/15	1500	1	√		√		
5/16	0845	2				√√	√√
5/16	1030	1		√√√	√	√√√	
5/16	1400	1					
5/16	1545	2	√	√√√√√	√	√	√√

MINI-CASE

Tip Top Markets

Tip Top Markets is a regional chain of supermarkets. On July 28, Karen Martin, manager of one of the stores, was disturbed by the large number of recent complaints from customers at her store, particularly on Tuesdays, so she obtained complaint records from the store's customer service desk for the last three Tuesdays. These are shown below.

Analyze the data and make a recommendation to Karen.

July 13

wrong price on spaghetti	overcharged
water on floor	out of brown rice
store looked messy	out of mushrooms
store too warm	overcharged
checkout lines too long	checkout wait too long
cashier not friendly	shopping cart broken
out of feta cheese	couldn't find Aspirin
overcharged	out of brown lunch bags
out of Saran Wrap	out of straws
out of Dove Bars	

July 20

out of low-salt pickles	out of large eggs
checkout lines too slow	out of cranapple juice
found keys in parking lot	out of pretzels
lost keys	out of apricot jam
wrong price on sale item	telephone out of order
overcharged on corn	out of cocktail sauce
wrong price on baby food	water on floor
out of 500-mL Tide	out of frozen onion rings
out of green tea	out of frozen squash
checkout lines too long	out of powdered sugar
out of romaine lettuce	out of nonfat peanut butter

July 27

out of dill pickles	wanted to know who won the lottery
reported accident in parking lot	store too warm
wrong price on cranapple juice	oatmeal spilled in bulk section
out of carrot juice	telephone out of order
out of licorice sticks	out of Lava soap
out of chocolate milk	water on floor
out of Dove Bars	out of glazed doughnuts
windows dirty	out of baby carrots
out of iceberg lettuce	spaghetti sauce on floor
dislike store decorations	out of Peter Pan crunchy peanut butter
out of St. John's wort	
out of vanilla soy milk	

SELECTED BIBLIOGRAPHY AND FURTHER READING

Besterfield, Dale H., Carol Besterfield-Micha, Glen Besterfield and Mary Besterfield-Sacre. *Total Quality Management*, 2nd ed. Englewood Cliffs, NJ: Prentice Hall, 1999.

Brassard, Michael, and Diane Ritter. *The Memory Jogger II: A Pocket Guide of Tools for Continuous Improvement and Effective Planning*. Methuen, MA: Goal/QPC, 1994.

Brunetti, W. "Reaching for the Prize: A Lesson in Quality," *Public Utilities Fortnightly*, April 12, 1990, pp. 9–16.

Cappels, Thomas. *Financially Focused Quality: TQM in the 21st Century*. Boca Raton, FL: St. Lucie Press, 1999.

Dale, Barrie G., ed. *Managing Quality*, 3rd ed. Oxford, UK: Blackwell Publishers, 1999.

Foster, Thomas A. *Managing Quality: An Integrative Approach*. Englewood Cliffs, NJ: Prentice Hall, 2001.

Garvin, David A. *Managing Quality*. New York: Free Press, 1988.

Giffith, Gary K. *The Quality Technician's Handbook*. 4th ed. Upper Saddle River, NJ: Prentice Hall, 2000.

Gitlow, Howard, Alan Oppenheim, and Rosa Oppenheim. *Quality Management: Tools and Methods for Improvement*. 2nd ed. Burr Ridge, IL: Irwin, 1995.

Goetsch, David L., and Stanley B. Davis. *Quality Management: Introduction to Total Quality Management for Production, Processing, and Services*, 3rd ed. Englewood Cliffs, NJ: Prentice Hall, 2000.

Gryna, Derek S., and Frank M. Gryna. "Quality in Banking Starts with Four Assessments." *Quality Progress*, August 1999, pp. 27–34.

Harrington, H. James, Erik K. C. Esseling, and Harm Van Nimwegen. *Business Process Improvement Workbook: Documentation, Analysis, Design, and Management of Business Process Improvement*. New York: McGraw-Hill, 1997.

Harry, Mikel, and Richard Schroeder. *Six Sigma: The Breakthrough Management Strategy Revolutionizing the World's Top Corporations*. New York: Currency, 2000.

Hendricks, Kevin B., and Vinod R. Singhal. "Don't Count TQM Out." *Quality Progress*, April 1999, pp. 35–41.

Ireland, Samuel. "Quality and Nonprofit Organizations." *Quality Progress*, March 1999, pp. 96–99.

Jacques, March Laree. "The Call of Quality: Doing Right Things Right." *Quality Progress*, September 1999, pp. 48–54.

Juran, Joseph M. *Juran's Quality Handbook.* New York: McGraw-Hill, 1999.

La Lopa, Joseph M., and Richard F. Marecki. "The Critical Role of Quality in the Tourism Industry." *Quality Progress,* August 1999, pp. 37–41.

Lientz, B. P., and P. Rea. *How to Plan and Implement Business Process Improvement.* San Diego, CA: Harcourt Brace Professional Publications, 1998.

Lynch, R. L., and K. F. Cross. *Measure Up! Yardsticks for Continuous Improvement.* 2nd ed. Cambridge, MA: Blackwell, 1995.

Mears, P. *Quality Improvement Tools and Techniques.* New York: McGraw-Hill, 1995.

Milakovich, M. E. *Improving Service Quality: Achieving High Performance in the Public and Private Sectors.* Delray Beach, FL: St. Lucie Press, 1995.

Mitra, Amitava. *Fundamentals of Quality Control and Improvement.* 2nd ed. Englewood Cliffs, NJ: Prentice Hall, 1998.

Oppenheim, Bohdan W., and Zbigniew H. Przasnyski. "Total Quality Requires Serious Training." *Quality Progress*, October 1999, pp. 63–73.

Pyzdek, Thomas. "Quality Profession Must Learn to Heed Its Own Advice." *Quality Progress*, June 1999, pp. 60–64.

Ross, Joel E. *Total Quality Management: Text, Cases, and Readings*, 3rd ed. Boca Raton, FL: St. Lucie Press, 1999.

Salegna, Gary, and Farzaneh Fazel. "Obstacles to Implementing Quality." *Quality Progress*, July 2000, pp. 53–57.

Scherkenbach, W. W. *The Deming Route to Quality and Productivity: Roadmaps and Roadblocks.* Rockville, MD: Mercury Press/Fairchild Publications, 1990.

Smith, Gerald. *Statistical Process Control and Process Improvement.* 3rd ed. Englewood Cliffs, NJ: Prentice Hall, 1997.

Stamatis, D. H. *Documenting and Auditing for ISO 9000 and QS-9000: Tools for Ensuring Certification or Registration.* Burr Ridge, IL: Irwin, 1996.

Stamatis, D. H. *Total Quality Services: Principles, Practices, and Implementation.* Delray Beach, FL: St. Lucie Press, 1996.

Stevenson, William J. "Supercharging Your Pareto Analysis." *Quality Progress*, October 2000, pp. 51–55.

Steeples, Marion M. "The Quality–Ethics Connection." *Quality Progress*, June 1994, pp. 73–75.

Straker, D. *A Toolbook for Quality Improvement and Problem Solving.* New York: Prentice Hall, 1995.

Summers, Donna. *Quality.* 2nd ed. Upper Saddle River, NJ: Prentice Hall, 2000.

Zuckerman, A. *ISO 9000 Made Easy: A Cost-Saving Guide to Documentation and Registration.* New York: AMACOM, 1995.

Zuckerman, A. *International Standards Desk Reference: Your Passport to World Markets, ISO 9000, CE Mark, QS-9000, SSM, ISO 14000, Q 9000, American, European, and Global Standards Systems.* New York: AMACOM, 1997.

CHAPTER 10

Quality Control

LEARNING OBJECTIVES

After completing this chapter, you should be able to:

1 List and briefly explain the elements of the quality control process.
2 Explain how control charts are designed to monitor a process, and the concepts that underlie their use.
3 Assess process capability.
4 Describe six sigma.

G E is one of the largest companies in the world and continues to grow. Harley Davidson is the only U.S. motorcycle company left. How do companies such as these survive and grow? While some other factors are also relevant, quality control is certainly an important contributor.

T his chapter covers quality control. The purpose of quality control is to ensure that processes are performing in an acceptable manner. Companies accomplish this by monitoring and inspecting the product during the production process, sometimes using sampling and statistical techniques. **Quality control** measures quality characteristics relative to standards and acts when they do not meet standards. If the results are acceptable, no further action is required; unacceptable results call for corrective action.

quality control An activity that evaluates quality characteristics relative to a standard, and takes corrective action when they do not meet standards.

INTRODUCTION

The best companies emphasize *designing quality into the process*, thereby greatly reducing the need for inspection/tests or control efforts. As you might expect, different business organizations are in different stages of this evolutionary process: the least progressive rely heavily on receiving and shipping inspection/tests. Many occupy a middle ground that involves some receiving and shipping inspection/tests and some process control (i.e., inspection during the process). The most progressive have achieved an inherent level of quality that is sufficiently high that they can avoid wholesale inspection/test and process control. That is the ultimate goal. Figure 10–1 illustrates these phases of quality assurance.

Quality assurance that relies primarily on inspection/tests of previously produced items is referred to as *acceptance sampling*. It is described in the chapter supplement, which can be found on the DVD or Online Learning Centre at www.mcgrawhill.ca/olc/stevenson in Student Edition under "Additional Content." Quality control efforts that occur during production are referred to as (*statistical*) *process control*, and these we examine in the following sections (see Figure 10–2). First some comments about inspection follow.

INSPECTION

Inspection is an appraisal activity that compares goods or services to a standard. To determine whether a process is functioning as intended or to verify that a batch or lot of raw materials or final products does not contain more than a specified percentage of

inspection Appraisal of goods or services against standards.

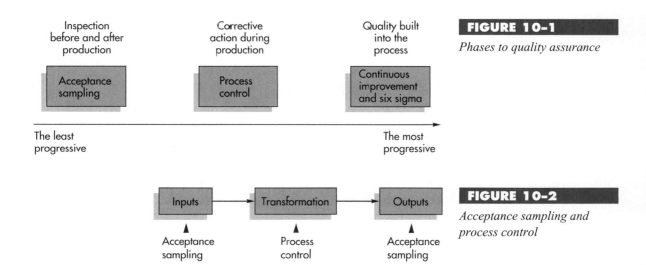

FIGURE 10-1

Phases to quality assurance

FIGURE 10-2

Acceptance sampling and process control

Process Control in Pulp and Paper Mills

Paper is made from wood pulp, which in turn is made from wood chips. Both pulp making and paper making processes are continuous. Therefore, it is important to continuously control the quality of pulp and paper. The quality of paper includes tensile strength, tear resistance, weight, and colour. These characteristics are influenced by the type of wood used, the processes used during pulp making, and the paper machine. Paper machines are huge integrated automated equipment as large as 10 m wide by 10 m high by 100 m long. Pulp making involves breaking the wood chips into fibres, performed either mechanically (grinding), chemically (dissolving in acid), or thermo-mechanically (grinding with steam added). In recent years, the paper makers have been under pressure to include recycled paper as part of the raw material input. However, recycled paper, mainly newsprint, requires de-inking and changes the process characteristics.

Abitibi-Consolidated's Alma, Quebec, paper mill produces newsprint and telephone directory papers, mostly for the U.S. market. Under pressure from the U.S. phone companies in the mid-1990s, the plant built a de-inking facility and started using the minimum required recycled newsprint (40 percent of input). Also, it replaced its very old chemical/mechanical pulp process with thermo-mechanical. These changes caused instability in the quality control. But the quality testing equipment was old and slow, providing only one test per paper machine per shift (Alma has three paper machines). More frequent tests were needed if the process were to be improved. The Alma mill installed an automated paper-testing machine: a sample strip from each paper machine's output reel is wound around a small cylinder and inserted in the machine. The machine automatically selects 10 random locations across the paper strip and measures 9 characteristics such as tensile strength and tear resistance. The results are available in 14 minutes and are used to adjust the mix of pulp (called "furnish") used for the next reel of paper (approximately 46 tests per day).

Pulp and paper mills constantly upgrade their quality control equipment. For example, the Abitibi-Consolidated's Belgo mill in Shawinigan, Quebec, recently installed online measuring instruments that stabilized the consistency of the whitewater (the water that is drained from wet pulp in the paper machine) routed back into the pulp mill process.

Sources: M. Williamson, "Automated Testing Helps Abitibi Mill Implement Furnish Management Plan," *Pulp & Paper* 70(9), September 1996, pp. 135–36; M. Williamson, "Wet End Sensors Improve Quality, Cut Costs for Abitibi-Consolidated," *Pulp & Paper* 74(12), December 2000, pp. 55–57.

defective goods, it is necessary to physically examine at least some of the items in question. The purpose of inspection is to provide information on the degree to which items conform to a standard. There are various kinds of testing equipment and software available, depending on the nature of the product. Some examples of these are given in the readings, "Delphi," "Retaining Rings," "Roctel Manufacturing," "Crown Cork and Seal," and "Hughes Bros.," which appear throughout the chapter. For an application of process control, see the above reading on pulp and paper.

Some basic decision-making issues are:

1. How much to inspect and how often.
2. At what points in the process inspection should occur.
3. Whether to inspect in a centralized location or on-site.

How Much to Inspect

The amount of inspection can range from no inspection whatsoever to inspection of each item. Low-cost, high-volume items such as paper clips, nails, and pencils often require little inspection because (1) the cost associated with passing defective items is quite low and (2) the processes that produce these items are usually highly reliable, so that defects are rare. Conversely, items that have large costs associated with passing defective products

READING

Delphi

The Delphi plant in Brookhaven, Mississippi, makes fuse and relay boxes for GM trucks and SUVs. The plastic fuse tray is produced by injection-molding presses. The rectangular holes on the tray and holes for terminals must have tolerance of 0.3 mm in order to hold fuses and metal terminals in place, and they must be located correctly on the tray. To check the accuracy of the trays, each molding press's output is tested every two hours by sampling one tray. The tray is put in a vision inspection machine and secured into a fixture. The machine magnifies the image 12 times, digitizes it, and compares it with a good tray. The positions of fuse holes and terminal holes are checked. The vision system is Smartscope Flash by Optical Gaging Products. It uses the Measure-X software to perform the analysis, and reports the results to the QC-Calc SPC software which produces control charts, etc. The fixture was carved out from acrylic material using laser to maximize its accuracy (5–7 percent tolerance), thus reducing measurement errors.

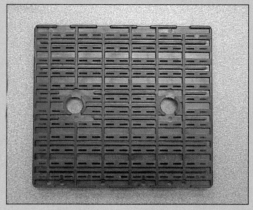

A plastic tray for fuse box of GM trucks and SUVs.

Sources: L. Adams, "Making Complex Parts That Fit Together," *Quality* 41(1), January 2002, pp. 24–26; www.ogpnet.com.

require inspection. Thus, critical components of a vehicle are closely scrutinized. In high-volume systems, *automated* inspection is one option that may be employed.

The majority of quality control applications lie somewhere between the two extremes. Most require some inspection, but it is neither possible nor economically feasible to examine every part of a product or every aspect of a service. The cost of inspection and resulting interruptions of a process typically outweigh the benefits of 100-percent inspection. However, the cost of letting undetected defects slip through is sufficiently high that inspection cannot be completely ignored. The amount of inspection needed is governed by the costs of inspection and the expected costs of passing defective items.

As illustrated in Figure 10–3, if inspection activities increase, inspection costs increase, but the costs of undetected defects decrease. The traditional goal was to minimize the sum of these two costs. In other words, it may not pay to attempt to catch every defect, particularly if the cost of inspection exceeds the penalties associated with letting some defects get through. Current thinking is that every reduction in defective output reduces total costs because the cost of passing defectives is usually underestimated.

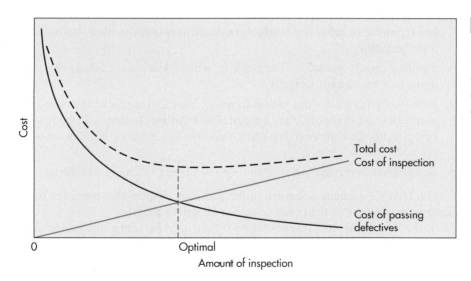

FIGURE 10-3

Traditional view:
The amount of inspection is optimal when the sum of the costs of inspection and passing defectives is minimized

Retaining Rings

Rotor Clips Company (RC), located in Somerset, New Jersey, is a large manufacturer of retaining rings. RC measures the thickness of the rings using micrometers. However, the diameter of very small rings is hard to measure manually by calipers because the operator either squeezes the ring or leaves a gap. Recently RC bought an In-Sight 1,000 vision sensor from Cognex Corp. The vision system magnifies the image of the ring, digitally measures the dimensions, compares these with the CAD specified dimensions of the ring, and notifies the operator if any specification is violated. Characteristics measured include the inside and outside diameters, width, lug size, and lug hole diameter. Accuracy has increased and inspection time for six rings has decreased from 20 to 5 minutes.

A visions sensor being used to measure dimensions of a retaining ring.

Sources: "Vision Sensor Improves Ring Measurement Process," *Quality*, 44(1), January 2005, pp. 80–83; www.cognex.com.

As a rule, operations with a high proportion of human involvement necessitate more inspection effort than mechanical operations which tend to be more reliable. For continuous process/assembly lines, the frequency of inspection depends largely on the rate at which a process may go out of control. A stable process will require only infrequent checks, whereas an unstable one or one that has recently given trouble will require more frequent checks. Likewise, many small lots will require more samples than a few large lots because it is important to obtain sample data from each lot.

Where to Inspect in the Process

Many operations have numerous possible inspection points. Because each inspection adds to the cost of the product or service, it is important to restrict inspection efforts to the points where they can do the most good. In manufacturing, some of the typical inspection points are:

1. *At the beginning of a process.* There is little sense in paying for goods that do not meet quality standards and in expending time and effort on material that is bad to begin with.
2. *At the end of a process.* Customer satisfaction and the firm's image are at stake here, and repairing or replacing products in the field is usually much more costly than doing it at the factory.
3. *Before a costly operation.* The point is to not waste costly labour or machine time on items that are already defective.
4. *Before an irreversible operation.* In many cases, items can be reworked up to a certain point; beyond that point they cannot. For example, pottery can be reworked prior to firing. After that, defective pottery must be discarded or sold as seconds at a lower price.
5. *Before a covering operation.* Painting and plating often mask defects.

The HACCP system described in the previous chapter also provides some guidelines for determining the critical control points for safety hazards.

In the service sector, inspection points include personnel/customer interfaces (e.g., service counter) and the facility. Table 10–1 illustrates a number of service examples.

Type of Business	Inspection Points	Quality Characteristics
Fast food	Server	Appearance, friendliness, waiting time
	Eating area	Cleanliness
	Kitchen	Cleanliness, purity of food, food storage, temperature and time of cooking, health regulations and hygiene
Supermarket	Cashiers	Accuracy, courtesy, waiting time
	Aisles and stockrooms	Clutter
	Shelf stock	Ample supply, rotation of perishables, appearance

TABLE 10-1

Examples of inspection points and quality characteristics inspected in two types of service organizations

Centralized versus On-Site Inspection

Some situations require that inspections be performed *on site*. For example, inspecting the hull of a ship for cracks requires inspectors to visit the ship. At other times, specialized tests can best be performed in a lab (e.g., medical tests, analyzing food and water samples, testing metals for hardness, running viscosity tests on lubricants).

The central issue in the decision concerning on-site or lab inspections is whether the advantages of specialized lab tests are worth the time and interruption needed to obtain the results. Specialized equipment, skilled quality control inspectors, and a more favourable test environment (less noise, vibrations, and dust) offer strong arguments for using a lab. More companies are now relying on self-inspections by operators on-site.

STATISTICAL PROCESS CONTROL

Process quality control is concerned with the quality of conformance of a process: the degree to which the output of a process conforms to the intent of design. Toward that end, managers sometimes use **statistical process control (SPC)** to evaluate the output of a process to determine its acceptability. To do this, they take periodic samples from the process and compare them with predetermined limits. If the sample results fall outside the limits, they stop the process and take corrective action. If the sample results fall within the limits, they allow the process to continue.

statistical process control
Statistical evaluation of the output of a process during production.

The Quality Control Steps

Effective quality control requires the following steps:

1. Define the quality characteristics to monitor.
2. Measure the characteristics.
3. Compare to a standard and evaluate.
4. Take corrective action if necessary.

The first step is to define, in sufficient detail, what is to be controlled. It is not enough, for example, to simply refer to a painted surface. The paint can have a number of important characteristics such as its colour, gloss, thickness, and resistance to fading or chipping. Different characteristics may require different approaches for control purposes.

Only those characteristics that can be measured are candidates for control. Thus, it is important to consider how measurement will be accomplished.

There must be a standard of comparison that can be used to evaluate the measurements. This will relate to the level of quality being sought.

When a process is judged out of control, the process should be stopped and corrective action must be taken. This involves uncovering the cause (e.g., worn toolbits, or failure

Roctel Manufacturing

A division of Linamar Corporation (www.linamar.ca), Roctel Manufacturing of Guelph, Ontario, is a small manufacturer of valve housing for automobile steering mechanisms. Roctel operators used to collect data on dimensions of parts and construct control charts manually. With an average time of 20 seconds per observation and approximately 2,000 observations per day, approximately 300 hours of machine and labour time per month was lost for acquiring data manually, choosing the right control chart, plotting, entering times and dates, and doing mathematical calculations. In addition, Roctel couldn't provide the quality control information required by its customers fast enough. Therefore, it installed 31 automated fixture gauges (fixed in position) connected to a computer running control chart plotting software. This has accelerated data

collection and plotting activities. Quality has also improved (customer complaints have been cut in half), and operators find it easier to work on different machines.

Source: M. Litsikas, "Roctel's Machine Operators Seek More Knowledge," *Quality* 34(5), May 1995, pp. 40, 42, 44.

Crown Cork and Seal

C rown Cork and Seal (CCS), Sandston, Virginia, makes plastic bottle caps. When sales doubled in the late 1990s, CCS had to increase its inspection speed. The coordinate measuring machine (CMM) was manual and could only be used to inspect one cap from four of the 22 injection-molding machines each hour. The new CMM made by Mitutoyo is computer numerically controlled and can inspect 196 caps at the same time. There is a stationary aluminum fixture plate which holds the caps with a vacuum. The inspection takes only 40 minutes: 10 minutes to collect the samples from the 22 injection molding machines, 20 minutes to place them on the fixture and index them, and 10 minutes to run the measurements. Both inside and outside dimensions of each cap is measured—3 to 5 different measurements per cap.

The coordinate measuring machine fixture holding several plastic bottle caps.

Source: "Bottle Closure Capacity Increases with CMM," *Quality* 40(6), June 2001, pp. 54, 56.

to follow specified procedures) and correcting it. Also, any potentially off-spec (i.e., defective) parts or products should be tested, and if defective, should be either reworked or scrapped. To ensure that corrective action is effective, the output of a process must be monitored for a sufficient period of time to verify that the problem has been eliminated.

Types of Variations

All processes that provide a good or a service exhibit a certain amount of "natural" variation in their output. The variations are created by the combined influences of countless minor factors, each one so unimportant that even if it could be identified and eliminated, the decrease in process variability would be negligible. In effect, this variability is inherent in the process. It is often referred to as *chance* or **random variation**. In Deming's terms, this is referred to as *common variability* (common across different operators of the same process). The amount of inherent variability differs from process to process.

random variation Natural variations in the output of a process, created by countless minor factors.

For instance, older machines generally exhibit a higher degree of natural variability than newer machines, partly because of worn parts and partly because new machines may incorporate design improvements that lessen the variability in their output.

A second kind of variability in process output is nonrandom and is called **assignable variation**. In Deming's terms, this is referred to as *special variation*. Unlike natural variation, the main sources of assignable variation can usually be identified (assigned to a specific cause) and eliminated. Excessive tool wear, equipment that needs adjustment, defective materials, and human errors (e.g., failure to follow correct procedures) are typical sources of assignable variation.

The main task in quality control is to distinguish assignable from random variation. Usually, taking a sample of two or more observations, calculating a sample statistic such as sample mean, and using this sample statistic makes the task easier. This is because random variations are reduced in sample statistics. The variability of a sample statistic is described by its *sampling distribution*, which is the theoretical distribution of the values of the statistic for all possible samples of a given size from the process. Note that assignable causes usually shift the whole distribution of the process, and this shift will be wholly duplicated in the sampling distribution of sample statistic (e.g., the sampling distribution of sample mean will shift in the same direction and for the distance).

Consider the process for filling bottles with soft drink. If the amount of soft drink in a large number of bottles is measured accurately, we would discover slight differences among the bottles. If these amounts were arranged on a graph, the frequency distribution would reflect the *process variability*. The values would be clustered close to the process average (e.g., 2 litres), but some of the values would vary somewhat from the mean.

If we return to the process and take *samples* of three bottles each and compute the *mean* amount of soft drink in each sample, we would discover that these values also vary, just as the *individual* values varied. However, the distribution of sample mean is more concentrated around process mean (e.g., two litres) than the distribution of process (i.e., individual bottles).

If the process contained *only* random variability, the distribution of process values would represent the inherent process variability, and the distribution of sample means would represent only the random variability of all possible sample means.

The two distributions are illustrated in Figure 10–4. The sampling distribution exhibits less variability (i.e., it is less spread out) than the process distribution. This reflects the *averaging* that occurs in computing the sample means: high and low values in samples tend to offset each other, resulting in less variability among sample means than among individual values. Note that both distributions have the same mean; the mean of the sampling distribution is exactly equal to the mean of the process. Finally, note that most process distributions and sampling distributions are approximately *Normal*. Furthermore, the *central limit theorem* implies that the sampling distribution will be Normal, even if the population (i.e., the process) is not.

The distribution of sampling distribution (of sample mean) can be used to help judge whether a process mean has changed (i.e., there is an assignable cause).If the process has only random variability, then the sample mean should most likely fall between ±2 (with 95.5 percent probability for Normal distribution) or ± 3 (with 99.7 percent probability for Normal distribution) standard deviations of the process mean (see Figure 10–5).

assignable variation
Non-random variability in process output, a variation whose cause can be identified.

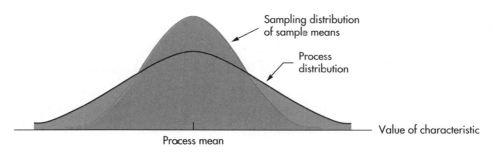

FIGURE 10-4

The sampling distribution of sample means has less variability than the process

Percentage of values within given ranges in a Normal sampling distribution of sample mean

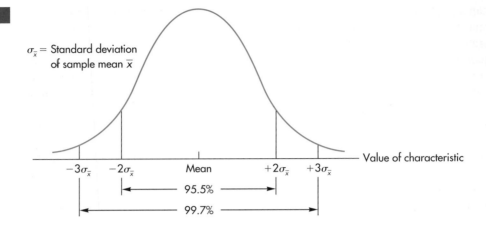

If it doesn't, then we can conclude that the process mean most likely has changed, and hence there is most likely an assignable cause.

Control Charts

control chart A time-ordered plot of a sample statistic with limits, used to distinguish between random and non-random variability.

A **control chart** is a *time-ordered* plot of a sample statistic with limits. It is used to distinguish between random variability and nonrandom (assignable) variability. The basis for a control chart is the sampling distribution. We will illustrate this concept by focussing on the sample mean control chart. As mentioned before, because sampling distribution of sample mean will be Normal, 99.7 percent of the sample means will fall within ±3 standard deviations of the mean of the distribution. Therefore, we could decide to set the limit separating random and nonrandom variation at ±3 standard deviations from the mean, and conclude that any value that was farther away from the mean than these limits is a nonrandom variation. In effect, these limits are called **control limits**. Figure 10–6 illustrates how control limits for sample mean control chart are based on the sampling distribution of sample mean.

control limits The dividing lines between random and nonrandom deviations.

Control charts have two limits that separate random variation and nonrandom variation. The larger value is the *upper control limit* (UCL), and the smaller value is the *lower control limit* (LCL). A sample statistic that falls between these two limits suggests randomness while a value outside or on either limit suggests nonrandomness (i.e., the deviation from the process mean is so large that the process mean most likely has changed).

Note that the control limits are not directly related to design specification limits. Control limits are based on the characteristic of the process, whereas the design specification limits are based on the desired characteristic of the product. The process is capable if the process values fall within the design specification limits. However, control limits are for sample statistics, so they will fall well within the design specification limits. This will be further explained in the Process Capability section later.

Control limits are based on the sampling distribution

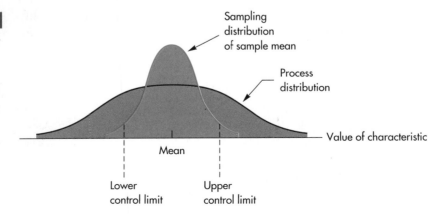

It is important to recognize that because any control limits will leave some area in the *tails* of the distribution, there is a small probability that a value will fall outside the limits *even though only random variations are present.* For example, if ±2 sigma (standard deviation) limits are used, they would include 95.5 percent of the values. Consequently, the complement of that number (100 percent − 95.5 percent = 4.5 percent) would not be included. That percentage (or *probability*) is sometimes referred to as the probability of a **Type I error**, where the "error" is concluding that a process has changed (nonrandomness is present) when it has not (only randomness is present). It is also referred to as *alpha risk*, where alpha (α) is the sum of the probabilities in the two tails. Figure 10–7 illustrates this concept.

Using wider limits (e.g., ±3 sigma limits) reduces the probability of a Type I error because it decreases the area in the tails. However, wider limits make it more difficult to detect nonrandom variations *if* they are present. For example, the mean of the process might shift (an assignable cause of variation) enough to be detected by two-sigma limits, but not enough to be readily apparent using three-sigma limits. That could lead to a second kind of error, known as a **Type II error**, which is concluding that a process has not changed (i.e., only randomness is present) when it has (nonrandomness is present). In theory, the costs of making each error should be balanced by their probabilities. However, in practice, two sigma limits and three sigma limits are commonly used without specifically referring to the probability of a Type II error.

The sample statistic values are usually plotted against time, together with upper and lower control limits. This produces a record of the quality control activity, as well as helping to prevent the process from going out of control. Figure 10–8 illustrates the components of a sample mean control chart. Each sample mean is represented by a single red dot on the chart. Moreover, each sample mean is compared to the extremes of the

Type I error Concluding that a process has changed (nonrandomness is present) when it has not (i.e., only randomness is present).

Type II error Concluding that a process has not changed (i.e., only randomness is present) when it has (nonrandomness is present).

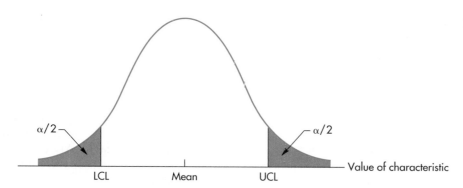

α = Probability of a Type I error

FIGURE 10-7

The probability of a Type I error

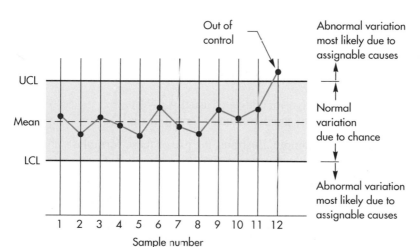

FIGURE 10-8

Example of a sample mean control chart

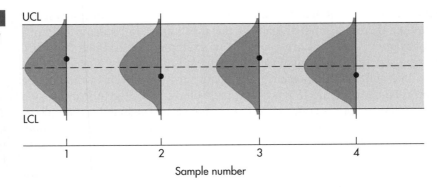

sampling distribution (i.e., the control limits) to judge if it is within the acceptable (random) range. Figure 10–9 illustrates this concept.

The design of control charts is described in detail below.

Designing Control Charts

The following steps are usually taken to design control charts:

1. Determine a sample size n (usually between 2 and 20). The choice of n depends on cost of inspection versus expected cost of Type I and Type II errors. The larger n, the smaller the probability of Type I and Type II errors.

2. Obtain 20 to 25 samples. Compute the appropriate sample statistic for each sample (e.g., sample mean).

3. Establish preliminary control limits using the following formulas, and graph them.

4. Plot the sample statistic values on the control chart, and note whether any points fall outside the control limits.

5. If you find no points outside control limits, assume that there is no assignable cause and therefore the process is stable and in control. If not, investigate and correct assignable causes of variation; then resume the process and collect another set of 20 to 25 samples upon which control limits can be based.

sample mean control chart
Control chart used to monitor the mean of a process.

Sample Mean Control Chart. A **sample mean control chart**, sometimes referred to as an $\bar{x}$ ("x-bar") chart, is used to monitor mean of a process. It can be constructed in one of two ways. The choice depends on what information is available. Although the value of the standard deviation of a process, σ, is often unknown, if a reasonable estimate is available, one can calculate control limits using these formulas:

$$\text{Upper control limit (UCL):} = \bar{\bar{x}} + z\sigma_{\bar{x}} \tag{10–1}$$

$$\text{Lower control limit (LCL):} = \bar{\bar{x}} - z\sigma_{\bar{x}}$$

where

$\sigma_{\bar{x}} =$ Standard deviation of sampling distribution of sample means $= \sigma/\sqrt{n}$
$\sigma \ =$ Process standard deviation
$n \ =$ Sample size
$z \ =$ Standard Normal deviate (usually $z = 3$)
$\bar{\bar{x}} =$ Average of sample means $=$ grand mean

The following example illustrates the use of these formulas.

Example 1

A quality inspector took five samples, each with four observations, of the length of a part (in cm). The analyst computed the mean of each sample and then computed the grand mean.

a. Use the following data to obtain three sigma (i.e., $z = 3$) control limits for means of future sample lengths. Is the process in control?

b. If a new sample has values 12.10, 12.10, 12.09, 12.12, and 12.14, using the control chart in part *a*, has the process mean changed (i.e., there is nonrandomness)?

It is known from previous experience that the standard deviation of the process is .02 cm.

		Sample				
		1	**2**	**3**	**4**	**5**
	1	12.11	12.15	12.09	12.12	12.09
Observation	**2**	12.10	12.12	12.09	12.10	12.14
	3	12.11	12.10	12.11	12.08	12.13
	4	12.08	12.11	12.15	12.10	12.12
	$\bar{x}$	12.10	12.12	12.11	12.10	12.12

Solution

a. $\bar{\bar{x}} = \dfrac{12.10 + 12.12 + 12.11 + 12.10 + 12.12}{5} = 12.11\,\text{cm}$

Using formula 10–1, with $z = 3$, $n = 4$ observations per sample, and $\sigma = .02$, we find

$$\text{UCL}:\quad 12.11 + 3\left(\frac{.02}{\sqrt{4}}\right) = 12.14$$

$$\text{LCL}:\quad 12.11 - 3\left(\frac{.02}{\sqrt{4}}\right) = 12.08$$

Because all sample means fall between the control limits (12.08 and 12.14), the process is in control.

b. $\bar{x}_6 = \dfrac{12.10 + 12.10 + 12.09 + 12.12 + 12.14}{5} = 12.11\,\text{cm}$

Because $12.08 < 12.11 < 12.14$, the process mean has not changed (i.e., there is only randomness).

Note: The fact that some of the *individual* measurements fall outside of the control limits (e.g., the first observation in Sample 2 and the last observation in Sample 3) is irrelevant. You can see why by referring back to Figure 10–6: *individual* values are represented by the process distribution, a large portion of which lies outside of the control limits for sample *means*.

A second approach (to calculate the control limits) is to use the sample *range* (i.e., maximum value − minimum value in sample) as a measure of process variability. The appropriate formulas for sample mean control limits in this case are

$$\text{UCL} = \bar{\bar{x}} + A_2\bar{R}$$

$$\text{LCL} = \bar{\bar{x}} - A_2\bar{R} \tag{10–2}$$

where

A_2 is from Table 10–2

$\bar{R}$ = Average of sample ranges

Example 2

Twenty samples of $n = 8$ have been taken of the weight of a part. The average of sample ranges for the 20 samples is .016 kg. and the average of sample means is 3 kg. Determine three sigma control limits for sample mean of this process.

Solution

$\bar{\bar{x}} = 3$, $\bar{R} = .016$, $A_2 = .37$ for $n = 8$ (from Table 10–2)

$$\text{UCL} = \bar{\bar{x}} + A_2\bar{R} = 3 + .37(.016) = 3.006\,\text{kg}$$

$$\text{LCL} = \bar{\bar{x}} - A_2\bar{R} = 3 - .37(.016) = 2.994\,\text{kg}$$

TABLE 10-2

Factors for three sigma control limits for x̄- and R-charts

Number of Observations in Sample, n	Factor for x̄ Charts, A_2	FACTORS FOR R-CHARTS Lower Control Limit, D_3	FACTORS FOR R-CHARTS Upper Control Limit, D_4
2	1.88	0	3.27
3	1.02	0	2.57
4	0.73	0	2.28
5	0.58	0	2.11
6	0.48	0	2.00
7	0.42	0.08	1.92
8	0.37	0.14	1.86
9	0.34	0.18	1.82
10	0.31	0.22	1.78
11	0.29	0.26	1.74
12	0.27	0.28	1.72
13	0.25	0.31	1.69
14	0.24	0.33	1.67
15	0.22	0.35	1.65
16	0.21	0.36	1.64
17	0.20	0.38	1.62
18	0.19	0.39	1.61
19	0.19	0.40	1.60
20	0.18	0.41	1.59

Source: Adapted from Eugene Grant and Richard Leavenworth, *Statistical Quality Control,* 5th ed. (New York: McGraw-Hill, 1980).

sample range control chart
Control chart used to monitor process dispersion.

Sample range control chart. Sample Range control chart (*R*-chart) is used to monitor process dispersion or spread. Although the underlying sampling distribution is not Normal, the concepts for design and use of sample range control charts are much the same as those for design and use of mean charts. Control limits for sample range control charts are found using the average of sample ranges from these formulas:

$$UCL_R = D_4\bar{R}$$
$$LCL_R = D_3\bar{R}$$
(10–3)

where values of D_3 and D_4 are obtained from Table 10–2.

Example 3

Twenty-five samples of $n = 10$ observations have been taken from a milling process. The average of sample ranges was .01 centimetre. Determine upper and lower control limits for sample range.

Solution

$\bar{R} = .01$ cm, $n = 10$

From Table 10–2, for $n = 10$, $D_4 = 1.78$ and $D_3 = .22$.

$UCL_R = 1.78(.01) = .0178$ cm

$LCL_R = .22(.01) = .0022$ cm

In Example 3, a sample range of .0178 centimetre or more would suggest that the process variability had increased. A sample range of .0022 cm or less would imply that the process variability had decreased. In the former case, this means that the process is producing too much variation; we would want to investigate this in order to remove the cause of variation. In the latter case, even though decreased variability is desirable, we would want to determine what is causing it: Perhaps an improved method has been used, in which case we would want to identify it.

If the standard deviation of process σ is not known but the average of sample ranges $\bar{R}$ is known, then σ can be estimated as follows: Equate the two UCLs in formulas 10–1 and 10–2, replace 3 for z, and simplify:

$$\bar{\bar{X}} + 3\sigma_{\bar{x}} \approx \bar{\bar{X}} + A_2\bar{R}$$

$$3\sigma_{\bar{x}} \approx A_2\bar{R}$$

$$3\frac{\sigma}{\sqrt{n}} \approx A_2\bar{R}$$

$$\sigma \approx \frac{\sqrt{n}}{3} A_2\bar{R} \tag{10-4}$$

Individual Unit and Moving Range Charts

When the rate of production is low, testing is expensive, or there is no reason to expect additional information by taking more observations, only one unit is used for inspection. In this case, the sample mean control chart reduces to X-chart:

$$\text{UCL}_x = \bar{X} + z\sigma \tag{10-5}$$

$$\text{LCL}_x = \bar{X} - z\sigma$$

where $\bar{X}$ is the mean of individual observations (i.e., process mean), σ is the process standard deviation, and z is the standard Normal deviate. It is important to note that the above formulas assume a Normal process distribution.

However, the "sample" range cannot be calculated in the usual way because there is only one observation in each sample. Instead, the differences between consecutive observations (called "moving range") are calculated and used. We can still use the formulas for sample range control limits:

$$\text{UCL}_{MR} = D_4\bar{R} \tag{10-6}$$

$$\text{LCL}_{MR} = D_3\bar{R}$$

where D_4 and D_3 can be obtained from Table 10–2 using $n = 2$, and $\bar{R}$ is the average of moving ranges (the absolute value of the difference between two consecutive observations). It is important to note that consecutive moving range values are not independent and that this fact has to be considered when analyzing the moving range chart.

The following data are the (Brinell) hardness measures of 10 individual steel screws produced by a screw machine.

Example 4

a. Determine the three sigma control limits for the X-chart and the moving range chart. Is the process in control (i.e., there is only randomness; process has not changed)?

Sample No.	Hardness
1	36.3
2	28.6
3	32.5
4	38.7
5	35.4
6	27.3
7	37.2
8	36.4
9	38.3
10	30.5

b. If the 11th observation is 38.7, using the control charts in part a, is the process still in control?

Solution

a. We have to compute the average and standard deviation of the individual observations. Also, we need to find the difference in the consecutive observations and take the absolute value to derive the moving ranges. These calculations are done using Excel and are displayed below:

Sample No.	Hardness	Moving Range
1	36.3	—
2	28.6	7.7
3	32.5	3.9
4	38.7	6.2
5	35.4	3.3
6	27.3	8.1
7	37.2	9.9
8	36.4	0.8
9	38.3	1.9
10	30.5	7.8
Average =	34.12	5.51
Std dev =	4.11	

The control limits for X-chart are:

$$\text{UCL}_x = \bar{X} + z\sigma = 34.12 + 3(4.11) = 46.45$$

$$\text{LCL}_x = \bar{X} - z\sigma = 34.12 - 3(4.11) = 21.79$$

The control limits for moving range chart are:

$$\text{UCL}_{MR} = D_4\bar{R} = 3.27(5.51) = 18.02$$

$$\text{LCL}_{MR} = D_3\bar{R} = 0(5.51) = 0$$

All 10 hardness values fall within the X-chart limits and all nine moving range values fall within the moving range chart limits. Therefore, the process is in control.

b. $21.79 < 38.7 < 46.45$, therefore the individual value is within its control limits. The moving range $= 38.7 - 30.5 = 8.2$. Because $0 < 8.2 < 18.02$, the moving range is also within its control limits. Therefore, the process is still in control.

Note that if formula 10–2 were used to estimate σ from $\bar{R}$ instead of calculating it directly, we would have obtained:

$$\sigma \approx \frac{\sqrt{n}}{3} A_2\bar{R} = \frac{\sqrt{2}}{3}(1.88)(5.51) = 4.88.$$

The relatively large discrepancy between 4.88 and 4.11 (σ derived directly) is due to the fact that the data are not distributed Normally, as evident from the histogram below (note that formula 10–4 assumes that process distribution is Normal).

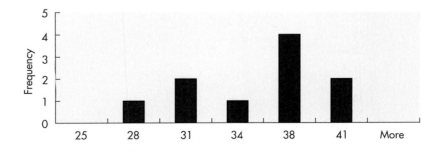

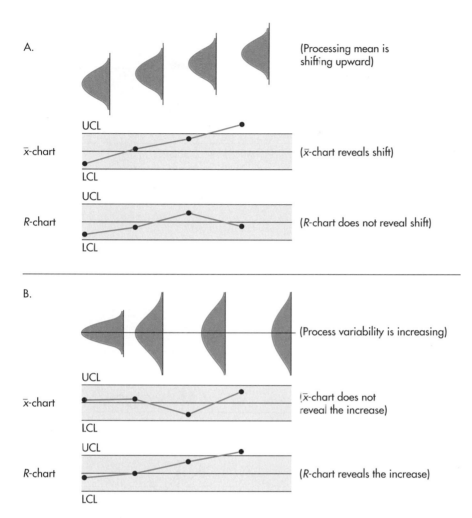

Using Sample Mean and Range Control Charts. Sample Mean and range control charts provide different perspectives on a process. Sample mean control charts are sensitive to shifts in the process mean, whereas sample range control charts are sensitive to changes in process dispersion. Because of this difference in perspective, both types of charts might be used to monitor the same process. The logic of using both is readily apparent in Figure 10–10. In 10–10A, the sample mean control chart picks up the shift in the process mean, but because the dispersion is not changing the sample range control chart fails to indicate a problem. Conversely, in 10–10B, a change in process dispersion is less apt to be detected by the sample mean control chart than by the sample range control chart. Thus, use of both charts provides more complete information than either chart alone.

Once control charts have been set up, they can serve as a basis for deciding when to interrupt a process and search for assignable causes of variation. A process should be investigated when sample statistic falls outside the control limits, and when the line plot has a trend or cycle(s) (i.e., the process is not stable). See Figure 10–11. For an application of control charts, see the reading, "Harley-Davidson" near the end of the chapter.

Control Charts for Attributes

Control charts for attributes are used when the process characteristic is *counted* rather than measured, i.e., an item in a sample is either defective or not. There are two types of attribute control charts, one for the fraction of defective items in a sample (*p*-chart) and one for the number of defects per unit (*c*-chart).

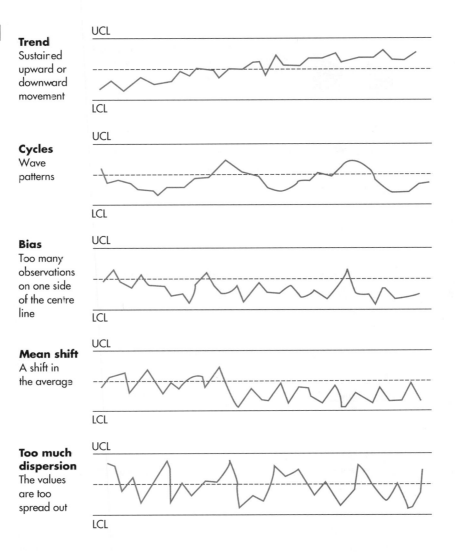

Trend
Sustained
upward or
downward
movement

Cycles
Wave
patterns

Bias
Too many
observations
on one side
of the centre
line

Mean shift
A shift in
the average

**Too much
dispersion**
The values
are too
spread out

p-**control chart** Control chart
for attributes, used to monitor
the proportion of defective
items in a process.

***p*-Control Chart.** A *p*-**control chart** is used to monitor the proportion of defective items generated by a process. The theoretical basis for *p*-chart is the Binomial distribution, although for large sample sizes the Normal distribution provides a good approximation to it. Conceptually, *p*-chart is constructed and used in much the same way as sample mean control chart.

The centre line on a *p*-chart is the average fraction defective in the population, *p*. The standard deviation of the sampling distribution of sample proportion, when *p* is known is

$$\sigma_p = \sqrt{\frac{p(1-p)}{n}}$$

Control limits are computed using the formulas

$$\text{UCL}_p = p + z\sigma_p \qquad\qquad (10\text{–}7)$$
$$\text{LCL}_p = p - z\sigma_p$$

If *p* is unknown, it can be estimated from samples. That estimate, $\bar{p}$, replaces *p* in the preceding formulas, as illustrated in Example 5.

Note: Because the formula is an approximation, sometimes the computed LCL_P is negative. In this case, zero is used as the lower control limit.

An inspector counted the number of defective parts a prototype machine made over 20 hours, taking a sample of 100 every hour.

Example 5

a. Using the following data, construct a three sigma control chart for the sample proportion of defectives.

b. Is the machine producing a stable proportion of defectives?

Sample	Number of Defectives	Sample	Number of Defectives
1	4	11	8
2	10	12	12
3	12	13	9
4	3	14	10
5	9	15	21
6	11	16	10
7	10	17	8
8	22	18	12
9	13	19	10
10	10	20	16
			220

a. $\bar{p} = \dfrac{\text{Total number of defectives}}{\text{Total number of observations}} = \dfrac{220}{20(100)} = .11$

Solution

$$\sigma_p = \sqrt{\frac{\bar{p}(1-\bar{p})}{n}} = \sqrt{\frac{.11(1-.11)}{100}} = .03$$

Control limits are:

$$\text{UCL}_p = \bar{p} + z(\hat{\sigma}_p) = .11 + 3(.03) = .20$$

$$\text{LCL}_p = \bar{p} - z(\hat{\sigma}_p) = .11 - 3(.03) = .02$$

b. Plotting the control limits and the sample fraction defectives, you can see that the process is not in control: sample 8 ($^{22}/_{100} = .22$) and sample 15 ($^{21}/_{100} = .21$) are above the upper control limit. Therefore, the machine operation should be investigated for assignable causes, and after corrective action, new data should be collected and new p-control limits should be calculated.

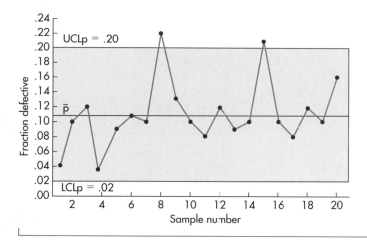

c-Control Chart. When the goal is to control the number of *occurrences* (e.g., defects) *per unit*, a *c*-**control chart** is used. Units might be automobiles, hotel rooms, typed pages, or rolls of carpet. In this case, there is no sample size, only occurrences may be counted: the

c-control chart Control chart for attributes, used to monitor the number of defects per unit.

nonoccurrences cannot be. The underlying sampling distribution is the Poisson distribution. Use of the Poisson distribution assumes that defects occur over some *continuous* region and that the probability of more than one defect at any particular spot is negligible. The mean number of defects per unit is c and the standard deviation is $\sqrt{c}$. For practical reasons, the Normal approximation to the Poisson is used. The control limits are

$$\mathrm{UCL}_c = c + z\sqrt{c}$$

$$\mathrm{LCL}_c = c - z\sqrt{c}$$

(10–8)

If the value of c is unknown, as is generally the case, the sample estimate, $\bar{c}$, is used in place of c, where $\bar{c}$ = number of defects ÷ number of samples.

When the computed lower control limit is negative, it is set to zero.

Example 6

Rolls of coiled wire are monitored using a c-chart. Eighteen rolls have been examined, and the number of defects per roll has been recorded in the following table.

a. Is the process in control? Plot the values on a c-control chart using three standard deviation control limits.

b. Suppose a new roll has seven defects. Using the c-control chart of part a, is the process producing the same average number of defects?

Sample	Number of Defectives	Sample	Number of Defectives
1	3	10	1
2	2	11	3
3	4	12	4
4	5	13	2
5	1	14	4
6	2	15	2
7	4	16	1
8	1	17	3
9	2	18	1
			45

Solution

a. $\bar{c} = 45/18 = 2.5$

$$\mathrm{UCL}_c = \bar{c} + 3\sqrt{\bar{c}} = 2.5 + 3\sqrt{2.5} = 7.24$$

$$\mathrm{LCL}_c = c - 3\sqrt{\bar{c}} = 2.5 - 3\sqrt{2.5} = -2.24 \to 0$$

As shown in the *c*-control chart below, the process is in control.

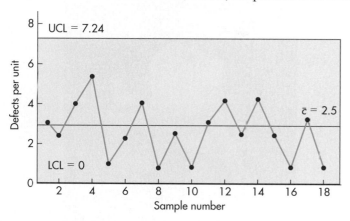

b. Because $0 < 7 < 7.24$, the process is still producing a stable number of defects.

Managerial Considerations Concerning Control Charts

Using control charts adds to the cost and time needed to obtain output. Ideally a process is so good that the desired level of quality could be achieved without the use of any control charts. The best organizations strive to reach this level, but many are not yet there, so they employ control charts at various points in their processes. In those organizations, managers must make a number of important decisions about the use of control charts:

1. At what points in the process to use control charts.
2. What type of control chart to use.

The decision about where to use control charts should focus on those aspects of the process that (1) have a tendency to go out of control and (2) are critical to the successful production of the good or service.

In some instances, a manager can choose between using a sample mean control chart and a *p*-control chart. If the manager is monitoring the diameter of a drive shaft, either the diameter could be measured and a sample mean chart used for control, or the shafts could be inspected using a *go, no-go gauge*—which simply indicates whether a particular shaft is within specification without giving its exact dimensions—and a *p*-control chart could be used. Measurement is more costly and time-consuming per unit than the yes–no inspection using a go, no-go gauge, but because measuring supplies more information than merely counting items as good or bad, one needs a much smaller sample size for a sample mean control chart than a *p*-control chart. Hence, a manager must weigh the time and cost of sampling against the information provided.

PROCESS CAPABILITY

The variability of a process can significantly impact quality. Three commonly used terms relate to the variability of process output. Each term relates to a slightly different aspect of that variability, so it is important to differentiate these terms.

Design specification is established by engineering design or customer requirements. It indicates a range of values in which *individual units* of output must fall in order to be acceptable.

Standardization is the key component of McDonald's strategy and all foods are prepared according to a strict reference manual. Farmers even have special guidelines to follow in growing potatoes for french fries. Here, quality assurance staff check all aspects of french fries, from the taste to the length of the fries.

www.mcdonalds.com

design specification A range of acceptable values established by engineering design or customer requirements.

Hughes Bros.

A small Manufacturer of parts for Boeing, Hughes Bros. of Southgate, California, had a problem. Boeing claimed that the part they recently received was off-spec by .1 inch whereas the allowed tolerance was only .03. Hughes used their FaroArm portable Coordinate Measuring Machine to measure the dimensions of part and compared it with the CAD data it had received from Boeing. The maximum deviation was only .01 inch. FaroArm's accuracy is .002 inch. The measurements exonerated them. The culprit was a mating part from another supplier.

Sources: "CMM Arm Proves Specifications Are Correct," *Quality* 40 (9), September 2001, pp. 60–62; www.faro.ccm/products/faroarm.asp.

A portable coordinate measuring system.

Control limits are statistical limits that reflect the extent to which *sample statistics* such as mean and range can vary due to randomness alone.

Process variability is the actual variability in a process (individual units).

process variability Actual variability in a process.

Control limits and process variability are directly related: control limits are based on sampling distribution variability, and sampling distribution variability is a function of process variability. On the other hand, there is no direct link between design specification and either control limits or process variability. Design specification is given in terms of a product or service, not in terms of the *process* by which the product or service is generated. Hence, in a given instance, the output of a process may or may not conform to design specification, even though the process may be statistically in control. That is why it is also necessary to take into account the *capability* of a process. The term **process capability** refers to the variability of process output *relative to* the variation allowed by the design specification. The following section describes capability analysis.

process capability The variability of process output relative to the variation allowed by the design specification.

Capability Analysis

Capability analysis is the determination of whether the variability of the process output falls within the acceptable range of variability allowed by the design specification. If it is within the design specification, the process is said to be "capable." If it is not, process is incapable and the manager must decide how to correct the situation.

Consider the three cases illustrated in Figure 10–12. In case A, process variability and design specification are well matched, so that nearly all of the process output can be expected to meet the design specification. In case B, the process variability is less than what is called for, so that 100 percent of the output will be within tolerance. In case C, however, the design specification is tighter than what the process is capable of, so that even when the process is functioning as it should, a sizable percentage of the output will fail to meet the design specification.

FIGURE 10–12

Process variability and design specification may or may not match

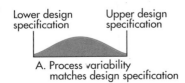

Lower design specification   Upper design specification

A. Process variability matches design specification

Lower design specification   Upper design specification

B. Process variability is well within design specification

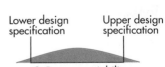

Lower design specification   Upper design specification

C. Process variability exceeds design specification

Harley-Davidson has recently implemented a PC-based networked statistical process control system in two of its power-train plants. Harley controls approximately 500 critical dimensions such as bore diameter, hole location, flatness, and surface finish of motorcycle parts. Upgrading from paper control charts, Harley installed more than 60 personal computers in strategic locations throughout both plants and connected the on-site coordinate measuring machines and other gauges into the network. As soon as an operator completes a measurement,

an updated control chart is displayed on the monitor. If the process is out of control but the part's characteristic is still within tolerance, a yellow status flag is shown. If it is outside the specification limits, a red flag is displayed.

Whenever a process goes out of control, or a part is produced outside specification limits, a dialogue box pops up and the operator is prompted to enter an assignable cause. In many cases the cause of the problem is readily apparent to the operator and immediately fixable. If the operator can't find the cause of the problem, he/she contacts the workgroup quality adviser. If additional assistance is needed, then a manufacturing engineer is brought in.

Source: R. Della, "Harley Rides High on SPC Changes," *Quality* 39(1), January 2000, pp. 40–43.

In instances such as case C in Figure 10–12, a manager might consider a range of possible solutions: (1) redesign the process or reduce the variability by, e.g., performing experiments to find the best setting for controllable factors, (2) use an alternative process that can achieve the desired output, (3) retain the current process but attempt to eliminate unacceptable output using 100-percent inspection, and (4) examine the design specification to see whether it is necessary or could be relaxed without adversely affecting customer satisfaction.

Process variability is typically measured as the interval ± 3 standard deviations from the process mean. To determine whether the process is capable, compare this ± 3 standard deviations value to acceptable range of variation (i.e., tolerance) from an ideal value (i.e., target or nominal value). For example, suppose that the ideal length of time to perform a service is 10 minutes, and an acceptable range of variation around this time is ± 1 minute. If the process has a standard deviation of .5 minute, it would not be capable because ± 3 standard deviations would be ± 1.5 minutes, which exceeds the specification of ± 1 minute.

An alternative way is to compare 6 standard deviation of process with the design specification range (upper design specification–lower design specification).

A *manager* has the option of using any one of three machines for making a part. The machines and their standard deviations of outputs are listed below. Determine which machines are capable if the design specification is for part lengths of between 101.00 mm and 101.60 mm.

Example 7

Machine	Standard Deviation (mm)
A	.10
B	.08
C	.13

Determine the capability of each machine (i.e., 6 standard deviations) and compare that value to the specification *difference* of .60 mm.

Solution

Machine	Standard Deviation (mm)	Machine Variability
A	.10	.60
B	.08	.48
C	.13	.78

READING

Imperial Bondware

Imperial Bondware of Kenton, Ohio, makes paper cups for hot and cold drinks. It has 62 large automated machines, each making cups starting from rolls of printed paperboard strip. The dimensions (rim diameter, rim thickness, and cup height) are important because the cups have to work flawlessly in automated drink machines (i.e., they must be released from the stack just before a drink is poured). Before automating the data gathering and analysis, it used to take four hours just to print the quality control charts. After installing automated laser gauges and Zontec's Synergy software, the manager can access the performance of each machine quickly. Of particular interest is the process capability of each machine. Two examples of the charts used by Imperial Bondware are on the right. The individual unit chart (without showing the control limits but showing the design specification limits) is displayed on the top, and a process distribution with the design specification limits are given in the bottom. This particular machine makes cups that have diameters 97.7 percent within specification.

Question

Using the information given in the charts, can you verify the value of $C_p = 0.875$ and $C_{pk} = 0.6656$?

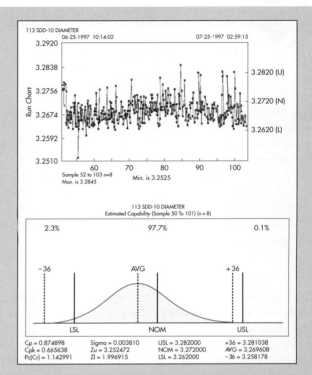

Source: K. Aldred, "Paper Cup Manufacturer Slashes Report Time," *IIE Solutions* 30(8), August 1998, pp. 44–45. Reprinted with permission of the Institute of Industrial Engineers, 3577 Parkway Lane, Suite 200, Norcross, GA, 720-449-0461.

We can see that both machine A and machine B are capable of producing output that is within the specification, but that machine C is not, because its machine variability exceeds the design specification width of .60. See Figure 10–12 for a visual portrayal of these results.

C_p

To express the capability of a machine or process, some companies use the ratio of the design specification width to the process width. It can be computed using the following formula:

$$\text{Process capability ratio, } C_p = \frac{\text{Design specification width}}{\text{Process width}}$$

$$= \frac{\text{Upper design specification} - \text{Lower design specification}}{6\sigma}$$

(10–9)

Example 8

Compute the process capability index for each machine in Example 7.

Solution

The specification width in Example 7 is .60 mm. Hence, to determine the capability index for each machine, divide .60 by the process width (i.e., 6 standard deviations) of each machine. The results are:

Machine	Standard Deviation (mm)	Machine Capability	C_p
A	.10	.60	.60/.60 = 1.00
B	.08	.48	.60/.48 = 1.25
C	.13	.78	.60/.78 = 0.77

Using the capability ratio, you can see that for a process to be capable, it must have a capability ratio of at least 1.00. A ratio of 1.00 implies that 99.74 percent of the output of a process can be expected to be within the specification limits, hence only 0.26 percent, or 2,600 units per million, fall outside the design specification zone. Moreover, the greater the capability ratio, the greater the probability that the output of a machine or process will fall within design specification.

C_{pk}

If a process is not centred between specification limits, or if there is no specification limit on one side, a slightly different measure is used to calculate its capability. This ratio is represented by the symbol C_{pk}. It is calculated by finding the difference between each of the specification limits and the mean, dividing that difference by three standard deviations of the process and identifying the smaller ratio. Thus, C_{pk} is equal to the *smaller* of

$$\frac{\text{Upper design specification} - \text{Process mean}}{3\sigma} \qquad (10\text{--}10)$$

and

$$\frac{\text{Process mean} - \text{Lower design specification}}{3\sigma}$$

Example 9

A process's output has a mean of 9.20 kg and a standard deviation of .30 kg. The lower design specification is 8.00 kg and the upper design specification is 10.00 kg. Compute the C_{pk}.

1. Compute the ratio for the lower design specification:

$$\frac{\text{Process mean} - \text{Lower design specification}}{3\sigma} = \frac{9.20 - 8.00}{3(.30)} = \frac{1.20}{.90} = 1.33$$

2. Compute the ratio for the upper design specification:

$$\frac{\text{Upper design specification} - \text{Process mean}}{3\sigma} = \frac{10.00 - 9.20}{3(.30)} = \frac{.80}{.90} = .89$$

The smaller of the two ratios is .89, so this is the C_{pk}. Because the C_{pk} is less than 1.00, the process is *not* capable. Note that if C_p had been used, it would have given the false impression that the process was capable.

$$C_p = \frac{\text{Upper design specification} - \text{Lower design specification}}{6\sigma} = \frac{10.00 - 8.00}{6(.30)} = \frac{2.00}{1.80} = 1.11$$

See the readings, "Imperial Bondware" and "Timex" earlier in the chapter for the application of process capability analysis.

SIX SIGMA

The Motorola Corporation is well known for its use of the term **six sigma**, which refers to its goal of achieving a process variability so small that the design specification half-width represents six standard deviations of the process. That means a process capability ratio equal to 2.00, resulting in an extremely small probability (.00034 percent, or 3.4 units per million) of getting any output not within the design specification. This is illustrated in Figure 10–13.[1]

six sigma A methodology created by Motorola Inc. to manage process variations that cause defects, defined as unacceptable deviation from the mean or target; and to systematically work towards managing variation to eliminate those defects.

---

[1]Actually 3.4 defects per million corresponds to 4.5σ. The other 1.5σ is for the process mean being off centre by up to 1.5σ.

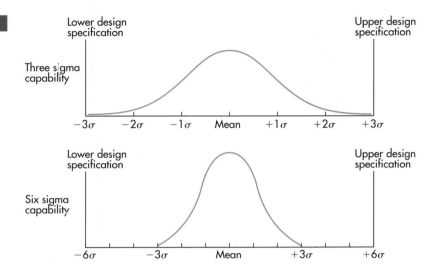

FIGURE 10-13

Three sigma versus six sigma capability

Achieving six sigma is similar to Continuous Improvement of TQM, but there are some differences:[2]

	Six Sigma	**Continuous Improvement of TQM**
Objective	Product and process perfection	Product and process improvement
Tools	Statistical, e.g., design of experiments and analysis of variance	Simple data analysis, e.g., Pareto chart, cause-and-effect diagram
Methodology	Define, measure, analyze, improve, control (DMAIC)	Plan, do, study, act (PDSA)
Team leader	Black belt	Champion
Training	Long/formal	Short/informal
Culture change	Usually enforced	Sometimes enforced
Project time frame	Months/years	Days/weeks

The six sigma improvement methodology DMAIC involves

Define	Determine the customers and critical-to-quality procedures
Measure	Identify and measure the quality problem, determine the baseline sigma, and identify possible influencing factors
Analyze	Test the influencing factors and identify the vital few
Improve	Select the solution method, prove its effectiveness, and implement it
Control	Develop process control plan

Example 10

The North Shore-Long Island Jewish Health System[3] consists of several hospitals and nursing homes around New York City. There is a central lab which performs blood tests for the health system as well as for other private clinics. The six sigma consultants are housed in the Center for Learning and Innovation of the health system. Although the health system has a very large and capable Quality Management Department, the six sigma group decided to remain separate. The six sigma group focuses on chronic issues which cannot be solved easily and uses systematic statistical and change management techniques.

One project the six sigma group worked on in 2002/2003 was the labelling of test specimens in the central lab. The tests are done by automated machines, so the most errors occur before the test. The critical-to-quality procedures for labelling are (*a*) receiving the requisition of blood test and specimen, (*b*) entering patient information into

[2]"Baldrige, Six Sigma, & ISO: Understanding Your Options," www.baldrige.nist.gov/Issue_Sheet_Options.htm, Summer 2002; J. Bossert et al., "Your Opinion: Are Six Sigma and Lean Manufacturing Really Different?", *ASQ Six Sigma Forum Magazine* 2(1), November 2002, pp. 38–43.

[3]N. B. Riebling et al., "Toward Error Free Lab Work," *ASQ Six Sigma Forum Magazine* 4(1), 2004, pp. 23–29.

the computer, (c) delivering the specimen to the automated machines, (d) obtaining results, and (e) sending the results to the requisitioner.

The six sigma team consisted of some members of the six sigma group, lab management, and representatives from Compliance, Quality, and Marketing. The objective was to reduce the errors and missing data. The data accompanying the specimens were: patient's name, social security number, date of birth, gender, physician's name, name of test, and a code name for the diagnosis.

The percentage of errors and omissions was 5 percent. The major problem was identified to be omission of the code name for diagnosis. The solution was rather simple: a pocket guide to the diagnosis code. This reduced the error and omission rate to 0.7 percent.

To further reduce labelling errors and omissions, the next common error (approximately 50 percent of remaining errors or omissions) was identified as the social security number. A pattern was easily found: most of these errors originated from units that used a special set of codes (called addressograph) which presented the information in a confusing way. Again, an easy solution was discovered: peel off the bar code in the bottom of patient's chart and attach it to the requisition.

The team also performed a benchmarking study of the productivity of the labelling staff (accessioners). A labeller prepared an average of 17 labels per hour, whereas the industry norm was 20. Although some workers were faster than others, there was no statistically significant difference in their productivity. The team decided to look at the method of labelling. A meeting of all staff was called. Their opinion was that there was quite a bit of walking and moving involved and sometimes it was confusing to find the right machines for the particular test needed for a specimen. Solutions suggested were (a) provide a colour-coded book of tests and machines that perform each, (b) put up same colour signs over machines, and (c) employ a runner to move the batch of specimens to the machines. The team decided to try these and also to create a position of lead labeller who would take 20 requisitions/ specimen per hour to each labeller and answer any questions they might have.

An experiment was designed to measure the influence of (a) using barcodes, (b) expertise of individual labellers (accessioners), and (c) the new work process (called distribution) on the productivity of labellers. This is done by collecting data under various levels of the factors above. The results are shown in the figure below.

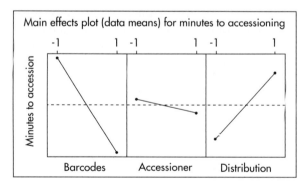

Figure reprinted with permission from Six Sigma Forum Magazine © 2004 American Society for Quality.

As can be seen, the use of barcodes (barcodes = 1) and the new work process (distribution = −1) reduces minutes to accession, i.e., increases productivity. Finally, the individual value and moving range control charts were constructed to monitor the productivity of each labeller. Productivity has been improving and has exceeded 20 labels per hour.

DESIGN OF EXPERIMENTS

A common method to increase the accuracy of a process (i.e., reduce the variations) is to perform experiments. First, one should identify the controllable factors that could influence the variation. Then, each factor is set to 2 or more levels, and the variation in

design of experiments
Performing experiments by changing levels of factors to measure influences and thus reduce the variation.

the process is measured. However, if this is done by changing the level of one factor at a time, while keeping the levels of other factors constant, then an extremely large number of experiments will be required.

Taguchi suggested a more concise set of experiments by changing the level of more than one factor at a time. For example, suppose we have three factors, each having two levels. Then, if we change one factor's level at a time, in order to determine the best levels for each factor, we will need $2^3 = 8$ different experiments. However, Taguchi suggested that, in this case, the following four experiments are adequate (the body of table shows the level of each factor):[4]

Factor	Experiment			
	(i)	(ii)	(iii)	(iv)
a	1	1	2	2
b	1	2	1	2
c	1	2	2	1

Example 11

In the early 1990s, Navistar's Indianapolis engine plant had a problem with the flatness of cylinder heads (the top part of engines). The specification width was a lot smaller than process variability, rendering the process incapable. The final machining operation shaved a small amount of metal from the base of cylinder heads. The variation in the flatness resulting from this operation needed to be reduced. Possible factors were thought to be:

a. feed rate for broach that shaved the metal

b. the thickness of metal removed

c. the pressure of clamp holding the cylinder head down

For each factor, two levels were determined:

a. (1 = 80 feet/minute, 2 = 120 feet/minute)

b. (1 = .020 inch, 2 = .0028 inch)

c. (1 = 600 pounds, 2 = 500 pounds)

The above four experiment designs were used. Each experiment (i) to (iv) was repeated six times in order to improve the accuracy of the results. For example, in the first experiment, all factors were set to level 1. For each cylinder head produced, the height of 32 points on the flat surface was measured and the difference between the maximum height and the minimum height was calculated. This high-low difference was averaged over the six pieces produced using the same experiment. The results are:

	Experiment			
	(i)	(ii)	(iii)	(iv)
Average high-low difference (in 1/10,000 inch):	33.32	45.93	25.88	27.17

From these results, the influence of each level of each factor can be determined. For example, Factor 1, level 1 was used in experiments (i) and (ii). Therefore, its average high-low difference is $(33.32 + 45.93)/2 = 39.62$. The other results were calculated in a similar manner:

Factor	Level 1	Level 2
a	39.62	26.52
b	29.60	36.55
c	30.24	35.90

---

[4]G. S. Peace, *Taguchi Methods* (Reading, Massachusetts: Addison-Wesley, 1993).

It can be shown that the levels of all three factors have significant influence on average high-low difference. Therefore, to reduce the variation in cylinder head flatness, this operation should use Level 2 of factor a (i.e., 120 feet/minute tool speed), Level 1 of Factor b (i.e., remove .020 inch metal), and Level 1 of Factor c (i.e., use 600 pounds of pressure). This will reduce the variation in flatness as much as possible.

Source: Based on R. W. Schmenner, Production/Operations Management, 5th ed. (New York: MacMillan, 1993).

SUMMARY

This chapter describes inspection, statistical process control, and process capability. Inspection means examining the output of a process to determine whether it is acceptable. Key issues in inspection include where to inspect in the process, how much to inspect, and whether to inspect on-site or in a laboratory.

Statistical process control focuses on detecting departures from randomness in a process. Control charts are commonly used for this. The theory behind control charts is discussed, and several types of control charts are described in the chapter. Process capability studies are used to determine if the output of a process will satisfy design specification. Six sigma is the approach which improves process capability to very high levels (3.4 defects per million). Table 10–3 provides a summary of formulas.

TABLE 10–3

Summary of formulas

CONTROL CHARTS		
Name	**Symbol**	**Control Limits**
Sample mean	$\bar{x}$	$\bar{\bar{x}} \pm z\dfrac{\sigma}{\sqrt{n}}$ or $\bar{\bar{x}} \pm A_2\bar{R}$
Sample range	R	$UCL = D_4\bar{R},\ LCL = D_3\bar{R}$
Sample fraction defective	p	$\bar{p} \pm z\sqrt{\dfrac{\bar{p}(1-\bar{p})}{n}}$
Sample number of defects	c	$\bar{c} \pm z\sqrt{\bar{c}}$

PROCESS CAPABILITY		
Name	**Symbol**	**Formula**
Capability index for a centred process	C_p	$\dfrac{\text{Design specification width}}{6\sigma \text{ of process}}$
Capability index for a noncentred process	C_{pk}	Smaller of $\begin{cases}\dfrac{\text{Mean} - \text{Lower design specification}}{3\sigma}\\[2mm]\dfrac{\text{Upper design specification} - \text{Mean}}{3\sigma}\end{cases}$

KEY TERMS

assignable variation, 357
c-control chart, 367
control chart, 358
control limits, 358
design of experiments, 375
design specification, 369
inspection, 351
p-control chart, 366
process capability, 370
process variability, 370
quality control, 351
random variation, 356
sample mean control chart, 360
sample range control chart, 362
six sigma, 373
statistical process control, 355
Type I error, 359
Type II error, 359

Solved Problems

Problem 1

Process distribution and sampling distribution. An industrial process that makes 3-foot sections of plastic pipe produces pipe with an average inside diameter of 1 inch and a standard deviation of .05 inch.

a. If you randomly select one piece of pipe, what is the probability that its inside diameter will exceed 1.02 inches, assuming that the process distribution is Normal?

b. If you select a random sample of 25 pieces of pipe, what is the probability that the sample mean will exceed 1.02 inches?

Solution

$\mu = 1.00, \sigma = .05$

a. $z = \dfrac{x - \mu}{\sigma} = \dfrac{1.02 - 1.00}{.05} = .4$

Using Appendix B, Table A, $P(z > .4) = .5000 - .1554 = .3446$.

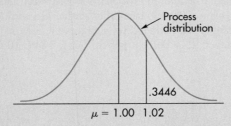

b. $z = \dfrac{\bar{x} - \mu}{\sigma / \sqrt{n}} = \dfrac{1.02 - 1.00}{.05 / \sqrt{25}} = 2.00$

Using Appendix B, Table A, $P(z > 2.00) = .5000 - .4772 = .0228$.

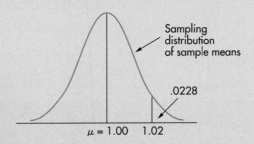

Problem 2

Control charts for sample mean and range. Processing new accounts at a bank is intended to average 10 minutes each. Five samples of four observations each have been taken. Use the sample data below in conjunction with Table 10–2 to construct upper and lower control limits for both sample mean and sample range control charts. Do the results suggest that the process is in control?

	Sample 1	Sample 2	Sample 3	Sample 4	Sample 5
	10.2	10.3	9.7	9.9	9.8
	9.9	9.8	9.9	10.3	10.2
	9.8	9.9	9.9	10.1	10.3
	10.1	10.4	10.1	10.5	9.7
Totals	40.0	40.4	39.6	40.8	40.0

Solution

a. Determine the mean and range of each sample.

$\bar{x} = \dfrac{\sum x}{n}$, Range = Largest − Smallest

Sample	Mean	Range
1	$40.0/4 = 10.0$	$10.2 - 9.8 = .4$
2	$40.4/4 = 10.1$	$10.4 - 9.8 = .6$
3	$39.6/4 = 9.9$	$10.1 - 9.7 = .4$
4	$40.8/4 = 10.2$	$10.5 - 9.9 = .6$
5	$40.0/4 = 10.0$	$10.3 - 9.7 = .6$

b. Compute the average sample mean and average sample range:

$$\overline{\overline{X}} = \frac{10.0 + 10.1 + 9.9 + 10.2 + 10.0}{5} = \frac{50.2}{5} = 10.04$$

$$\overline{R} = \frac{.4 + .6 + .4 + .6 + .6}{5} = \frac{2.6}{5} = .52$$

c. Obtain factors A_2, D_4, and D_3 from Table 10–2 for $n = 4$: $A_2 = .73$, $D_4 = 2.28$, $D_3 = 0$.

d. Compute upper and lower limits:

$$\text{UCL}_{\overline{x}} = \overline{\overline{x}} + A_2\overline{R} = 10.04 + .73(.52) = 10.42$$
$$\text{LCL}_{\overline{x}} = \overline{\overline{x}} - A_2\overline{R} = 10.04 + .73(.52) = 9.66$$
$$\text{UCL}_R = D_4\overline{R} = 2.28(.52) = 1.19$$
$$\text{LCL}_R = D_3\overline{R} = 0(.52) = 0$$

e. Plot sample means and ranges on their respective control charts, or otherwise verify that points are within limits.

The smallest sample mean is 9.9, and the largest is 10.2. Both are well within the $\overline{X}$ control limits. Similarly, the largest sample range is .6, which is also within the R-control limits. Hence, the results suggest that the process is in control.

Problem 3

Type I error (alpha risk). After several investigations of points outside control limits revealed nothing, a manager began to wonder about the probability of a Type I error for the control limits used which were based on $z = 1.90$.

a. Determine the alpha risk for this value of z.

b. What z would provide an alpha risk of about 2 percent?

a. Using Appendix B, Table A, we find that the area under the curve between $z = 0$ and $z = +1.90$ is .4713. Therefore, the area (probability) of values *within* -1.90 to $+1.90$ is $2(.4713) = .9426$, and the area *beyond* these values is $1 - .9426 = .0574$. Hence, the alpha risk is 5.74%.

b. Because half of the risk lies in each tail, the area under the curve between $z = 0$ and the value of z you are looking for is .49. The closest value is .4901 for $z = 2.33$. Thus, control limits based on $z = \pm 2.33$ provide an alpha risk of about 2 percent.

Problem 4

Sample p-control chart and c-control chart. Using the appropriate control chart, determine two-sigma control limits for each case:

a. An inspector found an average of 3.9 scratches in the exterior paint of each of the automobiles being prepared for shipment to dealers.

b. Before shipping lawn mowers to dealers, an inspector attempts to start each mower and notes the ones that do not start on the first try. The lot size is 100 mowers, and an average of 4 did not start on the first try (4 percent).

Solution

The choice between these two types of control charts relates to whether *two* types of results can be counted (*p*-chart) or whether *only occurrences* can be counted (*c*-chart).

a. The inspector can only count the scratches that occurred, not the ones that did not occur. Consequently, a *c*-chart is appropriate. The sample average is 3.9 scratches per car. Two-sigma control limits are found using the formulas

$$\text{UCL} = \bar{c} + z\sqrt{\bar{c}}$$

$$\text{LCL} = \bar{c} - z\sqrt{\bar{c}}$$

where $\bar{c} = 3.9$ and $z = 2$. Thus,

$$\text{UCL} = 3.9 + 2\sqrt{3.9} = 7.85 \text{ scratches}$$

$$\text{LCL} = 3.9 - 2\sqrt{3.9} = -.05, \text{ so the lower limit is 0 scratches}$$

*b.*The inspector can count both the lawn mowers that started and those that did not start. Consequently, a *p*-chart is appropriate. Two-sigma control limits can be computed using the following:

$$\text{UCL} = \bar{p} + z\sqrt{\frac{\bar{p}(1-\bar{p})}{n}}$$

$$\text{LCL} = \bar{p} - z\sqrt{\frac{\bar{p}(1-\bar{p})}{n}}$$

where

$$\bar{p} = .04$$
$$n = 100$$
$$z = 2$$

Thus,

$$\text{UCL} = .04 + 2\sqrt{\frac{.04(.96)}{100}} = .079$$

$$\text{LCL} = .04 - 2\sqrt{\frac{.04(.96)}{100}} = .001$$

DISCUSSION AND REVIEW QUESTIONS

1. List the steps in the quality control process.
2. What are the key concepts that underlie the construction and interpretation of control charts?
3. What is the purpose of a control chart?
4. Why is order of observation important in process control?
5. Briefly explain the purpose of each of these control charts:
   a. *x*-bar
   b. Range
   c. *p*-chart
   d. *c*-chart
6. Define and contrast control limits and design specification limits.
7. A customer has recently tightened the design specification for a part your company supplies. The design specification is now much tighter than the machine being used for the job is capable of. Briefly identify alternatives you might consider to resolve this problem.
8. If all observations are within control limits, does that guarantee that the process variation contains only randomness?
9. Answer these questions about inspection:
   a. What level of inspection is optimal?
   b. What are the main considerations in choosing between centralized inspection and on-site inspection?
   c. What points are potential candidates for inspection?
10. Classify each of the following as either a Type I error or a Type II error:
    a. Putting an innocent person in jail.
    b. Releasing a guilty person from jail.
11. What is six sigma and how does it differ from continuous improvement (PDSA)?

TAKING STOCK

1. What trade-offs are involved in each of these decisions?
   a. Deciding whether to use two sigma or three sigma control limits.
   b. Choosing between a large sample size and a smaller sample size.
2. Who needs to be involved in quality control?
3. Name two ways that technology has had an impact on quality control.

CRITICAL THINKING EXERCISE

Analysis of the output of a process has suggested that the variability was nonrandom on several occasions recently. However, each time an investigation has not revealed any assignable causes. What are some of the possible explanations for not finding any causes? What should the manager do?

INTERNET EXERCISES

1. Visit http://jobs.isixsigma.com, choose a job announcement for a Black Belt, and describe his/her duties.
2. Visit www.qualitymag.com, choose a case study from the current digital issue of *Quality Magazine* (in the bottom right of the page) and summarize it.
3. Visit www.mitutoyo.com/template1.aspx?id=168, choose a case study, and summarize it.

PROBLEMS

1. Design specification for a motor housing states that it should weigh between 24 and 25 kg. The process that produces the housing yields a mean of 24.5 kg and a standard deviation of .2 kg. The distribution of output is Normal.
   a. What percentage of housings will not meet the weight design specification?
   b. Within what values should 95.44 percent of sample means of this process fall if samples of $n = 16$ are taken?
2. An automatic filling machine is used to fill two-litre bottles of cola. The machine's output is known to be approximately Normal with a mean of 2.0 litre and a standard deviation of .01 litre. Output is monitored using means of samples of five observations.
   a. Determine upper and lower control limits that will include roughly 95.5 percent of the sample means.
   b. Given these sample means: 2.005, 2.001, 1.998, 2.002, 1.995, and 1.999, is the process in control?
3. Process time at a workstation is monitored using sample mean and range control charts. Six samples of $n = 10$ observations have been obtained and the sample means and ranges computed (in minutes):

Sample	Mean	Range
1	3.06	.42
2	3.15	.50
3	3.11	.41
4	3.13	.46
5	3.06	.46
6	3.09	.45

   a. Using the factors in Table 10–2, determine upper and lower limits for sample mean and range control charts.
   b. Is the process in control?
4. Six samples of five observations each have been taken of 80-kg concrete slabs produced by a machine, and the results are displayed on the next page.
   a. Using factors from Table 10–2, determine upper and lower control chart limits for sample mean and range control charts, and decide if the process is in control.
   b. Suppose that these control charts are being used. A new sample results in the following slab weights: 81.0, 81.0, 80.8, 80.6, and 80.5. Use the control limits determined in part *a* to decide if process is still in control.

		Sample			
1	2	3	4	5	6
79.2	80.5	79.6	78.9	80.5	79.7
78.8	78.7	79.4	79.4	79.6	80.6
80.0	81.0	80.4	79.7	80.4	80.5
78.4	80.4	80.3	79.4	80.8	80.0
81.0	80.1	80.8	80.6	78.8	81.1

5. In a refinery the octane rating of gasoline produced is measured by taking one observation from each batch. Twenty observations follow.

   a. Construct three sigma control charts for the individual unit and moving range. Is the process in control?[5]

   b. A new batch has octane rating of 94.0. Using the control charts in part *a*, is the process still in control?

Observation number	Octane rating	Observation number	Octane rating
1	89.2	11	85.4
2	86.5	12	91.6
3	88.4	13	87.7
4	91.8	14	85.0
5	90.3	15	91.5
6	87.5	16	90.3
7	92.6	17	85.6
8	87.0	18	90.9
9	89.8	19	82.1
10	92.2	20	85.8

6. Using four samples of 200 credit card statements each, an auditor found the following number of erroneous statements in each sample:

	SAMPLE			
	1	2	3	4
Number of errors　..	4	2	5	9

   a. Determine the fraction defective in each sample.

   b. If the true fraction defective for this process is unknown, what is your best estimate of it?

   c. What is your estimate of the mean and standard deviation of the sampling distribution of fraction defective for samples of 200?

   d. What control limits would give an alpha risk of .03 for this process?

   e. What alpha risk would control limits of .047 and .003 provide?

   f. Using control limits of .047 and .003, is the process in control?

   g. Suppose that the long-term fraction defective of the process is known to be 2 percent. What are the values of the mean and standard deviation of the sampling distribution?

   h. Construct a *p*-control chart for the process, assuming a fraction defective of 2 percent, using two sigma control limits. Is the process in control?

7. A medical facility does MRIs for sports injuries. Occasionally a test yields inconclusive results and must be repeated. Using the following 13 sample results in $n = 200$ observations each, construct a control chart for the fraction of retests using two sigma limits. Is the process in control?

	SAMPLE												
	1	2	3	4	5	6	7	8	9	10	11	12	13
Number of retests　..	1	2	2	0	2	1	2	0	2	7	3	2	1

---

[5]Adapted from Amitava Mitra. *Fundamentals of Quality Control and Improvement*, 2nd ed. (Englewood Cliffs, NJ: Prentice Hall, 1998).

8. The Administrator of a small town received a certain number of complaints during the last two weeks.

   a. Construct a control chart with three sigma limits for the number of complaints each day using the following data. Is the process in control?

   b. If 16 complaints are received today, using the control chart of part *a*, is there a change in average number of complaints?

	DAY													
	1	2	3	4	5	6	7	8	9	10	11	12	13	14
Number of complaints ..	4	10	14	8	9	6	5	12	13	7	6	4	2	10

9. *a.* Construct a control chart with three sigma limits for the number of defects per spool of cable given in the following data. Is the process in control?

   b. If a new spool has five defects, using the control chart of part *a*, has the process changed?

Observation	Number of Defects	Observation	Number of Defects
1	2	8	0
2	3	9	2
3	1	10	1
4	0	11	3
5	1	12	1
6	3	13	2
7	2	14	0

10. After a number of complaints about its directory assistance, a telephone company examined samples of calls to determine the frequency of wrong numbers given to callers. Each sample consisted of 100 calls. The manager stated that the error rate is about 4 percent. Construct a control chart using 95 percent limits using $\overline{P} = .04$. Is the process in control? Is the manager's assertion about the error rate correct? Explain.

Sample	Number of Errors	Sample	Number of Errors
1	5	9	5
2	3	10	9
3	5	11	3
4	7	12	4
5	4	13	5
6	6	14	6
7	8	15	6
8	4	16	7

11. Specification for the diameter of a metal shaft are much wider than the machine used to make the shafts is capable of. Consequently, the decision has been made to allow the cutting tool to wear a certain amount before replacement. The tool wears at the rate of .004 centimetre per piece. The process has a natural variation, σ, of .01 centimetre and is Normally distributed. Specification is 15.0 to 15.2 centimetres, and $n = 1$. For three sigma limits, how many shafts can the process turn out before tool replacement becomes necessary (i.e., before the process makes an out-of-spec shaft)? (See diagram below.)

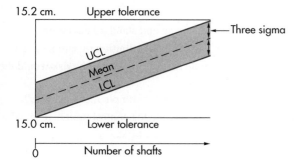

12. Designer specification for the concrete slabs in Problem 4 is between 78 and 81 kg.

    a. Based on the data given in the problem, is the specification being met?

    b. Estimate the process standard deviation from the average range using Formula 10–4. Then, calculate the C_p index. Is the process capable? Compare your answer to your answer to part *a.*

13. The time needed for performing a machining operation is to be investigated. Historically, the process has had a standard deviation equal to .146 minute. The means (in minutes) of 39 samples of $n = 6$ are:

Sample	Mean	Sample	Mean	Sample	Mean
1	3.86	14	3.81	27	3.81
2	3.90	15	3.83	28	3.86
3	3.83	16	3.86	29	3.98
4	3.81	17	3.82	30	3.96
5	3.84	18	3.86	31	3.88
6	3.83	19	3.84	32	3.76
7	3.87	20	3.87	33	3.83
8	3.88	21	3.84	34	3.77
9	3.84	22	3.82	35	3.86
10	3.80	23	3.89	36	3.80
11	3.88	24	3.86	37	3.84
12	3.86	25	3.88	38	3.79
13	3.88	26	3.90	39	3.85

    Construct an $\bar{x}$-chart for this process with two sigma limits. Is the process in control?

14. A company has just negotiated a contract to produce a part for another company. In the process of manufacturing the part, the inside diameter of successive parts becomes smaller and smaller as the cutting tool wears. However, the spec is so wide relative to machine capability that it is possible to set the diameter initially at a large value and let the process run for a while before replacing the cutting tool.

    The inside diameter decreases at an average rate of .001 cm per part, and the process has a standard deviation of .01cm. The variability is approximately Normal. Assuming three sigma control limits, how frequently must the tool be replaced if the design specification is between 3 cm and 3.5 cm, and the initial setting of the UCL is at the upper design specification? Use $n = 1$.

15. (Refer to Solved Problem 2.) Suppose that the design specification is between 9.65 and 10.35 minutes. Based on the data given, does it appear that the design specification is being met? If not, what should one do?

16. A technician in a quick oil change shop had the following service times (in minutes) for 20 randomly selected cars:

SAMPLE			
1	2	3	4
4.5	4.6	4.5	4.7
4.2	4.5	4.6	4.6
4.2	4.4	4.4	4.8
4.3	4.7	4.4	4.5
4.3	4.3	4.6	4.9

    a. Determine the mean of each sample.

    b. If the process parameters are unknown, estimate its mean and standard deviation.

    c. Estimate the mean and standard deviation of the sampling distribution of sample mean.

    d. What would three sigma control limits for the sample mean be? What alpha risk would they provide?

    e. What alpha risk would control limits of 4.14 and 4.86 for the sample mean provide?

    f. Using limits of 4.14 and 4.86, are any sample means beyond the control limits? If so, which one(s)?

g. Construct control charts for sample means and sample ranges using Table 10–2. Are any sample means and ranges beyond the control limits? If so, which one(s)?

h. Explain why the control limits are different for sample mean in parts *d* and *g*.

i. If the process has a known mean of 4.4 and a known standard deviation of .18, what would three sigma control limits be for a sample mean chart? Are any sample means beyond the control limits? If so, which one(s)?

17. A process screens a certain type of potash grains resulting in a mean diameter of .03 cm and a standard deviation of .003 cm. The allowable variation in grain diameter is from .02 to .04 cm.

a. Calculate the capacity ratio C_p for the process.

b. Is the process capable?

18. Given the following list of machines, the standard deviation for their output, and specification half-width for a job that may be processed on that machine, using C_p determine which machines are capable of performing the given jobs.

Machine	Standard Deviation (cm)	Job Half-Width Specification ($\pm$ cm)
001	.02	.05
002	.04	.07
003	.10	.18
004	.05	.15
005	.01	.04

19. Suppose your manager presents you with the following information about machines that could be used for a job, and wants your recommendation on which one to choose. The design specification width is .48 mm. Calculate the C_p index for each machine, and explain what additional information you need to make a choice.

Machine	Cost per Unit ($)	Standard Deviation (mm)
A	20	.079
B	12	.080
C	11	.C84
D	10	.081

20. Each of the processes listed below is noncentred with respect to the design specification. Calculate the C_{pk} index for each, and decide if the process is capable.

Process	Process Mean	Process Standard Deviation	Lower Design Specification	Upper Design Specification
H	15.0	.32	14.1	16.0
K	33.0	1.00	30.0	36.5
T	18.5	.50	16.5	20.1

21. Can the value of the C_{pk} exceed the value of C_p for the same process and specification? Explain.

22. As part of an insurance company's training program, participants learn how to conduct a fast but effective analysis of clients' insurability. The goal is to have participants achieve a time less than 45 minutes. There is no minimum time, but the quality of assessment should be acceptable. Test results for three participants were: Armand, a mean of 38 minutes and a standard deviation of 3 minutes; Jerry, a mean of 37 minutes and a standard deviation of 2.5 minutes; and Melissa, a mean of 37.5 minutes and a standard deviation of 2.5 minutes.

Which of the participants would you judge to be capable? Explain.

23. The following data (in ohms) are the resistance of resistors made on an automated machine. The mean and range of each sample are given in the right two columns, and the mean of sample means and the mean of sample ranges are given below these.

a. Develop sample mean and sample range control charts for resistance of resistors using the first 10 samples. Is the process in control?

b. Use the control charts developed in part *a* to decide if the eleventh sample (also given below) indicates an out-of-control situation.

Resistance of Resistors (in Ohms)

Sample	Obs 1	Obs 2	Obs 3	Obs 4	Mean	Range
1	1,010	991	985	986	993.00	25
2	995	996	1,009	994	998.50	15
3	990	1,003	1,015	1,008	1,004.00	25
4	1,015	1,020	1,009	998	1,010.50	22
5	1,013	1,019	1,005	993	1,007.50	26
6	994	1,001	994	1,005	998.50	11
7	989	992	982	1,020	995.75	38
8	1,001	986	996	996	994.75	15
9	1,006	989	1,005	1,007	1,001.75	18
10	992	1,007	1,006	979	<u>996.00</u>	<u>28</u>
					1,000.03	22.30
11	996	1,006	997	989		

24. Essex Corp. of St. Louis is a small manufacturer of parts for Boeing's Aircraft and Missile Systems. In the late 1990s, Essex was trying to establish a SPC program. Part no. 528003-N was typical. The following samples[6] of two were observed for a critical dimension of the part (in inches). The lower specification, nominal, and upper specification values are .4160, .4185, .4210 inches, respectively.

a. Is the process capable?

b. Construct sample mean and sample range control charts. Is the process in control?

Sample

1	2	3	4	5	6	7	8	9	10
.4190	.4190	.4180	.4180	.4175	.4180	.4175	.4173	.4183	.4185
.4190	.4185	.4180	.4179	.4175	.4179	.4175	.4176	.4184	.4185

25. When Polaroid reduced the number of quality inspectors and increased operator responsibility for quality control in its R2 plant (which made instant film cartridges with 10 films in each) in Waltham, Massachusetts, in 1985, it encountered an unexpected result.[7] Instead of quality improving, it actually got worse. To identify the problem, Bud Rolfs, quality control manager, asked an operator from each shift to sample six observations of the critical characteristics of the product and report these to him. One important characteristic of instant films is the pod weight. A pod is a small capsule at the end of each film that contains chemicals. When the film is pulled out, the pod bursts and releases the chemicals which will develop the film. Too much chemical overdevelops the film and too little underdevelops it.

a. Use the following three samples of six observations each (in grams) from the first day of the data collection period to develop a sample mean and sample range control chart for the pod weight. Is the process in control?

b. The first sample from the second day is: 2.841, 2.802, 2.802, 2.806, 2.807, and 2.807. Is the process still in control?

Sample	Shift	1	2	3	4	5	6	Average
1	A	2.800	2.799	2.760	2.802	2.805	2.803	2.795
2	B	2.750	2.820	2.850	2.740	2.850	2.790	2.800
3	C	2.768	2.807	2.807	2.804	2.804	2.803	2.799

---

[6]Data retrieved from S. K. Vermani, "SPC Modified with Percent Tolerance Pre-control Charts," *Quality Progress* 33(10), October 2000, pp. 43–48.

[7]Process Control at Polaroid (A), 1987, HBS case: 9-693-047.

MINI-CASE

Quality Control at Ingersoll-Rand

www.ingersollrand.com

The Ingersoll-Rand plant in Davidson, North Carolina, assembles air compressors for air tools. A few years ago it installed an SPC software that collects critical information about the quality of its air compressors. This made tracking of the percentage of defectives (for each compressor type, components in each compressor, and parts of each component) much easier. It also made it possible to monitor these percentages using *p*-control charts. Using the previous month's percentage defective *p*, Ingersoll-Rand monitored the percentage of defective compressors that it made on each day; if this number was larger than two standard deviations above *p*, Ingersoll-Rand would try to identify the cause of the most frequent defect and find a solution for it. For example, the portable line showed an increased percentage of defectives on January 6. First the 69 defects were classified according to defect types (see Exhibit 1): air leaks (30), motors (15), pumps (3), pressure switch (14), cosmetic (2), miscellaneous (3), and bad check valve (2). Given that each of these defects had a control chart in the software, they found out that air leaks' defective percentage was more than two standard deviations above its previous month's percentage defective (3%). Then, they classified the 30 air leak defects by location of air leak (see Exhibit 2): tanks weld (5), manifold (12), discharge elbow (1), discharge tube (11), and drain valve (1). Using the control charts for each of these, manifold defective percentage was more than two standard deviations above its previous month's percentage defective (0.7%). Having identified the most frequent defect source (air leak from manifold), Ingersoll-Rand contacted the manifold manufacturer and provided this information. The manufacturer found the root cause and fixed the problem. Use of SPC in Ingersoll-Rand facilities continues.

Questions

1. Verify that the percentage of defective portable compressors produced on January 6 was more than twice its standard deviation above the expected proportion (*Hint*: use $\bar{p} = 8\%$ and $n = 578$).
2. Do the same for air leaks (*Hint*: use $\bar{p} = 3\%$ and $n = 578$).
3. Do the same for manifolds (*Hint*: use $\bar{p} = .7\%$ and $n = 578$).

Sources: P. J. Cooper and N. Demos, "Losses Cut 76 Percent with Control Chart System," *Quality*, April 1991, pp. 22–24. Reprinted with permission from *Quality Magazine*.

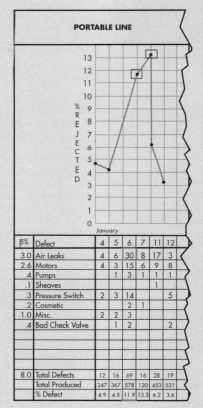

$\bar{p}$%	Defect	4	5	6	7	11	12
3.0	Air Leaks	4	6	30	8	17	3
2.6	Motors	4	3	15	6	9	8
.4	Pumps		1	3	1	1	1
.1	Sheaves					1	
.3	Pressure Switch	2	3	14			5
.2	Cosmetic			2	1		
1.0	Misc.	2	2	3			
.4	Bad Check Valve		1	2			2
8.0	Total Defects	12	16	69	16	28	19
	Total Produced	247	367	578	120	453	531
	% Defect	4.9	4.5	11.9	13.3	6.2	3.6

Exhibit 1

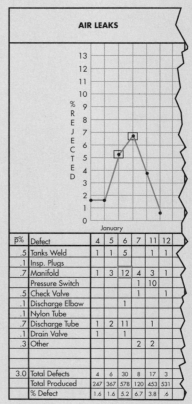

$\bar{p}$%	Defect	4	5	6	7	11	12
.5	Tanks Weld	1	1	5		1	1
.1	Insp. Plugs						
.7	Manifold	1	3	12	4	3	1
	Pressure Switch				1	10	
.5	Check Valve				1		1
.1	Discharge Elbow			1			
.1	Nylon Tube						
.7	Discharge Tube	1	2	11		1	
.1	Drain Valve	1		1			
.3	Other				2	2	
3.0	Total Defects	4	6	30	8	17	3
	Total Produced	247	367	578	120	453	531
	% Defect	1.6	1.6	5.2	6.7	3.8	.6

Exhibit 2

SELECTED BIBLIOGRAPHY AND FURTHER READING

Besterfield, Dale H., Carol Besterfield-Micha, Glen Besterfield, and Mary Besterfield-Sacre. *Total Quality Management*, 2nd ed. Englewood Cliffs, NJ: Prentice Hall, 1999.

Derman, C., and S. M. Ross. *Statistical Aspects of Quality Control*. San Diego: Academic Press, 1997.

Evans, James R., and W. M. Lindsay. *The Management and Control of Quality*. Cincinnati: South-Western College Publications, 1999.

Gitlow, Howard, Alan Oppenheim, and Rosa Oppenheim. *Quality Management: Tools and Methods for Improvement*, 2nd ed. Burr Ridge, IL: Irwin, 1995.

Goetsch, David L., and Stanley B. Davis. *Quality Management: Introduction to Total Quality Management for Production, Processing, and Services*, 3rd ed. Upper Saddle River, NJ: Prentice Hall, 2000.

Grant, Eugene L., and Richard Leavenworth. *Statistical Quality Control*. New York: McGraw-Hill, 1996.

Griffith, Gary K. *The Quality Technician's Handbook*, 4th ed. Upper Saddle River, NJ: Prentice Hall, 2000.

Gyrna, Frank, Jr. *Quality Planning and Analysis*. New York: McGraw-Hill, 2001.

Juran, Joseph M. *Juran's Quality Handbook*. New York: McGraw-Hill, 1999.

Kolarik, William J. *Creating Quality Process Design for Results*. New York: McGraw-Hill, 1999.

Mitra, Amitava. *Fundamentals of Quality Control and Improvement*, 2nd ed. Englewood Cliffs, NJ: Prentice Hall, 1998.

Montgomery, Douglas C. *Introduction to Statistical Quality Control*, 4th ed. New York: John Wiley and Sons, 2001.

Ott, Ellis, Edward G. Schilling, and Dean Neubauer. *Process Quality Control*. New York: McGraw-Hill, 2000.

Smith, Gerald. *Statistical Process Control and Process Improvement*, 3rd ed. Englewood Cliffs, NJ: Prentice Hall, 1997.

Summers, Donna. *Quality*, 2nd ed. Upper Saddle River, NJ: Prentice Hall, 2000.

To access "Acceptance Sampling," the supplement to Chapter 10, please visit the student **DVD** packaged with the text or the Online Learning Centre at
www.mcgrawhill.ca/olc/stevenson

PART FIVE

Operations Planning

T he chapters in this part relate to the management and control of inventories, planning, and scheduling; often key factors in the success or failure of operations management to achieve profit and/or cost objectives while satisfying customers. The basic issues are how much to order and when to order to effectively match supply and demand.

The chapters in this part cover the following topics:

Inventory Management

LEARNING OBJECTIVES

After completing this chapter, you should be able to:

1. Define the term *inventory* and list the major reasons for holding inventory.

2. Discuss the objectives of inventory management.

3. List the main requirements for effective inventory management.

4. Describe A-B-C classification and explain how it is useful.

5. Describe the basic EOQ model and solve typical problems.

6. Describe the economic production quantity model and solve typical problems.

7. Describe the quantity discount model and solve typical problems.

8. Describe the planned shortage model and solve typical problems.

9. Describe how to determine the reorder-point and solve typical problems.

10. Describe the fixed order-interval model and solve typical problems.

11. Describe the single-period model and solve typical problems.

CHAPTER OUTLINE

A grocery and hardware distributor such as Federated Co-op and retail co-op stores hold tens of thousands of parts and products. They compete with grocery chains such as Loblaw, hardware stores such as Home depot, and general merchandise stores such as Wal-Mart. It is costly to carry excess inventory and poor customer service to not carry enough. How has Federated Co-op remained competitive? One important factor is good inventory management.

G ood inventory management is important for the successful operation of most businesses and their supply chains. Operations, marketing, and finance have interests in good inventory management. Poor inventory management hampers operations, diminishes customer satisfaction, and increases operating costs.

This chapter describes management of finished goods, some raw materials, supplies and spare parts, and retail items. Management of manufacturing parts will be described in a later chapter on material requirements planning. Topics in this chapter include functions of inventory, the objectives, requirements for effective inventory management, and models for determining *how much* to order and *when* to order. Emphasis is on inventory analysis.

INTRODUCTION

An **inventory** is any material or product sitting idle, not being used, usually in a warehouse or store and kept for use or sale in the future. Companies typically stock hundreds or even thousands of items in inventory, ranging from small things such as pencils, paper clips, screws, nuts, and bolts to large items such as machines, trucks, construction equipment, and airplanes. Naturally, many of the items a company carries in inventory relate to the kind of business it engages in. Thus, manufacturing companies carry supplies of raw materials, purchased parts, partially finished items (i.e., work-in-progress, or, WIP), and finished goods, as well as spare parts for machines, tools, and other supplies. Stores carry items for sale. Hospitals stock drugs, surgical supplies, life-monitoring equipment, sheets and pillow cases, and more. Supermarkets stock foods and other items.

inventory An idle material or product.

Importance of Inventories

Inventories are a vital part of business. Not only are they necessary for operations, but also they contribute to customer satisfaction. To get a sense of the significance of inventories, consider the following: Although the amounts and dollar values of inventories carried by different types of companies vary widely, a typical company probably has about 30 percent of its current assets and perhaps as much as 90 percent of its working capital invested in inventories. One widely used measure of managerial performance relates to *return on investment* (ROI), which is profit after taxes divided by total assets. Because inventories may represent a significant portion of total assets, a reduction of inventories can result in a significant increase in ROI.

The major source of revenues for retail and wholesale businesses is the sale of merchandise (i.e., inventories). In fact, in terms of dollars, the inventory of goods held for sale is one of the largest assets of a merchandising business.

Service companies do not carry these kinds of inventories, although they do carry inventories of supplies and equipment. To understand why organizations have inventories at all, you need to be aware of the various functions of inventory.

Functions of Inventory

Inventories serve a number of functions. Among the most important are the following:

1. To meet expected sales or usage.
2. To wait while being transported.

3. To protect against stockouts.

4. To take advantage of economic lot size and quantity discount.

5. To smooth seasonal production requirements.

6. To decouple operations.

7. To hedge against price increases.

Let's take a closer look at each of these.

1. *To meet expected sales or usage.* Because purchase or production takes time (called lead time) and demand may not wait, companies need to hold some inventory of the average demand for finished goods and average usage of raw materials and parts.

2. *To wait while being transported.* Raw materials and parts from suppliers, and finished goods from manufacturers heading to markets need to be transported. This is usually done by ship, rail, truck, or planes. Depending on the mode of transportation, the freight could take up to a month to reach its destination. Also, there are sometimes long waits in the distribution centres, terminals, and borders. Items being transported are called in-transit inventory.

3. *To protect against stockouts.* Delayed deliveries and unexpected increases in demand increase the risk of shortages. Delays can occur because of weather conditions, supplier stockouts, deliveries of wrong materials, quality problems, and so on. The risk of shortages can be reduced by holding *safety stocks,* which are stocks in excess of average demand to compensate for *variabilities* in demand and lead time.

4. *To take advantage of economic lot size and quantity discount.* To minimize purchasing and Accounts Payable costs, an organization often buys in quantities that exceed immediate requirements. This necessitates storing some or all of the purchased goods for later use. Similarly, it is usually economical to produce in large rather than small quantities. Again, the excess output must be stored for later use. Thus, inventory storage enables an organization to buy or produce in *economic lot sizes.* This results in consecutive orders occurring after some interval of time, called *order* or *replenishment cycle.* The resulting stock is hence known as *cycle stock.* The ability to store extra goods also allows a firm to take advantage of price discounts for larger orders.

5. *To smooth seasonal production.* Firms that experience seasonal patterns in demand (e.g., icecream or beer manufacturers) often build up inventories during off-season periods to meet high requirements during peak seasons. These inventories are aptly named *seasonal inventories.* Also, when supply is seasonal such as in grain, fruit, and vegetable production and processing, there will be seasonal inventories.

6. *To decouple operations.* Historically, manufacturing firms have used inventories as buffers between successive operations to maintain continuity of production that would otherwise be disrupted by events such as breakdowns of equipment and accidents that cause a portion of the operation to shut down temporarily. The work-in-process buffers

---

READING

Decoupling Inventory of Ford Windstar

www.ford.ca

An example of decoupling inventory is the inventory of painted bodies of Ford Windstar minivans in Ford's Oakville, Ontario, assembly plant. A new "in-line vehicle sequencing" (ILVS) building was built in 1999 next to the assembly plant, which accommodates approximately 425 painted bodies. The paint operation is efficient only when

batches of the same colour bodies are painted: the setup time is rather long, involving washing the paint spray hoses thoroughly. However, one dealer's order generally has a combination of colours. So, even though painting is done in batches of six of the same colour, it is desirable that the assembly sequence reflect each dealer's order (this will reduce the number of assembled inventory and accelerates the shipment to each dealer). Using the ILVS building, Ford can now promise 15-day production/delivery lead times.

Source: L. Wichmann, "Auto Assemblers Put Their Houses in Order: Sequencing Tightens the Supply Chain and Gets Product Out Faster," *Plant* 59(2), February 14, 2000, p. 18.

Catalyst's Item Master

A good but inexpensive manufacturing software is Catalyst Manufacturing®. The first step to use the software is to define the inventory items. This is done in the Item Master under Data Maintenance menu. Each item will have a file. The typical information needed are: short description, stock and purchase units of measure, warehouse and location in it, whether manufactured or purchased, purchase lead time, or manufacturing lead time (setup time plus processing time per unit), cost, and supplier information.

Reprinted by permission from Catalyst Manufacturing®.
www.mfgcatalyst.com

permit other operations to continue temporarily while the problem is resolved. For an application, see the reading, "Decoupling Inventory of Ford Windstar."

7. *To hedge against price increases.* Occasionally a buyer or manager will suspect that a substantial price increase is about to occur and will purchase larger-than-normal amounts to avoid the increase.

Objectives of Inventory Control

Inadequate control of inventories can result in both under- and overstocking of items. Understocking results in missed deliveries, lost sales, dissatisfied customers, and production stoppage; overstocking unnecessarily ties up funds that might be more productive elsewhere. Although overstocking may appear to be the lesser of the two evils, the price tag for excessive overstocking can be staggering. It is not unheard of for managers to discover that their firm has a 10-year supply of some item. (No doubt the firm got a good buy on it!)

Inventory management has two main concerns. One is the *level of customer service;* that is, to have the right goods, in sufficient quantities, in the right place, at the right time. The other is the *costs of ordering and holding inventories.*

Eli Lilly Canada

www.lilly.ca

E li Lilly Canada manufactures pharmaceuticals and medical devices. From its Scarborough, Ontario, distribution centre, Eli Lilly ships products to 200 wholesale and key accounts across Canada. In order to improve lot traceability, inventory record accuracy, customer service, and to eliminate time-consuming paper procedures, in 1997 Eli Lilly installed a radio-frequency-based (wireless, using bar codes and scanners) warehouse management system (WMS), which is integrated with its manufacturing software.

As a product enters the warehouse, an employee uses an RF terminal's scanner to read the lot number and item code, and enters the quantity. This information is transmitted instantly to the computer, where it is immediately entered into the inventory database. Upon verification, the WMS generates a bar-code label that provides product tracking as it is stored.

In the picking function, the software first assigns a box number to a specific customer order. Once an operator logs on to the system, the box number label is first printed and attached to a box. The software then directs the picker to retrieve the order in the sequence which minimizes total distance travelled. Once at the picking location, the picker scans the bar-code location ID to confirm the location, and then confirms the product before picking the quantity requested. Once the WMS confirms a correct pick, it directs the picker to the next pick location until the order is filled. The order is then conveyed to a packing station where weight of the order is determined. Upon verification of the weight, the order box number is scanned and assigned to a specific carrier for shipment to the customer.

Source: "A Remedy for Inventory Ailments," *AS/400 Systems Management* 26(2), February 1998, pp. 46–47.

READING

MHR Warehouse

McGraw-Hill Ryerson, the publisher of this book, moved from a manually operated 100,000-square-foot warehouse in Scarborough into its new warehouse in Whitby, Ontario, in the early 1990s. The 80,000-square-foot warehouse, storing 25,000 stock-keeping units (SKUs), is divided into two areas; 80 percent of SKUs are in boxes on pallets and are kept on three-level pallet racks (over 8,000 racks) separated by very narrow aisles; 20 percent of SKUs are on shelves (out of box) and are placed on 12 horizontal (multishelf) carrousels. Raymond wire-guided turret trucks are used to put away pallets and retrieve pallets from the very narrow aisle storage racks. There is a wire running along the centre of each aisle which electronically keeps the equipment centred along the aisle. Every group of four carrousels leads into a manned workstation. The carrousels are "velocity-zoned": fast-moving SKUs are placed in the middle shelves, medium-moving SKUs in the bottom shelves, and slow-moving SKUs in the top shelves. A tote box is used to collect the book(s) ordered from the carrousel system, which is then moved to packing and shipping on conveyors. The mechanized warehouse has reduced order filling time from 3 days to 1 day and increased productivity from 30 SKUs per hour to 100. The operating and building costs have been reduced by $1 million per year.

Source: L. Gould, "New Warehouse Payoff: A 200% Jump in Productivity," *Modern Material Handling*, March 1993, pp. 40–42.

The overall objective of inventory management is to achieve satisfactory levels of customer service while keeping inventory costs within reasonable bounds. Toward this end, the buyer or inventory analyst tries to achieve a balance in stocking. He or she must make two fundamental decisions: the *timing* and *size* of orders (i.e., when to order and how much to order). The greater part of this chapter is devoted to models that can be applied to assist in making those decisions.

Managers have a number of measures of performance they can use to judge the effectiveness of inventory management. The most obvious, of course, is customer satisfaction, which they might measure by the in-stock (or fill) rate, or the number of back orders. Another measure is related to inventory costs: **inventory turnover**, which is the ratio of annual cost of goods sold to average inventory investment. The inventory turnover ratio indicates how many times a year the inventory is sold. Generally, the higher the ratio the better, because that implies more efficient use of inventories. A benefit of this measure is that it can be used to compare companies of different size in the *same* industry. A related measure is days of inventory on hand, a number that indicates the expected number of days of sales or usage that can be supplied from existing inventory.

inventory turnover Ratio of annual cost of goods sold to average inventory investment.

REQUIREMENTS FOR EFFECTIVE INVENTORY MANAGEMENT

Management has two basic functions concerning inventories. One is to establish a system to safely store and use inventories, and the other is to accurately keep track of levels of inventories, and make decisions about how much and when to order. These require the following:

1. A system to *safely store* and *use inventories*.
2. A system to *keep track of inventories,* and replenishment models.
3. Reliable *forecasts of demands* and knowledge of *lead times*.
4. Reasonable estimates of inventory *holding*, *ordering*, and *shortage costs*.
5. A-B-C *classification*.

Let's take a closer look at each of these requirements.

A System to Safely Store and Use Inventories

Most inventory items need to be protected from harsh outdoor environments such as rain and snow. Therefore, inventory is usually stored indoors, in a warehouse or storeroom. Depending on the nature of the item, racks, shelves, or bins may be used to hold them.

Heavy items or fast-moving items are stored on the floor. To save moving items long distances, warehouses usually use the vertical space, i.e., they are as high as a three - or four-story building. Forklifts and reach industrial trucks are used to access the top locations.

A warehouse/storeroom should not be cluttered so that items can be stored and retrieved easily. In addition to difficulty in finding a particular item, a cramped warehouse/store will result in excessive damage to stocks. Depending on the flow of items into and out of the warehouse/store, the right level of automation should be used. Most warehouses use forklifts which move items piled on pallets (called *unit loads*). Some use conveyors and some use carrousels. For an application, see the reading, "MHR Warehouse."

Inventory items are usually expensive, so access to the building should be controlled, and items which are prone to theft (e.g., small valuable items such as batteries) should be locked up in secure areas. Also, because full pallets are heavy, some racks in the warehouse are high, and equipment such as forklifts and pallet jacks are large and fast-moving, safety is an important issue in warehouse management.

A common problem in most warehouses/storerooms is the existence of a considerable amount of obsolete items. These include parts for machines that no longer exist, wrong parts, excess material, used machines, etc. To be efficient, outdated items should be either sent back to the supplier (called restocking) or sold at a discount (salvaged). Obsolete items are a drag on company's assets and take space in the warehouse.

Inventory Counting and Replenishment Models

Inventory counting can be periodic or perpetual. Under **periodic counting** or review, a physical count of items in inventory is made at periodic intervals (e.g., weekly, monthly) in order to decide how much of each item to order. Many small retailers use this approach: a manager periodically checks the shelves and stockroom to determine the quantities on hand. Then, the manager estimates how much of it will be demanded prior to the next delivery and bases the order quantity on this information. This replenishment model is called the fixed order-interval model. An advantage of this type of system is that orders from the same supplier can be issued at the same time, which can result in economies in processing and shipping. There are also several disadvantages of periodic reviews. One is a possibility of stockout between reviews. To protect against these, extra stock should be carried. The other is the time and cost of a physical count.

Perpetual tracking (also known as *continual* system) keeps track of removals from and additions to inventory on a continuous basis, so the system can provide information on the current level of inventory for each item. Usually, a **fixed order-quantity/reorder-point model** is used with perpetual tracking. When the amount on hand reaches a predetermined minimum (called the reorder point), a fixed quantity, Q, is ordered. An obvious advantage of this system is that shortages can be avoided. Another advantage is the fixed order quantity; management can determine an optimal order quantity and use it for every order (provided demand does not vary seasonally). Disadvantages of this approach are the added costs of continual record keeping, and possibly frequent orders. Bank accounts are kept using this system, i.e., transactions such as customer deposits and withdrawals are instantly recorded and balance is determined continually. All business and manufacturing software keeps track of inventories. For example, see the reading, "Catalyst's Item Master."

A simple implementation of a fixed order-quantity/reorder-point model which does not require inventory counting is the **two-bin system**. Items are withdrawn from the first bin until its contents are exhausted. It is then time to reorder. Sometimes an order card is placed at the bottom of the first bin. The second bin contains enough stock to satisfy expected demand until the order is filled plus an extra cushion of stock that will reduce the chance of stockouts if the order is late and/or if usage is greater than expected. The advantage of this system is that there is no need to record each withdrawal from inventory or keep track of inventory on hand; the disadvantage is that the reorder card may not be turned in.

Most warehouse and stores use laser scanning devices that read **bar codes** assigned to items, cases, pallets, etc., and the storage location (rack, shelf, bin, etc.). There are

periodic counting Physical count of items in inventory made at periodic intervals (e.g., weekly, monthly).

perpetual tracking System that keeps track of removals from and additions to inventory continuously, thus providing current levels of each item.

fixed order-quantity/reorder-point model An order of a fixed size, usually equal to the economic order quantity, is placed when the amount on hand drops to or below a minimum quantity called the *reorder point*.

two-bin system Two containers of inventory; reorder when the first is empty; use the second bin until order arrives.

bar code A number assigned to an item or location, made of a group of vertical bars of different thickness that are readable by a scanner.

approximately five different types of bar codes. A typical grocery universal product code (UPC) is illustrated above. The zero on the left of the bar code identifies this as a grocery item, the first five numbers (14800) indicate the manufacturer, and the last five numbers (23208) indicate the specific item (natural-style applesauce). Bar-code scanners represent a major change in the inventory systems of warehouses and stores because they have increased the speed and accuracy of transactions.

For applications of warehouse management systems, see the readings, on "Eli Lilly Canada," "Mississauga Hydro," "B.C. Hot House," and "Toyota's Parts Distribution and Information System."

Demand Forecasts and Lead-Time Information

Inventories are used to satisfy future demand requirements, so it is essential to have reliable estimates of the amount and timing of demand. Also, it is essential to know the **purchase lead time**, the time it will take for orders to be delivered. Similarly, manufacturing lead time is the time it will take for a batch of a product to be manufactured. In addition, managers need to know the extent to which demand and lead time might vary: the greater the potential variability, the greater the need for additional safety stock to reduce the risk of a shortage between deliveries. Thus, there is a crucial link between forecasting and inventory management.

Point-of-sale (POS) systems electronically record actual sales and updating inventory levels at the time and location of sale, which, after accumulation into daily or weekly sales for each stock-keeping unit (SKU), are used in forecasting.

Cost Information

Three basic costs are associated with inventories: holding, ordering, and shortage costs.

Holding or **carrying cost** relates to physically having items in storage. Costs include warehousing costs (heat, cooling, light, rent, security) and the opportunity cost associated with having funds, that could be used elsewhere, tied up in inventory. Other holding costs include insurance, obsolescence, spoilage, pilferage, and breakage.

The significance of some of the components of holding cost depends on the type of item involved. Items that are easily concealed or are fairly expensive are prone to theft and need to be locked up. Items such as meats and dairy are subject to rapid spoilage and need freezing or cooling.

Holding costs are stated in either of two ways: as a percentage of unit cost or as a dollar amount per unit. Typical annual holding cost rates range from 20 percent to 40 percent of the value of an item. In other words, to hold a $100 item for one year could cost from $20 to $40.

Ordering cost is the cost of the actual placement of an order (not including the purchase cost). These include the time of purchasing/inventory control staff determining how much is needed, periodically evaluating sources of supply, preparing purchase orders; and the fixed-cost portion of transportation, receiving, inspecting, and moving the goods to storage. It also includes the cost of time spent paying the invoice. Ordering costs are generally expressed as a fixed dollar amount per order, regardless of order size.

When a firm produces its own inventory, instead of ordering it from a supplier, the cost of machine **setup** is analogous to ordering cost; that is, it is expressed as a fixed charge per production run, regardless of the size of the run.

Shortage cost results when demand exceeds the supply of inventory on hand. These costs can include the opportunity cost of not making a sale (i.e., unrealized profit), loss of

---

purchase lead time Time interval between ordering and receiving the order.

point-of-sale (POS) system Software for electronically recording sales and updating inventory levels at the time and location of sale.

holding (carrying) cost Cost to keep an item in inventory.

ordering cost Cost of determining order quantity and preparing purchase orders; the fixed-cost portion of receiving, inspection, and material handling; and paying the invoice.

setup Time spent preparing equipment for the job by adjusting the machine, changing cutting tools, etc.

shortage cost Cost resulting when demand exceeds the supply of inventory on hand; often unrealized profit per unit.

customer goodwill, late charges, and expediting costs. Furthermore, if the shortage occurs in an item carried for internal use (e.g., to supply an assembly line), the cost of lost production or downtime is considered a shortage cost. Such costs can easily run into hundreds of dollars a minute or more.

A-B-C Classification

An important aspect of inventory management is that items held in inventory are not of equal importance in terms of dollars invested, profit potential, sales or usage quantity, or stockout penalties. For instance, a producer of electrical equipment might have electric generators, coils of wire, and miscellaneous nuts and bolts among the items carried in inventory. It would be unrealistic to devote equal attention to each of these items. Instead, a more reasonable approach would be to allocate control efforts according to the *relative importance* of various items in inventory.

The **A-B-C classification** groups inventory items to three classes according to some measure of importance, usually annual dollar value (i.e., dollar value per unit multiplied by annual usage or sale quantity), and then allocates control efforts accordingly. The three classes are: A (very important), B (moderately important), and C (least important). A items generally account for about 15 to 20 percent of the *number* of items (SKUs, not counting multiples of the same part/product) in inventory but about 70 to 80 percent of the annual *dollar value*. At the other end of the scale, C items might account for about 50 to 60 percent of the number of SKUs but only about 5 to 10 percent of the annual dollar value of inventory. These percentages vary from company to company, but in most instances a relatively small number of items will account for a large share of the annual dollar value of inventory, and these items should receive a greater share of control efforts. For instance, A items should receive close attention through better forecasting, more frequent replenishments, and better safety stock determination. The C items should receive only loose control (e.g., use a two-bin system, bulk orders), and the B items should have controls that lie between the two extremes.

A-B-C classification Grouping inventory items to three classes according to some measure of importance, and allocating control efforts accordingly.

READING

Mississauga Hydro

www.enersource.com

Mississauga Hydro's warehouse stores supplies (such as reels of cable) and equipment (such as transformers) that company's line workers need. The warehouse contains more than $5 million in inventory and processes orders worth $1 million a month. When the facility was run by manual paperwork, crews often lined up for two hours for materials. To make matters worse, it was operating at an accuracy rate of only 60 percent.

Ted Zlotnik, purchasing manager, found a solution in computers. The system's price tag of $100,000 included hardware, software, installation fees, training, and ongoing support. The utility's system comprises six radio frequency wireless Intermec JR2020 portable computers and scanners, five desktop computer terminals that are integrated into the utility's computer network, and two printers—one for printing bar codes and the other for printing reports. The system was operating and all users were trained in approximately 10 weeks.

The utility's system increased inventory accuracy rates to 98.6 percent. The 1.4-percent error comes from vendors short-shipping the quantities.

The beauty of the system is that it is partially self-service. The order entry room is designed for the approximately 150 line workers who are not computer literate. They can scan from order books or from the array of products and photos with accompanying bar codes mounted on the wall. Users also scan a bar code on their security badge, which gives them access to the system. Their badge identification and order is downloaded into a PC, and storekeepers, who are responsible for picking items, then retrieve the inventory items and scan them before they are removed from the warehouse. A packing slip is immediately generated that illustrates who ordered what material.

As a result, one data entry clerk position has been eliminated and annual overtime is reduced by $10,000 because line workers wait less.

Source: "Turning into New Automated Warehouse Technology: Radio Frequency Has Improved Inventory Management and Slashed Costs at Mississauga Hydro Facility," *Plant* 55(6), April 22, 1996, pp. 10–11.

Example 1

Classify the following inventory items as A, B, or C based on annual dollar value:

Item	Annual Demand	×	Unit Cost	=	Annual Dollar Value (ADV)
1	3,000	$	10	$	30,000
2	9,000		3		27,000
3	1,000		710		710,000
4	2,500		250		625,000
5	1,900		500		950,000
6	400		200		80,000
7	500		100		50,000
8	1,000		4,300		4,300,000
9	200		210		42,000
10	5,000		720		3,600,000
11	2,500		192		480,000
12	1,000		35		35,000

Solution

Sort the rows by increasing values of ADV, total, and calculate the percentage of total ADV for each SKU:

Item	Annual Demand	×	Unit Cost	=	Annual Dollar Value (ADV)	% of Total ADV	
8	1,000		$4,300		$4,300,000	39.3	A
10	5,000		720		3,600,000	32.9	
5	1,900		500		950,000	8.7	
3	1,000		710		710,000	6.5	B
4	2,500		250		625,000	5.7	
11	2,500		192		480,000	4.4	
6	400		200		80,000	.7	
7	500		100		50,000	.5	
9	200		210		42,000	.4	C
12	1,000		35		35,000	.3	
1	3,000		10		30,000	.3	
2	9,000		3		27,000	.3	
					$10,929,000	100.0	

Proceed down the list, adding ADVs until we get close to 80 percent of total ADV. The first two items have 72.2 percent of total annual dollar value and 2/12 = 17 percent of number of SKUs, so it seems reasonable to classify them as A items. (Also note the sharp drop in ADV from the second to third rows.) The next four items have moderate ADV (25.3 percent of total annual dollar value and 4/12 = 33 percent of number of SKUs) and should be classified as B items. (Also note the sharp drop in ADV between the sixth and seventh rows.) The remainder are C items, based on their relatively low annual dollar value (2.5 percent of total annual dollar value and 6/12 = 50 percent of number of SKUs).

Although annual dollar value may be the primary factor in classifying inventory items, a manager may take other factors into account in making exceptions for certain items (e.g., changing the classification of a C item to A). Factors may include the risk of obsolescence, the consequence of a stockout, the distance of a supplier, and so on.

Managers use the A-B-C concept in many different settings to improve operations. In fact, A-B-C classification is related to the 80–20 rule and Pareto analysis discussed in Chapter 9.

An application of the A-B-C concept is to guide **cycle counting**, which is a regular count of the items in inventory on a cyclic schedule rather than once a year. The purpose of cycle counting is (*a*) to reduce discrepancies between the amounts indicated by inventory records and the actual quantities of inventory on hand, (*b*) to investigate the cause of inaccuracy and fix it. Accuracy is important because inaccurate records can lead to wrong decisions leading to disruptions in production, poor customer service, and unnecessarily high inventory carrying costs.

cycle counting Regular physical count of the items in inventory on a cyclic schedule.

The key questions concerning cycle counting for management are:

1. How much accuracy is needed?
2. What counting cycle should be used?
3. Who should do it?

APICS, the American Production and Inventory Control Society, recommends the following guidelines for inventory record accuracy: ± 0.2 percent for A items, ± 1 percent for B items, and ± 5 percent for C items.

A items should be counted more frequently than C items. For example, A items should be counted every month, B items quarterly, and C items annually.

www.apics.org

Some companies use regular stockroom personnel to do cycle counting during periods of slow activity, while others contract with outside companies to do it on a periodic basis. Use of an outside company provides an independent check on inventory and may reduce the risk of problems created by dishonest employees.

FIXED-ORDER-QUANTITY/REORDER POINT MODEL: DETERMINING ECONOMIC ORDER QUANTITY

In this model, a fixed-order quantity is determined and used for an item in inventory when the amount on hand drops to or below the reorder point (quantity). The order quantity used is usually the optimal or **economic order quantity (EOQ)**. EOQ is determined by minimizing the sum of annual holding and ordering costs. Four models are described here:

economic order quantity (EOQ) The order size that minimizes total cost.

1. Basic economic order quantity
2. Economic production quantity
3. EOQ with quantity discounts
4. EOQ with planned shortages

Basic Economic Order Quantity (EOQ)

The basic EOQ model is used to identify the order size that will minimize the sum of the annual costs of holding and ordering inventory. The annual purchase price of units is not included in the total cost in this case because purchase price is unaffected by the order size.

The basic EOQ model involves a number of assumptions. They are listed in Table 11–1.

TABLE 11-1
1. Only one product is involved.
2. Annual demand requirements are known.
3. Demand is spread evenly throughout the year so that the demand rate is reasonably constant.
4. Lead time does not vary.
5. Each order is received in a single delivery.
6. There are no quantity discounts.

Assumptions of the basic EOQ model

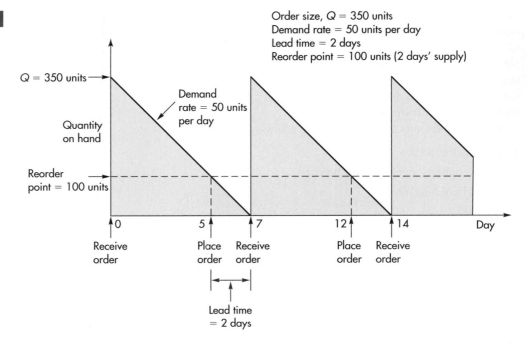

FIGURE 11-1

The inventory cycle: profile of inventory level over time

Order size, $Q = 350$ units
Demand rate $= 50$ units per day
Lead time $= 2$ days
Reorder point $= 100$ units (2 days' supply)

$Q = 350$ units

Demand rate $= 50$ units per day

Quantity on hand

Reorder point $= 100$ units

0   5   7   12   14   Day

Receive order   Place order   Receive order   Place order   Receive order

Lead time $= 2$ days

Inventory ordering and usage occur in cycles. Figure 11–1 illustrates several inventory cycles. A cycle begins with receipt of an order of another Q units, which are then withdrawn at a constant rate over time. When the quantity on hand is just sufficient to satisfy demand during lead time, an order for another Q units is submitted to the supplier. Because it is assumed that both the demand rate and the lead time do not vary, the order will be received at the precise instant that the inventory on hand falls to zero. Thus, orders are timed to avoid both excess stock and stockouts.

READING

B.C. Hot House

www.bchothouse.com

Vancouver's B.C. Hot House Foods works with 50 local growers of cucumbers, tomatoes, and peppers who bring their produce to the company so that they can be graded, packaged, sold, and distributed. B.C. Hot House moved into a 127,000-square-foot facility in the late 1990s. Until then, it was manually tracking the inventory. The new technology, including 15 Intermec hand-held scanners, has improved put-away, processing, and inventory counting.

When produce is received, a tag printer prints a bar-code label for each pallet, storing the SKU, product description, and date in a database. When the labels are scanned later, the hand-held terminals tell employees in which warehouse location to place the pallets. The system directs staff to the three best locations. Before the new system, employees had to search the racks for empty slots.

After grading the produce and putting it in cartons, roller encoders apply a bar code to the bottom of each carton indicating the product's originating lane (one of 32). Once on the main conveyor, this internally used bar code is scanned at the inkjet print station and the appropriate human-readable text is printed on the carton. Because the staff know which products are assigned to which lanes, they can identify each carton's contents at a glance.

B.C. Hot House performs daily inventory counting. It used to take two people a full day to count 70,000 to 80,000 cases. Because of the company's growth, 130,000 to 140,000 cases must now be counted, and yet inventory counting now takes one person just three hours daily with a hand-held terminal. The employee scans a bar-coded tag attached to each location, which identifies the location and its product on his or her hand-held terminal's screen display. Then the employee compares the screen information to the quantity of product actually found at the scanned location. If it matches, he or she moves on to the next location. If it doesn't match, he or she updates the screen display for that location. This new inventory counting system has resulted in labour savings of more than $20,000 annually.

Another benefit of the computerized inventory system is that the salespeople can find out what products are available in the warehouse and what date code is on them.

Source: A. Loudin, "A Greener Garden," *Automatic I.D. News* 14(2), February 1998, p. 26ff.

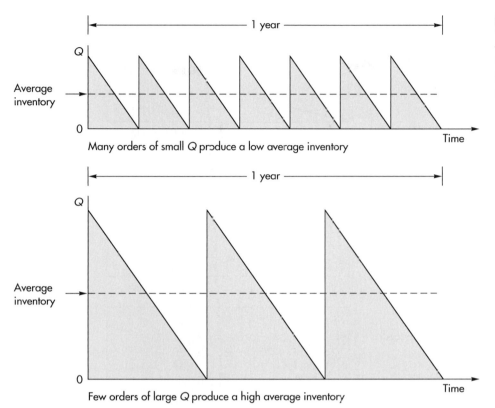

The optimal order quantity reflects a trade-off between holding cost and ordering cost: As order size varies, one type of cost will increase while the other decreases. For example, if the order size is relatively small, the average inventory will be low, resulting in low holding cost. However, a small order size will necessitate frequent orders, which will drive up annual ordering cost. Conversely, ordering large quantities at infrequent intervals can reduce annual ordering cost, but that would result in higher average inventory levels and therefore increased holding cost. Figure 11–2 illustrates these two extremes.

Thus, the ideal solution is an order size that causes neither few very large orders nor many small orders, but one that lies somewhere in between. The exact amount to order will depend on the relative magnitudes of holding and ordering costs.

Annual holding cost is computed by multiplying the average amount of inventory on hand by the cost to hold one unit for one year (even though any given unit would not necessarily be held for a year). The average inventory is simply half of the order quantity: The amount on hand decreases steadily from Q units to 0, for an average of $(Q + 0)/2$, or $Q/2$. Using the symbol H to represent the average annual holding cost per unit, the *total annual holding cost* is

$$\text{Annual holding cost} = \frac{Q}{2} H$$

where

Q = Order quantity in units

H = Holding (carrying) cost per unit per year

Annual holding cost is thus a linear function of Q: it increases or decreases in direct proportion to changes in the order quantity Q, as Figure 11–3A illustrates.

On the other hand, annual ordering cost will decrease as order quantity increases, because for a given annual demand, the larger the order quantity the fewer the number of

A. Annual holding
   cost is linearly
   related to
   order quantity.

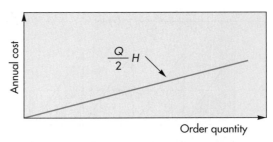

B. Annual ordering
   cost is inversely
   and nonlinearly
   related to
   order quantity.

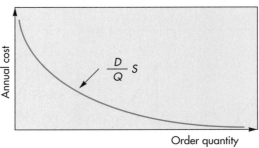

C. The total annual
   inventory cost
   curve is U-shaped.

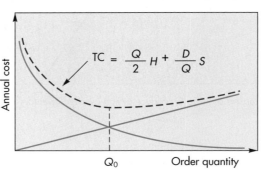

orders needed. For instance, if annual demand is 12,000 units and the order quantity is 1,000 units per order, there will be 12 orders during the year. But if $Q = 2,000$ units, only six orders will be needed; if $Q = 3,000$ units, only four orders will be needed. In general, the number of orders per year will be D/Q, where D = annual demand. Because ordering cost per order is relatively insensitive to order quantity, *annual ordering cost* equals the number of orders per year times the ordering cost per order:

$$\text{Annual ordering cost} = \frac{D}{Q} S$$

where

D = Demand, units per year

S = Ordering cost per order

Because the number of orders per year, D/Q, decreases as Q increases, annual ordering cost is inversely related to order quantity, as Figure 11–3B illustrates.

The total annual inventory cost of holding and ordering inventory, when Q units are ordered each time is

$$\text{TC} = \begin{array}{c}\text{Annual} \\ \text{holding} \\ \text{cost}\end{array} + \begin{array}{c}\text{Annual} \\ \text{ordering} \\ \text{cost}\end{array} = \frac{Q}{2}H + \frac{D}{Q}S \tag{11-1}$$

Figure 11–3C reveals that the total-cost curve is U-shaped (i.e., convex, with one minimum) and that *it reaches its minimum at the quantity where holding and ordering costs are equal.* An expression for the optimal order quantity, Q_0, can be obtained using calculus.[1] The result is the formula

$$EOQ = Q_0 = \sqrt{\frac{2DS}{H}} \tag{11-2}$$

Thus, given annual demand, the ordering cost per order, and the holding cost per unit per year, one can compute the optimal (economic) order quantity. The minimum total cost is then found by substituting Q_0 for Q in Formula 11–1.

The length of an order cycle (i.e., the time between orders, if Q_0 is used) is

$$\text{Length of order cycle} = \frac{Q_0}{D} \quad \text{(years)} \tag{11-3}$$

A tire store expects to sell approximately 9,600 steel-belted radial tires of a certain size and tread design next year. Annual holding cost is $16 per tire, and ordering cost is $75 per order. The store operates 360 days a year.

Example 2

a. What is the EOQ?

b. How many times per year would the store reorder if the EOQ is ordered?

c. What is the length of an order cycle if the EOQ is ordered?

d. What is the total annual inventory cost if the EOQ is ordered?

Solution

$D = 9,600$ tires per year

$H = \$16$ per unit per year

$S = \$75$ per order

a. $Q_0 = \sqrt{\dfrac{2DS}{H}} = \sqrt{\dfrac{2(9,600)75}{16}} = 300$ tires

b. Number of orders per year: $D/Q_0 = \dfrac{9,600 \text{ tires/yr}}{300 \text{ tires}} = 32$ per year

c. Length of order cycle: $Q_0/D = \dfrac{300 \text{ tires}}{9,600 \text{ tires/yr}} = \dfrac{1}{32}$ of a year, which is $\dfrac{1}{32} \times 360$, or 11.25 workdays.

d. TC = Annual holding cost + Annual ordering cost
$$= (Q_0/2)H + (D/Q_0)S$$
$$= (300/2)16 + (9,600/300)75$$
$$= \$2,400 + \$2,400$$
$$= \$4,800.$$

Note that annual ordering and holding costs are equal at the EOQ, as illustrated in Figure 11–3C.

---

[1]We can find the minimum point of the total-cost curve by differentiating TC with respect to Q, setting the result equal to zero, and solving for Q. Thus,

1. $\dfrac{d\text{TC}}{dQ} = \dfrac{dQ}{2}H + d(D/Q)S = H/2 - DS/Q^2$

2. $H/2 - DS/Q^2 = 0$, so $Q^2 = \dfrac{2DS}{H}$ and $Q = \sqrt{\dfrac{2DS}{H}}$

Note that the second derivative $\left(\dfrac{2DS}{Q^3}\right)$ is positive, which indicates a minimum has been obtained.

Holding cost is sometimes stated as a percentage of the purchase price of an item rather than as a dollar amount per unit. However, as long as the percentage is converted into a dollar amount, the EOQ formula is still appropriate.

| **Example 3** | A security company purchases 3,600 black-and-white monitors a year at $65 each. Ordering cost is $31 per order, and annual holding cost per unit is 20 percent of the purchase price. Calculate the optimal order quantity and the total annual cost of ordering and holding the inventory. |

Solution

D = 3,600 monitors per year

S = $31

i = holding cost rate per unit per year = 20%

$H = iR = .20(\$65) = \$13$

$$Q_0 = \sqrt{\frac{2DS}{H}} = \sqrt{\frac{2(3,600)(31)}{13}} = 131 \text{ monitors}$$

TC = Annual holding cost + Annual ordering cost

$\quad = (Q_0/2)H + (D/Q_0)S$

$\quad = (131/2)13 + (3,600/131)31$

$\quad = \$852 + \$852 = \$1,704$

Comment. Holding cost per unit per year, ordering cost per order, and annual demand are typically estimated values rather than values that can be precisely determined from, say, accounting records. Holding and ordering costs are sometimes *designated* rather than computed by managers. Consequently, the EOQ should be regarded as an *approximate* quantity rather than an exact quantity. Thus, rounding the calculated value is perfectly acceptable; stating a value to several decimal places would tend to give an unrealistic impression of the precision involved. An obvious question is: How good is this "approximate" EOQ in terms of minimizing cost? The answer is that the EOQ is fairly robust; the total cost curve is relatively flat near the EOQ, especially to the right of the EOQ. In other words, even if the approximate EOQ differs from the actual EOQ, total cost will not increase much at all. This is particularly true for quantities larger than the real EOQ (see Figure 11–4). Also note that annual demand D is usually estimated by multiplying next month's forecast of demand by 12 or next week's forecast of demand by 52. If there is seasonality in demand, a lot sizing technique, described in Chapter 13, will be more appropriate than EOQ.

Economic Production Quantity (EPQ)

Batch production is widely used. The reason for this is that in certain instances, the capacity to produce a part exceeds the part's usage or demand rate. As long as production

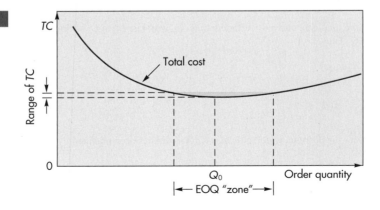

FIGURE 11–4

The total-cost curve is relatively flat near the EOQ

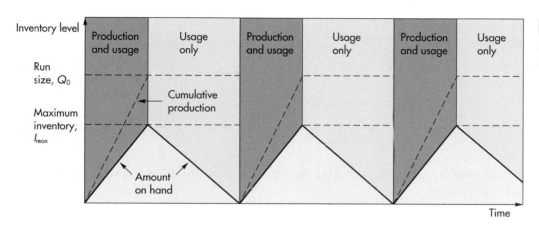

FIGURE 11-5

EOQ with incremental inventory replenishment

continues, inventory will continue to grow. In such instances, it makes sense to periodically produce such items in batches or *lots*.

The assumptions of the EPQ model are similar to those of the EOQ model, except that instead of orders being received in a single delivery, units are received incrementally during production; that is, the production rate is finite.

Figure 11–5 illustrates how inventory level is affected by periodically producing a batch of a particular item.

During the production phase of the cycle, inventory builds up at a rate equal to the difference between production and usage rates. For example, if the daily production rate is 20 units and the daily usage rate is 5 units, inventory will build up at the rate of $20 - 5 = 15$ units per day. As long as production occurs, the inventory level will continue to grow; when production ceases, the inventory level will begin to decrease. Hence, the inventory level will be maximum, denoted by I_{max}, when production ceases. When the amount of inventory on hand is exhausted, production is resumed and the cycle repeats itself. It can be seen that the average inventory on hand is $.5I_{max}$.

Because the company makes the product itself, there is no ordering cost as such. Nonetheless, with every production run (batch), there is setup cost—the cost to prepare the equipment for the job, such as cleaning, adjusting, and changing tools and fixtures. Setup costs are analogous to ordering costs because they are independent of the lot (run) quantity. They are treated in the formula in exactly the same way, and we use the same symbol, S, to denote setup cost per production run. The larger the run quantity, the fewer the number of runs needed and, hence, the lower the annual setup cost. The number of runs or batches is D/Q, and the annual setup cost is equal to the number of runs per year times the setup cost per run: $(D/Q)S$.

Total annual inventory cost is

$$TC = \text{Annual holding cost} + \text{Annual setup cost} = \left(\frac{I_{max}}{2}\right)H + (D/Q)S \qquad (11\text{–}4)$$

where

   I_{max} = Maximum inventory

   Q = Run quantity

   S = Setup cost per production run

Let

   p = Production rate

   d = Usage or demand rate

The run quantity Q is consumed at the rate of d during the cycle length (the time between the beginnings of two consecutive runs). Therefore,

$$\text{Cycle length} = \frac{Q}{d} \qquad (11\text{–}5)$$

The run quantity Q is produced at the rate of p during the run length (the production phase of the cycle). Therefore,

$$\text{Run length} = \frac{Q}{p} \tag{11–6}$$

Therefore, the maximum inventory level I_{max} is

$$I_{max} = Q - d\left(\frac{Q}{p}\right) = \frac{Q}{p}(p-d) \tag{11–7}$$

Substituting (11–7) in (11–4), taking derivatives with respect to Q, and setting it equal to zero, we will get

$$Q_0 = \sqrt{\frac{2DS}{H}}\sqrt{\frac{p}{p-d}} \tag{11–8}$$

| **Example 4** | A toy manufacturer uses 48,000 rubber wheels per year for its popular dump truck series. The firm makes its own wheels at a rate of 800 per day. The toy trucks are assembled uniformly over the entire year. Holding cost is \$1 per wheel per year. Setup cost for a production run of wheels is \$45. The firm operates 240 days per year. Determine the: |

a. Optimal run quantity

b. Minimum total annual cost for holding and setup

c. Cycle length for the optimal run quantity

d. Run length for the optimal run quantity

Solution

D = 48,000 wheels per year

S = \$45 per run

H = \$1 per wheel per year

p = 800 wheels per day

d = 48,000 wheels per 240 days, or 200 wheels per day

a. $Q_0 = \sqrt{\dfrac{2DS}{H}}\sqrt{\dfrac{p}{p-d}} = \sqrt{\dfrac{2(48,000)45}{1}}\sqrt{\dfrac{800}{800-200}} = 2,400$ wheels

b. TC_{min} = Annual holding cost + Annual setup cost $= \left(\dfrac{I_{max}}{2}\right)H + (D/Q_0)S$

Thus, you must first calculate I_{max}:

$$I_{max} = \frac{Q}{p}(p-d) = \frac{2,400}{800}(800-200) = 1,800 \text{ wheels}$$

$$TC_{min} = \frac{1,800}{2} \times \$1 + \frac{48,000}{2,400} \times \$45 = \$900 + \$900 = \$1,800$$

Note again the equality of costs (in this example, setup and holding costs) at the EPQ.

c. Cycle length $= \dfrac{Q}{d} = \dfrac{2,400 \text{ wheels}}{200 \text{ wheels per day}} = 12$ days

Thus, a run of wheels will be made every 12 days.

d. Run length $= \dfrac{Q}{p} = \dfrac{2,400 \text{ wheels}}{800 \text{ wheels per day}} = 3$ days

Thus, each production run is three days.

EOQ with Quantity Discounts

Quantity discounts are price reductions for large orders offered to customers to induce them to buy in large quantities. For example, a surgical supply company publishes the price list shown in Table 11–2 for boxes of gauze strips. Note that the price per box decreases as order quantity increases.

quantity discounts Price reductions for large orders.

If quantity discounts are offered, the buyer must weigh the potential benefits of reduced purchase price and fewer orders that will result from buying in large quantities against the increase in holding cost caused by higher average inventory. The buyer's goal is to select the order quantity that will minimize total annual cost, where total cost is the sum of annual holding cost, ordering cost, *and* purchasing cost:

$$TC = \text{Annual holding} + \text{Annual ordering} + \text{Annual purchasing}$$
$$\text{cost} \qquad\qquad \text{cost} \qquad\qquad \text{cost}$$

$$= \left(\frac{Q}{2}\right)H \quad + \quad \left(\frac{D}{Q}\right)S \quad + \quad RD \qquad\qquad (11\text{–}9)$$

where

$R = $ Unit price

Recall that in the basic EOQ model, determination of order quantity does not involve the purchasing cost. The rationale for not including purchasing cost there is that under the assumption of no quantity discounts, annual purchasing cost is not affected by order quantity. A graph of total annual purchase cost versus quantity would be a horizontal line. Hence, including purchasing cost would merely raise the total-cost curve (in Figure 11–3C) by the same amount (*RD*) at every point. That would not change the EOQ (see Figure 11–6).

Order Quantity	Price per Box	**TABLE 11-2**
1 to 44	$2.00	
45 to 69	1.70	
70 or more	1.40	

Price list for extra-wide gauze strips

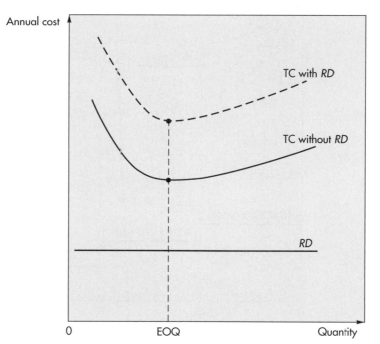

FIGURE 11-6

Adding RD doesn't change the EOQ if there is no quantity discount

When quantity discounts are offered, there is a separate U-shaped total-cost curve for each unit price, because *H* will be different. Again, including total purchase price merely raises each curve by a constant amount. However, because the unit prices are all different, each curve is raised by a different amount: Smaller unit prices will raise a total-cost curve less than larger unit prices. Note that no one curve applies to the entire range of quantities; each curve applies to only a *portion* of the range (see Figure 11–7). Hence, the applicable or *feasible* total cost is initially on the curve with the highest unit price and then drops down, curve by curve, at the *minimum price break quantities*. Note that from Table 11–2, the minimum price break quantities for gauze strips are at 45 and 70 boxes. The result is a total-cost curve with *steps* at the minimum price break quantities.

Even though each curve has a minimum, those points are not necessarily feasible. For example, the minimum point for the $1.40 curve in Figure 11–7 appears to be around 65 units. However, the price list shown in Table 11–2 indicates that an order size of 65 boxes will receive a unit price of $1.70. The actual total-cost curve is denoted by the solid lines; only those price–quantity combinations are feasible. The objective of the quantity discount model is to identify an order quantity that will represent the lowest total cost for the entire set of curves. The minimum point of each curve can be found by using the associated holding cost in the EOQ formula.

Note that because holding cost is a percentage of price, lower prices will mean lower holding cost and larger minimum points. Thus, as price decreases, each curve's minimum point will be to the right of the next higher curve's minimum point (see Figure 11–7).

We can determine the best purchase quantity with the following procedure:

1. Beginning with the lowest unit price, calculate the EOQ for each price until you find a feasible EOQ (i.e., until an EOQ falls in the quantity range for its price).

2. If the EOQ for the lowest unit price is feasible, it is the optimal order quantity. If not, compare the total cost at the minimum price break quantity for all *lower* prices with the total cost of the feasible EOQ. The quantity that yields the lowest total cost is optimum.

FIGURE 11-7

The total-cost curve with quantity discounts is composed of a portion of the total-cost curve for each price

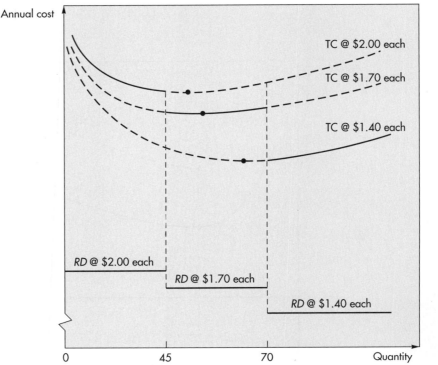

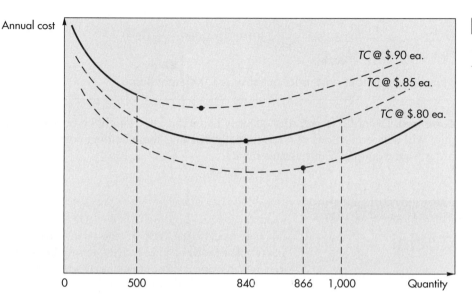

FIGURE 11-8

Total-cost curves for Example 5

A factory uses 4,000 light bulbs a year. Light bulbs are priced as follows: 1 to 499, 90 cents each; 500 to 999, 85 cents each; and 1,000 or more, 80 cents each. It costs approximately $30 to prepare a purchase order and receive it, and holding cost is 40 percent of purchase price per unit on an annual basis. Determine the optimal order quantity and the total annual cost.

Example 5

See Figure 11–8:

$D = 4,000$ light bulbs per year $S = \$30$ $H = .40R$ $R =$ unit price

Solution

Range	Unit Price R	H
1 to 499	$.90	.40(.90) = .36
500 to 999	$.85	.40(.85) = .34
1,000 or more	$.80	.40(.80) = .32

Find the EOQ for each price, starting with the lowest price, until you locate a feasible EOQ.

$$EOQ_{.80} = \sqrt{\frac{2DS}{H}} = \sqrt{\frac{2(4,000)30}{.32}} = 866 \text{ light bulbs}$$

Because an order size of 866 light bulbs will cost $.85 rather than $.80 each, 866 is not feasible for $.80 per light bulb. Next, try $.85 per unit.

$$EOQ_{.85} = \sqrt{\frac{2(4,000)30}{.34}} = 840 \text{ light bulbs}$$

This is feasible; it falls in the $.85-per-light-bulb quantity range (500 to 999).

Now calculate the total cost for 840, and compare it to the total cost of the minimum quantity necessary to obtain a price of $.80 per light bulb (i.e., 1,000 units).

$$TC = \text{Holding cost} + \text{Ordering cost} + \text{Purchasing cost}$$

$$= \left(\frac{Q}{2}\right)H + \left(\frac{D}{Q}\right)S + RD$$

$$TC_{840} = \frac{840}{2}(.34) + \frac{4,000}{840}(30) + .85(4,000) = \$3,686$$

$$TC_{1,000} = \frac{1,000}{2}(.32) + \frac{4,000}{1,000}(30) + .80(4,000) = \$3,480$$

Thus, the minimum-cost order quantity is 1,000 light bulbs.

Comment. Even if a large order quantity is purchased, it might be possible that the supplier will deliver portions of it at a time, thus saving some holding cost. A type of blanket order is an example of this arrangement.

READING

Min/Max Model

Another popular inventory model is the min/max model. It is very similar to the fixed order-quantity/reorder point model, with the difference that if at the time of order the quantity on hand is less than min (ROP), then the order quantity will be set equal to (max – quantity on hand). The max is approximately equal to the EOQ + ROP. One facility using min/max model is the Telus warehouse in Calgary which carries telephones and supplies such as tools for line workers. The system automatically issues purchase orders for most items, but for more expensive items the approval of the purchaser is required.

Source: J. Fulcher, "Chain of Events," *Manufacturing Systems* 17(1), January 1999, pp. 85–90.

EOQ WITH PLANNED SHORTAGES

When holding cost is high and the demand can wait, a company may decide to intentionally allow shortages (also called back orders). We assume that the back-ordered demand will "cost" the company in customer goodwill, and this cost will be proportional to the length of time a unit is back-ordered (similar to inventory holding cost). We represent this cost and the number of units back-ordered as:

B = back-order cost per unit per year

Q_b = quantity back-ordered per replenishment cycle

We also make the same assumptions as in basic EOQ model, except that we allow back orders. The inventory on hand can be represented by Figure 11–9.

where

T = order interval = length of a replenishment cycle (in days)

FIGURE 11-9

EOQ with planned shortages

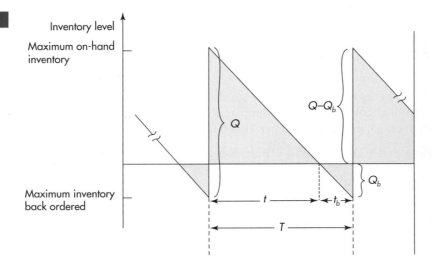

t = time period (during an order interval) when inventory on hand is non-negative

t_b = time period (during an order interval) when inventory on hand is negative (i.e., back-order occurs).

When the next order arrives, the back-ordered demand is satisfied first. Let d = demand rate per day. Because $Q - Q_b$ is used up at the rate of d units per day, then $Q - Q_b = d \times t$ or

$t = \dfrac{Q - Q_b}{d}$. Similarly, $t_b = \dfrac{Q_b}{d}$ and $T = \dfrac{Q}{d}$. Hence,

$$\frac{t}{T} = \frac{\dfrac{Q - Q_b}{d}}{\dfrac{Q}{d}} = \frac{Q - Q_b}{Q} \text{ and } \frac{t_b}{T} = \frac{\dfrac{Q_b}{d}}{\dfrac{Q}{d}} = \frac{Q_b}{Q}.$$

Therefore, average level of inventory during the year is:

$$\frac{Q - Q_b}{2} \times \frac{t}{T} + 0\left(\frac{t_b}{T}\right) = \frac{(Q - Q_b)^2}{2Q},$$

and average level of back orders during the year is:

$$\frac{Q_b}{2} \times \frac{t_b}{T} + 0\left(\frac{t}{T}\right) = \frac{Q_b^2}{2Q}.$$

The total annual inventory cost

TC = annual ordering cost + annual holding cost + annual back-order cost

$$= \left(\frac{D}{Q}\right)S + \left(\frac{(Q - Q_b)^2}{2Q}\right)H + \left(\frac{Q_b^2}{2Q}\right)B$$

Taking derivative of TC with respect to Q_b and setting it equal to zero, we get

$$Q_b = Q\left(\frac{H}{H + B}\right). \tag{11–10}$$

Taking derivative of TC with respect to Q and setting it equal to zero, multiplying by $2Q^2$ and rearranging, we get

$$-2DS + Q^2 \times H - Qb^2(H + B) = 0 \tag{11–11}$$

Substituting (11–10) in (11–11) and solving for Q, we get

$$Q = \sqrt{\frac{2DS}{H}\left(\frac{H + B}{B}\right)} \tag{11–12}$$

Annual demand for a particular model of a refrigerator at an appliance store is 50 units. The holding cost per unit per year is $200. The back-order cost per unit per year is estimated to be $500. Ordering cost from the manufacturer is $10 per order. Determine the order quantity and the back-order quantity per replenishment cycle.

Example 6

Solution

$D = 50$

$H = \$200$

$B = \$500$

$S = \$10$

$$Q = \sqrt{\frac{2DS}{H}\left(\frac{H+B}{B}\right)} = \sqrt{\frac{2(50)(10)}{200}\left(\frac{200+500}{500}\right)} = 2.65, \quad \text{round to 3 units.}$$

$$Q_b = Q\left(\frac{H}{H+B}\right) = 3\left(\frac{200}{200+500}\right) = 0.86, \quad \text{round to 1.}$$

FIXED ORDER-QUANTITY/REORDER POINT MODEL: DETERMINING THE REORDER POINT

reorder point (ROP) When the quantity on hand of an item drops to this amount, the item should be reordered.

The **reorder point (ROP)** is that level of quantity on hand at which an order should be issued.

If demand and lead time are both constant, the reorder point is simply

$$ROP = d \times LT \tag{11–13}$$

where

d = Demand rate (units per day or week)

LT = Lead time (in days or weeks)

Note: Demand and lead time must have the same time units.

Example 7	A person takes two special tablets per day, which are delivered to his home seven days after an order is called in. At what point should the person reorder?

Solution

Usage = 2 tablets a day

Lead time = 7 days

ROP = Usage × Lead time

= 2 tablets per day × 7 days = 14 tablets

Thus, the person should reorder when 14 tablets are left.

---

safety stock Stock that is held in excess of expected demand due to variable demand rate and/or variable lead time.

When variability is present in demand or lead time, it creates the possibility that actual demand during lead time will exceed expected demand. Consequently, it becomes necessary to carry additional inventory, called **safety stock**, to reduce the risk of running out of inventory (a stockout) during lead time. The reorder point then increases by the amount of the safety stock:

$$ROP = \frac{\text{Expected demand}}{\text{during lead time}} + \text{Safety stock}$$

For example, if expected demand during lead time is 100 units, and the desired amount of safety stock is 10 units, then the ROP would be 110 units.

Figure 11–10 illustrates how safety stock can reduce the risk of a stockout during lead time (LT). Note that stockout protection is needed only during lead time.

Because it costs money to hold safety stock, a manager must carefully weigh the cost of holding safety stock against the reduction in stockout risk it provides. The customer *service level* increases as the risk of stockout decreases. **Service level** for this model can be defined as the probability that demand will not exceed supply during lead time (i.e., that the amount of stock on hand will be sufficient to meet lead time demand). Hence, a service level of 95 percent implies a probability of .95 that demand will not exceed supply during lead time. The risk of a stockout is the complement of service level; a service level of 95 percent implies a stockout risk of 5 percent. That is,

service level Probability that demand will not exceed supply during lead time.

Service level = 100 percent − Stockout risk

The amount of safety stock that is appropriate for a given situation should depend on the following factors:

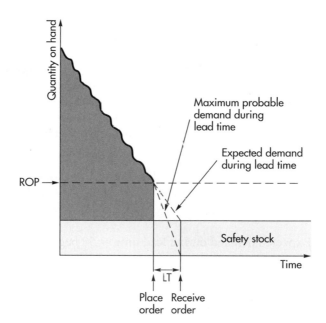

FIGURE 11-10

Safety stock reduces risk of stockout during lead time

1. Demand and lead time variability.
2. The desired service level.

Selection of a service level may reflect stockout costs (e.g., lost sales, customer dissatisfaction) or it might simply be a policy variable (e.g., the manager wants to achieve a specified service level for certain groups of SKUs).

Let us look at several models that can be used to determine ROP in cases when variability is present. The first model is used if an estimate of expected demand during lead time and its standard deviation are available. The formula is

$$\text{ROP} = \frac{\text{Expected demand}}{\text{during lead time}} + z\sigma_{d\text{LT}} \qquad (11\text{--}14)$$

where

$z =$ Safety factor; number of standard deviations above the expected demand

$\sigma_{d\text{LT}} =$ The standard deviation of demand during lead time

The models generally assume that any variability in demand rate or lead time can be adequately described by a Normal distribution. However, this is not a strict requirement; the models provide approximate reorder points even where actual distributions depart from Normal.

The value of z (see Figure 11--11) used in a particular instance depends on the stockout risk that the manager is willing to accept. Generally, the smaller the risk the manager

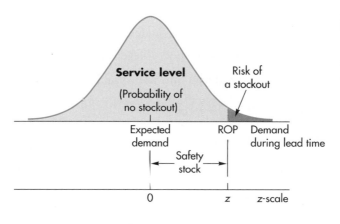

FIGURE 11-11

The ROP based on a Normal distribution of demand during lead time

is willing to accept, the greater the value of z. Use Appendix B, Table B to obtain the value of z, given a desired service level.

| **Example 8** | The manager of a Home Depot store has determined from historical records that demand for a type of bagged cement during its lead time could be described by a Normal distribution that has a mean of 50 bags and a standard deviation of 5 bags. Answer these questions, assuming that the manager is willing to accept a stockout risk of no more than 3 percent: |

    a. What value of z is appropriate?

    b. How much safety stock should be held?

    c. What reorder point should be used?

Solution

Expected demand during lead time = 50 bags

    $\sigma_{d\text{LT}}$ = 5 bags

    Risk = 3 percent

a. From Appendix B, Table B, using a service level of $1 - .03 = .97$, you obtain a value of $z = +1.88$.

b. Safety stock = $z\sigma_{d\text{LT}} = 1.88(5) = 9.40$ bags

c. ROP = Expected demand during lead time + Safety stock = $50 + 9.40 = 59.40$ bags

When data on demand during lead time are not readily available, Formula 11–14 cannot be used. Nevertheless, data are generally available on daily or weekly demand, and on the length of lead time. Using those data, a manager can determine whether demand and/or lead time is variable, and if variability exists in one or both, the related standard deviation(s). For those situations, one of the following formulas can be used:

If only demand is variable, then $\sigma_{d\text{LT}} = \sqrt{\text{LT}}\sigma_d$, and the reorder point is

$$\text{ROP} = \bar{d} \times \text{LT} + z\sqrt{\text{LT}}\sigma_d \tag{11–15}$$

where

    $\bar{d}$ = *Average* daily or weekly demand

    σ_d = Standard deviation of daily or weekly demand

    LT = Lead time in days or weeks

If only lead time is variable, then $\sigma_{d\text{LT}} = d\sigma_{\text{LT}}$, and the reorder point is

$$\text{ROP} = d \times \overline{\text{LT}} + zd\sigma_{\text{LT}} \tag{11–16}$$

where

    d = Daily or weekly demand

    $\overline{\text{LT}}$ = *Average* lead time in days or weeks

    σ_{LT} = Standard deviation of lead time in days or weeks

If both demand and lead time are variable, then it can be shown that

$$\sigma_{d\text{LT}} = \sqrt{\overline{\text{LT}}\sigma_d^2 + \bar{d}^2\sigma_{\text{LT}}^2}$$

and the reorder point is

$$\text{ROP} = \bar{d} \times \overline{\text{LT}} + z\sqrt{\overline{\text{LT}}\sigma_d^2 + \bar{d}^2\sigma_{\text{LT}}^2} \tag{11–17}$$

Note: Each of these models assumes that demands and lead times are *independent*.

Toyota's Parts Distribution and Information System

www.toyota.ca

Since there is very little that Toyota can do to shorten the distance between its manufacturing plants in Japan and its distribution centres in Canada and the U.S., it has invested in improving the speed of its ordering and distribution processes. Shipping cartons are bar-coded in Japan and information is pre-sent by electronic data interchange (EDI) to the main warehouse in Ontario, California. Approximately 32 sea-freight containers of inventory (approximately 19,000 line items) are received and tracked on a daily basis. Four hundred radio frequency data communication (RFDC) terminals mounted on forklifts and pallet jacks swap approximately 250,000 transmissions with a warehouse management system (WMS), which tells workers where to store the parts. The warehouse also receives orders by EDI and distributes approximately 37,000 line items to 1,400 dealers in the 11 regional centres throughout North America on a daily basis.

This streamlined process has reduced distribution lead times from 22–25 days to seven days, according to Charles Emery of Toyota's information systems staff. As well, the real-time inventory information provided by the new process has allowed the 11 regional centres to reduce their safety stock from three months to one month, and cross-docking of cartons (30 percent of the parts centre's receipts) allows the 760,000-square-foot warehouse to save space. Cross-docking is to prepare the received shipment for immediate distribution rather than placing it on racks, shelves, or bins.

The warehouse is divided into 12 zones—three made up of receiving, shipping, and cross-docking, and nine zones

managing a standard set of stock-keeping units (SKUs). Some 243,000 SKUs pass through the facility, which stores approximately 3.5 million parts at any one time.

For order picking, a worker scans a bar-coded assignment worksheet and radios the data to the WMS. All pertinent picking information (what items and how many units) is sent back to the worker's RFDC terminal. After the order picker gets to the bin/shelf location, the accuracy of pick is ensured by scanning the bar codes on the part and storage location. The items are then delivered to designated shipping lane.

By comparing the EDI information about receipts and the day's orders, the WMS determines which cartons should be moved to the cross-dock area where cartons and pallet loads are prepared for transport. Again, lift trucks with RFDC terminals handle the cross-dock cartons, updating the WMS with scanned data that are used to prepare the EDI message sent to each regional centre about the shipments.

Source: "Bar Codes, Wireless Terminals Cut Waste from Toyota's Supply Chain," *Modern Materials Handling* 53(2), February 1998, pp. S6–S7.

A wireless handheld Psion Teklogix Scanner.

Example 9

A restaurant uses an average of 50 jars of a special sauce each week. Weekly usage of sauce has a standard deviation of 3 jars. The manager is willing to accept no more than a 10 percent risk of stockout during lead time, which is two weeks. Assume the distribution of usage is Normal.

a. Which of the above formulas is appropriate for this situation? Why?

b. Determine the value of z.

c. Determine the ROP.

Solution

$\bar{d} = 50$ jars per week   LT = 2 weeks

$\sigma_d = 3$ jars per week   Acceptable risk = 10 percent, so service level is .90

a. Because only demand is variable (i.e., has a standard deviation), Formula 11–15 is appropriate.

b. From Appendix B, Table B, using a service level of .90, you obtain $z = +1.28$.

c. $\text{ROP} = \bar{d} \times \text{LT} + z\sqrt{\text{LT}}\sigma_d = 50 \times 2 + 1.28\sqrt{2}(3) = 100 + 5.43 = 105.43$ jars.

FIGURE 11-12

Demand during lead time

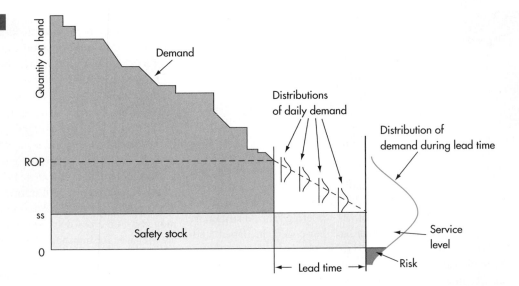

Comment. The logic of the three formulas for the reorder point may not be immediately obvious. The first part of each formula is the expected demand, which is the product of daily (or weekly) demand and the number of days (or weeks) of lead time. The second part of the formula is z times the standard deviation of demand during lead time. For the formula in which only demand is variable, daily (or weekly) demand is assumed to be Normally distributed and has the same mean and standard deviation (see Figure 11–12). The standard deviation of demand for the entire lead time is found by summing the *variances* of daily (or weekly) demands and then finding the square root of that number. Note that unlike variance, standard deviation is not additive. Hence, if the daily standard deviation is σ_d, the *variance* is σ_d^2, and if lead time is four days, the variance of demand during lead time will equal the sum of the four variances, which is $4\sigma_d^2$. The standard deviation of demand during lead time will be the square root of this, which is equal to $2\sigma_d$. In general, this becomes $\sqrt{LT}\sigma_d$ and, hence, the last part of Formula 11–15.

When only lead time is variable, the explanation is much simpler. The standard deviation of lead time demand is equal to the constant daily demand multiplied by the standard deviation of lead time.

When both demand and lead time are variable, the formula appears truly impressive. However, it is merely the result of squaring the standard deviations of the two previous formulas to obtain their variances, summing them, and then taking the square root.

Also note that average demand is usually estimated using forecast of demand, and standard deviation of demand is usually estimated using standard deviation of forecast error (square root of MSE or 1.25 × MAD).

Amount of Shortage and Annual Service Level

The ROP calculation does not reveal the expected *amount* of shortage for a given lead time service level. The expected number of units short can, however, be very useful to a manager. This quantity can easily be determined from the same information used to calculate the ROP, with one additional piece of information (see Table 11–3). Use of the table assumes that the distribution of demand during lead time can be adequately represented by a Normal distribution. If it can, the expected number of units short in each order cycle is given by this formula:

$$E(n) = E(z)\sigma_{d\text{LT}} \tag{11-18}$$

where

$E(n)$ = Expected number of units short per order cycle

$E(z)$ = Standardized expected number of units short obtained from Table 11–3

$\sigma_{d\text{LT}}$ = Standard deviation of demand during lead time

TABLE 11-3

Normal distribution service levels and standardized expected number short

z	Lead Time Service Level	E(z)	z	Lead Time Service Level	E(z)	z	Lead Time Service Level	E(z)	z	Lead Time Service Level	E(z)
−2.40	.0082	2.403	−.80	.2119	.920	.80	.7881	.120	2.40	.9918	.003
−2.36	.0091	2.363	−.76	.2236	.889	.84	.7995	.112	2.44	.9927	.002
−2.32	.0102	2.323	−.72	.2358	.858	.88	.8106	.104	2.48	.9934	.002
−2.28	.0113	2.284	−.68	.2483	.828	.92	.8212	.097	2.52	.9941	.002
−2.24	.0125	2.244	−.64	.2611	.798	.96	.8315	.089	2.56	.9948	.002
−2.20	.0139	2.205	−.60	.2743	.769	1.00	.8413	.083	2.60	.9953	.001
−2.16	.0154	2.165	−.56	.2877	.740	1.04	.8508	.077	2.64	.9959	.001
−2.12	.0170	2.126	−.52	.3015	.712	1.08	.8599	.071	2.68	.9963	.001
−2.08	.0188	2.087	−.48	.3156	.684	1.12	.8686	.066	2.72	.9967	.001
−2.04	.0207	2.048	−.44	.3300	.657	1.16	.8770	.061	2.76	.9971	.001
−2.00	.0228	2.008	−.40	.3446	.630	1.20	.8849	.056	2.80	.9974	.0008
−1.96	.0250	1.969	−.36	.3594	.597	1.24	.8925	.052	2.84	.9977	.0007
−1.92	.0274	1.930	−.32	.3745	.576	1.28	.8997	.048	2.88	.9980	.0006
−1.88	.0301	1.892	−.28	.3897	.555	1.32	.9066	.044	2.92	.9982	.0005
−1.84	.0329	1.853	−.24	.4052	.530	1.36	.9131	.040	2.96	.9985	.0004
−1.80	.0359	1.814	−.20	.4207	.507	1.40	.9192	.037	3.00	.9987	.0004
−1.76	.0392	1.776	−.16	.4364	.484	1.44	.9251	.034	3.04	.9988	.0003
−1.72	.0427	1.737	−.12	.4522	.462	1.48	.9306	.031	3.08	.9990	.0003
−1.68	.0465	1.699	−.08	.4681	.440	1.52	.9357	.028	3.12	.9991	.0002
−1.64	.0505	1.661	−.04	.4840	.419	1.56	.9406	.026	3.16	.9992	.0002
−1.60	.0548	1.623	.00	.5000	.399	1.60	.9452	.023	3.20	.9993	.0002
−1.56	.0594	1.586	.04	.5160	.379	1.64	.9495	.021	3.24	.9994	.0001
−1.52	.0643	1.548	.08	.5319	.360	1.68	.9535	.019	3.28	.9995	.0001
−1.48	.0694	1.511	.12	.5478	.342	1.72	.9573	.017	3.32	.9995	.0001
−1.44	.0749	1.474	.16	.5636	.324	1.76	.9608	.016	3.36	.9996	.0001
−1.40	.0808	1.437	.20	.5793	.307	1.80	.9641	.014	3.40	.9997	.0001
−1.36	.0869	1.400	.24	.5948	.290	1.84	.9671	.013			
−1.32	.0934	1.364	.28	.6103	.275	1.88	.9699	.012			
−1.28	.1003	1.328	.32	.6255	.256	1.92	.9726	.010			
−1.24	.1075	1.292	.36	.6406	.237	1.96	.9750	.009			
−1.20	.1151	1.256	.40	.6554	.230	2.00	.9772	.008			
−1.16	.1230	1.221	.44	.6700	.217	2.04	.9793	.008			
−1.12	.1314	1.186	.48	.6844	.204	2.08	.9812	.007			
−1.08	.1401	1.151	.52	.6985	.192	2.12	.9830	.006			
−1.04	.1492	1.117	.56	.7123	.180	2.16	.9846	.005			
−1.00	.1587	1.083	.60	.7257	.169	2.20	.9861	.005			
− .96	.1685	1.049	.64	.7389	.158	2.24	.9875	.004			
− .92	.1788	1.017	.68	.7517	.148	2.28	.9887	.004			
− .88	.1894	.984	.72	.7642	.138	2.32	.9898	.003			
− .84	.2005	.952	.76	.7764	.129	2.36	.9909	.003			

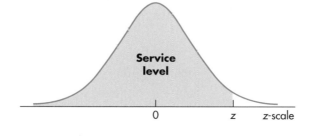

| **Example 10** | Suppose that the standard deviation of demand during lead time for an item is known to be 20 units and demand during lead time is approximately Normal. |

a. For a lead time service level of 90 percent, determine the expected number of units short for an order cycle.

b. What lead time service level would an expected shortage of 2 units imply?

Solution

$\sigma_{dLT} = 20$ units

a. Lead time (cycle) service level = .90. From Table 11–3, $E(z) = .048$. Using Formula 11–18, $E(n) = .048(20) = .96$, or about 1 unit.

b. For the case where $E(n) = 2$, you must solve for $E(z)$ and then use Table 11–3 to determine the lead time service level. Thus, $E(n) = E(z)\sigma_{dLT}$, so $E(z) = E(n)/\sigma_{dLT} = 2/20 = .100$. From Table 11–3, this implies a service level of approximately 81.5 percent (interpolating).

The expected number of units short is just that—an expected or *average* amount; the exact number of units short in any given cycle will be an amount close to that. Moreover, if discrete items are involved, the actual number of units short in any cycle will be an integer.

Having determined the expected number of units short for an order cycle, you can determine the expected number of units short per year. It is simply the expected number of units short per cycle multiplied by the number of cycles (orders) per year. Thus,

$$E(N) = E(n)\frac{D}{Q} \tag{11–19}$$

where

$E(N)$ = Expected number of units short per year

| **Example 11** | Given the following information, determine the expected number of units short per year. |

$$D = 1{,}000 \qquad Q = 250 \qquad E(n) = 2.5$$

Solution

Using the formula $E(N) = E(n)\dfrac{D}{Q}$,

$$E(N) = 2.5\left(\frac{1{,}000}{250}\right) = 10.0 \text{ units per year}$$

annual service level The percentage of demand filled directly from inventory during the whole year.

It is sometimes convenient to think of service level in annual terms. One definition of **annual service level** is the percentage of demand filled directly from inventory during the whole year. This is also known as the *fill rate*. Thus, if $D = 1{,}000$, and 990 units were filled directly from inventory (shortages totalling 10 units during the year were recorded), the annual service level (fill rate) would be $990/1{,}000 = 99$ percent. The annual service level and the lead time service level are related as follows. First, we have

$$SL_{annual} = 1 - \frac{E(N)}{D} \tag{11–20}$$

Using Formulas 11–19 and 11–18,

$$E(N) = E(n)\frac{D}{Q} = E(z)\sigma_{dLT}\frac{D}{Q}$$

Thus,

$$SL_{annual} = 1 - \frac{E(z)\sigma_{dLT}}{Q} \tag{11–21}$$

Given a lead time service level of 90 percent, $D = 1,000$, $Q = 250$, and $\sigma_{dLT} = 16$, determine (a) the annual service level, and (b) the amount of cycle safety stock that would provide an annual service level of .98.

Example 12

a. From Table 11–3, $E(z) = .048$ for a 90 percent lead time service level. Using Formula 11–21:

Solution

$$SL_{annual} = 1 - \frac{.048(16)}{250} = .997$$

b. Using Formula 11–21, and an annual service level of .98, solve for $E(z)$:

$$.98 = 1 - \frac{E(z)(16)}{250}$$

Solving, $E(z) = .312$. From Table 11–3, with $E(z) = .312$, you can see that this value of $E(z)$ is a little more than the value of .307. So it appears that an acceptable value of z might be .19. The necessary safety stock to achieve the specified annual service level is equal to $z\sigma_{dLT}$. Hence, the safety stock is .19(16) = 3.04, or approximately 3 units.

Note that in the preceding example, a lead time service level of 90 percent provided an annual service level of 99.7 percent. Naturally, different values of D, Q, and σ_{dLT} will tend to produce different results for a cycle service level of 90 percent. Nonetheless, the annual service level will always be greater than the cycle service level. In addition, since the annual service level or fill rate is often the measure used in practice, it makes sense to base cycle service level on a specified annual service level. This means first setting the annual level, next using Formula 11–21 to solve for $E(z)$, and then using Table 11–3 to obtain the service level for the order cycles.

A commonly used variation of the fixed-order-quantity/reorder point model is the min/max model—see the reading, "Min/Max Model" for a brief description.

FIXED-ORDER-INTERVAL MODEL

The **fixed-order-interval (FOI) model** is used when orders are placed at fixed time intervals (weekly, twice a month, etc.): Fixed-interval ordering is widely used by wholesale and retail businesses. The question to be answered at each order point is: How much should be ordered for the next (fixed) interval? If demand is variable, the order size will tend to vary from interval to interval. This is quite different from an EOQ/ROP model in which the order size remains fixed from cycle to cycle while the length of the cycle varies (shorter if demand is above average, and longer if demand is below average).

fixed-order-interval (FOI) model Orders are placed at fixed time intervals; usually all items from the same supplier are ordered at the same time.

In some cases, a supplier's policy might encourage orders at fixed intervals. Even when that is not the case, grouping orders for items from the same supplier can produce savings in ordering and shipping costs. Furthermore, some situations do not readily lend themselves to continuous monitoring of inventory levels. Many retail operations (e.g., small drugstores, small grocery stores) fall into this category. The alternative for them is to use fixed-interval ordering, which requires only periodic checks of inventory levels.

The order interval can be determined by minimizing total annual holding and ordering costs of all the SKUs received from a particular supplier. The complication is that there are two components to the ordering cost: the cost of issuing a purchase order and the cost of ordering each line item (SKU) in it. Also, not every SKU will be required at every order time. The calculation of the optimal order interval is complex and will be left to specialized inventory control books.

Determining the Amount to Order

If both the demand rate and lead time are constant, the fixed-order-interval model and the fixed-quantity (EOQ/ROP) model function identically. The differences in the two models become apparent only when examined under conditions of variability. Like ROP, the

FIGURE 11-13

Comparison of fixed-quantity (EOQ/ROP) and fixed-order-interval models

Fixed quantity (EOQ/ROP)

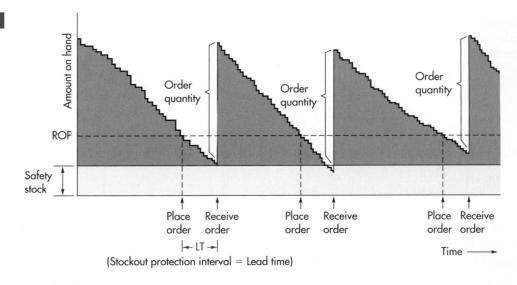

Fixed-order interval

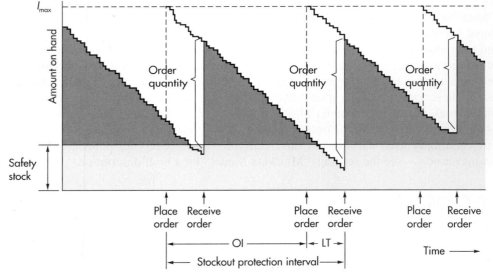

fixed-order-interval model can have variations in demand only, in lead time only, or in both demand and lead time. However, for the sake of simplicity and because it is perhaps the most frequently encountered situation, the discussion here will focus only on *variable demand* and *constant lead time case*.

Figure 11–13 provides a comparison of the fixed-quantity (EOQ/ROP) and fixed-order-interval models. In the fixed-quantity (EOQ/ROP) model, orders are triggered by a *quantity* (ROP), while in the fixed-order-interval model orders are triggered by a *time*. Therefore, the fixed-order-interval model must have stockout protection until the next order arrives (which is an order interval plus a lead time away), but the fixed-quantity (EOQ/ROP) model needs protection only during lead time because additional orders can be placed at any time and will be received shortly (lead time) thereafter. Consequently, there is a greater need for safety stock in the fixed-order-interval model than in the fixed-quantity (EOQ/ROP) model.

Order size Q in the fixed-order-interval model is determined as follows:

$$Q = I_{max} - \text{Amount on hand}$$

$$I_{max} = \begin{array}{c}\text{Expected demand} \\ \text{during protection} \\ \text{interval}\end{array} + \text{Safety stock}$$

$$= \bar{d}(\text{OI} + \text{LT}) + z\sigma_d\sqrt{\text{OI} + \text{LT}} \qquad (11\text{--}22)$$

where

OI = Order interval (length of time between orders)

I_{max} = Maximum amount of inventory (also called order-up-to-level point)

Note that I_{max} is fixed; so it does not have to be recalculated at each order time.

As in previous models, we assume that demand during the protection interval is Normally distributed.

Given the following information, determine the amount to order.

Example 13

$\bar{d}$ = 30 units per day   Desired service level = 99 percent

σ_d = 3 units per day   Amount on hand at reorder time = 71 units

LT = 2 days   OI = 7 days

z = 2.33 for 99-percent service level (from Appendix B, Table B)   *Solution*

$$I_{max} = \bar{d}(OI + LT) + z\sigma_d\sqrt{OI + LT}$$
$$= 30(7 + 2) + 2.33(3)\sqrt{7 + 2} = 291 \text{ units}$$

Amount to order = I_{max} − amount on hand = 291 − 71 = 220 units

---

Note that average demand is usually estimated using forecast of demand, and the standard deviation of demand is usually estimated using standard deviation of forecast error (square root of MSE or 1.25 × MAD).

Benefits and Disadvantages

When two or more items come from the same supplier, grouping orders can yield savings in ordering, packing, shipping costs, and paying invoices. Moreover, it may be the only practical approach if inventory withdrawals cannot be closely monitored.

On the negative side, the fixed-order-interval model necessitates a larger amount of safety stock for a given risk of stockout because of the need to protect against shortages during an entire order interval plus lead time (instead of lead time only), and this increases the holding cost.

Also note that not all items from the same supplier need to be ordered at each ordering opportunity. It might cost less to order some items every two, three, or more order intervals.

THE SINGLE-PERIOD MODEL

The **single-period model** (sometimes referred to as the *newsboy problem*) is used to handle ordering of perishables (e.g., fresh fruits and vegetables, baked goods, seafood, cut flowers) and other items that have a limited useful life (e.g., newspapers, magazines, spare parts for specialized equipment). The *period* for spare parts is the life of the equipment, assuming that the parts cannot be used for other equipment. What sets unsold or unused goods apart is that they are not typically carried over from one period to the next, at least not without penalty. Day-old baked goods, for instance, are often sold at reduced prices, leftover seafood may be discarded, and out-of-date magazines may be offered to used bookstores at bargain rates. There may even be some cost associated with disposal of leftover goods.

single-period model Model for ordering of perishables and other items with limited useful lives.

Analysis of single-period situations generally focuses on two costs: shortage and excess. Shortage cost may include a charge for loss of customer goodwill as well as the opportunity cost of lost sales. Generally, shortage cost is simply unrealized profit per unit. That is,

$$C_{shortage} = C_s = \text{Revenue per unit} - \text{Cost per unit}$$

excess cost Difference between purchase cost and salvage value of items left over at the end of a period.

We assume $C_s \geq 0$. If a shortage or stockout relates to an item used in production or to a spare part for a machine, then shortage cost refers to the actual cost of lost production.

Excess cost pertains to items left over at the end of the period. In effect, excess cost is the difference between purchase cost and salvage value. That is,

$$C_{\text{excess}} = C_e = \text{Original cost per unit} - \text{Salvage value per unit}$$

If there is cost associated with disposing of excess items, the salvage will be negative and will therefore *increase* the excess cost per unit. If salvage value is larger than original cost, then C_e will be negative. However, in this case $C_s + C_e > 0$ because salvage value is less than revenue per unit.

The goal of the single-period model is to identify the order quantity, or stocking level, that will minimize the long-run total excess and shortage cost.

There are two general categories of problems that we will consider: those for which demand can be approximated using a continuous distribution (perhaps a theoretical one such as Uniform or Normal distribution) and those for which demand can be approximated using a discrete distribution (say, historical frequencies or a theoretical distribution such as Poisson). The kind of inventory can indicate which type of model might be appropriate. For example, demand for liquids (such as petroleum, liquids, and gases) and items whose individual units are small but whose demand is large (such as muffins or cans of coke), tends to vary over some *continuous scale*, thus lending itself to description by a continuous distribution. Demand for tractors, cars, and computers is expressed in terms of the *number of units* demanded and lends itself to description by a discrete distribution.

Continuous Stocking Levels

The concept of identifying an optimal stocking level is perhaps easiest to visualize when demand is *Uniform*. Choosing the stocking level is similar to balancing a seesaw, but instead of a person on each end of the seesaw, we have excess cost per unit (C_e) on one end of the distribution and shortage cost per unit (C_s) on the other. The optimal stocking level is analogous to the fulcrum of the seesaw; the stocking level equalizes the cost weights, as illustrated in Figure 11–14. If actual demand exceeds S_o, there is shortage; hence, C_s is on the right end of the distribution. Similarly, if demand is less than S_o, there is excess, so C_e is on the left end of the distribution. When $C_e = C_s$, the optimal stocking level is halfway between the endpoints of the distribution. If one cost is greater than the other, S_o will be closer to the larger cost.

The *service level* is the *probability* that demand will not exceed the stocking level, and calculation of service level is the key to determining the optimal stocking level, S_o. It can be shown that in order to balance the seesaw on the fulcrum, service level should be chosen so that:

$$\text{Service level} = \text{SL} = \frac{C_s}{C_s + C_e} \tag{11–23}$$

where

$C_s = $ Shortage cost per unit

$C_e = $ Excess cost per unit

Then, optimal stocking level, S_o, can be easily determined from the demand distribution.

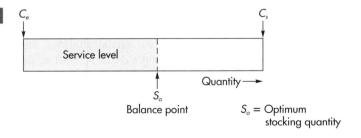

Muffins are delivered daily to Cindy's Cafeteria. Demand varies Uniformly between 30 and 50 muffins per day. Cindy pays 20 cents per muffin and charges 80 cents for it. Unsold muffins have no salvage value and cannot be carried over into the next day due to spoilage. Find the optimal stocking level and its stockout risk for that quantity.

Example 14

C_e = Cost per unit − Salvage value per unit

Solution

$\quad$ = $.20 − $0

$\quad$ = $.20 per unit

C_s = Revenue per unit − Cost per unit

$\quad$ = $.80 − $.20

$\quad$ = $.60 per unit

$$\text{SL} = \frac{C_s}{C_s + C_e} = \frac{\$.60}{\$.60 + \$.20} = .75$$

Thus, the optimal stocking level must satisfy demand 75 percent of the time. For the Uniform distribution, this will be at a point equal to the minimum demand plus 75 percent of the difference between maximum and minimum demands:

$$S_o = 30 + .75(50 − 30) = 45 \text{ muffins}$$

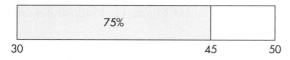

The stockout risk is $1.00 − .75 = .25$.

A similar approach can be applied when demand is Normally distributed.

Suppose the demand distribution for muffins in the previous example was approximately Normal with a mean of 40 per day and a standard deviation of 5 per day. Find the optimal stocking level for the muffins.

Example 15

Recall that C_s = $.60, C_e = $.20, and SL = .75

Solution

This indicates that 75 percent of the area under the Normal curve must be to the left of the stocking level. Appendix B, Table B shows that a value of z between +.67 and +.68, say, +.675, will satisfy this. Thus,

$$S_o = 40 + .675(5) = 43.375 \quad\quad \text{or 43 muffins.}$$

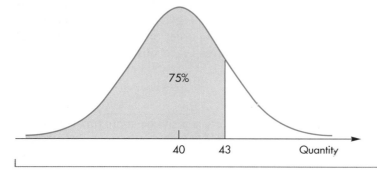

Discrete Stocking Levels

When stocking levels are discrete rather than continuous, the service level computed using the ratio $C_s/(C_s + C_e)$ usually does not coincide with a feasible stocking level (e.g., the optimal amount may be *between* five and six units). The optimal solution in this case

FIGURE 11-15

The service level for discrete stocking level must equal or exceed the ratio $C_s/(C_s + C_e)$

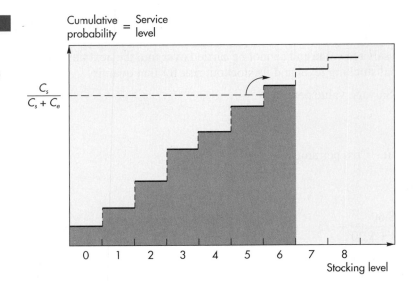

is to stock at the *next higher level* (e.g., six units). In other words, choose the stocking level so that the desired service level is equalled or *exceeded*. Figure 11–15 illustrates this concept.

| **Example 16** | Historical record on the use of a spare part for an old press serves as an estimate of usage for the spare in a similar new press. Stockout costs involve downtime expenses and special ordering costs. These average $4,200 per unit short. Spares cost $1,200 each, and unused parts have $400 salvage value. Determine the optimal stocking level. |

Number of Spares Used	Relative Frequency	Cumulative Frequency
0	.20	.20
1	.40	.60
2	.30	.90
3	.10	1.00
4 or more	.00	
	1.00	

Solution

$$C_s = \$4,200 \quad C_e = 1200 - 400 = \$800 \quad SL = \frac{C_s}{C_s + C_e} = \frac{\$4,200}{\$4,200 + \$800} = .84$$

The cumulative-frequency column indicates the percentage of time that demand was equal to or less than some amount. For example, demand $\le$ one spare 60 percent of the time, or two spares 90 percent of the time. Thus, in order to achieve a service level of 84 percent, it will be necessary to stock two spares (i.e., choose the higher stocking level).

| **Example 17** | Demand for long-stemmed red roses at a small flower shop can be approximated using a Poisson distribution that has a mean of four dozen per day. Profit on the roses is $3 per dozen. Leftover flowers are marked down and sold the next day at a loss of $2 per dozen. What is the optimal stocking level? |

$$C_s = \$3 \quad C_e = \$2 \quad SL = \frac{C_s}{C_s + C_e} = \frac{\$3}{\$3 + \$2} = .60$$

Solution

Obtain the cumulative probabilities from the Poisson table (Appendix B, Table C) for a mean of 4.0:

Demand (dozen per day)	Cumulative Probability
0	.018
1	.092
2	.238
3	.434
4	.629
5	.785
⋮	⋮

Compare the service level to the cumulative probabilities. Go down the table until cumulative probability just exceeds SL = .60. This is .629 which relates to 4 dozen (which is the average demand; *Note* C_s is almost equal to C_e).

SUMMARY

Inventory levels must be planned carefully in order to minimize the total cost of holding and ordering, but provide reasonable levels of customer service. Inventories serve different functions, including meeting seasonal demand, decoupling operations, protection against stockout, and allowing economic lot size. Successful inventory management requires a system to keep track of inventory transactions, accurate information about demand and lead times, realistic estimates of inventory costs, and a priority system for classifying the items in inventory and allocating control efforts.

Three classes of models are described: economic order quantity (EOQ)/reorder point (ROP), fixed-order-interval, and the single-period model. The first two are appropriate if unused items can be carried over into subsequent periods. The single-period model is appropriate when items cannot be carried over. EOQ models address the question of how much to order. They include the basic EOQ, economic production quantity, quantity discounts, and planned shortages models. The ROP models address the question of when to order and are particularly helpful in dealing with situations that include variations in either demand rate or lead time. They involve service level and safety stock considerations. When the time between orders is fixed, the fixed order-interval model is useful. The models presented in this chapter are summarized in Table 11–4.

KEY TERMS

A-B-C classification, 397
annual service level, 418
bar code, 395
cycle counting, 399
economic order quantity (EOQ), 399
excess cost, 422
fixed-order-interval (FOI) model, 419
fixed-order-quantity/reorder-point model, 395
holding (carrying) cost, 396
inventory, 391
inventory turnover, 394
ordering cost, 396

periodic counting, 395
perpetual tracking, 395
point-of-sale (POS) system, 396
purchase lead time, 396
quantity discounts, 407
reorder point (ROP), 412
safety stock, 412
service level, 412
setup, 396
shortage cost, 396
single-period model, 421
two-bin system, 395

Model	Formula		Symbols
1. Basic EOQ	$EOQ = Q_0 = \sqrt{\dfrac{2DS}{H}}$	(11–2)	Q_0 = Economic order quantity
	$TC = \dfrac{Q}{2}H + \dfrac{D}{Q}S$	(11–1)	D = Annual demand S = Ordering cost per order
	Length of order cycle $= \dfrac{Q_0}{D}$	(11–3)	H = Annual holding cost per unit
2. Economic production quantity	$Q_0 = \sqrt{\dfrac{2DS}{H}}\sqrt{\dfrac{p}{p-d}}$	(11–8)	Q_0 = Optimal run or order quantity p = Production rate
	$TC = \dfrac{I_{max}}{2}H + \dfrac{D}{Q}S$	(11–4)	d = Usage or demand rate I_{max} = Maximum inventory level
	Cycle length $= \dfrac{Q}{d}$	(11–5)	
	Run length $= \dfrac{Q}{p}$	(11–6)	
	$I_{max} = \dfrac{Q}{p}(p-d)$	(11–7)	
3. Quantity discounts	$TC = \dfrac{Q}{2}H + \dfrac{D}{Q}S + RD$	(11–9)	R = Unit price
4. Planned shortage	$Q_b = Q\left(\dfrac{H}{H+B}\right)$	(11–10)	Q_b = Quantity backordered in an order cycle
	$Q = \sqrt{\dfrac{2DS}{H}\left(\dfrac{H+B}{B}\right)}$	(11–12)	B = Annual backorder cost per unit
5. Reorder point under:			ROP = Quantity on hand at reorder point
a. Constant demand and lead time	$ROP = d(LT)$	(11–13)	d = Demand rate
b. Variable demand rate	$ROP = \bar{d}(LT) + z\sqrt{LT}(\sigma_d)$	(11–15)	LT = Lead time $\bar{d}$ = Average demand rate
c. Variable lead time	$ROP = d(\overline{LT}) + zd(\sigma_{LT})$	(11–16)	σ_d = Standard deviation of demand rate
d. Variable lead time and demand	$ROP = \overline{dLT} + z\sqrt{\overline{LT}\sigma_d^2 + \bar{d}^2\sigma_{LT}^2}$	(11–17)	z = Standard Normal deviate $\overline{LT}$ = Average lead time σ_{LT} = Standard deviation of lead time
6. Amount of shortage *a.* Units short per cycle	$E(n) = E(z)\sigma_{dLT}$	(11–18)	$E(n)$ = Expected number short per cycle
b. Units short per year	$E(N) = E(n)\dfrac{D}{Q}$	(11–19)	$E(z)$ = Standardized expected number short
c. Annual service level	$SL_{annual} = 1 - \dfrac{E(z)\sigma_{dLT}}{Q}$	(11–21)	σ_{dLT} = Standard deviation of demand during lead time $E(N)$ = Expected number short per year SL_{annual} = Annual service level
7. Fixed-order-interval	$Q = I_{max} - $ Amount on hand $I_{max} = \bar{d}(OI + LT) + z\sigma_d\sqrt{OI + LT}$	(11–22)	OI = Order interval I_{max} = Maximum inventory or order-up-to-level point
8. Single period	$SL = \dfrac{C_s}{C_s + C_e}$	(11–23)	SL = Service level C_s = Shortage cost per unit C_e = Excess cost per unit

TABLE 11–4

Summary of inventory formulas

Solved Problems

Basic EOQ. A toy manufacturer uses approximately 32,000 silicon chips annually. The chips are used at a steady rate during the 240 days a year that the plant operates. Annual holding cost is 60 cents per chip, and ordering cost is $24 per order. Determine:

a. The optimal order quantity.

b. The number of workdays in an order cycle.

Problem 1

D = 32,000 chips per year $\qquad S = \$24$

H = \$.60 per unit per year

Solution

a. $Q_0 = \sqrt{\dfrac{2DS}{H}} = \sqrt{\dfrac{2(32,000)\$24}{\$.60}} = 1,600$ chips.

b. $\dfrac{Q_0}{D} = \dfrac{1,600 \text{ chips}}{32,000 \text{ chips/yr}} = \dfrac{1}{20}$ year (i.e., $1/20 \times 240$ days), or 12 days.

Economic production quantity. The Dine Corporation is both a producer and a user of brass couplings. The firm operates 220 days a year and uses the couplings at a steady rate of 50 per day. Couplings can be produced at a rate of 200 per day. Annual holding cost is $1 per coupling, and machine setup cost is $35 per run.

Problem 2

a. Determine the economic production quantity.

b. Approximately how many runs per year will there be?

c. Calculate the maximum inventory level.

d. Determine the length of the *pure consumption* portion of the cycle.

D = 50 units per day $\times$ 220 days per year = 11,000 units per year

$S = \$35$

$H = \$1$ per unit per year

$p = 200$ units per day

$d = 50$ units per day

Solution

a. $Q_0 = \sqrt{\dfrac{2DS}{H}} \sqrt{\dfrac{p}{p-d}} = \sqrt{\dfrac{2(11,000)35}{1}} \sqrt{\dfrac{200}{200-50}} = 1,013$ units.

b. Number of runs per year: $D/Q_0 = 11,000/1,013 = 10.86$, or 11.

c. $I_{max} = \dfrac{Q_0}{p}(p-d) = \dfrac{1,013}{200}(200-50) = 759.75$ or 760 units.

d. Length of cycle $= \dfrac{Q_0}{d} = \dfrac{1,013 \text{ units}}{50 \text{ units per day}} = 20.26$ days

Length of run $= \dfrac{Q_0}{p} = \dfrac{1,013 \text{ units}}{200 \text{ units per day}} = 5.06$ days

$\begin{array}{l}\text{Length of pure} \\ \text{consumption portion}\end{array}$ = Length of cycle − Length of run

$= 20.26 - 5.06 = 15.20$ days.

Quantity discounts. A small manufacturing company uses roughly 3,400 kg of chemical dye a year. Currently the company purchases 300 kg per order and pays $3 per kg. The supplier has just announced that orders of 1,000 kg or more will be filled at a price of $2 per kg. The manufacturing firm incurs a cost of $100 each time it submits an order and assigns an annual holding cost of 17 percent of the purchase price.

Problem 3

a. Determine the order quantity that will minimize the total cost.

b. If the supplier offered the discount at 1,500 kg instead of 1,000 kg, what order quantity would minimize total cost?

Solution

$D = 3{,}400$ kg per year $S = \$100$ $H = .17R$

a. Calculate the EOQ for \$2 per kg

The quantity ranges are

Range	Unit Price
1 to 999	\$3
1,000+	\$2

$$Q_{\$2} = \sqrt{\frac{2DS}{H}} = \sqrt{\frac{2(3{,}400)100}{.17(2)}} = 1{,}414 \text{ kg}$$

Because this quantity falls in the \$2 per kg quantity range, it is optimal.

b. If the discount is offered at 1,500 kg, the EOQ for the \$2 per kg price is no longer feasible. Consequently, it becomes necessary to calculate the EOQ for \$3 per kg and compare the total annual cost for that order quantity with the total annual cost using the minimum price break quantity (i.e., 1,500).

$$Q_{\$3} = \sqrt{\frac{2DS}{H}} = \sqrt{\frac{2(3{,}400)100}{0.17(3)}} = 1{,}155 \text{ kg}$$

$$TC = \left(\frac{Q}{2}\right)H + \left(\frac{D}{Q}\right)S + RD$$

$$TC_{1,155} = \left(\frac{1{,}155}{2}\right).17(3) + \left(\frac{3{,}400}{1{,}155}\right)100 + 3(3{,}400)$$

$$= \$294{,}53 + \$294.37 + \$10{,}200 = \$10{,}789$$

$$TC_{1,500} = \left(\frac{1{,}500}{2}\right).17(2) + \left(\frac{3{,}400}{1{,}500}\right)100 + 2(3{,}400)$$

$$= \$255 + \$226.67 + \$6{,}800 = \$7{,}282$$

Because it would result in a lower total annual cost, 1,500 kg is the optimal order quantity (see the following figure).

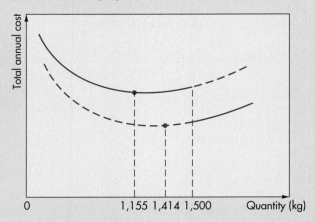

Problem 4

ROP for variable demand and constant lead time. The housekeeping department of a motel uses approximately 400 towels per day. The actual number tends to vary with the number of guests on any given night. Usage can be approximated by a Normal distribution that has a mean of 400 and a standard deviation of 9 towels per day. A linen services company washes the towels with a lead time of three days. If the motel policy is to maintain a stockout risk of 2 percent, what is the minimum number of towels that must be on hand at reorder time, and how much of that amount can be considered safety stock?

Solution

$\bar{d} = 400$ towels per day $LT = 3$ days

$\sigma_d = 9$ towels per day   Risk = 2 percent, so service level = 98 percent

From Appendix B, Table B, the z value that corresponds to an area under the Normal curve to the left of z for 98 percent is about $+2.055$.

$$\text{ROP} = \bar{d}\text{LT} + z\sqrt{\text{LT}}\sigma_d = 400(3) + 2.055\sqrt{3}(9)$$

$$= 1,200 + 32.03, \text{ or approximately } 1,232 \text{ towels}$$

Safety stock is approximately 32 towels.

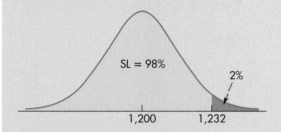

ROP for constant demand and variable lead time. The motel in the preceding example uses approximately 600 bars of soap each day, and this tends not to vary by more than a few bars either way. Lead time for soap delivery is Normally distributed with a mean of six days and a standard deviation of two days. A service level of 90 percent is desired. Find the ROP.

Problem 5

$\bar{d} = 600$ bars per day

$\text{SL} = 90$ percent, so $z = +1.28$ (from Appendix B, Table B)

$\overline{\text{LT}} = 6$ days

$\sigma_{\text{LT}} = 2$ days

$$\text{ROP} = \bar{d}\overline{\text{LT}} + zd(\sigma_{\text{LT}}) = 600(6) + 1.28(600)2$$

$$= 5,136 \text{ bars of soap}$$

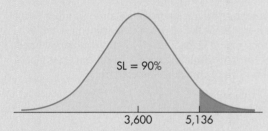

ROP for variable demand rate and variable lead time. The motel replaces broken glasses at a rate of 25 per day. In the past, this quantity has tended to vary Normally and has a standard deviation of 3 glasses per day. Glasses are ordered from a distant supplier. Lead time is Normally distributed with an average of 10 days and a standard deviation of 2 days. What ROP should be used to achieve a service level of 95 percent?

Problem 6

$\bar{d} = 25$ glasses per day $\overline{\text{LT}} = 10$ days

$\sigma_d = 3$ glasses per day $\sigma_{\text{LT}} = 2$ days

$\text{SL} = 95$ percent, so $z = +1.65$ (Appendix B, Table B)

Solution

$$\text{ROP} = \bar{d}\,\overline{\text{LT}} + z\sqrt{\overline{\text{LT}}\sigma_d^2 + \bar{d}^2\sigma_{\text{LT}}^2}$$

$$= 25(10) + 1.65\sqrt{10(3)^2 + (25)^2(2)^2} = 334 \text{ glasses}$$

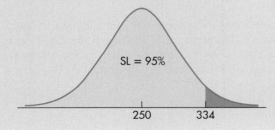

Problem 7

Amount of shortage and annual service level. The manager of a store that sells office supplies has decided to set an annual service level of 96 percent for a certain model of telephone answering equipment. The store sells approximately 300 of this model a year. Holding cost is $5 per unit annually, ordering cost is $25, and standard deviation of demand during lead time is 7.

a. What average number of units short per year will be consistent with the specified annual service level?

b. What average number of units short per cycle will provide the desired annual service level, assuming EOQ is used as order quantity?

c. What lead time service level is necessary for the 96-percent annual service level?

Solution

$SL_{annual} = 96$ percent $D = 300$ units $H = \$5$ $S = \$25$ $\sigma_{dLT} = 7$

a. $E(N) = (1 - SL_{annual}) D = (1 - .96)(300) = 12$ units.

b. First, we need to calculate the EOQ:

$$Q = \sqrt{\frac{2DS}{H}} = \sqrt{\frac{2(300)(25)}{5}} = 54.77 \text{ (round to 55)}$$

$E(N) = E(n)\dfrac{D}{Q}$. Solving for $E(n)$, you have

$$E(n) = E(N) \div \left(\frac{D}{Q}\right)$$

$$= 12 \div \left(\frac{300}{55}\right) = 2.2.$$

c. In order to find the lead time service level, you need the value of $E(z)$. Because the value of $E(n)$ is 2.2 and $E(n) = E(z)\sigma_{dLT}$, you have $2.2 = E(z)(7)$ or $E(z) = 2.2 \div 7 = .314$. Interpolating in Table 11–3 gives the approximate lead time service level of .57.

Problem 8

Fixed order-interval model. A lab orders a number of chemicals from the same supplier every 30 days. Lead time is five days. The assistant manager of the lab must determine how much of one of these chemicals to order. A check of stock revealed that eleven 25-mL jars are on hand. Daily usage of the chemical is approximately Normal with a mean of 15.2 mL and a standard deviation of 1.6 mL. The desired service level for this chemical is 95 percent.

a. What is the amount of safety stock of the chemical?

b. How many jars of the chemical should be ordered?

Solution

$\bar{d} = 15.2$ mL per day, OI = 30 days, SL = 95% or $z = 1.65$
$\sigma_d = 1.6$ mL per day, LT = 5 days, Amount on hand = 11 jars × 25 mL per jar = 275 mL

a. Safety stock $= z\sigma_d\sqrt{OI + LT} = 1.65(1.6)\sqrt{30 + 5} = 15.62$ mL.

b. Amount to order $= I_{max} -$ Amount on hand

$I_{max} = \bar{d}(OI + LT) + z\sigma_d\sqrt{OI + LT}$
$= 15.2(30 + 5) + 15.62 = 547.62$ mL

Amount to order $= 547.62 - 275 = 272.62$ mL

Convert this to number of jars:

$$\frac{272.62 \text{ mL}}{25 \text{ mL per jar}} = 10.90 \text{ or } 11 \text{ jars}$$

Problem 9

Single-period model. A company that installs cable TV systems uses a certain piece of equipment for which it carries two units of spare part. The part costs $500 and has no salvage value. Part failures can be modelled by a Poisson distribution with a mean of two failures during the useful life of the equipment. Estimate the range of shortage cost for which stocking two units of this spare part is optimal.

C_s is unknown $C_e = \$500$ *Solution*

The Poisson table (Appendix B, Table C) provides these values for a mean of 2.0:

Number of Failures	Cumulative Probability
0	.135
1	.406
2	.677
3	.857
4	.947
5	.983
⋮	⋮

For the optimal stocking level, the service level must be rounded up. Hence, you know that the service level must have been between .406 and .677 in order to make two units the optimal level. By setting the service level first equal to .406 and then to .677, you can establish bounds on the possible range of shortage cost.

$$\frac{C_s}{C_s + \$500} = .406, \text{ so } C_s = .406(\$500 + C_s)$$

Solving, you find $C_s = \$341.75$.

Similarly,

$$\frac{C_s}{C_s + \$500} = .677, \text{ so } C_s = .677(\$500 + C_s)$$

Solving, you find $C_s = \$1,047.99$. Hence, the range of shortage cost is \$341.75 to \$1,047.99.

DISCUSSION AND REVIEW QUESTIONS

1. What are the primary reasons for holding inventory?
2. What are the requirements for effective inventory management?
3. Briefly describe each of the costs associated with inventory.
4. Why might it be inappropriate to use inventory turnover ratios to compare inventory performance of companies that are in different industries?
5. How would you respond to the criticism that EOQ models tend to provide misleading results because values of *D*, *S*, and *H* are, at best, educated guesses?
6. Explain briefly how a higher holding cost can result in more frequent orders.
7. What is safety stock, and what is its purpose?
8. Under what circumstances would the amount of safety stock held be
   a. Large?   *b.* Small?   *c.* Zero?
9. What is meant by the term *service level*? Generally speaking, how is service level related to the amount of safety stock held?
10. Describe briefly the A-B-C classification.
11. The purchasing agent for a company that assembles and sells air-conditioning equipment in a Latin American country has noted that the cost of compressors has increased significantly each time they have reordered. What are the implications of this price escalation with respect to order size? What factors other than price must be taken into consideration?
12. Explain how a decrease in setup time can lead to a decrease in the average amount of inventory a company holds, and why that would be beneficial.
13. What is the single-period model, and under what circumstances is it appropriate?
14. Can the optimal stocking level in the single-period model ever be less than median (i.e., 50th percentile) demand? Explain briefly.
15. What are some ways that a company can reduce the need for inventories?
16. Why would any company intentionally plan for shortage? Give an example.

TAKING STOCK

1. What trade-offs are involved in each of these aspects of inventory management?
   a. Buying additional amounts to take advantage of quantity discounts.
   b. Conducting physical inventory counts once a quarter instead of once a year.
2. Who needs to be involved in inventory decisions?
3. How has technology aided inventory management?

CRITICAL THINKING EXERCISE

To be competitive, many fast-food chains began to expand their menus to include a wider range of foods. Although contributing to competitiveness, this has added to the complexity of operations, including inventory management. Specifically, why has the expansion of menu offerings created problems for inventory management?

INTERNET EXERCISES

1. Visit www.inventoryops.com, choose one of the topics below, find the relevant information in the Web page, and write a brief summary.
   a. Order picking methods
   b. RFID
2. Visit www.centor.ulaval.ca/MHMultimediaBank/general.asp, choose a category, click on "videos," pick a video and view it, and describe the equipment and its advantages.

PROBLEMS

1. The manager of an automobile repair shop hopes to achieve a better allocation of inventory control efforts by adopting A-B-C classification. Given the monthly usages in the following table, classify the items in A, B, and C categories according to monthly dollar value.

Item	Usage	Unit Cost
4021 ...	50	$1,400
9402 ...	300	12
4066 ...	40	700
6500 ...	150	20
9280 ...	10	1,020
4050 ...	80	140
6850 ...	2,000	15
3010 ...	400	20
4400 ...	7,000	25
2307 ...	1,958	14

2. The following table contains figures on the monthly volume and unit costs for a random sample of 15 items from a list of 2,000 inventory items at a health care facility.

Item	Unit Cost	Usage
K34	10	200
K35	25	600
K36	36	150
M10	16	25
M20	20	80
Z45	80	700
F14	20	300
F95	30	800
F99	20	60
D45	10	550
D48	12	90
D52	15	110
D57	40	120
N08	30	40
P05	16	500

   a. Develop an A-B-C classification for these items.
   b. How could the manager use this information?

   c. After reviewing your classification scheme, suppose that the manager decides to place item P05 into the A category. What are some possible explanations for this decision?

3. A large bakery buys flour in 25-kg bags. The bakery uses an average of 4,860 bags a year. Preparing an order and receiving a shipment of flour involves a cost of $10 per order. Annual holding cost is $5 per bag.

   a. Determine the economic order quantity.

   b. What is the average number of bags on hand?

   c. How many orders per year will there be?

   d. Calculate the total cost of ordering and holding flour.

   e. If ordering cost were to increase by 50 percent per order, what percentage would the EOQ change?

4. A large law firm uses an average of 10 packages of copier paper a day. Each package contains 500 sheets. The firm operates 260 days a year. Storage and handling costs for the paper are $1 a year per package, and it costs approximately $10 to order and receive a shipment of paper.

   a. What order quantity would minimize total annual ordering and holding costs?

   b. Calculate the total annual inventory cost using your order size from part *a*.

   c. Except for rounding, are annual ordering and holding costs always equal at the EOQ?

   d. The office manager is currently using an order quantity of 100 packages. The partners of the firm expect the office to be managed "in a cost-efficient manner." Would you recommend that the office manager use the optimal order quantity instead of 100 packages? Justify your answer.

5. Garden Variety Flower Shop uses 250 clay pots a month. The pots are purchased at $2 each. Annual holding cost is estimated to be 30 percent of purchase cost, and ordering cost is $20 per order. The manager has been using an order quantity of 250 flower pots.

   a. Calculate the EOQ.

   b. Calculate EOQ's total annual cost.

   c. What additional annual cost is the shop incurring by staying with the current order quantity?

6. A produce distributor uses 800 non-returnable packing crates a month, which it purchases at a cost of $5 each. The manager has assigned an annual holding cost of 25 percent of the purchase price per crate. Ordering cost is $28 per order. Currently the manager orders once a month. How much could the firm save annually in ordering and holding costs by using the EOQ?

7. Demand for an item is projected to be 100 units per month. The monthly holding cost is $2 per unit, and it costs an estimated $55 to process an order.

   a. Determine the EOQ.

   b. If the vendor is willing to offer the manager a discount of $10 *per order* for ordering in multiples of 50 units (e.g., 50, 100), would you advise the manager to take advantage of the offer? If so, what order quantity would you recommend?

   c. Alternatively, if demand can wait at the cost of $5 per unit per month, what should the order quantity and the maximum amount short per order cycle be?

8. A food processor uses approximately 27,000 non-returnable glass jars a month for its fruit juice product. Because of storage limitations, a lot size of 4,000 jars has been used. Monthly holding cost is one cent per jar, and ordering cost is $20 per order.

   a. What penalty is the company incurring by using its present order quantity?

   b. The manager would like to justify the present order quantity. One possibility is to simplify order processing to reduce the ordering cost. What ordering cost would enable the manager to justify current ordering?

9. The Friendly Sausage Factory (FSF) can produce European wieners at a rate of 500 kg per day. FSF supplies wieners to local stores and restaurants at a steady rate of 100 kg per day. The cost to prepare the equipment for producing wieners is $12. Annual holding cost is $4 per kg of wiener. The factory operates 300 days a year. Find

   a. The optimal run quantity.

   b. The number of runs per year.

   c. The length (in days) of a run.

10. A chemical company produces sodium bisulfate in 100-kg bags. Demand for this product is 20 tonnes per day. The capacity for producing the product is 50 tonnes per day. Setup costs are $400, and storage and handling costs are $200 per tonne a year. The company operates 200 days a year. (Note: 1 tonne = 1,000 kg.)

  a. How many bags per run are optimal?
  b. What would the average inventory be for this lot size?
  c. Determine the approximate length of a production run, in days.
  d. About how many runs per year would there be?
  e. How much could the company save annually if the setup cost could be reduced to $200 per run?

11. A company is about to begin production of a new product. The manager of the department that will produce one of the components for the product wants to know how often the machine to be used to produce the item will be available for other work. The machine will produce the item at a rate of 200 units a day. Eighty units will be used daily in assembling the final product. The company operates five days a week, 50 weeks a year. The manager estimates that it will take almost a full day to get the machine ready for a production run, at a cost of $300. Inventory holding cost will be $10 per unit a year.

  a. What run quantity should be used to minimize total annual setup and holding cost?
  b. What is the length of a production run in days?
  c. During production, at what rate will inventory build up?
  d. If the manager wants to run another job between runs of this item, and needs a minimum of 10 days per cycle for the other work, will there be enough time?

12. A company manufactures hair dryers. It buys some of the components, but it makes the heating element, which it can produce at the rate of 800 per day. Hair dryers are assembled daily, 250 days a year, at a rate of 300 per day. Because of the disparity between the production and usage rates, the heating elements are periodically produced in batches of 2,000 units.

  a. Approximately how many *batches* of heating elements are produced annually?
  b. If production on a batch begins when there is no inventory of heating elements on hand, how much inventory will be on hand *two days later*?
  c. What is the average inventory of the element, assuming each production cycle begins when there are none on hand?
  d. The same equipment that is used to make the heating element could also be used to make a component for another of the company's products. That job would require four days per cycle, including setup. Setup time for making a batch of the heating elements is a half day. Is there enough time to do this job between production of batches of heating element? Explain.

13. A mail-order company uses 18,000 boxes a year. Holding cost rate is 20 percent of unit cost a year, and ordering cost is $32 per order. The following quantity discounts are available. Determine:

  a. The optimal order quantity.
  b. The number of orders per year.

Number of Boxes	Price per Box
1,000 to 1,999	$1.25
2,000 to 4,999	1.20
5,000 to 9,999	1.15
10,000 or more	1.10

14. A jewellery manufacturer buys semi-precious stones to make bracelets and rings. The supplier quotes a price of $8 per stone for quantities of 600 stones or more, $9 per stone for orders of 400 to 599 stones, and $10 per stone for lesser quantities. The jewellery manufacturer operates 200 days per year. Usage rate is 25 stones per day, and ordering cost is $48 per order.

  a. If annual holding cost is 30 percent of unit cost, what is the optimal order size?
  b. If lead time is six working days, at what point should the company reorder?

15. A manufacturer of exercise equipment purchases pulleys from a supplier who lists these prices: less than 1,000, $5 each; 1,000 to 3,999, $4.95 each; 4,000 to 5,999, $4.90 each; and

6,000 or more, $4.85 each. Ordering cost is $50 per order, annual holding cost is 20 percent of purchase cost, and annual usage is 4,900 pulleys. Determine an order quantity that will minimize total cost.

16. A company will begin stocking remote control devices. Expected monthly demand is 800 units. The controllers can be purchased from either supplier A or supplier B. Their price lists are as follows:

SUPPLIER A		SUPPLIER B	
Quantity	Unit Price	Quantity	Unit Price
1–199	$14.00	1–149	$14.10
200–499	13.80	150–349	13.90
500+	13.60	350+	13.70

Ordering cost is $40 per order and annual holding cost is 25 percent of unit price. Which supplier should be used and what order quantity is optimal if the intent is to minimize total annual cost?

17. A manager just received a new price list for boxes from a supplier. It will now cost $1.00 a box for order quantities of 801 or more, $1.10 a box for 200 to 800, and $1.20 a box for smaller quantities. Ordering cost is $40 per order and holding cost rate is 40 percent of unit cost a year. The firm uses 3,600 boxes a year. The manager has suggested a "round number" order quantity of 800 boxes. The manager's rationale is that total annual inventory cost is U-shaped and fairly flat at its minimum. Therefore, the difference in total annual cost between 800 and 801 units would be small anyway. How would you reply to the manager's suggestion? What order quantity would you recommend?

18. A newspaper publisher uses roughly 800 metres (m) of baling wire each day to secure bundles of newspapers while they are being distributed to carriers. The paper is published Monday through Saturday. Lead time for purchase of wires is six workdays. What is the appropriate reorder point given that the company desires a service level of 95 percent? The stockout risk for various levels of safety stock are as follows: 1,500m, .10; 1,800m, .05; 2,100m, .02; and 2,400m, .01?

19. Given this information:

Expected demand during lead time = 300 units

Standard deviation of demand during lead time = 30 units

Determine each of the following, assuming that demand during lead time is distributed Normally:

a. The safety stock needed to attain a 1 percent risk of stockout during lead time.

b. Would a stockout risk of 2 percent require more or less safety stock than a 1 percent risk? Explain.

20. Given this information:

Expected demand during lead time = 600 kg

Standard deviation of demand during lead time = 52 kg

Acceptable stockout risk during during lead time = 4 percent

a. What amount of safety stock is appropriate?

b. When should this item be reordered?

21. Demand for vanilla ice cream at a grocery store can be approximated by a Normal distribution with a mean of 21 litres per week and a standard deviation of 3.5 litres per week. The new department manager desires a service level of 90 percent. Lead time from the producer is two days. The store is open seven days a week.

a. If the (EOQ, ROP) model is used, what ROP would be consistent with the desired service level?

b. If a fixed-order-interval model is used instead, what order quantity would be needed with an order interval of 7 days and 8 litres on hand at the order time?

c. Suppose that the department manager is using the (EOQ, ROP) model described in part *a*. One day after placing an order with the supplier, the manager receives a call from the supplier that the order will be delayed because of problems at the supplier's plant. The supplier promises to have the order there in two days. After hanging up, the manager checks the supply of vanilla ice cream and finds that 2 litres have been sold since the order was placed. Assuming that the supplier's promise is valid, what is the probability that the store will run out of this flavour before the shipment arrives?

22. The injection moulding department of a company uses an average of 30 litres of special lubricant a day. The supply of the lubricant is replenished when the amount on hand is 170 litres. It takes four days for an order to be delivered. The current stockout risk is 9 percent. What amount of safety stock would be needed if the acceptable risk of stockout is to be reduced to 3 percent?

23. A company uses 85 circuit boards a day in an assembly process. The person who orders the boards follows this rule: Order when the amount on hand drops to 625 boards. Orders are delivered approximately six days after being placed. The delivery time is Normal with a mean of six days and a standard deviation of 1.10 days. What is the probability that the supply of circuit boards will be exhausted before the order is received?

24. One item a computer store sells is supplied by a vendor who handles only that item. Demand for that item recently changed, and the store manager must determine when to replenish it. The manager wants a probability of at least 96 percent of not having a stockout during lead time. The manager expects demand to average a dozen units a day and have a standard deviation of two units a day. Lead time is variable, averaging four days with a standard deviation of one day. Assume demand during lead time is Normal. When should the manager reorder to achieve the desired probability?

25. The manager of a car wash has received a revised price list from the vendor who supplies soap, and a promise of a shorter lead time for deliveries. Formerly the lead time was four days, but now the vendor promises a reduction of 25 percent in that time. Annual usage of soap is 4,500 litres. The car wash is open 360 days a year. Assume that daily usage is Normal, and that it has a standard deviation of two litres per day. The ordering cost is $10 per order and annual holding cost rate is 40 percent of unit cost. The revised price list (cost per litre) is shown below.

Quantity	Unit Price
1–399	$2.00
400–799	1.80
800+	1.60

   a. What order quantity is optimal?

   b. What ROP is appropriate if the acceptable risk of a stockout is 1.5 percent?

26. Experience suggests that usage of copy paper at a small copy centre can be well approximated by a Normal distribution with a mean of five boxes per day and a standard deviation of one-half box per day. Two days are required to fill an order for paper. Ordering cost is $10 per order, and annual holding cost is $10 per box.

   a. Determine the economic order quantity, assuming 250 workdays a year.

   b. If the copy centre reorders when the paper on hand is 12 boxes, calculate the risk of a stockout.

   c. If a fixed-order-interval of seven days, instead of the (EOQ, ROP), is used for reordering, what shortage risk does the copy centre incur if it orders 36 boxes when the amount on hand is 12 boxes?

27. Ned's Natural Foods sells unshelled peanuts by the kilogram. Historically, Ned has observed that daily demand is Normally distributed with a mean of 8 kg and a standard deviation of 1 kg. Lead time also appears Normally distributed with a mean of eight days and a standard deviation of one day.

   a. What ROP would provide stockout risk of 10 percent during lead time?

   b. What is the associated expected number of units (kg) short per cycle?

28. A supermarket is open 360 days per year. Daily use of cash register tape averages 10 rolls. Usage appears Normally distributed with a standard deviation of two rolls per day. The cost of ordering tapes is $10 per order, and holding cost is 40 cents per roll a year. Lead time is three days.

   a. What is the EOQ?

   b. What ROP will provide a lead time service level of 96 percent?

   c. What is the expected number of units short per cycle with 96 percent lead time service level? Per year?

   d. What is the annual service level?

29. A service station uses 1,200 cases of oil a year. Ordering cost is $20 per order, and annual holding cost is $3 per case. The station owner has specified an *annual* service level of 99 percent.

  a. What is the EOQ?

  b. What level of safety stock is appropriate if demand during lead time is Normally distributed with a mean of 80 cases and a standard deviation of 5 cases?

  c. What is the risk of a stockout during lead time?

30. A school bus depot operates 250 days a year. Daily demand for diesel fuel at the depot is Normal with an average of 250 litres and a standard deviation of 14 litres. Holding cost for the fuel is $.30 per litre per year, and it costs $10 in administrative time to submit an order for more fuel. It takes one day to receive a delivery of diesel fuel.

  a. Calculate the EOQ.

  b. Determine the amount of safety stock that would be needed if the manager wants

    i. An annual service level of 99.5 percent.

    ii. The expected amount of fuel short per order cycle to be less than 5 litres.

31. A drugstore uses fixed order-interval model for many of the items it stocks. The manager wants a service level of .98. Determine the order size for the items in the following table if the order interval is 14 days and lead time is 2 days:

Item	Average Daily Demand	Daily Standard Deviation	Quantity on Hand
K033	60	5	420
K144	50	4	375
L700	8	2	160

32. A manager must set up inventory ordering systems for two new production items, P34 and P35. P34 can be ordered at any time, but P35 can only be ordered once every four weeks. The company operates 50 weeks a year, and the weekly usage rates for both items are Normally distributed. The manager has gathered the following information about the items:

	Item P34	Item P35
Average weekly demand	60 units	70 units
Standard deviation	4 units per week	5 units per week
Unit cost	$15	$20
Annual holding cost	30%	30%
Ordering cost per order	$70	$30
Lead time	2 weeks	2 weeks
Acceptable cycle stockout risk	2.5%	2.5%

  a. When should the manager reorder P34?

  b. Calculate the order quantity for P34.

  c. Calculate the order quantity for P35 if 110 units are on hand at the time the order is placed.

33. Given the following list of items,

  a. Classify the items as A, B, or C.

  b. Determine the economic order quantity for each item.

Item	Estimated Annual Demand	Ordering Cost	Holding Cost (%)	Unit Price
H4-010	20,000	50	20	2.50
H5-201	60,200	60	20	4.00
P6-400	9,800	80	30	28.50
P6-401	16,300	50	30	12.00
P7-100	6,250	50	30	9.00
P9-103	4,500	50	40	22.00
TS-300	21,000	40	25	45.00
TS-400	45,000	40	25	40.00
TS-041	800	40	25	20.00
V1-001	26,100	25	35	4.00

34. Demand for jelly doughnuts on Saturdays at Don's Doughnut Shoppe is shown in the following table. Determine the optimal number of doughnuts, in dozens, to make each Saturday morning if labour, materials, and overhead are estimated to be $3.20 per dozen, doughnuts are sold for $4.80 per dozen, and leftover doughnuts at the end of each day are sold the next day at half price. What is the *resulting* service level?

Demand (dozens)	Relative Frequency
19	.01
20	.05
21	.12
22	.18
23	.13
24	.14
25	.10
26	.11
27	.10
28	.04
29	.02

35. A public utility intends to buy a turbine as part of an expansion plan and must now decide on the number of spare parts to order. One part, no. X135, can be purchased for $100 each. Holding and disposal costs are estimated to be 145 percent of the purchase price over the life of the turbine. A stockout would cost roughly $8,000 due to downtime, ordering, and "special purchase" factors. Historical records based on the performance of similar equipment operating under similar conditions suggest that demand for the spare part will tend to approximate a Poisson distribution with a mean of 3.2 units for the useful life of the turbine.

    a. What is the optimal number of units of this spare part to order?

    b. Carrying six spare parts would be the best strategy for what range of shortage cost?

36. Skinner's Fish Market buys fresh tuna daily for $4.20 per kg and sells it for $5.70 per kg. At the end of each day, any remaining tuna is sold to a producer of cat food for $2.40 per kg. Daily demand can be approximated by a Normal distribution with a mean of 80 kg and a standard deviation of 10 kg. What is the optimal stocking level?

37. A small grocery store sells fresh produce, which it obtains from local farmers. During the strawberry season, demand for fresh strawberries can be reasonably approximated using a Normal distribution with a mean of 40 litres per day and a standard deviation of 6 litres per day. Excess costs is 35 cents per litre. The grocer orders 49 litres per day.

    a. What is the implied cost of shortage per litre?

    b. Why might this be a reasonable figure?

38. Demand for devil's food whipped-cream layer cake at a local pastry shop can be approximated using a Poisson distribution with a mean of six per day. The manager estimates it costs $9 to prepare each cake. Fresh cakes sell for $12. Day-old cakes sell for $7 each. What stocking level is appropriate?

39. Burger Prince buys top-grade ground beef for $3 per kg. A large sign over the entrance guarantees that the meat is fresh daily. Any leftover meat is sold to the local high school cafeteria for $2 per kg. Eight hamburgers can be prepared from each kilogram of meat. Burgers sell for $2 each. Labour, overhead, meat, buns, and condiments cost $1 per burger. Demand is Normally distributed with a mean of 400 kg per day and a standard deviation of 50 kg per day. What daily order quantity is optimal?

40. Daily demand for rug-cleaning machines at Clyde's U-Rent-It is shown in the following table. Machines are rented by the day only. Profit on a rug cleaner is $10 per day. Clyde has four rug-cleaning machines.

Demand	Frequency
0	.30
1	.20
2	.20
3	.15
4	.10
5	.05
	1.00

a. Assuming that Clyde's stocking decision is optimal, what is the implied range of excess cost per machine per day?

b. Your answer from part *a* has been presented to Clyde, who protests that the amount is too low. Does this suggest an increase or a decrease in the number of rug machines he stocks? Explain.

41. A manager is going to purchase new processing equipment and must decide on the number of spare parts to order with the new equipment. The spares cost $200 each, and any unused spares will have an expected salvage value of $50 each. The probability of usage of parts can be described by the following distribution:

Number	0	1	2	3
Probability	.10	.50	.25	.15

If a part fails and a spare is not available, it will take two days to obtain a replacement and install it. The cost for idle equipment is $500 per day. What quantity of spares should be ordered?

42. A Las Vegas supermarket bakery must decide how many wedding cakes to prepare for the upcoming weekend. Cakes cost $33 each to make, and they sell for $60 each. Unsold cakes are reduced to half-price on Monday, and typically one-third of those are sold. Any that remain are donated to a nearby senior centre. Analysis of recent demand resulted in the following table:

Demand	0	1	2	3
Probability	.15	.35	.30	.20

How many cakes should be prepared to maximize expected profit?

43. The South Texas Center for Pediatric Care in San Antonio wants to reduce its inventory replenishment costs. The Center carries vaccines (e.g., for whooping cough), non-injectable medical supplies (such as examining-table paper, alcohol swabs, tongue depressors), and office supplies (stationery, paper, and forms). Out of the 113 inventory items, the seven vaccines account for approximately 70 percent of annual dollar value of $225,000. Approximately 210 whooping cough vaccines are needed per month. An office manager spends a total of approximately one half-hour finding out how much inventory of whooping cough vaccine is on hand and actually placing an order. She is paid approximately $17 an hour. The cost of capital for the centre is 8 percent per year, and the storage cost (including freezers for some items) are estimated to be approximately 8 percent of item cost per year. A lot of 10 whooping cough vaccines costs an average of $160.[2]

a. Calculate the EOQ for whooping cough vaccines.

b. Suppose that the purchase lead time is two days and daily demand for whooping cough vaccines is Normally distributed with a mean of seven vaccines and a standard deviation of two vaccines. Calculate the reorder point if a service level of 98 percent is desired.

c. Suppose that the office manager wants to make the replenishment of whooping cough vaccines easier for herself by ordering them every two weeks.
   i. Using the information in part *b*, what should the order-up-to-level point (I_{max}) be?
   ii. Suppose that the Center has 34 whooping cough vaccines on hand. What should the order quantity be, given your answer to (i)?

---

[2]D. M. Burns, M. J. Cote, and S. L. Tucker, "Inventory Analysis of a Pediatric Care Center," *Hospital Materiel Management Quarterly* 22(3), February 2001, pp. 84–90.

44. The owner of a health food store has decided to intentionally allow shortage of a food supplement. The annual demand is 500 bottles, the ordering cost is $10 per order, and the holding cost is $1 per bottle per year. Cost of back-ordering one bottle is estimated to be $10 per bottle per year.

    a. What should the order quantity be?

    b. How many bottles will be short per order cycle?

45. Hallmark[3] sells "personal expression" cards and gifts worldwide through either their own stores or other retailers. Hallmark was founded over 100 years ago in Kansas City, and now has over $4.4 billion of sales per year (www.hallmark.com). Hallmark introduces thousands of new products each year based on current social interests. Most products are single runs. Unsold products are either discounted and sold to discount retailers, or are discarded. In the 1980s, Hallmark had very high volumes of unsold products. Order/production quantities were determined based on sale of similar products in the past. Demand was forecasted and used without consideration of its variability. Also, salvage and shortage costs were ignored. Hallmark brought in a consultant to teach the product managers, and inventory controllers and managers how to use the single-period (newsboy) ordering model.

    A typical problem Hallmark faces is as follows: A Barbie Stationary Gift set, containing 16 notes, envelopes, and foil seals, is to be produced and marketed to celebrate the 45th year of Barbie. The price will be set at $12.99 per unit. The cost of production to Hallmark will be approximately $6 per unit. The product manager, based on previous sales of Barbie stationery products, estimates that demand and its probability for this product will be as follows:

Demand (in 1000s)	90	100	110	120	130
Probability	.1	.2	.4	.2	.1

    Any units not sold through regular channels will be sold to discount retailers at $1 less than cost (i.e., $5 per unit). There is no penalty cost for being short. Determine the optimal order quantity for the Barbie Stationery Gift set.

46. Cominco[4] is a Canadian metal mining and processing company with mines in B.C., Quebec, Alaska, Washington, and Peru, and processing (smelting) plants in Trail (B.C.) and Peru. Cominco's revenue is mainly derived from zinc and copper. In 2001, Teck-Hughes Gold Mines Ltd. and Cominco merged to form Teck-Cominco. They also started coal production in 2003 through Elk Valley Coal Partnership. The company runs two warehouses in Trail to store thousands of parts and supplies for the machines and equipment used in its mines and operations in western Canada and Alaska. Until a few years ago, the stocks in the warehouses were controlled using an IBM mainframe computer and IBM application software called Inventory Management Program and Control Techniques, IMPACT. IMPACT keeps track of each part, its usage (withdrawal from the warehouse) over time, and triggers replenishment (addition to the warehouse) from the suppliers. IMPACT determines the reorder point (and the size of next order) primarily based on the forecast for usage of the part in the future. The forecasting technique used is Exponential Smoothing. For each inventoried part the smoothing constant is found by trial and error. For the order quantity, IMPACT uses the Economic Order Quantity (EOQ). The new version of IMPACT, called INFOREM, is used by many companies such as Federated Cooperatives Ltd. and Mark's Work Wearhouse.

    For illustration, consider a specific part which is kept in stock. The following data is the usage of the part during a nine-month period:

Jan	Feb	Mar	Apr	May	Jun	Jul	Aug	Sep
2	5	10	4	12	0	8	16	4

    Suppose that now is the end of September and the next reorder point is coming up. Using Exponential Smoothing with $\alpha = 0.2$, the forecast for October will be 6.7 units. The part costs Cominco $15/unit. Holding cost rate is 20 percent of unit cost per year. Ordering cost is $2/order. Purchase lead-time for this part is 20 days. Assume 30 days in a month.

---

[3]Based on F. H. Barron, "Payoff Matrices Pay off at Hallmark," *Interfaces* 15(4), July/August 1985, pp. 20–25.
[4]K. B. Hustwick and J. W. Merkley, "Cominco's Computerized Inventory Control System," *Canadian Institute of Mining Bulletin*, July 1982.

a. What should the EOQ be? *Hint*: Use the forecast for October $\times$ 12 to estimate next year's demand.

b. For how many days is the EOQ enough (time supply)?

c. Calculate the total annual inventory cost of the EOQ.

d. Suppose now this part is ordered once a month. How much more expensive is this?

e. Suppose there was no variability in demand or lead-time. Determine the reorder point.

f. Suppose a 95 percent service level is required. From the forecasting module, the standard deviation of monthly demand = 5.14 units. Determine the reorder point.

47. Federated Cooperatives Limited (FCL) is the largest wholesaler/distributor of food and hardware in western Canada. FCL uses the Inforem forecasting and inventory software and the fixed-order-interval model to order products to its four warehouses. As illustration, consider the ordering of Energizer batteries. Based on experience, FCL orders Energizer batteries every 14 days. The purchase lead time is approximately 15 days. Consider one type of energizer battery, the 6V lantern battery, item #0378422CA in FCL's stock. The demand last year for this battery was 5,767 units and the unit cost was $3.85. The forecasted demand for this battery is 138 units per week for the next few weeks and the standard deviation of demand is estimated to be 37 units per week. Currently there are 555 units on hand in the warehouse. The service level for batteries is desired to be 98.5 percent.

a. Calculate the I_{max} (order up-to-level point) for this battery.

b. Determine the quantity to order.

c. If the demand forecast for the next five weeks was 144.2, 144.2, 133.1, 133.1, and 122 units, respectively, how would your answer to part a change? Assume that the standard deviation of demand remains at 37 units per week.

48. Sterling Pulp Chemicals in Saskatoon produces chemicals for processing of pulp such as caustic soda. In its maintenance warehouse, it keeps all the spare parts for its equipment as well as supplies such as light bulbs. For inventory control, it uses a Min/Max model which is basically the (EOQ, ROP) model. Every day, the computer system identifies those stock which have reached their minimum (ROP) level, and the inventory staff orders those items. For illustration, consider the usage of item #14-46-506: four-foot supersaver fluorescent light bulbs in Sterling Pulp Chemicals in the first ten months of 1998: 10, 10, 66, 32, 34, 18, 24, 9, 14, and 48. The forecast for November using Exponential Smoothing with α = .3 is 27.48 units, and the standard deviation of monthly demand for these bulbs is 18.84 units. The lead time from the supplier, EECOL Electric, is 14 days, and the unit cost is $1.40. Holding cost rate for Sterling is estimated to be 20 percent of unit cost per year and ordering cost $1 per order. Assume 30 days in a month.

a. Calculate the EOQ for this item. (*Hint*: D = forecast for November $\times$ 12.)

b. For how many months is the EOQ enough (time supply)?

c. Calculate the total annual inventory cost of the EOQ.

d. Suppose now this part is ordered once every two months. How much more costly is this?

e. Calculate the reorder point of these bulbs. Use a 95 percent service level.

f. Suppose that the fixed-order-interval model is used to order these bulbs. Given an order interval of two months, calculate the order up-to-the-level point (I_{max}) for these bulbs. Use a 95 percent service level.

49. The usage of a Male Cord End (#4867), purchased from EECOL Electric Ltd, by Sterling Pulp Chemicals during the June to October period of 1998 were: 5, 1, 5, 9, and 8. Using Exponential Smoothing with α = .5, the forecast usage for November can be shown to be 7.25 units, and the standard deviation of monthly usage, using the above numbers, can be shown to be 3.13 units. The price of one unit is $2.48. Suppose Sterling uses 20 percent as its holding cost rate per year, purchase lead time is approximately 14 days, and desired service level is 95 percent. Assume 30 days in a month.

a. If this item is ordered individually using the (EOQ, ROP) model, and ordering cost is $1 per order, calculate the ROP and the EOQ for it.

b. If this item is ordered as part of a group of items from EECOL once a month, and currently there are 13 units on hand, how many should be ordered?

50. A franchisee of Fuddruckers,[5] a hamburger restaurant chain based in Texas, has contracted to supply food for a day-long music festival. Fuddruckers distinguishes itself from other hamburger joints with on-premise butcher shop and bakery. Fuddruckers' only Canadian restaurant is located in Saskatoon. It is now the Wednesday before the Saturday festival. Approximately 5,000 tickets have been sold so far, and this number should increase because it is predicted that Saturday will be sunny. The manager, based on previous experience, believes that the eventual number of people who will attend the festival, and the associated probabilities, are:

Numbers	6,000	7,000	8,000	9,000	10,000
Probability	.1	.2	.4	.2	.1

The manager expects that on average, each person will eat one meal during the seven-hour festival. She has decided to limit the menu to just two meals: one-third-pound burgers and quarter-pound hot dogs. She estimates, based on regular restaurant sales, that 60 percent of people will buy the burger and 40 percent will buy the hotdog. The cost of one burger will be $2.25 and it will sell for $5, whereas the hot dog will cost $1.34 and will sell for $4. Unused food has to be discarded, and there is no penalty for being short. The meat, hot dogs, buns, and vegetables need to be ordered today (three days before the festival so that they will arrive the day before the festival). Determine the optimal order quantities for burgers and hotdogs.

MINI-CASE

Bike Friday

www.bikefriday.com

Bike Friday is a small manufacturer of high-end folding travel bicycles located in Eugene, Oregon. The bikes can be folded and carried in a suitcase. In the late 1990s, the controller of Bike Friday was looking into ways to cut costs. At that time, they purchased the suitcases in lot sizes of 100, at a unit price of $65 plus $4.50 for shipping expense. A lot would last a little more than one month. The purchase lead time was six to eight weeks. The controller discovered that if they ordered a full truckload of 500 suitcases at a time, the unit price would be $50 plus $2.50 for shipping expense. However, Bike Friday would need a bigger storage space (350 square feet) which was not available in-house. Assuming that a nearby storage space could be leased for $400 a month, holding cost rate of 20 percent per unit per year, and order cost of $50 per order, determine if buying a truckload of suitcases would have a lower total cost.

Sources: G. A. Horsfall, "How to Leverage a Bad Inventory Situation," *Hospital Materiel Management Quarterly* 20(2), November 1998, pp. 40–46; www.bikefriday.com.

MINI-CASE

Alberta Wheat Pool

Alberta Wheat Pool (AWP, now part of Agricore United) sells chemicals and seeds to Alberta farmers and buys their grains. The chemicals are sold at several elevators which are located near the farms. Before the 1990s, each elevator manager (approximately 300) independently made decisions about the amount of chemicals they needed during the coming year. Because the elevator manager was only evaluated based on sales, he ordered the maximum probable amount. Excess chemicals were transported back to a heated regional warehouse.

---

[5] Based on S. M. Shafer, "Fuddruckers and the Crystal Coast Music Festival," *Case Research Journal* 22(2), 2002.

In the early 1990s, AWP changed the performance measure in order to cut costs of excess transportation and holding costs over the winter. A position was created: Coordinator of Regional Finance and Accounting to assist with coordination across elevators. A tool used was the single-period (newsboy) inventory model which was to assist elevator managers make better decisions. To illustrate, consider the ordering of a particular herbicide by a specific elevator. Each unit weighs 50 kg. The selling price is $56.93 per unit, and the purchase price (including transportation cost) is $45.54. Any excess herbicide is transported to the Calgary Warehouse at the cost of $1.09 per unit. The holding cost rate is 10 percent of unit cost

per year, charged only for half a year (approximate length of winter). It is estimated that 10 percent of shortage will be lost. The rest incur $2.19 per unit in expediting cost from the Calgary warehouse. The elevator manager estimates that the demand for this herbicide can take values 100, 400, and 1,500 units with probabilities of .1, .5, and .4, respectively. What is the best order quantity?

Source: D. J. Raby et al., "Inventory Management of Chemical Supplies at Alberta Wheat Pool," *Production and Inventory Management Journal* 32(1), First Quarter, 1991, pp. 1–6.

UPD Manufacturing

UPD Manufacturing produces a range of health-care appliances for hospital as well as for home use. The company has experienced a steady demand for its products, which are highly regarded in the health-care field. Recently the company has undertaken a review of its inventory ordering procedures as part of a larger effort to reduce costs.

One of the company's products is a blood-pressure testing kit. UPD manufactures all of the components for the kit in-house except for the digital display unit. The display units are ordered at six-week intervals from the supplier. This ordering system began about five years ago, because the supplier insisted on it. However, that supplier was bought out by another supplier about a year ago, and the six-week ordering requirement is no longer in place. Nonetheless, UPD has continued to use the six-week ordering policy. According to

purchasing manager Tom Chambers, "Unless somebody can give me a reason for changing, I'm going to stick with what we've been doing. I don't have time to reinvent the wheel."

Further discussions with Tom revealed a cost of $32 to order and receive a shipment of display units from the supplier. The company assembles 89 kits a week. Also, information from Sara James in Accounting indicated a weekly holding cost of $.08 for each display unit.

The supplier has been quite reliable with deliveries; orders are received five working days after they are faxed to the supplier. Tom indicated that as far as he was concerned, lead time variability is virtually nonexistent. Assume the company works 50 weeks a year.

Question
Would using an order interval other than every six weeks reduce costs? If so, what order interval would be best, and what order size would that involve?

Mark's Work Wearhouse

www.marks.com

From genteel downtown Toronto to the oil fields of Alberta, Mark's Work Wearhouse caters to customers with very different definitions of work wear.

"We're fashion followers, not fashion leaders," comments Colin Laker, VP of systems. We let the customers decide what we should be stocking in our stores. In downtown Toronto, work wear is khaki pants and a golf shirt, but in the oil fields

around Edmonton, guys will jump out of pickups covered head-to-foot in oil in search for new clothes.

We call ourselves a pull organization. We allow the stores to reorder basic commodities. We want them to do that because we want our stores to reflect Canada's regional differences. We sell a lot more rainwear in Vancouver than we do in Saskatoon.

Sizes also vary regionally. Mark's stores in British Columbia cater to a significant Asian population, and smaller sizes are a steady part of the mix in the stores. In Gallic Quebec, customers tend to be of average stature, while in the prairie and mountain provinces, they "grow 'em big."

Tailoring such refined, store-specific merchandising mixes is tough, but Laker says an inventory forecasting and replenishment system, Inforem, is letting the retailer do just that. Mark's installed Inforem/400 in December of 1995. The system, which runs on the IBM AS/400 platform, is allowing the chain to maintain its long-standing commitment to locally defined product mixes.

"We allow Inforem to compute the reorders, and then the store managers can review those suggested orders on their screens in the stores," Laker explains.

If the store managers don't alter the suggested order within 24 hours, the system automatically finalizes the order and sends it off to the manufacturer.

"The store managers also have input in setting different service-level parameters for their stores. You can tell the system that a specific store needs to be 99 percent in stock on a particular SKU at all times. Or you can set that parameter at 75 percent.

But the system is not only an inventory replenishment system, it's also a robust forecasting package. "For the past three years, we've been capturing historical data at 16 different levels of hierarchy in each of our stores," Laker says. "We accumulate that information on a store-by-store basis and we use it to do a store-specific forecasting plan twice a year, spring and fall. We call that our merchandising plan."

Mark's is feeding all that historical data into the Inforem/400 system. The chain is building a sort of "mini-data warehouse" on the AS/400. Inforem will allow the company to compare profiles of individual stores and clusters of stores. It is expected to make the forecasting process more consistent across stores.

The retailer also shares forecasting data with suppliers, where prudent. "If a vendor can manage inventory better than we can, we have no qualms about sharing forecasting information with that vendor," Laker says. "We supply them with sales information and model stock information. It's weekly, store-specific information, by style, by size."

"The problem with the concept of vendor-managed inventory in the past was that it didn't take into account the peaks and valleys in the sales patterns of individual stores," he continues. "The kind of forecasting information Inforem will allow us to offer the manufacturers will help them respond to those changes."

Mark's work wearhouse was bought by Canadian Tire in 2001.

Source: "Information Is Hard at Work at Mark's Work Wearhouse," *Chain Store Age,* November 1996, pp. 14A–16A.

Questions

1. How is Inforem helping Mark's Work Wearhouse?
2. What kind of service level, lead time, or annual, does Mark's use?

OPERATIONS TOUR

The Great Canadian Bagel

www.greatcanadianbagel.com

The Great Canadian Bagel bakeries make and sell a variety of bagels, including plain, rye, poppy-seed, sourdough, and cinnamon raisin, as well as an assortment of flavoured cream cheese spreads, including vegetable and fruit flavours. Bagels, however, are the major source of income for each outlet.

Bagel production is done in batches according to flavour, with each flavour being produced on a daily basis. Each Great Canadian Bagel store produces approximately 18 core varieties of bagels and approximately 12 extra varieties, depending on customer tastes at a particular location.

Production of bagels at a Great Canadian Bagel outlet begins on the premises as early as 4 A.M., where the basic ingredients of flour, water, yeast, and flavourings are combined in a special mixing and kneading machine manufactured to The Great Canadian Bagel's specification by Global Equipment (http://globalbakery.com).

After the dough has been thoroughly mixed and kneaded, it is transferred to another machine that forms the dough into individual shapes. Then, the bagels are stored in a special walk-in cooler to rise. Bagels that are ready to be baked are placed on large trays that hold 24 bagels. The next step occurs in a turntable steam oven specially designed for The Great Canadian Bagel. Cold water is sprayed on hot stainless steel pads located on the back of the oven. As the tray holding the bagels turns, the bagels are cooked evenly by wafts of steam for 15 to 20 minutes. Once the bagels are ready, they are sprayed with water to cool them off, and then are placed in baskets that go in the display case.

Each morning there are typically two to three "full bakes" at each outlet. A full bake provides enough bagels to fill between 12 and 18 baskets of bagels with two dozen bagels each. At busier outlets, an owner may produce three to four bakes to keep up with the demand. The goal of The Great Canadian Bagel is to offer its customers a dozen bagels of any flavour at any one time. At the end of the day, leftover bagels are often donated to shelters or are discarded.

Quality specifications and recommended sources of supplies and ingredients are provided by the company to each outlet.

Each outlet operates with minimal inventories of raw materials on site to maintain a high degree of freshness in the final product. A typical outlet may receive two to three shipments of flour per week (in 20 kg bags) for a total of approximately 60 bags of flour per week.

Questions

1. What inventory model should be used for each bagel type? Why?

2. Suppose a bagel costs the company an average of 15 cents, and it is sold for an average of 75 cents. What service level should the company provide in order to minimize the long-run total excess and shortage cost? Interpret your result.

SELECTED BIBLIOGRAPHY AND FURTHER READING

Brooks, Roger B., and Larry W. Wilson. *Inventory Record Accuracy: Unleashing the Power of Cycle Counting.* Essex Junction, VT: Oliver Wight, 1993.

Fogarty, Donald W., John H. Blackstone, and Thomas R. Hoffmann. *Production and Inventory Management.* 2nd ed. Cincinnati, OH: South-Western Publishing Co., 1991.

Hopp, Wallace J., and Mark L. Spearman. *Factory Physics.* 2nd ed. New York: Irwin/McGraw-Hill, 2001.

Peterson, R., and E. A. Silver. *Decision Systems for Inventory Management and Production Planning.* 2nd ed. New York: John Wiley & Sons, 1998.

Tersine, Richard J. *Principles of Inventory and Materials Management.* 4th ed. New York: Elsevier North-Holland, 1994.

Vollman, Thomas E., William L. Berry, and D. Clay Whybark. *Manufacturing Planning and Control Systems.* 5th ed. Burr Ridge, IL: Richard D. Irwin, 1997.

Zipkin, Paul. *Foundations of Inventory Management.* New York: Irwin/McGraw-Hill, 2000.

CHAPTER 12

Aggregate Operations Planning

LEARNING OBJECTIVES

After completing this chapter, you should be able to:

1 Explain what sales & operations planning is.
2 Explain what aggregate operations planning is and how it is useful.
3 Identify the variables decision makers have to work with in aggregate planning and some of the possible strategies they can use.
4 Describe some of the techniques planners use for aggregate operations planning.
5 Prepare aggregate operations plans and compute their costs.
6 Explain what master production scheduling is and how to do it.

CHAPTER OUTLINE

When Dupont and Merck started a joint venture in early 1990s, the marketing and manufacturing functions of the resulting company had little interaction. Then came the implementation of a software whose main function is to facilitate sales & operations planning. This brought marketing and operations closer. As a result, inventories and lead times have decreased and customer service has improved. What is sales & operations planning and how do companies perform operations planning? That is the subject of this chapter.

INTRODUCTION

The purpose of this chapter is to introduce sales & operations planning, the concept of aggregate operations planning, discuss the pertinent variables and possible strategies, and illustrate some of the different approaches currently in use. Also, master scheduling is described.

Sales and Operations Planning

Sales & operations planning (S&OP) is the process of integrating customer-focused marketing plans for new and existing products with the management of operations. It is usually performed once a month and the information is reviewed by the top management at an aggregate (product family) level. The process must reconcile all supply, demand, and new-product plans at both the detail and aggregate level and tie them to the business plan. It is for the near to intermediate term, covering a horizon sufficient to plan for resources and to support the annual business planning process. It links the strategic plan for the business with its execution (see Figure 12–1).

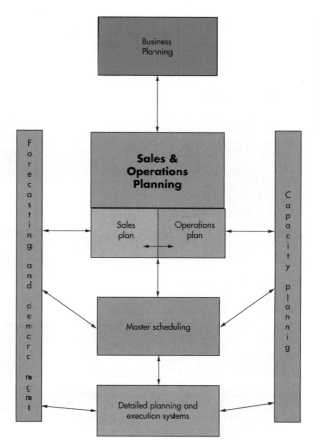

FIGURE 12-1

Sales & operations planning process

Source: T. F. Wallace, *Sales & Operations Planning* (Cincinnati: T. F. Wallace & Co., 2001). Figures reprinted courtesy of T. F. Wallace & Co.

The process of S&OP begins with recording the sales and production of the previous month, updating forecasts for the next 12 months or so, seeing if the necessary production changes are feasible, and providing a summary of information to top management for making decisions. See the Dupont Merck and the Ocean Spray readings in this chapter for more details.

In top management's S&OP meeting, the executives have time only to review a summary of sales, operations, and inventory plans of a limited number (e.g., 6 to 12) of families of products. An example of the summary information for a product family is shown in Figure 12–2. In Location A, the target file rate of 99 percent and finished goods inventory target of 10 days of supply are shown. Note that make-to-stock companies need to keep safety stocks of finished goods to meet demand variability. The level of finished goods inventory directly affects customer service through fill rate.

Locations B and E show the forecast sales for the past three months, and old and new (after update) forecasts for the next six months and the four quarters after that. Locations C and F show the operations plan and actual production during the past three months, and the old and new (after update) production plan for the next six months and four quarters after that. Locations D and G show the inventory plan and actual levels during the past three months, and the projected inventory levels resulting from the given forecasts and production plans (and the equivalent days of supply) during the next six months and two quarters after that. Also shown are file rate performance during the past three months. Finally, in Locations H and J, any major demand and operations issues are pointed out.

We will focus on (aggregate) operations planning in this chapter.

Aggregate Operations Planning

aggregate operations planning Intermediate-term capacity and production planning, usually covering the next 12 months.

In the spectrum of operations planning, **aggregate operations planning** is the intermediate term that typically covers a time horizon of the next 12 months, although in some companies it may extend to as much as 18 months. It plans the production of families of products, each represented by one aggregate measure. It is particularly useful for organizations that experience seasonal or other fluctuations in demand and/or supply. The goal

FIGURE 12-2

An example of the sales & operations planning spreadsheet

Source: T. F. Wallace. *Sales & Operations Planning* (Cincinnati: T. F. Wallace & Co., 2001). Figures reprinted courtesy of T. F. Wallace & Co.

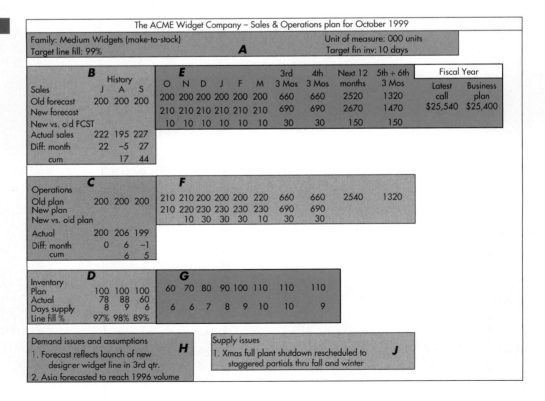

of aggregate operations planning is to achieve a production plan that will effectively utilize the organization's resources to satisfy expected demand. Planners must make decisions on output rates, employment levels and changes, inventory levels and changes, back orders, and possibly subcontracting.

Why do organizations need to do planning? The answer is that it takes time to implement plans. For instance, if plans call for hiring (and training) new workers, that will take time.

Intermediate Operations Planning in Perspective

Organizations make capacity and production decisions on three levels: long term, intermediate term, and short term. Long-term decisions relate to product and service selection (i.e., determining which products or services to offer), facility size and location, equipment decisions, and layout of facilities. These long-term decisions essentially define the capacity constraints within which intermediate planning must function. Intermediate decisions, as noted above, relate to general levels of employment, output, and inventories, which in turn define the boundaries within which short-range capacity and production decisions must be made. Thus, short-term decisions essentially consist of deciding the best way to achieve desired results within the constraints resulting from long-term and intermediate-term decisions. Short-term decisions involve scheduling jobs, workers and

READING

DuPont Merck's Production Planning Process

With three plants in North America and sales offices in eight countries, DuPont Merck Pharmaceutical Company was formed in 1991 as a joint venture between DuPont and Merck.

Business (Strategic) Planning

At DuPont Merck, the strategic planning process involves both Marketing and Manufacturing. The one-year and five-year objectives of strategic planning are supported by both divisions.

Sales and Operations Planning

This process involves monthly review of plans by senior management; this is where overall levels of manufacturing output and sales are set. Sales and Operations Planning (S&OP) process reviews recent past performance and is a forum for confirming or changing future plans, weighing the impact of changes in the market on supply and demand, and deciding how the business will adjust.

The monthly meetings are a touchstone in the cycle of events that make up the S&OP process. The cycle begins with extraction and review of sales history from the previous month by demand managers, and forecasting future months. A series of marketing meetings adjusts the aggregate sales forecasts in view of all internal and external factors.

Then, aggregate sales plan data are transmitted to the manufacturing planning groups which perform reviews and adjust production plans for the future. Simultaneously, master schedulers plan the production of each product in concert with demand managers.

Pre-S&OP meetings are held in the middle of each month, where key members of support teams like customer service, distribution, and quality, as well as marketing and production managers, meet to jointly review aggregate past sales and production (with particular attention to the performance metrics such as fill rate, finished goods inventory levels, and lead times) and review sales and operations plans for the coming 39 months. These meetings form the basis for the S&OP meetings, where company resources are committed by senior management.

Marketing is accountable for implementing the approved sales plans and Manufacturing for the approved production plans.

Results

The cooperation between Marketing and Manufacturing has had quantifiable results. The U.S. inventory and manufacturing lead times have been reduced by half, while unit sales have grown over 15 percent annually. With one product alone, more than $500,000 in business was taken away from a competitor who could not supply the surge in demand—a direct result of the cooperation between divisions. Dupont Merck was bought by Bristol-Myers Squibb in 2001.

Source: J. R. Dougherty and W. Lerner, "Sales and Marketing's Partnership Role in Class A MRPII," *Hospital Materiel Management Quarterly* 16(1), August 1994, pp. 40–46.

READING

Ocean Spray

Ocean Spray's monthly sales & operations planning (S&OP) process is typical: after all new sales data become known from the previous month, in the first week of the month, new forecasts are made by local sales managers for the next six months. For the top 75 customers, subjective forecasts, based on customer information, are made, whereas for other customers time series techniques are used. These forecasts are received by demand planners and aggregated to national category levels. In the next five days, sales and marketing managers meet to compare last month's sales with forecasts, and to possibly modify forecasts based on information such as national promotions. The updated forecasts for the next six months and four quarters after that, plus any sales and customer service (fill rates) issues are passed to the operations function around the eleventh of the month. Operations managers and production controllers compare their actual production last month with the planned production, and compare the planned production over the next six months with the new sales forecasts, also considering any fill rate and inventory issues. If there will be any production problems with the sales forecasts, these are pointed out, as well as problems meeting fill rate and inventory level targets. The summary of sales forecasts and issues, operations plans and issues, and inventory and fill rate performance of the company is communicated to the executives who deal with them in the

The Calendar of Sales & Operations Planning Activities in Ocean Spray

Day 1	Day 2	Day 3	Day 4	Day 5
		All forecast reports received from field sales managers		Final forecast entered into Manugistics Distribute Divisional Rollups (include regional totals)
←		Develop Customer Level Forecast		
Day 6	**Day 7**	**Day 8**	**Day 9**	**Day 10**
Distribute Aggregated Forecast	Division Changes finalized	Pre-Alignment Meetings (2) Final Alignment Meeting Packet Distributed	Alignment Team Reviews Packet	Forecast Alignment Mtg. (Monthly 1–6) (Quarterly 1–18)
←		Forecast Consensus		
Day 11	**Day 12**	**Day 13**	**Day 14**	**Day 15**
				Supply alignment Mtg. (2–6 months) Formalize and Communicate supply issues
←		Develop Supply Plans & Options → ←	Supply Alignment	
Day 16	**Day 17**	**Day 18**	**Day 19**	**Day 20**
Generate S&OP Pre-read Packet and review			S & OP Meeting (Monthly 2–6) (Quarterly 2–18)	
←		Sales & Operations Planning		

S&OP Meeting around the nineteenth of the month. Some companies also have a pre-S&OP meeting of operations, sales and marketing, finance, and other managers, who sort out the issues before the executive receives a summary report and alternatives for decision making.

Source: P. Gelly, "Managing Bottom-up and Top-down Approaches: Ocean Spray's Experience," *Journal of Business Forecasting Methods & Systems* 18(4), Winter 1999/2000, pp. 3–6.

equipment, and the like. The three levels of capacity and production decisions are depicted in Table 12–1. Long-term capacity decisions were covered in Chapter 5, and scheduling and related matters will be covered in Chapter 15. This chapter covers intermediate capacity and production decisions.

TABLE 12-1

Overview of planning levels (chapter numbers are shown)

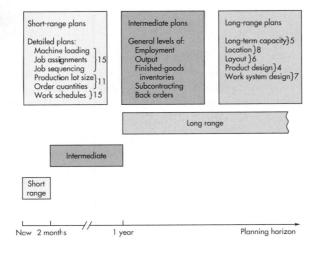

NATURE OF AGGREGATE OPERATIONS PLANNING

The Concept of Aggregation

Aggregate operations planning is essentially a "big picture" approach to planning. Planners usually try to avoid focusing on individual products or services—unless of course the organization has only one major product or service. Instead, they focus on a group of similar products or services, or sometimes an entire product or service line. For example, for purposes of aggregate operations planning, planners in a company producing television sets would not concern themselves with 21-inch sets versus 25-inch or 27-inch sets. Instead, planners would lump all models together and deal with them as though they were a single product; hence, the term *aggregate.* If the products are different, a typical product can be chosen and all other products can be represented in equivalent units of the chosen product. For example, a fast-food restaurant may use a hamburger as a typical burger produced. This average burger is called the "equivalent" unit because other burgers are measured in proportion to it. For example, a Big Mac may be counted as two hamburgers.

Now, consider how aggregate planning might work in a large department store. Space allocation is often an aggregate decision. That is, a manager might decide to allocate 20 percent of the available space in the clothing department to women's wear, 30 percent to juniors, and so on, without regard for what brand names will be offered or how much of juniors will be slacks. The aggregate measure or equivalent unit might be racks of clothing.

In each of these examples, an aggregate approach permits managers to make general decisions about intermediate-term capacity and production without having to deal with highly specific details. They can instead concern themselves with overall decisions on levels of output, employment, and inventories. They do this by lumping demand for all products into one or a few categories, and planning on that basis.

Sometimes, determining an aggregate measure or "equivalent unit" is difficult. In this case, the level of production and capacity can be measured in terms of a major input to operation such as labour hours or machine hours per period.

An Overview of Aggregate Operations Planning

Aggregate planning begins with a forecast of aggregate demand for the intermediate term. This is followed by a general plan to meet demand requirements by setting output, employment, and finished-goods inventory levels. Managers might consider a number of plans, each of which must be examined in light of feasibility and cost. If a plan is reasonably good but has minor difficulties, it may be reworked. Conversely, a poor plan should be discarded and alternative plans considered until an acceptable one is uncovered.

Aggregate plans are updated periodically, often monthly, to take into account updated forecasts and other changes. This results in a *rolling planning horizon* (i.e., the aggregate plan always covers the next 12–18 months).

Demand and Capacity

Aggregate operations planning is concerned with the *quantity* and the *timing* of forecast of demand. If total forecast of demand during the planning horizon is much different from available capacity over that same period, the major approach will be to try to achieve a balance by altering capacity. Even if capacity and demand are approximately equal for the planning horizon as a whole, planners may still be faced with the problem of dealing with seasonal demand *within* the planning horizon. In some periods, demand may be high and in others it may be low. The task of aggregate operations planning is to achieve rough equality of demand and capacity over the entire planning horizon and to achieve this while minimizing the total cost.

Inputs	Outputs
Resources	Total cost of a plan
Workforce/production rates	Projected levels of
Facilities and equipment	Inventory
Demand forecast	Output
Policy statements	Employment
Subcontracting	Subcontracting
Overtime	Backordering
Workforce changes, temp workers	
Inventory levels/changes	
Back orders	
Costs	
Inventory holding	
Back order	
Hiring/firing	
Wage rates	
Overtime	
Subcontracting	

Inputs to Aggregate Operations Planning

Effective aggregate operations planning requires good *information*. First, the available resources over the planning period must be known. Then, a forecast of demand must be available. Finally, planners must take into account company policies, for example regarding changes in employment levels (e.g., some organizations view layoffs as extremely undesirable, so they would use that only as a last resort). Costs of various variables should also be determined.

Table 12–2 lists the major inputs to and outputs from aggregate operations planning.

DEMAND AND CAPACITY OPTIONS

Management has a wide range of decision options at its disposal for purposes of sales & operations planning. These include demand-influencing actions such as changing prices, promotion, back orders, and producing complementary products during slack times, and capacity-influencing actions such as hiring and firing workers, using overtime/slack time, using part-time/temp workers, stockpiling inventories, and subcontracting.

Demand Options. The basic demand options, usually handled by marketing, are the following:

1. *Pricing.* Pricing differentials are commonly used to shift demand from peak periods to off-peak periods. For example, long-distance phone rates are lower after 6 p.m. and on the weekends.

2. *Promotion.* Advertising and other forms of promotion, such as displays and direct marketing, can sometimes be very effective in shifting demand so that it conforms more closely to capacity.

3. *Back orders.* An organization can shift demand to future periods by using back orders. That is, orders are taken in one period and deliveries promised for a later period. The success of this approach depends on how willing customers are to wait for delivery. Moreover, the costs associated with back orders can be difficult to pin down since it could include lost sales, annoyed or disappointed customers, and perhaps additional paperwork. Back orders can be thought of as negative inventory. Make-to-order companies carry an "inventory" of (back) orders as opposed to finished goods inventory carried by make-to-stock companies. A form of back order is the appointment system, which is an acceptable way to regulate demand in services such as health care.

4. *New/complementary products.* Many organizations are faced with the problem of having to provide products or services for peak demand in situations where demand is very uneven. For instance, demand for bus transportation tends to be more intense during the morning and late afternoon rush hours but much lighter at other times. Creating new

demand for buses at other times (e.g., trips by schools, clubs, and senior citizen groups) would make use of the excess capacity during those slack times. Similarly, many fast-food restaurants are open for breakfast to use their capacities more fully. Manufacturing firms that experience seasonal demands for certain products (e.g., snowblowers) are sometimes able to develop a demand for a complementary product (e.g., lawn mowers, garden equipment) that makes use of the same production processes. They thereby achieve a more constant use of labour, equipment, and facilities.

Capacity Options. The basic capacity options are the following:

1. *Hire and lay off workers.* Given the operating hours, number of shifts, and size of facility, companies may hire and fire a limited number of permanent full-time workers. The nature of operation determines the impact that changes in the workforce level will have on capacity. For instance, if a factory usually has 10 of 14 production lines operating, crews for an additional four lines could be added. Conversely, there may be a lower limit on the number of workers needed to maintain a viable operation (e.g., a skeleton crew).

Furthermore, a company may be able to add or reduce the number of shifts. For example, instead of working 8 hours a day (i.e., one shift), a company can double its workforce and operate in two shifts (i.e., work 16 hours a day).

Union contracts may restrict the amount of hiring and laying off a company can do. Moreover, because laying off can present serious problems for workers, some firms have policies that either prohibit or limit downward adjustments to a workforce. On the other hand, hiring presumes an available supply of workers. This may change from time to time and, at times of low labour supply, has an impact on the ability of an organization to pursue this approach. Another consideration is the skill level of workers. Highly skilled workers are generally more difficult to find than lower-skilled workers, and recruiting them involves greater costs. So the usefulness of this option is limited for highly skilled workers.

Use of hiring and laying off entails certain costs. Hiring costs include recruitment, screening, and training costs to bring new workers "up to speed." And quality may suffer. Some savings may occur if workers who have recently been laid off are rehired. Layoff costs include severance pay, the cost of realigning the remaining workforce, potential bad feelings toward the firm on the part of workers who have been laid off, and some loss of morale for workers who are retained (i.e., in spite of company assurances, some workers will believe that in time they too may be laid off).

An increasing number of organizations view workers as assets rather than as variable costs, and would not consider this approach. Instead, they might use overtime/slack time.

2. *Overtime/slack time.* Use of overtime or slack time (i.e., nonproductive employment or idle time) is a less severe method for changing capacity than hiring and laying off

---

READING

Capacity Strategies for Railway Car Builders

When faced with an increase in business, rail-car companies prefer to use overtime before they would increase the number of workers or start a second shift. The following are comments by top managers of some rail-car manufacturers.

Dick Brown of Trinity Railcar Co. (with facilities in seven U.S. states, five countries in Europe, and Mexico) says that "new people need to be trained to our quality standards and this isn't an overnight accomplishment." What's more, a company doesn't lightly take on new employees with an eye to shedding them when a bulge in business is over. "It takes time to train a workforce, and you like to do it gradually. And the costs of downsizing a workforce are just as formidable as growing one."

Bill Galbraith, senior vice-president, Marketing and Sales, The Greenbrier Companies (which includes TrentonWorks of Nova Scotia and facilities in Oregon, Mexico, and Europe), indicates that their preferred strategy to deal with capacity constraints is to place the existing workforce on overtime rather than build up additional workforces that the market might not support over the long run. Capacity increases of 12 to 15 percent are possible with this technique.

National Steel Car of Hamilton, Ontario, has the capacity for three shifts, but is operating a single shift. While extra shifts are possible, their preference, from the standpoint of manpower, is to develop a competent workforce and maintain employment at a consistent level (we call this level *output strategy*).

Source: A. Kruglinski, "How Tight is 'Capacity' for Car Builders?" *Railway Age* 195(1), January 1994, pp. 16ff.

Huronia

When in the late 1990s, the staff payroll cost of the intensive care/coronary care unit of Huronia District Hospital, part of North Simcoe Hospital Alliance, was exceeding its budget by more than 10 percent, the hospital administration decided to take action. The unit had only eight intensive care beds, and the budget was for six full-time registered nurses (RNs) and approximately eleven part-time RNs (counting as eight full-time equivalents). Nurses worked 12-hour shifts, and three RNs worked at any time (including nights). However, sometimes more RNs were needed because of the one-to-one care required by a critically ill patient. The overrun of budget was because of these cases and because the additional RNs' work was frequently overtime work (paid at 1.5 times the

regular pay). The administration decided that they could reduce the payroll costs by replacing some of the RNs (with wage rate of almost $30 per hour) with some registered practical nurses (RPN) who received almost half the wage of an RN. However, this initiative failed because RPNs were not qualified to do some of the tasks of RNs such as looking after critically ill patients or installing pacemakers. This resulted in having to have almost the same number of RNs working as before and some RPNs being idle at times. The unit laid off the RPNs after six months and reverted back to the old staffing plan. The following year, the unit's budget was increased by 1.6 RN FTE, and the budget overrun was almost eliminated.

Sources: www.nsha.on.ca/mservice.htm; Denis S. Lahaie, "Financial Challenges and Complexity in the Management of an Intensive Care/Coronary Care Unit: a Case Study," *International Journal of Health Care Quality Assurance* 17(2/3), 2004, pp. IX–XVI.

permanent, full-time workers. It can also be implemented more quickly than hiring and laying off and allows the company to maintain a steady base of employees. Organizations use slack time for training, performing maintenance, problem solving, and process improvement. Overtime also permits the employees to increase their earnings (overtime pay is usually 1.5 times the regular-time pay).

On the other hand, overtime often results in lower productivity, poorer quality, more accidents, and increased payroll costs, and idle (slack) time results in less efficient use of resources.

3. *Part-time/temp workers.* In certain instances, the use of part-time/temp workers is a viable option—much depends on the nature of the work, training and skills needed, and union agreements. Seasonal work requiring low-to-moderate job skills lends itself to temp workers, who generally cost less than permanent workers in hourly wages and fringe benefits. However, unions may regard such workers unfavourably because they typically do not pay union dues and may lessen the power of unions. Stores and restaurants make use of part-time/temp workers. So do parks and recreation departments, resorts, travel agencies, hotels, and other service organizations with seasonal demands. In order to be successful, these organizations must be able to hire part-time/temp employees when they are needed.

Although they are not permanent employees, often part-time/temp workers work alongside permanent workers. In addition to having different pay scales and few benefits, they can be added or subtracted from the workforce with greater ease than permanent workers, giving companies great flexibility in adjusting the size of the workforce.

4. *Inventories.* The use of finished-goods inventories allows companies to produce goods in one period and sell or distribute them in a future period. The holding cost includes not only storage costs and the cost of money tied up in inventory, but also the cost of obsolescence, spoilage, and so on. Inventories can be built up during periods when production capacity exceeds demand and drawn down in periods when demand exceeds production capacity. This method is suitable for make-to-stock manufacturing.

5. *Subcontracting.* Subcontracting enables a company to acquire temporary capacity by buying the goods or services from another company. It affords less control over the output and may lead to higher costs and quality problems. The question of whether to make or buy (or outsource) generally depends on factors such as available capacity, relative expertise, quality considerations, cost, and the amount and stability of demand. For two applications of capacity options, see the readings, "Capacity Strategies for Railway Car Builders" and "Huronia."

BASIC STRATEGIES FOR MEETING UNEVEN DEMAND

As you saw above, managers have a wide range of decision options they can consider for achieving a balance of demand and capacity in aggregate operations planning. We will concentrate on the options that directly affect production, such as capacity options and the use of back orders.

Aggregate operations planners might adopt a number of strategies. Some of the more prominent ones are:

1. Maintain a level output rate.

2. Match demand period by period.

3. Use a combination of decision variables.

The first two strategies are "pure" strategies because each has a single focus; the third strategy is "mixed." Under the **level output strategy**, variations in demand are met by using some combination of inventories, subcontracting, and back ordering. This strategy usually uses a fixed number of permanent workers (with no overtime). It may also use a fixed number of part time/temp workers.

Matching capacity to demand is **chase demand strategy**; the planned output for any period is equal to forecast of demand for that period. Chase demand strategy may or may not use a fixed number of permanent workers. Usually, the hours of part-time/temp workers are changed over time to meet the changing demand.

Level output strategy assumes that products have long shelf life. This is true for some products such as durable goods, but not for others such as groceries. Similarly, the use of backordering is usually limited to products which are custom-built.

Many organizations regard having a fixed number of permanent workers very appealing. Because workforce changes through hiring and firing can have a major impact on the lives and morale of employees and can be disruptive for managers, organizations often prefer to handle uneven demand in other ways. Moreover, changes in permanent workforce size can be very costly, and there is always the risk that there will not be a sufficient pool of workers with the appropriate skills when needed.

Permanent workers are often more dedicated to their employers. They are better qualified and more knowledgeable/skillful than part-time/temp workers. For this reason, many companies have policies regarding the ratio of permanent workers to part time/temp workers; for example, no less than 70% of personnel (measured as full-time equivalent) should be permanent.

A chase demand strategy presupposes a great deal of ability and willingness on the part of managers to be flexible in adjusting to demand. A major advantage of this approach is that inventories can be kept relatively low, which can yield substantial savings for an organization. A major disadvantage is the lack of stability in operations—the atmosphere is one of dancing to demand's tune. Service organizations that cannot regulate their demand have to use chase demand strategy. Figure 12–3 provides a comparison of the two strategies, using a varying demand pattern to highlight the differences in the two approaches.

A mixed strategy uses a combination of decision variables, e.g., a company can have two levels of operations, low in off season, and high in busy season using overtime and/or temp workers. For an application of chase demand strategy, see the reading, "Workforce Planning at Lands' End."

Choosing a Strategy

Whatever strategy an organization is considering, two important factors are *company policy* and *costs*. Company policy may set constraints on the available options or the extent to which they can be used. For instance, company policy may discourage layoffs except under extreme conditions. Subcontracting may not be a viable alternative due to the desire to maintain secrecy about some aspect of the manufacturing of the product (e.g., a secret formula or blending process). Union agreements often impose restrictions. For example, a union contract may specify both minimum and maximum numbers of hours part-time/temp workers can be used.

As a rule, aggregate planners seek to match supply and demand within the constraints imposed on them by policies or agreements and at minimum cost. They usually evaluate alternatives in terms of their overall costs. In the next section, a number of techniques for aggregate operations planning are described and presented with some examples of cost evaluation of alternative plans.

level output strategy
Maintaining a steady rate of output while meeting variations in demand by a combination of inventory, subcontracting, and back orders.

chase demand strategy
Matching capacity to demand; the planned output for a period is set at the forecast of demand for that period.

FIGURE 12-3

Comparison of chase and level output strategies

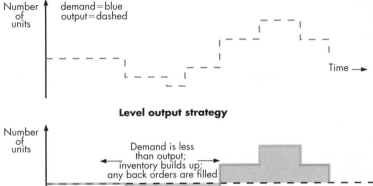

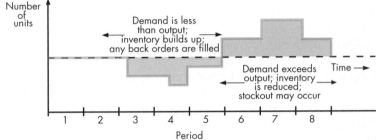

TECHNIQUES FOR AGGREGATE OPERATIONS PLANNING

Two different approaches are used: informal trial-and-error and optimization. In practice, trail-and-error is more frequently used.

A general procedure for aggregate operations planning consists of the following steps:

1. Determine demand forecast for each period.

2. Determine capacities and production rates (regular time, overtime, part-time/temp, subcontracting).

3. Identify company or departmental policies that are pertinent (e.g., maintain a safety stock of 5 percent of demand, maintain a reasonably stable workforce).

4. Determine unit costs for regular time, overtime, part-time/temp, subcontracting, holding inventory, back order, hiring and layoff.

READING

Workforce Planning at Lands' End

www.landsend.com

Lands' End is a major mail-order distributor of clothing and sewn goods located in the small town of Dodgeville, Wisconsin (population 4,000). Sales of Lands' End peak in November and December each year, much like other retailers, due to the holiday shopping season. Lands' End does 40 percent of its business during the fourth quarter. The number of phone calls received jumps from 40,000 a day to more than 100,000 on the busiest days. During the other three quarters, there is also some variation in sales. Lands' End employs customer sales (for phone orders), mail-order workers, warehouse workers, customer-service workers, and sewers who perform alterations. Lands' End employs approximately 3,500 permanent and 1,000 temporary/part time workers year round. How does the company meet its

excess demand for labour hours during November and December? First, it employs approximately 2,000 more temporary/part time workers. The supply of temporary/part time workers comes from high school, college, and university students who can work a six-hour shift after school (three times a week), and from workers from some local cheese factories who end their busy season in October. Second, Lands' End encourages its workers to cross train so that they can work in other jobs when they are needed (called job sharing). Third, employees can work extended schedules during November and December, up to 12 hours a day (the portion above eight hours is performed in a different department and is considered overtime). Approximately one-third of temporary/part time workers return to work for Lands' End again the following year or later. A new hire receives six hours of orientation/training, but a rehire may only receive up to two hours of retraining.

Sources: J. J. Laabs, "Strategic Holiday Staffing at Lands' End," *Personnel Journal* 73(12), December 1994, pp. 28ff; K. Haegele, "Gearing Up for the Holiday Rush," *Target Marketing* 23(6), June 2000, pp. 44–48ff.

5. If using trial-and-error, develop alternative feasible plans, compute the total cost for each, and select the one with lowest total cost. If using optimization, the lowest total cost feasible plan will be determined by the software.

Trial-and-Error

Trial-and-error consists of developing simple tables (worksheets) or graphs that enable managers to visually compare projected demand requirements with existing capacity. The chief disadvantage of such techniques is that they do not necessarily result in a good aggregate plan.

Very often, graphs can be used to guide the development of alternatives. The obvious advantage of a graph is that it provides a visual portrayal of a plan. Some planners prefer cumulative graphs while others prefer to see a period-by-period breakdown of a plan (Figure 12–3 is an example of a period-by-period graph). Figure 12–4 shows a cumulative graph for a plan with level output (the slope of the dashed line represents the production rate) and inventory absorption of demand variations. The preference of the planner determines which of the two types of graphs is chosen.

Three examples below illustrate the development and comparison of aggregate operations plans using worksheets. In the first example output is held level, with inventory absorbing demand variations. In the second example, a lower rate of regular output is used, supplemented by use of overtime. The third example is similar, but uses part-time/temp workers instead of overtime. In all three examples, some back orders are allowed to build up.

These and other examples and problems in this chapter are based on the following assumptions:

1. No allowance is made for holidays and different numbers of workdays in different months. This assumption simplifies computations.

2. We present all production in terms of number of units of the aggregate measure (equivalent unit), not number of labour hours or workers.

3. Each total cost (regular production, overtime production, back order, inventory, subcontracting, hire/layoff), is a linear function of number of units; that is, it equals a constant unit cost times number of units.

Unit cost of labour should be calculated using the wage rate and number of hours each unit will take a worker to make. The hiring cost per unit is the hiring cost per worker divided by the number of units a worker can make during one period, charged to the first period of employment. Laying off cost per unit is determined in the same way, but is charged to the period after the layoff. Cost is charged to the average level of inventory during a period, but to the amount of back order carried to the next period. The following relationships are used.

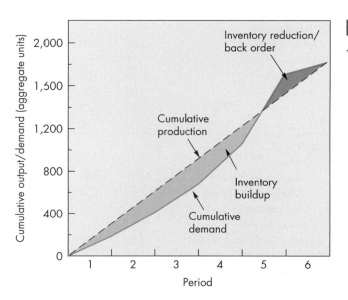

FIGURE 12-4

A cumulative graph

1. To determine the ending inventory and back order in any period i, first calculate

$$X = \text{Beginning inventory}_i + (\text{Output} - \text{Forecast})_i - \text{Back order}_{i-1},$$

where output is the sum of regular, overtime, part-time/temp, and subcontracting production.

If $X \geq 0$, then ending inventory$_i = X$ and back order$_i = 0$; whereas if $X < 0$, then ending inventory$_i = 0$ and back order$_i = -X$.
2. The average inventory for a period is equal to (Beginning inventory + Ending inventory)/2.
3. Beginning inventory$_i$ = ending inventory$_{i-1}$

Example 1

Planners for a company that makes several models of toy tractors are about to prepare an aggregate production plan that will cover the next six months. They have assembled the following information:

Month	1	2	3	4	5	6	Total
Forecast	200	200	300	400	500	200	1,800

Costs

Output

Regular time	= $2 per tractor
Overtime	= $3 per tractor
Subcontract	= $6 per tractor
Inventory	= $1 per tractor per month (on average inventory)
Back orders	= $5 per tractor per month

They now want to evaluate a plan that calls for level output, using inventory to absorb the uneven demand but allowing some back order. They start with zero inventory on hand in the first month. Prepare an aggregate production plan and determine its total cost. Assume that the planned ending inventory and back order at the end of the sixth month is zero.

Solution

To meet total demand, the total regular-time output should be 1,800 units. Hence, output per month should be $1,800 \div 6 = 300$ units. The filled worksheet for this level-output strategy is deployed below. The computations are explained below the worksheet.

Month	1	2	3	4	5	6	Total
Forecast	200	200	300	400	500	200	1,800
Output							
Regular	300	300	300	300	300	300	1,800
Overtime	—	—	—	—	—	—	
Subcontract	—	—	—	—	—	—	
Output − Forecast	100	100	0	−100	−200	100	0
Inventory							
Beginning	0	100	200	200	100	0	
Ending	100	200	200	100	0	0	
Average	50	150	200	150	50	0	600
Back order	0	0	0	0	100	0	100
Costs							
Output							
Regular (at $2/unit)	$600	600	600	600	600	600	$3,600
Overtime (at $3/unit)	—	—	—	—	—	—	
Subcontract (at $6/unit)	—	—	—	—	—	—	
Hire/Lay off	—	—	—	—	—	—	
Inventory (at $1/unit/month)	$50	150	200	150	50	0	$600
Back order (at $5/unit/month)	$0	0	0	0	500	0	$500
Total	$650	750	800	750	1,150	600	$4,700

Starting from month 1, (Output − Forecast)$_1$ = 300 − 200 = 100,

$$X = \text{Beginning inventory}_1 + (\text{Output} - \text{Forecast})_1 - \text{Back order}_0$$
$$= 0 + 100 - 0 = 100.$$

Therefore, ending inventory$_1$ = 100 and back order$_1$ = 0. Also,

$$\text{Average inventory}_1 = (\text{Beginning inventory}_1 + \text{Ending inventory}_1)/2$$
$$= (0 + 100)/2 = 50.$$

Then, beginning inventory$_2$ = ending inventory$_1$ = 100. Continue with the same formulas, but note that in month 5,

$$X = \text{Beginning inventory}_5 + (\text{Output} - \text{Forecast})_5 - \text{Back order}_4$$
$$= 100 + (-200) - 0 = -100.$$

Therefore, ending inventory$_5$ = 0 and back order$_5$ = −(−100) = 100. Also, in month 6,

$$X = \text{Beginning inventory}_6 + (\text{Output} - \text{Forecast})_6 - \text{Back order}_5$$
$$= 0 + 100 - 100 = 0.$$

Therefore, ending inventory$_6$ = 0 and back order$_6$ = 0.

The costs were computed as follows. Regular cost in each month equals 300 units × $2 per unit, or $600. Inventory cost equals average inventory × $1 per unit. Back-order cost is $5 per unit times number of back orders. The total cost for this plan (either sum the row totals of costs or sum the column totals of costs) is $4,700.

Example 2

After reviewing the plan developed in the preceding example, planners have decided to develop an alternative plan. They have learned that one person is about to retire from the company. There are currently 15 workers. Rather than replace that person, they would like to stay with the smaller workforce and use overtime to make up for the lost output. The reduced regular-time output is 280 units per month. It is the policy of the company that the maximum amount of overtime output per month is 40 units. Develop an aggregate production plan and compare it to the previous one.

Solution

The amount of overtime that must be scheduled has to make up for the reduction in regular output of 20 units per month for six months, which is 120. This should be scheduled toward the centre of the planning horizon since that is where the bulk of demand occurs. Scheduling it earlier would increase inventory holding costs; scheduling it later would increase the back order costs. That is why the maximum permitted overtime production is used in months 3 to 5. The completed worksheet is given below.

Month	1	2	3	4	5	6	Total
Forecast	200	200	300	400	500	200	1,800
Output							
Regular	280	280	280	280	280	280	1,680
Overtime	0	0	40	40	40	0	120
Subcontract	—	—	—	—	—	—	
Output − Forecast	80	80	20	−80	−180	80	0
Inventory							
Beginning	0	80	160	180	100	0	
Ending	80	160	180	100	0	0	
Average	40	120	170	140	50	0	520
Back order	0	0	0	0	80	0	80
Costs							
Output							
Regular (at $2/unit)	$560	560	560	560	560	560	$3,360
Overtime (at $3/unit)	0	0	120	120	120	0	$360
Subcontract (at $6/unit)	—	—	—	—	—	—	
Hire/Lay off	—	—	—	—	—	—	
Inventory (at $1/unit/month)	40	120	170	140	50	0	$520
Back order (at $5/unit/month)	$0	0	0	0	400	0	$400
Total	$600	680	850	820	1,130	560	$4,640

Overall, the total cost for this plan is $4,640, which is $60 less than the previous plan. Total regular-time production cost, total inventory cost, and total back order cost are down, but there is overtime cost.

Example 3

A third option is to use temp workers during months of high demand. Recall that a worker is to retire. Suppose that it costs an additional $100 to hire and train a temp worker and nothing to lay off a temp worker, and that a temp worker can produce at the rate of 15 units per month (compared with 20 units per month for permanent workers). Their pay is less, and results in the same unit cost ($2) per tractor. Develop an aggregate production plan in this case.

Solution

Dividing the number of units needed (120) by the output rate of 15 per temporary worker, you find that eight temp worker-months are needed (e.g., two temp workers for four months each, or four temp workers for two months each).

Noting that months 4 and 5 have the heaviest demand, using four temporary workers for months 4 and 5 seems to be reasonable. The completed worksheet is given below.

Month	1	2	3	4	5	6	Total
Forecast	200	200	300	400	500	200	1,800
Output
Regular	280	280	280	280	280	280	1,680
Temp				60	60		120
Overtime	—	—	—	—	—	—	
Subcontract	—	—	—	—	—	—	
Output − Forecast	80	80	−20	−60	−160	80	0
Inventory
Beginning	0	80	160	140	80	0	
Ending	80	160	140	80	0	0	
Average	40	120	150	110	40	0	460
Back order	0	0	0	0	80	0	80
Costs
Output
Regular (at $2/unit)	$560	560	560	560	560	560	$3,360
Temp (at $2/unit)				120	120		$240
Overtime (at $3/unit)	—	—	—	—	—	—	
Subcontract (at $6/unit)	—	—	—	—	—	—	
Hire/Lay off (Temp)	$0	0	0	400	0	0	$400
Inventory (at $1/unit/month)	$40	120	150	110	40	0	$460
Back order (at $5/unit/month)	$0	0	0	0	400	0	$400
Total	$600	680	710	1,190	1,120	560	$4,860

Overall, the total cost for this plan is $4,860, making it the most expensive of the three alternatives examined.

Trade-off Analysis. It is possible to use trade-off analysis using the unit costs in order to make good production planning decisions, without having to recalculate the total plan cost. Let's look at some of the decisions made in the above three examples. In Example 2, overtime should be used in the months when back orders will occur without overtime and, if more overtime production is needed, in the month(s) before them, not after because back order cost per unit ($5) is larger than inventory holding cost per unit ($1). Also, because holding inventory costs money, overtime should be used as close to the months with peak demand as possible.

Trade-off analysis would have been able to save us the trouble of completing the third option. This is because the cost of a unit made during overtime is $3, whereas the cost of a unit made by a temp worker (employed for two months) is $2 + hiring cost/no. of units produced = $2 + $100/(15[2]) = $5.33. So, even if a unit is made during overtime (by a regular worker) and carried in inventory for up to two months (at an extra cost of $2), its unit cost ($3 + $2) is less than $5.33, the cost of a unit made by a temporary worker who is employed for two months.

Another example is the question of how to use the temp workers: two temp workers for four months versus four temp workers for two months. As derived above, the cost of a unit produced by a temp worker employed for two months is $5.33. However, the cost of a unit produced by a temp worker employed for four months is only $2 + $100/(15[4]) = $3.67. However, because a unit needs to be carried in inventory for two more months, its total unit cost is $3.67 + $2 = $5.67 > $5.33. Therefore, using four temp workers for two months is cheaper than using two temp workers for four months.

The following example further illustrates trade-off analysis.

Example 4[1]

Bradford Food Co. makes small puddings. It sells the puddings in cases (a case contains 48 puddings). Bradford has potentially 15 parallel production lines. The regular operating hours is 8 hours a day, 5 days a week, 13 weeks a quarter. Each line is automated but needs 6 workers to operate it and can produce 200 units of output (each unit = 1,000 cases) per quarter. Currently, only 11 production lines are used, for a total quarterly output of 2,200 units. The sales department has forecasted demand for puddings for the next five quarters and they are given in the following worksheet (in units). Currently, there are no puddings in the warehouse. Bradford can change production by changing workforce level but needs to hire or lay off a group of six workers, i.e., by opening or shutting down one production line. Hiring or laying off one worker costs approximately $1,000. Each worker is paid an average of $19.23 per hour. Overtime labour costs 1.5 times regular-time wages, and is limited to a maximum of 20 percent of regular-time production in any quarter. Holding inventory of a unit for a quarter will cost $50 (charged on average level of inventory in the quarter). Back order per unit per quarter is estimated to cost $200. Assume maintenance costs are negligible.

a. Determine all the relevant unit costs.

b. If the current number of workers is kept for the next five quarters, how many units will Bradford be short of at the end of Quarter 5?

c. Meet the forecast demand at minimum cost by

  i. Adding another production line for three consecutive quarters

  ii. Using overtime

  iii. Adding any number of production lines and/or using overtime

You may use the trade-off analysis to limit the production plan choices.

a. Labour cost per unit during regular time **Solution**
  = Labour cost of one line for one quarter/production of the line in quarter
  = # of workers for a line × cost per worker per quarter/200
  = 6 × wage per hour × hours per quarter/200
  = 6 × $19.23 × hours per day × days per week × weeks per quarter/200
  = 6 × $19.23 × 8 × 5 × 13/200
  = $300

[1]Based on case in R. B. Chase, N. J. Aquilano, and F. R. Jacobs, *Operations Management for Competitive Advantage,* 9th ed. (New York: McGraw Hill/Irwin, 2001).

Labour cost per unit during overtime
= proportion of regular time cost × regular time cost
= 1.5 × $300 = $450

Hiring cost per unit (charged to the first quarter hired)
= Hiring cost per worker × no. of workers per line/production per line per quarter
= $1,000 × 6/200
= $30

Layoff cost per unit (charged to the quarter after layoff) = same = $30

b. No. short during five quarters
= total demand forecast − 5 × production per quarter
= 11,600 − 5(2,200)
= 600 units

c.

i. Note that the quarters with higher-than-average demand are Q3 and Q4. Therefore, the twelfth production line should include Q3 and Q4. This would relieve 400 units of back order. The period of hiring the extra workers is required to be three consecutive quarters, therefore the third quarter has to be either Q2 or Q5. The choice between Q2 and Q5 should be broken in favour of Q2 because holding a unit in inventory for two quarters (from Q2 to Q4) costs 2 × $50 = $100 < $200 = cost of back-ordering a unit for a quarter (from Q5 back to Q4). The completed worksheet is displayed below. Note that we have used a new row called "Temp" to show the output of the twelfth production line.

Aggregate plan for Bradford using an additional production line.

Quarter	1	2	3	4	5	Total
Forecast	2,000	2,200	2,500	2,700	2,200	11,600
Output						
Permanent	2,200	2,200	2,200	2,200	2,200	11,000
Temp		200	200	200		600
Overtime						0
Output − Forecast	200	200	−100	−300	0	0
Inventory						
Beginning	0	200	400	300	0	
Ending	200	400	300	0	0	
Average	100	300	350	150	0	900
Back order	0	0	0	0	0	0
Costs						
Permanent @ 300	660,000	660,000	660,000	660,000	660,000	3,300,000
Temp @ 300	0	60,000	60,000	60,000	0	180,000
Overtime @ 450	0	0	0	0	0	0
Hire/unit @ $30	0	6,000	0	0	0	6,000
Lay off/unit @ $30	0	0	0	0	6,000	6,000
Inventory @ 50	5,000	15,000	17,500	7,500	0	45,000
Back order @ 200	0	0	0	0	0	0
Total	665,000	741,000	737,500	727,500	666,000	$3,537,000

ii. Maximum overtime production is 20 percent of regular time production = 0.20 × 2,200 = 440 units. To avoid holding cost, we should use the overtime production when we need it (i.e., Q4 and Q3). If we use the maximum of 440 units in Q4, we will still need 160 units which we will plan to make in Q3. The completed worksheet is displayed below. The total cost in this case is larger than C−*i*.

Aggregate plan for Bradford using overtime.

Quarter	1	2	3	4	5	Total
Forecast	2,000	2,200	2,500	2,700	2,200	11,600
Output						
Permanent	2,200	2,200	2,200	2,200	2,200	11,000
Temp						0
Overtime			160	440		600
Output — Forecast	200	0	−140	−60	0	0
Inventory						
Beginning	0	200	200	60	0	
Ending	200	200	60	0	0	
Average	100	200	130	30	0	460
Back order	0	0	0	0	0	0
Costs						
Permanent @ 300	660,000	660,000	660,000	660,000	660,000	3,300,000
Temp @ 300	0	0	0	0	0	0
Overtime @ 450	0	0	72,000	198,000	0	270,000
Hire/unit @ $30	0	0	0	0	0	0
Lay off/unit @ $30	0	0	0	0	0	0
Inventory @ 50	5,000	10,000	6,500	1,500	0	23000
Back order @ 200	0	0	0	0	0	0
Total	665,000	670,000	738,500	859,500	660,000	$3,593,000

iii. First we will show that using temp workers is cheaper than using permanent workers during overtime:

> Unit cost of a unit made by a temp worker hired and laid off after one quarter = $300 + $30 + $30 = $360
>
> < $450 = unit cost of a unit produced by a permanent worker during overtime.

Now, given C-*i*, the only way to reduce the total cost more is to use two extra production lines during Q4. As you can see below, the total cost in this case is lower than C-*i*. In fact, this production plan is optimal.

Aggregate plan for Bradford using two additional production lines.

Quarter	1	2	3	4	5	Total
Forecast	2,000	2,200	2,500	2,700	2,200	11,600
Output						
Permanent	2,200	2,200	2,200	2,200	2,200	11,000
Temp			200	400		600
Overtime						0
Output — Forecast	200	0	−100	−100	0	0
Inventory						
Beginning	0	200	200	100	0	
Ending	200	200	100	0	0	
Average	100	200	150	50	0	500
Back order	0	0	0	0	0	0
Costs						
Permanent @ 300	660,000	660,000	660,000	660,000	660,000	3,300,000
Temp @ 300	0	0	60,000	120,000	0	180,000
Overtime @ 450	0	0	0	0	0	0
Hire/unit @ $30	0	0	6,000	6,000	0	12,000
Lay off/unit @ $30	0	0	0	0	12,000	12,000
Inventory @ 50	5,000	10,000	7,500	2,500	0	25000
Back order @ 200	0	0	0	0	0	0
Total	665,000	670,000	733,500	788,500	672,000	$3,529,000

Optimization

Linear Programming. A linear programming model is a mathematical representation of the aggregate operations planning problem. A variable is assigned to each output in each month. The total cost formula, consisting of the unit costs times the variables, is the linear objective function. The ending inventory, back order formulas, beginning inventories, and other policy requirements are represented as linear equations and inequalities. Once the model is entered in a linear programming software, it first adds more variables to made the inequalities into equations, then it iteratively chooses a subset of the variables, solves them using the equations, computes the total cost, and improves the solution by changing the subset one variable at a time in order to reduce the total cost. After some iterations, the optimal solution is found. Excel has an add-on program called Solver which solves linear programs. See the supplement to Chapter 6 for more information on linear programming.

Transportation Model. When there are no hires or layoffs, the problem can be formulated as a transportation model which is even simpler to solve than a linear programming model. See the supplement to Chapter 8 for more information on the transportation model. In order to use this approach, planners must identify capacity (maximum supply) of regular time, overtime, part-time/temp, and subcontracting, and demand for each period, as well as related costs of production and inventory.

Table 12–3 shows the notation and setup of a transportation table. There are n (e.g., 12) set of production rows and n consumption (demand) columns. There is also a row for the initial inventory (at the top). The production quantities, to be determined by the software, will be in each cell. Unit costs are in the little squares in the top right of each cell. Note the systematic way that costs change as you move across a row from left to right. Regular cost, overtime cost, and subcontracting cost are at their lowest when the output is consumed (i.e., delivered) in the same month it is produced. If goods are produced in one month but carried over to later months (i.e., moving across a row to the right), holding costs are incurred at the rate of h per month. Conversely, with back orders, the unit cost increases as you move across a row to the left. For instance, if some goods are produced in month 3 to satisfy back orders from month 2, a unit back-order cost of b is incurred. Unused capacity is generally given a unit cost of 0. Finally, beginning inventory is given a unit cost of 0 if it is used to satisfy demand in month 1. However, if it is held over for use in later months, a holding cost of h per unit is added for each month.

TABLE 12-3

Transportation notation for aggregate production planning

Consumption Month

Production Month		Month 1	Month 2	Month 3	. . .	Month n	Unused capacity	Capacity
Month	Beginning inventory	0	h	$2h$	. . .	nh	0	I_0
1	Regular time	r	$r+h$	$r+2h$	. . .	$r+nh$	0	R_1
	Overtime	t	$t+h$	$t+2h$	. . .	$t+nh$	0	O_1
	Subcontract	s	$s+h$	$s+2h$	. . .	$s+nh$	0	S_1
2	Regular time	$r+b$	r	$r+h$	. . .	$r+(n-1)h$	0	R_2
	Overtime	$t+b$	t	$t+h$	. . .	$t+(n-1)h$	0	O_2
	Subcontract	$s+b$	s	$s+h$	. . .	$s+(n-1)h$	0	S_2
3	Regular time	$r+2b$	$r+b$	r	. . .	$r+(n-2)h$	0	R_3
	Overtime	$t+2b$	$t+b$	t	. . .	$t+(n-2)h$	0	O_3
	Subcontract	$s+2b$	$s+b$	s	. . .	$s+(n-2)h$	0	S_3
	⋮	⋮	⋮	⋮	⋮	⋮	⋮	⋮
	Demand							Total

Example 5 illustrates the setup and final solution of a transportation model of an aggregate production planning problem.

Example 5

Given the following information, set up the aggregate production planning problem in a transportation table and solve it for the minimum cost plan:

MONTH

	1	2	3
Demand	550	70C	750
Capacity (maximum)			
Regular	500	500	500
Overtime	50	50	50
Subcontract	120	120	100
Beginning inventory	100		
Costs			
Regular time	$60 per uni⁻		
Overtime	$80 per unit		
Subcontract	$90 per unit		
Inventory holding cost	$1 per unit per month		
Back order cost	$3 per unit per month		

Solution

The transportation table and an optimal solution (using Excel's Solver) are shown in Table 12–4.

Thus, the demand of 550 units in period 1 will be met using 100 units from beginning inventory and 450 units obtained from regular-time output in month 1. The 700 units demanded in month 2 is met by 50 units produced during regular time, 50 units during overtime, and 30 units of subcontract in month 1 all carried to month 2; and 500 units produced during regular time, 50 units during overtime, and 20 units of subcontract in month 2. The 750 units demanded in month 3 is met by 100 units of subcontract in month 2 carried to month 3, and 500 units produced during regular time, 50 units during overtime, and 100 units of subcontract in month 3. It can be shown that the total cost for this solution is $124,730.

TABLE 12-4

Transportation table and solution for example 5

		Demand for				Total capacity
	Supply from	Month 1	Month 2	Month 3	Unused capacity	available (supply)
Month	Beginning inventory	[0] 100	[1]	[2]	[0]	100
1	Regular time	[60] 450	[61] 50	[62]	[0]	500
	Overtime	[80]	[81] 50	[82]	[0]	50
	Subcontract	[90]	[91] 30	[92]	[0] 90	120
2	Regular time	[63]	[60] 500	[61]	[0]	500
	Overtime	[83]	[80] 50	[81]	[0]	50
	Subcontract	[93]	[90] 20	[91] 100	[0]	120
3	Regular time	[66]	[63]	[60] 500	[0]	500
	Overtime	[86]	[83]	[80] 50	[0]	50
	Subcontract	[96]	[93]	[90] 100	[0]	100
	Demand	550	700	750	90	2,090

READING

Linear Programming at Shell Chemicals

www.shellchemicals.com

Some companies are using the linear programming method to determine a master production schedule that is feasible for the resources available (capacity); that is, the *disaggregation* of the aggregate plan. Shell Chemicals is an example. Shell used the MIMI software from Chesapeake Decision Sciences in Ottawa to improve the production planning and scheduling of its 12 U.S. facilities. The software uses an Oracle database that is also accessed by SAP's ERP system.

Each of the 11 product families, such as solvents, base chemicals, and resins, is planned separately. The output of MIMI is a "planning board" that specifies how many units of each product are to be made and when, and how the product is to be distributed over the next 12 to 18 weeks. The supply manager then transmits this information to each plant's scheduler, who will decide the plant's detailed schedule over the next two weeks. Because of timely and accurate information, the company can respond more quickly to a customer inquiry and can provide a more reliable delivery commitment. Software such as MIMI is referred to as Advanced Planning and Scheduling (APS) software.

Source: K. Parker, "Ready to Go," *Manufacturing Systems*, June 1996, pp. 18Aff.

Where back orders are not permitted, the cell costs for the back orders can be made prohibitively high so that no back orders will appear in the solution.

The main limitation of linear programming and transportation models is the assumption of linear terms and relationships among variables.

AGGREGATE PLANNING FOR SERVICES

 Aggregate planning for manufacturing and aggregate planning for services share similarities, but there are some important differences:

1. *Services occur when they are rendered.* Unlike manufacturing output, most services can't be inventoried or back ordered. Consequently, it becomes important to be able to match capacity and demand during any month (i.e., use chase demand strategy).

2. For labour-intensive services, it may be easier to measure the aggregate plan in terms of time (e.g., hours) or number of workers instead of an aggregate measure of output. See the following reading, "Some Examples of Aggregate Planning at Hospitals" and Example 6.

READING

Some Examples of Aggregate Planning at Hospitals

Hospitals are generally busier during the winter. In order to meet this seasonal variation, each unit of a hospital may use a combination of (*a*) having some extra nurses (temp and part time), (*b*) using some standby (per diem) employees, and (*c*) asking permanent staff to put in some overtime hours. In order to reduce costs, the extra nurses from all units of the hospital usually form a float pool and are traded between units when there is a short-term imbalance between units in nurse requirements. Even though this arrangement is satisfactory for

most hospitals, the nurses may find their float work in other units unsettling, having to work with other patients, nurses, and supervisors.

One such case occurred in the infant/toddler unit of the Children's Hospital Medical Center in Cincinnati in the early 1990s. This unit usually had approximately 25 patients to look after, but the number went up to approximately 40 patients during peak season. The unit had 45 permanent nurses, equivalent to five full-time (called FTE) float pool nurses, and equivalent to nine full-time standby nurses. The majority of nurses in the unit decided that a self-staffing system (i.e., not trading the float pool nurses with other units), with agreed-on flexibility, would be better. The flexibility is in various forms. For example, a .7 FTE nurse (i.e., a nurse who usually works 70 percent of full-time or 28 hours a week) would work .8 FTE (i.e., 32 hours a week) during winter and .6 FTE (i.e., 24 hours a week) during summer. Another example is that staff agreed to allow short-notice changes in the schedule, such as going home early or returning to work on a day off if needed. After one year, the results showed reduced total overtime cost (from $71,000 to $45,000) and happier staff who called in sick less often (280 person-days down to 207 person-days).

Good Samaritan Medical Center in Phoenix, Arizona, a 571-bed hospital, was in a different situation in the early 1990s. Its nursing budget was based on a level workforce (approximately 1,000 FTEs) throughout the year. Because there was little allowance for seasonality, the staff had idle time (approximately 20 percent) during summer months and hospital employed temporary nurses, hired from external nursing agencies, during winter months. Overtime was also used in winter at 1.5 times regular wage rate plus a premium of $7 per hour. These arrangements cost the hospital a great deal. In addition, the nurses were reluctant to serve as floats. Finally, in 1992—when these extra costs reached $10 million—a consultant was employed to assist the new senior administrator for nursing. Data were gathered on patient days during the year, and a time standard was set for the nursing hours required per patient day. Five levels of work for registered nurses (RNs) were established. Level 1 RNs, comprising the majority of RNs, only work in one unit (do not float). The number of RNs in Level 1 was based on annual patient days divided by 365. Level 2 RNs, also full time, work in three to four units that share similar skill requirements and are used to meet increases in patient numbers or acuity. Level 2 RNs are

paid $.75 per hour more. Level 3 RNs work in many units and are primarily per diem employees. They are used to fill in when regular RNs are sick or if help is needed during winter. Level 4 RNs are part time, filling in shifts of two hours' duration. Level 5 RNs comprise external agency nurses. Further efforts to reduce the permanent nurses' availability in the summer months were instituted in the form of career enhancement programs and voluntary leaves of absence. The new staffing system has been very successful. By 1995, the cost of external agency temp nurses and overtime declined to $2 million, flexibility increased, patient care improved, and nurses were happier.

Another hospital that started to use nurses as floats in order to reduce costs is North Oaks Medical Center in Hammond, Louisiana. Some RNs and assistant nurses are part of the Flex-Ability Nurse (FAN) program. A FAN participant is cross-trained to perform non-intensive nursing functions, and augments regular nurses during periods of high demand including winter peak months and during unpopular shifts such as weekends and Fridays. In return, the nurse is paid $5 per hour more and receives broad experience. The program continues to be well received.

Sources: J. Hausfeld et al., "Self-staffing: Improving Care and Staff Satisfaction," *Nursing Management* 25(10), October 1994, pp. 74–80; S. Hollabaugh and S. Kendrick, "Staffing: The Five-level Pyramid," *Nursing Management* 29(2), February 1998, pp. 34–36; E. T. Tate et al., "A Flex-Ability Nurse (FAN) Program," *Nursing Management* 29(5), May 1998, pp. 46ff.

The director of nursing of a hospital needs to plan the nursing levels for each quarter of next year. She has forecasted the average number of patients per day in each of the hospital wards throughout each quarter of next year. Then, she multiplied these by 90 days a quarter $\times$ 24 hours a day and divided by the number of patients to be assigned to each nurse in each ward (e.g., three patients per nurse in intensive care, etc.) to obtain the aggregate forecast for hours of nursing required in each quarter. These numbers are displayed as forecast (hours) in the following worksheet. There are currently 140 permanent nurses, each working 480 hours a quarter, and being paid $14 an hour. Overtime is allowed at up to 50 percent of regular hours and is compensated at 1.5 times the regular wage rate. Temp nurses are available but hospital policy dictates that the maximum hours for temp nurses be, at most, 20 percent of total hours of permanent nurses. Temp nurses are paid $17 per hour, but no overtime is permitted. The hiring cost is $480 and layoff cost is $240 per temp nurse. Being a service, there is no inventory of work hours and no shortage (back order) of hours is permitted.

Example 6

a. Determine all the relevant costs per hour.

b. If the 140 permanent nurses are employed throughout next year, calculate the regular permanent hours they will supply per quarter. Calculate the total hours short.

c. Suppose one temp nurse is hired and laid off after one quarter. Would this be cheaper than using a permanent nurse during overtime?

d. Determine the best (feasible) aggregate service plan, and fill the whole worksheet.

Solution

Note: The unit of product here is an hour of nursing service.

a. Regular permanent wage rate = $14/hour; temp nurse wage rate = $17/hour; overtime wage rate = $1.5 \times 14 = \$21$/hour. Hiring cost per hour (charged to the first quarter hired) is $480/480 hours = $1. Similarly, layoff cost per hour (charged to the quarter after lay off) is $240/480 hours = $0.50.

b. Total hours per quarter supplied by 140 permanent nurses = $480 \times 140 = 67{,}200$. Total hours short = total demand − total regular permanent hours = $307{,}196 - 4(67{,}200) = 38{,}396$.

c. Cost per hour of using a temp nurse in a quarter = $1 + $0.5 + $17 = $18.5 < $21 = cost per hour of overtime by a permanent nurse. Yes, using temp nurses is cheaper than using permanent nurses during overtime.

d. Given the result in part *c*, use up to the maximum hours of temp nurses in each quarter. Recall that maximum hours of temp workers = $0.20 \times 67{,}200 = 13{,}440$ hours in any quarter. If there is any more need for nursing hours, use permanent nurses during overtime. The following service plan results:

Quarter	1	2	3	4	Total
Forecast (hours)	80,326	71,953	75,627	79,290	307,196
Output (hours)					
Reg. perm.	67,200	67,200	67,200	67,200	268,800
Reg. temp.	13,126	4,753	8,427	12,090	38,396
Overtime					
Output − Forecast	0	0	0	0	
Costs per hour					
Reg. perm. @ 14	940,800	940,800	940,800	940,800	3,763,200
Reg. temp. @ 17	223,142	80,801	143,259	205,530	652,732
Overtime @ 21	0	0	0	0	0
Hire @ $1.00	13,126	0	3,674	3,663	20,463
Layoff @ $0.50	0	4,187	0	0	4,187
Total	1,177,068	1,025,788	1,087,733	1,149,993	$4,440,582

DISAGGREGATING THE AGGREGATE PLAN

For the aggregate production plan to be translated into meaningful terms for production, it is necessary to *disaggregate* the aggregate plan. This involves breaking down the aggregate plan into specific product's production schedule to determine labour requirements (skills, size of workforce), materials, and machine requirements.

For example, a lawn mower manufacturer may have an aggregate plan to produce 200 lawn mowers in January, 300 in February, and 400 in March. That company may produce push mowers, self-propelled mowers, and small riding mowers. Although all the mowers contain some of the same parts and involve some similar or identical operations for fabrication and assembly, there would be some differences in the materials, parts, and operations that each lawn mower type requires. Hence, the 200, 300, and 400 aggregate lawn mowers that are to be produced during those three months must be translated into specific numbers of mowers of each type and model prior to actually scheduling operations and planning inventory requirements.

master production schedule (MPS) The result of disaggregating an aggregate plan; shows quantity and timing of specific end items for the next 12 weeks or so.

The result of disaggregating the aggregate plan is **master production schedule (MPS)** showing the quantity and timing of *specific* end items for about 12 weeks ahead.

rough-cut capacity planning Approximate balancing of short-term capacity and production requirements to test the feasibility of a master schedule.

Once a *tentative* MPS has been developed, a planner can do **rough-cut capacity planning** to test the feasibility of a proposed MPS relative to available capacities, to ensure that no obvious capacity violations exist. This means checking capacities of production and warehouse facilities, labour, and vendors to ensure that no gross deficiencies exist

Aggregate plan	Month Planned output*	Jan.	Feb.	Mar.
		200	300	400

*Aggregate units

FIGURE 12-5

Concept of disaggregating the aggregate plan

Master production schedule	Month Planned output*	Jan.	Feb.	Mar.
	Push	100	100	100
	Self-propelled	75	150	200
	Riding	25	50	100
	Total	200	300	400

*Actual units—need to further disaggregate into weekly planned output.

that will render the MPS unworkable. The MPS then serves as the basis for *short-term* planning. It should be noted that whereas the aggregate plan covers an interval of, say, 12 months, the MPS covers only a portion of this. In other words, the aggregate plan is disaggregated in stages, or phases, that may cover, say, 12 weeks. Moreover, the MPS must be updated weekly.

Figure 12–5 illustrates the concept of disaggregating the aggregate plan. The process of determining the MPS is called *master production scheduling*. Master Production Scheduling is usually challenging because each product's forecast and committed orders should be satisfied, and the sum of resource requirements of MPS and inventories resulting from MPS should be close to those determined in the aggregate plan.

Like aggregate planning, master production scheduling can be done using linear programming. The type of software used for this is called advanced planning and scheduling (APS). See the readings, "Linear Programming at Shell Chemicals," and "Kellogg's."

Master Production Scheduling

The inputs and outputs of master production scheduling for each product can be shown in the form of a table.

Inputs. Master production scheduling has three inputs for each product: the beginning inventory, which is the actual quantity on hand from the preceding week; forecasts for each week of the schedule (next 12 weeks or so); and customer orders, which are quantities already *committed* to customers.

READING

Kellogg's

Kellogg's uses linear programming to perform both aggregate planning and master production scheduling. The Kellogg Planning System (KPS) was written in-house in 1990 to plan production/packaging and distribution of Kellogg's products (hundreds of SKUs). The operational version of KPS plans the next 30 weeks of production/packaging (in five plants and by many subcontractors called co-packers) and distribution (seven distribution centres DCs) for master scheduling (minimizing production, inventory, and transportation costs subject to safety stocks and meeting the demand at the plants and DCs), used by plant managers to schedule their production lines and for logistics managers to schedule inventories and transportation. The tactical version of KPS plans the next 18 months of production/packaging and distribution for aggregate planning. However, the products are not aggregated in the software (they are as in the operational version), but the results are aggregated manually to determine plant budgets, inventory spaces required in distribution centres, etc. Production of a product over time or in different plants is combined if its batch sizes are small. Software such as KPS is referred to as Advanced Planning and Scheduling (APS) software.

Sources: G. Brown et al., "The Kellogg Company Optimizes Production, Inventory, and Distribution," *Interfaces* 31(6), November/December 2001, pp. 1–15. www.kellogg.com

The master production scheduler should work closely with the demand manager to obtain the customer order and forecast information and to cooperatively determine the MPS.

Consider the following example. A company that makes industrial pumps wants to prepare a master production schedule for June and July. Marketing has forecasted demand of 120 pumps for June and 160 pumps for July for its major product. These will be evenly distributed over the four weeks in each month: 30 per week in June and 40 per week in July, as illustrated in Figure 12–6.

Now, suppose that there are currently 64 pumps in inventory (i.e., beginning inventory is 64 pumps), and that there are customer orders that have been committed (booked) and must be filled (see Figure 12–7).

Outputs. The master production scheduling process uses the inputs on a week-by-week basis for each product to determine the projected inventory, planned production, and the resulting uncommitted inventory, which is referred to as **available-to-promise (ATP) inventory**. Knowledge of the uncommitted inventory can enable marketing to make realistic promises to customers about deliveries of new orders. The set of planned productions for all the products is the MPS.

The first step is to calculate for each product the projected on-hand inventory, one week at a time, until it falls below a specified limit (safety stock). In the above example, the specified limit is assumed to be zero. Hence, we will continue until the projected on-hand inventory becomes negative.

The projected on-hand inventory is calculated as follows:

$$\begin{array}{c}\text{Projected on-hand} \\ \text{inventory}\end{array} = \begin{array}{c}\text{Inventory from} \\ \text{previous week}\end{array} - \begin{array}{c}\text{Current week's} \\ \text{requirements}\end{array} \qquad (14\text{–}1)$$

where the current week's requirements is the *larger* of forecast and customer orders (committed).

For the first week, projected on-hand inventory equals beginning inventory minus the larger of forecast and customer orders. Because customer orders (33) is larger than the forecast (30), the customer orders amount is used. Thus, for the first week, we obtain:

Projected on-hand inventory = 64 − 33 = 31

available-to-promise (ATP) inventory Uncommitted planned inventory.

FIGURE 12-6

Weekly forecast demand for the pumps

		Weeks						
		June				July			
	1	**2**	**3**	**4**	**5**	**6**	**7**	**8**
Forecast	30	30	30	30	40	40	40	40

FIGURE 12-7

The table for the pump showing forecasts, customer orders, and beginning inventory for eight weeks

Beginning inventory **64**		Weeks							
		June				July			
	1	**2**	**3**	**4**	**5**	**6**	**7**	**8**
Forecast	30	30	30	30	40	40	40	40
Customer orders (committed)	33	20	10	4	2			

FIGURE 12-8

Projected on-hand inventory is calculated week by week until it becomes negative

Weeks

Beginning inventory **64**

	Week 1	2	3	4	5	6	7	8
	June				July			
Forecast	30	30	30	30	40	40	40	40
Customer orders (committed)	33	20	10	4	2			
Projected on-hand inventory	31	1	−29					

Customer orders are larger than forecast in week 1; projected on-hand inventory is 64 − 33 = 31

Forecast is larger than customer orders in week 2; projected on-hand inventory is 31 − 30 = 1

Forecast is larger than customer orders in week 3; projected on-hand inventory is 1 − 30 = −29

FIGURE 12-9

Determining the planned production and projected on-hand inventory

Week	Inventory from Previous Week	Require-ments*	Net Inventory before Planned Production	(70) Planned Production			Projected Inventory
1	64	33	31				31
2	31	30	1				1
3	1	30	−29	+	70	=	41
4	41	30	11				11
5	11	40	−29	+	70	=	41
6	41	40	1				1
7	1	40	−39	+	70	=	31
8	31	40	−9	+	70	=	61

*Requirements equals the larger of forecast and customer orders in each week.

Projected on-hand inventories are shown in Figure 12–8 for the first three weeks (i.e., until the projected on-hand amount becomes negative). When the projected on-hand inventory becomes negative, this is a signal that production will be needed to replenish inventory. Hence, a negative projected on-hand inventory will require planned production. Suppose that an economic production quantity of 70 pumps is used, so that whenever production is called for, 70 pumps will be produced. (The determination of economic production quantity was described in Chapter 11.) Hence, the negative projected on-hand inventory in the third week will require production of 70 pumps, which will meet the projected shortfall of 29 pumps and leave 41 (i.e., 70 − 29 = 41) pumps for future demand.

These calculations continue for the entire master production scheduling horizon. Every time projected on-hand inventory becomes negative, another production lot of 70 pumps is added to the table. Figure 12–9 illustrates the calculations. The result is the planned production for each week. These can now be added to the table and projected on-hand inventories updated (see Figure 12–10).

It is now possible to determine the amount of inventory that is uncommitted and hence available to promise. Several methods are used in practice. The one we shall employ involves a "look-ahead" procedure: Sum booked customer orders week by week until

Planned productions are added and projected on-hand inventories are updated

Weeks

64	June				July			
	1	**2**	**3**	**4**	**5**	**6**	**7**	**8**
Forecast	30	30	30	30	40	40	40	40
Customer orders (committed)	33	20	10	4	2			
Projected on-hand inventory	31	1	41	11	41	1	31	61
Planned production			70		70		70	70

The available-to-promise inventory quantities have been added to the table

Weeks

64	June				July			
	1	**2**	**3**	**4**	**5**	**6**	**7**	**8**
Forecast	30	30	30	30	40	40	40	40
Customer orders (committed)	33	20	10	4	2			
Projected on-hand inventory	31	1	41	11	41	1	31	61
Planned production			70		70		70	70
Available-to-promise inventory (uncommitted)	11		56		68		70	70

(but not including) a week in which there is a planned production amount. For example, in the first week, this procedure results in summing customer orders of 33 (week 1) and 20 (week 2) and subtracting this from the beginning inventory of 64 pumps plus the planned production (zero in this example). Thus, ATP for week 1 is:

$$64 + 0 - (33 + 20) = 11$$

This inventory is uncommitted and can be delivered in weeks 1 and 2. Note that the ATP quantity is calculated only for the first week and for other weeks in which there is a positive planned production quantity. See Figure 12–11.

For weeks other than the first week, the beginning inventory drops out of the calculation, and ATP is the look-ahead customer orders subtracted from the production plan quantity. Thus, for week 3, the promised amounts are $10 + 4 = 14$ and the ATP is $70 - 14 = 56$. For week 5, customer orders are 2 (future orders have not yet been booked), and the ATP is $70 - 2 = 68$. For weeks 7 and 8, there are no customer orders, so for the present all of the planned production amount is available to promise. As additional orders are booked, these would be entered in the table, and the ATP amounts would be updated to reflect those orders. Marketing can use the ATP amounts to provide realistic delivery dates to customers.

Period

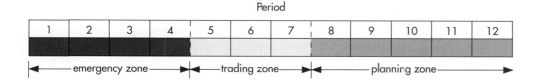

1	2	3	4	5	6	7	8	9	10	11	12

|←———— emergency zone ————→|←——— trading zone ———→|←—————— planning zone ——————→|

FIGURE 12-12

Examples of zones in the MPS

Stabilizing the Master Production Schedule

Changes to a master production schedule (i.e., the set of planned productions for all the products) can be disruptive, particularly changes to the near-future portions of the schedule. Typically, the further out in the future a change is, the less the tendency to cause problems.

Master production schedules are often divided into three zones. The dividing lines between zones are sometimes referred to as **time fences**. The emergency zone (see Figure 12–12) is closest to present time and is affected only when something unforeseen and unplanned has happened, such as sudden shifts in demand, or manufacturing problems. Changes in the emergency zone may affect commitment of key resources and therefore require top management level of approval. In addition, such changes should be discouraged unless no other alternatives exist. Next is the trading zone, when changes can be approved at a middle management level and generally involve trading one planned production for another, as opposed to the emergency change that usually sacrifices something in the short term. In the last and farthest forward timeframe, the planning zone, changes are managed without management approval, usually by the demand manager and scheduler.

time fences Points in time that separate zones of a master production schedule.

SUMMARY

Sales and operations planning is the process of integrating sales plans and forecasts with operations plans. This is done monthly when aggregate information is reviewed by top management.

Aggregate operations planning establishes general levels of employment, output, and inventories for the next 12 months or so. In the spectrum of planning, it falls between the broad decisions of long-term planning and the very specific and detailed short-term planning.

A basic requirement of aggregate planning is the aggregation of a category or family of products or services into one "product" or "service," called the "equivalent" unit. This permits planners to consider overall levels of employment and inventories without having to become involved with specific details that are better left to short-term planning. The planning variables are hire/lay off workers, overtime, part-time/temp workers, subcontracting, carrying inventory and allowing back orders. Planning strategies range from level output to chase demand production. Planners often use informal (trial-and-error) graphic and worksheet techniques to develop plans, although various mathematical optimization techniques are also used.

After the aggregate plan has been developed, it is disaggregated or broken down into specific product plans. This leads to a master production schedule, which indicates the planned quantities and timing of specific outputs. Inputs to the master production scheduling are on-hand inventory amount, forecasts of demand, and committed orders. The outputs are planned production, projected on-hand inventory, and uncommitted inventory (available-to-promise).

KEY TERMS

aggregate operations
   planning, 448
available-to-promise (ATP)
   inventory, 470
chase demand strategy, 455
level output strategy, 455

master production schedule
   (MPS), 463
rough-cut capacity planning, 468
time fences, 473

Solved Problems

Problem 1

A manager is attempting to put together an aggregate production plan for the coming nine months. She has obtained forecasts of aggregate demand for the planning horizon. The plan must deal with highly seasonal demand; demand is relatively high in months 3 and 4, and again in month 8, as can be seen below:

Month	1	2	3	4	5	6	7	8	9	Total
Forecast	190	230	260	280	210	170	160	260	180	1,940

The department has 20 permanent employees, each of whom can produce 10 units of output per month at a cost of $6 per unit. Inventory holding cost is $5 per unit per month, and back order cost is $10 per unit per month. The manager is considering a plan that would involve hiring two people to start working in month 1, one on a temporary basis who would work only through month 5. The hiring of these two and laying off of one later would cost $500 in addition to production costs.

a. What is the rationale for this plan?

b. Determine the total cost of the plan, including production, inventory, and back-order costs.

Solution

a. With the current workforce of 20 people each producing 10 units per month, regular capacity is $20 \times 10 \times 9 = 1,800$ units. That is 140 units less than total demand. Adding one worker would increase regular capacity to $1,800 + 10 \times 9 = 1,890$ units. That would still be 50 units short, or just the amount one temporary worker could produce in five months. Since one of the two seasonal peaks is quite early, it would make sense to start the temporary worker right away to avoid some of the back-order cost.

b. The production plan for this strategy is as follows:

Month	1	2	3	4	5	6	7	8	9	Total
Forecast	190	230	260	280	210	170	160	260	180	1,940
Output										
Regular	220	220	220	220	220	210	210	210	210	1,940
Overtime	—	—	—	—	—	—	—	—	—	—
Subcontract	—	—	—	—	—	—	—	—	—	—
Output − Forecast	30	−10	−40	−60	10	40	50	−50	30	0
Inventory										
Beginning	0	30	20	0	0	0	0	20	0	
Ending	30	20	0	0	0	0	20	0	0	
Average	15	25	10	0	0	0	10	10	0	70
Back order	0	0	20	80	70	30	0	30	0	230
Costs										
Output										
Regular @ $6	$1,320	1,320	1,320	1,320	1,320	1,260	1,260	1,260	1,260	$11,640
Overtime										
Subcontract										
Inventory @ $5	$75	125	50	0	0	0	50	50	0	$350
Back order @ $10	0	0	200	800	700	300	0	300	0	$2,300
Total	$1,395	1,445	1,570	2,120	2,020	1,560	1,310	1,610	1,260	$14,290

The total cost for this plan is $14,290 plus the $500 cost for two hirings and for one layoff, giving a total of $14,790. This plan may or may not be good. The manager would need to evaluate other alternative plans before settling on one plan.

You can also use the Excel template on the DVD to obtain the solution:

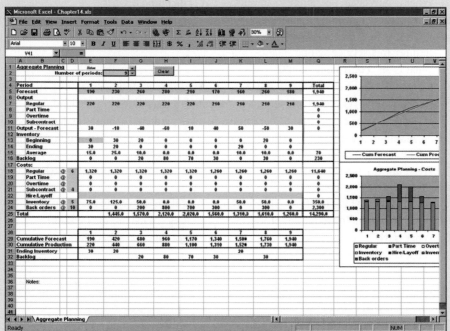

Prepare a table like that shown in Figure 12–11 for the following situation. The forecast for each week is 70 units. The starting inventory is zero. The MPS rule is to schedule production if the projected inventory on hand will be negative. The production lot size is 100 units. The following table shows customer (committed) orders.

Problem 2

Week	Customer Orders
1	80
2	50
3	30
4	10

Solution

Week	(A) Inventory from Previous Period	(B) Require-ments*	(C = B – A) Net Inventory before Planned Production	Planned Production	(Planned Production + C) Projected Inventory
1	0	80	(80)	100	20
2	20	70	(50)	100	50
3	50	70	(20)	100	80
4	80	70	10	0	10

*Requirements equals the larger of forecast and customer orders in each week.

	Week			
Starting Inv. = 0	**1**	**2**	**3**	**4**
Forecast	70	70	70	70
Customer orders	80	50	30	10
Projected on-hand inventory	20	50	80	10
Planned production	100	100	100	
ATP	20	50	60	

DISCUSSION AND REVIEW QUESTIONS	1. What is sales & operations planning?

1. What is sales & operations planning?
2. What is aggregate operations planning? What is its purpose?
3. Why is there a need for aggregate operations planning?
4. What are the most common decision variables for aggregate planning in a manufacturing setting? In a service setting?
5. What is an "equivalent" unit?
6. Briefly discuss the advantages and disadvantages of each of these planning strategies:
   a. Maintain level output and let inventories absorb fluctuations in demand.
   b. Vary the size of the workforce to correspond to predicted changes in demand requirements.
   c. Maintain a constant workforce size, but vary hours worked (through overtime and idle time) to correspond to predicted demand requirements.
7. What are the primary advantages and limitations of trial-and-error worksheet approach for aggregate operations planning?
8. Briefly describe the use of the transportation model for aggregate planning.
9. What are the inputs to master production scheduling? What are the outputs?
10. What is MPS and how is it different from master production scheduling?
11. What is rough-cut capacity planning?

TAKING STOCK

1. What general trade-offs are involved in master production scheduling in terms of the length of emergency zone of the schedule?
2. Who needs to interface with the master production schedule and why?
3. How has technology had an impact on master production scheduling?

CRITICAL THINKING EXERCISE

Contrast disaggregating aggregate operations planning in services versus manufacturing.

INTERNET EXERCISE

Briefly summarize the features of Interlace software described in www.interlacesystems.com/download/Interlace_ProductDataSheet_June_06.pdf

PROBLEMS

1. Refer to Example 1. Suppose that the president of the company is thinking about shutting down the plant for vacation and installing new equipment in month 4. After installation, the cost per unit will remain the same, but the output rate for regular time will be 450. Regular output will be the same as in Example 1 for months 1, 2, and 3; 0 for month 4; and 450 for each of the remaining months. Note, though, that the forecast of 400 units in month 4 must be dealt with. Prepare the aggregate production plan, and compute its total cost.
2. Refer to Example 1. Suppose that the regular output rate has dropped to 290 units per month due to an unexpected change in production requirements. Costs have not changed. Prepare a minimum-cost aggregate production plan and compute its total cost for each of these alternatives:
   a. Use overtime at a fixed rate of 20 units per month as needed. Plan for an ending inventory of zero with no back order for month 6.
   b. Use subcontracting at a maximum rate of 50 units per month; subcontracting need not be the same in every month used. Have an ending inventory of zero with no back ordering in the last month. Compare these two plans.
3. Refer to Example 2. Suppose that you can use a combination of overtime and subcontracting, but you cannot use subcontracting in more than two months. Up to 50 units of subcontracting and either 0 or 20 units of overtime production are allowed per month. Plan for an ending inventory of 0 with no back orders for month 6. Prepare a plan that will minimize total cost.
4. Refer to Example 2. Determine whether a plan to use subcontracting at a maximum rate of 50 units per month as needed with no overtime would achieve a lower total cost than the plan shown in Example 2. Again, plan for zero inventory and no back order at the end of month 6.

5. A manufacturer of heavy truck engines must develop an aggregate production plan, given the forecasts for engine demand shown in the following table. The company currently has 13 workers and makes 130 engines per month. Regular labour cost is $600 per engine. The beginning inventory is zero. Overtime labour costs $900 per engine. Hiring cost is $1,000 per worker and layoff cost is $2,000 per worker.

Inventory holding cost is $100 per engine per month, and back-order cost is $500 per engine per month. Develop the minimum cost aggregate production plan.

Month	1	2	3	4	5	6	7	8	Total
Forecast	120	135	140	120	125	125	140	135	1,040

6. A fabric mill has developed the forecasts shown in the table below for bolts of cloth it sells. The figures are in hundreds of bolts. The mill has a normal capacity of 275(00) bolts per month, employing 275 workers. Regular labour cost is $2,000 per hundred bolts and overtime labour cost is $3,000 hundred bolts. The beginning inventory is zero. Hiring cost is $500 per worker and layoff cost is $1,000 per worker. The inventory holding cost is $1,000 per hundred bolts per month, and back-order cost is $5,000 per hundred bolts per month.

a. Develop a level output plan.

b. Develop the minimum cost aggregate production plan.

Month	1	2	3	4	5	6	7	Total
Forecast	250	300	250	300	280	275	270	1,925

7. A small company produces a variety of recreation and leisure vehicles. The marketing manager has developed the following aggregate forecasts:

Month	Mar	Apr	May	Jun	Jul	Aug	Sep	Total
Forecast	50	44	55	60	50	40	51	350

Use the following information:

Regular labour cost	$240 per unit
Overtime labour cost	$360 per unit
Regular capacity	40 units per month, using 5 workers
Overtime capacity	8 units per month
Subcontracting cost	$400 per unit
Subcontracting capacity	12 units per month
Holding cost	$30 per unit per month
Back-order cost	$100 per unit per month
Beginning inventory	0 units
Desired ending inventory	0 units (and no back order)
Hiring cost	$2,000 per worker
Layoff cost	$4,000 per worker

Develop the minimum cost aggregate production plan and compute its total cost.

8. A small company produces whisky. The sales person has developed the following aggregate forecasts for demand (in cases) for the next six months.

Month	May	Jun	Jul	Aug	Sep	Oct
Forecast	4,000	4,800	5,600	7,200	6,400	5,000

Use the following information:

Regular labour cost	$20 per case
Regular labour capacity	5,000 cases per month using 50 workers
Overtime labour cost	$30 per case

Subcontracting cost	$40 per case
Holding cost	$2 per case per month
Back-order cost	$10 per case per month
Beginning inventory	0

Develop a close-to minimum cost aggregate production plan using a level output plan, supplemented with each of the following variables and compute the total cost for each plan. Which plan has the lower total cost?

a. Use overtime (up to 1,000 cases per month).

b. Use a combination of overtime (500 cases per month maximum) and subcontracting (500 cases per month maximum).

9. A company produces a variety of sofas. The manager wants to prepare an aggregate production plan for the next six months using the following information:

	MONTH					
	1	**2**	**3**	**4**	**5**	**6**
Forecast Demand	160	150	160	180	170	140

Cost Per Unit	
Regular time	$100
Overtime	$150
Subcontract	$180
Inventory, per month	$20
Back order, per month	$100
Hiring cost	$1,500 per worker
Firing cost	$1,500 per worker

There are 5 workers, each making 30 sofas a month. The maximum number of sofas during overtime is 10 per month. Subcontracting can handle a maximum of 10 units per month. Beginning inventory is zero. Develop a plan that minimizes total cost. No ending inventory or back orders are allowed at month 6.

10. Refer to Solved Problem 1. Prepare two additional aggregate plans which have minimum cost given the conditions below. Call the one in the solved problem plan A. For plan B, hire one more worker at a cost of $200. This would increase the number of employees to 21. Make up any shortfall using subcontracting at $8 per unit, with a maximum of 20 units per month (must use subcontracting for at least three consecutive months). Note that the ending inventory in month 9 should be zero. Leave no back orders at the end of month 9. For plan C, assume no new workers are hired (so regular output is 200 units per month instead of 210 as in plan B). Use subcontracting as needed, but no more than 20 units per month and must use subcontracting for at least three consecutive months. Leave no back orders or ending inventory at the end of month 9. Compute the total cost of each plan. Which plan has the lowest cost?

11. Refer to Solved Problem 1. Keep the regular workers at 20. Suppose another option is to use part-time workers to assist during seasonal peaks. The cost per unit, including hiring, training, and firing is $11. A maximum of 100 units can be made by part-time workers in any month, but the same number must be made in any month part-time workers are used and the months should be consecutive. The ending inventory in month 9 should be zero with no back orders allowed at the end. Determine a minimum cost aggregate plan in this case and compute its total cost.

12. Refer to Solved Problem 1. Keep the regular workers at 20. Prepare a minimum cost aggregate plan that uses overtime ($9 per unit, maximum output 25 units per month). The ending inventory in month 9 should be zero, with no back orders at the end. Compute the total cost of your plan.

13. Refer to Solved Problem 1. Start with 20 workers. Prepare a minimum cost aggregate plan that may use some combination of hiring ($200 per worker), laying off ($100 per worker), subcontracting ($8 per unit, maximum of 20 units per month, must use for at least three

consecutive months), and overtime ($9 per unit, maximum of 25 per month). The ending inventory in month 9 should be zero with no back orders at the end. Compute the total cost.

14. Refer to Example 5. Suppose that an increase in warehousing and other costs brings up the inventory holding costs to $2 per unit per month. All other costs and quantities remain the same. Determine a revised solution to this transportation problem.

15. Refer to Example 5. Suppose that regular-time capacity will be reduced to 440 units in month 3 to accommodate a companywide safety inspection of equipment. What will the additional cost of the optimal plan be as compared to the one shown in Example 5? Assume all input data are the same as given in Example 5 except for the regular-time capacity in month 3.

16. Solve Problem 15 using a holding carrying cost of $2 per unit per month.

17. A small company manufactures bicycles in two different sizes. David Dundas, the firm's owner-manager, has just received the forecasts for demands for the next six months.

	16-inch	20-inch
Nov.	1,000 units	500 units
Dec.	900	500
Jan.	600	300
Feb.	700	500
Mar.	1,100	400
Apr.	1,100	600

a. Under what circumstances will it be possible for David to develop just one aggregate production plan rather than two (one for each size bike)?

b. Suppose the forecasted demands for the two sizes of bikes are summed to obtain one aggregate forecast for each month. Currently Dundas employs 27 full-time, highly skilled employees, each of whom can produce 50 bikes per month. Because skilled labour is in short supply in the area, David would like to keep his 27 workers permanently with overtime. There is no inventory of finished bikes on hand at present, but David would like to have 300 on hand at the end of April. A maximum of 200 bikes can be produced during overtime each month. Determine a minimum cost aggregate plan and compute the total cost of your plan using these costs:

Regular	$50 per unit	Inventory	$2.00 per unit per month
Overtime	$75 per unit	Back order	$10.00 per unit per month

18. Prepare a table for the pumps of Figure 12–11; use the same inputs as the example, but change the Master Production Scheduling rule from "schedule production when the projected on-hand inventory would be negative without production" to "schedule production when the projected on-hand inventory would be less than 10 units without production."

19. Update the table shown in Figure 12–11 given these updated inputs: It is now the end of week 1; customer orders are 35 for week 2, 16 for week 3, 11 for week 4, 8 for week 5, and 3 for week 6. Inventory on hand is now 33 units. Use the Master Production Scheduling rule of ordering production when projected on-hand inventory would be negative without production.

20. Prepare a table like that shown in Figure 12–11 given the following information: The forecast for each week of an eight-week schedule is 50 units. The Master Production Scheduling rule is to schedule production if the projected on-hand inventory would be negative without it. Customer orders (committed) are:

Week	Customer Orders
1	52
2	35
3	20
4	12

Use a production lot size of 75 units and no beginning inventory.

21. Verify the available-to-promise (ATP) quantities for each period for the Solved Problem 2.

22. Prepare a table like that shown in Figure 12–11 for the following situation: The forecast is 80 units for each of the first two weeks and 60 units for each of the next three weeks. The starting inventory is 30 units. The company uses the lot size of 150 units. Also, the desired safety stock is 20 units. Committed orders are:

Week	Customer Orders
1	82
2	80
3	60
4	40
5	20

23. Minco Inc. is a small company in Midway, Tennessee, which makes fused magnesia and fused silica.[2] In the beginning of 1990s, Minco's continuous improvement efforts led it to look for a capacity and production planning software. To prepare for the use of software, a spreadsheet was first used to determine the capacity requirements for the main equipment (the fusion furnaces) and the production schedule for the main products. One major product had the following forecast sales and outstanding orders (all in thousand pounds):

	January			February			
Week	2	3	4	1	2	3	4
Forecast	56	56	56	66	66	66	66
Outstanding order	44	0	18				

The initial inventory is 119,000 pounds. If the scheduler has decided to use a lot size of 100,000 pounds per week and the minimum safety stock at the end of each week is to be 83,000 pounds, perform master production scheduling for this product.

24. Owens Corning makes different size Fiberglas mats in its composite materials facility in Anderson, S. Carolina.[3] For simplicity, consider only two products: light (3/4 ounce per square foot; 76 inches wide), and heavy (1.5 ounces per square foot; 76 inches wide) mats. Both are made on one production line. The line can make 370,000 pounds of light or 185,000 pounds of heavy mats per week. The forecast weekly demand for the next eight weeks for light mats is 110,000 pounds, and for heavy mats is 120,000 pounds. The economic production quantity (EPQ) for light mats is 370,000 pounds (one week of production), and for heavy mats is 555,000 pounds (three weeks of production). There are 120,000 pounds of inventory of each product currently on hand. Starting with light mats in week 1, determine the planned production for the two products so that neither product's projected on hand becomes negative, but their production lot sizes are close to their EPQ. If one of the products will be short, interrupt the production of the other and start making the first product.

		Week							
Light mats	0	1	2	3	4	5	6	7	8
Forecast		110	110	110	110	110	110	110	110
Committed									
Projected on hand	120								
Planned production (lot size = 370)									

		Week							
Heavy mats	0	1	2	3	4	5	6	7	8
Forecast		120	120	120	120	120	120	120	120
Committed									
Projected on hand	120								
Planned production (lot size = 185 × 3)									

---

[2]W. S. Beversluis and H. H. Jordan, "Using a Spreadsheet for Capacity Planning and Scheduling," *Production and Inventory Management Journal* 36(2), Second Quarter, 1995, pp. 12–16.

[3]M. D. Oliff and E. E. Burch, "Multi-period Production Scheduling at Owens-Corning Fiberglas," *Interfaces*, September/October 1985, pp. 25–34.

MINI-CASE

Eight Glasses a Day

The EGAD Bottling Company has recently expanded its bottled springwater operations to include several new flavours. Marketing manager Georgianna Mercer is predicting an upturn in demand based on the new offerings and the increased public awareness of the health benefits of drinking more water. She has prepared aggregate forecasts for the next six months, as shown below (quantities are in tankloads):

Month	May	Jun	Jul	Aug	Sept	Oct	Total
Forecast	50	60	70	90	80	70	420

Production manager Mark Mercer (no relation to Georgianna) has developed the following information:

Regular production cost	$1,000 per tankload
Regular production capacity	60 tankloads using 20 employees
Overtime production cost	$1,500 per tankload
Subcontracting cost	$1,800 per tankload
Holding cost	$200 per tankload per month
Back-order cost	$5,000 per tankload per month
Beginning inventory	0 tankload

Among the strategies being considered are:

1. Maximum regular production supplemented by up to 10 tankloads a month from overtime.

2. Same as 1 but subcontracting of a maximum of 10 tankloads per month is also allowed.

3. Same as 1 but can use overtime for up to 15 tankloads a month.

The objective is to choose the plan that has the lowest total cost. Which plan would you recommend?

MINI-CASE

Welch's

Welch's, the producer of grape juice, packages a few families of the products on each line. In order to prepare the master production schedule, the planner first aggregates the demand and required safety stock of each product in each family during the next four weeks. She also aggregates the initial inventory of each product to obtain the family initial inventory. Then, given the production hours available during the regular time and overtime, the production rates and the setup time for each family, and some other cost data, she uses a linear programming software to determine the production quantity of each family during the next four weeks in order to minimize the total costs of holding inventory, setup time, and overtime, such that after satisfying the demand, the ending inventories each week are greater or equal to the safety stocks.

On a particular line, four families are packaged. One of the families has three products in it. The forecast demand (in 1,000 cases), the required safety stock, and the beginning inventory for each product during the next four weeks are as follows:

Demand Forecast

	Week 1	Week 2	Week 3	Week 4
Product 1	6.7	6.78	6.78	6.78
Product 2	.5	1.48	1.48	1.48
Product 3	2.0	1.88	1.88	1.88

Minimum Safety Stock

	Week 1	Week 2	Week 3	Week 4
Product 1	17.99	19.03	17.12	16.73
Product 2	.93	.98	3.16	3.60
Product 3	3.02	3.16	5.72	6.23

Initial inventory

Product 1	12.89
Product 2	2.66
Product 3	4.45

a. Determine the aggregate forecasts and aggregate safety stock for each week; and the aggregate initial inventory.

b. Using the result of part a, and available hours during regular time (80 hours per week) and overtime (36 hours per week), production rate of 1.14 hours per unit, setup time of eight hours, holding cost per unit per week of $150, setup cost of $400, and overtime cost of $212 per unit, and similar information about the other families, the linear programming software has determined the following quantities for this family for Weeks 1 to 4: 11.14, 14.00, 10.34, and 10.70 units. Determine the aggregate ending inventory each week, and verify that the aggregate minimum safety stock levels are satisfied.

The aggregate production quantities are next disaggregated by also using linear programming for each family. Given the production rates and setup time for each product, and some other cost data, the linear programming software determines the production quantity for each product during the next four weeks in order to minimize the total cost of holding inventory and setup time and the deviation of total production quantity from that derived in the aggregate model for each week, such that after satisfying the demand, the ending inventories each week are greater or equal to the safety stocks.

c. Using the aggregate production quantities given in part *b*, production rates of 1.10, 1.21, and 1.12 hours per unit for products 1 to 3, respectively, setup time of 0.5 hour for each production run, holding cost per unit per week of $150, setup cost of $100 per product run, the linear programming software has determined the following quantities for Weeks 1 to 4. Determine the ending inventories for each

product in each week, and verify that the minimum safety stock levels are satisfied for each product.

Production	Week 1	Week 2	Week 3	Week 4
Product 1	12.44	7.24	5.43	5.77
Product 2	0	1.42	4.95	0
Product 3	1.69	5.34	0	5.00

Sources: Based on S. J. Allen and E. W. Schuster, "Practical Production Scheduling with Capacity Constraints and Dynamic Demand: Family Planning and Disaggregation," *Production and Inventory Management Journal* 35(4), Fourth Quarter, 1994, pp. 15–21; www.welchs.com.

SELECTED BIBLIOGRAPHY AND FURTHER READING

Brandimarte, P., and A. Villa (eds). *Modeling Manufacturing Systems: From Aggregate Planning to Real-Time Control.* New York: Springer, 1999.

Buxey, G. "Production Planning for Seasonal Demand." *International Journal of Operations and Production Management* 13(7), July 1993, pp. 4–21.

Fogarty, Donald W., John H. Blackstone Jr., and Thomas R. Hoffmann. *Production and Inventory Management.* Cincinnati: South-Western Publishing, 1991.

Hopp, Wallace J., and Mark L. Spearman. *Factory Physics.* 2nd ed. New York: Irwin/McGraw-Hill, 2001.

Silver, E. A., D. F. Pyke, and R. Peterson. *Inventory Management and Production Planning and Scheduling.* New York: Wiley, 1998.

Sipper, Daniel, and Robert Bulfin Jr. *Production: Planning, Control, and Integration.* New York: McGraw-Hill, 1997.

Vollmann, Thomas E., William L. Berry, and D. Clay Whybark. *Manufacturing Planning and Control Systems.* 4th ed. Burr Ridge, IL: Richard D. Irwin, 1997.

Material Requirements Planning and Enterprise Resource Planning

LEARNING OBJECTIVES

After completing this chapter, you should be able to:

1 Describe MRP and the conditions under which it is most appropriate.

2 Describe the inputs and calculation of MRP.

3 Describe lot sizing methods.

4 Explain capacity requirements planning.

5 Describe MRP II and how it relates to MRP.

6 Describe ERP.

Wescast is a large car exhaust-manifold manufacturer based in Brantford, Ontario. To meet the needs of its just-in-time big car manufacturer customers, Wescast had to become more efficient and effective in its operations. It needed to be able to track its production and inventories, and to reduce manufacturing lead times and work-in-progress inventories. How did Wescast achieve this? The answer to questions like this is given in this chapter.

INTRODUCTION

This chapter describes MRP (material requirements planning) and ERP (enterprise resource planning). MRP is a planning and scheduling technique used for batch production of assembled items. ERP involves the use of extensive software to integrate record keeping and information sharing throughout an organization.

First we will show why purchasing or production of manufacturing parts requires a different treatment than finished goods or supplies. Then MRP inputs and calculations are presented. Next, some lot-sizing techniques for MRP are described. Then, production planning is related to the use of resources, a process called *capacity requirements planning*. Next, MRP II, an expanded version of MRP, is presented and contrasted with MRP. Finally, ERP is described and contrasted with MRP II.

Dependent versus Independent Demand

A major distinction in the way inventories are managed results from the nature of demand for those items. When demand for items is derived from plans to make certain products, as it is with raw materials, parts, and subassemblies used in producing a finished product, those items are said to have **dependent demand**. The parts and materials that go into the production of a particular type and model of automobile have dependent demand because the amount of parts and raw materials needed is a function of the number of cars that is planned to be produced. Conversely, demand for the *finished* cars is independent. The customer demand is not known.

Independent demand is fairly steady once allowances are made for seasonal variations, but dependent demand tends to be sporadic or "lumpy"; large quantities are used at specific points in time with little or no usage at other times. For example, a company that produces lawn and garden equipment might make a variety of items, such as trimmers, lawn mowers, and small tractors but these are usually made in batches. Suppose that the various products are produced as follows—in one month, push mowers; in the next month, mulching mowers; and in the third month, tractors. Some components may be used in most of the items (e.g., nuts and bolts, screws). It makes sense to have a continual inventory of these parts because they are always needed. On the other hand, some parts might be used for only one item. Consequently, demand for those parts occurs only when that item is being produced, which might be once every few months; the rest of the time, demand is zero. Thus, demand is "lumpy." Because of these tendencies, independent-demand items must be carried on a continual basis, but dependent-demand items need only be stocked just prior to the time they will be needed in the production process. Moreover, the predictability of usage of dependent-demand items means that there is little or no need for safety stock.

Figure 13–1 illustrates key differences in independent- and dependent-demand inventories. The inventory control techniques of Chapter 11 are used for purchasing or production of items with independent demand. In this chapter, we will use MRP for planning purchasing or production of dependent-demand items.

dependent demand Demand for subassemblies, parts, or raw materials which are derived from the plan for production of finished goods.

AN OVERVIEW OF MRP

Material requirements planning (MRP) is the process to determine ordering and scheduling of dependent-demand components (e.g., raw materials, parts, and subassemblies). A production plan for a specified number of each finished product is translated into

material requirements planning The process to determine the ordering and scheduling of dependent-demand components.

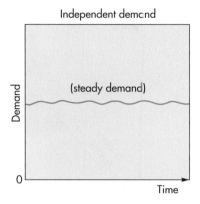

Independent demand

(steady demand)

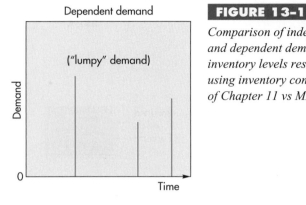

Dependent demand

("lumpy" demand)

FIGURE 13-1

Comparison of independent and dependent demand, and inventory levels resulting from using inventory control models of Chapter 11 vs MRP.

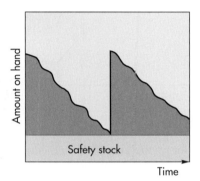

Safety stock

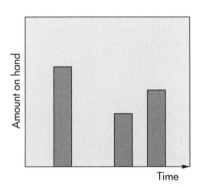

requirements for subassemblies, parts, and raw materials, working backward from the due dates, using lead times and other information to determine when and how much to order each component. Hence, requirements for end items generate requirements for lower-level components, so that ordering, fabrication, and assembly can be scheduled for timely completion of end items while inventory levels for components are kept reasonably low.

Historically, ordering and scheduling of components for assembled products suffered from two difficulties. One was the enormous task of setting up production schedules, keeping track of large numbers of parts and subassemblies, and coping with schedule and order changes. The other was a lack of differentiation between independent demand and dependent demand items. All too often, techniques designed for independent-demand items were used to handle dependent-demand items, which resulted in excessive inventories.

In the 1970s, manufacturers began to recognize the importance of the distinction between independent- and dependent-demand items and to approach these two categories in different ways. Much of the burden of record keeping and determining material requirements in many companies has now been transferred to computers, using techniques

READING

Futuretek-Bathurst

Futuretek-Bathurst Tool Inc. is a 50-employee machine shop in Oakville, Ontario, that makes tools and components for aerospace, power generation, and telecom companies. In the early 2000s, Futuretek needed to improve its control over customer orders and to be able to change orders as requested, and to also plan the process for each order. Further, Futuretek wanted in-process job tracking in order to prepare for ISO 9000 standards. Futuretek installed the IndustriOS ERP from IndustriOS Software Inc. of Oakville. The software has met Futuretek's objectives and also has increased staff communication. Lead times have decreased and capacity has increased. IndustriOS, like most other ERP software, uses Crystal Reports. Crystal Reports is a reporting tool kit that helps the user to rapidly create flexible, feature-rich reports and integrate them into Web and Windows applications.

Sources: www.industrios.com. Look in "Success Stories"; www.fbtmfg.com.

FIGURE 13-2

Overview of MRP

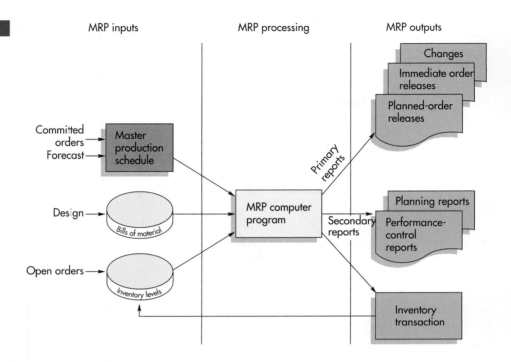

such as MRP. A great deal of the credit for publicizing MRP and educating potential users about MRP goes to Joseph Orlicky,[1] George Plossl, Oliver Wight, and APICS.

MRP begins with the production schedule for the finished goods that is converted into requirements for the subassemblies, parts, and raw materials needed to produce the finished items. Thus, MRP is designed to answer three questions: *what* is needed? *how much* is needed? and *when* is it needed?

The primary inputs to MRP are bills of material, which tell the composition of each assembled subassembly and product; master production schedule, which tells how many finished products are desired and when; and inventory levels, lead times, and any open shop or purchase orders (being executed). The planner processes this information to determine the *net* requirements for subassemblies, parts, and materials for each period (week or day) of the planning horizon (e.g., next 12 weeks).

Outputs from MRP include planned order releases and various reports. Figure 13–2 provides an overview of an MRP system. For applications of MRP, see the readings, "Futuretek-Bathurst," "Aerospace Welding," "Sunrise," "City of Edmonton," and "Wescast."

MRP INPUTS

An MRP system has three major sources of information: the master production schedule, bills-of-material, and inventory level, lead times, and open orders. Let's consider each of these inputs.

The Master Production Schedule

master production schedule
States which end items are to be produced, when, and in what quantities.

The **master production schedule (MPS),** as described in the previous chapter, states which end items are to be produced, when and in what quantities. Figure 13–3 illustrates a portion of an MPS that shows planned output for end item X for the planning horizon. The schedule indicates that 100 units of X will be needed (e.g., for shipments to customers) at the *start* of week 4 and that another 150 units will be needed at the *start* of week 8.

The quantities in an MPS come from a number of different sources, including customer orders and forecasts.

---

[1]Orlicky is the author of *Material Requirements Planning* (New York: McGraw-Hill, 1975).

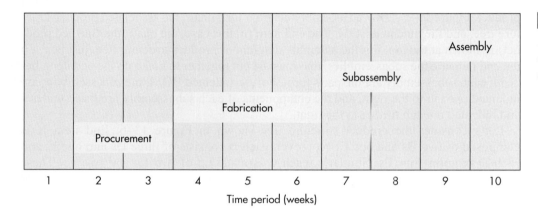

FIGURE 13-3

A portion of the master production schedule for end item X

FIGURE 13-4

The planning horizon must be longer than the cumulative lead time

The MPS separates the planning horizon into a series of time periods or *time buckets*, which are expressed in weeks or days. However, the time buckets need not be of equal length. In fact, the near-term portion of an MPS may be in days, but later portions may be in weeks or months. Usually, plans for those more distant time periods are more tentative than near-term requirements.

Although a master production schedule has no set time period that it must cover, most managers like to plan far enough into the future so that they will have some general idea of upcoming demands for the near term. It is important, though, that the planning horizon be longer than the *stacked* or **cumulative lead time** necessary to produce the end items. This amounts to the sum of the lead times that sequential phases of the production or assembly process require, as illustrated in Figure 13–4, where a total of nine weeks of lead time is needed from ordering parts and raw materials until final assembly is completed.

Some subassemblies are also included in the MPS if the production system involves making that subassembly to stock (and later using it to assemble the final product to order).

cumulative lead time The sum of the lead times that sequential phases of a process require, from ordering of parts and raw materials to completion of final assembly.

READING

Catalyst

Catalyst Manufacturing® software is a low-cost MRP software which is rather easy to use. To use the software, the suppliers, work centres/operations, all the parts/subassemblies/products, and customers first must be defined. Then, the configuration of each subassembly and product which has components needs to be defined. This involves listing each operation to be performed on the item and the materials used in that operation. Using the product configurations, customer orders or master production schedule, and inventories, Catalyst determines the material requirements. To the right is the BOM for a metal shelf which also shows the operations necessary for each subassembly. An evaluation version of Catalyst can be downloaded free from www.mfgcatalyst.com.

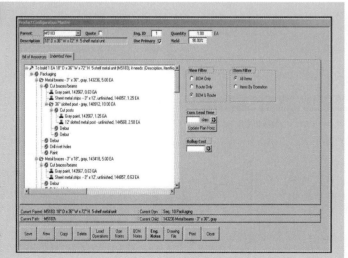

Reprinted by permission from Catalyst Manufacturing.®

Bills of Material

bill of material (BOM) A listing of all of the raw material, parts, and subassemblies needed to produce one unit of a product.

A **bill of material (BOM)** contains a listing of all of the subassemblies, parts, and raw material that are needed to produce *one* unit of a finished product. Thus, each finished product has its own bill of material.

assembly diagram and product structure tree Visual depiction of the requirements in a bill of material, where components are shown by levels.

A bill of material is related to the **assembly diagram and product structure tree**, which provide a visual hierarchical depiction of the components needed to assemble a product. Figure 13–5 shows an assembly diagram for a chair, the associated product structure tree, and the indented BOM. The end item (in this case, the chair, the finished product) is shown at the top. For the assembly diagram or product structure tree, just beneath the end item are the subassemblies, that must be put together to make up the end item; beneath each subassembly are the parts for it. For the indented BOM, the subassemblies are indented one tab to the right, and the components of each subassembly are listed under it and indented one tab further to the right.

Let's consider the product structure tree shown in Figure 13–6. End item X is composed of two Bs and one C. Moreover, each B consists of three Ds and one E, and each D requires four Es. Similarly, each C is made up of two Es and two Fs. These *requirements* are listed by *level*, beginning with level 0 for the end item, then level 1 for the next level, and so on. The items at each level are *components* of the next level up and,

FIGURE 13-5

Assembly diagram, product structure tree, and indented BOM for a chair

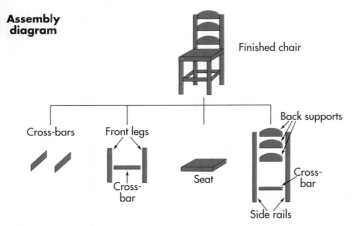

FIGURE 13-6

A product structure tree for end item X

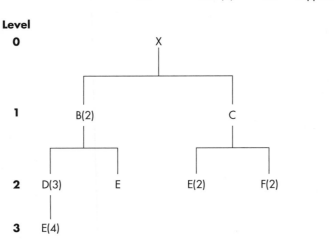

Aerospace Welding

Aerospace Welding of Blainville, Quebec, with approximately 150 employees, repairs and manufactures aircraft engine parts. Aerospace has used COSS Manufacturing System, an ERP software, since 1995. The original version ran under Unix, but the new version runs under Windows XP. The software is integrated with ACCPAC accounting system. Besides the basic functions, COSS has sophisticated modules such as product configurator, estimating and quoting, and

advanced shop floor scheduling. It also uses Crystal Reports. The 50-user system cost Aerospace $45,000, with $9,000 annual maintenance cost. Using the software has made Aerospace more efficient and effective. It can make better-informed sales decisions and quotes. Tracking of job times have resulted in some employees being identified for further training. The software keeps the records of parts repaired for 10 to 15 years, as required by regulation. COSS Systems Inc. is based in Mississauga, Houston, and Charlotte.

Sources: www.aerospacewelding.com; www.coss-systems.com under Info Center, then Case Studies.

as in a family tree, are *parents* of their respective components. Note that the quantities of each item in the product structure tree refer only to the amounts needed to complete one unit of the parent at the next higher level. For a software use of BOM, see the reading, "Catalyst," and for two applications, see the readings, "Planning Bills at SeaQuest," and "AccuRate."

Use the information presented in Figure 13–6 to do the following:

Example 1

a. Determine the quantities of B, C, D, E, and F needed to assemble one X.

b. Determine the quantities of these components that will be required to assemble 10 Xs, taking into account the following quantities on hand (i.e., in inventory) of various components:

Component	On Hand
B	4
C	10
D	8
E	60
F	5

a.

Solution

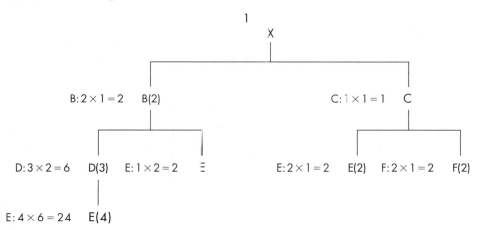

Thus, one X will require:

    B: 2
    C: 1
    D: 6
    E: 28 (Note that E occurs in three places, with requirements of 24 + 2 + 2 = 28)
    F: 2

b.

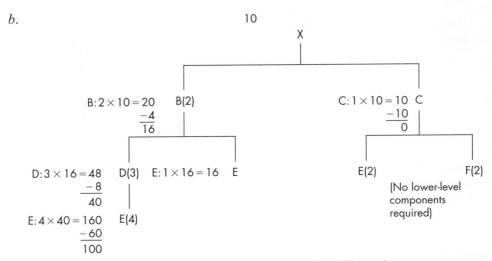

Thus, given the amounts of on-hand inventory, 10 Xs will require:

B: 16
C: 0
D: 40
E: 116 (100 + 16)
F: 0

Note that the amounts on hand are *netted out* (i.e., subtracted from the requirements) to determine the net requirements.

Determining net requirements is usually more complicated than Example 1 might suggest. The issue of *timing* is essential (i.e., when must the components be ordered or made) and must be included in the analysis.

Comment. It is extremely important that the bill of material accurately reflect the composition of a product, particularly since errors at one level become magnified by the multiplication process used to determine quantity requirements. As obvious as this might seem, many companies find themselves with incorrect bills of material. These make it

 READING

Planning Bills at SeaQuest

When there are very similar end products with only minor differences, such as different-colour trims, and if the final assembly can be postponed until late in production, then it is possible to simplify the planning process by combining similar end products into an artificial product grouping with a BOM called a planning bill. For example, SeaQuest, now part of AquaLung, a manufacturer of scuba diving equipment and wet suits in California, used the planning bill shown to the right for its Spectrum wet suit.

Each suit required 2 yards (1.8 metres) of fabric. Roughly 75 percent of suits were black and 25 percent were blue. Therefore, in the planning bill 1.5 yards of black and 0.5 yards of blue fabric were specified.

Component	Description	Unit	Qty	Level
1-7001	Fabric, Black	YD	1.5	1
1-7002	Fabric, Blue	YD	.5	1
1-7500	Bind Tape, Black	IN	300	1
1-7600	Bind Tape, Blue	IN	100	1
1-1410	Velcro Hook, Black	IN	33	1
1-1420	Velcro Hook, Blue	IN	11	1
2-3510	Airway Assembly	EA	1	1
2-8-228	Tank Band Assembly	EA	1	1
1-2567	Foam Pad	EA	1	1
1-9001	Box, Spectrum	EA	1	1

Sources: G. H. French, "Linking Design, Marketing, and Shipping for Success: A Case Study in Integration," *Production and Inventory Management Journal*, Third Quarter, 1992, pp. 44–48; www.aqualung.com/home.html.

READING

Sunrise

Sunrise Spas is a small (50–75 employees, 45,000 square feet) manufacturer of whirlpool spas in Grimsby, Ontario. It had installed Visual Manufacturing from Lilly Software in 2001, but was not happy with it. The problems included lack of flexible pricing (C$, US$, Euro, and quantity discount prices). Also, Sunrise was looking for a product configurator to customize options for some customers. This activity took the time of two order-taking clerks. Sunrise had recently used the consulting, support, and software company MDKS of Waterloo to install its new computers, so MDKS was consulted. In 2003 MDKS installed their own ERP software called MDKS Infinity on Sunrise's computers. This is integrated with the ACCPAC Advantage accounting software. Because Infinity does not have a product configurator either, MDKS wrote a separate program to perform this function. Sixteen users use the software at the cost of $50,000 plus $700 per month for support.

Sources: www.sunrisespas.com; www.mdksinfinity.com/pdf/InfinityBottomLineArticle.pdf.

impossible to effectively determine material requirements; moreover, the task of correcting these records can be complex and time-consuming. Accurate records are a prerequisite for effective MRP.

Inventory Levels, Lead Times, and Open Orders

Each item in stock (product, subassembly, part, or raw material) should have a separate description file that contains information about the item as well as the quantity on hand and, if purchased, the purchase lead-time. Each manufactured or assembled item will have a configuration file which shows the operations necessary and the materials or parts used. Each operation will have a standard time for setup and per unit operation time. Using these and the number of items to be produced, the total manufacturing lead time for the item can be calculated. Each open shop and purchase order (i.e., currently being executed) has a quantity and due date (called scheduled receipt date).

MRP CALCULATIONS

MRP processing takes the end item requirements specified by the MPS and "explodes" them into *time-phased* requirements for fabrication or assembly of subassemblies, and fabricated parts, and purchase of purchased parts and raw materials using the bills of

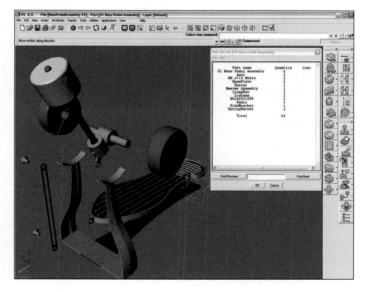

VX Corporation's CAD/CAM software can be used not only for product design, but also to prepare parts lists. This screen shows a parts lists for a bass drum pedal along with a three-dimensional view of the product subassemblies. www.vx.com

FIGURE 13-7

Assembly time chart showing material purchase order points and production start times needed to meet scheduled delivery of 100 units of the end item

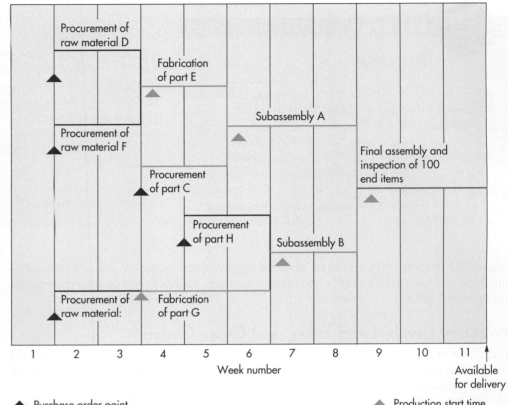

material, offset by the lead times and netted for any inventory on hand or scheduled receipts (on order). You can see the time-phasing of requirements in the assembly time chart in Figure 13–7. For example, raw materials D, F, and I must be ordered at the start of week 2, part C at the start of week 4, and part H at the start of week 5 in order for 100 units of the end item to be available for delivery at the start of week12. The figure also shows the planned fabrication or assembly start times of other items.

Note that the length of horizontal lines represents the lead times. For example, the purchase lead time for raw material D is two weeks, and the manufacturing lead time for 100 units of part E has been calculated to be two weeks. This is based on the speed of the operation(s) involved.

The quantities that are generated by exploding the bills of material are *gross requirements*; they do not take into account any inventory that is currently on hand or due to be received. The materials that a company must actually acquire to meet the demand generated by the MPS are the *net requirements*.

The determination of the net requirements (*netting*) is the core of MRP processing. One accomplishes this by subtracting from gross requirements the sum of inventory on hand and any scheduled receipts, and then adding in safety stock requirements, if applicable:

$$
\begin{array}{c}
\text{Net} \\
\text{requirements} \\
\text{in period } t
\end{array}
=
\begin{array}{c}
\text{Gross} \\
\text{requirements} \\
\text{in period } t
\end{array}
-
\begin{array}{c}
\text{Projected inventory} \\
\text{at the start of} \\
\text{period } t
\end{array}
-
\begin{array}{c}
\text{Scheduled} \\
\text{receipts}
\end{array}
+
\begin{array}{c}
\text{Safety} \\
\text{stock}
\end{array}
\qquad (15\text{–}1)
$$

If the formula gives a negative value, then there is no net requirements. For simplicity, we will omit safety stock from computations in the examples and most problems. Net requirements are sometimes adjusted to include an allowance for waste; but for simplicity, this too will not be included in the examples or most problems.

Lectronic is a small Mississauga-based company with an innovative product: a radio-controlled golf caddy. Lectronic has been using the full version (including the MRP module) of the Business System from Minotaur Software of Brampton for 12 years.

Sources: www.kaddy.com; www.minotaursoftware.com/studies/lectronic.htm.

The timing and sizes of orders (i.e., materials ordered from suppliers or work started within the company) are determined by *planned-order releases*. The timing of the receipts of these quantities is indicated by *planned-order receipts*. Depending on ordering policy, the planned-order releases may have a minimum level, may be multiples of a specified quantity (e.g., 50 units), or be equal to the quantity needed at that time (called lot-for-lot ordering). Example 2 will illustrate the difference between these ordering policies as well as the general concept of time-phasing material requirements in MRP. As you work through the example, you may find the following list of terms helpful.

Gross requirements. The total demand for an item *during* each time period without regard to the amount on hand. For end items, these quantities are shown in the MPS; for components, these quantities are equal to the planned-order releases of their immediate "parents" multiplied by number of each item in one parent.

Scheduled receipts. Open orders scheduled to arrive from vendors or shop floor in the *beginning* of a period.

Projected on-hand. The amount of inventory that is expected to be on hand at the *beginning* of each time period: it equals the scheduled receipts this period plus any ending inventory expected from the last period.

Net requirements. The actual amount needed in each time period.

Planned-order receipts. The quantity planned to be received in the *beginning* of each period. Under lot-for-lot ordering, these quantities will equal net requirements. Under lot-size ordering, these quantities may exceed net requirements. We assume that any excess is added to available inventory in the beginning of the *next* time period, although in reality it would be available in this period.

Planned-order releases. Indicates a *planned* amount to order in each time period; equals planned-order receipts offset by lead time. This amount generates gross requirements at the next level in the BOM. When an order is executed (i.e., the planned-order release of

gross requirements Total demand for an item in each time period.

scheduled receipts Open orders scheduled to arrive from vendors or shop floor.

projected on-hand Expected amount of inventory that will be on hand at the beginning of a time period.

net requirements The actual amount needed in each time period.

planned-order receipts Quantity planned to be received in the beginning of each period.

planned-order releases Planned amount to order in each time period; that is, planned-order receipts offset by lead time.

week 1 is released), it is removed from planned-order releases and receipts, and entered in scheduled receipts, lead-time periods later.

These quantities are used in a time-phased plan in the following format. The column for period 0 is used to show beginning on-hand inventory.

Week or day number	0	1	2	3	4	5	6	7	8
Item:									
Gross requirements									
Scheduled receipts									
Projected on-hand									
Net requirements									
Planned-order receipts									
Planned-order releases									

Example 2

A company that produces wood shutters has received two orders for a particular model of wood shutters: 100 units are due for delivery at the start of week 4 and the 150 units are due for delivery at the start of week 8. Each shutter consists of two frames and four slatted wood sections. The wood sections are ordered, and purchase lead time is one week for lot sizes between 300 and 700 wood sections. The frames are also ordered, and purchase lead time is two weeks for lot sizes of 200 to 400 frames. Assembly of the shutters requires one week for lot sizes of 100 to 200 shutters. There is a scheduled receipt of 70 wood sections from the vendor at the beginning of week 1. Currently, there is no on-hand inventory. Determine the size and timing of planned-order releases necessary to meet delivery requirements under each of these conditions:

1. Lot-for-lot ordering (i.e., order sizes equal to net requirements).

2. Lot-size ordering with a minimum lot size of 320 units for frames and multiples of 70 units for wood sections.

Solution

a. Develop a production schedule for shutters:

Week number:	1	2	3	4	5	6	7	8
Quantity:				100				150

b. Develop a product structure tree:

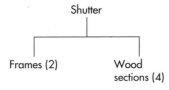

c. The production schedule gives the gross requirements for shutters. Next, compute net requirements. Using *lot-for-lot ordering*, determine planned-order receipt quantities and the planned-order release timing to satisfy the production schedule (see Figure 13–8).

The production schedule calls for 100 shutters to be ready for delivery, and no shutters are projected to be on hand at the start of week 4, so the net requirements are also 100 shutters. Therefore, planned receipt for week 4 equals 100 shutters. Because shutter assembly for 100 units requires one week, this means a planned-order release at the start of week 3. Using the same logic, 150 shutters must be assembled during week 7 in order to be available for delivery at the start of week 8.

The planned-order release of 100 shutters at the start of week 3 means that 200 frames (gross requirement) must be available at that time. Because none are expected to be on

Production schedule for shutters:

Week number	Beg. Inv.	1	2	3	4	5	6	7	8
Quantity					100				150

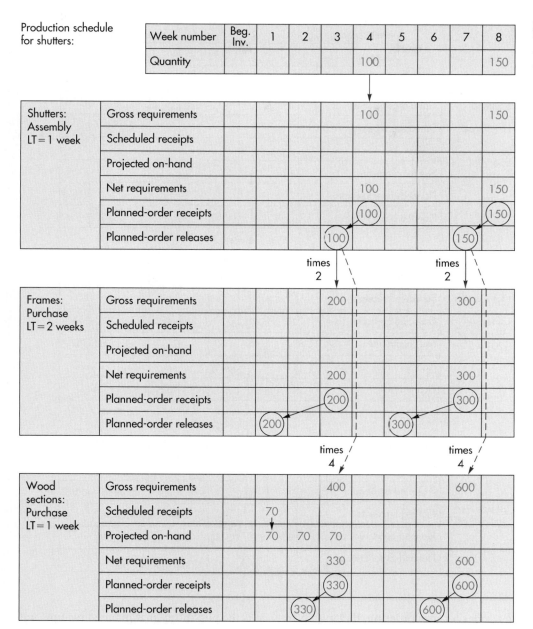

FIGURE 13-8

MRP tables with lot-for-lot ordering for Example 2

hand, this generates net requirement of 200 frames and necessitates planned receipt of 200 frames by the start of week 3. With a two-week purchase lead time, this means that the company must order 200 frames at the start of week 1. Similarly, the planned-order release of 150 shutters at the start of week 7 generates gross and net requirements of 300 frames for week 7 as well as planned receipt for that time. The two-week purchase lead time means that the firm must order frames at the start of week 5.

The planned-order release of 100 shutters at the start of week 3 also generates gross requirement of 400 wood sections at that time. However, because 70 wood sections are expected to be on hand, net requirement is $400 - 70 = 330$. This means a planned receipt of 330 by the start of week 3. Since purchased lead time is about one week, the purchase order must be issued (planned-order release) at the beginning of week 2.

Similarly, the planned-order release of 150 shutters in week 7 generates gross requirement of 600 wood sections at that point. Because no on-hand inventory of wood sections is projected, net requirement is also 600, and planned-order receipt is 600 units. Again, the approximate one-week purchase lead time means 600 sections should be scheduled for purchase at the start of week 6.

FIGURE 13-9

MRP tables with lot-size ordering for Example 2.

MPS for shutters:

Week number	Beg. Inv.	1	2	3	4	5	6	7	8
Quantity					100				150

Shutters: LT = 1 week, Lot size = lot-for-lot

		1	2	3	4	5	6	7	8
Gross requirements					100				150
Scheduled receipts									
Projected on-hand									
Net requirements					100				150
Planned-order receipts					(100)				(150)
Planned-order releases				(100)				(150)	

times 2   times 2

Frames: LT = 2 weeks, Lot size = minimum of 320

		1	2	3	4	5	6	7	8
Gross requirements				200				300	
Scheduled receipts									
Projected on-hand					120	120	120	120	140
Net requirements				200				180	
Planned-order receipts				(320)				(320)	
Planned-order releases		(320)				(320)			

times 4   times 4

Wood sections: LT = 1 week, Lot size = multiples of 70

		1	2	3	4	5	6	7	8
Gross requirements				400				600	
Scheduled receipts		70							
Projected on-hand		70	70	70	20	20	20	20	50
Net requirements				330				580	
Planned-order receipts				(350)				(630)	
Planned-order releases			(350)				(630)		

d. Under lot-size ordering, the only difference is the possibility that planned receipts will exceed net requirements. The excess is recorded as projected on hand inventory in the beginning of the following week. For example, in Figure 13–9, the minimum order size for frames is 320 units, net requirement for week 3 is 200; thus, there is an excess of 320 − 200 = 120 units, which become projected on hand inventory in the start of next week. Similarly, net frame requirement of 300 − 120 = 180 units in week 7 is 140 less than the 320 minimum order size; again, the excess becomes projected on hand inventory in the start of week 8. The same thing happens with wood sections; an excess of planned-order receipts in weeks 3 and 7 is added to projected inventory in the start of weeks 4 and 8. Note that the order size for wood sections must be in *multiples* of 70; for week 3 it is 5 times 70, and for week 7 it is 9 times 70.

Example 2 is useful for describing some of the main features of MRP processing, but it understates the enormousness of the task of keeping track of material requirements, especially in situations where the same subassemblies, parts, or raw materials are used in a number of different products. Differences in timing of demands, revisions caused by late deliveries, high scrap rates, and cancelled orders all have an impact on processing.

Consider the two product structure trees shown in Figure 13–10. Note that both products have D as a component. Suppose we want to develop a material requirements plan for D given this additional information: the demand for A is 80 units at the start of week 4 and the demand for C is 50 units at the start of week 5; there is a beginning inventory of 110 units of D on hand, all items have manufacturing or purchase lead times of one week, and we order D using lot-for-lot ordering. The plan is shown in Figure 13–11. Note that requirements for B and E are not shown because they are not a "parent" of D.

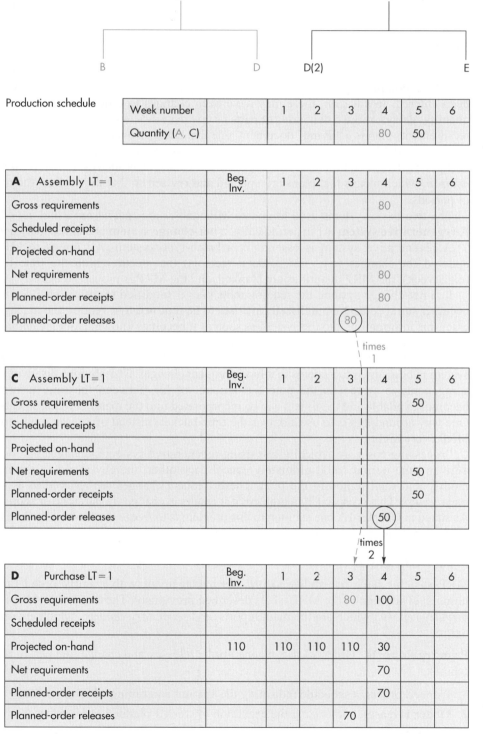

Production schedule

Week number		1	2	3	4	5	6
Quantity (A, C)					80	50	

A Assembly LT=1	Beg. Inv.	1	2	3	4	5	6
Gross requirements					80		
Scheduled receipts							
Projected on-hand							
Net requirements					80		
Planned-order receipts					80		
Planned-order releases				80			

times 1

C Assembly LT=1	Beg. Inv.	1	2	3	4	5	6
Gross requirements						50	
Scheduled receipts							
Projected on-hand							
Net requirements						50	
Planned-order receipts						50	
Planned-order releases					50		

times 2

D Purchase LT=1	Beg. Inv.	1	2	3	4	5	6
Gross requirements				80	100		
Scheduled receipts							
Projected on-hand	110	110	110	110	30		
Net requirements					70		
Planned-order receipts					70		
Planned-order releases				70			

pegging The process of identifying the parent items that have generated a given set of requirements for an item.

The term **pegging** denotes working this process in reverse; that is, identifying the parent items that have generated a given set of requirements for some item such as D. Although the process may appear simple enough given the product structure trees and tables shown in this chapter, when multiple products are involved, the process is more complex. Pegging enables managers to determine which product(s) will be affected if an order for an item is late.

The importance of the computer becomes evident when you consider that a typical company would have not one but hundreds of end items for which it needs to develop material requirements plans, each with its own set of components. Inventories on hand and on order, order releases, and so on must all be updated as changes and rescheduling occur. Without the aid of a computer, the task would be hopeless.

Updating the System

A material requirements plan is not a static document. As time passes, some orders will have been completed, other orders will be nearing completion, and new orders will have been entered. In addition, there may have been changes to orders, such as changes in quantity, delays, missed deliveries of parts or raw materials, and so on. Hence, a material requirements plan is a "living" document, one that changes over time. And what we refer to as "Period 1" (i.e., the current period) is continually moving ahead; so what is now Period 2 will soon be Period 1. In a sense, requirements plans such as these have *a rolling horizon*, which means that plans are updated and revised so that they reflect the next set of periods.

The two basic systems used to update MRP tables are *regenerative* and *net change*. A **regenerative system** is run periodically; a **net-change system** is continuously updated.

regenerative system Recalculates all the MRP quantities periodically.

A regenerative system is essentially a batch-type system. All inputs to MRP are updated for changes (e.g., new orders, receipts) that occur within the time interval (e.g., week), the MRP quantities are blanked, and the MRP is processed again.

net-change system Updates only MRP tables affected by a change immediately.

In a net-change system, the requirements plan is modified to reflect changes as they occur. If some defective purchased parts had to be returned to a vendor, the manager can enter this information into the system as soon as it becomes known. Only the *changes* are exploded through the system, level by level; the entire plan would not be regenerated.

The regenerative system is best suited to fairly stable systems, whereas the net-change system is best suited to systems that have frequent changes. The obvious disadvantage of a regenerative system is the potential amount of lag between the time information becomes available and the time it can be incorporated into the material requirements plan. One way around this is to use a day as the time bucket (instead of a week) and rerun the MRP every night.

Processing costs are typically less using regenerative systems; changes that occur in a given time period could ultimately cancel each other, thereby avoiding the need to modify and then remodify the plan. These frequent changes are referred to as system *nervousness*. This is especially a problem if it results in changes in purchase or shop orders. As stated in Chapter 12, one solution to this problem is to freeze the master schedule for the near future (e.g., next four weeks).

MRP Outputs

MRP systems have the ability to provide management with a fairly broad range of outputs, in addition to the MRP tables described previously. These are often classified as *primary reports*, which are the main reports, and *secondary reports*, which are optional outputs.

order releases Authorization for the execution of week 1 planned-order releases.

Primary Reports. Order release, planned-order releases, and changes are part of primary reports:

1. Planned orders, a schedule indicating the amount and timing of future orders.

2. **Order releases**, authorizing the execution of week 1 planned-order releases.

changes Revisions of dates or quantities of open orders.

3. **Changes** to open orders: revisions to due dates and quantities.

Secondary Reports. Performance-control and planning reports belong to secondary reports.

1. **Performance-control reports** evaluate system operation. They aid managers by measuring deviations from plans, including missed deliveries and stockouts, and by providing information that can be used to assess cost performance.

2. **Planning reports** are useful in forecasting future inventory requirements. They include net requirements and other data that can be used to assess future material requirements.

The wide range of outputs generally permits users to tailor MRP to their particular needs.

performance-control reports Evaluation of system operation, including deviations from plans and cost information.

planning reports Data useful for assessing future material requirements.

OTHER CONSIDERATIONS

Safety Stock

Theoretically, inventory systems with dependent demand should not require safety stock below the end item level. This is one of the main advantages of an MRP approach. Supposedly, safety stock is not needed because the manager can project the requirements once the MPS has been established. Practically, however, there may be exceptions.

READING

AccuRate

AccuRate of Whitewater, Wisconsin, is a manufacturer of dry feeders used, for example, to accurately feed chocolate chips into cookie mix, or dry chemicals into water treatment facilities. When its business was booming in the 1980s, AccuRate started to incur more inventory shortages. To alleviate this, AccuRate installed an MRP system. MPS is compiled by heads of sales, manufacturing, and engineering on a weekly basis. It includes a production plan for items such as the basic subassemblies, end products, and special items. Each Friday night, the MRP program explodes the BOMs, and supplies picking lists (used to pick components held in the warehouse), work orders, and MRP sheets (purchase orders). An example of a BOM is as follows:

Description	Part No.	Quantity
Dryfeeder, Final Assembly	602-087	
Key, SAE 1035 HPRO	M-1505	3
Clamp Hose, 2.50 dia	M-1003	2
Common Parts	602-177	1
Bracket & Brg. Assy.	602-165	2
Outer Bearing Sup.	600-516	1
Skid	602-032	1
Panel, Front Outside	602-031	1
Panel, Back Outside	602-029	1
Quill Assy.	602-017	1
Link & Brg. Assy.	602-016	1
Hopper Assy.	602-010	1
Lever Assy.	602-004	1
Main Frame Weldment	602-602	1
Blade Assy., LH	602-002	1

Description	Part No.	Quantity
Blade Assy., RH	602-001	1
Spacer	600-045	1
Spacer	600-044	1
Shaft, Eccentric	600-038	1
Cover Panel, Drive Box	600-031	2
Filler, Corner Post	600-025	2
Hold Down	600-011	4
Saddle	600-002	1

On Monday morning, the MRP detailed report is reviewed, and the buyer forwards the purchase orders to the vendors. Cooperation of vendors and all functional areas of the company are needed to provide accurate data. The result of MRP usage was a 10-percent reduction in inventory (despite increased sales) and better on-time delivery.

Sources: J. R. Biggs and E. J. Long, "Gaining the Competitive Edge with MRP/MRPII," *Management Accounting*, May 1988, pp. 27–32; www.accuratefeeders.com.

FIGURE 13-12

Demand for a part

	Period				
	1	2	3	4	5
Demand	70	50	1	80	4
Cumulative demand	70	120	121	201	205

For example, a bottleneck process or one with varying scrap rates can cause shortages in downstream operations. Furthermore, shortages may occur if orders are late or fabrication or assembly times are longer than expected.

MRP systems deal with these problems in several ways. The manager's first step is to identify activities or operations that are subject to variability and to determine the extent of that variability. When lead times are variable, the concept of safety *time* instead of safety *stock* is often used. This results in scheduling orders for arrival or completion sufficiently ahead of the time they are needed in order to eliminate or substantially reduce the element of chance in waiting for those items. It is important in general to make sure that lead times are accurate. If safety stock is needed because of possible quality problems resulting in scrap, planned order release amounts can be increased by a percentage.

Lot Sizing

lot sizing Choosing a lot size for ordering or production.

Determining a lot size to order or to produce is an important issue in inventory management for both independent- and dependent-demand items. This is called **lot sizing**. For independent-demand items, managers often use economic order quantity and economic production quantity. For dependent-demand systems, however, a much wider variety of models is used to determine lot sizes, mainly because no single model has a clear advantage over the others. Some of the most popular models for lot sizing are described in this section.

A primary goal of inventory management for both independent- and dependent-demand systems is to minimize the sum of annual ordering cost (or setup cost) and holding cost. With independent demand, the demand is frequently distributed uniformly throughout the year. Demand tends to be much more lumpy for dependent demand, and the planning horizon is shorter (e.g., three months), so that economic lot sizes are usually much more difficult to identify. Consider the situation depicted in Figure 13–12. Period demands vary from 1 to 80 units, and no demand size repeats over the horizon shown.

Managers can realize economies by grouping orders. This would be the case if the additional cost incurred by holding the extra units until they were used led to a savings in setup or ordering cost. This determination can be very complex at times, for several reasons. First, combining period demands into a single order, particularly for middle-level or end items, has a cascading effect down through the product structure tree; that is, in order to achieve this grouping, you must also group items at lower levels in the tree and incorporate their setup and holding costs into the decision. Second, the uneven period demand and the relatively short planning horizon require continual recalculation and updating of lot sizes. Not surprisingly, the methods used to handle lot sizing range from the simple to the complex.

The choice of a lot-sizing technique must take into account the nature of demand (degree of uniformity), the relative importance of holding cost versus ordering (or setup) cost, and any other considerations that affect ordering. It appears that no single method is suited to all conditions.

Regardless of the lot-sizing method in use, there is always the possibility of adjustments in order sizes due to allowance for shrinkage or scrap, minimum and maximum order quantities established by management (e.g., do not order more than five months' supply), and operating or shipping constraints (e.g., 200 pieces per run or 12 dozen per shipment).

Lot-for-Lot Ordering. The purchase order or run size for each period is set equal to net requirement for that period. Example 2, part 1, demonstrated this method. Not only is the order size obvious, it also eliminates holding costs. Its chief drawback is that it may require too many orders or production runs.

Economic Order Quantity. This can lead to minimum total annual ordering and holding cost if usage is fairly uniform. This is sometimes the case for lower-level items that are common to different parents and for raw materials.

Fixed-Period Ordering. This type of ordering provides coverage for some predetermined number of periods (e.g., two or three). In some instances, the span is simply arbitrary; in other cases, a review of historical demand patterns may lead to a more rational designation of a fixed period length. The rule can be modified when common sense suggests a better way. For example, take a look at the demands shown in Figure 13–12. Using a two-period rule, an order size of 120 units would cover the first two periods. However, the demand in period 3 is so small that it would make sense to combine it with the demand during the first two periods; that is, order 121 units for the first three periods. The following method provides a better way to determine the number of periods to order for at the same time.

Part-Period Method. The part-period method represents another attempt to balance setup (or ordering) and holding costs. The term *part period* refers to holding a part or parts over a number of periods. For instance, if 10 parts were held for two periods, this would be $10 \times 2 = 20$ part periods. The economic part period (EPP) can be calculated as the ratio of setup (or ordering) cost to the cost to hold a unit for one period. Thus, the formula for calculating the EPP is:

$$EPP = \frac{\text{Setup (or ordering) cost}}{\text{Unit holding cost per period}} \tag{15–2}$$

To determine an order size that is consistent with the EPP, various order sizes are examined for a planning horizon, and each one's number of part periods is determined. The one that comes closest to the EPP is selected as the best lot size. The order sizes that are examined are based on cumulative demand. Example 3 will illustrate this approach.

Use the part-period method to determine order sizes for the following demands (i.e., net requirements) for a manufactured part:

Example 3

				Period				
	1	**2**	**3**	**4**	**5**	**6**	**7**	**8**
Demand	60	40	20	2	30	—	70	50
Cumulative demand	60	100	120	122	152	152	222	272

Setup cost is $80 per run for this item, and unit holding cost is $.95 per period.

1. First calculate the EPP: EPP = $80/$.95 = 84.21, which rounds to 84 part periods. This is the target.

Solution

2. Next, try the cumulative lot sizes, beginning with 60, until the part periods approximate the EPP. Continue this process for the planning horizon. This leads to the following:

Period When Order Is Placed	Lot Size	Extra Inventory Carried	× Periods Carried	= Part Periods	Cumulative Part Periods
1	60	0	0	0	0
	100	40	1	40	40
	120	20	2	40	80
	122	2	3	6	86*
5	30	0	0	0	0
	100	70	2	140	140*
8	50	0	0	0	0

*Closer to 84 (than 80).

The calculations of part periods indicate that 122 units should be ordered to be available at period 1, and 100 units should be ordered to be available at period 5. The next lot will be ordered for period 8, but there is insufficient information now to determine its size.

The lot sizes considered for period 1 correspond to cumulative demand. Once the best lot size has been identified, the cumulative demand is set equal to zero and then summed beginning with the next order period. In this case, the lot size of 122 covers the first four periods, so cumulative demand is started next for period 5. The next lot size covers through period 7, and the count begins again at period 8.

The process works well for the first lot size because the cumulative number of part periods is close to the EPP, but the effect of lumpy demand is apparent for the second lot size of 100 (140 part periods is not very close to 84 part periods).

Capacity Requirements Planning

One of the most important features of MRP is its ability to aid managers in capacity planning.

capacity requirements planning The process of determining short-term capacity requirements.

Capacity requirements planning is the process of determining short-term capacity requirements. The necessary inputs include planned-order releases of MRP for manufactured or assembled items, the current shop load, routing information, and job times. Key outputs include load reports for each work centre. When underloads or overloads are projected, managers might consider remedies such as alternative routings, changing lot sizing, and lot splitting. Moving production forward or backward can be extremely challenging because of possible unavailability of subassemblies, parts, or raw materials.

A firm usually generates an MPS initially in terms of what is needed and not what is possible. The initial production schedule may or may not be feasible given the capacities of the production system. It is often necessary to run a proposed MPS through MRP processing in order to obtain a clearer picture of actual requirements, which can then be compared to available capacity. If it turns out that the current MPS is not feasible, management may make a decision to either increase the capacity (e.g., through overtime) or to revise the MPS. In the latter case, this may entail several revisions, each of which is run through the MRP system until a feasible plan is obtained. At that point, the master production schedule is *frozen*, at least for the near term, thus establishing a firm schedule from which to plan requirements.

Figure 13–13 presents an overview of the capacity requirements planning process. The process begins with a proposed or tentative master production schedule that must be tested for feasibility and possibly adjusted before it becomes permanent. The proposed schedule is processed using MRP to ascertain the material requirements the schedule would generate. These are then translated into resource (i.e., capacity) requirements for items made in-house involving assembly or fabrication. This is often in the form of a

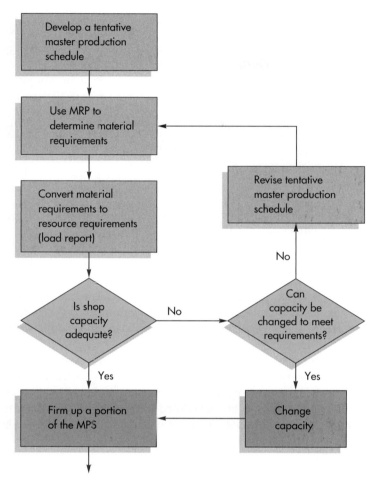

FIGURE 13-13

Using MRP to assist in capacity requirements planning

Source: Stephen Love, *Inventory Control* (New York: McGraw-Hill) 1979), p. 164. Reprinted by permission.

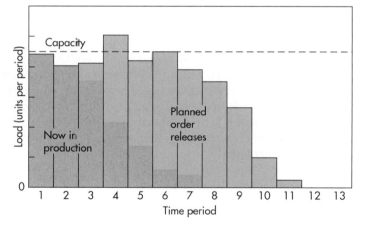

FIGURE 13-14

A hypothetical department load report

series of **load reports** for each department or work centre, which compares known and expected future capacity requirements with projected capacity availability. Figure 13–14 illustrates the nature of a load report. It shows expected resource requirements (i.e., usage) for jobs currently being worked on and planned orders for the planning horizon. Given this sort of information, the manager can more easily determine whether capacity is sufficient to satisfy these requirements. In the load report illustrated in Figure 13–14, planned-order releases in time period 4 will cause an overload. However, it appears possible to accommodate demand by shifting some orders to adjacent periods. In cases where capacity is insufficient, a manager may be able to increase capacity by scheduling overtime or transferring personnel from other areas if this is possible and economical

load reports Department or work centre reports that compare known and expected future capacity requirements with projected capacity availability.

READING

Wescast

Wescast is a large Brantford-based car exhaust manifold manufacturer. In the late 1990s, Wescast was looking for a software to integrate its various functions of business including order-taking, production-scheduling, and EDI, under pressure from its big automaker customers who demanded JIT delivery. Wescast bought TRANS4M ERP from Agilisys (now called Infor Global Solutions) and implemented it in phases. TRANS4M receives orders from automakers, schedules the orders, releases purchase orders to suppliers, and releases shop orders automatically. As a result, inventories have been cut down from 10 days to 3–4 days of supply.

Sources: "Supplier Slashed Inventory," *Manufacturing Systems*, October 1999, pp. 25A–28A; www.wescast.com; http://www.infor.com/infor/company_pressreleases_694.htm

or else revise the master production schedule and repeat the process until an acceptable master production schedule is obtained.

If the master production schedule must be revised, this generally means that the manager must assign priorities to orders if some orders will be finished later than originally planned.

One note of caution is in order concerning capacity load reports. Often, the load reports are only approximations, and they may not give a true picture because the loading does not take into account scheduling and queuing delays. Consequently, it is possible to experience system backups even though a load report implies sufficient capacity to handle projected loads.

An important aspect of capacity requirements planning is the conversion of quantity requirements into time requirements. One accomplishes this by multiplying each period's quantity requirements by standard time per unit plus a setup time per run. For instance, if 10 units of product A are scheduled in the fabrication department, and each unit has a standard time of 2 hours plus a set-up time of 8 hours for the batch, then 10 units of A converts into:

$$10 \text{ units} \times 2 \text{ hours/unit} + 8 = 28 \text{ hours}$$

By the way, this is the manufacturing lead time for fabricating 10 units of A.

MRP II

manufacturing resource planning (MRP II) Expanded system for production planning involving sales & operations planning, MPS, MRP, and detailed scheduling and control.

In the early 1980s, material requirements planning was expanded into a broader system for planning and scheduling the resources of manufacturing firms. This expanded system has been dubbed **MRP II**, which refers to **manufacturing resource planning**. MRP II is a closed-loop MRP which means that it involves the whole production planning process, starting with sales & operations planning, then MPS and MRP, and finally detailed scheduling and control, with feedback going back up to planning (see Figure 13–15).

The DuPont Merck reading in the previous chapter was actually an example of the MRP II implementation.

ERP

enterprise resource planning (ERP) Integration of sales/marketing, finance accounting, manufacturing and materials management, and human resources functions on a single computer system.

ERP (enterprise resource planning) involves *standardized* record keeping using one database that will permit *information sharing* among different functions (finance accounting, manufacturing and materials management, marketing and sales, and HR) and branches of an organization in order to manage the system more effectively. The reading, "The ABCs of ERP" and the newsclip on SAP further describe ERP.

ERP became popular in the 1990s as MRP II began to fade. ERP software are both loved and hated. Two major problems with top tier ERP software such as SAP are their high cost and complexity (see the reading on "Some Implementations of ERP" for both advantage and disadvantages of ERP). Note that not every ERP software package includes MRP. In fact, most are expanded versions of accounting or business software.

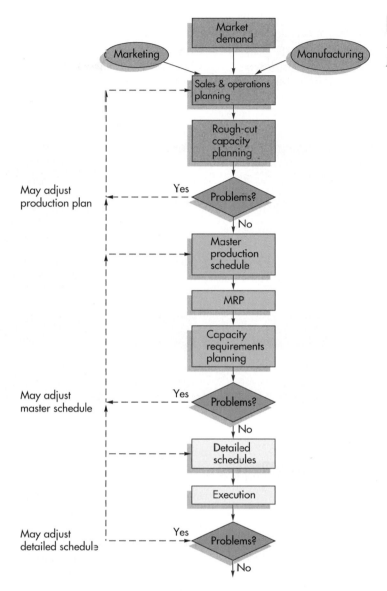

FIGURE 13-15

An overview of MRP II process

Recently, some mid-market accounting software, such as Axapta, have caught up with top tier ERP software in terms of functionality, while costing much less (see the reading, "ERP versus Accounting Software").

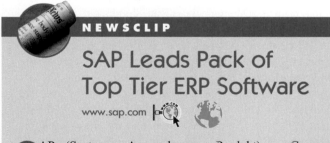

NEWSCLIP

SAP Leads Pack of Top Tier ERP Software

www.sap.com

SAP (Systeme, Anwendungen, Produkt), a German company, produces software designed to fully link all functional areas within a company, from financial accounting to sales and human resource planning, including many of the manufacturing, planning and control functions.

According to SAP, the Production Planning and Control module can draw forecast demand data directly from the S&OP (sales & operations planning) module, which can then be used to create MPS. Most types of production processes are covered within the production planning and control program, from flow/process type systems to repetitive manufacturing and a kanban-specific support system that actually links to a bar-code reader. The MRP system will calculate quantities and dates down to the raw material level.

The ERP idea is also reflected in the Product Data Management part of SAP, which is a database system containing a "material master record" for parts and products. This record would typically include part number or component data and design information—possibly including CAD drawings. This data object is central to the SAP system. Below are the major processes in SAP.

Source: SAP company press releases.

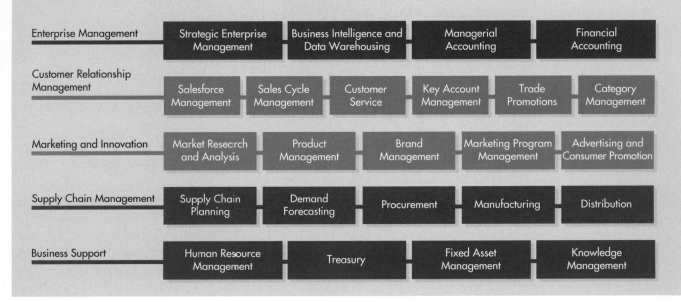

Enterprise Management	Strategic Enterprise Management	Business Intelligence and Data Warehousing		Managerial Accounting		Financial Accounting
Customer Relationship Management	Salesforce Management	Sales Cycle Management	Customer Service	Key Account Management	Trade Promotions	Category Management
Marketing and Innovation	Market Research and Analysis	Product Management	Brand Management	Marketing Program Management	Advertising and Consumer Promotion	
Supply Chain Management	Supply Chain Planning	Demand Forecasting	Procurement	Manufacturing	Distribution	
Business Support	Human Resource Management	Treasury		Fixed Asset Management	Knowledge Management	

READING

The ABCs of ERP

What Is ERP?

ERP attempts to integrate all departments and functions across a company onto a single computer system that can serve all those different departments' particular needs.

It's a tall order, building a single software program that serves the needs of the people in finance as well as it does the people in human resources and in the warehouse. Each of those departments typically has its own computer system, each optimized for the particular ways that the department does its work. But ERP combines them all into a single, integrated software program that runs off a single database so that the various departments can more easily share information and communicate with each other, and also to reduce redundant data entry.

The integrated approach can have a tremendous payback if companies install the software correctly. Take a customer order, for example. Typically, when a customer places an order, that order begins a mostly paper-based journey from in-basket to in-basket around the company, often being keyed and rekeyed into different departments' computer systems along the way. All that lounging around in in-baskets causes delays and lost orders, and all the keying into different computer systems invites errors. Meanwhile, no one in the company truly knows what the status of the order is at any given point because there is no way for the finance department, for example, to get into the warehouse's computer system to see whether the item has been shipped. "You'll have to call the warehouse," is the familiar refrain heard by frustrated customers.

How Can ERP Improve a Company's Business Performance?

ERP automates the tasks involved in performing a business process—such as order fulfillment, which involves taking an order from a customer, making it, shipping it, and billing for it. With ERP, when a customer service representative takes an order from a customer, he or she has all the information necessary to complete the order (the customer's credit rating and order history, the company's MPS and inventory levels, and the shipping trucking schedule). Everyone else in the company sees the same computer screen and has access to the single database that holds the customer's new order. When one department finishes with the order it is automatically routed using the ERP system to the next department. To find out where the order is at any point, one needs only to log on to the

ERP system and track it down. Customers get their orders faster and with fewer mistakes than before. ERP can apply that same magic to the other major business processes, such as employee benefits or financial reporting.

That, at least, is the dream of ERP. The reality is much harsher. Let's go back to those in-baskets. That process may not have been efficient, but it was simple. Finance did its job, the warehouse did its job, and if anything went wrong outside of the department's walls, it was somebody else's problem. Not anymore. With ERP, the customer service representatives are no longer just typists entering someone's name into a computer and hitting the return key. The ERP screen makes them business people. It flickers with the customer's credit rating from the finance department and the product inventory levels from the warehouse. Will the customer pay on time? Will we be able to ship the order on time? These are decisions that customer service representatives have never had to make before and that affect the customer and every other department in the company. But it's not just the customer service representatives who have to wake up. People in the warehouse who used to keep inventory in their heads or on scraps of paper now need to put that information online. If they don't, customer service will see low inventory levels on their screens and tell customers that their requested item is not in stock. Accountability, responsibility, and communication have never been tested like this before.

To do ERP right, the ways you do business will need to change and the ways people do their jobs will need to change too. Real transformational ERP efforts usually run between one and three years.

Will ERP Fit the Ways I Do Business?

It's critical for companies to figure out if their ways of doing business will fit within a standard ERP package before the cheques are signed and the implementation begins. The most common reason that companies walk away from multi-million dollar ERP projects is that they discover that the software does not support one of their important business processes. At that point there are two things they can do: They can change the business process to accommodate the software, which will mean deep changes in long-established ways of doing business and shaking up important people's roles and responsibilities. Or they can modify the software to fit the process, which will slow down the project, introduce dangerous bugs into the system, and make upgrading the software difficult.

What Does ERP Really Cost?

Meta Group recently did a study looking at the total cost of ownership (TCO) of ERP, including hardware, software, professional services, and internal staff costs. The TCO numbers include getting the software installed and the two years afterward, which is when the real costs of maintaining, upgrading,

and optimizing the system for your business are felt. Among the 63 companies surveyed—including small, medium, and large companies in a range of industries—the average TCO was $15 million (the highest was $300 million and the lowest was $400,000).

The Hidden Costs of ERP

ERP pros vote the following areas as most likely to result in budget overrun.

1. *Training.* Training expenses are high because workers almost invariably have to learn a new set of processes, not just a new software interface.

2. *Integration and testing.* A typical manufacturing company may have add-on applications for logistics, production planning and bar coding. If this laundry list also includes customization of the core ERP package, expect the cost of integrating, testing, and maintaining the system to skyrocket.

3. *Data conversion.* It costs money to move corporate information, such as customer and supplier records, product design data and the like, from old systems to new ERP system.

4. *Data analysis.* Often, the data from the ERP system must be combined with data from external systems for analysis purposes. Users with heavy analysis needs should include the cost of a data warehouse in the ERP budget—and they should expect to do quite a bit of work to make it run smoothly.

5. *Consultants ad infinitum.* When users fail to plan for disengagement, consulting fees run wild.

How Do You Configure ERP Software?

The packages are built from database tables, thousands of them, that information systems programmers and end users must set to match their business processes; each table has a decision "switch" that leads the software down one decision path or another. By presenting only one way for the company to do each task—say, run the payroll or close the books—a company's individual operating units and far-flung divisions are integrated under one system. But figuring out precisely how to set all the switches in the tables requires a deep understanding of the existing processes being used to operate the business. As the table settings are decided, these business processes are reengineered, ERP's way. Most ERP systems are preconfigured, allowing just hundreds—rather than thousands—of procedural settings to be made by the customer.

Questions

1. What is ERP?

2. How can ERP help a business organization?

3. What are some obstacles to implementing ERP?

Source: Adapted from C. Koch, "The ABCs of ERP," *www.CIO.com/ research/erp/edit/erpbasics.html*

Some Implementations of ERP

SMED International

Calgary-based SMED International custom builds modular office furniture and wall systems. It has sales of $200-million-plus a year and employs 1,700 people. In 1997 SMED decided to replace a homegrown legacy system with ERP from Baan. It hoped to improve customer service by tracking the status of orders better and to increase profit by more closely tracking costs. SMED began implementing major distribution, manufacturing, and finance modules in 1998. It turned the system on in one part of the firm (representing about 30 percent of revenues) in 1999. The implementation went "fairly smoothly." The reason was that customization of software was kept to a minimum. There was some user resistance, because the integration of front-end and back-end processes meant that salespeople could no longer count on engineers in manufacturing to fill in the blanks in specifications for custom orders, and if an order isn't entered completely the system kicks it out, which is frustrating for users.

Honda Canada

Honda Canada Inc. is the $5-billion-a-year Canadian subsidiary of the Japanese auto giant. It employs 3,200 people. The company manufactures Civics and Odyssey minivans at its two plants in Alliston, Ontario, north of Toronto. In 1997 Honda decided to implement the finance, payroll, and HR modules of PeopleSoft's ERP. Honda's legacy HR and finance systems were 10 years old, and its U.S. sister company was implementing PeopleSoft. One reason the implementation was a success was that Honda, like SMED, kept customizations to a minimum. Its basic strategy was to get the ERP system up and running first, and then work on refining it later.

University of Toronto

In 1995 U of T turned to SAP for its major financial and administrative modules. Most recently it added a payroll system too. One mistake the university made was to do the training sequentially, in small groups, one after the other, starting relatively early in the implementation process. By the time the system was actually up and running, the first users trained had forgotten what they had learned. This situation was exacerbated by the fact that it took longer than expected to get the system up and running. Unfortunately, hiring consultants didn't turn out to be a one-year scenario, but rather three years. Perhaps U of T would have been wiser to hire outside people on long-term contracts. The University also had difficulty hanging on to full-time IT staff once they were fully trained on SAP.

High Liner Foods

After Atlantic fish stocks disappeared in the early 1990s, seafood processor High Liner Foods of Lunenburg, N.S., saw its annual revenues plummet from more than $700 million to barely $200 million. In order to survive, the company went through an intense period of process redesign. At the end of the process, High Liner realized it didn't have the systems it needed to streamline its processes and reduce head count. It ended up selecting an ERP system from J. D. Edwards to replace a mix of disjointed homegrown and off-the-shelf software. High Liner made the buying decision in late 1993, began implementation in 1994, and has now installed finance, sales order processing, logistics, distribution, manufacturing, and most recently warehousing modules. The system is delivering exactly what the company wanted, and the project has come in on time and on budget.

This success is attributed to two main factors: J. D. Edwards' "conference-room pilot" methodology, and high-level management support for the project within High Liner. In the J. D. Edwards methodology, senior managers from operational departments should get involved in defining company processes and adapting them to the practices incorporated in the ERP system. Later they're involved in testing the system with real data—the conference-room pilot—and, ultimately, with training users. When the VP of finance is leading the training, it makes it awfully hard for an accountant not to play along. Another factor in High Liner's success was the decision to make virtually no changes to the J. D. Edwards system.

Sobeys

Sobeys chose SAP to upgrade its human resources and financial systems in the latter half of 1990s. These projects were successful. Later, SAP was asked to install its transaction-processing module in Sobeys' Atlantic and company-owned Ontario stores. However, after two years of implementation problems, Sobeys new CEO, Bill McEwan, announced in January 2001 that the SAP system caused Sobeys' IBM DB2 database to crash during the past December, leaving it unable to process transactions moving through the stores' systems for five days—creating a five-week backlog just before the busy holiday shopping period. This caused Sobeys a great deal of extra cost (processing the transactions manually) and many stockouts. McEwan decided that SAP's transaction processing function was unable to effectively deal with the extremely high number of transactions and products in the Sobeys retail operation environment. Sobeys took a $90-million write-off to phase out SAP from its retail stores.

Ikon Office Solutions

Ikon, based in Pennsylvania with branches in Canada, other U.S. locations, Mexico, and Europe, is in the business of helping companies with their copying, imaging, and storage of documents. Ikon asked SAP to set up its ERP in Ikon's northern California region branches as a pilot project in 1994. After two years of using a 50-member project team from Ikon, and 40 to 50 outside consultants, the ERP was operational. However, the total cost reached $25 million, double the planned budget. Most of the cost went to pay consultants: IBM alone received $8 million. The consultants charged $300 an hour, and there was no knowledge transfer to Ikon's staff so consultants' involvement after ERP startup still continued. In 1997, the new corporate chief information officer decided that the cost of ERP exceeded its benefit, and that it would be

dismantled from the northern California region. Besides excessive costs, the software did not sufficiently address the needs of a service company like Ikon: it didn't have an adequate feature for tracking service calls.

Sources: T. Martell, "Scaling the ERP Mountain," *CIO Canada* 7(5), May 1999, pp. 16–20; D. Steinhart, "Sobeys Takes One-time $50M Write-down to Phase Out SAP Software System That Failed in December," *Financial Post (National Post)*, January 26, 2001, p. C4; J. Brown, "Sobeys Fires SAP over ERP Debacle," *Computing Canada* 27(3), February 9, 2001, pp. 1,2ff; M. Kolbasuk McGee, "Ikon Writes Off $25M in Costs on SAP Pilot," *Informationweek* 627(25), April 21, 1997, pp. 25ff

READING

ERP versus Accounting Software

The boom time for ERP software was in the middle to late 1990s when enterprises were revamping their legacy mainframe computer systems in anticipation of possible Year 2000 (Y2K) problems. Tier 1 ERPs, such as SAP, PeopleSoft, J. D. Edwards, BAAN, and Oracle cost million of dollars to buy and implement, and had a high annual maintenance fee. But top managers felt that they had no choice and jumped on the bandwagon. Because of complexity, the implementation took many years. The complexity was due to the fact that the software had hundreds of features. For example, Tier 1 ERPs are multi-currency and multi-language.

However, Tier 1 ERPs offered capabilities not offered by accounting software such as Great Plains which primarily kept track of transactions. These included high-volume fast databases which could be connected directly to supplier systems, and modules to perform HR, manufacturing planning and control, materials management, customer relationship

management (CRM), and e-commerce including Web stores directly connected to the database. They also provided industry-specific solutions and the ability to control work flow such as enforcing the authorization requirement for a high-dollar purchase by a buyer.

Since the mid-1990s, many midmarket accounting software have moved closer to become a complete business system, even including manufacturing modules. Microsoft has also got into this market by buying Great Plains, Navision, and Solomon accounting software, and even introducing their own Axapta. The difference between Tier 1 ERPs and these software has shrunk. At the same time, many companies have realized that the high cost and complexity of Tier 1 ERPs is not worth it. Nowadays, companies are hardly buying Tier 1 ERPs. As a result, ERP companies such as SAP are providing midmarket products such as SAP Business One. Also, there has been heavy consolidation (e.g., Peoplesoft bought J. D. Edwards in 2003 and Oracle bought Peoplesoft in 2004). There is also more emphasis on e-commerce.

Source: www.180systems.com/erp-systems.php.

Material requirements planning (MRP) is a process to determine the ordering of dependent-demand items (i.e., components of assembled products). The planning process begins with master production schedule. The end items are exploded using the bills of material, and material requirements plans are developed that show quantity and timing for ordering or producing components.

SUMMARY

Various lot-sizing rules are used in MRP, but the main one is lot-for-lot ordering. Capacity requirements planning uses the MRP shop order releases and standard operations times to determine the capacity requirements from each work centre.

MRP II is a second-generation MRP that adds a broader scope to planning because it links sales & operations planning, MPS, MRP, and detailed scheduling.

ERP systems build even further on these linkages by integrating all functions of business on a single common data base.

Solved Problems

Problem 1

The following product structure tree shows the components needed to assemble one unit of product W. Determine the quantities of each component needed to assemble 100 units of W.

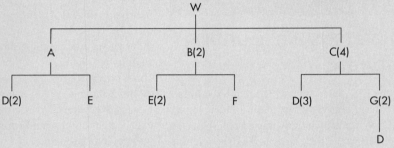

Solution

An easy way to calculate and keep track of component requirements is to do it right on the tree, as shown in the following figure.

Level

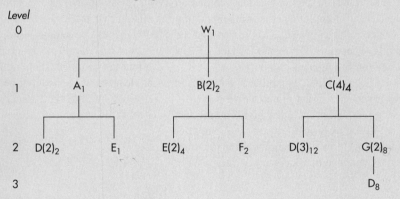

Summary:

Level	Item	(1 W) Quantity	(100 W) Quantity
0............	W	1	100
1............	A	1	100
	B	2	200
	C	4	400
2............	E	5 = (1 + 4)	500
	F	2	200
	G	8	800
3............	D	22 = (2 + 12 + 8)	2,200

Note: An item's level is considered to be the lowest level that it appears in the BOM. In this case, D is in Level 3.

Problem 2

The product structure tree for end item E follows. The manager wants to know the material requirements for ordered part R that will be needed to complete 120 units of E by the start of week 5. Manufacturing lead times for items of this order are one week for level 0 and level 1 items, and purchase lead time is two weeks for level 2 items. There is a scheduled receipt of 60 units of M at the *end* of week 1 and 100 units of R at the *start* of week 1. Lot-for-lot ordering is used, and there are no inventories on hand.

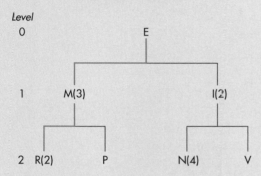

Solution

A partial assembly time chart that includes R and leads to completion of E by the start of week 5 looks like this:

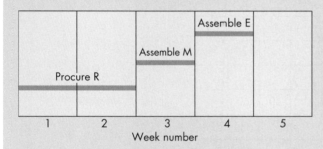

The table entries are arrived at as follows:

Production schedule: 120 units of E to be available at the start of week 5.

Item E: Gross requirements equal the quantity specified in the production schedule. Since there is no on-hand inventory, net requirements also equal 120 units. Using lot-for-lot ordering, 120 units must be scheduled to be available at the start of week 5. Because there is a one-week lead time for assembly of 120 units of Es, shop order will need to be released (i.e., work started) at the beginning of week 4.

Item M: The *gross* requirements for M are three times the planned-order releases for E, because each E requires three Ms. These must be available at the start of week 4. The net requirements are 60 units less due to the 60 units expected to be on hand at that time. Note that the 60 units expected at the end of week 1 are entered in week 2 because, according to our convention, scheduled receipts occur at the start of the week. Also note that according to our convention, the scheduled receipt goes into projected on-hand immediately. Hence, 300 additional units of M must be available at the start of week 4. With the one-week lead time, there must be an order release at the start of week 3.

Item R: Because each M requires two units of R, 600 Rs will be needed to assemble 300 units of M. However, 100 units will be on hand, so only 500 need to be ordered. Because there is a purchase lead time of two weeks, the 500 Rs must be ordered at the start of week 1.

The production schedule for E and requirements plans for E, M, and R follow.

Production schedule for E

Week number	Beg. Inv.	1	2	3	4	5
Quantity						(120)

Item: E LT=1 week		1	2	3	4	5
Gross requirements						(120)
Scheduled receipts						
Projected on-hand						
Net requirements						120
Planned-order receipts						(120)
Planned-order releases					(120)	

Multiplied by 3
(see product tree)

Item: M LT=1 week		1	2	3	4	5
Gross requirements					(360)	
Scheduled receipts			(60)			
Projected on-hand			(60)	60	60	
Net requirements					300	
Planned-order receipts					(300)	
Planned-order releases				(300)		

Multiplied by 2
(see product tree)

Item: R LT=2 weeks		1	2	3	4	5
Gross requirements				(600)		
Scheduled receipts		(100)				
Projected on-hand		(100)	100	100		
Net requirements				500		
Planned-order receipts				(500)		
Planned-order releases		(500)				

Problem 3   *Capacity requirements planning.* Given the following production schedule and the production standard times for this product at a bottleneck work centre, determine the labour hour requirements for each week. Is the production schedule feasible if capacity is 120 labour hours per week at the work centre?

Production Schedule:

Week	1	2	3	4
Quantity	200	300	100	150

Standard Times:

Labour	.5 hour/unit
Machine setup	10 hours (assume one run per week)

Convert the quantity requirements into labour requirements by multiplying the quantity requirements by the respective standard times and adding the setup time:

Solution

Week	1	2	3	4
Quantity	200	300	100	150
Operating hours	100	150	50	75
Setup hours	10	10	10	10
Total	110	160	60	85

Capacity in week 2 is insufficient.

---

1. Contrast independent and dependent demand.
2. When is MRP appropriate?
3. Briefly define or explain each of these terms.
   a. Master production schedule
   b. Bill of material
   c. Manufacturing lead time
   d. Gross requirement
   e. Net requirement
4. How is safety stock included in a material requirements plan?
5. What is meant by the term *safety time*?
6. Contrast *net-change* and *regenerative* systems for MRP.
7. What is CRP?
8. What is the difference between the treatment of purchased parts and manufactured parts in MRP?
9. How can the use of MRP contribute to productivity?
10. Briefly describe MRP II and indicate how it relates to MRP.
11. What is lot sizing and what is its goal?
12. Contrast planned-order receipts and scheduled receipts.
13. If seasonal variations are present, is their incorporation into MRP fairly simple or fairly difficult? Explain briefly.
14. How does an ERP system differ from MRP II software?
15. What are some unforeseen costs of ERP?

---

1. What trade-offs are involved in the decision to purchase an ERP software package?
2. Who in the organization needs to be involved in MRP? Who needs to be involved in ERP?
3. How important are each of the following considerations in a software such as an MRP or ERP?
   a. Ease of use
   b. Complete integration
   c. Data reliability

Lead time (in days) for all items is a function of each order size and is shown below. Prepare a material requirements plan for all components using lot-for-lot ordering.

Quantity	Lead Time (days)
1–200	1
201–550	2
551–999	3

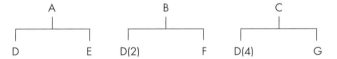

Table: Wood sections (2), Braces (3), Legs (4)

7. Eighty units of product X are needed at the beginning of week 6, and another 30 units are needed at the beginning of week 8. Prepare a material requirements plan for component D and its parents. D can be ordered only in whole cases (50 units per case). One case of D is automatically received every other week, beginning in week 1 (i.e., week 1, 3, 5, 7). Also, there are 30 units of B and 20 units of D on hand now. Lead times for all items are a function of quantity: one week for up to 100 units, two weeks for 101 to 200 units, three weeks for 201 to 300 units, and four weeks for 301 or more units.

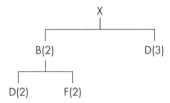

8. Oh No!, Inc., sells three models of radar detector units. It buys three basic units (E, F, and G) from a Japanese manufacturer and adds one, two, or four lights (component D) to further differentiate the models. D is bought from a domestic producer.

```
      A              B              C
   ┌──┴──┐        ┌──┴──┐        ┌──┴──┐
   D     E      D(2)    F      D(4)    G
```

Lead times are one week for all items except C, which is two weeks. There are ample supplies of the basic units (E, F, and G) on hand. There are also 10 units of B, 10 units of C, and 25 units of D on hand. Lot sizing rules are lot-for-lot ordering for all items except D, which must be ordered in multiples of 100 units. There is a scheduled receipt of 100 units of D at the start of week 1.

The production schedule calls for 40 units of A to be available at the start of week 4, 60 units of B at the start of week 5, and 30 units of C at the start of week 6. Prepare a material requirements plan for D and its parents.

9. Assume that you are the manager of a shop that assembles power tools. You have just received an order for 50 chain saws, which are to be shipped at the start of week 8. Pertinent information on the saw is:

Item	Lead Time (weeks)	On Hand	Components
Saw	2	15	A (2), B (1), C (3)
A	1	10	E (3), D (1)
B	2	5	D (2), F (3)
C	2	30	E (2), D (2)
D	1	20	
E	1	10	
F	2	30	

a. Develop a product structure tree and an assembly time chart.

b. Develop the material requirements plan for component E and its parents using lot-for-lot ordering.

c. Suppose that capacity to produce part E is limited to a maximum of 100 units per week. Revise the planned-order releases for weeks 1–4 so that the maximum is not exceeded in any period, keeping in mind the objective of minimizing holding costs. The quantities need

Production Schedule:

Week	1	2	3	4
Quantity	200	300	100	150

Standard Times:

Labour   .5 hour/unit
Machine setup   10 hours (assume one run per week)

Convert the quantity requirements into labour requirements by multiplying the quantity requirements by the respective standard times and adding the setup time:

Solution

Week	1	2	3	4
Quantity	200	300	100	150
Operating hours	100	150	50	75
Setup hours	10	10	10	10
Total	110	160	60	85

Capacity in week 2 is insufficient.

---

1. Contrast independent and dependent demand.
2. When is MRP appropriate?
3. Briefly define or explain each of these terms.
   a. Master production schedule
   b. Bill of material
   c. Manufacturing lead time
   d. Gross requirement
   e. Net requirement
4. How is safety stock included in a material requirements plan?
5. What is meant by the term *safety time*?
6. Contrast *net-change* and *regenerative* systems for MRP.
7. What is CRP?
8. What is the difference between the treatment of purchased parts and manufactured parts in MRP?
9. How can the use of MRP contribute to productivity?
10. Briefly describe MRP II and indicate how it relates to MRP.
11. What is lot sizing and what is its goal?
12. Contrast planned-order receipts and scheduled receipts.
13. If seasonal variations are present, is their incorporation into MRP fairly simple or fairly difficult? Explain briefly.
14. How does an ERP system differ from MRP II software?
15. What are some unforeseen costs of ERP?

---

1. What trade-offs are involved in the decision to purchase an ERP software package?
2. Who in the organization needs to be involved in MRP? Who needs to be involved in ERP?
3. How important are each of the following considerations in a software such as an MRP or ERP?
   a. Ease of use
   b. Complete integration
   c. Data reliability

CRITICAL THINKING EXERCISE	Suppose you work for a furniture manufacturer, one of whose products is the chair depicted in Figure 13–5. Finished goods inventory is held in a central warehouse in anticipation of customer orders. Finished goods are controlled using (EOQ, ROP) model. The warehouse manager, Juan Villa, has suggested using the same model for controlling component inventory. Write him a brief memo outlining your opinion on doing that.

INTERNET EXERCISE	For each of the following applications of ERP, determine what the benefit of using the software is for the company:

    a. www.coss-systems.com under Info Center, then Case Studies, All Stick Label.

    b. www.industrios.com under Success Stories

        i. Cam Tran

        ii. Leicatex

        iii. Frank Zamboni

PROBLEMS	1. *a.* Given the following product structure tree for product E, determine the quantity of each component required to assemble one unit of E.

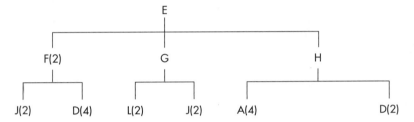

    b. Draw a product structure tree for a stapler using the indented BOM below:

Item

Stapler
Top assembly
  Cover
  Spring
  Slide assembly
    Slide
    Spring
Base assembly
  Base
  Strike plate
  Rubber pad (2)

2. The following list shows the components needed to assemble an end item, their manufacturing or purchase lead times for typical lot sizes, and quantities on hand, and the following product structure tree shows the number of each component per parent.

Item	End	B	C	D	E	F	G	H
LT (wk)	1	2	3	3	1	2	1	2
Amount on hand	0	10	10	25	12	30	5	0

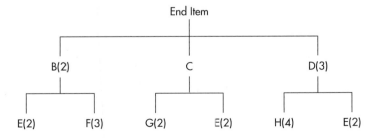

a. If 20 units of the end item are to be assembled, how many additional units of E are needed? (You don't need to develop MRP tables to determine this.)

b. An order for the end item is scheduled to be shipped at the start of week 11. What is the latest week that production or purchasing of the components of the order can be started and the order still be ready to ship on time? (You don't need to develop MRP tables for this part either.)

3. The following table lists the components needed to assemble an end item, manufacturing or purchase lead times (in weeks) for typical lot sizes, and quantities on hand.

Item	Lead Time	Amount on Hand	Direct Components
End	1	—	L(2), C(1), K(3)
L	2	10	B(2), J(3)
C	3	15	G(2), B(2)
K	3	20	H(4), B(2)
B	2	30	
J	3	30	
G	3	5	
H	2	—	

a. Draw the product structure tree.

b. If 40 units of the end item are to be assembled, how many additional units of B are needed? (You don't need to develop MRP tables.)

c. An order for 40 units of the end item is scheduled to be shipped at the start of week 8. What is the latest week that the components of the order can be started and the order still be ready to ship on time? (You don't need to develop MRP tables.)

4. Eighty units of product E are needed at the beginning of week 6. Three cases (30 units per case) of J have been ordered and one case is scheduled to arrive in week 3, one in week 4, and one in week 5. Note: *J must be ordered by the case*, and B must be produced in multiples of 120 units. There are 60 units of B and 20 units of J on hand now. Manufacturing lead times are two weeks each for E and B for these lot sizes, and purchase lead time is usually one week for J.

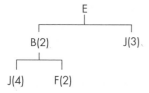

a. Prepare a material requirements plan for component J and its parts.

b. Suppose that now is week 4 and the quantity of E needed in week 6 is changed from 80 to 70. The planned order releases through week 3 and scheduled receipts have all been executed as in part a. How many more Bs and Js will be on hand in week 6?

5. Product P is composed of three subassemblies: K, L, and W. K is assembled using 3 Gs and 4 Hs; L is made of 2 Ms and 2 Ns; and W is made of 3 Zs. On-hand inventories are 40 Gs, and 200 Hs. Scheduled receipts are 10 Ks at the start of week 3 and 30 Ks at the start of week 6.

One hundred Ps must be shipped at the start of week 6, and another 100 at the start of week 7. Manufacturing lead times are usually two weeks for subassemblies for these lot sizes and purchase lead times are one week for the components. Final assembly of P requires one week for 100 units. Include an extra 10-percent scrap allowance in each planned order of G. The minimum order size for H is 200 units. For other items, use lot-for-lot ordering. Develop each of the following:

a. A product structure tree.

b. A material requirements plan for K, G, and H.

6. A table is assembled using three components, as shown in the following product structure tree. The company that makes the table wants to ship 100 units at the beginning of day 4, 150 units at the beginning of day 5, and 200 units at the beginning of day 7. Receipts of 100 wood sections are scheduled at the beginning of day 2. There are 120 legs on hand. An additional 10 percent of the order size on legs is added for safety stock. There are 60 braces on hand.

Lead time (in days) for all items is a function of each order size and is shown below. Prepare a material requirements plan for all components using lot-for-lot ordering.

Quantity	Lead Time (days)
1–200	1
201–550	2
551–999	3

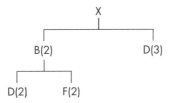

7. Eighty units of product X are needed at the beginning of week 6, and another 30 units are needed at the beginning of week 8. Prepare a material requirements plan for component D and its parents. D can be ordered only in whole cases (50 units per case). One case of D is automatically received every other week, beginning in week 1 (i.e., week 1, 3, 5, 7). Also, there are 30 units of B and 20 units of D on hand now. Lead times for all items are a function of quantity: one week for up to 100 units, two weeks for 101 to 200 units, three weeks for 201 to 300 units, and four weeks for 301 or more units.

8. Oh No!, Inc., sells three models of radar detector units. It buys three basic units (E, F, and G) from a Japanese manufacturer and adds one, two, or four lights (component D) to further differentiate the models. D is bought from a domestic producer.

Lead times are one week for all items except C, which is two weeks. There are ample supplies of the basic units (E, F, and G) on hand. There are also 10 units of B, 10 units of C, and 25 units of D on hand. Lot sizing rules are lot-for-lot ordering for all items except D, which must be ordered in multiples of 100 units. There is a scheduled receipt of 100 units of D at the start of week 1.

The production schedule calls for 40 units of A to be available at the start of week 4, 60 units of B at the start of week 5, and 30 units of C at the start of week 6. Prepare a material requirements plan for D and its parents.

9. Assume that you are the manager of a shop that assembles power tools. You have just received an order for 50 chain saws, which are to be shipped at the start of week 8. Pertinent information on the saw is:

Item	Lead Time (weeks)	On Hand	Components
Saw	2	15	A (2), B (1), C (3)
A	1	10	E (3), D (1)
B	2	5	D (2), F (3)
C	2	30	E (2), D (2)
D	1	20	
E	1	10	
F	2	30	

a. Develop a product structure tree and an assembly time chart.

b. Develop the material requirements plan for component E and its parents using lot-for-lot ordering.

c. Suppose that capacity to produce part E is limited to a maximum of 100 units per week. Revise the planned-order releases for weeks 1–4 so that the maximum is not exceeded in any period, keeping in mind the objective of minimizing holding costs. The quantities need not be equal in every period. Note that the gross requirements for E will remain the same. However, quantities in some of the other rows will change. Determine the new cell values for those rows.

10. Assume that you are the manager of Assembly, Inc. You have just received an order for 40 units of an industrial robot, which is to be delivered at the start of week 7. Using the following information, determine how many units of part G to order and the timing of those orders, given that part G must be ordered in multiples of 80 units and all other components are ordered lot-for-lot.

Item	Lead Time (weeks)	On Hand	Components
Robot	2	10	B, G, C(3)
B	1	5	E, F
C	1	20	G(2), H
E	2	4	—
F	3	8	—
G	2	15	—
H	1	10	—

11. Determine material requirements plans for parts N and V and subassembly I as described in Solved Problem 2 for each of the following situations:

    a. Assume that there are currently 100 Ns on hand and scheduled receipts of 40 Is and 10 Vs are expected at the beginning of week 3. 120 Es are needed at the start of week 5.

    b. Assume on-hand and scheduled receipts are as in part a. Now suppose that 100 Es are needed at the start of week 5 and 50 at the start of week 7. Also, use multiples of these order sizes: N, 800; V, 200. Use lot-for-lot ordering for I and E.

    c. Using your answer to part a, update the MRP for I, N, and V, using the following additional information for each of these cases: (1) one week has elapsed (making it the start of week 2), and (2) three weeks have elapsed (making it the start of week 4). *Note*: Start your revised plans so that the updated time in each case is designated as week 1. The updated production schedule now has an order for 100 units of E in week 8 of case 1 and in week 6 of case 2 (i.e., week 9 under the former master schedule). Assume all orders are released and received as planned.

12. Information concerning the product structure, lead times, and quantities on hand for an electric golf cart is shown in the following table. Use this information to do each of the following:

    a. Construct a product structure tree.

    b. Construct an assembly time chart.

    c. Develop a material requirements plan that will provide 200 golf carts at the start of week 8 assuming lot-for-lot ordering.

Parts List for Electric Golf Cart	Lead Time	Quantity on Hand
Electric golf cart	1	0
Top	1	40
Base	1	20
Top		
Supports (4)	1	200
Cover	1	0
Base		
Motor	2	300
Body	3	50
Seats (2)	2	120
Body		
Frame	1	35
Controls	1	0
Wheels (4)	1	240

13. Refer to Problem 12. Assume that unusually mild weather has caused a change in the quantity and timing of orders for golf carts. The revised plan calls for 100 golf carts at the start of week 6, 100 at the start of week 8, and 100 at the start of week 9.

 a. Determine the timing and quantities for orders for tops and bases.

 b. Assume that equipment problems have reduced the firm's capacity for assembling bases to 50 units per week. Revise your material requirements plan for bases to reflect this, but still meet delivery dates.

14. A manufacturing company buys a certain part in varying quantities throughout the year. Ordering cost is $11 per order, and holding cost is $0.14 per piece per month. Given the following demand (net requirements) for the part for the next eight months, what order sizes would be indicated using the part-period method? When should each order be received?

Month	Demand
1	—
2	80
3	10
4	30
5	—
6	30
7	—
8	30

15. A company periodically produces a part that is a basic component of an assembled product it makes. Each time the part is run, a fixed cost of $125 is incurred. The cost to hold one unit for a week is estimated to be $1.65. For the demand (net requirement) shown below, determine the quantity and timing of runs that would be consistent with the part-period method.

Week	Demand
1	40
2	20
3	100
4	20
5	—
6	20
7	80

16. A company that manufactures paving material for driveways and parking lots expects the following demand for its product for the next four months.

Month number	1	2	3	4
Material (tonnes)	40	80	60	70

 The company's machine standard time and available capacity are:

Production standard (hours per tonne)	3
Monthly production capacity (hours)	200

 a. Determine the capacity requirement for each of the four months.

 b. In which months do you foresee a problem? What options would you suggest to resolve any problems?

17. The Systems Department has a problem. Its computer died just as it spit out the following information: Planned-order release for item J27 = 640 units in Week 2. The company has been able to reconstruct all the information they lost except the production schedule for end item 565. The company is fortunate because J27 is used only in 565s. Given the following product structure tree and associated inventory and lead time information, determine what production schedule entry for item 565 was exploded into the material requirements plan that killed the computer.

Part Number	On Hand	Lot Size	Lead Time
565	0	Lot-for-lot	1 week
X43	60	Multiples of 120	1 week
N78	0	Lot-for-lot	2 weeks
Y36	200	Lot-for-lot	1 week
J27	0	Lot-for-lot	2 weeks

```
                    565
        ┌────────────┼────────────┐
       X43        Y36(2)         N78
                ┌───┴───┐
             J27(4)    X43
```

18. Using the diagram below, do the following:

    a. Draw a product structure tree for the scissors.

    b. Prepare an MRP for scissors. Lead times are one day for buying each type of blade, assembling the blades with grips, and for final scissor assembly, but two days for buying each type of plastic grip. Six hundred pairs of scissors are needed on Day 6. *Note:* there are 200 straight blades, 350 bent blades, and 40 top blade assemblies on hand. Also note that screws are bought in large quantities outside the MRP system.

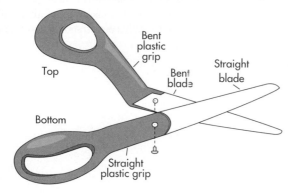

19. A small furniture maker has just received an order to deliver 250 chairs at the beginning of week 6. The production/purchase planner needs to arrange for the assembly of subassemblies and purchase of parts required for the order. The product structure tree for the chair is displayed below. The chairs, leg assemblies, and back assemblies are to be assembled by one worker each. During an eight-hour day, 25 chairs and 25 legs assemblies can be assembled, whereas 50 back assemblies can be assembled. The company operates five days a week. The seats, spindles, tops, legs, and rails are purchased from another company. Purchase lead time for this size order for each part is one week. The company has some inventory of parts from previous productions: 40 seats, 100 rails, 150 legs, 30 tops, and 80 spindles.

    a. Calculate assembly lead times for chairs, leg assemblies, and back assemblies required for this order. Assume that chair assembly will start only after the whole batch of its components is available.

    b. Develop material requirements plans for this order. Use lot-for-lot assembly and ordering. What action should you take now?

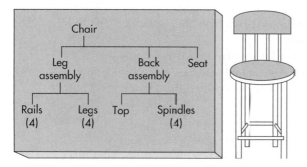

20. You have received an order for 100 units of a simple kitchen table to be delivered at the beginning of Week 6. The table consists of one top and four legs. The top is made from 1.5 units of lumber, each unit being 2 inches thick by 6 inches wide by 6 feet long. The lumber is first cut thicknesswise, then lengthwise, then glued and clamped together, and finally sanded and finished. The legs are made from a two-thirds unit of the same lumber by first cutting it widthwise, then lengthwise, then lathe work, and finally sanding and finishing. Suppose that manufacturing lead time for 100 tops is approximately three weeks and for 400 legs is approximately two weeks. Also, final assembly of four legs to a top will take approximately one week for 100 tables, and purchase lead time for lumber is one week. Currently we have 20 units of lumber in stock. Draw the product structure tree and perform material requirements planning for this order. Assume table assembly only starts after the whole batch of its components is available.

21. You wish to plan the assembly and purchase of the components for an order of 4,800 side tables due in the beginning of week 7. See the product structure tree below.

    a. Suppose that the assembly of two leg assemblies to a top will take approximately one minute, and the assembly of two leg braces to a WIP will take approximately 1.5 minutes. Assuming that the company works 40 hours a week, calculate the assembly lead time for these two operations for assembling 4,800 tables. Assume that the whole 4,800 unit batch of WIP is completed before the table assembly starts.

    b. Suppose that the tops, leg assemblies, and leg braces are purchased from a vendor, and that purchase lead time is one week each. We have 100 units of top, 200 leg assemblies and 300 leg braces on hand. A purchase order was released last week for 5,000 tops in anticipation of this order (scheduled receipt = week 1). The leg braces have to be purchased in multiples of 500. Otherwise use lot-for-lot ordering. Develop the MRP tables. What action should you take now?

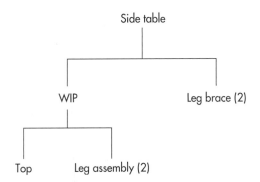

22. Restaurants need to plan the purchase and production of the food ingredients and components based on the forecast of demand for each meal. Consider the following example for veal picante with linguini in a New Orleans restaurant.[2]

    The forecasts for demand for veal picante with linguini during each of the next four days are: Thursday, 6; Friday, 10; Saturday, 9; and Sunday, 8. The product structure tree of one veal picante with linguini is as follows: The chef assembles the dish from one serving of cooked linguini and one piece of grilled veal steak. The assistant chef boils the linguini using approximately 100 grams of linguini (takes approximately 15 minutes). The chef grills the veal steak from a marinated piece of veal (takes approximately 17 minutes). Marinating of a raw veal steak needs to be done the day before (by assistant chef) using some picante sauce, lime juice, oil, salt, and pepper (takes approximately 5 minutes but needs to rest in the fridge overnight). On hand, we have 1 kg of (uncooked) linguini, six marinated veal steaks and thirteen unmarinated veal steaks. All production times are negligible (zero day), except marinating which takes one day. All purchase lead times are one day. The restaurant orders linguini in 10 kg bags and veal steaks in 20 piece boxes.

    a. Draw the product structure tree for a veal picante with linguini.

    b. Develop MRP tables for all the required activities and purchase of raw veal steaks and (uncooked) linguini. (The restaurant buys all the other ingredients in bulk.)

---

[2]Based on John G. Wacker, "Effective Planning and Cost Control for Restaurants: Making Resource Requirements Planning Work," *Production and Inventory Management Journal*, First Quarter, 1985, pp. 55–70.

DMD Enterprises

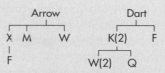

After the dot-com bust, David "Marty" Dawkins decided to pursue his boyhood dream of owning a bike factory. After several false starts, he finally got the small company up and running. The company currently assembles two models Marty designed: the Arrow and the Dart. The company hasn't turned a profit yet, but Marty feels that once he resolves some of the problems he's having with inventory and scheduling, he can increase productivity and reduce costs.

At first, he ordered enough bike parts and subassemblies for four months' worth of production. Parts were stacked all over the place, seriously reducing work space and hampering movement of workers. And no one knew exactly where anything was. In Marty's words, "It was a solid mess!"

He and his two partners eventually managed to work off most of the inventory. They hope to avoid similar problems in the future by using a more orderly approach. Marty's first priority is to develop an MRP plan for upcoming periods. He wants to assemble 15 Arrows and 10 Darts each week, for weeks 4 through 8. The product structure trees for the two bikes follow.

One of Marty's partners, Ann, has collected the following information on lead times, inventory on hand, and lot-sizing rules (established by suppliers):

Item	Lead Time (weeks)	On Hand	Lot-Sizing Rule
Arrow	2	5	Lot-for-lot
Dart	2	2	Lot-for-lot
X	1	5	Q = 25
W	2*	2	Multiples of 12
F	1	10	Multiples of 30
K	1	3	Lot-for-lot
Q	1	15	Q = 30
M	1	0	Lot-for-lot

*LT = 3 weeks for orders of 36 or more units.

Scheduled receipts are:

Week 1:   20 Arrows, 18 Ws
Week 2:   20 Darts, 15 Fs
Develop the material requirements plan.

Stickley Furniture

www.stickley.com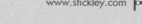

Introduction

L & J. G. Stickley was founded in 1900 by brothers Leopold and George Stickley. Located just outside of Syracuse, New York, the company is a producer of fine cherry, white oak, and mahogany furniture. In the late 1980s, the company reintroduced the company's original line of mission oak furniture, which now accounts for over 50 percent of the company's sales.

Over the years, the company experienced both good and bad times, and at one point it employed over 200 people. But by the early 1970s, the business was in disarray: there were only about 20 full-time employees, and the company was on the brink of bankruptcy. The present owners bought the ailing company in 1974, and under their leadership the company has prospered and grown, and now has 900 employees. Stickley has five retail showrooms in New York State, and its furniture is sold in the U.S. by some 100 dealers. In 1994, sales were about $65 million.

Production

The production facility is a large, rectangular building with a 9-metre ceiling. Furniture making is labour intensive, although

saws, sanders, and other equipment are very much a part of the process. In fact, electricity costs average $40,000 to $50,000 a month. The company has its own toolroom where cutting tools are sharpened and replacement tools are produced as needed.

Worker skills range from low-skilled material handlers to highly skilled craftsmen. For example, three master cabinet makers handle customized orders.

The process (see the floor layout diagram on the next page) begins with various sawing operations where planks received from the lumber mills are cut into smaller sizes. The company recently purchased a computer-controlled "optimizer" saw that greatly improves sawing productivity and eliminates some waste. Workers inspect and mark knot locations and other defects they find on each piece of lumber before feeding it into the saw. The computer then determines the optimal set of cuttings, given the location of knots and other defects, and standard lengths needed for subsequent operations. Approximately 29,000 board feet are cut each day. A board foot is lumber equivalent to 1" thick by 1' wide by 1' long. Subsequent sawing operations provide additional cuts for specific jobs.

Workers then glue some of the pieces together that will end up as tops of tables, desks, dressers, or similar items. Large presses hold 20 to 30 glued sections at a time. Other pieces that will become table or chair legs, chair backs or other items go through various shaping operations. Next comes a series of sanding operations, which remove excess glue from the glued sections and smooth the surface of both glued pieces and other pieces.

Some of the pieces may require drilling or *mortising*, an operation in which rectangular holes and other shapes are cut into the wood. The company has two CNC (computer numerically controlled) routers that can be programmed to make grooves and other specialty cuts. Some items require carving, which involves highly skilled workers.

Next, workers assemble the various components, either into subassemblies or sometimes directly to other components to obtain completed pieces. Each item is stamped with the date of

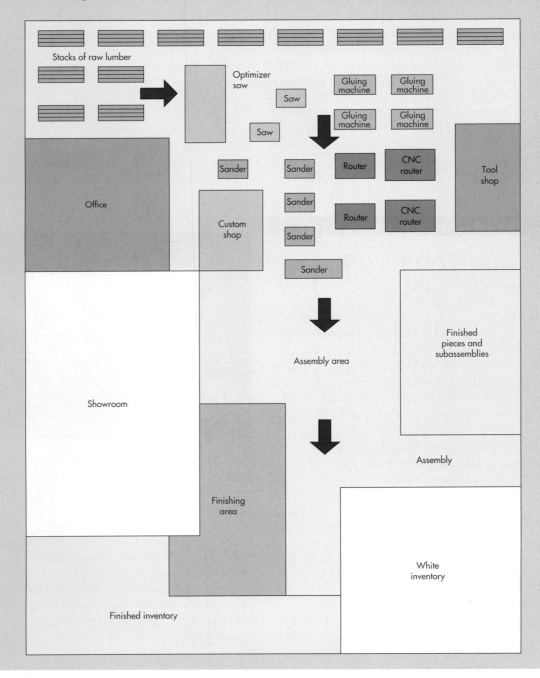

production, and components such as dresser drawers, cabinet doors, and expansion leaves of tables also are stamped to identify their location (e.g., top drawer, left door) Careful records are kept so that if a piece of furniture is ever returned for repairs, complete instructions are available (type of wood, finish, etc.) to enable repair people to closely match the original piece.

The furniture items then usually move to the "white inventory" (unfinished) section, and eventually to the finishing department where workers apply linseed oil or another finish before the items are moved to the finished goods inventory to await shipment to stores or customer locations.

Aggregate Production Planning

The company uses a level output plan (maintains steady labour force). Demand is seasonal; it is highest in the first and third quarters. During the second and fourth quarters, excess output goes into inventory; during the first and third quarters, excess demand is met using these inventory. The production scheduler uses a schedule that is set for the next 8 to 10 weeks.

Production Scheduling and Control

Job sequence is determined by the amount of remaining inventory (days' supply on hand) and processing time. Lot sizes are determined by factoring in demand, setup costs, and holding costs. Typical lot sizes are 25 to 60 pieces. There are many jobs (lots) being produced concurrently. Each job (lot) is accompanied by a set of bar codes that identify the job and the operation. As each operation is completed, the operator removes a bar-code sticker and delivers it to the scheduling office where it is scanned into the computer, thereby enabling production control to keep track of progress on a job and to know its location in the shop.

Inventory

In addition to the "white" inventory and a small finished-goods inventory, the company maintains inventories of finished parts

(e.g., table and chair legs) and partially assembled items. This inventory serves two important functions. One is to reduce the amount of time needed to respond to customer orders rather than having to go through the entire production process to obtain needed items, and the other is that it helps to smooth production and utilize idle machinery/workers. Because of unequal job times on successive operations, some workstations invariably have slack time while others work at capacity. Slack times are used to build inventories of commonly used pieces and subassemblies. Moreover, because pieces are being made for inventory, there is flexibility in sequencing. This permits jobs that have similar setups to be produced in sequence, thereby reducing setup time and cost.

Quality

Each worker is responsible for checking his or her quality, as well as the quality of materials received from preceding operations, and to report any deficiencies. In addition, on several difficult operations quality control people handle inspections and work with operators to correct any deficiencies. The company is considering a TQM approach (see Chapter 9), but has not yet made a decision on whether to go in that direction. For a virtual tour of Stickley's plant, go to www.stickley.com/tour.

Questions

1. Which type of production process—job shop, batch, repetitive, or continuous—is the primary mode of operation at Stickley Furniture?

2. Suppose that the company has just received an order for 40 mission oak dining room sets. Briefly list the kinds of information the company will need to plan, schedule and process this job.

3. Can you suggest any planning tools that might be beneficial to the company? Explain.

SELECTED BIBLIOGRAPHY AND FURTHER READING

Bennett, Wayne D. "The Big Risk for Small Fry." *CIO Magazine*, May 15, 2000.

Davenport, Tom. *Mission Critical: Realizing the Promise of Enterprise Systems*. Boston: Harvard Business School Press, 2000.

Hopp, Wallace, and Mark L. Spearman. *Factory Physics*. 2nd ed. New York: Irwin/McGraw-Hill, 2001.

Jacobs, Robert F., and D. Clay Whybark. *Why ERP? A Primer on SAP Implementation*. New York: Irwin/McGraw-Hill, 2000.

Jeffery, Bill, and Jim Morrison. "ERP, One Step at a Time." *CIO Magazine*, September 1, 2000.

Kapp, Karl M., Bill Latham, and Hester-Ford Latham. *Integrated Learning for ERP Success*. Boca Raton, FL: St. Lucie Press, 2001.

Orlicky, Joseph. *Material Requirements Planning*. New York: McGraw-Hill, 1975.

Ptak, Carol A., and Eli Schragenheim. *ERP: Tools, Techniques, and Applications for Integrating the Supply Chain*. Boca Raton, FL: St. Lucie Press, 1999.

Slater, Derek. "The Hidden Costs of Enterprise Software." *CIO Enterprise*, January 15, 1998.

Vollmann, Thomas E., William L. Berry, and D. Clay Whybark. *Manufacturing, Planning and Control Systems*. 4th ed. Burr Ridge, IL: Richard D. Irwin, 1997.

Wheatley, Malcolm. "ERP Training Stinks." *CIO Magazine*, June 1, 2000.

Wight, Oliver W. *The Executive's Guide to Successful MRP II*. Williston, VT: Oliver Wight Limited Publications, 1982

CHAPTER 14

Just-in-Time and Lean Manufacturing

Celestica is a major Electronic Manufacturing Services provider (i.e., manufactures components for computer and telecom equipment manufacturers), fast replacing Nortel Networks as Canada's largest high-tech company. Celestica needs to be flexible and fast, but at the same time low cost. How do Celestica and other progressive manufacturers achieve these competitive requirements? That is the subject of this chapter.

INTRODUCTION

The term **just-in-time (JIT)**, in a narrow sense, refers to a production system in which both the movement of goods during production and deliveries from suppliers are carefully timed so that at each step of the process, the next (usually small) batch arrives for processing just as the preceding batch is completed—thus the name, *just-in-time*. The result is a system with few idle items waiting to be processed and a balanced, rapid flow.

In a broader sense, JIT is a philosophy of "waste" reduction, be it inventory or resources such as workers, equipment, or floor space. In this sense, JIT is identical to **lean manufacturing**. This system requires the highest levels of quality in parts and products, short lead times and machine setup times (flexibility), and a program of continuous improvement to improve efficiency and quality and eliminate disruptions.

JIT, in the narrow sense, is sometimes contrasted with MRP. MRP systems are fairly complex, requiring extensive and detailed shop floor controls. JIT systems are much simpler, involving only minimal shop floor controls. Moreover, MRP relies on a computer-based *component-scheduling* system to trigger production and deliveries, whereas JIT mostly relies on visual signals to trigger production and deliveries.

The JIT approach was developed at the Toyota Motor Company by Taiichi Ohno (who eventually became vice-president of manufacturing) and several of his colleagues. The development of JIT in Japan was probably influenced by Japan being a crowded country with few natural resources. Not surprisingly, the Japanese are very sensitive to waste and inefficiency. They regard rework as waste and excess inventory as an evil because it takes up space and ties up resources.

Just like awards for quality, there is a prize for world-class lean manufacturing, called the Shingo Prize. The criteria for judging lean achievement are summarized in the following reading.

The design and operation of a system provide the foundation for lean manufacturing. The foundation is made up of four building blocks:

1. Product design
2. Process design
3. Personnel/organizational elements
4. Manufacturing planning and control

Figure 14–1 displays the goals and building blocks of lean manufacturing. We will describe each building block below.

PRODUCT DESIGN

Four elements of product design are important for JIT:

1. Standard parts
2. Modular design
3. Quality
4. DFMA

The use of *standard parts* means that workers have fewer parts to deal with, and training times and costs are reduced. Purchasing, handling, and checking quality are more

just-in-time (JIT) Production system in which processing and movement of materials and goods occur just as they are needed, usually in small batches.

lean manufacturing A system requiring high levels of quality, flexibility, and a program of continuous improvement.

FIGURE 14-1

An overview of the goals and building blocks of lean systems

Source: Adapted from Thomas E. Vollmann, William L. Berry, and D. Clay Whybark. *Manufacturing Planning and Control Systems*, 3rd ed. Copyright 1992 Irwin/McGraw-Hill Companies, Inc. Used with permission.

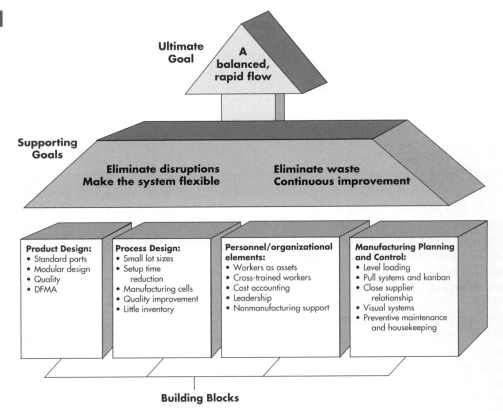

Ultimate Goal — A balanced, rapid flow

Supporting Goals — Eliminate disruptions / Make the system flexible — Eliminate waste / Continuous improvement

Product Design:
• Standard parts
• Modular design
• Quality
• DFMA

Process Design:
• Small lot sizes
• Setup time reduction
• Manufacturing cells
• Quality improvement
• Little inventory

Personnel/organizational elements:
• Workers as assets
• Cross-trained workers
• Cost accounting
• Leadership
• Nonmanufacturing support

Manufacturing Planning and Control:
• Level loading
• Pull systems and kanban
• Close supplier relationship
• Visual systems
• Preventive maintenance and housekeeping

Building Blocks

READING

Shingo Prize

The Shingo Prize was established in 1988 to recognize the achievement of companies in the United States, Canada, or Mexico which implemented lean manufacturing well. It is named after the Japanese guru on lean manufacturing Dr. Shigeo Shingo. The criteria used and their weight are given below.

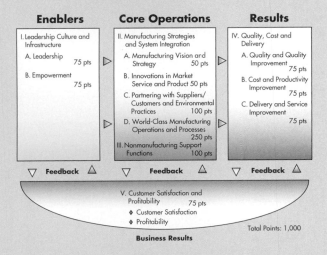

Enablers

I. Leadership Culture and Infrastructure

A. Leadership 75 pts

B. Empowerment 75 pts

Core Operations

II. Manufacturing Strategies and System Integration

A. Manufacturing Vision and Strategy 50 pts

B. Innovations in Market Service and Product 50 pts

C. Partnering with Suppliers/Customers and Environmental Practices 100 pts

D. World-Class Manufacturing Operations and Processes 250 pts

III. Nonmanufacturing Support Functions 100 pts

Results

IV. Quality, Cost and Delivery

A. Quality and Quality Improvement 75 pts

B. Cost and Productivity Improvement 75 pts

C. Delivery and Service Improvement 75 pts

▽ Feedback △   ▽ Feedback △   ▽ Feedback △

V. Customer Satisfaction and Profitability 75 pts
♦ Customer Satisfaction
♦ Profitability

Total Points: 1,000

Business Results

Leadership means adoption and deployment of lean goals through resource allocation, encouragement, and communication.

Empowerment means employee participation in teams and suggestion systems, which are facilitated through training, recognition/rewarding of contribution, and clean/safe/ergonomic environment.

Manufacturing vision and strategy includes selection and use of methods, processes, and systems for deploying lean manufacturing.

Innovations in market service and product design include QFD, concurrent engineering, benchmarking, DFMA, and use of e-commerce.

Partnering with suppliers/customers and environmental practices includes integration of product development and production. It also includes environmental initiatives and unions/community involvement.

World-class operations and processes include waste reduction, process (value stream) mapping, value analysis, 5S, standardized work, total preventive maintenance, SMED, poka-yoke, visual workplace, cellular manufacturing, jidoka (stopping the line if defect occurs), kanbans, load leveling, six sigma or SPC, theory of constraints (described in the next chapter), kaizen (continuous improvement) events, quality tools, and production process preparation (redesign of the process).

Nonmanufacturing support functions such as sales/marketing, accounting/finance, HR, purchasing, quality, and MIS must support and integrate with manufacturing. They also must have waste reduction programs.

Quality and quality improvement is measured by extent of rework, customer rejects, scraps, and process variation.

Cost and productivity improvement involves increasing inventory turns, reducing manufacturing lead time, increasing labour productivity, and reducing changeover and product cost.

Delivery and service improvement is measured by fill rate, expediting costs, and backorders.

Customer satisfaction and profitability are measured by net margin, ROA, cash flow, customer surveys, and market share.

Source: www.shingoprize.org/AwardInfo/BusPrize/BusinessGuide lines.pdf.

routine and lend themselves to continual improvement. Another important benefit is the ability to use standard processing.

Modular design is an extension of standard parts. Modules are clusters of parts treated as a single unit. This greatly reduces the number of parts to deal with, simplifying purchasing, handling, training, assembly, and so on.

Quality is crucial to JIT systems because poor quality can create major disruptions. Quality must be designed in goods and processes. QFD should be used to capture the "voice" of customer and deploy it in the product design. Concurrent engineering should be used to increase functional communication, reduce the need for engineering changes, and speed up the design process.

Products should be designed for easy manufacturing and assembly (DFMA). This speeds up the operations. Value analysis may be used to identify the necessary functions of the product and cut down product features not valued by customers. For more information on these elements, see Chapter 4 on Product Design.

PROCESS DESIGN

Five aspects of process design are particularly important for JIT systems:

1. Small lot sizes
2. Setup time reduction
3. Manufacturing cells
4. Quality improvement
5. Little inventory

Small Lot Sizes. In the JIT philosophy, the ideal lot size is one unit, a quantity that may not always be realistic owing to practical considerations requiring minimum lot sizes (e.g., machines that process multiple items simultaneously, and machines with very long setup times). Nevertheless, the goal is still to reduce the lot size as much as possible. Small lot sizes in both the production process and deliveries from suppliers yield a number of benefits that enable JIT systems to operate effectively. First, with small lots moving through the system, in-process inventory is considerably less than it is with large lots. This reduces holding cost, space requirement, and clutter in the workplace. Second, inspection and rework costs are less when problems with quality occur, because there are fewer items in a lot to inspect and rework.

Small lots also permit greater flexibility in scheduling. Repetitive systems typically produce a small variety of products. In traditional systems, this usually means long production runs of each product, one after the other. Although this spreads the setup cost for a run over many items, it also results in long cycles over the entire range of products. For instance, suppose a firm has three product models, A, B, and C. In a traditional system, there would be a long run of model A (e.g., covering two or three days or more), then a long run of model B, followed by a long run of model C before the sequence would repeat. In contrast, a JIT system, using small lots, would frequently shift from producing A to producing B and C. This flexibility enables JIT systems to respond more quickly to changing customer demands: JIT systems can produce just what is needed, when it is needed. The contrast between small and large lot sizes is illustrated in Figure 14–2.

FIGURE 14-2

Small-lot JIT versus large-lot run sizes

A = units of product A
B = units of product B
C = units of product C

JIT approach

AAA   BBBBBBB   CC   AAA   BBBBBBB   CC   AAA   BBBBBBB   CC   AAA   BBBBBBB   CC

Time ⟶

Large-lot approach

AAAAAAAAAAA   BBBBBBBBBBBBBBBBBBBBBBBBBB   CCCCCCCCC   AAAAAAAAAA

Time ⟶

It is important to note that the use of small lot sizes is not in conflict with the EOQ approach. The fact is that in JIT there is an emphasis on reducing the setup cost, which reduces the optimal lot size.

Setup Time Reduction. Small lots and changing product mixes require frequent machine setups. Example of a machine setup is putting in a different fixture in a machine to hold a different part or is putting in a different die in a press to "stamp" a different part. Another example of a machine setup is adjusting the heights of fillers and labellers on a bottling line to fill different size bottles. Unless these are quick and relatively inexpensive, the time and cost to accomplish them can be prohibitive. In JITsystems, workers are often trained to do their own setups. Moreover, techniques to reduce setup time and cost are used to achieve the desired results.

READING

Celestica

Celestica is a large electronic manufacturing services company based in Toronto, with 47,000 employees in 40 plants located in 19 countries. Celestica manufactures complex printed circuit assemblies such as PC motherboards and networking cards on contract for computer and communication equipment manufacturers including Dell, IBM, Lucent, and Cisco. Celestica was formed in 1996 and has quickly grown to have over $10 billion in annual revenue. Celestica started lean manufacturing initiatives in the Americas plants in 1999. The objective is waste reduction, including defects, overproduction, transportation, waiting, inventory, motion, and any other non-value-adding activity. This is done by kaizen teams from each work area, each over a short period of time, e.g., a week. A kaizen team includes most operators in an area and the management representatives and facilitators.

An example of a kaizen team in Celestica's Toronto plant is the rework group. When the kaizen blitz started, the rework area had no organized process flow with lead time for rework being approximately 14 days. The team rearranged the area into a U-shaped manufacturing cell, cutting travel distances three-fold and number of benches by half (from seven to four). The team wrote standard operating procedures including rules for rejecting a circuit board (previously done by an engineer from outside the group). As a result, the lead time has decreased to two days.

Celestica's Toronto factory.

Sources: www.advancedmanufacturing.com/Dec04/coverstory.htm; www.celestica.com

READING

Kubota

Single Minute Exchange of Die (SMED) is a set of methods and tools for reducing setup time to less than 10 minutes, developed by Shigeo Shingo. When Kubota, a Japanese tractor manufacturer wanted to implement SMED, it started with redesigning of fasteners that are used to hold a part to a fixture and/or a fixture (or a die) to a platform (or a press). To the right are some of the fast ways of temporarily joining two items.

Sources: www.kubota.com/f/home/home.cfm; S. Shingo, *A Revolution in Manufacturing: The SMED System* (Cambridge, Massachusetts: Productivity Press, 1985).

[1] Reduce number of screws — 4 screws are enough	[2] C-washer method — Don't remove the C-washer! hinge
[3] Pear-shaped hole method — tighten here, attach and remove here	[4] U-slot method — clamp, fixture
[5] Variation of pear-shaped hole method — bushing cap	[6] Wing nut method
[7] Cam method	[8] Snap method (for restraining work) — clamp, ball-and-spring stop screws
[9] Magnets — contact with workpiece, Magnet	[10] Toggle clamp — can apply pressures of over 500 kg
[11] Taper-type U-slot collar — taper-type U-slot collar, rotating stop	[12] Gear slippage prevention [A] using gear box cover — stops [B] one-touch stopper ring

Setup tools, equipment, and procedures must be simple and standardized. Multipurpose equipment or attachments can help reduce setup time. For instance, a machine with multiple spindles that can easily be rotated into place for different job requirements can drastically reduce changeover time. Moreover, *group technology* may be used to reduce setup cost and time. For instance, parts that are similar in shape, materials, and so on require similar setups.

Another method for setup time reduction is to separate the internal setup activities (i.e., those that cannot be done off line in advance) from the external setup activities (i.e., those that can be done off line in advance), and to make as many setup activities as possible external. For example, bringing the tools and fixtures to the machine before the setup, or preheating the injection mold. Yet, another technique is to streamline the setup. For example, preset the desired settings, use location pins to prevent misalignment, reduce tools, and make movement easier.

Setup time reduction methods for using presses and dies have been advanced by Shigeo Shingo under the name, "Single Minute Exchange of Die." One approach is to make loading parts and using fixtures faster. For some examples of this, see the reading, "Kubota."

Manufacturing Cells. One characteristic of many JIT systems is multiple *manufacturing cells*. The cells contain the machines and tools needed to process families of parts having similar processing requirements. In essence, the cells are highly specialized and efficient production centres.

For an example of a manufacturing cell, see the mini-case, "Airline Manufacturing," at the end of this chapter. Conversion to manufacturing cells requires

- mapping the current process for major products
- determining the operations and standard work required
- grouping similar products together
- determining the capacity requirements
- rearranging the layout and bringing the necessary machines closer together, usually in U-shaped configuration
- determining the capacity of the cell
- upgrading the machines if the capacity is inadequate
- balancing the cell and determining labour requirements
- determining the minimum WIP required between the machines in the cell

The advantages of manufacturing cells include faster throughput (i.e., shorter manufacturing lead times), less material handling, and more flexibility to increase/decrease the capacity by adding/subtracting workers to reducing the severity of bottlenecks. The disadvantage of manufacturing cells is that the machines may not be fully utilized.

Quality Improvement. Because of low inventories in JIT, it is important to prevent defects from occurring. Thus, the importance of SPC (e.g., control charts) to control the process, six sigma to reduce its variability, and poka-yoke to fool-proof it. Another tool is **autonomation** (note the extra syllable *no* in the middle of the word), also referred to as **jidoka**. It involves the automatic detection of defects during production and can be used with machines or manual operations. It consists of two mechanisms: one for detecting defects when they occur and another for stopping production in order to correct the cause of the defects.

The occurrence of quality defects during the process can disrupt the orderly flow of work. Consequently, problem solving is important when defects occur. Moreover, there is continuous improvement or Kaizen, a never-ending quest for *quality improvement*, which often focuses on finding and eliminating the causes of problems so they do not continually crop up. For an example, see the "Celestica" reading.

Little Inventory. JIT systems are designed to *minimize* inventory. Recall that in the JIT philosophy, inventory is a waste. Inventories are buffers that tend to cover up recurring problems that are never resolved, partly because they aren't obvious and partly because the presence of inventory makes them seem less serious. When a machine breaks down, it won't disrupt the system if there is sufficient inventory of the machine's output to feed into the next workstation. The use of inventory as the "solution" can lead to increasing amounts of inventory if breakdowns increase. A better solution is to investigate the *causes* of machine breakdowns and focus on eliminating them. Similar problems with quality, unreliable vendors, and scheduling can also be solved by having ample inventories to fall back on. However, holding all that extra inventory creates a tremendous burden in cost and space, and allows problems to go unresolved.

The JIT approach is to pare down inventories gradually in order to uncover the problems. Once they are uncovered and solved, the system removes more inventory, finds and solves additional problems, and so on. A useful analogy is a boat on a pond that has large, hidden rocks (see Figure 14–3). The rocks represent problems that can hinder production (boat' movement). The water in the pond that covers the rocks is the inventory in the system. As the water level is slowly lowered, the largest rocks are the first to appear (those problems are the first to be identified). At that point, efforts are undertaken to remove these rocks from the water (resolve these problems). Once that has been accomplished, additional water is removed from the pond, revealing the next layer of rocks, which are then worked on. As more rocks are removed, the need for water to cover them diminishes. Likewise, as more of the major production problems are solved, there is less need to rely on inventory.

One way to minimize inventory of raw materials/purchase parts in a JIT system is to have deliveries from suppliers go directly to the production floor, which completely eliminates the need to store incoming parts and materials. At the other end of the process, completed units are shipped out as soon as they are ready, which minimizes

FIGURE 14-3

Large rocks (problems) are hidden by a high water level (inventory) in A. Lower water level (B) reveals rocks. Once the large rocks are removed, the lower water level (inventory) is adequate (C).

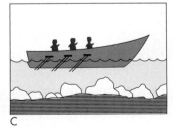

A   B   C

READING

Dana

When Toyota decided to build a truck assembly plant in Princeton, Indiana, to make Tundra and Sequoia in the late 1990s, it chose Dana Corporation to build its truck frames. Dana built a 129,000-square-foot plant employing about 300 people 73 miles away in Owensboro, Kentucky. To be as lean as possible, Dana makes the frames to the sequence of trucks planned in the Toyota Plant. There are 14 frame models which are sequenced in batches of one. Therefore, the Dana plant has to be very flexible: it takes a maximum of three seconds to change over from one model to the next in any work centre on the production line. The order information comes via Internet (FTP) from the Toyota plant and is displayed on every work centre. About nine hours later, after operations such as welding, machining, and painting, the frames are trucked to the Toyota plant in batches of 25, about one truck every half hour.

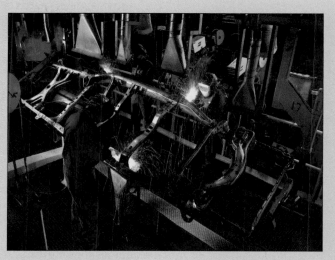

Sources: www.dana.com/centennial/images.asp; T. Vinas, "In Sync with the Customer," *Industry Week* 252(10), October 2002, pp. 46–48.

storage of finished goods. Coupled with small manufacturing lot sizes resulting in low work-in-process inventory, these features result in systems that operate with very little inventory.

PERSONNEL/ORGANIZATIONAL ELEMENTS

There are five elements of personnel and organization that are particularly important for JIT systems:

1. Workers as assets
2. Cross-trained workers
3. Cost accounting
4. Leadership
5. Nonmanufacturing support

Workers as Assets. A fundamental tenet of the JIT philosophy is that *workers are assets*. Well-trained and motivated workers are the heart of a JIT system. They are given more authority (empowered) to make decisions than their counterparts in more traditional systems, but they are also expected to do more. Workers are expected to participate in continuous improvement (kaizen) teams and suggestion systems. In return, their contribution will be recognized and rewarded.

Cross-Trained Workers. Workers are *cross-trained* to perform several parts of a process and operate a variety of machines. This adds to system flexibility because workers are able to help one another when bottlenecks occur or when a co-worker is absent. It also helps line balancing.

Cost Accounting. Another feature of some JIT systems is the method of allocating overhead. Traditional accounting methods sometimes distort overhead allocation because they allocate it on the basis of direct labour hours. However, that approach does not always accurately reflect the consumption of overhead by different jobs. In addition, the number of direct labour hours in some industries has declined significantly over the years and now frequently accounts for a relatively small portion of the total cost. Conversely, other costs now represent a major portion of the total cost. Therefore, labour-intensive jobs (i.e., those that use relatively large proportions of direct labour) may be assigned a disproportionate share of overhead, one that does not truly reflect actual costs. That in turn can cause managers to make poor decisions. Furthermore, the need to track direct labour hours can itself involve considerable effort.

activity-based costing
Allocation of overhead to specific jobs based on the percentage of activities they consume.

One alternative method of allocating overhead is **activity-based costing**. This method is designed to more closely reflect the actual amount of overhead consumed by a particular job or activity. Activity-based costing first identifies traceable costs and then assigns those costs to various types of activities such as machine setups, inspection, machine hours, direct labour hours, and movement of materials. Specific jobs are then assigned overhead based on the percentage of activities they consume.

Leadership. Top management takes leadership in conversion to lean manufacturing because it involves culture change, i.e., the way workers do their job. Goals are set to progress towards world-class JIT status, and resources are allocated. Employees are both directed and encouraged to assist in selecting and using methods, processes, and systems of lean manufacturing. On the other hand, managers are expected to be facilitators, not just order givers. JIT encourages two-way communication between workers and managers. For an application, see the reading, "Exide's Lean Manufacturing."

Nonmanufacturing Support. Clearly support is needed from Sales/Marketing for product design, from Accounting for product costing, from HR for hiring and training good employees, and from Quality Assurance and Control for improving the quality of products and processes. Further, Finance needs to provide the cash for faster but more flexible equipment, Purchasing needs to identify qualified JIT suppliers and maintain close relationships, and MIS needs to provide the information required to track performance measures and to provide data gathering/communication links. In addition, all these functions should reduce their own department's "wastes."

MANUFACTURING PLANNING AND CONTROL

Five elements of manufacturing planning and control are particularly important for JIT systems:

1. Level loading
2. Pull system and kanban
3. Close supplier relationship
4. Visual systems
5. Preventive maintenance and housekeeping

Level Loading

JIT systems place a strong emphasis on achieving stable, level daily mixed-model schedules. Also, the master production schedule is developed to provide *level capacity loading*.

When a company produces different products or product models, it is desirable to produce in small lots (to minimize the work-in-process inventory of both itself and all its components, and to maintain flexibility) and to spread the production of the different products throughout the day to achieve smooth production. The ideal case would be to produce one unit of one product, then one of another, then one of another, and so on.

The simplest method for determining a level mixed-model sequence is as follows:[1]

a. determine a "due date" for each unit of each model so that the units of the model are evenly distributed during the day.

b. sequence the units of all models based on their "due dates" (smallest to largest).

---

[1]R. R. Inman and R. L. Bulfin, "Sequencing JIT Mixed-model Assembly Lines," *Management Science* 37(7), July 1991, pp. 901–904.

The "due dates," based on demand for each model are as follows:

Daily Demand	Due Dates (whole day = 1)
1	1/2
2	1/4, 3/4
3	1/6, 3/6, 5/6
4	1/8, 3/8, 5/8, 7/8
5	1/10, 3/10, 5/10, 7/10, 9/10
6	1/12, 3/12, 5/12, 7/12, 9/12, 11/12
7	1/14, 3/14, 5/14, 7/14, 9/14, 11/14, 13/14
8	1/16, 3/16, 5/16, 7/16, 9/16, 11/16, 13/16, 15/16
⋮	

In general, if daily demand is n, the due dates will be: $\dfrac{1}{2n}, \dfrac{3}{2n}, \dfrac{5}{2n}, \cdots \dfrac{2n-1}{2n}$.

Example 1

Determine a level mixed model sequence if daily demand for A = 7, B = 16, and C = 5 units.

Solution

The due dates are:

A: $1/14 = .071$, $3/14 = .214$, $5/14 = .357$, $7/14 = .5$, $9/14 = .643$, $11/14 = .786$, $13/14 = .929$

B: $1/32 = .031$, $3/32 = .094$, $5/32 = .156$, $7/32 = .219$, $9/32 = .281$, $11/32 = .344$, $13/32 = .406$, $15/32 = .469$, $17/32 = .531$, $19/32 = .594$, $21/32 = .656$, $23/32 = .719$, $25/32 = .781$, $27/32 = .844$, $29/32 = .906$, $31/32 = .969$

C: $1/10 = .1$, $3/10 = .3$, $5/10 = .5$, $7/10 = .7$, $9/10 = .9$

Now, sequence by sorting the dues dates from the smallest to the largest. The smallest "due date" is .031 for a B, so the first unit to produce is B. The next smallest due date is .071 for an A, so the second unit to produce is A, and so on. The level mixed model sequence is:

B-A-B-C-B-A-B-B-C-B-A-B-B-A-C-B-B-A-B-C-B-B-A-B-C-B-A-B

Hyundai's Mixed-Model Sequencing. Hyundai uses a more sophisticated method for its mixed model sequencing.[2] On any production line, only one model of Hyundai car is assembled, but there are many model types, each having a particular set of options. For example, on an Accent line, the options are shown in Table 14–1.

Given next month's production plan for each model type, daily production plans are determined by dividing the monthly numbers by the number of working days in the month. Given the number of working minutes in a day, the cycle time is determined by

---

[2]E. A. Duplaga et al., "Mixed-Model Assembly Line Sequencing at Hyundai Motor Company," *Production and Inventory Management Journal,* Third Quarter 96, 37(3), pp. 20–26.

TABLE 14-1

Options available for the Hyundai Accent (note: these are not for the current models)

Characteristics	Options
1. Door Type:	3-Door (3DR), 4-Door (4DR), 5-Door (5DR)
2. Engine:	1300 cc (13), 1500 cc (15)
3. Trim Level:	L, GL, GLS (most luxurious)
4. Transmission (T/M):	Manual (5), Automatic (A4)
5. Drive Type	Right-Hand Drive (RH), Left-Hand Drive (LH)
6. Region:	Domestic, Export
7. Air Bag System:	Yes (O), No
8. Power Steering:	Yes (O), No
9. Anti-Lock Brakes	Yes (O), No
10. Rear Spoiler:	Yes (O), No
11. Delivery Wrapping:	California, Canada, Puerto Rico, Other
12. Driving Instruction Vehicle:	Yes (O), No

dividing it by the total number of cars planned for the day. The number of workers and workstations are determined using the weighted average of task times and the assembly line balancing method.

The sequence of model types is determined one position at a time, starting from the first position. Each model type is tried and the one which gives the lowest value for the square root of the sum (over options) of the square of the difference of the expected number of an option used so far and the actual number of the option used so far is chosen. This would give level production of options, thus minimizing the total WIP.

To clarify the method, it may help to introduce some notation:

$$i = \text{index of model type}, \quad i = 1, \ldots, I$$
$$j = \text{index of option}, \quad j = 1, \ldots, J$$
$$k = \text{index of position in the sequence, with a particular value } K$$
$$P_j = \text{proportion of option } j \text{ in the daily demand}$$
$$N_{j,K-1} = \text{total number of option } j \text{ used before the current position } K$$
$$I_{ij} = 1 \text{ if model type } i \text{ has option } j; 0 \text{ otherwise}$$
$$I_{ik} = 1 \text{ if model type } i \text{ has been chosen for position } k; 0 \text{ otherwise}$$
$$D_{iK} = \text{square root of the sum (over options) of the square of the difference of the expected number of an option used up to position } K \text{ and the actual number of the option used up to position } K \text{ if model type } i \text{ is used in position } K.$$

Mathematically,

$$D_{iK} = \sqrt{\sum_{j=1}^{J} (K.p_j - N_{j,K-1} - I_{iK}I_{ij})^2} \quad \text{where} \quad N_{j,K-1} = \sum_{k=1}^{K-1} \sum_{i=1}^{I} I_{ik}I_{ij}$$

The solution method starts with position $k = 1$, computes D_{i1} for all model types i, and chooses the model type with smallest D_{i1}. Then, this is repeated for position $k = 2$, given the model type selected for position 1, and so on, until all daily demand is sequenced.

Example 2

Suppose that there are only five model types with the options and daily "units required" below. Determine a level mixed-model sequence according to Hyundai's method.

Model Type	Door Type	Engine	Trim Level	T/M	Drive Type	Air Bag	Units Required
A	4DR	13	GLS	A4	LH	O	4
B	3DR	13	GLS	5	RH	O	2
C	3DR	13	GL	A4	LH		3
D	4DR	15	L	5	LH	O	3
E	5DR	15	GL	A4	RH		1

Solution

The expected number of options during a day is:

1300 cc	9/13
3 Door	5/13
4 Door	7/13
Auto T/M	8/13
GLS Trim	6/13
GL Trim	4/13
Air Bag	9/13
LH Drive	10/13

If the first model type in the sequence is A, then the difference between expected and actual number of options used will be:

1300 cc	$1 \times 9/13 - 0 - 1 = -4/13$
3 Door	$1 \times 5/13 - 0 - 0 = 5/13$
4 Door	$1 \times 7/13 - 0 - 1 = -6/13$
Auto T/M	$1 \times 8/13 - 0 - 1 = -5/13$
GLS Trim	$1 \times 6/13 - 0 - 1 = -7/13$
GL Trim	$1 \times 4/13 - 0 - 0 = 4/13$
Air Bag	$1 \times 9/13 - 0 - 1 = -4/13$
LH Drive	$1 \times 10/13 - 0 - 1 = -3/13$

where the second term (0 in this case) is the actual number of options used before the current position, and the third term is 1 if model type A has this option (otherwise, it is 0). Now, squaring these differences, adding, and taking the square root, we get:

$$D_{A1} = \sqrt{(-4/13)^2 + (5/13)^2 + (-6/13)^2 + (-5/13)^2 + (-7/13)^2 + (4/13)^2 + (-4/13)^2 + (-3/13)^2}$$

$$= 1.066$$

Similarly, we can calculate $D_{B1} = 1.488$, $D_{C1} = 1.462$, $D_{D1} = 1.294$, and $D_{E1} = 1.682$. The smallest of these is 1.066 for A; therefore sequence A first.

Now, to determine the choice of the second position in the sequence, calculate the new differences if A is second (given that A has already been chosen to be first):

1300 cc	$2 \times 9/13 - 1 - 1 = -8/13$
3 Door	$2 \times 5/13 - 0 - 0 = 10/13$
4 Door	$2 \times 7/13 - 1 - 1 = -12/13$
Auto T/M	$2 \times 8/13 - 1 - 1 = -10/13$
GLS Trim	$2 \times 6/13 - 1 - 1 = -14/13$
GL Trim	$2 \times 4/13 - 0 - 0 = 8/13$
Air Bag	$2 \times 9/13 - 1 - 1 = -8/13$
LH Drive	$2 \times 10/13 - 1 - 1 = -6/13$

Squaring these differences, summing and taking the square root results in $D_{A2} = 2.132$. Similarly, we will calculate $D_{B2} = 1.643$, $D_{C2} = 1.243$, $D_{D2} = 1.619$, and $D_{E2} = 1.389$. The smallest of these is 1.243 for C; therefore sequence C second.

This process is continued until all model types demanded during the day are sequenced:

A-C-D-B-A-E-D-C-A-B-D-C-A.

Pull System and Kanban

The terms *push* and *pull* are used to describe two different systems for moving work through a production process. In traditional production environments, a **push system** is used: When work is finished at a workstation, the output is *pushed* to the next station; or, in the case of the final operation, it is pushed on to finished goods inventory. Consequently, work may pile up at workstations. Conversely, in a **pull system,** control of moving the work rests with the following operation; each workstation *pulls* the output from the preceding station as it is needed; output of the final operation is pulled by customer demand or the master production schedule.

push system Work is pushed to the next station as it is completed.

JIT system communication moves backward through the system from station to station. Each workstation (i.e., "customer") communicates its need for more work to the preceding workstation (i.e., "supplier"), thereby ensuring that supply equals demand. Work moves "just in time" for the next operation; the flow of work is thereby coordinated, and the accumulation of excessive inventories between operations is avoided. Of course, some inventory is usually present because operations are not instantaneous. If a workstation waited until it received a request from the next workstation before starting its work, the next station would have to wait for the preceding station to perform its work. Therefore, there is a small buffer of stock between stations; when the buffer decreases to a certain level, this signals the preceding station to produce enough output to replenish the

pull system A workstation pulls output from the preceding station as it is needed.

buffer supply. The size of the buffer supply depends on the cycle time at the preceding workstation. If the cycle time is short, the station will need little buffer; if the cycle time is long, it will need a considerable amount of buffer.

A system can communicate the next-step demand in a variety of ways, including a shout or a wave, but by far the most commonly used device is the **kanban** card. *Kanban* is a Japanese word meaning "signal" or "visible record." When a worker needs materials or work from the preceding station, he or she uses a kanban card. In effect, the kanban card is the *authorization* to move or work on parts. In kanban systems, no part or lot can be moved or worked on without one of these cards.

kanban Card or other device that communicates demand for work or materials to the preceding station.

The system works this way: A kanban card is affixed to each container. When a workstation needs to replenish its supply of parts, a worker goes to the area where these parts are stored and withdraws one container of parts. Each container holds a predetermined quantity. The worker removes the kanban card from the container and posts it in a designated spot where it will be clearly visible, and the worker moves the container to the workstation. The posted kanban is then picked up and another container of the same part is fabricated or replenished. Usually because of significant setup time required and high utilization of the producing work centre, a batch of kanbans are accumulated before production is triggered. Similar withdrawals and replenishments—all controlled by kanbans—occur all the way up and down the line from vendors to finished-goods inventories. If supervisors decide the system is too loose because inventories are building up, they may decide to tighten the system and withdraw some kanbans. Conversely, if the system seems too tight, they may introduce additional kanbans to bring the system into balance. Vendors can also influence the number of containers. Trip times will affect the number: longer trip times will lead to more containers.

It is apparent that the number of kanban cards in use is an important variable. One can calculate the ideal number of kanban cards using this formula:

$$N = \frac{DT(1+X)}{C} \tag{14-1}$$

where

N = Total number of containers (1 card per container)

D = Average usage rate of using work centre

T = Average waiting time for replenishment of one container (includes wait before production, setup, production, and transport times): production or purchase lead time

X = Policy variable set by management that represents safety stock (as a proportion of average usage during lead time T)

C = Capacity of a standard container

Note that D and T must use the same unit of time (e.g., hours, days).

| **Example 3** | Usage at a work centre is 300 parts per day, and a standard container holds 25 parts. It takes an average of .12 day for a container to complete a circuit from the time a kanban card is received until the container is returned full. Compute the number of kanban cards (containers) needed if X = .20. |

Solution

N = ?
D = 300 parts per day
T = .12 day
C = 25 parts per container
X = .20

$$N = \frac{300(.12)(1+.20)}{25} = 1.728 \text{ (round to two containers)}$$

Note: Rounding up will cause the system to be looser, and rounding down will cause it to be tighter. Usually, rounding up is used.

READING

Use of Kanbans by Waterville TG

www.wtg.ca

Exhibit 1

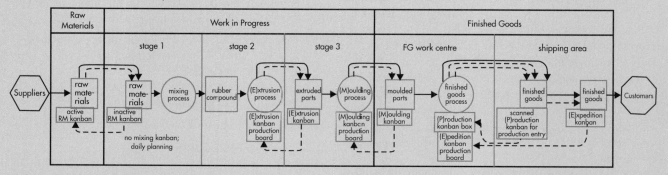

Waterville TG (WTG), of Quebec, designs and manufactures weather strips for cars from various types of rubber. Waterville TG is part of Toyoda Gosei Co. Ltd., a division of Toyota Motor Company. WTG has close to 385 different models of weather strips designed for almost all types of automobiles. The raw material is synthetic powder rubber. The production process is four stages: mixing, extrusion, moulding, and finishing. WTG uses kanbans for pulling material through most of the production process, as shown in Exhibit 1 above.

There are raw material (RM) kanbans, WIP extrusion (E) and moulding (M) kanbans, finished goods production (P) kanbans, and shipping or expedition (E) kanbans. An example of an RM kanban is shown in Exhibit 2 below:

pouch. This pouch is then attached to a container. Soon after a full container is moved to its point of use, the kanban is detached and moved back to the originating area. The punched hole in the top left corner is used to hang the card on the kanban boards.

Exhibit 3 shows an example of a WIP E kanban. A Ziplock-type seal was added to the pouch for easier maintenance. After trying out several versions of this card, WTG found that kanban maintenance was easier when cards included only information that changed little or not at all over time.

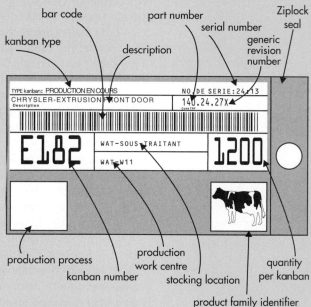

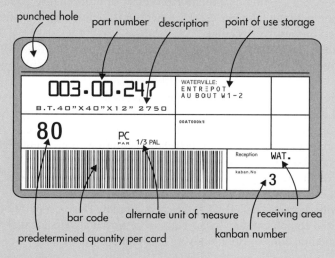

Exhibit 2

The use of bar codes on a kanban is unusual. WTG uses the computer (an MRP software) and bar codes to keep track of inventories and changes the number of active kanbans as demand varies. The bar codes make this easier. The card itself is printed on plain white paper and inserted in a protective clear plastic pouch that in turn is placed in a self-adhesive

Exhibit 3

At the finished goods level, two cards are used instead of one to allow some excess production (relative to shipment). These kanbans are similar to the WIP kanbans.

Source: S. Chausse, S. Landry, F. Pasin, and S. Fortier, "Anatomy of a Kanban: A Case Study," *Production and Inventory Management Journal* 41(4), Fourth Quarter 2000, pp. 11–16.

McDonnell & Miller

McDonnell & Miller (M&M) is a small manufacturer of boiler controls, such as valves and switches, in Chicago. The mechanical part of these products is made from small pieces of cast iron by machining operations. In the early 1990s, the company started a JIT program which involved grouping similar products together and forming manufacturing cells for each group. In designing the cell, the capacity of the bottleneck operation was matched with the average total daily demand for the group. The demand was fairly stable. M&M had to upgrade some of its machines to achieve this capacity and the flexibility required. For example, a semiautomated NC lathe and a multi-spindle drill machine replaced the machines in one cell. However, the setup times were still significant.

To determine the WIP after the machining (bottleneck) operation, M&M used a simple method: First they determined a production cycle interval during which a batch of each product in the group is made. Then they set the WIP equal to the demand during the cycle interval. For example, a group of valves consisted of 10 different products. The total setup time for all 10 valves was two days (eight hours of work per day). The average total daily demand for the group was 200 units. The production rate at the bottleneck machine was 300 per day. Then, the cycle time was determined as follows:

Demand during cycle time = Supply during cycle time
$$200 \text{ (Cycle Time)} = 300 \text{ (Cycle Time } - 2 \text{ days)}$$
$$100 \text{ Cycle Time} = 600 \text{ days}$$
$$\text{Cycle Time} = 6 \text{ days}$$
$$\text{WIP} = 6 (200) = 1{,}200 \text{ units.}$$

Using WIP, the number of kanbans was then set.

Sources: www.mcdonnellmiller.com, A. Soni, "Eight Steps to a JIT-focused Factory," *Manufacturing Systems* 10(2), February 92, pp. 46–52.

For an application, see the reading, "Use of Kanbans by Waterville TG." When the setup time is significant, production waits for a batch of containers to accumulate before producing the part. For two similar solutions to this problem, see the reading, "McDonnell & Miller" and Problem 9 at the end of this chapter.

Close Supplier Relationship

JIT companies typically have *close relationships with their suppliers*, who are expected to provide frequent small deliveries of high-quality goods on time. Buyers work with suppliers to help them achieve the desired quality and on-time delivery and to impress upon them the importance of consistent, high-quality goods to be delivered on time. The ultimate goal of the buyer is to be able to *certify* a supplier as a reliable producer of high-quality goods. The implication of certification is that a supplier can be relied on to deliver high-quality goods on time without the need for buyer inspection.

In effect, the supplier becomes part of an extended JIT system that integrates the facilities of buyer and supplier. Integration is easier when a supplier is dedicated to only one or few buyers.

Because of the need for frequent, small deliveries, many buyers attempt to find local suppliers to shorten the lead time for deliveries and to reduce lead time variability. An added advantage of having suppliers nearby is quick response when problems arise.

Price often becomes secondary to other aspects of the relationship (e.g., consistent high quality, flexibility, frequent small deliveries, and quick response to problems).

For some applications, see the readings, "Dana," "Mackie," and "Raymond's JIT System & Supplier Certification."

A very close cooperation with suppliers, called JIT II, has been used by Bose Corporation, the manufacturer of luxury audio equipment, in which a supplier representative is located in Bose's facility and performs the functions of Bose's buyer. This reduces lead times.

Visual Systems

JIT is a visual system. Kanbans are visual production control tools. Visual systems are simpler to operate than computer-based systems. Other visual techniques in JIT are point-of-use inventories and tools which are openly displayed, located in specified places.

Some companies use a light system to signal problems; in Japan, such a system is called **andon**. Each workstation is equipped with a set of three lights. A green light means no problems, an amber light means a worker is falling a little bit behind, and a red light indicates

andon System of lights used at each workstation to signal problems or slowdowns.

READING

Mackie

When a new car is ordered, the customer makes a number of decisions—colour, upholstery, automatic versus standard transmission, clear versus tinted windows…. It's called build-to-order and customers are demanding more of it every day. But can assemblers build a nearly infinite variety of the same car without stashing floor-to-ceiling inventory? If not, it might be time to turn to a "Tier Zero" integrator for help.

Nebe Tamburro, president of Oshawa, Ontario–based Mackie Automotive Systems, describes Tier Zero as "the final integration of complete modules or assemblies…it's that final movement and management of (parts) into an assembly plant."

Mackie Automotive receives parts from various manufacturers and assembles them into modules such as bumpers and complete instrument panels. One of Mackie's main customers is the GM plant located only a few minutes away.

A steady stream of products is fed into the GM plant—as much as 400 truckloads every day. Mackie trucks run back and forth to the GM plant every hour, ensuring modules are delivered just in time and in the right sequence (the order in which they're needed).

"Every time a car comes out of the GM paint system, that sends a trigger which tells you what type of car it is, the colour and the model. And from that, we know exactly what it is they need," Tamburro explains. At that point, work orders are issued to the various locations within the Mackie plant, then the subassemblies are made and whisked out the door. In some cases, the window of time between the trigger and the deadline to get the module to GM's plant can be as little as one hour.

Part of the company's success as a just-in-time sequencer goes back to Mackie's roots as a transportation company. "In the 1980s, when sequencing began, trucking companies were responsible for making it happen, doing the sequencing in their trucking facilities," Tamburro says. Seats were the first to be outsourced, because they take up so much space and are so labour-intensive. As manufacturers began to outsource more modules, many trucking companies decided sequencing on a just-in-time basis was too much of a challenge.

It was then that the trucking industry realized sequencing was a separate operation, requiring separate subassembly plants. So in 1987, the Mackie family's transportation firm merged with an automotive engineering company to form Mackie Automotive Systems, a distinct and separate company. But the transportation roots have allowed Mackie Automotive to maintain its own private fleet.

"Right from the beginning, we've maintained that if we have the responsibility to bring (modules) right to the plant, and in some cases right to the assembly line, we'd run our own trucks. That way, you don't have a third-party you can blame for a problem," says Tamburro. Controlling both the assembly and transportation allows Mackie to be the ultimate just-in-time supplier. Mackie Automotive was bought by TDS Automotive, a multi-national subassembly, sequencing, and logistics provider, based in Mississauga, in 2001.

Source: Excerpted from "Tier Zero—Mackie Automotive Systems' Supply Chain Message," *Materials Management and Distribution*, Maclean Hunter Publishing Ltd., September 1999.

a serious problem. The purpose of the light system is to keep others informed and to enable workers and supervisors to immediately see when and where problems are occurring.

Preventive Maintenance and Housekeeping

Because JIT systems have very little work-in-process inventory, equipment breakdowns can be extremely disruptive. To minimize breakdowns, companies use **preventive maintenance** programs, which emphasize maintaining equipment in good operating condition and replacing parts that have a tendency to fail before they fail. Workers are often responsible for maintaining their own equipment.

preventive maintenance Maintaining equipment in good operating condition and replacing parts that have a tendency to fail before they actually do fail.

Even with preventive maintenance, occasional equipment failures will occur. Companies must be prepared for this, so they can quickly return equipment to working order. This may mean maintaining supplies of critical spare parts and making other provisions for emergency situations, perhaps maintaining a small force of repair people or training workers to do certain repairs themselves.

Housekeeping involves keeping the workplace clean as well as keeping it free of any materials that are not needed for production, because those materials take up space and may cause disruption to the work flow.

housekeeping Maintaining a workplace that is clean and free of unnecessary materials.

The 5S principles for housekeeping have been used by most JIT companies (e.g., Pratt & Whitney Canada). The five words that start with S and their meanings are:

- SORT: remove all objects that do not need to be in the workstation or area.
- STRAIGHTEN: tidy up the objects needed and organize them such that they can be found quickly.

www.pwc.ca/en/4_0/4_0_1/4_0_1_4_1.asp

Raymond's JIT System & Supplier Certification

www.Raymondcorp.com

Raymond Industrial Equipment (RIE) of Brantford, Ontario, a subsidiary of Raymond Corporation of Greene, New York, is a leader in North America's electric narrow aisle lift truck industry. Over half of all reach trucks sold in North America are built in Brantford, so it's not surprising that the company has invested $10 million to expand its facility and potentially double its production.

Raymond began to adopt JIT in 1989 because the more traditional method of batch manufacturing was inefficient and too many resources were wrapped up in inventory. "During production, parts flow through the plant synchronized, so that one part meets with its counterpart at precisely the right moment," explains Jim Locker, vice-president and general manager of RIE.

When an order is placed with Raymond, it is entered into the MRP system (MAPICS/XA). From the MRP, it is moved into the Manufacturing Execution System (MES), which constructs a daily schedule at each workstation throughout the plant. Parts, triggered by kanbans, are delivered to the plant daily and placed in carts waiting to be called into use. In some instances, parts are delivered directly to the workstation. "The system is very visual. A lot of our parts are quite large, so we use a cart system. When an empty cart comes back from the upstream station, that is a visual signal that the next guy is ready, and you can send the next piece," says Locker.

With the new integrated system, a reach truck that took 20 days in manufacturing now takes only four. And a "walkie"-type truck (electric pallet jack) that took 10 days is now complete in two. "That doesn't mean a customer gets it in four days, because we can only produce so many trucks per day—but traditionally Raymond has the most competitive lead times in the business. We aim to deliver a walkie truck in four to six weeks and reach truck in about 10 to 12 weeks," says Locker. Raymond has seen a significant reduction in overall costs, and increased its inventory turns from 11 in 1989 to more than 30 in 2000.

Supplier Certification

Having a reliable supply base, with many suppliers strategically located within an 80-kilometre radius of the plant, has allowed the company to adopt the JIT system. Raymond's supplier certification program is based on two elements—assessment and performance. "Prior to being accepted as a Raymond supplier, an on-site assessment is conducted by our certification team," says Reg Lewicki, materials manager at Raymond in Brantford. "This assessment evaluates various aspects of the supplier's operations, including facilities, quality systems, business systems, and operating procedures."

The minimum grade is 90 percent. Any operational weaknesses or shortcomings are noted and corrective action is requested. Inspections are followed up at six-month intervals. Once a supplier has been accepted, its performance is monitored on a continuous basis and "report cards" are issued monthly. Supplier standing is determined based on three categories: quality, 45 percent; on-time delivery, 35 percent; and service, 20 percent. Suppliers that fall below 90 percent are put on probation until they can re-prove their capabilities. But suppliers who meet Raymond's demanding expectations will score long-term agreements and sourcing preference.

Take Wilson Machine, based in Cathcart, Ontario. Located about 20 minutes from Raymond, between Brantford and Woodstock, Wilson is a machine fabrication shop that has been a RIE supplier since 1967. Wilson delivers parts to Raymond on a daily basis and twice on Mondays and Tuesdays. "Things have really progressed over the last several years. At one time we'd send them a box of this, a box of that. Now we kit them. They just send the kit up to the machine and pull them off in sequence," says Dave Wilson, president of Wilson Machine.

Raymond's goal over the past decade has been to reduce its supplier base and use only those meeting all the company's requirements. "Today we have about 135 active suppliers, less than one third of what we had 10 years ago," says Lewicki. "But the ones we do have we consider to be the very best available in our specific industry."

Source: C. McLean, "Raymond Is Going with the Flow: Winning Supply Chain Strategy Drives Productivity," *Plant* 59(9), June 23, 2000, pp. 18–19.

- SHINE: clean the workstation completely and eliminate all signs of dust or grime on the floor, machines, and equipment.
- STANDARDIZE: Set standards in cleanliness and organization, and audit the area for compliance.
- SUSTAIN: train personnel to perform the house keeping and continuously improve on standards; make 5S part of the work culture.

JIT systems have been described and compared with traditional manufacturing systems in the preceding pages. Table 14–2 provides a brief overview of those comparisons.

Factor	Traditional	JIT
Inventory	Much, to offset forecast errors, late deliveries	Minimal necessary to operate
Deliveries	Few, large	Many, small
Lot sizes	Large	Small
Setups, runs	Few, long runs	Many, short runs
Vendors	Long-term relationships are unusual	Partners
Workers	Necessary to do the work	Assets

TABLE 14-2

Comparison of JIT/lean and traditional production philosophies

READING

Exide's Lean Manufacturing

When Exide, a major lead-acid battery manufacturer, was facing bankruptcy in the beginning of the 2000s, it turned to lean manufacturing. It brought in leaders with experience in just-in-time from Pratt & Whitney who had implemented JIT a few years before. Because of shortage of time, JIT was implemented simultaneously in all 60 Exide plants, located mainly in North America and Europe. The program is called Exide's Customer-Focused Lean Leadership (EXCELL). EXCELL has a central office with lean agents who train and assist each plant's lean leader and champions (hourly workers taking a leading role in lean implementation in their own work centres). After one week of training and one week of participation in a sister plant's kaizen (team-based process improvement effort), champions would lead their own kaizen. One of the benefits of kaizen is that by participation, team members learn from each other. As a result of EXCELL, all Exide employees have learned lean manufacturing. There is one kaizen per month per plant.

But EXCELL is not just process improvement. It is tied to ambitious strategic goals. Each plant has been given annual targets for improvement depending on their current performance. For example, if the fill rate is 70 percent for a plant, its target after one year is 85 percent, whereas if the fill rate is 90 percent, its target would be 95 percent. About 10 key performance indicators are measured, including manufacturing lead time, cost, inventories, quality (scrap rate, etc), safety (number of accidents, blood lead levels), and machine downtime. When a plant achieves its first year goals, it is "certified" to copper status. The second target level is bronze, then silver, next gold, and finally platinum. Each plant manager is responsible for achieving these goals. Some managers have been replaced for not fully cooperating with EXCELL. But, overall the results have been impressive. Most plants have copper status and some have bronze. The move towards perfection (platinum) is on-going. Exide is profitable again.

Sources: B. Weiner et al., "Charged with Change," *Industrial Engineering* 35(1), January 2003, pp. 34–37; www.exide.com/pdf/going_lean.pdf; www.exide.com/pdf/stone_age.pdf.

SUMMARY

Just-in-time (JIT) is a system of lean production in which goods move through the system and tasks are completed just in time. JIT systems require very little inventory because successive operations are closely coordinated.

The goal of a JIT system is eliminating waste, especially setup and lead times, and inventories. The building blocks of a JIT system are product design, process design, personnel and organization, and manufacturing planning and control.

Products should be made of standard parts of the highest quality, and products should be simple to make and assemble, using modular design. Concurrent engineering and QFD should be used to ensure a fast product design process and that the voice of the customer is reflected in the product's quality.

Small production lot sizes should be used in order to reduce the WIP, increase flexibility, and facilitate defect detection. Setup times should be reduced to render small lot sizes economical. Product families should be identified and produced in dedicated manufacturing cells; this would reduce material handling and manufacturing lead times. JIT requires the highest quality products because there is little safety stock. The raw material and finished good inventories should also be minimized.

Workers should be empowered in order to participate in teams and suggestion systems; this will assist in conversion to JIT and continuous improvement (kaizen). Activity-based costing should be used in order to determine the true cost of manufacturing. Top management should assign the necessary resources and direct the JIT conversion process. Other functions of business should support manufacturing to become lean, and they should also initiate waste reduction programs within their departments.

To reduce inventories, production of various products should be level; this will match demand which is also required to be level. Level loads are achieved by mixed-model sequencing. Production is synchronized to demand by using kanbans which pull the minimum amount of parts and material through the manufacturing process and from the suppliers. There is a need to integrate production planning with the suppliers; hence, the number of suppliers should be reduced in order to establish closer relationships and partnerships. Other than kanbans, examples of visual techniques include easy-to-see and organized inventories, tools, and lights to show work-centre status (called *andon*). Preventative maintenance is crucial for JIT operations, again because machine downtime may stop the whole plant's production. The 5S housekeeping method is also important because organized and clean workstations operate fast.

KEY TERMS		
activity-based costing, 532		kanban, 536
andon, 538		lean manufacturing, 525
autonomation, 530		preventive maintenance, 539
jikoda, 530		pull system, 535
housekeeping, 539		push system, 535
just-in-time (JIT), 525		

Solved Problems

Problem 1

Determine the number of containers needed for a workstation that uses 100 parts per hour if the time for a container to complete a cycle (move, wait, fill, return) is 90 minutes and a standard container holds 84 parts. A safety factor of .10 is currently being used.

Solution

$N = ?$
$D = 100$ parts per hour
$T = 90$ minutes (1.5 hours)
$C = 84$ parts
$X = .10$

$$N = \frac{D(T)(1 + X)}{C} = \frac{100(1.5)(1 + .10)}{84} = 1.96 \text{ (round to 2) containers}$$

Problem 2

Determine a level mixed-model sequence for the following set of products and demand. The department operates five days a week.

Product	Weekly Quantity
A	20
B	40
C	30
D	15

Solution

Convert weekly quantities to daily quantities:

Product	Daily Quantity = Weekly Quantity ÷ 5
A	20 ÷ 5 = 4
B	40 ÷ 5 = 8
C	30 ÷ 5 = 6
D	15 ÷ 5 = 3

The due dates are:

A: 1/8 = .125, 3/8 = .375, 5/8 = .625, 7/8 = .875
B: 1/16 = .0625, 3/16 = .1875, 5/16 = .3125, 7/16 = .4375, 9/16 = .5625, 11/16 = .6875, 13/16 = .8125, 15/16 = .9375

C: $1/12 = .083, 3/12 = .25, 5/12 = .417, 7/12 = .583, 9/12 = .75, 11/12 = .917$
D: $1/6 = .167, 3/6 = .5, 5/6 = .83$

Sort the due dates from smallest to largest. The smallest "due date" is .0625 for B, so the first unit in sequence is B. The next smallest is .083 for C, so the second unit in sequence to produce is C, and so on:

B-C-A-D-B-C-B-A-C-B-D-B-C-A-B-C-B-D-A-C-B

DISCUSSION AND REVIEW QUESTIONS

1. Explain briefly how JIT systems differ from traditional production systems.
2. What is the goal of a JIT system? What are the building blocks?
3. Contrast the elements of the Shingo prize with the building blocks of JIT.
4. Briefly discuss supplier relations in JIT systems in terms of the following issues:
    a. Why are they important?
    b. How do they tend to differ from the more adversarial relations of the past?
    c. Why might suppliers be hesitant about JIT purchasing?
5. What is SMED?
6. What is a kanban?
7. Contrast push and pull systems of moving goods and materials through production systems.
8. What are the main benefits of a JIT system?
9. What is the benefit of level mixed-model sequencing?
10. What are the benefits of small lot sizes?

TAKING STOCK

1. What trade-offs are involved in shifting from a traditional operations system to a JIT/lean system for a manufacturing firm?
2. Who in the organization is affected by a decision to shift from a traditional operations system to a JIT/lean system?
3. To what extent has technology had an impact on JIT/lean systems?

CRITICAL THINKING EXERCISE

What are the key enablers for successful implementation of JIT/lean manufacturing?

INTERNET EXERCISE

Visit www.shingoprize.org, choose a recent recipient of the Shingo prize, and briefly summarize its JIT program.

PROBLEMS

1. A manager wants to determine the number of containers to use for a kanban system to be installed next month. The process will have a usage rate of 80 pieces per hour. Because the process is new, the manager has assigned a safety factor of 1.0. Each container holds 45 pieces and will take an average of 75 minutes to complete a cycle. How many containers should be used? As the system improves, will more or fewer containers be required? Why?
2. A JIT system uses kanban cards to authorize production and movement of materials. In one portion of the system, a work centre uses an average of 100 pieces per hour while running. The manager has assigned a safety factor of .50 to the centre. Standard containers are designed to hold six dozen parts each. The cycle time for part containers is about 105 minutes. How many containers are needed?
3. A machine cell uses 90 kg of a certain material each day. Material is transported in vats that hold 54 kg each. Cycle time for the vats is about two hours. The manager has assigned a safety factor of .50 to the cell. The plant operates on an eight-hour day. How many vats are needed?

4. Determine a level of mixed-model sequence, given the following data:

Product	Daily Quantity
A	1
B	2
C	3
D	5

5. Determine a level mixed-model sequence, given the following data:

Product	Daily Quantity
A	2
B	12
C	4
D	5
E	9

6. Determine a level mixed-model sequence, given the following data:

Product	Daily Quantity
F	9
G	8
H	5
K	6

7. Toyota has recently decided to make its minivan, the Sienna, in the same plant as the Camry and the Avalon. Suppose that during a half-hour period 12 Camrys, 9 Avalons, and 6 Siennas are to be produced. Determine a level mixed-model sequence.

8. Perform level mixed-model sequencing using Hyundai's method, given the following data:

Model Type	Door Type	Engine	Trim Level	TIM	Drive Type	Air Bag	Units Required
A	4DR	13	GLS	A4	LH	O	4
B	3DR	13	GLS	5	RH	O	2
C	3DR	13	GL	A4	LH		3

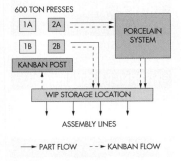

600 TON PRESSES

1A 2A → PORCELAIN SYSTEM

1B 2B

KANBAN POST

WIP STORAGE LOCATION

ASSEMBLY LINES

→ PART FLOW   - - ► KANBAN FLOW

Figure reprinted with permission of APICS The Association for Operations Management. *Production and Inventory Management Journal* 39(1), First Quarter, 1998, pp. 17–22.

9. The whirlpool factory in Oxford, Mississippi, makes built-in kitchen ovens.[3] In the 1990s, this plant re-engineered its processes to become lean. One of the parts of a particular oven, Part A, goes through two 600 ton presses (in series), and then goes through a porcelain system to be coated. Then, it is stored in the WIP storage location until it is used by the assembly lines. As a container of Part A is used, the kanban is taken to the press area and posted on the Kanban Post. Demand for Part A is 175 units per workday. A workday is 19 hours. The container size is 30 units. The setup time is 1 hour. Because of the large setup time, 5 kanbans are accumulated before production of A begins on the presses (approximately 16 hours of wait time). [The number of kanbans required to trigger a run of A is determined by optimization with the objective of minimizing the trigger values for all the products produced by the presses subject to meeting products' demand and not exceeding 80 percent utilization for the presses.] Production rate for A is 120 units per hour. The safety factor is 120 percent. Determine the number of kanbans required for Part A.

---

[3]Based on J. D. Hall et al., "An Optimizer for the Kanban Sizing Problem: A Spreadsheet Application for Whirlpool Corporation," *Production and Inventory Management Journal* 39(1), First Quarter, 1998, pp. 17–22.

MINI-CASE

Airline Manufacturing

Airline Manufacturing is a 250,000-square-foot, 160-employee wood component manufacturer supplying upholsterers (e.g., sofa manufacturers), located in Columbus, Mississippi. When Judy Dunaway took the helm of the company following her father in 2000, the company had used a batch production system for 40 years. However, the threat of competition led her to start lean manufacturing in Airline. High run (quantity) products were identified and grouped together if their required sequence of operations were identical. The machines required for each group were located close together in a dedicated manufacturing cell (flow line). As a result, the amount of WIP inventory has been cut by more than half, the number of material-handling carts has been reduced from 3,000 to 1,000, and the number of material handlers has been reduced by half. Also, manufacturing lead time is down from 4 weeks to less than a week.

A high run product is part #146-3843. Consider the production of a 2,900-unit customer order. Before the layout change, batches of approximately 1,000 units were transported from the warehouse to the CNC Router, and from there batches of approximately 380 units were carried, when ready, from one machine to another by two workers using heavy carts. These workers returned the empty cart to the originating machine. After the final operation, Dowel, the finished product was transported in batches of approximately 380 units to the Finished Goods Warehouse using forklifts. The total worker-feet of movement using the forklifts (including the return to their origin) was approximately 5,300.

After the layout change, the only transport is by forklifts bringing in and taking out the product. The total worker-feet of movement using the forklifts has remained at approximately 5,300. However, the amount of machine-to-machine material handling has been greatly reduced because the machines are located close to each other. Due to elimination of delays waiting for material handling, the company can now make the 2,900-unit customer order in one day whereas it used to take six days.

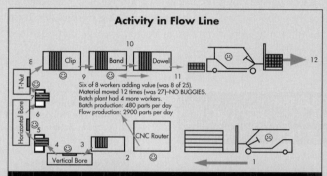

Figure 2. Airline's new flow-line includes all the operations required to complete the product-group parts.

Question

List the benefits of the manufacturing cell to airline manufacturing.

Vertical boring machine.

Sources: W. Duane Motsenbocker et al., *Wood Furniture Components: Implementation of Flow-Line Technology Based on Lean Manufacturing Concepts*, Research Bulletin, Forest and Wildlife Centre, Mississippi State University; www.airlinemfg.com/capabilities.html. Figures courtesy of Mississippi State University.

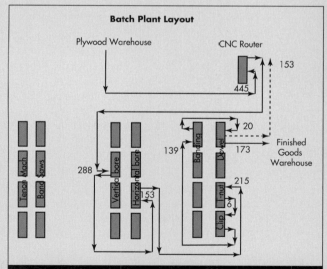

Figure 1. Airline's original batch processing flow for part number 146-3843. Only a small portion of the plant is shown. Numbers represent actual distance travelled in feet and are not to scale.

MINI-CASE

Level Operations

Level Operations is a small company that produces a variety of security devices and safes. The safes come in several different designs. Recently, a number of new customers have placed orders, and the production facility has been enlarged to accommodate increased demand for safes. Production manager Stephanie Coles is currently working on a production plan for the safes. She has obtained the following information from the marketing department on projected average daily demand for each model:

Model	Avg. Daily Quantity
A	4
B	3
C	10
D	12
E	5

Question

What might Stephanie determine as the level mixed-model sequence for each day?

SELECTED BIBLIOGRAPHY AND FURTHER READING

Benton, W. C., and Hojung Shin. "Manufacturing Planning and Control: The Evaluation of MRP and JIT Integration." *European Journal of Operational Research* 110 (1998), pp. 411–40.

Blackburn, Joseph D. *Time-Based Competition*. Burr Ridge, IL: Business One Irwin, 1991.

Hopp, Wallace J., and Mark Spearman. *Factory Physics: Foundations of Manufacturing Management*. 2nd ed. New York: Irwin/McGraw-Hill, 2001.

"JIT Manufacturing Is Working Overtime." *Business Week*, November 8, 1999.

Monden, Yasuhiro. "What Makes the Toyota Production System Really Tick?" *Industrial Engineering* 13(1) January 1981, pp. 38–46.

Spencer, Michael S., and V. Daniel Guide. "An Exploration of the Components of JIT." *International Journal of Operations and Production Management* 15(5) 1995, pp. 72–83.

Sriparavastu, Loknath, and Tarun Gupta. "An Empirical Study of JIT and Total Quality Management Principles Implementation in Manufacturing Firms in the USA." *International Journal of Operations and Production Management* 17(12) 1997, pp. 1215–32.

Swanson, Christine A., and William M. Lankford. "JIT Manufacturing." *Business Process Management Journal* 4(4) 1998, pp. 333–41.

White, Richard E., and John N. Pearson. "JIT Manufacturing: A Survey of Implementations in Small and Large U.S. Manufacturers." *Management Science* 45(1) January 1999, pp. 1–15.

Vollman, Thomas E., William L. Berry, and D. Clay Whybark. *Manufacturing Planning and Control Systems*. 4th ed. New York: Irwin/McGraw-Hill, 1997.

Zipkin, Paul H. *Foundations of Inventory Management*. New York: Irwin/McGraw-Hill, 2000.

Scheduling and Control

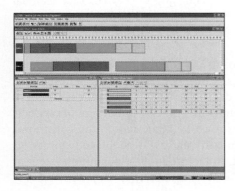

LEARNING OBJECTIVES

After completing this chapter, you should be able to:

1 Explain scheduling and control.

2 Discuss scheduling needs in high-volume and intermediate-volume systems.

3 Discuss scheduling needs in job shops.

4 Use and interpret Gantt charts, and input/output control for loading.

5 Discuss and use commonly used priority rules for sequencing.

6 Perform one-machine and two-machines sequencing.

7 Describe the Theory of Constraints.

8 Describe some of the approaches used for scheduling service systems.

9 Schedule full-time employees with two consecutive days off.

10 Describe part-time staff scheduling.

When Herman Miller, the major office furniture manufacturer, started the new division Miller SQA (Simple, Quick, Affordable), it tried to change its production system so that it could meet customer orders in two days. How did Miller SQA achieve this? McDonald's is in a competitive market with low margins. How can McDonald's keep its labour costs down? These are the kind of questions answered in this chapter.

INTRODUCTION

scheduling Establishing the timing of the use of equipment, facilities, and human activities in an organization.

Within an organization, **scheduling** pertains to establishing the timing of the use of specific resources or activities of that organization. It relates to the use of equipment, facilities, and human activities. Scheduling occurs in every organization, regardless of the nature of its activities. For example, manufacturers must schedule production, which means developing schedules for workers, equipment, purchases, maintenance, and so on. Hospitals must schedule admissions, surgery, nurses, and support services such as meal preparation, security, maintenance, and cleaning. Educational institutions must schedule classrooms, instructors, and students. And lawyers, doctors, dentists, hairdressers, and auto repair shops must schedule appointments.

In the decision-making hierarchy, scheduling decisions are the final step in the transformation process before actual output occurs. Many decisions about system design and planning have to be made long before scheduling decisions. They include the capacity of the system, equipment selection, selection and training of workers, and design of products and services. Consequently, scheduling decisions must be made within the constraints established by many other decisions, making them fairly narrow in scope and latitude.

Figure 15–1 depicts the location of scheduling in the production planning system of Black & Decker. It is called *dynamic scheduler*. We will also refer to *shop-floor control* which relates to execution of the schedule and involves monitoring the material, orders, and process, and taking any necessary actions.

Generally, scheduling involves trade-offs among conflicting goals, which include efficient utilization of staff, equipment, and facilities, and minimization of customer waiting time, inventories, and production times.

This chapter covers scheduling in both manufacturing and service environments. Although the two environments have many similarities, there are some differences. We begin with manufacturing environment.

SCHEDULING IN MANUFACTURING

Scheduling tasks are largely a function of the volume of system. High-volume systems require approaches that are substantially different from those required by job shops, and projects require a different approach still. In this chapter, we will consider scheduling for high-volume, intermediate-volume, and low-volume (job shop) systems. Project scheduling is discussed in Chapter 17.

Scheduling in High-Volume Systems (Continuous and Assembly Line)

flow system High-volume system with one main flow of material movement, using standardized equipment and activities.

flow-shop scheduling Scheduling for flow systems.

Scheduling encompasses allocating workloads to specific work centres and determining the sequence in which operations are to be performed. High-volume systems are characterized by standardized equipment and activities that provide identical or highly similar operations on products as they pass through the system. The goal is to obtain a constant rate of flow of goods through the system in order to get high utilization of labour and equipment. High-volume systems are often referred to as **flow systems**; scheduling in these systems is referred to as **flow-shop scheduling**, although flow-shop scheduling can also be used in medium-volume systems. An example of a high-volume product in

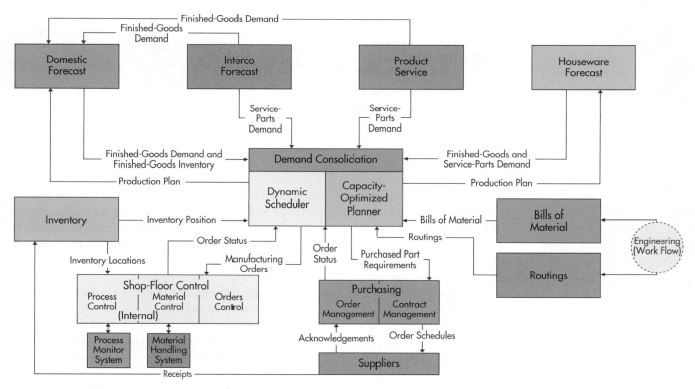

B&D implemented rhythm from i2 Technologies[1] in the early 1990s. The demand consolidation module (used for forecasting) is now called Demand Management; Capacity-Optimized Planner (advanced planning and scheduling which performs the function of MRP but keeps within machine capacities) is now called Factory Planner; and Dynamic Scheduler (the topic of this chapter) is now called Production Scheduler. Rhythm has hundreds of installations around the world. A recent example is the implementation of Factory Planner in all five manufacturing plants of 3M Canada.

Source: R. Eade, "Cutting Lead Time through Smart Scheduling," *Manufacturing Systems* 11(11), November, 1993, pp. 76–80; http://www.i2.com/assets/pdf/DD9F7212-997B-4525-A13F6247C9002D53.pdf.

FIGURE 15-1

Black & Decker's Production Planning System

Source: R. Eade, "Cutting Lead Time through Smart Scheduling," *Manufacturing Systems* 11(11), November, 1993. Figure reprinted with permission.

Rhythm (Demand Consolidation, Capacity Optimized Planner, and Dynamic Scheduler) is at the core of Black & Decker's computer-integrated manufacturing system.

repetitive systems is automobiles. In process industries (continuous flow), examples include petroleum refining, sugar refining, and water treatment. Because of the highly repetitive nature of these systems, many of the loading and sequencing decisions are determined during the design of the system. The use of highly specialized tools and equipment, the arrangement of equipment, the use of specialized material-handling equipment, and the division of labour are all designed to enhance the flow of work through the system, because all items follow virtually the same sequence of operations.

A major aspect in the design of flow systems is *line balancing*, which concerns allocating the required tasks to workstations so that they satisfy technical (sequencing) constraints and are balanced with respect to equal work times among stations. Highly balanced systems result in the maximum utilization of equipment and personnel as well as the highest possible rate of output. Line balancing was discussed in Chapter 6.

In spite of the built-in attributes of flow systems related to scheduling, a number of scheduling problems remain. One stems from the fact that few flow systems are *completely* devoted to a single product or service; most must handle a variety of sizes and models. Thus, an automobile manufacturer will assemble many different combinations of cars—two-door and four-door models, some with air-conditioning and some not, and so on. In these cases, in order to keep the line fairly balanced, longer-taking activities are interspaced as evenly as possible among other activities.

Scheduling in Intermediate-Volume Systems (Batch)

Intermediate-volume (or batch) system outputs fall between the standardized type of output of the high-volume systems and made-to-order output of job shops. Like the high-volume systems, intermediate-volume systems typically produce standard outputs. The

Taylor Software

Taylor Software of Edmonton makes various types of advanced planning and scheduling software. In particular, the Taylor Scheduler (TESS) has been used by several companies. This software uses optimization techniques. In the laser-printer toner plant of LexMark in Boulder, Colorado, TESS has reduced the scheduling task from 12 to 14 hours a week, using manual method, down to minutes. Instead of once every week, now TESS is run after every shift (eight hours).

Sources: www.taylor.com/downloads/Brochure.pdf; www.taylor.com/about/news.php?&flag=3&news=41.

products are for stock rather than for special order. However, the volume of each product is not large enough to justify continuous production. Instead, it is more economical to process these items *intermittently*. Thus, intermediate-volume work centres or lines periodically shift from one product to another. In contrast to a job shop, the run sizes are relatively large. Examples of products made in these systems include canned foods, baked goods, beer, and cosmetics.

The three basic issues in these systems are the *run size* of batches, the *sequence* in which batches should be processed, and the *timing* of batches.

Sometimes, the issue of run size can be determined by using a model such as the economic production quantity model discussed in Chapter 11 on inventory management. The run size (production quantity) that would minimize setup and inventory holding costs is

$$Q_0 = \sqrt{\frac{2DS}{H}} \sqrt{\frac{p}{p-d}} \tag{15-1}$$

However, setup costs may depend on the order in which batches are processed: similar products may require less setup change between them. For example, batches in a paint shop of a car assembly plant are usually sequenced by colour to reduce the number of setups needed.

Another difficulty arises because usage is not always as smooth as assumed in the model. Some products will tend to be used up faster than expected and have to be replenished sooner. Therefore, it is not always possible to schedule production to correspond with optimum run intervals.

Usually the runout time method is used to choose the next product to make; runout time for each product is the number of days the amount of inventory can supply the demand for the product; the product with the smallest run-out time is chosen for production next.

Another approach to scheduling a batch process is to produce according to the MRP schedule. However, MRP cannot handle changes to the plans easily and does not

Mitsubishi

Companies need a tool to monitor the production floor (e.g., for downtime tracking) and collect workstation information as well as reschedule jobs on a real time basis. These systems are called Manufacturing Execution Systems (MES). Mitsubishi Electric Automotive America's Maysville, Kentucky, plant is such a case. The management wanted to be able to communicate with eight coil-assembly lines wirelessly, using an Internet Web page interface. They chose ProductionIQ software from Rocky River, Ohio. The software can even provide visual information of the shop floor using a Webcam. The system can recalculate target production values on line, a feature which has increased productivity, acting as a motivational tool.

Sources: www.productioniq.com; "Mitsubishi Goes Beyond MES to Incorporate Lean," *Quality* 43(10), October 2004, pp. 48–49.

READING

U.S. Air Force Depot

The Warner Air Logistics Center in Robins, Georgia, is one of five U.S. Air Force's manufacturing and repair centres. In the CNC machine shop which makes parts, there are 15 CNCs with different levels of flexibility. For example, a five-axis CNC is more flexible that a four-axis CNC. Approximately half the jobs are repeat jobs whose manufacturing program is already stored in the machine that ran it before. The other jobs need to be assigned to a CNC. Before the mid-1990s a new job was assigned to a feasible CNC with the lowest flexibility. Because a program had to be written for the job before the CNC would be set up and operate many days later, the impact of this decision was not apparent. However, the centre started to receive complaints about late jobs. This prompted a simulation study into its operations. The recommendation was that assigning a job to a feasible work centre with the lowest amount of WIP, instead of the lowest flexibility, would reduce the lateness problem. This was done and the number of late jobs was reduced significantly.

Sources: www.acq.osd.mil/log/mppr/depot_partnerships/depot_capabilities_brochure_8-28-03.pdf; D. J. McFeely et al., "Scheduling to Achieve Multiple Criteria in an Air Force Depot CNC Machine Shop," *Production and Inventory Management Journal*, First Quarter 1997, 38(1), pp. 72–79.

consider resource capacities. Therefore, many companies are using Advanced Planning and Scheduling (APS) systems. APS uses the linear programming method and ensures that resource capacities are not violated. For example, see the "Taylor Software" reading.

SCHEDULING IN LOW-VOLUME SYSTEMS (JOB SHOP)

The characteristics of low-volume systems (job shops) are considerably different from those of high- and intermediate-volume systems. Products are made to order, and orders usually differ considerably in terms of materials needed, processing time, and processing sequence and setups. Because of these circumstances, **job-shop scheduling** is usually fairly complex. This is compounded by the difficulty of establishing firm schedules prior to receiving the actual jobs.

> **job-shop scheduling** Scheduling for low-volume systems with many variations in requirements.

Job-shop processing gives rise to two basic issues for schedulers: how to distribute the workload among work centres and what job processing sequence to use.

Loading

Loading refers to the assignment of jobs to work centres and to various machines in the work centres. In cases where a job can be processed only by a specific machine, loading presents little difficulty except for timing of the operation. However, problems arise when two or more jobs are to be processed and there are a number of work centres capable of performing the required work. In such cases, the operations manager needs some way of assigning jobs to the centres.

> **loading** The assignment of jobs to processing centres.

When making an assignment, managers often choose a machine that will minimize processing and setup costs (usually the least sophisticated machine that can do the job), minimize idle time among work centres, allow an operator to run two machines simultaneously, or minimize job completion time, depending on the situation. For an example, see the "U.S. Air Force Depot" reading above.

Gantt Charts. Visual aids called **Gantt charts** are used for a variety of purposes related to loading and scheduling. They derive their name from Henry Gantt, who pioneered the use of these charts for industrial scheduling in the early 1900s.

> **Gantt chart** Chart used as a visual aid for loading and scheduling purposes.

There are a number of different types of Gantt charts. Two of the most commonly used are the *load chart* and the *schedule/control chart*.

A **load chart** depicts the loading and idle times for resources such as machines, facilities, or workers. These charts are used in services as well. Two examples are illustrated in Figure 15–2, which shows scheduling classrooms for a university and scheduling hospital operating rooms.

> **load chart** A Gantt chart that shows the loading and idle times for a resource.

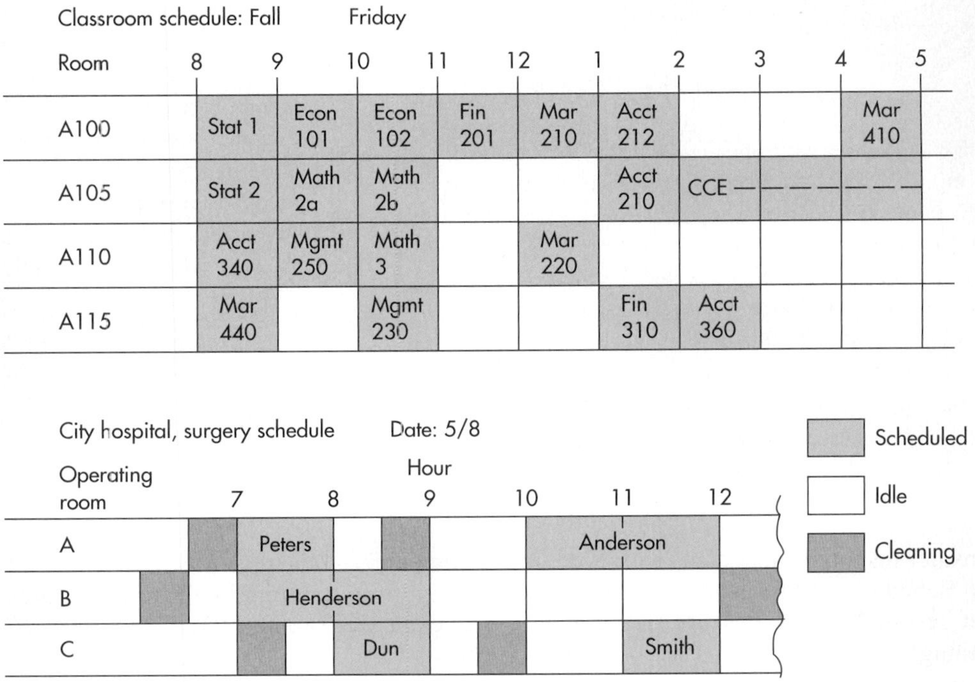

FIGURE 15-2

FIGURE 15-2

Examples of load charts used for scheduling in services

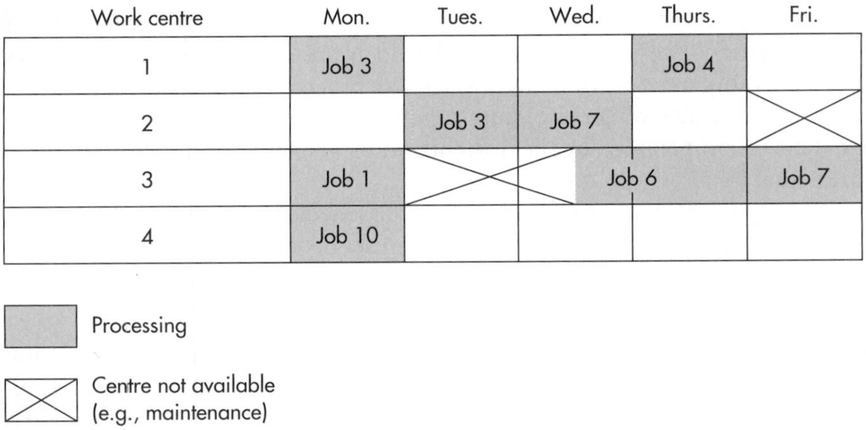

Classroom schedule: Fall   Friday

Room	8	9	10	11	12	1	2	3	4	5
A100	Stat 1	Econ 101	Econ 102	Fin 201	Mar 210	Acct 212				Mar 410
A105	Stat 2	Math 2a	Math 2b			Acct 210	CCE — — — — — —			
A110	Acct 340	Mgmt 250	Math 3		Mar 220					
A115	Mar 440		Mgmt 230				Fin 310	Acct 360		

City hospital, surgery schedule   Date: 5/8

Operating room / Hour

Operating room	7	8	9	10	11	12
A		Peters			Anderson	
B		Henderson				
C		Dun			Smith	

☐ Scheduled
☐ Idle
☐ Cleaning

FIGURE 15-3

A load chart in manufacturing

Work centre	Mon.	Tues.	Wed.	Thurs.	Fri.
1	Job 3			Job 4	
2		Job 3	Job 7		✕
3	Job 1	✕	Job 6	Job 7	
4	Job 10				

☐ Processing

✕ Centre not available (e.g., maintenance)

The purpose of a Gantt chart is to organize and clarify the actual or intended use of resources over *time*. Time scale is represented horizontally, and resources to be scheduled are listed vertically. The use of the resources is reflected in the body of the chart.

Managers may use the charts for trial-and-error schedule development to get an idea of what different arrangements would involve. Thus, a tentative surgery schedule might reveal insufficient allowance for surgery that takes longer than expected and can be revised accordingly. Use of the chart for classroom scheduling would help avoid assigning two different classes to the same room at the same time. Another example of a load chart is given in Figure 15–3. This chart indicates that work centre 3 is completely loaded for the entire week, centre 4 will be available on Tuesday, and the other two centres have idle time scattered throughout the week. This information can help a manager rework loading assignments to better utilize the centres. For instance, if all centres perform the same kind of work, the manager might want to free one centre for a long job or a rush order. The chart also shows when certain jobs are scheduled to start and finish, and when to expect idle time.

Sometimes it is advantageous to schedule jobs without capacity considerations. An example is MRP scheduling. This is called *infinite loading*. **Infinite loading** assigns jobs to work centres without regard to the capacity of the work centre. One possible result of infinite loading is the formation of queues.

Most scheduling is done by finite loading. **Finite loading** projects actual job starting and stopping times at each work centre, taking into account the capacity of each work centre and the processing times of jobs, so that capacity is not exceeded. One output of finite loading is a detailed projection of hours each work centre will operate. Schedules based on finite loading may have to be updated often, perhaps daily, due to processing delays at work centres and the addition of new jobs or cancellation of current jobs. The following diagram illustrates these two approaches.

infinite loading Jobs are assigned to work centres without regard to the capacity of the work centre.

finite loading Jobs are assigned to work centres taking into account the work centre capacity and job processing times.

Infinite loading

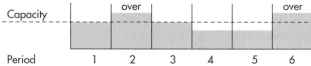

Finite loading

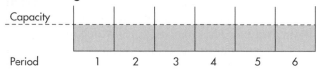

With infinite loading, a manager may need to make some response to overloaded work centres. Among the possible responses are shifting work to other periods or other centres, working overtime, or contracting out a portion of the work. Note that the last two options in effect increase capacity to meet the workload. For an application, see the following reading, "Robert Bowden."

READING

Robert Bowden

Robert Bowden Inc. (RBI) is a small manufacturer of doors and windows, including custom orders, based in Marietta, Georgia. In the mid 1990s, RBI was under competitive pressure because its lead time of six to eight weeks for custom millwork was three weeks longer than its competition. The millwork shop employed 20 workers with four skill levels: 11 low-skilled apprentice I and II, and 9 high-skilled journeymen and mill-workers. The millwork shop was laid out as a process (i.e., func-tional) layout. The customer orders were assigned to the shop by the purchasing department after a brief make-or-buy analysis. The order was then released to the shop on the same day as the assistant operations manager (OM) assigned it to a skilled worker. This worker managed the order all the way, getting assistance from low-skilled workers as needed. The problem with this system was that the skilled workers were overloaded with work. The assistant OM was also overwhelmed because he had to assist the skilled workers with the orders (approximately 20 at any time), such as interpreting the drawings.

The president of RBI brought in a professor of OM from a nearby university to help solve the problems. The professor suggested a manufacturing cell layout with five cells, each with four workers having mixed-skill levels. Also, the load in each cell was determined to be one order per day, and the amount of orders waiting to be released to each cell was determined to be about three weeks' work. The purchasing de-partment automatically outsourced the customer order if all cells had more than three weeks of orders waiting for them. This system was implemented in RBI. Three skilled workers left because they did not like to work in cell teams. These were replaced with low-skilled workers (RBI could not find high-skilled workers). Nevertheless, the productivity went up 20 percent, training of low-skilled workers accelerated, and the assistant OM's job became easier because there were only five active jobs at any time.

Sources: www.robertbowden.com; S. S. Chakravorty, "Robert Bowden Inc.: A Case Study of Cellular Manufacturing and Drum-Buffer-Rope Implementation," *Production and Inventory Management Journal* 37(3), Third Quarter, 1996, pp. 15–19.

When the capacity of a work centre is fixed (i.e., overtime or subcontracting is not used), then finite loading is used. This requires giving priorities to jobs as it may involve shifting work.

vertical loading Loading jobs at work centres independently.

Finite loading can be done in various ways. **Vertical loading** refers to loading the work centres independently. In contrast, **horizontal loading** involves loading first the job that has the highest priority on all work centres it will require, then the job with the next highest priority, and so on. One possible result of horizontal loading, assuming that a job cannot be split, is keeping jobs waiting at a work centre, even though that centre is idle, so the centre will be ready to process a higher-priority job that is expected to arrive shortly. That would not happen with vertical loading; the work centre would be fully loaded, and a higher-priority job would have to wait if it arrived while the work centre was busy. So horizontal loading takes a more *global* approach to scheduling, while vertical loading uses a *local* approach. Which approach is better? That depends on the relative costs of keeping higher-priority jobs waiting versus the cost of having work centres idle. Usually horizontal loading is used.

horizontal loading Loading each job on all work centres it will require, one job at a time, according to some priority rule.

Most scheduling is done starting from the present time and working forward into the future. This is called **forward scheduling**. However, it is sometimes necessary to do **backward scheduling**, starting from the due date and working backwards. This is to determine the start date of a job. MRP uses backward scheduling.

forward scheduling Scheduling ahead, starting from the start date of a job.

A manager often uses a **schedule/control (Gantt) chart** to monitor the progress of jobs. The vertical axis on this type of Gantt chart shows the jobs or components in progress, and the horizontal axis shows the time. The chart indicates which jobs or components are on schedule and which are behind or ahead. A typical schedule/control chart is illustrated in Figure 15–4 for a service. It shows the current status of a landscaping job with planned and actual starting and finishing times for the five components of the job. The chart indicates that approval and the ordering of trees and shrubs was on schedule. The site preparation was a bit behind schedule. The trees were received earlier than expected, and planting is ahead of schedule. However, the shrubs have not yet been received. The chart indicates some slack between scheduled receipt of shrubs and shrub planting, so if the shrubs arrive by the end of the week, it appears that the schedule can still be met.

backward scheduling Scheduling by working backwards from the due date.

schedule/control (Gantt) chart A Gantt chart that shows the jobs or components in progress and whether they are on schedule.

input/output (I/O) control Managing work flow and queues at each work centre.

Input/Output Control. **Input/output (I/O) control** refers to monitoring and managing the work flow and queue lengths at each work centre. The purpose of I/O control is to manage work flow so that queues and waiting times are kept under control. Without I/O control, demand may exceed processing capacity, causing an overload at the centre. Conversely, work may arrive slower than the rate a work centre can handle, leaving the work centre underutilized. Ideally, a balance can be struck between the input and output rates, thereby achieving effective use of work centre capacities without experiencing excessive queues at the work centre.

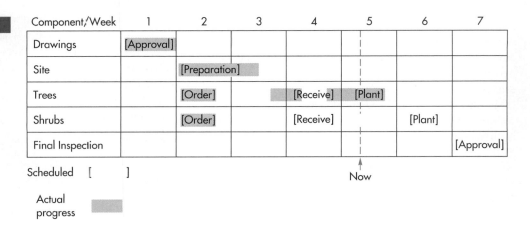

FIGURE 15–4

Schedule/control chart for a landscaping job

Component/Week	1	2	3	4	5	6	7
Drawings	[Approval]						
Site		[Preparation]					
Trees		[Order]		[Receive]	[Plant]		
Shrubs		[Order]		[Receive]		[Plant]	
Final Inspection							[Approval]

Now

Scheduled [   ]

Actual progress

FIGURE 15-5

An input/output report for a work centre

		Period (weeks)					
		1	2	3	4	5	6
Input	Planned	100	100	90	90	90	90
	Actual	120	95	80	88	93	94
	Deviation	+20	-5	-10	-2	+3	+4
	Cum. dev.	+20	+15	+5	+3	+6	+10

		1	2	3	4	5	6
Output	Planned	110	110	100	100	100	95
	Actual	110	105	95	101	103	96
	Deviation	0	-5	-5	+1	+3	+1
	Cum. dev.	0	-5	-10	-9	-6	-5

WIP	40	50	40	25	12	2	0

Note: Figures represent standard hours of processing time.

Figure 15–5 illustrates an input/output report for a work centre. A key portion of the report is the WIP waiting to be processed. The report highlights deviations-from-planned for both inputs and outputs, thereby enabling a manager to determine possible sources of problems.

The deviations in each period are determined by subtracting "planned" from "actual." For example, in the first period, subtracting the planned input of 100 hours from the actual input of 120 hours produces a deviation of +20 hours. Similarly, in the first period, the planned and actual outputs are equal, producing a deviation of 0 hours.

The WIP for each period is determined by subtracting the "actual output" from the "actual input" and adjusting the WIP from the previous period by that amount. For example, in the second period actual output exceeds actual input by 10 hours. Hence, the previous WIP of 50 hours is reduced by 10 hours to 40 hours.

The objective is to plan the output based on labour/equipment capacity, then plan the input so that desired WIP is maintained, and monitor deviations from planned input and output to identify any problems and fix them. The functioning of the input/output control is similar to keeping an unplugged sink at a desired level. In the above example, it appears that the production controller planned inputs lower than outputs, therefore reducing the WIP to zero, which is not usually desirable in a job shop.

Another tool for shop-floor control is the Anticipated Delay Report which lists late parts, cause of delay, actions taken, and new due dates. Manufacturing Execution Systems (MES) usually generate both these reports, as well as assist in scheduling. See, for example, the "Mitsubishi" reading earlier in the chapter and the "Pfaudler" reading later.

Sequencing

Although loading decisions determine the machines or work centres that will be used to process specific jobs, they do not necessarily indicate the *order* in which the jobs waiting at a given work centre or workstation are to be processed. **Sequencing** is concerned with determining job processing order at various work centres and stations/machines.

If work centres or stations/machines are lightly loaded and if jobs all require the same amount of processing time, sequencing presents no particular difficulties. However, for heavily loaded work centres or stations/machines, especially in situations where relatively lengthy jobs are involved, the order of processing can be very important in terms of costs associated with jobs waiting for processing and in terms of idle time at the work centres/stations/machines. In this section, we will examine some of the ways in which jobs are sequenced.

sequencing Determining the order in which jobs will be processed.

TABLE 15-1 *Common priority rules*	**FCFS (first come, first served):** Jobs are processed in the order in which they arrive at a machine/station/centre. **SPT (shortest [imminent] processing time):** Jobs are processed according to processing time at a machine/station/centre, shortest job first. **SRPT (shortest remaining processing time):** Jobs are processed according to smallest sum of the processing times at all the remaining centres/stations/machines for this job. **EDD (earliest due date):** Jobs are processed according to due date, earliest due date first. **MST (minimum slack time):** Jobs are processed according to their slack time (time until due date minus remaining processing time), minimum first. **CR (critical ratio):** Jobs are processed according to smallest ratio of time until due date to remaining processing time. **Rush:** Emergency or preferred customers first.

priority rules Simple heuristics used to select the order in which jobs will be processed.

Typically, a number of jobs will be waiting for processing. **Priority rules** are simple heuristics used to select the order in which jobs will be processed. Some of the most common are listed in Table 15–1. The rules generally rest on the assumption that job setup time is *independent* of processing sequence, and processing time usually includes setup time. Due dates may be the result of delivery times promised to customers, MRP processing, or managerial decisions. They are subject to revision and must be kept current to give meaning to sequencing choices. For two applications, see the "Miller SQA" reading and the "Macronix International" reading.

The effectiveness of any given sequence is judged in terms of one or more *performance measures*. The most frequently used performance measures are:

Job flow time. This is the length of time a job is at a particular station/machine/centre or shop. It includes not only actual processing time but also any time waiting to be processed, and transportation time between operations. The average flow time for a group of jobs is equal to the total flow time for the jobs divided by the number of jobs.

Job lateness. This is the length of time the job completion date exceeds the date the job was due or promised to a customer. We assign zeros to jobs that are early. The average lateness for a group of jobs is equal to the total job lateness for the jobs divided by the number of jobs.

makespan Total time needed to complete a group of jobs from the beginning of the first job to the completion of the last job.

Makespan. **Makespan** is the total time needed to complete a *group* of jobs. It is the length of time between the start of the first job in the group and the completion of the last job in the group.

Average WIP. Jobs that are in a shop are considered to be work-in-process inventory. The average work-in-process for a group of jobs can be computed using the following formula if the jobs represent equal amounts of inventory:

Average WIP = Total flow time/Makespan

READING

Miller SQA

Miller SQA, a subsidiary of office furniture giant Herman Miller Inc., is one of the fastest-growing companies in the office furniture industry. The initials SQA stand for "simple, quick, affordable." The company sells customized products, so the make-to-order production system has to be fast.

When Miller SQA was a smaller company, it just used its MRP system to plan fabrication and assembly operations. It offered a premium two-day and a regular two-week delivery service. When a wholesaler or retailer placed an order, the order and its delivery date/time were either electronically (via EDI) or manually entered into Miller SQA's Symix ERP system. The enhanced MRP module produced a daily schedule based on capacity and materials. Then the supervisors used their experience to sequence the jobs for each work centre. Miller SQA used expediters to accelerate the movement of high-priority late jobs through the operations. But as product demand grew, so did their coordination and execution need.

Therefore, Miller SQA reorganized its 27,000-m^2 manufacturing plant in Holland, Michigan, into 19 workgroups, or "cells." Each cell specializes in a particular product line and oversees its assembly from start to finish, with little WIP inventory.

Because a customer order typically involves many products that are made in different cells, Miller SQA also needed to ensure that all cells were working on the same order at the same time. The company chose SynQuest's Synchronized Manufacturing to do this. SynQuest combines an MES (manufacturing execution system) with a finite capacity scheduler to calculate schedules for all orders through the cells. Orders are frequently downloaded from the MRP system into SynQuest, where it prioritizes each order according to its slack time (i.e., due hour—remaining production hours). The order with the least slack time jumps to the top of the dispatch list (i.e., it uses the MST rule). The system distributes this dispatch list across the network of 65 PCs located throughout the manufacturing floor.

SynQuest's MES module provides shop-floor operators, planners, schedulers, managers, buyers, and shippers with up-to-the-minute information on job status, projected job completion times, and any problems. SynQuest's scheduler is

continually running in the background adjusting production schedules based on any job status changes. The MES module immediately reflects these changes and shop-floor dispatch lists are adjusted accordingly. If jobs are late, the system warns all users by displaying late jobs in red.

Miller SQA has succeeded in reducing its manufacturing lead times from two weeks to two days, and has cut its work-in-process inventory to about eight hours' supply.

SynQuest is now part of Viewlocity.

Sources: "Software Boosts Manufacturing Process," *FDM, Furniture Design & Manufacturing* 70(4), April 1998, pp. 116–124; "Miller SQA Powers up with Quick Response Manufacturing," *Modern Materials Handling*, 53(2), February 1998, pp. 44–46.

Note that average WIP and average flow time are closely related. If a priority rule results in small average flow time, it will also result in small average WIP and vice versa. Of the priority rules, the FCFS and rush priority rules are quite simple and need no explanation. The other rules and performance measures are illustrated in the following one-workstation example.

Example 1

Processing times (including setup times) and due dates for six jobs waiting to be processed at the only workstation in a shop are given in the following table. Determine the sequence of jobs, the average flow time, average days late, and average WIP at the workstation for each of these rules:

a. SPT

b. EDD

c. MST

d. CR

Job	Processing Time (days)	Due Date (days)
A	2	7
B	8	16
C	4	4
D	10	17
E	5	15
F	12	18

READING

Pfaudler

Pfaudler is a Rochester, New York, manufacturer of customized glass-lined vessels such as reactors. A typical vessel has approximately 1,000 parts, 100 of which are especially made. At any time 3,200 work orders are active in 140 work centres. Before 1994, Pfaudler had manual shop floor control which was ineffective. A customer order would take 10–14 weeks and there were frequent raw material shortages. In 1994, Pfaudler installed the Factory System MES from FACTS. This software was chosen because it was easy to use and was windows-based. The MES keeps track of jobs and performs dynamic finite-scheduling for each work centre. The supervisors can see the jobs coming to their work centre, thus can shift a worker to avoid a bottleneck. Pfaudler uses EDD in the assembly area, and if there is a tie, the longest job is chosen. Work on various parts of a job are now coordinated. All shop floor departments use the same priority for the jobs. The system collects labour times which are used to set standard times. The MES allows the specification of types of any problem with a job, e.g., wrong material, difficulty reading the drawing, setup problem, etc. A record of material and processes used to make a vessel is available if the customer needs to see it. As a result of the MES implementation, jobs of dispatchers (who scheduled work orders) were eliminated, overtime of shop workers was reduced, and production lead time was decreased.

Sources: www.pfaudler.com; D. Davis, "The Same Sheet of Music," 12(10), October 1994, pp. 32–34.

Solution

a. Using the SPT rule, the job sequence is A-C-E-B-D-F. See the calculations below. The completion time column indicates *cumulative* processing time, so summing these times and dividing by the total number of jobs processed indicates the average time each job spends at the workstation. Similarly, we calculate the average WIP at the station by summing the completion times and dividing by the makespan (i.e., the last job's completion time). The resulting values for the three measures of effectiveness are:

(1) *Average flow time*: 108/6 = 18 days.

(2) *Average days late*: 40/6 = 6.67 days.

(3) *Average WIP at the workstation*: 108/41 = 2.63 jobs.

Job Sequence	(1) Processing Time	(2) Completion Time	(3) Due Date	(2) − (3) Days Late [0 if negative]
A	2	2	7	0
C	4	6	4	2
E	5	11	15	0
B	8	19	16	3
D	10	29	17	12
F	12	41	18	23
		108		40

b. Using earliest due date (EDD) rule as the selection criterion, the job sequence is C-A-E-B-D-F. The measures of effectiveness are (see table below):

(1) *Average flow time*: 110/6 = 18.33 days.

(2) *Average days late*: 38/6 = 6.33 days.

(3) *Average WIP at the workstation*: 110/41 = 2.68 jobs.

Job Sequence	(1) Processing Time	(2) Completion Time	(3) Due Date	(2) − (3) Days Late [0 if negative]
C	4	4	4	0
A	2	6	7	0
E	5	11	15	0
B	8	19	16	3
D	10	29	17	12
F	12	41	18	23
		110		38

c. Using minimum slack time (due date – processing time) rule as the selection criterion, the job sequence is C-A-F-D-B-E (see the slack times in the table below), and the resulting values for the measures of effectiveness are:

(1) *Average flow time:* $133/6 = 22.17$ days

(2) *Average days late:* $57/6 = 9.5$ days

(3) *Average WIP at the workstation:* $133/41 = 3.24$ jobs

Job Sequence	**(1)** Slack Time	**(2)** Processing Time	**(3)** Completion Time	**(4)** Due Date	**(3) – (4)** Days Late (0 if negative)
C	0	4	4	4	0
A	5	2	6	7	0
F	6	12	18	18	0
D	7	10	28	17	11
B	8	8	36	16	20
E	10	5	41	15	26
			133		57

d. Using the critical ratio (due date ÷ processing time), the job sequence is C-F-D-B-E-A (see the critical ratios in the table below), and the resulting values for the measures of effectiveness are:

(1) *Average flow time:* $160/6 = 26.67$ days.

(2) *Average days late:* $85/6 = 14.17$ days.

(3) *Average WIP at the workstation:* $160/41 = 3.90$.

Job Sequence	**(1)** Critical Ratio	**(2)** Processing Time	**(3)** Completion Time	**(4)** Due Date	**(3) – (4)** Days Late (0 if negative)
C. 1.0		4	4	4	0
F. 1.5		12	16	18	0
D. 1.7		10	26	17	9
B. 2.0		8	34	16	18
E. 3.0		5	39	15	24
A. 3.5		2	41	7	34
			160		85

The results of these four rules are summarized in Table 15–2.

In this example, the SPT rule is the best according to two of the measures of effectiveness and a little worse than the EDD rule on average days late. The CR rule is the worst in every case. For a different set of numbers, the performance of priority rules may be different. However, the following results can be shown for every one machine/station shop: SPT is always superior in terms of minimizing average flow time and, hence, average WIP at the workstation; if all jobs are late, the SPT rule will always minimize average days late as well; however, EDD always minimizes the maximum days late.

Rule	Average Flow Time (days)	Average Days Late	Average WIP at the Workstation
SPT	18.00	6.67	2.63
EDD	18.33	6.33	2.68
MST	22.17	9.5	3.24
CR	26.67	14.17	3.90

TABLE 15–2

Comparison of the four rules for Example 1

In general, the primary limitation of the FCFS rule is that long jobs may delay the following jobs. If a process consists of work on a number of machines, machine idle time for downstream workstations/centres will increase. However, for service systems in which customers are directly involved, the FCFS rule is by far the dominant priority rule, mainly because of the inherent fairness but also because of the inability to obtain realistic estimates of processing time for individual jobs. The FCFS rule also has the advantage of simplicity.

Because the SPT rule results in low average flow time, and because it often provides low average days late, it can result in high customer service levels. In addition, since it involves low average WIP in the shop, there tends to be less congestion in the work area. SPT also minimizes downstream idle time. However, due dates are often uppermost in managers' minds, so they may not use SPT or SRPT because it doesn't incorporate due dates. The major disadvantage of the SPT rule is that it tends to make long jobs wait, perhaps for rather long times (especially if new, shorter jobs are continually added to the system). Various modifications may be used in an effort to avoid this. For example, after waiting for a given time period, a long job is automatically moved to the head of the line.

The EDD rule directly addresses due dates and usually results in low maximum days late. Although it has intuitive appeal, its main limitation is that it does not take processing time into account. One possible consequence is that it can result in a long job being processed first, resulting in other jobs waiting a long time, which adds to both in-process inventories and shop congestion.

The MST and CR rules have intuitive appeal. Both use both the due dates and remaining processing times. Although they had the poorest showing in Example 1 for all three measures, they usually do quite well in terms of minimizing average days late and average flow time.

Any particular dispatching rule may lead to schedules that are far from optimal. Each company should determine the rule that works best for its circumstances.

The following section describes a special-purpose algorithm that can be used to sequence a set of jobs that must all be processed at two machines/workstations/centres in series.

Sequencing Jobs through Two Machines/Stations/Centres

Johnson's rule Technique for minimizing makespan for a group of jobs to be processed on two successive machines/workstations/centres.

Johnson's rule is a technique that schedulers can use to minimize the makespan for a group of jobs to be processed on two successive machines/workstations/centres (sometimes referred to as a two-machine flow shop).[1] It also minimizes the total idle time at the machines/workstations/centres. For the technique to work, several conditions must be satisfied:

1. Job time (setup and processing) must be known for each job at each machine/workstation/centre.
2. Job times must be independent of the job sequence.
3. All jobs must follow the same two-step work sequence.
4. All units in a job must be completed at the first machine/station/centre before the job moves on to the second machine/station/centre.
5. There is adequate space for WIP in front of the second machine/station/centre.

Determination of the optimum sequence involves these steps:

1. Determine the jobs and their times at each machine/station/centre.
2. Select the job with the shortest time. If the shortest time is at the first machine/station/centre, schedule that job first; if the time is at the second machine/station/centre, schedule the job last. Break ties arbitrarily.
3. Eliminate the job and its time from further consideration.
4. Repeat steps 2 and 3, working toward the centre of the sequence, until all jobs have been scheduled.

---

[1]S. M. Johnson, "Optimal Two- and Three-Stage Production with Setup Times Included," *Naval Research Quarterly* 1, March 1954, pp. 61–68.

READING

Macronix International

www.macronix.com

A wafer consists of several copies of an integrated circuit chip, used in computers. The lithography process is the critical step in wafer production and includes coating, exposure, developing, inspection, alignment, and measurement. The exposure is performed by machines called steppers, which work like cameras, exposing chemicals on wafers to light through masks which contain outlines of circuits. Steppers are generally considered the bottleneck of the lithography process, so providing efficient scheduling for them is important. The process is performed on a batch of wafers at a time, and each wafer requires a few layers of exposure. Issues to be considered for lot scheduling in the lithography area include mask availability, dedication of a particular product or layer to a stepper, mask change time, line balance, WIP level, loading on downstream equipment, lot grade, variation of process and equipment conditions, and flow time.

In 1998, Macronix International's facility in Hsinchu, Taiwan, focused its efforts on reducing the mean and variance of flow times. Shorter flow times lead to lower WIP levels, reduced chance of particle contamination, and the ability to respond quickly to market-demand changes. Lowering the variance of flow times enables better process control and predictability.

The integrated scheduling system developed by Macronix includes a manufacturing execution system (MES), a recipe distribution management system (RDMS), and a real-time dispatcher (RTD). All the production data of lots, products, routes, operations, and tools are stored and updated in the MES. The RDMS allows users to query available steppers by a particular product or layer, and check the limitations of products and layers by a specific stepper. When an operator triggers dispatching through the MES on any operation or tool, the RTD calculates lot priority and informs the operator which lot is to be next.

The shortest remaining processing time (SRPT) rule sums the processing times of the remaining steps along the route of each queued lot and picks the lot with the shortest remaining processing time first. SRPT is the best rule for reducing average flow time, but the resulting flow times will have unacceptably high variation. For this reason, the minimum slack time (MST) rule (i.e., time till due date minus remaining processing time) is applied instead as one of the general rules of dispatching. MST performs well in reducing average flow time and its variance.

Macronix also uses the next queue (NQ) rule. For each lot, NQ = (current WIP) ÷ (standard WIP), where WIP is the work-in-process of the next major machine on the route of the lot. A low NQ implies higher priority for the lot. Using the next-queue rule keeps the line balanced and protects the bottleneck machines from "starvation." However, the rush orders (two categories: super hot and hot) and lots with wafers having critical layers (e.g., metal, or with tight specs) get even higher priority.

In summary, when a stepper becomes idle, an operator triggers dispatching. All lots available are searched by the dispatcher and filtered by RDMS limitation table. If the status of the lot is on-hold, it will have the lowest priority. Super-hot lots have the highest priority, and the hot lots have the second level of priority. If there is a tie in priority, jobs will be ranked by slack time. Lots needing a critical-layer process have the third level of priority, and finally come the normal jobs. These jobs are ranked by NQ ratio (lowest first), and in the case of a tie by slack time (lowest first).

As a result of using the above dispatching rule, there have been continuous reductions in the mean and variance of flow times, from an average of 2.5 days to an average of 1.7 days.

Source: Y.-J. Chen, Y.-J. Su, M.-S. Hong, and I. Wang, "Real-time Dispatching Reduces Cycle Time," *Semiconductor International* 23(3), March 2000, pp. 109–112.

A group of six jobs is to be processed through a two-workstation flow shop. The first operation involves cleaning and the second involves painting. Determine a sequence that will minimize the makespan for this group of jobs. Processing times (including setups) are expected to be as follows:

Example 2

PROCESSING TIME (HOURS)

Job	Workstation 1	Workstation 2
A	5	5
B	4	3
C	8	9
D	2	7
E	6	8
F	12	15

Solution

    a. Select the job with the shortest processing time. It is job D, with a time of two hours.

    b. Since the time is at the first station, schedule job D first. Eliminate job D from further consideration.

    c. Job B has the next shortest processing time. Since it is at the second workstation, schedule it last and eliminate job B from further consideration. We now have

1st	2nd	3rd	4th	5th	6th
D					B

    d. The remaining jobs and their times are

Job	1	2
A	5	5
C	8	9
E	6	8
F	12	15

Note that there is a tie for the shortest remaining time: job A has the same time at each workstation. It makes no difference whether we place it toward the beginning or the end of the sequence. Suppose A is placed arbitrarily toward the end and eliminate job A's time. We now have

1st	2nd	3rd	4th	5th	6th
D				A	B

    e. The shortest remaining time is six hours for job E at workstation 1. Thus, schedule that job toward the beginning of the sequence (after job D) and eliminate job E's time. Thus,

1st	2nd	3rd	4th	5th	6th
D	E			A	B

    f. Job C has the shortest time of the remaining two jobs. Since it is for the first workstation, place it third in the sequence. Finally, assign the remaining job (F) to the fourth position and the result is

1st	2nd	3rd	4th	5th	6th
D	E	C	F	A	B

    g. One way to determine the makespan and idle times at the workstations is to construct a Gantt (load) chart:

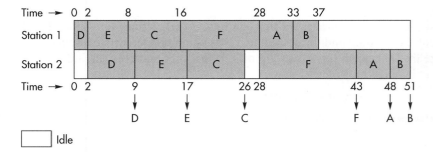

Thus, the group of jobs will take 51 hours to complete. The second workstation will wait two hours for its first job and also wait two hours after finishing job C. Station 1 will be finished in 37 hours.

You can use the Lekin Scheduling software on your DVD to solve this (or any other scheduling) problem. To enter the above problem in Lekin, in the main menu, "Flow Shop" was chosen, then in the pop-up window, number of work centres (2) and jobs (6) were set. In the pop-up windows, names of workstations were changed, and the name of each job was changed, and time of each job was changed by clicking on "Edit Route." The problem is solved by choosing "Heuristic" under "Schedule," and then "Shifting Bottleneck/Tmax." The result is given below.

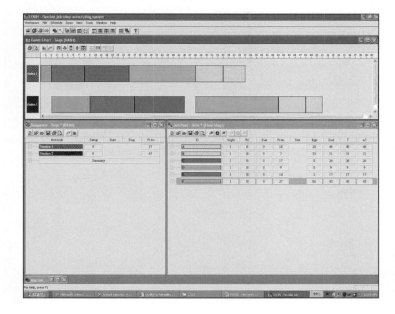

Source: Lekin® Flexible Job Shop Scheduling System. Leonard N. Stern School of Business, New York University.

When significant idle time at the second workstation occurs, job splitting at the first station just prior to the occurrence of idle time may alleviate some of the problem and also shorten throughput time. The use of transfer batches (i.e., splitting jobs) is an important tool in the Theory of Constraints described later. The last solved problem at the end of this chapter illustrates the use of job splitting.

Sequencing Jobs When Setup Times Are Sequence-Dependent

The preceding discussion and examples assumed that machine setup times are independent of processing order, but in many instances that assumption is not true. Consequently, a manager may want to schedule jobs at a workstation taking those dependencies into account. The goal is to minimize total setup time.

Consider the following table, which shows workstation/machine setup times based on job processing order. For example, if job A is followed by job B, the setup time for B will be 6 hours. Furthermore, if job C follows job B, it will have a setup time of 4 hours. If a job is done first, its setup time will be the amount shown in the setup time column to the right of the job. Thus, if job A is done first, its setup time will be 3 hours.

		Setup time (hours)	Resulting following job setup time (hours) is		
			A	**B**	**C**
If the	**A**	**3**	–	6	2
preceding	**B**	**2**	1	–	4
job is	**C**	**2**	5	3	–

The simplest way to determine which sequence will result in the lowest total setup time is to list each possible sequence and determine its total setup time. In general, the number

READING

Valmont

almont Industries Inc. is a multinational manufacturer of light, traffic, and utility poles and irrigation systems. The Brenham, Texas, branch had about 40 work centres and 7,000–8,000 parts. Before early 1990s, Brenham Valmont used a push batch system which was scheduled using an MRP system with weekly time-buckets based on demand forecasts. This system produced a 78 percent fill rate with large amounts of WIP. Then, the system was changed to incorporate the

Drum-Buffer-Rope pull system. First, the bottleneck work centres were identified (the fit-up and weld work). Then, these were loaded with customer orders and scheduled daily. Next, a five-day WIP buffer before these bottleneck stations was used. Finally, the MRP system was used to schedule the feeding (subordinate) work centres such as small parts. The fill rate went up to 95 percent and amount of WIP almost halved.

Sources: www.valmont.com/asp/poles/poles.shtml; G. Reimer, "Material Requirements Planning and Theory of Constraints: Can They Coexist? A Case Study," *Production and Inventory Management Journal* 32(4), Fourth Quarter, 1991, pp. 48–52.

of different alternatives is equal to $n!$, where n is the number of jobs. Here, n is 3, so $n! = 3 \times 2 \times 1 = 6$. The six alternatives and their total setup times are:

Sequence	Setup Times	Total
A-B-C	$3 + 6 + 4 =$	13
A-C-B	$3 + 2 + 3 =$	8
B-A-C	$2 + 1 + 2 =$	5 (best)
B-C-A	$2 + 4 + 5 =$	11
C-A-B	$2 + 5 + 6 =$	13
C-B-A	$2 + 3 + 1 =$	6

Hence, to minimize total setup time, the scheduler would select sequence B-A-C.

This procedure is relatively simple to do manually when the number of jobs is two or three. However, as the number of jobs increases, the list of alternatives quickly becomes larger. For example, six jobs would have 720 alternatives. In such instances, a scheduler would employ a computer to generate the list and identify the best alternative.

Why Scheduling Can Be Difficult

Scheduling can be difficult for a number of reasons. One is that in reality, an operation must deal with variability in setup times, processing times, interruptions, and changes in the set of jobs. Another major reason is that, except for very small problems, there is no practical method for identifying the optimal schedule, and it would be virtually impossible to sort through the vast number of possible alternatives to obtain the best schedule. As a result, scheduling is far from an exact science.

Job shops where each job may have a different sequence of operations are especially hard to schedule. See the following example for an illustration.

Example 3

Job Scheduling in a Machine Shop

For simplicity, assume that there are exactly one lathe, mill, grind, and vertical drill machine in the shop. Suppose that the following five jobs should be processed in the machine sequence given (top down) with standard times given in front of the machine name. For example, for job 1, first one hour of drill is required, then two hours of lathe, etc. To simplify the problem, suppose that the four machines are available starting tomorrow morning and there are no WIP. Also, suppose that the due hours are all at the end of tomorrow, i.e., the end of hour 8. Hours 9 to 14 correspond to the first six hours of the day after tomorrow. For simplicity we assume that setup times are included in the operation times and that it is possible to split the processing of a job on a machine into two nonconsecutive hours, but half a job cannot be transferred to the next operation. Determine the schedule which meets the due hours.

	Job 1		**Job 2**		**Job 3**		**Job 4**		**Job 5**	
1.	Drill	1	Lathe	2	Grind	2	Drill	1	Mill	1
2.	Lathe	2	Mill	2	Drill	2	Grind	2	Drill	1
3.	Grind	1	Grind	1	Mill	2	Lathe	1	Lathe	1
4.	Mill	2	Drill	2	Lathe	2			Grind	2
Total (hours)		6		7		8		4		5

All five jobs have the same due hour, so EDD will not provide a sequence. The shortest remaining processing time (SRPT) rule results in the sequence 4-5-1-2-3. In the following schedule, first job 4 is scheduled all the way on all machines (i.e., horizontal loading), then job 5, etc: *Solution*

4-5-1-2-3   **Hours**

	1	2	3	4	5	6	7	8	9	10	11	12	13	14
Lathe	2	2	5	4	1	1							3	3
Mill	5		2	2			1	1		3	3			
Grind	3	4	4	5	5	2	1	3						
Drill	4	5	1				2	2	3	3				

We observe that the above schedule results in job 3 being six hours late, and job 1 one hour late. The minimum slack time (MST) rule results in the opposite sequence: 3-2-1-5-4, with the following schedule:

3-2-1-5-4   **Hours**

	1	2	3	4	5	6	7	8	9	10	11	12	13	14
Lathe	2	2	1	1	5		3	3			4			
Mill	5		2	2	3	3	1	1						
Grind	3	3			2	1	5	5	4	4				
Drill	1	5	3	3	4	2	2							

Even though the MST rule performs better than the SRPT rule, its schedule still results in job 4 being three hours late.

As you can see, scheduling in a job shop is generally very difficult. One needs to try various sequences and choose the best. The problem is that there are too many sequences. Note that we made many simplifying assumptions. In general, there are WIP in the shop, the processing time estimates may be inaccurate, a machine could break down, an operator may become ill, set up times may be sequence dependent, and jobs could be split and transferred to the next operation in smaller batch sizes. By the way, Example 3 can be solved by switching a pair of jobs in the MST sequence.

Computer technology such as Lekin scheduling software reduces the burden of scheduling and makes real-time dynamic scheduling possible.

Things a Scheduler Can Do to Achieve Good Scheduling Results

There are a number of actions that schedulers can consider to minimize scheduling problems, such as:

- Setting realistic due dates.
- Focusing on bottleneck operations: schedule the bottleneck operations first, and then schedule the nonbottleneck operations around the bottleneck operations.
- Considering lot splitting for large jobs, i.e., transfer a portion of the job to the next operation.

The Theory of Constraints

This approach to scheduling was developed and promoted by Eli Goldratt in the 1980s.[2] He avoided much of the complexity often associated with scheduling problems by simply focusing on *bottleneck* operations (i.e., those for which there is insufficient capacity—in effect, a work centre with zero idle time). He reasoned that the output of the system was limited by the output of the bottleneck operation(s); therefore, it was essential to schedule the nonbottleneck operations in a way that minimized the idle time of the bottleneck operation(s). Thus, idle time of nonbottleneck operations was not a factor in overall productivity of the system, as long as the bottleneck operations were used effectively. The result was a technique for scheduling intermittent production systems that was simpler and less time-consuming to use.

The technique uses the *drum-buffer-rope* conceptualization to manage the system. The "drum" is the master schedule; it sets the pace of production of bottleneck operation(s). The "buffer" refers to inventory just before the bottleneck operation. The "rope" represents the synchronizing of nonbottleneck operations before bottleneck operation(s) to ensure that these nonbottleneck operations produce the right quantities and at the right times. The goal is to avoid costly and time-consuming multiple setups at bottleneck operation(s).

Goldratt also developed a system of varying batch sizes to achieve the greatest output of bottleneck operations. He used the term *process batch* to denote the production lot size for a job and the term *transfer batch* to denote a portion of the production lot that could be moved to the bottleneck operation. In effect, a lot could be split into two or more portions. Splitting a large lot at one or more operations preceding a bottleneck operation would reduce the waiting time of the bottleneck operation. The following reading on Oregon Freeze Dry and the earlier reading on Valmont are applications of drum-buffer-rope techniques.

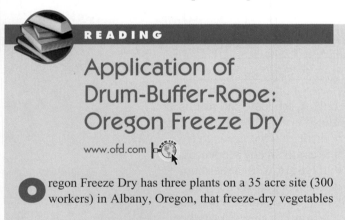

READING

Application of Drum-Buffer-Rope: Oregon Freeze Dry

www.ofd.com

Oregon Freeze Dry has three plants on a 35 acre site (300 workers) in Albany, Oregon, that freeze-dry vegetables and other items by removing their water at low temperature and pressure. In the low-pressure chambers, ice is evaporated without melting into water. Freeze drying retains the flavour, and the natural structure of the food is regained by adding water at the time of consumption. Production begins with the wet processing of products—a labour-intensive technique involving activities such as cooking or heating. The next step is freezing. This is a capital-intensive operation that uses one of the six very large freezers. The product is then processed through one of 32 dryers. The drying operation is also capital-intensive and may take from 8 to 50 hours (depending on the

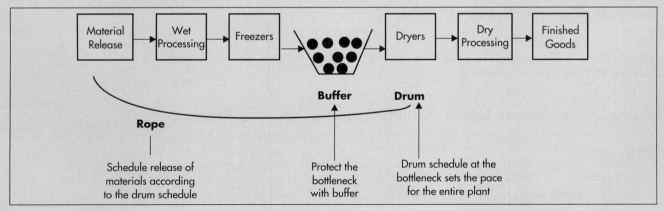

[2]Eli Goldratt, *The General Theory of Constraints* (New Haven, CT: Avraham Y. Institute, 1989).

product), although 14 to 20 hours is typical. The final step is dry processing—a labour-intensive step including activities such as blending, packaging, and boxing.

Before 1998 the production was scheduled on a make-to-stock basis according to predetermined batch sizes and sequence. This resulted in large inventories of finished goods and WIP in freezers which increased the production lead times and caused the company to be slow in responding to customer orders that could not be satisfied from finished goods. In addition, it resulted in extensive costly overtime and disruptive expediting efforts. Meanwhile, the plants were overstocked with products for which there were no current orders.

Specifically, materials were released for processing according to production schedule, available wet processing capacity, and available storage space for the accumulated WIP (in freezers). The wet processing schedule drove all other operations as in a push system. There were no formal schedules for the freezers, dryers, or dry processing. Typically, about six to eight weeks' worth of demand for each product were processed. The highly variable product times created a "feast or famine" environment in which periods of work overload were followed by periods in which there was nothing to do. The freezers were used as a queuing area for the dryers. The primary operational measurements were dryer utilization and labour efficiency.

In 1998, the company implemented the drum-buffer-rope technique. The capacity analysis clearly indicated that wet processing and dry processing were not constraints. The constraint (i.e., bottleneck) was drying. The dryer schedule was set based on market demand and dryer capacity. All other departments' schedules were subordinated to support the dryer

Bank of dryers at Oregon Freeze Dry.

schedule, which fully utilized dryer capacity. Specifically, materials were released to wet processing at the rate dictated by the dryer schedule (offset by leadtimes). As a result, the wet processing department could not overproduce and cause excess WIP inventory in the freezers. Furthermore, having a set schedule at the dryers resulted in a predictable product flow to downstream operations at dry processing. The dryer schedule provided greater visibility to future work schedules in wet and dry processing and made the labour requirements in these departments smoother and predictable. Monitoring the buffer inventory in the freezers for the timely arrival of materials highlights when the system is having a problem.

Source: M. Umble, E. Umble, and L. Von Deylen, "Integrating Enterprise Resources Planning and Theory of Constraints: A Case Study," *Production and Inventory Management Journal* 42(2), Second Quarter 2001, pp. 43–48.

SCHEDULING SERVICES

Scheduling services presents certain problems not generally encountered in manufacturing. This is due primarily to (1) the inability to store or inventory services, and (2) the random nature and timing of customer requests for service.

An important goal in service systems is to match the flow of customers and service capabilities. An ideal situation is one that has a smooth flow of customers through the system. This would occur if each new customer arrives at the precise instant that the preceding customer's service is completed, as in a physician's office with punctual patients and physicians. In this situation customer waiting time is minimized, and the service system staff and equipment would be fully utilized. Unfortunately, the appointment system is not practical or possible for many services, e.g., supermarkets, gas stations, hospital emergency rooms, and repair of equipment breakdowns. Chapter 18 on waiting lines focuses on those kinds of situations. There, the emphasis is on intermediate and short-term questions related to required service capacity. In this section, we will concern ourselves with short-term *scheduling*, in which the required capacity of a system has been determined, and the goal is to provide that required capacity at minimum cost (i.e., schedule the staff and equipment to meet demand efficiently).

Scheduling in service systems may involve scheduling (1) customers, (2) workforce, and (3) multiple resources.

READING

Royal Bank

Royal Bank, like most banks in North America, is using a workforce management software called Planet from GMT to determine the staffing level and the schedule for the (transactional) tellers in its approximately 1,350 branches. The software is used centrally by a group under the Manager of Operations and Resource Optimization. The staffing is done once a year, using forecasts based on historical data collected on customer arrivals and transaction times taken every 15 minutes in each branch. Every month, the actual data is compared with forecasts, and the performance of the software is evaluated. If there is a significant deviation, changes are made to the staffing of the branch.

Sources: www.rbc.com; K. Nelson, "Royal Bank of Canada Optimizes Work Force," *Bank Systems & Technology* 39(6), June 2002, p. 42; www.gmt.com.

Appointment Systems

Appointment systems are intended to control the timing of customer arrivals in order to minimize customer waiting while achieving a high degree of capacity utilization. Even with appointments, however, problems can still arise due to lack of punctuality on the part of patients or clients, no-shows, and the inability to completely control the length of contact time (e.g., a dentist might run into complications in filling a tooth, thus backing up later appointments). Some of this can be avoided by trying to match the time reserved for a patient or client with the specific needs of that case rather than setting appointments at regular intervals. Other useful practices include leaving extra time for emergencies, not seeing a patient who is more than ten minutes late, dealing with no-shows by charging them the second time, and being aware of and keeping pace with the slotted time during the service.[3] Even with the above-mentioned problems the appointment system is a tremendous improvement over random arrivals.

Scheduling the Workforce

For many services, demand can be predicted with reasonable accuracy. This is often true for restaurants, grocery stores, hospitals, police, call centres, banks, theatres, and rush-hour traffic. See, for an example, the reading "Royal Bank." An additional consideration is the extent to which variations in customer demands can be met with workforce flexibility. Thus, capacity can be adjusted by having cross-trained workers who can be temporarily assigned to help out on bottleneck operations during periods of peak demand. Various constraints can affect workforce scheduling flexibility, including legal, behavioural, technical—such as workers' qualifications to perform certain operations—and budget constraints. Union contracts may provide still more constraints.

Cyclical Scheduling for Full-Time Staff (Two Consecutive Days Off). Many services are offered seven days a week. Full-time employees must be assigned to work shifts usually eight hours a day and have days off, on a repeating or cyclical basis. Here is a method for determining a schedule using the minimum number of workers needed.

Generally a basic work pattern is set (e.g., work five consecutive days, then have two consecutive days off), and a list of staffing needs for the schedule cycle (usually one week) is given. For example:

Day	Mon	Tue	Wed	Thu	Fri	Sat	Sun
Staff needed	2	4	3	4	6	5	5

---

[3]See Dr. W. B. Schafer, "Keep Patients Waiting? Not in My Office," *Medical Economics*, May 12, 1986, pp. 137–141.

A fairly simple but effective approach for determining the minimum number of workers needed is the following:[4]

1. Make the first worker's assignment such that the two days with the lowest maximum daily need are designated as days off. Here Mon–Tue, Tue–Wed, and Wed–Thu have a maximum of four staff needs. Among these three pairs, choose the one with minimum sum of staff needs: min (6, 7, 7) = 6. Therefore, Mon–Tue should be the two days off for worker 1. Circle those days. (Note, in case of a further tie, pick the pair whose previous day is not part of pairs in the tie. If there is still a tie, break it arbitrarily.)

Day	Mon	Tue	Wed	Thu	Fri	Sat	Sun
Staff needed	**2**	**4**	**3**	**4**	**6**	**5**	**5**
Worker 1	(2	4)	3	4	6	5	5

2. Subtract one from each day's need, except for the circled days, and write them in front of worker 2. Assign worker 2's days off using the lowest maximum remaining need of two consecutive days. Wed–Thu has the lowest (3). Circle those days.

Day	Mon	Tue	Wed	Thu	Fri	Sat	Sun
Staff needed	**2**	**4**	**3**	**4**	**6**	**5**	**5**
Worker 1	(2	4)	3	4	6	5	5
Worker 2	2	4	(2	3)	5	4	4

3. Subtract one from each day's remaining needs, except for the circled days, and write them in front of the next worker. Assign the next employee's days off, using the lowest maximum remaining need of two consecutive days. In this case, Mon–Tue, Tue–Wed, Wed–Thu, Sat–Sun, and Sun–Mon all have a maximum remaining need of three employees. The sum of Mon–Tue and Sun–Mon is the smallest (4) among these five pairs. The day before Sun (i.e., Sat) is not part of these two tied pairs. Therefore, circle Sun–Mon as the third employee's days off, and repeat the preceding step for each additional worker until all staffing needs have been met. However, don't subtract from a value of zero.

Day	Mon	Tue	Wed	Thu	Fri	Sat	Sun
Staff needed	**2**	**4**	**3**	**4**	**6**	**5**	**5**
Worker 1	(2	4)	3	4	6	5	5
Worker 2	2	4	(2	3)	5	4	4
Worker 3	1)	3	2	3	4	3	(3
Worker 4	(1	2)	1	2	3	2	3
Worker 5	1	2	(0	1)	2	1	2
Worker 6	0	1	0	1	(1	0)	1
Worker 7	0	0	0	0	1	(0	0)
No. working:	**4**	**5**	**5**	**5**	**6**	**5**	**5**

To identify the days each worker is working, go across each worker's row to find the values that are not circled. Similarly, to find the workers who are assigned to work for any particular day, go down that day's column to find the values that are not circled. Note: Worker 6 is only needed to work three days, and worker 7 is only needed *one* day.

---

[4]R. Tibrewala et al., "Optimal Scheduling of Two Consecutive Idle Periods," *Management Science* 19(1), September, 1972, pp. 71–75.

The maximum need of pairs and the sum of needs of pairs can easily be computed using Excel. These computations for the above problem are shown below:

| | | | | | | | | | | | | | Max | | | | | | | Sum | | | |
							(the minimum are shaded)								(the minimum are shaded)					
M	T	W	Th	F	Sa	Su	MT	TW	WTh	ThF	FSa	SaSu	SuM	MT	TW	WTh	ThF	FSa	SaSu	SuM
2	4	3	4	6	5	5	4	4	4	6	6	5	5	6	7	7	10	11	10	7
2	4	2	3	5	4	4	4	4	3	5	5	4	4	6	6	5	8	9	8	6
1	3	2	3	4	3	3	3	3	3	4	4	3	3	4	5	5	7	7	6	4
1	2	1	2	3	2	3	2	2	2	3	3	3	3	3	3	3	5	5	5	4
1	2	0	1	2	1	2	2	2	1	2	2	2	2	3	2	1	3	3	3	3
0	1	0	1	1	0	1	1	1	1	1	1	1	1	1	1	1	2	1	1	1
0	0	0	0	1	0	0	0	0	0	1	1	0	0	0	0	0	1	1	0	0

Scheduling Part-Time Employees. Part-time employees usually work shorter shifts in a day than full-time employees and tend to work less than five days a week, so that the total hours of their work is usually not greater than 20 hours a week. Part-time employees are usually used to meet peaks in demand, e.g., to receive periodic supplies or meet peak weekend demand in grocery stores. Similarly, in restaurants part-time workers are used to meet peak lunch and supper demands.

Part-time staff scheduling usually involves the following steps:

1. Determine the requirements (i.e., the number) for each category of staff needed to meet the forecast of customer demand during each operating hour of each near-future day.

2. Cover these needs with shifts that use a minimum number of staff (i.e., at minimum cost), subject to constraints on minimum/maximum length of shifts, etc.

3. Put the shifts up for bids, allowing the staff to maximize their time preferences.

We will illustrate staff scheduling in fast-food restaurants. A fast-food restaurant typically employs hourly employees, paying wages between $7 and $9 per hour. Most staff are under 20 years old and are female. Some are full-timers, but most work part time. Crew selection, hiring, and scheduling are usually the responsibility of one of the managers or assistant managers. The schedule for the following week will be made up a few days earlier; for example, on Tuesday or Wednesday for the following Monday through Sunday.

The steps taken to make up the staff schedule are as follows. First, the hourly sales are forecasted for each day of the following week. The sales dollars are surprisingly consistent; that is, the same hour of the same day this week and next week will usually have very close sales. Second, corporate standards for labour hours per sales dollar (called *manning charts*) are used to determine hourly staffing needs for the following week (note that in addition to crew, at least one manager or assistant manager, who work eight-hour shifts, is always present). Third, shifts are scheduled to satisfy the labour needs, subject to constraints of minimum (usually three-hour) and maximum (eight-hour) shift lengths. Finally, staff are assigned to shifts, trying to satisfy each person's availability as to time of day or evening or weekend work.

The following example illustrates this. McDonald's uses a more sophisticated solution technique programmed into the ESP software by ThoughtWorks (see the reading "ESP" following the example).

| **Example 4** | Erindale McDonald's in Saskatoon uses the following manning chart (positional guide) for regular menu (there are two others for breakfast and for night times): |

Sales/Hour	Counter	Drive Thru	CSA	Assembly Board	Grill	French Fries
0–$162	1	1			1	
163–223	1	1		1	1	
224–338	1	2		1	1	
339–395	1	2		2	1	
396–492	2	2		2	1	
493–542	2	2		2	1	1
543–621	2	2		3	1	1
622–723	2	3		3	1	1
724–905	2	3	1	4	1	1
906–1,109	3	3	1	4	1	1
>1,110	3	3	1	5	1	1

The hourly forecast sales for May 21, 2004, starting from 5 a.m. was:

5–6	6–7	7–8	8–9	9–10	10–11	11–noon	noon–1	1–2	2–3	3–4
$20	$90	$180	$320	$410	$410	$920	$1,260	$630	$420,	$360

4–5	5–6	6–7	7–8	8–9	9–10	10–11
$590	$1,040	$1,040	$810	$390	$340	$240.

a. Determine the number of drive-thru (DT) staff required during each hour.

b. Determine shifts (three to eight hours) and number of DT staff on each using the following heuristic. (McDonald's uses a more sophisticated solution technique programmed into the ESP software by Thoughtworks. See the ESP reading next.)

1. Start from opening hour:
   - Determine the length of shift: begin with three hours; increase it by one hour at a time until the number of staff required (still not met) at its end decreases.
   - Set the number of workers on this shift equal to the number of staff required at the opening hour.

2. Move to the next hour with the positive number of staff required (still not met).
   - Determine length of shift as in Step 1.
   - Set the number of workers on this shift equal to the number of staff required (still not met) during this hour.

3. Continue until a shift passes the mid-point of the operating hours (e.g., 4 p.m.). Then jump to the closing hour and work backwards repeating steps 1 and 2 until all staff required is met.

First the number of DT staff required during each hour is determined based on the hour's forecast sales and the manning chart (see the following diagram, the second column from the left). For example, between 8 and 9 a.m., the forecast sales are $320, which falls within the $224–$338 range. Therefore, 2 DT workers are required then.

Second, shifts s_1, s_2, … are created to meet or exceed these requirements. S_1's length is the maximum 8 hours because the number of DT staff required is not decreasing from 5 a.m. until 1 p.m. The number of DT staff on s_1 = the requirement between 5 and 6 a.m. = 1.

Shift 2 (s_2) starts at 8 a.m. because the one person on s_1 would cover the requirements from 6 to 8 a.m. The length of s_2 is only 6 hours because the requirement, still not met, starts decreasing after 2 p.m. The number of DT staff on s_2 = the requirement, still not met, between 8 and 9 a.m. After s_3, s_4 starts from 11 p.m., working backwards, because s_3 reached midpoint at 4 p.m.

Length of s_4 is only 4 hours because the requirement, still not met, between 6 and 7 p.m. (2) is less than the requirement between 7 and 8 p.m. (3). The numbers of DT staff on S_4 = requirement between 10 and 11 p.m. = 2, and so on.

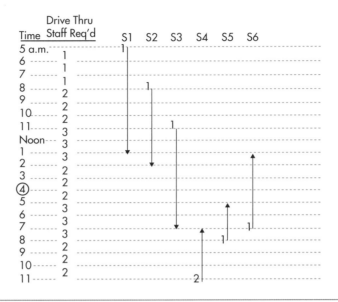

Time	Drive Thru Staff Req'd	S1	S2	S3	S4	S5	S6
5 a.m.	1	1					
6	1						
7	1						
8	2		1				
9	2						
10	2						
11	3			1			
Noon	3						
1	3						
2	2						
3	2						
4	2						
5	3						
6	3						
7	3			1			
8	2					1	
9	2						
10	2						
11	2				2		

Scheduling Multiple Resources

In some situations, it is necessary to coordinate the use of more than one resource. For example, hospitals must schedule surgeons, operating room, special equipment, nursing staffs, and so on. Educational institutions must schedule faculty, classrooms, and students. As you might guess, the greater the number of resources to be scheduled, the greater the complexity of the problem and the less likely that an optimal schedule can be achieved. Some schools and hospitals are using computer programs to assist them in devising acceptable schedules, although many appear to be using intuitive approaches with varying degrees of success.

Airlines are another example of service systems that require the scheduling of multiple resources. Flight crews, aircraft, baggage handlers, ticket-counter staff, gate personnel, and maintenance personnel all have to be coordinated. Furthermore, government regulations on the number of hours a pilot can spend flying place an additional restriction on the system. Another interesting variable is that, unlike most systems, the flight crews and the

READING

ESP

The Employee Scheduling Program (ESP) of Thought-Works Software Solutions, Dundas, Ontario, is used by major fast food chains such as McDonald's. ESP allows the restaurant manager to enter information on:

- each employee including their skill level and qualifications to work at one or more of the stations (e.g., front counter, assembly board, fries), hours and days available, and maximum hours in a day or in a week

- staffing requirements for each station based on expected sales during each hour (called *positioning guide* or *manning chart*)

- any fixed shifts as deemed necessary by the manager

- operating hours, shift lengths and their desirability during various times of the day, and preferences such as desired

average skill level for a station during a particular period, and fairness (giving part-time workers approximately equal number of hours in a week)

- sales each hour of last week

ESP will use the history of sales from the past few weeks or year to forecast next week's sales on an hourly basis (using e.g., the moving average method). Then, using the positioning guide it will determine the number of staff (excluding the managers) required in each station. Next, using an iterative solution technique ESP determines feasible shifts close to the required staff every hour. Finally, ESP will assign employees to the chosen shifts according to their availability and the objectives of the manager. ESP will report this as daily schedules for each day of the following week and will allow their modification if necessary.

Source: www.thoughtworksinc.com.

planes do not remain in one location. Moreover, the crews and the planes are not usually scheduled as a single unit. Flight crews are often scheduled so that they return to their base city every two days or so. On the other hand, the aircraft may be in almost continuous use except for periodic maintenance and repairs. Consequently, flight crews commonly follow different trip patterns than that of the aircraft.

SUMMARY

Scheduling involves the timing of use of resources. Scheduling problems differ for high volume, intermediate volume, or low volume systems. Scheduling problems are particularly complex for job shops (low volume system) because of the variety of jobs these systems are required to process.

The two major problems in job-shop scheduling are assigning (loading) jobs to machines/workstations/centres, and designating the sequence of job processing at a given machine workstation/centre. Gantt load charts are frequently employed to help managers visualize workloads, and they are useful for describing and analyzing sequencing alternatives. Input/output control is used to monitor the work flows and WIP at a machine/workstation/centre; priority rules are used to develop sequencing plans.

Customer requirements in services generally present very different circumstances than those encountered in manufacturing systems. Some services can use appointments and reservations for scheduling purposes, although not all systems are amenable to this. Staff scheduling is a common problem in services. Determining two consecutive days off for full-time and daily shifts for part-time employees are common staff scheduling problems. When multiple resources are involved, the task of coordinating the system can be complex.

KEY TERMS

backward scheduling, 554
finite loading, 553
flow-shop scheduling, 548
flow system, 548
forward scheduling, 554
Gantt chart, 551
horizontal loading, 554
infinite loading, 553
input/output (I/O) control, 554
job-shop scheduling, 551
Johnson's rule, 560
load chart, 551
loading, 551
makespan, 556
priority rules, 556
schedule/control (Gantt) chart, 554
scheduling, 548
sequencing, 555
vertical loading, 554

Solved Problems

Problem 1

Priority rules. Job times (including setup) and due hours are shown in the following table for five jobs waiting to be processed at a workstation:

Job	Job Time (hours)	Due Hour
a	12	15
b	6	24
c	14	20
d	3	8
e	7	6

Determine the processing sequence that would result from each of these priority rules:

a. SPT
b. EDD

Solution

Job	a. SPT Job Time	Processing Order	b. EDD Due Hour	Processing Order
a	12	4	15	3
b	6	2	24	5
c	14	5	20	4
d	3	1	8	2
e	7	3	6	1

Problem 2

Priority rules. Using the job times and due dates from Solved Problem 1 above, determine each of the following performance measures for first-come, first-served processing order (a-b-c-d-e):

a. Makespan

b. Average flow time

c. Average hours late

d. Average WIP at workstation.

Solution

Job	Job Time	Completion Time	Hour Due	Hours Late
a	12	12	15	0
b	6	18	24	0
c	14	32	20	12
d	3	35	8	27
e	7	42	6	36
Total		139		75

a. Makespan $= 42$ hours

b. Average flow time $= \dfrac{\text{Total completion time}}{\text{Number of jobs}} = \dfrac{139}{5} = 27.80$ hours

c. Average hours late $= \dfrac{\text{Total hours late}}{\text{Number of jobs}} = \dfrac{75}{5} = 15$ hours

d. Average WIP at workstation $= \dfrac{\text{Total completion time}}{\text{Makespan}} = \dfrac{139}{42} = 3.31$ jobs

Problem 3

Sequencing jobs through two workstations. Use Johnson's rule to obtain the sequence with minimum makespan for processing the jobs shown below through workstations A and B.

	JOB TIMES (HOURS)	
Job	Workstation A	Workstation B
a	2.50	4.20
b	3.80	1.50
c	2.20	3.00
d	5.80	4.00
e	4.50	2.00

Solution

a. Identify the smallest time: job b (1.50 hours at workstation B). Because the time is for B, schedule this job last, and eliminate B times.

b. The next smallest time is job e (2.00 hours at B). Schedule job e next to last, and eliminate e times.

c. Identify the smallest remaining job time: job c (2.20 hours at station A). Because the time is in the A column, schedule job c first and eliminate c times. At this point, we have:

c, _____, _____, e, b

d. The smallest time for remaining jobs is 2.50 hours for job a at station A. Schedule this job after job c. The one remaining job (job d) fills the remaining slot. Thus, we have:

c-a-d-e-b

For Solved Problem 3, determine what effect splitting jobs c, d, e, and b in workstation A would have on the idle time of workstation B and on the makespan. Assume that each job can be split into two equal parts.

Problem 4

We assume that the processing sequence remains unchanged and proceed on that basis. The solution from the previous problem is shown in the following Gantt chart. The bottom chart shows reduced idle time at station B when splitting is used.

Solution

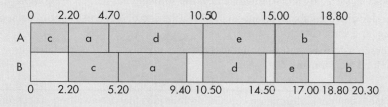

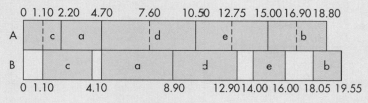

An inspection of these two charts reveals that makespan has decreased from 20.30 hours to 19.55 hours. In addition, the original idle time was 5.6 hours. After splitting c, d, e, and b, idle time was reduced to 4.85 hours, so some improvement was achieved. Note that processing times at B are generally less than at A for jobs toward the end of the sequence. As a result, jobs e and b at B were scheduled so that they were *centred* around the finishing times of e and b, respectively, at A, to avoid having to break the jobs due to waiting for the remainder of the split job from A.

1. Why is scheduling fairly simple for repetitive systems but fairly complex for job shops?
2. What are the main decision areas of job-shop scheduling?
3. What are Gantt charts? How are they used in scheduling? What are the advantages of using Gantt charts?
4. Briefly describe each of these priority rules:
   a. FCFS   *b.* SPT   *c.* EDD   *d.* MST   *e.* Rush
5. Why are priority rules needed?
6. What problems, not generally found in manufacturing systems, do service systems present in terms of scheduling the use of resources?
7. Doctors' and dentists' offices frequently schedule patient visits at regularly spaced intervals. What problems can this create? Can you suggest ways to reduce these problems?
8. What is the input/output control?
9. What factors would you take into account in deciding whether or not to split a job?
10. Explain the term *makespan*.
11. What steps is used for staff scheduling?

DISCUSSION AND REVIEW QUESTIONS

1. What general trade-offs are involved in sequencing decision?
2. Who needs to be involved in setting job schedules?
3. How has technology had an impact on scheduling?

TAKING STOCK

CRITICAL THINKING EXERCISE

One approach that can be effective in reducing the impact of production bottlenecks in a job shop or batch operations is to use smaller lot sizes as in the Theory of Constraints. Explain how small lot sizes can reduce the impact on bottleneck operations.

INTERNET EXERCISES

1. Visit www.matrikonopc.com/resources/case-studies.asp, the site of Matrikon, an Edmonton-based process control company. Choose a project and summarize it.

2. Visit www.asprova.com/en/case/index.html, the site of a Japanese scheduling software company. Choose a case study and summarize how the software has helped the company.

3. Visit www.wonderware.com/about_us/success/videos, the site of a process control company. Choose a project and summarize it.

4. Visit www.i2.com/customers, choose an industry, then a company, and summarize how the software has helped the company.

PROBLEMS

1. The following table contains information concerning four jobs that are awaiting processing at a workstation.

Job	Job Time (days)	Due Date (days)
A	14	20
B	10	16
C	7	15
D	6	17

   a. Sequence the jobs using (1) MST, (2) SPT, (3) EDD, and (4) CR.

   b. For each of the priority rules in part a, determine (1) the average flow time, (2) the average days late, and (3) the average WIP at the workstation.

   c. Is one priority rule superior to the others? Explain.

2. Using the information presented in the following table, identify the processing sequence that would result using (1) MST, (2) SPT, (3) EDD, and (4) CR. For each priority rule, determine (1) average flow time, (2) average hours late, and (3) average WIP in the system. Is one priority rule superior to the others? Explain. (*Hint*: First determine the total job time for each job by calculating the total processing time for the job and then adding in the setup time. All times are in hours.)

Job	Processing Time per Unit	Units per Job	Setup Time	Due Hour
a	0.14	45	0.7	4
b	0.25	14	0.5	10
c	0.10	18	0.2	12
d	0.25	40	1.0	20
e	0.10	75	0.5	15

3. The following table shows orders to be processed at a machine as of 8 a.m., Monday. Jobs are listed in order of arrival.

   a. Determine the processing sequence using each of these rules: (1) CR, (2) MST, (3) SPT, (4) EDD.

   b. Determine the effectiveness of each rule using each of these measures: (1) average flow time, (2) average days late.

   c. Is one rule superior to the others?

Job	Processing Time (days)	Due Date (days)
A	8	20
B	10	18
C	5	25
D	11	17
E	9	35

4. A production process uses a two-step process. Tomorrow's work will consist of seven orders shown below. Determine a job sequence that will minimize the total time required to fill the orders (i.e., makespan).

TIME (HOURS)

Order	Step 1	Step 2
A	1.20	1.40
B	0.90	1.30
C	2.00	0.80
D	1.70	1.50
E	1.60	1.80
F	2.20	1.75
G	1.30	1.40

5. The times required to complete each of eight jobs in a two-machine flow shop are shown in the table that follows. Each job must follow the same sequence, beginning with machine A and moving to machine B.

   a. Determine a sequence that will minimize makespan.

   b. Construct a Gantt chart for the resulting sequence, and find machine B's idle time.

   c. For the sequence determined in part a, how much would machine B's idle time be reduced by splitting the last two jobs in the sequence in half?

TIME (HOURS)

Job	Machine A	Machine B
a	16	5
b	3	13
c	9	6
d	8	7
e	2	14
f	12	4
g	18	14
h	20	11

6. Given the operation times below:

   a. Develop a job sequence that minimizes total idle time at the two workstations.

   b. Construct a Gantt chart for the activities at the two stations, and determine each station's idle time.

JOB TIMES (MINUTES)

	A	B	C	D	E	F
Station 1	20	16	43	60	35	42
Station 2	27	30	51	12	28	24

7. A two-man shoe repair operation uses a two-step sequence that all jobs follow. For the group of jobs listed below,

   a. Find the sequence that will minimize makespan.

   b. Determine the amount of idle time for workstation B.

   c. What jobs are candidates for splitting? Why? If b and c are split in half, how much would idle time be reduced?

JOB TIMES (MINUTES)

	a	b	c	d	e
Workstation A	27	18	70	26	15
Workstation B	45	33	30	24	10

8. The following schedule (in hours) was prepared by the production manager of Marymount Metal Shop.

Job	CUTTING		POLISHING	
	Start	Finish	Start	Finish
A	0	2	2	5
B	2	6	6	9
C	6	11	11	13
D	11	15	15	20
E	15	17	20	23
F	17	20	23	24
G	20	21	24	28

Determine a schedule that will result in a shorter makespan.

9. A production manager must determine the processing sequence for seven jobs through the grinding and deburring departments. The same sequence will be followed in both departments. The manager's goal is to move the jobs through the two departments as quickly as possible. The site supervisor of the grinding department wants the SPT rule to be used to minimize the work-in-process inventory in his department.

Job	PROCESSING TIME (HOURS)	
	Grinding	Deburring
A	3	6
B	2	4
C	1	5
D	4	3
E	9	4
F	8	7
G	6	2

a. Prepare a schedule using SPT for the grinding department (using the grinding times).

b. What is the total flow time in the grinding department for the SPT sequence? What is the makespan needed to process the seven jobs in both the grinding and deburring departments (using the same sequence found in part a)?

c. Determine a sequence that will minimize the makespan in both departments. What total flow time will result for the grinding department?

10. A foreman has determined expected processing times at a workstation for a set of jobs and now wants to sequence them. Given the information shown below, do the following:

a. Determine the processing sequence using (1) MST, (2) SPT, (3) EDD, and (4) CR. For each sequence, calculate the average days late, the average flow time, and the average WIP at the workstation.

b. Which rule is best?

Job	Job Time (days)	Due Date (days)
a	4.5	10
b	6.0	17
c	5.2	12
d	1.6	27
e	2.8	18
f	3.3	19

11. Given the information in the following table, determine a processing sequence that would minimize average flow time.

Job	Processing Time (days)	Due Date
a	5	8
b	6	5
c	9	10
d	7	12
e	8	10

12. Given the following information on job times and due hours, determine the processing sequence using (1) MST, (2) SPT, (3) EDD, and (4) CR. For each method, find the average job flow time and the average hours late. Which rule is best?

Job	Job Time (hours)	Due Date (hours)
a	3.5	7
b	2.0	6
c	4.5	18
d	5.0	22
e	2.5	4
f	6.0	20

13. The Budd Gear Co. specializes in heat-treating gears. At 8 a.m., when Budd's shop opened today, five orders were waiting to be processed. Assume that only one unit at a time can be heat treated.

Order	Order Size (units)	Per Unit Time in Heat Treatment (minutes/unit)	Due Date (min. from now)
A	16	4	160
B	6	12	200
C	10	3	180
D	8	10	190
E	4	1	220

   a. If the earliest due date (EDD) rule is used, what sequence should be used?
   b. What will be the average minutes late?
   c. What will be the average WIP in the system?
   d. Would the SPT rule produce better results in terms of minutes late?

14. The following table contains order-dependent setup times for three jobs. Which processing sequence will minimize the total setup time?

		Setup Time (hours)	Following Job's Setup Time (hours)		
			A	**B**	**C**
Preceding Job	**A**	2	–	3	5
	B	3	8	–	2
	C	2	4	3	–

15. The following table contains order-dependent setup times for three jobs. Which processing sequence will minimize the total setup time?

		Setup Time (hours)	Following Job's Setup Time (hours)		
			A	**B**	**C**
	A	2.4	–	1.8	2.2
Preceding Job	**B**	3.2	0.8	–	1.4
	C	2.0	2.6	1.3	–

16. The following table contains order-dependent setup times for four jobs. For safety reasons, job C cannot follow job A, nor can job A follow job C. Determine the processing sequence that will minimize the total setup time. (*Hint:* There are 12 alternatives.)

		Setup Time (hours)	Following Job's Setup Time (hours)			
			A	**B**	**C**	**D**
	A	2	–	5	x	4
Preceding Job	**B**	1	7	–	3	2
	C	3	x	2	–	2
	D	2	4	3	6	–

17. Given the following standard hours of planned and actual inputs and outputs for a work centre, determine the WIP for each period. The beginning WIP is 12 hours of work.

		Period				
		1	**2**	**3**	**4**	**5**
Input	Planned	24	24	24	24	20
	Actual	25	27	20	22	24

Output	Planned	24	24	24	24	23
	Actual	24	22	23	24	24

18. During each four-hour period, the Smalltown police force requires the following number of on-duty police officers: eight from midnight to 4 a.m.; seven from 4 a.m. to 8 a.m.; six from 8 a.m. to noon; six from noon to 4 p.m.; five from 4 p.m. to 8 p.m.; and four from 8 p.m. to midnight. Each police officer works two consecutive four-hour shifts. Determine how to minimize the number of police officers needed to meet Smalltown's daily requirements.

19. Determine the minimum number of workers needed, and a schedule for the following staffing requirements, giving workers two consecutive days off per week.

Day	Mon	Tue	Wed	Thu	Fri	Sat	Sun
Staff needed	2	3	1	2	4	3	1

20. Determine the minimum number of workers needed, and a schedule for the following staffing requirements, giving workers two consecutive days off per week.

Day	Mon	Tue	Wed	Thu	Fri	Sat	Sun
Staff needed	3	4	2	3	4	5	3

21. Determine the minimum number of workers needed, and a schedule for the following staffing requirements, giving workers two consecutive days off per week.

Day	Mon	Tue	Wed	Thu	Fri	Sat	Sun
Staff needed	4	4	5	6	7	8	4

22. Refer to Example 4. Determine shifts for
   a. Counter
   b. Assembly Board

CASE

Staff Requirements and Scheduling in Browns Restaurants

Bass PLC, the owner of the seven-unit Browns Restaurant Group in London, England, was concerned that the restaurants were not achieving their full potential for service speed and efficiency. A consulting team was brought in to look at the operations and improve them. The following activities were undertaken:

1. Identify the components of the restaurant production and service-delivery system;
2. Measure the capacity requirements of each component using time study;
3. Measure the historical demand for each component by operating environment (e.g., meal period by day of week);
4. Calculate ideal capacity-use levels by factoring steps 2 and 3;
5. Compare current usage with ideal capacity-use levels, determine reasons for the variance, and improve the system.

The project team's first step was to document the details of an ideal experience from the guest's perspective (Exhibit 1). Creating the process map allows one to start defining the activities of each staff position (who does what, when, and for whom).

By using a stopwatch, the team conducted a time study for each service and production function. For the kitchen functions, the activities were separated into hands-on assembly and cooking times in order to identify the sequential or parallel nature of activities. Adding the hands-on production time to the elapsed cooking time yields the total production time for each menu item.

The production time was multiplied by historical menu-mix data to determine the workload distribution of cooking effort by cook–function location (e.g., grill, fry). The result was that work was reallocated in a manner that levelled workloads, and bottlenecks plaguing the operation were removed. This line balancing resulted in a reduction of peak-period cooks from 10 to 7.

Browns was staffing its kitchens in a fairly traditional fashion. Day cooks handled the bulk of daily prep work each morning prior to opening. All day cooks arrived at the same time (8 a.m.) and left at the same time (4 p.m.). Because the restaurant was open from noon to midnight, the full complement of evening cooks arrived and departed following a similar eight-hour shift (4 p.m. to midnight). Because the number of customers peaked for lunch around 1:30 p.m. and for dinner around 8:30 p.m., but dipped between 2:30 and 5:30 p.m., the

Exhibit 1

Process Map—Ideal Customer Experience

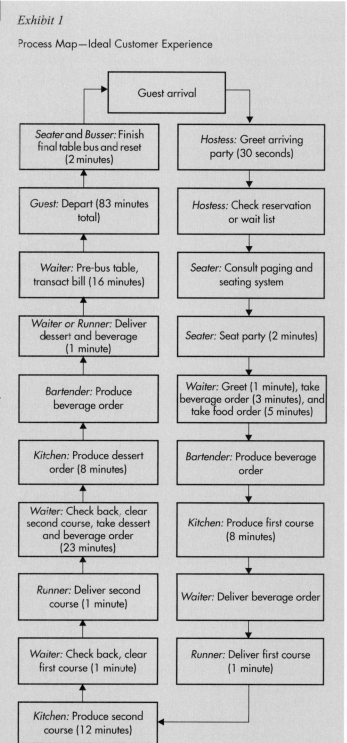

analysis showed that Browns was able to save more than four cooks by shifting the prep work to the middle of the day and staggering the start of the shifts. In effect, no shift before noon was required.

Exhibit 2
Server Time Analysis

Process step (per shift)	Time (minutes)	Time (percentage)	Time per table	Number of occurrences	Time per occurrence
Idle	195.6	–	–	91	2.1
Table clearing and bussing	87.3	20%	3.0	78	1.1
Order delivery	77.1	18%	3.3	47	1.6
Beverage delivery	65.3	15%	2.2	42	1.6
Taking order	46.0	11%	1.5	44	1.0
POS operation	45.6	10%	1.6	72	0.6
Silverware setup	36.7	8%	1.2	31	1.2
Transact bill	31.0	7%	1.1	22	1.4
Greet	17.9	4%	0.6	25	0.7
Condiments	13.0	3%	0.4	15	0.9
Print bill	12.3	3%	0.4	21	0.6
Check back	2.8	<1%	0.1	10	0.3
Total	630.6	–	15.3		
Work minutes	435.0	69%			
Idle minutes	195.6	31%			

Total tables attended during study = 29.
Total guests attended during study = 93.
Average guests per table = 3.2.
Target table turns = 4.2 (assuming an 85-minute turn and 75-percent staff-time efficiency).
Suggested section size = 5.

Browns used to assign each server a section comprising six to seven tables. Time studies of service steps revealed that the servers could properly handle just five tables each (Exhibit 2). While management augmented the service coverage with runners, the fact that only two runners supported 15 servers during peak times meant that food often sat in the service window getting cold. Attempting to make up for the labour shortage, the floor managers employed a policy of having the first available server deliver food items as they came up—and frequently the managers themselves had to run food to the guests. With so many service providers delivering orders in such a hurried fashion, guests weren't sure who exactly was the server, were hard pressed to know whom to call for what, and couldn't be sure that their requests would ever be fulfilled if they did ask for something. Moreover, servers rarely had the chance to check back to make sure the customers were satisfied with their entrées. The service studies resulted in a reduction of server sections to five tables to improve service delivery quality, as well as increasing sales potential and tips for servers.

The team also analyzed bar staffing requirements based on historical beverage demand and work effort required for each drink (e.g., bottled beer, premium spirit, wine by the glass and bottle, blended drinks). An example of time study results is shown in Exhibit 3.

Exhibit 3
Beverage-Service Time Analysis (sample)

Product	Process steps	Work time (seconds)
Premium spirit	Take order	7.0
	Stage glass to bar, fill with ice	3.5
	Measure premium spirit to glass	11.1
	Fill glass with post mix	6.0
	Garnish to glass	1.5
	Transact cash	18.2
	Total	47.3

The outcome of the whole study is a graphic overview of the restaurant capacity requirements as a function of guest demand (Exhibit 4). The graph displays the required capacity of each component as a function of guest demand (in number of tables). For example, during peak hours (50 tables/hour or 71 tables for 85-minute turns), a total of 15 wait staff, 2 host staff, and 7 cooks are required.

Following the modelling exercise, staff schedules were reworked to better fit the restaurants' business patterns. The

Exhibit 4

Staff Requirements as a Function of Guest Demand (Number of Tables)

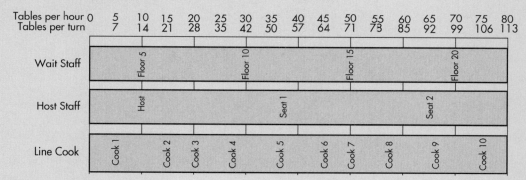

revised schedule increased the number of servers by two per shift and reduced the kitchen staffing by 5 cooks per week. Scheduling is assisted by a forecasting system, and a spreadsheet connected to the point-of-sale system facilitates daily transfers of data on guest demand that is used as part of a four-week weighted moving average forecast for demand.

Questions

1. Each guest table takes approximately 15 minutes of a waiter's time. The waiter works with 75-percent staff-time efficiency (i.e., 25 percent allowance factor). Customers spend an average of 85 minutes in the restaurant. How many tables can a waiter be assigned to?

2. The forecast for the number of new tables (guest groups) on a specific day during every half hour from noon to 3 p.m. is 8, 13, 28, 31, 14, and 11. Assuming each table stays 1.5 hour and we assign one waiter to 5 tables, how many waiters would Browns need every half hour between this noon and 3 p.m. period?

3. Suppose that the hourly number of waiters needed on a specific day from noon to midnight is 5, 15, 15, 6, 1, 3, 9, 11, 12, 13, 9, and 6. Determine 4-hour shifts to cover these needs with minimum waiter numbers. *Hint*: Start with noon and use the minimum number of waiters required, still not met, at the start of each shift. No need for backward shifts. However, the last shift should employ the number of waiters required, not still met, during any hour of that shift.

Source: Based on B. Sill and R. Decker, "Applying Capacity-Management Science: The Case of Browns Restaurants," *Cornell Hotel & Restaurant Administration Quarterly* 40(3), June 1999, pp. 22–30.

SELECTED BIBLIOGRAPHY AND FURTHER READING

Baker, K. R. *Introduction to Sequencing and Scheduling*. New York: Wiley, 1974.

Fogarty, D. W., J. H. Blackstone Jr., and T. R. Hoffman. *Production and Inventory Management*, 2nd ed. Cincinnati: South Western, 1991.

Goldratt, Eli, and Jeff Cox. *The Goal: A Process of Ongoing Improvement*. Great Barrington, MA: North River Press, 1992.

Hopp, Wallace J., and Mark L. Spearman. *Factory Physics*. 2nd ed. New York: Irwin/McGraw-Hill, 2001.

Metters, Richard, and Vicente Vargus. "A Comparison of Production Scheduling Policies on Costs, Service Levels, and Scheduling Changes." *Production and Operations Management* 17(8) 1999, pp. 76–91.

Pinedo, M., and X. Chao. *Operations Scheduling with Applications in Manufacturing and Services*. New York: McGraw-Hill/Irwin, 1999.

Silver, E. A., D. F. Pyke, and R. Peterson. *Inventory Management and Production Planning and Scheduling*. New York: Wiley, 1998.

Vollman, Thomas E., William L. Berry, and D. Clay Whybark. *Manufacturing Planning and Control Systems*. 4th ed. Burr Ridge, IL: Irwin, 1997.

To access "Maintenance," the supplement to Chapter 15, please use the student **DVD** packaged with the text or visit the Online Learning Centre at **www.mcgrawhill.ca/olc/stevenson.**

PART SIX

Supply Chain Management

Supply chain management refers to management of all of the functions, facilities, and activities, both within and external to a business organization, that make up a value chain, starting from raw materials to the ultimate consumption of the finished product, linking across supplier–user companies.

Supply Chain Management

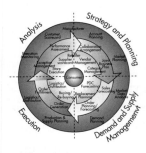

CHAPTER OUTLINE

LEARNING OBJECTIVES

*After completing this chapter, you
should be able to:*

1　Explain what a supply chain is.

2　Explain the need to manage a
　　supply chain and potential
　　benefits of doing so.

3　Identify the strategic and
　　tactical/operational issues in
　　supply chain management.

4　Describe what logistics is.

5　Evaluate shipping alternatives.

6　Discuss the importance of
　　information exchange across a
　　supply chain.

7　Discuss the importance of
　　supply chain management for
　　e-commerce.

8　Outline the key steps and
　　potential challenges in creating
　　an effective supply chain.

9　Explain the importance of the
　　purchasing function in business
　　organizations.

10　Describe purchasing's internal
　　customers and suppliers.

11　Describe a purchasing cycle.

12　Explain the term *value analysis*.

13　Explain how to make a
　　make-or-buy decision.

14　Explain how price is determined.

15　Compare the advantages of
　　centralized purchasing with those
　　of decentralized purchasing.

16　Identify several guidelines for
　　ethical behaviour in purchasing.

17　List several important factors in
　　choosing suppliers.

18　Explain how supplier
　　partnerships can be
　　advantageous to an organization.

ygard International is the largest ladies wear manufacturer in Canada, based in Winnipeg. Nygard has been very successful and is continuously expanding. When FTA and NAFTA were being agreed upon, Nygard was one of the few Canadian clothing manufacturers that supported them. Now, when competition from the Far East has threatened most other apparel makers, Nygard is able to compete. How does Nygard do this? It is not just the design of the clothing, the workmanship, or the quality of fabric. It is Nygard's supply chain management.

This chapter covers supply chain management, logistics, and purchasing. You will learn what a supply chain is, why there is a need for managing supply chains, what the key issues in managing a supply chain are, what is logistics and how to evaluate shipping alternatives, what the role of the supply chain is in e-commerce, what steps are necessary in creating an effective supply chain, and what some of the challenges are in supply chain management.

You will also learn about the purchasing function and supplier management. In particular, you will learn what purchasing managers do, the importance of purchasing, its internal customers and suppliers, the purchasing cycle, value analysis, make-or-buy decisions, how price is determined, centralization vs. decentralization, guidelines for ethical behaviour in purchasing, and various aspects of supplier management, including vendor analysis, supplier audits, and strategic partnering.

INTRODUCTION

A **supply chain** is the sequence of organizations—their facilities, functions, and activities— that are involved in producing and delivering a product or service. The sequence begins with suppliers of raw materials and extends all the way to the final customer. Facilities include factories, processing centres, warehouses, distribution centres, retail outlets, and offices. Functions and activities include forecasting, purchasing, inventory management, information management, quality assurance, scheduling, production, distribution, delivery, and customer service. There are two kinds of movement in these systems: the physical movement of material (generally toward the end of the chain) and the exchange of information (mainly toward the beginning of the chain).

supply chain Sequence of organizations—their facilities, functions, and activities—that are involved in producing and delivering a product or service.

The term chain in supply chain signifies the importance of close relationship between suppliers and buyers (i.e., inseparable as in a chain). This is a relatively new term, first used approximately two decades ago when quick replenishment systems such as Quick Response were introduced between some retail companies and their suppliers (i.e., manufacturers).

Every business organization is part of at least one supply chain, and many are part of multiple supply chains. The number and type of organizations in a supply chain are determined by whether the supply chain is manufacturing- or service-oriented. Figure 16–1 illustrates typical supply chains for a manufacturer and a service provider. In Chapter 1, a typical supply chain for bread was displayed.

Supply chains are sometimes referred to as **value chains**, a term that reflects the concept that value is added as goods progress through the chain. Supply or value chains are typically comprised of separate business organizations, rather than just a single organization. Moreover, the supply or value chain has two components for each organization: a supply component and a demand component. The supply component starts at the beginning of the chain and ends with the internal operations of the organization. The demand component of the chain starts at the point where the organization's output is delivered to its immediate customer and ends with the final customer in the chain. The length of each component depends on where a particular organization is in the chain; the closer the organization is to the final customer, the shorter its demand component and the longer its supply component.

value chain A supply chain.

FIGURE 16-1

Typical supply chains
a. Manufacturer
b. Service provider

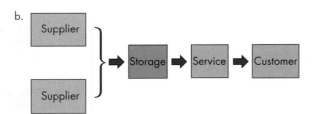

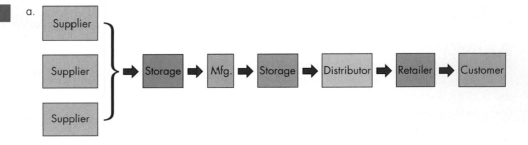

READING

Warburtons Ltd.

One reason for a company to partner with its raw material supplier(s) is to preserve the quality of raw material. A case in point is Warburtons Ltd., Britain's largest bakery, which emphasizes the quality of its bread. A few years ago, Warburtons determined that the most suitable wheat for its bread and processes is Canada Western Red Spring wheat. Warburtons partnered with Manitoba Pool Elevators (now called Agricore United, after merger with Alberta Pool and

United Grain Growers), which selects and contracts with farmers to grow the specified wheat ordered by Warburtons. In return, the farmers are paid a premium. The extra cost of the premium and the cost of segregating the wheat in transportation to Warburtons are evidently less than the cost of regular careful purchases of the same grade of wheat in the grain markets using quality control lab tests.

Source: J. Kennett, M. Fulton, P. Molder, and H. Brooks, "Supply Chain Management: The Case of a UK Baker Preserving the Identity of Canadian Milling Wheat," *Supply Chain Management* 3(3), 1998, pp. 157ff.

All organizations, regardless of where they are in the chain, must deal with supply and demand issues. The goal of supply chain management is to link all components of the supply chain so that market demand is met as efficiently and effectively as possible across the entire chain. This requires matching supply and demand at each stage of the chain. Note that except for the beginning supplier(s) and the final customer(s), the organizations in a supply chain are both customers and suppliers. An unusual example of a supply chain with quality objectives is described in the "Warburtons Ltd." reading above.

THE NEED FOR SUPPLY CHAIN MANAGEMENT

In the past, most organizations did little to manage their supply chains. Instead, they tended to concentrate on their own operations. However, a number of factors make it desirable for business organizations to actively manage their supply chains. The major factors are:

1. *The need to improve operations.* During the last two decades, many organizations adopted practices such as just-in-time and TQM. As a result, they were able to achieve improved quality while wringing much of the excess costs out of their systems. Although there is still room for improvement, for many organizations the major gains have been realized. Opportunity now lies largely with procurement, distribution, and logistics—the supply chain.

2. *Increasing levels of outsourcing.* Organizations are increasing their levels of **outsourcing**, buying goods or services instead of producing or providing them themselves. As outsourcing increases, organizations are spending increasing amounts on supply-related activities (purchasing and transportation). Some of the cost and time spent on these activities may be unnecessary.

outsourcing Buying goods or services instead of producing or providing them in-house.

3. *Competitive pressures.* Competitive pressures have led to an increasing number of new products, shorter product-development cycles, and increased demand for customization. Uncertainty in demand has increased, resulting in greater need for risk-sharing. The emphasis on quality has led some companies to ensure material quality starting from the beginning of the supply chain. And in some industries, most notably computers and consumer electronics, product life cycles are becoming shorter. Added to this are adoption of just-in-time and quick-response strategies and efforts to reduce lead times.

4. *Increasing globalization.* Increasing globalization has expanded the physical length of supply chains, and the quantity of materials and products being transported.

5. *Increasing e-commerce.* Increasing e-commerce has stimulated commerce, and business-to-business e-commerce has required new technology and closer relationship between buyers and sellers.

6. *The complexity of supply chains.* Supply chains are complex; they are dynamic, and they have many inherent uncertainties that can adversely affect the supply chain, such as inaccurate forecasts, late deliveries, substandard quality, equipment breakdowns, and cancelled or changed orders. A change in one part of a supply chain may have a large impact on the whole supply chain.

7. *The need to manage inventories across the supply chain.* Inventories play a major role in the success or failure of a supply chain, so it is important to coordinate inventory levels throughout a supply chain. Shortages can severely disrupt the timely flow of work and have far-reaching impacts, while excess inventories add unnecessary costs. It would not be unusual to find inventory shortages in some parts of a supply chain and excess inventories in other parts of the same supply chain.

Effective supply chain management offers numerous benefits. For example, Campbell Soup doubled its inventory turnover rate; Hewlett-Packard cut deskjet printer supply costs by 75 percent.[1] And effective supply chain management helped Wal-Mart become the largest and most profitable retailer in the world!

www.campbellsoups.com
www.hp.com
www.walmart.com

READING

HP's CD-RW

In the late 1990s, Hewlett-Packard was under competitive pressure in its CD-RW (CD-rewriter) markets. The supply chain from the manufacturers of the CD-RWs in Japan and Malaysia to the customers (computer resellers) in Americas or Europe took approximately 126 days: the shipment of the base units from the Far East took about 30 days; there was a 75-day supply kept in the three regional localization and conversion centres (Singapore, U.S., Netherlands) in order to hedge against the variability of supply lead time; localization and conversion, i.e., adding a case for external units and putting on labels and packaging in various languages, took only 1 day; 15 days of finished good inventory was kept to hedge against demand variability; and ground transportation within North America or Europe took 5 days on average. The total of 126 days cost HP 8 percent per year in holding cost, which amounted to $5.50 per unit (using a unit selling price of $200).

HP's Strategic Planning and Modelling Group was asked to redesign the supply chain. They evaluated eight different supply networks and found the lowest cost one. The localization and conversion activities have been centralized in one place (Singapore), and air freight, instead of ships, is used to transport the CD-RWs to Singapore. Also, air freight is used to transport the finished CD-RWs to regional distribution centres. The use of air has resulted in elimination of safety stocks at the localization and conversion centre in Singapore. The supply chain cycle time is reduced to approximately eight days.

Other advantages of a single worldwide centre are that forecasting is brought under one roof and the variation in aggregate demand is less (called *risk pooling*). Another advantage of the new supply chain is that HP can introduce new products to markets faster. HP also reduced the number of suppliers of CD-RWs from eight down to one, and got into partnership and collaborative planning, forecasting, and replenishment (CPFR) with the supplier which has reduced the manufacturing lead time significantly. HP is using the same supply chain for the new DVD-RWs.

Source: T. Hammel et al., "The Re-engineering of Hewlett-Packard's CD-RW Supply Chain," *Supply Chain Management* 7(3/4), 2002, pp. 113–118.

---

[1]Marshall Fisher, "What Is the Right Supply Chain for Your Product?" *Harvard Business Review,* March/April 1997, pp. 105–16.

READING

Midas Canada

www.midas.ca

Midas Canada's approximately 240 auto service shops, mostly franchises, repair mainly mufflers. The mufflers are mainly produced in Midas factories in the U.S. and trucked to Canada. Midas has three distribution centres (DC), in Toronto, Montreal, and Vancouver, and two third-party-operated DCs in Edmonton and Moncton. Before 1997, Toronto's DC, located in Agincourt under the same roof as the national headquarters, supplied all the other DCs as well as repair shops in Ontario and Manitoba. In 1997, the installation of better forecasting/inventory control software enabled Midas Canada to have most manufacturers ship directly to the other four DCs. This reduced the total shipment cost by 12 percent and speeded up deliveries to the other four DCs. Direct shipment is an example of "disintermediation," one way to reduce costs in some supply chains.

Source: G. Guidoni, "Midas Touch: Forecasting Software Installation Pays Off for Auto Service Giant," *Materials Management & Distribution* 42(5), May 1997, pp. 16–19.

MANAGING THE SUPPLY CHAIN

supply chain management
Designing, planning, coordinating, and controlling the facilities, functions, and activities across the supply chain.

Supply chain management involves designing, planning, coordinating, and controlling the facilities, functions, and activities across the supply chain.

Strategic Design Issues. Strategic decisions generally have long-term impacts on a supply chain. Goals and competitive characteristics such as quality, cost, flexibility, speed, customer service, and fill rate should be determined. Then, a supply chain is designed to achieve the objectives. This involves determining the number, location, and capacity of facilities. For examples of redesign of supply chains, see the readings, "HP's CD-RW," "Midas Canada," and "Couche-Tard." Also, the information systems, database, and software architecture and operation have to be determined.

Determining the extent of vertical integration (i.e., the ownership of a segment of supply chain), which is affected by make-or-buy and outsourcing decisions, is a related

READING

Couche-Tard

Couche-Tard is the second largest chain of convenience stores in North America. Headquartered in Laval, Quebec, Couche-Tard includes Mac's stores and recently bought the Circle K chain in the U.S. Before 2002, Couche-Tard used wholesale distributors and suppliers to directly deliver the products it sells, 2,500 SKUs, to its stores. However, because of the variety of products it carries, there were some 50 different delivery trucks dropping their goods off at any store which caused parking problems and interfered with business. Because most of Couche-Tard's stores were in Montreal, it decided to start a distribution centre close by in Laval. Then, the recent purchase of the Circle K chain added the Circle K's distribution centre in Arizona. Couche-Tard has reorganized into eight regions (see to the right: squares are company-owned and circles are franchises). The challenging logistics problem is currently under review.

Sources: www.couchetard.com/en/index.sn; J. Shanahan, "Making Distribution More Convenience," *Logistics Management* 43(2), February 2004, p. 57; T. Keller, "Alain Bouchard, CEO, Alimentation Couche-Tard," *National Post Business*, March 2004, p. 16.

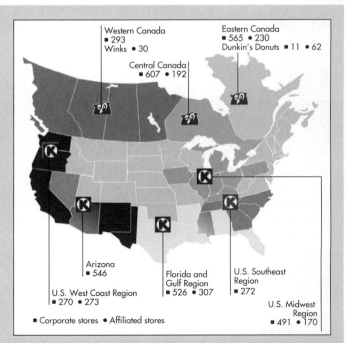

Regions where Couche-Tard stores are located. Figure courtesy of Alimentation Couche-Tard Inc. Reprinted with permission.

READING

Cami Automotive

Because companies operating under a JIT system don't carry much inventory and have high production rates, they need to bring in purchased parts and components frequently and in small quantities. They also need to partner with suppliers that are located close by and that can accommodate their special needs. Also, in order to accelerate the transportation and handling activities, special returnable containers are usually used instead of cardboard boxes. As well, there is usually a need for a cross-dock or staging facility near the assembly plant, which allows "breaking" the shipments for various parts of the assembly line and sequencing each according to the line sequence. Because of the frequency of deliveries to the assembly plant, the arrivals of trucks to the plant must be highly coordinated and be on time. Usually one trucking company is partnered to perform "milk runs" to supplier plants. An example of this supply chain is that used by Cami Automotive of Ingersoll, Ontario (a GM and Suzuki joint venture now making the Chevy Equinox and Pontiac Torrent); Cami uses Transfreight Inc. as its logistics partner. Transfreight has 8 to 10 semi trailers dedicated to Cami and runs a cross-dock facility in London, 30 minutes from Ingersoll and another in Windsor, and cross docking in Dayton, Ohio. A Transfreight contract manager is located in Cami's plant and works closely with Cami's manager of logistics and material handling. Seventy percent of Cami's suppliers are located less than 500 km away.

Source: L. Young, "Rev Up—Cami Shapes Cutting-edge Supply Chain," *Materials Management & Distribution*, September 1998, pp. 20–21.

issue. Customer–supplier partnerships are becoming more widespread as business organizations reduce the number of suppliers they use to move in the direction of just-in-time.

Tactical/Operational (Planning, etc.) Issues. The important tactical/operational decisions in supply chain management relate to production planning and control, including forecasting, purchasing, transportation of material, inventory control, and scheduling of production and deliveries, and movement of products (replenishment). Questions such as "should a product be manufactured at this plant, today or later, or shipped from another location, today or later?" should be answered.

LOGISTICS

Logistics refers to the movement of materials/products and information within a facility and outside. In addition to raw materials and manufacturing parts and components, incoming materials include maintenance, repair, and operating (MRO) supplies such as fuels, spare parts, lubricants, and office supplies.

logistics The movement of materials/products and information within a facility and outside.

READING

Saturn

www.saturn.com

Another example of a JIT system is the Saturn operation in Spring Hill, Tennessee. So well does the automaker manage its supply chain that in four years it has had to halt production just once—for only 18 minutes—because the right part was not delivered at the right time. Saturn maintains almost no inventory of parts and components. Instead, a central computer directs trucks to deliver preinspected and presorted parts and components at precise times to the factory's 56 receiving docks, 21 hours a day, six days a week. Especially striking about this just-in-time system is that most of Saturn's 339 suppliers aren't located anywhere near the plant. They are in 39 states and an average of 900 km away from Spring Hill.

Charged with making the Saturn network run on schedule is Ryder Trucks, the Miami transportation service company that has become the biggest logistics management firm. Tractors, pulling trailers that are, on average, 90 percent full (an exceptionally high ratio), arrive daily at Ryder's command post some 3 km from the Saturn factory. There the drivers uncouple the trailers.

Then a driver picks up and plugs a key, loaded with electronic data, into his onboard computer. The screen then tells him which empty trailer to hitch to, exactly where to go, which route to take, and how much time to spend getting there.

Specially designed shuttle tractors then take the trailers, which contain bar-coded, reusable plastic bins full of parts, and deliver them to the plant as needed. See the illustration on the next page.

Source: Based on R. Henkoff, "Delivering the Goods," *Fortune*, November 28, 1994, © 1994 Time, Inc.

1. *Thursday, 9 A.M.: A Ryder truck (labelled Saturn) arrives at a Saturn supplier for speedometers and odometers.*

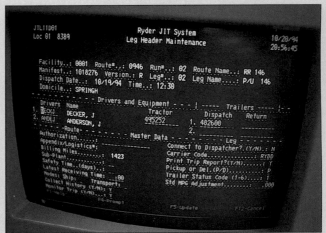

4. *The driver plugs the key-shaped floppy disk into his on-board computer, which tells him which empty trailer to hitch into, where to go next, which route to take, and how much time to spend getting there.*

2. *After loading, the driver enters some information into the onboard computer, which provides routing information back to the Saturn plant along with estimated travel times.*

5. *12:50 P.M.: A shuttle tractor takes the trailer of speedometers and odometers to the Saturn plant.*

3. *Friday, 3 A.M.: After parking the trailer in a computer-assigned spot in Ryder's switching yard 3 km from the Saturn plant, the driver picks up a plastic key-shaped floppy disk with his name on it.*

6. *12:53 P.M.: The trailer arrives at one of the plant's 56 receiving docks just in time for Saturn workers to unload the bins and unwrap the pre-inspected instruments to ready them for the production line.*

www.ryder.com

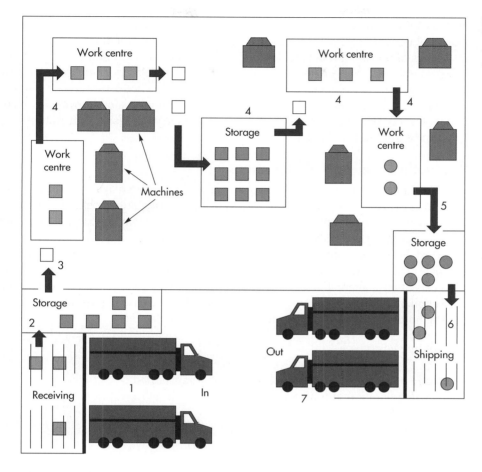

FIGURE 16-2

Movement of goods within a facility

Movement within a Facility

Movement of goods within a manufacturing facility is part of production control. Depending on the nature of goods, the volume, and production process, different material handling equipment is used. Common equipment includes forklifts, carts, baskets, and bins. Figure 16–2 shows the movement of parts in a batch manufacturing facility:

1. From incoming vehicles to receiving.
2. From receiving to storage.
3. From storage to the point of use (e.g., a work centre).
4. From one work centre to the next or to temporary storage.
5. From the last operation to final storage.
6. From storage to packaging/shipping.
7. From shipping to outgoing vehicles.

Shipping is the term used for the act of sending goods out for delivery. In an assembly line/JIT system, there are less or no storage/inventories. In a continuous process, there are more receiving and shipping inventories. In a job shop, there are more WIP inventories.

Movement of materials must be coordinated so that they arrive at the appropriate destinations at appropriate times. Workers and supervisors must take care so that items are not lost, stolen, or damaged during movement.

Incoming and Outgoing Deliveries

Overseeing the delivery of incoming and outgoing goods comes under the heading of **traffic management**. This function handles schedules and decisions on delivery methods and times, taking into account costs of various alternatives, government regulations, the

traffic management
Overseeing the shipment of incoming and outgoing goods.

needs of the organization relative to quantities and timing, and external factors such as potential delivery delays or disruptions (e.g., highway construction, truckers' strikes).

Modes of transportation include ships, trains, trucks, and air. Some logistics companies use a combination of these modes. For example, parcel delivery companies such as FedEx use air and trucks. Computer tracking of deliveries often helps to maintain knowledge of the current status of goods as well as to provide other up-to-date information on costs and schedules. For two examples of JIT deliveries, see the readings, "Cami Automotive," and "Saturn" earlier in the chapter.

Evaluating Delivery Alternatives

A situation that often arises in some businesses is the need to make a choice between rapid (but more expensive) delivery alternatives such as overnight or second-day air and slower (but less expensive) alternatives such as using trucks. In some instances, an overriding factor justifies sending the goods by the quickest means possible, so there is little or no choice involved. However, in other instances urgency is not the primary consideration, so there is a choice. The decision in such cases often focuses on the total transport and inventory holding costs of each alternative. An important assumption is that the buyer takes ownership at the supplier's location and pays for delivery, which is the case in most business purchases.

The holding cost incurred by an alternative is calculated as

$$\text{Holding cost} = \frac{H(d)}{365} \qquad (16\text{--}1)$$

where H = annual holding cost of items being transported
d = duration of transport (in days)

$$\text{Total delivery cost} = \text{transportation cost} + \text{holding cost}$$
$$= \text{transportation cost} + H(d)/365$$

Example 1	Determine which delivery alternative, one day or three days, is best when the holding cost of the item is $1,000 per year, the one-day delivery transportation cost is $40, and the three-day delivery transportation cost is: *a.* $35 *b.* $30

Solution

$H = \$1,000$ per year
Total cost of 1-day delivery $= \$40 + \$1000(1/365)$
$\qquad\qquad\qquad\qquad\qquad\quad = \$42.74$
Total cost of 3-day delivery

a. $= \$35 + \$1000(3/365)$
$\quad = \$43.22 > \$42.74$
Therefore, 1-day delivery is cheaper.

b. $= \$30 + \$1000(3/365)$
$\quad = \$38.22 < \$42.74$
Therefore, 3-day delivery is cheaper.

Electronic Data Interchange

electronic data interchange (EDI) The direct transmission of interorganizational transactions, computer-to-computer, including purchase orders, advance shipping notices, and invoices.

Electronic data interchange (EDI) is the direct, computer-to-computer transmission of interorganizational transactions, including purchase orders, sales data, advance shipping notices, invoices, engineering drawings, and more. Among the reasons companies are increasingly using EDI (especially the Internet-based version of it; see "L'eBiz" reading later in the chapter) are:

- Increased productivity.
- Reduction of paperwork.

READING

Source Medical

www.sourcemedical.com

Source Medical Corporation, Canada's largest national distributor of medical and surgical products, uses its supply chain as a competitive weapon. A hospital transmits its order through EDI to one of Source Medical's five regional distribution centres (50,000 stock-keeping units from 300 manufacturers), which will deliver the order direct to the user department in the hospital on a just-in-time basis (this is called *stockless purchasing*).

For York Central Hospital in Richmond Hill, Ontario, this arrangement has reduced handling of products from nine times to two times and has enabled the hospital to reduce its inventories. The result: $2.5 million in savings. The EDI allows York Central Hospital not only to communicate its orders electronically, but also receive its invoices electronically.

Another group of hospitals that uses Source Medical is Chinook Health Region, in and around Lethbridge, Alberta. Chinook Health Region also benefits from EDI, but the main cost-savings came as a result of centralizing the purchasing and inventory of the 10 health-care facilities in one hospital. This allowed reduction of inventory by half, reduction of purchasing staff, and enabled price breaks for larger pooled purchases. The deliveries by Source Medical are cross-docked at the main facility and distributed to the rural facilities by truck.

Source: L. Young, "Finding the Right Supply Chain Medicine," *Data Capture Communications & Commerce*, April 1999, pp. DC9–DC10.

- Lead time and inventory reduction.
- Facilitation of just-in-time (JIT) system.
- Electronic transfer of funds.
- Improved control of operations.
- Reduction in clerical labour.
- Increased accuracy.

The use of EDI linkages with other organizations can be part of a strategy to achieve a competitive advantage by leveraging logistics performance. In addition, in some JIT systems, EDI serves as the signal for replenishment to the supplier. For two applications, see the readings, "Source Medical" and "Abitibi Consolidated."

There are many applications of EDI in retailing involving electronic communication between retailers and vendors. Wal-Mart has a satellite network for EDI that allows retail store point-of-sale data to be downloaded every night to the Wal-Mart main database, which vendors can also access. This enables the vendors to improve their forecasting, production scheduling, and inventory management, and Wal-Mart saves money on carrying inventory, and fill rate goes up.

Dubbed **quick response**, this JIT approach involves making sales information available to vendors. The purpose is to create a just-in-time replenishment system that is keyed to customer buying as opposed to periodic orders by buyers. Quick response was initiated in 1984 in the soft goods and apparel industries. Another name for it is *continuous product replenishment*.

quick response Just-in-time inventory replenishment system in retailing using EDI.

Quick-response has several benefits. Among them are reduced dependency on forecasts and the ability to achieve a closer match between supply and demand. In addition, there are

READING

Abitibi Consolidated

www.abitibiconsolidated.com

Another example of a company using EDI is Abitibi Consolidated, the forest-products company, which had GE Information Services implement an EDI service with its major spare-parts and logistics suppliers. This led to savings of $3.5 million per year in purchasing-department costs. Abitibi's goal was to have approximately 300 of its suppliers on the EDI system. Although some (such as railways) were connected to EDI, many other smaller suppliers have been reluctant. Abitibi is trying to reduce its number of suppliers (approximately 6,000 in 1997) and work with only preferred suppliers.

Source: "Paper Trail: Abitibi-Price Uses EDI to Revamp Purchasing Process and Lower Overall Supply Chain Costs," *Material Management & Distribution* 41(7), July 1996, p. 14.

efficient consumer response (ECR) An expanded quick response initiative in the grocery industry, including some collaboration.

savings on inventory holding costs. For applications, see the readings on Sears Canada, Reckitt Benckiser (Canada), Campbell Soup, and Nygard (later in this chapter).

Efficient consumer response (ECR), initiated in 1992, is an expanded quick response in the grocery industry. In addition to continuous replenishment, ECR includes some collaboration on replenishment, forecasting, and planning store assortments, promotions, and product introductions.

Vendor-Managed Inventory (VMI) is another initiative that reduces the inventories in the supply chain. In VMI, the vendor's employee periodically comes on the buyer's premise, counts the inventories of his/her company on the buyer's shelves, replenishes them up to the previously agreed upon level, and issues an invoice later. VMI has been used by soft drink companies supplying convenience stores, electrical distributors supplying small maintenance warehouses, etc. A version of VMI is co-managed inventory where the buyer assists the vendor in planning, forecasting, and replenishment.

Distribution Requirements Planning

distribution requirements planning (DRP) A system for distribution planning.

Distribution requirements planning (DRP) is a system for distribution planning. It is especially useful in multi-echelon warehousing systems (hierarchial levels of factory, regional warehouses, and local warehouses). It uses a concept similar to material

---

READING

Sears Canada's Quick Response

www.sears.ca

Sears Canada has two words of advice for retailers who spend a lot of time trying to forecast sales of specific items, seeking to avoid out-of-stocks: Don't bother.

This is what you'd have to infer from the success the Toronto-based division of Chicago-based Sears, Roebuck and Co. has achieved by implementing new procurement processes founded on Quick Response.

In doing so, the retailer has effectively removed the burdens of forecasting from itself and placed them squarely on the shoulders of its suppliers.

Sears Canada, with 124 department stores, 39 furniture and appliance stores, and 2,150 catalogue pick-up locations, is the highest-volume retailer in Canada. In 1994, with the help of Andersen Consulting, the chain began an initiative to re-design its merchandise procurement processes, seeking to streamline activities from purchase to delivery to payment.

There was ample reason to move quickly. Wal-Mart had entered Canada, acquiring 120 former Woolco stores, and other competitors including The Home Depot and Costco were expanding their Canadian presence.

Sears Canada had been proud of its sophisticated but often complex procurement capabilities. Many different methods were employed to accomplish the same basic business functions.

In simplifying, they went from 37 distinct procurement methods to four standard models; from many distribution methods to total flow-through (the name sometimes used for quick response); and from 31 ways to pay to one.

Other changes included using more negotiations, cross-docking, Advance Shipping Notices (ASNs), and Electronic Fund Transfer.

For example, under the old approach there were large monthly shipments of large appliances from suppliers to Sears' warehouses, from where customer orders were filled. This required a large, expensive inventory, high storage costs, and extensive handling with the commensurately higher possibility of damage.

Now, when a customer in a store decides to buy a Whirlpool dishwasher, for example, the sales associate connects on-line to Whirlpool via a store terminal to confirm the availability of the item. The associate then places the order (via EDI) and commits to a fast and firm delivery date.

Whirlpool then sends an ASN and ships the next day. The product is cross-docked at a Sears warehouse and put on an outbound route. Nearly 100 big-ticket suppliers, including Whirlpool, GE, Sanyo, and Goldstar, had been converted to the new approach as of 1994.

Results include $65 million in inventory take out and an 11 percent improvement in the customer fill rate.

ASNs have become a vital part of the overall supply chain process vision, with the top 700 suppliers—representing 85 percent of all purchases—converted in the first six months.

Gone with this new approach are attempts by Sears Canada to forecast customer demand. Instead, the chain agrees to provide to its suppliers its sales information and its promotional marketing plans. The suppliers then must agree to decrease lead-time and be responsive to actual demand by replacing what is sold.

Question

How did Sears Canada's supply chain reduce its costs?

Source: Based on "Sears Canada on Forecasts: Let the Manufacturer Do It," from *Chain Store Age* 71(8), August 1995, pp. 44–46.

Reckitt Benckiser (Canada) Quick Response

Reckitt Benckiser (Canada), a manufacturer of food and household products such as French's, Lysol, Easy-off, Veet, and Air Wick, partnered with two of its major customers, the food and merchandise distributors Oshawa Foods and Hudon & Deaudelin (both now part of Sobeys), to provide Quick Response. This involved EDI connections to the distributors and required provision of demand history and valid

inventory data by the distributors. Reckitt Benckiser monitors the inventories of its products in the distributors' warehouses and replenishes them very frequently to maintain the inventory levels required by the distributors. Distributor fill rates have gone up to 99 to 100 percent, inventory turns have increased, and invoice accuracy has gone up (because Reckitt Benckiser creates both the orders and the invoices). The access to the distributors' data has also reduced the average demand forecast errors (MAPE) from 48 to 27 percent.

Source: "CPR at Work: Reckitt & Colman Canada Makes the Most of Continuous Replenishment to Get Its Products to Retail Distributors," *Materials Management & Distribution* 41(5), May 1996, pp. 19–20.

Campbell Soup's Quick Response

In the early 1990s, Campbell Soup adopted the Quick Response (QR) system with 30 percent of its major customers (approximately 80 distribution centres) by establishing EDI with them via a high-speed network. Before that, Campbell's restocked customer warehouses based on information punched into its computer system after it was received from its salespeople dealing directly with the stores' buyers. But the

forecast was inaccurate and ignored demand patterns. Now, the participating customers use EDI to send daily updates of how many of Campbell's products were bought the day before and how many were left in inventory. After comparing these numbers with historical patterns, the mainframe computer tells Campbell's plants how many of each product to deliver and on what day. In return for using QR, participating customers buy at reduced prices. The frequent replenishment has also allowed customers to reduce their inventories by 50 percent.

Source: N. Byrnes, "Inventory Management: Campbell Soup," *Financial World* 162(19), September 28, 1993, pp. 52ff.

requirements planning (see Chapter 13) for distribution, starting with demand at the end of the channel and working back through the network to obtain time-phased replenishment schedules for moving goods from the factory through each level of the distribution network.

Note that the DRP structure is like the product structure tree but upside down: the children are on the top and the factory is at the bottom. Moreover, the same time-phasing and inventory netting as in MRP is used. Also note that the DRP is a push system (works based on forecasts and planning) whereas quick response is a pull system (works based on actual demand and fast). For an application, see the reading, "Good Humor Breyers' DRP."

JIT Delivery Problems

JIT systems such as quick response often require frequent deliveries of small shipments. This can place a tremendous burden on the delivery system in several respects. One is the increased traffic that results. Instead of one large delivery per week, a company switching to JIT may require many smaller loads every day. Multiply that by the number of parts obtained from various suppliers, and you can begin to appreciate the potential traffic nightmare and, resulting delays in the receiving area. Also, there is the likely increase in transportation cost per unit. There is often a fixed cost per delivery (e.g., per truck), even if only a partial load is delivered. Smaller trucks are one possibility, but that, too, will generate a fixed cost. There is always a chance of disruption of deliveries due to labour strikes, equipment problems, etc. Because of these factors, it is necessary to carefully weigh the costs and benefits of using frequent, small deliveries, and select a lot size that *balances* all relevant costs.

READING

Good Humor Breyers' DRP

G ood Humor Breyers was formed when Unilever Canada bought the ice cream businesses of Beatrice and Natrel and joined them to Popsicle Industries and Dickie Dee Ice Cream. Good Humor Breyers has a plant in Simcoe, Ontario, and another in Montreal, but the warehousing and distribution is contracted out to third-party regional distributors. In 1998 Good Humor Breyers installed an ERP software to automate and integrate its newly combined businesses. The first process to be redesigned was the order fulfillment and inventory replenishment. Before this change, the third-party distributors each would place their own replenishment orders. Although this worked most of the time, sometimes inventory was deployed to the wrong regional warehouse. A multifunctional team redesigned the inventory replenishment process based on DRP as follows: sales information for each regional warehouse is received and accumulated on a daily basis by Breyers, and forecasts for each regional warehouse are made periodically using historical demand data and information on promotions provided by sales and marketing departments. The consolidated requirements, net of projected inventories, are used for production planning at the supplying plants. The planned shipments are sent to regional warehouses for review. Once approved, Breyers produces and delivers the ice cream to the warehouse.

Source: S. Leith and M. Birkenhauer, "Good Humor Breyers Speeds Ice Cream to Market Using ERP," *Food in Canada* 58(7), September 1998, pp. 37–39.

Third Party Logistics

Some companies are outsourcing their logistics and inventory management, turning over warehousing and deliveries to companies that specialize in these areas such as Purolator, UPS, FedEx, PBB Global Logistics, and Ryder Trucks. This is called *third-party logistics*. One possible reason for this is a desire to concentrate on the core business. Employing a company that specializes in logistics provides other benefits such as a well-developed logistics information system, experienced logistics personnel, customs facilities, foreign locations, and the ability to provide lower transportation rates. For two applications, see the readings, "Purolator" and "PBB Global Logistics."

The Global Supply Chain

As international trade barriers fall, more companies are expanding global operations. This is presenting tremendous opportunities and opening up previously untapped markets for raw materials, products, and services. It has also increased the number of competitors, and even companies that operate only within a single country are faced with increased foreign competition.

Managing a global supply chain that may have far-flung customers and/or suppliers magnifies some of the challenges of managing a domestic supply chain. Obviously, distances and lead times increase as the supply chain becomes longer. In addition, there is the possibility of having to deal with different languages and cultures, currency fluctuations, and possibly additional modes of transportation.

READING

Purolator

C ustomers want a package delivery company (such as Purolator) to do more than delivery, including warehousing and customs brokerage. For example, Purolator has a growing business with U.S. companies selling products in Canada: Purolator consolidates the shipments destined to Canada of such companies as Victoria's Secret, transports them to the border, clears them through Canada Customs, and distributes them in Canada. To address customer needs, there have been some vertical acquisitions and partnerships. For example, Purolator has partnered with Burnham Logistics (a logistics services provider).

Source: A. Jones, "Fast and Curious: Now That They've Mastered Express Delivery Through Extensive Infrastructure, Couriers Are Intrigued about the Possibilities of Handling Your Total Supply Chain," *Canadian Transportation Logistics* 103(4), April 2000, pp. 30, 32ff.

The ability to export to other countries, as opposed to make the product there, has allowed multinational companies to centralize the production of families of their products in one location. This allows economies of scale, but requires localization of the product for different markets which have different feature preferences. For example, most people buy front-load washing machines in the U.K., whereas in North America, top-loading washing machines are popular.

E-COMMERCE

E-commerce refers to the use of computers and telecommunication technologies to conduct buying and selling. E-commerce involves business to business (B2B) and business to customers (B2C) commerce. Delivery firms have seen the demand for their services increase dramatically due to e-commerce. Among them are UPS, FedEx, and Purolator. Table 16–1 lists some of the numerous advantages of e-commerce.

There are two essential features of e-commerce businesses: the Web site, and order fulfillment. Companies may invest considerable time and effort in front-end design (the Web site), but the back end (order fulfillment) is at least as important. It involves order processing, inventory management, warehousing, packing, shipping, billing, and delivery.

Many of the problems that occur with Internet selling are supply-related. The ability to order quickly creates an expectation in customers that the remainder of the process will proceed smoothly and quickly. But the same capability that enables quick ordering also enables demand fluctuations that can inject a certain amount of chaos into the system, almost guaranteeing that there won't be a smooth or quick delivery. Not too long ago, Toys "R" Us had this experience during the busy Christmas season; it ended up offering thousands of disappointed customers a $100 coupon to make up for it.

In the early days of Internet selling, many organizations thought they could avoid bearing the costs of holding inventories by acting solely as intermediaries, having their suppliers ship directly to their customers. Although this approach worked for some companies, it failed for others usually because suppliers ran out of certain items. This led

e-commerce The use of computers and telecommunication technologies to conduct buying and selling.

www.ups.com/canada
www.fedex.com/ca_english
www.purolator.ca

www.amazon.com

TABLE 16-1
Advantages of e-commerce

Companies have a global presence and the customer has global choices and easy access to information.

Companies can improve competitiveness and quality of service by allowing access to their services, any time.

Companies can analyze the interest in various products based on the number of hits and requests for information.

Companies can collect detailed information about clients' choices, which enables mass customization and personalized products. An example is the purchase of PCs over the Web, where the buyer specifies the final configuration.

Supply chain response times are shortened. The biggest impact is on products that can be delivered directly on the Web, such as software distribution.

The roles of the intermediary and sometimes the traditional retailer or service provider are reduced or eliminated entirely in a process called *disintermediation*. This process reduces costs and adds alternative purchasing options.

Substantial cost savings and substantial price reductions related to the reduction of transaction costs can be realized. Companies that provide purchasing and support through the Web can save significant personnel costs.

E-commerce allows the creation of virtual companies that distribute only through the Web, thus reducing costs. Amazon.com and other net vendors can afford to sell for a lower price because they do not need to maintain retail stores and, in some cases, warehouse space.

The playing field is leveled for small companies which lack significant resources to invest in infrastructure and marketing.

Source: Reprinted by permission from David Simchi-Levi, Philip Kaminsky, and Edith Simchi-Levi, *Designing and Managing the Supply Chain: Concepts, Strategies, and Case Studies,* New York: Irwin/McGraw-Hill, 2000, p. 235.

some companies to rethink the strategy. Industry giants such as Amazon.com built huge warehouses so they could maintain greater control over their inventories. Still others are outsourcing fulfillment, turning over that portion of their business to third-party fulfillment operators. Order-fulfillment operators perform third-party logistics functions as well as take customer orders and fill the order from their warehouse.

Using third-party fulfillment means losing control over fulfillment. It might also result in fulfillers substituting their standards for the company they are serving, and using the fulfiller's shipping price structure. On the other hand, an e-commerce company may not have the resources or infrastructure to do the job itself. Another alternative might be to form a strategic partnership with a bricks-and-mortar company. This can be a quick way to jump-start an e-commerce business. In any case, somewhere in the supply chain there has to be a bricks-and-mortar facility.

To facilitate e-commerce, including finding a buyer or a seller, e-marketplaces or exchanges are being created. Table 16–2 describes some mainly B2B e-exchanges. For an example of a software which can be used to set up private exchanges, see the "Ariba" reading later in this chapter.

CREATING AN EFFECTIVE SUPPLY CHAIN

Creating an effective supply chain requires linking the market, distribution channel, production, and suppliers. It should enable all participants in the chain to achieve significant gains, hence giving them an incentive to cooperate.

Keys to Effective Supply Chains

Successful supply chain management requires integration of all aspects of the supply chain: suppliers, warehouses, factories, distributors, and retail outlets. This requires cooperation among supply chain partners in planning, coordination of activities, and information sharing, which, in turn, requires partners to agree on common goals. Trust and a willingness to cooperate are necessary to achieve the common goals. Coordination and information sharing are critical to the effective operation of a supply chain.

TABLE 16-2	Type	Description	Web site
Examples of e-exchanges	**Buyer-initiated exchanges**		
	CareNet Services Inc.	Has over 260 hospitals using EDI for ordering and receiving invoices from more than 100 healthcare vendors.	www.carenet.ca
	Covisint	Set up by the Big Three automobile manufacturers for buying and selling auto parts, and using auctions.	www.covisint.com
	Quadrem	Set up by 14 large mining companies to facilitate their purchasing transactions.	www.quadrem.com
	Global Net Xchange	Set up by Sears and France's Carrefour for retailers	www.gnx.com
	Avendra	Set up by Marriott and Hyatt; buys for about 2,800 hotels	www.avendra.com
	Seller-initiated exchanges		
	Global Healthcare Exchange	Set up by a few large pharmaceutical and medical/surgical equipment suppliers.	www.ghx.com
	Transora	Set up by few large manufacturers of consumer packaged goods.	www.transora.com
	Bank-sponsored exchange		
	TD Online Mart	TD Bank's small-business storefront; it provides a safe marketplace for a variety of products.	www.onlinemart.ca

READING

PBB Global Logistics

www.pbb.com

PBB Global Logistics is a third-party logistics provider. It provides warehousing services to customers (e.g., a manufacturer) in addition to distribution. It also offers e-fulfillment, which consists of Internet-based order taking and need-fulfillment of customers and/or the customer's customers. One of PBB's customers is Calgary-based Sanmina Canada, an electronics contract manufacturer. Sanmina has a limited space for storage (it has only a total of 6,750 square metres in floor space), so the company hired PBB to store its inventory and manage it. PBB uses a 9,290 square metre facility in Calgary dedicated almost entirely to Sanmina. Both parts and finished goods are stored there. Sanmina, using the Internet, is able to place an order with PBB destined to one of its customers, and track shipments and inventories in PBB's warehouse. PBB is able to ship fast; for example, shipments to the Nortel plant in Calgary, Sanmina's biggest customer, can reach Nortel by shuttle trailers in four hours. Raw material shipments to Sanmina from the PBB warehouse are also fast. One of the features of the system is that each morning a report of the previous day's incoming and outgoing shipments is provided by PBB to Sanmina's logistics coordinator. PBB's e-fulfillment system also offers a secure Web-based store-front service for any e-tailer in the business-to-customer environment.

Source: C. McLean, "A Window into the Warehouse: E-fulfillment System Streamlines Ordering, Inventory Management," *PurchasingB2B*, July/August 2001, p. 26.

Information exchange must be reciprocal: Partners share forecasts and sales data, as well as information on inventory quantities, impending shortages, breakdowns, delays, quality problems, and other problems that could impact the timely flow of products and services through the chain. Thus, instead of each organization in a supply chain making plans based on a combination of actual orders plus forecasts of demand of its immediate customer, by sharing data on end-customer sales and production/inventory on a real-time basis each organization in the chain can develop plans that contribute to synchronization across the chain.

This cooperation requires forming *strategic partnerships*. **Strategic partnering** occurs when two or more business organizations agree to collaborate so that each may realize a strategic benefit. A simple example occurs when a supplier agrees to hold inventory for a customer, thereby reducing the customer's cost of holding the inventory in exchange for the customer agreeing to a long-term commitment, thereby relieving the supplier of the costs that would be needed to continually find new customers, negotiate prices and services, and so on. It is important that the number of partners in a supply chain be small and the number of chains a company belongs to be limited so that working relationships and trust can be established.

strategic partnering Two or more business organizations collaborate so that each may realize a strategic benefit.

Collaborative Planning, Forecasting, and Replenishment (CPFR)

CPFR is the latest effort to increase the effectiveness and efficiency of supply chains. It moves quick response one step further by establishing a process for communicating and agreeing on forecasts and plans between the manufacturer and the customer (the distributor). The two parties exchange data and written comments electronically—for example, they communicate the reasons for their forecast or reasons for disagreeing with the partner's forecast. Some companies such as Wal-Mart, HP, Procter & Gamble, Kimberly-Clark, and Nabisco are currently involved in pilot tests of CPFR.[2]

Below is a summary of the implementation guideline prepared by the Voluntary Inter-Industry Commerce Standards Association (VICS):[3]

CPFR An effort to increase the effectiveness and efficiency of supply chains by establishing a process for communicating and agreeing on forecasts between the manufacturer and the customer (distributor).

- Planning
  - Decide which product category to collaborate on, the objectives, resources, information sharing, forecast horizon, promotions, minimum order size, lead time, review period.

[2]Sources: J. W. Verity, "Clearing the Cobwebs from Stockroom," *Business Week*, October 21, 1996, pp. 140ff; www.vics.org/committees/cpfr.

[3]www.vics.org/committees/cpfr/voluntary_v2/CPFR_Tabs_061802.pdf.

- Forecasting
  - Buyer collects POS data, forecasts sales, shares with supplier (including promotion plans).
  - Supplier compares with capacity. Any significant shortage?
  - Supplier tries to resolve the difference; may contact buyer
  - Buyer/supplier jointly create order forecasts (taking inventory into account).
- Replenish
  - Buyer generates order for next week.
  - Supplier issues acknowledgement; executes delivery.

For two applications, see the "Whirlpool" and "Canadian Tire" readings.

Performance Metrics

The following performance drivers may represent the goals and measure performance of a supply chain:

1. Quality.
2. Cost (Supply chain management costs, warrantee costs).
3. Flexibility (production and product changes).
4. Velocity (response time, lead time).
5. Customer service (fill rate, on-time delivery).

Quality, cost, flexibility, and customer service are perhaps obvious. Velocity refers to the rate or speed of travel through the system. Velocity is important in two areas: materials and information. **Inventory velocity** refers to the rate at which inventory (material) goes through the system. Faster is better: The quicker materials pass through the supply chain, the lower inventory costs will be, and the quicker products and services will be delivered to the customer. **Information velocity** refers to the speed at which information is transferred within a supply chain. Again, faster is better: the quicker information is transmitted, the faster the actions in the supply chain.

inventory velocity The rate at which inventory (material) goes through the supply chain.

information velocity The rate at which information is communicated in a supply chain.

Challenges

Barriers to Integration of Separate Organizations. Organizations, and their functional areas, have traditionally had an inward focus. They set up buffers between them and their suppliers. Changing that attitude can be difficult.

Another barrier is that different components of the supply chain often have conflicting objectives. For example, to reduce their inventory holding costs, some companies opt for frequent small receipts of supplies. This can result in increased holding costs for suppliers, so the cost is merely transferred to suppliers. Similarly, within an organization functional areas often make decisions with a narrow focus, doing things that "optimize" results under their control; in so doing, however, they may suboptimize results for the overall organization. To be effective, organizations must adopt a *systems approach* to both the internal and external portions of their supply chains, being careful to make decisions that are consistent with optimizing the supply chain.

Another difficulty is that for supply chain management to be successful, organizations in the chain must allow other organizations access to their data. There is a natural reluctance to do this in many cases. One reason can be lack of trust, especially over cost information; another can be unwillingness to share proprietary information, especially when the partner is also a member of another chain which contains competitors.

READING

Whirlpool's CPFR

In 2002 Whirlpool's Logistics Department was reorganized into the Supply Chain Department so that it could improve its customer service performance. As part of that, Whirlpool tested CPFR with two of its major customers (retail chains). Even though there was informal collaboration before, the lack of a shared-files database and a predetermined collaboration schedule (specific hourly and daily plan in a weekly cycle) meant that the process of forecast reconciliation was not effective. After getting internal and external buy in, the project manager formed two separate CPFR teams, one for each customer, and prepared a training manual on CPFR.

The teams included Whirlpool's demand managers dealing with each customer, some production planners, deployment planners (responsible for inventory levels in Whirlpool's regional distribution centres), and marketing forecast managers (who generated top-down forecasts based on industry trends and market shares). The customers each also formed a team including Inventory Managers/Planners, Buyers, and Information System staff. One team chose i2 Technologies' Supply Chain Collaborator (now called Collaborative Supply Execution), while the other used another software which was used by the customer with another supplier.

The CPFR process actually affected Whirlpool's internal forecasting and planning process. Instead of monthly sales and operations planning, Whirlpool executives review the weekly forecast generated jointly with the customer. Sales and Marketing are alerted with short-supply and excess-supply SKUs in order to shape the demand.

After only a few months, the forecast inaccuracy has significantly decreased (MAPE for SKUs at store-level have decreased from an average of 69 percent to 44 percent) and the order quantities and units shipped are closer together and to the store sales (see Figure 1 below). Also, CPFR has given better understanding of Whirlpool-customer problems. The improvement process continues.

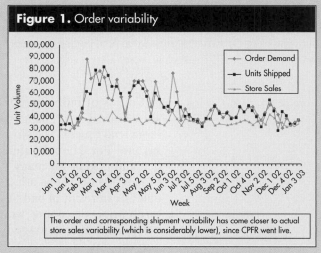

Figure 1. Order variability

The order and corresponding shipment variability has come closer to actual store sales variability (which is considerably lower), since CPFR went live.

Figure reprinted with the permission of the Institute of Business Forecasting.

Source: N. Sagar, "CPFR at Whirlpool Corporation: Two Heads and an Exception Engine," *Journal of Business Forecasting Methods & Systems* 22(4), Winter 2003/2004, pp. 3–10.

Dealing with Trade-offs.[4] A number of trade-offs must be taken into account in a supply chain:

1. *Lot size–inventory trade-off.* Ordering large lot sizes yields benefits in terms of quantity discounts and lower annual ordering cost, but it increases the holding cost of the ordering company and the amount of safety stock carried by the supplier and, hence, its holding and production costs. It also can contribute to what is known as the *bullwhip effect*. On the other hand, ordering very small lots results in higher prices, higher ordering cost, and a jammed receiving department.

Bullwhip effect or demand amplification is the phenomenon in supply chains in which the demand variability increases for companies upstream in the supply chain, i.e., while the demand at a retail store for a particular product is fairly stable, the demand at the wholesaler/distribution centre (DC) is more variable, containing large spikes and wave-like patterns (called *rogue seasonality*). These variations are even more magnified at the manufacturer. Clearly, bullwhip effect causes inefficiencies at the manufacturer and DC, such as excess inventory holding cost and overtime, and leads to lower customer service.

bullwhip effect Demand variability is progressively larger moving backward through a supply chain.

---

[4]Hau L. Lee and C. Billington, "Managing Supply Chain Inventory: Pitfalls and Opportunities," *Sloan Management Review*, Spring 1992, pp. 65–73.

READING

Canadian Tire's CPFR

When Canadian Tire (CT) wanted to improve its supply chain in 1996, one of the actions it took was to turn to Manugistics Inc of Rockville, Maryland. (The other action was to build a distribution centre in Montreal and another in Calgary to supplement its two Toronto distribution centres). Manugistics software allowed CT to forecast the demand for its approximately 100,000 SKUs for the next 26 weeks and send it to its major suppliers through (one-way) EDI lines. The following year, CT used the software to plan its transportation

requirements. Finally, in 2000 CT decided to use the CPFR module to be able to communicate with its major suppliers, reach consensus, get a commitment, and discuss promotions and seasonal products. The communication takes place in Manugistics hosted solutions, a trading network. Manugistics is used by several major retailers. CT's inventory turns have doubled since 1997 while sales have almost gone up by 30 percent.

Sources: P. Sinnott, "Canadian Tire's Engine for Growth," *Optimize*, March 2005, pp. 62–65; www.manu.com/news/press_detail.aspx?id=14.

Causes of bullwhip effect range from using large order quantities downstream to slow reactions to changes in demand upstream (due to lack of demand visibility and large lead times). The slow reactions can be part of the demand forecasting/production system. For example, time series methods have a lag and the effect of one jump in demand is kept for many future periods (this is called the *feed-forward effect*). Also, production decisions are effected by inventory on hand, which together with lead time delays can result in bad timing (called the *feedback effect*). Other causes are manufacturer price discounts which lead to surges in demand, and gaming by retailers when there is a shortage by inflating their orders in anticipation of receiving only a portion of it.

The solutions to bullwhip effect include sharing customer POS information upstream in the supply chain such as is done in JIT systems, quick response, vender managed inventory, and CPFR systems. These also reduce lead times. The solution to surges in demand as a result of price discounts is to not use discounts, as is done in the everyday low-pricing policy used by Wal-Mart and Loblaw. The solution to gaming in shortage situations is to base allocation decisions on past demand.

Figure 16–3 shows the orders received at a Distribution Centre (DC) from retailers and the orders placed by the DC to the manufacturer for a prepared salad meal in Europe. It can be observed that while the demand for salads is fairly stable, the orders placed to the manufacturer have a wave-like cycle of one week and there is some demand amplification.

FIGURE 16-3

Orders Placed and Orders Received at a Distribution Centre

Figure reprinted with the permission of Emerald Group Publishing Limited.

Sources: P. McCullen and D. Towill, "Diagnosis and Reduction of Bullwhip in Supply Chains," *Supply Chain Management* 7(3/4), 2002, pp. 164–179; J. C. Fransoo and M. J. F. Wouters, "Measuring the Bullwhip Effect in the Supply Chain," *Supply Chain Management* 5(2), 2000, pp. 78–89.

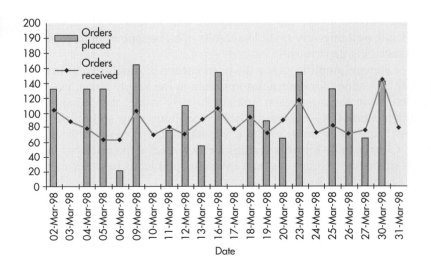

2. *Inventory/lead time–transportation cost trade-off.* Similarly, it is cheaper to ship full truckloads instead of partial loads in order to spread fixed transport costs over as many units as possible. However, this leads to higher holding costs and increased lead times. Solutions include downsizing truck capacity and *cross-docking.* **Cross-docking** is a technique whereby goods arriving at a warehouse from a supplier are unloaded from the supplier's truck and loaded on one or more outbound trucks to major retailers or other warehouses, thereby avoiding storage at the warehouse. Wal-Mart initiated this technique to reduce inventory holding costs and to reduce lead times, while minimizing transport cost.

3. *Product variety–lot size trade-off.* Higher product variety generally means smaller lot sizes, which results in higher setup costs as well as higher transportation and ordering costs. One possible means of reducing some costs is **delayed differentiation** or **postponement**, which means producing standard components and products, then waiting until late in the process to add differentiating features. For example, in the paint industry manufacturers send white base paint to retail stores, where a small quantity of colour paint is mixed into white to get the customer desired colours. Another example is in making products for global markets: standard base units are made-to-stock, such as disk drives, and then localized for each market as demand arises.

cross-docking Goods arriving at a warehouse from a supplier are directly loaded onto outbound trucks, thereby avoiding warehouse storage.

delayed differentiation Production of standard components and products, and waiting until late in the process to add differentiating features. Also called **postponement**.

Variability and Uncertainty. In addition to demand, timing and quantity of incoming shipments from suppliers and internal operations are subject to variability and uncertainty. Increases in product and service variety also add to this problem. Unfortunately, variability and uncertainty are detrimental to scheduling, leading to various undesirable occurrences including inventory buildups (safety stocks), delays, missed delivery dates, and frustration for employees and customers at all stages of a supply chain. Solutions include shorter lead times, process variability reduction as in continuous improvement and six sigma, process control, EDI, closer suppliers, good communication, and reduced product variety.

PURCHASING

Purchasing is responsible for obtaining the raw materials, parts, supplies, machines and equipment, and services needed to produce a product or provide a service. You can get some idea of the importance of purchasing when you consider that in manufacturing most of the cost of finished goods comes from purchased parts and materials. Furthermore, all goods sold by retail and wholesale companies have to be purchased first. Nonetheless, the importance of purchasing is more than just the cost of goods purchased; other important

READING

L'eBiz

L'eBiz is a supply chain collaboration software by Toronto's QLogitek, which also provides hosting (private trading exchange) service. L'eBiz uses Microsoft's BizTalk software which allows a company to communicate with its suppliers over the Internet, instead of using EDI on a dedicated value-added network (VAN).

One company that uses L'eBiz is HMV. L'eBiz allows HMV's approximately 100 stores to send purchase orders to and receive invoices from its small suppliers (the larger suppliers and all the stores are connected using a VAN and

EDI). Use of L'eBiz has reduced the purchasing/accounts payable staffing needs of HMV by 75 percent.

Another company that uses L'eBiz is Hudson's Bay Company (HBC), where it is used to receive advance shipping notices and invoices from small suppliers. Before L'eBiz, HBC had 57 receiving schedulers in its seven distribution centres making appointments for approximately 3,000 weekly deliveries with 2,000 suppliers and 100 common carriers using phone/fax/e-mail. The L'eBiz has made three-quarters of the schedulers redundant.

Sources: G. Hilson, "Harmonious Supply Chain," *Computing Canada* 28, January 18, 2002, p. 19; www.qlogitek.com/files/HMV%20Case%20Study.pdf; www.qlogitek.com/files/ims_brochure.pdf; www.qlogitek.com/files/L'eBIZ%20FAQ%20-%20Zellers%20Zoom.doc.

factors include the *quality* of goods and services and *timing* of deliveries of goods or services, both of which can have a significant impact on operations. Also, purchasing plays the central role in forming partnerships.

The basic goal of purchasing is to develop and implement purchasing plans for products and services that support operations strategies. Among the duties of purchasing are identifying sources of supply, negotiating contracts, maintaining a database of suppliers, obtaining goods and services that meet operations requirements in a timely and cost-efficient manner, managing suppliers, establishing partnerships, and acting as liaison between suppliers and various internal departments.

Purchasing is taking on increased importance as organizations place greater emphasis on supply chain management, quality improvement, just-in-time, and outsourcing. It is also changing strategically. See the reading, "Examples of Strategic Changes to the Purchasing Function."

Purchasing's Interfaces

Purchasing interfaces with a number of other functional areas, as well as with outside suppliers. Purchasing is the connecting link between the organization and its suppliers. In this capacity, it exchanges information with suppliers and with functional areas.

Operations constitute the main source of requests for purchased materials (manufacturing parts and operating supplies), and close cooperation between these units and the purchasing department is vital if quality, quantity, and delivery goals are to be met. Cancellations, changes in specifications, or changes in quantity or delivery times must be communicated to the other side, the requisitioner or supplier, immediately. Another user of purchasing services is the *maintenance* department, which requires spare parts and repair supplies. New machines and equipment are also needed.

The purchasing department may require the assistance of the *legal* department in interpreting regulations, writing up contracts, and providing advice in case of a dispute.

READING

Nygard

Nygard International is the largest ladies wear manufacturer in Canada (revenues of $300 million). Its main manufacturing facilities are in Winnipeg, California, and Mexico. The founder, Peter J. Nygard, is considered a visionary in the apparel industry. In the early 1990s, he computerized the design and production activities in his Winnipeg facilities using CAD, CAM (computerized cutting and planning/control systems) with a computer at every work centre, and computerized receiving and shipping using bar codes and software to ensure accuracy. All the programming, equivalent to a full-blown ERP, was done in-house. By 2000, the entire operation was paperless.

In the mid-1990s, Nygard turned his attention to the supply chain. He asked his major customers, such as HBC, to let an EDI software be installed on their system so that when an item was sold at a store, this information was immediately relayed to a Nygard factory and routed to the right work centre to start production. Nygard guarantees 24-hour response time,

Peter J. Nygard, founder of Nygard International.

from the time of receiving an order to shipment. This is revolutionary in the apparel industry where the usual lead time is at least two weeks. Nygard's system also has EDI connection to its major suppliers of fabric, zipper, buttons, etc. Nygard has spent approximately $50 million on its information technology during the last two decades.

Sources: www3.nygard.com/corporate/company_profile.html.

Accounting is responsible for handling payments to suppliers. In many firms, *data processing* is handled by the accounting department, which keeps inventory records and checks invoices.

Design engineering usually prepares material/part specifications, which must be communicated to suppliers. On the other hand, because of its contacts with suppliers, purchasing is often in a position to pass information about product and material improvements on to design personnel. Also, design and purchasing people may work closely to determine whether changes in specifications, design, or materials can reduce the cost of purchased items (see the later section on value analysis).

Receiving checks incoming shipments, and material handling moves the goods to their destination (the requisitioner). Accounting must be notified when shipments are received so that payments can be made.

Marketing/sales staff sometimes needs products for resale. In this case, Purchasing and marketing should have close relations in order to satisfy the customer. In retail/wholesale, this relationship is vital. In fact in many retail/wholesale companies, the job of marketing and purchasing are combined into one job. Merchandise buyers should have a good sense of marketing in order to buy items which will be purchased by companys' customers.

Suppliers or vendors work closely with purchasing to learn what materials/parts will be purchased and their cost, quality, quantity, and deliveries. Purchasing must rate vendors on cost, quality, reliability, and so on (see the later section on choosing suppliers). Good supplier relations can be important in rush orders and changes.

Figure 16–4 summarizes purchasing's interfaces.

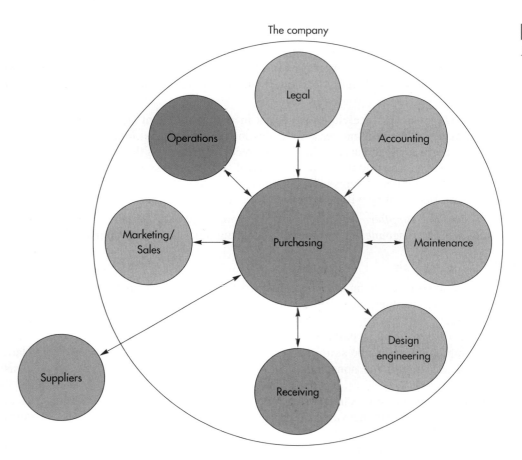

FIGURE 16–4

Purchasing's Interfaces

The Purchasing Cycle

purchasing cycle A series of steps that begins with a request for purchase and ends with paying the supplier.

The **purchasing cycle** begins with a request from within the organization to purchase material, equipment, supplies, or other items, and ends with paying the supplier. The main steps in the cycle are these:

1. *Purchasing receives the requisition.* The requisition includes (*a*) a description of the item desired, (*b*) the quantity and quality necessary, and (*c*) desired delivery dates. Having a catalogue of approved products will accelerate the purchasing cycle.

2. *Purchasing selects a supplier.* The purchasing department must identify suppliers who have the capability of supplying the desired goods. If no suppliers are currently in the files, new ones must be sought. Trade directories may be referenced. If used before, vendor ratings may be referred to in choosing among vendors. Usually potential suppliers are asked to quote a price (more on this in the following section on determining price). If the order involves a large expenditure, particularly for a one-time purchase of equipment, for example, vendors will usually be asked to put in a proposal saying how they will meet the need, and operating and design personnel will be asked to assist in the purchase.

3. *Purchasing places the order with the supplier.* Large-volume, continuously used manufacturing-parts purchases are negotiated using long-term contracts. Large-volume, continuously used supplies may be covered by blanket purchase orders, which often involve annual negotiation of prices with deliveries subject to operating units' direct request throughout the year. Many companies have an established EDI connection with some of their suppliers, which has reduced the cost and time of procurement. Moderate-volume items may also have blanket purchase orders, or they may be handled on an individual basis. Small purchases should be handled directly between the operating unit requesting a purchased item and the supplier. Using corporate credit cards simplifies paying the suppliers because there is only one bill per requisitioner per month.

4. *Monitoring orders* (and expediting). Routine follow-up on orders, especially large orders or those with lengthy lead times, allows the purchasing department to prevent delays.

5. *Receiving orders.* Receiving must check incoming shipment against purchase order, and material handling moves it to its destination (the requisitioner). Receiving must notify purchasing and accounting using a receiving report. If the quality of the incoming shipment is in doubt, the quality control staff must inspect the shipment. If there are a large number of items in the shipment, sampling should be used. If the goods are not satisfactory, they will be returned to the supplier for credit or replacement.

6. *Paying the supplier.* Accounts payable, upon receipt of shipment, must pay the invoice. If a discount is given for early payment, this should be taken advantage of.

Value Analysis

value analysis Examination of the function of purchased parts/components/products in an effort to reduce their cost.

Value analysis refers to an examination of the *function* of parts/components/products in an effort to reduce their cost. Typical questions that would be asked as part of the analysis include: Could a cheaper part or material be used? Is the function necessary? Can the function of two or more parts be performed by a single part for a lower cost? Can a part/component/product be simplified? Could specifications be relaxed? Could standard parts be substituted for nonstandard parts? Table 16–3 provides the value analysis process.

Naturally, purchasing cannot perform value analysis each time items are ordered. However, it should conduct value analysis periodically on large annual dollar-value items because of the potential savings.

Although purchasing does not ordinarily have the authority to implement changes on the basis of a value analysis, it can make suggestions to operating units and designers, which may lead to reduction of the cost of those goods. Purchasing can offer a different

1. Select an item that has a high annual dollar value. This can be a part, component, or product.
2. Identify the function of the item (in a verb–noun form, e.g., a bolt "joins things.")
3. Obtain answers to these kinds of questions:
   a. Can the function be performed in another way?
   b. Could another material or part/product be used instead?
   c. Can specifications be less stringent to save cost or time?
   d. Can two or more parts of the item be combined?
   e. Can a different process be used on the item to save cost or time?
   f. Do suppliers/providers have suggestions for improvement?
   g. Can packaging be improved or made less costly?
4. Evaluate the answers obtained, and make recommendations.

TABLE 16-3

Overview of value analysis

READING

Examples of Strategic Changes to the Purchasing Function

Hiram Walker & Sons

Fierce retail competition and taxation on spirits as high as 83 percent have caused revenue for Hiram Walker (the maker of Canadian Club whiskey) to remain static at a time when shareholders expect profits to rise by 10 percent per year. To meet this challenge, Martin Williams, the director of supply management, began restructuring his purchasing department with a strategic analysis of each purchased item to discover opportunities for savings and how to achieve them. For example, a team of purchasing staff is involved in redesigning packaging. Another team is looking at suppliers' internal costs to see where they can trim costs (this is called *cost analysis*).

At the same time, Williams led a team of purchasing managers from across the parent company (Allied Domecq PLC)'s wines and spirits division to identify the new-staff competencies that would be required. These were, they concluded, the ability to form strategic visions, to make business decisions about supply management, and to overcome barriers to change. In 1995, the department was restructured around these new requirements and skills, while traditional purchasing activities were transferred to internal users, allowing purchasing to concentrate on long-term strategic planning. Williams now reports directly to the president of Hiram Walker. Deliveries are now brought in just-in-time. The next stage will be for Hiram Walker to forecast its needs precisely for suppliers to eliminate their warehousing costs. A computer network throughout the parent company and subsidiaries worldwide enables staff to examine and compare prices for any purchased item to a level of detail not available before.

Air Canada

With pressure to reduce airfares, the prime objective of Air Canada's purchasing department is to keep cost increases below inflation. The airline's centralized material management —whose staff has been downsized by 40 percent—is organized into teams dedicated to particular products (such as the Airbus aircraft). A product manager directs purchasing specialists, inventory controllers, and material planners who are responsible for determining material requirements, purchasing the material, managing the inventory level, and ensuring the supply to internal customers. During major purchases, the team approach is widened to include the internal customers and the suppliers. This has helped overcome resistance from some users who may find their favoured suppliers being changed.

Air Canada has pursued closer relationships with fewer suppliers since the early 1990s. It reduced the number of plastic-bag vendors from 20 to 2 and reduced the number of types of bags from 65 to 23, resulting in a 40-percent cost reduction. Air Canada has used EDI within the aircraft industry for several years, but in 1995 a new purchasing and inventory management system extended EDI to other suppliers. The intention is to deal with vendors totally electronically.

Petro-Canada

When Petro-Canada became a public company in 1995, its new shareholders had expectations for profitability that added to the bottom-line pressures exerted by competition. Cost control was re-emphasized throughout the corporation and especially in purchasing, where a decentralized department was reorganized into a supply chain group that is distributed across Canada but is centrally driven.

Computer software is being installed for all the downstream businesses (i.e., from refineries to service stations) to create a single common database of purchasing and inventory control information. This will enable staff to access supplier profiles quickly and obtain other information. It will be used by people outside the supply chain to order using standing or blanket orders.

Hewlett-Packard (Canada)

Value-added is how David Lansley, the operations manager of the Mississauga, Ontario, facility describes the new role of purchasing. Once decentralized and concerned with the buying of commodity items, it's now centralized and far more concerned with assisting end users make their own purchases while developing long-term supplier relationships. Products such as furniture, automobiles, and telephone equipment are no longer sourced through competitive bidding, but are evaluated according to the added services the suppliers can offer. This doesn't necessarily mean that HP has lost the benefits of competition. Purchasing staff periodically audits its suppliers, which includes comparisons with market prices. When a vendor's performance starts to deteriorate, Hewlett-Packard works with the vendor to improve it—in the past, the company might simply have sought another vendor.

Users are encouraged to purchase their own commodities, and orders of less than $500 can be paid for by corporate credit cards. Although HP's business in Canada has doubled over the past five years, the number of purchasing people has remained the same—but the required competencies have grown considerably. Staff are trained in the company's internal facilities. Courses on purchasing are also offered, such as negotiation skills. In filling a need for a buyer recently, Lansley was looking for a university graduate with a commerce or business degree. "Ten years ago," he said, "we would not have had that expectation."

Interuniversity Services

The biggest challenge facing all universities (as well as all other public organizations) is the reduction in transfer payments from Ottawa and provincial government funding. For universities, where students are also being hit with higher tuition fees, this makes cost control of small-dollar purchases of paramount importance, said Ron MacDonald, CEO of Interuniversity Services Inc., which purchases major commodities and services for 17 Atlantic-region universities. To reduce the cost of administering purchases, organizations have started to use purchasing cards, increased the use of computers in purchasing, standardized the items they buy, and reduced the supplier base. While MacDonald recognizes the basic importance of technical purchasing skills, he has ensured his staff's capabilities have evolved to embrace strategic thinking, customer focus, and people skills.

Source: "Putting Purchasing in the Profit Picture: Senior Supply Management Executives Describe How Their Departments Play a More Strategic Role," *Modern Purchasing* 38(2), January/February 1996, pp. 18–24.

READING

Ariba

Ariba is a major purchasing and business-to-business software company producing software that costs between $1 and $4 million, created primarily for large enterprises. Ariba's software is written in computer languages (Java and XML), which makes it compatible with the Internet and different computer systems. Ariba can create a private supplier network, an exchange for a buying company used to house supplier catalogues, conduct auctions, and send and receive purchasing documents. In addition to automating basic purchasing activities (e.g., creating a requisition and purchase order, transmitting it to a supplier, and receiving and paying invoices),

Ariba's software modules assist in purchasing-data collection and analysis in order to identify major types of purchases and amount purchased from each supplier (called *visibility*), sourcing activities including conducting online auctions, and collaborative purchasing (e.g., in requisitioning) involving suppliers. Ariba also has the Ariba Supplier Network, consisting of over 120,000 suppliers in 115 countries, an exchange used primarily for small- to medium-size buyers to find and do business with suppliers.

Sources: J. Kerstetter, "How Ariba Got Airborne: Timely Acquisitions Have Made the Upstart a Leader in B2B E-commerce," *Business Week* 36, September 18, 2000, p. 126; www.ariba.com/solutions/solutions_datasheets.cfm.

perspective to the analysis, because of its association with suppliers. If a fair amount of technical knowledge is required to review a part or service, a team can be formed with representatives from design engineering, operations, and cost accounting to work with purchasing to conduct the analysis.

Make or Buy

Business organizations do not typically own all of the resources or provide all of the parts necessary to produce a product or service: that would be prohibitively expensive. There are other organizations that focus on a particular portion of the process or product.

READING

Challenger 300

The Challenger 300 business jet is the result of a partnership between Bombardier, Mitsubishi, and Taichung, the three main structural manufacturers. Each company makes a piece of the plane, which is then assembled in just four days in Bombardier's Dorval facility in Quebec. Mitsubishi makes the wings; Taichung makes the tail. The mid-fuselage is made at the Belfast site of Bombardier and the front is made at the Montreal site. The engines are made by Honeywell, the avionics by Rockwell Collins, and there are another 30 suppliers of the interior equipment. The Challenger 300 is a super midsize business jet which seats 8–9 people. Normally, small planes are made by one facility. However, Bombardier wanted to integrate the operations of its different facilities—most were bought in the late 1980s as different companies: the Montreal site was Canadair, the Belfast branch site was Short Brothers, and the Kansas City site is Learjet. The reason for outsourcing parts of the plane to Japanese and Taiwanese companies was that they agreed to incur the development cost.

Sources: www.bombardier.com/en/3_0/3_2/pdf/challenger_300_fact sheet.pdf; P. Siekman, "The Snap-Together Business Jet," *Fortune* 145(2), January 21, 2002, pp. 104Aff.

Challenger 300.

Some companies do little outsourcing, preferring to do almost everything themselves, whereas others engage in extensive outsourcing. For example, some personal computer companies buy most or all of the parts from suppliers and merely assemble the computers. Services can also be outsourced, and it is not unusual for companies to outsource data processing, payroll and benefits, maintenance, field service and repair, food services, security, legal, and accounting.

Companies may outsource for a variety of reasons. Chief among them is the ability of the outside source to provide better materials, parts, or services more cheaply. For example, a large supplier of a certain part or service can—because of economies of scale—provide the part or service at a lower cost than the buying company can achieve. Expertise and knowledge are other key reasons for outsourcing. Or a supplier may hold a patent on a necessary part. Using outsourcing gives a company added flexibility. Or the demand may be temporary or seasonal. Or the company may not have idle capacity. Outsourcing often increases when companies downsize, as they narrow their focus to core activities and subcontract the other activities. See the reading, "Challenger 300," for yet a different reason.

Outsourcing carries risks as well as benefits. Among the risks are loss of control, greater dependency on suppliers, and loss of the expertise to make or perform it in-house. Strategic considerations may outweigh other factors in some instances. Should the knowledge of how to make the part be developed in-house? Are there adequate suppliers available in the long run? In some cases, a firm might choose to make a portion of the quantity needed itself and let a supplier handle the rest in order to maintain expertise, flexibility, and hedge against loss of a supplier. Moreover, this provides a bargaining tool in negotiations with the supplier.

The following simple example illustrates how one might compare the costs of make versus buy.

Example 2

Analyze the following data to determine the total annual cost of making and of buying.

	Make	**Buy**
Expected annual volume	20,000 units	20,000 units
Variable cost per unit	$5.00	$6.00
Annual fixed costs	$30,000	

Solution

Total annual cost = Fixed cost + Variable cost per unit $\times$ Estimated annual volume

Make: $30,000 + $5 \times 20,000 = $130,000

Buy: $0 + $6 \times 20,000 = $120,000

In this instance, buying would save $10,000 a year. This information should be combined with information on other relevant factors to decide which alternative would be better.

Determining Prices

Organizations typically determine prices in one of three ways: published price lists, competitive bidding, and negotiation.

In many instances, organizations buy products and services that have fixed or *predetermined prices*. This is generally the case for standard items that are bought infrequently and/or in small quantities.

For large orders of standard products and services, getting quotes or *competitive bidding* are common. The purchasing department calls (in the informal version) or sends written requests (in the formal version) for bids to potential suppliers, asking vendors to quote a price for a specified quantity and quality of items or for a specified service to be performed. Large government purchases of goods or services are usually made through formal competitive bidding. Usually, the lowest quote or bid wins the contract. Large orders usually receive price breaks (called quantity discounts).

Negotiated purchasing is used for special purchasing situations—when specifications are vague, when one or a few customized products or services are involved (e.g., building a new all-purpose military jet), and when few potential sources exist. Several myths concerning negotiated purchasing should be recognized:

1. Negotiation is a win–lose confrontation.
2. The main goal is to obtain the lowest possible price.
3. Each negotiation is an isolated transaction.

No one likes to be taken advantage of. Furthermore, contractors and suppliers need a reasonable profit to survive. Therefore, a take-it-or-leave-it approach or one that capitalizes on the weaknesses of the other party will serve no useful purpose and may have detrimental effects that surface later. The most reasonable approach is one of give and take, with each side giving and receiving some concessions.

Centralized versus Decentralized Purchasing

Purchasing can be centralized or decentralized. Centralized purchasing means that purchasing is handled by the purchasing department. Decentralized purchasing means that individual departments or separate locations handle their own purchasing requirements.

centralized purchasing
Purchasing is handled by the purchasing department.

Centralized purchasing may be able to obtain lower prices than decentralized units if the higher volume created by combining orders enables it to take advantage of quantity discounts offered on large orders. Centralized purchasing may also be able to obtain

Supply Chain Medicine

www.chr.ab.ca

When Chinook Health Region around Lethbridge, Alberta, centralized the purchasing and inventory warehousing functions of its 10 facilities in one location in the late 1990s, inventory was reduced by half and the number of purchasing staff was reduced, which reduced the materials management's budget by 20 percent. The centralization permitted the smaller rural hospitals to take advantage of quantity discount buying, up to five to six times cheaper! Among the items centralized were medical supplies, laundry services, and sterilization of surgical equipment.

Source: L. Young, "Finding the Right Supply Chain Medicine," *Data Capture Communications & Commerce*, April 1999, pp. DC9–DC10.

Mountain Equipment Co-op

Mountain Equipment Co-op (MEC) was established in 1971 by a small group of outdoor enthusiasts in Vancouver who wanted to have quality outdoor equipment available for sale in Canada. MEC now has stores in 10 Canadian cities and two million members. MEC designs and manufactures approximately 60 percent of the items it sells. Other items are purchased from manufacturers. MEC has a strong ethical sourcing policy which requires suppliers to have respect for the environment and the health/safety/dignity of their workers. It requires that a supplier not employ children under 15 or forced labour such as prisoners. The supplier should not abuse its workers, prevent unions, force its workers to work more than 48 hours regular-time and 12 hours overtime per week. Workers should have at least one in seven days off and should be paid fairly. There should be no discrimination or harassment. New potential suppliers and current suppliers (annually) get audited by an MEC team or external auditors. This entails a one-day visit and a 200-question survey.

Sources: www.mec.ca, ABOUT MEC, sustainability, Sourcing and Factory Conditions. R. Shaw, "Peak Performance [Mountain Equipment Co-op]," *Alternatives Journal* 31(1), January/February 2005, p. 19.

better service and closer attention from suppliers. In addition, centralized purchasing often enables companies to assign certain categories of items to specialists, who tend to be more efficient because they are able to concentrate their efforts on relatively few items instead of spreading themselves across many items. See the reading, "Supply Chain Medicine."

Decentralized purchasing has the advantage of awareness of differing "local" needs and being better able to respond to those needs. Decentralized purchasing usually can offer quicker response than centralized purchasing. Where locations are widely scattered, decentralized purchasing may be able to save on transportation costs by buying locally, which has the added attraction of creating goodwill in the community.

decentralized purchasing
Individual departments or separate locations handle their own purchasing requirements.

Some organizations manage to take advantage of both centralization and decentralization by permitting individual units to handle certain items while centralizing purchases of other items. For example, small orders and rush orders may be handled locally or by departments, while centralized purchases would be used for high-volume, high-value items for which discounts are applicable.

Ethics in Purchasing

Ethical behaviour is important in all aspects of business. This is certainly true in purchasing, where the temptations for unethical behaviour can be enormous. Buyers often hold great power, and salespeople are often eager to make a sale. Unless both parties act in an ethical manner, the potential for abuse is very real. Furthermore, with increased globalization, the challenges are particularly great because a behaviour regarded as customary in one country might be regarded as unethical in another country.

TABLE 16-4

Norms of ethical behaviour and code of conduct in purchasing

1. To consider first the interests of one's organization in all transactions and to carry out and believe in its established policies.
2. To be receptive to competent counsel from one's colleagues and to be guided by such counsel without impairing the responsibility of one's office.
3. To buy without prejudice, seeking to obtain the maximum value for each dollar of expenditure.
4. To strive for increased knowledge of the materials and processes of manufacture, and to establish practical procedures for the performance of one's responsibilities.
5. To participate in professional development programs so that one's purchasing knowledge and performance are enhanced.
6. To subscribe to and work for honesty in buying and selling, and to denounce all forms of improper business practice.
7. To accord a prompt and courteous reception to all who call on a legitimate business mission.
8. To abide by and to encourage others to practise the Professional Code of Ethics of the Purchasing Management Association of Canada and its affiliated institutes and corporation.
9. To counsel and assist fellow purchasers in the performance of their duties.
10. To cooperate with all organizations and individuals engaged in activities that enhance the development and standing of purchasing and materials management.

Source: Adapted from Purchasing Management Association of Canada—Manitoba Institute, www.mipmac.com/profile/ethics.html.

The Purchasing Management Association of Canada has established a set of guidelines for ethical behaviour and code of conduct. (See Table 16–4.) As you read through the list, you get insight into the scope of ethical issues in purchasing. A company known for its ethical purchasing is Mountain Equipment Co-op (see the reading on the preceding page).

SUPPLIER MANAGEMENT

Reliable and trustworthy suppliers are a vital link in an effective supply chain. Timely deliveries of goods or services and high quality are just two of the ways that suppliers can contribute to effective operations. A buyer may function as an "external operations manager," working with suppliers to coordinate the supplier operations and buyer needs.

In this section, various aspects of supplier management are described, including choosing suppliers, supplier audits, supplier certification, supplier relations, and supplier partnerships.

Choosing Suppliers

In many respects, choosing a supplier involves taking into account many of the same factors associated with making a major purchase (e.g., a car or stereo system). A person considers price, quality, availability of product or timely delivery, the supplier's capability and reputation, past experience with the supplier, and service after the sale. The main difference is that a company, because of the quantities it orders and production requirements, often provides suppliers with quantities, delivery dates, and detailed specifications of the materials or parts it wants instead of buying items off the shelf. Also, the items are usually delivered to the buyer's location later, and the invoice can be paid a few weeks later. The main factors a company takes into account when it selects a supplier and typical questions to ask are outlined in Table 16–5.

supplier analysis Evaluating the source of supply in terms of factors such as price, quality, delivery, and service.

Because different factors are important for different situations, purchasing must decide, with the help of the requisitioner, the importance of each factor (i.e., how much weight to give to each factor), and then rate potential suppliers according to how well they can be expected to perform against this list. This process is called **supplier analysis**.

Factor	Typical Questions
Quality and quality assurance	Is the supplier technically capable to achieve the desired quality? What procedures does the supplier have for quality control and quality assurance?
Flexibility	How flexible is the supplier in handling changes in delivery schedules, quantity, and product or service?
Location	Is the supplier nearby?
Price	Are prices reasonable given the entire package the supplier will provide? Is the supplier willing to cooperate to reduce costs?
Reputation and financial stability	If used previously, how was the supplier's performance? What is the reputation of the supplier? Is the supplier financially stable?
Lead times and on-time delivery	What lead times can the supplier provide? What policies does the supplier have for keeping items in stock? Is the supplier reliable?
Other accounts	Is the supplier heavily dependent on other customers, causing a risk of giving priority to those needs over ours?
Service after sale	How much after-sale support does the supplier provide?

TABLE 16-5

Choosing a supplier

Supplier Audits

Periodic audits of major suppliers are a means of keeping current on suppliers' production (or service) capabilities, quality and delivery problems and resolutions, and suppliers' performance on other criteria. If an audit reveals problem areas, a buyer can attempt to find a solution before more serious problems develop. Supplier audits are also an important first step in supplier certification programs.

Supplier Certification

Supplier certification is a detailed examination of the policies, capabilities, and performance of a supplier. The certification process verifies that a supplier meets or exceeds the requirements of a buyer. This is particularly important when buyers are seeking to establish a long-term relationship with suppliers. One advantage of using certified suppliers is that the buyer can eliminate much or all of the inspection and testing of delivered goods.

Rather than develop their own certification program, some companies rely on standard industry certifications such as ISO 9000, perhaps the most widely used international certification.

Supplier Relations

Purchasing has the ultimate responsibility for establishing and maintaining good supplier relations. The type of relationship is often related to the length of a contract between buyers and sellers. In short-term contracts, suppliers are kept at arm's length and the relationship is minimal. Medium-term contracts often involve ongoing relationships. Long-term contracts may evolve into partnerships, with buyers and sellers cooperating on various *strategic* issues that tend to benefit both parties.

North American companies have become increasingly aware of the importance of building good relations with their suppliers. In the past, too many companies regarded their suppliers as adversaries and dealt with them on that basis. One lesson learned from the Japanese is that numerous benefits derive from good supplier relations, including supplier flexibility in terms of accepting changes in delivery schedules, quality, and

Grand & Toy

Grand & Toy Company provides office supplies, paper, furniture, and computer supplies to Canadian companies. It carries approximately 6,000 stock-keeping units in its eight regional distribution centres. It also has 75 retail locations and 21 sales offices. The new Toronto distribution centre, 230,000 square feet, has state-of-the-art automated carousels and sorting capability using bar codes, controlled by a warehouse management system (WMS) software. Grand & Toy provides EDI service to its customers, using its own wide area network, IBM AS/400 computer, and ERP software. Now, it also allows its customers to order over the Internet (using its OrderPoint system), where they can use Grand & Toy's electronic catalogue. For example, Nova Corp. of Calgary, the natural gas producer, buys its stationery from Grand & Toy over the Internet. Grand & Toy also keeps records of customer purchase quantities and allows them to access this data, in effect providing inventory record-keeping

for its customers. Grand & Toy provides next-day delivery in major cities, and has an in-stock rate of 98 percent. Grand & Toy also helps organizations develop EDI connection with their other suppliers. For example, the University of Calgary is now connected to 25 of its largest suppliers using Grand & Toy's EDI network, which also provides a Web-based catalogue for the university buyers who now buy 50 to 60 percent of their purchases using it. In 1996, Grand & Toy was purchased by Boise Cascade, the large U.S. office supplies distributor and paper/lumber producer. This development provides Grand & Toy with paper and preferred pricing on its other purchases.

Sources: "Gearing up for Full Value: Grand & Toy's Value-added Supply Chain Solution," *Modern Purchasing*, 41(8), July/August 1999, pp. S1–S28; "Grand & Toy: Your Partner in the Supply Chain," *Modern Purchasing* 41(2), January/February 1999, pp. S1–S34; "Grand & Toy: A Boise Cascade Office Products Company," *Modern Purchasing* 38(8), July/August 1996, pp. S1–S18; and T. Venetis, "Office Supplies Online: Internet Ordering Cuts Time, Paperwork," *PurchasingB2B*, September 2000, p. 43ff.

quantities. Moreover, suppliers can often help identify improvements in the design of an item purchased from them or suggest better substitutes (i.e., value analysis). In fact, they can be involved in the design of new products (called *early supplier involvement*). Thus, simply choosing and switching suppliers on the basis of price is a very shortsighted approach to handling an ongoing need.

Many Japanese companies rely on one or two suppliers to handle their needs for a group of items. In contrast, many U.S. firms deal with numerous suppliers. Perhaps they want to remain flexible, and possibly there are advantages in playing off one against the others. The advantages of single-sourcing include lower numbers of orders, deliveries, and invoices, and being able to work with the supplier to reduce lead time, for example. However, North American companies are moving in the direction of reducing the number of suppliers.

Supplier Partnerships

More and more business organizations are seeking to establish partnerships with their suppliers. This implies fewer suppliers, longer-term relationships, sharing of information (forecasts, sales data, replenishments, problem alerts), and cooperation in planning. Assistance from suppliers could:[5]

1. Reduce the cost of making a purchase.
2. Reduce transportation costs.
3. Reduce production costs.
4. Improve product quality.
5. Improve product design.
6. Reduce time to market.

---

[5]Jim Morgan, "Nine Ways Suppliers Can Improve Competitiveness," *Purchasing*, November 24, 1994, pp. 7–9.

READING

St. Mary's Hospital

Purchasing function can provide cost savings and improved services for an organization. When St. Mary's Hospital Centre of McGill University wanted to save costs, it got into a five-year contract to buy all its intravenous (IV) products requirements from Baxter Corp. Even before the contract, Baxter was the major supplier of IVs to the hospital for many years. As part of the partnership, Baxter provided a nurse who communicated with the hospital nurses in order to find suitable substitutes for the non-Baxter-supplied IVs. The standardization process took approximately four months.

Sources: www.smhc.qc.ca/english1/About/about-en.htm; M. S. Kamel, "Montreal Hospital Gets Shot in the Arm," *Summit* 3(4), December 2000, pp. 42–43.

7. Improve customer satisfaction.

8. Reduce inventory costs.

9. Introduce new products or services.

The organizations that stand the best chance of tapping into these ideas are those that have good supplier relations and are genuinely open to supplier input. Supplier partnerships are required for JIT relationships and initiatives such as quick response and CPFR. For examples of partnership, see the readings, "Grand & Toy" and "St. Mary's Hospital."

SUMMARY

A supply chain consists of all the organizations, facilities, and activities involved in producing and delivering a product or service, from the initial suppliers to the final customer. Supply chain management is designing, planning, coordinating, and controlling the supply chain.

Supply chain management represents a shift in focus for many business organizations. Until recently companies tended to focus mainly on their own operations as they attempted to cut costs, improve quality, and meet delivery schedules. But because effective supply chain management offers the benefits of lower operating costs, reduced inventories, better product availability, and customer satisfaction, more and more companies are using supply chains to meet their objectives.

Problems in supply chain management can be classified into strategic (e.g., partnering, network design), and tactical/operational (e.g., production planning and control, replenishment).

Logistics involves the movement of goods, material, and information in a supply chain. This includes incoming materials, movement within a facility, and outgoing goods. A major operational decision in supply chain management is to determine the shipping mode: the faster mode results in higher shipping cost, but the slower mode results in higher inventory holding cost.

Retailers/wholesalers and manufacturers have initiated quick (JIT) replenishment systems with their supplier partners under the names of *quick response* and *efficient consumer response*. Electronic data interchange is being increasingly used for purchasing, order confirmation and payment, and arranging shipment.

The explosion of e-commerce has introduced tremendous opportunities, and it underscores the importance of effective supply chain management.

The key to an effective supply chain is to link companies and share information. Collaborative planning, forecasting, and replenishment (CPFR) is a new initiative that links planning, forecasting, and replenishment activities of the company and its major suppliers.

One of the objectives of supply chain management is to be efficient and fast across the entire supply chain. Among the difficulties in achieving this objective are organizational barriers to integration, the need to deal with numerous trade-offs, bullwhip effect, and variability of demand and lead times.

The purchasing function in business organizations is becoming increasingly important. Among the reasons are increased levels of outsourcing, greater emphasis on supply chain management, globalization, and continuing efforts to reduce costs and increase quality.

Among purchasing responsibilities are obtaining the materials, parts, supplies, equipment and machines, and services needed to produce a product or provide a service. Price, quality, and timely delivery are important variables. Purchasing selects suppliers, negotiates contracts, establishes alliances, and acts as liaison between suppliers and various internal departments. It also is involved in value analysis, make-or-buy decision, supplier analysis, supplier audits, and supplier certification.

An underlying consideration in purchasing, as in all areas of business, is maintaining ethical standards.

In many business organizations there is a move to reduce the number of suppliers and to establish and maintain longer-term relationships with suppliers. Supplier partnerships may involve cooperation that takes the form of sharing of information, quality control, JIT, and perhaps cooperation in product and process design.

KEY TERMS

bullwhip effect, 603	outsourcing, 588
centralized purchasing, 612	postponement, 605
CPFR, 601	purchasing cycle, 608
cross-docking, 605	quick response, 595
decentralized purchasing, 613	strategic partnering, 601
delayed differentiation, 605	supplier analysis, 614
distribution requirements planning (DRP), 596	supply chain, 587
e-commerce, 599	supply chain management, 590
efficient consumer response (ECR), 596	traffic management, 593
electronic data interchange (EDI), 594	value analysis, 608
information velocity, 602	value chain, 587
inventory velocity, 602	
logistics, 591	

Solved Problem

Problem 1

Determine which shipping alternative is best if the annual holding cost of an item is 25 percent of its unit price, and a single unit with a price of $6,000 is to be delivered, either by two-day freight at a cost of $400 or five-day freight at a cost of $350.

Solution

$H = .25(\$6,000) = \$1,500$ per year

Total two-day delivery cost $= \$400 + \$1,500(2/365)$
$\qquad\qquad\qquad\qquad\quad = \$408.22$

Total five-day delivery cost $= \$350 + \$1500(5/365)$
$\qquad\qquad\qquad\qquad\quad = \$370.55 < \$408.22$

Hence, use the five-day alternative.

DISCUSSION AND REVIEW QUESTIONS

1. What is a supply chain?
2. What factors have made it desirable to manage supply chains? What are some potential benefits of doing so?
3. What are the strategic and tactical/operational issues in supply chain management?
4. What is logistics?
5. What is the bullwhip effect, and why does it occur? How can it be overcome?
6. Explain how the need to ensure quality of raw materials would be a good reason for a manufacturer to form a supply chain, and give an example.
7. What is meant by the term *inventory velocity* and why is this important? What is *information velocity*, and why is it important?
8. Explain the term *quick response*.
9. What impact has e-commerce had on supply chain management?
10. What are some of the advantages of e-commerce?
11. What are some of the supply chain trade-offs?
12. What is EDI?
13. What is CPFR?
14. Explain the importance of the purchasing function in business organizations.

15. Describe what a business buyer does.
16. Describe how purchasing interacts with two other functional areas of an organization.
17. Describe value analysis.
18. Discuss centralization versus decentralization in purchasing. What are the advantages of each?
19. Describe supplier analysis.
20. Describe supplier certification and explain why it is important.
21. Why is good supplier relations important?
22. What are the advantages of partnership to the buyer? To the supplier?
23. When should a company outsource the production of a part or performance of a service?

---

1. What trade-offs are involved in sharing information with a supplier? With a customer?
2. Who needs to be involved in supply chain management?
3. Name two different ways that technology has improved the ability to manage supply chains.

TAKING STOCK

Explain why each of these is important for successful supply chain management:
a. Integrated technology
b. Information sharing
c. Trust among trading partners

CRITICAL THINKING EXERCISE

---

1. Visit www.manu.com/company/collateral.aspx, choose a client company, and briefly describe how the Manugistics software is helping the company.
2. Visit www.manufacturing.net/scm, the Web site of *Supply Chain Management Review*, find an application article, and summarize how the supply chain members are benefiting from close linkage.
3. Visit www.varsitylogistics.com/customers, pick a customer, and describe how it has benefited from the shipping software.

INTERNET EXERCISES

---

1. A manager at Strateline Manufacturing must choose between two delivery alternatives: two-day freight and five-day freight. Using five-day freight would cost $135 less than using two-day freight for the shipment of 2,000 units. Another consideration is holding cost, which is $10 per unit per year. Which alternative would you recommend? Explain.
2. Determine which delivery alternative would be most economical for 80 boxes of parts. Each box has a price of $200 and annual holding cost is 30 percent of price. Freight costs are:

PROBLEMS

Alternative	Freight Cost (for all 80)
Overnight	$300
Two-day	260
Six-day	180

3. A manager must make a decision on delivery mode. There are two shippers, A and B. Both offer a two-day rate. In addition, A offers a three-day rate and a nine-day rate, and B offers a four-day rate and a seven-day rate. Three hundred boxes are to be delivered and the delivery costs for the whole lot for each option are given below. Annual holding cost is 35 percent of unit price, and each box has a price of $140. Which delivery alternative would you recommend?

Shipper A		Shipper B	
Options	Cost	Options	Cost
2 days	$500	2 days	$525
3 days	460	4 days	450
9 days	400	7 days	410

4. An appliance manufacturer has a plant near Toronto that receives small electric motors from a manufacturer located in Winnipeg. The demand for motors is 120,000 units per year. The cost of each motor is $120. The motors are purchased in lots of 3,000 units. The ownership of motors transfers to the appliance manufacturer in Winnipeg. The question is which mode of transportation, truck or train, the appliance manufacturer should use to bring the motors from Winnipeg to Toronto. The railroad company charges $0.65 per motor (based on its weight) as long as there are at least 2,000 motors in the rail car, and it takes four days by train. The trucking company charges $0.75 per motor (based on weight) for lots of at least 1,000 motors, and it takes only two days. If the holding cost rate is 25 percent of unit cost per year, and the appliance manufacturer transports 3,000 motors at a time, which mode of transportation will minimize total transportation and holding cost?

5. Pratt & Whitney, a major aircraft engine manufacturer, wants to re-evaluate the transportation mode it uses to send unfinished parts to its joint-venture facility in Chengdu, China, and receive them back finished.[6] At present they use air freight. It takes approximately six days from Los Angeles to Chengdu (due to pickup and delivery and customs delays). There are 20 parts in a lot, each weighing 30 kilograms. The air freight cost per part is $30. The pickup and delivery charges at origin and destination add up to $3 per part. The alternative is to use an ocean liner to ship the parts to Shanghai and from there to either use a truck or a train (a 1,000 kilometre distance). The ocean freight for this lot size will cost $10 per part and will take 15 days. The truck from Shanghai to Chengdu will cost $10 per part and will take six days (due to pickup and delivery and customs delays). By rail will cost $5 per part and will take 14 days (due to pickup and delivery, customs, and transfer delays). In addition, for rail there is a $4 per part charge for pickup and delivery. The company's inventory holding cost rate is 12 percent per year, and the value of each part is about $1,000. Determine the cheapest (total freight, delivery, and inventory holding cost) mode of transportation for these parts.

6. Given the following data, determine the total annual cost of making and of buying from each of vendor A and B. Estimated demand is 15,000 units a year. Which alternative is best?

	Make	Vendor A	Vendor B
Variable cost per unit	$8	$11	$10
Annual fixed costs	$20,000	$0	$5,000 (annual charge)

7. Given the following data, determine the total annual cost of making with each of process A and B and of buying. Estimated demand is 10,000 units a year. Which alternative is best?

	MAKE		Buy
	Process A	Process B	
Variable cost per unit	$50	$52	$51
Annual fixed costs	$40,000	$36,000	
Transportation cost per unit			$2

8. For the previous problem, suppose that the operations manager has said that it would be possible to achieve a 10-percent reduction in the fixed cost of Process B and a 10-percent reduction in B's variable cost. Would that be enough to change your answer if the estimated annual cost to achieve those savings was $8,000? Explain.

[6]Based on A. Z. Zeng and C. Rossetti, "Developing a Framework for Evaluating the Logistics Costs in Global Sourcing Processes," *International Journal of Physical Distribution & Logistics Management* 33(9/10), 2003, pp. 785–803.

MINI-CASE

Crusty Cargo

www.clearwater.ca

In the late 1990s, Clearwater Fine Foods of Bedford, Nova Scotia, the supplier of live lobsters to many of North America's finest restaurants, was seriously considering opening a large live-lobster holding facility (with a capacity of 22,500 lobsters) in Louisville, Kentucky. Clearwater was experiencing some difficulties shipping lobsters from Bedford to the U.S., because of delays due to paperwork mix-ups, technology interruptions, and customs backlogs. The idea was to

truck live lobsters once or twice a week from Bedford to Louisville on special trucks, hold the lobsters in Louisville waiting for customer orders, and then courier them via UPS. Louisville is the main U.S. air hub for UPS.

Question

What are the advantages and disadvantages of opening up a Louisville warehouse/distribution centre versus shipping via courier from Halifax (within 20 km of Bedford)?

Source: Based on P. C. Pethick, "Crusty Cargo—Clearwater Fine Foods Scores with Fishy Supply Chain," *Materials Management & Distribution*, August 2001, p. 27.

MINI-CASE

Bank of Montreal

www2.bmo.com

In 2001, Bank of Montreal (BMO) wanted to automate its procurement system for small-value purchases such as office supplies, estimated at around $2 billion a year, in order to improve purchasing, find out its total purchases on items (to consolidate purchases and get quantity discounts), and find out its vendors service (fill) rate. A full automation requires electronic connection with suppliers. However, BMO had a dilemma. Most of its suppliers were reluctant to install EDI on their systems (because of complexity and expense), but were willing to give the Internet-based EDI a try. Unfortunately, BMO's legacy (old) mainframe computer and database were not suitable for running Web-based e-purchasing software. One seriously considered option was using an Application Service Provider (ASP) to host the services needed—that is, using the

host's e-procurement software and accounts payable—including creation of an e-catalogue. The user (bank employees) would log in to an account at the host's Website, choose a product, and issue the purchase order, which would be sent to suppliers using Web-based EDI. Suppliers could also log into the account, send invoices, and get paid electronically. The BMO database on the mainframe computer could still be used (by connecting it to the host), provided the database was upgraded.

Question

What are the advantages and disadvantages of outsourcing the purchasing of office supplies?

Sources: Based on M. MacMillan, "Driving Out Inefficiencies: Bank of Montreal Puts Its Money on Oracle to Meet Its Customization Requirements and Cut Costs," *Computing Canada* 27(14), June 29, 2001, p. 19; J. Middlemiss, "BMO Employs Supply Chain Management," *Bank Systems & Technology* 38(8), August 2001, pp. 24ff.

READING

E-Commerce and Supply Chain Management at Amazon.com

by Romulus Cismaru

It is universally accepted that Amazon.com is the company that is most closely associated with the e-commerce

phenomenon. Based in Seattle, Amazon.com started as an online retailer of books in July 1995. Since opening for business as "Earth's Biggest Bookstore," Amazon.com has quickly become one of the most widely known, used, and cited commerce sites on the Web. The company has grown at a tremendous rate with revenues rising from about $150 million in 1997 to $6.9 billion in 2004. Amazon.com's customer base grew from 1.5 million in December 1997 to 24.7 million in December 2001. However, the rise in revenue and number of customers was not accompanied by a rise in profits. After several years in which large operational losses were accumulated, it was only in the fourth quarter of 2001 that the company made its first quarterly profit of $5.8 million and this was achieved during the holiday season.

The company was founded by Jeff Bezos, a computer science and electrical engineering graduate from Princeton University. After seeing a statistic about the unprecedented growth rate of 2,300 percent in the number of Internet users, he quit his job as senior vice president of a Wall Street investment bank and decided to pursue the business opportunity of selling books solely on the Web. He started the company out of his garage in a Seattle suburb, packing orders and then delivering them to the post office in the family car. Jeff Bezos understood immediately the huge growth opportunity of Internet retailing: "Look at e-tailing. The key trade that we make is that we trade real estate for technology. Real estate is the key cost of physical retailers. That's why there's the old saying: location, location, location. Real estate gets expensive every year, and technology gets cheaper every year."

Initially, Amazon.com was only selling books. Selling books on the Internet makes sense for three reasons: books are easy to ship (reduced bulkiness), books are reasonably low value items (low risk to ship), and many online features such as sample chapters and editorial and customer reviews make books suitable for online sales. As an online seller, Amazon.com has virtually unlimited online shelf space and can offer a vast selection through an efficient search and retrieval interface. Amazon.com offers a huge selection of 3.1 million books, while the biggest brick and mortar stores can offer a maximum of 175,000 titles.

Initially Amazon.com was intended to be a "virtual retailer" with no inventory, no warehouses, and no overhead, just a network of computers taking orders and asking others to fill them, but the reality turned out to be quite different. In order to satisfy a huge increase in demand and offer a reliable delivery schedule, Amazon.com could not rely entirely on the wholesaler, Ingram Books, and decided to build its own regional warehouses. Currently, it has six warehouses, three as large as 800,000 square feet.

The following factors gave Amazon.com a competitive advantage over the physical bookstores:

1. Having only a few warehouses, its inventory turnaround was much quicker than that of a brick and mortar store.
2. Designing an efficient supply network, Amazon.com reduced book return rates from about 30 percent, the industry average, to only 3 percent, with a huge impact on profitability.
3. Retailers bear the cost of displaying the product in a brick and mortar book store, while Amazon.com passes these cost savings in the form of price reductions to customers.

4. Physical stores have to stock up to 160 days' worth of inventory to provide a reasonable in-store selection for the customers; they have to pay the publishers and distributors 45 to 90 days after they buy the books, thus, on average, they carry the cost of the books for up to four months. On the other hand, Amazon.com carries only 15 days' worth of inventory which is paid immediately by credit card. So, Amazon.com can use the money for one month interest free.

The domination of Amazon.com in the online book market became clear in 2001 with the capitulation of a major competitor, Borders. Borders had become a force in book retailing due to its superior computerized inventory management system and had sought in vain to offer a Web site that would effectively compete with Amazon.com. In 2001, Borders eliminated all staff positions in Borders.com and announced that Amazon.com will handle its online bookselling.

Buoyed by early successes in the bookselling business, Amazon.com has decided to diversify its offerings and to expand internationally. In 1998, Amazon.com started selling music, DVDs and videos, toys, electronics, home improvement products, software, and video games. In 2005, Amazon.com also started selling apparel and accessories, jewellery and watches, shoes, musical instruments, gourmet food, health and personal care products, beauty products, computers, cell phones and service, automotive accessories, and even pet supplies.

Amazon.com has also launched international operations in France, the United Kingdom, Japan, Germany, China, and Canada. The company already had strong sales in Canada through its U.S. site, and Canada is the retailer's largest export destination.

The major argument for the expansion was a technological one. The company has already incurred the fixed costs of developing software for the online storefronts. Expanding into other categories would only allow spreading those fixed costs across a larger number of transactions, leading to greater profits through economies of scale. Says Bezos: "When we open a new category, we use basically the same software. We get to leverage the same customer base, our brand name, and the infrastructure. It's very low-cost for us to open a new category, whereas to have a pure-play single line store is very expensive. Other companies will end up spending much more on technology and other fixed costs than we will, just because our earlier stores are already covering those costs."

However, Amazon.com's diversification plans put the company at a crossroads. New products led to new challenges. Many of the new offerings were bulky products that are expensive to stock, ship, and return. Moreover, in the electronics business, leading manufacturers have stringent requirements on how the retailer will display and sell their products. Large manufacturers did not want to jeopardize existing relationships with retailers by selling through Amazon.com whom they feared will sell at lower prices. At the same time, many manufacturers wanted to set up their own online stores. By moving into new products, Amazon.com exposed itself to new levels of competition creating new vulnerabilities. Many established brick and mortar players (Best Buy, Circuit City, and JC Penny) had decided to be present in the online arena, too. It has become clear that, by increasing the complexity of the business, even if the technological cost has remained the same, the cost of handling the physical goods and the cost of inventory has increased, pulling the company down to some degree.

Amazon.com strives to offer its customers compelling value through innovative use of technology, broad selection, high-quality content, high level of customer service, competitive pricing and personalized service. The following features are intended to enhance the shopping experience: One-Click Shopping (the Web site interface remembers all relevant information about the customer and reduces the transactional burden), product review information, purchase circles (identifies items that are most popular with each specific group of population), e-mail alerts, recommendations, wish list (list of items that each individual would like to acquire), and The Page You Made

(recently viewed portions of the site by each customer). As Jeff Bezos stated, "Ultimately, Amazon.com is an information broker. On the left side, Amazon.com has lots of products, on the right side, it has lots of customers. Amazon.com is in the middle, making the connections."

Today, Amazon.com is recognized as a virtual Wal-Mart of the Web industry. While the general view is that Amazon.com is the vanguard of a new breed of companies which lead industries into the economy of the new millennium, it is almost certain that the future of the company will prove to be at least as interesting as its past.

Questions:

1. Should Amazon.com have remained an online bookstore? What are the advantages and disadvantages of diversification?

2. Identify the strategic issues of supply chain management for Amazon.com and explain how each was used to achieve competitive advantage over a brick-and-mortar store.

Sources: Sandeep Krishnamurthy, "Amazon.com—A business History," in *E-commerce Management: Text and Cases*, September 27, 2002, pp. 1–45; available electronically in www.swlearning.com/marketing/krishnamurthy/first_edition/case_updates/amazon_final.pdf

SELECTED BIBLIOGRAPHY AND FURTHER READING

Anders, George. "Virtual Reality: Web Firms Go On Warehouse Building Boom." The *Wall Street Journal*, September 8, 1999, p. B1.

Ballou, Ronald H. *Business Logistics Management*, 4th ed. Englewood Cliffs, NJ: Prentice Hall, 1999.

Bender, Paul S. "Debunking 5 Supply Chain Myths." *Supply Chain Management Review* 4(1) March 2000, pp. 52–58.

Bender, Paul S. "How to Design an Optimum Worldwide Supply Chain." *Supply Chain Management Review*, Spring 1997, pp. 70–81.

Bhatnagar, Rohit, and S. Viswanathan. "Re-engineering Global Supply Chains: Alliances between Manufacturing Firms and Global Logistics Services Providers." *International Journal of Physical Distribution and Logistics Management* 30(1), 2000, pp. 13–14.

Blackwell, Roger D., and Kristina Blackwell. "The Century of the Consumer: Converting Supply Chains into Demand Chains." *Supply Chain Management*, Fall 1999.

Bovet, David, and Yossi Sheffi. "The Brave New World of Supply Chain Management." *Supply Chain Management Review*, Spring 1998, pp. 14–20.

Chopra, Sunil, and Peter Meindl. *Supply Chain Management: Strategy, Planning, and Operation*. Upper Saddle River, NJ: Prentice Hall, 2001.

Copacino, William C. *Supply Chain Management: The Basics and Beyond*. Boca Raton, FL: St. Lucie Press, 1997.

Dornier, Phillippe-Pierre, Ricardo Ernst, Michel Fender, and Panos Kouvelis. *Global Operations and Logistics: Text and Cases*. New York: Wiley, 1998.

Fisher, Marshall. "What is the Right Supply Chain for Your Product?" *Harvard Business Review*, March–April 1997.

Fitzgerald, Kevin R. "Purchasing Occupies Key Position in Supply Chains." *Supply Chain Yearbook 2000*, New York: Cahners Business Information, 2000, p. 21.

Handfield, Robert B., and Ernest L. Nichols Jr. *Introduction to Supply Chain Management*. Englewood Cliffs, NJ: Prentice Hall, 1999.

Harvard Business Review on Managing the Value Chain. Boston: Harvard Business School Press, 2000. A collection of articles, some of which are listed separately in this section.

Hill, Terry. *Manufacturing Strategy: Text and Cases*. New York: McGraw-Hill, 2000.

Lee, Hau L., and C. Billington, "Managing Supply Chain Inventory: Pitfalls and Opportunities." *Sloan Management Review*, Spring 1992, pp. 65–73.

Lee, Hau L., V. Padmanaghan, and Seunjin Whang. "The Paralyzing Curse of the Bullwhip Effect in Supply Chains." *Sloan Management Review*, Spring 1997, pp. 93–102.

Leenders, M. R., H. E. Fearon, A. E. Flynn, and P. F. Johnson. *Purchasing and Supply Management* 12th ed. New York: McGraw-Hill, 2002.

Margretta, Joan. "The Power of Virtual Integration: An Interview with Dell Computer's Michael Dell." *Harvard Business Review*, March–April 1998, pp. 73–84.

Margretta, Joan. "Fast, Global, and Entrepreneurial: Supply Chain Management, Hong Kong Style." *Harvard Business Review*, September–October 1998, pp. 102–14.

Martin, Justin, "Are You as Good as You Think You Are?" *Fortune*, September 30, 1996, pp. 145–46.

Metz, Peter J. "Demystifying the Supply Chain." *Supply Chain Management Review*, Winter 1998, pp. 46–55.

Pooler, Victor H., and David J. Pooler. *Purchasing and Supply Chain Management: Creating the Vision*. New York: Chapman and Hall, 1997.

Ptak, Carol A., and Eli Schragenheim. *ERP: Tools, Techniques, and Applications for Integrating the Supply Chain*. Boca Raton, FL: St. Lucie Press, 1999.

Ross, D. F. *Competing through Supply Chain Management*. New York: Chapman and Hall, 1998.

Schorr, John E. *Purchasing in the 21st Century: A Guide to State-of-the-Art Techniques and Strategies*. Essex Junction, VT: Oliver Wight Companies, 1992.

Silverstein, Judith. "Desperately Seeking E-Fulfillment." *Digital Chicago*, November/December 1999, pp. 22–47.

Simchi-Levi, David, Philip Kaminsky, and Edith Simchi-Levi. *Designing and Managing the Supply Chain: Concepts, Strategies, and Case Studies*. Irwin/McGraw-Hill, 2000.

Supply Chain Linkages. An entire issue of *Decision Sciences* 29(3), Summer 1998, with a research focus on supply chain linkages.

Walker, William T., and Karen Alber. "Understanding Supply Chain Management." *APICS—The Performance Advantage*, January 1999.

PART SEVEN

Project Management

The chapter in this section covers various topics related to successfully managing projects.

CHAPTER 17

Project Management

When HP took over Compaq Computers in the early 2000s, it had to merge the two organizations, including computer systems such as the two PeopleSoft Human Resources software packages. There were hundreds of projects to undertake, but HP did not have a systematic way to manage them. Fortunately, Compaq had an effective project organizer, the Program Management Office (PMO). A program is a collection or series of projects. Using Compaq's PMO, HP managed to merge efficiently and effectively with Compaq. By just discontinuing redundant projects, HP saved $110 million. The PMO is only one way to manage projects. This chapter describes this and other methods for managing projects efficiently and effectively.

READING

Olympics

Olympic Games are huge projects. Every two years, the Winter and Summer Olympic Games alternate. They are held in various cities. Winter Games are smaller than Summer Games. For example, in the Salt Lake 2002 Winter Games, 2,400 athletes from 77 countries participated in 78 events, with 8,700 media people reporting the games and 22,000 volunteers helping with the operations. In contrast, at the Athens 2004 Summer Games, 11,000 athletes from 201 countries participated in 301 events, with 21,500 media people reporting the games and 45,000 volunteers helping with the operations.

The process for organization of an Olympic Games is as follows: The International Olympic Committee (IOC) awards the Games to a city based on the merits of the application. Because holding such an event is a large expense ($2 billion for Summer and $1 billion for Winter Olympics), the application team should include members of the city, province/state, and country's government, as well as their National Olympic Committee (NOC). This is done about seven years before the event is to be held in order to leave enough time for any necessary constructions. Then, an organizing committee is formed of people from the application team and others who will be in charge of all the planning and management of activities (e.g., asking for construction bids, etc). IOC also forms a team called the Coordination Commission to assist the organizing committee. After the Sidney Summer Olympics, a company, the Olympics Games Knowledge Services, was formed which also assists the organizing committee with the procedures and systems they need to manage the project.

The organizing committee is responsible for all the venues (competition stadium and training halls), scheduling the

The 2010 Winter Olympics will be held in Vancouver and Whistler.

competitions, arranging for necessary equipment, lodging for athletes/entourage/officials, organizing medical services, solving transportation problems, meeting the requirements of media, and organizing cultural events such as the opening and closing shows.

The 2010 Winter Olympics will be held in Vancouver and Whistler. Awarded in 2003, the Vancouver Organizing Committee had to prepare a proposal outlining its plans for the venues, accommodation, transport, cultural events, and more. The venues are a combination of existing facilities, those to be renovated, and new facilities. The work on the venues started in 2005 and is planned to be completed by 2008.

Sources: www.olympic.org/uk/games/past/index_uk.asp?OLGT=2& OLGY=2002; www.olympic.org/uk/games/past/index_uk.asp? OLGT=1&OLGY=2004; www.olympic.org/uk/organisation/index_ uk.asp; www.vancouver2010.com

INTRODUCTION

Employees typically perform a variety of operations. Some of these involve routine, repetitive activities, but others involve nonroutine activities. Under the latter heading are **projects**: unique, one-time operations designed to accomplish a set of objectives in a limited time frame. Examples of projects include constructing a shopping complex, launching the space shuttle, redesigning a business process, merging two companies,

projects Unique, one-time operations designed to accomplish a specific set of objectives in a limited time frame.

putting on a play, planning and running a political campaign, designing new products or services, planning advertising campaigns, and designing information systems. A very complex project is an Olympic Games (see the reading on the preceding page).

Projects may involve considerable cost. Some have a long time horizon, and some involve a large number of activities that must be carefully planned and coordinated. All are expected to be completed within time, cost, and performance guidelines. To accomplish this, projects must be authorized, objectives and scope must be established, a project manager should be appointed, and the project must be planned. Tasks must be identified and time estimates made. Resource requirements also must be projected and budgets prepared. Once underway, progress must be monitored to ensure that project goals and objectives will be achieved. For an example of how a company estimates and controls costs of a project, see the reading, "General Dynamics Land Systems—Canada."

This chapter introduces the basic concepts of project management. It begins with a brief discussion of the nature of project management, organization, and the difficulties project managers are likely to encounter. The main portion of the chapter is devoted to project planning, and a description of a solution technique that is used for scheduling projects. Project execution and control is also discussed. Finally, a description of how to use Microsoft Project is given, and two other software are described.

READING

General Dynamics Land Systems—Canada

An important part of a project is budgeting for the costs, especially if the company has to bid for the job. GDLS-Canada in London, Ontario, manufactures light armoured vehicles for armies around the world. There is some customization involved, so GDLS needed a project scheduling software. It chose Deltek's (Welcom) Software Technology's Open Plan for scheduling and Deltek's (Welcom) Cobra for cost management and estimating.

The company uses Cobra to develop a resource-loaded schedule for the project. Once the work breakdown structure and cost class breakouts are defined according to project requirements, GDLS loads a skeleton into its Basis-of-estimate Input Device (BID) system, which computes labour and other direct cost estimates.

Sometimes the process involves several phases of corrections and negotiations, but eventually a baseline "budgeted cost of work scheduled" is established. Then, individuals charge work orders to the project.

"Being able to compare budgeted cost of work scheduled, budgeted cost of work performed, and actual costs allows the project analysis team to generate cost/schedule status reports at the project and enterprise levels," explains Gary Caryn, GDLS's senior scheduler/coordinator.

Source: www.welcom.com/documents/userstories_GeneralDynamics landsystems.pdf.

THE NATURE OF PROJECT MANAGEMENT

Projects go through a series of stages—a life cycle—which include project initiation, planning, execution, control, and closeout. During this life cycle, a variety of skill requirements are involved. The circumstances are analogous to constructing a house. Initially an idea is presented and its feasibility is assessed, then plans must be drawn up by an architect, and approved by the owner and possibly a town building permits department. Then a succession of activities occurs, each with its own skill requirements, starting with the site preparation, then laying the foundation, erecting the frame, roofing, constructing exterior walls, wiring and plumbing, installing kitchen and bathroom fixtures and appliances, interior finishing work, and painting and carpeting work. Similar sequences occur on large construction projects, in R&D work, information technology projects, and in virtually every other instance where projects are being carried out.

In a company, the project initiator/sponsor is usually a senior manager. Project output or deliverable is a product such as a building/software or a service such as merging two databases.

A project is influenced by the company policies and procedures, and "environment" (e.g., culture, information systems, human resources). The major documents used in

READING

SNC-Lavalin

SNC-Lavalin is a large design, engineering, construction, and project management company, based in Montreal, with 30 international offices. Founded in 1911, SNC-Lavalin has performed hundreds of large projects. Some examples are:

Project	Location	Customer Name	Type of Work
Aluminum Smelter	Alma, Quebec	Alcan	Design, engineering
Hockey rink	Montreal	Bell Centre	Construction
Sorting plants	Eastern Canada	Canada Post	Facilities management
Oil rig	Newfoundland	Hibernia	Engineering, buying, project management
Bridge	Montreal	Jacque-Cartier	Redecking
La Grande Dams	Northern Quebec	James Bay	Engineering and project management
Relocation of Production lines	Montreal	Johnson & Johnson	Cost estimating and project management
Uranium processing mill	McLean Lake, SK	Cogema	Engineering and procurement
Power plant expansion	Saskatoon	Sask Power	Installed six gas turbines
Bitumen plant expansion	Mildred Lake, AB	Syncrude	Design, engineering project management
Train lines and stations	Vancouver	SkyTrain	Design, construction, project management

Source: www.snclavalin.com/en/8_0/8_7.aspx, project browser.

project initiation are the project charter (i.e., authorization) and project scope (the work that needs to be accomplished to deliver a product or service with the specified features and functions).

Project planning determines how the project is to be undertaken, including breaking down the work into smaller components, called Work Breakdown Structure (WBS), determining the resources needed and estimating their costs, scheduling the activities involved or subcontracting the work, risk management planning, and planning material purchases.

Project execution involves purchasing materials, and using the team members and subcontractors to perform the work, while assuring quality. Project monitoring and control involves observing the project's progress, issuing performance reports on scope/schedule/cost/quality/risk, and making any necessary changes to the project.

Projects bring various people together, both from inside and from outside the company. These stakeholders include the project team who perform the activities, project sponsor/initiator who initiates and approves funding for the project, and customer/users. The project is headed by a project manager, guided by the sponsor.

Most team members, who have diverse knowledge and skills, will remain associated with the project for less than its full life. Some people go from project to project as their contributions become needed, and others are "on loan," either on a full-time or part-time basis, from their regular jobs.

Certain kinds of organizations are involved with projects on a regular basis; examples include consulting firms, architects, writers and publishers, and construction companies. For example, see the reading, "SNC-Lavalin." In these organizations, it is not uncommon for some individuals to spend virtually all of their time on projects. These companies have a pure *project organization*. However, most organizations use a **matrix organization** that allows them to integrate the activities of a variety of specialists within a functional framework. Each staff member, for example a structural engineer or an accountant, works on one or more project(s) part time, but permanently belongs to his or her department.

Finally, some companies have set up a Project Management Office (PMO) which acts as a department, housing project managers who use team members from functional departments just as in the matrix organization structure. See the readings, "EMCO" and "HP."

Deciding which projects to implement involves factors such as budget, availability of personnel with appropriate knowledge and skill, cost–benefit considerations, financial benefits e.g., return on investment and net present value, and how the project will contribute to the company's strategy.

matrix organization An organizational structure which temporarily groups together specialists from different departments to work on special projects. The project manager and the functional managers share the responsibility of assigning priorities and directing the work.

Project Manager's Job

project manager The person responsible for the planning, execution, and controlling of a project from inception to completion, meeting the project's requirements and ensuring completion on time, within cost, and to the required quality standards.

The **project manager** bears the ultimate responsibility for the success or failure of the project. He or she must be capable of working through others to accomplish the objectives of the project. The project manager is responsible for effectively managing each of the following:

1. The *work*, so that all of the necessary activities are accomplished in the desired sequence and performance goals are met.

2. The *human resources*, so that those working on the project have direction and motivation.

3. *Communications*, so that everybody has the information they need to do their work, and the customer/user are well informed.

4. *Quality*, so that performance objectives are realized.

5. *Time*, so that the project is completed on schedule.

6. *Costs*, so that the project is completed within budget.

To effectively manage a project, a project manager must employ a certain set of skills. The skills include the ability to motivate and direct team members, make trade-off decisions, expedite the work when necessary, put out fires, and monitor time, budget, and technical details. For projects that involve fairly well-defined work, those skills will often suffice. However, for projects that are less well defined, and thus have a higher degree of uncertainty, the project manager must also employ strong leadership skills. These include the ability to adapt to changing circumstances that may involve changes to project goals, technical requirements, and project team composition. He/she must recognize the need for change, decide what changes are necessary in consultation with stakeholders, and work to accomplish them.

The job of project manager can be both difficult and rewarding. He/she must coordinate and motivate people who sometimes owe their allegiance to other managers in their

READING

EMCO

www.emcoltd.com

E MCO is one of Canada's leading distributors and manufacturers of building products for residential, commercial, and industrial construction markets.

Before 1998, EMCO's information systems department had trouble estimating internal project durations, progress, and end dates. Red flags often came up too late to have a meaningful impact. Managing multiple projects simultaneously was difficult at best, posing serious resource allocation problems. The upshot: dissatisfied information systems customers.

In 1998, EMCO created a Project Management Office (PMO). Fardin Maknoni, Senior Analyst, Project Management, heads up this department, which handles implementation and support of telecommunications, transaction processing (such as EDI), data processing, systems conversions, and financial systems projects for the entire company.

The PMO adopted Deltek's (Welcom) Open Plan. According to Maknoni, "Open Plan was flexible and easy for everyone

to use, and it had the features we needed. It allowed us to control and centralize all of our projects." Here are some of the ways EMCO uses Open Plan:

- Before a project begins, managers create six to ten "what-if" scenarios in Open Plan. These allow them to effectively plan ahead, resolve schedule conflicts, and make baseline determinations (such as a project's start date).

- During a project, EMCO generates weekly progress reports that include time sheets, action items, and project status.

- Time sheet information is uploaded to Open Plan from three sources: an internal data management system, Excel, and manual input.

- Various Gantt, PERT, and spreadsheet reports are created and filtered by criteria meaningful to different tiers of users.

- Progress-analysis reports give critical information to senior management to monitor projects and construct new project proposals.

Source www.welcom.com/documents/userstories_EMCO.pdf.

functional areas. In addition, the people who work on a project possess specialized knowledge and skills that the project manager lacks. Nevertheless, he/she is expected to guide and evaluate their efforts. Project managers must often function in an environment that is beset with uncertainties. Even so, budgets and time constraints are usually imposed, which can create additional pressures on project personnel.

Ethical issues often arise in connection with projects. Examples include the temptation to understate costs or to withhold information in order to get a project approved, pressure to alter or make misleading statements on status reports, falsifying records, compromising workers' safety, and approving substandard work. It is the responsibility of project managers to maintain and enforce ethical standards.

PROJECT PLANNING

Project planning involves further elaboration of the project scope (the work to be done) including breaking down the project into smaller components (deliverables, subprojects, work packages, and activities), risk management planning (the identification, analysis, and response plans to what may go wrong), estimating the required activity resources (employees, equipment, material), cost estimation (for each activity) and budgeting (calculating total cost per unit time, including subcontracting costs), human resource planning (including assigning team member roles and responsibilities), project scheduling (estimating activity durations, sequencing, and scheduling), quality planning, communications planning, and purchase planning.

project planning Involves analyzing the project into work packages and activities, estimating resources needed and durations, scheduling, etc.

It is important to determine the details of work to be done (scope), to formally obtain acceptance of the detailed scope from project customer/user, and later during execution and control, to control the changes to the project scope. We will describe risk management planning, work breakdown structure (WBS), and project scheduling in more detail in the following sections.

Quality planning involves determining how product quality is to be assured and controlled. Quality planning involves deciding quality policy, objectives, responsibilities, metrics, and quality tools such as checklists.

Communications planning involves determining the nature of information needed by stakeholders and how to satisfy these needs. It involves plans for information collection/storage, the technology and media used, nature of information distributed (e.g., project performance reports), and methods for accessing and updating the information.

Purchase planning involves determining what to purchase (using make-or-buy analysis), contract statement of work (the portion of project scope dealing with the specific purchase), the type of contract to be used, the contract form (purchase order), and supplier evaluation and selection. The actual purchasing and monitoring/controlling of supplier performance are part of the execution and control of the project.

READING

HP

When HP took over Compaq in 2002, it adopted its global project management system which included a standard approach to projects, administered by a global Program Management Office (PMO) using the Primavera software. Before this, HP's project management was ineffective. The PMO examined all HP's current projects and also proposed some new ones. It determined approximately 200 projects as Must-Start (e.g., merging the two PeopleSoft HR software), approximately 300 Must-Do projects (to start within

the first 100 days of takeover, e.g., integration of the supply chain systems), and approximately 115 Must-Stop projects (e.g., duplicate Customer Relationship Management software). The savings of Must-Stop projects alone were approximately $110 million. HP has over 3,000 active IT projects involving over 10,000 IT professionals. Every six months, HP reassesses the worthiness of all its projects. About 70 percent of the strategic projects are on track.

Sources: www.primavera.com/customer/conference/documents/PRV_ UC2002_Award_04.mpeg; www.primavera.com/successes, accessed August 2005.

Iris' Risk

When in the late 1990s Xwave, the Canadian systems integrator and software company, got involved with Project Iris, the Canadian Forces' new digital radio and computer voice and data communication system, it was only a subcontractor. Xwave managed the risk of the project by identifying potential risks, categorizing them according to their impact and probability (Priority 1 = most important, ... , Priority 5 = least important), tried to mitigate their effect, and monitored them throughout the four-year project. Most risks involved were external to Xwave such as changing customer-furnished equipment and software (that Xwave had to integrate), resulting in changing project scope. Also, army personnel got reassigned frequently, delaying information on user requirements. In addition, there was a project management risk due to the tight schedule.

Xwave could not do much about the risks because it was just a subcontractor. Staff recruitment and training plans were put in place to have excess manpower available for the project. Xwave monitored the risks throughout the project. The risk of customer-furnished equipment and software went up in the middle of project because the Canadian Forces decided to use updated equipment and software. The risk of inconsistent client involvement went down after the first year as the requirements/specifications of the operators were fully determined. The risk of tight schedule remained high throughout the project.

Sources: J. Pyra and J. Trask, "Risk Management Post Analysis: Gauging the Success of a Simple Strategy in a Complex Project," *Project Management Journal* 33(2), June 2002, pp. 41–48; www.army.forces.gc.ca/lf/English/2_0_62_1.asp?FlashEnabled= 1&uSubSection=62&uSection=5.

Risk Management Planning

Risks are inherent in projects. They relate to the occurrence of events that can have undesirable consequences, such as delays, increased costs, and an inability to meet technical specifications. In some instances, there is the risk that events will occur that will cause a project to be terminated. Although careful planning can reduce risks no amount of planning can eliminate chance events due to unforeseen or uncontrollable circumstances.

The probability of occurrence of risk events is highest near the beginning of a project and lowest near the end. However, the cost associated with risk events tends to be lowest near the beginning of a project and highest near the end.

Good risk management entails identifying as many potential risks as possible, analyzing and assessing those risks, and planning a response to avoid, transfer, or mitigate the risk. Much of this takes place during planning of a project, although it is not unusual for this process to be repeated during the execution of project as experience grows and new information becomes available.

The first step is to identify the risks. Typically, there are numerous sources of risks, although the more experience an organization has with a particular type of work, the fewer and more identifiable the risks will be. Everyone associated with the project should have responsibility for the task of identifying risks. Brainstorming sessions and questionnaires can be useful in this regard. Another approach to risk identification is to review the documents and analyze the assumptions, looking for inaccuracies, inconsistencies, and incompleteness. The list of risks and other information obtained in the following steps is usually stored in a *risk register*.

Once risks have been identified, each risk must be evaluated to determine its probability of occurrence and the potential consequences if it does occur. Both quantitative and qualitative approaches have merit. All stakeholders can contribute to this effort, and experts might also be called on. Experience with previous projects can be useful. Many tools might be applied, including scenario analysis, simulation, decision trees, sensitivity analysis, and probabilistic PERT (described later in the chapter). There should be a response to risks with high probability and impact.

Risk response can take a number of forms. Much depends on the nature and scope of a project. First, the root cause of a risk is identified. It will help to categorize risks by either their source (risk breakdown structure) or by the area of work (using the WBS). Risk response includes:

- Redundant (backup) systems, for example, an emergency generator could supply power in the event of an electrical failure.
- Using a less complex process or a more stable supplier.
- Frequent monitoring of critical project aspects with the goal of catching and eliminating problems in their early stages, before they cause extensive damage.
- Transferring risks, say by outsourcing a particular component of a project and requiring performance bonds.
- Risk-sharing.
- Partnering, for example, as in an oil and gas consortium.
- Extending the schedule, creating contingency funds, reducing project scope, clarifying the requirements, obtaining information, and improving communication.

For an application, see the reading, "Iris' Risk."

Work Breakdown Structure

Because large projects usually involve large amount of work, the project is decomposed into smaller components. **Work breakdown structure (WBS)** is a hierarchical listing of what must be done during the project (see Figure 17–1); it is for the project what the product structure tree is for a product. The first step in developing the work breakdown structure is to identify the major components of the project. These could be the phases of project, deliverables or subprojects. The next step is to identify the major supporting subcomponents for each of the major components. This process is repeated until a component is decomposed into a work package which can be performed by a worker, team, or subcontractor. Then, each work package is broken down into a list of the activities that will be needed to accomplish it.

A company can use its past experience to determine the WBS. Progressive elaboration can be pursued as the details of activities become known (this is also called rolling wave planning). Each component in a WBS should be assigned a code for purposes of monitoring its performance. Performing WBS may require changing the project scope.

work breakdown structure (WBS) A hierarchical listing of what must be done during a project.

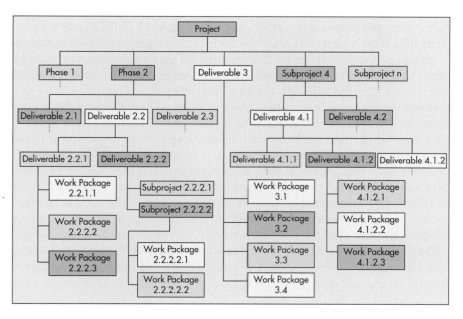

FIGURE 17-1

Schematic of work breakdown structure

Source: Project Management Institute, *A Guide to the Project Management Body of Knowledge* (PMBOK® Guide), third edition, 2004. Copyright and all rights reserved. Material from this publication has been reproduced with the permission of PMI.

PROJECT SCHEDULING

project scheduling
Determining the timing of
performance of activities of the
project.

Project scheduling involves determining the timing of performing the activities which comprise the project. It starts with activities which have been defined in the WBS, including their attributes (e.g., physical location to be performed, person/group/subcontractor responsible) and whether an activity is a milestone activity (signifying a review/test/approval decision).

Then, the logical sequence of activities, i.e., their dependencies, should be identified. A precedence network diagram is used to display the dependencies.

Next, the resources (employees or subcontractors, equipment, material) needed for each activity should be identified for the chosen method of performing the activity, given the availability of the resources (using the resource calendar). If the needed resources cannot be identified, the activity should be further decomposed.

Then, duration of each activity can be estimated using information on the availability of resources, the risk register (which could possibly add some contingency time to the duration), and the chosen method of performing the activity. As work is undertaken, more accurate estimates of costs and times become available. Analogous activities in the past, in conjunction with numerical estimation techniques such as regression, can be used to estimate the activity duration. The Three-point Estimates method, described later under Probabilistic Activity Durations, can also be used to estimate the activity's average and standard deviation of duration.

Finally, the schedule is developed using the activity duration estimates, and the precedence network diagram. The PERT/CPM technique (described later), for both one-point estimate (deterministic times) and three-point estimates (probabilistic times) is used to schedule the activities. Attempts may be made to modify the schedule so that a more level use of resources takes place. If the project will be late, schedule compression methods such as activity crashing (accelerating activities) and fast tracking (overlapping predecessor-successor activities) will be performed. The schedule will be displayed graphically using Gantt and PERT/CPM charts. For two applications, see the "Tembec" and "Electramedia" readings later in the chapter.

We will describe Gantt charts, the PERT/CPM technique, including the precedence network diagram, using both deterministic and probabilistic times, and activity crashing below.

Gantt Charts

Gantt chart A horizontal bar
chart that depicts activities
as blocks over time. The
beginning and end of the block
correspond to the beginning
and end date of the activity.

The (schedule) **Gantt chart** is a popular tool for scheduling *simple* projects. It enables a manager to schedule project activities and then to monitor its progress over time by comparing planned progress to actual progress. Figure 17–2 illustrates a (schedule) Gantt chart for a bank's plan to establish a new branch. To prepare the chart, the vice-president in charge of the project had to first identify the major activities that would be required. Next, time estimates for each activity were made, and the sequence of activities was determined. Once completed, the chart indicated which activities were to occur, their planned duration, and when they were to occur. Then, as the project progressed, the manager was able to see which activities were ahead of schedule and which were behind. This enabled the manager to direct attention where it was needed most in order to finish the project on schedule.

Aside from being a visual tool, an advantage of a Gantt chart is its simplicity. However, Gantt charts fail to reveal certain relationships among activities that can be crucial to effective project management. For instance, if one of the early activities in a project suffers a delay, it would be important for the manager to be able to easily determine which later activities are affected. Conversely, some activities may safely be delayed without affecting the overall project schedule. The Gantt chart does not directly reveal this. On more complex projects, a *precedence network diagram*, described later, is used for scheduling purposes.

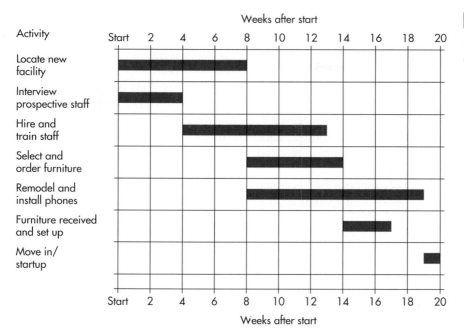

FIGURE 17-2

(Schedule) Gantt chart for a new bank branch

PERT/CPM Technique

PERT (program evaluation and review technique) and **CPM** (critical path method) are two of the most widely used techniques for scheduling and control of large-scale projects. By using PERT or CPM, managers are able to obtain:

1. A graphical display of project activities.
2. An estimate of how long the project will take.
3. An indication of which activities are the most critical to timely project completion.
4. An indication of how long any activity can be delayed without delaying the project.

PERT *Program evaluation and review technique,* used for scheduling and control of large projects.

CPM *Critical path method,* used for scheduling and control of large projects.

PERT and CPM were developed independently during the late 1950s. PERT evolved through the joint efforts of Lockheed Aircraft, the U.S. Navy Special Projects Office, and consulting firm of Booz, Allen & Hamilton, in an effort to speed up the Polaris missile project. At the time, the U.S. government was concerned that the Soviet Union might be gaining nuclear superiority over the U.S., and it gave top priority for the early completion of the project by the U.S. Department of Defense. The project was a huge one, with more than 3,000 contractors and thousands of activities. PERT was quite successful and was generally credited with shaving two years off the length of the project.

CPM was developed by J. E. Kelly of the Remington Rand Corporation and M. R. Walker of DuPont to schedule and control maintenance projects in chemical plants.

Although PERT and CPM were developed independently, they have a great deal in common. Moreover, many of the initial differences between them have disappeared as users borrowed certain features from one technique for use with the other. For example, PERT originally stressed probabilistic activity duration estimates because the environment in which it developed was characterized by high uncertainty. In contrast, the tasks for which CPM was developed were less uncertain, so CPM originally made no provision for variable duration estimates. At present, either technique can be used with deterministic or probabilistic activity durations. Other initial differences concerned the mechanical aspects of developing precedence network diagrams. However, from a conceptual standpoint, most of these differences were relatively minor. To avoid confusion, we will not delve into the differences. For practical purposes, the two techniques are the same; the comments and procedures described will apply to CPM analysis as well as to PERT analysis of projects.

The Precedence Network Diagram

precedence network diagram
Diagram of project activities that shows sequential relationships by use of arrows and nodes.

One of the main features of PERT and CPM is their use of a **precedence network diagram** to depict project activities and their sequential relationships. There are two slightly different conventions for constructing these diagrams. Under one convention, the *arrows* designate activities; under the other convention, the *nodes* designate activities. These conventions are referred to as **activity-on-arrow (AOA)** and **activity-on-node (AON)**.

activity-on-arrow (AOA)
Network diagram convention in which arrows designate activities.

Both conventions are illustrated in Figure 17–3, using the new bank branch example that was depicted in the Gantt chart in Figure 17–2. Compare the two. In the AOA network diagram, the arrows represent activities and they show the sequence in which certain activities must be performed (e.g., Interview precedes Hire and Train); in the AON network diagram, the arrows show only the sequence in which certain activities must be performed, while the nodes represent the activities. Only AON precedence network diagrams are used in this chapter.

activity-on-node (AON)
Network diagram convention in which nodes designate activities.

Note that the AON network diagram has a starting node, S, which is actually not an activity but is added in order to have a single starting node. Also, a project should have one ending node.

The relationships shown in Figure 17–3 are of the finish-to-start type (i.e., an activity must finish before its immediate successor can start). Sometimes other types of relationships exist, such as start-to-start (an activity can start only after another has started), finish-to-finish, and start-to-finish. Also, it is possible to require a prespecified minimum delay (time buffer) in any of these relationships. In addition, some dependencies may be discretionary. Further, there may be external dependencies, e.g., an externally determined start or finish time for an activity. We will consider only finish-to-start mandatory relationships, which are most common, in this chapter. Developing and interpreting AON precedence network diagrams require some familiarity with network conventions. Figure 17–4 illustrates some of the most basic and common features of AON precedence network diagrams.

path A sequence of activities that leads from the starting node to the ending node.

Of particular interest to managers are the *paths* in a precedence network diagram. A **path** is a sequence of activities that leads from the starting node to the ending node. For example, in the AON diagram of Figure 17–3, S-1-2-6-7 is a path. Note that there are three paths in this

FIGURE 17–3

Precedence network diagrams of a new bank branch

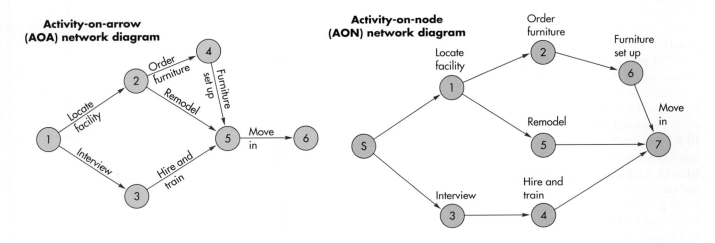

INTERPRETATION	NETWORK RELATIONSHIP

FIGURE 17–4

AON precedence network conventions

Activities must be completed in sequence: first a, then b, and then c.

Both a and b must be completed before c can start.

Activity a must be completed before b or c can start.

Both a and b must be completed before c or d can start.

diagram. One reason for the importance of paths is that they reveal *sequential relationships*. If one activity in a sequence is delayed (i.e., is late) or done incorrectly, the start of all the following activities on that path will be delayed.

Another important aspect of paths is the length (duration) of a path: How long will a particular sequence of activities take to complete? The length of any path can be determined by summing the expected duration of the activities on that path. The path with the largest duration is of particular interest because it governs project completion time. In other words, expected project duration equals the expected duration of the longest path. Moreover, if there are any delays along the longest path, there will be corresponding delays in project completion time. Attempts to shorten project completion must focus on the longest sequence of activities. Because of its influence on project completion time, the longest path is referred to as the **critical path**, and its activities are referred to as **critical activities**.

Paths that are shorter than the critical path can experience some delays and still not affect the overall project completion time as long as the ultimate path duration does not exceed the length of the critical path. The allowable slippage for any path is called **path slack**, and it reflects the difference between the length of a given path and the length of the critical path. The critical path, then, has zero path slack time.

Deterministic Activity Durations

The main determinant of the way PERT/CPM networks are analyzed and interpreted is whether activity durations are *probabilistic* or *deterministic*. If durations are fairly certain, we say that the durations are **deterministic**. If durations are subject to variation, we say that the durations are **probabilistic**. Probabilistic durations must include an indication of the extent of probable variation.

This section describes analysis of procedure network diagrams with deterministic activity durations. A later section deals with probabilistic activity durations.

One of the best ways to gain an understanding of the nature of a precedence network diagram and the critical path is to consider a simple example using an intuitive solution approach.

critical path The longest path from start to end; determines expected project duration.

critical activities Activities on the critical path.

path slack Allowable slippage for a path; the difference between the length of a path and the length of the critical (longest) path.

deterministic Durations that are fairly certain.

probabilistic Durations that allow for variation.

The Rogers Centre is one of the few stadiums in the world with a fully retractable roof. It was built in the late 1980s by general contractor Ellis-Don Ltd. The project scheduler used Primavera's Project Planner to schedule and control thousands of activities of different tradespeople working on this fast-track project. Despite problems with accessibility and a labour strike, the $400-million project was completed on time.

Source: S. Wintrob, "Project Management Helps Build the SkyDome," *Computing Canada* 15(2), January 18, 1989, pp. 1ff.

Example 1

Given the information provided in Figure 17–5 below:

FIGURE 17-5

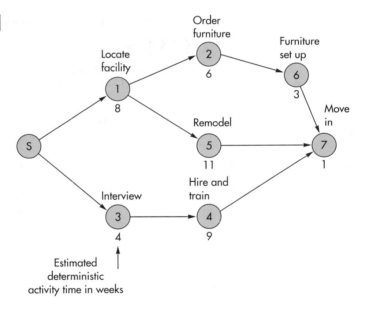

Determine:

a. The length (duration) of each path.

b. The critical path.

c. The expected length (duration) of the project.

d. Amount of slack time for each path.

Solution

a. As shown in the table on page 639, the path lengths (durations) are 18 weeks, 20 weeks, and 14 weeks.

b. The longest path (20 weeks) is S-1-5-7, so it is the critical path.

c. The expected length (duration) of the project is equal to the length of the critical path (i.e., 20 weeks).

d. We find the slack for each path by subtracting its length from the length of the critical path, as shown in the right column of the table. (*Note*: It is sometimes desirable to know the slack time associated with activities. The next section describes a method for obtaining those slack times.)

Path	Length (weeks)	Path Slack (weeks)
S-1-2-6-7	8 + 6 + 3 + 1 = 18	20 − 18 = 2
S-1-5-7	8 + 11 + 1 = 20*	20 − 20 = 0
S-3-4-7	4 + 9 + 1 = 14	20 − 14 = 6

*Critical path length.

READING

Tembec

When Tembec Paperboard Group decided to build a board mill in Tamiscaming, Quebec, in the late 1980s, Primavera project management software was used to plan the construction and purchase of equipment. The work breakdown structure was set up by area (e.g., unloading, board machine) and, within each area by discipline. Milestones were established for the start and end of project and each area. A Gantt chart was developed, acting as the master project schedule.

A detailed work breakdown was then done within each area and discipline using information provided by the subcontracts. Even though the budget was very detailed, the schedule contained only major activities. The following information was entered in the software: activity times and a precedence network diagram; a project calendar (workdays, holidays); activity codes for each activity including responsibility (e.g., Al Jo: mechanical), area (e.g., coating preparation),

accounting code, instrumentation, subcontracts, and milestones. The board machine area was broken down further into segments such as head-box, press, dryer, cylinder, and coater. Approximately 750 activities were entered in the software.

After the schedule was verified through discussions with subcontractors, a resource dictionary was set up and the schedule was loaded by labour requirements. A labour histogram was verified with the superintendents, and some activities were rescheduled because the labour requirement was higher than was available. The final labour histogram was resource-levelled using slack times.

The schedule was the basis of construction-level schedules and also used to monitor the progress of the job. The progress was compared with the master schedule on a monthly basis. A progress curve compared the work hours used per discipline with the budgeted work hours.

Source: R. Singh, "Computerized Planning/Scheduling on a Board Machine," *AACE Transactions*, 1990, pp. I.2.1–I.2.4.

Solution Technique

Many real-life precedence network diagrams are much larger than the simple network diagram illustrated in the preceding example; they often contain hundreds or even thousands of activities. Because the necessary calculations can become exceedingly complex and time-consuming, large network diagrams are generally analyzed by computer programs instead of manually. Planners use a solution technique to develop four values for each activity:

- ES, the *earliest* time the activity can *start* (assuming all preceding activities start as early as possible).
- EF, the *earliest* time the activity can *finish*.
- LS, the *latest* time the activity can *start* and not delay the project.
- LF, the *latest* time the activity can *finish* and not delay the project.

Once these values have been determined, they can be used to find:

1. Expected project duration.
2. Activity slack times.
3. The critical path.

The three examples that follow illustrate how to calculate these values using the precedence network diagram of Example 1.

Example 2	Calculate the earliest start time and earliest finish time for each activity in the diagram shown in Figure 17–5.

Solution

Begin by enlarging each node and placing activity number and duration inside it as follows:

We determine and place inside the node for each activity the earliest start time, ES, and the earliest finish time, EF, for the activity as follows:

Do this, beginning at the left side of the precedence network diagram and moving to the right side. Once ES has been determined for each activity, EF can be found by adding the activity duration, t, to ES: $ES + t = EF$.

Use an ES of 0 for the start node. The start node in this example has zero duration. Therefore, $EF_S = ES_S + t = 0 + 0 = 0$. The EF time of the start node becomes the ES time of the nodes immediately following it. Thus, $ES_1 = 0$ and $ES_3 = 0$.

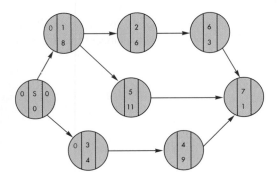

Next, $EF = ES + t$ for each of the nodes 1 and 3; i.e., $EF_1 = 0 + 8 = 8$ and $EF_3 = 0 + 4 = 4$.

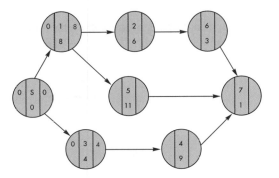

Now, because activity 1 has an EF time of 8, both activities 2 and 5 will have ES times of 8. Similarly, activity 4 will have an ES time of 4.

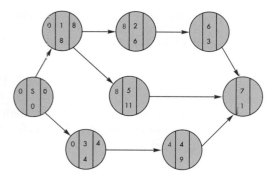

This permits calculation of the EF times for these activities: $EF_2 = 8 + 6 = 14$, $EF_5 = 8 + 11 = 19$, and $EF_4 = 4 + 9 = 13$.

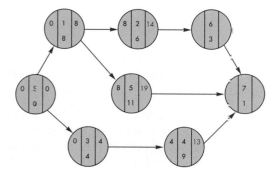

The ES for activity 6 is the EF time of activity 2 which is 14. Using this value, we find $EF_6 = 14 + 3 = 17$.

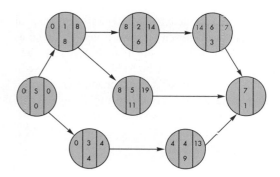

In order to determine the ES for activity 7, we must realize that activity 7 cannot start until *every* activity that immediately precedes it is finished. Therefore, the *largest* of the EF times for the three activities that immediately precede activity 7 determines ES_7. Hence, the ES for activity 7 is 19 (i.e., max (17, 19, 13)).

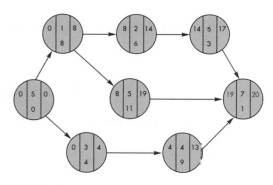

Then the EF for the last activity, 7, is 20; $EF_7 = 19 + 1 = 20$. Note that the latest EF is the project duration. Thus, the expected length of the project is 20 weeks.

Calculate the earliest start and finish times, aided by the following two simple rules:

1. The earliest finish time for any activity is equal to its earliest start time plus its expected duration, t:

$$EF = ES + t \qquad (17\text{--}1)$$

2. ES for an activity with one immediate preceding node is equal to EF of the immediately preceding node. ES for an activity with multiple immediate preceding nodes is equal to the largest EF of the immediately preceding nodes.

Calculation of the latest start and finish times is aided by the use of the following two rules:

1. The latest start time for any activity is equal to its latest finish time minus its expected duration:

$$LS = LF - t \qquad (17\text{--}2)$$

2. For a node with one immediate succeeding node, LF equals the LS of the immediately succeeding node. For a node with multiple immediate succeeding nodes, LF equals the smallest LS of immediately succeeding nodes.

Finding ES and EF times involves a *forward pass* through the precedence network diagram; finding LS and LF times involves a *backward pass* through the network. To calculate the latest time, we must begin with the EF of the last activity (end note) and use that time as the LF for the last activity. Then we obtain the LS for the last activity by subtracting its expected duration from its LF.

Example 3

Calculate the latest finish and start times for the precedence network diagram shown in Figure 17–5.

Solution

We will add the LS and LF times to the nodes just below the ES and EF determined in Example 2.

Begin by setting the LF time of the last activity equal to the EF of that activity. Thus,

$$LF_7 = EF_7 = 20 \text{ weeks}$$

Obtain the LS time for activity 7 by subtracting the activity duration, t, from the LF time:

$LS_7 = LF_7 - t = 20 - 1 = 19.$

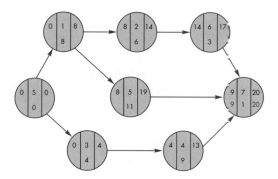

The LS time of 19 for activity 7 now becomes the LF time for each of the activities that immediately precede activity 7. Thus, $LF_6 = LF_5 = LF_4 = 19$. Now subtract the activity time from the LF to obtain the LS time for these activities. The LS time for activity 4 is $19 - 9 = 10$, for activity 5 is $19 - 11 = 8$, and for activity 6 is $19 - 3 = 16$.

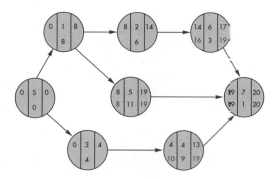

Next, the LS for activity 6, which is 16, becomes the LF for activity 2, and the LS for activity 4, which is 10, becomes the LF for activity 3. Using these values, you find the LS for each of these activities by subtracting the activity time from the LF time. Therefore, LS for activity 2 is $16 - 6 = 10$, and for activity 3 is $10 - 4 = 6$.

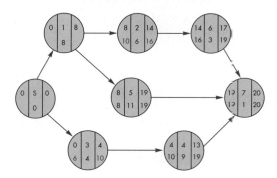

The LF for activity 1 is the *smaller* of the two LS times of the activities that immediately succeed it. Hence, the LF time for activity 1 is 8 (i.e., min (8, 10)). The reason you use the smaller time is that activity 1 must finish at a time that permits all the following activities to start no later than their LS times.

Once you have determined the LF time of activity 1, find its LS time by subtracting the activity time of 8 from the LF time of 8. Hence, its LS time is 0.

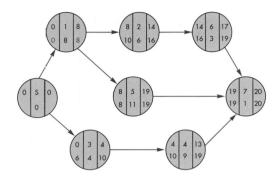

Next, the LF time of activity S is the smaller of LS times of activities 1 and 3, i.e., $LF_S = \min (0, 6) = 0$. Finally, $LS_S = LF_S - t = 0 - 0 = 0$.

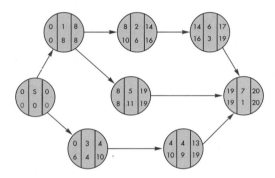

The rules for the solution technique are reiterated below.

Calculating Activity Slack Times. Activity slack times can be calculated in either of two ways:

$$\text{Slack} = \text{LS} - \text{ES} \quad \text{or} \quad \text{LF} - \text{EF} \tag{17–3}$$

The critical path consists of activities with zero slack time. Thus, the table in the following Example 4 indicates that activities S, 1, 5, and 7 are all critical activities, which agrees with the results of the intuitive approach demonstrated in Example 1.

Rules for the Solution Technique

Forward Pass

Start at the left side of the precedence network diagram and work toward the right side.

For the start activity: ES = 0.

For each activity: ES + Activity duration = EF.

For the unique immediate following activity: ES = EF of the immediately preceding activity.

Note: If an activity has multiple immediate preceding activities, set its ES equal to the largest EF of its immediate predecessors.

Backward Pass

Start at the right side of the precedence network diagram and work toward the left side.

Use the EF as the LF for the ending activity.

For each activity: LS = LF − Activity time.

For the unique immediate preceding activity: LF = LS of the immediately following activity.

Note: If an activity has multiple immediately following activities, set the activity's LF equal to the smallest LS of the immediately following activities.

Calculate activity slack times for the procedure network diagram of Figure 17–5.

Example 4

Either the start times or the finish times can be used. Suppose we choose the start times. Using ES times calculated in Example 2 and LS times calculated in Example 3, activity slack times are:

Solution

Activity	LS	ES	(LS – ES) Slack
S	0	0	C
1	0	0	C
3	6	0	6
2	10	8	2
5	8	8	0
4	10	4	6
6	16	14	2
7	19	19	0

Knowledge of activity slack times provides managers with information for planning allocation of scarce resources and for directing control efforts toward those activities that are most susceptible to delaying the project. In this regard, it is important to recognize that the activity slack times are based on the assumption that all of the activities on the same path will be started as early as possible and not exceed their expected times. Furthermore, if two activities are both on the same path (e.g., activities 2 and 6 in the preceding example) and have the same slack (e.g., two weeks), this will be the *total* slack available to both. In essence, the activities have *shared slack*. Hence, if the first activity uses all the slack, there will be zero slack left for all the following activities on that same path.

As noted earlier, this solution technique lends itself to computerization. This problem will be solved using Microsoft Project at the end of chapter.

Probabilistic Activity Durations

The preceding discussion assumed that activity durations were known and not subject to variation. While that assumption is appropriate in some situations, there are many others where it is not. Consequently, those situations require a probabilistic approach.

The probabilistic approach, called the **3-Point Estimates method**, involves *three* duration estimates for each activity instead of one:

1. **Optimistic duration:** The length of time under the best conditions; represented by t_o.
2. **Pessimistic duration:** The length of time under the worst conditions; represented by t_p.
3. **Most likely duration:** The most probable amount of time; represented by t_m.

Managers or others with knowledge about the project can make these duration estimates.

The **Beta distribution** is a family of continuous positive distributions used to describe the inherent variability in activity durations (see Figure 17–6). Although there is no real theoretical justification for using the Beta distribution, it has certain features that make it attractive in practice: The distribution can be symmetrical or skewed to either the right or the left depending on its shape parameters; the mean and variance of the distribution can be readily obtained from the three estimates listed above; and shape parameters can be chosen so that the distribution is unimodal with a high concentration of probability surrounding the most likely duration estimate.

3-Point Estimates method PERT when the activity durations are variable and are determined using three estimates: optimistic, most likely, and pessimistic.

optimistic duration The length of time under the best conditions (t_o).

pessimistic duration The length of time under the worst conditions (t_p).

most likely duration The most probable length of time (t_m).

Beta distribution A family of continuous positive distributions used to describe the inherent variability in activity durations.

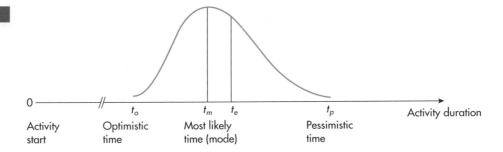

Of special interest in probabilistic PERT analysis are the average or expected duration for each activity t_e, and the variance of each activity duration, σ^2. The expected duration of an activity, t_e, is an unequally weighted average of the three estimates:

$$t_e = \frac{t_o + 4t_m + t_p}{6} \tag{17–4}$$

The expected (mean) duration of a path is equal to the sum of the expected duration of the activities on that path:

$$\text{Path mean} = \Sigma \text{ expected duration of activities on the path.} \tag{17–5}$$

The standard deviation of each activity's duration is estimated as one-sixth of the difference between the pessimistic and optimistic estimates. (Analogously, almost all of the area under a Normal distribution lies within three standard deviations of the mean, which is a range of six standard deviations.) We find the variance by squaring the standard deviation. Thus,

$$\sigma^2 = \left[\frac{(t_p - t_o)}{6} \right]^2 \quad \text{or} \quad \frac{(t_p - t_o)^2}{36} \tag{17–6}$$

The size of the variance reflects the degree of uncertainty associated with an activity's duration: The larger the variance, the greater the uncertainty.

It is also desirable to calculate the standard deviation of the total duration for *each path*. We can do this by summing the variances of the activity durations on the path and then taking the square root of that number; that is,

$$\sigma_{\text{path}} = \sqrt{\Sigma (\text{variances of activity durations on path})} \tag{17–7}$$

Example 5 illustrates these calculations.

Example 5

The precedence network diagram for a project is shown below, with three duration estimates for each activity (in weeks) over each hole. Do the following:

a. Calculate the expected duration for each activity and the expected duration for each path.

b. Identify the critical path (based on expected durations).

c. Calculate the variance of each activity and the standard deviation of each path.

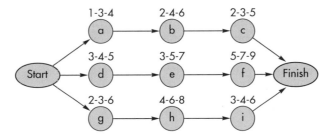

a. Because the start and finish activities do not take any time in this example, we can   ***Solution***
ignore them in the following calculations:

Path	Activity	DURATIONS t_o	t_m	t_p	$t_e = \dfrac{t_o + 4t_m + t_p}{6}$	Path Total
a-b-c	a	1	3	4	2.83 ⎫	
	b	2	4	6	4.00 ⎬	10.00
	c	2	3	5	3.17 ⎭	
d-e-f	d	3	4	5	4.00 ⎫	
	e	3	5	7	5.00 ⎬	16.00
	f	5	7	9	7.00 ⎭	
g-h-i	g	2	3	6	3.33 ⎫	
	h	4	6	8	6.00 ⎬	13.50
	i	3	4	6	4.17 ⎭	

b. The path that has the largest expected duration is the critical path. Because path d-e-f
has the largest expected path total, it is the critical path.

c.

Path	Activity	DURATIONS t_o	t_m	t_p	$\sigma^2_{act} = \dfrac{(t_p - t_o)^2}{36}$	σ^2_{path}	σ_{path}
a-b-c	a	1	3	4	$(4-1)^2/36 = 9/36$		
	b	2	4	6	$(6-2)^2/36 = 16/36$	$34/36 = 0.944$	0.97
	c	2	3	5	$(5-2)^2/36 = 9/36$		
d-e-f	d	3	4	5	$(5-3)^2/36 = 4/36$		
	e	3	5	7	$(7-3)^2/36 = 16/36$	$36/36 = 1.00$	1.00
	f	5	7	9	$(9-5)^2/36 = 16/36$		
g-h-i	g	2	3	6	$(6-2)^2/36 = 16/36$		
	h	4	6	8	$(8-4)^2/36 = 16/36$	$41/36 = 1.139$	1.07
	i	3	4	6	$(6-3)^2/36 = 9/36$		

Knowledge of the path's expected duration and standard deviation enables a manager
to compute probabilistic estimates of the project completion time, such as these:

The probability that the project will be completed by a specified time.

The probability that the project will take longer than its scheduled completion time.

These estimates can be derived from the probability that various paths will be
completed by the specified time or take longer than the scheduled completion time.
Although activity durations are represented by Beta distribution, the path duration distribution is represented by a Normal distribution. The summing of activity duration random
variables results in a Normal distribution. This concept, called the central limit theorem,
is illustrated in Figure 17–7.

FIGURE 17-7

*Activity duration distributions
and the path duration distribution*

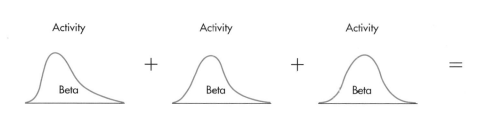 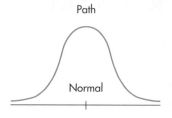

FIGURE 17-8

The path probability is the area under a Normal curve to the left of z

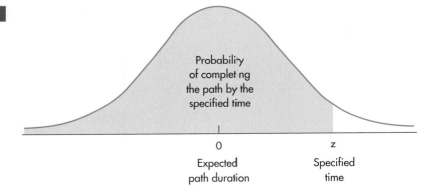

FIGURE 17-8

The path probability is the area under a Normal curve to the left of z

Determining Path Probabilities

The probability that a given path will be completed in a specified length of time can be determined using the following formula:

$$z = \frac{\text{Specified length of time} - \text{Expected path duration}}{\text{Standard deviation of path duration}} \qquad (17\text{--}8)$$

The resulting value of z indicates how many standard deviations of the path duration the specified length of time is beyond the expected path duration. (A negative value of z indicates that the specified time is *earlier* than the expected path duration.) Once the value of z has been determined, it can be used to obtain the probability that the path will be completed by the specified time from Appendix B, Table B. Note that the probability is equal to the area under the Normal curve to the left of z, as illustrated in Figure 17–8.

A project is not completed until *all* of its activities have been completed, not only those on the critical path. It sometimes happens that another path ends up taking more time to complete than the critical path, in which case the project runs longer than expected. Hence, it can be risky to focus exclusively on the critical path. This requires determining the probability that *all* paths will finish by a specified time. To do that, find the probability that each path will finish by the specified time, and then multiply those probabilities. The result is the probability that the *project* will be completed by the specified time. This assumes independence of path durations. In practice, for a large project which contains a lot of paths, up to 10 longest paths are examined.

The assumption of **independence** of path durations requires two things: activity durations are independent of each other, and each activity is on only one path. For activity durations to be independent, the duration for one must not be a function of the duration of another; if two activities were always early or late together, they would not be considered independent. The assumption of independent *paths* is usually considered to be met if only a *few* activities in a large project are on multiple paths. Even then, common sense should govern the decision of whether the independence assumption is justified.

independence Assumption that path durations are independent of each other, requiring that activity durations be independent and that each activity be on only one path.

Example 6

Using the information from Example 5, answer the following questions:

a. Can the paths be considered independent? Why?

b. What is the probability that the project can be completed within 17 weeks of its start?

c. What is the probability that the project will be completed within 15 weeks of its start?

d. What is the probability that the project will *not* be completed within 15 weeks of its start?

Solution

a. Yes, the paths can be considered independent, since no activity is on more than one path and you have no information suggesting that activity durations are interrelated.

b. To answer questions of this nature, you must take into account the degree to which the path duration distributions "exceed" the specified completion time. This concept is illustrated in the following figure which shows the three path duration distributions, each centred on that path's expected duration, and the specified completion time of 17 weeks.

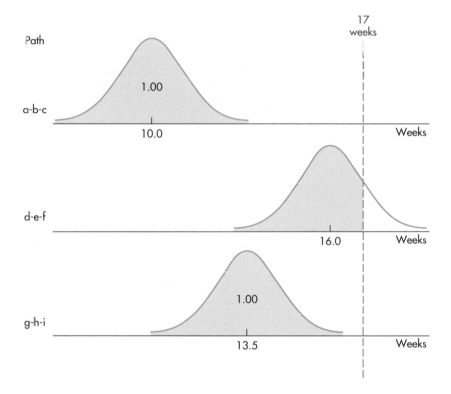

The coloured portion of each distribution corresponds to the probability that the path will be completed within the specified time. Observe that paths a-b-c and g-h-i are well enough to the left of the specified time so that it is highly likely that both will be finished by week 17. In such cases, you essentially need to consider only the distribution of path d-e-f in assessing the probability of completion by week 17. To do so, you must first calculate the value of z using formula 17–8 for this path:

$$z = \frac{17 - 16}{1.00} = +1.00$$

Turning to Appendix B, Table B with $z = +1.00$, you will find that the area under the curve to the left of z is .8413. To check our intuition, the probabilities for the other two paths are also calculated, and all three are summarized in the following table. Note: If the value of z exceeds $+3.50$, treat the probability of completion as being equal to 1.

Path	$z = \dfrac{17 - \text{Expected path duration}}{\text{Standard deviation of path duration}}$	Probability of Completion in 17 Weeks
a-b-c	$\dfrac{17 - 10}{.97} = +7.22$	1.00
d-e-f	$\dfrac{17 - 16}{1.00} = +1.00$	.8413
g-h-i	$\dfrac{17 - 13.5}{1.07} = +3.27$	.9995

Thus, Prob(finish by week 17) = Prob(path a-b-c finish by week 17) × Prob(path d-e-f finish week 17) × Prob(path g-h-i finish by week 17)

$$= 1.00 \times .8413 \times .9995 = .8409 \sim 84\%$$

c. For a specified time of 15 weeks, the z values are:

Path	$z = \dfrac{15 - \text{Expected path duration}}{\text{Standard deviation of path duration}}$	Probability of Completion in 15 Weeks
a-b-c	$\dfrac{15 - 10}{.97} = +5.15$	1.0000
d-e-f	$\dfrac{15 - 16}{1.00} = -1.00$	.1587
g-h-i	$\dfrac{15 - 13.5}{1.07} = +1.40$	.9192

Paths d-e-f and g-h-i have z values that are less than $+2.50$. From Appendix B, Table B, the area to the *left* of $z = -1.00$ is .1587, and the area to the *left* of $z = +1.40$ is .9192. The path distributions are illustrated in the following figure. The joint probability of all paths finishing before week 15 is the product of their probabilities: $(1.00)(.1587)(.9192) = .1459$.

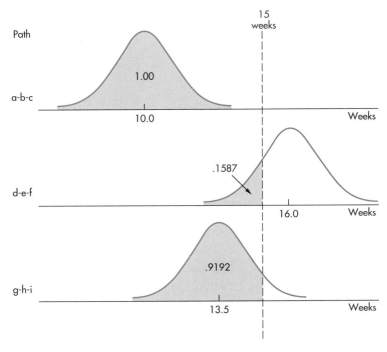

d. The probability of not finishing before week 15 is the complement of the probability obtained in part c: $1 - .1459 = .8541$.

READING

Toronto Transit Commission

www.city.toronto.on.ca/ttc

The Toronto Transit Commission (TTC) is responsible for running the buses, subway, and light rail system in the Toronto area. It employs approximately 9,000 people, and there are approximately 60 engineering and construction projects underway at any time. Each project has a budget of $2 million to $100 million, lasts approximately five years, and involves an average of 100 to 150 activities. The projects are managed by the Engineering and Construction branch, which employs approximately 300 people. Head scheduler Vince Carroll says, "Engineering managers need to see how other projects may impact their own. Senior managers need to communicate with city government to secure funding. Marketing and public relations people need the latest information to set public expectations." The above is the main reason why TTC purchased Primavera Project Planner. TTC produces a master schedule that summarizes the status of each project using bar charts and also shows the links between projects. The 90-page summary used to take 10 times longer to prepare manually.

Source: www.primavera.com/files/customers/tortransit.pdf, accessed 2002.

Simulation. The above discussion assumed that the paths of the project were *independent*, which requires that the same activities not be on more than one path. If an activity were on more than one path and it happened that the completion time for that activity far exceeded its expected time, all paths that include that activity would be affected and, hence, their durations would not be independent. If only a few activities are on multiple paths, particularly if the paths are *much* shorter than the critical path, the independence assumption may still be reasonable.

Otherwise project planners often use *simulation*. It amounts to a form of repeated sampling wherein many passes are made through the precedence network diagram. In each pass, a random value for each activity duration is selected from the activity durations probability distribution. After each pass, the project duration is determined by adding the times along each path and designating the time of the longest path as the project duration. After a large number of such passes (e.g., several hundred), there is enough information to prepare a frequency distribution of the project duration. Project scheduler can use this distribution to make a probabilistic assessment of the actual project duration.

ACTIVITY CRASHING

Estimates of activity durations for projects usually are made for some given level of resources. In many situations, it is possible to reduce the length of a project by using additional resources. The impetus to shorten projects may reflect efforts to avoid late penalties, to take advantage of monetary incentives for timely or early competition of a project, or to free resources for use on other projects. In new product development, shortening the time may lead to a strategic benefit: beating the competition to the market. In some cases, however, the desire to shorten the length of a project merely reflects an attempt to reduce the indirect costs associated with running the project, such as facilities and equipment costs, supervision, and personnel costs.

Managers often have certain options at their disposal that will allow them to shorten, or **crash**, certain activities. Among the most obvious options are the use of additional funds to support additional personnel or more efficient equipment, and the relaxing of some work specifications (reducing the scope). Hence, a project manager may be able to shorten a project by increasing *direct* expenses to speed up the project, thereby realizing savings on indirect project costs. Time–cost trade-off can be used to identify those activities that will reduce the sum of the indirect and direct project costs.

crash Shortening activity duration.

Activities on the critical path are potential candidates for crashing, because shortening noncritical activities would not have an impact on total project duration. From an economic standpoint, activities should be crashed according to crashing cost per period: crash those with the lowest crash cost per period first. Moreover, crashing should continue as long as the cost to crash is less than the benefits derived from crashing.

FIGURE 17-9

*Crashing activities**

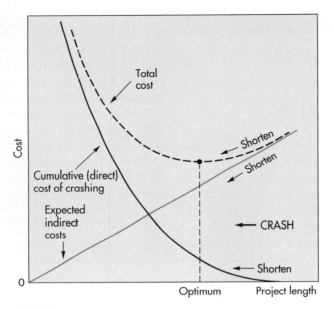

* Crashing activities reduces indirect project costs (minus incentives) but increase direct costs; the optimum amount of crashing results in minimizing the sum of these two types of costs.

We assume that the indirect costs (minus the incentive payments) are a linear function of project length. Also, we assume (direct) crashing cost per period increases faster the more you crash the project. Figure 17–9 illustrates the basic relationship between indirect, direct, and total project costs due to crashing.

The general procedure for crashing is:

1. Obtain estimates of regular and crash durations and direct and indirect costs per period for each activity.

2. Determine the lengths of all paths.

3. Determine which are the critical activities.

4. Crash critical activities, starting from the cheapest, as long as crashing cost per period does not exceed the benefits. Note that two or more paths may become critical as the original critical path becomes shorter, so that subsequent improvements will require simultaneous shortening of two or more paths. In some cases, it will be more economical to shorten an activity that is on two (or more) of the critical paths than two (or more) activities on each critical path.

Example 7

Using the following information and precedence network diagram, develop the optimal activity crashing. Indirect project costs are $1,000 per day.

Activity	Normal Duration (days)	Crash Duration (days)	Cost per Day to Crash
a	6	6	—
b	10	8	$500
c	5	4	300
d	4	1	700
e	9	7	600
f	2	1	800

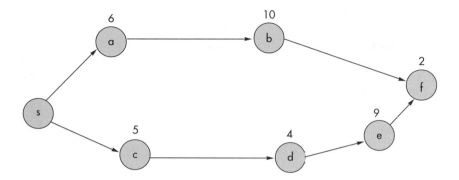

a. Determine which activities are on the critical path, its length, and the length of the   **Solution**
other path:

Path	Length
s-a-b-f	18
s-c-d-e-f	20 (critical path)

b. Rank the critical-path activities in order of crashing cost per day, starting from the lowest, and determine the number of days for which each can be crashed.

Activity	Cost per Day to Crash	Available Days to Crash
c	$300	1
e	600	2
d	700	3
f	800	1

c. Begin shortening the project, one day at a time, and check after each reduction to see if the other path becomes critical. (After a certain point, the other path's length may equal the length of the shortened critical path.) Thus:

(1) Shorten the activity with cheapest crash cost per day, activity *c*, one day at a cost of $300. The length of the critical path now becomes 19 days.

(2) Activity *c* cannot be shortened any more. Shorten the activity with next cheapest crash cost per day, activity *e*, one day at a cost of $600. The length of path *s-c-d-e-f* now becomes 18 days, which is the same as the length of path s-a-b-f.

(3) The paths are now both critical; further improvements will necessitate shortening both paths.

The remaining activities for crashing and their costs are:

Path	Activity	Crash Cost (per day)	Available Days
s-a-b-f	a	–	0
	b	$500	2
	f	800	1
s-c-d-e-f	c	–	0
	e	$600	1
	d	700	3
	f	800	1

At first glance, it would seem that crashing f would not be advantageous, because it has the highest crashing cost per day. However, f is on both paths, so shortening f by one day would shorten *both* paths (and hence, the project) by one day for a cost of $800. The option of shortening the least expensive activity on each path would cost $500 for b for s-a-b-f and $600 for e for s-c-d-e-f, or $1,100 in total. Thus, shorten f by one day. The project duration is now 17 days.

(4) At this point, no additional crashing is cost-effective. The cost to crash b and e is a total of $1,100, and that would exceed the indirect project costs of $1,000 per day.

The crashing sequence is summarized below:

	LENGTH AFTER CRASHING *n* DAYS:			
Path	***n* = 0**	**1**	**2**	**3**
s-a-b-f	18	18	18	17
s-c-d-e-f	20	19	18	17
Activity crashed		c	e	f
Cost		$300	$600	$800

PROJECT EXECUTION

project execution Involves performance of activities planned.

Project execution involves the actual performance of the activities planned in project planning. The project manager directs, coordinates, and manages project activities and team members. The budgeted funds are expended to accomplish the project objectives. Resources are obtained, managed, and used. The planned methods and standards are implemented to create deliverables.

During execution, quality of the product is assured by applying the planned systematic quality activities to ensure that the project will employ all processes needed to meet its requirements.

Team members who are not yet assigned are chosen, their skills are assessed, needed training instituted, and ground rules for team participation is set.

Any purchases or subcontracting plans, whose supplier is not determined yet, is finalized, and contracts are negotiated.

The plan for information collection and distribution is executed using clear and timely information in appropriate form (written, oral, formal, informal, using software, manual, etc). Unexpected requests for information by stakeholders are responded to.

PROJECT MONITORING AND CONTROL

project control Involves comparing project's progress against plans and taking corrective action if necessary.

Project monitoring involves observing a project's progress, and **project control** involves assessing these observations against plans and taking corrective actions, if necessary, in order to bring the project on track. Forecasts of costs, completion time, etc., are generated using trend analysis to determine the need for action.

Project control also involves controlling the changes to the project, e.g., to the project scope. Replanning is usually necessary, but it should be kept to a minimum. Changes to the project scope should be tightly controlled. If acceptable to the project's management, a change to the scope should be formally verified (i.e., authorized by the customers/users/sponsor). A common problem is that the customers/users tend to frequently demand changes to the work required. The problem of uncontrolled changes to the project scope is called *scope creep*.

To monitor and control a project's cost and schedule, various measures are used. Work performance information includes the completed and uncompleted deliverables, ongoing and completed activities, percentage of each activity completed, costs authorized/incurred, cost estimates to (project) completion time, and so on.

A common technique used for cost control is *earned value analysis*. After the project time and cost are planned (called schedule baseline and cost baseline or budget), the

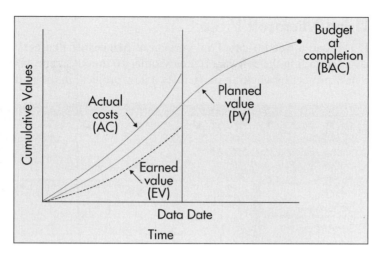

FIGURE 17-10

Cumulative cost values for a project that is overbudget and behind schedule.

Source: Project Management Institute, *A Guide to the Project Management Body of Knowledge* (PMBOK® Guide), third edition, 2004. Copyright and all rights reserved. Material from this publication has been reproduced with the permission of PMI.

progress of the project is measured, not by the budgeted cost of work scheduled (BCWS; also known as planned value, PV), but by budgeted cost of work performed (BCWP; also known as earned value, EV). The scheduled time overrun is measured by schedule "variance" = PV – EV, and the cost overrun is measured by cost "variance" = actual cost – EV. See Figure 17–10 for an overbudget project which is also behind schedule. Also, forecasts of cost estimate to completion (ETC) and estimate at completion (EAC) are made.

Quality monitoring and control involves using quality tools such as control charts and cause and effect diagrams in order to identify quality "variance," find its cause, and implement corrective actions.

Project team is monitored and controlled by measuring team performance, providing feedback, resolving issues, and recognizing and rewarding good performance.

Software, e-mail, status review meetings, etc., are used to collect and report performance of project in the form of status reports, progress measurements, and forecasts. Communication with project stakeholders is monitored and controlled by resolving issues promptly.

Risks are tracked, reassessed, and the response plans evaluated. Reserve analysis is performed to determine the adequacy of the contingency fund.

Contracts are administered by measuring the performance of supplier, comparing it with the contract requirements, and taking corrective actions if necessary. The relations with suppliers are managed by quickly resolving issues such as contested changes or late payments.

PROJECT MANAGEMENT SOFTWARE

Many project management software packages are available such as Microsoft Project, Primavera Project Planner, and Open Plan by Deltek (Welcom) Software Technology.

There are many advantages to using a project management software package. Among them are the following:

- It imposes a methodology and a common project management terminology.
- It provides a logical planning structure.
- It can enhance communication among team members.
- It can flag the occurrence of constraint violations.
- It automatically formats reports.
- It can generate multiple levels of summary reports and detailed reports.
- It enables "what-if" scenarios.
- It can generate various chart types, including basic Gantt charts.

Using Microsoft Project

Microsoft Project A project management software from Microsoft Corp.

Download a free 60-day Trial version of **Microsoft Project**[1] (takes about 10 minutes). After installing the software (takes another 10 minutes approximately), open it, and create a new project by clicking on "Create a new project" in the middle of the left column:

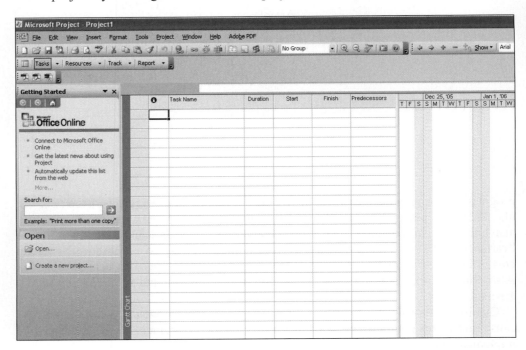

Then, click on "Tasks" in the top menu to get a list of tasks (in blue) on the left:

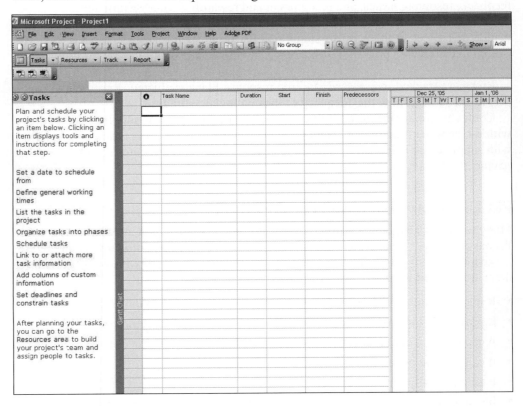

You can leave "Set a date to schedule from" as is (if project will start today). However, you should click on "Define general working times," then press "Save and go to step . . ."

---

[1]www.microsoft.com/office/project/prodinfo/trial.mspx#ECAA.

in the bottom left twice until you get to step 3, "Set holidays and days off." Here, click on "Change working time …" to have a small window open:

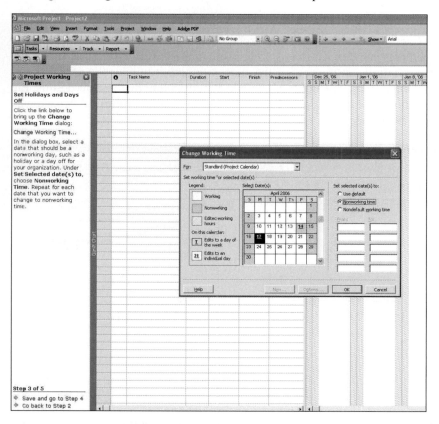

Next, assign the public holidays during the length of your project as "Nonworking time" (these squares will turn grey). This is done by clicking on the holiday and then clicking on the "Nonworking time" button on the top right on the small window. You can move to the next month by pressing the arrow-down blue square in the small window, and repeat. Finally, press OK. Press the Save button in the bottom of left column (of the large window) three times to get back to the list of tasks.

Press the "List the tasks in the project," and enter the activities and their duration. Microsoft Project will assign numbers to the activities starting with 1 (for the top row). Use "w" if the duration is in weeks; e.g., enter 8w for 8 weeks. As you enter an activity and its duration, the Gantt chart on the right assigns a horizontal bar to the activity. After you have entered all the activities, press "Done" in the middle of the left column. We have entered the data from Example 1 below:

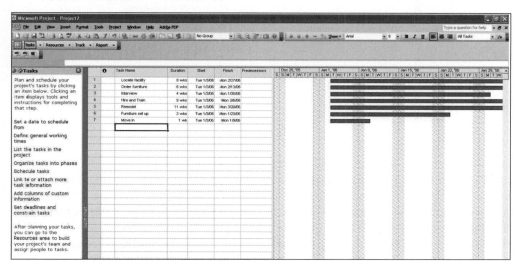

In order to see the whole Gantt chart, press the "Zoom Out" icon (i.e., the icon on the top showing a magnifying glass with a minus sign in it). Note that all the activities start at the current date.

In order to give the precedence relationships, press the "Schedule tasks" on the left, then select two activities with finish-start relationship (by keeping the control key pressed), and then pressing the "finish to start link" on the left. This will write the number of the predecessor activity in the row of the successor activity under the predecessors column. Alternatively, one can enter this number directly. Note that as you do this, the Gantt chart will move the successor's bar to the right. Continue until all precedence relationships have been specified.

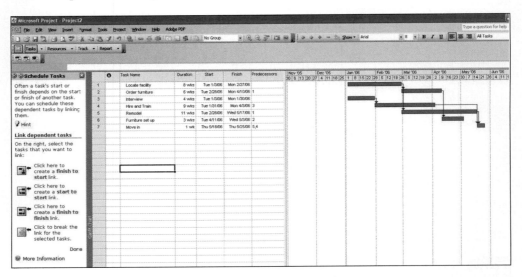

To see the precedence network diagram, under the "View" pull-down menu choose "Network diagram":

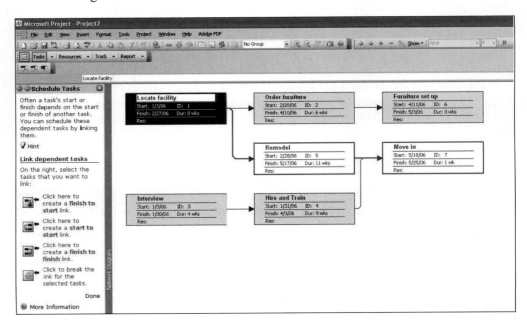

As you can see, the box for critical activities has red border lines.

Microsoft Project also permits us to define resources (i.e., employees and equipment) and to assign these to the activities. This is done by pressing the "Resources" button just to the right of "Tasks" button on the top left. Also, Microsoft Project allows us to track the progress of activities. This is done by pressing the "Track" button just to the right of the "Resources" button. As days pass, team members should enter the percentage of each activity completed. The software will indicate if any activity is behind schedule.

Deltek (Welcom)[2]

The Deltek (Welcom) Project Portfolio Management (PPM) software suite is an integrated toolset with modules supporting portfolio analysis, risk management, planning and scheduling, project collaboration, and complete earned value management (EVM). This modular, integrated toolset provides timely and selective information to all project participants from chief executives to project managers to team members.

Five products support the Deltek PPM suite: WelcomPortfolio™, WelcomRisk™, WelcomHome™, Open Plan®, and Cobra®. Each product can be used standalone or configured in combination to meet customer requirements. The complete suite supports the full project life cycle from conception through to closure.

Deltek's WelcomPortfolio is a portfolio analysis tool that provides a structured approach to evaluating, selecting, and prioritizing projects so that resources are invested in the projects that best fit current business or organizational strategy. Scoring criteria such as net present value and return on investment are included in a library with the ability to edit or create new ones. Users can also utilize project risk scores generated in Deltek's WelcomRisk as additional scoring criteria.

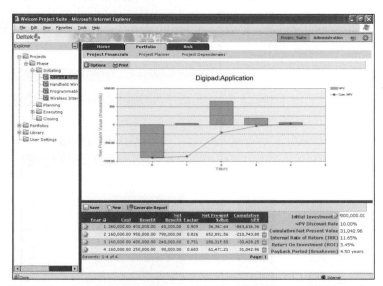

Typical project financial analysis with user-defined reporting criteria in WelcomPortfolio.

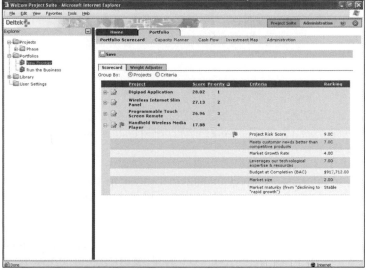

A typical portfolio of potential new projects with respective scores. Note the project risk score from Deltek's WelcomRisk is being used as a ranking criterion.

[2]Deltek section courtesy of Deltek staff.

Deltek's WelcomRisk is a risk management solution for the systematic identification, mitigation, and reporting of organizational and project risk on both threats and opportunities. Graphical reports allow executives to assess risk exposure across projects and track mitigation efforts. Project risks are identified, quantified, and tracked to increase project control and minimize risk exposure. Team members play a collaborative role in identifying and mitigating risks using a formalized process.

WelcomRisk supports a typical five-step process to reduce risk and increase control. Risk planning is supported by identifying risk categories (in development, production, technical, political), risk assessment is done by identifying impact types (on cost, quality, schedule, safety), the probability and severity impact of each risk, risk mitigation, and risk monitoring and control.

Risk identification involves determining a risk breakdown structure (also called a Risk Tree) and using it to calculate the risk of a project, working from bottom up using the risk scores. Risk assessment uses each risk, its cause, and potential consequences. The probability and impact severity is estimated and a risk score is generated for each risk event. The risk score is tracked overtime and is expected to be reduced as a result of risk mitigation. Risk mitigation involves the approach and steps to reduce the risk score. WelcomRisk has a library of generic response types, and can also recalculate the risk score given the mitigation steps undertaken. Risk Monitoring and Control uses reports such as Risk Tree and "waterfall" diagrams.

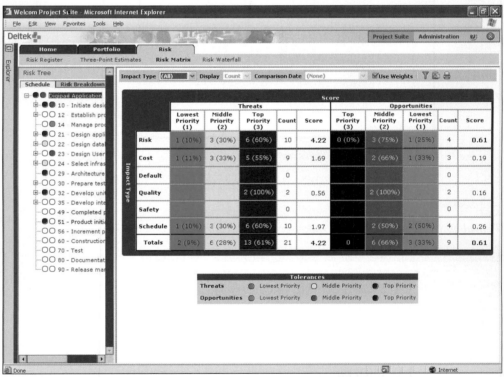

Typical risk tree (on the left) built from a project schedule with corresponding matrix showing threats and opportunities on a project.

Deltek's Open Plan is an enterprise project management system that improves an organization's ability to complete multiple projects on time and on budget. Multi-project analysis, critical path planning and resource management are supported.

Inter-project constraints are easily modeled in Open Plan. Resource constraints and relationships can be created either at a high level between projects or at a more detailed level between specific activities in different projects. The relative priority of projects can be adjusted to ensure that important projects have access to resources first.

Deltek Open Plan's views can be tailored to create custom reports. For flexible program analysis, projects can be grouped into multi-projects, with the ability for a project to belong to more than one multi-project.

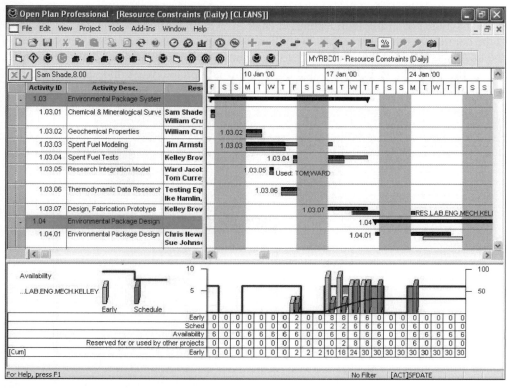

Open Plan's advanced Gantt chart view automatically showing constraining resources.

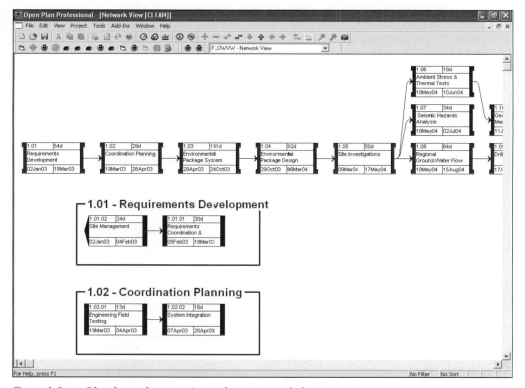

Typical Open Plan logic diagram (precedence network diagram).

Deltek's Cobra is a robust cost management tool for managing project costs, measuring earned value, and analyzing budgets, actuals and forecasts. Earned value is a means of putting a dollar value on project status. This allows one to formulate a three-way comparison between budget, actual costs, and project status in order to evaluate the true health of project. Simply analyzing budget versus actual costs often gives an incorrect picture of project status. For example, if a contract is 10 percent under budget, this might appear as if the contract is doing very well. Yet, when the project status or earned value is added to the analysis, it shows that only half of the originally planned work has been performed. Thus, the contract is behind schedule and the completed work has cost more than originally planned!

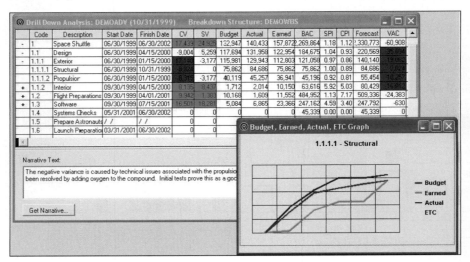

Cobra drill down report highlighting problem areas and an earned value curve.

Deltek's WelcomHome is a Web-based project management portal that provides all project participants with easy access to project information. It provides live access to schedules, budgets, action items, and project documents. WelcomHome also allows submission of progress and timesheet information using only a browser.

Graphical dashboards provide executives with high-level summaries at the program level. These views include cost, schedule, and outstanding item metrics in the form of bar charts, line graphs, and pie charts.

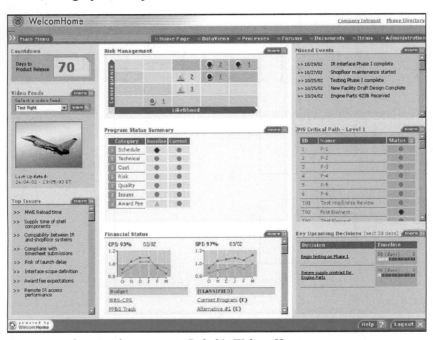

A customized project homepage in Deltek's WelcomHome.

Such instruments grouped together within a dashboard provide the user with an easy means of obtaining a high-level status overview of a project or program. Dashboards can also serve as an early warning system for potential problems (e.g. red, yellow, green indicators), helping busy executives make timely decisions and take corrective action. Each instrument can be expanded to show additional detailed metric information and can report at a project or program level.

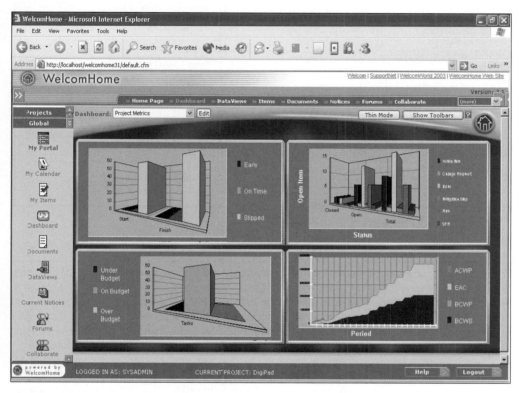

Sample project metrics dashboard in WelcomHome.

Primavera

Primavera[3] is a project and portfolio management software which can be used by various stakeholders for information technology (IT), construction, new product development, and other projects.

Every project participant is able to access the information in the form that he/she needs. For example, the executives/project sponsor can access high-level portfolio status displays. Chief information officers (for IT projects) can access programmers' availability and requirement charts. If there is a Project Management Office (PMO), its staff can use process flow diagrams for project administration. Project managers use the project information to manage and control the project and generate summary reports. There may be project controllers/cost managers/resource managers who estimate project costs and monitor the expenses. There may be a contract manager who tabulates the bids, negotiates contracts, and manages submittals (requests for a change/clarification/material approval) from the subcontractors. The scheduler draws the Gantt/PERT chart and updates it. Supervisors can enter project progress information into the system using hand-held devices. Subcontractors also report their progress to the project manager. Team members can see their assigned activities and schedule in the software. For an application, see the "Toronto Transit Commission" reading earlier in this chapter.

---

[3]www.primavera.com/customer.

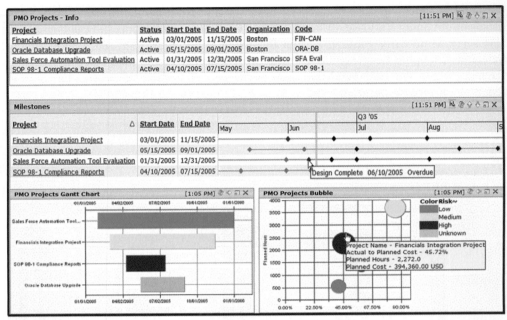

Example of a high level view of some projects.

SUMMARY

Projects are unique operations established to realize a given set of objectives in a limited time span. Projects go through a life cycle that involves initiation, planning, execution, control, and closeout. Most project teams organize as a matrix, with members working for both the project and a functional department. The non-routine nature of project activities places a set of demands on the project manager that are different in many respects from those the manager of more routine operations experiences, both in planning and control of the work and in the human problems encountered.

Project planning involves finalizing the project scope, creating the work breakdown structure, risk management planning, scheduling, cost estimation and budgeting, and quality, communication, and purchase planning. Risk management planning involves risk identification, assessment, and response planning. Gantt charts are used to schedule simple projects.

PERT/CPM is used to schedule and control complex projects. It depicts the sequential relationships that exist among activities and reveals to managers which activities must be completed on time to achieve timely project completion. Managers can use that information to direct their attention and resources toward the most critical activities.

For projects with variable activity durations, the 3-point Estimates method can be used.

In some instances, it may be possible to shorten, or crash, the length of a project by shortening one or more of the activities. Typically, such gains are achieved by the use of additional resources, although in some cases it may be possible to transfer resources among project activities.

Project execution involves putting the project plans into action, buying materials and assigning team members, or subcontracting the work. Project monitoring and control means taking measurements of project performance, using corrective actions, and replanning if necessary. Microsoft Project, Deltek's (Welcom), and Primavera are widely used project management software.

KEY TERMS

activity-on-arrow (AOA), 636
activity-on-node (AON), 636
Beta distribution, 645
CPM, 635
crash, 651
critical activities, 637
critical path, 637
deterministic, 637
Gantt chart, 634

independence, 648
matrix organization, 629
Microsoft Project, 656
most likely duration, 645
optimistic duration, 645
path, 636
path slack, 637
PERT, 635
pessimistic duration, 645

The following table contains information related to the major activities of a research project. Use the information to do the following:

a. Draw a precedence network diagram.

b. Find the critical path by identifying all the start to end paths and calculating their lengths.

c. What is the expected duration of the project?

Activity	Immediately Precedes	Expected Duration (days)
a	c, b	5
c	d	8
d	i	2
b	i	7
e	f	3
f	m	6
i	m	10
m	End	8
g	h	1
h	k	2
k	End	17

Solution

a. In constructing precedence network diagrams, these observations can be useful.

(1) Activities with no predecessors are at the beginning (left side) of the network, immediately after the start node S.

(2) Activities with multiple predecessors are located at path intersections.

Complete the diagram in sections. Go down the activity list in order to avoid overlooking any activities.

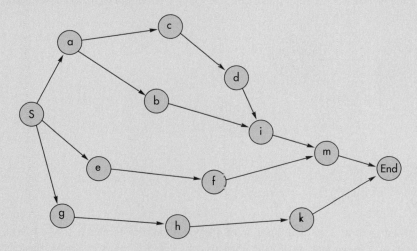

Here are some additional hints for constructing a precedence network diagram.

(1) Use pencil.

(2) Start and end with a single node.

(3) Try to avoid having paths cross each other.
(4) Have arrows go from left to right.

b. and *c.*

Path	Length (days)
s-a-c-d-i-m-End*	$5 + 8 + 2 + 10 + 8 = 33^†$
s-a-b-i-m-End	$5 + 7 + 10 + 8 = 30$
s-e-f-m-End	$3 + 6 + 8 = 17$
s-g-h-k-End	$1 + 2 + 17 = 20$

*Critical path.
†Expected project duration.

Problem 2

Using the PERT/CPM solution technique, determine the slack times for the following precedence network diagram (durations are in days). Identify the activities that are on the critical path.

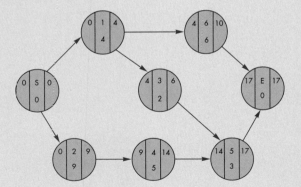

Solution

The task of determining ES, EF, LS, and LF times can be greatly simplified by first setting up a large circle for each node:

Then determine the earliest start and finish times, working from left to right, as shown in the following diagram.

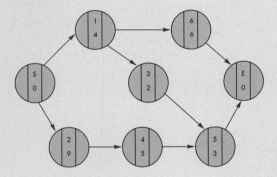

Thus, activity 1 can start at 0. With a duration of 4 days, it can finish after $0 + 4 = 4$ days. Hence, activity 6 and 3 can start no earlier than day 4. Activity 6 has an early finish of $4 + 6 = 10$ days, and activity 3 has an early finish of $4 + 2 = 6$ days. At this point, it is impossible to say what the earliest start is for activity 5; that will depend on which activity, 4 or 3, has the larger EF. Consequently, it is necessary to calculate ES and EF along the lower path. Using an ES of 0 for activity 2, its EF will be 9, so activity 4 will have an ES of 9 and an EF of $9 + 5 = 14$.

Considering that the two activities entering node 5 have EF times of 6 and 14, the earliest that activity 5 can start is the *larger* of these, which is 14. Hence, activity 5 has an ES of 14 and an EF of $14 + 3 = 17$.

Now compare the EFs of the activities entering the End node. The larger of these, 17, is the ES_{End}, and $EF_{End} = 17 + 0 = 17$. This is also the expected project duration.

The LF and LS times for each activity can now be determined by working backward through the network (from right to left). The LF for the End node is 17—the project duration. Then, $LS_{End} = LF_{End} - 0 = 17 - 0 = 17$.

Now, $LF_6 = LF_5 = LS_{End} = 17$. In the case of activity 5, the LS necessary for an LF of 17 is $17 - 3 = 14$. This means that both activities 3 and 4 must finish no later than 14 days. Hence, their LF times are 14. Activity 4 has an LS time of $14 - 5 = 9$, making the LF of activity 2 equal to 9, and its LS equal to $9 - 9 = 0$.

Activity 3, with an LF time of 14, has an LS time of $14 - 2 = 12$. Activity 6 has an LF of 17 and therefore an LS of $17 - 6 = 11$. Thus, the latest activity 6 can start is 11, and the latest 3 can start is 12 in order for the project to finish by week 17. Since activity 1 precedes *both* of these activities, it can finish no later than the *smaller* of 11 and 12, which is 11. Hence, activity 1 has an LF of 11 and an LS of $11 - 4 = 7$.

The ES, EF, LF, and LS times are shown on the following precedence network diagram.

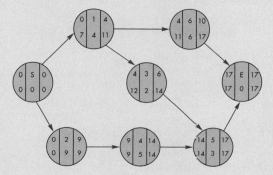

The slack time for any activity is the difference between *either* LF and EF *or* LS and ES. Thus,

Activity	LS	ES	Slack	or	LF	EF	Slack
1	7	0	7		11	4	7
6	11	4	7		17	10	7
3	12	4	8		14	6	8
2	0	0	0		9	9	0
4	9	9	0		14	14	0
5	14	14	0		17	17	0

The activities with zero slack times indicate the critical path. In this case the critical path is S-2-4-5-E.

When working on problems of this nature, keep in mind the following:

a. The ES time for a node with multiple immediate predecessors is the largest EF of the immediate predecessors.

b. The LF for a node with multiple immediate successors is the smallest LS of the immediate successors.

Problem 3

Expected durations (in weeks) and variances for the major activities of an R&D project are depicted in the following precedence network diagram chart. Determine the probability that project completion time will be

a. Less than 50 weeks.

b. More than 50 weeks.

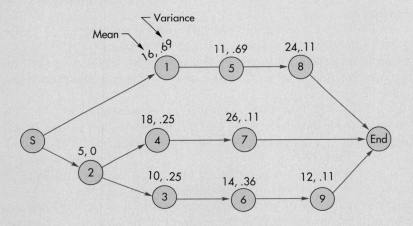

Because S and End have zero durations, we can ignore them in the following calculations. The mean and standard deviation for each path are:

Solution

Path	Expected Time (weeks)	Standard Deviation (weeks)
S-1-5-8-End	$16 + 11 + 24 = 51$	$\sqrt{.69 + .69 + .11} = 1.22$
S-2-4-7-End	$5 + 18 + 26 = 49$	$\sqrt{.00 + .25 + .11} = .60$
S-2-3-6-9-End	$5 + 10 + 14 + 12 = 41$	$\sqrt{.00 + .25 + .36 + .11} = .85$

a. Calculate the z value for each path for the length specified. Use

$$z = \frac{50 - t_{path}}{\sigma_{path}}$$

The probability that each path will be completed in 50 weeks or less is shown in the following charts. (Probabilities are from Appendix B, Table B.) The probability that the project will be completed in 50 weeks or less depends on all three paths being completed in that time. Because z for path S-2-3-6-9-End is greater than $+3.50$, it is treated as having a probability of completion in 50 weeks of 100 percent. It is less certain that the other two paths will be completed in that time. The probability that *both* will not exceed 50 is the *product* of their individual probabilities of completion within 50 weeks. Thus, $(.2061)(.9525) = .1963$.

b. The probability that the project *will* exceed 50 weeks is the complement of this number, which is $1.000 - .1963 = .8037$. (Note that it is *not* the product of the path probabilities of exceeding 50 weeks.)

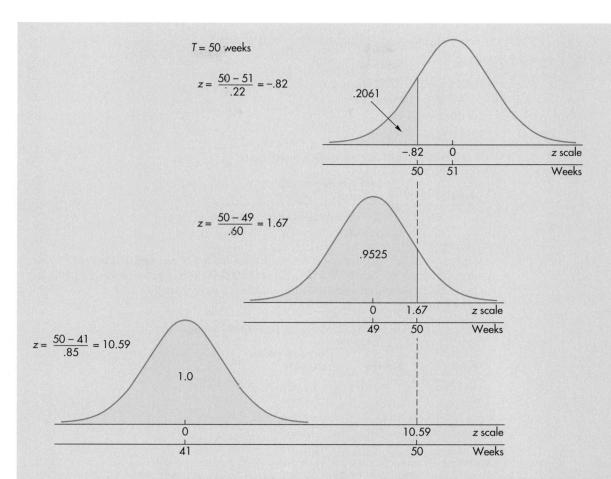

$T = 50$ weeks

$$z = \frac{50 - 51}{.22} = -.82$$

.2061

−.82   0   z scale
50   51   Weeks

$$z = \frac{50 - 49}{.60} = 1.67$$

.9525

0   1.67   z scale
49   50   Weeks

$$z = \frac{50 - 41}{.85} = 10.59$$

1.0

0   10.59   z scale
41   50   Weeks

Indirect cost for a project is \$12,000 per week for as long as the project lasts. The project manager has supplied the cost and time information and precedence network diagram shown below. Use the information to:

Problem 4

a. Determine an optimum crashing plan.

b. Graph the total costs for the plan.

Activity	Crashing Potential (weeks)	Cost per Week to Crash
a	3	\$11,000
b	3	3,000 first week, \$4,000 after that
c	2	6,000
d	1	1,000
e	3	6,000
f	1	2,000

10 weeks   14
(a) → (b)

13   6
(s) → (c) → (d) → (End)

15   8
(e) → (f)

Solution

a. (1) Calculate path lengths and identify the critical path:

Path	Duration (weeks)
s-a-b-End	24 (critical path)
s-c-d-End	19
s-e-f-End	23

(2) Rank critical activities according to crash costs:

Activity	Cost per Week to Crash
b	$3,000 first week, $4,000 after that
a	11,000

Activity b should be shortened one week since it has the lower crashing cost per week. This would reduce indirect costs by $12,000 at a cost of $3,000, for a net savings of $9,000. At this point, paths s-a-b-End and s-e-f-End would both have a length of 23 weeks, so both would be critical.

(3) Rank activities by crashing cost on the two critical paths:

Path	Activity	Cost per Week to Crash
s-a-b-End	b	$4,000
. . . .	a	11,000
s-e-f-End	f	2,000
. . . .	e	6,000

Choose one activity (the least costly) on each path to crash: b on s-a-b-End and f on s-e-f-End, for a total cost of $4,000 + $2,000 = $6,000 and a net savings of $12,000 − $6,000 = $6,000. Note: There is no activity common to the two critical paths.

(4) Check to see which path(s) might be critical: s-a-b-End and s-e-f-End would be 22 weeks in length, and s-c-d-End would still be 19 weeks.

(5) Rank activities on the critical paths:

Path	Activity	Cost per Week to Crash
a-b	b	$4,000
. . . .	a	11,000
e-f	e	6,000
. . . .	f	(no further crashing possible)

Crash b on path s-a-b-End and e on s-e-f-End for a cost of $4,000 + $6,000 = $10,000, for a net savings of $12,000 − $10,000 = $2,000.

(6) At this point, no further reduction is cost-effective: paths s-a-b-End and s-e-f-End would be 21 weeks in length, and one activity from each path would have to be shortened. This would mean activity a at $11,000 and e at $6,000 for a total of $17,000, which exceeds the $12,000 potential savings in indirect costs. Note that no further crashing for activity b is possible.

b. The following table summarizes the results, showing the length of the project after crashing n weeks:

Path	n = 0	1	2	3
s-a-b-End	24	23	22	21
s-c-d-End	19	19	19	19
s-e-f-End	23	23	22	21
Activity crashed		b	b,f	b,e
Crashing costs ($000)		3	6	10

A summary of costs for the preceding schedule would look like this:

Project Length	Cumulative Weeks Shortened	Cumulative Crashing Costs ($000)	Indirect Costs ($000)	Total Costs ($000)
24	0	0	24(12) = 288	288
23	1	3	23(12) = 276	279
22	2	3 + 6 = 9	22(12) = 264	273
21	3	9 + 10 = 19	21(12) = 252	271
20	4	19 + 17 = 36	20(12) = 240	276

The graph of total cost is as follows.

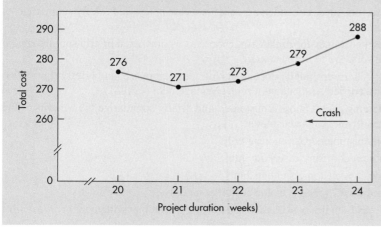

1. What skills would a project manager need?
2. Explain the term matrix organization.
3. List the steps in risk management planning.
4. What are the phases of project management?
5. What does project planning involve?
6. What is a work breakdown structure, and how is it useful for project planning?
7. Identify the term used for each of the following:
   a. A sequence of activities in a project.
   b. The longest sequence of activities in a project.
   c. The technique used for probabilistic activity durations.
   d. The difference in time length of any path and the critical path.
   e. The statistical distribution used to describe variability of an activity's duration.
   f. The statistical distribution used to describe variability of project duration.
   g. Shortening an activity by allocating additional resources.
8. Describe project execution.
9. Why might a probabilistic estimate of a project's completion time based solely on the variance of the *critical path* using expected activity durations be misleading? Under what circumstances would it be acceptable?
10. Define each of these terms used in the 3-Point Estimates method, and indicate how each is determined.
    a. Expected activity duration.
    b. Variance of activity duration.
    c. Standard deviation of a path's duration.
11. What does project control involve?
12. How can Microsoft Project help to manage a project?
13. What are some aspects of the project manager's job that make it more demanding than the job of a manager working in a more routine organizational framework?
14. How can Primavera help to manage a project?

DISCUSSION AND REVIEW QUESTIONS

1. What trade-offs are associated with duration and cost of an activity?
2. Who needs to be involved in project management?
3. Explain briefly how Deltek's (Welcom) software assists in project management.

Project management techniques have been used successfully for a wide variety of efforts, including the many NASA space missions, huge construction projects, implementation of major systems such as ERP, production of movies, development of new products and services, theatrical productions, and much more. Why not use them for managing the operations function of any business?

1. Download a trial version of Primavera's SureTrak 3.0 from www.primavera.com/customer/products/suretrak.asp and compare it with Microsoft Project.
2. Visit www.primavera.com/successes/index.asp, choose a case study, and briefly summarize its benefits to the customer.
3. Visit www.deltek.com/customers/openplan.asp, choose a customer, and briefly summarize the benefits of using the software to the customer.
4. Visit www.pmi.org/prod/groups/public/documents/info/pdc_capm.asp, and briefly summarize the requirements for Certified Associate in Project Management (CAPM).
5. Visit one of the following sites, choose a customer, and briefly summarize the benefits of the project management software to the customer:
   a. www.innotas.com/customers/casestudies.html
   b. www.pertmaster.com/company/caseStudy.htm
   c. www.amsrealtime.com/customers/clients.htm
   d. www.aisc.com/industry/2 (choose a blue customer name)
   e. www.astaus.com/case_studies/construction.asp (choose a customer with *more detailed* info.)

1. For each of the following precedence network diagrams, determine both the critical path and the project duration by determining the length of each path. The numbers above the nodes represent activity durations (in days).

a.

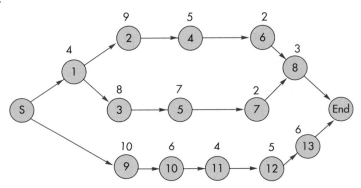

b.

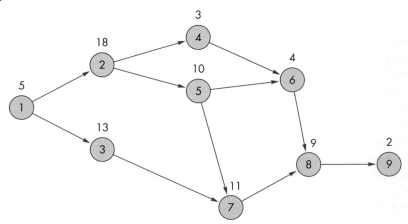

c.

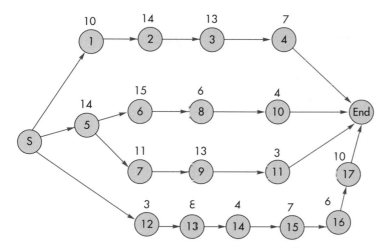

2. Chris received a new word-processing software program for her birthday. She also received a cheque, with which she intends to purchase a new computer. Chris's university instructor assigned a paper due next week. Chris decided that she will prepare the paper on the new computer. She made a list of the activities and their estimated durations. Chris's friend has offered to shop for, select and purchase a computer, and install the software.

   a. Arrange the activities into two logical sequences.

   b. Construct a precedence network diagram.

   c. Determine the critical path and its expected duration.

   d. What are some possible reasons for the project to take longer than the expected duration?

Estimated Time (hours)	Activity (abbreviation)
.8	Install software (Install)
.4	Outline the paper (Outline)
.2	Submit paper to instructor (Submit)
.6	Choose a topic (Choose)
.5	Use grammar-checking routine and make corrections (Check)
3.0	Write the paper using the word-processing software (Write)
2.0	Shop for a new computer (Shop)
1.0	Select and purchase computer (Select)
2.0	Library research on chosen topic (Library)

3. The information in the following table pertains to a project that is about to commence. As the project manager, which activities would you be concerned with in terms of timely project completion? Explain.

Activity	Precedes	Estimated Duration (days)
A	B	15
B	C, D	12
C	E	6
D	End	5
E	End	3
F	G, H	8
G	I	8
H	J	9
I	End	7
J	K	14
K	End	6

4. Construct a precedence network diagram for each of the following two cases.

(1) Activity	Precedes Activity	(2) Activity	Precedes Activity
A	D	J	L, N
B	E, F	K	R
C	G	L	M
D	K	M	End
E	K	N	P
F	H, I	P	End
G	I	Q	S, T
H	End	R	V
I	End	S	V
K	End	V	End
		T	V, W
		W	End

5. For each of the problems listed below, determine the following values for each activity: the earliest start time, earliest finish time, latest finish time, latest start time, and activity slack time. Identify the critical activities, and determine the expected duration of the project.

   a. Problem 1a.

   b. Problem 1b.

   c. Problem 3.

6. Reconsider the precedence network diagram of Problem 1a. Suppose that after 12 days, activities 1, 9, and 2 have been finished; activity 3 is 75 percent finished; and activity 10 is half finished. How many days after the original start time would the project finish?

7. Three recent university graduates have formed a partnership and have opened an advertising firm. Their first project consists of activities listed in the following table.

   a. Draw the precedence network diagram.

   b. What is the probability that the project can be completed in 24 days or less? In 21 days or less?

   c. Suppose it is now the end of the seventh day and that activities a and b have been completed while activity d is 50 percent completed. Three-point Estimates for the completion of activity d are now 5, 6, and 7 days. Activities c and h are ready to begin. Determine the probability of finishing the project by day 24 and the probability of finishing by day 21.

Activity	Precedes	DURATION IN DAYS Optimistic	Most Likely	Pessimistic
a. c		5	6	7
b. . . . . h		8	8	11
c. . . . . e		6	8	11
d. . . . . f		9	12	15
e. . . . . End		5	6	9
f. . . . . g		5	6	7
g. . . . . End		2	3	7
h. i		4	4	5
i. . . . . End		5	7	8

8. The new director of special events at a large university has decided to completely revamp graduation ceremonies. Toward that end, a precedence network diagram of the major activities has been developed. The chart has five paths with expected durations and variances as shown in the following table. Graduation day is 16 full weeks from now. Assuming that the project begins now, what is the probability that the project will be completed before:

   a. Graduation time?

   b. The end of week 15?

   c. The end of week 13?

Path	Expected Duration (weeks)	Variance
A	10	1.21
B	8	2.00
C	12	1.00
D	15	2.89
E	14	1.44

9. What is the probability that the following project will take more than 10 weeks to complete if the activity means and standard deviations (both in weeks) are as shown below?

Activity	Mean	Standard Deviation
a	5	1.3
b	4	1.0
c	8	1.6

10. The project described in the following table and precedence network diagram has just begun. It is scheduled to be completed in 11 weeks.

   a. If you were the manager of this project, would you be concerned? Explain.

   b. If there is a penalty of $5,000 a week for each week the project is late, what is the probability of incurring a penalty of at least $5,000?

Activity	Expected Duration (weeks)	Standard Deviation (weeks)
a	4	.70
b	6	.90
c	3	.62
d	9	1.90

11. The following precedence network diagram reflects 3-Point Estimates for each activity. Determine:

   a. The expected completion time for each path and its variance.

   b. The probability that the project will require more than 49 weeks.

   c. The probability that the project can be completed in 46 weeks or fewer.

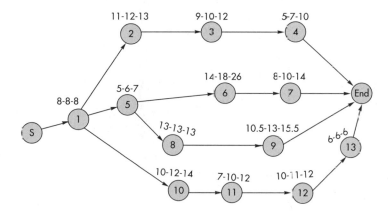

12. A project manager has compiled a list of major activities that will be required to install a computer information system in her company. The list includes 3-Point Estimates of durations (optimistic, most likely, pessimistic) for activities and precedence relationships.

Activity	Precedes	3-Point Estimates (weeks)
a	d, f	2-4-6
d	e	6-8-10
e	h	7-9-12
h	End	2-3-5
f	g	3-4-8
g	End	5-7-9
b	i	2-2-3
i	j	2-3-6
j	k	3-4-5
k	End	4-5-8
c	m	5-8-12
m	n	1-1-1
n	o	6-7-11
o	End	8-9-13

If the project is finished within 26 weeks of its start, the project manager will receive a bonus of $1,000; and if the project is finished within 27 weeks of its start, the bonus will be $500. Find the probability of each bonus.

13. The project manager of a taskforce planning the construction of a domed stadium had hoped to be able to complete construction prior to the start of the next season. After reviewing construction duration estimates, it now appears that a certain amount of crashing will be needed to ensure project completion before the season opener. Given the following information, determine a minimum-cost crashing schedule that will shave five weeks off the project length.

Activity	Precedes	Normal Duration (weeks)	CRASHING COSTS First Week	CRASHING COSTS Second Week
A	B	12	$15,000	$20,000
B	K	14	10,000	10,000
C	D, E, F	10	5,000	5,000
D	G	17	20,000	21,000
E	H	18	16,000	18,000
F	I	12	12,000	15,000
G	M	15	24,000	24,000
H	N, P	8	—	—
I	J	7	30,000	—
J	P	12	25,000	25,000
K	End	9	10,000	10,000
M	End	3	—	—
N	End	11	40,000	—
ɔ	End	8	20,000	20,000

14. A construction project has indirect costs totalling $40,000 per week. Major activities in the project and their expected durations are shown in the following precedence network diagram:

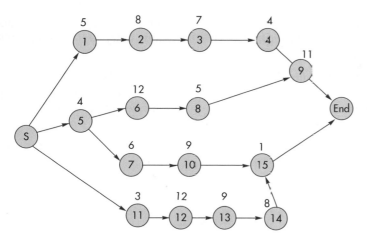

Crashing costs for each activity are:

	CRASHING COSTS [$000)		
Activity	**First Week**	**Second Week**	**Third Week**
1	$18	$22	$—
2	24	25	25
3	30	30	35
4	15	20	—
9	30	33	36
5	12	24	26
6	—	—	—
8	40	40	40
7	3	10	12
10	2	7	10
15	26	—	—
11	10	15	25
12	8	13	—
13	5	12	—
14	14	15	—

a. Determine a minimum-cost crashing plan that will take off six weeks from the project duration.

b. Plot the total-cost curve from part *a* against project duration. What is the optimum number of weeks to crash?

15. Chuck's Custom Boats (CCB) builds luxury yachts to customer order. CCB has landed a contract with a Vancouver businessman (Mr. P). Relevant data are shown below. The complication is that Mr. P wants delivery in 32 weeks or he will impose a penalty of $375 for each week his yacht is late.

		Normal Duration	**CRASHING COSTS**	
Activity	**Precedes**	**(weeks)**	**1st Week**	**2nd Week**
K	L, N	9	$410	$415
L	M	7	125	—
N	J	5	45	45
M	Q	4	300	350
J	Q	6	50	—
Q	P, Y	5	200	225
P	Z	8	—	—
Y	End	7	85	90
Z	End	6	90	—

Develop a minimum cost crashing schedule.

16. The following is the list of activities and their expected duration, used by a component supplier to automobile manufacturers, to plan for QS9000 (the auto industry version of ISO9000) certification (registration).[4]

A List of Activities in a QS-9000 Registration Project

Activity	Description	Immediate Predecessor(s)	Estimated time*
A	Appointment of QS-9000 taskforce	none	1 week
B	Preparation of a feasible plan	A	1 week
C	Delegation of authority responsibilities	B	1 week
D	Searching for a QS-9000 registrar	C	1 week
E	Preparation of three levels of documentation	C	12 weeks
F	QS-9000 awareness training	C	6 weeks
G	QS-9000 training of auditors and quality personnel	F	6 weeks
H	Preparing the plant for QS-9000 registrar	C	24 weeks
I	Conference with lead auditor	D	1 week
J	Examination of documentation	E,I	3 weeks
K	Internal audit of plant sections	G,H,J	12 weeks
L	Corrective actions of plant sections	K	12 weeks
M	Lead auditor and audit team audit plant	L	1 week
N	Audit conference and corrective action plan	M	2 weeks
O	Implementation of corrective action plans	N	12 weeks
P	Lead auditor re-audit corrective actions	O	2 weeks
Q	Lead auditor's recommendation	P	1 week

*These are estimates of time and may vary based upon situation, company and registrar.

a. Draw the precedence network diagram.

b. Determine the earliest and latest times, and identify the critical activities and the project duration.

MINI-CASE

Time, Please

B "Smitty" Smith is a project manager for a large consumer electronics corporation. Although she has been with the company only four years, she has demonstrated an uncanny ability to bring projects in on time, meet technical specifications, and be close to budget.

Her latest assignment is a project that will involve merging two existing technologies. She and her team have almost finished developing the proposal that will be presented to a management committee for approval. All that remains to be done is to develop a time estimate for the project. Smitty wants an estimated time that will have a probability of completion of at least 95 percent. The team has constructed a precedence network diagram for the project. It has three paths. The expected durations and standard deviations for the paths are listed below.

Path	Expected Duration (weeks)	Standard Deviation (weeks)
A	10	4
B	14	2
C	13	2

What project duration (in weeks) should Smitty include in the proposal?

---

[4] J. K. Bandyopadhyay, "The CPM/PERT Project Scheduling Approach to QS-9000 Registration: A Case Study at a United States Auto Parts Company," *International Journal of Management* 19(3), September 2002, pp. 455–463. Figure reprinted with permission.

CASE

Fantasy Products

Company Background

The Fantasy Products Company (disguised name) is a manufacturer of high-quality small appliances intended for home use. Their current product line includes irons, a small hand-held vacuum, and a number of kitchen appliances such as toasters, blenders, waffle irons, and coffeemakers. Fantasy Products has a strong R&D department that continually searches for ways to improve existing products as well as developing new products.

Currently, the R&D department is working on the development of a new kitchen appliance that will chill foods quickly much as a microwave oven heats them quickly, although the technology involved is quite different. Tentatively named The Big Chill, the product will initially carry a price tag of around $125, and the target market consists of upper-income consumers. At this price, it is expected to be a very profitable item. R&D engineers now have a working prototype and are satisfied that, with the cooperation from the production and marketing people, the product can be ready in time for the all-important Christmas buying season. A target date has been set for product introduction that is 24 weeks away.

Current Problem

Fantasy Products' Marketing Vice-President Vera Sloan has recently learned from reliable sources that a competitor is also in the process of developing a similar product, which it intends to bring out at almost exactly the same time. In addition, her source indicated that the competitor plans to sell its product, which will be smaller than The Big Chill, for $99 in the hope of appealing to more customers. Vera, with the help of several of her key people who are to be involved in marketing The Big Chill, has decided that in order to compete, the selling price for The Big Chill will have to be lowered to within $10 of the competitor's price. At this price level, it will still be profitable, although not nearly as profitable as originally anticipated.

However, Vera is wondering whether it would be possible to expedite the usual product introduction process in order to beat the competition to the market. If possible, she would like to get a six-week jump on the competition; this would put the product introduction date only 18 weeks away. During this initial period, Fantasy Products could sell The Big Chill for $125, reducing the selling price to $109 when the competitor's product actually enters the market. Since forecasts based on market research show that sales during the first six weeks will be about 400 per week, there is an opportunity for $25 per unit profit if the early introduction can be accomplished. In addition, there is a certain amount of prestige involved in being first to the market. This should help enhance The Big Chill's image during the anticipated battle for market share.

Data Collection

Since Fantasy Products has been through the product-introduction process a number of times, Vera has developed a list of the tasks that must be accomplished and the order in which they must be completed. Although the duration and costs vary depending on the particular product, the basic process does not. The list of activities involved and their precedence relationships are presented in Table 1. Duration and cost estimates for the introduction of The Big Chill are presented in Table 2. Note that some of the activities can be completed on a crash basis, with an associated increase in cost. For example, activity B can be crashed from 8 weeks to 6 weeks at an additional cost of $3,000 (i.e., $12,000–$9,000). Assume that if B is crashed to 7 weeks, the additional cost will be $1,500 (i.e., $3,000/2).

Table 1
List of activities and precedence relationships

Activity	Description	Immediate Predecessor
A	Select and order equipment	–
B	Receive equipment from supplier	A
C	Install and set up equipment	B
D	Finalize bill of materials	–
E	Order component parts	D
F	Receive component parts	E
G	First production run	C, F
H	Finalize marketing plan	–
I	Produce magazine ads	H
J	Script for TV ads	H
K	Produce TV ads	J
L	Begin ad campaign	I, K
M	Ship product to consumers	G, L

Table 2
Duration and cost estimates

Activity	Normal Duration (weeks)	Normal Cost	Crash Duration (weeks)	Normal & Crash Cost
A	3	$2,000	2	$4,400
B	8	9,000	6	12,000
C	4	2,000	2	7,000
D	2	1,000	1	2,000
E	2	2,000	1	3,000
F	5	0	5	0
G	6	12,000	3	24,000
H	4	3,500	2	8,000
I	4	5,000	3	8,000
J	3	8,000	2	15000
K	4	50,000	3	70,000
L	6	10,000	6	10,000
M	1	5,000	1	5,000

Questions

Fantasy Products needs to decide whether to bring The Big Chill to market 18 weeks from now as Vera Sloan is recommending. As the project management specialist in the R&D department, you have been asked to answer the following questions:

1. When would the project be completed using normal durations?

2. Is it possible to complete the project in 18 weeks? What would the associated additional cost be? Which activities would need to be completed on a crash basis?

3. Is there some time frame shorter than the 18 weeks Vera has recommended that would make more sense in terms of profits?

Source: Adapted from an original case by Robert J. Thieraus, Margaret Cunningham, and Melanie Blackwell, Xavier University, Cincinnati, Ohio.

SELECTED BIBLIOGRAPHY AND FURTHER READING

Angus, Robert B., Norman A. Gundersen, and Thomas P. Cullinane. *Planning, Performing, and Controlling Projects: Principles and Applications.* 2nd ed. Upper Saddle River, NJ: Prentice Hall, 2000.

Chapman, Chris, and Stephen Ward. *Project Risk Management.* New York: John Wiley & Sons, 1997.

Cleland, David I. *Project Managers' Portable Handbook.* New York: McGraw-Hill, 2000.

DeWeaver, Mary Feeherry, and Lori Ciprian Gillespie. *Real World Project Management.* New York: Quality Resources, 1997.

Ghattas, R. G., and Sandra L. McKee. *Practical Project Management.* Upper Saddle River, NJ: Prentice Hall, 2001.

Gido, Jack, and James P. Clements. *Successful Project Management.* Cincinnati: South-Western, 1999.

Graham, Robert J., and Randall L. Englund. *Creating an Environment for Successful Projects: The Quest to Manage Project Management.* San Francisco: Jossey-Bass, 1997.

Gray, Clifford F., and Erik W. Larson. *Project Management: The Managerial Process.* New York: McGraw-Hill, 2000.

Kanabar, Vijay. *Project Risk Management: A Step-by-Step Guide to Reducing Project Risk.* Boston: Copley Publishing Group, 1997.

Kerzner, Harold. *Project Management: A Systems Approach for Planning, Scheduling, and Controlling.* 7th ed. New York: Wiley, 2001.

Larson, Melissa. "Manage Your Projects before They Manage You." *Quality,* September 1997, pp. 64–67.

Lientz, Bennet P., and Kathryn P. Rea. *Breakthrough Project Managent.* New York: Academic Press, 1999.

Mantel, Samuel, Jack R. Meredith, Scott M. Shafer, and Margaret Sutton. *Project Management in Practice.* New York: Wiley, 2001.

Matta, Nadim F., and Ronald N. Ashkenas. "Why Good Projects Fail Anyway." *Harvard Business Review,* September 2003, pp. 109–114.

Project Management Institute. *A Guide to the Project Management Body of Knowledge.* 3rd ed. 2004.

Smith-Daniels, Dwight. "Teaching Project Management to MBAs: The Means to How Many Ends?" *Decision Line,* May 1997, pp. 11–13.

Stevenson, William J. *Introduction to Management Science.* 3rd ed. New York: McGraw-Hill/Irwin, 1998.

PART EIGHT

Waiting Lines Analysis

The chapter in this part covers the analysis of waiting lines. The occurrence of waiting lines in service systems indicates a temporary imbalance between demand and capacity. Waiting Lines analysis can help managers reduce the impact of waiting lines on system cost and effectiveness.

CHAPTER 18

Waiting Lines Analysis

LEARNING OBJECTIVES

After completing this chapter, you should be able to:

1 Explain why waiting lines form.
2 Identify the goal of queuing (waiting line) analysis.
3 List the measures of system performance that are used in queuing.
4 Discuss the basic queuing models presented.
5 Solve typical problems.

CHAPTER OUTLINE

Amusement parks such as Disney World and Six Flags, like many other services, need to keep patrons waiting in line in order to maximize the utilization of their resources. However, it is hard to wait an hour in line in the heat to take a less-than-a-minute ride. How does Disney or Six Flags manage its rides so that just the right number of people will be willing to wait in line? Services such as a bank or call centre face variations in customer arrivals during the same hour from day to day. How are they able to determine the right level of staffing? These are some questions answered in this chapter.

INTRODUCTION

Those waiting in line would all agree that the solution to the problem is obvious: simply add more servers or else do something to speed up service. Although both ideas may be potential solutions, there are certain subtleties that must be dealt with. For one thing, most service systems have the capacity to process customers over the long run. Hence, the problem of customers waiting is a short-term phenomenon. And at certain times the servers are idle, waiting for customers. Thus, by increasing the service capacity, the server idle time would increase even more. Consequently, in designing service systems, the designer must weigh the cost of providing a given level of service capacity against the cost of having customers wait for service. This planning and analysis of service capacity frequently lends itself to **queuing theory**, which is a mathematical approach to the analysis of waiting lines.

queuing theory Mathematical approach to the analysis of waiting lines.

The modern queuing theory is based on studies about automatic dialling equipment made in the early part of the twentieth century by Danish telephone engineer A. K. Erlang. Prior to the Second World War, very few attempts were made to apply queuing theory to business problems. Since that time, queuing theory has been applied to a range of problems.

The mathematics of queuing can be complex; for that reason, the emphasis here will not be on the mathematics but the concepts that underlie the use of queuing in analyzing waiting line problems. We shall rely on the use of formulas and tables for analysis.

Waiting lines are commonly found wherever customers arrive *randomly* for services. Some examples of waiting lines we encounter in our daily lives include the lines at supermarket checkouts, fast-food restaurants, hospital registration, college and university registration, airport ticket counters, theatres, post offices, and banks. In many situations, the "customers" are not people but orders waiting to be filled, trucks waiting to be unloaded, jobs waiting to be processed, equipment awaiting repairs, planes waiting to land or take off, and cars waiting at a traffic light or traffic jam.

One reason that queuing analysis is important is that customers tend to associate waiting with poor service quality, especially if the wait is long. Similarly, for an organization having employees wait is a waste.

Why Is There Waiting?

Many people are surprised to learn that waiting lines tend to form even though a system is basically underloaded. For example, a fast-food restaurant may have the capacity to handle an average of 200 orders per hour and yet experience waiting lines even though the number of orders is only 150 per hour. In reality, customers arrive at random rather than at evenly spaced intervals and some orders take longer to fill than others. In other words, both arrivals times and service durations exhibit a high degree of variability. As a result, the system at times becomes temporarily overloaded, giving rise to waiting lines; at other times, the system is idle because there are no customers. Thus, although a system may be *underloaded* from a *macro* standpoint, variabilities in arrivals times and service durations imply that at times the system is *overloaded* from a *micro* standpoint. It follows that in systems where variability is minimal or nonexistent (e.g., because arrivals can be scheduled and service durations are constant), waiting lines do not ordinarily form.

READING

Bank Teller Staffing

Most banks have a table that suggests the minimum number of tellers required based on the forecast of number of customers expected (i.e., arrival rates) during each half-hour of each day of the following week. These tables are derived by entering the following data into queuing theory formulas: forecast of arrival rates, the average customer service duration, and a customer service goal (such as an average wait time of approximately four minutes). From branch to branch, the average customer service duration varies because of type of transactions performed (e.g., retail vs. commercial), demographics, and the experience level of tellers. Most of these factors, and the time of day, affect the customer arrival pattern at each branch during each half-hour. In addition, both service durations and arrival rates change over the years because of technological improvements. For example, Internet/telephone banking has reduced the need of customers to personally visit their bank.

To check the model assumptions, a sufficiently long data collection period is required; for example, the number of arrivals during each 15-minute period, the queue length at the end of each 15-minute period, and the number of tellers providing service could be recorded. Also, the service durations of at least 1,000 customers needs to be measured. Usually the distributions of number of arrivals and service durations match the assumed shapes (presented later).

The staffing requirements determined for each half-hour during each day of the following week are used to form feasible shifts and staff schedules (discussed in Chapter 15 on Staff Scheduling).

Source: H. Deutsch and V. A. Mabert, "Queuing Theory and Teller Staffing; A Successful Application," *Interfaces* 10(5), October 1980, pp. 63–67.

Goals of Waiting Line Analysis

The goal of queuing analysis is essentially to minimize total costs. There are two basic categories of cost in a queuing situation: those associated with customers waiting for service and those associated with providing capacity. Capacity decision examples include the number of checkouts and cashiers used at a supermarket, the number of repair people to handle equipment breakdowns, and the number of lanes on a highway. When a service facility is idle, capacity is lost because it cannot be stored. The cost of customers waiting, in addition to loss of goodwill, includes any loss of business due to customers refusing to wait and possibly going elsewhere in the future. Also, if the "customers" are employees, the salaries paid to employees while they wait for service (e.g., mechanics waiting for tools, drivers of trucks waiting to unload), are part of the cost of customers waiting.

Figure 18–1 shows the two costs and the total cost as a function of service capacity. Note that as capacity increases, its cost increases. For simplicity, the increase is shown as a linear relationship. As capacity increases, the number of customers waiting and the time they wait tend to decrease at a faster rate; also the dissatisfaction of a typical customer is a nonlinear function of the waiting time (initially it is insignificant but increases at a faster rate as the wait time increases past a threshold which depends on the situation); therefore waiting cost decreases in a nonlinear way. For the role of perception, see the reading, "Waiting-Time Perception Management" at the end of this chapter. Total cost is a U-shaped curve, and the goal of queuing analysis is to identify the level of service capacity that will minimize total cost. (Unlike the situation in the inventory EOQ model, the minimum point on the total cost curve is *not* necessarily where the two cost lines intersect.)

A practical difficulty frequently encountered is pinning down the cost of customers waiting because this cost is not a part of accounting data. One approach often used is to treat waiting times or line lengths as a policy variable: a manager simply specifies an acceptable level of waiting and directs that capacity be established to achieve that level (e.g., average wait time of four minutes before service at a bank).

For an example of queuing analysis, see the reading, "Bank Teller Staffing." For an example of a device assisting in data collection, see the "Q-MATIC" reading later in this chapter.

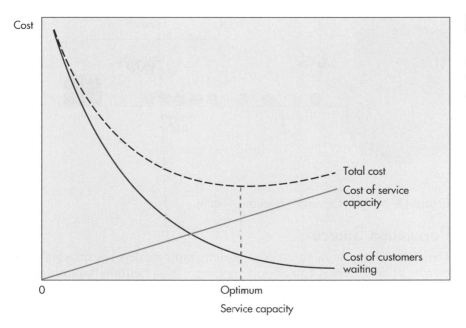

FIGURE 18-1

The goal of queuing is to minimize the sum of two costs: customers waiting cost and service capacity cost

Visitors wait to ride the Big Thunder Mountain Railroad at Disney World in Florida. Disney can predict how many people will be drawn to which rides. To make the wait more palatable, waiting times are often posted, and many of the more popular rides include entertainment and snack vendors along the way. A new feature, "Fastpass," allows guests to get a designated ride time ticket for use later on during the day for some of the most popular attractions. This results in little waiting if the person returns during the specified time.

Disneyworld.disney.go.com

SYSTEM CHARACTERISTICS AND PERFORMANCE MEASURES

There are numerous queuing models from which an analyst can choose. Naturally, much of the success of the analysis will depend on choosing the appropriate model. Model choice is affected by the characteristics of the system under investigation. The main characteristics are:

1. Population source.
2. Number of servers and structure of queuing system.
3. Arrival and service patterns.
4. Queue discipline (order of service).

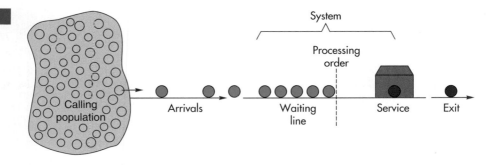

FIGURE 18-2

A simple queuing system

Figure 18–2 depicts a simple queuing system.

Population Source

The approach to use in analyzing a queuing problem depends on whether the potential number of customers is limited or is very large. In an **"infinite"-source** situation, the potential number of customers greatly exceeds system capacity. Examples are supermarkets, drugstores, banks, restaurants, theatres, amusement parks, and call centres. Theoretically, large numbers of customers from the "calling population" can request service at any one time. When the potential number of customers is limited, a **finite-source** situation exists. An example is the maintenance of machines in a company. The potential number of machines that might need repair at any one time is limited. A similar waiting situation occurs when an operator is responsible for loading and unloading four machines and a nurse is responsible for answering patient calls for a eight-bed ward.

"infinite"-source Potential number of customers greatly exceeds system capacity.

finite-source The number of potential customers is limited.

Number of Servers and Structure of Queuing Systems

The capacity of queuing systems is a function of the capacity of each server and the number of servers being used. Each server can handle one customer at a time. Systems can have either *single-* or *multiple-servers.* Sometimes, these are called single and multiple-channel systems. A group of servers working together as a team such as a surgical team is treated as a single-server system. Other examples of single-server systems are small grocery stores with one checkout counter, some theatres, single-bay car washes, and drive-in banks with one teller. Multiple-servers systems are commonly found in banks, at airline ticket counters, and at call centres as a phone wait line.

A related distinction is the number of steps or *phases* in a queuing system. For example, at a fast-food drive-through, cars first wait to order at the menu board, and then wait to pay at the window and pick up the order at the next window. Each stage constitutes a separate phase where queues form.

Figure 18–3 illustrates some of the most common queuing systems. Because it would not be possible to cover all of these cases in sufficient detail in the limited amount of space available here, our discussion will focus on *single-phase* systems.

If the customers are homogeneous, then a single line feeding into multiple servers is usually preferred to multiple independent lines each feeding to its own server. The reasons for this are as follows: First, the average wait time will be less because if there is an idle server, the customer waiting at the top of the line will be directed to him/her right away. This does not happen in independent lines, especially if the other lines cannot be observed. Even if a customer can see and jump to a shorter queue, this process will consume some time and does not guarantee getting to the server first. Secondly, the customers will be served first-come, first-served which is more equitable and preferred by most customers.

The disadvantages of a joint line are that the joint line might appear too long for some customers, the time for a customer to move to an idle server is longer, the server may not

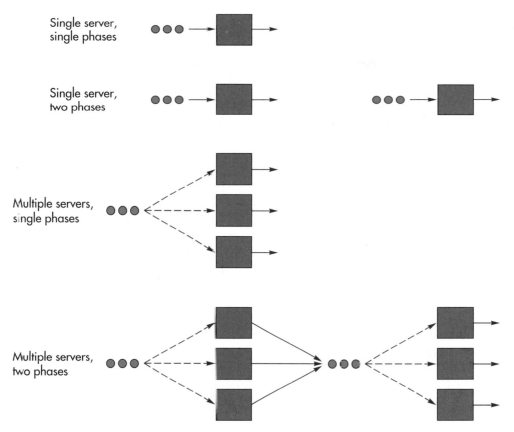

FIGURE 18-3

Four common variations of queuing systems

work as fast as if he/she was responsible for his/her line, and customers cannot choose their favourite server.

Also, if the customers are heterogeneous, then separate lines would be more preferred by customers. For example, a line for 10 items or less in a grocery store moves faster, resulting in shorter wait times, which are expected by customers who do not buy a lot. This is also a way to reduce the total variability of service durations, resulting in reduced average wait time. In addition, the servers can become more efficient at providing more homogeneous service, reducing the average service time and, hence, the average wait time. In some cases, the company can charge a higher price for providing a faster line (with more capacity) to those who do not want to wait much; for example, the one-hour photo developing service is more expensive than five-day economy service in the Superstore.

Arrival and Service Patterns

Waiting lines are a direct result of arrival and service variability. They occur because random, highly variable arrival and service patterns cause systems to be temporarily overloaded. In many instances, the variabilities can be described by theoretical distributions. In fact, the most commonly used models assume that the customer arrival *rates* (i.e., the number of arrivals per time unit) can be described by a **Poisson distribution** and that the service *durations* can be described by an **Exponential distribution**. Figure 18–4 illustrates these distributions.

Poisson distribution often provides a reasonably good description of customer arrivals per time unit (e.g., per hour). Figure 18–5A illustrates how Poisson-distributed arrivals (e.g., accidents) might occur during a three-day period. In some hours, there are three or four arrivals, in other hours one or two arrivals, and in some hours no arrivals.

Poisson distribution A one-parameter, discrete frequency distribution giving the probability that *n* events will occur in an interval of time, provided that these events are independent and that the number occurring in a subinterval does not influence the number occurring in any other subinterval.

Exponential distribution A continuous frequency distribution that is often used to model the time between events that happen at a constant average rate.

FIGURE 18-4

Poisson and Exponential distributions

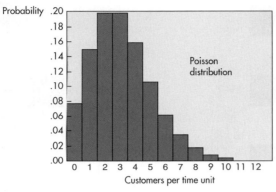
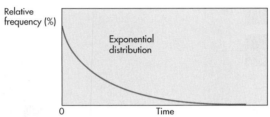

FIGURE 18-5

Examples of Poisson arrivals and Exponential service durations

A. Customer Arrivals

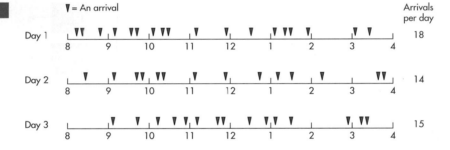

B. Service Durations

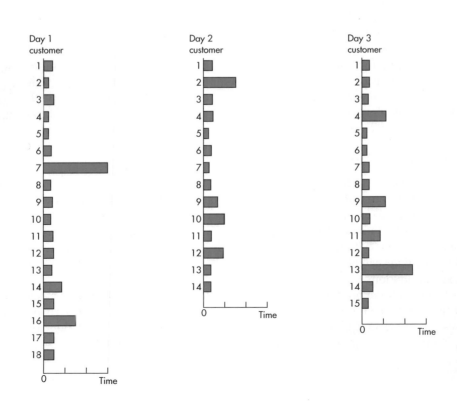

The Exponential distribution often provides a reasonably good description of service durations. Figure 18–5B illustrates how Exponential service durations might appear for the customers whose arrivals are illustrated in Figure 18–5A. Note that most service durations are very short—some are close to zero—but a few require a relatively long service duration. That is typical of an Exponential distribution.

Waiting lines are likely to occur when arrivals are bunched up or when service durations are particularly lengthy, and they are very likely to occur when both factors are present. For instance, note the long service duration of customer 7 on day 1 in Figure 18–5B. In Figure 18–5A, the seventh customer arrived just after 10 o'clock and the next two customers arrived shortly after that, making it very likely that a waiting line would form. A similar situation occurred on day 3 with the last three customers: the relatively long service duration for customer 13 (Figure 18–5B) and the short time before the next two arrivals (Figure 18–5A, day 3) would create (or increase the length of) a waiting line.

It is interesting to note that the Poisson and Exponential distributions are alternate ways of presenting the same basic information. That is, if service durations are Exponential, then the service rates (i.e., the number of services per time unit) are Poisson. Similarly, if the customer arrival rates are Poisson, then the interarrival durations (i.e., the time between two consecutive arrivals) are Exponential. There is an inverse relationship between the means of these two distributions. For example, if a service facility can process 12 customers per hour, average service duration is five minutes. And if the arrival rate is 10 per hour, then the average duration between two consecutive arrivals is six minutes.

The models described here generally require that arrival and service rates be approximately Poisson or, equivalently, that interarrival and service durations be approximately Exponential. In practice, it is necessary to verify that these assumptions are met. Sometimes this is done by collecting data and plotting them, although the preferred approach is to use a chi-square goodness-of-fit test for that purpose. A discussion of the chi-square test is beyond the scope of this text, but most basic statistics textbooks cover the topic.

Research has shown that these assumptions are often appropriate for customer arrivals but less likely to be appropriate for service durations. In situations where the assumptions are not reasonably satisfied, the alternatives would be to (1) use a better (and usually more complex) model, or (2) resort to computer simulation. Both of these alternatives require much effort and cost.

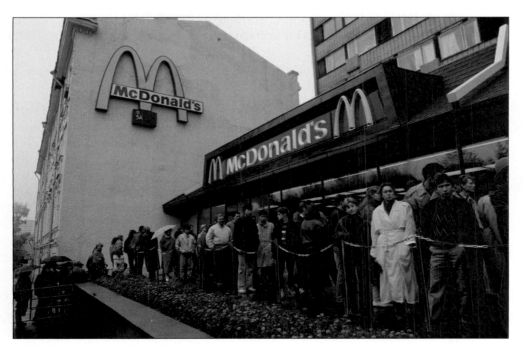

The first McDonald's in Russia opened in Pushkin Square in 1990. It is the largest McDonald's restaurant in the world, but it is also the busiest. The waiting line usually stretch outside the restaurant and average waiting time is 45 minutes! However, this is considered acceptable to Russian customers who are used to waiting in line.

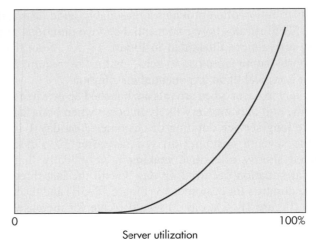

Queue Discipline (Order of Service)

Queue discipline refers to the order in which customers are processed. All but one of the models to be described shortly assume that service is provided on a *first-come, first-served* (FCFS) basis. This is perhaps the most commonly encountered rule, for example, at banks, stores, theatres, restaurants, four-way stop signs, registration lines, and so on. Examples of systems that do not serve on a FCFS basis include hospital emergency rooms, rush orders in a factory, and mainframe computer processing of jobs. In these and similar situations, customers do not all represent the same waiting costs; those with the highest cost (e.g., the most seriously ill) are processed first, even though other customers may have arrived earlier.

Performance Measures

Operations managers typically look at four measures when evaluating existing or proposed queuing systems. Those measures are:

1. The average number of customers waiting, either in line (not counting those being served) or in the system (including those being served).

2. The average length of time customers wait, either in line or in the system.

3. Server utilization, which refers to the average percentage of the time server(s), is (are) busy with service.

4. The probability that an arriving customer will have to wait for service or will have to wait more than a specified length of time.

Of these measures, server utilization bears some elaboration. It reflects the extent to which the servers are busy rather than idle. On the surface, it might seem that the operations manager would want to seek 100 percent utilization. However, as Figure 18–6 illustrates, increases in server utilization are achieved at the expense of increases in the average waiting time. In fact, these values become exceedingly large as utilization approaches 100 percent. Also, 100-percent utilization of service personnel is not good; they need some slack time. Instead, a utilization of 80 to 90 percent is appropriate for most systems.

QUEUING MODELS: "INFINITE"-SOURCE

Many "infinite"-source queuing models are available for a manager or analyst to choose from. The discussion here includes four of the most basic and widely used models. The purpose is to provide an exposure to few models rather than an extensive coverage of the field. All models discussed assume Poisson arrival rates. Moreover, the "infinite"-source

Symbol	Represents
λ	Average arrival rate
μ	Average service rate
L_q	Average number of customers waiting for service
L_s	Average number of customers in the system (waiting and/or being served)
ρ	Server utilization
W_q	Average length of time customers wait in line
W_s	Average length of time customers spend in the system (waiting in line and being served)
$1/\mu$	Average service duration
P_0	Probability of zero customers in the system
P_n	Probability of n customers in the system
M	Number of servers
r	Average number of customers being served at any time

TABLE 18-1

"Infinite"-source models symbols

models assume stable conditions; that is, they assume that the average arrival and service rates are constant. If they are not, then the operating hours should be divided into sub-periods within which the rates are fairly constant. For example, each hour or half-hour may have a different average arrival rate. In addition, the results are for the steady state condition, i.e., the transient behaviour of the queuing system at the opening hour are ignored. For an application in which the transient behaviour of queuing system was deemed important, see the reading, "Bell Canada" near the end of this chapter. The four "infinite"-source models described are:

1. Single server, Exponential service durations.
2. Single server, constant service durations.
3. Multiple servers, Exponential service durations.
4. Multiple-servers with priority, Exponential service durations.

To facilitate your use of queuing models, Table 18–1 provides a list of the symbols used for the "infinite"-source models.

Basic Relationships

There are certain basic relationships that hold for all "infinite"-source queuing models. Knowledge of these can be very helpful in deriving desired performance measures, given a few key values. Here are the basic relationships. Some are intuitive, others complex. For the latter, proof is omitted here.

> Note: The average arrival and service rates, represented by λ and μ, must be in the same time units (e.g., per hour or per minute).

Server utilization: Also called *system utilization*; reflects the ratio of demand (as measured by the average arrival rate) to capacity (as measured by the product of the number of servers, M, and the average service rate, μ).

server utilization
The proportion of time a server will be busy.

$$\rho = \frac{\lambda}{M\mu} \qquad (18\text{--}1)$$

The average number of customers being served (at any point in time):

$$r = \frac{\lambda}{\mu} \qquad (18\text{--}2)$$

Six Flags is using a ticketing system, called Fast Lane, in 18 of its U.S. amusement parks. Fast Lane is like Disney's Fastpass except that all of the advance tickets are purchased at the Guest Relations office at the park entrance ($15 for four rides) and it does not require reservation or predetermined arrival time. Another innovation is undertaken by Six Flags Over Georgia, west of Atlanta, which is using a virtual queuing system by Lo-Q company. Each customer can rent a pager at the entrance. Then, at some popular rides, the pager can be used to reserve the person's spot in line. The person can go away and enjoy other rides. Ten minutes before his or her actual turn, he or she will be notified via the pager.

Source: T. O'Brien, "Six Flags Debuts Queue Management," *Amusement Business* 113(9), March 5, 2001, pp. 1, 26.

The average *number* of customers

waiting in line for service: L_q [Model dependent. Obtain using a table or formula.]

in the system (line plus being served): $L_s = L_q + r$ (18–3)

The average length of *time* customers

wait in line: $W_q = \dfrac{L_q}{\lambda}$ [Little's Formula]   (18–4)

spend in the system: $W_s = W_q + \dfrac{1}{\mu} = \dfrac{L_s}{\lambda}$ [Little's Formula]   (18–5)

All "infinite"-source models require that server utilization be less than 1.0; the models apply only to underloaded systems.

The average number of customers waiting in line, L_q, is a key value because it is a determinant of the other measures of system performance. Hence, L_q will usually be one of the first values you will want to determine in problem solving.

Example 1

Customers arrive at a bakery at an average rate of 18 per hour on weekday mornings. The arrival distribution can be described by a Poisson distribution. Each server can serve a customer in an average of four minutes; service durations can be described by an Exponential distribution.

a. What are the average arrival and service *rates*?

b. Calculate the average number of customers being served at any time (assuming that at least two servers will be working, resulting in server utilization <100 percent).

c. Suppose that it has been determined that the average number of customers waiting in line is 3.6. Calculate the average number of customers in the system (i.e., waiting in line or being served), the average length of time customers wait in line, and the average length of time customers spend in the system.

d. Determine the server utilization if there are $M = 2$, 3, or 4 servers.

Solution

a. The average arrival rate is given in the problem: $\lambda = 18$ customers per hour. Change the average service duration to a comparable *hourly* rate by first restating the duration in hours and then taking its reciprocal. Thus, (4 minutes per customer)/(60 minutes per hour) = $1/15 = 1/\mu$. Its reciprocal is $\mu = 15$ customers per hour.

b. $r = \dfrac{\lambda}{\mu} = \dfrac{18}{15} = 1.2$ customers

c. Given: $L_q = 3.6$ customers,

$L_s = L_q + r = 3.6 + 1.2 = 4.8$ customers

$W_q = \dfrac{L_q}{\lambda} = \dfrac{3.6}{18} = .20$ hour per customer, or .20 hour × 60 minutes/hours
      = 12 minutes

$$W_s = W_q + \frac{1}{\mu} = .20 + \frac{1}{15} = .267 \text{ hour, or 16 minutes}$$

d. Server utilization is $\rho = \dfrac{\lambda}{M\mu}$.

For $M = 2$, $\rho = \dfrac{18}{2(15)} = .60$

For $M = 3$, $\rho = \dfrac{18}{3(15)} = .40$

For $M = 4$, $\rho = \dfrac{18}{4(15)} = .30$

Hence, as the system capacity, as measured by $M\mu$, increases, the server utilization (for a given arrival rate) decreases.

Model 1: Single Server, Exponential Service Durations

The simplest model involves a system that has one server (or a single crew). The queue discipline is FCFS, and it is assumed that the customer arrival rates can be approximated by a Poisson distribution and service durations by an Exponential distribution. There is no limit on length of queue.

Table 18–2 lists some formulas for this basic single-server model, which should be used in conjunction with formulas 18–1 through 18–5.

Performance Measure	Equation	
Average number in line	$L_q = \dfrac{\lambda^2}{\mu(\mu - \lambda)}$	(18−6)
Probability of zero customers in the system	$P_0 = 1 - \left(\dfrac{\lambda}{\mu}\right)$	(18−7)
Probability of n customers in the system	$P_n = P_0\left(\dfrac{\lambda}{\mu}\right)^n$	(18−8a)
Probability of fewer than n customers in the system	$P_{<n} = 1 - \left(\dfrac{\lambda}{\mu}\right)^n$	(18−8b)
Probability that a customer waits at least t time units in queue	$P_{W \text{ in } Q > t} = \dfrac{\lambda}{\mu}e^{-(\mu - \lambda)t}$	(18−8c)

TABLE 18-2

Formulas for basic single-server model

Example 2

A phone company is planning to open a kiosk in a new shopping mall, staffed by one sales agent. It is estimated that requests for phones, accessories, and information will average 15 per hour during peak period, and number of requests will have a Poisson distribution. Service durations are assumed to be Exponentially distributed. Previous experience with similar kiosks suggests that mean service duration should average about three minutes per request. Determine each of the following measures during the peak period:

a. Server utilization.

b. Percentage of time the sales agent will be idle.

c. The expected number of customers waiting to be served.

d. The average length of time customers will spend in the system.

e. The probability of zero customers in the system and the probability of four customers in the system.

f. The probability that a customer waits more than 5 minutes.

Solution

$$\lambda = 15 \text{ per hour}$$

$$\mu = \frac{1}{\text{Average service duration}} = \frac{1 \text{ customer}}{3 \text{ minutes}} \times 60 \text{ minutes per hour}$$

$$= 20 \text{ customers per hour}$$

a. $\rho = \dfrac{\lambda}{M\mu} = \dfrac{15}{1(20)} = .75$

b. Percentage idle time $= 1 - \rho = 1 - .75 = .25$, or 25 percent

c. $L_q = \dfrac{\lambda^2}{\mu(\mu - \lambda)} = \dfrac{15^2}{20(20 - 15)} = 2.25$ customers

d. $W_s = \dfrac{L_q}{\lambda} + \dfrac{1}{\mu} = \dfrac{2.25}{15} + \dfrac{1}{20} = .20$ hour, or 12 minutes

e. $P_0 = 1 - \dfrac{\lambda}{\mu} = 1 - \dfrac{15}{20} = .25$ and $P_4 = P_0 \left(\dfrac{\lambda}{\mu}\right)^4 = .25 \left(\dfrac{15}{20}\right)^4 = .079$

f. $P_{W \, in \, Q \, > \, t} = \dfrac{\lambda}{\mu} e^{-(\mu - \lambda)t}$

$$= \frac{15}{20} e^{-(20 - 15)(5/60)}$$

$$= .494$$

Note that t should be in the same time unit as λ and μ. Also, it appears that almost half the customers during the peak time will be waiting too long. In reality, most will not join the line or will leave the line after joining.

READING

Q-MATIC

Q-MATIC, based in Sweden, is an international company which produces hardware and software for queue and customer flow management. When a customer comes in, she receives a ticket which puts her on a queue. Then, she can sit down (or go away and return later) until the ticket number is displayed on a LED display. The ticket number could also be called out. From management's point of view, Q-MATIC's major advantage is that it automatically collects data such as the number of customers arriving per period, waiting and trans-action (service) durations, and the number of customers waiting. It also recommends the right number of servers to use. This allows the manager to add or remove servers as needed. Also, statistical data can be generated to devise better staffing plans and to measure employee productivity.

Q-MATIC is being used in thousands of companies where queues develop: banks; hospital receptions and phar-macies; government departments/agencies/institutions such as motor vehicle offices, post offices, embassies and consulates, colleges and universities, courts, and city hall; and retail stores and hotels.

A Q-Matic ticket printer and waiting line data collector

Sources: www.q-Matic.ca; www.navalhospitaljax.com/news/abc.asp.

Model 2: Single Server, Constant Service Durations

As noted previously, waiting lines are a consequence of random, highly variable arrival and service rates. If a system can reduce or eliminate the variability of either or both, it can shorten its waiting line noticeably. A case in point is a system with constant service durations (and Poisson arrial rates). The effect of constant service durations is to cut the average number of customers waiting in line in half:

$$L_q = \frac{\lambda^2}{2\mu(\mu - \lambda)} \qquad (18\text{–}9)$$

The average length of time customers wait in line W_q is also cut in half. Similar improvements can be realized by spreading out arrival times evenly (e.g., by use of appointments).

Wanda's Car Wash is an automatic, five-minute operation with a single bay. On a typical Saturday morning, cars arrive at a mean rate of eight per hour, with arrivals tending to follow a Poisson distribution. Find:

Example 3

a. The average number of cars in line.

b. The average length of time cars spend in line and service (i.e., system).

$\lambda = 8$ cars per hour

$\mu = 1$ per 5 minutes, or 12 per hour

Solution

a. $L_q = \dfrac{\lambda^2}{2\mu(\mu - \lambda)} = \dfrac{8^2}{2(12)(12 - 8)} = .667$ car

b. $W_s = \dfrac{L_q}{\lambda} + \dfrac{1}{\mu} = \dfrac{.667}{8} + \dfrac{1}{12} = .167$ hour, or 10 minutes

---

For a general service duration distribution with standard deviation $= \sigma_s$, it can be shown that

$$L_q = \frac{\lambda^2(\mu^2\sigma_S^2 + 1)}{2\mu(\mu - \lambda)}$$

Note that $\sigma_s = 0$ for Constant service durations, and $\sigma_s = \dfrac{1}{\mu}$ for Exponential service durations.

Model 3: Multiple Servers, Exponential Service Durations

A multiple-server system exists whenever there are two or more servers working individually to provide service to customers. Use of the model involves the following assumptions:

1. Poisson arrival rates with average λ and Exponential service durations with average $\dfrac{1}{\mu}$.

2. All M servers work at the same average rate (μ).

3. Customers form a single waiting line.

Formulas for this basic multiple-servers model are listed in Table 18–3. Obviously, the multiple-servers formulas are more complex than the single-server formulas for L_q and P_0. These formulas are shown primarily for completeness; you can actually determine their values using Table 18–4, given selected values of λ/μ and M.

To use Table 18–4, calculate the value of λ/μ and round it to two decimal places if $\lambda/\mu = <1$ and one decimal place if $\lambda/\mu = >1$. Then, simply read the values of L_q and P_0 for the appropriate number of servers, M. For instance, if $\lambda/\mu = 0.50$ and $M = 2$, the table provides a value of 0.033 for L_q and a value of .600 for P_0. These values can then be used to calculate other measures of system performance. Note also that Table 18–4 can also be used for the basic single-server (Model 1) problems (i.e., for $M = 1$).

Two new measures are given in Table 18–3: W_a and P_W. W_a is the average length of queue wait time for only those customers who have to wait. Note that $W_a > W_q$ because W_q also contains those customers who do not wait. P_W is the probability that a customer has to wait. These three terms are related through the following relationship:

W_q = avg. length of wait time if do not wait $\times$ probability of no wait + avg. wait time if have to wait $\times$ probability of wait

$$= 0(1 - P_W) + W_a P_W \ \ or, \ P_W = \frac{W_q}{W_a}.$$

TABLE 18–3	Performance Measure	Equation	
Formulas for basic multiple-servers model	Average number of customers in line	$L_q = \dfrac{\lambda\mu\left(\frac{\lambda}{\mu}\right)^M}{(M-1)!(M\mu-\lambda)^2} P_0$	(18–10)
	Probability of zero customers in the system	$P_0 = \left[\displaystyle\sum_{n=0}^{M-1} \frac{\left(\frac{\lambda}{\mu}\right)^n}{n!} + \frac{\left(\frac{\lambda}{\mu}\right)^M}{M!\left(1-\frac{\lambda}{M\mu}\right)} \right]^{-1}$	(18–11)
	Probability of n customers in the system	$P_n = \begin{cases} \dfrac{1}{n!}\left(\dfrac{\lambda}{\mu}\right)^n P_0 & \text{if} \ \ n \le M \\ \dfrac{1}{M! \, M^{n-m}}\left(\dfrac{\lambda}{\mu}\right)^n P_0 & \text{if} \ \ n > M \end{cases}$	(18–12)
	Average length of waiting time (before being served) for an arrival who is not immediately served	$W_a = \dfrac{1}{M\mu - \lambda}$	(18–13)
	Probability that an arrival will have to wait for service	$P_w = \dfrac{W_q}{W_a}$	(18–14)

TABLE 18–4	λ/μ	M	L_q	P_0	λ/μ	M	L_q	P_0	λ/μ	M	L_q	P_0
Basic multiple-servers model values for L_q and P_0, given values for λ/μ and M	0.15	1	0.026	.850	0.65	1	1.207	.350	1.0	2	0.333	.333
		2	0.001	.860		2	0.077	.509		3	0.045	.364
	0.20	1	0.050	.800		3	0.008	.521		4	0.007	.367
		2	0.002	.818	0.70	1	1.633	.300	1.1	2	0.477	.290
	0.25	1	0.083	.750		2	0.098	.481		3	0.066	.327
		2	0.004	.778		3	0.011	.495		4	0.011	.367
	0.30	1	0.129	.700	0.75	1	2.250	.250	1.2	2	0.675	.250
		2	0.007	.739		2	0.123	.455		3	0.094	.294
	0.35	1	0.188	.650		3	0.015	.471		4	0.016	.300
		2	0.011	.702	0.80	1	3.200	.200		5	0.003	.301
	0.40	1	0.267	.600		2	0.152	.429	1.3	2	0.951	.212
		2	0.017	.667		3	0.019	.447		3	0.130	.264
	0.45	1	0.368	.550	0.85	1	4.817	.150		4	0.023	.271
		2	0.024	.633		2	0.187	.404		5	0.004	.272
		3	0.002	.637		3	0.024	.425	1.4	2	1.345	.176
	0.50	1	0.500	.500		4	0.003	.427		3	0.177	.236
		2	0.033	.600	0.90	1	8.100	.100		4	0.032	.245
		3	0.003	.606		2	0.229	.379		5	0.006	.246
	0.55	1	0.672	.450		3	0.030	.403	1.5	2	1.929	.143
		2	0.045	.569		4	0.004	.406		3	0.237	.211
		3	0.004	.576	0.95	1	18.050	.050		4	0.045	.221
	0.60	1	0.900	.400		2	0.277	.356		5	0.009	.223
		2	0.059	.538		3	0.037	.383				
		3	0.006	.548		4	0.005	.386				

(continued)

TABLE 18-4

(continued)

λ/μ	M	L_q	P_0	λ/μ	M	L_q	P_0	λ/μ	M	L_q	P_0
1.6	2	2.844	.111	2.9	6	0.081	.054	4.1	5	2.703	.011
	3	0.313	.187		7	0.023	.055		6	0.668	.015
	4	0.060	.199	3.0	4	1.528	.038		7	0.212	.016
	5	0.012	.201		5	0.354	.047		8	0.070	.016
1.7	2	4.426	.081		6	0.099	.049		9	0.023	.017
	3	0.409	.166		7	0.028	.050	4.2	5	3.327	.009
	4	0.080	.180		8	0.008	.050		6	0.784	.013
	5	0.017	.182	3.1	4	1.902	.032		7	0.248	.014
1.8	2	7.674	.053		5	0.427	.042		8	0.083	.015
	3	0.532	.146		6	0.120	.044		9	0.027	.015
	4	0.105	.162		7	0.035	.045		10	0.009	.015
	5	0.023	.165		8	0.010	.045	4.3	5	4.149	.008
1.9	2	17.587	.026	3.2	4	2.386	.027		6	0.919	.012
	3	0.688	.128		5	0.513	.037		7	0.289	.130
	4	0.136	.145		6	0.145	.040		8	0.097	.013
	5	0.030	.149		7	0.043	.040		9	0.033	.014
	6	0.007	.149		8	0.012	.041		10	0.011	.014
2.0	3	0.889	.111	3.3	4	3.027	.023	4.4	5	5.268	.006
	4	0.174	.130		5	0.615	.033		6	1.078	.010
	5	0.040	.134		6	0.174	.036		7	0.337	.012
	6	0.009	.135		7	0.052	.037		8	0.114	.012
2.1	3	1.149	.096		8	0.015	.037		9	0.039	.012
	4	0.220	.117	3.4	4	3.906	.019		10	0.013	.012
	5	0.052	.121		5	0.737	.029	4.5	5	6.862	.005
	6	0.012	.122		6	0.209	.032		6	1.265	.009
2.2	3	1.491	.081		7	0.063	.033		7	0.391	.010
	4	0.277	.105		8	0.019	.033		8	0.133	.011
	5	0.066	.109	3.5	4	5.165	.015		9	0.046	.011
	6	0.016	.111		5	0.882	.026		10	0.015	.011
2.3	3	1.951	.068		6	0.248	.029	4.6	5	9.289	.004
	4	0.346	.093		7	0.076	.030		6	1.487	.008
	5	0.084	.099		8	0.023	.030		7	0.453	.009
	6	0.021	.100		9	0.007	.030		8	0.156	.010
2.4	3	2.589	.056	3.6	4	7.090	.011		9	0.054	.010
	4	0.431	.083		5	1.055	.023		10	0.018	.010
	5	0.105	.089		6	0.295	.026	4.7	5	13.382	.003
	6	0.027	.090		7	0.019	.027		6	1.752	.007
	7	0.007	.091		8	0.028	.027		7	0.525	.008
2.5	3	3.511	.045		9	0.008	.027		8	0.181	.008
	4	0.533	.074	3.7	4	10.347	.008		9	0.064	.009
	5	0.130	.080		5	1.265	.020		10	0.022	.009
	6	0.034	.082		6	0.349	.023	4.8	5	21.641	.002
	7	0.009	.082		7	0.109	.024		6	2.071	.006
2.6	3	4.933	.035		8	0.034	.025		7	0.607	.008
	4	0.658	.065		9	0.010	.025		8	0.209	.008
	5	0.161	.072	3.8	4	16.937	.005		9	0.074	.008
	6	0.043	.074		5	1.519	.017		10	0.026	.008
	7	0.011	.074		6	0.412	.021	4.9	5	46.566	.001
2.7	3	7.354	.025		7	0.129	.022		6	2.459	.005
	4	0.811	.057		8	0.041	.022		7	0.702	.007
	5	0.198	.065		9	0.013	.022		8	0.242	.007
	6	0.053	.067	3.9	4	36.859	.002		9	0.087	.007
	7	0.014	.067		5	1.830	015		10	0.031	.007
2.8	3	12.273	.016		6	0.485	.019		11	0.011	.077
	4	1.000	.050		7	0.153	.020	5.0	6	2.938	.005
	5	0.241	.058		8	0.050	.020		7	0.810	.006
	6	0.066	.060		9	0.016	.020		8	0.279	.006
	7	0.018	.061	4.0	5	2.216	.013		9	0.101	.007
2.9	3	27.193	.008		6	0.570	.017		10	0.036	.007
	4	1.234	.044		7	0.180	.018		11	0.013	.007
	5	0.293	.052		8	0.059	.018				
					9	0.019	.018				

(continued)

TABLE 18-4

(concluded)

λ/μ	M	L_q	P_0	λ/μ	M	L_q	P_0	λ/μ	M	L_q	P_0
5.1	6	3.536	.004	5.4	6	6.661	.002	5.7	6	16.446	.001
	7	0.936	.005		7	1.444	.004		7	2.264	.002
	8	0.321	.006		8	0.483	.004		8	0.721	.003
	9	0.117	.006		9	0.178	.004		9	0.266	.003
	10	0.042	.006		10	0.066	.004		10	0.102	.003
	11	0.015	.006		11	0.024	.005		11	0.038	.003
5.2	6	4.301	.003		12	0.009	.005		12	0.014	.003
	7	1.081	.005	5.5	6	8.590	.002	5.8	6	26.373	.001
	8	0.368	.005		7	1.674	.003		7	2.648	.002
	9	0.135	.005		8	0.553	.004		8	0.823	.003
	10	0.049	.005		9	0.204	.004		9	0.303	.003
	11	0.017	.006		10	0.077	.004		10	0.116	.003
5.3	6	5.303	.003		11	0.028	.004		11	0.044	.003
	7	1.249	.004		12	0.010	.004		12	0.017	.003
5.3	8	0.422	.005	5.6	6	11.519	.001	5.9	6	56.300	.000
	9	0.155	.005		7	1.944	.003		7	3.113	.002
	10	0.057	.005		8	0.631	.003		8	0.939	.002
	11	0.021	.005		9	0.233	.004		9	0.345	.003
	12	0.007	.005		10	0.088	.004		10	0.133	.003
					11	0.033	.004				
					12	0.012	.004				

Example 4

Alpha Taxi Company has seven cars stationed at the airport. The company has determined that during late evening hours on weeknights, customers request taxis at rates that follow Poisson distribution with a mean of 6.6 per hour. Service durations are Exponential with a mean of 50 minutes per customer (including the return time to the airport). Assume that there is one customer per taxi. Find each of the performance measures listed in Table 18–3, and each taxi's utilization.

Solution

$\lambda = 6.6$ per hour $M = 7$ taxis (servers)

$$\mu = \frac{1 \text{ customer per trip}}{50 \text{ minutes per trip} \div 60 \text{ minutes per hour}}$$

$$= 1.2 \text{ customers per hour per cab}$$

$\lambda/\mu = \dfrac{6.6}{1.2} = 5.5$. From Table 18–4, for $\dfrac{\lambda}{M} = 5.5$ and $M = 7$ we get $L_q = 1.674$

and $P_0 = .003$

$$P_1 = \frac{1}{1!}(5.5)^1(.003) = .0176$$

$$P_2 = \frac{1}{2!}(5.5)^2(.003) = .0484$$

$\ldots$

$$W_a = \frac{1}{M\mu - \lambda} = \frac{1}{7(1.2) - 6.6} = .556 \text{ hour, or } 33.36 \text{ minutes}$$

$$W_q = \frac{L_q}{\lambda} = \frac{1.674}{6.6} = .2536 \text{ hour, or } 15.22 \text{ minutes}$$

$$P_W = \frac{W_q}{W_a} = \frac{.2536}{.556} = .456$$

$$\rho = \frac{\lambda}{M\mu} = \frac{6.6}{7(1.2)} = .786$$

READING

Queuing for Toilets

The Building Industry Authority (BIA) in New Zealand sets building codes such as number of toilets (this depends on the number of people using the building). However, the codes were old and inconsistent. In 1994, BAI commissioned the New Zealand Works Consultancy Services to study this issue. Data from 27 locations representing 13 different types of buildings (such as offices, schools, swimming pools, and shopping malls) were collected in order to estimate the number of arrivals and occupancy duration of the toilets. Electronic data collection tools such as infrared beams and magnetic switches on the cubicle doors were used for three weeks.

The data fit "infinite"-source Model 3, multiple-servers, with Poisson arrivals and Exponential service durations. The customer length of wait time goal was set as follows: the 90th percentile of the length of waiting time distribution should not be larger than 60 seconds. Using the peak-period number of arrivals, the number of necessary toilets, based on building occupancy, was determined. The results differed markedly from the old building code for many types of buildings. Two examples are shown below. As it can be observed, the old standards for the number of men toilets in the offices were way more than sufficient, whereas those for women in theatres were inadequate.

Sources: Don McNickle, "Queueing for Toilets," *OR Insight*, April/June 1998, Figures reprinted with permission. Available at www.orsoc.org.uk.

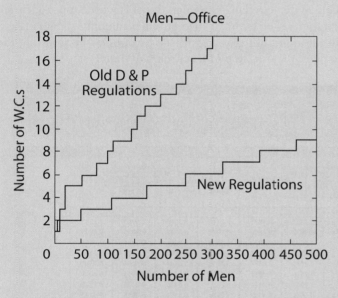

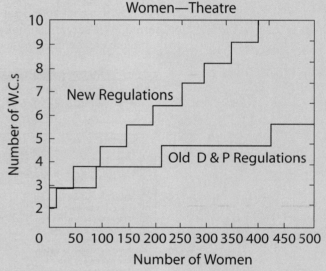

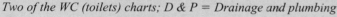

Two of the WC (toilets) charts; D & P = Drainage and plumbing

MINI-CASE

Phoenix Mutual

Call volumes to Phoenix Mutual, a life insurance company based in Hartford, Connecticut, doubled in 1981 and the service representatives could not answer the calls as quickly as their goal indicated they should. This occurred even though the company had installed an automatic call sequencer in 1979. Customers were on hold for too long and there were too many abandoned calls. Phoenix Mutual installed an automatic call distributor and started to analyze the work of service representatives and the queuing system. The goal was to answer 85 percent of the calls in 30 seconds. There also were other tasks required of a sales rep, such as making 150 to 200

outgoing calls per day. A 1.5-month study showed that only 38 percent of an employee's time was spent on answering calls, and another 31 percent of his or her time was classified as "available" for receiving calls. A graph of the number of incoming calls per half hour showed the peaks to be about 70 calls per half hour between 10:00 a.m.—noon and 1:00–4:00 p.m. Within each half-hour, the number of calls each day followed a Poisson distribution. Using the service goal of answering 85 percent of incoming calls within 30 seconds and the multiple-servers queuing model, Phoenix Mutual was able to determine the number of service representatives required to receive the forecasted incoming calls per half-hour of each day. These requirements were then increased to allow the service reps to also do the other required tasks. The result of the study was that the average service duration for incoming calls went down from approximately 4 minutes to 3.3 minutes, and the percentage of time a service representative was "available" to receive calls went down to approximately 20 percent. These are because the number of service representatives was reduced from 33 to 29 even though service was apparently improved.

template on the DVD. Does it appear that the service goal is satisfied?

Source: M. A. Yanke and J. D. Wehr, "The Queueing Method to Better Use of Your Phone System," *The Office* 96(5), November 1982, pp. 200, 204–5.

Question

Assuming that 38 percent of the sales reps are available at any time to take a call, determine W_a and P_W using the Excel

The Excel template on the DVD can also be used to solve Example 4. After entering $\lambda = 6.6$ and $\mu = 1.2$ at the top of the template, the queuing statistics for 7 servers are shown in Column D of the table in the template. Note that Excel is a little more accurate because it carries four decimal digits. The template also provides queuing statistics for 8 through 12 servers, although these are not required for this example. In addition, the template can be used to increment λ and μ, to perform sensitivity analysis.

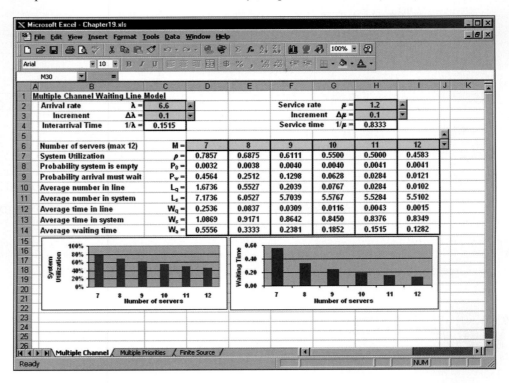

For an application of the basic multiple-servers model, see the reading, "Queuing for Toilets," and for a challenging mini-case, see "Phoenix Mutual."

Determining the Number of Servers

So far we have determined the performance measures using λ, μ and M. However, we can also do the reverse; that is, an analyst can determine the number of servers M needed to achieve specified levels of various performance measures. This approach is illustrated in the following example.

Alpha Taxi company also plans to have taxis at a new rail station. The expected arrival rate there is 4.8 customers per hour during non-peak times, and the average service rate (including the return time to the rail station) is expected to be 1.5 per hour. How many taxis will be needed to achieve an average customer wait time in line of close to but not exceeding 10 minutes?

Example 5

$\lambda = 4.8$ customers per hour

$\mu = 1.5$ customers per hour

$M = ?$

$W_q(\text{desired}) = 10$ minutes, or .167 hour

Using $L_q = \lambda \times W_q$, $L_q = (4.8/\text{hour})(.167 \text{ hour}) = .8$ customers. Thus, the average number waiting should be close to but not exceeding .8 customers. Referring to Table 18–4, with $\lambda/\mu = 4.8/1.5 = 3.2$, we obtain $L_q = 2.386$ for $M = 4$ and 0.513 for $M = 5$. Hence, five taxis will be needed.

Cost Analysis

Instead of achieving a goal in terms of a performance measure (e.g., the average wait time should be close to but not exceed 10 minutes), we can determine the number of servers by minimizing the sum of customer wait cost and servers cost. Thus, the goal is

Minimize total cost   =   Total wait cost   +   Servers cost

An iterative process is used to identify the number of servers that will minimize total cost. Number of servers is incremented one unit at a time and the total cost is calculated at each increment. Because the total cost curve is U-shaped, usually the total cost will initially decrease as number of servers is increased and then it will eventually begin to increase. The optimal capacity size is the number of servers just before the total cost increases.

Total average wait time in the system during an hour, say, is equal to average number of customers arriving during the hour multiplied by the average wait time per customer in the system; that is, $\lambda \times W_s$. But this equals L_s by Little's formula. To save on calculations, we will use the formula $L_s = L_q + \dfrac{\lambda}{\mu}$ to obtain the total average wait time in the system.

Trucks arrive at a warehouse at an average rate of 15 per hour during business hours. A crew can unload the trucks at an average rate of five per hour. (Both distributions are Poisson.) Recent changes in wage rates have caused the warehouse manager to re-examine the question of how many crews to use. The new rates are: a crew costs $100 per hour; truck and driver cost $120 per hour. Assuming that number of docks is not a constraint, how many crews should the manager use?

Example 6

Solution

(L_q values are from Table 18–4 using $\dfrac{\lambda}{\mu} = \dfrac{15}{5} = 3.0$.)

Crew size	Crew/ cost	$\left[L_s = L_q + \dfrac{\lambda}{\mu}\right]$ Total average wait time in system per hour	[$L_s \times$ \$120] Total average driver/truck wait cost per hour	Total cost
4	\$400	1.528 + 3.0 = 4.528	\$543.36	\$943.36
5	500	.354 + 3.0 = 3.354	402.48	902.48 (minimum)
6	600	.099 + 3.0 = 3.099	371.88	971.88
7	700	.028 + 3.0 = 3.028	363.36	1,063.36

Five crews will minimize the total cost. Because the total cost will continue to increase once the minimum is reached, it is not necessary to calculate total cost for crew sizes larger than six.

One additional point should be made concerning cost analysis. Because both customer wait cost and capacity cost often reflect estimated amounts, the apparent optimal solution may not represent the true optimum. This is compounded by the fact that arrival and service rates either may be approximations or may not be exactly represented by the Poisson/Exponential distributions. If cost estimates can be obtained as *ranges* (e.g., customer wait cost is estimated to range between \$40 and \$50 per hour), total cost should be computed using both ends of the range to see whether the optimal solution is affected. If it is, management must decide whether to expend additional effort to obtain more precise cost estimates or to choose one of the two indicated optimal solutions.

READING

Cardiac Care Network of Ontario

www.ccn.on.ca

In the late 1980s the waiting system for major heart surgeries in Ontario was under public criticism because of the impression of unfairness in the priorities for surgeries and deaths due to excessive waiting times. In 1990, the Ontario provincial government established the Cardiac Care Network (CCN) to improve the efficiency of the waiting system. CCN has established an Urgency Rating Score (URS), which is a guide to identifying a person's urgency for surgery and an estimate of the maximum time a person can "safely" wait for surgery. Also, for each cardiac hospital, the average current wait time for surgery is displayed on the CCN's Web site. Each cardiac hospital keeps a list of people on its waiting list and monitors their health. If a patient's condition worsens, the coordinator revises the patient's URS and hence the maximum wait time. This systematic priority setting process has reduced the percentage of deaths on the waiting list to approximately 0.3 percent. The urgent patients now wait an average of 3 days, the semi-urgent patients wait about 7 days, and elective (non-urgent) patients wait an average of 38 days.

Source: http://www.ccn.on.ca/pdfs/case-2.pdf.

Maximum Line Length

A question that often comes up in capacity planning is the amount of space to allocate for waiting lines. Theoretically, with an "infinite" population source the waiting line can become infinitely long. This implies that no matter how much space is allocated for a waiting line, one can never be completely sure that the space requirements won't exceed that amount. Nonetheless, as a practical matter, one can determine a line length that will not be exceeded a specified percentage of the time. For instance, an analyst may wish to know the length of line that will not be exceeded 98 percent of the time and use that number as a planning value.

The approximate line length n that will not be exceeded by a specified percentage of time can be determined by solving the following equation for n:

$$n = \frac{\log K}{\log \rho} \text{ or } \frac{\ln K}{\ln \rho} \qquad \text{where} \qquad K = \frac{1 - \text{Specified percentage}}{L_q(1 - \rho)} \qquad (18\text{–}15)$$

Determine the maximum length of a waiting line that will not be exceeded (a) 95 percent, (b) 98 percent of the time for a system in which $M = 2$, $\lambda = 8$ per hour, and $\mu = 5$ per hour.

Example 7

$$\frac{\lambda}{\mu} = \frac{8}{5} = 1.6 \quad \text{and} \quad \rho = \frac{\lambda}{M\mu} = \frac{8}{2(5)} = .80$$

From Table 18–4, $L_q = 2.844$ customers.

(*a*) For 95 percent probability of not exceeding the wait space, using formula 18–15:

$$K = \frac{1 - .95}{2.844(1 - .80)} = .088$$

$$n = \frac{\ln .088}{\ln .80} = \frac{-2.4304}{-.2231} = 10.89, \text{ which rounds to } 11$$

(*b*) For 98 percent:

$$K = \frac{1 - .98}{2.844(1 - .80)} = .035$$

$$n = \frac{\ln .035}{\ln .80} = \frac{-3.352}{-.2231} = 15.02, \text{ which rounds to } 15$$

Approximate Solution to the Multiple-Servers System with General Interarrival and Service Durations[1]

Let σ_A = standard deviation of interarrival durations,

and σ_S = standard deviation of service durations.

Then,

$$L_q \approx \frac{\rho^{\sqrt{2(M+1)}}}{1 - \rho} \times \frac{\mu^2 \sigma_S^2 + \lambda^2 \sigma_A^2}{2}$$

We will evaluate the performance of the above approximation by comparing it with the results of Examples 4 and 5.

In Example 4, $\lambda = 6.6$, $\mu = 1.2$, $M = 7$, and $\rho = .786$. It is well known that the standard deviation of an Exponential distribution equals its mean. Therefore, $\sigma_A = \frac{1}{\lambda}$ and $\sigma_S = \frac{1}{\mu}$. Substituting all these in the L_q formula above results in:

$$L_q = \frac{0.786^{\sqrt{2(7+1)}}}{1 - 0.786} \times \frac{1+1}{2} = 1.784, \text{ which is very close to } L_q = 1.674 \text{ value obtained}$$
in Example 4.

In Example 5, $\lambda = 4.8$, $\mu = 1.5$, $M = 5$, $\rho = \frac{4.8}{5(1.5)} = .64$. Substituting all these

in the L_q formula above results in: $L_q = \frac{.64^{\sqrt{2(5+1)}}}{1 - .64} \times \frac{1+1}{2} = .592$, which is very close

to $L_q = .513$ value obtained in Example 5 for $M = 5$.

Model 4: Multiple Servers with Priority, Exponential Service Durations

In many queuing systems, processing occurs on a first-come, first-served (FCFS) basis. However, there are situations in which FCFS is inappropriate. The reason is that

---

[1] R. B. Chase et al., *Operations Management for Competitive Advantage*, 10th ed. (Boston: Irwin, 2004).

the waiting cost or penalty incurred may not be the same for all customers. In a hospital emergency waiting room, a wide variety of injuries and illnesses need treatment. Some may be minor (e.g., sliver in finger) and others may be much more serious, even life threatening. It is more reasonable to treat the most serious cases first, letting the nonserious cases wait until all serious cases have been treated. Similarly, computer processing of jobs on mainframes often follows rules other than FCFS (e.g., shortest job first). In such cases, a **multiple-servers with priority model** is useful for describing customer waiting times. For an application, see the reading, "Cardiac Care Network of Ontario" earlier in this chapter.

multiple-servers with priority model Customers are processed according to some measure of importance.

This model incorporates all of the assumptions of the basic multiple-servers model except that it uses priority serving instead of FCFS. Arrivals to the system are assigned a priority as they arrive (e.g., highest priority = 1, next priority class = 2, next priority class = 3, and so on). Let λ_k be the average arrival rate of priority class K. We have $\lambda = \Sigma \lambda_k$. An existing queue might look something like this:

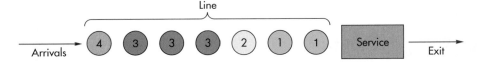

Within each class, waiting units are processed in the order they arrived (i.e., FCFS). Thus, in this sequence, the first 1 would be processed as soon as a server becomes available. The second 1 would be processed when that server or another one becomes available. We assume that each server can process any customer with any priority class and that the average service time is $\frac{1}{\mu}$ for any arrival. If, in the interim, another 1 arrived, it would be next in line *ahead of the first 2*. If there were no new arrivals, the only 2 would be processed by the next available server. At that point, if a new 1 or 2 arrived, it would be processed ahead of the 3s and the 4. We assume that any service already in progress would not be *preempted* or interrupted for another customer. Conversely, if a new 4 arrived, it would take its place at the end of the line.

Obviously, a unit with a low priority could conceivably wait a rather long time for processing. In some cases, units that have waited more than a specified time are reassigned a higher priority.

Table 18–5 gives the appropriate formulas for this multiple-servers with priority service model.

TABLE 18–5

Multiple-servers with priority service model

Performance Measure	Formula	Formula Number
Server utilization	$\rho = \dfrac{\lambda}{M\mu}$	(18–16)
Intermediate values (L_q from Table 18–4)	$A = \dfrac{\lambda}{(1-\rho)L_q}$	(18–17)
	$B_k = 1 - \displaystyle\sum_{c=1}^{k} \dfrac{\lambda_c}{M\mu}$ $(B_0 = 1)$	(18–18)
Average length of wait time in line for units in *k*th priority class	$W_k = \dfrac{1}{A \cdot B_{k-1} \cdot B_k}$	(18–19)
Average length of time in the system for units in the *k*th priority class	$W = W_k + \dfrac{1}{\mu}$	(18–20)
Average number of the *k*th priority class waiting in line	$L_k = \lambda_k \times W_k$	(18–21)

A machine shop handles tool repairs in a large company. As each job arrives in the shop, it is assigned a priority based on urgency of the need for that tool priority 1 is the highest and priority 3 is the lowest. Number of requests for repair can be described by a Poisson distribution. Average arrival rates are: $\lambda_1 = 2$ per hour, $\lambda_2 = 2$ per hour, and $\lambda_3 = 1$ per hour. The average service rate is one tool per hour for each mechanic, and service rate has Poisson distribution. There are six mechanics in the shop. Determine the value of the following measures:

Example 8

a. The server utilization.

b. The average length of time a tool in each of the priority classes will wait for repair.

c. The average length of time a tool spends in the system for each priority class.

d. The average number of tools waiting for repair in each class.

$\lambda = \Sigma \lambda_k = 2 + 2 + 1 = 5$ per hour

Solution

$M = 6$ servers

$\mu = 1$ tool per hour

a. $\rho = \dfrac{\lambda}{M\mu} = \dfrac{5}{6(1)} = .833$

b. Intermediate values. For $\lambda/\mu = 5/1 = 5$ and $M = 6$; from Table 18–4, $L_q = 2.938$

$A = \dfrac{5}{(1 - .833)2.938} = 10.19$

$B_0 = 1$

$B_1 = 1 - \dfrac{2}{6(1)} = \dfrac{2}{3} = .667$

$B_2 = 1 - \dfrac{2+2}{6(1)} = \dfrac{1}{3} = .333$

$B_3 = 1 - \dfrac{2+2+1}{6(1)} = \dfrac{1}{6} = .167$

$W_1 = \dfrac{1}{A \cdot B_0 \cdot B_1} = \dfrac{1}{10.19(1)(.667)} = .147$ hour

$W_2 = \dfrac{1}{A \cdot B_1 \cdot B_2} = \dfrac{1}{10.19(.667)(.333)} = .442$ hour

$W_3 = \dfrac{1}{A \cdot B_2 \cdot B_3} = \dfrac{1}{10.19(.333)(.167)} = 1.765$ hours

c. $W = W_k + 1/\mu$. In this case, $1/\mu = 1/1 = 1$. Thus:

Class	$W_k + 1 = W$ Hours
1	.147 + 1 = 1.147
2	.442 + 1 = 1.442
3	1.765 + 1 = 2.765

d. The average number of units waiting for repair in each class is $L_k = \lambda_k \cdot W_k$. Thus:

Class	$\lambda_k \cdot W_k = L_k$ Units
1	$2(.147) = .294$
2	$2(.442) = .884$
3	$1(1.765) = 1.765$

Using the Excel template on the DVD, the solution to Example 8 would appear as follows:

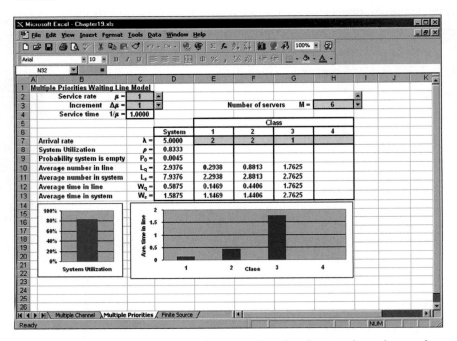

Note that the small differences between Excel and manual results are due to rounding.

Revising Priorities. If any of the wait times calculated in Example 8 are deemed too long by management (e.g., a wait time of .147 hour for tools in the first class might be too long), there are several options. One is to increase the number of servers. Another is to attempt to increase the service rate, say, by introducing new methods. If such options are not feasible, another approach is to re-examine the membership of each of the priority classifications because, if some repair requests in the first priority class can be reassigned to the second priority class, for example, this will tend to decrease the average length of

READING

Bell Canada

In a study by the Corporate Productivity Department of Bell Canada, a queuing model was developed to determine the required number of scheduled and standby Service Representatives (SR) in a Bell business office in order to obtain a desired average customer wait time. Standby SRs would answer calls if number of calls waiting reaches a maximum point and would stop answering if the number of calls waiting goes below this number. Because of the dynamic nature of capacity produced, a transient (not in equilibrium) technique was used to determine the number of scheduled and standby SRs.

Source: S. K. Mok and J. G. Shanthi Kumar, "A Transient Queuing Model for Business Office with Standby Servers," *European Journal of Operational Research* 28, 1987, pp. 158–174.

wait times for repair jobs in the highest priority classification simply because the arrival rate of those items will be lower.

The manager of the repair shop, after consulting with the managers of the departments that use the shop's services, has revised the list of tools that are given the highest priorities. This is reflected by revised average arrival rates. Suppose that the revised average arrival rates are: $\lambda_1 = 1.5$, $\lambda_2 = 2.5$, and λ_3 remains unchanged at 1.0. Determine the value of the following measures:

Example 9

a. The server utilization.

b. The average length of wait time for units in each priority class.

$\lambda = \Sigma\lambda_k = 1.5 + 2.5 + 1.0 = 5.0$

Solution

$M = 6$

$\mu = 1$

Note that these values are the same as in the previous example.

a. $\rho = \dfrac{\lambda}{M\mu} = 5.0/6(1) = .833$, the same as in the previous example.

b. The value of A, since it is a function of M, μ, and λ, is the same as in the preceding example because these values are the same. Therefore, $A = 10.19$ and

$B_0 = 1$ (always)

$B_1 = 1 - \dfrac{1.5}{6(1)} = .75$

$B_2 = 1 - \dfrac{1.5 + 2.5}{6(1)} = .333$

$B_3 = 1 - \dfrac{1.5 + 2.5 + 1.0}{6(1)} = .167$

Then

$W_1 = \dfrac{1}{10.19(1)(.75)} = .131 \text{ hour}$

$W_2 = \dfrac{1}{10.19(.75)(.333)} = .393 \text{ hour}$

$W_3 = \dfrac{1}{10.19(.333)(.167)} = 1.765 \text{ hours}$

Example 9 offers several interesting results. One is that through reduction of the average arrival rate of the highest priority class, the length of average wait time for units in that class has decreased. In other words, removing some members of the highest class and placing them into the next lower class reduced the length of average wait time for units that remained in the highest class. Note that the length of average wait time for the second priority class also was reduced, even though units were added to that class. Although this may appear counterintuitive, it is necessary to recognize that the *total* wait time (when all arrivals are taken into account) will remain unchanged. We can see this by noticing that the average *number* waiting (see Example 8, part *d*) is .294 + .884 + 1.765 = 2.943. In Example 9, using the average wait times just computed, the average number waiting in all three classes in total is

$$\sum_{k=1}^{3} \lambda_k W_k = 1.5(.131) + 2.5(.393) + 1.0(1.765) = 2.944.$$

Aside from a slight difference due to rounding, the totals are the same.

Another interesting observation is that the average wait time for customers in the third priority class did not change from the preceding example. The reason for this is that the *total* arrival rate for the two higher-priority classes did not change and the average arrival rate for this class did not change.

QUEUING MODEL: FINITE SOURCE

The finite-source model is appropriate for cases in which the calling population is limited. For instance, in a queuing system for breakdowns of five machines, the size of the calling population is five.

As in the "infinite"-source models, arrival rates are assumed to be Poisson and service durations Exponential. A major difference between the finite- and "infinite"-source models is that the arrival rate of customers (machines) in a finite situation is *affected by* the length of the waiting line; the arrival rate decreases as the length of the line increases simply because there is a decreasing proportion of the population that is out and can generate calls for service. The limit occurs when *all* of the population are waiting in line; at that point the arrival rate is zero since no additional units can arrive.

Because the mathematics of the finite-source model can be complex, analysts often use finite-source model table in conjunction with simple formulas to analyze these systems. Table 18–6 contains a list of the key formulas and definitions. The inputs to the model are the average service duration *T*, the average run duration *U*, the number of servers *M*, and total number of machines *N*. The desired quantities of interest are the average wait duration *W*, average number running *J*, the average number in line *L*, and the average number in service *H*. You will find it helpful to study the diagram of a run-wait-service cycle that is presented in the table.

Table 18–7 is an abbreviated finite-source model table used to obtain values of *D* and *F*. (Most of the formulas require a value for *F*.) In order to use the table, follow this procedure:

1. Identify the values for

   a. *N*, population size.

   b. *M*, number of servers.

   c. *T*, average service duration.

   d. *U*, average run duration.

2. Compute the service factor, $X = T/(T+U)$.

3. Locate the section of the finite-source model table for *N*. (Only values for $N = 5$ and 10 are shown here because of space limitation.)

4. Using the value of *X* as the point of entry, find the values of *F* and *D* that correspond to *M*.

5. Use the value of *F* to determine the values of the desired measures of system performance using the formulas in Table 18–6.

	Formulas		Notation†
Service factor	$X = \dfrac{T}{T+U}$	(18–22)	D = Probability that a machine will have to wait in line before service
Average number waiting	$L = N(1 - F)$	(18–23)	F = Efficiency factor: proportion of machines being serviced or running
Average waiting time	$W = \dfrac{L(T+U)}{N-L} = \dfrac{T(1-F)}{XF}$	(18–24)	H = Average number of machines being serviced
Average number running	$J = NF(1 - X)$	(18–25)	J = Average number of machines running
Average number being serviced	$H = FNX$	(18–26)	L = Average number of machines waiting for service
Number in population	$N = J + L + H$	(18–27)	M = Number of servers
			N = Number of machines
			T = Average service duration
			U = Average run duration
			W = Average wait duration
			X = Service factor; proportion of average service to total of average service and average run durations

Cycle

Running	Waiting	Being serviced

Average number:	J	L	H
Average time:	U	W	T

TABLE 18-6

Finite-source model formulas and notation

Source: †Adapted from L. G. Peck and R. N. Hazelwood, *Finite Queuing Tables* (New York: John Wiley & Sons, 1958). Reprinted by permission.

TABLE 18-7

Finite-source model table

X	M	D	F	X	M	D	F	X	M	D	F	X	M	D	F
Population 5				.062	2	.022	.999	.100	2	.054	.997	.145	3	.011	.999
.012	1	.048	.999		1	.245	.982		1	.386	.950		2	.109	.991
.019	1	.076	.998	.064	2	.023	.999	.105	2	.059	.997		1	.537	.892
.025	1	.100	.997		1	.253	.981		1	.404	.945	.150	3	.012	.999
.030	1	.120	.996	.066	2	.024	.999	.110	2	.065	.996		2	.115	.990
.034	1	.135	.995		1	.260	.979		1	.421	.939		1	.553	.885
.036	1	.143	.994	.068	2	.026	.999	.115	2	.017	.995	.155	3	.013	.999
.040	1	.159	.993		1	.268	.978		1	.439	.933		2	.123	.989
.042	1	.167	.992	.070	2	.027	.999	.120	2	.076	.995		1	.568	.877
.044	1	.175	.991		1	.275	.977		1	.456	.927	.160	3	.015	.999
.046	1	.183	.990	.075	2	.031	.999	.125	2	.082	.994		2	.130	.988
.050	1	.198	.989		1	.294	.973		1	.473	.920		1	.582	.869
.052	1	.206	.988	.080	2	.035	.998	.130	2	.089	.933	.165	3	.016	.999
.054	1	.214	.987		1	.313	.969		1	.489	.914		2	.137	.987
.056	2	.018	.999	.085	2	.040	.998	.135	2	.095	.933		1	.597	.861
	1	.222	.985		1	.332	.965		1	.505	.907	.170	3	.017	.999
.058	2	.019	.999	.090	2	.044	.998	.140	2	.102	.992		2	.145	.985
	1	.229	.984		1	.350	.960		1	.521	.900		1	.611	.853
.060	2	.020	.999	.095	2	.049	.997								
	1	.237	.983		1	.368	.955								

(continued)

TABLE 18-7

(continued)

X	M	D	F
.180	3	.021	.999
	2	.161	.983
	1	.683	.836
.190	3	.024	.998
	2	.117	.980
	1	.665	.819
.200	3	.028	.998
	2	.194	.976
	1	.689	.801
.210	3	.032	.998
	2	.211	.973
	1	.713	.783
.220	3	.036	.997
	2	.229	.969
	1	.735	.765
.230	3	.041	.997
	2	.247	.965
	1	.756	.747
.240	3	.046	.996
	2	.265	.960
	1	.775	.730
.250	3	.052	.995
	2	.284	.955
	1	.794	.712
.260	3	.058	.994
	2	.303	.950
	1	.811	.695
.270	3	.064	.994
	2	.323	.944
	1	.827	.677
.280	3	.071	.993
	2	.342	.938
	1	.842	.661
.290	4	.007	.999
	3	.079	.992
	2	.362	.932
	1	.856	.644
.300	4	.008	.999
	3	.086	.990
	2	.382	.926
	1	.869	.628
.310	4	.009	.999
	3	.094	.989
	2	.402	.919
	1	.881	.613
.320	4	.010	.999
	3	.103	.988
	2	.422	.912
	1	.892	.597
.330	4	.012	.999
	3	.112	.986
	2	.442	.904
	1	.902	.583
.340	4	.013	.999
	3	.121	.985
	2	.462	.896
	1	.911	.569
.360	4	.017	.998
	3	.141	.981
	2	.501	.880
	1	.927	.542

X	M	D	F
.380	4	.021	.998
	3	.163	.976
	2	.540	.863
	1	.941	.516
.400	4	.026	.997
	3	.186	.972
	2	.579	.845
	1	.952	.493
.420	4	.031	.997
	3	.211	.966
	2	.616	.826
	1	.961	.471
.440	4	.037	.996
	3	.238	.960
	2	.652	.807
	1	.969	.451
.460	4	.045	.995
	3	.266	.953
	2	.686	.787
	1	.975	.432
.480	4	.053	.994
	3	.296	.945
	2	.719	.767
	1	.980	.415
.500	4	.063	.992
	3	.327	.936
	2	.750	.748
	1	.985	.399
.520	4	.073	.991
	3	.359	.927
	2	.779	.728
	1	.988	.384
.540	4	.085	.989
	3	.392	.917
	2	.806	.708
	1	.991	.370
.560	4	.098	.986
	3	.426	.906
.560	2	.831	.689
	1	.993	.357
.580	4	.113	.984
	3	.461	.895
	2	.854	.670
	1	.994	.345
.600	4	.130	.981
	3	.497	.883
	2	.875	.652
	1	.996	.333
.650	4	.179	.972
	3	.588	.850
	2	.918	.608
	1	.998	.308
.700	4	.240	.960
	3	.678	.815
	2	.950	.568
	1	.999	.286
.750	4	.316	.944
	3	.763	.777
	2	.972	.532

X	M	D	F
.800	4	.410	.924
	3	.841	.739
	2	.987	.500
.850	4	.522	.900
	3	.907	.702
	2	.995	.470
.900	4	.656	.871
	3	.957	.666
	2	.998	.444
.950	4	.815	.838
	3	.989	.631

Population 10

X	M	D	F
.016	1	.144	.997
.019	1	.170	.996
.021	1	.188	.995
.023	1	.206	.994
.025	1	.224	.993
.026	1	.232	.992
.028	1	.250	.991
.030	1	.268	.990
.032	2	.033	.999
	1	.285	.988
.034	2	.037	.999
	1	.301	.986
.036	2	.041	.999
	1	.320	.984
.038	2	.046	.999
	1	.337	.982
.040	2	.050	.999
	1	.354	.980
.042	2	.055	.999
	1	.371	.978
.044	2	.060	.998
	1	.388	.975
.046	2	.065	.998
	1	.404	.973
.048	2	.071	.998
	1	.421	.970
.050	2	.076	.998
	1	.437	.967
.052	2	.082	.997
	1	.454	.963
.054	2	.088	.997
	1	.470	.960
.056	2	.094	.997
	1	.486	.956
.058	2	.100	.996
	1	.501	.953
.060	2	.106	.996
	1	.517	.949
.062	2	.113	.996
	1	.532	.945
.064	2	.119	.995
	1	.547	.940
.066	2	.126	.995
	1	.562	.936
.068	3	.020	.999
	2	.133	.994
	1	.577	.931

X	M	D	F
.070	3	.022	.999
	2	.140	.994
	1	.591	.926
.075	3	.026	.999
	2	.158	.992
	1	.627	.913
.080	3	.031	.999
	2	.177	.990
	1	.660	.899
.085	3	.037	.999
	2	.196	.988
	1	.692	.883
.090	3	.043	.998
	2	.216	.986
	1	.722	.867
.095	3	.049	.998
	2	.237	.984
	1	.750	.850
.100	3	.056	.998
	2	.258	.981
	1	.776	.832
.105	3	.064	.997
	2	.279	.978
	1	.800	.814
.110	3	.072	.997
	2	.301	.974
	1	.822	.795
.115	3	.081	.996
	2	.324	.971
	1	.843	.776
.120	4	.016	.999
	3	.090	.995
	2	.346	.967
	1	.861	.756
.125	4	.019	.999
	3	.100	.994
	2	.369	.962
	1	.878	.737
.130	4	.022	.999
	3	.110	.994
	2	.392	.958
	1	.893	.718
.135	4	.025	.999
	3	.121	.993
	2	.415	.952
	1	.907	.699
.140	4	.028	.999
	3	.132	.991
	2	.437	.947
	1	.919	.680
.145	4	.032	.999
	3	.144	.990
	2	.460	.941
	1	.929	.662
.150	4	.036	.998
	3	.156	.989
	2	.483	.935
	1	.939	.644

(continued)

TABLE 18-7

(concluded)

X	M	D	F	X	M	D	F	X	M	D	F	X	M	D	F
.155	4	.040	.998	.260	6	.013	.999	.380	7	.019	.999	.560	8	.044	.996
	3	.169	.987		5	.060	.996		6	.083	.993		7	.171	.982
	2	.505	.928		4	.205	.980		5	.247	.971		6	.413	.939
	1	.947	.627		3	.503	.919		4	.533	.906	.560	5	.707	.848
.160	4	.044	.998		2	.866	.732		3	.840	.758		4	.917	.706
	3	.182	.986		1	.998	.384		2	.986	.525		3	.991	.535
	2	.528	.921	.270	6	.015	.999	.400	7	.026	.998	.580	8	.057	.995
	1	.954	.610		5	.070	.995		6	.105	.991		7	.204	.977
.165	4	.049	.997		4	.228	.976		5	.292	.963		6	.465	.927
	3	.195	.984		3	.537	.908		4	.591	.887		5	.753	.829
	2	.550	.914		2	.886	.712		3	.875	.728		4	.937	.684
	1	.961	.594		1	.999	.370		2	.991	.499		3	.994	.517
.170	4	.054	.997	.280	6	.018	.999	.420	7	.034	.993	.600	9	.010	.999
	3	.209	.982		5	.081	.994		6	.130	.987		8	.072	.994
	2	.571	.906		4	.252	.972		5	.341	.954		7	.242	.972
	1	.966	.579		3	.571	.896		4	.646	.866		6	.518	.915
.180	5	.013	.999		2	.903	.692		3	.905	.700		5	.795	.809
	4	.066	.996		1	.999	.357		2	.994	.476		4	.953	.663
	3	.238	.978	.290	6	.022	.999	.440	7	.045	.997		3	.996	.500
	2	.614	.890		5	.093	.993		6	.160	.984	.650	9	.021	.999
	1	.975	.890		4	.278	968		5	.392	.943		8	.123	.988
.190	5	.016	.999		3	.603	.884		4	.698	.845		7	.353	.954
	4	.078	.995		2	.918	.672		3	.928	.672	.650	6	.651	.878
	3	.269	.973		1	.999	.345		2	.996	.454		5	.882	.759
	2	.654	.873	.300	6	.026	.998	.460	8	.011	.999		4	.980	.614
	1	.982	.522		5	.106	.991		7	.058	.995		3	.999	.461
.200	5	.020	.999		4	.304	.963		6	.193	.979	.700	9	.040	.997
	4	.092	.994		3	.635	.872		5	.445	.930		8	.200	.979
	3	.300	.968		2	.932	.653		4	.747	.822		7	.484	.929
	2	.692	.854		1	.999	.333		3	.947	.646		6	.772	.836
	1	.987	.497	.310	6	.031	.998		2	.998	.435		5	.940	.711
.210	5	.025	.999		5	.120	.990	.480	8	.015	.999		4	.992	.571
	4	.108	.992		4	.331	.957		7	.074	.994	.750	9	.075	.994
	3	.333	.961		3	.666	.858		6	.230	.973		8	.307	.965
	2	.728	.835		2	.943	.635		5	.499	.916		7	.626	.897
	1	.990	.474	.320	6	.036	.998		4	.791	.799		6	.870	.792
.220	5	.030	.998		5	.135	.988		3	.961	.621		5	.975	.666
	4	.124	.990		4	.359	.952		2	.998	.417		4	.998	.533
	3	.366	.954		3	.695	.845	.500	8	.020	.999	.800	9	.134	.988
.220	2	.761	.815		2	.952	.617		7	.093	.992		8	.446	.944
	1	.993	.453	.330	6	.042	.997		6	.271	.966		7	.763	.859
.230	5	.037	.998		5	.151	.986		5	.553	.901	.800	6	.939	.747
	4	.142	.988		4	.387	.945	.500	4	.830	.775		5	.991	.625
	3	.400	.947		3	.723	.831		3	.972	.598		4	.999	.500
	2	.791	.794		2	.961	.600		2	.999	.400	.850	9	.232	.979
	1	.995	.434	.340	7	.010	.999	.520	8	.026	.998		8	.611	.916
.240	5	.044	.997		6	.049	.997		7	.115	.989		7	.879	.818
	4	.162	.986		5	.168	.983		6	.316	.958		6	.978	.705
	3	.434	.938		4	.416	.938		5	.606	.884		5	.998	.588
	2	.819	.774		3	.750	.816		4	.864	.752	.900	9	.387	.963
	1	.996	.416		2	.968	.584		3	.980	.575		8	.785	.881
.250	6	.010	.999	.360	7	.014	.999		2	.999	.385		7	.957	.777
	5	.052	.997		6	.064	.995	.540	8	.034	.997		6	.995	.667
	4	.183	.983		5	.205	.978		7	.141	.986	.950	9	.630	.938
	3	.469	.929		4	.474	.923		6	.363	.949		8	.934	.841
	2	.844	.753		3	.798	.787		5	.658	.867		7	.994	.737
	1	.997	.400		2	.978	.553		4	.893	.729				
									3	.986	.555				

Source: L. G. Peck and R. N. Hazelwood, *Finite Queuing Tables* (New York: John Wiley & Sons, 1958). Reprinted by permission.

Example 10	One operator loads and unloads a group of five machines. Service durations (i.e., one unloading and loading) are Exponentially distributed with a mean of 10 minutes per machine. Machines run for an average of 70 minutes between loading and unloading, and this duration is also Exponential. Find:

a. The average number of machines waiting for the operator.

b. The expected number of machines running.

c. Average duration of downtime.

d. The probability that a machine will not have to wait for service.

Solution

$N = 5$

$T = 10$ minutes

$M = 1$

$U = 70$ minutes

$$\chi = \frac{T}{T+U} = \frac{10}{10+70} = .125$$

From Table 18–7, with $N = 5$, $M = 1$, and $X = .125$, we obtain $D = .473$ and $F = .920$.

a. Average number waiting, $L = N(1 - F) = 5(1 - .920) = .40$ machine.

b. Expected number running, $J = NF(1 - X) = 5(.92)(1 - .125) = 4.025$ machines.

c. Downtime = Waiting time + Service time:

$$\text{Average waiting time } W = \frac{L(T+U)}{N-L} = \frac{.40(10+70)}{5-.40} = 6.957 \text{ minutes}$$

Downtime = 6.957 minutes + 10 minutes = 16.957 minutes

d. Probability of not having to wait = 1 − Probability of having to wait

$$= 1 - D$$

$$= 1 - .473 = .527$$

Using the Excel template, the solution to Example 10 would appear as follows:

	A	B	C	D	E	F	G	H	I	J
1	**Finite Source Waiting Line Model**									
2										
3		Population Size	N =	5	5					
4		Number of servers	M =	1	2					
5		Average service time	T =	10	10					
6		Average time between service calls	U =	70	70					
7		P(wait) - from table	D =	0.4730	0.0820					
8		Efficiency factor - from table	F =	0.9200	0.9940					
9		Service factor	X =	0.125	0.125					
10		Average number waiting	L =	0.4000	0.0300					
11		Average waiting time	W =	6.9565	0.4829					
12		Average number running	J =	4.0250	4.3488					
13		Average number being serviced	H =	0.5750	0.6213					
14										
15			Per Time							
16			Unit							
17		Service cost =	10	10	20					
18		Downtime cost =	16	15.6	10.42					
19		Total Cost =		25.6	30.42					
20										
21										
22		Note: You must enter D and F (based on N, X, and M) from the table in the text.								
23										
24										
25										
26										

Multiple Channel / Multiple Priorities \ Finite Source /

READING

Waiting-Time Perception Management

I n 1988, Bank of Boston's branch at 60 State Street wanted to know if adding either an electronic board or a clock that displayed the expected wait time at the start of the waiting line would influence customers' opinion of waiting. Cameras were set up at the start and end of the waiting line, which also recorded the time of events. In addition, about a third of customers were interviewed after they saw the teller. The idea behind the board was that increased distraction may reduce the perception of waiting. The idea behind the clock was that if customers knew how long they would have to wait, they would be more satisfied. Three phases of data collection took place: Phase 1 (for comparison), Phase 2 (with the board), and Phase 3 (with the clock). Generally, the average customer who had to wait waited approximately four minutes, but perceived it as being five minutes. The average customer in Phase 3 (with the clock) actually estimated his/her wait time accurately. The average customer in Phase 2 (with the board) found the experience more interesting. However, the average customer found waiting somewhat stressful, and there was no difference in the overall satisfaction of customers among the three phases.

Some suggestions resulting from the above and other experiments:

- Determine the acceptable wait time for the operation.
- Install distractions that entertain and involve customers. For example, provide magazines, TV, mirrors in elevators, ask the customer to fill out a form, and use the lounge before eating.
- Inform the customer of the cause of an abnormal wait.
- Keep the line moving continuously.
- Use FCFS discipline (fairness is important).
- Make the wait comfortable.
- Allow customers to serve themselves.
- Prepare for service beforehand if possible.
- Make people conscious of time only if they overestimate the wait time.
- Keep staff who are not serving customers out of sight.
- Try to segment customers by personality; some customers, the "watchers," actually like to spend time in lines, whereas the "impatients" need shorter lines. Some airlines and hotels have club memberships that provide express check-in and check-out for those who want it.
- Never underestimate the power of a friendly server.

Source: K. L. Katz, B. M. Larson, and R. C. Larson, "Prescription for the Waiting-in-Line Blues: Entertain, Enlighten, and Engage," *Sloan Management Review*, Winter 1991, pp. 44–53.

Suppose that in Example 10, operators are paid $10 per hour and machine downtime costs $16 per hour. Should the department add another operator if the goal is total cost minimization?

Compare the total cost of the present system with the total cost of the proposed system:

Example 11

Solution

M	Average Number Down, N − J	Average Down Cost (per hour), (N − J) ($16)	Operator Cost (per hour)	Total Cost (per hour)
1	.975	$15.60	$10	$25.60
2	.651	10.42	20	30.42

where N − J for M = 2 is obtained from the Excel template on the previous page. Hence, the present system is superior because its total cost is less than the total cost using two operators.

SUMMARY

Analysis of waiting lines can be an important aspect of the design of service systems. Waiting lines have a tendency to form in such systems even though, in a macro sense, the system is underloaded. The arrival of customers at random times and variability of service durations combine to create temporary overloads. By the same token, at other times the servers are idle.

A major consideration in the analysis of queuing systems is whether the number of potential customers is limited (finite-source) or whether entry to the system is unrestricted ("infinite"-source).

Five basic queuing models are described, four dealing with "infinite"-source populations and one dealing with finite-source populations. In general, the models assume that customer arrival rates can be described by a Poisson distribution and that service durations can be described by an Exponential distribution.

KEY TERMS		
Exponential distribution, 687		Poisson distribution, 687
finite-source, 686		queue discipline, 690
"infinite"-source, 686		queuing theory, 683
multiple-servers with priority model, 704		server utilization, 691

Solved Problems

Problem 1

"Infinite"-source. One of the features of a new machine shop will be a well-stocked tool crib. The manager of the shop must decide on the number of attendants needed to staff the crib. Attendants will receive $9 per hour in wages and fringe benefits. Mechanics' time will be worth $30 per hour, which includes wages and fringe benefits. Based on previous experience, the manager estimates requests for tools will average 18 per hour with a service capacity of 20 requests per hour per attendant. How many attendants should be on duty in order to minimize total mechanics wait cost and attendants' wages? Assume that arrival and service rates will be Poisson. (Assume that the number of mechanics is very large, in order for the infinite-source model to be appropriate.)

Solution

$\lambda = 18$ per hour
$\mu = 20$ per hour

The solution requires an iterative approach that reveals the total cost of feasible alternatives (i.e., a utilization less than 100 percent) and selection of the lowest-cost alternative. Note that the total-cost curve will always be U-shaped; increase the number of servers until the total cost shows an increase over the previous value. The optimum will be the number of servers that produced the previous total cost value. Thus,

Number of Servers, M	L_q^*	$L_q + \dfrac{\lambda}{\mu} = L_s$	$9M:$ Server Cost (per hour)	$30L_s:$ Mechanic Cost (per hour)	Total Cost (per hour)
1 ..	8.1	8.1 + .9 = 9.0	$9	$270	$279
2 ..	.229	.229 + .9 = 1.129	$18	$33.87	$52[†]
3 ..	.03	.03 + .9 = .93	$27	$27.9	$55[†]

*L_q from Table 18–4, with $\lambda/\mu = 18/20 = .9$.
[†]Rounded.

Hence, two servers will produce the lowest total cost.

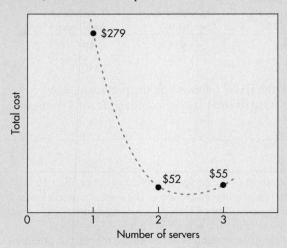

Infinite source. The following is a list of average service durations for three different operations: **Problem 2**

Operation	Average Service Duration
A	8 minutes
B	1.2 hours
C	2 days

a. Determine the average service rate for each operation.

b. Would the calculated rates be different if these were interarrival durations rather than service durations?

a. The average service rate is the reciprocal of average service durations. Thus, the rates are: **Solution**

  A: 1/8 per minute = .125 per minute, or .125/min. × 60 min./hr. = 7.5 per hour

  B: 1/1.2 per hour = .833 per hour

  C: 1/2 per day = .50 per day

b. No. In either case, the rate is simply the reciprocal of the duration.

Finite source. A group of 10 machines is loaded and unloaded by one of three servers. The   **Problem 3**
machines run for an average of six minutes per cycle, and average time to unload and reload is
nine minutes. Run and service durations can be described by Exponential distributions. While
running, the machines produce 16 units per hour if they did not have to pause to wait for a
server and be loaded and unloaded. What is the average hourly output of each machine when
waiting and serving are taken into account?

T = 9 minutes   **Solution**

U = 6 minutes; $X = \dfrac{T}{T+U} = \dfrac{9}{9+6} = .60$

N = 10 machines

M = 3 servers; from Table 18–7, we obtain F = .500, D = .996

Calculate the average number of machines running:

   $J = NF(1 - X) = 10(.500)(.40) = 2$

Determine the percentage of machines running, and multiply by output while running:

   $\dfrac{J}{N} \times (16 \text{ per hour}) = \dfrac{2}{10} \times (16 \text{ per hour}) = 3.2 \text{ per hour}$

1. Give some examples of services where waiting lines are used.   **DISCUSSION AND**
2. Why do waiting lines form even though a service system is underloaded?   **REVIEW QUESTIONS**
3. What are the most common measures of system performance in queuing analysis?
4. What effect would decreasing arrival and service variability have on the waiting line?
5. What approach do supermarkets use to reduce waiting times?
6. Contrast *finite* and *"infinite"* population sources.
7. Will doubling the service rate of a single-server system reduce the average waiting time in line by a factor of one-half? Explain briefly.
8. In a multiple-servers system, what is the rationale for having customers wait in a single joint line as is now being done in many banks, rather than in multiple lines?
9. What happens to the average wait time if a manager attempts to achieve a high percentage of capacity utilization?

<table>
<tr><td>

TAKING STOCK

</td><td>

1. What general trade-off is involved in waiting line decisions?
2. Who needs to be involved in assessing the cost of customers waiting for service if the customers are (a) the general public and (b) employees of the organization?
3. How has technology had an impact on analyzing waiting line systems? How has technology improved waiting line performance?

</td></tr>
<tr><td>

CRITICAL THINKING EXERCISE

</td><td>

The owner of Eat Now Restaurant implemented an expanded menu early last year. The menu was a success, drawing many more customers than the previous menu. But good news soon became bad news as long waiting lines began to deter customers, and business dropped off. However, because of space and other limitations, there didn't seem to be any viable options to consider. Then a customer mentioned a technique that was being used in the company he worked for, called mass customization. He said it really streamlined processing, and maybe it could work for the restaurant.

Describe how that approach might work at the restaurant and why that could be expected to reduce waiting times.

</td></tr>
<tr><td>

INTERNET EXERCISE

</td><td>

Visit www.Q-MATIC.CA/?id=1250, under "solutions," choose a sector, find a case study, and briefly describe how the Q-MATIC system helped the operation.

</td></tr>
<tr><td>

PROBLEMS

</td><td>

1. Repair calls for Xerox copiers in a small city are handled by one repairman. Repair duration, including travel time, is Exponentially distributed with a mean of two hours per call. Requests for copier repairs come in at a mean rate of three per eight-hour day (assume Poisson). Assume infinite source. Determine:
   a. The average number of copiers awaiting repairs.
   b. Server utilization.
   c. The amount of time during an eight-hour day that the repairman is not out on a call.
   d. The probability of two or more copiers in the system (waiting for or being repaired).
   e. The probability that a copier waits more than 4 hours for repair to begin.
2. A vending machine dispenses hot chocolate or coffee. Service duration is 30 seconds per cup and is constant. Customers arrive at a mean rate of 80 per hour and this rate is Poisson. Assume that each customer buys only one cup. Determine:
   a. The average number of customers waiting in line.
   b. The average time customers spend in the system.
   c. The average number of customers in the system.
3. Many of a bank's customers use its automated teller machine (ATM) to transact business. During the early evening hours in the summer months, customers arrive at the ATM at the rate of one every other minute. This can be modelled using Poisson distribution. Each customer spends an average of 90 seconds completing his or her transaction. Transaction times are Exponentially distributed. Determine:
   a. The average time customers spend at the machine, including waiting in line and completing transactions.
   b. The probability that a customer will not have to wait upon arrival at the ATM.
   c. Utilization of the ATM.
   d. The probability that a customer waits 4 minutes or more in the line.
4. A small town with one hospital has two ambulances. Requests for ambulances during weekday mornings average .8 per hour and tend to be Poisson. Travel and loading/unloading time averages one hour per call and follows an Exponential distribution. Find:
   a. Server utilization.
   b. The average number of patients waiting.
   c. The average time patients wait for an ambulance.
   d. The probability that *both* ambulances will be busy when a call comes in.

</td></tr>
</table>

5. The following information pertains to telephone calls to a call centre on a typical Tuesday. Assume Poisson arrivals and Exponential service durations.

Period	Average Incoming Rate (calls per minute)	Average Service Rate (calls per minute per operator)	Number of Operators
Morning 1.8	1.5	2
Afternoon 2.2	1.0	3
Evening 1.4	0.7	3

   a. Determine the average time callers wait to have their calls answered for each period and the probability that a caller will have to wait during each period.

   b. The call centre is installing a new call waiting system and needs to know how many lines it would require. For each case, determine the number of lines required which will be adequate 96 percent of the time.

6. Trucks are required to pass through a weighing station so that they can be checked for weight violations. Trucks arrive at the station at the rate of 40 an hour between 7 p.m. and 9 p.m. according to Poisson distribution. Currently two inspectors are on duty during those hours, each of whom can inspect 25 trucks an hour, according to an Exponential distribution.

   a. How many trucks would you expect to see at the weighing station, including those being inspected?

   b. If a truck were just arriving at the station, about how many minutes could the driver expect to wait?

   c. How many minutes, on average, would a truck that is not immediately inspected have to wait?

   d. What is the probability that both inspectors would be busy at the same time?

   e. What condition would exist if there were only one inspector?

   f. What is the maximum line length for a probability .97 of not exceeding it?

7. The manager of a regional warehouse must decide on the number of loading docks to request for a new facility in order to minimize the sum of dock–crew and driver–truck costs. The manager has learned that each driver–truck combination represents a cost of $300 per day and that each dock plus loading crew represents a cost of $1,100 per day.

   a. How many docks should be requested if trucks arrive at average rate of four per day, each dock can handle average of five trucks per day, and both rates are Poisson?

   b. An employee has proposed adding new equipment that would speed up the loading rate to 5.71 trucks per day. The equipment would cost $100 per day for each dock. Should the manager invest in the new equipment?

8. The parts department of a large automobile dealership has a counter used exclusively for mechanics' requests for parts. The length of time between requests can be modelled by an Exponential distribution that has a mean of five minutes. A clerk can handle requests at an average rate of 15 per hour, and this can be modelled by a Poisson distribution. Suppose there are two clerks at the counter.

   a. On average, how many mechanics would be at the counter, including those being served?

   b. If a mechanic has to wait, how long would the average wait be?

   c. What is the probability that a mechanic would have to wait for service?

   d. What percentage of time is a clerk idle?

   e. If clerks represent a cost of $20 per hour and mechanics a cost of $30 per hour, what number of clerks would be optimal in terms of minimizing total cost?

9. One field representative services five customers for a computer manufacturer. Customers request assistance at an average (Poisson-distributed) rate of once every four workdays. The field representative can handle an average (Poisson-distributed) of one call per day. Determine:

   a. The expected number of customers waiting.

   b. The average length of time customers must wait from the initial request for service until the service has been completed.

  c. The percentage of time the service rep will be idle.

  d. By how much would your answer to part *a* be reduced if a second field rep were added?

10. Two operators handle adjustments for a group of 10 machines. Adjustment time is Exponentially distributed and has a mean of 14 minutes per machine. The machines operate for an average of 86 minutes after an adjustment. While running, each machine can turn out 50 pieces per hour. Find:

  a. The probability that a machine will have to wait for an adjustment.

  b. The average number of machines waiting for adjustment.

  c. The average number of machines being serviced.

  d. The expected hourly output of each machine, taking adjustments into account.

  e. Machine downtime represents a cost of $70 per hour; operator cost (including wage and fringe benefits) is $15 per hour. What is the optimum number of operators?

11. One operator services a group of five machines. Machine run time and service durations are both Exponential. Machines run for an average of 90 minutes after a service, and service duration averages 35 minutes. The operator receives $20 per hour in wage and fringe benefits, and machine downtime costs $70 per hour per machine.

  a. If each machine produces 60 pieces per hour while running, find the average hourly output of each machine when waiting and service times are taken into account.

  b. Determine the optimum number of operators.

12. A milling department has 10 machines. Each machine operates an average of eight hours before requiring adjustment which takes an average of two hours. Both distributions are Exponential. While running, each machine can produce 40 pieces an hour.

  a. With one adjuster, what is the net average hourly output per machine?

  b. If machine downtime cost is $80 per hour and adjuster cost is $20 per hour, how many adjusters would be optimal?

13. Trucks arrive at the loading dock of a wholesale grocer at an average rate of 1.2 per hour in the mornings. A single crew consisting of two workers can load a truck in about 30 minutes. Crew members receive $10 per hour in wage and fringe benefits, and trucks and drivers reflect an hourly cost of $60. The manager is thinking of adding another member to the crew. The average service rate would then be 2.4 trucks per hour. Assume rates are Poisson.

  a. Would the third crew member be economical?

  b. Would a fourth member be justifiable if the resulting average service capacity were 2.6 trucks per hour?

14. Customers arriving at a service centre are assigned to one of three categories, with category 1 given the highest priority. Records indicate that an average of nine customers arrive per hour and that one-third are assigned to each category. There are two servers, and each can process customers at an average rate of five per hour. Arrival and service rates can be described by Poisson distributions.

  a. What is the utilization rate for a server?

  b. Determine the average length of wait time for units in each class.

  c. Find the average number of customers in each class that are waiting for service.

15. A priority system is used to process customers, who are assigned to one of two classes when they enter the processing centre. The highest-priority class has an average arrival rate of four per hour; the other class has an average arrival rate of two per hour. Both are Poisson. There are two servers, and each can process customers in an average of six minutes (Exponentially distributed).

  a. What is the server utilization?

  b. Determine the average length of wait time for each class.

  c. Determine the average number of customers of each class that would be waiting for service.

  d. If the manager could alter the assignment rules so that arrival rates of the two classes were equal, what would be the revised average length of wait time for each priority class?

16. A priority waiting system assigns arriving customers to one of four classes. Average arrival rates (Poisson) of the classes are:

Class	Average Arrivals per Hour
1	2
2	4
3	3
4	2

Five servers process the customers, and each can handle an average of three customers per hour (Exponential).

   a. What is the server utilization?

   b. What is the average length of wait time for service by customers in the various classes? How many are waiting in each class on average?

   c. If the average arrival rate of the second priority class could be reduced to three units per hour by shifting some arrivals into the third priority class, how would your answers to part *b* change?

   d. What observations can you make based on your answers to part *c*?

17. Referring to Problem 16, suppose that each server could handle an average of four customers per hour. Answer the questions posed in the problem. Explain why the impact of reassigning customers in part *c* is much less than in Problem 16.

18. During the morning hours at a catalogue sales department, telephone calls come in at the rate (Poisson) of 40 per hour on average. Calls that cannot be answered immediately are put on hold. The system can handle eight callers on hold. If additional calls come in, they receive a busy signal. The three customer service representatives who answer the calls spend an average of three minutes with a customer (Exponentially distributed).

   a. What is the probability that a caller will get a busy signal? (*Hint*: Use Formula 18–15 in reverse.)

   b. What is the probability that a customer will be put on hold?

19. After the terrorist attack of September 11, 2001, getting into the U.S. has become more difficult, and hence slower for Canadian cars and trucks at border crossings. This has resulted in long line-ups. One such case occurred on the Ambassador Bridge connecting Windsor to Detroit.[2] There were nine U.S. customs booths at the Detroit side of the bridge. Each truck took approximately two minutes to get cleared. During the busy hours, about 300 trucks (i.e., one every 12 seconds) arrived at the booths. Assuming that the standard deviation of getting cleared is 1 minute per truck and the standard deviation of interarrival durations is 6 seconds, how many more U.S. Customs Booths were needed at the Ambassador Bridge to provide a reasonable average wait time?

20. The number of customers coming to a branch of First National Bank of Philadelphia during the period 5:00 p.m. to 5:30 p.m. of a "normal" day had a Poisson distribution with an average of 39 persons during the half hour. The length of time each customer spent with a teller was Exponential with an average of 45.5 seconds. The average time a customer spent in the line waiting was desired to be just less than three minutes. The manager was wondering how many tellers were adequate during this time period.

21. Model 8300 Telemetry system used at Wesley Long Community Hospital, Greensboro, North Carolina, is a completely self-contained, wireless, one-patient cardiac monitor. The system provides wireless transmission of a patient's heartbeat to a receiver either at a central station or at the bedside. A study was undertaken to analyze the service provided by the 18 currently-held telemetry units and to investigate the cost/benefit of any additional telemetry units. During a 38-day reviewing period, there were 156 requests for service (telemetry units are requested and used 24 hours a day). The average service duration was 93.6 hours per patient. Both interarrival and service durations could be approximated by Exponential distributions.[3]

   a. What is the average arrival rate per day of patients needing telemetry?

   b. What is the average service rate per day of patients needing telemetry?

   c. If the length of average wait time before service is desired to be less than 5 hours, are 18 telemetry units enough? (*Hint*: For $\lambda/\mu = 16$ and $M = 18$, it can be shown that $Lq = 4.29$.)

22. Number of calls coming into the New York State Child Abuse Register during the 5 p.m. to 9 a.m. period on weekdays had approximately a Poisson distribution with an average of 1.67 calls per hour. Call lengths were distributed approximately as an Exponential distribution with average of 5.4 minutes. It is considered important that a very high percentage of calls get through to the operator right away (as opposed to having to wait). If only one person is assigned to answer the phones, what is the probability that a call will have to wait because the operator is busy?

---

[2]D. Battagello, *Windsor Star Border Reporter*, November 9, 2004, www2.uwindsor.ca/~hlynka/qreal.html.

[3]T. Scott and W. A. Hailey, "Queuing Model Aids Economic Analysis of Health Centre," *Industrial Engineering*, February 1981, pp. 56–61.

23. Becton-Dickinson manufactures medical supplies such as syringes. In one plant it had 10 parallel syringe manufacturing lines. The problem was that syringes kept getting stuck in the lines, shutting the lines down. On average, a line worked one minute after a blockage was fixed. One operator was assigned to five lines (i.e., a total of two operators). The average time it took the operator to walk to the blocked line and fix the problem was 10 seconds. The number of blockages per minute per line was Poisson and the service duration distribution was Exponential. How long was a line expected to be down per hour? Assume that the two operators do not help each other.

MINI-CASE

Nortel's Call-Centre Consolidation

www.nortel.com

In the late 1990s, Nortel was looking for a way to reduce the costs of running call centres and also to improve service. It had a call centre in Saint John, New Brunswick (servicing Canada), and a call centre in Dallas, Texas (servicing the U.S.). These two call centres performed the same sales/marketing jobs and handled enquiries from Nortel switches and equipment distributors and end-users. After a study, it was decided to consolidate both call centres in Saint John. Most Dallas employees were re-assigned and new employees were recruited in Saint John. Approximately the same total number of staff are now employed, but the annual costs have decreased by 20 percent and service has improved. The goal of answering 80 percent of calls within 20 seconds is being achieved, and fewer than 5 percent of callers abandon their call because of a long wait. The service improvement is the result of combining two separate waiting lines into one line.

Question

Can you explain why combining two separate waiting lines into one, while keeping the same total number of servers, could result in lower average wait times for callers?

Source: D. Hanson, "International Call Center Consolidation: A Real-life Example," *Call Center Solutions* 17(10), April 1999, pp. 64–70.

MINI-CASE

Adjusting Centralized Appointment Scheduling at Lourdes Hospital

www.lourdes.com

When doctors referred their patients to the Lourdes Hospital in Binghamton, New York, for various services such as X-rays, their office had a tough time getting through to the centralized appointment office of Lourdes. Most of the time, the line was busy. The installation of a call waiting system did not improve the situation, because callers were put on hold for indefinite lengths of time. The poor service had resulted in numerous complaints. One of the managers was put in charge of finding a solution, and a goal of answering at least 90 percent of calls without delay was set. The hospital was willing to employ more staff to receive calls. The manager studied this queuing problem by collecting data for 21 workdays during which additional staff were used to answer calls and no call received a busy signal or was put on hold. The number of calls per day ranged between 220 and 350, with no day-of-the-week seasonality. Most days, the number of calls was between 250 and 300. The average number of calls arriving during each 15-minute interval peaked at about 10 calls during 9:00–11:30 a.m. and 2:00–3:45 p.m. periods. The 944 service durations had a distribution similar to Exponential with a mean of 3.11 minutes. The manager also found out that previously the 6.5 full-time-equivalent employees usually spent half their time doing other tasks and turned off their phones while busy with other tasks. Using the multiple-servers queuing model and a service goal of at least 90-percent probability of not having to wait, the manager determined the number of staff required during each 15-minute interval. When the original staffing levels were compared with the model-determined ones, it was discovered that more staff were required earlier in the day and later in the afternoon, and fewer were needed around noon. The problem was solved by rearranging work shifts.

Question

During busy periods (9:00 a.m.–11:30 a.m. and 2:00 p.m.–3:45 p.m.), the central appointment office receives 40 calls per hour, on average. Each call takes an average of 3.15 minutes to serve. It is desired that at least 90 percent of calls is received without waiting. What is the minimum number of staff needed during these busy times?

Source: S. R. Agnihothri and P. F. Taylor, "Staffing a Centralized Appointment Scheduling Department in Lourdes Hospital," *Interfaces* 21(5), September–October 1991, pp. 1–11.

MINI-CASE

Surgery Wait Times

A major problem with Canada's health care system is the excessive wait times for non-life-threatening elective surgeries (even though a small percentage of people on the waiting list actually die while waiting for surgery). Although there has been much anecdotal evidence for this, according to the Fraser Institute, both federal and provincial governments have resisted collecting data on it. However, the Fraser Institute has been publishing the result of an annual survey of specialists (surgeons) for more than a decade. Two charts from their 2004 report are shown to the right. As can be observed, wait times have almost doubled since 1993!

The wait times actually consists of two parts: (a) waiting to see a specialist, and then (b) waiting for surgery. The relative size of these two waits varies by specialty and province.

Urgent life-threatening cases get higher priority (e.g., surgery is performed within 1 or 2 days). However, in many cases there is no objective way to measure the severity of a problem (i.e., the difference between an urgent and an elective surgery is not always evident). Attempts have been made to use a scoring system to measure this for some medical problems needing surgery, but so far there is no general agreement.

Another problem is that the queuing system is not coordinated within Canada or even within a province (i.e., the specialists act independently, each having their own queue). However, some provinces are making average wait times available, by city or region, and by specialty (so that patients could choose the minimum expected wait time option).

There is no question that a large percentage of people waiting for some surgeries are in pain. Specialists generally believe that a reasonable wait time for elective surgery is about six weeks.

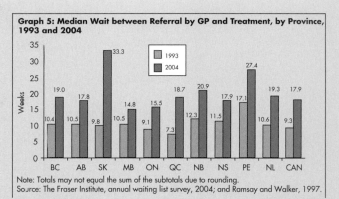

Graph 5: Median Wait between Referral by GP and Treatment, by Province, 1993 and 2004

Note: Totals may not equal the sum of the subtotals due to rounding.
Source: The Fraser Institute, annual waiting list survey, 2004; and Ramsay and Walker, 1997.

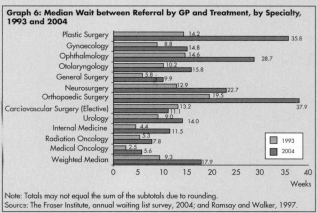

Graph 6: Median Wait between Referral by GP and Treatment, by Specialty, 1993 and 2004

Note: Totals may not equal the sum of the subtotals due to rounding.
Source: The Fraser Institute, annual waiting list survey, 2004; and Ramsay and Walker, 1997.

Figures from Nadeem Esmail and Michael Walker, *Waiting Your Turn: Hospital Waiting Lists in Canada*. The Fraser Institute, www.fraserinstitute.ca. Reprinted with permission.

Question

If you were a health minister, what would you do about this issue?

Source: www.fraserinstitute.ca/admin/books/chapterfiles/wyt2004.pdf#.

Buffa, Elwood. *Operations Management*. 3rd ed. New York: John Wiley & Sons, 1972.

Griffin, W. *Queuing: Basic Theory and Applications*. Columbus, OH: Grid Publishing, 1978.

Hillier, Frederick S., and Gerald J. Lieberman. *Introduction to Operations Research*, 3rd ed. San Francisco: Holden-Day, 1980.

Katz, K. L., B. M. Larson, and R. C. Larson. "Prescriptions for the Waiting-in-Line Blues: Entertain, Enlighten, and Engage." *Sloan Management Review* 32(2) Winter 1991, pp. 44–53.

Nahmias, S. *Production and Operations Analysis*, 3rd ed. Chicago: Irwin, 1997.

Stevenson, William J. *Introduction to Management Science*. 3rd ed. Burr Ridge, IL: Richard D. Irwin, 1998.

SELECTED BIBLIOGRAPHY AND FURTHER READING

To access "Simulation," the supplement to Chapter 18, please use the student **DVD** packaged with the text or visit the Online Learning Centre at **www.mcgrawhill.ca/olc/stevenson.**

Answers to Selected Problems

Chapter 2: Competitiveness, Strategy, and Productivity

2. A crew size of two had the highest productivity (250 m^2 per person per week installed).

3. Week 1: 5.62.
   Week 2: 5.45.
   Week 3: 5.20.
   Week 4: 5.01.
   Multifactor productivity is decreasing.

6. 4.3% increase.

Chapter 3: Forecasting

1. *a.* blueberry = 33, cinnamon = 35, cupcakes = 47.
   b. That demand did not exceed supply.

4. *a.* 22.   *b.* 20.75.   *c.* 20.72.

5. *a.* Increasing by 15,000 bottles per year.
   b. 275 (i.e., 275,000 bottles).

9. *a.* $Y_t = 195.47 + 7.00t$.
   $Y_{16} = 307.47$ $Y_{18} = 321.47$
   $Y_{17} = 314.47$ $Y_{19} = 328.47$
   b. 307.23.

12. Q_1: 157.85; Q_2: 175; Q_3: 126.3; Q_4: 325; Q_1 = 322.85.

13. *a.* Fri. = 0.79, Sat. = 1.34, Sun. = 0.87.

16.
Day	Relative
1	0.900
2	0.833
3	0.916
4	1.031
5	1.412
6	1.482
7	0.426

19. *b.* Jan. 800
    Feb. 810
    Mar. 900
    Apr. 809.6
    . . . . .

22. *b.* $700,000.

24. *b.* −0.985. A high negative relationship between sales and price.

29. *a.*

	MSE	MAD	MAPE
Forecast 1	9.4	2.8	.36%
Forecast 2	38.2	3.6	.46%

Forecast 1 is superior.

Chapter 4 Supplement: Reliability

2. .9033.

4. .93.

6. *a.* .7876.   *b.* .90 component, reliability = .8664.
   c. .90 component, reliability .86814.

9. .996.

12. *a.* (1) .2725.   *b.* (1) .6608.
    (2) .2019.   (2) .3935.
    (3) .1353.   (3) .1813.
    c. (1) 21 months.   (3) 90 months.
    (2) 57 months.   (4) 138 months.

16. *a.* .2266.   *b.* .4400.   *c.* .3830.

19. *a.* .93.   *b.* .98.

Chapter 5: Strategic Capacity Planning

4. *a.* A: 8,000 units.   *b.* 10,000 units.
   B: 7,500 units.
   c. A: $20,000.
   B: $18,000.
   A's profit would be higher.

6. *a.* A: $82.
   B: $92.
   C: $100.
   c. A: 0 to less than 178.
   B: Never.
   C: 178+.

7. Vendor best for $Q \le 63,333$. For larger quantities, produce in-house with process B.

9. 3 machines.

11. *a.* one machine: BEP = 80.   two: BEP = 152.
    b. one machine.

Chapter 6: Process Design and Facility Layout

1. *a.* Minimum cycle time is 2.4 minutes, maximum is 18 minutes.

   b. 25 units to 187.5 units.

   c. Eight.

   d. 3.6 minutes.

   e. (1) 50 units.

      (2) 30 units.

2. *a.*

Station	Tasks	Time
1	a	1.4
2	b, e	1.3
3	d, c, f	1.8
4	g, h	1.5

   b. 83.3%.

10.

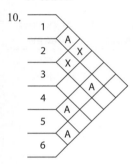

11.

4	3	1
5	8	6
7	2	

16. 3→A, 5→B, 1→C, 4→D, 6→E, 2→F.

Chapter 7: Design of Work Systems

2. *a.* 1.2 minutes.

   b. 1.14 minutes.

   c. 1.27 minutes.

4.

Element	OT
1	4.10
2	1.50
3	3.25
4	2.77

7. 5.85 minutes.

8. 7.125 minutes.

10. 57 observations.

11. 37 work cycles.

12. *a.* 12%.   *b.* 254 observations.

Chapter 8: Location Planning and Analysis

2. *a.* A: 16,854; B: 17,416; C: 17,753.   *b.* C: $14,670.

4. *a.* B: 0 to 33; C: 34 to 400; A: 400+.   *b.* C

   c. Expansion leads to more control, whereas subcontracting leads to more flexibility.

9. A (Score = 87.02).

11. (5,4).

Chapter 9: Management of Quality

2.

	Res.	Com.
Noisy	10	3
Failed	7	2
Odour	5	7
Warm	3	4

Chapter 10: Quality Control

1. *a.* 1.24%.   *b.* 24.4 kg and 24.6 kg.

2. *a.* LCL: 1.991 litres.   *b.* Yes, process is in control.
   UCL: 2.009 litres.

3. *a.* Mean: LCL is 2.96, UCL is 3.24.
   Range: LCL is .099, UCL is 0.801.

   b. Yes.

6. *a.*

1	2	3	4
.020	.010	.025	.045

   b. .025.

   c. Mean = .025, standard deviation = .011.

   d. LCL = .001, UCL = .049.

   e. .0456.

   f. Yes.

   g. Mean = .02, standard deviation = .0099.

   h. LCL = .0002, UCL = .0399. No.

8. *a.* UCL = 16.266, LCL = 0, Yes.   *b.* No change

11. 35 pieces.

16. *b.* 4.5, .192.

    c. 4.5, .086.

    d. 4.242 to 4.758.

    f. None.

17. *a.* 1.11.   *b.* Capable.

20. H: C_{pk} = .9375, incapable, k: C_{pk} = 1.0, capable, T: C_{pk} = 1.06, capable.

Chapter 11: Inventory Management

2. *a.*

Item	Class
Z45	A
F95	A
K35	A
P05	B
F14	B
D45	B
K36	B
D57	B
K34	C
D52	C
M20	C
F99	C
N08	C
D48	C
M10	C

4. *a.* 228 packages.

   b. $228

   c. Yes.

   d. Yes; TC = $310; save $82.

10. *a.* 1,633 bags.

    b. 490 bags.

    c. 3.27 days.

    d. 24.5 runs per year.

    e. $5,739.71

14. *a.* 600 stones (total cost = $41,120).

    b. 150 stones on hand.

18. 6,600 metres.

20. *a.* 91 kg.

    b. ROP = 691 kg.

29. *a.* EOQ = 126.5 cases.   *b.* SS = 1.6 cases.

    c. .3745.

31. K033:581; K144:458; L700:−16 (do not order).

34. 25 dozen, service level = 73%.

36. 78.85 kg.

Chapter 12: Aggregate Planning

2. *a.* $4,670. Use overtime: Month 3: 20 units; Month 4: 20 units; Month 5: 20 units.

   b. $4,800. Use subcontracting: Month 4: 10 units; Month 5: 50 units.

10. Plan B: $14,340.

    Plan C: $14,470.

14. Total cost = $124,960.

18. Projected on-hand, wk1 = 31, wk2 = 71, wk3 = 41, wk4 = 11, wk5 = 41, wk6 = 71, wk7 = 31, wk8 = 61.

Chapter 13: MRP and ERP

1. *a.* F = 2, G = 1, H = 1, J = 6, D = 10, L = 2, A = 4

2. *a.* E = 138.

   b. Week 5.

10. Order 160 units in Week 2; projected on-hand wk4 = 15, wk5 = 35, wk6 = 5, …

13. *b.* Production schedule for golf carts.

Week number	1	2	3	4	5	6	7	8	9
Quantity						100		100	100

Item: Golf cart LT = 1 week									
Gross requirements						100		100	100
Scheduled receipts									
Projected on-hand									
Net requirements						100		100	100
Planned-order receipts						100		100	100
Planned-order releases					100		100	100	

Item: Bases LT = 1 week									
Gross requirements						100		100	100
Scheduled receipts									
Projected on-hand	20	20	20	20	50	100	50	100	50	0
Net requirements									
Planned-order receipts				30	50	50	50	50	50
Planned-order releases			30	50	50	50	50	50	

14. EPP = 78.57. Order 120 units in Month 2 and 60 units in Month 6.

Chapter 14: Just-in-Time and Lean Operations

1. 4 or 5; less containers.
4. D, C, B, D, (C, D, A), D, B, C, D.

Chapter 15: Scheduling and Control

1. *a.* MST: A-B-C-D or
   B-A-C-D,
   SPT = D-C−B-A,
   EDD = C-B-D-A,
   CR = A-B-C-D.

   b.

	CR	SPT	EDD	MST (B–A–C–D)
Avg. flow time	26.5	19.75	21	25.5
Avg. days late	11	6	6	10
Avg. WIP	2.86	2.14	2.27	2.76

   c. SPT.
4. B-A-G-E-F-D-C.
14. A-B-C, total setup time = 7 hrs.

Chapter 16: Supply Chain Management

1. Use 2-day freight ($29.38 saving).

Chapter 17: Project Management

1. *a.* S-9-10-11-12-13-End: 31 days.
   b. 1-2-5-7-8-9: 55.
   c. 1-2-3-4-End: 44.

3. Concerned about critical path activities F, H, J, K.
8. *a.* .6881.
   b. .3978.
   c. .0203.
14. *a.* wk1: 4, wk2: 1, wk3: 4 and 13, wk4: 9 and 12, wk5: 9 and 11, wk6: 1, 5, and 13.

Chapter 18: Waiting Lines

5. *a.* M: .375 minute; .45.
   A: .678 minute; .54.
   E: .635 minute; .44.
   b. M: 4; A: 7; E: 5.
9. *a.* .995 customer.
   b. 2.24 days.
   c. 31.1 percent.
   d. .875 customer less.
15. *a.* 30.
   b. $W_1 = .52$ min.
   $W_2 = .74$ min.
   c. $L_1 = .034.$
   $L_2 = .025.$
   d. $W_1 = .49$ min.
   $W_2 = .69$ min.

B APPENDIX

Tables

A. Areas under the Standardized Normal curve, 0 to z, 727
B. Areas under the Standardized Normal curve
   1. From $-\infty$ to $-z$, $z < 0$ 728
   2. From $-\infty$ to $+z$, 729
C. Cumulative Poisson probabilities, 730

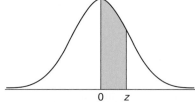

| TABLE A | | | *Areas under the Standardized Normal curve, 0 to z* | | | | | | |

z	.00	.01	.02	.03	.04	.05	.06	.07	.08	.09
0.0.	.0000	.0040	.0080	.0120	.0160	.0199	.0239	.0279	.0319	.0359
0.1.	.0398	.0438	.0478	.0517	.0557	.0596	.0636	.0675	.0714	.0753
0.2.	.0793	.0832	.0871	.0910	.0948	.0987	.1026	.1064	.1103	.1141
0.3.	.1179	.1217	.1255	.1293	.1331	.1368	.1406	.1443	.1480	.1517
0.4.	.1554	.1591	.1628	.1664	.1700	.1736	.1772	.1808	.1844	.1879
0.5.	.1915	.1950	.1985	.2019	.2054	.2088	.2123	.2157	.2190	.2224
0.6.	.2257	.2291	.2324	.2357	.2389	.2422	.2454	.2486	.2517	.2549
0.7.	.2580	.2611	.2642	.2673	.2703	.2734	.2764	.2794	.2823	.2852
0.8.	.2881	.2910	.2939	.2967	.2995	.3023	.3051	.3078	.3106	.3133
0.9.	.3159	.3186	.3212	.3238	.3264	.3289	.3315	.3340	.3365	.3389
1.0.	.3413	.3438	.3461	.3485	.3508	.3531	.3554	.3577	.3599	.3621
1.1.	.3643	.3665	.3686	.3708	.3729	.3749	.3770	.3790	.3810	.3830
1.2.	.3849	.3869	.3888	.3907	.3925	.3944	.3962	.3980	.3997	.4015
1.3.	.4032	.4049	.4066	.4082	.4099	.4115	.4131	.4147	.4162	.4177
1.4.	.4192	.4207	.4222	.4236	.4251	.4265	.4279	.4292	.4306	.4319
1.5.	.4332	.4345	.4357	.4370	.4382	.4394	.4406	.4418	.4429	.4441
1.6.	.4452	.4463	.4474	.4484	.4495	.4505	.4515	.4525	.4535	.4545
1.7.	.4554	.4564	.4573	.4582	.4591	.4599	.4608	.4616	.4625	.4633
1.8.	.4641	.4649	.4656	.4664	.4671	.4678	.4686	.4693	.4699	.4706
1.9.	.4713	.4719	.4726	.4732	.4738	.4744	.4750	.4756	.4761	.4767
2.0.	.4772	.4778	.4783	.4788	.4793	.4798	.4803	.4808	.4812	.4817
2.1.	.4821	.4826	.4830	.4834	.4838	.4842	.4846	.4850	.4854	.4857
2.2.	.4861	.4864	.4868	.4871	.4875	.4878	.4881	.4884	.4887	.4890
2.3.	.4893	.4896	.4898	.4901	.4904	.4906	.4909	.4911	.4913	.4916
2.4.	.4918	.4920	.4922	.4925	.4927	.4929	.4931	.4932	.4934	.4936
2.5.	.4938	.4940	.4941	.4943	.4945	.4946	.4948	.4949	.4951	.4952
2.6	.4953	.4955	.4956	.4957	.4959	.4960	.4961	.4962	.4963	.4964
2.7	.4965	.4966	.4967	.4968	.4969	.4970	.4971	.4972	.4973	.4974
2.8.	.4974	.4975	.4976	.4977	.4977	.4978	.4979	.4979	.4980	.4981
2.9.	.4981	.4982	.4982	.4983	.4984	.4984	.4985	.4985	.4986	.4986
3.0.	.4987	.4987	.4987	.4988	.4988	.4989	.4989	.4989	.4990	.4990

1. *Areas under the Standardized Normal curve, from $-\infty$ to z*

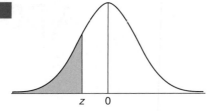

.09	.08	.07	.06	.05	.04	.03	.02	.01	.00	z
.0002	.0003	.0003	.0003	.0003	.0003	.0003	.0003	.0003	.0003	−3.4
.0003	.0004	.0004	.0004	.0004	.0004	.0004	.0005	.0005	.0005	−3.3
.0005	.0005	.0005	.0006	.0006	.0006	.0006	.0006	.0007	.0007	−3.2
.0007	.0007	.0008	.0008	.0008	.0008	.0009	.0009	.0009	.0010	−3.1
.0010	.0010	.0011	.0011	.0011	.0012	.0012	.0013	.0013	.0013	−3.0
.0014	.0014	0015	.0015	.0016	.0016	.0017	.0018	.0018	.0019	−2.9
.0019	.0020	.0021	.0021	.0022	.0023	.0023	.0024	.0025	.0026	−2.8
.0026	.0027	.0028	.0029	.0030	0031	.0032	.0033	.0034	.0035	−2.7
.0036	.0037	.0038	.0039	.0040	.0041	.0043	.0044	.0045	.0047	−2.6
.0048	.0049	.0051	.0052	.0054	.0055	.0057	.0059	.0060	.0062	−2.5
.0064	.0066	.0068	.0069	.0071	.0073	.0075	.0078	.0080	.0082	−2.4
.0084	.0087	.0089	.0091	.0094	.0096	.0099	.0102	.0104	.0107	−2.3
.0110	.0113	.0116	.0119	.0122	.0125	.0129	.0132	.0136	.0139	−2.2
.0143	.0146	.0150	.0154	.0158	.0162	.0166	.0170	.0174	.0179	−2.1
.0183	.0188	.0192	.0197	.0202	.0207	.0212	.0217	.0222	.0228	−2.0
.0233	.0239	.0244	.0250	.0256	.0262	.0268	.0274	.0281	.0287	−1.9
.0294	.0301	.0307	.0314	.0322	.0329	.0336	.0344	.0351	.0359	−1.8
.0367	.0375	.0384	.0392	.0401	.0409	.0418	.0427	.0436	.0446	−1.7
.0455	.0465	.0475	.0485	.0495	.0505	.0516	.0526	.0537	.0548	−1.6
.0559	.0571	.0582	.0594	.0606	.0618	.0630	.0643	.0655	.0668	−1.5
.0681	.0694	.0708	.0721	.0735	.0749	.0764	.0778	.0793	.0808	−1.4
.0823	.0838	.0853	.0869	.0885	.0901	.0918	.0934	.0951	.0968	−1.3
.0985	.1003	.1020	.1038	.1056	.1075	.1093	.1112	.1131	.1151	−1.2
.1170	.1190	.1210	.1230	.1251	.1271	.1292	.1314	.1335	.1357	−1.1
.1379	.1401	.1423	.1446	.1469	.1492	.1515	.1539	.1562	.1587	−1.0
.1611	.1635	.1660	.1685	.1711	.1736	.1762	.1788	.1814	.1841	−0.9
.1867	.1894	.1922	.1949	.1977	.2005	.2033	.2061	.2090	.2119	−0.8
.2148	.2177	.2206	.2236	.2266	.2296	.2327	.2358	.2389	.2420	−0.7
.2451	.2483	.2514	.2546	.2578	.2611	.2643	.2676	.2709	.2743	−0.6
.2776	.2810	.2843	.2877	.2912	.2946	.2981	.3015	.3050	.3085	−0.5
.3121	.3156	.3192	.3228	.3264	.3300	.3336	.3372	.3409	.3446	−0.4
.3483	.3520	.3557	.3594	.3632	.3669	.3707	.3745	.3783	.3821	−0.3
.3859	.3897	.3936	.3974	.4013	.4052	.4090	.4129	.4168	.4207	−0.2
.4247	.4286	.4325	.4364	.4404	.4443	.4483	.4522	.4562	.4602	−0.1
.4641	.4681	.4721	.4761	.4801	.4840	.4880	.4920	.4960	.5000	−0.0

(continued)

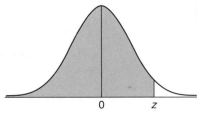

2. Areas under the Standardized Normal curve, from $-\infty$ *to z*

z	.00	.01	.02	.03	.04	.05	.06	.07	.08	.09
.0	.5000	.5040	.5080	.5120	.5160	.5199	.5239	.5279	.5319	.5359
.1 . . .	.5398	.5438	.5478	.5517	.5557	.5596	.5636	.5675	.5714	.5753
.2 . . .	.5793	.5832	.5871	.5910	.5948	.5987	.6026	.6064	.6103	.6141
.3 . . .	.6179	.6217	.6255	.6293	.6331	.6368	.6406	.6443	.6480	.6517
.4 . . .	.6554	.6591	.6628	.6664	.6700	.6736	.6772	.6808	.6844	.6879
.5 . . .	.6915	.6950	.6985	.7019	.7054	.7088	.7123	.7157	.7190	.7224
.6 . . .	.7257	.7291	.7324	.7357	.7389	.7422	.7454	.7486	.7517	.7549
.7 . . .	.7580	.7611	.7642	.7673	.7703	.7734	.7764	.7794	.7823	.7852
.8 . . .	.7881	.7910	.7939	.7967	.7995	.8023	.8051	.8078	.8106	.8133
.9 . . .	.8159	.8186	.8212	.8238	.8264	.8289	.8315	.8340	.8365	.8389
1.0 . . .	.8413	.8438	.8461	.8485	.8508	.8531	.8554	.8577	.8599	.8621
1.1 . . .	.8643	.8665	.8686	.8708	.8729	.8749	.8770	.8790	.8810	.8830
1.2 . . .	.8849	.8869	.8888	.8907	.8925	.8944	.8962	.8980	.8997	.9015
1.3 . . .	.9032	.9049	.9066	.9082	.9099	.9115	.9131	.9147	.9162	.9177
1.4 . . .	.9192	.9207	.9222	.9236	.9251	.9265	.9279	.9292	.9306	.9319
1.5 . . .	.9332	.9345	.9357	.9370	.9382	.9394	.9406	.9418	.9429	.9441
1.6 . . .	.9452	.9463	.9474	.9484	.9495	.9505	.9515	.9525	.9535	.9545
1.7 . . .	.9554	.9564	.9573	.9582	.9591	.9599	.9608	.9616	.9625	.9633
1.8 . . .	.9641	.9649	.9656	.9664	.9671	.9678	.9686	.9693	.9699	.9706
1.9 . . .	.9713	.9719	.9726	.9732	.9738	.9744	.9750	.9756	.9761	.9767
2.0 . . .	.9772	.9778	.9783	.9788	.9793	.9798	.9803	.9808	.9812	.9817
2.1 . . .	.9821	.9826	.9830	.9834	.9838	.9842	.9846	.9850	.9854	.9857
2.2 . . .	.9861	.9864	.9868	.9871	.9875	.9878	.9881	.9884	.9887	.9890
2.3 . . .	.9893	.9896	.9898	.9901	.9904	.9906	.9909	.9911	.9913	.9916
2.4 . . .	.9918	.9920	.9922	.9925	.9927	.9929	.9931	.9932	.9934	.9936
2.5 . . .	.9938	.9940	.9941	.9943	.9945	.9946	.9948	.9949	.9951	.9952
2.6 . . .	.9953	.9955	.9956	.9957	.9959	.9960	.9961	.9962	.9963	.9964
2.7 . . .	.9965	.9966	.9967	.9968	.9969	.9970	.9971	.9972	.9973	.9974
2.8 . . .	.9974	.9975	.9976	.9977	.9977	.9978	.9979	.9979	.9980	.9981
2.9 . . .	.9981	.9982	.9982	.9983	.9984	.9984	.9985	.9985	.9986	.9986
3.0 . . .	.9987	.9987	.9987	.9988	.9988	.9989	.9989	.9989	.9990	.9990
3.1 . . .	.9990	.9991	.9991	.9991	.9991	.9992	.9992	.9992	.9993	.9993
3.2 . . .	.9993	.9993	.9994	.9994	.9994	.9994	.9994	.9995	.9995	.9995
3.3 . . .	.9995	.9995	.9995	.9996	.9996	.9996	.9996	.9996	.9996	.9997
3.4 . . .	.9997	.9997	.9997	.9997	.9997	.9997	.9997	.9997	.9997	.9998

TABLE C

*Cumulative Poisson
probabilities*

$$P(x \le c) = \sum_{x=0}^{x=c} \frac{\mu^x \cdot e^{-\mu}}{x!}$$

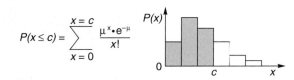

μ\x	0	1	2	3	4	5	6	7	8	9
0.05	.951	.999	1.000							
0.10	.905	.995	1.000							
0.15	.861	.990	.999	1.000						
0.20	.819	.982	.999	1.000						
0.25	.779	.974	.998	1.000						
0.30	.741	.963	.996	1.000						
0.35	.705	.951	.994	1.000						
0.40	.670	.938	.992	.999	1.000					
0.45	.638	.925	.989	.999	1.000					
0.50	.607	.910	.986	.998	1.000					
0.55	.577	.894	.982	.998	1.000					
0.60	.549	.878	.977	.997	1.000					
0.65	.522	.861	.972	.996	.999	1.000				
0.70	.497	.844	.966	.994	.999	1.000				
0.75	.472	.827	.960	.993	.999	1.000				
0.80	.449	.809	.953	.991	.999	1.000				
0.85	.427	.791	.945	.989	.998	1.000				
0.90	.407	.772	.937	.987	.998	1.000				
0.95	.387	.754	.929	.984	.997	1.000				
1.0	.368	.736	.920	.981	.996	.999	1.000			
1.1	.333	.699	.900	.974	.995	.999	1.000			
1.2	.301	.663	.880	.966	.992	.998	1.000			
1.3	.273	.627	.857	.957	.989	.998	1.000			
1.4	.247	.592	.833	.946	.986	.997	.999	1.000		
1.5	.223	.558	.809	.934	.981	.996	.999	1.000		
1.6	.202	.525	.783	.921	.976	.994	.999	1.000		
1.7	.183	.493	.757	.907	.970	.992	.998	1.000		
1.8	.165	.463	.731	.891	.964	.990	.997	.999	1.000	
1.9	.150	.434	.704	.875	.956	.987	.997	.999	1.000	
2.0	.135	.406	.677	.857	.947	.983	.995	.999	1.000	
2.2	.111	.355	.623	.819	.928	.975	.993	.998	1.000	
2.4	.091	.308	.570	.779	.904	.964	.988	.997	.999	1.000
2.6	.074	.267	.518	.736	.877	.951	.983	.995	.999	1.000
2.8	.061	.231	.470	.692	.848	.935	.976	.992	.998	.999

(continued)

TABLE C (concluded)

μ\x	0	1	2	3	4	5	6	7	8	9	10	11	12	13	14	15	16	17	18	19	20
3.0	.050	.199	.423	.647	.815	.916	.966	.988	.996	.999	1.000										
3.2	.041	.171	.380	.603	.781	.895	.955	.983	.994	.998	1.000										
3.4	.033	.147	.340	.558	.744	.871	.942	.977	.992	.997	.999	1.000									
3.6	.027	.126	.303	.515	.706	.844	.927	.969	.988	.996	.999	1.000									
3.8	.022	.107	.269	.474	.668	.816	.909	.960	.984	.994	.998	.999	1.000								
4.0	.018	.092	.238	.433	.629	.785	.889	.949	.979	.992	.997	.999	1.000								
4.2	.015	.078	.210	.395	.590	.753	.868	.936	.972	.989	.996	.999	1.000								
4.4	.012	.066	.185	.359	.551	.720	.844	.921	.964	.985	.994	.998	.999	1.000							
4.6	.010	.056	.163	.326	.513	.686	.818	.905	.955	.980	.992	.997	.999	1.000							
4.8	.008	.048	.143	.294	.476	.651	.791	.887	.944	.975	.990	.996	.999	.999	1.000						
5.0	.007	.040	.125	.265	.441	.616	.762	.867	.932	.968	.986	.995	.998	.999	1.000						
5.2	.006	.034	.109	.238	.406	.581	.732	.845	.918	.960	.982	.993	.997	.999	1.000						
5.4	.005	.029	.095	.213	.373	.546	.702	.822	.903	.951	.978	.990	.996	.999	1.000						
5.6	.004	.024	.082	.191	.342	.512	.670	.797	.886	.941	.972	.988	.995	.998	.999	1.000					
5.8	.003	.021	.072	.170	.313	.478	.638	.771	.867	.929	.965	.984	.993	.997	.999	1.000					
6.0	.002	.017	.062	.151	.285	.446	.606	.744	.847	.916	.957	.980	.991	.996	.999	.999	1.000				
6.2	.002	.015	.054	.134	.259	.414	.574	.716	.826	.902	.949	.975	.989	.995	.998	.999	1.000				
6.4	.002	.012	.046	.119	.235	.384	.542	.687	.803	.886	.939	.969	.986	.994	.997	.999	1.000				
6.6	.001	.010	.040	.105	.213	.355	.511	.658	.780	.869	.927	.963	.982	.992	.997	.999	.999	1.000			
6.8	.001	.009	.034	.093	.192	.327	.480	.628	.755	.850	.915	.955	.978	.990	.996	.998	.999	1.000			
7.0	.001	.007	.030	.082	.173	.301	.450	.599	.729	.830	.901	.947	.973	.987	.994	.998	.999	1.000			
7.2	.001	.006	.025	.072	.156	.276	.420	.569	.703	.810	.887	.937	.967	.984	.993	.997	.999	1.000			
7.4	.001	.005	.022	.063	.140	.253	.392	.539	.676	.788	.871	.926	.961	.980	.991	.996	.998	.999	1.000		
7.6	.001	.004	.019	.055	.125	.231	.365	.510	.648	.765	.854	.915	.954	.976	.989	.995	.998	.999	1.000		
7.8	.000	.004	.016	.048	.112	.210	.338	.481	.620	.741	.835	.902	.945	.971	.986	.993	.997	.999	.999	1.000	
8.0	.000	.003	.014	.042	.100	.191	.313	.453	.593	.717	.816	.888	.936	.966	.983	.992	.996	.998	.999	1.000	
8.2	.000	.003	.012	.037	.089	.174	.290	.425	.566	.692	.796	.873	.926	.960	.979	.990	.995	.998	.999	1.000	
8.4	.000	.002	.010	.032	.079	.157	.267	.400	.537	.666	.774	.857	.915	.952	.975	.987	.994	.997	.999	1.000	
8.6	.000	.002	.009	.028	.070	.142	.246	.373	.509	.640	.752	.840	.903	.944	.970	.985	.992	.996	.998	.999	1.000
8.8	.000	.001	.007	.024	.062	.128	.226	.348	.482	.614	.729	.822	.889	.935	.964	.981	.990	.995	.998	.999	1.000
9.0	.000	.001	.006	.021	.055	.116	.207	.324	.456	.587	.706	.803	.876	.926	.959	.978	.989	.995	.998	.999	1.000
9.5	.000	.001	.004	.015	.040	.089	.165	.269	.392	.522	.645	.752	.836	.898	.940	.967	.982	.991	.996	.998	.999

Photo Credits

Chapter 1
Page 26: Courtesy Sobeys, Inc.; **Page 27:** Courtesy Sobeys, Inc.

Chapter 2
Page 29: CP/Ottawa Citizen-Wayne Hiebert; **Page 30:** © 2003 Hertz System, Inc. Hertz is a registered service mark and trademark of Hertz System, Inc.; **Page 32:** CP/AP Photo-Atsushi Tsukada; **Page 54:** Courtesy WestJet.

Chapter 3
Page 58: © Bill Lai/The Image Works; **Page 61:** Photo courtesy of Ocean Spray Cranberries, Inc.; **Page 76:** Courtesy Bombardier Recreational Products; **Page 85:** Photodisc/Getty Images.

Chapter 4
Page 116: CP Photo; **Page 120:** Courtesy of Ford Motor Corporation; **Page 120:** Photo provided by the NHTSA; **Page 122:** The LUKE Parking Meter by Digital Technologies Corp.; **Page 125:** Courtesy Tesma/Magna; **Page 126:** Courtesy Garrison Guitars; **Page 128:** © Chris Jones/Corbis Stock Market; **Page 129:** Courtesy of Research In Motion (RIM); **Page 131:** © The McGraw-Hill Companies; **Page 140:** Photos and figures courtesy of Steve Copeland and Roger Ball.

Chapter 5
Page 159: CP/Ryan Remiorz; **Page 162:** Photodisc/Getty Images; **Page 173:** John Feingersh/Stock Market; **Page 181:** Photo courtesy of 3COM.

Chapter 6
Page 182: Courtesy Tate and Lyle; **Page 186:** Photos courtesy of the Great Western Brewing Company, Saskatoon, SK. Canada; **Page 189:** Courtesy Tate and Lyle; **Page 190:** Courtesy Tate and Lyle; **Page 193:** College-Industry Council on Material Handling Education, associated to Material Handling Industry of America; **Page 195:** Michael Rosenfeld/Tony Stone Images; **Page 204:** AP Photo/Al Goldis; **Page 206:** Photo Courtesy of Standard Aero; **Page 216:** Photos Courtesy of Mike Willis, Oakswings.com; **Page 237:** Images courtesy Harris Corporation; **Page 238:** Courtesy Jubilee Ford/Lori Leech; **Page 239:** Courtesy Steve Hunter, Mississippi State University.

Chapter 7
Page 242: © David Sams/Stock Boston; **Page 254:** Courtesy NexGen Ergonomics Inc. www.nexgenergo.com; **Page 263:** CP/Toronto Star-Rick Eglinton.

Chapter 8
Page 278: © 2006 MapInfo Corporation. All Rights Reserved; **Page 282:** © Corel Professional Photos; **Page 283:** Photo by Roger Lévesque; **Page 284:** Photo by Roger Lévesque; **Page 287:** Photodisc/Getty Images; **Page 288:** Images Courtesy of Globeco International; **Page 294:** Visualization: Chris Pelkie, Cornell Theory Center, for New York State GAP.

Chapter 9
Page 304: Courtesy Standard Aero; **Page 311:** Reprinted: Courtesy of Applied Precision Inc. (www.appliedprecision.ca)

Chapter 10
Page 350: © Charles Thatcher/Stone; **Page 352:** CP/AP Photo/The Lufkin Daily News—Joel Andrews; **Page 353:** Reprinted with permission of *Quality Magazine* 2001–2005; **Page 354:** Reprinted with permission of *Quality Magazine* 2001–2005; **Page 356:** Courtesy Roctel Manufacturing and Linamar Corporation; **Page 356:** Reprinted with permission of *Quality Magazine* 2001–2005; **Page 369:** Michael L. Abramson; **Page 370:** Reprinted with permission of *Quality Magazine* 2001–2005.

Chapter 11
Page 390: Courtesy of College-Industry Council on Material Handling Education, associated to Material Handling Industry of America; **Page 393:** Reprinted by permission from Catalyst Manufacturing®; **Page 415:** Photo courtesy of Psion Teklogix; **Page 442:** Picture provided by Green Gear (Bike Friday); **Page 443:** Courtesy Mark's Work Warehouse.

Chapter 12
Page 446: Photodisc/Getty Images.

Chapter 13
Page 483: with 3D CAD Solid Concept—www.solid-concept.com; **Page 487:** Reprinted by permission from Catalyst Manufacturing®; **Page 491:** Courtesy of VX Corporation, www.vx.com; **Page 493:** Photograph courtesy of Lectronic Kaddy Corporation; **Page 499:** Photo Courtesy of Schenck AccuRate; **Page 521:** Courtesy of Stickley Furniture, L & J.G. Stickley, Inc.

Chapter 14
Page 524: Courtesy Toyota Motor Mfg. Canada Inc.; **Page 528:** CP/Toronto Star/Dick Loek; **Page 531:** Photo courtesy of Dana Corporation; **Page 545:** James Williamson, Airline Manufacturing Company Inc.

Chapter 15
Page 547: Lenkin® Flexible Job Shop Scheduling System. Leonard N. Stern School of Business, New York University; **Page 557:** Courtesy Herman Miller Inc.; **Page 567:** © Oregon Freeze Dry Inc.

Chapter 16
Page 586: © Voluntary InterIndustry Commerce Standards Association, www.vics.org.; **Page 590:** Courtesy of Alimentation Couche-Tard Inc. Reprinted with permission.; **Page 592:** © JB Pictures, Ltd.; **Page 606:** Courtesy Nygard International; **Page 611:** Image provided courtesy of Bombardier Inc.

Chapter 17
Page 626: CP/Chuck Stoody; **Page 627:** CP/Richard Lam; **Page 638:** CP/Peter Bregg; **Pages 656–658:** Courtesy Microsoft Canada; **Pages 659–663:** Information courtesy of Deltek Systems, Inc.; **Page 664:** Photo courtesy of Primavera Systems Inc.

Chapter 18
Page 682: Photodisc/Getty Images; **Page 685:** Jeff Greenberg/PhotoEdit; **Page 689:** © Mark L Stephenson/CORBIS; **Page 694:** Courtesy Q-MATIC Canada Ltd.

Company Index

Subject Index

Areas under the Standardized Normal curve, from − ∞ to + z

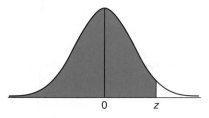

z	.00	.01	.02	.03	.04	.05	.06	.07	.08	.09
.0	.5000	.5040	.5080	.5120	.5160	.5199	.5239	.5279	.5319	.5359
.1	.5398	.5438	.5478	.5517	.5557	.5596	.5636	.5675	.5714	.5753
.2	.5793	.5832	.5871	.5910	.5948	.5987	.6026	.6064	.6103	.6141
.3	.6179	.6217	.6255	.6293	.6331	.6368	.6406	.6443	.6480	.6517
.4	.6554	.6591	.6628	.6664	.6700	.6736	.6772	.6808	.6844	.6879
.5	.6915	.6950	.6985	.7019	.7054	.7088	.7123	.7157	.7190	.7224
.6	.7257	.7291	.7324	.7357	.7389	.7422	.7454	.7486	.7517	.7549
.7	.7580	.7611	.7642	.7673	.7703	.7734	.7764	.7794	.7823	.7852
.8	.7881	.7910	.7939	.7967	.7995	.8023	.8051	.8078	.8106	.8133
.9	.8159	.8186	.8212	.8238	.8264	.8289	.8315	.8340	.8365	.8389
1.0	.8413	.8438	.8461	.8485	.8508	.8531	.8554	.8577	.8599	.8621
1.1	.8643	.8665	.8686	.8708	.8729	.8749	.8770	.8790	.8810	.8830
1.2	.8849	.8869	.8888	.8907	.8925	.8944	.8962	.8980	.8997	.9015
1.3	.9032	.9049	.9066	.9082	.9099	.9115	.9131	.9147	.9162	.9177
1.4	.9192	.9207	.9222	.9236	.9251	.9265	.9279	.9292	.9306	.9319
1.5	.9332	.9345	.9357	.9370	.9382	.9394	.9406	.9418	.9429	.9441
1.6	.9452	.9463	.9474	.9484	.9495	.9505	.9515	.9525	.9535	.9545
1.7	.9554	.9564	.9573	.9582	.9591	.9599	.9608	.9616	.9625	.9633
1.8	.9641	.9649	.9656	.9664	.9671	.9678	.9686	.9693	.9699	.9706
1.9	.9713	.9719	.9726	.9732	.9738	.9744	.9750	.9756	.9761	.9767
2.0	.9772	.9778	.9783	.9788	.9793	.9798	.9803	.9808	.9812	.9817
2.1	.9821	.9826	.9830	.9834	.9838	.9842	.9846	.9850	.9854	.9857
2.2	.9861	.9864	.9868	.9871	.9875	.9878	.9881	.9884	.9887	.9890
2.3	.9893	.9896	.9898	.9901	.9904	.9906	.9909	.9911	.9913	.9916
2.4	.9918	.9920	.9922	.9925	.9927	.9929	.9931	.9932	.9934	.9936
2.5	.9938	.9940	.9941	.9943	.9945	.9946	.9948	.9949	.9951	.9952
2.6	.9953	.9955	.9956	.9957	.9959	.9960	.9961	.9962	.9963	.9964
2.7	.9965	.9966	.9967	.9968	.9969	.9970	.9971	.9972	.9973	.9974
2.8	.9974	.9975	.9976	.9977	.9977	.9978	.9979	.9979	.9980	.9981
2.9	.9981	.9982	.9982	.9983	.9984	.9984	.9985	.9985	.9986	.9986
3.0	.9987	.9987	.9987	.9988	.9988	.9989	.9989	.9989	.9990	.9990
3.1	.9990	.9991	.9991	.9991	.9991	.9992	.9992	.9992	.9993	.9993
3.2	.9993	.9993	.9994	.9994	.9994	.9994	.9994	.9995	.9995	.9995
3.3	.9995	.9995	.9995	.9996	.9996	.9996	.9996	.9996	.9996	.9997
3.4	.9997	.9997	.9997	.9997	.9997	.9997	.9997	.9997	.9997	.9998

Areas under the Standardized Normal curve, 0 to z

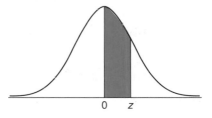

z	.00	.01	.02	.03	.04	.05	.06	.07	.08	.09
0.0	.0000	.0040	.0080	.0120	.0160	.0199	.0239	.0279	.0319	.0359
0.1	.0398	.0438	.0478	.0517	.0557	.0596	.0636	.0675	.0714	.0753
0.2	.0793	.0832	.0871	.0910	.0948	.0987	.1026	.1064	.1103	.1141
0.3	.1179	.1217	.1255	.1293	.1331	.1368	.1406	.1443	.1480	.1517
0.4	.1554	.1591	.1628	.1664	.1700	.1736	.1772	.1808	.1844	.1879
0.5	.1915	.1950	.1985	.2019	.2054	.2088	.2123	.2157	.2190	.2224
0.6	.2257	.2291	.2324	.2357	2389	.2422	.2454	.2486	.2517	.2549
0.7	.2580	.2611	.2642	.2673	2703	.2734	.2764	.2794	.2823	.2852
0.8	.2881	.2910	.2939	.2967	.2995	.3023	.3051	.3078	.3106	.3133
0.9	.3159	.3186	.3212	.3238	.3264	.3289	.3315	.3340	.3365	.3389
1.0	.3413	.3438	.3461	.3485	.3508	.3531	.3554	.3577	.3599	.3621
1.1	.3643	.3665	.3686	.3708	.3729	.3749	.3770	.3790	.3810	.3830
1.2	.3849	.3869	.3888	.3907	.3925	.3944	.3962	.3980	.3997	.4015
1.3	.4032	.4049	.4066	.4082	.4099	.4115	.4131	.4147	.4162	.4177
1.4	.4192	.4207	.4222	.4236	.4251	.4265	.4279	.4292	.4306	.4319
1.5	.4332	.4345	.4357	.4370	.4382	.4394	.4406	.4418	.4429	.4441
1.6	.4452	.4463	.4474	.4484	.4495	.4505	.4515	.4525	.4535	.4545
1.7	.4554	.4564	.4573	.4582	.4591	.4599	.4608	.4616	.4625	.4633
1.8	.4641	.4649	.4656	.4664	.4671	.4678	.4686	.4693	.4699	.4706
1.9	.4713	.4719	.4726	.4732	.4738	.4744	.4750	.4756	.4761	.4767
2.0	.4772	.4778	.4783	.4788	.4793	.4798	.4803	.4808	.4812	.4817
2.1	.4821	.4826	.4830	.4834	.4838	.4842	.4846	.4850	.4854	.4857
2.2	.4861	.4864	.4868	.4871	.4875	.4878	.4881	.4884	.4887	.4890
2.3	.4893	.4896	.4898	.4901	.4904	.4906	.4909	.4911	.4913	.4916
2.4	.4918	.4920	.4922	.4925	.4927	.4929	.4931	.4932	.4934	.4936
2.5	.4938	.4940	.4941	.4943	.4945	.4946	.4948	.4949	.4951	.4952
2.6	.4953	.4955	.4956	.4957	.4959	.4960	.4961	.4962	.4963	.4964
2.7	.4965	.4966	.4967	.4968	.4969	.4970	.4971	.4972	.4973	.4974
2.8	.4974	.4975	.4976	.4977	.4977	.4978	.4979	.4979	.4980	.4981
2.9	.4981	.4982	.4982	.4983	.4984	.4984	.4985	.4985	.4986	.4986
3.0	.4987	.4987	.4987	.4988	.4988	.4989	.4989	.4989	.4990	.4990

Stevenson 3CE DVD Content

- Added Content (supplements):

  Chapter 5 Supplement: Decision Theory

  Chapter 6 Supplement: Linear Programming

  Chapter 7 Supplement: Learning Curves

  Chapter 8 Supplement: The Transportation Model

  Chapter 10 Supplement: Acceptance Sampling

  Chapter 15 Supplement: Maintenance

  Chapter 18 Supplement: Simulation

- Data Sets
- Excel Templates
- Videos
- Study Outlines
- Link to OLC
- Lekin Scheduling Software – use in **Chapter 15, Scheduling and Control**
- Web Links
- Self Quizzes
- Screencam Tutorials